DEDICATION

This book is dedicated to all members of the British armed
forces, past, present and future.

Our thanks and gratitude is extended, to all those who have
served, for the services that they have provided to ensure the
welfare, independence and security of our nation.

FOR VALOUR

The Complete History of the Victoria Cross

VOLUME 2
The Indian Mutiny

Michael Charles Robson

Published in 2017 by
Uniform, an imprint of Unicorn Publishing Group LLP
101 Wardour Street
London W1F 0UG
www.unicornpublishing.org

ISBN 978 1 910500 91 0

Typeset in Minion Pro

Design by Nick Newton Design

Printed and bound in Poland

The author would be grateful for any information that may add to the further
enhancement, accuracy or development of this title or others in the series.
Please contact the publisher in the first instance.

CONTENTS

ILLUSTRATIONS

PART ONE

BACKGROUND

THE VICTORIA CROSS WARRANT CHANGES

Following public outrage at the treatment and management of troops during the Crimean War, the Victoria Cross was established by a Royal Warrant issued on 29th January 1856.

The Victoria Cross was the first British award for bravery in the face of the enemy that would be available to all members of all arms of the Military forces irrespective of rank, length of service or any other restriction.

Although the Crimean War was all but over by the time the Royal Warrant was issued, it had been agreed that deeds during the Crimean War would be considered for retrospective awards of the medal.

In all 111 Victoria Cross medals were awarded for actions during the Crimean War, following a protracted recommendation and selection process.

The Indian Mutiny was the first major conflict since the inception of the Victoria Cross and as such the intended recommendation and selection process was more closely followed as the powers that be were now fully aware that this preeminent award was now available to recognise the most gallant and brave deeds.

The Indian Mutiny also presented new circumstances that required some revisions to the Originating Warrant.

Eligibility of officers and men employed by Honourable East India Company

As a large number of the troops involved in quelling the Mutiny were not part of the British Army but were employed by the Honourable East India Company, a change to the original Victoria Cross warrant was necessary for these men to be eligible for an award of the medal.

The Indian native troops were not considered for the award of the Victoria Cross because, since 1837, they had been eligible for the award of the Indian Order of Merit, the oldest British gallantry award available to all ranks.

However, in October 1857, the Victoria Cross warrant was amended to extend the eligibility for the award to the European officers and men of the naval and military services of the Honourable East India Company, who were not eligible for the award of the India Order of Merit.

And whereas, by another Warrant under Our Royal Sign Manual, countersigned by one of Our Principal Secretaries of State and bearing date at Our Court at Windsor, the twenty-ninth day of October, one thousand eight hundred and fifty-seven, in the twenty-first year of Our reign, We thought fit to signify Our Royal Will and Pleasure, that the said decoration shall be conferred on the officers and men of the naval and military services of the East India Company, who may be qualified to receive the same in accordance with the rules and ordinances made, ordained and established by Us, for the government thereof, by Our first recited Warrant, aforesaid.

Forfeiture for misconduct

Clause 15 of the Originating Royal Warrant contained the rules for the forfeiture of the Victoria Cross Medal and pension in the case of subsequent serious misconduct by the recipient.

Although the first case of forfeiture, which occurred in 1861 had nothing to do with the Indian Mutiny, an Indian Mutiny recipient was the subject of forfeiture in 1872.

King George V was in complete opposition to this clause and in fact had stated *"... that even were a VC to be sentenced to be hanged for murder, he should be allowed to wear the VC on the scaffold"* and the clause was omitted from a revised warrant issued in 1920.

The men who had previously been the subject of forfeiture were reinstated to the roll and where appropriate their medal was returned and their pension reinstated.

Posthumous awards

The originating Warrant did not permit the award of the Victoria Cross posthumously.

In response to several requests for posthumous awards, forwarded by the government in India, Mr Pennington, the person responsible for the operation of the system of awards, did allow for a memorandum to be published in the London Gazette, indicating that the stated person would have received the award had he survived.

On 15th January 1907, King Edward VII issued a Royal Warrant that posthumously awarded the Victoria Cross to those persons who had been the subject of the *"had they survived"* memoranda.

Under this new warrant an Indian Mutiny recipient was the first to receive a posthumous award, some 50 years after his death.

Recognition of a posthumous award of the Victoria Cross was not made official until the Royal Warrant was completely rewritten by George V and reissued in June 1920. A new clause 4, stated that the award could be made posthumously.

Civilian awards

The Originating Victoria Cross Warrant did not anticipate the award of the medal to civilians, however, circumstances during the mutiny in India merited such awards and Queen Victoria issued a revision to the warrant on 13th December 1858 that allowed for awards to civilians.

2

THE HONOURABLE EAST INDIA COMPANY (HEIC)

Before we can consider the root causes of the Mutiny it is essential to form an understanding of the conditions of governance applicable to the Indian sub-continent and in order to do this we need to have a good understanding of the history of the 'Honourable Company of Merchants of England Trading to the East Indies' better known as the Honourable East India Company and popularly known as 'John Company'.

The development of 'John Company'

In the late 1500s Britain was vying with the Dutch and Portuguese for the trade in spices from India and the Far East.

Without the benefit of a 'Northwest Passage' sea route to the East (not established until 1903) an alternative was being sought to the long and hazardous sea journey via the Cape of Good Hope.

In 1581 the Turkey Company was founded with approval of the Sultan to establish trade with the Ottoman Empire. With access to the lands of the Sultan this gave rise to the thought of establishing an overland route to India and the east which would eventually evolve into the 'Spice Trail'.

With this overland route in mind the Turkey Company enhanced its scope of operation by obtaining a new charter, from Queen Elizabeth I, which allowed for the overland trade with India by the 'Governor and Company of the Merchants of Levant'.

Figure 1. East India Company Crest

Figure 2. Queen Elizabeth I

Not satisfied with the current situation and desiring a more exclusive arrangement a group of London merchants (some of whom were involved with both the Turkey Company and the Merchants of Levant) met up in London with a view to setting up a new company and to seek a patent of monopoly from the Queen.

The first formal meeting of the new company took place on 24th September 1599 where a draft patent was drawn up and 15 Directors were appointed to manage the company.

The Directors met with Queen Elizabeth I on 16th October and received a very positive reception from the Queen to their request for a patent of monopoly.

The Privy Council, however, was less enthusiastic and insisted on negotiations with Spain, who had a Papal Bull protecting their trade. These negotiations took some time and it was not until 23rd September 1600 that the 2nd meeting of the new company took place in Founder's Hall, confident that all objections to their patent of monopoly had been overcome.

At this meeting 17 Directors were appointed to oversee the management of the company and a new patent of privileges was drawn up in the name of 'The Society of Adventurers to the East Indies' and was submitted for approval.

At a meeting on 30th October, 24 Directors were appointed and Alderman Thomas Smythe was appointed as the first Governor of the company.

Figure 3. Thomas Smythe

On 31st December 1600, the new company was incorporated as the 'Honourable Company of Merchants of England Trading to the East Indies' with a Royal Charter that provided the company with powers for the unlimited purchasing of land in the East and with 15 years of exclusive trade "… *into the Countries and Ports of Asia and Africa and into all the Islands, Ports, Towns and Places of Asia, Africa and America, or any of them beyond the Cape of Buena Esperanza or the Straits of Magellan, where any traffic may be used*".

Thus was born what would become the most powerful commercial and military power, outside of a nation state, to have ever existed before or since.

The Company's first trading expedition to the East Indies, set sail from London on 13th February 1601 beginning a dominance that would last for almost 250 years.

In 1608 the Company's ships began to dock at Surat and established the port as a transit point and within two years had established its first factory in the town of Machilipatnam on the Coromandel Coast in the Bay of Bengal.

By 1609, with several profitable voyages behind them, the Company approached the King to address the 15 year limitation on their monopoly and on 31st May 1609 King James I granted the Company new letters-patent giving them "… *the whole entire and only trade and traffic to the East Indies … for ever*".

A proviso was added to the letters-patent such that the rights granted to the Company could be withdrawn, following three years notice, if the trade with India "… *should not prove to be profitable to the realm*".

During the early years the Company made a profitable trade in cotton, silk, indigo dye, salt, saltpetre and tea, however, it was not initially able to compete in the spice trade with the well established Dutch East India Company.

Although the Company had a monopoly of trade granted by the crown, it should be remembered that this monopoly only extended to other British companies and that their traders faced fierce competition from Dutch and Portuguese merchantmen which often led to hostilities in the Indian Ocean.

Realising that the best way to dominate the trade with India was to establish a substantial presence on the mainland, the Company petitioned King James I to send a diplomatic mission to India to secure a treaty in the favour of the Company.

In 1615, Sir Thomas Roe was duly despatched on a mission to visit the Mughal Emperor Jahangir, who ruled approximately 70% of the sub-continent, with the objective to secure a commercial treaty giving exclusive rights to the Company to build factories in Surat and other areas of India.

The mission was successful and in September 1618, the Emperor stated in a letter to King James that in return for goods

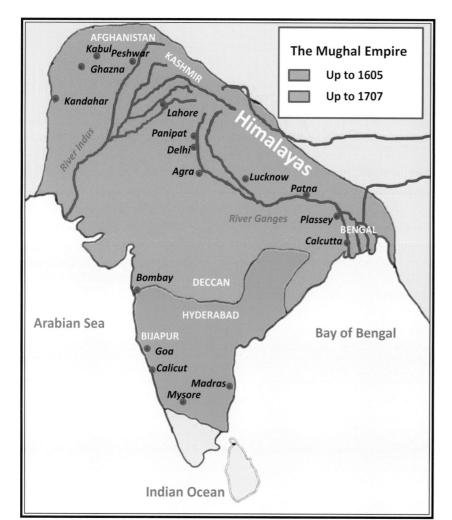

Figure 4. The Mughal Empire

The Mughal Empire
- Up to 1605
- Up to 1707

from the European market, "... *I have given my general command to all the kingdoms and ports of my dominions to receive all the merchants of the English nation as the subjects of my friend; that in what place so ever they choose to live, they may have free liberty without any restraint; and at what port so ever they shall arrive, that neither Portugal nor any other shall dare to molest their quiet; and in what city so ever they shall have residence, I have commanded all my governors and captains to give them freedom answerable to their own desires; to sell, buy, and to transport into their country at their pleasure.*"

With such obvious Royal patronage, the Company soon began to prosper and outstrip the Portuguese who had established bases at Goa and Bombay[1] and created strongholds at Surat, where they built a factory in 1612 and at Madras in 1639. By 1647 the Company had 23 factories and 90 employees in India.

Having established a dominant position in the East Indies during the 16th century, the Portuguese decline as a competitor to the Company accelerated when they were forcibly annexed with Spain in 1580, a situation which was to last until 1640. The Portuguese fleet was considerably reduced along with that

of their Spanish conquerors following the destruction of the 'Spanish Armada' during 1588.

Following the destruction of a Portuguese fleet off the coast of India in 1612, Portugal was a spent force in the competition for trade on the Indian sub-continent, this was extended to the East Indies following a defeat of their fleet in the Persian Gulf during 1620.

The position of Portugal regarding trade in India and the East Indies was finally formalised by a treaty between England and Portugal signed by Oliver Cromwell and King John IV of Portugal on 10th July 1654 which ceded to the English the rights to reside and trade in all of Portugal's Eastern possessions.

With the removal of Portugal as a threat to trade in the East, the Dutch remained the sole competitor to the Company, in particular for the lucrative trade in the Spice Islands.

The rise of the Dutch as a trading force was paralleled by her breaking free of the Spanish yoke which had been established in 1555. In 1566 the Dutch revolted against Spain and in 1581 declared their independence, following a truce with Spain in 1609 Dutch independence was finally formalised by the treaty of Westphalia which ended the 30 years war.

Initially there was an unofficial alliance between the Protestant Dutch and English with both trading companies directing

---

1 With the marriage of Catherine of Braganza to King Charles II, in 1662, the Portuguese base at Bombay was ceded to the British as part of her dowry.

their hostilities against the Spanish and Portuguese traders, however, this ended in 1604 following the treaty by King James I with Spain and Portugal.

Hostilities with the Dutch were briefly suspended by a treaty signed on 2nd June 1619 which allowed English trade in the Spice Islands, this agreement ended in 1623 following the notorious 'Amboyna' incident. The Dutch arrested, tried and on 9th March 1623 beheaded 20 men accused of conspiracy against the Dutch government, 10 of these men were employees of the Honourable East India Company.

Although they continued to maintain their factory at Bantam in Java, following the incident at Amboyna and the resultant termination of the 1619 trade agreement, the Company concentrated their efforts more on the Indian mainland rather than the Spice Islands.

Over the next century, the British would fight four wars against the Dutch (1652–54, 1665–67, 1672–74 and 1780–84) as the two nations vied for domination of world trade.

In 1634, the Mughal Emperor extended his hospitality to the British traders, to the region of Bengal.

In 1657, Oliver Cromwell, following a large loan to the Commonwealth, renewed the 1609 charter at a time when the Company was under immense pressure from adventurer merchants who were seeking to break their monopoly.

Following the ceding of Bombay to the British by the Portuguese, upon the marriage of Catherine de Braganza to King Charles II in 1662, the Company built a factory at Bombay in 1668. The major factories were fortified and became the walled forts at Fort William in Bengal, Fort St George in Madras and Bombay Castle.

During 1670 the Company obtained several new letters-patent from King Charles II which mightily extended their powers. These would now include; the rights to autonomous territorial acquisition, the right to mint money, the right to command fortresses and troops, the rights to make war and peace and form alliances and the right to exercise both civil and criminal jurisdiction over the acquired areas.

Surrounded by trading competitors from other imperial powers and at time opposed by hostile native rulers, the freedom to manage its own military affairs, granted by the acts of 1670, was most welcome and the Company rapidly raised armed forces during the 1680s, mainly manned by men from the local population with European officers.

By 1689, the Company was comparable to a nation on the Indian sub-continent, independently administering the huge presidencies of Bengal, Madras and Bombay supported by its own formidable army.

With huge profits being made from the trade in the East Indies, the excluded merchants formed a powerful political lobby with the intention to overturn the monopoly and eventually in 1694 their efforts were successful when the Deregulation Act allowed any British company to trade with India, unless specifically excluded by an act of Parliament. This act ended the monopoly that the Company had enjoyed for almost 100 years.

In 1698, an act of Parliament established a new company the "English Company Trading to the East Indies" to compete with the Honourable East India Company. The new company was floated with government securities of £2 million; at last the state was giving strong financial support to the lucrative trade in the East.

All did not go as planned for the new company; powerful stockholders of the Honourable East India Company purchased a significant portion of the stock and established a dominant position in the new company.

For several years the two companies seemingly vied with each other for trade in the East, however, in practice, such was the dominant position of the Honourable East India Company that they experienced very limited competition.

The two companies eventually merged in 1702, forming the "United Company of Merchants of England Trading to the East Indies". Providing the Treasury with a £3 million loan, secured the new company exclusive trade rights for three years, after which time the position was to be reviewed.

Ten years later in 1712, another act of Parliament renewed the Company position and a further act in 1730 extended their licence until 1766.

However, by this time frequent hostilities with the traditional enemy France were taking place over control of colonial possessions.

In 1664 the French East India Company was founded to compete with the British, Dutch and Portuguese for the spice trade in the east and by 1719 they had established a small presence in India at Pondicherry on the Coromandel Coast.

Joseph Francis Dupleix, who arrived in India during 1741 and by 1742 was governor of the French East India Company, had grand plans for greatly increasing the influence of the French in India.

By 1742 the risk of outright war with France prompted the British Government to further extend the Companies exclusive licence until 1783 in return for a loan of £1 million to help fund the cost of any upcoming war.

Despite the hostile relationship between their respective governments, the French and British traders in India had cordial relations, however, with the outbreak of the War of Austrian Succession in 1740 things were soon to change.

In 1744, Britain entered the war in opposition to France and her allies and despite orders to the French officials in India to

Figure 5. Joseph Francis Dupleix

avoid conflict, hostilities broke out in India after a Royal Navy fleet was despatched to the area and precipitated the 1st Carnatic War.

The French managed to capture Madras from the British on 21st September 1746, however, attempts to capture Cuddalore were successfully repulsed.

The British successfully besieged Pondicherry in late 1748 but with the onset of the monsoon season in October the siege was lifted.

The War of Austrian Succession was ended with the Treaty of Aix-la-Chapelle (Treaty of Aachen) which was signed on 18th October 1748 and this also ended the 1st Carnatic War.

Under the terms of the treaty the French returned Madras to the British in exchange for Fort Louisbourg in North America which had been captured by the British.

It should be noted that this war was the first active service experience for Robert Clive (Clive of India) who was captured at Madras but escaped and took part in the defence of Cuddalore and the siege of Pondicherry.

The death of Nizam-ul-Mulk the Nizam of Hyderabad on 1st June 1748 prompted a civil war for the succession which became known as the 2nd Carnatic War. The proponents were the Nizam's son Nasir Jung and his grandson Muzaffar Jung. Chanda Sahib saw the war as an opportunity to become the Nawab of Arcot and sided with Muzaffar Jung.

The French, seeking to extend their influence into the states of Hyderabad and Arcot allied themselves with Muzaffar Jung and Chanda Sahib and after some initial success had placed their men on the thrones of both states in 1749.

The British, seeking to offset the influence of the French, began supporting Nasir Jung and Muhammad Ali Khan Walajah, the son of the deposed and murdered Nawab of Arcot, Anwaruddin Muhammed Khan.

In 1751, Robert Clive led a small force of 500 and captured the Carnatic capital of Arcot on 1st September as a diversion to elicit a response from Chanda Sahib and the French forces which were besieging the British at Trichinopoly.

The ruse worked and a force of 10,000 men was sent from the siege at Trichinopoly to recapture Arcot.

A small force of about 300 men from Fort St David in Cuddalore and Fort St George in Madras was assembled and despatched to go to the aid of Robert Clive at Arcot, however, they were intercepted by a much larger force supported by French artillery and had to return to Madras.

The commander of the besieging force, concerned about a force of 6,000 Maharattas coming to the support of Clive, launched his final attack on the town on 14th November 1751 and when this failed he retired his forces and returned to the siege at Trichinopoly.

After surviving a siege of 50 days with only 500 men against 10,000 Clive was relieved by a force from Fort St George and returned to Madras.

In April 1752, after more than a year, the British finally broke the siege at Trichinopoly and Chanda Sahib was killed. Mohammed Ali had made a secret treaty with the Rajah of Mysore in which he promised the city of Trichinopoly as a reward for his support.

With the city now in the hands of Mohammed Ali, the Rajah quite rightly expected to receive his reward, however, this was refused and the Rajah of Mysore switched his allegiance to the French.

Figure 6. Robert Clive

In early 1753, the French again lay siege to Trichinopoly, however, this was dispersed in May 1753 with some ease.

By now the French had been ceded significant territory gaining the provinces of Ellore, Rajahmundry, Cicacole, Condapilly and Guntore (known as the Northern Circars) and were now in control of the Coramandel and Orissa coasts.

The French territorial gain was short lived, however, as in an effort by the British and French governments to avoid another war, as tensions continued to rise in Europe, the French agreed to withdraw from the Carnatic states in a treaty agreed on 26th December 1754.

A fresh bid to secure part of the trade in India was launched in 1756, when Germany, Russia, Portugal, Spain, Sweden and Denmark all created government supported East India Companies.

The conflict facing the company now moved to the state of Bengal. The death of the Nawab of Bengal Alivardi Khan on 9th April 1756, led to the succession of his grandson 20 year old Suraj-uh-Daulah who was less sympathetic to the Company. The new Nawab sought to demonstrate his power by an attack on Calcutta which he captured on 20th June 1756. The infamous "Black Hole of Calcutta" incident occurred during his occupation of the city.

Due to the distances involved and the slowness of communications it took the British some time to respond to the fall of Calcutta, however, on 2nd January 1757 a fleet and troops commanded by Clive arrived off Calcutta and after very little fighting recaptured the city.

A small battle was fought at Hugli on 10th January 1757, as a force of 40,000 men led by Suraj-uh-Daulah advanced on Calcutta but was easily repulsed by Clive and his men. Rather than chase down and destroy the Nawab and his men in revenge for the atrocities at Calcutta, much to his annoyance, Clive was ordered to conclude a treaty with the Nawab to prevent him from forming an alliance with the French.

In 1756, the 7 Years War in Europe, which had started two years earlier, resulted in renewed hostilities between the French and British East India Companies trading in India and the 3rd and final Carnatic War had begun.

With the French pressing around Madras, Clive was ordered by the Company to return from Bengal. Clive, who suspected, quite correctly, that the Nawab would make an alliance with the French as soon as his back was turned, with the danger of a repeat of the atrocities at Calcutta, decided to stay in Bengal.

On 23rd March 1757, the French trading centre of Chadernagore was captured by Clive for the British.

The Nawab Suraj-ud-Daulah was conducting secret negotiations with the French to expel the British from Bengal, however,

Clive heard of a plot by Mir Jafir (the son on the previous Nawab Alivardi Khan) and formed an alliance with the conspirators to move on the Nawab. Clive with a force of just 3,500 met the Nawab's army of 50,000 men at Plassey on 23rd June 1757 and while the forces of Mir Jafir just stood and watched, he completely routed the Nawab's force. After fleeing the battlefield, Suraj-ud-Daulah was killed by Mir Jafar's son and the French retired to Behar.

Despite his reluctance to get involved in the battle, Mir Jafir was placed on the throne of Murshedabad but was subject to the authority of the Company which annexed the Bengal, Behar and Orissa provinces.

In April 1758, the French were defeated in a major sea battle off Fort St David, but not before they landed their troops, who went on to capture Cuddalore and then on 2nd June 1758 captured Fort St David which they raised to the ground.

By December 1758, the French had gained much ground and were laying siege to Madras, however, the garrison at Fort St George managed to hold out until a fleet of 6 ships arrived with reinforcements in February 1759 and on 17th February the French abandoned their siege.

In 1759, the Dutch briefly tried to reassert influence in India when in response to secret negotiations with Mir Jafir at Chinsurah they sent a force which arrived at Huli in August 1759. The force sailed up river towards Calcutta where they were comprehensively defeated by Clive, ending their ambitions of a return to a position of influence in India.

On 22nd January 1760, Sir Eyre Coote defeated the French at the Battle of Wandiwash and they retired to their fortress at Pondicherry.

The earlier successes of the French were all reversed and the only significant French force was now besieged in Pondicherry. Following a protracted siege the French force, which was near to starvation, surrendered Pondicherry on 16th January 1761. The fort and town at Pondicherry were raised to the ground and by April 1761 and the French now did not have a single military post in all of India.

The 7 Years War in Europe finally ended with the Treaty of Paris on 10th February 1763 which confirmed all of the British acquisitions in India leaving them as the undisputed European power on the sub-continent.

The French were allowed to have trading posts in India, however, all of the territories were to be administered by the British East India Company.

In April 1764, Robert Clive was elected Chairman of the East India Company and over the next few years he did much to consolidate the Company's position with the acquisition of new territories and a reorganisation of the Company army.

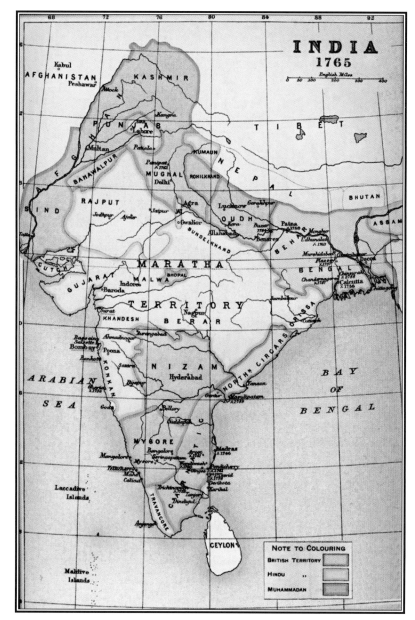

Figure 7. India 1765

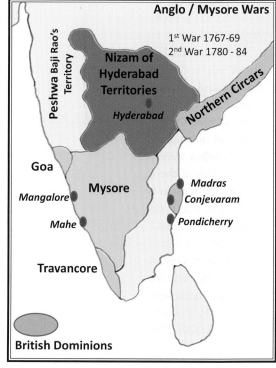

Figure 8. 1st & 2nd Mysore Wars

King George III, now sought to increase the authority of the Crown over the Company, he granted plenipotentiary rights to several of the ruling Princes thus inserting the Crown as a buffer between the Company and the Princes.

By 1765, the holdings of the East India Company were mainly in the east of the country with the isolated settlement at Madras subject of a treaty with Muhammed Ali Khan the Carnatic Nawab. Other influential leaders in the area were the Nizam of Hyderabad and the Sultan of Mysore, Hyder Ali. The Company also occupied the Northern Circars which they had secured in the recent wars with the French. In August 1765, the Mughal Emperor Shah Alam II had granted the Company rights to occupy this territory. Finally they had major holdings in the state of Bengal centred on their capital at Calcutta. In the west they had the isolated holding at Bombay. The settlements in Bombay and the Northern Circars were also largely dependent upon alliances with the Marathas.

Concerns regarding the expansionist desire of Hyder Ali, the Sultan of Mysore led to an alliance between the Company and the Nizam of Maratha, which in January 1767 led to the invasion of Mysore and the beginning of the 1st Anglo/Mysore war.

In May 1767, the British discovered that their Maratha allies had struck a deal with Hyder Ali, in which the invasion would end and they would advance against the British and install Hyder's son Tipu Sultan as Nawab of the Carnatic.

A combined Mysore and Hyderabad force moved against the Company at Changama, however, a British force of 7,000 men managed to repulse the 70,000 invaders and inflict heavy losses.

Kaveripattinam was captured after a two day siege and the British force commanded by Colonel Smith retired to Tiruvannamalai, for supplies and reinforcements, where on 26th September 1767 they again repulsed Hyder Ali's force.

In November the British were besieged at Ambur but the arrival of a relief force in December forced Hyder Ali to lift the siege. The failure of this campaign led to a split in the alliance between Hyder Ali and the Nizam who withdrew back to Hyderabad and negotiated a new treaty with the British. With this setback Hyder Ali tried to make his own treaty with the British but was rebuffed and the Company authorities in Bombay launched an expedition against Mysore's Malabar Coast territories.

In February 1768, the British captured Mangalore, a major port which was the home of Mysore's small fleet, which prompted Hyder Ali to abandon his activities in the Carnatic and proceed with purpose to Malabar.

Hyder Ali and his son Tipu Sultan managed to retake Mangalore and other ports which had been occupied by the over-extended British force, however, their absence from the Carnatic allowed the British to recapture their lost towns which had been left only lightly garrisoned.

The Marathas were once again convinced to join the conflict on the side of the British and in August a combined force began preparations to besiege Bangalore, however, before the siege could be put in place Hyder Ali arrived with a force from Malabar on 9th August 1768 and disrupted the plans.

After suffering heavy losses in a battle against a superior Maratha force at Ooscota on 22nd August, Hyder Ali retreated to Gurramkanda and tried to negotiate a peace with the British, however, due to his insistence that the Nizam be excluded from these talks they finally broke down.

On 3rd October 1768, Hyder Ali again advanced on Bangalore but made little progress and after receiving additional force from Malabar in November decided once again to go on the offensive against the Carnatic states.

Hyder Ali made good progress in the Carnatic, recovering many of the towns that had been recaptured by the British and advanced to the gates of Madras.

With Madras being only lightly defended it was now the turn of the British to seek a peace treaty, and this was signed on 29th March 1769 at Madras thus ending the 1st Anglo-Mysore War. The treaty included a pact of mutual protection, with each party agreeing to go to the aid of the other if its territory was invaded. In 1770, Hyder Ali, apparently comforted by the treaty with the British, engaged in war with the Marathas and when the Marathas invaded Mysore requested the help of the British to expel the invaders – despite the terms of the treaty this aid was refused.

In the early 1770s, despite an increase in their revenues, the Company were experiencing falling profits. This was probably due to officers of the Company, at all levels, accepting income as personal gifts rather than revenue to the Company but was also affected by the fall in sales of tea to America.

In order to reverse this trend the Company sacked the native revenue collectors and on 14th May 1772 established a Board of Revenue and native treasury at Calcutta.

In 1773 the Regulating Act was passed which imposed several important administrative and economic reforms which clearly established the British Governments sovereignty and control over the Companies affairs in India. The Act established the principle that all acquisitions of territory by the Company were on behalf of the Crown. The territory was then leased back to the Company on payment of a fee to the Crown.

Company dividend payments were limited to 6% until a substantial government loan had been repaid and all employees of the Company were prohibited from engaging in private trade or accepting presents and bribes from the natives.

To ensure that Government interests were looked after, a governing Council was established at Calcutta with three of the five members being appointed by the British Parliament. Warren Hastings who had been the Governor of Bengal since 1771, was elevated to the position of Governor-General of Bengal and the Madras and Bombay presidencies were declared to be subservient to Bengal.

The Act also declared that British India was to be administered according to British Law and a supreme court was established at Fort William in Calcutta by judges sent to India from England.

On 18th November 1772 the death of Madhavrao Peshwa led to a struggle for the control of the Maratha Empire with Raghunathrao Balaji eventually gaining the throne.

In the face of rising opposition, Raghunathrao sought the help of the British and signed the treaty of Surat on 6th March 1775 which ceded territories to the Bengal Presidency in return for help from British troops.

The governing Council in Calcutta was opposed to the treaty which was annulled and replaced by the treat of Purandar on 1st March 1776 under which the cause of Raghunathrao was abandoned, however, British troops continued to campaign against the Marathas.

On 12th January 1779, the British suffered a severe defeat by the Maratha army commanded by Mahadji Scindia at Wodgaon and 4 days later signed the Treaty of Wodgaon under the terms of which the Company was to relinquish all the territories that they had gained since 1773.

The governing Council in Calcutta again rejected this treaty and sent a new force against the Maratha army which experienced early victories capturing Ahmadabad on 15th February 1779, Gwalior on 4th August 1780 and Bassein on 11th December 1780.

After suffering several defeats in Central India and the Deccan during 1781, the governing Council decided to sue for peace and the 1st Anglo-Maratha War came to a close after the treaty of Salbai was signed on 17th May 1782.

In 1778, during the American War of Independence, after siding with the Americans the French declared war on England and once again conflict between the European powers spilt over into the sub-continent.

The Company, who took this opportunity to try and drive the French out of India once and for all, captured Pondicherry and other French outposts during 1778 and in 1779, captured the French port of Mahé on the Malabar Coast.

The capture of Mahé prompted Hyder Ali, who was already allied with the French, to form an alliance with the Marathas and the Nizam of Hyderabad in opposition against the British and launched the 2nd Anglo-Mysore War. In July 1780, Hyder Ali invaded the Carnatic and laid siege to the British forts at Arcot.

On 10th September 1780, a force commanded by Hyder Ali's son Tipu Sultan intercepted and defeated a British force at Pollilur, which was advancing to the relief of Arcot, making good use of Rocket Artillery. Following the defeat, the British returned to Madras but instead of capitalising on his victory and pursuing the British, Tipu Sultan returned to the siege at Arcot which was captured on 3rd November 1780.

In the summer of 1781, after the Dutch entered the American War of Independence on the side of the Americans, the Company was ordered to take action against the Dutch outposts in India and in November 1781, after a three week siege the British captured their base at Negapatam.

Following the ending of the American War of Independence, with the signing of the treaties of Versailles on 3rd September 1783 the British and French governments sought to end the war in India.

The 2nd Anglo-Mysore War came to an end with the signing of the treaty of Mangalore on 11th March 1784, under the terms of which all parties returned to the territories that they occupied at the start of the conflict.

The war with the Dutch (4th Anglo-Dutch War) came to an end on 20th May 1884, with the treaty of Paris which was signed at Negapatam. Ceylon was returned to the Dutch, however, the Company gained the valuable concession of free trade throughout the Dutch East Indies.

In August 1784, the East India Act 1784 (Pitt's India Act) was passed into law which further differentiated the Companies Commercial and Political activities.

In political matters the Company was to be totally subordinate to the British Government and to accomplish this, the Act established a Board of Commissioners for the Affairs of India (the Board of Control). The members of the Board were to be the Chancellor of the Exchequer, the Secretary of State and four

Privy Councillors nominated by the King. The Secretary of State was to be the President of the Board.

The Act stated that the Board would henceforth "superintend, direct and control" the government of the Company's possessions in India.

The Act also laid the foundations for the centralisation of the British administration of India with the presidency at Bengal having control over the Madras and Bombay presidencies.

Apart from three minor amendments enacted in 1786, the Act would form the basis for the government of India until repealed by the Government of India Act in 1916.

Despite the Act, the Company were still able to wage war in order to protect and expand its territory in India, however, from now on it would require the approval of the Board of Control (essentially the British Government) before it could do so.

In February 1786, General Charles Earl Cornwallis was appointed as Governor-General of India and Commander-in-Chief of the East India Company army.

In 1789, Tipu Sultan, who had ascended to the throne of Mysore on the death of his father Hyder Ali in December 1782, decided once again to direct his aggression against the British interests in India.

On 29th December 1789, Tipu Sultan launched an attack on Nedumkotta, the defensive line protecting the Kingdom of Travancore a British ally and precipitated the start of the 3rd Anglo-Mysore War.

In late April 1790, the forces of Tipu Sultan finally breached the Nedumkotta defences, however, suffered heavy losses and after hearing of a British relief force leaving Madras withdrew from Travancore.

The British force, commanded by General William Medows left Trichinopoly in late May and after meeting little resistance entered Coimbatore unopposed on 21st July 1790, Tipu Sultans forces having withdrawn to the comparative safety of the Mysore Highlands.

General Medows, consolidated his position in the Coimbatore district by occupying Palghat and Sathyamangalore.

On 2nd September 1790, Tipu Sultan with a force of 40,000 men left Srirangapatnam and advanced via the mountain passes to Sathyamangalore where on 13th September, after withstanding the initial assault, the garrison of 2,800 men commanded by Captain John Floyd were forced to withdraw and head for Coimbatore. Captain Floyd's force was pursued by 15,000 of Tipu Sultan's cavalry, however, after repulsing several attacks by this force they were rescued by a relief force sent out from Coimbatore by General Medows.

Thwarted in his attacks against Captain Floyd's men, Tipu Sultan turned his attention to disrupting the British lines of

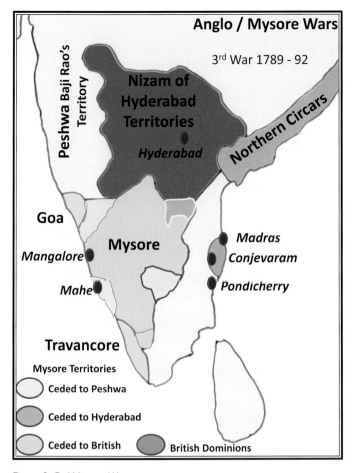

Figure 9. 3rd Mysore War

supply and communication until early November when he advanced against a smaller force of 9,000 men sent from Bengal.

By the time that Tipu Sultan caught up with the force from Bengal, which was commanded by Colonel Maxwell, they were firmly entrenched in fortified positions in the town of Kaveripattinam and were impossible to dislodge.

On learning that a force commanded by General Medows was on its way to the aid of Colonel Maxwell, Tipu Sultan broke the siege on 14th September and fled south towards Trichinopoly before going on a rampage in the Carnatic.

General Medows and his army returned to Madras where command of the army was handed over to General Charles Cornwallis.

Tipu Sultan arrived at the French outpost of Pondicherry in late 1790 and sought support from his former allies, however, as the French Revolution was in its early stages no assistance was provided by the French.

In December 1790, after battles at Calicut and Cannanore the British secured the Malabar Coast.

In the summer of 1790, the Maratha Empire entered the war as allies of the British and sent two armies to invade Mysore.

The first army commanded by Perseram Bhow and supplemented with Company troops from the Bombay army, besieged the city of Darwar in September 1790 and captured the city on 3rd April 1791.

The second army commanded by Hurry Punt and complemented by Company troops from the Madras army, captured Kurnool early in 1791 and after receiving news that General Cornwallis had captured Bangalore set off to join forces with him, which was achieved during May 1791.

The Nizam of Hyderabad also sent a force, commanded by Mahabat Jung, to invade Mysore and after a protracted siege which started in October 1790 managed to capture the town of Koppal in April 1791.

After capturing Bangalore in April 1791, General Cornwallis carried out operations in the surrounding area to secure his supply lines to Madras before embarking on an expedition to Seringapatam.

The Maratha and Hyderabad armies carried out independent operations in northern Mysore, seeking to secure territorial gains.

By December 1791, General Cornwallis was ready to go on the offensive and captured the towns of Nundydroog and Savendroog after brief sieges.

On 25th January 1792, General Cornwallis began his advance on Seringapatam, the Mysore capital and on 5th February started siege operations. On 12th February General Cornwallis was reinforced by a contingent from the Bombay Army led by General Abercrombie.

Recognising his perilous situation, Tipu Sultan began negotiations for a peace on 24th February and the Treaty of Seringapatam, which ended the 3rd Anglo-Mysore War, was signed on 18th March 1792.

Under the terms of the treaty, Mysore lost almost half of its lands, with territory being ceded to the Maratha Empire and the Kingdom of Hyderabad; the districts of Malabar, Salem, Bellary and Anatapur were annexed by the Madras presidency.

In 1793, the Company's charter was renewed for a further 20 years by an act of Parliament.

During the French Revolution and Napoleonic Wars (1793 1815), the Netherlands became a satellite state of France and after the British defeated the Dutch fleet at the Battle of Camperdown in 1797 they took over many of the Dutch colonial territories, notably Ceylon.

In 1798, Napoleon Bonaparte's landing in Egypt was thought to be a precursor to further French hostilities against British interests in India, however, the defeat of Napoleon at the Battle of the Nile on 1st to 3rd August 1798 brought an end to this ambition.

In a response to this perceived threat, the British invaded the Kingdom of Mysore, a long term ally of the French. After the Battle of Seedaseer on 8th March 1799, the British lay siege to the

Figure 10. Napoleon Bonaparte

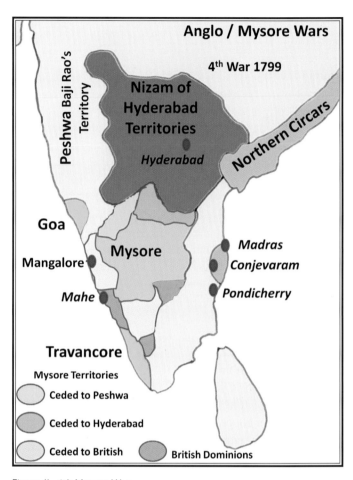

Figure 11. 4th Mysore War

Mysore capital city of Seringapatam which was captured on 4th May. During the final assault Tipu Sultan, the Mysore leader was killed. This ended the 4th and final Anglo-Mysore War.

Tipu Sultan's successor was sent into exile and much of the Mysore lands were distributed to the Maratha Empire and the Nizam of Hyderabad, with the districts of Coimbatore, Uttara Kannada and Dakshina Kannada being annexed by the Company.

The remaining core of land around Mysore and Seringapatam was established as a Princely State and restored to the rule of the Wodeyar dynasty, who had ruled the kingdom prior to the takeover by Hyder Ali.

With the fall of the Kingdom of Mysore, the Maratha Empire was the only major power outside of British control.

The Maratha Empire was a confederation of five chiefdoms; Peshwa at Poona, Gaekwad of Baroda, Sindhia of Gwalior, Holkar of Indore and Bhonsle of Nagpur.

The chiefs were often engaged in internal squabbles and when on 25th October 1802, Peshwa Baji Rao II was defeated by Yashwantrao Holkar the ruler of Indore at the Battle of Poona, he sought the protection of the British.

On 31st December 1802, Peshwa Baji Rao II signed the treaty of Bassein with the Company, ceding some of his territory in return for the British maintaining a protecting force on his lands.

The other Maratha chiefs were opposed to this treaty and Sindhia of Gwalior and Bhonsle of Nagpur decided to contest the issue and the 2nd Anglo-Maratha war commenced.

In September 1803, Scindia forces were defeated at Delhi and Assaye and at Laswari in November.

After Bhonsle forces were defeated at the Battle of Argaon on 29th November 1803, Holkar forces decided to enter the war which compelled the British to seek a peace.

On 17th December 1803, Rajhoji Bhonsle II of Nagpur signed the treaty of Deogaon and ceded the British the province of Cuttack and on 30th December Daulat Scindia of Gwalior signed the treaty of Surji-Anjangaon and ceded the British the districts of Rohtak, Gurgaon, Ganges-Jumna Doab, the

Delhi-Agra region, Broach, the fort of Ahmednagar and some parts of Gujarat and Bundelkhand.

After securing an alliance with the Raja of Bharatpur, Yashwantrao Holkar continued his hostilities against the British and it was not until 24th December 1805 that the 2nd Anglo-Maratha War came to a close with the signing of the Treaty of Rajghat. Under the terms of the treaty, Holkar regained much of his land and retained control over most of Rajasthan.

In 1810, the Company took advantage of the war against France to once again gain control of the Dutch Spice Islands. Amboyna which had been handed back to the Dutch (now a dependency of France) by the treaty of Amiens was invaded in February and by the end of the month was under the control of the Company together with the rest of the Banda Isles.

In August 1810, the Company captured Java and was now in control of the lucrative nutmeg trade, this good fortune was to be short lived as the British Government were soon to return the islands to the Dutch.

In 1813, with the 20 year charter coming to an end, a new act of Parliament was required to dictate the operations of the Company in India. Once again the British Crown asserted its sovereignty over the Company territories in India and renewed the charter for a further 20 years. However, the new act removed the Company monopoly in Indian trade except for the trade in tea and the trade with China. The Company was required to maintain separate accounts for its commercial and territorial dealings and India was opened up to missionaries.

The Company continued to expand its territories and after acquiring land from the Nawab of Awadh (Oudh) they had territory close to the region of Gorakhpur in the Kingdom of Nepal.

The Kingdom of Nepal was also expanding its territory and seized the lands of Butwal which was under British protection. The resulting border disputes led to a declaration of war by Britain against Nepal on 1st November 1814 and the start of the Anglo-Nepal (Gorkha) War.

After several battles in very inhospitable lands, the war was ended by the treaty of Sugauli which was ratified on 4th March 1816.

Under the terms of the treaty, Nepal ceded the regions of Sikkim (including Darjeeling), Kumaon, Garhwal and most of Butwal to the Company.

By 1815 a peace had existed between the Company and the Maratha Empire for 10 years, however, due to the actions of the Pindaris, this was soon to change. The Pindaris were a collection of tribes which occupied the Chambal and Malwa regions of central India and each tribe was allied to one or other of the Maratha leaders.

In 1815 a large force of Pindaris, acting as independent robber bands, entered lands under the control of the Madras Presidency and looted and destroyed over 300 villages on the Coramandel Coast. Other bands raided lands controlled by the Nizam of Hyderabad and in the province of Malabar.

The raids continued through 1816 and well into 1817, until the Marquis of Hastings, the Governor-General of India decided enough was enough and stated that the Pindaris would have to be destroyed if peace was to be restored.

Due to the Pindaris alliances with the Maratha leaders, the destruction of the Pindaris led to the start of the 3rd and final Anglo-Maratha (Pindari) War.

To address the problems with the Pindaris, the Marquis of Hastings assembled a large army comprising troops from the Bengal Army that he would command and troops from the Army of the Deccan under the command of General Hislop.

It was assumed that due to the guerrilla nature of the Pindaris warfare that they would never face up to the British in a set battle, the plan was therefore to advance on the Pindaris lands from the north and the south, surround their forces then close the net and destroy them.

In addition to the military offensive the British were involved in diplomatic activity, negotiating with the Maratha leaders to eliminate their support to the Pindaris.

On 13th June 1817 a treaty was signed with the Peshwar leader Baji Rao II at Poona which limited the involvement of the Peshwar for a short time.

The next target was the Shinde (the long time ruling family) of Gwalior and when the British discovered, by the interception of secret messages, that the Shinde were in negotiations with the Peshwa and the Kingdom of Nepal to form an alliance against the British, Daulat Rao Shinde was forced to sign the Treaty of Gwalior on 5th November 1817.

Under the terms of the treaty, the Shinde pledged to support the British and stop new Pindaris gangs being formed in their territory.

Amir Khan of Afghanistan agreed to disband his army and prevent the Pindaris from operating in his territory in return for possession of the Tonk principality in Rajputana.

Despite the diplomatic activity, the forces of Baji Rao II of Peshwar, Mudhoji II Bhonsle of Nagpur and Malharrao Holkar III of Indore did rise up against the British.

The Peshwa was defeated at the Battle of Khadki (Kirkee) on 5th November 1817 and the Battle of Koregaon (near Poona) on 1st January 1818. Baji Rao II was eventually captured and placed on a small estate at Bithoor (near Kanpur) and most of his lands were annexed and became part of the Bombay Presidency. The remaining Peshwar territory was formed as a

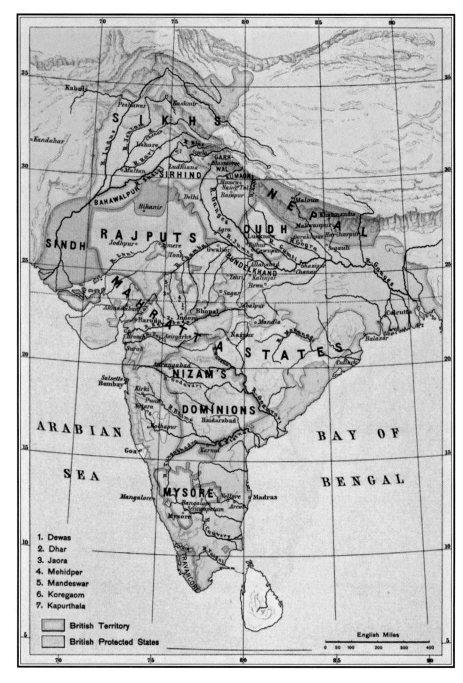

Figure 12. India 1823

princely state and the Maharaja of Satara was restored as the ruler.

The forces of Mudhoji II Bhonsle of Nagpur were decisively defeated at the Battle of Sitabuldi on 26th November 1817 by the British and much of the Bhonsle lands were ceded to the Company.

The forces of Malharrao Holkar III of Indore were defeated at Mahidpur in Malwa on 21st December 1817 by a British force commanded by General Sir Thomas Hislop. The treaty of Mandsaur signed on 6th January 1818 which ceded much of the Holkar lands to the Company was the end of the war.

The Pindaris, whose actions had sparked off the war, were surrounded by the British armies, many of their villages were destroyed and many of their warriors were killed.

The end of the war signalled the end of the Maratha Empire; the northern part of the Bhonsle territory in and around Nagpur, together with the Peshwar territories in Bundelkhand were annexed by the Company and became the Saugor and Nerbudda Territories.

The states of Gwalior from Shinde and Jhansi from Peshwar were also acquired by the Company and all of these territories were established as Princely States under British Control.

The Company trading activities had been in decline for some years and revenue from trade in India, since the loss of its monopoly in 1813 was dwarfed by that derived from its administrative duties on behalf of the Crown.

Trade from the Philippines, Java and especially China was still providing significant income, however, the purchase of tea from

China was dependent upon the export of Indian grown Opium to China which was being resisted by the Chinese Government and would eventually lead to the 1st Opium War in 1839.

With this background, the Government of India Act 1833, which became law on 28th August 1833, would result in a step change in the Company operations.

The act removed all of the Company's remaining trade monopolies and divested it of its commercial functions effectively bringing to an end the Company trading activities.

However, the act also renewed for a further 20 years the Company's political and administrative authority in India, which was still to be managed by a Board of Control that would be the final authority for all civil and military matters.

In 1835 the English Education Act was enacted by the Council of India, this redirected the funds that the Company was required to spend on education and literature in India from traditional Muslim and Hindu education and languages to a western curriculum with English as the language of instruction.

It was this act that led to English becoming the language of Administration and within the Law Courts in India and establishing English as one of the languages of the Indian people rather than just the language of its foreign rulers.

General Charles James Napier was appointed to the command of the Indian army in the Bengal Presidency during May 1842 and the following year, on the instruction of Lord Ellenborough the Governor-General of India, lead an invasion of the Sindh province.

The purpose of the invasion of Sindh was to quell the rebellion of some Muslim leaders who still remained hostile to Britain following the 1st Anglo-Afghan War.

The rebels were defeated at the Battle of Miani on 17th February 1843 and the Battle of Hyderabad on 24th March 1843 which brought the rebellion to an end.

Having defeated the rebels, General Napier went on to subdue the whole of the Sindh province whose lands were annexed by the Company.

In 1845, the British purchased the colony of Tranquebar on the east coast from the Danish and all of the Danish possessions in India were transferred to the Company.

In the late 1830s, the Sikh Kingdom of the Punjab was being expanded under the rule of Maharaja Ranjit Singh, who taking advantage of the disunity within Afghanistan, captured the provinces of Peshawar and Muttan and the states of Jammu and Kashmir from the Afghans and incorporated these territories within the Sikh Empire.

In the early 1840s the British were consolidating and expanding their territories which bordered the Punjab, establishing a large military presence at Ferozepur near the border with the Punjab and in 1843 they annexed the province of Sindh to the south of the Punjab.

These moves caused much distrust and concern between the two parties and when diplomatic relations broke down the British moved elements of the Bombay army to reinforce their troops at Ferozepur and in response the Sikh army crossed the Sutlej River on 11th December 1845.

The British viewed this move by the Sikh army to be an invasion of their territory and declared war, thus starting the 1st Anglo-Sikh War.

Elements of the Sikh army moved towards Ferozepur, where they did not engage with the British forces but maintained a watching brief. The remainder of the Sikh army moved towards the Bengal army commanded by Sir Hugh Gough and Sir Henry Hardinge which was moving to reinforce Ferozepur. These forces clashed and fought the Battle of Mudki on 18th December and a few days later at the Battle of Ferozeshah on 21st–22nd December, both of which were British victories.

A further force of the Sikh army crossed the Sutlej River and were engaged and defeated by troops commanded by Sir Harry Smith at the Battle of Aliwal on 28th January 1846.

After joining up with the force commanded by Sir Harry Smith, the army commanded by Sir Hugh Gough fought the decisive action of the war on 10th February 1846 when the Sikh army was defeated at the Battle of Sobraon.

The war was formally concluded with the treaty of Lahore which was signed on 9th March 1846, under the terms of which the Sikh Empire ceded the regions of Jullundur Doab, Kashmir and Hazarah to the Company.

A few days later on 16th March, under the terms of the treaty of Amritsar, Gulab Singh the Rajah of Jammu purchased Kashmir from the Company and was recognised as the Maharaja of Jammu and Kashmir.

The treaty of Bhyroval, which was signed on 16th December 1846 allowed the Maharaja Duleep Singh to remain as the ruler of the Punjab but established a British Resident at Lahore who had control over the government of the region.

On 18th December 1846, the Sultan of Borneo Omar Ali Saifuddin II ceded the islands of Labuan to the Company, to be used as a base to combat the Chinese pirates who were disrupting trade in the area.

Following the end of the 1st Anglo-Sikh war in 1846, there was much local resentment regarding British control over the Punjab by the installation of Sir Henry Lawrence as Resident at Lahore.

In early 1848, Sir Lawrence left for England on sick leave and was replaced by Sir Frederick Currie who, being based in

Calcutta, was unfamiliar with the delicate political and military situation in the region.

Sir Frederick Currie also had little confidence in his subordinate Residents and Political Agents and refused to act upon reports from James Abbott, the Political Agent for Hazara, who was convinced that the Governor of Hazara, Sardar Chattor Singh Attariwalla was actively planning rebellion.

There was also trouble at the City of Multan where the Hindu Viceroy, Dewan Mulraj, was trying to act independently from the Resident at Lahore and refused to pay an increase in taxes.

When Dewan Mulraj attempted to transfer his powers to his son, Sir Frederick Currie instead imposed a Sikh Governor, Sardar Khan Singh with a British Political Agent Lieutenant Patrick Vans Agnew to control the city.

On 18th April 1848, when Lieutenant Vans Agnew and Lieutenant William Anderson with a small escort, arrived at the city to assume control they were attacked and wounded by some of Dewan Mulraj's irregular troops and a mob from the city.

The British officers were rescued from the mob by men loyal to Sardar Khan Singh and moved to a mosque just outside the city. The next day both officers were murdered by the mob after their escort had fled. These actions prompted the start of the 2nd Anglo-Sikh war.

News of the murders fermented further unrest as it spread across the Punjab and prompted large numbers of Sikh soldiers to desert from regiments that stayed loyal to the British. Many of these men joined the army of rebels being assembled by Dewan Mulraj and other disaffected Sardars.

On hearing the news from Multan, Lieutenant Herbert Benjamin Edwardes, the Political Agent of nearby Bannu, raised a force of Pashtun irregulars and some units from the Sikh army and attacked Mulraj's army which he defeated at the Battle of Kineyri on 18th June 1848.

After the battle, Lieutenant Edwardes with his force chased the rebels back to the city of Multan but due to the lack of men was unable to storm the fortified city, which he besieged instead.

On learning of the situation at Multan, Sir Frederick Currie wrote to the Commander in Chief of the Bengal Army, Sir Hugh Gough, requesting that a large force be sent immediately to Multan.

However, General Gough, with the support of the Governor-General James Broun-Ramsey the 1st Marquis of Dalhousie, decided not to send any major units of the army to the Punjab until the end of the hot weather and the monsoon season, which would not be until November.

A small force under the command of General Whish was sent to Multan from the Bengal Army and with locally recruited irregulars and units from the Sikh Army they joined up with the force of Lieutenant Edwardes, in mid August, to enforce the siege.

Much to the consternation of the local Political Agents, a large contingent from the Sikh army was under the command of Sardar Sher Singh Attariwalla, the son of rebel leader Chattar Singh.

Political Agent Captain John Nicholson, leading irregular cavalry from Peshawar, seized the strategic fort at Attock before the Sikh garrison could join the rebellion and then joined up with the force of Political Agent James Abbott from Hazara and occupied the Margalla Hills which separated Hazara from the rest of the Punjab.

When the forces of Chattar Singh rebelled at Hazara in August 1848 the British occupation of the Margalla Hills was instrumental in keeping them confined to the city limits despite their attempts to break through to the rest of the Punjab.

On 14th September 1848, the contingent of the Sikh army commanded by Sher Singh revolted but instead of joining the forces of Dewar Malraj's force in Multan marched off into central Punjab and eventually joined up with the forces of Chattar Singh.

Due to the loss of a large part of his force, General Whish was forced to raise the siege of Multan and await the arrival of reinforcements.

In November 1848, with the arrival of the cold and dry season, the Company finally began to commit significant contingents from their armies to the conflict. A contingent was sent from the Bombay army to reinforce the troops of General Whish and re-establish the siege of Multan. A large force from the Bengal army, under the command of General Sir Hugh Gough, was sent to engage with Sher Singh's army which had established a defensive line on the banks of the Chenab River.

The armies of General Gough and Sher Singh fought the Battle of Ramnugger on 22nd November 1848. The outcome of the battle was inconclusive with both sides claiming some sort of victory, however, the Sikhs were forced to abandon their bridgehead which allowed General Gough to move his force across the River Chenab in early December.

In January 1849, Amir Dost Mohammed Khan, the leader of Afghanistan, joined the war on the side of the Sikh rebels and ceded the city of Peshawar to the Sikhs.

Afghan forces captured Fort Attock when the Muslim garrison installed by Captain John Nicholson defected. The loss of this strategically placed fort opened up an alternative route which allowed Chattar Singh to leave Hazara without having to cross the Margalla Hills; Chattar Singh's army was now free to try and join up with the Sikh army commanded by his son.

Following the fall of Fort Attock, instead of waiting for the fall of Multan and the opportunity to join up with the force of

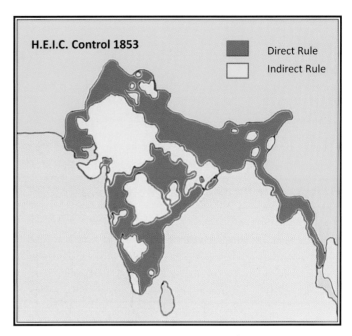

Figure 13. HEIC control 1853

General Whish, General Gough set off in pursuit of Sher Singh's army, the priority now being to destroy the army before it was joined by the army of Chattar Singh.

General Gough's army caught up with the army of Sher Singh near the Jhelum River on 13th January 1849 and although it was late in the day he decided to launch an attack against the Sikhs. The resulting Battle of Chillianwala was a hard fought affair with heavy losses on both sides. The battle was followed by three days of heavy rain, which prevented the forces re-engaging, following which each force withdrew. The battle was a strategic victory for the Sikhs as it allowed Sher Singh to continue his journey northwards to join forces with his father Chattar Singh.

After the city was pounded by heavy artillery and the defensive walls breached, the forces of General Whish stormed and captured the city of Multan on 22nd January 1849. The rebel leader Dewar Malraj was forced to surrender and was imprisoned for life by the Company.

With the end of the siege, General Whish was now able to join forces with General Gough, where the additional men and more importantly, heavy artillery would play a vital role in bringing the war to a close.

The combined force attacked the Sikh army on 13th February 1849 at the Battle of Gujrat, which began with a three hour bombardment of the Sikh position by 100 guns which had arrive with General Whish's force. In the four hour battle the Sikhs suffered heavy losses and were force to flee the battle field.

Gujrat proved to be the decisive battle of the war, Chattar and Sher Singh surrendered near Rawalpindi on 12th March 1849.

With the surrender of the Sikhs the Afghans withdrew from Fort Attock and the city of Peshawar and returned to Afghanistan. The Afghan leader Dost Mohammed Khan would later sign a treaty which acknowledged the British right to these possessions.

The war was formally ended on 29th March, when Maharaja Duleep Singh signed a treaty at Lahore where he ceded the whole of the Punjab to the Company ending the Sikh Empire; he was granted a pension for life to support himself and his family. He also handed over the famous Kohinoor diamond (Mountain of Light), which is now part of the British Crown Jewels.

In 1853, another Government of India Act was passed by the British Parliament; this extended the Company administration of India, on behalf of the Crown, for an indefinite period, until Parliament should decide otherwise. By this time almost all of India was under the direct or indirect control of the Honourable East India Company.

Under the Act, the legislative and executive powers of the Governor General's Council were separated for the first time and a system of open competition was introduced to be the basis for recruitment of the Company Civil Servants, in place of the previous system which was based upon patronage.

On 13th February 1856, one of the last actions of the outgoing Governor-General Lord Dalhousie was the annexation of the province of Oudh on the grounds that it was no longer capable of governing itself.

The events of the Indian Mutiny, which resulted in much devastation across India, signalled the death knell of the East India Company as it was concluded in many quarters that the Company was responsible for some of the conditions that led to mutiny and were ineffective in preventing such an outbreak to occur.

In the aftermath of the Mutiny, the government of Benjamin Disraeli enacted the Government of India Act 1858, which was given royal assent on 2nd August 1858 and Lord Canning was appointed as the first Viceroy of India by Queen Victoria.

Under the provisions of this Act, the East India Company was nationalised and the Crown took over total control of its possessions in India with the Company Administrative machinery (Civil Service) and armed forces.

The company remained in existence, managing the tea trade on behalf of the British Government until the end of 1873 when the East India Stock Dividend Redemption Act came into effect on 1st January 1874. This act formally dissolved the Company on 1st June 1874, after payment of a final dividend and redemption of stock.

On 18th April 1873, on the eve of the Act coming into law, *The Times* summarised the extraordinary accomplishments of the Company as follows: *"Now when it passes away with the solemnities of Parliamentary sepulchre, out of the land of the living, it is just as well, as becoming, to record that it accomplished a work such as in the whole history of the human race no other trading company ever attempted and as such as none surely is likely to attempt in years to come."*

Honourable East India Company training establishments

As the scale and nature of the Company's involvement in India changed, with their movement from being primarily a merchant trading concern to that of managing and expanding an Empire, there was an increasing need for a ready supply of appropriately trained young men to serve in the administration and army of the Company.

To secure this supply of new employees the Company established a training establishment in India and two training establishments in England.

College of Fort William

Fort William College was founded on 10th July 1800, by the then Governor-General Lord Wellesley as a training establishment aimed at training British officials in Indian Languages.

In addition to training in the official languages of Sanskrit and Hindi, the college also fostered the development of languages such as Bengali and Urdu. Other oriental languages such as Arabic, Chinese and Persian were also taught.

Employing around 100 Indian linguists, the college was also responsible for translating thousands of books written in Sanskrit, Arabic, Persian, Bengali, Hindi and Urdu into English.

The college, which was located within the Fort William military complex at Calcutta, was dissolved in 1854 by the Dalhousie administration.

Haileybury College

In 1806, the Company founded the East India College as a training establishment for "writers" (Clerks and Administrators) in the Company's service.

Initially the college was established in Hertford Castle but in February 1809 moved to purpose built premises at Haileybury, Hertford Heath in Hertfordshire.

Until 1856, when an open and competitive examination system was introduced, entrance to the college and the security of a sometimes lucrative employment with the Honourable East India Company was by patronage rather than ability. However, attendance at the college did result in employees who at least met the minimum standards required for Company employment.

In January 1858, after the British Government took over the administration of India in the wake of the Indian Mutiny, the college was closed.

In 1862, a public school was established in the HEIC buildings at Haileybury and in 1942 merged with the Imperial Service College to become the Haileybury and Imperial Service College.

Addiscombe College

The East India Company Military Seminary was opened at Addiscombe in Surrey on 21st January 1809 as a college to

Fig 14. Haileybury College

Figure 15. Addiscombe Military Seminary

train young officers for service in the Company's armies in India.

Prior to the opening of the college at Addiscombe, the Companies officers had been trained at the Royal Military Academy at Woolwich, the Royal Military College at Great Marlow or privately.

Addiscombe had a Junior Academy, which cadets entered at the age of 13½ and spent 6 months to prepare for entry into the Senior College. Cadets entered the Senior College between the ages of 14 and 16 and were required to pay annual fees of £30, raised to £50 in 1835. Admission examinations were held in January and July and the cadets usually remained at the college for two years with about 150 in residence at any one time.

Originally, the purpose of the college was to train cadets destined to be Engineering or Artillery officers but later this was changed to include all arms of the service.

The curriculum included instruction in the "sciences of Mathematics, Fortification, Natural Philosophy and Chemistry". Instruction in the art of Civil, Military and Lithographic Drawing and Surveying and the construction of gun-carriages and mortar beds as used in the Artillery was also provided together with a smattering of language skills in Hindustani, Latin and French.

Cadets passed out of the college after three weeks of examinations in July or December, which culminated in a 1 day public examination which include both academic and practical exercises.

In its 52 years of existence, 3,600 cadets passed through the college providing 500 Engineering Officers, 1,100 Artillery Officers and 2,000 Infantry officers; many of whom would go on to have distinguished military careers.

In 1855 the college name was changed to the East India Company Military College and in 1858, after the Company was nationalised, to the Royal India Military College and was finally closed in June 1861.

Other HEIC establishments in England
Company headquarters

The Company occupied premises in Philpot Lane, Fenchurch Street from 1600 until 1621 when it moved to Crosby House, Bishopsgate before moving to Leadenhall Street in 1638.

Figure 16. East India House (c. 1800)

In 1838 the London Headquarters, from which much of the Indian Empire would be governed, moved to Craven House in Leadenhall Street.

By 1661, this former Elizabethan mansion was known as East India House. The building was enlarged and completely rebuilt in 1726–29 and further remodelling and expansion was carried out from 1796–1800.

The building was finally vacated by the Company in 1860.

Shipbuilding

In 1607, the Company decided to start building its own ships and leased a shipyard at Deptford, on the River Thames for this purpose.

By 1614, the needs of the Company had outgrown the small yard at Deptford and new facilities were acquired at Blackwall which became fully operational in 1617.

For some years after moving to Blackwall, the Company still had ships built and repaired at Deptford, which had continued to operate under new ownership.

The ships which plied the Company Trade, known as East Indiamen, were generally of excellent construction, such that when they came available for resale they were often purchased by the Royal Navy.

Nemesis, which was built for the Company at the Birkenhead Ironworks, was the first British built iron clad ocean going warship and the first warship to be fitted with internal watertight bulkheads.

Dockyards

In 1803, following an Act of Parliament which gave the Company a 21-year monopoly for handling the trade with the East Indies, the Company formed the East India Dock Company, with the aim of establishing new docks (the East India Docks) to handle the trade.

The Brunswick Dock, which was part of the Company shipbuilding site at Blackwall, was used as the Export Dock and a new dock was built on the site which became the Import Dock.

Together with the West India Dock Company the East India Dock Company financed the construction of Commercial Road, to provide a suitable link between the docks and the city.

The traffic from the East India Docks was mainly to and from massive Company warehouse facilities at Cutler Street which covered 5 acres and employed 400 clerks and 4,000 warehousemen.

The docks were taken over by the Port of London Authority in 1909 and closed down in 1967.

Figure 17. East India Shipbuilding Yard at Deptford (c. 1660)

Figure 18. East India Docks (c. 1800)

Care of the insane

In 1818, the Company entered in an agreement with Pembroke House in Hackney (a private lunatic asylum) for the care of Company personnel who had been certified as insane in India.

The arrangement continued until 1870, at which time the India Office opened its own facilities, the Royal India Asylum at Hanwell in Middlesex.

Officers club

In 1849, the East India Club was opened in London for use by the officers of the Company. The club still exists as a private gentlemen's club with its premises at 16 & 17 St James's Square in London.

Figure 19. East India Club

PART TWO

WARS, BATTLES AND DEEDS

THE INDIAN MUTINY

The events of the Indian Mutiny unfold in many locations in a compressed time scale and if outlined in strict chronological sequence would result in an almost incomprehensive narrative.

I have therefore decided to describe the events, campaign by campaign which hopefully is more enjoyable for the reader, unfortunately this does mean that the Victoria Cross deeds are not described in chronological order.

The biographical summaries of each recipient, however, are in date order in the appendices of the final volume of this work.

3

INTRODUCTION

Territory at time of Mutiny

By the time of the Mutiny, the Honourable East India Company was administering much of the Indian sub-continent on behalf of the British Crown. The land was divided into; independent kingdoms, British dominions, British protected states and French and Portuguese trading posts.

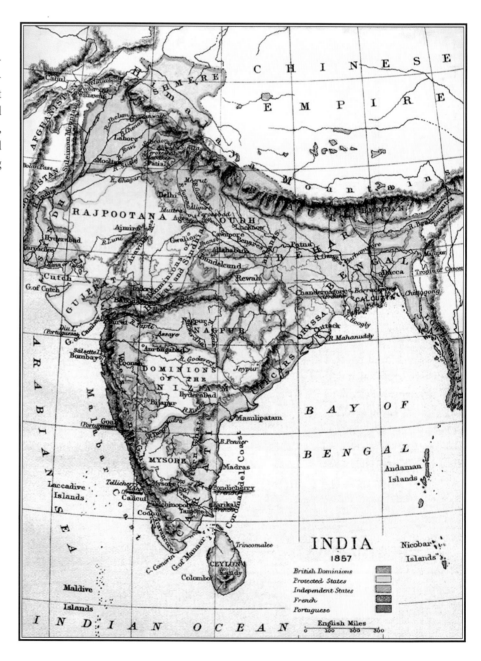

Figure 20. India 1857

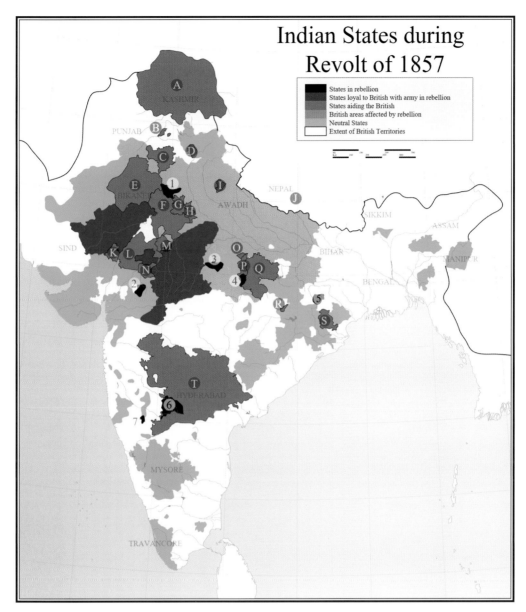

Figure 21. Extent of the Indian Mutiny

The French trading posts were at Mahé on the Malabar Coast; Pondicherry, Karikal and Yanaon on the Coromandel Coast and Chandemagor in Bengal.

The Portuguese trading posts were at Goa on the Malabar Coast and Diu in the state of Gujarat.

The independent kingdoms of Kashmir and Nepal, sided with the British during the time of the mutiny.

The following Princely States protected by the British also aided the British during the mutiny: Kapurthala, Patiala, Simur, Bikaner, Jaipur, Alwar, Bharathpur, Rampur, Sirohi, Mewar, Bundi, Jaora, Bijawar, Ajaigarh, Rewa, Udaipur, Keonjhar and Hyderabad.

Many other states remained neutral and were not involved in the mutiny.

The states that came out in open revolt against the British during the mutiny were: Jhajjar, Dadri, Farukhnagar, Bahadurgarh, Amjhera, Shagarh, Biaj Raghogarh, Singhbum, Nargund and Shorapur.

HEIC Army at start of Mutiny

By the time of the mutiny, the Honourable East India Company was no longer a trading company but was an agent of the British Government with responsibility for the government and administration of the British dominions in India.

To fulfil this role, the Company employed a large number of officials operating a centralised bureaucracy to administer the affairs of British India.

The Company responsibilities also extended to maintaining the peace and protecting the British territories and to meet this obligation they maintained their own armies.

The HEIC had three independent armies maintained by each of the Presidencies of Bengal, Madras and Bombay.

Employment as a soldier in the HEIC Army (infantrymen were known as Sepoys and cavalrymen as Sowars) was generally much valued by the Indian population as the soldier received an

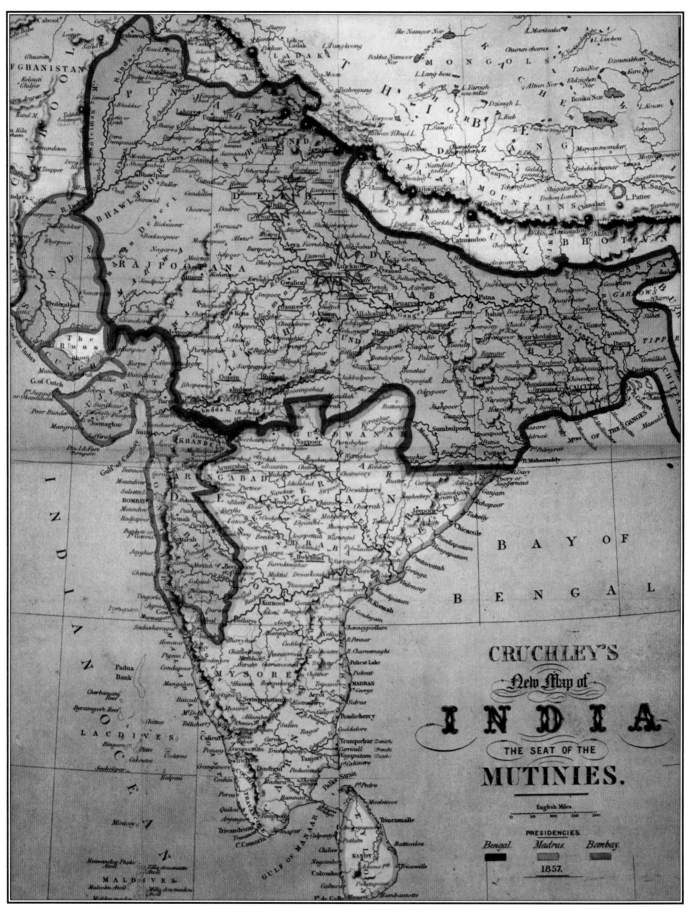

Figure 22. HEIC Presidencies

income greater than could be attained by most, they also received accommodation and food and at the end of their employment were guaranteed a pension.

Each army was made up of European Regiments and Native Regiments with Infantry, Engineers (Sappers & Miners), Cavalry and Artillery units.

Each Native regiment had both British and Indian Officers, however, the most senior Indian Officer was only on a par with the British Sergeant-Major.

Various regiments of the British Army (known as the Queen's Regiments) also served in India under the overall command of the Commander-in-Chief India to provide support to the HEIC Armies.

The normal ratio between the two forces was one British to every three native soldiers, however, at the time of the mutiny, due to the need to provide forces to the Crimean War and unrest in China and Burma, this had fallen to almost one to eight.

In April 1857, according to a return made to the Houses of Parliament, there were 299,545 troops in the army in India made up of: elements of 26 British Army regiments (Royal Troops) with 808 officers and 23,455 men; 214 regiments of Company Troops with a total of 253,481 troops made up from 5,362 European Officers, 16,331 European NCOs and other ranks and 227,639 native soldiers.

In total the combined armies in India amounted to almost 300,000 men; 46,000 Europeans and 254,000 Native soldiers.

4

THE SEEDS OF MUTINY

Previous mutinies

Although mutiny within the ranks of the Native Regiments of the HEIC armies was not an everyday occurrence, it was not unheard of, with several having occurred over the years.

Vellore 1806

On 10th July 1806, three Battalions of the Madras Native Infantry mutinied at Fort Vellore in the state of Mysore. The mutineers turned on four companies of the 69th Regiment of Foot who were also part of the forts garrison and after killing or wounding around 200 of the English soldiers, raised the flag of Mysore and declared Fateh Hyder to be their king.

The mutiny was very quickly subdued by a force of 19th Light Dragoons led by Sir Rollo Gillespie and supported by artillery that arrived from Arcot on the same day.

The main reason for the mutiny was put down to minor changes in the Sepoy dress code, introduced to give a more "soldierly appearance". These changes introduced a new headdress to replace the turban and prohibited Hindus from wearing religious marks on their forehead, Muslims were also required to shave of their beards and trim their moustaches.

Although there were valid religious reasons for concern, the flames of mutiny were undoubtedly fanned, if not instigated, by the sons of Tipu Sultan, the deposed sultan of Mysore.

Barrackpore 1824

In late 1824, troops were being assembled at Barrackpore, in preparation for a move to Chittagong and onward transportation to Rangoon (by sea) to take part in the 1st Anglo-Burmese War.

The 47th regiment of the Bengal Army comprised of mainly high caste men who were reluctant to go to Chittagong as a sea voyage to foreign lands was not permitted by their religion.

Another cause for concern was that, again for religious reasons, the men were required to take all their personal possession with them, however, the army would not provide bullock carts only knapsacks.

The men appointed Bindee Tiwari to represent their concerns, however, these were summarily dismissed by the authorities.

On hearing this news, the men mutinied and turned on the British Officers; after two days the rebellion was broken up by British artillery fired into the men.

Bindee Tiwari and other leaders were hung and the regiment was disbanded and removed from the army list.

This incident nearly led to the recall of the British Governor-General, Lord Amherst and the military authorities were heavily criticised for their handling of the affair and the harshness of the punishments handed out.

Bolarum 1855

Several other minor mutinies occurred in the 1840s and 1850s such as the mutiny at Bolarum in September 1855.

The causes of mutiny

The 1857 mutiny was different in two respects to all previous mutinies; the scale of the rebellion was very much larger than previous incidents and for the first time significant numbers from the civil population were involved in the unrest. Some of the causes had been the reasons for earlier mutinies which should have been resolved.

Like most children of my era who were educated in England, I was taught that the Indian Mutiny broke out due to religious reasons resulting from the requirement of the sepoys to use tallowed cartridges.

I now know that the reasons were far more complex than this, with: political, economic, military, religious and social issues, some of which only affected the military but others which also affected the civil population; also contributing to the reasons for mutiny.

Dalhousie's reforms

On 12th January 1848, James Broun-Ramsay, the Earl of Dalhousie took up his position as Governor-General of India and Governor of the Bengal Presidency and immediately he began a series of reforms and projects aimed at the modernisation and Europeanisation of British India.

New Engineering colleges and a Public Works department were established to create or upgrade; telegraphs, railways, ports and metalled roads. He also encouraged the tea plantations to provide the infrastructure needed to take away their products. The Ganges canal was built to irrigate large areas of central India. A postal system was also introduced.

These changes were introduced to help improve the efficiency of the operation of the colony, which they did, however, in some quarters they were viewed as attempts by the Company to erode the Indian culture.

The improved infrastructure and communications also had a negative effect on some Indian jobs and businesses mainly

Figure 23. Lord Dalhousie

in haulage and farming, where local monopolies were being challenged by cheaper imports from other parts of India or further afield.

The progress of the industrial revolution in Britain meant that many businesses were seeking worldwide markets for their cheap mass produced goods and India fitted the bill.

The short term investment cost, required to implement these changes also placed a higher burden on the already strained taxation system.

One of the new taxes was a tax on land ownership; failure to pay this tax resulted in the land being confiscated by the Company. This caused much hardship and resentment amongst the already hard pressed farming communities.

Lord Dalhousie also encouraged Christian missionaries and societies to set up missions to care for the needy and the low caste Indians.

Although well intentioned, this was viewed as an attempt by the Company to convert India into a Christian society. This problem was further exacerbated by some British Officers, who emboldened by the stance of Lord Dalhousie, began preaching to their sepoys.

The Company were also making changes to the conditions for women; the practice of Suttee, where a widow committed suicide by throwing herself on her husband's funeral pyre, was being outlawed and legislation was being introduced which allowed widows to remarry.

Together with changes that encouraged the education of women, these reforms were viewed as further evidence of the Company's intention to destroy the Indian culture and religions.

The Doctrine of Lapse

One of Lord Dalhousie's most controversial and divisive reforms was the "Doctrine of Lapse", which allowed the Company to annex the lands of any Indian ruler who died without natural heirs. It had long been the accepted practice that rulers without heirs would adopt an heir to avoid succession issues, however, this custom was outlawed by the doctrine of lapse.

The Company thought that this doctrine would be an easy way to increase territory and the attendant tax revenues, without having to go to the expense of military conquest.

Satara was the first state to be annexed under this doctrine, when the ruler Prince Shaji Raja died without a male heir in 1848; this was closely followed by the states of Nagpur in 1849, Bhagat and Sanbalpur in 1850 and Jaipur and Jhansi in 1853.

Land acquired by the Company in this way left behind many disaffected people, who had seen themselves deprived of their lands, many of whom would later cause disruption during the mutiny.

The doctrine of lapse also allowed the Company to annex lands where they determined that the current ruler was incompetent and or corrupt. In 1856, the state of Oudh was acquired in this way.

The annexing of the province of Oudh would prove to be a significant event in the lead up to the mutiny as it disaffected much of the local population and large numbers of the Bengal Army who came from Oudh.

Prophesies and rumours

Towards the end of 1856, rumours were spreading regarding a prophesy that foretold the Company rule would end after 100 years, on the centenary of the Battle of Plassey, on 23rd June 1857.

At about the same time, Chapattis and Lotus flowers began to be distributed between villages; this was a form of chain letter, with villages obliged to pass on to the next village to avoid the occurrence of calamitous events.

By many this was viewed as the harbinger of widespread violent disruption, which indeed proved to be the case.

Military issues and changing attitudes

For many years the British Officers had cultivated an excellent relationship with the Sepoys within their regiments which bred mutual respect and intense loyalty from the Sepoys. At this time many of the officers spoke the local languages, shared the same quarters and food as their men and importantly had fought side by side with them during many conflicts.

As the role of the Company changed and their armies expanded, the officers attracted to serve with the Company also changed, with many of the new men having previously served in the British Army.

Slowly the officers became more distant from their men, establishing separate officers quarters where increasing they resided with wives and family brought over from England. This had a seriously detrimental effect on the relationship between officers and their men.

One example of this was that, the long term custom and practice of the native soldiers, was that it was legitimate to withhold their service and refuse to perform duties as part of the process of resolving disputes.

This of course was anathema to the new breed of officers who viewed the refusal to obey orders as the most heinous crime of mutiny, which needed a harsh response rather than negotiation.

Over the years, the Sepoys and general native population's attitude to the Company had also deteriorated. For some time it had been viewed as being fair and benevolent as well as being invincible. However, recent events had slowly changed this attitude with the Company now being viewed as being unjust, uncaring and following some defeats in recent wars was no longer thought to be invincible.

In some quarters, the recent changes imposed on the Company by the British Government were thought to signal the possible demise of the Company.

At the time of the mutiny, the number of regular British Army troops in India was at a low point with very few resources in northern India.

Most of the British troops in Bengal had been moved west to secure the Punjab and the only remaining units were battalions at Calcutta and Dinapore and regiments at Agra and Lucknow.

A large proportion of the Bengal army had been recruited from high caste Bhumihor Brahmins and Rajputs from the Ganges valley and as such were from the landed gentry and were personally affected by Lord Dalhousie's reforms such as the doctrine of lapse and land taxation.

An unexpected effect of the doctrine of lapse was that with the acquisition of provinces like Sindh, Awadh and Punjab by the Company, Sepoys serving in these areas no longer received "Batta" the payment for service abroad, i.e. in lands beyond the borders of Company rule.

Tallow cartridges

In August 1856, the Company began to replace the India pattern musket "Brown Bess" with the Enfield 1853 pattern musket, which due to its rifled barrel had greater range and was more accurate.

Both muskets were muzzle loaders but the Enfield rifle used a new design of cartridge which contained a measured charge of powder and a bullet of the minié design.

To prepare the Enfield for firing, it was required to remove the end of the cartridge (the training manual recommended removal with the teeth), pour the powder into the barrel and then place the cartridge which now just contained the bullet into the barrel and using a ramrod tamp down onto the powder. In order to ease the passage of the cartridge down the barrel it was lubricated with tallow.

Almost as soon as the new weapon was distributed to centres for training in its use, rumours began to circulate that the new cartridges were greased with pig and cow fat, which if placed in the mouth of a devout Hindu or Muslim would invalidate their caste.

Figure 24. Tallow cartridge

Local British officers were quick to recognise this as an issue and the original batches of cartridges despatched from England with the new rifles were soon withdrawn. Facilities at the arsenal at Dum Dum, which were to be used for the continued production of cartridges, were used to create ungreased cartridges.

These ungreased cartridges were issued to replace the greased cartridges, with instructions that they should be greased by the Sepoys themselves using ghee, vegetable oil or any other material that they considered suitable. The Sepoys were also informed that they could use their fingers rather than teeth to tear off the end of the cartridge if they preferred.

Despite all of these measures, which should have nullified the issue, the cartridges were the spark that ultimately ignited the mutiny.

It is rather ironic that the mutineers had no trouble in using the new rifles and cartridges against the British forces during the mutiny.

5

THE OUTBREAK OF MUTINY

Rumours regarding the greased cartridges had been circulating since before the turn of the year, however, on 23rd January 1857 at Dum Dum, one of the three training centres for instruction in use of the new Enfield rifle, things were about to escalate.

Mutiny at Berhampore and Barrackpore

A low caste Lascar[2] asked a Brahmin Sepoy for a drink of water from his drinking vessel, when the Sepoy refused because of the difference in caste, the Laskar taunted the Brahmin that everyone would be reduced to the same low caste as himself because the British were requiring all soldiers to bite the end off cartridges smeared with cow and hog fat.

The Brahmin was devastated by the news and when he returned to his regiment based at nearby Barrackpore he informed his comrades of the news. Secret midnight meetings were held by the Sepoys to discuss the cartridges and as a protest they began to start fires at Company buildings, Officers bungalows and the telegraph station were burned down.

To try and resolve the problem, General Hearsey convened a special court of inquiry at Barrackpore on 6th February 1857. The inquiry heard evidence from Sepoys and their native officers regarding their concerns about the cartridges and provided information to the Sepoys about the actual situation and the fact that they could grease the cartridges themselves. The arguments failed to convince the Sepoys and hearing about the possibility of mutiny General Hearsey ordered a special parade for 9th February, at which he explained to the Sepoys, in their own language, that neither the Army nor Government had any intention of destroying their castes or trying to harm their religions or to convert them to Christianity.

General Hearsey's words seemed to have the desired effect, the tension was alleviated and the men quietened down,

unfortunately all of General Hearsey's good work was soon to be undone by events that occurred elsewhere.

At Berhampore, the 19th Regiment of Native Infantry, like many of the Sepoys in the army had heard the rumours regarding the cartridges, however, when a small detachment of the 34th Regiment arrived from Dum Dum on 24th February and confirmed the rumours; they started to take things more seriously.

On 26th February 1857, the 19th Regiment refused to accept blank ammunition being handed out at parade for use in an exercise later that day. Despite being informed of the serious nature of their action and the fact that the ammunition in question was actually nearly a year old and had been put together by men of 7th Native Infantry, the men still refused to accept the ammunition.

The men were dismissed while the commanding officer Lieutenant-Colonel Mitchell considered what action was to be taken against the men. The dispute escalated further that evening when the Sepoys broke into the armoury and retrieved their muskets and ammunition. Lieutenant-Colonel Mitchell turned out the Cavalry and Artillery and the men were eventually convinced to lay down their arms.

When news of the incident reached Calcutta on 4th March, the Governor-General decided that strong action should be taken against the mutineers, however, as there was only one British regiment between Calcutta and Dinapore (300 miles away) he despatched the steamer *Bentinck* to Rangoon to bring troops from the 84th Regiment of Foot.

A few days later two men from the 2nd Native Infantry Regiment, who were on duty as part of the guard at Fort William, tried to rally support for an uprising against the garrison. They were immediately arrested by native officers, tried by a native court martial and sentenced to 14 years hard labour.

On 17th March, General Hearsey again addressed the regiment at Barrackpore; after reconfirming all that was said during his previous address, the General informed the troops of the action to be taken against the 19th (i.e. that they were to be

---

2 Soldier

Figure 25. Mangal Pandy

By now General Hearsey had been informed and he sent off messages to Colonel Reed, Commanding Officer of the 84th Regiment of Foot at Chinsurah and Colonel Amsinck commanding officer at Dum Dum requesting help to put down an insurrection.

General Hersey, his two sons (who were also officers in the regiment) and Major Ross rode to the parade ground and when they confronted Mughal Pandy, he turned his rifle on himself and fired into his chest. Mangal Pandy was arrested and rushed to hospital where his wound was found to be not that serious.

On 31st March 1857, the 19th Native Infantry arrived at Barrackpore and with the help of; the 84th Regiment of Foot, a wing of the 53rd Regiment of Foot and two batteries of European Artillery; were disarmed and disbanded in front of the 34th Native Infantry.

Despite their crime, the men of the 19th were treated very leniently as they were allowed to keep their uniforms and were given a sum of money to pay for their travel home.

On 7th April 1857, Mangal Pandy was tried by a native court martial, found guilty of using violence against his officers, sentenced to death and was hanged the next day. An officer, Issuree Pandy, who had ordered men of the 34th not to go to the aid of their officers was also tried, convicted, sentenced to death and was also hanged, on 21st April at Barrackpore.

A special court of inquiry, into the behaviour of the 34th during the Pandy incident was held at Barrackpore, which found the 7 companies of the regiment stationed at Barrackpore complicit in the mutiny and on 6th May, these companies were disarmed and disbanded.

disbanded in front of other troops at Barrackpore) and that other British troops were coming to the station to ensure this was carried out safely. He also advised that they were not in trouble as they had done nothing wrong.

On 20th March 1857, the steamer *Bentinck* arrived back at Calcutta and the 84th Regiment of Foot was disembarked; the 19th Native Infantry had begun their march to Barrackpore but were not expected to arrive until 31st March.

On 29th March 1857, the first shots of the Mutiny were fired when a Sepoy Mangal Pandy, who was intoxicated with bhang,[3] turned out in front of the quarter-guard and after exhorting his comrades to take action in support of the 19th Native Infantry, fired a shot at Sergeant-Major James Hewson.

Having been informed of the event, Adjutant Lieutenant Henry Baugh rode up to the scene and Mangal Pandy fired another shot, which hit the Lieutenants horse and brought both to the ground.

Mangal Pandy, aided by another Sepoy, immediately set about Lieutenant Baugh and Sergeant-Major Hewson with his sword, severely injuring both and the pair were only saved from death by the intervention of Sepoy Shaik Puttoo.

Mutiny at Meerut

Meerut was a large British Cantonment some 36 miles from Delhi which was garrisoned by the; 1st Battalion 60th Rifles, the 6th Regiment of Dragoon Guards, a troop of Horse Artillery, a company of foot artillery, a light field battery and three native corps, the 3rd Light Cavalry and the 11th and 20th Native Infantry Regiments.

Like many others stations, Meerut was also beset by the rumours regarding the greased cartridges and displeasure had been shown by the native troops, with the usual sporadic outbreaks of arson and refusal to salute their officers.

In an attempt to offset the rumours, Lieutenant-Colonel George Carmichael-Smyth, commander of the 3rd Light Cavalry ordered a parade of his men on 24th April 1857, where a native officer, a Havildar-Major showed the assembled sepoys the

3 A native drink made from the leaves and flowers of the female cannabis plant

revised method of loading the musket, tearing rather than biting off the end of the cartridge.

At the end of the demonstration, the 90 assembled men (15 from each troop) were asked to take a cartridge and load their musket as shown. Only five men accepted the cartridges, the remainder refused; after repeated requests the men still refused so the parade was dismissed.

The 85 men were later tried by a native court martial, found guilty and sentenced to 10 years hard labour (11 of the younger Sepoys received a sentence of 5 years).

On 9th May, at a parade of all of the forces at Meerut, the outcome of the court martial and the sentence handed down was read out and the 85 convicted men were stripped of their uniforms and placed in shackles before being marched off to jail.

In the evening of the next day, which was a Sunday, the 3rd Light Cavalry decided to free their comrades from jail and choosing the time at which the European Officers and men would be unarmed as they assembled for church, rode to the jail.

The men from the 3rd Light Cavalry, who were guarded by a small number of native troops, were easily released, when Kotwal Dhan Singh Gurjar opened the gates to the jail, another 800 other prisoners were also released.

The 3rd Light Cavalry returned to the parade ground where they unexpectedly encountered armed Europeans making ready for a Church Parade which fortunately had been put back half an hour due to the excessive heat.

The rebels exhorted the men from the 11th and 20th Native Infantry to join them and despite the efforts of Colonel Finnis, the commander of the 11th, to keep his men loyal, both regiments joined the mutiny and the Colonel was shot down by men from the 20th.

Joined by a mob from the city, the Sepoys went on the rampage burning bungalows and killing every European that they could find,[4] however, with the Europeans still armed and able to put up resistance the rabble soon fled Meerut and headed down the Grand Trunk Road towards Delhi.

As this was the first occurrence of Sepoys turning their weapons en mass against their European officers, this event at Meerut is considered to be the start of the Indian Mutiny.

Although the cantonment at Meerut contained a high level of British troops, surprisingly no effort was made to rally a force and pursue the mutineers – if they had then the mutiny may have been nipped in the bud.

---

4 About 50 men, women and children were killed at Meerut

6

THE MUTINY DEEPENS

News of the mutiny at Meerut and the capture of Delhi spread rapidly throughout India, however, unlike the events at Meerut the Company was informed of the fall of Delhi as it happened, thanks to the dedication of the telegraph operators, who were able to issue warnings to the commanders of many other stations.

Of the three presidency armies, the Bengal Army was the largest with almost 169,000 men made up of 144,500 native troops and 24,500 European troops.

This army was also the most affected by the mutiny, with 54 of its 75 regular Native Infantry Regiments joining the mutiny and a number of the remaining 21 regiments being disarmed to prevent them joining the rebellion.

The Bengal Army also included irregular units with 42 infantry regiments and 29 cavalry regiments; these units included a large contingent from the recently annexed state of Oudh and another substantial contingent from the state of Gwalior, both joined the rebellion despite the rulers of those states remaining loyal to the Company.

Most of the remaining irregular units were ambivalent to the mutiny, however, 3 Ghurkha and 5 Sikh regiments actively supported the Company.

The mutiny was widespread throughout the Bengal Presidency and was to affect most of the states.

Mutinies in the Punjab

Meean Meer, Lahore

With the advanced warning, the 81st Regiment of Foot, supported by the Bengal Horse Artillery were able to prevent a mutiny at Meean Meer near Lahore when on 13th May they disarmed the 16th, 26th and 49th Bengal Native Regiments and the 8th Bengal Light Cavalry.

On the 30th July, Prakash Singh, a soldier in the 26th Bengal Native Regiment, incited his comrades to turn on their British Officers and armed with a sword he killed the commander Major Spencer.

Under the cover of a dust storm which was raging, the disarmed men of the 26th fled south to the river Ravi where on the following day, at Ajnala, they were attacked by the police who were assisted by the local villagers.

About 150 of the mutineers were killed during the attack and the remainder were forced into the river where a further 35 drowned, the survivors assembled on an island in the river and subsequently surrendered to Mr Francis Cooper, the Deputy Commissioner of the Punjab with a detachment of about 80 Sikh cavalry.

The surviving rebels were taken to the police station at Ujnalla, where 45 of them died of their wounds in the jail. On the next day, the 1st August, 237 of the rebels were executed by firing squad and the remaining 42 were sent to Lahore, where they were blown from guns as an example to the assembled native regiments.

Amritsar

On the 14th May, officers from Lahore with a detachment of men from the 81st Regiment of Foot went to Amritsar and disarmed the 59th Bengal Native Infantry Regiment.

Ferozepur

At the time of the mutiny, the station at Ferozepur was garrisoned by the 61st Regiment of Foot, two companies of European Artillery and the 45th and 57th Bengal Native Infantry.

On the 14th May, in an attempt to prevent mutiny, it was decided that the 61st Regiment of Foot supported by the artillery would disarm the native regiments.

The 57th Bengal Native Infantry were successfully disarmed, however, the 45th regiment did mutiny and after a failed attempt to seize the magazine fled with their weapons to join the rebels at Delhi.

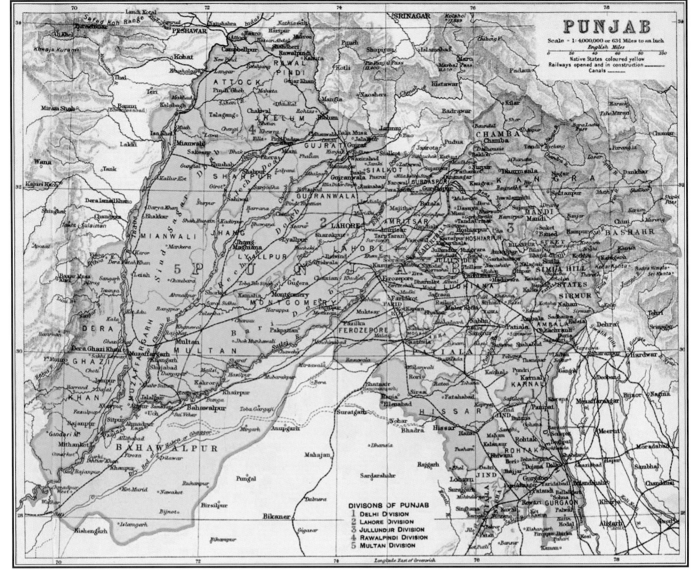

Figure 26. Punjab

Some of the rebels were killed and about 100 were captured, after a trial, 14 sepoys were sentenced to death, two were hanged with the remainder blown from cannon on 13th June.

On the 19th August, the 10th Light Cavalry, which had previously been disarmed but not dismounted, rebelled and headed off for Delhi.

Peshawar

Following news of the troubles at Delhi, on 22nd May the 24th, 27th and 51st Native Infantry together with the 5th Light Cavalry were disarmed at Peshawar as a precaution as they seemed to be on the verge of mutiny.

Three battalions at the station remained loyal to the British; the 7th and 18th Irregular Cavalry and the 21st Native Infantry; together with the 12th Pioneers (the Kalat-i-Ghilzai Regiment) and the Corps of Guides.

A minor mutiny occurred on the 28th August but was soon put down.

Hoti Mardan and Naushahra

On 23rd May the 55th Native Infantry together with elements of the 10th Irregular Horse mutinied at Hoti Mardan and Naushahra, when a force advanced against them they fled the station, heading for the Swat Hills.

On the 25th May, General Nicholson, with the Multan Horse chased down the mutineers, about 120 were killed and 150 captured, the remainder fleeing into the Swat Hills. Those who escaped to the hills either died of hunger or exposure or were hunted down by the local clans and taken prisoner – to be sent to the British.

The 150 prisoners were taken to Peshawar, where in the presence of the assembled troops 40 who were selected at random were blown from the guns, the remainder were hung.

Abazai

At Abazai, General Nicholson and the Multan Horse disarmed and disbanded the 64th Bengal Native Infantry who were also on the verge of mutiny.

Jullundur

On the 3rd of June, fire broke out in the lines of the 61st Bengal Native Infantry stationed at Jullundur which was a normal precursor to mutiny.

At 11 o'clock in the evening of the 7th June fires broke out in the lines of the 36th Bengal Native Infantry and the 6th Native Cavalry spurred the 36th and 61st regiments to threaten their British officers.

The whole of the native garrison was now on the verge of mutiny, with the exception of the Native Artillery which was closely entwined with the detachment of European Artillery and remained loyal.

The lack of artillery seemed to break the resolve of some of the natives and in the end only about half of their number joined the mutiny and fled with their arms towards Phillour on their way to Delhi. Those who remained behind were disarmed by men of the 8th Regiment of Foot.

Phillour

On the 8th June as the mutineers from Jullundur approached Phillour, the 3rd Bengal Native Infantry were assembled and the officers ordered them to make ready to defend the station against the rebels.

The regiment refused these orders and left to join the mutineers, while the British garrison of about 100 men from the 8th Regiment of Foot moved into the fort to protect the European residents and the magazine.

The combined force of rebels crossed the river Sutlej, via a bridge of boats, into the province of Sirhind and moved off to join the mutineers at Delhi.

Jhelum and Rawalpindi

The continued loyalty of the 14th Bengal Native Infantry Regiment had been a concern for some time so the chief commissioner made secret arrangements to disarm them before they could cause trouble.

Colonel Ellice, with a force of 285 men from the 24th Regiment of Foot and a detachment of Multan Irregulars with three guns was despatched from Rawalpindi towards Jhelum; his sealed orders were to be opened only when he was close to the station.

On opening his orders, Colonel Ellice found that he was part of a mission to simultaneously disarm the native troops at Jhelum and Rawalpindi; to ensure a coordinated operation, the Colonel was ordered to arrive at Jhelum in the early morning of 7th July.

Colonel Gerrard, the commanding officer of the station, was informed of the arrangements on the evening of the 6th July and he took the precaution of informing the European women that they should calmly make their way to the civil lines the next morning.

As planned, Colonel Ellice arrived at Jhelum just as the 14th Bengal Native Infantry were being assembled on parade and was joined by Colonel Gerrard with 150 men of the Police Battalion, 60 men of the Police Cavalry and 250 men of the Tewanah Horse.

As the British force advanced on the parade ground, some men of the 14th regiment fired their muskets at them and then took up concealed positions in and around the quarter guard which was a heavily fortified building.

Gunner William Connolly – Victoria Cross No. 138

In response to the rebel fire, Colonel Ellice advanced with his cavalry and artillery which was unlimbered and began to lay down fire on enemy lines.

When one of the sponge men operating a gun was wounded, Gunner Connolly stepped in to take his place but after a few moments was wounded by a bullet to the thigh. Soon afterwards, due to the ferocity of the rebel fire, the order was given to retreat and the guns were set up again at a range of about 500 yards.

Although wounded, Gunner Connolly continued to man his gun which kept up a constant fire on the quarter guard building, until he was once again wounded, this time in the hip.

When Lieutenant Cookes, in command of the battery, ordered Gunner Connolly to be removed he said *"No, Sir, I'll not go there while I can work here"* and continued to man his gun.

Colonel Ellice sent the Tewanah Horse to form a line at the church, to protect the building, which had been consecrated only three months earlier, and also to prevent the rebels escaping into the city.

The men of the 24th and the Police Battalion were sent into the rebel lines to drive them from their cover, which they did slowly due to the stiff resistance.

As his guns appeared to be having little effect on the position, Colonel Ellice led a charge against the rebels in the quarter guard building which although it was successful resulted in the Colonel being seriously wounded by shots to the neck and leg.

The rebels now left their position and moved down to the village of Saielah, about half a mile away on the river bank.

Colonel Gerrard, who was now in command, ordered the cavalry to pursue the rebels but they could not catch them before they took up positions in the village.

The village was surrounded and when the artillery was brought up it began to pound the village walls, Gunner Connolly was still manning his gun, despite his two wounds, however, when he received a third wound, this time to his right leg, and collapsed due to loss of blood, he was finally carried from the field.

For his part in the action, Gunner Connolly was later awarded the Victoria Cross.

After ordering his infantry to once again clear the native lines at Jhelum, of any remaining mutineers, Colonel Gerrard moved his force down to Saielah, where after a short rest they reinforced the encirclement of the village.

Running low on ammunition, the British force did not press ahead with an attack but made camp for the night to wait for a resupply in the morning.

During the night the main force of rebels escaped from the village and made their way towards the fort at Muglah and while trying to reach the fort by crossing the river in three boats, one overturned and 25 rebels were drowned.

The next day the mutineers were pursued by Lieutenant Lind and the Multan Irregulars, eventually 108 rebels were captured and later executed, however, 181 escaped but 138 of these were subsequently captured.

During the fighting nearly 160 rebels had been killed, so of the 500 men who mutinied very few were left to continue the fight against the British.

The situation at Rawalpindi was less of a problem, on the morning of the 7th July the 58th Bengal Native Infantry and two companies of the 14th were assembled at parade to hear the reading of a General Order.

Also at the parade were four companies of the 24th Regiment of Foot, three guns of horse artillery and a detachment of mounted Police. On the order of Colonel Campbell, in command of the station, the artillery was turned on the assembled native soldiers who immediately fled towards their lines.

The British officers followed their men and the 58th were convinced to give up their arms and surrender, however, the men from the 14th fled towards the town and were chased down by the mounted police.

Sealkote

On the 8th of July rumours were spread that a message had arrived from the King of Delhi urging the native troops to rebel.

A wing of the 9th Punjab Light Cavalry also arrived at the station on the 8th of July and reported that their column was coming down from Amritsar to disarm the native troops.

On the next day, the 9th Cavalry formed up near the jail and released 350 prisoners, blew up the magazine, ransacked houses and robbed the treasury.

Alerted by the noise of the mutiny the station commander Brigadier Frederick Brind led some of his officers to the lines of the 46th Bengal Native Infantry, his garrison troops, in an attempt to stop their rebellion. Unfortunately the party was shot at by men of the 46th and the Brigadier and some of his officers were killed.

The cavalry officers and most of the European civilians managed to make their way to the relative safety of the fort, however, the surviving officers of the 46th rode 40 miles to Gujranwala where they were well received by the local population.

After completely sacking the cantonment, the rebels moved off towards Hoshiapur and on the 12th of July, while trying to cross the river Ravi at Trimmoo Ghat were chased down by a column of men from the 52nd Regiment of Foot with some cavalry and artillery, commanded by Brigadier John Nicholson.

In the ensuing battle many of the mutineers were killed and some escaped across the river but due to a lack of cavalry Brigadier Nicholson was forced to call off the pursuit.

Mutinies in Rajputana
Nasirabad

On 28th May 1857 the two native regiments, the 15th and 30th Bengal Native Infantry, at Nasirabad mutinied, captured the Jellalabad battery of Native artillery and killed their British officers.

The 1st Bombay Lancers charged the guns but were unable to recapture them. With further resistance being impossible the Lancers escorted the women and children to safety at Bewar.

The rebels, after plundering the town marched off towards Delhi.

Neemuch

Colonel Abbott commanded the garrison at Neemuch which was made up of; the 4th troop of 1st Native Horse Artillery, the left wing of the 1st Light Cavalry, the 72nd Bengal Native Infantry and the 7th Regiment of the Gwalior Contingent.

On the 28th May, rumours that the bazaar was being plundered caused the 72nd and the 7th to take up their arms, however, order was established by their officers and at a parade the men took an oath of loyalty to the Crown.

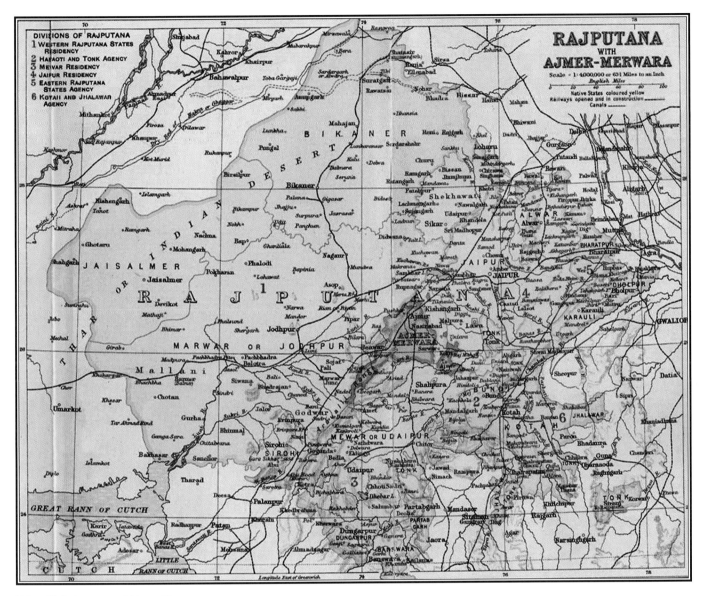

Figure 27. Rajputana and Ajmer-Merwara

On the 2nd June, when news of the mutiny at Nasirabad reached the station, the troops with the exception of the cavalry were mainly subdued, however, to protect against the possibility of mutiny, Captain Showers, the Agent for Marwar, Major Burton the political agent at Kotah and the superintendent at Neemuch, Captain Lloyd all thought it prudent to request troops from the Raja of Kotah and the Rana of Oodeypore.

In case of mutiny, it was also agreed that the European civilians should retire to the village of Dharroo, on the road to Oodeypore from where the Rana's troops would be approaching.

At about 11o'clock on the evening of the 3rd June, the 72nd Regiment mutinied and the cavalry headed off for the jail where they released all of the prisoners. After firing the officers' bungalows, the mutineers were joined by the artillery and all hope of establishing order was now abandoned.

At about 1 o'clock in the morning, Colonel Abbott with his 15 officers and the European civilians (three women and three children) set out to make their way across country to the Fort of Jawud, 12 miles away, which they reached at about 7 o'clock.

At the fort they were met by Major Burton, who had come down from Kotah with a force of about 1,500 men.

Later in the day, Major Burton led his troops to hunt down the mutineers but they had moved off in the direction of Agra.

Although Neemuch would not be relieved until 25th November 1857, by the Malwa field force led by Major Robertson, British forces remained in the area and continued to harass the mutineers who occupied the town.

Lieutenant James Blair – Victoria Cross No. 154

It was on the night of 12th August 1857 during such an operation that Lieutenant Blair volunteered to capture 7 or 8 mutineers who had barricaded themselves within a house.

Breaking down the door, the Lieutenant rushed in forcing the mutineers to escape through the roof. Despite being seriously wounded, Lieutenant Blair continued his pursuit of the rebels but lost them in the dark.

For this action Lieutenant Blair was later awarded the Victoria Cross.

His Victoria Cross citation, makes reference to a second act of bravery. On 23rd October (the day he received a promotion to the rank of Captain) at Jeerum, he fought his way through a band of rebels who surrounded him and despite having been badly wounded in his right arm by a sabre cut, led his men in a charge against the rebels and dispersed them.

———— ✠ ————

This second action took place during the advance of a column from Nasirabad which went to the relief of Neemuch.

Mutinies in North West Provinces and Oudh

Following the mutinies at Delhi and Lucknow, there was a rash of other mutinies throughout the province.

Lucknow

On 1 May sepoys of the 7th Oude Infantry at Moosa Bagh refused to handle the greased cartridges.

On the following day when confronted by loyal troops with loaded artillery, some of the men fled and some surrendered. Fifty mutineers were jailed and Lucknow remained quiet for the following three weeks.

Etawah

On 19th May a detachment of the 9th Bengal Native Infantry mutinied at Etawah and the magistrate Mr Alan Octavian Hume was forced to flee to nearby Jaswantnagar.

On 22nd May, Major Hennessy with the 1st Gwalior Contingent Infantry set out from Agra and on 24th May retook the town which had been abandoned by the rebels who had left to join the mutineers at Delhi.

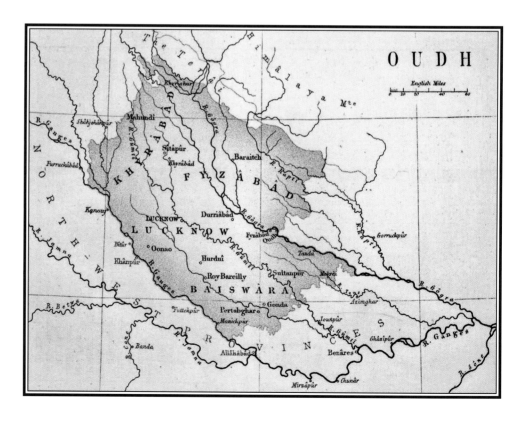

Figure 28. Oudh

Aligarh

On the 20th May, four companies of the 9th Bengal Native Infantry mutinied at Aligarh, plundered the treasury and broke open the jail.

Just after the outbreak, Lieutenant Cockburn arrived from Agra, with men from the 1st Irregular Gwalior Cavalry and was able to escort the Europeans to safety at the town of Hattras, however, on arrival some of the cavalry decided to mutiny and left to join the mutineers at Delhi.

Mynpoorie

On 23rd May, when news of the rebellion of their comrades at Aligarh reached Mynpoorie, three further companies of the Bengal Native Infantry mutinied, plundered the treasury and arsenal, carrying off large quantities of ammunition and treasure.

Lieutenant De Kantzow, a European officer of the 9th, did everything possible to dissuade the regiment from taking such drastic action but to no avail.

The assistant Magistrate Mr J. N. Power, escorted the European women and children to Agra.

Hansi

On 13th May, news of the mutiny at Delhi and the massacre of the European occupants, reached Hansi and raised the usual disquiet amongst the native troops.

On the 17th May, the adjutant Lieutenant Barwell had been dispatched to Hissar to help raise a body of Irregular Cavalry and on the 20th the 4th Irregular Cavalry had been sent to Karnal, which left Captain Stafford, commander of the Hurriana Light Infantry Battalion as the only European Officer at the station.

On the 29th May, after having handed out the men's pay, Captain Stafford had no indication of trouble, however, just after 11 o'clock in the evening his regiment mutinied. Some of the Captain's native officers, warned him that the men would plunder the town and that he should leave as they could not guarantee his life. After a short delay, Captain Stafford gathered the 32 Europeans at the station and escorted them to safety at Hissar.

Bareilly

While Brigadier Sibbald, commander of the station, was absent on inspection, tensions were noted in the 18th and 68th Native Infantry Regiments, such that Colonel Troup and Mr Alexander, the Commissioner of Rohilkhand, made efforts to contain the situation.

Captain Mackenzie was ordered to increase the establishment of his Irregular Cavalry to a strength of 1,000, which was completed very quickly due to the large number of men waiting to be enrolled.

The cavalry, which so far had demonstrated their loyalty, was deployed to protect the boundaries of the station, the guns, treasury and jail. As a further precaution the women and children were sent to Nainital, in the hills away from the station.

On his return to the station, Brigadier Sibbald addressed a general parade and the native soldiers expressed their loyalty, however, at 11 o'clock in the morning of Sunday 31st May they assembled on the parade ground without orders and captured the artillery.

A shot fired from one of the guns was the signal to start the mutiny and the men rushed the officers in their lines and began an intense fusillade at their bungalows, Brigadier Sibbald was one of the first to be killed during this initial act of treachery.

The surviving officers, mounted their horses and made for the cavalry parade ground, the previously agreed assembly point and after a further attempt to calm the mutineers, which was met with a volley of grape shot, rode off to Nainital.

Saharunpore

On 2nd June, the 5th Bengal Native Infantry, who had been showing discontent for some time, were assembled on parade and a proposition for their discharge was put forward by their officers. The offer of a formal discharge was thought to be preferable to mutiny, however, this was not the view of the assembled men who said they wanted to fight not be discharged.

The native infantry now turned their guns on the European officers and ransacked the station, fortunately the women and children had been sent to safety at Mussouree a few days earlier.

Azamgarh

On 3rd June 1857, the 17th Bengal Native Infantry mutinied at Azamgarh and when news of this reached Benares it was decided to disarm the 37th Bengal Native Infantry, however, when they were paraded they mutinied, together with the 13th Irregular Cavalry and a regiment of Sikh Infantry.

Towards the end of May, with the loyalty of many of the native troops in doubt, the Accountant of the North-West provinces decided that it was prudent to move treasure from Goruckpore and Azamgarh to the relative safety of Allahabad.

Lieutenant Palisser with a detachment of irregular horse was in charge of the operation and after picking up the treasure at

Goruckpore arrived at Azamgarh on the 2nd June where he picked up further treasure and two companies of the 17th Bengal Native Infantry were added to his escort. On the evening of 3rd June, Lieutenant Palisser continued on his journey towards Allahabad but was only about three hours down the road when the remaining companies of the 17th regiment mutinied at Azamgarh.

The rebels killed their commanding officer, Lieutenant Hutchinson, released the prisoners from the jail and then set off in pursuit of Lieutenant Palisser and the treasure. The mutineers caught up with Lieutenant Palisser and relieved him of the treasure but the Cavalry escort protected the Lieutenant and his fellow officers and escorted them to safety at Benares but the next day they also mutinied.

Most of the Europeans at Azamgarh fled to Ghazipore but some moved to the estate of the Indigo Planter, Mr Edward Venables who had armed his workers and was able to provide protection.

Sitapur

Sitapur was a major military cantonment, about 50 miles from Lucknow, which was garrisoned by the 41st Bengal Native Infantry, the 9th and 10th Oudh Irregular Infantry, the 15th Oudh Irregular Cavalry and a force of 250 Military Police.

On the 1st June, hearing that mutineers from Lucknow were advancing on the town, Colonel Birch set off with his regiment the 41st Bengal Native Infantry to intercept them, however, while on the road he received additional intelligence that the mutineers had diverted to Delhi so he returned to Sitapur on the following day.

Despite the 41st regiment's willingness to move against the mutineers, Mr Christian, the commissioner had doubts about the loyalty of the troops and on 2nd June ordered the European women and children to be moved into his house, for safety.

On the morning of 4th June, with increasing doubts about the loyalty of the troops, the guard on Mr Christian's house was increased, however, later in the morning four companies of the 41st regiment left their lines to plunder the treasury and release prisoners from the jail. When their commanding officer Colonel Birch and his adjutant Lieutenant Graves, tried to stop the rebels they were shot down. After the 9th Irregular Infantry took up fire against their officers, this signalled a general revolt of all the native troops, including the Military Police battalion.

The majority of the European officers and civilians were killed but a few did manage to escape and reach safety.

Benares

While the Delhi Field Force continued to advance on Delhi, significant events began to unfold at Benares an important station essential to securing road, river and telegraph links between Calcutta and upper India.

Reports of the various mutinies had caused great unrest in the civil population of the town where many of the civilians openly carried arms. Fearing a civil uprising Commissioner Henry Tucker and Colonel Patrick Gordon the temporary commander of the station initially proposed to evacuate the garrison to the nearby stronghold of Chungar, however, in light of the strategic importance of the station it was decided to send for reinforcements and remain in the town.

The garrison consisted of the 37th Native Infantry commanded by Lieutenant-Colonel Arthur Spottiswoode, elements of the Ludhiana Sikh Infantry regiment commanded by Colonel Gordon, a wing of the 13th Irregular Cavalry and a half battery of European Foot Artillery.

Sergeant Major Peter Gill – Victoria Cross No. 121
Sergeant Major Matthew Rosamund – Victoria Cross No. 122
Private John Kirk – Victoria Cross No. 123

The requested reinforcements, in the form of 150 men from the 10th Regiment of Foot and 60 men of 1st Madras Fusiliers, under the command of Lieutenant-Colonel James Neill arrived at Benares on 3rd June 1857.

Immediately upon his arrival Colonel Neill wanted to disarm the 37th Native Infantry but this was resisted by the British officers of the regiment, including the Commanding Officer Colonel Spottiswoode and Major Barrett who both thought that the regiment would remain loyal.

On the next day, after news of the mutiny of the 17th Native Infantry at Azamgarh reached Benares, Colonel Neill again pressed his case for the 37th to be disarmed; this time the commanding officer at Benares, Brigadier Ponsonby, acceded to his wishes and ordered a parade for 5:00 pm. Unfortunately, preparations for the disarming parade were so hurried that none of the supporting European troops were in position before the parade started.

One by one each company of the 37th was called forward and asked to surrender their weapons, however, as the 6th company came forward an advanced guard of the 10th Regiment of Foot accompanied by some artillery arrived at the parade ground. This created much panic amongst the men of the 37th and cries went up that they had been deceived by their officers to lay down their arms so that the Europeans could shoot them down.

The men, who had been disarmed, immediately retrieved their weapons and began to fire on the nearest European troops, who responded with accurate rifle and artillery fire.

Colonel Neill now took command of the situation and ordered the European and Sikh troops to fire on the assembled Sepoys, however, in the confusion the 13th Irregular Cavalry fired shots in the direction of the Sikhs who returned their fire. Seeing this exchange of fire between the Cavalry and Sikhs, the European gunners wrongly assumed that the Sikhs had mutinied and opened fire on them with their guns which scattered the regiment. Fighting continued into the evening with the mutineers setting fire to buildings and killing the Europeans, as they came across them.

On hearing that Captain Brown, the Pension Paymaster, and his family were cut off in an isolated bungalow which had been set on fire by the mutineers, Sergeant-Majors Peter Gill and Matthew Rosamund and Private John Kirk volunteered to go and rescue them. The three men were successful in their mission and brought Captain Brown and his family back to the safety of the barracks. All three were later awarded the Victoria Cross for their actions.

It was also reported that earlier in the evening Sergeant-Major Gill saved the life of a Quartermaster-Sergeant by decapitating a sepoy who had just bayoneted him. It is also said that he saved the life of Major Barrett on two occasions and defended himself against a group of 27 sepoys with only his sword.

Later in the day, Sergeant-Major Rosamund volunteered to go with Colonel Spottiswoode and set fire to the Sepoy lines.

---✠---

Despite the mutiny of the 37th Native Infantry, the confusion regarding the units of the Ludhiana Sikh Infantry was resolved and they remained loyal.

Allahabad

On the 1st of June the 6th Bengal Native Infantry based at Allahabad demonstrated their loyalty by volunteering to fight against the rebels at Delhi and on the 5th June their commanding officer Colonel Simpson gave public thanks to the regiment for their offer.

Despite the apparent loyalty of the garrison, when news of the mutiny at Benares reached the station many of the European civilian population were armed, formed into a militia and moved to the fort to help guard the women and children who had been moved there.

The militia supplemented the fort garrison under the command of Captain Hazelwood with about 400 Sikhs of the Ferozepur regiment and 80 men of the 6th Bengal Native Infantry who guarded the main gate.

Captain Harward with two companies of the 6th regiment and two guns was sent to guard the bridge of boats which crossed the river Ganges on the road to Benares and Captain Alexander with two squadrons of the 3rd Oude Irregular Cavalry was sent to the Alopee Bagh camping ground which commanded the station approach roads.

The main body of the 6th Bengal Native Infantry regiment remained in their lines which were about three miles from the fort.

All was quiet and seemingly under control until 9 o'clock in the evening of 6th June when to the dismay of their officers the regiment rose in mutiny. When a bugle was sounded as a signal to revolt, the European officers were dining in the mess and when they rushed out on hearing the alarm most were shot dead.

The detachment of the 6th at the bridge of boats seized the guns and Captain Harward was lucky to escape with his life.

When he heard the sounds of the uprising, Captain Alexander led his small band of troopers towards the native soldiers' lines but was ambushed by a large group of rebels and was shot down.

The mutineers released the prisoners from the jail, plundered the treasury and went on a rampage throughout the town killing all Europeans that they came across.

At the fort, Lieutenant Brasyer and his Sikhs managed to disarm the detachment from the 6th Bengal Native Infantry who were guarding the gate and expelled them before securing the fort against attack from the rebels.

On the evening of the 9th June, Lieutenant-Colonel James Neil, with one officer and 43 men of the Madras Fusiliers, left Benares to go to the rescue of the Europeans besieged in the fort at Allahabad some 75 miles away. On the same evening Major Stephenson, with almost 100 men set out on the same journey but as they were travelling by bullock carts his progress was slower than that of Colonel Neil. By the 11th June, Colonel Neil and his men reached the river Ganges and found that the partially destroyed bridge of boats was in the hands of the mutineers and the nearby villages were all occupied by the rebels. With some difficulty, Colonel Neil managed to find enough boats to ferry himself and his men across the river to the fort, where he immediately assumed command.

On the next morning, the Colonel led a party of Fusiliers and Sikhs to recapture the bridge of boats and drive the rebels from the villages to secure a route for Major Stephenson's force which arrived that evening.

With the arrival of a stronger British force, most of the rebels left to join the mutineers at Delhi.

Sultanpur

On the 5th June, Mr Block, the political agent at Sultanpur, received news that mutineers from Juanpore had reached nearby Chanda and as a precaution sent the women and children from the station to Allahabad.

Further news arrived on the 8th June to the effect that the mutineers who had sacked Chanda, were now on their way to Sultanpur and that their own men, the 15th Irregular Cavalry commanded by Colonel Fisher, could not be relied upon.

Early the next morning the 1st Regiment of Military Police, commanded by Captain Bunbury, rose in mutiny and Colonel Fisher at the head of the 15th Irregular Cavalry went down to their lines to try and regain order. As the Colonel approached the lines, he was shot in the back and killed by one of the policemen while his own regiment stood by as passive spectators although they allowed Lieutenant Tucker to tend to the Colonel during his last moments.

Following the death of their Colonel, the 15th Irregular Cavalry mutinied and shot Captain Gibbings the second in command of the regiment. The civil officers Mr Block and Mr Stoyan were also killed but several of the European officers and the doctor managed to reach safety at Benares.

Fyzabad

With news of nearby troubles many of the European civilians at Fyzabad were sent to safety under the protection of Rajah Maun Singh at Sheergunge on 8th June.

On the following day the 22nd Bengal Native Infantry, 6th Oudh Irregular Infantry and the 15th Irregular Cavalry all mutinied, however, the men of the 22nd voted to protect their British officers who were allowed to take a few private possessions before boarding four boats to take them down river to Ghogra.

Unfortunately a message was sent to the 17th Bengal Native Infantry that the British were escaping and they were intercepted with many of the British party being killed before the survivors reached Dinapore.

Saloni

Captain Barrow was the deputy commissioner at Saloni, which was served by six companies of the 1st Oudh Irregular Infantry under the command of Captain Thomson.

On the 9th June, news reached the station of the mutiny at Sultanpur and on the following day the 1st Oudh Irregular Infantry also joined the mutiny. The European officers managed to escape safely and made their way to the fort of Darapur, where they were sheltered by Rajah Hanmant Singh who later escorted them to a ferry which allowed them to reach Allahabad.

Mutinies in Bengal

Following the outbreak of mutiny at Meerut and the capture of Delhi by the mutineers, it was vital that no mutiny should occur at Patna or Dinapore. Both of these locations were strategically placed on the Grand Trunk road and River Ganges which were essential resupply routes from Calcutta to Lucknow and Delhi.

Dinapore

On 3rd June the 7th Bengal Native Infantry Regiment was paraded at Dinapore and addressed regarding their loyalty, in response, native officers presented a petition which not only expressed their allegiance but offered to take up arms against the mutineers.

On the 7th June, when news of the disarming of native troops at Benares reached Dinapore, it caused some disquiet amongst the men but this was contained by their officers.

On the evening of 7th June, Mr William Tayler, the Commissioner at Patna, received news of an impending mutiny at Dinapore and as no European regiments were stationed anywhere between Patna and Calcutta was reinforced the following day by a wing of Captain Rattray's Sikhs on the orders of the government at Calcutta.

On 12th June, a native officer of the local Behar Battalion was caught trying to incite some of Rattray's Sikhs to mutiny and following a trial was convicted and hung.

On 18th June, Mr Tayler invited local dignitaries to his home to discuss the current situation, amongst the many that attended were three of the spiritual heads of the Wahabees, a fanatical Mohammedan sect. These three men were arrested and held under guard in the Circuit House as a precautionary move as there was no evidence of them inciting rebellion.

On the day following the arrest of the Wahabee leaders, Mr Tayler made two further precautionary moves; he issued a proclamation ordering all citizens to hand in their arms within the next 24 hours, he also implemented a night time curfew which started at 9 o'clock in the evening.

On the evening of 2nd July, in contravention of the curfew, a large body of Mohammedans congregated in the town and marched on the Roman Catholic mission-house with the declared intent of murdering the priest, who fortunately managed to escape before they arrived.

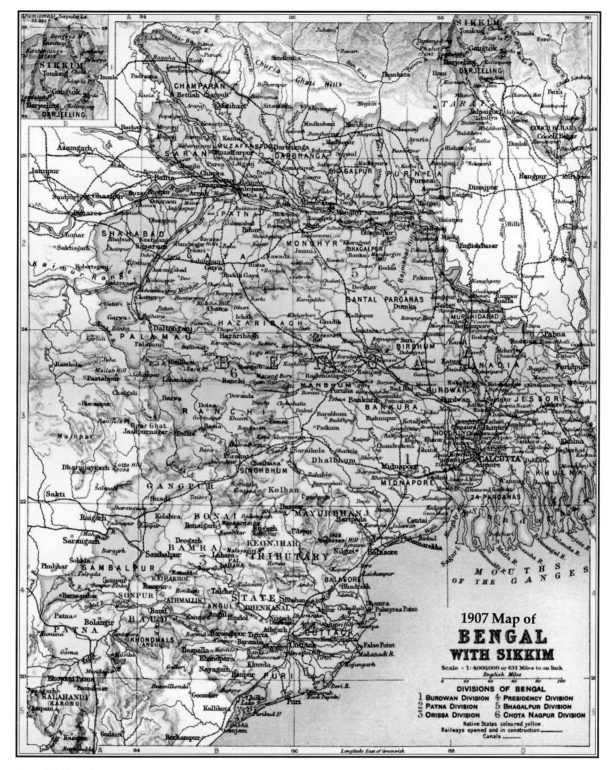

Figure 29. Bengal

Dr R. Lyell, an assistant to the Opium Agent, pulled together a small force of 50 native soldiers and accompanied by eight of Rattray's Sikhs went to quell the burgeoning riot but on approaching the group he was shot dead. As the native soldiers and Sikhs advanced towards the party of rebels they broke and one of their numbers was killed and another seriously wounded. The wounded man, Peer Ali Khan was arrested and a search of his home revealed a large quantity of arms and seditious material.

Peer Ali Khan was tried, convicted and hanged, together with 16 other rioters who had been previously convicted.

On the 5th of July the 5th Fusiliers with 800 men arrived at Calcutta and seven days later on 12th July they were despatched by river steamer up the Ganges.

The local Indigo planters petitioned Lord Canning, on 20th July, to land the 5th Fusiliers at Dinapore and together with the 10th Regiment of Foot disarm the native regiments.

On 22nd July a detachment of the 5th Fusiliers arrived at Dinapore, however, they did not disembark as they were being sent forward as urgent reinforcements to General Havelock's force.

Two days later on 24th July, two companies of the 37th Regiment of Foot were disembarked at Dinapore but instead of disarming the native troops, which he thought because of the disgrace would cause a revolt, the commanding officer General Lloyd decided to remove the percussion caps from the native magazines instead.

On the next morning, with the European troops on parade in the barrack square, two carts were used to collect the percussion caps from the native magazine, on their return journey men of the 7th and 8th Bengal Native Infantry caught sight of the carts and began yelling that their ammunition was being removed.

It was only the swift action of their officers that prevented the men from seizing the carts which were eventually allowed on their way; men from the 40th Bengal Native Regiment were ready to intervene and prevent the seizure.

General Lloyd, alarmed by the reaction of the native regiments, was now determined to remove the percussion caps held by each individual and ordered his native officers to parade the men for that purpose. The men from the 7th and 8th regiments refused to give up their caps but some men of the 40th complied.

The European officers of the regiments tried in vain to get their men to comply with the order, so the general assembly was sounded and the men and artillery of the 10th and 37th regiments who had been mustered in the barracks square advanced on the parade ground.

At the advance of the British troops the assembled native regiments took flight in mutiny. Without a suitable force of cavalry, General Lloyd attempted to pursue some of the rebels by river steamer, some of the mutineers were shot and some drowned, however, the majority managed to escape into the countryside.

Uncertain as to the intentions of the rebels, General Lloyd sent a detachment with two guns to protect Patna, leaving about 500 men with 4 guns at Dinapore, it later became apparent that the mutineers had headed for the Shahabad District about ten miles north of Dinapore.

Siege of Arrah

On 26th July under the leadership of Kunwar Singh, the Dinapore rebels lay siege to Arrah, the capital of the Shahabad district, besieging Mr Herwald Wake the magistrate of Howrah and a small band of men; about 50 men of Captain Rattray's Sikh police battalion and 17 civilians.

On 27th July a detachment of men from 5th Fusiliers, recently arrived from Calcutta, was sent via river steamer to go to the relief of Arrah but got stuck on a sandbank and waited all day for the arrival of a replacement steamer.

In the evening a steamer, bound for Calcutta, arrived at Dinapore from Allahabad. After the passengers were landed and accommodated in the church the steamer was requisitioned and it was planned that this would tow a barge with a force of 250 men from the 10th Regiment of Foot, together with some Sikhs all under the command of Colonel Fenwick down river where they would collect the stranded barge and proceed towards Arrah.

On the following morning the captain of the steamer decided that he could not tow two barges, so a reduced force of 100 men under the command of Captain Dunbar was sent instead. Six civilians, including Mr William McDonell the magistrate of Chuprah and Mr Ross Mangles the assistant magistrate at Patna volunteered to join the force and show them the way.

At about 2 o'clock in the afternoon of 29th July Captain Dunbar and his troops disembarked at a landing place chosen by Mr McDonell which was two miles from a stream that would have to be crossed in order to reach the road to Arrah. Mr McDonell volunteered to guide a party of 15 Sikhs commanded by Lieutenant Ingilby on a mission to secure boats for the crossing but on reaching the stream they found that all of the boats were on the other side guarded by a force of about 200 rebels. Lieutenant Ingilby sent a messenger back for the rest of his Sikhs (about 50 men) to return and help clear the rebels, this was soon accomplished and by 7 o'clock in the evening all of Captain Dunbar's men had crossed the stream and were ready to resume their march. The column set off with Lieutenant Ingilby and twenty Sikhs forming the vanguard, followed by 150 men of the 10th Regiment of Foot, a further 50 Sikhs and 200 men of the 37th Regiment of Foot bringing up the rear. The force halted at the Kainugger Bridge, about three miles from Arrah at about 10 o'clock in the evening and Captain Harrison, the second in command urged Captain Dunbar to call a halt for the night. After a short rest, Captain Dunbar, assured by a message from Mr Wake that his advance would be unopposed, decided to press ahead.

As the advance party, composed of Captain Dunbar, Lieutenant Ingilby and Mr McDonell with about 20 Sikhs proceeded down the road between an avenue of trees, they were assailed by volleys of musket fire. The fire killed many of the advanced party including Captain Dunbar and in the confusion of the attack the British force split into small units and returned fire but in the dark it was difficult to tell friend from foe and they often inflicted wounds on their own comrades. Captain Jones, with the help of a bugler, finally managed to get control of the situation and assembled the men in a small depression protected by a bank.

At daybreak on the 30th July, the British force, now down to 350 men, found the three mutinied regiments from Dinapore drawn up to their front, a total of about 2,000 men together with a further force of 1,000 rebels. In the face of such a formidable force, although they were only about half a mile outside Arrah, it was decided that the best course of action would be to retreat. As soon as the British began their retreat they were fired on by mutineers from every direction and many men were killed or wounded.

Private Denis Dempsey – Victoria Cross No. 155

During the retreat, Private Dempsey together with another Private carried Ensign Erskine, who had been badly wounded, for about five miles.

For this action, Private Dempsey was later awarded the Victoria Cross. Unfortunately, Ensign Erskine's wounds proved to be mortal.

✣

Civilian Ross Lowis Mangles – Victoria Cross No. 150

During the retreat from Arrah, Private Richard Taylor from the 37th Regiment , who had been badly wounded, begged not to be left to the mercy of the mutineers. Mr Mangles bandaged up Private Taylor's wounds as best as he could and then carried him on his back across swampy ground for about six miles.

At last he reached the river and swam, towing the Private, to the safety of a boat.

For this action, Mr Mangles was later awarded the Victoria Cross, one of only four civilians to receive the medal.

✣

Civilian William McDonell – Victoria Cross No. 151

On reaching the river the retreating British force was pleased to see that their boats were still in place on the river bank but had suffered some interference from the mutineers.

Captain Medhurst of the 60th Rifles, formerly of the 10th Foot, wrote in his official account as follows: *"On the ill-fated expedition retiring from Arrah on the morning of the 30th July 1857, and on arriving at the village and stream of Bherara, as is well known, the men, exhausted and dispirited, broke and made for the only six large country boats moored close to the right bank. After assisting some wounded men into the farthest boat, and being myself pulled in, I saw that Mr M'Donnell, who was one of our number, was exerting himself with a sergeant to move the boat*

into the stream. It being discovered that the boat was bound to the bank, one or two men jumped out and loosened the rope, and the boat moved. Assisted by the less exhausted of my party, I was keeping up a fire of Enfields on the enemy, whose musketry was very galling. Whilst so employed, I heard Mr M'Donnell call out for a knife to cut away some rope which bound the rudder to the right, causing the lumbering boat to veer round into the right shore again, and for a time causing it to stick fast. On looking round I saw him seated on the stern extremity of the boat in full view of the enemy, and quite exposed to their fire. He cut away the mentioned rope, and guiding the rudder himself, a fortunate breeze carried our boat across the stream, grounding at about ten yards from the left bank, whereby all those who were alive were enabled to jump out and reach the steamer in safety. The number of men thus saved was about thirty-five ; and during the passage across three men were shot dead, one was mortally, and two or three slightly, wounded. I may safely assert that it was owing to Mr McDonnell's presence of mind, and at his personal risk, that our boat got across on that day."

For this action, Mr McDonell was later awarded the Victoria Cross, one of only four civilians to have received the medal.

✣

Of the 450 men who had crossed the river the previous evening, only 250 managed to recross the river that morning and make their way to the steamer which took them back to Dinapore.

Relief of Arrah

Major Vincent Eyre landed at Calcutta on the night of 14th June, having arrived from Burma with his 60 European gunners and their Light Field Battery. On 10th June, the Major and his artillery boarded a barge under tow by the river steamer *Lady Thackwell* with orders to proceed to Allahabad as fast as possible.

On the evening of 25th July, Major Eyre saw flames rising above the town of Dinapore and learning that the garrison had mutinied he immediately offered his services to General Lloyd.

The Major set off upriver the next morning and by 28th July had arrived at Buxar where he found that the fort and old military station had been abandoned.

Captain Hastings, the superintendant at Buxar informed Major Eyre that the mutineers were besieging a small British force at Arrah so the next morning he continued his river journey to Ghazeepore an important town that was the centre of opium production for poppies grown in the upper provinces. Due to the high value of the opium stock held in the town it was guarded by a native regiment and a company of 78th Highlanders.

Major Eyre arrived at Ghazeepore on 29th July and after discussions with the commanding officer found all to be in order but landed two of his guns to assist and after boarding 25 men from the 78th Highlanders returned to Buxar. When he arrived at Buxar that evening, Major Eyre found that a detachment of 160 men from the 5th Fusiliers, commanded by Captain L'Estrange had just arrived on board the steamer *James Hume*. Major Eyre requested the help of Captain L'Estrange and his men in the mission to relieve Arrah and the next morning a field force comprising 40 artillerymen, 150 men of 5th Fusiliers, 14 mounted volunteers and 12 officers was formed to carry out the mission. Accompanied by Mr Bax, the assistant Magistrate at Ghazeepore, the small force set out and by the morning of 1st August had reached the village of Shahpoor where they learned of the ill fated action led by Captain Dunbar.

The column resumed their march that afternoon and made their way to the village of Gujrajegunge where they made camp for the night; a party of 50 men from the 5th Fusiliers was sent to guard a bridge leading to the village.

Early the next morning the force resumed its march and about a mile from the village came to a wood that surrounded the direct road to Arrah, Major Eyre halted his force and sent out skirmishers to reconnoitre the way ahead and discovered a force of mutineers waiting in ambush.

The Major deployed his guns and laid down fire to his front and flanks, which drew the mutineers out into the open, it was here that the superiority of the Enfield rifle showed itself to the full and under accurate British rifle fire the mutineers fell back into the shelter of the woods. With his artillery fire concentrated on the enemy centre, Major Eyre's force managed to move through the enemy positions and arrived at the village of Beebeegunje where the rebels had destroyed the bridge.

Finding no suitable ford to cross the river, Major Eyre continued his march along the river bank, and the mutineers followed along the opposite bank while a force of their Irregular Cavalry tried to harass their rear. When the force came to another wood they were again assailed by volleys of rebel musket fire from a large force of mutineers who were blocking the way to the Arrah road. Once again Major Eyre directed his artillery at the enemy and for over an hour managed to keep the rebels at bay, however, Captain Hastings rode up to the Major and informed him that the 5th Fusiliers were losing ground. Captain L'Estrange was ordered to charge the mutineers and with fixed bayonets he his men managed to turn the enemy right flank and with grape shot directed at their centre they abandoned their positions and Major Eyre's force cleared the woods and gained the road to Arrah.

After continuing their march they arrived at a stream, about four miles from Arrah, which they could not cross with their guns, so they halted for the night while the engineers constructed a temporary bridge from wagons. At 11 o'clock the next morning, the force managed to cross the stream with their guns and an hour later were in Arrah, where they found that the rebels had fled and the siege was lifted.

Kunwar Singh and the mutineers had fled to Jugdeespore where the rebel leader had a fortress.

On 11th August, Major Eyre, having been reinforced by 200 men from the 10th Regiment of Foot and 100 men from Rattray's Sikhs accompanied by Mr Wake at the head of his Sikh force set out for Jugdeespore. The force now numbering 522 men engaged the rebels on 12th August and after a fierce battle captured Kunwar Singh's citadel, unfortunately the rebel leader with a few of his men managed to escape.

After pursuing the rebels for a time Major Eyre was ordered to return to Arrah, which he reached on 19th August. The detachment of the 10th Regiment of Foot returned to Dinapore and Major Eyre with the rest of the force returned to Buxar.

Chittagong and Dacca

On 18th November 1857, detachments of the 34th Bengal Native Infantry mutinied at Chitragaon (Chittagong) and after plundering the treasury and releasing prisoners from the jail set off in the direction of the Tiparah hills.

Midshipman Arthur Mayo – Victoria Cross No. 233

Four days later on 22nd November, Lieutenant Lewis of the Indian Navy attempted to disarm detachments of the 73rd Bengal Native Infantry and Native Artillery, a total of 350 men, at Dacca. To accomplish this task, Lieutenant Lewis had at his disposal four officers and 85 British sailors of the Indian Naval Brigade plus 30 civilian volunteers.

Lieutenant Lewis managed to disarm the men guarding the public buildings and then preceded towards the main infantry lines, where in his own words;

I proceeded to disarm the sepoys stationed at Dacca. We marched down to the Lall Bagh and on entering the lines found the sepoys drawn up by their magazine with two 8-pounders in the centre.

Immediately after we deployed into line they opened fire on us from front and left flank with canister and musketry. We gave them one volley, and then charged with the bayonet up hill and carried the whole of the barracks on the top of it, breaking the doors with our musket-butts and bayoneting the sepoys inside. As soon as this was done, we charged downhill, and taking them in flank, carried both their guns and all the buildings, driving them into the jungle.

Everyone, both officers and men, behaved most gallantly, charging repeatedly in the face of most heavy fire without the slightest hesitation for a moment. I beg particularly to bring to notice the conduct of Mr. Midshipman Arthur Mayo, who led the last charge on their guns most gallantly, being nearly 20 yards in front of the men.

For his part in leading the charge on the guns, Midshipman Mayo was later awarded the Victoria Cross.

———— ✠ ————

After their guns were taken the mutineers broke ranks and fled, eventually finding temporary refuge in Bhutan.

Mutinies in Central India

On 16th May, news reached Gwalior of the mutiny at Meerut; this caused great concern to the small number of Europeans who lived in the city, as the city and the entire state was garrisoned solely by native troops.

The state was ruled by a young Maharaja, Jayajirao Scindia, with an army of 10,000 men, however, in addition to this army was the Gwalior Contingent, which was one of the bodies of troops that the British Government had insisted that certain native princes must maintain in addition to their own armies, these were to be used for the civil administration of their territory. Although these troops were paid for by the local ruler, he had no control over them as they were directed by the officers of the Company army.

At the time of the mutiny, the Gwalior Contingent was made up of; four artillery field batteries, a small siege train, two regiments of cavalry and seven infantry regiments; a total of over 8,300 men, commanded by Brigadier Ramsey. A large part of this force was stationed at Gwalior, the state capital, but outposts were also maintained at Sipri, Gwali, Agra, Mehidpur, Neemuch and Asirgarh.

During discussions with Major Charters Macpherson, the political Resident at Gwalior, about the worsening situation, the Maharaja promised the full support of his troops to suppress any revolt at Gwalior, if this should occur.

Also on the 16th May, Major Macpherson, received a request from John Russell Colvin, the Lieutenant-Governor of the North-West Provinces, for a brigade of troops from the Gwalior Contingent to bolster the forces at Agra. In response to this request Major Macpherson sent one and a half regiments of infantry, 100 cavalry and a battery of artillery, about half of the force currently at Gwalior. Prior to this, on the 13th May, Major Macpherson had despatched Lieutenant Cockburn with 200 men of the 18th Native Cavalry and a battery of six guns to Agra, following a previous request for aid.

Mutiny at Jhansi

On 21st November 1853, Gangadhar Rao the Raja of Jhansi died without an heir and under Dalhousie's Doctrine of Lapse the state of Jhansi now became crown territory. The territory was annexed despite the Raja adopting a son and heir on his death bed, as this was ruled to be illegal. The Ranee made several applications to have the decision overturned, however, all to no avail and had to settle for the generous pension which she had been granted.

When news of the mutiny at Meerut on 18th May reached Jhansi, the Ranee did much to promote discontent in the local populace mainly based upon British measures aimed at the eradication of their religious beliefs.

Despite being the capital of a recently annexed state, Jhansi had no British troops as part of its garrison; at the start of the mutiny it was defended by a detachment of foot artillery, the left wing of the 12th Regiment of Bengal Native Infantry and the right wing of the 14th Bengal Irregular Cavalry.

The garrison was commanded by Captain Dunlop and Captain Alexander Skene was the Political Officer acting as the British Superintendant for the state. The troops were stationed in the Town Fort, high on a rocky outcrop at a short distance from the walled town while the artillery was stationed in Star Fort which housed the treasury.

On the afternoon of 4th June 1857, a company of the 12th Regiment of Bengal Infantry mutinied and occupied Star Fort. Captain Dunlop immediately paraded the rest of the regiment and the cavalry and to a man they said that they would stand by him.

During the night Captain Burgess, Lieutenant Turnbull, Ensign Taylor and Quartermaster Sergeant Newton slept with the men of the 12th in their lines and Lieutenant Campbell slept in the lines with the cavalry.

The men were again paraded the next morning and renewed their loyalty to Captain Dunlop, who spent the rest of the morning preparing shells for an attack to dislodge the rebels from Star Fort. In the afternoon, while returning from the Post Office with Ensign Taylor, Captain Dunlop was shot dead by some men from his regiment and Ensign Taylor was seriously wounded.

Men from the cavalry, taking their lead from the infantry, shot Lieutenant Campbell but he managed to stay on his horse and reached the safety of the Town Fort.

Lieutenant Turnbull, who was making his way to the fort on foot, was not so lucky and after trying to take refuge up a tree he was shot dead.

The garrison was now in full revolt, and breaking into smaller bands the rebels began to set fire to the officers' bungalows and released the convicts from the jail. A rebel party of 50 cavalry and 300 infantry with two guns now approached the town, where the gates were thrown open to allow entry, and descended on the palace where the Ranee had placed guards on the gate.

Captain Gordon sent an urgent message to the Ranee, requesting help but this was refused as she was threatened with death by the mutineers if she came to the aid of the British.

The palace guards joined the mutineers and the large body of rebels moved off to attack the Town Fort.

At the first sign of trouble, Captain Dunlop had advised that all Europeans living outside the Town Fort, should come and join him there; so in addition to the normal garrison of 55, including wives and children, the fort now housed a total of 68 people.

On reaching the Town Fort, and being assailed by a fierce barrage of fire, the mutineers pulled back and laid siege to the fort and during the night brought up guns for their next assault.

On the morning of the 6th June, three men were sent out from the Town Fort (Messrs Andrews, Purcell and Scott) disguised as natives, to request the Ranee to provide assistance in ensuring

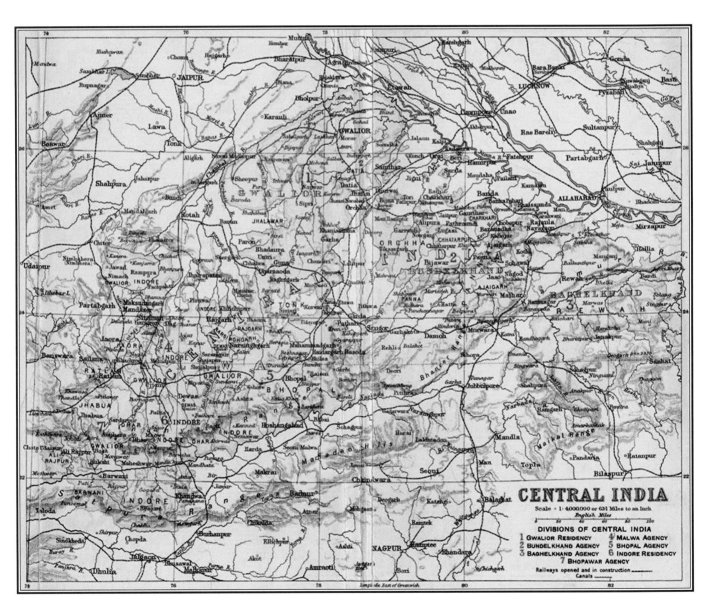

Figure 30. Central India

safe passage if they were to quit the Town Fort. The men were discovered, the Ranee would not grant them an audience and they were summarily executed.

In the afternoon the rebels made another attack on the fort and tried to breach a gate but this was repulsed by the garrison and the mutineers began an indiscriminate plunder of the town, sacking the houses of leading Bengalis as well as those of the Europeans.

The Ranee was again petitioned by the mutineers to join their cause and after being threatened with death, supplied 1,000 men and two heavy guns (which had been buried for three years) to help the rebels. During the night, these guns and others were brought to bear on the Town Fort and opened up a bombardment on the morning of 7th June but too little effect.

During the day, Captain Gordon was killed by a shot to the head when he raised it above the parapet. It was also discovered that there were traitors within the fort, Lieutenant Powys was wounded in the neck and the four natives that had attacked him were put to death.

By now the garrison was running short of ammunition and food so when after a parley, the rebels promised safe passage if they surrendered and laid down their arms, Captain Skene reluctantly complied and opened up the gates. The 27 men, 19 women and 20 children were taken from the Town Fort to the Jokan Bagh, just outside the town walls where they were all slaughtered. Having committed their foul deed, the mutineers moved off to Agra and Delhi to join up with the main rebel forces.

Mutiny at Nowgong

Nowgong was a station about 200 miles to the east of Jhansi garrisoned by the right wing of the 12th Bengal Native Infantry with 400 men, the left wing of the 14th Irregular Cavalry with 220 men and the 4th Company of the 9th Battalion of Native Artillery with 66 men.

On 23rd May, rumours began to spread regarding the slaughter of Europeans at Delhi which caused some disquiet amongst the native troops, to a large extent this was dispelled by the trust shown by the British officers who continued to sleep in the lines with their men.

On 30th May, Major Kirke, the garrison commander, received a report that mutiny was being plotted by his artillery; four men thought to be the ring leaders were dismissed and as a precaution the guns were moved to be guarded by the infantry each evening.

On 4th June, Major Kirke received a letter from Jhansi, where the other wings of his troops were stationed, informing him that the troops had mutinied and taken the Star Fort.

Major Kirke immediately summoned his native officers, who swore their allegiance and at a full parade the men did the same

saying that they would take up arms against the rebels if required to do so.

Major Kirke sent one party of the 14th Irregular Cavalry to Jhansi and another to Futtehpore to advise them of the loyalty of the Nowgong garrison.

On 10th June a letter arrived from the magistrate at Mowraneepore, stating that all the Europeans had been killed at Jhansi and that the Ranee had assumed the throne.

That evening, while the guard was being changed on the guns, the 12th Bengal Native Infantry decided to mutiny, seized the guns and turned them on the British Officers. Faced by a large rebel force, armed with artillery and with only a few of his troops remaining loyal, Major Kirke had little alternative but to abandon the station. With about 80 native soldiers who had remained loyal, Major Kirke and his officers escorted a large number of women and children on the road to Chutterpore. Thanks to taking a wrong turn in the failing light, the column managed to avoid the rebels who, after setting fire to the British bungalows at the station, were trying to chase them down. Marching through the night the column reached Chutterpore, where they were treated with kindness by the ruling Ranee. After a tortuous journey, during which many, including Major Kirke, died from sunstroke the party arrived at Nagode on 29th June where they received the protection of the Ranee of Adzighur.

Another band of 41 persons, drummers, buglers and their families, under the command of Captain Scot, made their way to the town of Banda where the Nawab provided them with care and protection.

Mutiny at Banda

Banda was a military station that was mainly garrisoned by detachments of regiments stationed at Cawnpore and at the time of the mutiny at Meerut, three companies of the 1st Regiment of Native Infantry had just arrived at the station.

On the 14th June, when news of the mutiny at Cawnpore reached the station, the troops at Banda made clear their intentions to join the mutiny. The Nawab, with his own loyal troops, tried to disarm the men but this failed and the native soldiers mutinied.

After sacking the station and plundering the treasury and armoury, the rebels fled to join their comrades at Cawnpore.

Mutiny at Gwalior

Towards the end of the month, Major Macpherson had another meeting with the Maharaja, during which he was informed that the Resident should no longer count on the loyalty of the

Gwalior Contingent and that he should move all Europeans to the Residency building – which the Maharaja would guard with his own loyal troops.

The next morning, with rumours of mutiny abounding, the Europeans were moved into the Residency, under the guard of the Maharaja's men. However, on the following day, when doubts about the loyalty of the Maharaja's troops, who had been recruited outside the province, were raised, the women were moved to the Maharaja's palace to be guarded by his personal bodyguard.

Despite the unrest, the British officers continued to sleep in the lines with their men and as a result of Brigadier Ramsey's confidence in the loyalty of his native troops, some of the officers' wives joined them.

On 7th June a request for aid was received from Jhansi and Captain Murray with a wing of the 4th Contingent Infantry together with a battery of artillery was despatched to provide the requested assistance. After three days march, Captain Murray received news that all Europeans at Jhansi had been murdered and returned to Gwalior on 13th June with the news, which was the cause of much concern. On the same day a wing of the 6th Regiment of the Gwalior Contingent mutinied at Lalitpur.

On the afternoon of 14th June, after the British attended church, the officers' bungalows and mess house were set on fire but by sunset the fires had been brought under control. At 9 o'clock when the evening gun was fired the native soldiers mutinied, killing all that crossed their path. Some of the native regiments were appalled at the revolt of their comrades and tried to protect their European officers but many were killed.

With the rebels running riot in the city, the occupants of the Residency were escorted by the Maharaja's bodyguard to his palace in Lashkar. At a meeting between the Maharaja and Major Macpherson, at the palace, it was decided that the safest course of action was to transport the Europeans to Agra, under the escort of the Maharaja's bodyguard.

It was also agreed that the Maharaja would make every effort to keep the Gwalior Contingent in the city, even to the extent of employing them in his service, if necessary.

After two days march, the column reached a village near the river Chumbul, which formed the border of the Maharaja's territory where they were unexpectedly met by Thakoor Buldeo Sing, the chief of a warlike clan that remained loyal to the British, with a large contingent of his men. When the Maharaja's bodyguard turned back at the river Chumbul, Thakoor Buldeo Sing and his men continued to escort the column until it reached Agra. The next day, the 19th June another column, composed of only women and children also arrived at Agra.

Mutinies in Indore

Like the Gwalior state, Indore state was ruled by a young Maharaja, Tookajee Rao Hulkar and on the 5th April 1857, Colonel Henry Marion Durand was appointed as agent in charge of the Central India Agency which had its headquarters at Indore.

Also like Gwalior, the state was garrisoned only by native troops; the Malwa Contingent was formed of regiments paid for by the various princes and chiefs of Malwa but was employed for the administration and protection of the state under the control of the political agent.

The Maharaja, also maintained his own army which consisted of 640 artillerymen, 3,820 cavalry and 3,145 infantry.

Mutiny at Indore

When news of the mutiny at Meerut reached Indore on 13th May, Colonel Durand was concerned that the discontent might spread to his troops stationed at Mhow. The Colonel's initial aim was to protect the considerable government treasury, which was located at Indore and was only protected by a small detachment of 200 men from the Malwa Contingent. To reinforce the garrison at Indore, the Colonel ordered 270 men of the Malwa Bhil Contingent, stationed at Sirdarpore, 40 miles from Indore, to come to Indore with utmost urgency. He also summoned, two troops of cavalry, 270 infantry and two guns from the Bhopal Contingent stationed at Sehore, about 100 miles from Indore.

On 15th May, Colonel Durand had a private meeting with the Maharaja and requested the help of his troops, in the event of a mutiny occurring before his reinforcements arrived. The Maharaja was happy to agree but as he reported that he was short of ammunition, the Colonel ordered a supply to be sent to him from the magazine at Mhow.

Mhow was a very important military station, about 13 miles from Indore where Colonel Platt, commanded the garrison of an artillery company, the right wing of the 1st Light Cavalry and the 23rd Bengal Native Infantry a total of 1,450 natives and 120 Europeans (officers and artillerymen).

On 30th May, the requested detachments from the Bohpal and Malwa Bhil Contingents arrived at Indore to reinforce Colonel Durand's forces and on the following day he received news of the mutiny at Nusseerabad in the adjoining state of Rajputana.

On 2nd June, Colonel Durant made a visit to Mhow with the intention of bringing the European artillery battery back to Indore, however, after Colonel Platt convinced him that things were under control and that in the event of a mutiny he would ensure it was quashed, the battery was left in place.

On the 6th June, news of the mutiny at Neemuch reached Indore, increasing the view that mutiny at Mhow was imminent. To counter the possible threat, Colonel Durand reinforced the defences of the Residency, moving up the guns of the Bhopal Contingent and placing the Bhopal Cavalry in the Residency stables. The Maharaja also provided three guns, a company of infantry and two troops of cavalry to bolster the defences.

On the 27th June, religious fanatics appeared at the native camp and began to ferment unrest and it was expected that an outbreak of trouble would only be a matter of time. On the 1st July, the expected trouble came from an unexpected quarter; the Maharaja's guns which had been sent to bolster the defences of the Residency were suddenly unlimbered and turned on the Bhopal Cavalry stationed in the stable block. After a few shots, the artillery was moved to a position where they began to fire grape-shot at the Residency.

Colonel James Travers – Victoria Cross No. 136

The two guns of the Bhopal Contingent, under the command of Captain Cobbe and manned by Sergeants Orr and Murphy and 14 loyal native gunners began to return the fire from the Maharaja's guns.

Colonel Travers, the commander of the Bohpal Contingent, tried to rally his cavalry for a charge at the guns, however, only five of his men accompanied him.[5] Despite his small force, Colonel Travers managed to reach the guns and drive the gunners away, in the process he wounded Saadat Khan, who had been the instigator of the mutiny and was able to guard the guns for a short time which created a useful diversion.

During the diversion, many Europeans managed to escape into the Residency and Colonel Durand was able to get the Residency guns into position.

Under heavy rebel musket fire, and after his horse was wounded, Colonel Travers was forced to retire back to the Residency where he helped to man the guns.

For this action, Colonel Travers was later awarded the Victoria Cross.

✠

In addition to the Maharaja's men, the infantry of the Bhopal and Malwa Contingents also joined in the mutiny.

With news that the Maharaja was advancing at the head of his troops to attack the Residency, Colonel Durant decided to evacuate the Residency and head for Simrol. After the women and children were loaded on ammunition wagons and bullock carts the Colonel set off guarded by Colonel Traver's cavalry and the Malwa Bhil Contingent who brought up the rear. On reaching the valley of Narbada, the force changed its destination to Sehore after receiving intelligence that the Maharaja's troops were guarding the road to Simrol. Colonel Durand and his column arrived at Sehore on the 4th July, however, the next day he set out for Hoshangabad with the hope of making contact with General Woodburn.

Mutiny at Mhow

News of the mutiny at Indore reached Mhow on 1st July and expecting that the Maharaja's troops would now advance on Mhow, Colonel Platt sent out a piquet of Light Cavalry to a point about five miles down the road to Indore. Another detachment was sent out to the north of the town to take up station near a ravine.

Inside Mhow, the women and children were moved to the refuge of the fort which served as the arsenal and the European Artillery Battery were posted to stand guard.

After taking dinner in the mess, the European officers of the 1st Cavalry were ordered to join their men in the lines but to be ready to return at a moment's notice.

The officers of the 23rd Bengal Native Infantry dined at the house of the Sergeant-Major which was close to the lines and were ready to go to their beds in the lines when a message was received that the regiment would mutiny at 10 o'clock that evening.

At about 10 o'clock, Captain Brooke's, in charge of the cavalry guard noticed that a bungalow was on fire and as he approached the guard to investigate was assailed by musket fire from the infantry who had mutinied.

On hearing the shots at the cavalry lines, the infantry officers ran to their units in the lines but were also fired upon by the rebels. In the face of such fire, both sets of officers decided to make for the fort which was about a mile from the lines and with some help from their men managed to reach safety. When the officers arrived at the fort, Colonel Platt decided to disarm the native guard and eject them from the fort and then called for the European Artillery Battery to be made ready for action.

After half an hour, the artillery was limbered up and Colonel Platt left the fort with his officers and artillery to go and try to stop the mutiny. When the force reached the infantry parade ground, the guns were unlimbered and several rounds of grape were fired into the infantry lines. The rebel infantry soon dispersed and headed off for Indore following the cavalry which had left earlier. The officers and artillery returned to the fort where they began to prepare the defences for an assault.

---

5 Nehal Singh and Harsa Singh, two of the men who accompanied Colonel Travers, were both awarded the Indian Order of Merit for their part in the action.

On the next morning, the mutilated bodies of Colonel Platt, Major Harris and Captain Fagan, who had become separated from the force during the night, were found in the lines.

On the 3rd of July, Captain Hungerford received news that the Maharaja's troops together with the Mhow mutineers intended to attack the fort and while every effort was made to prepare for the attack, he sent a letter to the Maharaja asking if indeed this was his intention. On the 5th July, the Maharaja's Prime Minister, Bhao Rao Ramchunder and his Treasurer, Khooman Sing accompanied by Captain Fenwick arrived at Mhow with a reply from the Maharaja. The Maharaja stated in his letter that he had been unable to control his troops, who fell under the influence of the mutineers, however, he did regret the actions that had taken place at Indore and had done all that he could to protect the Europeans. He also offered to forward the contents of the Company treasury, which arrived on the evening of the 6th July.

On the same day, the Maharaja intervened to rescue Lieutenant Hutchinson, assistant to the Resident at Indore, who had been captured by the Rajah of Amjhera.

Mutiny at Agra

After some of the rebels from Indore reached the town, the 5th Infantry Regiment of the Gwalior Contingent mutinied at Agra on the 4th July.

All of the Europeans at the station, except Dr James and his wife who were shot while mounting their horses for a morning ride, managed to escape with their lives; including those who had arrived from Sipri on 18th June. After trekking through the jungle for twelve days, the group managed to reach Hoshangabad.

Mutiny at Sehore

On hearing of the mutiny at Indore, Major Richards, the political agent at Bhopal, ordered a stockade to be built around the Agency with the hope that his men of the Bhopal Contingent would remain loyal.

On the 7th July, three companies of mutineers from Indore returned to Sehore, with their plunder and began to incite the local troops who were soon in revolt.

With little alternative, Major Richards was forced to abandon the town and led the European Officers and their families, some 23 persons, to Hoshangabad.

Mutinies in the Bombay Presidency

With news of the outbreak of mutiny at Meerut, Lord Elphinstone, the Governor of the Bombay Presidency acted swiftly to limit the impact on his Presidency.

After fortifying the Residency at Bombay, Lord Elphinstone chartered and despatched two ships, the *Pottinger* and *Madras*, to Mauritius and the Cape Colony for reinforcements of British Troops. The 33rd Regiment of Foot, together with some artillery was despatched on board *Pottinger* and another vessel from Mauritius and the 89th and 95th Regiments of Foot were sent from the Cape Colony on board *Madras*. Lord Elphinstone seemed to have little concern regarding the loyalty of his own troops, but was worried about the incursion of mutineers from Central India into his territory and used the British troops mainly to guard his borders against such an eventuality.

While waiting for the arrival of the reinforcements, a column under the command of Major-General Woodburn was formed between Bombay and Agra to combat any incursion. This column consisted of five troops of the 14th Light Dragoons, the 25th Bombay Native Infantry, Captain Woolcombe's horse-battery of artillery and a pontoon train.

Lord Elphinstone's confidence in the loyalty of his troops was justified; from the 29 regiments of the Bombay army only three regiments would join the mutiny. From the 52 regiments of the Madras army none would rebel, however, one refused to volunteer for service in Bengal to help quell the mutiny.

Aurangabad

At the time of the mutiny, the 1st and 3rd Cavalry Regiments and the 2nd Infantry of the Hyderabad Contingent were stationed at Aurangabad, together with a battery of artillery.

On 14th June, when the garrison learned that they would be joining a column from Bombay and Agra to march against the mutineers at Delhi, the native troops of the 1st Cavalry rebelled. The regiment's native officers promised that they and their men would remain loyal but would not take up arms against the mutineers. Captain Abbott was left with little choice but to relent and informed the troops that they would not be required to march to Delhi.

Although rebellion had been avoided, when General Woodburn arrived at the station with his column on 23rd June, all of the troops were ordered to surrender their arms as a precautionary measure.

All of the men complied with the order, except those of the 1st Cavalry who fled; four of the men were captured and executed by hanging the next day.

Satara

When news of the mutinies in Central India reached Satara, many of the local chiefs, who were angry about the possible loss of their lands under the doctrine of lapse, began to prepare for rebellion and pulled together a force of about 2,000 men.

On the 20th June a native officer of the 22nd Native Infantry was arrested and executed for urging his men to mutiny and again on 13th July another abortive mutiny was thwarted by troops newly arrived from Poona, six of the rebels leaders were tried and executed.

Kolapore

Kolapore was garrisoned by the 27th Bengal Native Infantry, commanded by Major Roland and a native corps commanded by Captain Schneider; Colonel Maughan was the political superintendant of the station.

Since the outbreaks of mutiny in Bengal, the attitude of the 29th Regiment at Belgaum, the 28th Regiment at Darwar and the 27th at Kolapore were being affected and the flames of mutiny were fanned by regular messages between the regiments.

It appears that, instead of agreeing a date and making a coordinated mutiny, it was agreed that the 27th would mutiny first, followed by the 29th and then the 28th.

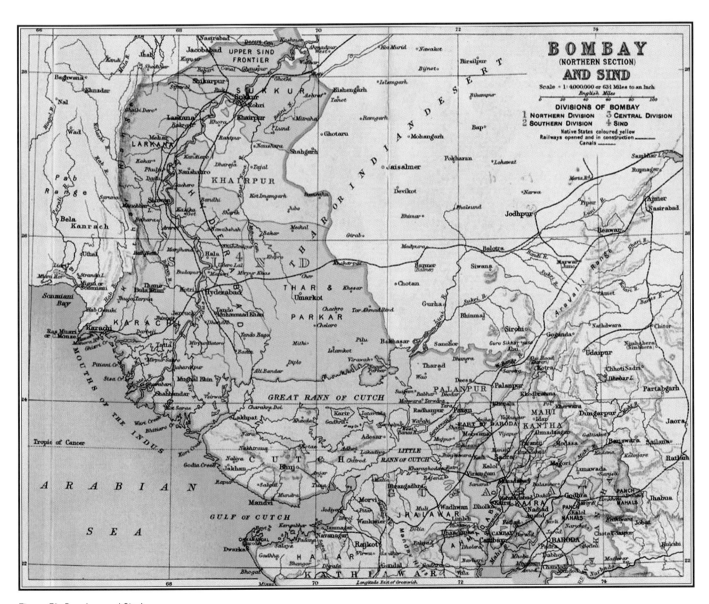

Figure 31. Bombay and Sind

During the night of the 8th July, the 27th Bengal Native Infantry mutinied and began to attack their officers bungalows, fortunately the native adjutant raised the alarm which allowed the women and children to escape from the houses before they were attacked.

Some of the European officers tried to quell the mutiny but to no avail and three who tried to escape into the country were shot down but the remainder managed to take refuge in the Residency protected by the local native Corps that remained loyal.

Mutinies at Belgaum and Darwar were forestalled following warning messages sent from Kolhapur via telegraph.

After turning on their officers, the rebels took time to fire the officers' bungalows, sack the treasury and plunder the station before moving off to plunder the town, however, Colonel Maughan had managed to close the town gates.

After spending the night locked out of the town, it appears that the majority of the mutineers came to their senses and returned to their duties, however, a small number of mutineers occupied a nearby fort.

Lieutenant William Alexander Kerr – Victoria Cross No. 143

When Lieutenant Kerr, adjutant of the South Mahratta Horse stationed at Satara, heard of the mutiny of the 27th Bombay Native Infantry at Kolapore, some 70 miles away, he immediately volunteered his services to go and help put down the mutiny.

With about 50 of his men, the Lieutenant set off on the 70 mile journey and 26 hours later arrived at the fort outside Kolapore after night had fallen on the 10th of July and immediately set about an attack on the mutineers. Without any artillery, the Lieutenant had to seek alternative means of breaching the fort gates which he did by leading a storming party of 17 men to the gates which he and a native soldier forced open with the aid of crowbars. As the British force entered the fort, the mutineers retreated to a loop holed house in the centre of the enclosure and barricaded themselves within to continue the fight.

Lieutenant Kerr led his small party to the door of the house and again forced entry using his crowbar, being first into the house he took the full blast of a musket shot and was wounded. Despite his wounds, Lieutenant Kerr participated in the ferocious

hand to hand fighting which followed; all of the 34 mutineers were either killed or captured. Of the 17 strong storming party 8 were killed in action, 4 subsequently died of their wounds and the remaining five were all seriously wounded, including Lieutenant Kerr.

For his part in this action, Lieutenant Kerr was later awarded the Victoria Cross.

Ahmadabad/Hyderabad

In September, mutinies at Ahmadabad and Hyderabad were forestalled when the garrisons were disarmed.

Karachi

On the 10th September, the 21st Bombay Native Infantry declared their allegiance to the rebels, however, British forces were soon able to restore order.

Bombay

When news of the mutinies in Central India reached Bombay, Mr Charles Forjett, the Superintendant of Police managed to keep matters in check by arresting anyone that his network of informers reported was expressing sympathy with the mutineers.

He also erected a scaffold near to the main police office and after summoning the leading civilians to a meeting, pointed to the scaffold telling them that anyone showing the slightest hint of rebellion would be hanged. This seemed to do the trick and major religious festivals, at the end of August and September, passed without incident.

A plan for a mutiny of the native soldiers during the festival of Diwali, on the 17th October, was uncovered and the two ring leaders, a native officer of the Marine Battalion and a Private of the 10th Bengal Native Infantry were tried by court martial, found guilty and blown from guns; six accomplices were transported for life.

7

THE DELHI CAMPAIGN

Delhi had long been the capital of the Mughal Empire and for centuries before that, a capital of importance to those of the Hindu faith.

The aged and blind Bahadur Shah Zafar, the last Mughal Emperor[6] occupied a fortified palace within the city walls where he existed with the benefit of a Company pension and the notional title of King of Delhi.

Although the city housed a magazine with one of the largest stores of powder and ammunition in the whole of India, the garrison was comprised of the 38th, 54th and 74th Native Infantry Regiments commanded by a small number of British Officers but no British or European Regiments.

The fall of Delhi

The mutineers from Meerut arrived at Delhi, soon after British Officers had read out the news of the hanging of Mughal Pandy to their assembled troops, who were greatly inflamed by the news.

A forward element of the mutineers arrived at the Salumgarh and entered the Palace via a bridge across the River Jumna and took up position outside the Emperors apartments where they shouted out requests for the Emperor to become their leader and the King of India. The Emperor immediately sent a message to Captain Douglas, commander of the Palace guard, who upon reaching the palace addressed the mutineers from a balcony and requested them to disperse in respect of the Emperors wishes. This they did but went on a rampage throughout the palace killing every European that they came across.

Responding to a request from Mr Simon Fraser, the Commissioner of Delhi, Captain Douglas proceeded to the Calcutta Gate and met with the Commissioner, Sir Thomas Theophilus Metcalfe the Magistrate of Delhi and Mr Hutchinson the Collector. From their position it was obvious that they had arrived too late as the mutineers were in possession of the gate and hordes of rebels were streaming into the city. The mutineers were also admitted to the city by the Rajghat Gate which was opened by supporters within the city.

Sir Thomas Theophilus Metcalf set off for the police headquarters at Chandney Chowk where he intended to turn out the police force and try to guard the other city gates.

Mr Fraser tried to reason with the mutineers but after shots were exchanged Mr Fraser, Mr Hutchinson and Captain Douglas were captured and carried to apartments above the gate. It was here together with the Chaplain Mr Jennings and his daughter, who were tending to their wounds, that they were butchered by the mutineers.

Defence of the Magazine[7]

On his way to Chandney Chowk, Sir Thomas Theophilus Metcalf stopped off at the Magazine to inform Lieutenant George Dobson Percival Willoughby, the commander in charge that the mutineers were streaming into the city.

Initially he sought to obtain two artillery pieces with a view to defending the bridge of boats and preventing access to the city, however, after assessing the situation Lieutenant Willoughby decided that this was no longer possible and instead set about the defence of the magazine.

At first, Lieutenant Willoughby was assisted by the native soldiers and workers under his command, however, in short order they climbed the high walls and defected to the rebels.

---

6 Having no male heirs, under the doctrine of lapse, his title would become defunct upon his death.

7 The magazine in question was a walled enclosure located within the walls of Delhi, another magazine with 3,000 barrels of gunpowder located 3 miles outside the city was siezed by the mutineers.

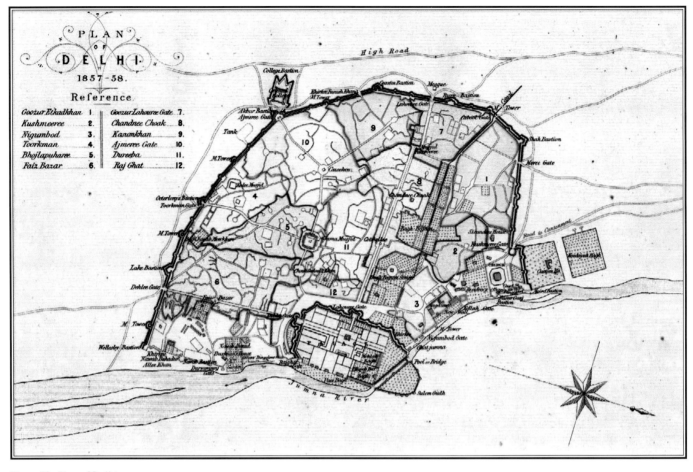

Figure 32. Plan of Delhi

Assistant Commissary John Buckley – Victoria Cross No. 116
Lieutenant George Forrest – Victoria Cross No. 117
Lieutenant William Raynor – Victoria Cross No. 118

Following the desertion of the native workers, Lieutenant Willoughby had at his disposal only a very small force to defend the magazine; Lieutenants William Raynor and George Forrest both from the Bengal Veteran Establishment, Conductors John Buckley and John Sculley from the Bengal Army Ordnance Department, Sub-Conductor William Shaw also from the Ordnance Department and Sergeants Bryan Edwards and Peter Stewart both with the Bengal Artillery.

The defensive measures implemented by Lieutenant Willoughby are best described by the words of Lieutenant George Forrest who later wrote about the event:

Figure 33. Magazine at Delhi

Inside the gate leading to the park we placed two six pounders double charged with grape, one under Acting Sub-Conductor Crow and Sergeant Stewart, with the lighted matches in their hands, and with orders that, if any attempt was made to force the gate, both guns were to be fired at once, and they were to fall back on that part of the Magazine in which Lt Willoughby and I were posted.

The principal gate of the Magazine was similarly defended by two guns, with the 'chevaux de frieze'[8] laid down on the inside. For the further defence of this gate and the Magazine in its vicinity there were two six pounders so placed as both to command the gate and a small bastion in its vicinity.

Within sixty yards of the gate, and in front of the office, and commanding two cross-roads, were three six pounders and one twenty four pounder howitzer which could be so managed as to act on any part of the Magazine in that neighbourhood.

After all these guns and howitzers had been placed in the several positions above named they were loaded with double charges of grape.

With measures now in place to defend the magazine, Lieutenant Willoughby made one final preparation to prevent the magazine falling into rebel hands in the event that they were overpowered.

A trail of gunpowder was laid from the foot of a large Lime tree in the enclosure into the magazine and Conductor Scully was stationed next to the tree with orders to ignite the powder when Conductor Buckley gave the signal by raising his hat.

Bahadur Shah Zafar, the King of Delhi, sent several messages to Lieutenant Willoughby, ordering him to surrender the magazine but these went unanswered.

Eventually the rebels used scaling ladders to breach the walls but were repulsed by fire of grapeshot from the gallant defenders.

Lieutenant Willoughby and his men managed to stand fast for five hours, until their ammunition was exhausted and the signal was given to Conductor Scully to fire the magazine. In the confusion from the tremendous explosion, which killed hundreds of mutineers, Lieutenants Willoughby, Forrest and Raynor together with Conductor Buckley managed to make their escape and eventually, with the exception of Lieutenant Willoughby managed to make their way back to Meerut. The remaining defenders were killed in the explosion and Lieutenant Willoughby was killed by villagers the next day while making his way to Meerut.

---

8 A defensive spiked barrier

The three surviving defenders were all awarded the Victoria Cross and the widow of Lieutenant Willoughby received a pension of £150 a year.

———— ✠ ————

Events at the Cashmere Gate

The Cashmere Gate was the entrance to Delhi from the cantonment some two miles from the city where the Company army had its barracks. It was guarded by about 50 men from the 38th Native Infantry Regiment with a few British Officers in command.

When news of the trouble in Delhi finally reached the cantonment, the commanding officer Brigadier-General Harry Graves ordered the 54th Native Regiment of Foot and two artillery pieces to proceed into the city by way of the Cashmere Gate.

As it was taking some time for the artillery pieces to be made ready, Colonel Ripley led an advanced party of men from the 54th towards the city. On reaching the Cashmere Gate, Colonel Ripley could see a mob and mutineers from Meerut congregating on the city side of the gate, face to face with men from the 38th who were guarding the gate. As his men from the 54th seemed to be loyal, Colonel Ripley entered the inner gate and confronted the mutineers, however, after issuing orders for the 38th and 54th to fire on the mutineers which were ignored, his troops turned on their officers and he and his fellow officers were all slaughtered.

The men from the 38th and 54th now joined the rebels in their rampage of killing and looting throughout the city.

Captain Wallace, who was in command of the detachment from the 38th which was manning the gate, did manage to escape and fled up the road back towards the cantonment. On his way back to the cantonment, Captain Wallace met up with Major Patterson, who was proceeding to the Cashmere Gate with 2 guns and two companies of the 54th, and after reporting the situation at the Gate continued to the cantonment to seek reinforcements. Major Patterson continued on to the Gate and when the mutineers saw his artillery pieces they dispersed to continue their rampage in the city. The action also prompted some of the men from the 54th to return to the ranks.

When Captain Wallace arrived at the cantonment and reported the situation to Major Abbott, the Major ordered the men of his regiment the 74th Native Infantry to assemble and mindful of the defection of the 38th and 54th Regiments informed his men of the situation in Delhi and stated that now was the time to demonstrate their loyalty.

Major Abbott called for volunteers to put down the insurgents at Delhi and to a man they stepped forward and following the

Figure 34. The Cashmere Gate

command to load their muskets did so obediently without any problems.

On reaching the Cashmere Gate, Major Abbott saw some men and officers of the 38th and 54th on guard at the gate but no sign of the mutineers, although he could hear the sounds of fierce fighting within the city.

At around noon there was the sound of a great explosion when the magazine was ignited, and soon afterwards the blackened and unrecognisable figures of Lieutenants Willoughby and Forrest appeared at the gate as they made their escape to Meerut.

By mid afternoon, Major Abbott received orders to return with his guns to the cantonment, however, before he could act on these orders some men and officers returned to the Gate from within the city with the news that the gunners had defected to the rebels with their guns.

By now the thought that a British relief force from Meerut might arrive to quell the rebellion had been dismissed by the up till now loyal men and they now decided to turn their guns on the British officers. The men of the 38th and 74th advised Major Abbott and his officers that they could no longer protect them and that they should flee in order to save their lives. Major Abbott, seeing the futility of further resistance ordered his officers to retreat back to the cantonment and escorted some women and children who had arrived at the Gate fleeing the carnage in the city.

About half of the European civilians managed to escape the city and made their way to the outskirts where they initially congregated at the Flagstaff Tower. The cantonment was finally abandoned at nightfall and with the civilians the survivors made their way to Meerut, Karnal and Umballa.

Atrocities after the fall of Delhi

On 12th May, despite his earlier reticence, the King of Delhi held his first formal audience for many years and declared his support for the mutineers.

Four days later on 16th May 1857, 52 European prisoners, who had been held in the palace, were murdered in front of the King to implicate him and make it impossible for him to reach a compromise with the Company.

Preparations to recapture Delhi

At the start of the mutiny, the Commander in Chief of forces in India, Major-General George Anson was at the hill station of Simla in the foothills of the Himalayas, recovering from a recent illness.

On 12th May, Captain Barnard, Aide-de-Camp to Sir Henry Barnard the commander of the Sirhind Division, arrived at Simla with news of the mutiny and massacre at Delhi.

General Anson immediately despatched orders to the 75th Regiment of Foot stationed at Kasauli and to the 1st European Fusiliers Regiment at Dugshai to move as soon as possible to

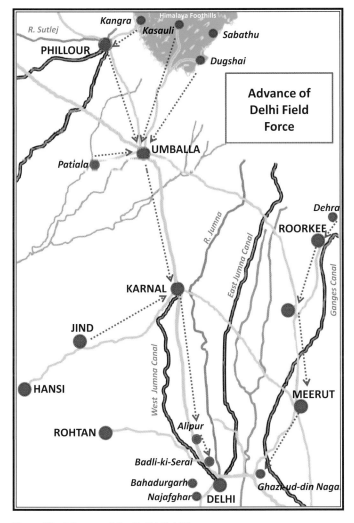

Figure 35. Advance of the Delhi Field Force

Having completed the initial deployments to protect strategic outposts and begin the assembly of a force to retake Delhi, General Anson left Simla on 14th May 1857 and proceeded to Umballa where he arrived the next day. After sending a small force to Karnal to keep open communications with Meerut, General Anson had little choice but to wait while his forces and supplies were assembled at Umballa.

By the 22nd May 1857, General Anson had formulated his plans for the attack on Delhi; these would require a force of three brigades; two from Umballa and one from Meerut.

The 1st Umballa brigade would be commanded by Brigadier Halifax and was made up of the 75th Queens Regiment, 1st Bengal European Fusiliers, 2 squadrons of the 9th Lancers and 1 troop of Horse Artillery.

The 2nd Umballa brigade would be commanded by Brigadier Jones and was made up of the 60th Native Infantry, 2nd Bengal European Fusiliers, 2 squadrons of the 9th Lancers, 1 squadron of 4th Bengal Lancers and one troop of Horse Artillery.

The Meerut brigade was initially commanded by Major-General W. H. Hewitt, however, due to illness, command was transferred to Brigadier Archdale Wilson and was made up of a wing of the 60th Royal Rifles, 2 squadrons of Carabineers, 1 unit of Field Artillery, 1 troop of Horse Artillery, some sappers and 120 Artillerymen.

The combined forces totalled 3,000 European and 1,000 Native soldiers with 22 field guns.

The plan was for the Umballa Brigades to be concentrated at Karnal by 30th May and then march together to Baghput where they would join up with the Meerut Brigade and advance on Delhi.

After communicating his plans to General Hewitt at Meerut, General Anson left Umballa for Karnal on 24th May and arrived the next day.

On 26th May 1857, General Anson was struck down by cholera and died a few hours later; with his death, command of the Delhi Field Force passed down to Major-General Sir Henry Barnard, who had only been in India for a few weeks.

Advance on Delhi

Despite this being the hottest season of the year, which required the men to march only at night, General Barnard decided to press on from Karnal and continue with the advance towards Delhi rather than wait for the arrival of his siege guns.

On 5th June, General Barnard and an advanced party of the Umballa brigades reached Alipur, only 10 miles from Delhi, where he decided to wait for the arrival of the rest of his men, the siege train and the Meerut Brigade.

Umballa. He also despatched messages informing units of the Sepoy mutiny and ordering the magazine at Ferozepur and the fort at Phillour to be secured with a European guard.

On the next day, having received details of the mutiny at Meerut, General Anson ordered the 2nd European Fusiliers based at Sabathu to also move to Umballa. An artillery officer was also despatched to Phillour with orders to assemble a siege train to take small arms ammunition to Umballa together with the Native Artillery units currently based at Nurpur and Kangra.

The Nasiri battalion of Ghurkhas, based at Jatogh, were ordered to Phillour to act as a guard for the siege train as it proceeded to Umballa together with a detachment of the 9th Irregular Cavalry.

The Simur battalion of Ghurkhas, based at Dehra, together with Sappers and Miners, based at Roorkee, were ordered to proceed to Meerut.

The Meerut Brigade, under the command of General Wilson began its journey towards Delhi on 27th May and by the 30th May had reached the village of Ghazi-ud-din Nagar on the banks of the River Hindun, about 10 miles from Delhi without any difficulty.

On reaching the village, the column was bombarded by artillery fire from a nearby ridge, however, after returned artillery fire the mutineers broke ranks and fled back to Delhi and the British captured five of their guns. The mutineers returned to their position the next day and began to fire on the column but were again driven off without much difficulty.

On the 3rd June, General Wilson's force was augmented by the arrival of the Simur Battalion of Ghurkhas, some 500 men, commanded by Major Charles Reid who had travelled from Bulandshahr.

On the next day, General Wilson received orders from General Bernard to join his force at Alipur and after crossing the River Jumna at Baghput arrived at Alipur on the 6th June 1857, as did the siege train with its much needed supply of ammunition and heavier guns.

With all his resources now in place, General Wilson renewed the advance to Delhi on 7th June, however, the force had not gone far before scouts reported that the mutineers had established a defensive position at Badli-ki-Serai only five miles from the city and spanning the main road.

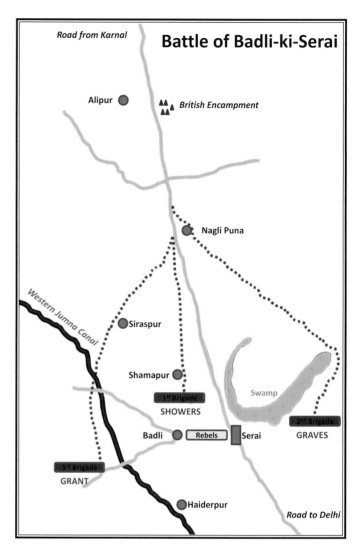

Figure 36. Battle of Badli-ki-Serai

Battle of Badli-ki-Serai

After further reconnaissance of the enemy position, General Bernard began positioning his troops for an attack during the early hours of 8th June.

The 1st Brigade, under the command of Brigadier Showers, with the support of artillery was to advance down the road, while the 2nd Brigade under the command of Brigadier Graves would attack the left flank and the 3rd Brigade commanded by Brigadier Grant would attack the right flank.

At daybreak, with the flanking forces in position, Brigadier Showers began his advance down the road and an artillery duel ensued, however, having smaller calibre guns the British artillery was having little impact on the enemy. With the British guns having little effect, the order was given and the men from the 75th Regiment of Foot charged the enemy artillery batteries head on with fixed bayonets.

Colour Sergeant Cornelius Coughlan – Victoria Cross No. 124

With the artillery duel at an end, the men from the 2nd Brigade attacked the enemy left flank which was protected by a walled and gated building (Serai). Men of the 75th Regiment of Foot stormed the Serai, bursting in the gates and attacked the defenders.

Colour Sergeant Coughlan rescued the severely wounded Private Corbett of the 75th and carried him to the rear under heavy fire, for treatment. For this selfless action, Colour Sergeant Coughlan was later awarded the Victoria Cross.

✠

Pensioned Sergeant Henry Hartigan – Victoria Cross No. 126

With the enemy under pressure to their front and left flank, Brigadier Hope Grant made the decisive move of the battle and launched his cavalry, the 9th Lancers, to attack the enemy rear.

During the mêlée, Sergeant Hartigan came across the wounded Sergeant Helstone who had been unseated from his horse and was surrounded by the enemy.

He drove into the crowd of Sepoys and rescued Sergeant Helstone from probable death and carried him to the rear for treatment.

For this action Sergeant Hartigan was later awarded the Victoria Cross.

After the charge of the cavalry, the battle was soon over and the mutineers fled their positions and made their way back towards Delhi.

Lieutenant Alfred Stowell Jones – Victoria Cross No. 125

Some of the mutineers were bravely trying to take their artillery pieces with them as they retreated back to Delhi.

Lieutenant Jones, in command of a troop of the 4th squadron of the 9th Lancers was leading his troop in pursuit of a column of dust thought to be retreating enemy guns, when he saw a 9 pounder off to his left being pulled by six horses with drivers. As his troop continued to chase the column of dust, Lieutenant Jones charged after the escaping gun that he had spotted and coming alongside he dismounted the first driver with a slash from his sword and managed to grab the horse bridle and bring the gun carriage to a stop. Having failed to catch up with the cloud of dust, the troop returned to Lieutenant Jones and the captured gun and after locating the ammunition fired off a few rounds at mutineers taking refuge in a nearby village.

The gun, which had belonged to Captain De Tessier's Field Battery that had mutinied at Delhi a month early was returned to the column's artillery force.

For capturing the gun, Lieutenant Jones was later awarded the Victoria Cross.

The siege of Delhi

After clearing the defensive positions at Badli-ki-Serai, General Bernard did not rest on his laurels, but instead pressed on towards Delhi, fearful that if he did not do so then the rebels would establish further defensive positions to halt his progress.

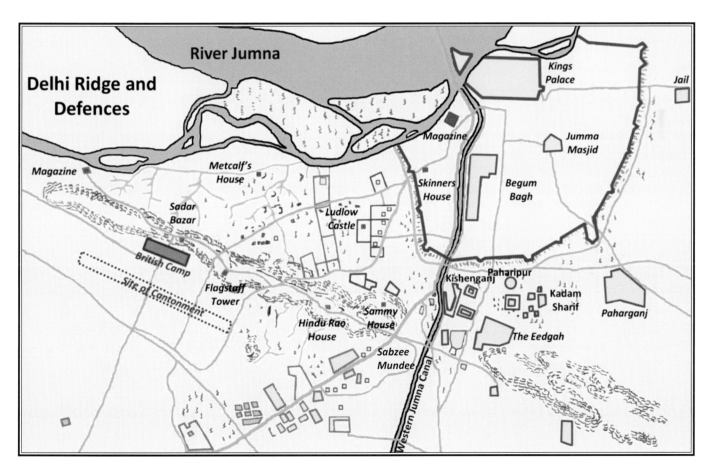

Figure 37. Delhi defences

Capture of the Delhi Ridge

Not far from Badli-ki-Serai, the road branches with one branch continuing on to the Sabzee Mundee suburb of Delhi while the branch off to the left led to the cantonment to the rear of the Delhi Ridge.

General Bernard split his force into two main columns, with the intention of mounting a simultaneous attack at both ends of the ridge.

The first column led by General Bernard consisted of the infantry brigade commanded by Brigadier Graves together with Captain Money's troop of Horse Artillery and a squadron of the 9th Lancers; would take the road to the cantonment and attack the river end of the ridge.

The second column commanded by Brigadier Wilson consisted of the infantry brigade commanded by Brigadier Showers and the remainder of the artillery and cavalry; would continue down the road to Delhi and then turn left at Sabzee Mundee and attack the city end of the ridge.

The Simur Battalion of Sikhs would act as a skirmishing line between the two main columns and attack the centre of the ridge.

As General Barnard's force approached the bridge across the Nujjufghur swamp drain, which gave access to the cantonment, they came under enemy artillery fire from a battery near the Flagstaff Tower on the ridge some 1,200 yards distant. In spite of the accurate fire, Captain Money managed to cross the bridge with his artillery and after reaching the parade ground set up his guns and soon silenced the mutineers' battery. The 60th Rifles and 2nd Bengal European Fusiliers now advanced up the slope of the ridge, captured the guns and began to force the mutineers back along the ridge towards Hindu Rao's House.

General Wilson's force passed through Sabzee Mundee after facing heavy fire from the houses and walled gardens and attacked the right most end of the ridge before advancing along the crest toward Hindu Rao's House where they met up with General Bernard's men.

As planned the Simur Battalion of Sikhs attacked the centre of the ridge and before long this strategic high ground was in the hands of the British, with the defenders having fled back to the city.

At the end of a very long day, with much fighting during the heat of the day, General Barnard had secured his objective and in the process had capture 13 enemy artillery pieces, including two 24 pounder guns and a quantity of much needed ammunition. The success however came at a cost, with 53 men killed and 130 men wounded or missing, it is believed that the mutineers lost about 1,000 men killed or wounded.

Defence of the Delhi Ridge

Delhi was a strongly fortified walled city with the length of the walls being about 7 miles. The wall itself was about 24 foot high with bastions at regular intervals, each of which contained between 10 and 14 artillery pieces; the wall also had many strongly fortified gates.

The external wall was fronted by a grass bank (glacis) for up to a third of its height in front of which was a wide ditch about 24 feet deep.

The eastern wall of the city faced the River Jumna and at this time of year the waters lapped right up to the wall.

At this stage of the campaign, General Barnard had neither the men nor equipment to mount a siege and any attempt to take the city would have been futile; therefore the General concentrated his efforts on securing and improving the defences of the Delhi Ridge which was of strategic importance to any future assault on the city.

Having cleared the Delhi Ridge of mutineers, General Barnard had two objectives; to establish defensive positions on the ridge to guard against attacks from the city and to establish an encampment for his men, equipment and materials. On the city of western end of the ridge the "Right Battery" was established, with a heavy mortar battery nearby, hidden in a hollow to the rear of the ridge. Further east along the ridge at Hindu Rao's House, which was a very substantial building, the main infantry piquet was set up with the "Centre Half Moon Battery" just in front of the house. About 300 yards further along the ridge was another substantial building, the Observatory, which was where the heavy battery was established. Yet further east was on old disused Pathan Mosque, whose strong walls were used to protect another piquet supported by two guns. The last piquet, for now, was set up at the Flagstaff tower, again supported by two guns.

In the circumstances, excellent defences were established in a very short period of time; the most vulnerable position was the area around the "Right Battery" which was closest to the city. It was in this area that the buildings and walled gardens of Sabzee Mundee and Kishengunge, together with wooded scrub land which extended almost to the city walls offered protection and concealment to any attacking force from Delhi.

An encampment was established in and around the original cantonment, many of the officer bungalows and other buildings had been burnt to the ground during the mutiny a month earlier and to prevent concealment for attackers the sepoy barracks were now burnt down.

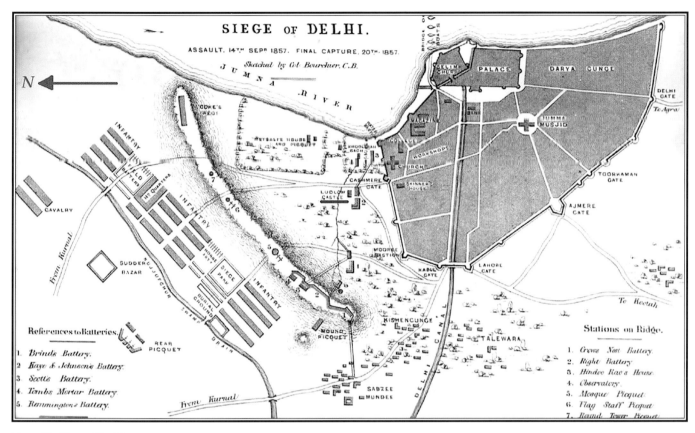

Figure 38. Siege of Delhi

Attacks on the Delhi Ridge

The first assault on the Delhi Ridge came on 9th June, the day after the British had secured their position on the Ridge. After a short bombardment the rebels attacked Hindu Rao's house in force, fortunately the position was one of those reinforced following the arrival that morning of Captain Morley with a force of Guides, comprising 3 troops of Cavalry and 7 companies of Infantry, and the attack was repulsed.

This force had marched from Mardan on the Yusufzai frontier, some 580 miles from Delhi, in only 22 days, a remarkable feat during the hot season.

The following day, on the 10th June 1857, a large force of 500 mutineers with support from Cavalry and two guns left the city by the Ajmer Gate with the apparent intention of attacking the British right flank on the ridge or their rear. Seeing the approach of this force, Major Reid immediately deployed a force of 7 companies from his Simur Battalion of Sikhs, 2 companies from the 60th Rifles and 150 men from the Guides, supported by 2 guns from Major Scott's battery. The opposing forces continued to close and at about 6:00 pm when they were within musket range

the British force unleashed such a withering fire that the mutineers retreated back within the city walls.

To help forestall a similar attack the "Mound Piquet" was established.

On 11th June the mutineers again mounted an attack on Hindu Rao's House, which had been identified as a key British position on the Ridge, and were yet again repulsed by Major Reid's Sikhs supported by men from the 60th Rifles.

Lieutenant Thomas Cadell – Victoria Cross No. 127

On 12th June, Lieutenant Cadell was part of an advanced piquet made up from men of his own unit the 2nd European Fusiliers a detachment from 75th Regiment of Foot and two guns, which was helping to protect the piquet at the Flagstaff Tower. The piquet was located near the River Jumna, within the grounds of Sir Theophilus Metcalfe's country retreat, surrounded by thickets of trees used by the mutineers to mask their attack.

When the mutineers attacked in force, the commander of the detachment Captain Knox was killed along with several of the gunners and the guns were in danger of being lost until the 75th managed to mount a charge at the rebels. Under heavy fire from the enemy, Lieutenant Cadell rescued a bugler from his regiment who had been seriously wounded and brought him back to safety. The piquet retired to the ridge pursued by the enemy, some of whom actually crested the ridge and were close to entering the British encampment.

With the arrival of reinforcements the mutineers were driven off the ridge and pursued for some way and when the call to retire was sounded Lieutenant Cadell, helped by three others, again advanced into the mutineers to rescue a severely wounded soldier from the 75th who had been left behind.

For these two acts of selfless bravery, Lieutenant Cadell was later awarded the Victoria Cross.

✠

To help prevent another surprise attack on their left flank a much larger piquet was established in the ruins of Sir Metcalfe's House.

Later in the day another attack on Hindu Rao's house was mounted by the mutineers by a force which had advanced through Sabzee Mundee which was easily repulsed by Major Jacob and units of the 1st Bengal European Fusiliers. It is probable that this attack was intended to be coordinated with the attack on the Flagstaff Tower but fortunately this did not happen.

Planned coup de main

Since arriving at the gates of Delhi, some days earlier, General Bernard had come under intense pressure from the powers that be, in distant Calcutta, to recapture the city. It was felt that a British victory could help to prevent any further mutinies of the Native regiments, however, equally a defeat or only partial success could have a very detrimental effect. Any enterprise therefore carried a high risk of causing immense harm to the British position in the whole of India.

It was clear to General Bernard that he could not effectively besiege the city, with only sufficient forces to establish a front at the northern end of the city, leaving the south, east and west boundaries open for the mutineers to come and go as they pleased. So far the mutineers had used this freedom to great effect being joined on a regular basis by new Native Regiments as they mutinied. They were also able to resupply with ammunition for their muskets and guns, which allowed them to bombard the British positions on an almost continual basis, while the British could only reply at intervals as they needed to conserve their ammunition. The lack of Sappers and men for working parties also limited the possibilities for establishing protected lines of approach to the city and the use of mines.

For some of General Barnard's staff officers this left only one alternative for a quick victory, a *coup de main*, a swift surprise attack in force.

Reluctantly, General Barnard agreed to a plan by which two of the Delhi gates would be blown up allowing his force of infantry (at this point only 1,800 men, which included all of the men on the ridge piquets) to enter the city in two columns. The attack was planned for the 13th June and at about 11:00 am, the officer of the day, General Graves, received orders to remove all the Europeans from the ridge for assembly as part of the attack force. As General Graves had not received a written order, for this most important command, he went to the tent of General Barnard for clarification. When asked by General Barnard of his opinion regarding success of the undertaking General Graves replied *"You may certainly take the city by surprise, but whether you are strong enough to hold it is another matter"*. This comment caused General Barnard to re-evaluate the matter and he finally decided to abandon the planned attack, a decision for which he was widely criticised. Future events, however, proved that this was a very wise decision.

Attacks on the Ridge resume

On the 17th June the mutineers mounted another attack on the Metcalfe piquet, supported by heavy artillery fire, the attack was driven back and fortunately it was realised that this was all a diversion, to conceal work taking place at Eidgha Mosque in the Kishgunge suburb of Delhi.

The mosque was a strong fortified position, on a knoll, within which the rebels were attempting to construct an artillery battery. If allowed to become operational this battery would be able to threaten the security of the right end of the Ridge. As soon as the seriousness of the threat was recognised, two columns led by Majors Reid and Tombs were sent out from the Ridge to deal with the threat; this was accomplished with heavy losses to the mutineers, the destruction of their battery and much of the mosque.

On 19th June the British received intelligence that the rebels intended to mount a large scale attack later in the day, so they reinforced the piquets on the Ridge leaving only cavalry and artillery in the camp. In the late afternoon, a large force of mutineers left Delhi via the Lahore Gate and began a frontal attack on the Ridge. It appears that the frontal attack may have been a diversion, or the first part of a two pronged attack as a small unit of cavalry on patrol to the rear of the city end of the ridge spotted a large enemy force advancing through the walled gardens of Sabzee Mundee intending to attack the British rear.

Private Thomas Hancock – Victoria Cross No. 128
Private John Purcell – Victoria Cross No. 129
Sowar Rooper Khan

When news of the danger to the rear reached the camp, Brigadier Hope Grant assembled a force of about 500 cavalry, supported by 12 guns and rode off to confront the enemy.

The mutineers had taken up position in walled gardens supported by artillery which were difficult to dislodge by the British artillery. Fierce fighting continued until the light began to fade, with several cavalry charges being needed to save the British guns from capture.

During one of these charges, when a British ammunition wagon exploded nearby, Brigadier Hope Grant's horse reared and was shot out from under him and he was pinned to the ground by his wounded horse.

Private Hancock and Private Purcell, who had also had his horse shot out from under him, both rushed to the aid of their fallen commanding officer. Private Hancock dismounted and offered his horse to the Brigadier which was refused and Sowar Rooper Khan from the 4th Irregular Cavalry rode up and made the same offer.

Again the offer was refused; the Brigadier did however grab the tail of Sowar Khan's horse and allowed himself to be dragged to safety.

Privates Hancock and Purcell were both awarded the Victoria Cross for their part in the action which saved the life of their commanding officer. During the action, Private Hancock was severely wounded in the arm, which was later amputated.

Sadly Private Purcell was killed in the action to take Delhi in September 1857.

Sowar Rooper Khan did not receive the award as he was not eligible,[9] however, he was offered a sum of money by Brigadier Grant. The Sowar refused the offer but requested the Brigadier to ask his commanding officer for a promotion.

Private Samuel Turner – Victoria Cross No. 130

During the attack Private Turner serving with the 60th Rifles, went into a mass of the enemy under heavy fire to rescue the wounded Lieutenant Humphreys and brought him back to safety, unfortunately the Lieutenant's wound proved to be mortal.

Private Turner, who was severely wounded by a sabre cut to his right arm, was later awarded the Victoria Cross for this action.

---

9 Native troops were only eligible for the award from 1867.

With nightfall the fighting stopped but both forces maintained their positions, however, when the British advanced the following morning, with the intention of driving the rebels back into Delhi, they found little resistance as the enemy had retired during the night.

To help guard against further attacks against their rear, the Rear Piquet was established with infantry and heavy guns and the Mound Piquet was also reinforced.

It was of little surprise to the British when they received intelligence of a major rebel attack planned for the 23rd June 1857. This was the centenary of the Battle of Plassey, for months rumours had been circulating, regarding a prophesy that British rule in India would end on this day. It was also *Ruth Juttra*; a high festival for Hindus and it was also to be a full moon which was seen as a good omen by Mohammedans. The mutineers in Delhi had also received reinforcements; three infantry and one cavalry regiments from those that mutinied at Jullundur and Phillour.

The British also received the good news that a reinforcement of over 700 men under the command of Major Olpherts was only 20 miles away. With news of the impending assault, General Barnard ordered Major Olpherts to advance to the city as soon as possible and they had just arrived in the early hours of the 23rd June when the rebels began an immense bombardment of the Ridge from the City bastions.

At first light a large force of mutineers, still supported by artillery fire from the city, advanced through Sabzee Mundee and attacked the "Mound Battery" at the city end of the Ridge. Despite being vastly outnumbered, Major Reid and his small group of men managed to fend off several attacks before reinforcements arrived and they were able to drive the rebels back to the outskirts of Sabzee Mundee. Major Reid requested further reinforcements so that he could drive the enemy back into the city, General Barnard acceded to this request and despatched a large force of Ghurkhas and men from the 1st European Fusiliers who had arrived that morning as part of Major Olpherts column.

Colour Sergeant Stephen Garvin – Victoria Cross No. 131

With the additional resources, the British force was now able to drive the enemy back into Sabzee Mundee, however, the rebels were able to take up positions in the many fortified houses of the suburb and put up a great resistance laying down heavy fire on the advancing British force.

The rebels' strongest position appeared to be at the old temple, known as "*Sammy House*" on the main street into the suburb and had to be cleared if the mutineers were to be dislodged. Colour Sergeant Garvin volunteered to lead a small party of men to clear the temple. Despite the intense enemy fire and facing a significantly larger force of rebels, Colour Sergeant Garvin and his small band of men were able to clear and secure the *"Sammy House"* which greatly reduced the enemy fire on the advancing British force.

For his action Colour Sergeant Garvin was later awarded the Victoria Cross.

With the *"Sammy House"* now in British hands the advance continued and by nightfall the rebels were finally driven back into the city.

Private John McGovern – Victoria Cross No. 132

During the action to clear Sabzee Mundee Private McGovern rescued a wounded comrade and under intense enemy artillery fire managed to bring him back to the safety of the camp.

For this action Private McGovern was later awarded the Victoria Cross.

With Sabzee Mundee in British hands it was decided that it was time to incorporate *"Sammy House"* and a walled building (Serai) on the other side of the road into the Ridge defences. Engineers immediately set about improving the defences of both buildings and as they were only 200 to 300 yards from the rightmost end of the Ridge connected them with a line of embrasures. A permanent piquet of almost 200 men was established in the buildings which greatly improved the defence against attacks to the rear and prevented the enemy use of Sabzee Mundee as an easy approach to the Ridge.

After the failure of the attacks on the 23rd June, the spirits of the mutineers seemed to fall and for the rest of the month there was little activity against the British positions.

At the beginning of July General Neville Chamberlain arrived at Delhi with reinforcements from the Punjab, however, the mutineer numbers were also increased with the arrival of 4 infantry and 1 Cavalry regiments supported by a battery of Horse Artillery from the mutinies in the Rohilkhand. These new arrivals brought the British forces up to 6,600 men, however, due to illness and wounds only 5,600 were effective, the remained being in hospitals which had been established in the old cantonment. In comparison the rebels had 30,000 men with many guns and an almost inexhaustible supply of ammunition. Despite the disparity in the size of the forces, the arrival of reinforcements prompted another *coup de main* to be planned, however, on hearing that the mutineers had knowledge of their plans and had reinforced the gates to be attacked the plan was abandoned.

It now became clear that the enemy had spies within their camp and it was determined that this was down to companies of Poorbeahs within some of their regiments. Some of these traitors were tried and executed and the remainder were disarmed and expelled from the ranks. A long held concern regarding the disproportionate loss of officers could now be explained, it appears that many had been killed or wounded by the Poorbeahs within their own ranks, not by the enemy forces that they faced.

On 5th July 1857, General Barnard died quite suddenly from cholera, after first showing signs of the illness, which had afflicted many men on the Ridge, in the morning he was dead by 3 o'clock in the afternoon; Major General Thomas Reed was appointed as his replacement.

General Reed's first actions following his appointment involved ordering the Engineers to destroy all but one of the bridges which crossed the Nujjufghur Canal, giving further protection to the British rear, the remaining bridge being protected by a piquet and battery. He also ordered the Engineers to destroy the Phoolchudder Aqueduct over which the waters from the Delhi Canal flowed into the city. On 8th July, Engineers with a large supporting force were sent to blow up the Bussaye Bridge, some two miles from the British Camp. The mutineers, seeing the departure of such a large force took the opportunity to mount a large scale assault on the British positions at Sabzee Mundee, however, within their recently improved positions the British easily fought off the attack and the mutineers suffered heavy losses.

Major Henry Tombs – Victoria Cross No. 140
2nd Lieutenant James Hills – Victoria Cross No. 141

On 9th July 1857, at about 10:00 am, during a period of heavy rain and the usual bombardment of guns from the city walls a surprise enemy cavalry attack was made against the "Mound Battery", this occurred during yet another attack on the Sabzee Mundee piquet.

Guarding the Mound was three heavy guns, a piquet of Infantry and 30 troopers from the 9th Lancers commanded by Lieutenant Martin. A little in front and to the right of the Mound piquet was a unit of Carabineers, a unit of the 9th Irregular Cavalry and two guns from Major Tomb's troop commanded by Lieutenant Hills.

A force of the 8th Irregular Cavalry which had mutinied but still wore the standard white uniform approached the British position but were initially mistaken for a friendly force until they charged, riding past the 9th Irregular Cavalry who did not intervene, their loyalty had long been suspect.

The prompt action of Major Olpherts artillery troop managed to drive off the rebel cavalry, killing many in the process and they fled the camp with many of the 9th Irregulars joining them.

Meanwhile, the remaining rebels charged the advanced piquet and guns of Lieutenant Hills; the inexperienced Carabineers fled in the face of this charge leaving their officer Lieutenant Stillman alone to protect the guns.

To give his gunners time to unlimber and prepare their guns for firing, Lieutenant Hills charged into the advancing rebel cavalry and managed to cut down two of the rebels before he was dismounted.

As he was on the ground searching for his sword, Lieutenant Hills was attacked by three rebels, two mounted and one on foot. He wounded one with his pistol and grabbing the lance of a second wounded him with his sword and then dispatched the man that he had wounded with his pistol, by another swipe of his sword. By now the man on foot had arrived and seized the sword from Lieutenant Hills hand and was about to kill him when Major Tombs rode up and shot the man with his pistol.

By now the rebel cavalry had moved on so Major Tombs and Lieutenant Hills walked over to the Mound to help their wounded gunners and as they neared the mound, Major Tombs spotted a dismounted rebel passing by with Lieutenant Hill's pistol in his hand. Both men approached the man and he began waving his sword about and launched blows against Major Tombs and Lieutenant Hills both of which were parried. The second attack against Lieutenant Hills was more successful and he fell to the ground with a bad sword cut to the head. Major Tombs rushed in to save the Lieutenant and after a cut to his head, from which he was saved serious injury by his heavily padded head dress, he killed the rebel with his sword.

For this action, during which each had saved the others life, both Major Tombs and Lieutenant Hills were later awarded the Victoria Cross.

A large column under the command of Brigadier W. Jones, comprising about 700 Infantry supported by 6 guns and two companies of the 60th Rifles was sent to the aid of the Sabzee Mundee piquet and by sunset the rebels had been driven back into the city.

Private James Thompson – Victoria Cross No. 142

During the attack on the Sabzee Mundee piquet, Private Thompson went to the aid of his commanding officer Captain Wilton who was surrounded by a party of mutineers. Private Thompson charged into the mutineers killing two of their number and held off the rest until assistance arrived.

For saving the life of Captain Wilton, Private Thompson was later awarded the Victoria Cross, under rule 13 of the originating warrant he was elected for the award by a ballot of the Privates of his regiment.

The events of the day had proved to be a major engagement with significant losses; 1 Officer and 40 men killed, 8 Officers and 160 men wounded and 11 men missing, however, about 500 mutineers were killed.

After the desertion of men from the 9th Irregular Cavalry there was a further clearout of Native Regiments from the British camp, the 9th and 17th Irregular Cavalry were sent back to the Punjab and the 1st was sent to Umballa. It was also decided that Native Regiments would not be allowed to man any of the piquets on their own and the 75th Regiment of Foot were despatched to man the Sabzee Mundee piquet.

Things were relatively quiet until 14th July, when yet another attack on the Sabzee Mundee piquet was mounted, again the rebels advanced under cover of the gardens and walled building. Behind their new defences, the British managed to hold the rebels at bay and remained on the defensive until mid afternoon when a column commanded by Brigadier Showers went on the offensive and began to drive the rebels back to the city. During this pursuit Brigadier Chamberlain, who was accompanying the force, was wounded by grapeshot to the shoulder. After pushing the rebels back to the Lahore Gate the call to retreat was sounded and a steady withdrawal began. At the sight of the withdrawal, the rebels began to reform and attack the British forces, however, after a charge by Hodson's Horse they abandoned the attempt and withdrew into the city.

On 17th July 1857, command of the Delhi Field force was passed to General Sir Archdale Wilson as General Thomas Reed had become too ill to continue in command and had gone to Simla on sick leave.

On the same day the British received intelligence about a rebel attack planned for the next day; a large force of 12,000 were to be sent to occupy Alipore and when the British responded by sending troops they would again mount an attack on the city end of the Ridge.

Lieutenant Richard Wadeson – Victoria Cross No. 147

On 18th July, for some reason the attack on Alipore was abandoned but the attack on Sabzee Mundee defences was still mounted. As had become the custom, fresh troops in the form of the mutineers from Jhansi; the 14th Irregular Cavalry, 12th Native Infantry and some light field batteries; were used in the attack. The attack took place during the hottest part of the day and men in the British lines were collapsing from the effects of the sun, where upon they were set about by a band of rebel cavalry.

It was during these attacks that Lieutenant Wadeson of the 75th Regiment of Foot saved the lives of two Privates of his regiment; Private Farrell and Private Barry; by rushing out and killing the horsemen who were attacking them.

For this action Lieutenant Wadeson was later awarded the Victoria Cross.

The events of the day unfolded in a similar fashion to those on the 14th July, however, after clearing the rebels from Sabzee Mundee they were not followed to the gates of the city.

For the next few days there was little activity from the mutineers, apart from occasional bombardments and minor forays.

Due to changes implemented by General Wilson, the men's health and general well being were slowly improving. A duty rota had been established so that all men at a piquet did not have to turn out for every alarm, this allowed the men on the rest rota to get longer periods of undisturbed sleep even though they still had to sleep fully dressed with arms nearby just in case. Sanitation and the distribution of food had also improved with the attendant reduction in illness, although cholera was still rife.

General Wilson had also pressed the Engineers to continue their improvements to the Ridge defences and an almost unbroken line of embrasures now led from one end of the Ridge to the other, houses and walled gardens near to the Sabzee Mundee piquet at 'Sammy House' had also been cleared to give improved fields of fire.

This relative period of calm was broken on 23rd July when the rebels left the Cashmere Gate and established a battery of guns in Ludlow Castle from where they began a bombardment of the Metcalfe House piquet. As the British artillery was having difficulty dislodging the rebels a force commanded by Brigadier Showers attacked the castle and drove them back into the city, they did however manage to retain their guns.

The 1st August is the Mohammedan festival of Bakra Eed and following prayers at the Jumna Musjid and other mosques in the city, where they had been whipped up to a religious frenzy, a large force of mutineers made an attack against the British lines in the afternoon. Wave after wave of mutineers threw themselves at the length of the British defences time after time, however, from their sound defensive line the British rained down heavy musket and grape shot fire inflicting heavy losses. The attacks continued through the night and did not end until mid-afternoon the next day when they retired back into the city having suffered significant casualties; in front of the 'Sammy House', 197 dead were counted after the battles.

At the beginning of August, after eight weeks of unrelenting defence against over 25 rebel attacks the momentum of the 'siege' appeared to be turning in the favour of the British forces.

Fighting had broken out within the city between different factions of the mutineers and rumours of a large British force advancing on the city caused much concern.

The rebel powder magazine within the city was accidentally blown up on 7th August and was a great loss to the mutineers.

On the same day the mutineers left the Cashmere Gate with four guns, supported by infantry skirmishers and began another bombardment of the Metcalfe House piquet from Ludlow Castle again the British artillery was ineffective in dislodging the rebels so Brigadier Showers mounted a surprise attack on the position. The attack was successful, with the four guns being captured, however, after advancing too close to the city walls the force suffered over 100 men wounded, including Brigadier Showers and Major Cole.

Later in the day, Brigadier General John Nicholson "Lion of the Punjab", rode into the camp in advance of his column of reinforcements which was closing on the city, having made their way down the Grand Trunk Road from the Punjab.

Brigadier Nicholson's column, consisting of the 52nd Light Infantry Regiment, 2nd Punjab Infantry, a wing of the 61st Regiment of Foot, a European Horse Artillery battery and 200 Cavalry, arrived in the British camp on 14th August 1857.

Despite the arrival of reinforcements the British still needed to wait for the arrival of the siege train from the Punjab, with the much needed ammunition, before they could risk going on the offensive against Delhi.

Soon after the arrival of Brigadier Nicholson's column, a large force of mutineers left the city with the intention of cutting the British communication lines with the Punjab. They were followed by a force of 360 cavalry, led by Major Hodson on 15th August 1857.

Major Charles Gough – Victoria Cross No. 156

Hodson's force was advancing slowly along the road between Delhi and Karnal, due to the flooded countryside, and in the afternoon they came across a large band of rebel Irregular Cavalry resting near the village of Kurkowdah, following a short engagement they managed to inflict heavy losses on the rebels.

It was during this engagement that Major Gough fought off two mutineers and saved the life of his wounded brother Lieutenant Hugh Gough,[10] for this action he would later be awarded the Victoria Cross.

---

10 Lieutenant Hugh Gough would also be awarded the Victoria Cross for deeds later on in the mutiny.

It was at Kurkowdah that Hodson received news that the rebels were assembling at Rohtuk and this is where he came across a large rebel force of 300 cavalry and 900 infantry, settled into enclosures in and around the town. Major Hodson determined that, with only a force of cavalry, it would be foolhardy to attack the rebels behind their strong defensive positions, however, he advanced on the city and then began to slowly retire in the hope that he could draw the rebel force out into the open. The ruse worked and the rebels left the town in pursuit of the retreating cavalry; when they were out in the open, the British cavalry turned and attacked with vigour inflicting very heavy losses. At nightfall, the rebels dispersed and the following day Hodson and his column returned to the camp at Delhi.

Battle of Najafgarh

News had been received that the Siege Train was now rapidly approaching Delhi and on 24th August a large force of 6,000 men comprising the recent mutineers from Neemuch and Rohilkhand, supported by 18 guns left Delhi with the intention of intercepting and destroying it.

To counter this move, General Nicholson set off the following day with a force of 2,000 men and 16 guns of horse artillery. Due to the heavy rain, that had turned the roads to quagmires, the going was slow and very hard work moving the guns. At midday the column was halted, however, when news arrived that the rebels were encamped only 12 miles away at the village of Najafgarh, General Nicholson decided to move off and try to engage with the enemy before nightfall.

By sunset the force had reached a branch of the Najafgarh canal with the enemy positions to their left, the enemy occupied positions from the bridge and on either side of the Delhi road

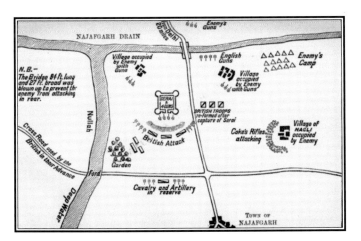

Figure 39. Battle of Najafgarh

with the town of Najafgarh some two miles further on. After crossing the river by a ford, under heavy enemy fire, General Nicholson decided to press ahead with the attack despite the advancing nightfall. Leaving a reserve of artillery and cavalry to their rear, after a brief artillery barrage, the force attacked the main enemy position in an old Serai defended by 4 guns. After an intense period of hand to hand fighting, the British took the Serai and now directed their attention to enemy positions in two villages close to canal. These villages were taken together with the village of Nagli to their rear and the Battle of Najafgarh was wound up in full darkness. The surviving mutineers took advantage of the dark and made their way back to Delhi during the night.

General Nicholson's force spent the night on the battlefield, where engineers blew up the bridge over the canal and several large carts of abandoned rebel powder was set on fire. The force returned to the British camp at Delhi on the following day with 13 captured enemy guns and large quantities of ammunition. Following their defeat at the Battle of Najafgarh, the rebels abandoned further attempts to destroy the siege train.

Preparations for assault on Delhi

The siege train arrived at the British camp on 3rd September 1857, with 30 pieces of heavy ordnance and copious supplies of ammunition; preparations could now proceed for an assault on the city.

The Engineers had been working for some days preparing embrasures for the heavy artillery. A battery (the Crows Nest) was formed at the end of a trench running from the left of Sammy House, which contained four 9 pounder and two 24 pounder howitzers. This was positioned to prevent enemy sorties from the Kabul and Lahore Gates and was also able to help suppress the enemy fire from the Moree Bastion.

Construction of this battery also gave the enemy the impression that the British were going to mount their assault on the city from this end of the Ridge, however, the attack was actually planned for the other end of the Ridge where the River Jumna would protect their left flank.

The attack would focus on the Water Bastion, Cashmere Gate and Moree Bastion which were the only positions where the enemy could not mount artillery; the curtain walls were only wide enough to support infantrymen.

By the 6th September 1857, all of the reinforcements had arrived at the city and the British had a force of 6,500 infantry, 1,000 cavalry and 600 artillerymen available for the assault, two thirds of which were loyal native troops. The British troops in the

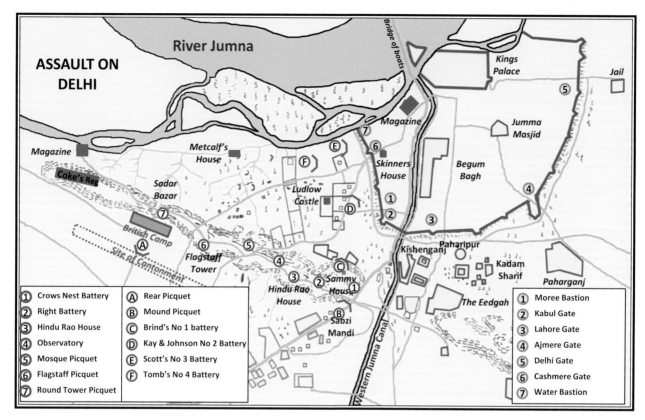

ASSAULT ON DELHI

River Jumna

Magazine

Metcalf's House

Coke's Reg

Sadar Bazar

Ludlow Castle

British Camp

Flagstaff Tower

Hindu Rao House

Sammy House

Sabzi Mandi

Bridge of boats

Magazine

Skinners House

Kishenganj Paharipur

The Eedgah

Kings Palace

Jail

Jumma Masjid

Begum Bagh

Kadam Sharif

Paharganj

①	Crows Nest Battery	Ⓐ	Rear Picquet
②	Right Battery	Ⓑ	Mound Picquet
③	Hindu Rao House	Ⓒ	Brind's No 1 battery
④	Observatory	Ⓓ	Kay & Johnson No 2 Battery
⑤	Mosque Picquet	Ⓔ	Scott's No 3 Battery
⑥	Flagstaff Picquet	Ⓕ	Tomb's No 4 Battery
⑦	Round Tower Picquet		

①	Moree Bastion
②	Kabul Gate
③	Lahore Gate
④	Ajmere Gate
⑤	Delhi Gate
⑥	Cashmere Gate
⑦	Water Bastion

Figure 40. Siege and assault on Delhi

European regiments had suffered many losses due to illness and had large numbers hospitalised.

Being short of men to man the available artillery and having little need of cavalry for the assault, volunteers from the cavalry were pressed in to assist the artillerymen.

On the evening of 7th September, the No. 1 (Brind's) Battery was established some 700 yards from the Moree Bastion, however, by daybreak only one gun had been mounted and in the daylight the enemy saw what was happening and began to lay down a murderous fire on the position.

Despite the heavy fire the battery was completed with five 18 pounders on the right commanded by Major Brind and four 24 pounders on the left commanded by Major Kaye. Once operational these batteries commenced their fire on the Moree Bastion and by afternoon all return fire had stopped and the bastion was in ruins.

On the 8th September a British party advanced on Ludlow Castle and with very little effort cleared out the enemy's advanced piquet and during the nights of 9th and 10th September established No. 2 (Kaye and Johnson's) battery in front of the castle some 500 yards from the Cashmere Gate.

Private John Divane – Victoria Cross No. 158

On the 10th September during an action to clear mutineers from positions close to where No. 2 battery was being established, there was a temporary pause as the force was fired on by a small battery that the rebels had established on a ridge in front of the city walls.

Private Divane rallied his comrades and led an attack on the enemy battery and reached the parapet before he was wounded in the right leg, which was subsequently amputated.

For his part in the action, Private Divane was later awarded the Victoria Cross, having been elected for the award by a ballot of the Privates of his regiment.

✠

The No.2 battery consisted of seven heavy howitzers and two 18 pounders on the right commanded by Major Kaye and nine 24 pounders on the left, originally commanded by Major Campbell but after he was seriously wounded, commanded by Captain Johnson.

On the evening of the 10th September, the No. 4 (Tombs) battery, consisting of ten heavy mortars, was established in the Kudsia Bagh gardens under the command of Major Tombs.

Also on the 10th September it was decided to relocate the No. 3 (Scott's) battery to a more favourable position and work was started to prepare the Old Custom House which was only 150 yards from the Water Bastion. Due to heavy enemy fire the work had to be stopped at first light on the 11th September but was resumed and completed in the evening when six 18 pounders were installed under the command of Major Scott.

Private Patrick Green – Victoria Cross No. 159

During the period when the four batteries were established, the mutineers did not meekly remain behind the walls of Delhi.

On the evening of 11th September, the rebels mounted an attack in force against the No. 4 battery and piquet in the Kudsia Bagh gardens. During the attack, Private Green rescued a comrade who had fallen wounded and was surrounded by the enemy. For his actions Private Green was later awarded the Victoria Cross.

At 8 o'clock on the morning of 11th September, all the batteries except No. 3 opened up on the northern city wall and defences. When the Cashmere Bastion began to return the fire it was quickly silenced and under the devastating fire soon collapsed, together with a portion of the curtain wall.

On 12th September, battery No. 3 also joined in the bombardment which continued throughout the day and night.

By midday on the 13th September, it was apparent that significant breaches in the defences had been made at the Water Bastion and Cashmere Gate but the scale of the breaches would need to be investigated.

Bugler William Sutton – Victoria Cross No. 152

The job of evaluating the two breaches fell to four young Engineering Lieutenants; Medley, Lang, Greathed and Home; who were ordered to investigate the nature of the breaches and report back.

At 10:00 pm the British guns stopped firing and the Engineers, together with small parties moved off to reconnoitre, with Medley, Lang and their party going to the Cashmere Gate while Greathed and Home headed for the Water Bastion.

Medley and Lang reached their objective and noted that the breach was satisfactory, however, as they moved to the crest of the rubble they had to retire at the sound of advancing enemy sentries.

On leaving the position they were fired upon by the sentries, however, escaped unharmed.

Bugler Sutton had volunteered for this mission and was later awarded the Victoria Cross for his part, having been elected by a ballot of the Privates of his regiment. An earlier action on the 2nd September when he killed an enemy bugler who was about to sound an order was also cited.

Greathed and Home also completed their mission and reported that the breach at the Water Bastion was also viable.

On their return, the bombardment was restarted and in light of their reports it was decided that the assault on Delhi would commence at 3 o'clock in the morning of the 14th September 1857.

Despite the fact that all of the Bastions on the northern city wall had been destroyed and the curtain wall had been breached in several places, the decision to mount an attack was a bold move as the attacking force of 6,500 (including only 1,700 British) would be outnumbered almost 5 to 1 by the 30,000 mutineers within the city.

Assault to recapture Delhi

The plan which had already been agreed, involved an assault by five columns.

The first column, commanded by Brigadier-General Nicholson; was comprised of 300 men of 75th Regiment of Foot, 250 men of 1st Bengal European Infantry and 450 men of 2nd Punjab Infantry with Engineering support from Medley, Lang and Bingham; had the objective of storming the breach near the Cashmere Bastion.

The second column, commanded by Brigadier Jones of the 61st Regiment of Foot; was comprised of 250 men of the 8th Regiment of Foot, 250 men of the 2nd Bengal European Fusiliers and 350 men of the 4th Sikh Infantry Regiment with Engineering support from Lieutenants Greathed, Hovenden and Pemberton; had the objective of storming the breach at the Water Bastion.

The third column, commanded by Colonel Campbell of 52nd Regiment of Light Infantry; was comprised of 200 men from 52nd Regiment of Light Infantry, 250 men of the Kumaon Sikh Battalion and 500 men from 1st Punjab Infantry with engineering support from Lieutenants Holm, Salkeld and Tandy; had the objective of assaulting the Cashmere Gate after it had been blown.

The fourth column, commanded by Major Reid the commander of the Simur Battalion; was comprised of the Simur battalion of Ghurkhas and Guides, 860 men gathered from the piquets near Hindu Rao's House and 1,200 men from the Cashmere Contingent; had the objective to attack the suburbs of Kissengunge and Paharipor and support the main attack by trying to gain access to the city via the Kabul Gate, engineering support was provided by Lieutenants Maunsell and Tennant.

The fifth column, commanded by Brigadier Longfield of the 8th Regiment of Foot; was comprised of 250 men from 61st Regiment of Foot, 450 men of 4th Punjab Infantry, 300 men of the Beluch battalion, 300 men of the Jhind Contingent and 200 men of the 60th Rifles, supported by engineers Lieutenants Ward and Thackeray; was the reserve column.

Columns 1 to 3, together with the reserve column assembled near Ludlow Castle and were all in place by 3 o'clock in the morning.

Column one moved off to its start point in the Kudsia Bagh Gardens, while column two moved down to the Custom House Garden and column three moved to the main road for a direct assault on the Cashmere Gate once it had been blown; the explosion of the gate was to be the signal for a simultaneous assault by all three columns.

At first light it became apparent that the mutineers had been busy during the night and had erected barriers of sandbags in each of the breaches. It was decided to halt the attack until the artillery had destroyed these temporary repairs. The British batteries opened fire and quickly reopened the breaches and stopped their fire which was the signal to start the assault.

Lieutenant Duncan Home – Victoria Cross No. 160
Lieutenant Philip Salkeld – Victoria Cross No. 161
Sergeant John Smith – Victoria Cross No. 164
Bugler Robert Hawthorne – Victoria Cross No. 166

As planned, the start of the assault was to be the blowing up of the Cashmere Gate; this important task was assigned to Lieutenants Salkeld and Home of the Engineers together with Sergeants Carmichael, Burgess and Smith of the Bengal Sappers and Miners and Bugler Hawthorne of the 52nd Regiment of Foot.

The party was accompanied by eight native sappers who were carrying some of the twelve 25 pound bags of gunpowder.

The story is best told in the words of Sergeant Smith, who was one of the party;

The party blowing in the gate, the 60th Rifles leading, went off at a double from the Ludlow Castle, until they arrived at the cross-road leading to the Customs, and the men, when they opened out right and left, the Sappers going to the gate led by Lieutenant Home, and one bugler (Hawthorne), Lieutenant Salkeld, with the party carrying the powder a few paces behind, the three European non-commissioned officers, and nine natives with twelve bags of twenty-five pounds each. My duty was to bring up the rear, and see that none of them remained behind. Lieutenant Salkeld had passed through the temporary Burn Gate with sergeants Carmichael and Burgess, but four of the natives had stopped behind the above gate and refused to go on. I had put down my bag and taken my gun, and threatened to shoot them, when Lieutenant Salkeld came running back and said, 'Why don't you come on?' I told him there were four men behind the gate, and that I was going to shoot them. He said; Shoot them d----n their eyes, shoot them!' I said 'You hear the orders, and I will shoot you,' raising the gun slowly to 'present' to give fair time, when two men went on. Lieutenant Salkeld said, 'Do not shoot; with your own bag it will be enough.' I went on, and

only Lieutenant Salkeld and Sergeant Burgess were there; Lieutenant Home and the bugler had jumped into the ditch, and Sergeant Carmichael was killed as he went up with his powder on his shoulder, evidently having been shot from the wicket while crossing the broken part of the bridge along one of the beams. I placed my bag, and then at great risk reached Carmichael's bag from in front of the wicket, placed it, arranged the fuses for the explosion, and reported all ready to Lieutenant Salkeld, who held the slow (not a port-fire, as I have seen stated). In stooping down to light the quick match, he put out his foot, and was shot through the thigh from the wicket, and in falling had the presence of mind to hold out the slow match, and told me to fire the charge. Burgess was next to him and took it. I told him to fire the charge and keep cool. He turned round and said, 'It won't go off, sir; it has gone out, sir (not knowing that one officer had fallen into the ditch). I gave him a box of Lucifers, and, as he took them, he let them fall into my hand, he being shot through the body from the wicket also, and fell over after Lieutenant Salkeld. I was then left alone, and keeping close to the charge, seeing from where the others were shot, I struck a light, when the port fire in the fuse went off in my face, the light not having gone out as we thought. I took up my gun and jumped into the ditch, but before I had reached the ground the charge went off, and filled the ditch with smoke, so that I saw no one. I turned while in the act of jumping so my back would come to the wall to save me from falling. I stuck close to the wall, and by that I escaped being smashed to pieces, only getting a severe bruise on the leg, the leather helmet saving my head. I put my hands along the wall and touched someone, and asked who it was. 'Lieutenant Home,' was the answer. I said, 'Has God spared you? Are you hurt?' He said 'No' and asked the same from me. As soon as the dust cleared a little we saw Lieutenant Salkeld and Burgess covered with dust; their lying in the middle of the ditch had saved them from being smashed to pieces and covered by the debris from the top of the wall, the shock only toppling the stones over, which fell between where we stood and where they lay. I went to Lieutenant Salkeld and called the bugler to help me to remove him under the bridge as the fire covered upon us, and Lieutenant Salkeld's arms were broken. Lieutenant Home came to assist, but I begged him to keep out of the fire and that (sic) we would do all that could be done. Lieutenant Salkeld would not let us remove him, so I put a bag of powder under his head for a pillow, and with the bugler's puggery bound up his arms and thigh, and I left the bugler to look to him and went to Burgess, took off his sword, which I put on, and done (sic) what I could for him. I got some brandy from Lieutenant Home and gave to both, also to a Havildar (Pelluck Singh), who had his thigh shot through, and was under the bridge by a ladder that had been put into the ditch, leaving me in charge of the wounded, and went to the front after the Rifles had gone in, and the 52nd followed them. I then went to the rear for three stretchers and brought them, one of which was taken from me an officer of the Rifles. I had to draw my sword and threaten to run any one through who took the other two. I put them into the ditch, and with the bugler's assistance got Lieutenant Salkeld into one and sent him, charging him strictly not to leave him until he had placed him in the hands of a surgeon, and with the assistance of a Naick who had come to the Havildar, got Burgess into one and sent the Naick with him, I being scarcely able to walk, and in a few minutes he returned to say he was dead, and asked for further orders. I told him to take him to the hospital. After assisting to clear away the gate and make the roadway again, I went on to the front to see what was going on.

The surviving Europeans in the party; Lieutenants Salkeld and Home, Sergeant Smith and Bugler Hawthorne were all awarded the Victoria Cross for their part in the action being nominated for the award by the commanding officer on the day.

Tragically both of the Lieutenants would never see their medal as Salkeld died from the wounds sustained during the attack and Home died on 1st October 1857 when a bomb that he was setting at Fort Malgurgh exploded prematurely.

Following the blowing of the Cashmere Gate, Bugler Hawthorne sounded the call to advance and Captain Bayley of the 52nd Light Infantry, with a storming party of 150 men advanced down the road under heavy fire and quickly took possession of the gate and main guard.

The remainder of column three commanded by Colonel Campbell followed the storming party into the city.

Lance Corporal Henry Smith – Victoria Cross No. 165

A detachment of the 60th Rifles with men from the 52nd Light Infantry and the 1st Bengal European Infantry were soon engaged with the rebels in hand to hand fighting in the streets of Delhi.

Finding themselves becoming isolated, the column began to retire across the Chandney Chowk and when a man from the 52nd fell wounded, Lance Corporal Smith, in the face of heavy enemy fire, picked him up and carried him to safety.

For this action Lance Corporal Smith was later awarded the Victoria Cross.

The first column, commanded by Brigadier-General Nicholson, despite very heavy fire from the walls of the city managed to storm the breach in the wall near the Cashmere Gate and re-formed at the main guard.

The second column, led by Colonel Jones, emerged from their position near the Custom House and advanced towards the breach at the Water Bastion.

Ensign Everard Lisle Phillipps – Victoria Cross No. 119

Almost as soon as they emerged from the protection of the No. 3 battery, Lieutenants Greathed and Ovenden from the Engineers who were leading an advanced party of men with scaling ladders were both severely wounded, as were 29 of the 39 men in their party.

Ensign Lisle Phillipps, however, leading a small group of men managed to scale the breach in the face of heavy fire and dislodge the mutineers. They then turned the rebel guns on the retreating mutineers and fired off several shots into their rear. The rest of the column advanced and secured the position that had been so bravely gained.

Ensign Lisle Phillipps was immediately given a commission as Lieutenant in the 60th Rifles, however, this was short lived as he was killed two days later during street fighting at the Delhi Bank House.

Fifty years after his death, Ensign Lisle Phillipps was eventually awarded the Victoria Cross for this action, following a change in the rules regarding posthumous awards.

The fourth column commanded by Major Reid advanced from their positions at Sabzee Mundee and began the attack to clear the rebels from Kissengunge. Almost at once they met strong resistance from rebels in a strongly defended Serai and Major Reid has hit in the head.

Lieutenant Robert Shebbeare – Victoria Cross No. 162

Lieutenant Shebbeare commanding a small party of Ghurkhas and Guides captured a nearby mosque and from here launched several attacks on the Seri, which due to the strength of the defenders were unsuccessful. Despite being wounded in the cheek and the back of his head, Lieutenant Shebbeare managed to safely withdraw his men from this impossible position.

For his part in this action Lieutenant Shebbeare was later awarded the Victoria Cross.

Major Lawrence, who assumed the command when Major Reid was wounded, called a general withdrawal of the column back to their start positions near the Ridge, as he feared that the mutineers were in danger of over running his men and capturing the batteries. This action, however, encouraged the mutineers who sent a large force out of the Lahore Gate which was kept at bay for some time by intense fire from the batteries at Hindu Rao's House. Brigadier Hope Grant quickly gathered together a force of Cavalry and Horse Artillery and managed to set up a battery near to the Moree Bastion from where he sent effective fire of grape shot into the mutineers.

Meanwhile, Brigadier Longfield and the reserve had been called forward and began to occupy the positions taken by the first three columns which allowed them to move along the Rampart Road and further into the city.

Colonel Campbell and the third column moved to the left of the Cashmere Gate to clear the Kutcheree and Church and were soon heavily engaged with the enemy.

Surgeon Herbert Reade – Victoria Cross No. 168

Surgeon Reade was treating numerous wounded at the end of a street when a party of advancing mutineers established themselves on the roofs of nearby houses and began to rain down heavy fire on him and his patients. The surgeon gathered up his sword and after assembling a small force of ten men set about clearing the enemy from the rooftops. The raid was successful, however, two of his men were killed and six wounded.

For his part in this action Surgeon Reade was later awarded the Victoria Cross, he was also cited for an action two days later when he stormed a magazine and spiked one of the guns.

The first column commanded by Brigadier-General Nicholson turned right down the Rampart Road and after clearing the Moree Bastion made their way towards the Kabul Gate.

Lieutenant George Waller – Victoria Cross No. 169

As the column approached the Kabul Gate, Lieutenant Waller led a charge which managed to capture the rebel guns guarding the gate.

For this action Lieutenant Waller was later awarded the Victoria Cross. He was elected for the award by a ballot of the officers of his regiment.

Lieutenant Waller was also cited for an action two days later when he helped fight back an enemy attack on British guns in Chandney Chowk.

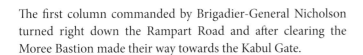

After reaching the Kabul Gate the column was called to a halt to await further orders.

Sergeant James McGuire – Victoria Cross No. 163
Drummer Miles Ryan – Victoria Cross No. 167

The column took advantage of the temporary halt to distribute ammunition to the men, for some unknown reason three of the boxes of ammunition exploded and another two caught fire. The explosion caused much confusion amongst the troops and they were running around aimlessly, many towards the ammunition which was now on fire. Sergeant McGuire and Drummer Ryan had the courage and foresight to grab the burning ammunition boxes and throw them over the parapet and into the ditch, saving the lives of many of their comrades.

For this action Sergeant McGuire and Drummer Ryan were later awarded the Victoria Cross.

The unfortunate but necessary delay of the first column at the Kabul Gate allowed the rebels to regroup and form a very good defensive position on the narrow rampart road which was the approach to the Lahore Gate. Sharpshooters were placed on the rooftops and ramparts lining the road where two field guns were placed at bends in the road about 60 yards apart just before the Burn Bastion, which was also guarded by heavy artillery pieces. The column mounted a charge against the first artillery piece and despite taking heavy losses managed to spike the gun before they had to retire. Two further charges were mounted against the second gun but the enemy fire was too intense to make much progress. Brigadier Nicholson came to the front to urge his men on for a further attack but was shot in the chest and mortally wounded, he would die from his wounds on 23rd September 1857.

Major Brookes of the 75th Regiment of Foot took command of the column and seeing the futility of further attacks without artillery support retired back to the Kabul gate where he joined up with the second column commanded by Brigadier Jones.

The third column, after clearing the Water Bastion pressed on to the Jumma Musjid mosque but without blasting powder or artillery were unable to breach the defences so retired to the Church where they united with the reserve that had occupied the Water Bastion, Cashmere Gate, Skinners House and other nearby buildings.

By the end of the day, the British forces had established a foothold in the city but this had been gained at a heavy loss with 1,104 men and 64 officers either killed or wounded (almost one third of the forces sent into the city). With such a loss of men and officers, the 15th September was used to regroup, reorganise and improve the defences of the ground so far taken. Sandbags were used to build breastworks on the flat roofs of Skinner's House, the Press House, the College and other buildings. The British mortar and heavy artillery batteries outside the city maintained a steady and devastating fire on the Palace, Jumma Musjid mosque and other rebel positions within the city. The British gains, limited though they were, had a significant effect on the moral of the mutineers and civilians within the city, who were soon leaving in large numbers via the Lahore and other gates.

On the 16th September, now armed with some artillery captured from the mutineers, the British once again went on the offensive and made an attack against the Magazine.

Lieutenant George Renny – Victoria Cross No. 170

After the magazine had been captured following fierce fighting, the rebels attempted to recapture it by advancing to the high walls under covering fire from nearby rooftops on the Salumgarh and the Palace.

Lieutenant Renny, climbed to the top of the magazine wall and threw live shells, which had been handed to him with their fuses lit, into the ranks of mutineers with devastating effect. He continued this hazardous task until the rebels were forced to retire.

For this action Lieutenant Renny was later awarded the Victoria Cross.

✠

2nd Lieutenant Edward Thackeray – Victoria Cross No. 171

During the attack on the magazine by the rebels, a shed containing powder was set on fire and Lieutenant Thackerey in the face of heavy fire and an imminent explosion rushed to the shed and managed to put out the fire.

For this action Lieutenant Thackerey was later awarded the Victoria Cross.

✠

With some surprise and gratitude, it became apparent that the attempt to destroy the magazine by Lieutenant Willoughby had been only partially successful as 171 large calibre guns were found undamaged, together with large amounts of ammunition. Mortars taken from the magazine were used to lay down fire on the Salumgarh and Palace.

On 17th and 18th September the street by street fighting continued, however, instead of marching down the narrow streets where they were exposed to rebel fire from within and on the rooftops of buildings on each side of the road, the British now adopted a new approach. The columns now used artillery to blast their way through houses and other buildings, clearing them of rebels as they moved forward. This approach was used on 19th September by men from the Kabul Gate for a surprise attack on the Burn Bastion which was captured and held.

On the following morning the column pressed on with their attack and finally took the Lahore Gate and Garstin Bastion; in the afternoon the gates to the palace were blown and the Palace was occupied by British troops. The Palace was practically deserted as most of the mutineers and citizens had fled the city by the southern gates.

At dawn on the 21st September, an artillery salute was fired which signalled the city was back in the hands of the British.

Lieutenant Alfred Heathcote – Victoria Cross No. 120

Lieutenant Heathcote served throughout the final six days of the assault on Delhi and volunteered on several occasions for hazardous tasks, despite having been wounded.

For his conduct Lieutenant Heathcote was later awarded the Victoria Cross, having been elected for the award by a ballot of the officers in his regiment.

✠

After a siege which had lasted from 30th May until 13th September followed by an assault which lasted six days, Delhi was back in the hands of the British, however, the level of casualties was the highest to be experienced during the rest of the Mutiny. Overall 3,854 men and officers were killed or wounded during the campaign with 1,347 of these occurring during the six days of the assault.

Acting on information received, Major Hodson and 50 of his men rode to Emperor Homayun's tomb a few miles outside the city and captured King Bahadur Shah who had escaped from his palace in the city. The King was accompanied by thousands of servants and supporters but agreed to come quietly if Major Hodson promised that his life would be spared. Followed by his vast entourage, the King was led back to Delhi as Hodson's prisoner. After gathering up a further 50 of his irregular cavalry, Major Hodson returned to Homayun's tomb, this time to take the three royal princes captive. After retrieving the princes from their hiding place, Major Hodson and his men were surrounded by a mob of royal retainers and supporters, some of whom were armed. The response of the Major was to summarily execute the three princes with his rifle; the shocked mob did nothing and Hodson was able to return to Delhi with the bodies which were dumped in the Palace, supposedly on the spot where the princes had participated in the murder of British civilians. After a trial the king was exiled for life to Rangoon in Burma.

Battle of Narnoul

On 22nd August 1857, the Jodhpur Legion mutinied at Erinpura and news reached Delhi in early November that the rebels, under the command of Sanand Khan, were heading towards the city. With this news, Lieutenant-Colonel John Grant Gerrard recently appointed to the command of the 1st Bengal European Fusiliers was appointed to head up a force of over 2,500 men to go and intercept the rebels. Colonel Gerrard with his force comprising men of the 1st Bengal European Fusiliers, 7th and 23rd Punjab Infantry and detachments of Guides and Lind's Multan Horse, left Delhi on the 10th November.

Lieutenant Francis David Millet Brown – Victoria Cross No. 212

On the 16th November, Colonel Gerrard and his force met and engaged the rebels near Narnoul where the rebels had occupied a strong fortress. After a strenuous battle, the rebels were defeated and dispersed, however, Colonel Gerrard was killed in the conflict. During the battle, while enemy cavalry were only 40 to 50 yards away, Lieutenant Brown under heavy rebel fire rushed to the aid of a wounded comrade and brought him to safety.

For this act Lieutenant Brown was later awarded the Victoria Cross.

At the end of the battle, having achieved their objective of dispersing the rebel force, the brigade now under the temporary command of Captain Caulfield returned to Delhi where they arrived on the 29th November 1857.

8

THE FIRST CAWNPORE CAMPAIGN

Cawnpore was a strategic and important garrison town, approximately 40 miles from Lucknow, 270 miles from Delhi and nearly 700 miles from Calcutta.

Located on the Grand Trunk Road and Grand Trunk Canal and close to the River Ganges the city was an important communications hub and lay on the main approach to the Punjab, Sindh and newly acquired Oudh provinces.

Prior to the mutiny, Cawnpore had been the headquarters of the Bengal Field Command and had a garrison of almost 40,000 men, with artillery, infantry and cavalry units from both the Company army and the Queen's army.

At the time of the mutiny the forces were much depleted, with many of the garrison having been sent to the Punjab, Sindh and Oudh provinces. Despite being of strategic importance and housing a major magazine the city was now occupied by just over 200 European soldiers; a company of artillery with 59 men and 6 guns, 60 men of the 84th Regiment of Foot, 65 men of the 1st Madras Fusiliers and 30 men of the 32nd Regiment of Foot who were invalids.

On the other hand the native troops in the city were almost 3,000 in number; 2nd Regiment of Light Cavalry, 1st, 53rd and 56th Bengal Native Infantry and native gunners attached to the British artillery batteries.

Since 1856, the garrison had been commanded by General Hugh Massy Wheeler of the East India Company Bengal army who had 50 years experience in India, was married to an Indian woman and spoke Hindi fluently. These attributes made the General very popular with the sepoys.

The town also contained about 750 European civilians; men (and their families) who worked for the Railway, Canal, Civil and

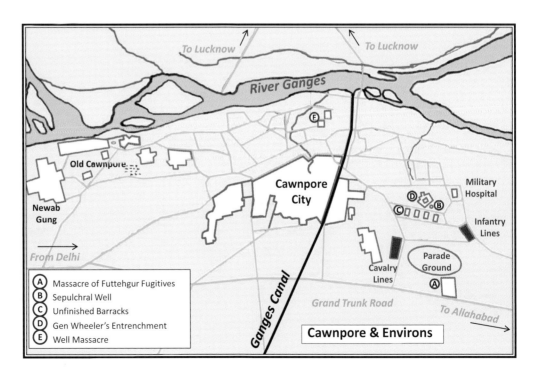

Figure 4I. Cawnpore

other departments together with the wives and families of the 32nd Regiment of Foot who were now stationed at Lucknow.

A complicating factor was the presence at nearby Bithoor of Nana Sahib the adopted son of the last Mahratta King Bajee Rao, who under the Company doctrine of lapse was not allowed to succeed his adopted father, whose title and pension died with him in 1852.

News of the mutiny at Meerut reached Cawnpore on 14th May 1857 and two days later General Wheeler sent the following telegraph to the Governor General in Calcutta; *"As far as I have means of judging, the troops here and at Allahabad are at present well disposed, however, there is much excitement in consequence of events elsewhere."*

The first sign of possible trouble occurred on the evening of 16th May when an unexplained fire in the lines of the 1st Native Infantry Regiment caused the artillery to be moved back to the barracks. At around the same time many of the civilians, including women and children were also moved into the barracks.

General Wheeler stated in another telegraph on 18th May; *"All at Cawnpore quiet, but excitement continues among the people."* General Wheeler was advised to move his troops and the civilians into the magazine, which with its strong walls would provide a very secure and easily defended position. The General put forward two reasons why he did not accede to this request; the first being that as the magazine was about six miles from the native lines, he would have to withdraw his officers (who were accommodated with their native troops) and lose their calming influence, secondly the removal of native soldiers from the magazine would demonstrate a mistrust which might spark off a revolt. As things turned out matters were taken from the General's hands when he received a telegraph from the Governor General on 19th May which ordered him to make ready for the arrival of a large European Force, which could only be accommodated in the barracks area, where several new barracks were under construction.

On 22nd May, 55 Europeans from the 32nd Regiment of Foot based at Lucknow arrived in the city, together with 240 troopers of the 2nd Oudh Irregular Cavalry.

Rumours began to circulate that at a parade to be held on the 23rd May, the 'unclean' cartridges were to be handed out and that the artillery would be used on those who refused. Tensions were so strained that on 24th May, the gun salute to celebrate the Queen's birthday was cancelled.

On 26th May, General Wheeler accepted the offer from Nana Sahib to protect the Treasury, in case trouble broke out and 2 guns and 200 of Nana's armed retainers were used to support a company of the 53rd Native Infantry Regiment to guard the Treasury.

On 2nd June, 71 men from the 84th Regiment of Foot and 15 men from the Madras Fusiliers arrived in the city as reinforcements, however, the next day General Wheeler sent 50 men and 2 officers from the 84th back to Lucknow as he thought that their need was greater.

Mutiny at Cawnpore

On 2nd June, a drunken Lieutenant Cox discharged his pistol towards his native troops and was arrested. At his court martial the next day he was found not guilty as it was judged that the discharge was accidental due to his drunken state. This caused much concern amongst the native troops and may have been the spark which provoked the mutiny.

On the 3rd of June, General Wheeler concentrated the Europeans in the "entrenchment" which was a poorly constructed

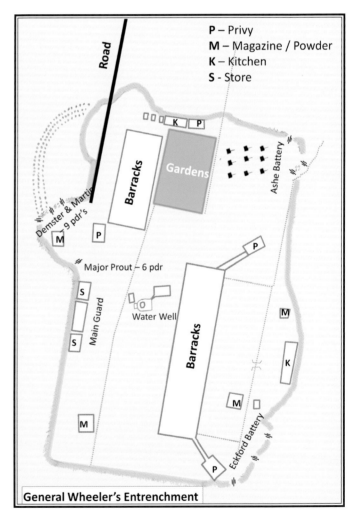

Figure 42. General Wheeler's entrenchment at Cawnpore

defensive position with mud walls and defended by only 10 light guns. Over 800 people, including 400 women and children were crowded into this area near the barracks which were under construction.

The General moved a month's worth of provisions into the entrenchment, however, inexplicably he did not move in a commensurate amount of ammunition from the magazine.

In the early hours of 5th June, the 2nd Irregular Cavalry decided to mutiny and rode out to loot the Treasury and Magazine and afterwards entered the jail, released the prisoners and burned down nearby public offices. The 1st Native Infantry regiment joined in with the mutiny and went on a rampage through the town, however, the 53rd and 56th Native Infantry hesitated and calmed by their officers, remained loyal until first light. At this time the mutineers returned to their lines, loaded down with booty and began extolling their comrades to join the mutiny. The matter was decided when a gun in the entrenchment fired rounds of grape shot at the rebels. After further looting in the city the rebels left the town on their way to join the mutineers in Delhi; many of the British officers and about 80 sepoys who remained loyal managed to join General Wheeler in the entrenchment.

With the rebels on their way to Delhi, this may have been the end of the violence at Cawnpore, however, Nana Sahib who had taken possession of a large portion of the Treasury saw the revolt as an opportunity to enhance his own position and rushed after the mutineers. Nana Sahib caught up with the mutineers at Kullumpore and convinced them that they should return to Cawnpore, under his leadership, where they would kill the British soldiers and all Europeans and establish rebel control of the city before then proceeding to Delhi.

Siege of Cawnpore

The mutineers returned to the city that evening and killed every European that they came across; by 10 am on the 7th June the rebels began a bombardment of the entrenchment with two guns provided by Nana Sahib and two heavier guns taken from the magazine. Before long the mutineers had 14 guns and mortars laying down a murderous fire on the inadequately defended entrenchment.

Conditions for the British soldiers and civilians were dire, with little shelter from the enemy fire and the elements. The two barracks within the enclosure were soon reduced to rubble and the only shelter from the musket fire and harsh sun was holes dug in the ground, covered with planks of wood. Food and ammunition were soon in short supply and water was critical, one of the two wells in the enclosure soon ran dry and was used to store the dead, the other well was in the open and only accessible during the night.

Despite all the disadvantages of their position the British gallantly defended the entrenchment against overwhelming odds, some of the fiercest fighting taking place in the new barrack buildings which were under construction.

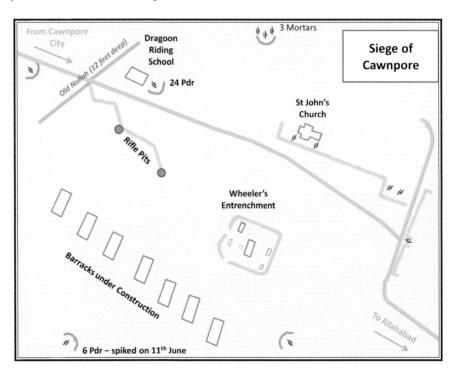

Figure 43. Siege of Cawnpore

On the 8th night of the siege, the thatched barracks being used as a hospital caught fire and burned to the ground. Most of the women and children sheltering in the barracks made their escape, however, many of the sick and wounded were not so fortunate and were burned to death.

The barracks were also used to accommodate the 80 loyal Sepoys, with their destruction the sepoys were allowed to leave the entrenchment and make their escape from the rebels.

Although the plight of the British was dire, they had inflicted heavy losses on the mutineers and their stout resistance was causing Nana Sahib some concern that his forces might give up his quest to take the city. With this in mind, on 24th June, 19 days into the siege, Nana Sahib sent a message with a captured English woman, Rose Greenway, to General Wheeler offering terms of surrender. The terms were not accepted, however, negotiations continued the following day and it was agreed that the British could leave with 60 rounds of ammunition per man and that they would be provided with carriages for the sick and wounded and boats stocked with food to take them to Allahabad. Nana Sahib's acceptance of the terms was conveyed to General Wheeler by another captured English woman Mrs Jacobi on 25th June.

Cawnpore Chowra Ghat massacre

After 24 hours to prepare, the 450 survivors of the 21 day siege left Cawnpore on the morning of 27th June in a column led by General Wheeler on their journey of about a mile to the landing on the Ganges where boats were awaiting for their onward journey to Allahabad. They crossed a small bridge to the landing at Sati Chowra where 40 boats were moored but as no planks were available to board the vessels, the able bodied had to get into the water and carry the sick, wounded and children to the boats.

At about 9 am an enemy bugle sounded and the native boatmen jumped off their boats into the river and swam to the bank, many knocking over the cooking fires and setting fire to the boats as they made their escape. With this signal the mutineers began to pour down artillery and musket fire, from both banks of the river, onto the boats loaded down with the British survivors, all being directed by Nana Sahib's general Tantia Topi from a small white temple on the river bank. Three boats out of the 40 did manage to escape down river, but two were caught almost immediately and the occupants were slaughtered.

The third boat, with about 100 people on board, was pursued by the rebels both on foot and by river but managed to get about 6 miles downriver before becoming grounded.

Lieutenants Delafosse and Thompson led a small party of 14 men to keep the rebels at bay until the boat was refloated, and managed to reach Mussapgurh before once again becoming grounded. The Lieutenants and their small party again charged the rebels to keep them from overwhelming the boat and during the night a severe storm managed to dislodge the boat which again floated downstream to Sooragpoor about 30 miles from Cawnpore where it became grounded for the final time. Once again Lieutenant Mobray Thompson, Lieutenant Delafosse and 12 men from the 82nd and 34th Regiments, left the boat to drive off the mutineers, however, this time they became separated from the boat and could not find it when they returned to the river bank. Unable to rejoin the boat the party made its way down the river bank towards Allahabad but after being steadily picked off by rebel fire, the men who could swim took to the water and swam for their lives.

Eventually four men survived and were dragged exhausted from the river by a party of Cavalry commanded by Raja Dirigibijah Singh who had remained loyal to the British. Lieutenants Delafosse and Thompson together with Privates Murphy and Sullivan would be the only male survivors of the Cawnpore massacre (Jonah Sheppard would also survive but he was captured and held prisoner before the massacre occurred). The men were looked after by Raja Dirigibijah's men until 28th July when they joined up with General Havelock's relief force at Allahabad (except for Private Sullivan who had died from his wounds).

The boat was captured by the mutineers at Sooragpoor and brought back up river to its start point near Cawnpore. The 60 wounded men on board, including General Wheeler were executed and the 25 women and four children were taken to Savada House in the city to be held prisoner with the other women and children.

On 1st July, the prisoners were moved to the Bibigarh a small house in the grounds of the residency of Sir George Parker.

Relief of Cawnpore

On hearing of the fall of Cawnpore, the authorities in Calcutta instigated the assembly of a relief force at Allahabad under the command of General Havelock.

The force of 1,900 men consisted of; 76 men of the Royal Artillery, 400 men of the Madras Fusiliers, 300 men of the 78th Regiment of Foot, 435 men of the 64th Regiment of Foot, 190 men of the 84th Regiment of Foot, 450 Sikhs, 50 men with the Irregular Cavalry and 20 Cavalry volunteers.

On 7th July the assembled force left Allahabad bound for Cawnpore and on 12th July inflicted a heavy defeat on a large body of mutineers in the Battle of Futtehgur after which they rested on 13th July before resuming their journey on the 14th July.

On the morning of the 15th July a large enemy force was defeated at Aong and in the afternoon another force was defeated at a main bridge over the river Pandoo Nuddee about 22 miles from Cawnpore

The Bibigarh massacre

During the afternoon of 15th July, Bala Raothe, the brother of Nana Sahib, who had been wounded in the shoulder, returned to Cawnpore from the battle at Pandoo Nuddee and discussions took place regarding what to do with the prisoners. Fear of retribution for the barbaric acts the prisoners had witnessed and would report if rescued led to the decision that all of the prisoners should be killed.

The prisoners numbered about 210 including five men, the men and a male youth of about 14 years old were led before Nana Sahib and killed by a hastily formed firing squad.

Later in the afternoon a woman from Nana Sahib's household went to the Bibigarh and told the officer of the men guarding the prisoners to kill all the prisoners. To his credit, the officer replied that he was a soldier and would not murder women and children, he later discussed this with his men and they all agreed that they would not kill the prisoners. Undaunted, Nana Sahib soon found five men willing to perform the task; two local peasants, two butchers and a man from his own body guard. At about 5 o'clock in the afternoon, the men entered the Bibigarh armed with swords and cleavers and mercilessly butchered the women and children.

Early the next day, the bodies of the dead and wounded were unceremoniously dumped in a disused well.

The recapture of Cawnpore

After the victory at Pandoo Nuddee, General Havelock allowed his men to rest at the battle site but at 3 o'clock in the morning he addressed his men with the news that it was believed that over 200 women and children were being held captive in the city.

Without waiting for orders the men immediately formed into column and began the 22 mile march to Cawnpore, intent on rescuing the prisoners.

As they approached the city, it became evident that Nana Sahib had assembled a considerable force of 7,000 men supported by heavy artillery to guard the approach to the city.

Facing such a formidable force and being armed with only light artillery, General Havelock had little chance of success with a traditional frontal attack, however, the General bravely decided on an attack in force on the enemy right flank.

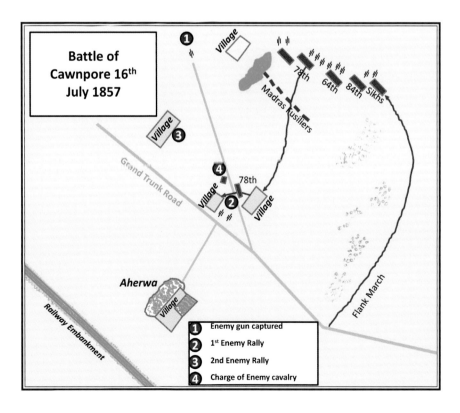

Figure 44. 1st Battle of Cawnpore

The mutineers were slow to react to this audacious move but soon managed to turn their artillery so that they could lay down fire on the advancing British troops. The 78th Regiment of Foot bravely charged the enemy line in the face of heavy artillery fire and managed to overwhelm the mutineers' batteries. Guns from the centre were now able to fire on the British troops but with further charges from the Highlanders and attacks on the enemy left flank and centre by the 64th and 84th Regiments the mutineers were pushed back from their positions and regrouped at a small village about a mile closer to Cawnpore. Pressing forward the British troops once again cleared the rebels from their positions and cleared the village.

Lieutenant Henry Havelock – Victoria Cross No. 146

For the third and last time Nana Sahib managed to regroup his troops and take up positions on either side of the Cawnpore road on the outskirts of the city. Again the enemy artillery was spread across the length of their front with a large 24 pounder in the centre.

This large gun was putting down devastating fire from round shot and as the British came closer from grape shot. The gun was in the direct path of the 64th Regiment being led on foot by Major Stirling who had been dismounted. With no other mounted officer being nearby, Lieutenant Havelock the son and Aide-de-Camp to General Havelock volunteered to lead the men and attack the gun. Riding his horse at walking pace, Lieutenant Havelock led the men right up to the gun and after a brief charge this was captured and the rebels were routed.

For his part in this action Lieutenant Havelock was later awarded the Victoria Cross.

✚

On the morning of 17th July, Havelock's force entered Cawnpore virtually unopposed as Nana Sahib with his commanders and men had fled after the previous day's battle and 5,000 men with 45 guns were now encamped at Bithoor.

As news of the fate of the women and children filtered down to the men they went on the rampage through the town killing soldiers and civilians as they found them; incensed by the atrocity their officers did little to stop them.

All of the captured Sepoys were executed, the majority were hanged, however, some were "cannoned"; tied across the muzzle of a loaded cannon such that when the cannon was fired they were blown apart.[11]

Figure 45. Blown from guns

---

11 This was a traditional Mughal punishment for mutiny.

9

THE LUCKNOW CAMPAIGN

Lucknow was the capital of the recently annexed province of Oudh and as such was the administrative centre of the region with a garrison of Queen's and Company troops.

At the time of the mutiny, the garrison comprised; 32nd Regiment of Foot, 7th Native Cavalry, 13th, 48th and 71st Bengal Native Infantry Regiments. The native troops outnumbered the European troops by a factor of ten to one.

Following the annexation of Oudh in 1856, the discontent amongst the Sepoys had been on the increase for some months. The majority of the native troops were from the region and most were directly affected by the change in rule; loss to them and their families of land rights, increased taxation and the loss to the troops of an allowance for foreign service now that the province was in the hands of the Company were a few of the more prominent concerns.

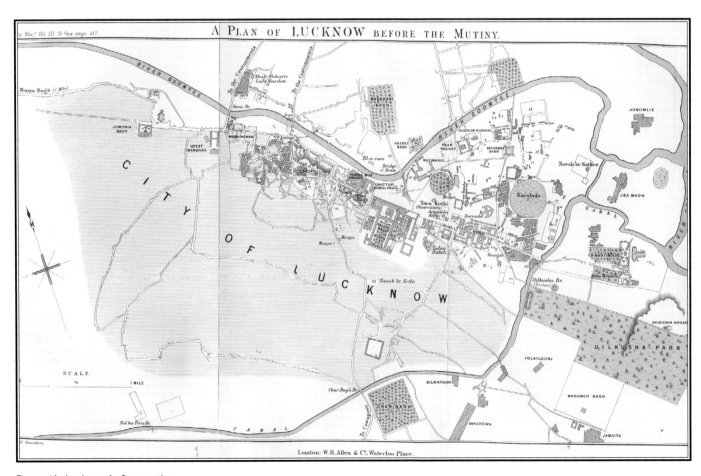

Figure 46. Lucknow before mutiny

On 20th March Brigadier-General Sir Henry Lawrence, a much respected and experienced officer was appointed as the Chief Commissioner for the Oudh province and he immediately set about implementing changes to try and diffuse the tensions.

In common with many other garrisons the issue with the greased cartridges also affected the mood of the native soldiers. The first actual trouble was on 1st May 1857 when the 7th Oudh Irregular Infantry based at Moosa Bagh, a suburb of Lucknow, refused to accept the new cartridges when they were issued. On the following day, the regiment was paraded and disarmed, about 50 mutineers thought to be the ringleaders were sent to prison, and those who remained loyal were rewarded with several being promoted.

By the 14th May 1857, General Sir Henry Lawrence was aware of the mutiny at Meerut and the situation at Delhi and decided to take actions to defend the city in the case of a mutiny at Lucknow.

Loyal troops were placed in the Macchi Bhawan, an old Sikh fort, and set about making repairs and improving the defences so that it could be used as a place of refuge. General Lawrence also split the British troops between the Murriaon Cantonement where most of the Sepoys were billeted and the Residency where he began to assemble the British families. For the next few days General Lawrence used his engineers to strengthen the Macchi Bhawan and the Residency and began to stockpile food and ammunition at both locations in anticipation of a rebellion at Lucknow.

Mutiny at Lucknow

The expected mutiny finally arrived on the evening of 30th May 1857, following the firing of the 9 o'clock gun, while General Lawrence was dining in Government House with his senior staff. The mutineers began setting fire to the officer houses and started firing shots into the British camp, however, not all of the native regiments were involved in the outbreak, the 13th and 71st Native Infantry remained loyal and marched to the British camp where they formed up with the 32nd Regiment of Foot. A detachment of the 13th Native Infantry moved to Government House in order to protect General Lawrence and his staff. The night passed with little activity and in the morning the mutineers were assembled in the cavalry lines at Moodkepore which they had burned the previous evening.

General Lawrence acted decisively and after leaving a detachment from the 32nd Regiment of Foot to guard the cantonments he launched an attack on the rebels who, after a brief fusillade from the British guns, were quickly dispersed. General Lawrence's men pursued the mutineers for about 6 miles, capturing

about 60 of their number, before returning to the city. On reaching the city the General established his head quarters in the Residency.

On the 1st July, elements of the civil population rioted, in sympathy with the mutineers, however, all of the disturbances were quelled by the city police under the command of Captain Carnegie.

Improving the defences of the Residency

Having knowledge of General Wheeler's experience at Cawnpore, General Lawrence correctly assumed that the mutineers would adopt similar tactics at Lucknow and besiege the town. With this in mind the decision was taken to concentrate their efforts on making the Residency defensible against an attack with artillery. Engineers began constructing ramparts to create a perimeter around the area of the Residency and large emplacements known as the Redan and Cawnpore Battery were constructed. To reduce the number of high points available to the rebels, the upper stories of nearby tall buildings were demolished and other buildings were destroyed in their entirety. Magazines were established throughout the Residency emplacement and stocked with ammunition and powder from the Macchi Bhawan fort. After 200 guns were found in an old arsenal within the city, these were incorporated into the defences. The Residency was now prepared to be the main place of refuge in the event of a siege.

Battle of Chinhut

So far the mutineers had shown no sign of advancing on Lucknow, however, with news of the fall of Cawnpore the rebels began to assemble at Nuwabgunge, 20 miles from the city and when intelligence of this move reached General Lawrence he sent out a small force of cavalry to reconnoitre the situation.

When the party returned with news that an advanced party of mutineers had reached the town of Chinhut, only eight miles from the Residency, General Lawrence decided to withdraw his troops from the Cantonments and concentrate his forces at the Residency and the Macchi Bhawan fort.

The General also decided that now was the time to go on the offensive and perhaps nip the siege in the bud before it actually started. The following force was assembled: Artillery; No.1 Horse Light Field Battery (4 Guns), No. 2 Oudh Field Battery (4 guns) and No. 3 Oudh Field Battery (2 guns and 8" Howitzer); Cavalry; volunteers from 1st, 2nd and 3rd Regiments of Oudh Irregular Cavalry; Infantry; 300 men from 32nd Regiment of Foot, 150

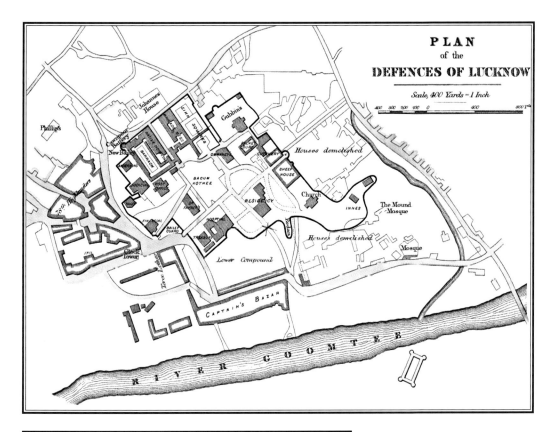

Figure 47. Lucknow defences

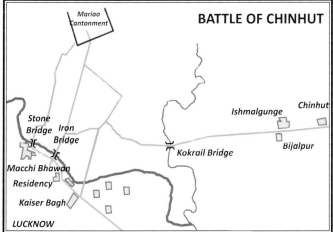

Figure 48. Battle of Chinhut

men from 13th Bengal Native Infantry, 60 men from 48th Bengal Native Infantry and 29 men from 71st Bengal Native Infantry. It should be noted that apart from the men of the No. 1 Horse Light Field Battery and the 32nd Regiment of Foot the remainder of the force was made up by native soldiers who had remained loyal to the crown. In all 800 natives had remained loyal after the mutiny, including 80 pensioners who were persuaded to come out of retirement.

On the morning of 30th June, General Lawrence accompanied the force under the command of Lieutenant-Colonel William Case as it advanced towards the village of Chinhut where it was expecting to intercept the advanced party of mutineers thought to be no more than 5,000 in number.

After crossing a bridge over the river Kukrail, the column was ordered to halt for a rest and something to eat, as they had not yet had breakfast. Before they could break their fast an order was given to about turn and return to Lucknow as there was no sign of the mutineers. This order was no sooner begun when it was reversed as a forward scouting party had located the mutineers just up the road near the village of Ishmalgunge.

As the party advanced on the village it became apparent that they were facing the full might of the rebel force of about 15,000 men, not just an advanced party, and they were entrenched in the village with about 40 artillery guns.

Despite being heavily outnumbered and outgunned, the British force advanced and managed to take a small hamlet on the right of the road but as they approached Ishmalgunge they were met with a withering fire of grape and musket fire.

The native artillery accompanying the British force abandoned their guns and fled to the rebels soon to be followed by the Sikh cavalry.

In the face of such overwhelming force it was necessary to retreat and in peril of being outflanked the force just managed to recross the bridge across the Kukrail River.

Lieutenant William Cubitt – Victoria Cross No. 133

During the retreat, the men exhausted by the intense heat and lack of food and water were often chased down by the rebels. Lieutenant Cubitt rescued three men from the 32nd Regiment of Foot by fighting off mutineers who had surrounded the exhausted men.

For this action Lieutenant Cubitt was later awarded the Victoria Cross.

＋

Having crossed the bridge over the Kukrail, the men of the Light Horse Artillery, bravely unlimbered their guns and laid down fire on the advancing mutineers giving protection to the retreating British forces. By 11:30 a.m. the force had crossed the Iron bridge over the River Gumti and was back within the relative safety of Lucknow where General Lawrence now congregated his forces within the defensive works of the Residency.

The British losses following the disastrous action at Chinhut was 118 European Officers Killed and 54 wounded with 182 native soldiers killed and 11 wounded.

Siege of Lucknow

Following the Battle of Chinhut, the mutineers continued their advance on Lucknow but were slowed at the River Gumti bridges by artillery fire from the Residency and the fort of Macchi

Bhawan, however, they managed to establish artillery positions and began their bombardment of the city – the siege of Lucknow had begun at 11:00 o'clock on 30th June 1857.

Corporal William Oxenham – Victoria Cross No. 134

One of the casualties of this first bombardment was the veranda of Anderson House which collapsed and buried Mr Capper, a civil servant.

Under heavy fire, Corporal Oxenham toiled for over ten minutes to dig out Mr Capper from beneath the rubble which he completed successfully, saving the life of the civil servant.

For this action Corporal Oxenham was later awarded the Victoria Cross.

＋

Lieutenant Robert Aitken – Victoria Cross No. 135

During the first hours of the bombardment, Lieutenant Aitken made three forays into the abandoned Residency Gardens, under direct fire from mutineers in the Captain's Bazaar and on two of these trips brought back a number of bullocks which had been left in the gardens.

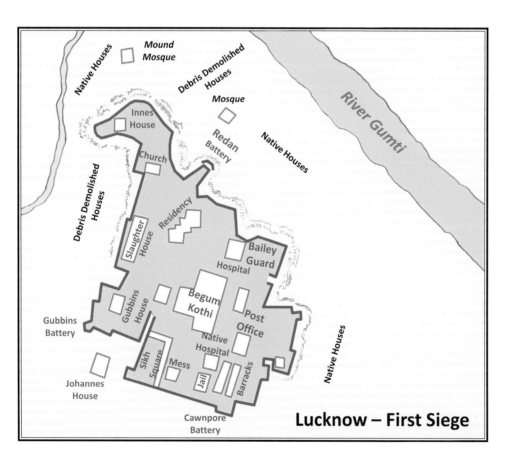

Figure 49. 1st siege of Lucknow

On 3rd July the enemy gunfire had set fire to a large stock of fodder for the animals which was stored within the compound. Lieutenant Aitken, noticed that the fire was in danger of spreading to a line of tents, which if ignited would risk setting fire to a nearby powder magazine, under heavy enemy fire he rushed across open ground and cut down the tents.

For these acts Lieutenant Aitken was later awarded the Victoria Cross, his citation also mentions four further acts of bravery.

On the night of 20th August, the mutineers set fire to the Bailey Guard Gate, Lieutenant Aitken opened the gate and under heavy musket fire removed the burning wood and straw piled in front of the gate, saving it from destruction.

On the evening of 25th September, Lieutenant Aitken led a small force to capture two guns which the mutineers were training on General Havelock's advancing second column. After successfully capturing the guns, the small force attacked and captured the Teree Kotee.

On the following morning, Lieutenant Aitken again led a small force and captured a gateway of the Furreed Buksh Palace, he personally kept open a small wicket gate which allowed his men to enter and capture the palace.

On 29th September, Lieutenant Aitken again distinguished himself when he led a party of four men to capture an enemy gun in the face of heavy fire from nearby houses. Despite the heavy fire the men held their position and with reinforcements managed to capture this and a further gun and return with them to the Residency.

On the 1st July, General Lawrence decided that it was time to abandon the Macchi Bhawan fort and destroy it, together with the remainder of its magazine contents which amounted to a large supply of ammunition and powder. After receiving a telegraph signal from the residency to this effect, Colonel Palmer of the 42nd Native Infantry who commanded the fort ordered the few guns that remained to be spiked and prepared the building for destruction. At midnight, the fuse was set and Colonel Palmer and his men evacuated the building and stealthily moved to the Residency gates some 1,000 yards distant, as they reached the gates the magazine exploded destroying the fort and its contents.

After the fort was abandoned, General Lawrence now had all his forces and non-combatants, a total of almost 3,000 people, concentrated within the entrenchment known as the "Residency".

The besieged

The besieged were comprised of; just over 600 European women and children, nearly 700 native servants, 700 Sepoys some of whose loyalty was questionable and a fighting force of just over 900 Europeans. The European fighting force was made up of; 535 men from the 32nd Regiment of Foot, 50 men of the 84th Regiment of Foot, 89 men manning the artillery, 100 British Officers who were mainly from regiments that had mutinied and 153 civilians mostly clerks who were pressed into service.

The "Residency" defences

The "Residency" was an area of 30 acres, ringed by trenches, earthworks and palisades which encircled several buildings including the actual Residency building with a perimeter of about 2,500 yards.

The fighting force was mainly distributed amongst 17 posts and batteries which protected the perimeter: Innes's Post was commanded by Lieutenant Laughnan and was manned by men of the 32nd and some clerks; the North Curtain was commanded by Colonel Palmer with a force of Sepoys; the Redan was commanded by Lieutenant Lawrence and men from the 32nd; the Hospital was commanded by Lieutenant Langmore with a force of Sepoys; the Bailey Guard was commanded by Lieutenant Aitken with a force of Sepoys; Dr Fayrer's House was commanded by Captain Weston and a force of Sepoy pensioners; Sago's House was commanded by Lieutenant Clery with men from the 32nd; the Financial Commissioners Office was commanded by Captain Saunders manned by men from the 32nd and some civilian clerks; the Judicial Commissioners Office was commanded by Captain Germon manned by Sepoys and some civilian clerks; Anderson's Garrison was commanded by Captain Anderson manned by men of the 32nd and some civilian volunteers; the Cawnpore Battery was manned by artillerymen and the command was changed daily; the Sikhs' square was commanded by Captain Harding with units of Sikh cavalry; Gubbin's Battery was commanded by Major Banks manned by Sepoy Pensioners, men from the 32nd and Native levies; the Racket Court, the Slaughter House, the Sheep Pen and St Mary's Church were all manned by men from the Commissariat department and finally the Residency where Captain Lowe commanded men from the 84th which were held in reserve.

The line was also defended by many other minor gun emplacements and piquets.

The women and children were housed in many buildings including the Residency, the hospital, Begum Kotee, St Mary's Church and the Thag Goal which also housed the boys from the Martinière College who were looked after by their Principal Mr Schilling.

The besieged were blessed with an abundant supply of food, including fresh meat from animals that had been brought into the enclosure. They also had an adequate supply of water.

Death of General Lawrence

On 2nd July an enemy shell exploded in a room in the Residency occupied by General Lawrence but he escaped injury, despite being advised to seek safer accommodation, the General returned to his room later in the day, when another shell exploded and caused mortal wounds to his left leg.

General Lawrence died two days later on 4th July and in accordance with his wishes, Major Banks was appointed as Chief Commissioner and Colonel Inglis was given command of the troops.

Rebel bombardment

As expected the mutineers employed tactics similar to those used at Cawnpore, from the start they kept up a sporadic artillery barrage on the "Residency" emplacement and where possible closed under cover to occupy houses from where they could support the artillery with musket fire.

Despite their large numbers of over 30,000 men, due to a lack of overall command these resources were thankfully never effectively deployed to the full.

British tactics

With an adequate supply of food, water and munitions the British strategy was to withstand the siege until relief arrived once the situations at Delhi and Cawnpore had been resolved.

To implement this strategy the British forces would use their artillery to reduce the enemy bombardment by destroying their guns and also to repel any enemy attacks. Commandants were instructed that no man was to leave his post without permission and everyone was told to keep under cover, always be on the alert and never to fire a shot unless he could see his man.

These instructions were hard to enforce as in the words of a soldier of the 32nd "It's not the way of the English to fight behind walls" and almost from the start the men carried out "local sorties". Small groups of soldiers, normally less than 10 would appoint their own leader and raid one of the houses occupied by the mutineers, killing the occupants and spiking any guns before returning to their positions in the "Residency".

Private William Dowling – Victoria Cross No. 137

On 4th July Private Dowling, together with two other men was involved in a "local sortie" where he spiked a gun and killed a mutineer. He was involved in similar escapades on 9th July and 27th September. For these actions Private Dowling was later awarded the Victoria Cross.

Sometimes the sorties were more formal, supported by Engineers who would blow up the enemy position with bags of gun powder.

Johannes House

Johannes House was a building just outside the "Residency" entrenchment which had been occupied by a small band of mutineer marksmen who were causing much disruption by firing from the roof where they had commanding views of the Cawnpore Battery.

The commander of the group was one of the ex-Viceroy's African eunuchs known as "Bob the Nailer" by the British troops, due to his prowess as a sniper.

It was also thought that due to its proximity to the "Residency" defences, the building was also being used for mining operations.

Lieutenant Samuel Lawrence – Victoria Cross No. 139

On 7th July, just after noon, when a short barrage was fired at the building to distract the occupants, a small party exited the "Residency" enclosure by a small hole made in the wall near the Martinière quarters with the intent of eliminating the Johannes House nuisance.

The party consisted of Captain Mansfield, Lieutenant Lawrence and Ensign Studdy of the 32nd Regiment of Foot, Ensign Green of the 13th Native Infantry accompanied by 50 men from the 32nd and 20 Sikhs. Lieutenant Lawrence was the first man to enter the house via a window which he entered from a ladder. Just as he stepped off the ladder his pistol was knocked from his hand by a mutineer, however, he prevailed in the ensuing fight and the party managed to kill about 15 to 20 mutineers and spike a gun before they had to retire in the face of rebel reinforcements.

Unfortunately, "Bob the Nailer" managed to escape and the party were unable to lay their charges and demolish the house.

For his part in the action Lieutenant Lawrence was later awarded the Victoria Cross. He was also cited for an action on 26th September when he led a party that captured three enemy guns.

The siege continues

On the 9th July a party of about 300 mutineers made an attack on the Bailey Guard, however, this was easily repulsed. Further attacks on the Bailey Guard and on Gubbin's Post took place on 12th July but again were repulsed with little difficulty. On 14th July the Brigade Mess was the target of a heavy bombardment and much damage was caused to the building. On the same day it was noticed that there was much enemy activity near to a mosque close to the Captain's Bazaar, it was thought that this was the construction of a mine[12] aimed at the Redan defence.

The first concerted enemy attack on the British positions took place on the evening of 20th July, the start of the assault was signalled by the explosion of a mine at 10:15 p m , this was close to the Redan but fell about 30 yards short so did little damage. Following the explosion of the mine, under a heavy barrage from their artillery and supported by musket fire, the mutineers launched simultaneous assaults in force at several points in the Residency defences. A mass attack took place on the Redan and Innes's Post but the mutineers soon retreated when they came under heavy fire from the Redan, which had escaped damage from the mine, and also from Evans's guns. Other attacks took place at Anderson's Post, Germons Post and Gubbins Bastion and although the rebels reached the walls all of these attacks were repulsed. The enemy kept up a continuous barrage until 4:00 a.m. when the attacks ended. British spirits were high, having repulsed a major enemy attack in force with minimal losses; 4 men were killed and 12 wounded.

The success of the 20th July was marred by the death of Major Banks, the High Commissioner, on the following day, who was shot through the head while inspecting an outpost. With the death of Major Banks, the civil post of High Commissioner was left vacant and sole command of Lucknow was given to the military commander Colonel Inglis.

On the evening of 22nd July, Angad Tewari a native pensioner, who had left the city as a messenger at the end of June, returned with the news that General Havelock had recaptured Cawnpore and had defeated Nana Sahib at three battles. With this good news, Angad Tewari was immediately sent out again, this time with a letter from Colonel Inglis requesting assistance. Angad Tewari returned to Lucknow on 25th July, with a reply from Colonel B. Fraser Tyler, the assistant Quartermaster-General to General Havelock's force, which stated: *"We have two-thirds of our force across the river and eight guns in position already. The rest will follow immediately. I will send over more news to-night or to-morrow. We have ample force to destroy all who oppose us. Send us a sketch of your position in the city, and any directions for entering it or turning it that may strike you. In five or six days we shall meet. You must threaten the rear of the enemy if they come out, and we will smash them."* The next evening, Angad Tewari

___

12 Mining was the process of digging a tunnel to a point directly under your objective, where explosives were then placed and exploded to destroy the target. Initially used during the Crimean War, the tactic was used by both the British and Mutineer forces during the Mutiny and was of course used extensively during the trench warfare of the Great War.

once again left the city with Colonel Inglis's reply, which suggested a route into the city and concluded with the request, *"If you have rockets with you, send up two or three at 8 p.m. on the night before you intend entering the city, by way of warning to us, at which signal we will begin shelling the houses on both sides of the road … with the assurance that the utmost our weak and harassed garrison is capable of, shall be done to cause a diversion in your favour as soon as you are sufficiently near."*

Following the repulse of the enemy attack on 20th July, it was determined that the best chance of success for the mutineers would be to breach the defences with mining operations. Throughout the siege the rebels constructed over 30 mines, however, only one was successful in causing a breach. To counter this threat, British engineers carried out their own very successful counter-mining operations and with the 32nd being a Cornish regiment, there was no shortage of experienced miners.

During the nights of 22nd and 23rd July, 240 barrels of powder were moved to a new magazine which had been established in underground rooms of the Begum Kothi, safeguarding this precious resource which had nearly been blown up earlier in the month.

Since the arrival of the message from Colonel Tyler a watch was kept each day for the signal which would announce the arrival of Havelock's relief force, however, to no avail.

On 6th August a British spy, Aodhan Singh who was an orderly to Brigadier Grey, returned to the city with news that General Havelock had fought two successful engagements on the Lucknow side of the River Ganges but due to cholera had been force to halt at Mangalwar.

Soon after receiving this unfortunate news, the rebels launched their second full scale attack on the city on 10th August, however, sentries had noticed the mutineers preparations and all posts were fully manned in expectation of an assault.

In a similar fashion to the attack of 20th July, the attack was launched following the detonation of two mines; one directed at the Martinière to the south and the other towards Sago's House on the east of the defences. Both mines fell short of their intended position and caused no breach to the defences, again accompanied by heavy artillery and musket fire a large force of mutineers charged these two positions but finding the defences intact had to retire in the face of heavy fire from the British defences. Attacks were also launched against, Innes's Post, Gubbins Bastion, the Cawnpore Battery and Andersons Post. The mutineers, who carried scaling ladders, were repulsed with heavy losses unable to get close enough to the defences to deploy their ladders.

Again the British losses were light, with five killed and 12 wounded; on the other hand the rebels experienced greater losses than they had on the 20th July.

Unfortunately, the Chief Engineer Major Anderson died on this day from dysentery which he had been fighting since the beginning of the siege. He was succeeded by Captain Fulton.

On 12th August, the mutineers launched an intense bombardment and musket fire against the Cawnpore Battery, mainly from the area of Johannes House. The fire was so intense that the occupants together with their guns had to be withdrawn from the battery.

On the night of the 15th August, the native pensioner Angad Tewari once again arrived at the Residency with a letter from Colonel Tyler. The letter was dated 4th August, Angad Tewari had been briefly captured by the mutineers, hence the delay. In the letter Colonel Tyler stated *"We march to-morrow morning for Lucknow, having been reinforced. We shall push on as speedily as possible. We hope to reach you in four days at furthest. You must aid us in every way, even to cutting your way out, if we can't force our way in. We have only a small Force."* After being released by the mutineers, Angad Tewari retraced his steps to Mangalwar but found the place to have been abandoned by our force. Further enquiries determined that General Havelock and his force had recrossed the Ganges and moved to Cawnpore where Nana Sahib was once again threatening the city. It was also reported that General Havelock had defeated the mutineers again at Busherut-gunge and moved his force into the city.

On 16th August, Colonel Inglis sent out Angad Tewari once again with a letter to General Havelock *"My dear General, — A note from Colonel Tytler to Mr. Gubbins reached me last night, dated Mungulwar, 4th instant, the latter part of which is as follows: 'You must aid us in every way, even to cutting your way out, if we can't force our way in; we have only a small force.' This has caused me much uneasiness, as it is quite impossible with my weak and shattered force that I can leave my defences. You must bear in mind how I am hampered, that I have upwards of 120 sick and wounded, and at least 220 women, and about 230 children, and no carriage of any description, besides sacrificing 23 lakhs of treasure and about 30 guns of sorts. In consequence of the news received, I shall soon put this force on half rations until I hear again from you. Our provisions will last us then till about the 10th of September*.[13] If you hope to save this force, no time must be lost in pushing forward. We are daily being attacked by the enemy, who are within a few yards of our defences. Their mines have already weakened our posts, and I have every reason to believe they are carrying on others. Their 18-pounders are within 150 yards of some of our batteries, and from their position and our inability to form working parties we cannot reply to them, and therefore the damage hourly is* very great. *My strength now in Europeans is 350, and 300 Natives, and the men dreadfully harassed, and, owing to part of the Residency having been brought down by round shot, many are without shelter. If our Native forces, which are losing confidence, leave us I do not know how the defences are to be manned. Did you receive a letter and plan from me? Kindly answer this question. — Yours truly, (Signed) "J. Inglis."*

Following the second general attack by the mutineers, the mining contest continued at a pace and during the next few weeks the rebels completed 14 mines, however, all but one of these was destroyed by British counter measures. The successful mine was exploded on 18th August and was directed towards the defences at the front of Sikh Square on the south of the city where it caused a breach of 10 yards. Thinking that this may be a prelude to another general attack, the 18 men of the 84th who were held in reserve were called out for the first and only time to help defend the breach while it was being repaired.

No general attack ensued, however a group of mutineers did try to storm the breach, in fact one man actually reached the British side of the defences, the only man to do so during the whole siege, but was killed and the attack was repulsed. The breach was then repaired.

Lieutenant Henry Gore-Browne – Victoria Cross No. 157

In addition to mining counter measures, the British engineers were also carrying out their own mining operations and on 21st August they exploded a mine directed at Johannes House. The house was destroyed and in the process the notorious rebel sniper known as "Bob the Nailer" was amongst those killed in the explosion. As part of the operation against Johannes House, two British sorties were directed on rebel gun batteries on either side of the house. The assault parties were led by Captain McCabe and Lieutenant Gore-Brown. Lieutenant Gore-Brown was the first man to enter his battery where he killed the gunners and spiked their guns; during the attacks over 100 mutineers were killed.

For this action Captain Gore-Brown was later awarded the Victoria Cross.

✛

Towards the end of the month the rebels established a new battery within the grounds of the Buland Bagh, armed with 24 and 12 pounder guns this battery caused substantial damage to Gubbins Battery and forced the defenders to remove their guns until the battery could be reinforced.

On the night of 28th August, Angad Tewari once again returned to the Residency with a letter from General Havelock *"I have your letter of the 16th. Sir Colin Campbell, who came*

---

13 Colonel Inglis's estimation of the food supply was based upon only a quarter of the food that was actually available due to the fact that an accurate and complete inventory of food had not been compiled.

out at a day's notice to command on hearing of General Anson's death, promises me fresh troops, and you shall be my first care. The reinforcements may reach me in about twenty to twenty-five days, and I will prepare everything for a march on Lucknow. Do not negotiate, but rather perish sword in hand."

On 31st August the mutineers established a new battery within the Lutkun Durwaza (Clock Tower), manned with a formidable 32 pounder gun which was only 100 yards from the Bailey Guard Gate. To counter this new threat, the British established a new battery at the Treasury Post which was completed on 4th September and was manned with an 18 pounder gun and 24 pounder howitzer.

On the 5th September the rebels began their fourth and final general assault on the Residency, as with the previous assaults the mutineer preparations as they assembled about 8,000 men were most apparent to the British and the men were all at their posts ready for the assault to begin. The assault began at around 10 o'clock, again triggered by the explosion of a mine, this time in the direction of Gubbins Bastion; yet again the mutineers had miscalculated the distances and the mine fell short leaving the defences undamaged. Under heavy fire the mutineers did manage to get some ladders up against the defences and tried to scale the walls, however, the defenders managed to prevent any of the enemy gaining entry to their domain. Soon after the Gubbins Bastion mine exploded, another mine was exploded towards the Brigade Mess; again this fell short and caused no damage to the defences. Despite the lack of a breach, the mutineers threw themselves at the defences and were killed in great numbers. The new British Battery at the Treasury Post was used to good effect and destroyed many of the guns at the Clock Tower battery. Several attacks were mounted at other parts of the Residency defences, however they were all repulsed with heavy losses incurred by the mutineers.

Again the British losses were minimal with 3 killed and one wounded, however, the rebels experienced their heaviest losses of all of the assaults.

Captain Fulton, the brave and capable Chief Engineer was killed by a round shot while on duty at the Gubbins Bastion on 14th September.

On 16th September, the pensioner Angad Tewari was once again sent out[14] with a letter from Colonel Inglis to General Havelock "Since the date of my last letter, the enemy have continued to persevere unceasingly in their efforts against this position, and the firing has never ceased either day or night. ... I shall be quite out of rum for the men in eight days; but we have been living on reduced rations, so I hope to be able to get on pretty well until the 18th

14 The pensioner Angad Tewari was paid the astronomical sum of £500 for each of these dangerous missions.

proximo. If you have not relieved us by that time, we shall have no meat left, as I must keep some bullocks to move my guns about the position; as it is, I have had to kill nearly all the gun bullocks, as my men could not perform the hard work without animal food. I am most anxious to hear of your advance to reassure the native soldiers." Colonel Inglis was correct in assertion that the native soldiers needed reassurance; rumours had been circulating for days that the letters brought by Angad Tewari were fabrications and that their position was untenable as no reinforcements were on their way.

The defenders position was indeed becoming dire, repeated bombardment by the rebels had reduced many of the buildings to rubble so shelter for the women, children, sick and wounded was in short supply. The health of the garrison was being steadily eroded by sickness from cholera and dysentery and some of the food stock was becoming short in supply.

On 18th September there was a partial eclipse of the sun, perhaps this was a good omen as four days later on the evening of 22nd September, Angad Tewari arrived back at the Residency with good news of an approaching relief force.

The good news was in the form of a letter from General Outram dated 20th September which stated

> The army crossed the river yesterday, and all the material being over now, marches towards you tomorrow, and with the blessing of God will now relieve you. The rebels, we hear, intend making one desperate assault on you as we approach the city, and will be on the watch in expectation of your weakening your garrison to make a diversion in our favour as we attack the city. I beg to warn you against being enticed to venture far from your works. When you see us engaged in your vicinity, such diversion as you could make without in any way risking your position should only be attempted.

On the 23rd September, gunfire could be heard in the distance toward the direction of Cawnpore, heralding the arrival of the relief force, however, it was not until the evening of the 25th September that Generals Outram and Havelock entered the Residency compound via the Bailey Guard Gate.

After 87 days the first stage of the Lucknow siege was at an end, reinforcements had at long last arrived to bolster the small force of defenders. During this stage of the siege, only 577 Europeans and men of the East India Company were still alive from the 927 who were present on the 1st July, but many of these were sick or wounded. Of the native soldiers, only 395 men remained alive of the 765 present on the 1st of July, 130 had been killed and 230 had deserted; again many of the survivors were sick or wounded.

Havelock's expedition to relieve Lucknow

After the recapture of Cawnpore, Brigadier-General J. G. Neill left Allahabad on 16th July and joined General Havelock at Cawnpore on 20th July. With the arrival of General Neill, General Havelock established some defensive works near the River Ganges and left the General with a small garrison of about 300 men to guard the city while he prepared to go to the relief of Lucknow.

Havelock's 1st Advance

Havelock's expeditionary force was made up of about 1,200 Europeans, comprising; men from the 64th Regiment of Foot, 78th Highlanders, 84th Regiment of Foot, 1st Madras Fusiliers and Royal Artillery (with 10 light guns) supported by a small force of Cavalry volunteers. The native troops, numbering about 300, comprised the 1st Sikh Irregulars and some cavalry.

The force started to cross the River Ganges on 21st July, however, following the monsoon rains the river had to be crossed by ferry which was a slow process. A steamer was used to tow five or six ferry boats at a time across the river but each journey took about 4 hours. By 25th July most of the men had been ferried across the river and by 26th July General Havelock had established a camp at Mangalwar where the troops rested while the baggage was transported across the river. While waiting for the baggage at Mangalwar, the troops were inflicted with an outbreak of cholera, however, at 5 o'clock in the morning on 29th July they once again began their advance on Lucknow.

Battle of Oonoa

Lieutenant Andrew Bogle – Victoria Cross No. 148

At a point about nine miles from the River Ganges, the force came upon the village of Oonoa, with the town of Oonoa a short distance further on.

Mutineers from the Oudh Irregular Infantry occupied each house in the village which were prepared as defensive positions, with loopholes cut to allow them to pour fire on any British advance. The ground to either side of the village was swampy due to the heavy rains, so there was no alternative other than a frontal assault.

The infantry had arrived at the village well ahead of their artillery but rather than wait they were eager to get at the enemy and wreak revenge for the atrocities that had been inflicted at Cawnpore.

The 78th Highlanders were unleashed on the village and with fierce hand to hand fighting began to clear and then set fire to each house in the village.

During this action Lieutenant Bogle led the attack on one particularly heavily defended house which was laying down murderous fire on the advance and managed to take his objective despite suffering a serious wound.

For his part in this action, Lieutenant Bogle was later awarded the Victoria Cross.

After the charge of the highlanders on the village, the 64th Regiment of Foot was sent in to assist with mopping up operations and after clearing the village the force assembled on the town side of the village.

The surviving mutineers fled to the town where their artillery started to lay down fire on the only clear approach to the town. By this time the British artillery had arrived and began a barrage of the enemy guns and the town.

Sergeant Major George Lambert – Victoria Cross No. 149

It was obvious that the town of Oonoa had to be cleared of the rebels, so the British force advanced and captured the 15 enemy guns and drove the mutineers from the town.

During this action Sergeant-Major Lambert acted with great courage and was later awarded the Victoria Cross for his efforts.

He was also cited for bravery at the Battle of Bithoor on 16th August and also during the entry to Lucknow on 25th September.

After clearing the town, the British force was allowed 3 hours of rest and the opportunity to take a meal before they once again began their advance on Lucknow.

First Battle of Busherut-gunge

The column marched on for a further six miles before reaching the walled town of Busherut-gunge which straddled the road. This time General Havelock decided to wait for his guns to arrive before pressing ahead with an attack, however, he did send the 64th Regiment to flank the town and gain the rear of the mutineers' position in order to be ready to cut off their retreat. Things did not go as planned as the British artillery quickly demolished the gates to the town and the 78th Highlanders, supported by the 1st Madras Fusiliers advanced so rapidly that the mutineers retreated before the 64th could gain the position to prevent their retreat.

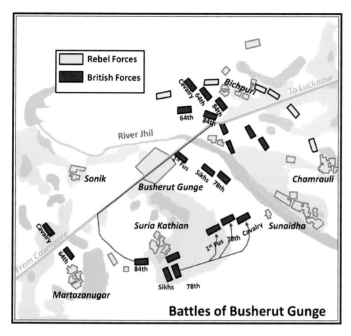

Figure 50. Battles of Busherut-gunge

Having successfully defeated the mutineers at two battles during the long day, Havelock ordered his troops to rest up at Busherut-gunge.

On the following morning, General Havelock received the news that the garrison at Dinapore had joined the mutiny and that he would be unlikely to receive any reinforcements for at least two months. It was also thought that these new rebels could threaten General Neill at nearby Cawnpore. After taking stock of his own position; he had already expended about a third of his ammunition and was down to about 850 effective infantry due to losses from combat and disease. He also had insufficient transport to take his sick and wounded on any further march towards Lucknow. For all of these reasons, General Havelock issued the painful order to return to Mangalwar from where he could send the sick and wounded to Cawnpore and be ready to provide General Neill with assistance if required.

General Havelock arrived at Mangalwar on 31st July where he remained for four days, on 3rd August he received a small reinforcement of a half battery of artillery and a company of men from the 84th Regiment.

Second Battle of Busherut-gunge

After hearing that the rebels were once again congregating at Busherut-gunge he set off on 4th August 1857 and engaged the enemy in the 2nd Battle of Busherut-gunge on the following day. The General adopted the same plan used at the first battle

and it was just as effective and after a short fight the mutineers once again fled after having lost 300 of their men. The losses to Havelock's force were minor, just two killed and 17 wounded, however, 75 men succumbed to the rigours of cholera and Havelock was once again forced to return to Mangalwar.

Havelock planned to let his men rest until the 14th August when it was intended that they would cross the Ganges over a bridge of boats which was now being built, however, he received intelligence that the mutineers were once again congregating at Busherut-gunge with the intention of launching an attack against the force as it crossed the river.

With the improved river crossing complete, General Havelock sent his sick, wounded and baggage train back to Cawnpore.

Third Battle of Busherut-gunge

Knowing that his force would be exposed while they crossed the river, General Havelock had no alternative but to once again set off towards Busherut-gunge.

On 11th August the force reached the town of Oonoa where they rested for the night after clearing the town of an advanced party of mutineers.

On the following morning the force moved on and at the village of Boorhya-ka-Chowkee, on the main road about a mile and a half on from the previous battle sites, they found the mutineers entrenched in well defended positions.

The rebels had gun batteries to the left and right of their position which were joined by a ditch with breastworks, behind which were their infantry. Cavalry guarded their left flank.

Lieutenant Joseph Crowe – Victoria Cross No. 153

Havelock sent men of the 78th Highlanders and the 1st Madras Fusiliers to attack the enemy left flank and within five minutes the men were engaged in fierce hand to hand combat with the mutineers.

Lieutenant Crowe led an attack on a strong redoubt and was the first to enter the enclosure, where all of the mutineers were either killed or captured. For his part in this action Lieutenant Crowe was later awarded the Victoria Cross.

Men from the 84th Regiment of Foot, supported by heavy artillery attacked the right flank and soon the mutineers broke and fled the field with losses of over 200 men killed or wounded; the British losses were 35, however, once again due to the ravages of cholera, Havelock's effective force was reduced by a quarter.

Having once again defeated the mutineers, Havelock fell back leisurely to his position at Mangalwar and covered by the 1st

Madras Fusiliers, 4 guns and the volunteer cavalry, crossed the River Ganges on 13th August and returned to Cawnpore.

Battle of Bithoor

After allowing his men a few days rest, General Havelock decided to act against the 4,000 mutineers gathered at Bithoor, before they could advance against Cawnpore. The battle was fought on 16th August, the British force of about 1,000 (750 Europeans and 250 Sikhs) launched a frontal attack on the enemy positions after a bombardment by their artillery. After fierce hand to hand combat the British force managed to drive the rebels from the town with losses of about 250 and the capture of their guns. British casualties were 70, 10 being due to sunstroke.

Return to Cawnpore

After the battle the force returned to Cawnpore and received the news that mutineers were assembling at Dalamow in preparation for an assault across the river at Futtehpore in an attempt to cut the British lines of communication between Cawnpore and Allahabad. To counter this threat General Havelock despatched Captain Gordon with a force of 120 men and three guns up river by steamer. The expedition was extremely successful as they prevented a river crossing by destroying every boat that they came across.

The General also received news, not by any official communication but by reading an announcement in the Calcutta Gazette, that the divisions of Dinapore and Cawnpore were to be amalgamated under the command of General Outram to whom he would now report. With this change in the command structure, General Havelock was forced to cease all but the most urgent operations and wait at Cawnpore for further orders. As he was waiting, the General received news that, following the defeat of the mutineers at Jugdeespore, Major Eyres and his seven battalions were approaching Allahabad and would soon be able to join him at Cawnpore.

The General later received the unwanted news that Major Eyre's troops had been diverted to Juanpore by General Outram

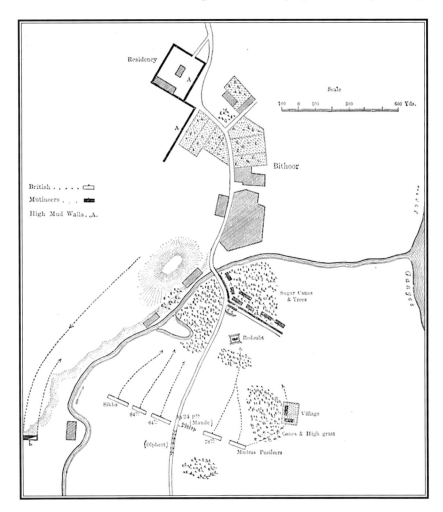

Figure 51. Battle of Bithoor

from where he intended to launch an advance on Lucknow under his own command.

General Havelock was expected to advance as before, across the River Ganges, and join up with General Outram's force near Lucknow.

From this news, it was apparent that General Outram was not aware of the situation at Cawnpore so on 20th August General Havelock sent a telegraph to the Commander in Chief, Sir Colin Campbell, at Calcutta, reiterating his position that he could not advance without reinforcement. He further explained that without reinforcements, in the face of Cawnpore being threatened by three large forces of mutineers, he may in fact have to abandon Cawnpore and retreat to Allahabad. The reply from Sir Colin Campbell was in full support of Havelock's position and he promised to send elements of the 5th Fusiliers and 90th Regiment of Foot to reinforce the position at Cawnpore as soon as possible.

General Outram proceeds to Cawnpore

On 28th August, General Outram reached Benares where he was brought up to date with recent events; he was indeed ignorant of the plight of Havelock at Cawnpore and agreed totally with the proposal of Sir Colin Campbell to send reinforcements to Cawnpore. With news that Havelock was only limited by the lack of men he abandoned his plan for a separate approach from Juanpore and set out at once for the city.

General Outram reached Allahabad on 1st September, closely followed by the 5th Fusiliers who arrived on the 4th September and the 90th Light Infantry who arrived the next day; both regiments were immediately sent forward to Cawnpore.

On 9th September a force of about 400 mutineers, together with four guns, crossed the Ganges. Thought to be the advanced guard of a much larger force intent on disrupting the arrival of British reinforcements it had to be countered. Major Eyre, with a detachment of the 5th Fusiliers and some of the other reinforcements marched 40 miles, engaged with the enemy on 11th September and managed to drive them back across the river and destroy their boats.

General Outram reached Cawnpore on 15th September and soon afterwards the remaining reinforcements arrived bringing the total of new men to almost 1,500.

Outram and Havelock march to Lucknow

General Outram, somewhat embarrassed by his appointment as Havelock's commander was quick to assure General Havelock that although he would be present with the force going to the relief of Lucknow, he would do so in his civil capacity as the Commissioner of Oudh and that Havelock would have military command.

On 19th September, General Havelock began the crossing of the River Ganges with a force of over 3,000 men made up of: one heavy and two light batteries of Artillery with 282 men; 168 Cavalry mainly volunteers but including 59 loyal natives, men of the 11th Irregulars; the Infantry numbered 2,729 including 341 Sikhs. The artillery was under the command of Colonel Cooper and comprised the Heavy Battery of Major Eyre and the field batteries of Maude and Olpherts. General Neill was in command of the first brigade which included men from the 1st Madras Fusiliers, 5th Fusiliers, 84th Regiment of Foot and two companies of the 64th Regiment of Foot. The second brigade was under the command of Colonel Hamilton and consisted of the 78th Highlanders, 90th Light Infantry and Brasyer's Sikhs.

The men camped on the Lucknow side of the river until all were across, which with the artillery and baggage took until late on 20th September.

Battle of Mangalwar

On the morning of 21st September, the force set out for Lucknow in heavy rain and came across a large body of mutineers at Mangalwar.

Sergeant Patrick Mahoney – Victoria Cross No. 172

The rebels included men from the 1st, 53rd and 56th Native Infantry and the 2nd Cavalry who had mutinied at Cawnpore.

General Havelock sent part of his force, led by the cavalry, to turn the right flank of the enemy and after a brief bombardment by his artillery ordered a frontal attack by the rest of his infantry.

With the rapid advance of the British forces the mutineers broke and were pursued through Oonoa and Busherut-gunge, during this operation the colours of the 1st Native Infantry were captured by Sergeant Mahoney.

For this action Sergeant Mahoney was later awarded the Victoria Cross.

Lieutenant William Rennie – Victoria Cross No. 173

During the advance on the enemy positions, Lieutenant Rennie advancing ahead of his skirmishers led a charge against the guns and prevented one of them being carried away by the mutineers.

For this action Lieutenant Rennie was later awarded the Victoria Cross.

His citation mentions a second act which occurred on 25th September when he again led a charge against enemy guns forcing them to be abandoned.

After the battle, General Havelock's troops made camp at a serai on the Lucknow side of Busherut-gunge.

The next morning the expedition continued along the road to Lucknow and at about 3 o'clock in the afternoon reached the River Sye which they crossed by the bridge at Bunnee; the mutineers having failed to destroy the bridge in their haste to retreat. The force rested for the night at Bunnee, but due to the continued heavy rain they spent a miserable night.

Battle of the Alum Bagh

At 8 a.m. on the 23rd September the force continued on its march to Lucknow until at 2 p.m., after having covered 10 miles, cavalry scouts returned to the column with news that a large enemy force was entrenched at the Alum Bagh, some three miles further down the road.

The Alum Bagh was a walled garden palace which had been built by one of the Princes of Oudh for his favourite wife. This was a large enclosure, about 500 yards square, with high walls each of which contained a heavy gate protected by high towers at each corner. Located at the centre of the enclosure was the Bara Dari palace.

The enemy commanded a superior position on an elevated plateau with a front of almost two miles, while the British force was

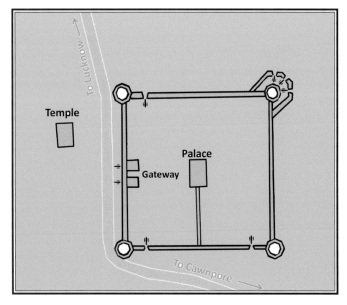

Figure 52. Plan of the Alum Bagh

confined to the narrow road, bordered by swamps. With 10,000 to 12,000 men the enemy also had the superiority of numbers with larger numbers of artillery and cavalry as well as infantry.

As soon as the column came within range the enemy artillery fired down the road and such was their accuracy that three officers of the 90th Light Infantry who were at the head of the column were shot down; all three later died from their wounds.

There was a short delay while the 2nd Brigade was moved ahead of the 1st Brigade to lead the advance and after a short distance came to dry land to the left of the road where both brigades were deployed facing the enemy lines. By this time the British artillery had deployed and their intense fire soon dispersed the enemy cavalry and silenced their guns. The British line continued their advance and cleared the rebels from their lines around the Alum Bagh.

It was left to the 5th Fusiliers to storm the Alum Bagh and after only 10 minutes, they managed to clear the fortified position, the 78th Highlanders also entered the Alum Bagh soon afterwards.

With the rebels in flight back towards Lucknow, the small force of British cavalry with the support of guns from Olpherts battery pursued the mutineers to the "Yellow House" close to the Char Bagh Bridge.

However, finding this position strongly defended they retired back to join the main force now encamped near the Alum Bagh. On his return to the camp, General Outram received a letter from a messenger which incorrectly stated that the city of Delhi had been recaptured nine days earlier. This news did much to raise the spirits of the men.

Having fought long and hard over the past three days, in pouring rain, General Havelock decided on a rest day for his men while he finalised his plans for the final stage of his approach to the Residency which was now only four miles distant.

Corporal Robert Grant – Victoria Cross No. 174

It was decided to use the Alum Bagh as a place of refuge for the sick and wounded and to store the reserves of food and ammunition as well as the men's baggage. Defence of the Alum Bagh was delegated to the command of Colonel McIntire with 6 officers, 42 NCOs and 250 men.

During the rest day of the 24th September a force of enemy cavalry made an attack against the baggage train but this was fought off by men from the 90th Light Infantry.

An attack on the camp was also made by guns and men from the rebel position at the "Yellow House".

A reconnoitring party from the Alum Bagh under the command of Lieutenant Brown was sent out but soon came under heavy fire from the rebels so the party began to retreat.

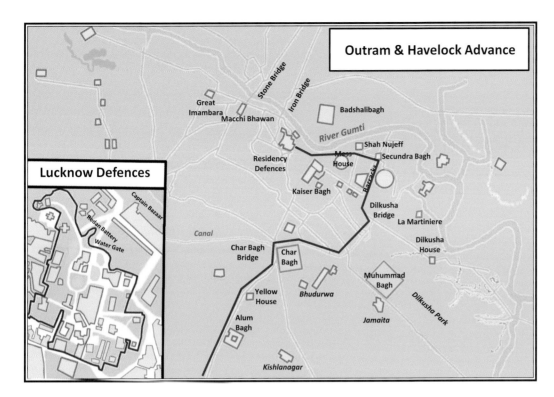

Outram & Havelock Advance

Lucknow Defences

Figure 53. Advance on Lucknow – 1st relief

Private E. Deveney had his leg shot off by a cannonball and Corporal Grant returned to rescue him; aided by Lieutenant Brown, Private Deveney was brought back to the safety of the camp.

For this deed which was accomplished under heavy fire, Corporal Grant was later awarded the Victoria Cross.

✠

Final advance on the Residency

After considering several different routes to the Residency, it was finally decided that the most expedient route was to cross the canal by the Char Bagh Bridge, to then turn right and advance along a winding lane along the north bank of the canal before turning left and advancing across the plain between the canal and the Kaiser Bagh.

This would avoid the need for street by street fighting in the heart of the city, however, due to the heavy ground it would not be possible to take the heavy guns of Eyre's battery.

At 8 a.m. on 25th August, the column was formed in front of the Alum Bagh, with Colonel Neill's brigade leading the way, headed by two companies of the 5th Fusiliers and Maude's field battery. Almost immediately after leaving the vicinity of the Alum Bagh, the column came under furious musket fire from nearby houses and from enemy artillery placed in the "Yellow House". The column briefly came to a halt, apparently on the orders of General Havelock, which only increased the effectiveness of the rebel fire during which General Outram and his aid were both wounded in the arm by musket balls.

Battle of Char Bagh Bridge

Fortunately the impromptu halt was of short duration as General Havelock's galloper Major Battine soon came forward with the order to advance.

Captain Maude's battery was deployed and helped clear the way and the column was soon past the "Yellow House" and on the approaches to the Char Bagh Bridge which was guarded by a high palisade and heavy guns.

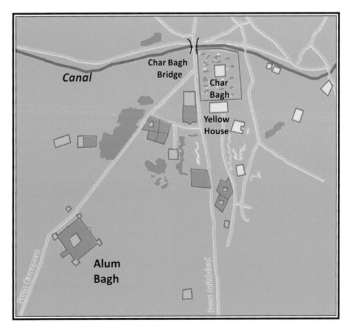

Figure 54. Battle of Char Bagh Bridge

Lieutenant Arnold with men from the 1st Madras Fusiliers were sent to the left of the bridge to hold the canal bank, while General Outram with men from the 5th Fusiliers advanced on the walled garden of the Char Bagh, from where they would be able to lay down fire on the bridge.

Captain Francis Maude – Victoria Cross No. 177
Private Joel Holmes – Victoria Cross No. 180

Two of Captain Maude's guns were unlimbered and placed at the bend in the road to bombard the bridge; there was only space for two guns, but almost immediately one was disabled by enemy artillery fire and the crew were all killed or wounded.

Volunteers were called for to man a replacement gun and Private Holmes was the first man to come forward, his example led to other men coming forward. Operation of the guns was extremely hazardous due to the intense enemy musket and artillery fire which mowed down many of the volunteer gunners almost as soon as they took their place.

For this action, Private Holmes was later awarded the Victoria Cross.

For his bravery in continuing to ensure the operation of his battery in the face of heavy fire, Captain Maude was also later awarded the Victoria Cross for his part in this action, which enabled the Char Bagh bridge to be taken and allowed the advance into Lucknow to proceed.

Lieutenant-Colonel Fraser-Tytler, Deputy Assistant Quartermaster to the expedition, under heavy fire from the enemy, reconnoitred the area close to the bridge and came to the opinion that it could be carried by a bayonet charge. After obtaining permission from General Neill for the charge, Colonel Tytler together with Lieutenants Havelock and Arnold led men from the 1st Madras Fusiliers and men from the 84th regiment in the charge. Lieutenant Arnold fell having been shot through both thighs and Colonel Tytler fell when his horse was shot out from under him, leaving Lieutenant Havelock and Corporal Jacques to continue the charge, which carried the bridge.

Lance Corporal Abraham Boulger – Victoria Cross No. 144

Lance-Corporal Boulger was one of the men who charged and captured the bridge; he killed a gunner before he was able to discharge his piece at the British soldiers. He was also the first man to enter a masked enemy battery.

For his part in this action Lance-Corporal Boulger was later awarded the Victoria Cross.

General Outram emerged from the Char Bagh just as the bridge was taken and proceeded to clear the houses on either side of the bridge which allowed the rest of the column to move forward.

Surgeon Joseph Jee – Victoria Cross No. 175

During the attack on the bridge, Surgeon Jee was very active in retrieving the wounded men and bringing them to safety.

After the bridge was taken, he arranged for the wounded to be carried towards the Residency where they were initially held in the Moti Mahal. He tended the wounded in the Moti Mahal throughout the night and in the morning helped transport many into the Residency despite heavy enemy fire.

For these actions, Surgeon Jee was later awarded the Victoria Cross.

On getting to his feet, Colonel Tytler noticed that two guns at the "Yellow House" had started to pour down fire on the bridge, now that it was in British hands, and brought this to the attention of General Havelock.

Captain William Olpherts – Victoria Cross No. 178

Being unable to bring his own artillery to bear on the rebel guns, General Havelock despatched Colonel Campbell with men of the 90th Light Infantry to deal with the matter.

The force, accompanied by Captain Olpherts, rushed the mutineers' position in the face of intense grape shot fire and captured the guns. Despite heavy musket fire from surrounding mutineers, Captain Olpherts, returned with horses, limbered up the two guns and carried them off.

For his part in this action Captain Olpherts was later awarded the Victoria Cross.

With the Char Bagh bridge now in British hands, General Havelock ordered the 78th Highlanders to hold the bridge and adjacent houses until all of the troops and baggage had crossed and then to follow the column acting as a rear guard.

The main column turned to the right over the bridge and advanced along a narrow lane which bordered the canal, but they had great difficulty in moving the guns across the soft ground. At the Dilkusha road, near the hospital, the force left the road and headed across open ground towards the Secundra Bagh, passing the barracks of the 32nd on their left. After the barracks they again turned left and approached the Moti Mahal (Pearl Palace) which was an imposing structure comprising three buildings surrounded by a high wall.

The mutineers must have been surprised by the relief forces route through the city, as since leaving the Char Bagh Bridge they had proceeded unmolested.

As they approached the Moti Mahal, things suddenly changed and they came under fire from four guns placed in front of the Kaiser Bagh (Caesars Garden) and heavy musket fire from the Kursheed Manzil (Palace of the Sun) which was being used as the mess house by the 32nd Regiment of Foot. The column was halted and two British guns were deployed which soon silenced the Kaiser Bagh battery. While they rested, a message arrived that the 78th, who were acting as rear guard, were being heavily pressed by the rebels.

While the main column was still in sight, the 78th were left alone by the mutineers and they occupied themselves by throwing the captured enemy guns into the canal. The 78th were surprised by an attack down the Cawnpore road and with the mutineers holed up in a little temple the fight continued for three hours until the 78th went on the offensive and successfully stormed the temple.

Lieutenant Herbert MacPherson – Victoria Cross No. 179

Not giving up, the mutineers brought forward some field guns and fought for a further hour.

Lieutenant MacPherson led a charge against two 9 pounder cannons that the mutineers had set up on the road. The cannons were successfully captured and thrown in the canal.

For his part in this action Lieutenant McPherson was later awarded the Victoria Cross.

✠

While this fight was going on the column managed to cross the bridge with the 90th Light Infantry taking over the role of rear guard.

The last hour of fighting meant that when the 78th finally crossed the bridge the column was no longer in sight and instead of taking the road to the Secundra Bagh, they took the Huzerutgungh which led them directly to the Kaiser Bagh. A party was sent out to locate the Highlanders and guide them back to the main column, however, they arrived back without having managed to locate the Highlanders. At about 3 o'clock in the afternoon, the 78th were spotted on the left flank of the main column advancing on a parallel path towards the Kaiser Bagh.

After leaving behind the wounded, baggage and heavy guns the main column once again began to advance and after skirting the Moti Mahal reached one of the main roads into the city, where once again they came under heavy musket and artillery fire and were halted by a massive gate that blocked the way

ahead. It took some time for Captain Olpherts guns to destroy the gate but eventually the column moved on until they reached the Chatter Manzil (Umbrella House) where it was decided to wait for the 78th to rejoin the column.

While waiting for the 78th and with night closing in, Generals Outram and Havelock discussed their next move; Outram was for resting for a few hours and then gaining the residency by way of nearby houses and palaces which would provide cover; on the other hand Havelock was keen to make a more direct approach through the Khas Bazaar to the Bailey Gate which was only 500 yards distant. In the end it was agreed to make for the Bailey Gate which they did once they had been joined by the 78th. The way through the Khas Bazaar was fraught with danger due to the heavy musket fire that the mutineers could rain down from the nearby buildings. Artillery fire from the Kaiser Bagh also began to rain down on the column.

The approach to the Khas Bazaar was through a narrow archway and General Neill positioned himself such that he could control the men's passage, so that they would not be slowed down; working in such an exposed position General Neill was soon killed, shot through the head.

Despite the heavy enemy fire, a large portion of the relief force managed to gain access to Lucknow via the Bailey Guard Gate which had been opened by Lieutenant Aitken with a party of sepoys. Unfortunately, the sepoys were thought to be mutineers by the advancing relief force and three were bayoneted before they were told that they were part of the defending force.

The goal of the relief force had now been achieved, however, many of the men still remained outside the gates until the next morning.

The losses to the relief column were 196 killed and 339 wounded.

Private Patrick Mylott – Victoria Cross No. 145

Private Mylott distinguished himself in all of the actions fought during Havelock's march to Lucknow and notably rushed across an open road in the face of heavy fire to capture an enclosure.

For these deeds, Private Mylott was later awarded the Victoria Cross, having been elected for the award by a ballot of the Privates of his regiment.

✠

Despite having gained the city, many of the British force still remained outside the gates. The sick and wounded were in a makeshift hospital which had been set up in the Moti Mahal where they were being protected by a force of men from the 90th Light Infantry under the command of Colonel Campbell.

Assistant Surgeon Valentine McMaster – Victoria Cross No. 176

During the night, Assistant Surgeon McMaster tended the wounded in the Moti Mahal and made several excursions under heavy enemy fire to bring in the wounded.

For these actions Assistant Surgeon McMaster was later awarded the Victoria Cross.

✠

Private Henry Ward – Victoria Cross No. 181

In his attempt to gain the Residency, Captain Havelock was seriously wounded and was placed on a dhoolie by Private Ward who remained to guard him throughout the night.

In the morning, Private Thomas Pilkington was wounded and placed in the same dhoolie as Captain Havelock. Private Ward escorted the dhoolie through fierce fire into the Bailey Guard Gate supporting the bearers in their efforts to carry the heavy load.

For this action, Private Ward was later awarded the Victoria Cross.

✠

Evacuation of the Moti Mahal

When the majority of the main column made their bid for entry into the city, via the Bailey Guard Gate, the wounded together with the heavy artillery and several ammunition wagons were left behind in the Moti Mahal. Colonel Campbell and about 100 men from the 90th Regiment of Foot, who had acted as rear guard for the final push into the city, were left to provide a guard at the Moti Mahal.

During the night of 25th September, the mutineers lay siege to the Moti Mahal but Colonel Campbell was able to get a message into the Residency informing them of the situation and that he would be unable to move from his position without reinforcements.

On the morning of the 26th September, a force under the command of Major Simmons, consisting of 250 men from 5th Fusiliers and some Sikhs commanded by Captain Brasyer, were sent out to go to the relief of the men besieged in the Moti Mahal. The force manage to get half way to the Moti Mahal before they were forced to take shelter in Martin's house after coming under intense fire, including artillery fire from the Kaiser Bagh.

As this relief force was now halted, a second force commanded by Colonel Napier was sent out to go to their assistance. This force was made up of 100 men from the 78th Highlanders commanded by Colonel Stisted with a band of Sowars under the

Figure 55. The Moti Mahal

command of Captain Hardinge. Initially Captain Olpherts was asked to take along two of his guns but after his objection they were left behind, and the Captain went with the force as a volunteer. Mr Kavanagh, a member of the Bengal Civil Service, also accompanied this party as a guide and they managed to join up with Major Simmons force.

General Outram sent a further force out comprising 150 men of the 32nd Regiment commanded by Captain Lowe, some more Sikhs and 50 men of the 78th under the command of Captain Haliburton on a mission to secure the river bank from the Iron Bridge to the Chatter Manzil. Captain Lowe and his force left from Innes's Post and made their way towards the river where they encountered a large force of mutineers. Some of Captain Lowe's men swept to the left and drove the mutineers towards the Iron Bridge but were unable to push them beyond the bridge.

The remainder of the force move along the river bank to the right up to the Tehri Kothi and joined up with a detachment of Lieutenant Aitken's men who had spent the night there.

All of the relieving forces had now joined up and after capturing two 18 pounder and several lighter guns cleared and occupied the Furhut Buksh Palace and enclosure, leaving only the Chatter Manzil building occupied by the mutineers, between them and the Moti Mahal.

Colour Sergeant Stewart McPherson – Victoria Cross No. 138

During the fighting, Colour Sergeant McPherson saw Private James Lowther, from his regiment, lying badly wounded and under heavy musket and artillery fire managed to carry him back to safety.

For this action Colour Sergeant McPherson was later awarded the Victoria Cross. Tragically, Private Lowther died soon afterwards as a result of his wounds.

During the previous day, in the rush to gain the Residency a 24 pounder gun had been abandoned and left in an exposed position. Captain Olpherts was determined that the gun should be retrieved, however, due to the heavy enemy musket fire this was not possible to attempt during daylight.

Private Thomas Duffy – Victoria Cross No. 185

Under the cover of darkness, Private Duffy, acting under the direction of Captain Olpherts, crept forward unobserved by the enemy and succeeded in attaching two drag ropes to the gun carriage.

These ropes were then fastened to the limbers where bullocks were yoked and the gun was pulled clear and back into the hands of the British.

During the operation, Captain Crump, who was helping Private Duffy, was killed.

For his part in this action, Private Duffy was later awarded the Victoria Cross.

Now that night had fallen, the force managed, after a fierce battle, to clear and occupy the Chatter Manzil and with a path now clear along the river bank to the Residency, began to escort some of the wounded, ammunition wagons and guns back to safety.

Colonel Purnell and men from the 90th Light Infantry continued around the Chatter Manzil and eventually came to the rescue of Surgeon Home's party.

Assistant Surgeon William Bradshaw – Victoria Cross No. 183

At around mid-morning, the force of men from the 5th Fusiliers, commanded by Major Simmons, arrived at the Moti Mahal to escort the wounded to the Residency. The wounded, under the care of Assistant Surgeon Bradshaw and Surgeon Home, were loaded onto dhoolies (litters) and in a long column began their journey to the Residency. For the first 200 yards, until they left the Moti Mahal square, they proceeded in safety but as they were crossing a small stream they came under intense fire from across the River Gumti. Keeping the native dhoolie-bearers under control was not easy, however, the column managed to gain the shelter of a building where they were able to be reorganised. Moving out once again, the column began to cross another square which appeared to be deserted, however, after the first few dhoolies had crossed the square the column came under very heavy fire from mutineers lodged in the surrounding buildings. Many of the dhoolie-bearers were killed and the remainder dropped their charges and fled for cover from the fire, the wounded being killed in great numbers as they lay helpless on the ground.

Assistant Surgeon Bradshaw managed to round up about 20 dhoolie-bearers who picked up some of the dhoolies and he led them out of the square, eventually finding a path to the river bank and then bringing them into the safety of the Residency.

For this action, during which he was wounded, Assistant Surgeon Bradshaw was later awarded the Victoria Cross.

Surgeon Anthony Home – Victoria Cross No. 182

Meanwhile, Surgeon Home, with a party of about 14, comprising some walking wounded and remnants of the escort managed to gain entry to a small one storied house which had many doors and windows. The house was soon surrounded by about 1,000 mutineers who made several charges at the house each of which were repulsed by the fire from within.

The remained of the account is best told in Surgeon Home's own words, taken from a letter that he wrote soon after the events took place.

They were not more than five yards off, but round the corner and sheltered from our fire. At this time we expected instant death; it seemed incredible that ten effective men could resist a thousand, who were firing a fearful hail of shot through the windows. Three of our number inside were struck down wounded, and this diminished our fire. The Sepoys all this time were massacring the wounded men in the dhoolies (we rescued two more wounded officers and five more wounded men); perhaps they killed forty by firing volleys at the dhoolies.

The rebels now gave up the attempt to storm us, but crept up to the windows and fired in on us, so we had to lie down on the ground for a time, and let them fire over us; there was no door to the doorway, so we made a barricade of sandbags by digging the floor with bayonets, and using the dead Sepoys' clothes to hold the sand; we also piled up the dead so as to obstruct the men rushing on us.

My duties as the only unwounded officer were to direct and encourage the men, – as a surgeon, to dress the wounded, as a man, to use a rifle belonging to a wounded man when he fell.

After a while we saw that the enemy were tired of rushing on us; we had killed over twenty of them, and must have wounded many more: this dampened them. We now told off one man to fire from each window, and three from the door. My post was at a window. I had my revolver, but only five shots left in it. I had no second, and, worst of all, no fresh charges. I must tell you that an eastern window means a latticework. At this I kept watch and ward.

After a time a Sepoy crept up very cautiously to fire, as usual through the window, quite unconscious that at this time a Feringhee had him covered with a revolver. When he got about three yards from me, I shot him dead and another who was coming up was shot by one of the men. For nearly an hour now they were very quiet, only firing at a distance. All at once we heard in the street a dull rumbling noise which froze me to the very heart. I jumped up, and said 'Now, men, now or never. Let us rush out and die in the open air, and not be killed like rats in a hole. They are bringing a gun on us.' The men were quite ready, but we saw that it was not a gun, but something on wheels, with a heavy planking in front too thick for our shot to enter. They

brought it to the very window I was firing at. I could touch it, but my shots were useless.

To shorten my story, after half an hour they set the house in flames, and we were enabled to escape by breaking through into the second room, which opened into a large square, where we found a large shed, with large doorways at intervals; into this we got, carrying our wounded, who strange to say were the only ones hurt. Three of them were mortally wounded whilst we carried them; we sound men did not get a scratch.

It was a complete surprise to the enemy; they expected us by the door, and not by the way we came, so the pleasure of shooting us as we ran from the burning house was denied them, and when they did see us, they, with at least 600 men, only shot three already wounded men.

It was now three in the afternoon, and our position seemed hopeless. We thought up to this time that the General would never leave us without succour, but now we thought that the Sepoys must have quite hemmed in our army. Imagine our horror when we found that the shed we were in was loop holed everywhere; it had been used the day before as a place to fire on our army from, and the Sepoys came creeping up now to the loopholes, firing in suddenly and off again. We now put a man at every loophole as far as they would go; even wounded were put to watch; and this soon checked the bold, brave Sepoys, for whom one British soldier is an object of terrible dread.

We soon had a worse alarm. The Sepoys got on the roof, bored holes through it, and fired down on us. The first two shots were fired at me, the muzzles of the pieces being perhaps four feet from me, and neither shot hurt me beyond a lot of stuff from the roof being sent with force into my face, and a trifling hurt in my hand.

Nothing more wonderful in the way of narrow escapes was ever seen. This could not last, so we bored through the wall of the shed into the courtyard behind, and two of us went out to reconnoitre. For some time the Sepoys did not seen us, as it was getting dark. About fifty yards off was a mosque, with no one in it, as I found by creeping on all-fours into it; but before we could get the wounded out we were discovered. We now ran back to the shed. However, we had in the interval secured a chatty of excellent water belonging to the Sepoys. And what a prize it was! The wounded were dying with thirst, and we, who had been biting cartridges all day, were just as bad. It gave us one good draught all round, and after it we felt twice the men we did before.

Being a long shed, we had a great deal to defend; but luckily the Sepoys found out that if they could fire through the roof, so could we, with the advantage of knowing exactly where they were by the noise of their feet; so they kept off the roof.

We now organised our defence, told off each man to his alarm-post, and told off the sentries and reliefs.

Including wounded, there were nine men for sentry, seven men fit to fight, and of these six unhurt, including myself. It was agreed that if the Sepoys forced the shed, we would rush out and die outside.

By this time all our wounded were in their possession, and they were put to death with horrible tortures, actually before our faces; some were burnt alive in the dhoolies; the shrieks of these men chilled one's blood.

The terrors of that awful night were almost maddening; raging thirst, fierce rage against those who, as we thought, had without an attempt at succour left us to perish; uncertainty as to where the Sepoys would next attack us; add to this the exhaustion produced by want of food, heat and anxiety.

I now proposed to our men either to fight our way back to the rear-guard, or forward to the entrenched camp; but there were only two who would go, and so I refused to go, as we could not for shame desert eight wounded men; still I tried to persuade all to make the trial: someone might escape; as it was, no one could.

Day broke soon after, and we had fallen into perfect apathy; our nerves, so highly strung for twenty hours, seemed now to have gone quite the other way. Suddenly a few shots were fired outside; then more; then we heard the sharp crack of our own Enfield rifles. Ryan, who was sentry, now shouted, 'Oh, boys, them's our own chaps.' Still, we were uncertain, till presently we heard a regular rattling volley, such as no Sepoys could give. Oh, how our hearts jumped into our mouths then! Up we got; now I said, 'Men, cheer together'. Our people outside heard us, and sent a cheer back. We replied like madmen, and shouted to them to keep off our sides. We also fired through all the loopholes at the Sepoys, to keep them from firing at our men advancing. In five minutes we were all rescued, and in the midst of our own people; half an hour later we were settled down in the King of Oudh's palace – conquerors.

After a brave defence of their position for over 22 hours against incredible numbers of mutineers, the force was finally rescued by Colonel Parnell and men from the 90th Light Infantry and brought safely to the Residency.

For his part in this action, which saved the lives of wounded men, Surgeon Home was later awarded the Victoria Cross.

In addition to Surgeon Home, three other men were recognised for their bravery during this effort to save the wounded.

Private James Hollowell – Victoria Cross No. 186

Private Hollowell was one of Surgeon Home's party who behaved in the most admirable manner during the day directing, encouraging and leading the men in the defence of the shed, constantly exposing himself to danger.

For his part in this action, Private Hollowell was later awarded the Victoria Cross.

Private Peter McManus – Victoria Cross No. 187

When Surgeon Home's party first occupied the house, Private McManus remained outside hidden behind a pillar from where he kept up a continuous fire on the mutineers keeping them in check. He continued to occupy this post until he was wounded.

For his part in the action Private McManus was later awarded the Victoria Cross.

Private John Ryan – Victoria Cross No. 188

While holed up in the house with Surgeon Home's party, Private Ryan showed great bravery and on several occasions went forth into the square, under heavy fire to bring back wounded men. On one occasion, accompanied by Private McManus he rescued Captain Arnold of the 1st Madras Fusiliers, unfortunately the Captain was wounded again during the rescue and died a few days later from his wounds.

For his part in the action Private Ryan was later awarded the Victoria Cross.

Sorties to secure the enlarged perimeter

Since the relief force first gained access to the city, the palaces from the Kaiser Bagh down to the River Gumti had gradually been secured by the British forces to give the Residency a much enlarged perimeter. Although this provided much needed accommodation for the increased number of inhabitants the new territory was not easily defended due to a large exposed face of buildings subject to fire from adjacent buildings held by the mutineers.

In order to improve the security of these new positions a number of sorties were carried out.

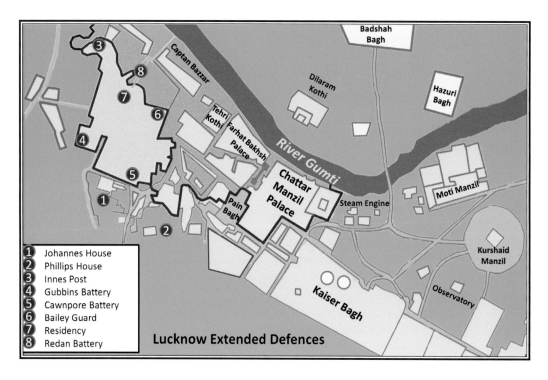

Figure 56. Enlarged Lucknow perimeter

Lucknow Extended Defences

1. Johannes House
2. Phillips House
3. Innes Post
4. Gubbins Battery
5. Cawnpore Battery
6. Bailey Guard
7. Residency
8. Redan Battery

Bombardier Jacob Thomas – Victoria Cross No. 189

At 2 o'clock in the afternoon on 27th September, men of the Madras Fusiliers under the command of Major Stephenson were assembled for a sortie against the Garden Battery which the rebels were operating opposite the Cawnpore Battery.

The force, which was accompanied by some artillerymen under the command of Captain Evans, made its way through the Tehri Kothi and crossed the road to the rear of the Clock Tower. On reaching the road, the party was exposed to heavy fire from a large house which they attacked and cleared. On leaving the house, they came face to face with a small battery which immediately let loose with grapeshot, the battery was charged, taken and the guns were spiked. A 24 pounder and 18 pounder gun were found abandoned in a nearby enclosure and were also spiked.

At this time the enemy fire became so fierce that it was necessary to withdraw, during the retreat a man from the Madras Fusiliers was disabled by a musket shot. Bombardier Thomas picked up the Fusilier and carried him back to the safety of the Residency, thus saving his life.

For this act Bombardier Thomas was later awarded the Victoria Cross.

On 28th September, Captain Morrison with a party of 50 men taken from the 90th Light Infantry and 5th Fusiliers carried out another sortie to explore the palace buildings in the direction of the Khas Bazaar. The party came across several mutineers, who were driven out of the buildings at bayonet point with many of them being killed.

To secure the new position that they had reached, Captain Morrison left a piquet in a house with commanding lines of fire to the Cheena and Khas Bazaars,

On 29th September, three sorties were launched simultaneously, two from the area of the Brigade Mess and the third from Innes's Post towards the Iron Bridge. The two sorties from the Brigade Mess successfully cleared the positions to their front for a width of about 300 yards; blowing up and destroying the houses and batteries that they came across, including those that had been causing so much trouble to Gubbins Bastion. The most important of the sorties, however, was the third which had the objective of securing the Iron Bridge to open up a communications route ready for a future relief and food from sympathisers within the city. Unfortunately this sortie was less successful as it only got as far as Hill's shop, where it captured and destroyed an enemy 24 pounder gun that had been causing much disruption.

General Outram, who by now had assumed command of the city, received news from his detachment at the Alum Bagh that they were in urgent need of supplies. To try and establish a line of communication with the detachment, the General sent out a force of cavalry, however, in the face of an overwhelming force of rebels they were unable to complete their mission.

Determined to reach the Alum Bagh, General Outram decided that the route along the Cawnpore road would have to be cleared, house by house if necessary. However, before this could be attempted it would be necessary to clear Phillips House and garden which contained the large enemy battery that faced the Cawnpore Battery.

The task was given to Colonel Napier and on the afternoon of 1st October he set out with a force of 568 men, made up of detachments from the 5th Fusiliers, 32nd, 64th, 78th and 90th Regiments and men from the Madras Fusiliers together with some engineers and artillery men. The party set out from the Pacen Bagh and made their way via various buildings near the jail until they reached a position near to Phillips House. The road was blocked by a sturdy barricade and nearby houses which were also stoutly defended; many had had their doorways bricked up. With the falling light, Colonel Napier decided to wait for first light before pressing home the final attack and the men rested in nearby houses.

Private Patrick McHale – Victoria Cross No. 199

At first light the next morning, following a brief bombardment of the house and gardens by British artillery Colonel Napier launched his attack.

Lieutenant Creagh and men from the Madras Fusiliers managed to outflank the barricade and head for the house while men from the 5th Fusiliers and 64th Regiment forced their way through a stockade and advanced on the battery forcing them out. Phillips House was taken without much opposition and after leaving a piquet as guard, the remainder of the force advanced on the enemy guns which had been withdrawn to the end of the garden and adjacent street.

Private McHale led the 5th Fusiliers in a charge on the battery and was the first man into the enclosure where he bayoneted several of the gunners.

For this act Private McHale was later awarded the Victoria Cross, his citation also mentions a second episode on 22nd December during the attack on the Alum Bagh when he again led a charge on a battery, captured the gun and turned it on the rebels.

Private McHale was elected for the award by a ballot of the Privates of his regiment.

✠

The guns were all captured and destroyed, Phillips House was also blown up and a permanent outpost was established in the gardens by men from the 78th Highlanders.

The second defence of Lucknow

Almost from the time that the relief force gained entry to the city, it became obvious to Generals Outram and Havelock that their mission had changed from one of relief to one of reinforcement.

This was largely due to the lack of transport and the number of troops required to ensure a safe passage through almost five miles of suburbs, while escorting large numbers of women, children and wounded who totalled about 1,500.

The decision was therefore taken to improve the defences of the expanded "Residency" enclosure and to wait for a further relief force to arrive. It was also decided that it would be best to leave the 300 men at the Alum Bagh to their own devices as the

effort to return them to the "Residency" would probably result in heavy losses with no advantage to be gained. As a result of this decision the work to clear the houses bordering the Cawnpore road was suspended.

Mining operations

During the clearance operations of late September, six enemy mines were uncovered and destroyed, however, once the new British lines had been established the mutineers began new mining operations directed at their new positions.

On the 3rd and 5th November the mutineers exploded two mines directed at the gardens of the Chattar Manzil palace. The first caused no damage as it fell short, however, the second made a large breach. This was immediately assaulted by a large rebel force which was repulsed by men of the 90th Light Infantry, causing heavy casualties. The mutineers, despite having their attack repulsed were able to retain possession of the Hirum Khana (Deer House) and a nearby mosque from where they continued to pour down musket fire on the gardens of the palace, making it necessary for the British to dig trenches to provide some protection.

Lance Corporal John Sinnott – Victoria Cross No. 200

On the 6th November, Lance Corporal Sinnott, together with Lieutenant Gibaut repeatedly carried water under heavy fire to extinguish a fire which had broken out in the breastworks.

When Lieutenant Gibaut was seriously wounded, Lance Corporal Sinnott, together with Sergeants Glynn and Mulling and Private Mulling went out and carried the Lieutenant to safety; unfortunately the Lieutenant's wounds proved to be fatal.

For his part in this action, during which he was twice wounded, Lance Corporal Sinnott was later awarded the Victoria Cross having been elected for the award by a ballot of the NCOs of his regiment.

✠

On the same day, another mine was exploded against our piquet near the Cheena and Khas bazaars which resulted in three of our men being killed. In the ensuing confusion the piquet was stormed but the enemy was repulsed with losses of about 450 men.

On the 8th October the mutineers launched another attack on the piquet at the junction of the Cheena and Khas bazaars, this time from the mosque near the Hirum Khana; this attack was again repulsed and the enemy suffered heavy losses.

In order to eliminate the threat to the piquet, Colonels Napier and Purcell together with Captain Moorsam undertook a reconnaissance of the buildings connected to those occupied by the rebels and discovered a vault underneath the Hirum Khana. Lieutenant Russell of the Bengal Engineers placed two barrels of powder in the vault which were exploded with devastating effect. With the Hirum Khana destroyed, Captain Crommelin immediately began to erect barricades to improve the defence of the piquet.

Colonel Napier and Colonel Purcell leading men from the 90th Light Infantry and the 1st Madras Fusiliers carried out a surprise attack and managed to capture the mosque and established an outpost which was again defended by barriers erected by Captain Crommelin and his men.

During this second phase of the Defence of Lucknow, almost all of the enemy activity was directed at mining, against the newly established British positions. The mining by the rebels towards Lockart's Post, which was occupied by the 78th Highlanders, was particularly extensive, however, the British counter mining operations were so effective that not a single mine was exploded against the defences. The rebels also expended a lot of energy in mining operations against the Chatter Manzil palace but yet again this was ineffective due to the British counter mining efforts.

The Alum Bagh

The troops at the Alum Bagh, under the command of Major McIntyre, continued to hold their own but their position was considerably improved when Major Bingham, arrived from Cawnpore on 7th October, with a column of 250 men of the 64th Regiment, two guns and supplies.

The position was further improved when another column of 500 men, 50 cavalry and two guns under the command of Colonel Wilson arrived from Cawnpore, which allowed the garrison to extend their foraging activities.

The defence continues

Apart from the mining activities, the enemy action against the "Residency" during this second phase of the defence was considerably less than during the first phase and no significant enemy attacks were made against the defences.

Due to the increased perimeter and the British clearance operations, the rebels had been forced to pull back their batteries and due to the increased range these were less effective and caused fewer casualties.

The garrison took the opportunity to improve the defences; rebuilding the Cawnpore Battery and completing the batteries at the Slaughter House and Sheep House, a series of zig zag

trenches were also dug on the mound near Innes Post to give a better command of the Iron Bridge.

Despite the improved situation, rations were still a matter of concern and on 26th October they were once again reduced, so that the remaining food could last for another month.

Improved communications allowed the besieged to be constantly updated on the improving situation outside of the city and following the receipt of news that Delhi had been retaken and that a relief force was on its way to Lucknow, spirits rose accordingly.

Second relief of Lucknow

On 11th July 1857, when news reached London of the death of General Anson, Lord Panmure offered Sir Colin Campbell the command of forces in India. Jumping at the opportunity, to serve his country, the 65 year old veteran General left for India that same afternoon and landed at Calcutta on 13th August.

After Delhi was recaptured, the General was intent on the relief of Lucknow, however, he remained in Calcutta for some time resolving issues concerned with the organisation of troops in India.

In the meanwhile, troops were being positioned to be part of the eventual relief force.

Figure 57. General Sir Colin Campbell

Delhi Field Force

After the recapture of Delhi on 20th September 1857, Sir Archdale Wilson sent a column, under the command of Colonel E. H. Greathed, to clear the province of rebels and restore British control to the area between Delhi and Cawnpore.

The force of 2,790 men was comprised of: 700 Cavalry, with the 9th Lancers and detachments of Hodson's Horse, the 1st, 2nd and 5th Punjab Cavalry; 1,650 Infantry, with the 8th and 75th Regiments of Foot and the 1st and 4th Punjab Infantry; 240 Artillerymen with 16 guns from Captain Remmington and Captain Blunt's Horse Artillery with Bourchier's battery and 200 native sappers.

On 27th September, the column rested overnight at Secundra and in the morning of 28th an advanced party arrived at a crossroads where the roads led to Bulandshahr and Fort Malgurgh which was held by the rebel leader Walidad Khan.

Battle of Bulandshahr

With the approach of the British advance party, a rebel cavalry piquet stationed at the crossroads fled towards the city of Bulandshahr.

British scouts pressed ahead to determine the exact enemy positions and reported back that the mutineers had established artillery and infantry in buildings and a walled serai within the town with units of cavalry patrolling in advance of the town where a line of infantry had been established at a crossroads with an artillery battery at the centre.

A reserve under the command of Major Turner was left at the crossroads to guard the baggage train, while the column advanced led by Captain Remmington and his horse artillery which was soon laying down fire on the enemy positions. The column lined up on both sides of the road with infantry, artillery and cavalry to the right and cavalry to the left and with the horse artillery on the road; a cross fire was established against the enemy guns in the city.

Sergeant Bernard Diamond – Victoria Cross No. 191
Gunner Richard Fitzgerald – Victoria Cross No. 194

The Horse Artillery was instrumental in suppressing the fire of the enemy guns but being in an exposed position on the roadway took heavy fire from the enemy and suffered many casualties.

Sergeant Diamond and Gunner Fitzgerald continued to man and fire their gun by themselves, despite the heavy fire and the loss of their comrades.

For this action Sergeant Diamond and Gunner Fitzgerald were later awarded the Victoria Cross.

With the enemy artillery fire now being less fierce, the British began to attack the city from both flanks; canister and grape shot from the horse artillery cleared the enemy lines in the centre and the 75th Regiment of Foot advanced and captured two guns. The 9th Lancers advanced and took another gun and before long both cavalry and infantry were engaged with the enemy in the city.

Lieutenant Robert Blair – Victoria Cross No. 190

After the enemy guns had been captured, Lieutenant Blair, accompanied by a Sergeant and 12 troopers, advanced to retrieve an abandoned ammunition wagon, thinking the area was clear of mutineers.

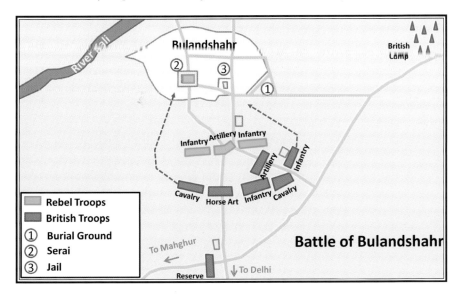

Figure 58. Battle of Bulandshahr

The party was unexpectedly surrounded by about 50 or 60 enemy cavalry who came out from behind a house. Without hesitation, Lieutenant Blair charged the enemy cavalry breaking through their ranks killing four mutineers in the process and led his men to safety unharmed.

For his part in this action, during which he was severely wounded by a sword cut to the shoulder, Lieutenant Blair was later awarded the Victoria Cross.

Private Patrick Donohoe – Victoria Cross No. 193

During the action above, Private Donohoe went to the rescue of his wounded commander, Lieutenant Blair and fighting off several enemy cavalry helped escort him to safety.

For his part in this action Private Donohoe was later awarded the Victoria Cross.

The mutineers' stronghold in the city was centred on a walled serai and the jail, both of which were substantial buildings.

Lance Corporal Robert Kells – Victoria Cross No. 192

After capturing the gun, the 9th lancers continued to pursue the mutineers through the streets of the city, when Captain Drysdale who was commanding the Lancers had his horse shot out from under him causing him to fall heavily to the ground breaking his collar bone. Lance-Corporal Kells immediately went to the help of his stricken commander and fought off several mutineers before being able to carry the Captain to safety.

For this action Lance-Corporal Kells was later awarded the Victoria Cross.

Private James Roberts – Victoria Cross No. 195

In a similar fashion, Private Roberts rode through heavy enemy fire in the streets of Bulandshahr to rescue a fallen and wounded comrade and bring him out to safety.

Private Roberts who was wounded during the incident was later awarded the Victoria Cross for his action, unfortunately the man that he rescued later died from his wounds.

Captain Augustus Anson – Victoria Cross No. 196

Having ridden through the town, the 9th Lancers moved into a serai to reform, however, the mutineers began to move carts across the entrance in a move to contain them.

Seeing the danger posed by such a manoeuvre, Captain Anson grabbed a lance from one of his men and charged at the carts dislodging their drivers with his lance.

For this prompt and brave action Captain Anson was later awarded the Victoria Cross.

Having been assailed by the British on both flanks, and under heavy artillery fire from the British guns the mutineers began their retreat and after a fight of three hours the battle was won.

During the battle the British losses were six men killed, 6 officers and 35 men wounded with the enemy losses being over 300.

A large quantity of ammunition was seized together with a lot of baggage which had been plundered from European civilians.

On the 1st October the force moved a short distance to the Fort of Malgurgh, which they found abandoned. As the British force did not intend to occupy the fort it was decided to reduce its defensive capability, during the demolition of one of the bastions a premature explosion took the life of Lieutenant Home who had acted so bravely in blowing up the Cashmere Gate during the final assault on Delhi.

Continuing down the trunk road towards Cawnpore, Colonel Greathed's column passed through and destroyed villages at Koorjah, Allygurh and Akarabad where two rebel leaders were killed on 7th October.

It was here that the Colonel received news of the plight of the garrison at Agra, causing a change in plans as they now went off to give assistance. There was also intelligence that many of the mutineers displaced from Delhi were congregating at nearby Muttra, together with the 1st Bengal Light Cavalry and 23rd Bengal Native Infantry.

Passing through Hattras and crossing the River Jumna by a bridge of boats, the column arrived at the outskirts of Agra on 10th October.

Battle of Agra

When news of the outbreak of mutiny reached Agra, the native garrison of 44th and 67th Bengal Native Infantry were disarmed as a precautionary measure, even though they had shown no signs of dissent.

With news of the worsening situation at Delhi, 6,000 refugees (comprising British civilians with their families and servants) from the surrounding districts began to converge on Agra, seeking protection in the old fort.

Following an uprising in the city in June, the British were besieged in the fort, however, with the arrival of Greathed's column, the besiegers drifted away.

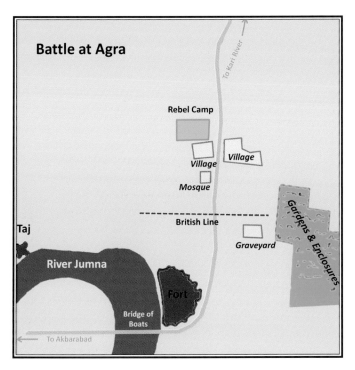

Figure 59. Battle of Agra

Private John Freeman – Victoria Cross No. 201

The cavalry attacked an artillery battery and killed the gunners who were still trying to make their guns ready, however, a squadron of the 9th Lancers led by Captain Lucius John French charged and dispersed the rebels. Unfortunately Captain French was killed in the charge and Lieutenant Alfred Stowell Jones[16] was dangerously wounded with 22 sabre cuts to his head and arms.

Seeing his badly wounded Lieutenant lying on the ground and likely to be killed by the encircling rebels who were still striking at him with their swords, Private Freeman rode into the horde, killed the leader of the group and remained guarding the Lieutenant until help arrived.

For this act, Private Freeman was later awarded the Victoria Cross.

The charge bought the British force some time to assemble and soon the 8th Regiment of Foot together with the 1st and 4th Punjab Infantry were at arms and ready for the fight, the remaining British cavalry were rapidly being saddled up, Pearson's 9 pounder battery was also now manned up.

Major Henry Aime Ouvry with the 9th lancers together with Lieutenant Hugh Gough's squadron of Hodson's horse and three squadrons of Punjab Cavalry commanded by Lieutenants Probyn, Watson and Younghusband attacked the left flank of the enemy.

Captain Dighton Macnaghten Probyn – Victoria Cross No. 115

Lieutenant Probyn's squadron began to outflank the rebel infantry and well ahead of his squadron, he charged a group of about 6 rebels, killing two before the rest of his troop arrived.

Soon afterwards, while fighting a most determined mutineer, Lieutenant Probyn received a bayonet wound to the chest but Probyn managed to slay his foe.

He next charged a rebel standard bearer, about whom a number of mutineers were collecting and as he raised his sword to cut him down another rebel made a strike at the Lieutenant fortunately his orderly, an aging Sikh, deflected the blow with his arm which was nearly severed (he died of this wound two days later) saving his life.

For these and other deeds, Lieutenant Probyn was later awarded the Victoria Cross.

With the cavalry already engaged and the infantry and artillery assembled and ready for act, Colonel Greathed arrived on the

With the threat to the city having dispersed, many of the troops went to sleep on the parade ground to the south west of the city, to recover from their exhausting march; having covered 44 miles in 28 hours. Others settled down to breakfast and Colonel Greathed and some of his officers went into the fort to dine with the local command; tradesmen came out of the city to ply their wares and entertain the troops. It was assumed that the rebels were leaving the area and on their way to Gwalior so no piquets were posted and no patrols were sent out.

Suddenly the quiet of the day was broken by a surprise attack from mutineers, supported by artillery, who were hidden in the high crops which surrounded the parade ground. Four men dressed as jugglers attacked the sentry guard, and began laying into Sergeant Crews who was in charge. Sergeant Hartigan,[15] who was unarmed, ran to the assistance of Sergeant Crews and punching one of the rebels in the mouth, disarmed him and then used his sword to defend himself against the other three, killing one and wounding the other two. During this action he received disabling wounds. Soon afterwards a large band of 2nd Gwalior Cavalry appeared from nowhere and began to attack the resting British force.

---

15 Sergeant Hartigan was awarded the Victoria Cross for deeds at the Battle of Budle-ke-Serai on 8th June, this action was also noted in his citation.

16 Lieutenant Jones was awarded the Victoria Cross for deeds at Delhi on 8th June and received a second mention in his citation for this action.

field and launched an infantry attack at the rebel centre which was supported by the artillery. In the face of this determined assault the mutineers soon left the field abandoning two of their guns.

Colonel Greathed wanted to pursue the rebels, however, he had to await the arrival of Lieutenant-Colonel Cotton, the commander of the Agra garrison, who was the senior officer, for orders to do so. When Lieutenant-Colonel Cotton arrived with the 3rd Europeans, he assumed command and fully in agreement with Colonel Greathed's wishes the force set off in pursuit of the rebels. Despite the delay, the mutineers were soon caught up, about four miles down the road to Gwalior, at the Kari Nadi stream which they were trying to cross. The rebels tried to make a stand, however, accurate fire from the British artillery soon dispersed the rebels who abandoned all of their guns and supplies, in all the British captured 15 artillery pieces and vast supplies of ammunition.

During the battle the British losses were comparatively light with 12 killed, 54 wounded and 2 missing in action, the rebel losses were considerably higher.

Greathed's advance towards Cawnpore continues

After the battle, the force returned to their camp at Agra where they rested up for the next three days, the wounded were sent to a hospital which had been established in the Moti Musjid mosque in Agra.

On the morning of 14th October the column left Agra to continue its journey towards Cawnpore, at the end of the day's march they camped at Ram Bagh where they were reinforced by two siege guns and detachments of men from the 8th and 75th Regiments of Foot.

By the 16th October, the column had reached Firozabad where Colonel James Hope Grant joined the column and assumed the command. After having had Colonel Greathed appointed to the command of the column over his head, Colonel Hope Grant remained in Delhi until this decision was overturned and he was appointed to the command.

On 19th October the column reached Mynpoorie and the on the 21st arrived at Bewar which was an important junction on the Grand Truck road where the roads from Meerut, Agra, Futtehgur and Cawnpore all met.

It was while at Bewar that a letter arrived from General Outram at Lucknow begging for aid to be sent as soon as possible as their provisions were running out.

Action at Kanauji

The urgency was communicated to the men who responded with a 28 mile march the next day, and arrived near the ruined Hindu city of Kanauji on the morning of the 23rd November. Lieutenant Roberts, assistant Quartermaster General to the force, was fired on by a party of mutineers from across the river, while reconnoitring with his staff. The small force of mutineers consisting of about 300 cavalry and 500 infantry, were working to get their four field guns across the river. Colonel Hope Grant sent a force two horse artillery guns and a platoon of Dragoons, under the command of Lieutenant Murray to disperse the enemy. The group quickly set up their guns on the river bank and were soon firing grape and shot into the mutineers who turned and fled. The Dragoons, now supported by platoons of Punjab cavalry commanded by Lieutenants Probyn and Watson were soon in pursuit of the rebels and chased them to the banks of the River Ganges.

Arrival at Cawnpore

After the action at Kanauji, the column resumed their march and arrived at Cawnpore on 26th October where a force was being assembled to go to the relief of Lucknow. Here they expected to await the arrival of the new Commander in Chief before continuing to Lucknow.

Conductor James Miller – Victoria Cross No. 202

Meanwhile back at Agra, on 28th October, Colonel Cotton was leading an attack against mutineers who had established a position in a serai at Futtehpore.

Conductor Miller was looking after the ordnance stores for the heavy howitzers deployed against the serai when he saw Lieutenant Glubb wounded and lying in an exposed position. Without any thought for his own safety, Conductor Miller, under heavy fire, went out and carried Lieutenant Glubb back to safety.

For this action Conductor Miller was later awarded the Victoria Cross.

On 27th October, news reached Cawnpore that the Commander-in-Chief General Sir Colin Campbell had left Calcutta and was making his way to Cawnpore to lead the force to relieve Lucknow.

Colonel Hope Grant also received orders to advance to the Alum Bagh and send the sick and wounded back to Cawnpore.

General Hope Grant's advance to the Alum Bagh

On 30th October, General Hope Grant's force, reinforced by 4 companies of 93rd Highlanders and some other infantry, left Cawnpore and crossed the River Ganges into the province of Oudh. The next day, while at Bunnee Bridge, news reached the column that the Commander-in-Chief General Sir Colin Campbell had arrived at Cawnpore. By 2nd November, the force had reached Buntera, a village about 6 miles from the Alum Bagh, from here Colonel Hope Grant sent out a force which retrieved the sick and wounded from the Alum Bagh who were then sent back to Cawnpore under a heavy escort. As instructed, the Colonel stayed at Buntera with his force, awaiting the arrival of General Sir Colin Campbell.

The Naval Brigade's journey to Cawnpore

Soon after their arrival at Hong Kong, in the summer of 1857, *HMS Pearl*, *HMS Sanspareil* and *HMS Shannon* were despatched to Calcutta by Rear Admiral Sir Michael Seymour to assist with subduing the mutiny. *HMS Sanspareil* returned back to Chinese waters after two or three months, taking no part in the suppression of the mutiny, however, officers and men from *HMS Pearl* and *HMS Shannon* would be involved as part of the Naval Brigade.

HMS Shannon arrived off the mouth of the Ganges on 6th August and Captain Peel immediately offered the services of his men and guns.

On 14th August, Captain Peel with several of his officers and 390 seamen and marines set out up river, on towed barges, to join the Lucknow Relief Force. Four days later on 18th August, a second detachment from *HMS Shannon* also set out up river, this force comprised 5 officers and 120 men, some of whom had been recruited from merchant ships moored at Calcutta. The *Shannon* was left under the command of Master George A. Waters with a crew of 140 men. Progress up river was slow, due to the fact that the barges were loaded with heavy guns and howitzers from *HMS Shannon*, and did not reach Allahabad until mid-October; by 20th October, the Naval Brigade with 516 men of all ranks, had been assembled, Lieutenants Wilson and Wratislaw with 240 men were left to supplement the Garrison at Allahabad but Lieutenants Vaughan and Salmon with 100 men set out for Cawnpore on 23rd October with 4 siege train 24 pounder guns. This column arrived safely in Cawnpore without incident.

Captain Peel with a further 103 men, four 24 pounder guns and two 8" howitzers left Allahabad on 28th October and soon afterwards joined up with a column, under the command of Colonel Powell, which consisted of; 162 men of the 53rd Regiment under Major Clark, 68 men of the Royal Engineers under Captain Gierke, 70 men of a depot detachment under Lieutenant Fanning, who were also on the way to Cawnpore.

After resting up at Thuree, a village about half way to Cawnpore, the column received intelligence from Futtehpore that a large force of mutineers comprising about 2,000 men from the Dinapore regiment with 3 guns and about a further 2,000 men from the surrounding area, were seen to be assembling at Jumna.

It was assumed that the force was either going to attack Futtehpore or cross the river into the province of Oudh. Colonel Powell decided that this threat to the forces at Cawnpore needed to be urgently addressed, so ordered camp to be struck and immediately set out for Futtehpore, which was reached at midnight.

Battle of Khujwa

On the following morning, having been joined by, 100 men of the 93rd Highlanders under Captain Cornwall, two 9 pounder guns and men of the Bengal Artillery under Lieutenant Anderson from the garrison at Futtehpore, the force moved out to engage the enemy who by now were reported to be at Khujwa.

After a march of 16 miles the column briefly halted for refreshments at the village of Binkee and then continued their march to the village of Khujwa, where the rebels were posted on embankments at either side of the road with their guns in the centre, on the road. The British force advanced in skirmishing order against both enemy flanks; Colonel Powell on the left of the road managed to capture two enemy guns but was killed when shot in the head by musket fire and Captain Peel assumed command of the column. With the flanks having been pushed in, the British force was in danger of being encircled and attacked from the rear. Captain Peel collected together a force and attacked the enemy centre, dividing their force and rolling back the flanks. In the confusion, the rebels retired from the field leaving behind two of their guns.

As the men were exhausted from the fight and their marches, Captain Peel decided not to pursue the enemy but set up camp and gathered in the dead and wounded.

The British losses amounted to 95 killed or wounded, however, the rebel casualties were thought to be over 300.

On the following day, Captain Peel and the column resumed their march to Cawnpore.

The two detachments of the Naval Brigade would eventually be reunited before Lucknow on 12th November.

The 53rd Regiment of Foot's journey to Cawnpore

At the start of the mutiny, the 53rd Regiment was based at Fort William in Calcutta and for the first few weeks were involved in disarming several native regiments in and around the arsenal at Dum Dum; they also spent some time guarding commercial and public buildings in Calcutta.

On 27th August, following the spread of mutiny, the left wing of the regiment with 374 officers and men marched to Raniganj and from there along the Grand Trunk road towards Allahabad, where troops were being concentrated. As they continued their march, mutiny broke out in the Chota Nagpur district to the West of their route to Allahabad.

The 7th, 8th and 40th Bengal Infantry Regiments mutinied at Dinapore and marched off to join the rebel leader Kunwar Singh.

At Hazaribagh, part of the 8th Native Infantry had turned on their British officers and fled to the surrounding countryside.

The Ramghur Battalion mutinied at Ranchi and plundered the town of Duranda where they sacked the treasury, opened the jails and set fire to the church.

The European residents of the district fled towards Hazaribagh for safety, where the Commissioner Captain Dalton, aided by the Raja of Ramghur, who remained loyal to the British, tried to maintain order.

Concerned that the large concentration of mutinied regiments would combine and launch an attack on Hazaribagh, Captain Dalton made an urgent request to Calcutta for assistance.

Some units of the Madras army, which remained unaffected by the mutiny, were sent to his aid, however, they failed to locate and engage the powerful Ramghur Battalion, which Captain Dalton was sure intended to attack Hazaribagh, so further requests were made to Calcutta for assistance.

In response to these further requests, in late September the 53rd Regiment of Foot were ordered to divert from their march to Allahabad and go to the assistance of Hazaribagh.

Battle of Chattra (Chota Behar)

Following intelligence received from Colonel Fischer of the 18th Madras Infantry, that the Ramghur Battalion were camped near the village of Chattra, a village about 35 mile from Hazaribagh, Major English with a detachment from the column set out to engage the enemy.

Corporal Denis Dynon – Victoria Cross No. 197
Lieutenant John Daunt – Victoria Cross No. 198

Colonel Fischer and the 18th Madras Infantry were deployed to guard the Grand Trunk Road, while Major English with a force of about 350 men; 180 men from the 53rd, 150 Sikh soldiers, mainly from the 11th Bengal Infantry and two guns; advanced on Chattra.

On the morning of 2nd October, Major English and his small force arrived at Chattra to find that 3,000 rebels of the Ramghur Battalion were camped to the west of the village, while other mutineers occupied the village itself. Despite the overwhelming odds, Major English decided on an immediate attack and for the next hour his force was engaged in fierce hand to hand fighting in the village. During the fighting, two enemy field guns opened up with well directed and lethal fire on the attacking force, firing grapeshot at close range killing or wounding about a third of Lieutenant Daunt's company of 11th Bengal Infantry, which was attacking towards the guns.

One of the guns was destroyed by British artillery fire and Lieutenant Daunt together with Corporal Dynan led a direct assault on the other, which they captured and killed the gunners.

For this action Lieutenant Daunt and Corporal Dynan were both later awarded the Victoria Cross.

Lieutenant Daunt's citation mentions a second incident when on 2nd November; he led a small party of Rattray's Sikhs and chased mutineers from the 32nd Bengal Native Infantry driving them from an enclosure. During this action he was dangerously wounded.

By the time that the mutineers broke off the action and fled, Major English had lost 42 men killed or wounded but had capture 40 cartloads of ammunition, 10 elephants, 20 teams of gun bullocks, several boxes of "treasure" and four field guns.

For a while Major English and his men carried out operations against local mutineers from the 32nd Bengal Native Infantry before continuing their journey towards Cawnpore where they met up with the rest of the wing of the 53rd commanded by Colonel Powell which had joined up with Captain Peel at Allahabad on 28th October.

General Sir Colin Campbell's journey to Cawnpore

After arriving in Calcutta on 13th August, Sir Colin Campbell assumed the command of the army in India on 17th August and, surprised at the lack of preparations for the soon to arrive new troops, set about reorganising the administrative departments.

Sir Colin spent the next few weeks making preparations for the assembly of men and equipment and the means of transporting them to the theatre of war. His success in this endeavour was demonstrated by the fact that once new troops began arriving from England and China during October they were almost immediately sent off to the war zone.

With all preparations now complete, General Campbell was at last able to leave Calcutta and on the evening of 27th October, he made his way to the war zone.

When he reached Allahabad on the 1st November, he received a letter from General Outram which stated that following a further reduction in rations he expected to be able to last out until the end of November. The letter also contained directions for a suggested route into the city, which was the same route used by General Outram's column.

General Sir Colin Campbell arrived at Cawnpore on 3rd November, after having completed a journey of 620 miles in six days.

The General spent the next few days making arrangements for the protection of the city, which was still under threat from the Gwalior contingent of mutineers. Major-General Charles A. Windham was left in charge of the defence of the city with a garrison of about 500 Europeans comprising; 450 men from the 64th Regiment and the men of the Depot detachment, 49 men from the Naval Brigade under the command of Lieutenant Hay and 20 artillerymen. There was also a small force of Sikhs who manned a 4 gun field battery. General Windham was ordered to send on towards Lucknow any newly arriving troops, with the exception of the Madras Infantry, expected to arrive at Cawnpore on 10th November, which would be used to supplement the garrison.

Advance on Lucknow

On 9th November, having completed the arrangements for the security of Cawnpore, General Sir Colin Campbell moved to Buntera where his forces for the advance on Lucknow were being assembled.

On the following day, a European man, disguised as a native was brought before the General, this was the civilian Mr Kavanagh, who had managed to escape through the enemy lines to bring news from Lucknow and to provide assistance to the relief force by guiding them by the best route to the Residency.

Civilian Thomas Kavanagh – Victoria Cross No. 203

Mr Kavanagh was a civilian clerk in the employ of the East India Company civil service who, as he had been based at Lucknow for some time, had an intimate knowledge of the city.

At about 10 a.m. on the 9th November, Mr Kavanagh became aware that a spy, Kunoujee Lall, had arrived from Cawnpore and was intending to go to the Alum Bagh with despatches from General Outram to General Campbell, that evening. It occurred to Mr Kavanagh that if he went with Kunoujee Lall, he would be able to act as a guide to the relief column and help them advance to the Residency by the safest route. With the help of Colonel Napier, Mr Kavanagh gained an audience with General Outram and volunteered his services and although initially reticent, the General eventually agreed to the plan.

Mr Kavanagh disguised himself as an irregular native soldier and blackened his face and arms with lamp black painted on with a cork dipped in oil. At about 9 p.m. Mr Kavanagh with Kunoujee Lall was escorted down to the river Gumti by Captain Harding of the Irregular Cavalry and after undressing the pair waded across the river. After dressing once again, the pair proceeded down the river bank towards the Iron Bridge; Mr Kavanagh had a native sword held over his shoulder and had a small double barrelled pistol concealed about his person.

At the Iron Bridge, the pair was stopped by a native cavalry officer who was in charge of a piquet, however, after explaining that they had come from Mundeon and were on their way back home, they were left to go on their way.

They next recrossed the Gumti via the stone bridge and emerged onto the Chowk, which was one of the main streets of the city and made their way into the open countryside.

For a time they lost their way and ended up in the Dilkusha Park, which was heavily occupied by the mutineers but eventually found their way to the Char Bagh. At about 1 o'clock it was decided to press on to the camp at Buntera, rather than the Alum Bagh which was surrounded by mutineers.

At 4 o'clock, after having been stopped by several Sepoy piquets, the pair finally came across an advanced British piquet and Mr Kavanagh was escorted by an officer of the 9th Lancers to General Campbell's camp. At noon a flag was raised on the Alum Bagh, as a sign to the command in Lucknow that Mr Kavanagh had been successful in his mission.

For making this hazardous journey, Mr Kavanagh was later awarded the Victoria Cross only the second civilian to receive the award.

On 11th November, General Campbell inspected his troops assembled at Buntera, the force was made up of the remnants of regiments that had already blooded themselves against the mutineers and were all seasoned troops.

Advance to the Alum Bagh

On the 12th November, the force set out for the Alum Bagh, from where Sir Colin Campbell intended to launch his attack on Lucknow. Proceeding down the road, the advanced guard had only progressed a short way before they came under fire from about 2,000 mutineers with two guns, who were positioned on the right of the road near the old Jellalabad fort.

Lieutenant Hugh Gough – Victoria Cross No. 204

Fire from the battery of Captain Bouchier, soon silenced the enemy guns, however, Lieutenant Gough, commanding Hodson's Irregular Horse, had managed to gain the flank of the enemy force unseen, by way of some fields of cane.

An extensive swamp protected the enemy flank but Lieutenant Gough and his men went through the tall reedy grass at a trot and when they came into the open, the Lieutenant gave the order *"Form Line! Charge!"*

In Lieutenant Gough's own words – *"My men gave a ringing cheer and were into the masses. The surprise was complete, and owing to its suddenness they had no conception of our numbers; and so the shock to them and victory to us was as if it had been a whole brigade. It seemed like cutting one's way through a field of corn, and I had to make a lane for myself as I rode along. The men followed me splendidly, and in a very short time the affair was over, — the guns were captured, the enemy scattered, and the fight became a pursuit."*

For this action, Lieutenant Gough, who was wounded twice during the engagement, was later awarded the Victoria Cross.

His citation refers to a second act of bravery when on 25th February 1858 he charged enemy guns and engaged in several single handed combats at Jellalabad, having two horses shot out from under him before he was shot in the leg and disabled while charging Sepoys with fixed bayonets.

Sir Colin Campbell and the relief force managed to reach the Alum Bagh without further incident and camped at some distance to the rear, just outside the range of the enemy artillery.

With the help of instructions brought by Mr Kavanagh, a semaphore system was set up and a short communication with the Residency took place.

For 49 days, since 25th September, the Alum Bagh had been held by Major McIntyre, initially with a garrison of only 280 men, however, by the time of the arrival of Campbell's relief force the garrison had grown to 930 Europeans, some Sikhs and 8 guns; augmented by men arriving from Cawnpore with supplies. Although the position had been under constant fire from rebel batteries, the garrison had only lost one man killed and two wounded, however, the native camp followers and cattle had suffered badly.

With the arrival of General Campbell, Major McIntyre was relieved of his command of the Alum Bagh and together with the able men of the garrison, was assigned as part of the relief force. About 300 men of the 75th Regiment, which had suffered badly during their journey, were assigned to take over the duties

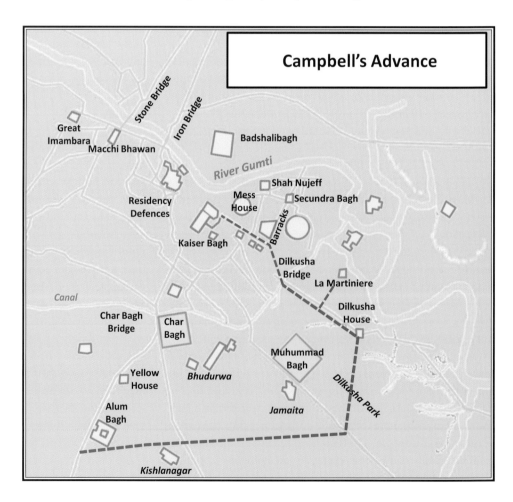

Figure 60. General Campbell's advance on Lucknow

as garrison together with about 50 Sikhs and a small detachment of artillery, all under the command of Captain Moir.

On the 13th November, the relief force rested at the Alum Bagh, while General Sir Colin Campbell finalised his plans for the advance on Lucknow.

With help from Mr Kavanagh, the route was decided; this was a revision of the route suggested by General Outram. The force was to proceed to Dilkusha Park, then to the Martinière then moving towards the river to the barracks at the Secundra Bagh and then onwards to the Residency.

This route was intended to minimise the street by street fighting which had been so costly during General Outram's approach to the Residency.

On the morning of the 13th November, Brigadier Adrian Hope with men from the 93rd Highlanders was directed to seize the old Jellalabad fort as if it was occupied by mutineers it would be a threat to communications. On reaching the fort, it was found to be deserted, so one wall was demolished to render it useless as a defensible position.

In the afternoon, a reconnaissance in force was made towards the Char Bagh Bridge in an attempt to deceive the mutineers as to the real line of advance.

Having received further reinforcements during the day, General Campbell completed the final organisation of his relief force on the evening of the 13th November.

The infantry was organised into three nominal brigades, under Hope Grant with the rank of Brigadier-General: the strongest Commanded by Brigadier Adrian Hope was comprised of; 934 men and 48 officers of the 93rd Highlanders, a wing of the 53rd Regiment of Foot and the 4th Punjab Infantry: the brigade commanded by Brigadier Greathed was comprised of; the 8th Regiment of Foot, the 2nd Punjab Infantry and a battalion of detachments: the last brigade, commanded by Brigadier Russell was comprised of; a wing of the 23rd Royal Welsh Fusiliers and two companies of the 82nd Regiment of Foot.

The artillery brigade, commanded by Brigadier Crawford, was comprised of two companies of Royal Artillery under Captains Travers and Longden, equipped with 18 pounder guns; two troops of Bengal Horse Artillery under Captains Remmington and Blunt; two guns of the Madras Native Horse Artillery under Captain Bridge; a horse battery of the Royal Artillery commanded by Captain Middleton and the Bengal Field Battery under Captain Bourchier.

The Naval Brigade, commanded by Captain Peel, augmented the army infantry and artillery brigades with their six 24 pounder guns, two howitzers, two rocket tubes and 250 seamen and marines.

The Cavalry Brigade, commanded by Brigadier Little, was comprised of: 2 squadrons of 9th Lancers, commanded by Major Audry; detachments of the 1st, 2nd and 5th Punjab Cavalry led by Lieutenants Watson, Probyn and Younghusband; Hodson's Horse led by Lieutenant Gough and two squadrons of cavalry from the military train commanded by Major Robertson.

The force was completed by a small brigade of Engineers under the command of Lieutenant Lennox of the Royal Engineers and comprised: a company of Royal Engineers, a company of Madras Sappers, some Bengal Sappers and two companies of Punjab Pioneers.

For the assault, General Campbell had a force of almost 4,500 men at his disposal, however, these would be pitted against about 60,000 mutineers who were besieging the city.

At 9 o'clock on the morning of 14th November 1857, General Sir Colin Campbell's relief force began its advance on Lucknow. As planned the column headed off to the right almost due east, towards the Dilkusha Park rather than, as the rebels expected, towards the Char Bagh bridge which was the direct route.

Colonel Greathed with his infantry and guns kept to the left, towards the canal and acted as a guard for the left flank and rear of the advancing column.

Not hampered by the boggy ground, now that the monsoon season was over, which had prevented Generals Outram and Havelock from using this route, the force was able to progress without difficulty and managed to march three miles before they met any resistance.

Taking of Dilkusha Park and the Martinière

On reaching the wall which bordered the Dilkusha Park, the advanced guard was met with fierce rebel musket fire and until reinforced by Captain Remmington's horse artillery and men from the 5th Fusiliers, 64th Foot and 78th Highlanders commanded by Lieutenant-Colonel Hamilton, was temporarily halted.

The British cavalry and infantry rushed through a hole in the wall and the rebels fled in disarray down the slope to the Martinière and the Dilkusha House (Hearts Delight), which had been erected as a hunting lodge for the Nawabs of Oudh, was taken.

As the British arrived at the crest of the hill, they were assailed by artillery and musket fire from the Martinière but before this had any appreciable effect the guns of Captain Bourchier and Captain Remmington's troop had opened up. This fire was soon followed by fire from Captain Travers's 18 pounders and a heavy howitzer brought forward by Captain Hardy.

The infantry now rushed down the hill and quickly took the Martinière, chasing the rebels off towards the canal and the river, where they were pursued by the cavalry.

Figure 61. La Martinière College

Figure 62. Dilkusha House

Lieutenant John Watson – Victoria Cross No. 205

In the course of the pursuit, Lieutenant Watson, commander of the 1st Punjab Cavalry, who was ahead of his troop, charged into the midst of a group of six fleeing enemy cavalry.

Making directly for the group's leader, a native officer from the 15th Irregular Cavalry, he was quickly engaged in hand-to-hand combat and killed him with his sword; in the encounter he had a narrow escape when the rebel discharged a pistol at him from only a few feet but escaped injury.[17]

Despite being knocked off his horse, Lieutenant Watson continued the fight with the remaining rebels and received sword blows to the head, both arms and a leg (which left him lame for a few days).

Lieutenant Watson was rescued from his plight by Lieutenant Probyn, who arrived with two squadrons of his men and chased the assailants off.

For this action, Lieutenant Watson was later awarded the Victoria Cross.

By noon, having taken these two important positions, General Sir Colin Campbell now began making arrangements to secure them and the ground down to the canal. Brigadier Hope's brigade was brought forward and together with Captain Remmington's troop of horse artillery took up positions in the gardens of the Martinière. Brigadier Russell and his brigade were posted on the left in front of the Dilkusha House and Brigadier Little with his brigade of cavalry and Captain Bourchier's battery took up positions on the plain in front of the Martinière. Later in the afternoon, Russell sent several companies of his men to occupy two villages down by the canal, to provide cover to the extreme left of the British positions.

These moves by General Sir Colin Campbell were most fortuitous, as soon after they were completed it became clear that the

enemy were going to attack, as they began massing forces against the centre of the British positions. The first attack, however, came from the west when the rebels came down to the canal near the villages just occupied by Russell's men. Russell's men managed to hold off the assault long enough for the guns of Bourchier's battery to come into play and in the face of heavy artillery fire, the attack from this direction was soon put down. At about 5 o'clock in the afternoon, the mutineers launched an attack from the direction of the Dilkusha Bridge but Brigadier Hope pushed men from the 93rd and 53rd Regiments of foot, the 4th Punjab Infantry and the guns of Captain Remmington's troop, to occupy an embankment to the left and right of the bridge. The fire from these men prevented the mutineers from crossing the canal and the enemy was soon under fire from Bourchier's battery and the 24 pounder guns from the Naval Brigade which were located on high ground to the left of the bridge. Under the intense artillery fire, which caused heavy casualties, the mutineers fled back to the city and the British established positions to secure the far end of the bridge.

Since leaving the Alum Bagh, Lieutenant-Colonel Ewart and men of the 93rd Highlanders had acted as the rearguard, escorting the baggage train, which also included the reserves of food and ammunition. Thought to be an easier target than the main force, the rearguard was constantly harassed by the enemy throughout the day and their progress was slow.

The 15th November was a day of preparation for the final assault while, General Sir Colin Campbell awaited the arrival of the rearguard and the baggage train.

Once the baggage train arrived, the supplies together with the sick and wounded were moved into the Dilkusha House and Brigadier Little with a force of 300 men; comprising five field-guns, half of the 9th Lancers, a squadron of Punjab cavalry, men of the 8th Regiment of Foot and the military train; were delegated to form the garrison.

An enemy attack in strength against the extreme right took place at about midday but this was fought off with heavy artillery fire.

---

17 It is believed that the bullet must have fallen out of the barrel before the pistol was discharged.

In an attempt to disguise the direction of his planned attack, General Campbell moved all of his artillery to the left of his position and during the night unleashed a bombardment on rebel positions to the west, as if in preparation for an advance across the Dilkusha Bridge.

Before the light faded, the semaphore post established on the roof of the Dilkusha House was used to signal the Residency that the relief force would be coming to their rescue on the following day.

Advance on the Secundra Bagh

Early on the morning of 16th November, the heavy guns were withdrawn from the advanced piquets on the canal and the detachments from Brigadier Adrian Hope's brigade were recalled and rejoined their regiments.

After breakfast, the men were issued with three days rations, which they carried in their knapsacks as, for speed of movement, the column would be advancing without a baggage train.

With an advanced guard formed from Cavalry, Blunt's horse artillery and men from the 53rd Regiment of Foot, the relief force resumed their advance and headed north with their first objective being to take the Secundra Bagh.

The Secundra Bagh was a heavily fortified enemy position, formerly the summer residence of the Nawab of Oudh, possibly named after Alexander the Great. The fortress had a high wall about 150 yards long on each side, pierced by loopholes and with large bastions at each corner. The wall surrounded a central pavilion with gardens and another single story building with its own courtyard to the rear. The only entrance to the Secundra Bagh was a fortified gate in the southern wall.

The relief force advanced across the dry canal bed behind the Martinière and when they reached the River Gumti took a sharp left turn to proceed along the river bank. Advancing through wooded enclosures, they crossed the canal again at a point opposite the village of Jagrauli on the other side of the river.

The force then advanced down a sunken lane between rows of native houses for an approach parallel to the eastern wall of the Secundra Bagh.

The brigade of Brigadier Hope marched behind the advanced guard followed by Russell's brigade and then the engineers with the ammunition wagons.

Greathed's brigade remained at the canal crossing until midday, providing protection to the left rear of the column and then followed behind the main force, acting as the rear guard.

General Campbell's diversion of the previous evening had proved to be successful, as the advanced guard was only spotted by the mutineers after they had gained the sunken road near the Secundra Bagh, however, once spotted they came under heavy musket fire from the walls of the Secundra Bagh.

Figure 63. The Secundra Bagh

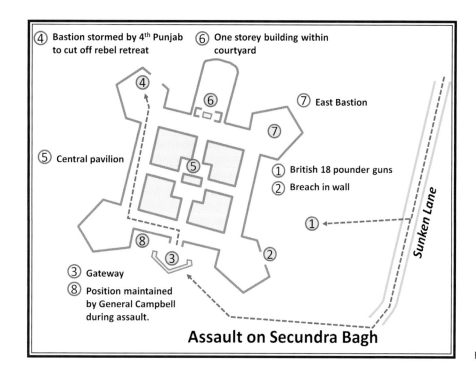

Figure 64. Assault on the Secundra Bagh

The Secundra Bagh is taken

For a time, the column was in a visible position, with their flank exposed to the enemy fire for a length of almost 150 yards. The force was hemmed in by the high banks to the side of the road and from this position it was not possible to bring their guns to bear on the enemy, urgent action was required to allow the force to break out from their precarious position. Seeing the predicament, Captain Blunt with his horse artillery managed to struggle with their pieces up the steep bank and gain open ground between the Secundra Bagh and a serai off to the left. Despite being assailed by fierce musket fire from the walls of the Secundra Bagh and the serai, Blunt's men unlimbered their pieces and began a rapid fire against both targets and also against the Kaiser Bagh off to the centre which was now beginning to lay down fire from the battery placed there. General Sir Colin Campbell, also rushed up the slope on his horse and bravely took up a position next to the artillery as it commenced its fire, it was not long before he was wounded by a musket ball which passed through his thigh.

Captain William Steuart – Victoria Cross No. 211

As Captain Blunts battery began to lay down its fire, Captain Steuart with some men from the 93rd Highlanders and men from the 53rd Regiment of Foot, launched an attack on the serai, from where the mutineers were sending a murderous fire down the length of the sunken road.

Having chased the rebels from the serai, Captain Steuart and his force, now supported by two field pieces from Blunt's battery, advanced on the Chauper Istanbul (the king's stables) which had been the barracks of the 32nd regiment, to attack two guns which were laying down heavy flanking fire.

Captain Steuart led his men in a charge against these guns, which were captured at bayonet point and then turned on the fleeing mutineers and together with Captain Cornwall and his men pressed on and captured the barracks.

For his part in this action, Captain Steuart was later awarded the Victoria Cross having been nominated for the award by a ballot of the officers of his regiment.

While the attacks on the serai and barracks were taking place, two of Travers's 18 pounder guns were brought forward and after sappers had cut down part of the embankment of the sunken road, these were hauled by soldiers to the open ground and set up next to Blunt's guns.

The infantry had now moved to a wooded copse where, from the shelter of a low mud bank, they were able to keep up a fierce suppressing fire against the mutineers on the ramparts of the Secundra Bagh.

The 18 pounders were now firing at the almost point blank range of 60 yards, at the wall of the south east bastion and after about 30 minutes had blasted a small hole, about 3 foot square and 3 feet of the ground, in the wall.

It is unclear whether or not a signal was given for the charge on the opening; some sources say the charge was spontaneous, some say a trumpet was sounded and some say that General Campbell doffed his bonnet which was taken as the signal to charge.

Lieutenant Alfred Ffrench – Victoria Cross No. 213
Private Charles Irwin – Victoria Cross No. 220

Irrespective of whether ordered to or not, almost as soon as the breach was made, several men rushed forward towards the hole. This gallant band consisted of men from the 93rd

Highlanders commanded by Lieutenant-Colonel Ewart, the 4th Punjab Rifles led by Lieutenant Paul, the 53rd Regiment led by Lieutenant-Colonel Gordon and men of the detachments led by Major Barnston.

Again the records are unclear as to who was first through the breach but accepted accounts put forward the following scenario.

A native officer Gotal Singh led the Sikhs forward and it was one of his men who was first through the breach, but he was killed in the process. He was closely followed by men from the Highlanders (thought to be Sergeant-Major Murray and Lance-Corporal Donnelly), who were also killed, the first named man, to make the breach, is thought to have been Lieutenant Richard Cooper who dived through the hole like a gymnast.

Colonel Ewart, Captain Lumsden and about a dozen men from the Highlanders and Sikhs were next through the breach.

Lieutenant FFrench and Private Irwin were later awarded the Victoria Cross for being amongst the first to enter the Secundra Bagh, having been elected for the award by a ballot of the Officers or Privates of their regiments, as appropriate.

During the attack, Private Irwin was severely wounded in the right shoulder.

Having gained the enclosure, Colonel Ewart, Captain Lumsden, Lieutenant Cooper and the group of 12 privates, turned right along the road towards the north east bastion. Surprised by the appearance of British Officers and men approaching their position, the mutineers assumed that the main gate had been breached and fled to establish positions in the building and courtyard at the north of the Secundra Bagh. During a fight with the retreating rebels Lieutenant Cooper was killed by a sword blow to his head and Captain Lumsden was killed by musket fire.

Lance Corporal John Dunlay – Victoria Cross No. 218

Soon after the first entry was made Captain Burroughs, Corporal Fraser, Lance-Corporal Dunlay (who was wounded in the leg) and Private Nairn also forced the breach and turned to their left towards the main gateway.

The party was rushed by a small force of rebels from the gate house and as he had such a small force Captain Burroughs halted his advance but began to lay down fire, which delayed the rebels.

For being amongst the first men to enter the Secundra Bagh, Lance-Corporal Dunlay was later awarded the Victoria Cross, having been elected for the award by a ballot of the NCOs of his regiment.

When more men arrived through the breach, Captain Burroughs once again advanced on the gate house where his small force became engaged in hand to hand fighting with the rebels.

Because the breach in the wall of the south east bastion was so small, it could only allow entry at a slow rate, one man at a time. Seeking a faster means of entry, men of the 93rd Highlanders and 4th Punjab rifles headed for the main gate which was guarded by a traverse and earthworks.

Private John Smith – Victoria Cross No. 223

The gateway was charged and the mutineers guarding the traverse were forced back through the gates. Before the gates could be fully closed, Mukurrab Khan,[18] a native soldier, forced his left arm through the gap to prevent the gate being closed. When this arm had been repeatedly struck by swords he withdrew it but replaced it with his right arm which again was struck by blows which nearly severed his hand at the wrist.

This gallant action allowed the press of the British forces to push open the gate and swarm into the enclosure; men of the 53rd also gained entry by a window to the right of the gate.

Private Smith was later awarded the Victoria Cross for being one of the first men to enter the Secundra Bagh via the north gate. Despite being wounded by a sword blow to the head and a bayonet wound to the side, Private Smith continued to fight during the rest of the day.

With the gates now forced, the relief force gained entry to the Secundra Bagh in great numbers, many of the mutineers fled to the pavilion in the centre of the gardens and put up stiff resistance, however, this was soon stormed and cleared.

The surviving rebels fled to join their comrades in the north building and courtyard while others occupied the towers of the north east and north west bastions.

With the gate clear, it was now possible to bring artillery into the Secundra Bagh and this was used to force entry into the buildings and towers.

With thoughts of the rebel atrocities at Cawnpore fresh in their minds, the British troops showed no quarter and at the end of the battle, which lasted for about three hours, all 2,200 mutineers who had occupied the Secundra Bagh had been killed. The mutineers were mainly from the 71st Bengal Native Infantry and the Oudh Irregulars.

Lieutenant Frederick Roberts (later to become Lord Roberts) who witnessed the assault later recalled: *"Inch by inch they were forced back to the pavilion, and into the space between it and the*

---

18 Not eligible for the Victoria Cross, Mukurrab Khan was awarded the Order of Merit.

north wall, where they were all shot or bayoneted. There they lay in a heap as high as my head, a heaving, surging mass of dead and dying inextricably entangled. It was a sickening site, one of those which even in the excitement of battle and the flush of victory, make one feel strongly what a horrible side there is to war. The wounded men could not get clear of their dead comrades, however great their struggles, and those near the top of this ghastly pile vented their rage and determination on every British officer who approached, by showering upon him abuse of the foulest description".

During the final phase of the battle for the Secundra Bagh, several acts of bravery were singled out for recognition:

Colour Sergeant James Munro – Victoria Cross No. 216

Captain Walsh had fallen severely wounded and was in danger of being killed by the rebels when Colour-Sergeant Munro rushed to his rescue and carried him to a place of safety, thus saving his life.

Soon afterward, having himself been seriously wounded Colour-Sergeant Munro was also brought to safety.

For this action Colour-Sergeant Munro was later awarded the Victoria Cross, having been elected for the award by a ballot of the NCOs of his regiment.

Private Peter Grant – Victoria Cross No. 219

During the battle Colonel Ewart observed two rebel officers go into a room with their colours, without hesitation, the Colonel rushed into the room and captured the colours after killing the two officers but was wounded by two sabre cuts.

After he returned to the main enclosure with the colours, Colonel Ewart was defended against five mutineers by Private Grant who killed the five with a sword that he had taken from one of them.

For this action Private Grant was later awarded the Victoria Cross, having been elected for the award by a ballot of the Privates of his regiment.

Private James Kenny – Victoria Cross No. 221

During the battle, Private Kenny volunteered to go out into a heavy enemy cross fire and bring back a fresh supply of ammunition for his company.

For this act, Private Kenny was later awarded the Victoria Cross, having been elected for the award by a ballot of the Privates of his regiment.

Private David Mackay – Victoria Cross No. 222

In the face of heavy enemy fire, Private Mackay managed to capture one of the mutineers' standards.

For this action Private Mackay was later awarded the Victoria Cross, having been nominated for the award by a ballot of the Privates of his regiment.

Later in the day, during the capture of the Shah Najaf mosque, he was severely wounded.

Major John Guise – Victoria Cross No. 226
Sergeant Samuel hollis – Victoria Cross No. 227

During the battle the pair saved the life of Captain Irby and under heavy fire went to the assistance of two wounded men.

For this action they were both later awarded the Victoria Cross, having been elected for the award by a ballot of respectively, the officers and the NCOs of their regiments.

Storming of the Shah Najaf Mosque (Imambara)

By the late afternoon, a detachment of men under the command of Brigadier Hope disengaged from the Secundra Bagh and made for the Shah Najaf Mosque which was the next objective on the road to the Residency.

The Shah Najaf Mosque, more correctly an Imambara not a mosque, was built by Nawab Ghazi-ud-Din Haider, the last Nawab Wazir and first King of the state of Awadh, as his mausoleum. The tombs of the Nawab and his three wives are contained within a central domed building that had small bastions at its corners and was surrounded by a strong wall enclosing the tombs and garden.

After advancing for about 350 yards, Brigadier Hope's force reached a village, at the road side with the Kadam Rasul (Prophets Footprint)[19] Mosque further off to the right; Lieutenant-Colonel Gordon and his men cleared the village while the Sikhs cleared the mosque.

With the village clear, Captain Peel brought the guns of the Naval Brigade forward and began a bombardment of the Shah Najaf which was about 250 yards ahead of his position and about 100 yards to the right of the road.

Almost as soon as the British were in position, they were assailed by musket, grape and cannon fire from the heavily

---

19 So called because it contained a stone brought from Arabia, said to have been imprinted by the footstep of the prophet Mohammed.

Figure 65. The Shah Najaf Mosque (Imambara)

fortified Shah Najaf, which was supported by cannon fire from the Kaiser Bagh and batteries from the other side of the River Gumti. After almost three hours of bombardment by the British guns, there was no sign of a breach and due to their exposed position the relief force was suffering heavy losses. Almost in desperation, Captain Peel brought some of his guns up to within 20 yards of the Shah Najaf and began to fire at point blank range, although somewhat sheltered by nearby buildings the gun crew were suffering heavy losses from sharpshooters on the walls who were also throwing grenades.

Lieutenant Nowell Salmon – Victoria Cross No. 214
Leading Seaman John Harrison – Victoria Cross No. 224

When Captain Peel called for volunteers to climb a tree and dislodge the mutineers from the wall Lieutenant Salmon and another man climbed the tree and began firing on the mutineers.

When the first volunteer was killed, Leading Seaman Harrison stepped forward and began handing loaded rifles up to Lieutenant Salmon. When Lieutenant Salmon was wounded by a bullet through the thigh, Leading Seaman Harrison climbed the tree and continued firing against the mutineers greatly reducing their effectiveness.

For this action both men were later awarded the Victoria Cross.

Lieutenant Thomas James Young – Victoria Cross No. 215
Able Seaman William Hall – Victoria Cross No. 225

Able Seaman Hall was one of the first men to volunteer to man the guns that Captain Peel had brought close to the Shah Najaf,

due to the musket fire and grenades launched from the wall of the mosque, all the crew of one gun had been killed. When Able Seaman Hall was the only member of the other gun still fit to fire the gun, the others being either killed or wounded, Lieutenant Young, despite being seriously wounded, stepped up to help Able Seaman Hall with the loading and firing of the gun. They carried out this task until the wall was finally breached.

For this action Lieutenant Young and Able Seaman Hall were both later awarded the Victoria Cross.

With darkness rapidly approaching and little progress having been made, the British force was on the verge of withdrawing – General Campbell had approved the withdrawal once the dead and wounded had been recovered.

Sergeant John Paton – Victoria Cross No. 217

Brigadier Hope and about 50 men decided to have one last look to find an alternative entry into the Shah Najaf, before they implemented the withdrawal. This party was just moving off towards the rear of the enclosure when Sergeant Paton ran up with news of a small fracture in the wall; on his own initiative Sergeant Paton had set off to reconnoitre the rear of the Shah Najaf.

Sergeant Paton led Brigadier Hope and his men to the fissure in the wall, which was later widened by sappers, and the men gained entry and ran to open the gates.

It would appear that the mutineers believed that the British were on the verge of breaching their defences because as Brigadier Hopes men entered the enclosure, they viewed the last of the mutineers leaving it.

For his part in this action Sergeant Paton was later awarded the Victoria Cross, having been nominated for the award following a ballot of the NCOs of his regiment.

With the gates now open, the rest of Brigadier Hope's men entered the Shah Najaf unopposed and with the position in British hands, General Sir Colin Campbell was using the mosque as his headquarters by nightfall.

Lucknow Garrison's diversion

After receiving the signal, on the evening of the 15th November, that the relief force would advance in the morning; General Outram and General Havelock finalised plans for a diversion to assist them with their advance.

On the morning of 16th November, the Generals with their staff took up a position in the upper storey of the Chattar Manzil, from where they could observe the advance of General Campbell and his men.

Three days earlier, two mines had been laid to the garden wall of the Chattar Manzil, which formed the eastern most boundary of the Residency defences and behind this wall, two substantial gun emplacements were erected. At 11 o'clock, when the relief force was observed to be attacking the Secundra Bagh, the mines were exploded but failed to destroy the wall as intended. Not deterred, the British batteries opened up at point blank range and soon reduced the wall to rubble leaving them with a clear field of fire on the nearby enemy positions at the Hiram Khana (Deer House) and the Steam Engine House. Almost as soon as the wall was destroyed, the breach became the target of intense enemy musket fire from the nearby buildings and cannon fire from the Kaiser Bagh.

The batteries of Major Eyre and Captain Olpherts, aided by 6 mortars set up in the Palace courtyard, commanded by Captain Maude, were soon laying down a heavy return fire against the buildings as well as the battery at the Kaiser Bagh.

At 3:15 in the afternoon, two British mines to the Hirum Khana were exploded with good effect and troops which had been assembled in the Palace courtyard rapidly advanced on this building and the Steam Engine House, taking both positions after a short fight. Despite several attacks by the mutineers, these new positions were held throughout the night and heavy guns were brought forward to be directed against the Kaiser Bagh which was now within breaching distance.

The Mess House and the Moti Mahal were now the only enemy positions between the advanced force of the Lucknow Garrison and the Relief Force, however, the Kaiser Bagh could still direct dangerous flanking fire against any force attempting to reach the Residency.

Capture of the Mess House and Moti Mahal

Early in the morning of 17th November, General Campbell direct the Naval Brigade and Mortar Batteries to begin a bombardment of the Kursheed Manzil (Mess House) which was a strongly fortified building, surrounded by a 12 foot earth and masonry embankment, located about mid way between the Kaiser Bagh and the Shah Najaf mosque.

Figure 66. The Mess House

General Campbell was eager for his artillery to do much of the work, before risking his infantry.

At first light Lieutenant McBean, Sergeant Hutchinson and a 12 year old drummer boy named Ross, climbed onto the roof of the Shah Najaf and raised the regimental colours of the 93rd to signal their position to the Residency; this was answered by a colour raised on the Chatter Manzil palace.

Although somewhat protected by the forces in the barracks and surrounding buildings, General Campbell felt that his left flank was still threatened by an enemy attack from the direction of the hospital. To eliminate this threat, the General sent Brigadier Russell with detachments from the 23rd, 82nd and 93rd regiments to secure Banks's House and four bungalows near to the point where the road to Dilkusha House crossed the canal. The bungalows with their enclosure were eventually captured and occupied, after some difficulty, and Lieutenant Keen with a detachment of the 2nd Punjab Infantry managed to clear and occupy Banks's House.

After three hours of continuous bombardment, the rebel musket fire at the Mess House began to diminish and General Campbell now considered that it was safe to storm the position without too much risk to his troops. The storming party consisted of: Captain Wolseley with a company of men from the 90th Foot; Captain Hopkins with men from the 53rd Foot; Major Barnston's battalion of detachments under Captain Guise and some men of the Punjab Infantry under Lieutenant Powlett. Captain Hopkins with the 53rd led the way, gaining entry via a drawbridge over the embankment and ditch, which the rebels had fortunately left in the lowered position. The Mess House was quickly cleared and occupied by the storming party and in accordance with General Campbell's wishes, Lieutenant Roberts assisted by Sir David Baird and Captain Hopkins, raised a regimental colour on one of the turrets to once again signal their position to the Residency. The flag was twice shot down by enemy fire, however, after the third time it was raised, it remained in position.

Captain Hopkins was given command of the Mess-House until he was relieved by Captain Rolleston of the 84th, on the next day.

Sergeant Major Charles Pye – Victoria Cross No. 228

During the battle for the Mess House, Sergeant-Major Pye showed great courage in bringing forward ammunition for his comrades in the face of heavy enemy fire.

For this action Sergeant-Major Pye was later awarded the Victoria Cross, having been nominated for the award by a ballot of the NCOs of his regiment.

Figure 67. The Moti Mahal

Private Patrick Graham – Victoria Cross No. 229

During the fighting at the Mess-House, Private Graham brought in a wounded comrade in the face of heavy enemy fire.

For this action Private Graham was later awarded the Victoria Cross, having been nominated for the award by a ballot of the Privates of his regiment.

With the Mess-House now in British hands, the Moti Mahal remained the last significant place of refuge for the mutineers trying to stop the garrison and relief forces joining up.

The Tara Kothi (observatory) had been stormed and occupied at the same time that the Mess-House was taken by Captain Irby and his men.

The troops in the Mess-House were now lining the wall facing the Moti Mahal, waiting to be unleashed on the enemy. Captain Wolseley ordered sappers to blow holes in the walls and the troops were soon storming the buildings of the Moti Mahal. The rebels fought vigorously but were steadily driven back at bayonet point and room by room they were eventually expelled from the complex.

Garrison and relief force meet

With the Moti Mahal now taken, the garrison and relief force were separated by only a strip of open ground about 450 yards wide, however, this was exposed to musket and cannon fire from the Kaiser Bagh as well as cannon fire from the Badshah Bagh on the other side of the river.

Despite the heavy fire, Generals Outram and Havelock were eager to join up with General Campbell, so with some of their staff; Colonels Napier, Eyre and Hodgson and Lieutenants Sitwell and Havelock; they made a dash to the Moti Mahal. Colonel Napier and the two Lieutenants were wounded and did not complete the journey, but the rest managed to get to the relative safety of the Moti Mahal buildings; while proceeding through the buildings to the Mess House they had a narrow escape when an enemy shell burst nearby blowing General Havelock off his feet. The meeting between the three Generals took place in the Mess-House and was initially joyous.

With the first part of the relief having been successful, friendships were renewed and General Havelock was informed that like Outram and Campbell he was now also a knight of the realm having been appointed so on 26th September. The meeting was tempered by General Campbell reporting the losses of the relief force so far; 43 officers and 450 men killed or wounded. It was also agreed that even with their combined strength they had insufficient force to completely break the siege and must plan instead for an extraction of all of the Lucknow occupants. After the meeting, Generals Outram and Havelock, together with their staff and some officers from the relief force, returned to the Residency lines.

The biggest challenge still lay ahead of them, to safely extract their forces, 600 women and children and about 1,000 sick and wounded and cover the six miles to the relative safety of Dilkusha House.

Evacuation of Lucknow

With the decision taken to evacuate the Residency, General Campbell set about implementing plans to allow this to be done safely. High on his priorities was to somehow nullify the impact of the disruptive enemy fire from the Kaiser Bagh and also to develop a second escape route over the Dilkusha Bridge.

Instrumental to the success of opening out the second escape route was Brigadier Russell's force which had capture Banks House and bungalows to the left of the British line. This force had been under constant attack from the mutineers and through the night of 17th November and into the 18th November had been heavily bombarded by an enemy 18 pounder gun. Before Brigadier Russell could advance on the hospital, which was his next objective, it was essential that this gun was silenced, but to do this he required artillery.

Colonel Biddulph and Major Bourchier carried out a reconnaissance of the roads leading to the barracks and canal to find a route suitable for bringing heavy guns down to aid Brigadier Russell.

Having found a suitable route, Colonel Biddulph and Major Bourchier returned to the bungalows with a 9 pounder gun, 24 pounder howitzer and four 5½ inch mortars which were soon laying down a heavy fire on the enemy 18 pounder gun. Soon after the arrival of the artillery, Brigadier Russell was wounded and his command was handed over to Colonel Biddulph who, after the mutineers withdrew their 18 pounder, began preparations for an attack on the hospital. Before the attack could begin, Colonel Biddulph was killed by a shot to the head and Lieutenant-Colonel Hale assumed the command. At 4 o'clock in the afternoon, Colonel Hale led the attack against the hospital, supported by fire from the 24 pounder howitzer, however, having suffered heavy losses and after the rebels set fire to the roof of the hospital, the force retired to their previous positions.

Lieutenant Hastings Harington – Victoria Cross No. 206

During the withdrawal back to the bungalows, a man from the storming party who had been wounded and left in a garden tended by a drummer boy, was rescued by Lieutenant Harrington, accompanied by another officer and a gunner, who left the cover of the bungalows and under heavy fire brought him back to safety.

For this action, Lieutenant Harrington was later awarded the Victoria Cross, having been elected for the award by a ballot of the officers of his regiment.

Thinking that the attack on the hospital must have weakened the British position at the centre of their line, the mutineers mounted a fierce attack against the barracks and the Secundra Bagh. This was immediately countered by General Campbell, who personally led a force comprising; Captain Remmington's troop of Horse Artillery, a company of men from the 23rd and a company of men from the 53rd; against the attack which was repulsed.

Lieutenant Thomas Hackett – Victoria Cross No. 230
Private George Monger – Victoria Cross No. 231

During the attack, Lieutenant Hackett and Private Monger went to the aid of a young Corporal who was dangerously wounded and lying in a position exposed to heavy enemy fire.

The pair brought the Corporal back to safety and secured the urgent medical attention which saved his life.

For this action both men were later awarded the Victoria Cross.

Later in the day, Lieutenant Hackett climbed onto the roof of a burning bungalow under heavy enemy fire and tore away the thatch to prevent the fire spreading.

On the evening of 18th November, having failed to capture the hospital, General Campbell was forced to abandon plans to use his preferred route of escape along the wide metalled road just to the east of the barracks and the hospital. The General now began to look for a route from the Secundra Bagh, further to the east of his preferred route, however, as the start of this route from the Chattar Manzil to the Moti Mahal would leave the column exposed to fire from the Kaiser Bagh he arranged for a earth embankment to be constructed along the road side from the Steam-Engine House to Mr Martin's House to provide some protection.

After reconnoitring the new route on the morning of the 19th November and finding it to be viable, General Campbell sent a message to General Outram informing him that arrangements had now been completed for the evacuation of the women, children, sick and wounded and that transport would be sent for them.

A 24 pounder gun from the Naval Brigade, under the command of midshipman Lord Arthur Clinton, was placed on the road midway between the Moti Mahal and the Secundra Bagh to provide additional covering fire.

At noon, the evacuees were packed into horse drawn carriages and native oxen carts and began their journey to freedom after a five month siege. Leaving by the Bailey Guard Gate, the column made their way through the Farhat Bukhsh and Chattar Manzil palaces until they came to the road by the Hiram Khana, from here until they reached the Moti Mahal the column was under intense fire from the Kaiser Bagh. Leaving the Moti Mahal, the column gained the road to the Secundra Bagh; on this part of their journey they were under fire from rebel batteries on the other side of the river. After a hazardous journey of about an hour, the column reached the Secundra Bagh where they were allowed to rest until nightfall. At about 11 o'clock in the evening, the column now set out for Dilkusha House which they had reached by 2 o'clock in the morning.

General Havelock, who had been sick for some time and whose condition had worsened since his exertions to meet up with General Campbell, was one of the sick who were evacuated.

On the early morning of 20th November, the heavy guns from Captain Peel's Naval Brigade were established in a battery near Mr Martin's house and began an intense bombardment of the Kaiser Bagh. The battery kept up their bombardment of the Kaiser Bagh, with ever increasing intensity, for the next three days until on the evening of the 22nd November the palace defences were breached in three places. With their defences breached, the mutineers expected an imminent attack on the Kaiser Bagh, however, this was not the British plan as they now intended to withdraw the Residency garrison under the cover of darkness.

After receiving a message from General Campbell, to coordinate the timing, General Outram slowly began to withdraw his garrison from the Residency at midnight. Graciously, General Outram allowed Colonel Inglis, who had commanded the garrison during the first defence of Lucknow, to be the last man to leave the Residency by the Bailey Guard Gate; which he ceremoniously closed behind him. Leaving via the Bailey Guard Gate, General Outram's men made their way past the clock tower, through the Tehri Kotee and the palaces all the way back to the Secundra Bagh, collecting up their men on the way. Brigadier Hope's men, with 15 artillery pieces were stationed at the Secundra Bagh ready to defend the withdrawal, should they have been pursued by the rebels, however, this was not necessary.

The ploy of the decoy assault on the Kaiser Bagh had proved so successful that the mutineers continued to bombard the Residency for nearly four hours after it had been evacuated.

Rough Rider Edward Jennings – Victoria Cross No. 207
Gunner Thomas Laughnan – Victoria Cross No. 208
Gunner Hugh McInnes – Victoria Cross No. 209
Gunner James Park – Victoria Cross No. 210

The above men were all noted for their conspicuous bravery throughout the nine days of General Campbell's relief of Lucknow and were subsequently awarded the Victoria Cross.

They were all elected for the award after a ballot of the men of their regiments.

Shortly before dawn on the 23rd November, the withdrawal was complete and all the British forces were now gathered at the Dilkusha House or Martinière, according to their assignments. On the 24th November, under a heavy escort, the women, children, sick and wounded were transported to the Alum Bagh. On the morning of the 24th November, with his son by his side, General Havelock finally succumbed to the dysentery from which he had suffered for some time and his body was transferred to the Alum Bagh, where on 25th November, under the shade of a mango tree in the enclosure, he was laid to rest. General Outram carved a cross on the tree as a temporary marker as, not wishing his body to be disturbed by the mutineers his grave had been otherwise left unmarked.

Return to Cawnpore

Having successfully relieved Lucknow, General Sir Colin Campbell now had three urgent objectives, two of which involved a return to Cawnpore.

The return to Cawnpore was needed to get the evacuated women, children, sick and wounded to a place of safety where their ailments could be cared for.

It was also urgent to get back to support General Windham, who had been left at Cawnpore with a small force of just 500 men to defend the city against a possible attack from the Gwalior Contingent of mutineers commanded by Tantia Topi with a force of 25,000 men.

The third objective was to leave a strong garrison force at the Alum Bagh, to maintain a British presence in the province of Oudh and also to provide a stronghold from which an attack to recapture Lucknow, at some time in the future, could be launched. To satisfy this objective, General Campbell left General Outram with a force of 4,000 men and 25 guns and howitzers and ten mortars to garrison the Alum Bagh. A force of 500 European troops was also sent to reinforce the detachment of Madras Fusiliers at the Bunnee Bridge to maintain communications between the Alum Bagh and Cawnpore.

10

THE SECOND CAWNPORE CAMPAIGN

When General Campbell left Cawnpore to go to the relief of Lucknow, he left General Windham in charge of a garrison of 500 men made up of convalescent artillerymen, some sailors and four companies from the 64th Regiment of Foot.

General Windham was left with clear instructions; to hold the bridge at all cost, to keep an eye on the movements of the Gwalior Contingent but not to advance against them and to send forward reinforcements as soon as they arrived at Cawnpore.

To guard the bridge across the Ganges, General Windham erected defensive earthworks; these provided some protection, however, fell far short of providing an easily defensible position.

Reinforcements were dutifully sent forward, as instructed, however, when it became clear that the Gwalior Contingent, now strengthened by Nana Sahib and his men, were closing in on his position General Windham began to hold back the reinforcements to bolster his own force.

This was done after receiving the approval of General Campbell, which was received on 14th November; with men from the Madras Brigade and detachments from the 34th, 82nd and 88th Regiments of Foot and men from the Rifle Brigade General Windham's force now numbered 1,700 men.

On 17th November, after having left 300 men to guard the Ganges River crossing, General Windham moved the rest of his force to the junction of the Delhi Kalpi roads, ready to attack Tantia Tope's force if they chose to advance.

Second siege of Cawnpore

By 19th November, General Windham had received intelligence that the mutineers were distributed in a rough semicircle to the north and west of the city; the advanced units were at a distance of about 15 miles while the main body of the force was 25 miles out.

On 23rd November, after hearing news that the rebels had taken the bridge at Bunnee and were threatening the rear of General Campbell's force, General Windham sent the 27th Madras Native Infantry to retake the bridge.

On 26th November, rather than wait to be attacked, but against his expressed orders, General Windham decided to take the fight to Tantia Topi and launched an attack.

The attack, at the Pandoo Nadi, against the forward columns of 2,500 men supported by 500 cavalry and artillery, met with some success and two guns were captured, however, as the main columns pressed forward, General Windham was forced to retire with his men to the outskirts of the city.

The force of the mutineers was such that the British continued to fall back and soon became besieged, once again, within the enclosure in Cawnpore.

The mutineers soon occupied the city and found a great bounty, General Windham had failed to move the stores and baggage left behind by General Campbell and this together with large amounts of ammunition, paymaster's chests and regimental mess silver was seized by the rebels.

Although surrounded by the enemy and being hard pressed by the mutineers, General Windham still attempted to take the fight to the rebels. He sent out a force of 100 men of the 64th with some sailors, to retrieve a gun which had overturned and been abandoned in the city during the rush to the enclosure.

Drummer Thomas Flynn – Victoria Cross No. 234

In a similar vein, on the morning of 28th November, General Wilson with two companies of the 64th was sent on an audacious raid to capture a battery of enemy guns.

During the action General Wilson was killed, together with Major Stirling and Lieutenant McCrae who were both cut down while spiking one of the enemy guns.

Also during this action, despite himself being wounded, Drummer Flynn engaged in hand to hand fighting with two of the enemy gunners. For his part in the action Drummer Flynn was later awarded the Victoria Cross at the age of 15 years and three months one of the two youngest recipients.[20]

---

20 The other being Andrew Fitzgibbon, also aged 15 years and three months.

General Sir Colin Campbell arrives at Cawnpore

After leaving the Alum Bagh on 27th November, General Campbell rested for the night at the Bunnee Bridge where the distant sound of cannon fire could be clearly heard.

Fearing a threat to the bridge over the Ganges, General Campbell set off early the next morning with his cavalry and horse artillery, leaving the infantry to continue to escort the women and children and the sick and wounded.

By noon, messengers arrived from General Windham with news that he was being pressed by the mutineers and urgently required assistance. On reaching Mangalwar, General Campbell ordered General Hope Grant to establish camp and then set off with some of his staff for the banks of the Ganges, four miles further ahead.

On reaching the banks of the Ganges, the General was relieved to see that the bridge of boats was still intact and guarded by British units; seeing the British forces beleaguered in the Cawnpore entrenchment he continued across the bridge and gained entry to the British position.

After a brief meeting with General Windham, during which he outlined his plans for a relief the next day, General Campbell returned to Mangalwar.

During the night the convoy of evacuees continued to arrive at the camp at Mangalwar but it was not until dawn that the heavy guns of the Naval Brigade, commanded by Captain Peel, arrived at the camp.

Almost as soon as they arrived, the Naval Brigade heavy guns began a bombardment of the rebel artillery and infantry positions and the battery which had finally been brought to bear on the bridge was soon silenced. At 9 o'clock in the morning, after artillery fire had driven back the advanced rebel batteries, Colonel Campbell with his cavalry, horse artillery and Brigadier Hope's brigade crossed the Ganges while Brigadier Adrian Hope's men were left behind to guard the convoy. At 3 o'clock in the afternoon of the 29th November, the convoy began to cross the bridge and this continued unabated until 6 o'clock in the evening of the 30th November; the rebels tried, unsuccessfully, to disrupt their progress by sending fire-rafts down the river.

For the next three days, preparations were made to transport the convoy of the women, children, sick and wounded to Allahabad; the convoy left on their journey to safety on the evening of 3rd December 1857.

Before beginning his attack on the mutineers at Cawnpore, General Campbell wanted to wait a few days to be sure that the column of evacuees were well clear of the area before hostilities renewed in earnest.

General Campbell now had a force of about 5,000 men and 600 sailors, supported by 35 guns at his disposal to face the mutineers who were thought to number about 25,000 men, supported by 40 guns.

Nana Sahib, with a large force of rebels occupied the right flank, to the north between the city and the River Ganges. Tantia Topi and his men of the Gwalior Contingent occupied the enemy centre and left flank with men occupying the city and to the south down to the canal.

During the early days of December, the action was limited to minor skirmishes and an artillery duel between the opposing forces.

This changed on the afternoon of the 5th December, when following an intense artillery bombardment; the mutineers followed up with a concerted infantry attack against the British left flank in an attempt to turn them, however, in the face of equally intense British artillery fire, the attack came to nothing.

Second Battle of Cawnpore

With the women, children, sick and wounded now well on their way to safety and about to complete their journey by rail; General Campbell was ready to do battle.

The enemy right flank between the city and the river was on easily defended ground which was covered by trees, ruined bungalows and public buildings; and as such was a strong position.

Likewise the rebel centre, which was in the city with the buildings and narrow winding streets, was also a strong position.

The enemy left flank, however, situated as it was on the open plain and only protected to the front by the canal, was a relatively weak position so was chosen by General Campbell to be the focus of his attack.

On the evening of the 5th December, General Campbell outlined his plans for the attack and discussed the troop deployments with his senior officers.

Brigadier Greathed's Brigade; the 8th Regiment of Foot and the 2nd Punjab Infantry; were detailed to hold the ground to the front of the rebel centre, a position that they had held since the 2nd of December.

Walpole's Brigade; the 2nd and 3rd battalions, Rifle Brigade, a detachment of the 38th Regiment of Foot and Captain Smith's battery of field artillery; were directed to cross the bridge immediately to the left of Brigadier Greathed's position and skirt the walls of the city to prevent reinforcements coming through the gates to aid their comrades.

General Hope Grant's Brigade; the 42nd, 53rd and 93rd Regiments of Foot and the 4th Punjab Infantry; together with Inglis's

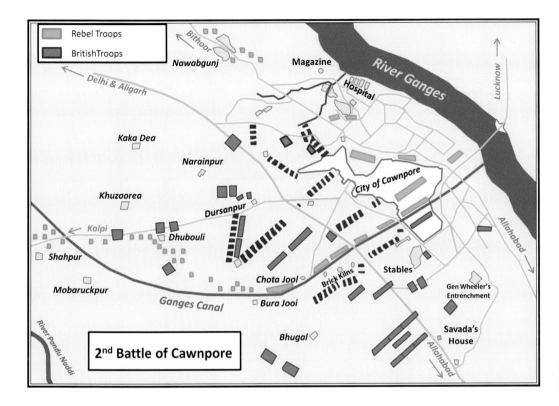

Figure 68. 2nd Battle of Cawnpore

Brigade; 23rd Fusiliers, 32nd and 82nd Regiments of Foot; would attack the rebels at the brick kilns and force the bridge over the canal at the Allahabad road crossing. They would then press on and assume a position across the Kalpi road to cut off the mutineers' main route of escape.

General Windham in the entrenchment was to direct a heavy bombardment against the enemy centre and right flank to disguise the intended direction of attack.

On the morning of 6th December at 9 o'clock, as planned, General Windham began the bombardment of the city and the rebel positions on the left next to the river; the British artillery caused heavy casualties to the mutineers massed in the narrow city streets.

At 11 o'clock, Brigadier Greathed's men began a steady fire against the rebel centre, from their positions in the General Gunge south of the canal. This signalled the advance of Walpole's brigade which, supported by heavy artillery fire, crossed the canal and blocked the city gates along the south west wall.

The brigades of General Hope Grant and Brigadier Inglis drove the rebels at the brick kilns back across the canal and towards their camp, which was soon captured together with all of their guns.

With the left wing of the mutineers now in full flight back along the road to Kalpi, General Hope Grant with the cavalry and horse artillery set off in pursuit.

General Campbell, as ever leading from the front, directed General Mansfield; with men from the 93rd Regiment of Foot and Rifle Brigade, supported by field artillery from Captain Longden and Captain Middleton's batteries; towards the north of the city against the retreating right wing. General Mansfield and his force hoped to intercept the retreating mutineers at Subadar's Tank, however, by the time that he reached the village the head of the rebel column had already passed and was heading up the road towards Bithoor. General Mansfield engaged the retreating rebels with his artillery but was unable to stop the rebels retiring with their guns. With his rear exposed to the city, which still contained large numbers of mutineers, General Mansfield chose not to pursue the retreating rebels choosing instead to camp for the night at Subadar's Tank.

On the morning of 7th December, when cavalry was sent to reconnoitre the city they found it to be deserted, the mutineers had melted away during the night; Cawnpore was back in British hands.

Pursuit of Nana Sahib

After the Gwalior Contingent retired towards Kalpi, it soon became widely dispersed so was thought not to be worth pursuing.

The forces of Nana Sahib, which had occupied the right and centre, and who were moving off together towards Bithoor, were thought to be worth chasing; General Campbell was reluctant to let such a large force of rebels retire unchallenged. At 1 o'clock in the afternoon of 8th December, a force under the command of General Hope Grant was sent off in pursuit of the rebel army. General Hope Grant's force of 2,800 men with 11 guns consisted of; 220 artillerymen, Captain Middleton's Field Battery and Captain Remmington's Horse Artillery; 2,000 men of the 4th Infantry Brigade, 42nd and 93rd Highlanders, 53rd Regiment of Foot and the 4th Punjab Rifles; 520 Cavalry, 9th Lancers, 5th Punjab Cavalry and Hodson's Horse with 100 sappers in support.

By evening, the force had reached a branch in the road about 13 miles from Cawnpore where they halted for the night. During the night a spy brought news that Nana Sahib had headed for the ferry crossing at Serai Ghat where he hoped to cross the Ganges into the province of Oudh. With this news, General Hope Grant changed his direction of march, headed for Serai Ghat and by nightfall was camped at the village of Sheorajpore, about three miles from the ferry crossing.

Battle of Serai Ghat

At first light on the morning of 10th December, the force advanced on the river crossing, however, as soon as they came within range they came under a heavy bombardment from 13 enemy guns. In the face of heavy fire, the advanced units of British Artillery managed to set up their batteries on the banks of the Ganges and began to put down return fire against the enemy artillery and the ferry being used to transport the enemy guns across the river. As more British artillery was deployed, the rebel guns were soon silenced and the enemy cavalry was sent against the British guns.

Brigadier Little led his force of cavalry into the charging rebels and drove them off; this prompted the remaining rebels to flee for their lives towards Bithoor having failed to escape into Oudh, leaving 14 guns which were captured.

Following this success, General Hope Grant returned with his men to Cawnpore.

11

THE DUAB CAMPAIGN

Having completed the relief of Lucknow and regained possession of Cawnpore, General Campbell was now free to carry out the plan which had been agreed in Calcutta; namely to secure the routes of communication between Delhi and the Punjab.

Although Allahabad and Agra were under British control, for complete control over the Duab it was necessary to gain possession of Futtehgur, which being situated at the junction of the Oudh and Rohilkhand provinces, was of strategic importance. To accomplish this task, General Campbell's plan was to utilise three columns; a column from Delhi under the command of Colonel Seaton would head south sweeping the rebels in the Duab valley before him; General Walpole would head north west and after joining up with Colonel Seaton the conjoined force would head toward Futtehgur; General Campbell would lead the third column and head directly for Futtehgur.

Colonel Seaton with a force of almost 2,000 men left Delhi on 6th December 1857 and headed south towards the district of Aligarh. His column consisted of; a squadron of Carabineers,

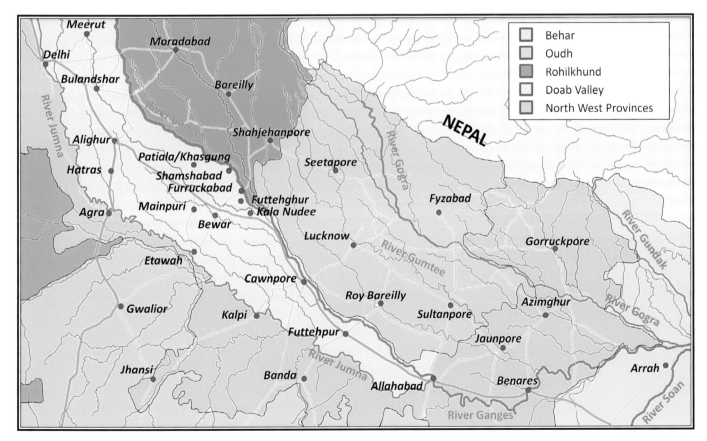

Figure 69. The Duab valley

Hodson's Irregular Horse, a wing of 1st Bengal Fusiliers, the 7th Punjab Infantry, a troop of Horse Artillery and two companies of Sappers and Miners, escorted a large convoy of grain and stores.

Battle of Khasgunge (Kasganj)

The column attacked and defeated a force of mutineers at the Battle of Khasgunge on 14th December, capturing three guns.

On 17th December, the force came across a large rebel force partially dug in before the town of Patiala on the Futtehgur road. After a half hour artillery duel, Colonel Seaton ordered his infantry to advance and at the head of his cavalry mounted a charge against the enemy position. The rebels did not wait to receive the charge but broke and fled and were pursued through their camp and the town. All their guns, ammunition and baggage were captured.

Colonel Seaton's force also fought an action against mutineers at Mynpoorie on 27th December and arrived at Bewar on 31st December where he waited to join up with General Walpole's force.

General Walpole left Cawnpore on 18th December 1857 with a force comprising; 2nd and 3rd Battalions, Rifle Brigade, a detachment of 30th Regiment of Foot, Captain Bourchier's Field Battery, Captain Blunt's troop of Horse Artillery and one company of Sappers.

This force, headed west towards Kalpi and then along the left bank of the River Jumna, sweeping the lower Duab and after encountering little opposition met up with Colonel Seaton's force at Bewar (on the road to Futtehgur, about 15 miles from Mynpoorie) on 3rd January 1858.

General Campbell's advance from Cawnpore was delayed due to the lack of transportation, the available wagons and carriages had been given to General Walpole's column, and the wagons and carriages used to transport the Lucknow evacuees had not yet returned. The wagons and carriages arrived back at Cawnpore on 23rd December and the next day General Campbell set out on the road to Futtehgur, clearing the country on his flanks as he advanced. On Christmas day, after his journey to Bithoor to burn Nana Sahib's palace, General Hope Grant and his force of cavalry and artillery rejoined General Campbell's force, leaving his infantry to search the nearby ferry crossings and destroy any boats that could be found.

General Windham with his brigade left the main force on 28th December to go out and destroy a nearby rebel fort, while General Campbell waited at Miran-ki-Serai for General Hope Grant's infantry brigade to catch up with the main column.

At 4 o'clock in the morning of 30th December, Major Hodson (of Hodson's Horse) together with Lieutenant McDowell arrived in the camp with despatches from Colonel Seaton. The pair had completed a memorable journey of 55 miles, through rebel strewn territory, in a matter of ten hours without having had the opportunity to change their mounts.

After a few hours rest, they started out on their return journey to Colonel Seaton at Bewar at 8 o'clock that same evening, on what proved to be another extraordinary venture.

On 1st December, General Windham returned to the main column with his brigade and early in the afternoon, General Hope Grant's infantry brigade; supplemented by a squadron of cavalry, four field guns and a company of engineers; set off to reconnoitre the bridge over the Kala Nuddee.

General Campbell's converging columns had been steadily driving the rebels in the Doab down towards Futtehgur and the suspension bridge across the Kala Nuddee which was a main access route into the town.

On reaching the bridge, General Hope Grant discovered that the rebels had removed the plank floor of the bridge and had caused some damage to the structure but the main suspension chains were still intact.

The engineers and some sailors, under the command of Major Nicholson, immediately set about making repairs to the bridge, working through the day and night, while a detachment of the 53rd Regiment of Foot established a position on the rebel side to guard the work.

On the morning of 2nd January 1858, General Campbell and his chief-of-staff rode down to inspect the work and rode across the bridge to test that it was ready for his column to advance and found that the bridge, although passable, still required some work to be completed.

Battle of Kala Nuddee (Khodagunge)

General Campbell had just returned across the bridge when a rebel force began to lay down artillery fire from the nearby village of Khodagunge and under heavy musket fire managed to bring down two more guns to intensify the fire.

The remainder of the 53rd Regiment together with some heavy guns managed to cross the bridge and establish a more secure bridgehead on the rebel side of the river and their fire began to suppress that of the enemy.

Before committing more men to the attack, General Campbell decided to wait for the arrival of the main column.

At 11 o'clock the column began to arrive with Greatham's brigade to the fore, the 8th and 64th Regiments of Foot immediately crossed the bridge to strengthen the bridge head together with Lieutenant Vaughan, and three guns from Peel's Naval Brigade, who set up a battery in the shelter of a yellow bungalow.

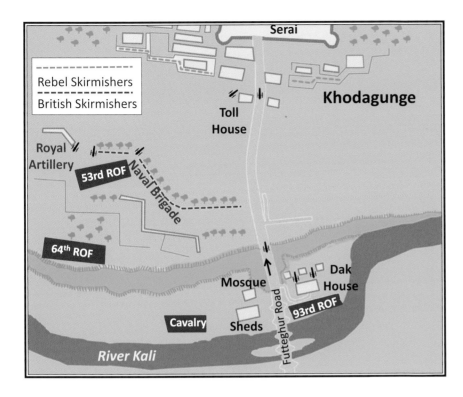

Figure 70. Battle of Kala Nuddee

At about 2 o'clock, the mutineers sent forward a heavy gun which was established in the shelter of the Toll House but this was soon silenced with the accurate fire by Lt Vaughan, using a 24 pounder brought up earlier by Captain Peel.

Generals Campbell and Hope Grant were both wounded but not seriously as they were struck by bullets that were nearly spent.

As the bridge was not yet fully repaired, it took some time for the main column to cross with their cavalry and artillery; the 93rd Highlanders were the last to cross, having been held back to have a meal before taking up their position at the head of the column, where they relieved the 53rd Regiment.

Not wishing to be deprived of a chance to get at the enemy, the 53rd, in response to an unordered bugle call, launched a fierce attack on the mutineers at the Toll House and drove them back into the village.

The whole of the force now began to advance on the village and the rebels began to retire along the road to Futtehgur rather than face this determined British attack.

General Hope Grant led the cavalry in pursuit of the mutineers for five miles along the road, the harassment causing them to abandon some of their wagons and guns.

Lieutenant Frederick Roberts – Victoria Cross No. 235

As the light was starting to fade, the order was given for the cavalry force to wheel about and re-form on the road in preparation for their return to the main column. Before the manoeuvre could be completed, a group of mutineers stopped and fired a volley into the cavalry, mortally wounding Lieutenant Younghusband.

Lieutenant Roberts could not go to his aid as his path was blocked by a native Sowar of his regiment being attacked by a rebel on foot armed with a rifle with bayonet fixed. Lieutenant Roberts went to the Sowar's aid killing the rebel with one stroke of his sword.

He then saw two mutineers making off with a standard and rode after them *"... while wrenching the staff out of the hands of one of them, whom I cut down, the other put his musket close to my body and fired : fortunately for me it missed fire, and I carried off the standard."*

For these two acts, Lieutenant Roberts was later awarded the Victoria Cross.

Now that night was approaching, General Hope Grant and his cavalry returned to the main column, proudly displaying their captured colours.

The next day, on the 3rd January 1858, General Campbell advanced with his troops into Futtehgur and found the place deserted; the rebels had fled in such haste that they had failed to destroy the bridge or the gun carriage factory in the nearby fort and instead made their escape across the River Ganges into the province of Rohilkhand.

On the 6th January, the column of Colonel Seaton and General Walpole's men finally joined up with General Campbell's main column, however, their services were not immediately needed as Sir Colin's objectives had already been achieved. Communications between Delhi had been restored and the Duab rebels had been chased across the River Ganges into Rohilkhand. For some days the rebels were pursued by a force commanded by General James Hope Grant.

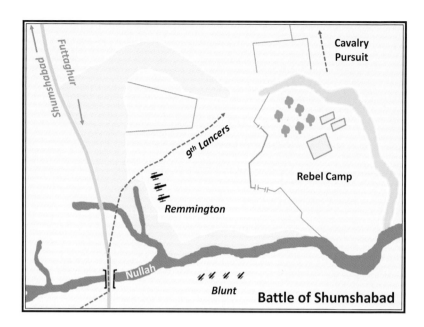

Figure 71. Battle of Shumshabad

Battle of Shumshabad

On the 17th January, after marching all night, at about 8 o'clock in the morning, the column confronted a rebel force of about 10,000, encamped in the village of Suita about half a mile from Shumshabad.

Sergeant Major David Spence – Victoria Cross No. 237

During the battle, Sergeant-Major Spence became separated from his men after a charge and when he heard a cry for help discovered one of his men, Private Kidd, lying wounded and pinned down by his wounded horse.

Despite the private being surrounded by a group of rebels, Sergeant-Major Spence did not hesitate but lowered the point of his lance and galloped into the bunch of mutineers. Alone and outnumbered the Sergeant-Major cut his way to the wounded soldier and extricated him from beneath his horse and carried him to safety.

For this act, Sergeant-Major Spence was later awarded the Victoria Cross.

✠

After the battle, General Hope Grant and his force moved off to Lucknow, where General Campbell was assembling his troops for the final assault to recapture the city.

12

WHAT NEXT, ROHILKHAND OR OUDH?

With three months of ideal cold campaigning weather still remaining, General Campbell was in favour of continuing the pursuit of the rebels into Rohilkhand and subduing that province. This would greatly assist in bringing the whole of the North West provinces back under British control. He thought that the subjugation of Oudh could wait until the start of the next cold weather season, as he did not wish to expose his mainly European troops to the rigours of a hot season campaign and the autumn monsoon.

Lord Canning and the governing Council of India in Calcutta, however, had other views which pointed them to the recapture of Lucknow and the conquest of Oudh as being of the higher priority.

Lucknow and Oudh were of greater political and strategic importance than Rohilkhand without any doubt, however, a deciding factor was that Jang Bahádur, the Prime Minister of Nepal, had offered to lead a force of 10,000 men to help the British subdue Oudh but if this was to be accepted then it must be done soon.

Another consideration was the situation of General Outram, who with a force of 4,000 men was still manfully holding the Alum Bagh despite being strongly pressed by the rebels whose number were increasing by thousands as each day passed.

In the face of these arguments and in line with the wishes of Lord Canning, General Campbell agreed that his next objective was the relief of Lucknow and the suppression of the rebels in the province of Oudh and began to make his plans accordingly.

13

THE OUDH CAMPAIGN

The forces that General Campbell hoped to have at his disposal for the campaign in Oudh were: the forces that he currently had under his command in the Doab; newly arrived troops that were still due to arrive from Calcutta; the siege train and attendant troops from Agra; a detachment from the Punjab promised by General Sir John Lawrence; General Outram's force at the Alum Bagh; a division commanded by General Franks which was currently holding the eastern frontier of Oudh and the Nepalese army commanded by Jung Bahádur which was approaching from the east.

The Nepalese contingent

At the start of the mutiny, Jung Bahádur the prime minister of Nepal offered to place the total military resources of his country at the disposal of the British Government to suppress the disorder taking place near his borders. After some hesitation, Lord Channing accepted a contingent of 3,000 Ghurkhas who in June 1857 left Kathmandu and entered the Goruckpore district in the province of Oudh. By the end of the month, this force had occupied the civil station of Goruckpore, ending the rule of the local

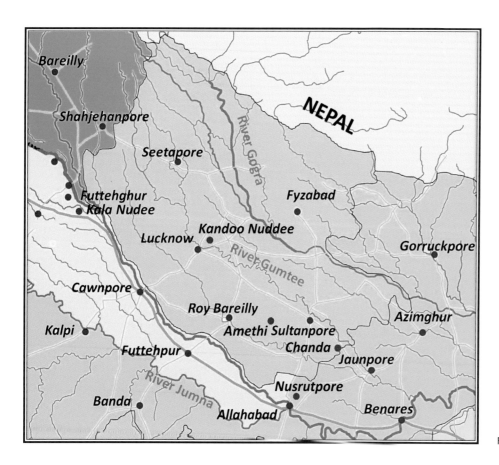

Figure 72. The Province of Oudh

Figure 73. Jung Bahádur

chief appointed by the King of Oudh. The Nepal force moved on to Azamgarh, which they reached on 13th July and then on to the British garrison town of Juanpore where they arrived on the 17th July.

At Juanpore, some British officers were assigned to the Nepalese force and helped train them in the European methods of drill.

When Colonel Wroughton, who commanded the station at Juanpore, received news that Azamgarh was under threat from a large force of mutineers he despatched a regiment of Nepalese under their commander Colonel Shumshere Sing to provide assistance. After a march of 36 hours, having covered 50 miles, the force arrived at Azamgarh on the evening of 19th September.

On the next morning it was confirmed that the rebels were congregating at the nearby village of Mundoree and Captain Boileau was placed in command of a force which consisted of the Ghurkha regiment and some irregular horse raised by Mr Venables a local Indigo planter. As the force approached the village they came under a heavy rebel bombardment, however, the Ghurkhas mounted a charge and soon dispersed the mutineers and captured 3 of their guns.

Having received news that a large rebel force was being assembled at Chanda, probably with the intention of mounting an attack against Juanpore, Colonel Wroughton once again despatched the Ghurkhas to deal with the matter. On 31st October, after having marched 15 miles the 1,100 Ghurkhas found, 5,000 mutineers dug into strong defensive positions supported by five artillery pieces. Again the Ghurkhas distinguished themselves with a frontal attack, which after some fierce fighting dislodged the enemy from their positions with the loss of most of their guns and ammunition.

On 2nd November, Colonel Longdon with a force comprising; 320 men of the 10th Regiment of Foot, a detachment of European Artillery with two field guns and 170 men of the Madras Native Infantry; arrived at Juanpore from Benares.

Two days after their arrival Colonel Longdon's force together with the Ghurkha regiment were deployed to push back a rebel force that had crossed the border into the Oudh province.

To help prevent future incursions, the force at Juanpore was reinforced to brigade strength and placed under the command of Brigadier-General Franks.

On the 21st December, the main Nepalese force of 14 regiments with four batteries of artillery, a total of 10,000 men, reached the Oudh border where it was met by Brigadier-General G. H. Macgregor who had been appointed as Military Commissioner to the force commanded by Jung Bahádur.

The General was supported by a small staff of British officers; Lieutenant J. F. MacHowden with the role of Military Secretary and Aide-de-Camp to the General, Major G. F. C. Fitzgerald, Captain A. C. Plowden, Captain F. N. Edmonstone, Lieutenant F. R. Foote, Lieutenant A. Cory and Lieutenant G. E. Hill.

A joint force of 1,100 British and Nepalese troops was formed in western Behar on 25th December, under the command of Colonel Rowcraft, with 500 Ghurkhas from Jung Bahádur force it also included 130 men of the Naval Brigade from *HMS Pearl*. On 26th December, this small force engaged 5,000 mutineers with a large artillery train at Sohanpore. After turning the rebels left flank, Colonel Rowcrafts men drove the enemy from the village and chased them for 6 miles until they were driven back across the River Gandak.

On 13th January, Jung Bahádur's main force was in action for the first time when they came across a large rebel force in the jungle near Goruckpore, after a short artillery duel, the Ghurkhas launched a charge against the mutineers who fled and were pursued into the jungle for about two miles. Many of the enemy were driven into the River Gogra with estimated losses of between 300 to 400 men.

Jung Bahádur's force proceeded to the Burkai Ghat on the River Gogra where on 19th February they were joined by Colonel Rowcraft's force.

While Jung Bahádur's force would now cross the river into the province of Oudh and march towards Lucknow, it was agreed that Colonel Rowcraft and his force would remain at Goruckpore to secure the district and to protect Jung Bahádur's lines of communication.

Battle of Kandoo Nuddee

On 25th February 1858, Jung Bahádur's force attacked and captured the fort at Ambarpore; General Franks column having cleared the way. This was the only significant interaction with the rebels until the Battle of Kandoo Nuddee on 5th March.

Unusual in battles with the mutineers, at this battle the forces were almost numerically identical with about 4,000 men on each side. The Nepalese army however inflicted a severe defeat upon the enemy as demonstrated by their respective losses. The Nepal army lost 1 killed and 16 wounded, however, enemy losses were estimated at 600 killed.

After the battle, the Nepal Contingent continued their march and arrived at Lucknow on 11th March, a week after the arrival of General Franks force.

General Franks's Field Force

The force at Juanpore, which had been increased to brigade strength and placed under the command of Brigadier-General Franks now numbered just over 5,700 men, with a large contingent of Nepalese troops commanded by General Pulivan Sing.

The brigade was composed of: Artillery 370 men made up from two companies of Royal Artillery, a company from the Madras Artillery, a company from the Bengal Artillery and a detachment of artillery from the Nepal army; Infantry of 5,300 men made up of, 2,108 men from the 10th, 20th and 97th Regiments of foot and six battalions numbering 3,193 men from the Nepal army.

The main limitation of General Franks's force was the lack of cavalry, which initially was only 38 mounted policemen of the Benares Horse, commanded by Captain Matheson. In an attempt to bolster this force 25 men from the 10th Regiment of Foot were mounted and placed under the command of Lieutenant Tucker of the Bengal artillery.

Battle of Nusrutpore

The force left Juanpore in early January 1858 and on 23rd January, the left wing under the command of Colonel Ingram was involved in the Battle of Nusrutpore.

With just over 1,400 men, a mix of men from the 97th Regiment and twice as many Ghurkhas from the Nepal army, supported by six field guns, Colonel Ingram's force faced 8,000 mutineers led by Nazim Fuzil Azeem.

This first battle of the field force was a comprehensive victory for Colonel Ingram whose force only suffered 6 wounded while the rebel casualties were estimated at 500 killed or wounded.

The main forces opposing General Franks consisted of 10,000 men under the command of rebel leader Mehndee Hussan and another 8,000 men under the command of Bunda Hussan, one of Mehndee Hussan's sub-Lieutenants.

Battle of Chanda

On the morning of 19th February 1858, General Franks force came upon Bunda Hussan's force at Chanda where they occupied a mud fort and a large serai, both of which were heavily defended with supporting artillery.

Without hesitation, Franks's men charged and soon carried the positions and captured six guns. The rebels were pursued through the village and beyond and only halted as night began to fall, when at sunset they began to make camp.

No sooner had they started preparations for their overnight halt, than Mehndee Hussan's force appeared on their right front; the British force immediately formed up, faced the enemy, charged and quickly dispersed the mutineers. After the mutineers had been put to flight, they were not pursued due to the growing darkness and the troops completed their preparations for their overnight bivouac.

On the following morning General Franks decided to remain at Chanda for the day, to give his men a rest and to allow the baggage train to catch up.

While resting at Chanda, General Franks received news that the rebels were intending to block his passage by occupying Fort Budhayon, nine miles to his front, which guarded a deep and difficult ravine. Not to be outdone, on the morning of 21st February, General Franks assembled his force in battle order, as if he was going to make an attack to his front, however, his baggage train moved off to his right rear towards a village half way to the fort. The escort for the baggage was in fact General Franks advance guard, which once out of sight overtook the baggage train and seized the fort before it could be occupied by the mutineers.

Having failed to take the fort, the rebel leader Mirza Gaffoor Bey and his men headed for Sultanpore instead, where again he hoped to forestall the British progress.

With a force said to be 25,000, made up of 5,000 Sepoys, 1,100 cavalry and 25 guns, the former General of Artillery to the king of Oudh occupied a formidable position at the town; positioned behind a deep and winding ravine which ran down to the river Gumti his line ran for a mile and a half along a plain with his left at the Sultanpur bazaar and his right covered by low hills at the village of Badshahgunge.

At the point where the main road to Lucknow crosses the ravine the mutineers placed their main batteries.

Battle of Sultanpore

At 6 o'clock, on the morning of 23rd February, General Franks force broke camp and headed down the main road towards Lucknow, three hours later his cavalry scouts spotted enemy piquets near a village on the road.

General Franks immediately formed up his force into battle order and advanced down the road and through the village, clearing the enemy piquets as he proceeded.

After advancing with his small mounted detachment to the ravine, taking advantage of a thick belt of trees which concealed his movements, he went down into the ravine and reconnoitred to his left, where as he suspected the ravine came out onto the plain. Using this route, the General was able to navigate the ravine with his men and guns, out of sight and range of the enemy forces. When he emerged from the ravine, near where it is crossed by the Allahabad road he was still concealed from his enemy by mango groves.

General Franks was able to deploy his troops to attack the mutineers left flank and it was not until he emerged from the trees that the rebels were able to deploy their artillery but due to the range their shot fell short.

Lieutenant James Innes – Victoria Cross No. 239

Skirmishers, with light artillery, were deployed to close on the enemy positions; Lieutenant Innes riding well in advance of the skirmishers, was first to capture a gun which the rebels were abandoning.

Moving on from this gun Lieutenant Innes advanced alone against another gun which had been brought to bear on the advancing British force, just before the gun was fired he shot the gunner who had lit his match and was about to fire the piece.

Lieutenant Innes remained in position, despite heavy musket fire from mutineers in nearby huts, and kept the artillerymen at bay until help arrived.

For this action, Lieutenant Innes was later awarded the Victoria Cross.

With the gun having been captured, the British forces gradually circled the rebels and drove them from their positions and into the ravine. The advance was stopped by the five guns that the enemy had placed on the Lucknow road. It was not until General Franks, leading some men from the 10th Regiment of Foot, captured these guns, after a desperate fight with their gunners, that the battle was finally over; with the mutineers fleeing in all directions.

General Franks was unable to pursue the rebels due to the lack of a suitable cavalry force, however, 21 guns (9 of large calibre) and large amounts of ammunition were captured.

After the battle, the force set up camp to rest for the night and during the evening their small cavalry unit was reinforced by the arrival of the Lahore Light Horse and the Pathan Horse under the command of Captain Balmain.

On the next morning the 3rd Sikh Jalandhar Cavalry, commanded by Lieutenant Aikman also arrived at the camp, having ridden 25 miles that day.

On 25th February, the force resumed its march.

Battle of Amethi

Lieutenant Frederick Aikman – Victoria Cross No. 240

On the morning of 1st March, just as the force was about to break camp, Lieutenant Aikman who was in command of the advanced piquets received news that a body of mutineers was camped three miles away on the banks of the River Gumti, near the village of Amethi.

The rebel force was thought to be 500 infantry and 200 cavalry supported by two artillery pieces. Although his force only amounted to 100 men, Lieutenant Aikman, after sending a rider to General Franks requesting cavalry and artillery reinforcements, decided to press ahead with an attack.

On coming across the rebel force, Lieutenant Aikman led his men in a charge and was soon engaged in desperate hand to hand combat during which the Lieutenant received a severe sword cut to the face.

Lieutenant Aikman and his gallant troopers managed to drive the mutineers back across the river and captured their two guns.

For his part in the action Lieutenant Aikman was later awarded the Victoria Cross.

General Franks continued his advance and by 4th March was only eight miles from Lucknow, however, just off his route was the Fort of Dhowara which was occupied by a large force of mutineers. Not wanting to leave such a significant threat to his rear and baggage train, as he continued his advance, General Franks decided that the fort must be taken and while his main force continued their advance he led a small force against the fort.

This force consisted of Lieutenant Arbuthnot, commanding two Horse Artillery guns and cavalry from the 9th Lancers and Sikh/Pathan Horse commanded by Captain Coles.

On reaching the fort, General Franks's men were immediately under fire from two guns in the fort, this was soon answered by the horse artillery guns but despite being brought forward to close range they were ineffective because of their light calibre.

General Franks sent word back to the main column and ordered up companies of marksmen from the regiments commanded by Lieutenant-Colonel Longden and two 24 pounder howitzers from the Madras battery under Major Cotter. The howitzers soon did their job and cleared the outer enclosure of the fort and the defenders retired to the inner keep; this was stormed by men from the 20th and 97th regiments, led by Captain Middleton and Ensign Elton, who drove the rebels out and captured their guns.

Some of the rebels fled to a strongly defended house which despite several attempts could not be breached, when Lieutenant Innes, the only engineering officer present was severely wounded, General Franks decided to withdraw and return to the main column where he was urgently needed.

In the evening, after a march of 130 miles in 13 days, General Franks force reached General Campbell's camp on the outskirts of Lucknow.

Kemaon Defence Force

The Kemaon Field Force was charged with guarding the border with Nepal in the province of Uttakakhand. The bulk of the force was composed of the Nasiri battalion of the 66th (Goorkha) Bengal Native Infantry Regiment based at Almorah, with detachments at Nainital and Bhim Tal in the foothills near Bareilly.

The force was placed under the command of Lieutenant-Colonel John Kennedy McCausland who, due to the small size of his force, restricted his operations to the area around Haldwani and the Kemaon Hills.

Two large bodies of rebel troops threatened the region; one under the leadership of Fuzul Huq consisted of 4,000 men and was based at Sunda on the Sookee River, the other under Khali Khan consisted of 5,000 men based at Churpurah on the Paha Nuddee. It appeared that these 9,000 men were planning a combined attack on Haldwani so that they could force the hill passes.

To combat this threat, Lieutenant-Colonel McCausland had a force of 700 infantry, 200 cavalry and 2 field guns. Despite his small force Colonel McCausland decided to go on the offensive and on 9th February 1858 move off towards the camp of Khali Khan to prevent a junction of the two rebel forces.

Battle of Churpurah

At daybreak on the 10th February, the Colonel's force came across the rebels occupying a very strong position. Their rear and

left flank was protected by the Paha Nuddee River and the right flank was covered by a small village that was full of infantry. The front of their position was covered by rough ground intersected with ditches and tall jungle grass; the road was protected by four artillery pieces.

The enemy was initially surprised by the appearance of the British cavalry and at first thought that it was the arrival of Fuzul Huq and his forces, whose arrival was expected.

Colonel McCausland decided that it would be best to attack the enemy right flank and directed the fire of his two guns, under the command of Captain Ross, against that position.

Lieutenant John Tytler – Victoria Cross No. 238

As the troops and cavalry were advancing on the village to the enemy right, an intense artillery duel was being fought and the British guns managed to knock out the heaviest rebel gun.

Lieutenant Tytler, rode ahead into the enemy gun placements where he was engaged in hand to hand fighting until the guns were carried by the advancing British forces.

For his part in the action, during which he was seriously wounded by a shot to the left arm and a spear wound in the chest, Lieutenant Tytler was later awarded the Victoria Cross.

The enemy defeat at Churpurah was very severe, with 300 killed, 600 wounded and all their guns, ammunition and baggage captured. The rebel survivors escaped back to Bareilly and after the battle the British forces returned to Haldwani. After the defeat the rebels seemed to lose heart and were only involved in minor skirmishes in the area afterwards.

On the 10th May 1858, with their job done, the Kumaon Brigade was broken up and the 66th Goorkha regiment returned to their base at Almorah.

General Outram at the Alum Bagh

While the forces were slowly being assembled for the final assault to recapture Lucknow, General Outram was left to guard the Alum Bagh and maintain a British position on the outskirts of the city.

General Outram's force was too large for all of his men to be accommodated in the Alum Bagh so a strong piquet was established there with the main force taking up positions about a mile to the rear.

The main British force was established on the plain, across the main Cawnpore road, with one flank extending to a village on the left of the road and the other to the old Jellalabad fort on the extreme right. The positions were protected by gun batteries and small defensive works which utilised the nearby swamps.

Against a rebel force estimated at about 95,000 men General Outram had a force of just under 4,000 men to maintain his position.

At first rebel opposition was slight, probably due to the after effects of the defeats caused by General Campbell during his relief of the garrison, however, skirmishes against General Outram's forward positions were steadily increased.

On 21st December, the General received news from his spies that the mutineers were planning to surround his position in order to cut off his supply route and communications and prevent any foraging expeditions. In the evening, news arrived that the rebels had established a force of 4,000 men, 400 cavalry and 8 field guns at the village of Guilee about three miles from the British camp and near the Dilkusha road.

At 5 o'clock in the morning of 22nd December, General Outram set out with a force to carry out a surprise attack at daybreak. His force consisted of 1,227 infantry under the command of Brigadier Stisted, 190 cavalry under Major Robertson and artillery with six 9 pounders guns commanded by Captains Olpherts and Maude.

The right wing consisting of detachments from the 78th and 90th Regiments and Sikhs from the Ferozepur Regiment, commanded by Lieutenant-Colonel Purnell, charged at the enemy position with such ferocity that the enemy were soon put to flight. The left wing consisting of 400 men of the 5th Fusiliers, commanded by Colonel Guy, carried out a simultaneous attack on the village of Guilee where they also put the rebels to flight and captured two guns. The cavalry under Captain Barrow chased the fleeing mutineers until they took refuge in another village where they mounted a desperate rear guard action but were soon dislodged by fire from Captain Olpherts' guns and headed off for the Dilkusha. The rebels were now pursued by the military train commanded by Major Robertson, who dispersed their cavalry and drove their artillery into a ravine where it was captured.

When a strong force came out of the city in support of their comrades the British forces retired back to their positions at the Alum Bagh.

Apart from the road back to Cawnpore, the mutineers had effectively blocked all other routes of supply and communications for General Outram's force, so every two weeks a strongly escorted convoy was sent by this route for the purpose of resupply. In early January, General Outram received news that Mansoob Ali was collecting together a force to attack the next convoy, so to protect it; it was sent with a larger escort than usual.

Taking advantage of this reduction in the British forces, at sunrise on 12th January the mutineers mounted an attack with 30,000 men against the British lines at the Alum Bagh. Despite a spirited attack in numbers, the rebels were driven back by the well placed British artillery, and after suffering a large number of casualties, by 5 o'clock in the afternoon they had dispersed back to the city.

Four days later, on 16th January, the rebels mounted another attack, which on this occasion was more focused, being concentrated on the piquet at the old Jellalabad fort on the extreme right of the British line. Again this attack was repelled by the British artillery which caused large enemy casualties but when night had fallen they followed up the assault on the right with an attack on the villages at the left of the line, these attacks were also repelled by the British artillery and cavalry.

On the 15th February, as a convoy was approaching the Alum Bagh, the rebels used the cover of a dust storm to try and seize the convoy by an attack in strength from the rear of the British lines, however, this move was spotted and the force was dispersed by the British cavalry.

On the next day the mutineers made another attack on the left wing of the Alum Bagh, but this was repelled by the 200 man piquet of the 90th Light Infantry, supported yet again by heavy artillery fire.

The next rebel attack on the Alum Bagh positions took place on 21st February; again this was prompted by General Outram having sent out a strong escort of his cavalry to a convoy that was approaching from Cawnpore. The attack was also in response to the news that two British columns were advancing from eastern Oudh and that General Campbell at Cawnpore was also making preparations for an advance on Lucknow. Another reason for choosing the 21st February to attack was because it was a Sunday and the rebels expected that General Outram and his officers would be attending church, however, late on Saturday evening the General was informed by his spies that the mutineers were planning an attack for the next morning.

At day break about 20,000 men with a large number of artillery pieces mounted an attack across the whole of the British front, with the bulk of the forces concentrated against the extreme flanks. General Outram was quick to reinforce his flanks and again, the determined British artillery fire caused much devastation and the attack was repelled.

On 25th February, the mutineers launched their final attempt to dislodge the British forces from the Alum Bagh, this time it was witnessed by the Queen Regent, her son, the Prime Minister and other notables who came out of the city mounted on elephants.

At about 9 o'clock in the morning, a strong force of infantry and cavalry with the support of some artillery advanced against the British left while an even stronger force accompanied by the royal procession advanced on the right wing. Part of the rebel force on the right massed at their forward entrenchments while the remainder swung around to the rear of the Jellalabad fort and occupied some mango groves and began to pour artillery fire into the old fort. General Outram, immediately countered this threat by directing some of his cavalry to attack their rear while he led another force of cavalry and artillery to make a more direct assault, almost as soon as his horse artillery unlimbered and began laying down fire, the royal entourage fled from the field. The two forces of British cavalry then made a combined attack on the rebel column at the old Jellalabad fort from the front and rear and quickly put them to flight. While the cavalry harried them on both flanks, the retreating rebel force was cut down in large numbers by the British artillery which put up a continuous fire into their masses. Later in the afternoon the mutineers mounted another attack at the British left wing, but yet again this was repelled by heavy musket and artillery fire.

After enduring a strenuous three month holding action at the Alum Bagh, General Outram and his men were now only a few days from being joined by General Campbell and his relief force.

Mutineers improve Lucknow defences

As well as mounting attacks against the Alum Bagh, the mutineers spent the three months since the evacuation of the garrison in improving the defences of the city.

Lucknow was a large city with widely distributed native houses, mosques and other buildings covering an area with a circumference of more than 20 miles.

As the two previous British assaults on the city had entered from the eastern side, the mutineers assumed that any future attacks would take the same line of approach so they endeavoured to block this path with three lines of defence.

The new defences took the form of three concentric roughly semicircular lines to the east of the city, progressively getting closer to the heart of Lucknow.

The outermost defence utilised the canal, at the end closest to the river they deepened the channel and from the River Gumti to the Char Bagh they destroyed bridges and raised an escarpment on the city side of the canal. The canal now formed a formidable wet ditch barrier with an earth rampart dotted with bastions, and to support this line, a battery of three guns was established in the buildings at the Hazarat Gunge, the junction of the three main city roads.

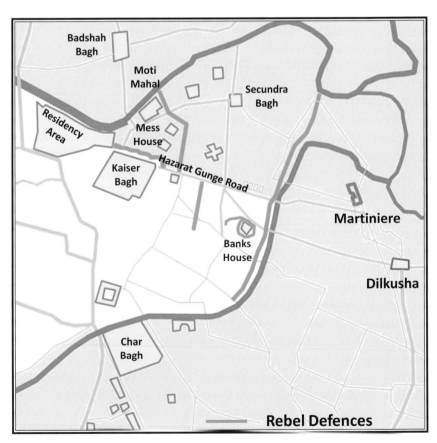

Figure 74. Improved rebel defences at Lucknow

The second line also started at the river, passed in front of the Moti Mahal, encircled the Mess House and joined the Hazarat Gunge main road near some mosques.

The third line, which was at right angles to the first two, protected the Kaiser Bagh, which was the main citadel for the rebels.

These defences were protected by about 130 guns and mortars of various calibres, mounted in fortified enclosures.

In addition to these main lines of defence, almost every house was fortified with loop holes cut to allow protected musket fire and most of the main streets had been barricaded, with guns positioned to fire along their length.

Formidable as they were, the defences had a critical design flaw; one flank was based upon a river that could be crossed with ease, allowing any attacker to bypass the defences and attack their positions from the rear. This was soon to be exploited by General Campbell.

General Campbell's force advances

Having cleared the Duab of rebels, General Campbell was now ready to begin the reconquest of the province of Oudh and to recapture Lucknow, the state capital.

Before setting out on the road to Lucknow, General Campbell first wanted to secure his conquests and to confuse the enemy regarding his intended movements.

To guard his position at Futtehgur and the surrounding districts, General Campbell assigned Colonel Seaton with the 82nd Regiment of Foot, 7th Punjab Infantry, a 9 pounder field battery and 350 recently raised irregular cavalry.

To confuse the rebels in the Rohilkhand, regarding his intentions, General Campbell sent a force commanded by Brigadier Adrian Hope to reconnoitre the country in the direction of Bareilly as if this would be the focus of his next attacks.

On his return to Futtehgur, Brigadier Hope reported that a large enemy force of about 15,000 men was being assembled at Allahganj on the banks of the River Ramganga. To continue the charade of a planned attack on Bareilly, General Campbell sent General Walpole's Brigade towards their position but with orders not to engage with them. To enforce the deception, Walpole's sappers repaired the bridge across the river which the rebels had destroyed. The deception worked for a while and the rebels remained encamped across the river, however, a band of about 5,000 rebels eventually crossed the river further upstream and occupied the village of Shumshabad.

On the evening of 26th January, Brigadier Hope's brigade was sent against these rebels and on the morning of 27th January they pressed ahead with an attack. After a protracted artillery exchange the mutineers finally broke and were pursued for about eight miles by the British cavalry who caused great casualties and drove the survivors back across the River Ganges into Rohilkhand.

With preparations now completed and the siege train well on the way to Cawnpore, having reached the station at Oonoa, General Campbell with his cavalry and horse artillery left Futtehgur on 1st February and arrived at Cawnpore on 4th February.

On the 10th February 1858, with his troops being assembled at Cawnpore, General Campbell issued a general order which announced the organisation of the Army of Oudh into Brigades and Divisions; Major-General Archdale Wilson was appointed to command the Artillery Division, Brigadier Robert Napier was appointed to the command of the Engineer Brigade and General Hope Grant was appointed to command the Cavalry Division.

The Infantry was divided into three divisions with Major-General Sir James Outram commanding the first, Brigadier-General Sir Edward Lugard the second and Brigadier-General Robert Walpole the third.

Brigadier Hope's brigade, together with the artillery also left Cawnpore on 1st February, however, General Walpole's brigade left a few days later and by 23rd February all of General Campbell's troops had crossed the Ganges into the province of Oudh and by 1st March were on the outskirts of Lucknow.

14

THE RECAPTURE OF LUCKNOW

On the 1st of March, General Campbell met up with General Outram and outlined the general plan of attack that had been formulated with the help of Brigadier Napier: a strong artillery battery would be formed near Dilkusha House to bombard the canal defences and the Kaiser Bagh; a division would cross the River Gumti, proceed along the northern bank establishing batteries to fire at the rear of the enemy defences and then recross the River Gumti at the Iron and Stone bridges and enter the city to the west of the Residency and attack the rebels from behind.

After these moves had suitably softened up the mutineers, the main force would cross the canal near Banks House, outflanking the enemy forces, and attack the Kaiser Bagh.

A point of discussion was whether or not to wait for the Army of Nepal, however, as it was proposed that they would be part of the main force attacking over the canal, it was agreed that the initial stages of the plan could start immediately.

Capture of Dilkusha House

Early on the morning of 2nd March, General Campbell began the execution of his plan by leading a force to capture Dilkusha House. The force consisted of: the Artillery HQ (General Wilson and Colonel Wood) with Colonel D'Aguilar's, Major Tombs's and

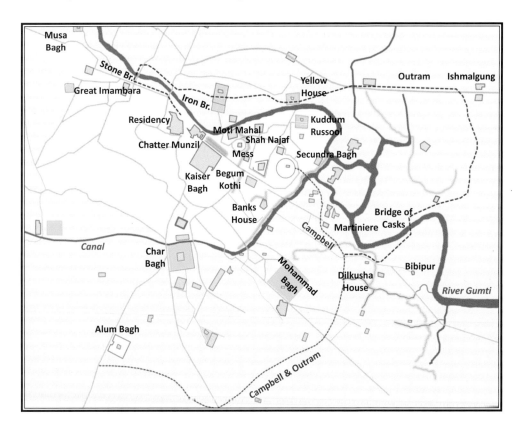

Figure 75. Recapture of Lucknow

Major Bishop's troops of Horse Artillery, Captain Peel with two 24 pounder guns and two 8" howitzers of the Naval Brigade and two companies of Sappers and Miners; the Cavalry HQ (General Hope Grant) with Little's cavalry brigade, 9th Lancers, 2nd and 5th Punjab Cavalry and 1st Sikh Irregulars; Infantry 2nd Division (General Lugard) with 3rd brigade under Brigadier Guy, 35th, 38th and 53rd Regiments of Foot and the 4th brigade under Brigadier Hope, 42nd and 93rd Regiments and the 4th Punjab Rifles.

The force advanced from the Alum Bagh past the old Jellalabad fort and on through the Dilkusha Park, pushing the advanced piquets of the enemy ahead of them. With little effort they managed to occupy Dilkusha House and the Muhammad Bagh, a nearby walled garden. Due to the intense rebel artillery fire from across the canal, General Campbell withdrew the majority of his troops out of range while his own artillery batteries were being established.

On the morning of 3rd March, the British batteries, which had been established at Dilkusha House and the Muhammad Bagh, opened up their barrage on the rebel guns and soon the enemy fire began to diminish. It was not long before the mutineers had to withdraw their guns and when they resumed their fire it was largely ineffective due to the increased range.

Also on 3rd March, General Campbell's force was joined by three regiments from the Alum Bagh and the Engineering Division established their headquarters in the Bibipur Park, below the Dilkusha House near to the river.

By the 4th of March, the remainder of the siege train and Brigadier Walpole's division had moved up to the Dilkusha House and General Campbell had established his headquarters at a chateau in the Bibipur Park.

Bridge of casks

On the night of 4th March, the engineers started work on two bridges across the River Gumti, the basic construction was beer casks lashed by rope to timber cross members which were floated into position and then connected by a plank floor which was lashed on top. Once the river was bridged a strong piquet was established on the northern bank and earthworks were constructed to provide a defensible bridgehead.

Throughout the night the construction work was unobserved by the enemy, however, at first light they spotted the works and tried to stop construction. A large column of rebel horse, with three artillery pieces advanced on the bridge piquet and began to fire on the working parties; a gun near the Martinière also began to fire on the bridge construction. The two British guns with the

bridge piquet managed to disperse the horse artillery but the gun at the Martinière carried on firing throughout the construction which continued during the 5th March and was completed at midnight.

Arrival of General Franks

During the 5th March, General Franks arrived at Lucknow with his column and was assigned as the 4th Infantry Division of the Army of Oudh.

With the arrival of General Franks's men, General Campbell now had at his disposal an army of nearly 25,700 men and 164 artillery pieces and Jung Bahádur's army of Nepal with 8,000 men were expected to arrive in the next few days.

General Outram crosses the Gumti

After leaving Brigadier Franklin with the 5th and 78th Regiments of Foot in charge of the Alum Bagh, General Outram with his division advanced down to the bridge of casks and at 4 o'clock in the morning on 6th March began the crossing over to the north bank of the Gumti which was completed just before daybreak.

General Outram's force consisted of: the 4th Company of Royal Engineers with 254 Bengal Sappers, Lieutenant-Colonel D'Aguilar's troop of horse artillery, Captain Mackinnon's and Captain Remmington's troops of Bengal Artillery, 2nd Dragoon Guards, 9th Lancers, detachments of 1st, 2nd and 5th Punjab Cavalry, 23rd Royal Welsh Fusiliers, 79th Highlanders, 1st Bengal Fusiliers, 2nd and 3rd battalion of the Rifle Brigade and 2nd Punjab Infantry.

As soon as General Outram's force had crossed the bridge, he started his march to the north as planned but was soon approached by a large body of rebel cavalry, however, this was soon dispersed by the approach of Outram's cavalry who gave chase.

Lance Corporal William Goate – Victoria Cross No. 241

During the chase, due to the broken ground the British cavalry was split into small groups who cut down the rebels as they were caught, however, as they got closer to the rebel infantry lines they were assailed by musket and artillery fire and had to withdraw.

While returning to the British lines, Lance-Corporal Goate was riding next to Major Percy Smith of the 2nd Dragoon Guards when the Major received a musket shot to the body.

Lance-Corporal Goate tried in vain to prevent the Major from being dismounted but the Major fell to the ground seriously wounded. The Lance-Corporal reigned in his horse, dismounted and after placing the Major on his back began to carry him off the field leading his own horse behind him.

After carrying the Major for several hundred yards, Lance-Corporal Goate heard the rebel cavalry closing in behind him; reluctantly he placed the Major on the ground and remounted.

Rather than race back to his own lines, Lance-Corporal Goate turned to face the enemy, shot one with his pistol and unhorsed another with his now empty pistol before drawing his sword to defend himself against the encircling Sowars. In his own words *"… I cannot tell you how many saddles I must have emptied; the enemy didn't seem to know how to parry; taking advantage of this, I settled accounts with a jolly lot"*.

Lance-Corporal Goate was determined not to be taken alive and desperately continued his fight until help arrived and the rebels were dispersed.

After the action Lance-Corporal Goate continued to look for Major Smith but could not find him, unfortunately the Majors headless and mutilated body was found the next day.

For his action, Lance-Corporal Goate was later awarded the Victoria Cross.

After the enemy had been dispersed, General Outram continued his advance and made his camp on the Fyzabad road, near the village of Ishmalgunge, about four miles from the city.

Early the next morning on 7th March, the mutineers made a spirited attack on General Outram's advanced piquets, aided by several guns which they had brought up under the cover of nearby ravines. Following fire from the British Horse Artillery and Captain Middleton's field battery the rebel force was dispersed.

During the day, one of the cask bridges, which had been dismantled the previous evening, was re-erected at a point downstream near Bibipur, where it could not be observed by the rebels holding the Martinière. In the evening, the new bridge was crossed by the siege train which arrived at General Outram's camp the next morning.

New Dilkusha batteries

On 8th March, native sappers constructed a new battery to the front and left of the Dilkusha House, the battery was manned by six guns from the Naval Brigade which were brought to bear

on the Martinière. Two more batteries, each with four guns, were established to the right front of the Dilkusha House and the Mohammed Bagh, which were also brought to bear on the Martinière.

General Outram's attack across the Gumti

Having decided to attack the enemy positions the next day, General Outram also constructed a gun emplacement near his camp which was built during the evening and with the use of elephants, was populated with eight 24 pounder guns and three 8" mortars by day break. As soon as General Outram's heavy guns were in position, they began a bombardment of the enemy positions to their front.

After a short time the Rifle Brigade were sent out as skirmishers to probe the enemy front lines advancing across broken ground towards a thick wood. After advancing for about three quarters of a mile, the Rifle Brigade came under heavy musket fire from the jungle which they had now reached. With the Rifle Brigade temporarily halted, the heavy guns restarted their barrage now concentrating their fire on the forest. Following this barrage, the Rifle Brigade, now followed by the rest of the right column which included the Highlanders and Sikhs drove the mutineers through the trees and on emerging rejoined the Fyzabad road.

The left column of the attack; comprising 1st Bengal Fusiliers with two companies of the 79th Highlanders, supported by Brigadier Wood with his horse artillery; mounted a coordinated attack with the right column on the Chukkur Kotee (Yellow House)[21] which was a key rebel position. In the face of the British attack, which assailed both the front and rear of the building, most of the occupants fled but those that remained put up a stiff fight killing three officers and nine men. Not wishing to sacrifice more of his men, General Outram brought up artillery which drove out the rebels. With the Yellow House now occupied, General Outram ordered that the colours of the Bengal Fusiliers be flown from the roof, as a signal to General Campbell at the Dilkusha that the objective had been taken.

After taking the Yellow House, General Outram's force continued its advance and captured the Badshah Bagh and from the batteries established at both locations was now able to lay down fire on the exposed rear of the rebels first and second lines of defence.

21 The grandstand of the King of Oudh's racecourse.

Lieutenant Thomas Butler – Victoria Cross No. 242

After taking the Badshah Bagh a battery of three heavy guns and two howitzers was installed in the gardens and began a heavy fire to the rear of the Martinière, another battery of two 24 pounder guns and two 8" mortars was established near the river bank and began to bombard the town and the Kaiser Bagh.

After some considerable fire, Major Nicholson who was in command of the first battery thought that the enemy had abandoned their first lines of defence, information that would be valuable to Brigadier Hope and his men who were advancing on the positions on the south bank of the river.

Lieutenant Butler and four privates volunteered to go down to the river edge and signal to Brigadier Hope but due to his being over 600 yards away they were unable to attract his attention. Knowing the importance of the intelligence and despite the dangers involved, as the rebel positions may not have been abandoned, Lieutenant Butler decided to swim across the river and deliver the news.

At this point the river was about 60 yards wide, very deep and with a strong current but Lieutenant Butler managed to swim across and arrived at the rear of the enemy batteries which he fortunately found to have been abandoned.

Cold and wet from his swim, Lieutenant Butler climbed the parapet at the front of the emplacement and signalled to Brigadier Hope's men. Despite being under enemy fire he remained in the battery until some men from the Highlanders and 4th Punjab Rifles arrive to occupy the battery and relieve him. Following the relief, Lieutenant Butler swam back across the river to rejoin his men.

For this action Lieutenant Butler was later awarded the Victoria Cross.

Battle of La Martinière

To assist the progress of General Outram's Division along the north bank of the River Gumti and as part of the preparations for his own assault over the canal it was essential for General Campbell to capture the Martinière.

On the morning of the 9th March, while General Outram's force was engaged on the north bank of the Gumti, General Campbell's batteries at the Dilkusha House stepped up their bombardment against the Martinière, using rockets as well as traditional artillery.

In response to a request from Colonel Napier to breach a particular wall, Captain Peel went out to direct the fire of his guns

– *"Peel, with his usual indifference to danger, thinking only of the effects of his shot against the breach he was making, and taking no notice of the bullets which were buzzing about our ears, was standing upon a little knoll, a fair target to the marksmen. One could see the fellows lay their muskets along the top of the rifle-pit; then puff, a little white smoke; then bang and whew-ew-iz, then sput against some stone as the bullet fell flattened close to our feet. At last one bullet, more true than the others, struck him, and he fell saying, 'Oh, they have hit me!'"[22]*

The wound to Captain Peel's thigh, by a bullet which missed the bone and was soon extracted at the aid station in Dilkusha House, was not serious, however, due to unfortunate circumstances it would lead to his death. For his evacuation to Cawnpore he was placed in a litter that was contaminated by a previous occupant with smallpox and after contracting the disease Captain Peel VC died at Cawnpore on 27th April 1858.

After their gallant Captain had been carried from the field, the men of the Naval Brigade continued their barrage of the Martinière.

At about 1 o'clock in the afternoon, Brigadiers Lugard and Hope began to assemble their men for the attack and at 2 o'clock after seeing General Outram's signal on the Yellow House the attack was launched.

Lieutenant Francis Farquharson – Victoria Cross No. 243

Brigadier Lugard, with the Highlanders advance on the Martinière from the right and after taking the building continued on towards the canal, to clear the remaining enemy positions still active in their first line of defence.

Lieutenant Farquharson led men from his company against an enemy bastion, killed the gunners and spiked their guns, helping to secure the advanced British position against artillery fire during the evening.

For this action Lieutenant Farquharson was later awarded the Victoria Cross. He was seriously wounded during the next day while he was holding a forward position.

Brigadier Hope's men approached the Martinière from the left and again after the building was taken turned down to the canal to clear any rebels from their first line of defence.

By the end of the day the canal had been secured from the river down to Banks's House but, due to the lack of heavy guns, the force did not attempt to assault Banks House and instead rested up for the evening.

---

22 "Recollections of a Winter Campaign in India in 1857–58," by Captain Oliver J. Jones, R.N., p. 173.

Capture of Banks's House

Early on the morning of 10th March, a battery of four large guns, one howitzer and three 8" mortars was established at the corner of the Martinière Park and was soon directing a heavy fire against Banks's House.

Breaches were soon evident and the forces of Lugard and Hope advanced and took the position, the first part of General Campbell's plan had now been accomplished, the canal defences were now totally under British control.

Preparations for the next phase of attack

Having now captured and secured the first line of the rebel defences, General Campbell spent the next day the 10th March, making preparations for the next stage of the offensive, an attack on the second line of defences.

Banks's House was fortified and a gun battery to house four large guns and eight mortars was constructed nearby. This battery was used to bombard the Begum Kothi, a large collection of buildings and enclosures that anchored the extreme left of the 2nd line of defence and provided protection to the Kaiser Bagh immediately to its rear.

Another battery consisting of two large guns and six mortars, manned by the Naval Brigade, was established near the bungalows to the right of Banks's House. These batteries began a bombardment of the Begum Kothi and the buildings along the Hazarat Gunge, which was General Campbell's intended route into the city.

On the other side of the River Gumti, General Outram's force spent the day consolidating and strengthening their positions.

Figure 76. Major Banks's House

Roads were improved to the Badshah Bagh to bring up heavy guns and the Dilarum Kothi (Heart's Rest) building was seized and fortified, these actions were carried out under heavy fire from the mutineers across the river in the Chattar Manzil.

Throughout the night, General Campbell's batteries kept up their bombardment of the Begum Kothi, Mess House and Kaiser Bagh, while from across the river General Outram's guns were able to fire into the rear of these positions.

During these operations, Jung Bahádur arrived at Lucknow with his 9,000 Ghurkhas of the Nepal army.

Battle of Begum Kothi

The battery of the enemy defences continued throughout the morning and until the early afternoon of 11th March when Brigadier Napier reported that two suitable breaches had been made in the Begum Kothi defences and the attack could now take place.

The storming party, commanded by Brigadier Hope, consisted of the 93rd Highlanders, 4th Punjab Rifles supported by a detachment of Ghurkha troops. The right wing commanded by Lieutenant-Colonel Leith Hay was to attack the central breach while the left wing would attack the breach on the flank towards the direction of Banks's House. At 4 o'clock in the afternoon the guns became silent, the rebel musket fire diminished and both wings of the storming party launched their attack.

The right wing were confronted by an earth parapet and a ditch 18 foot wide and 10 foot deep in front of the central breach and in the face of heavy musket fire had to scale this obstacle before gaining access to the Begum Kothi via the small breach in the wall.

Lieutenant William McBean – Victoria Cross No. 245

On entering the palace, the attacking force was confronted with a confusing array of interconnecting buildings, each of which needed to be cleared room by room with vicious hand to hand fighting.

Lieutenant McBean single handed killed 11 of the rebels armed only with his sword and bare fists, at one time he was surrounded by 5 rebels one of whom was said to be 6'7" tall and weighed 265 pounds.

For this action, Lieutenant McBean was later awarded the Victoria Cross.

The left wing of the storming party also entered via their assigned breach and drove large numbers of mutineers from the buildings and towards the nearby Kaiser Bagh.

Figure 77. The Begum Kothi

After about two hours of intense hand to hand fighting, the palace was finally in British hands.

Secundra Bagh and Shah Najaf taken

While Brigadier Hope's men were engaged on the British left flank, Brigadier Lugard's division made advances on the right flank.

During the morning two engineers crept up on the Kuddum Russool and after finding it unoccupied gained entry, from where they were able to look down on the nearby Shah Najaf which also looked to be deserted. One of the engineers went back to the main force, returned with 100 men and 50 sappers and found that the Shah Najaf was indeed abandoned, so set about trying to make the building into a defensible position. The building was later reinforced with an additional 100 men.

Outram advances on the Iron and Stone Bridges

While General Campbell was making his advances on the south of the river, General Outram was continuing his operations on the north side of the river and began to advance his men towards the Stone and Iron bridges.

Brigadier-General Walpole, in command of the right wing of the division; comprising the 79th Highlanders, 1st Bengal Fusiliers, 2nd and 3rd Battalions of the Rifle Brigade and supported by a battery of Light Field Artillery commanded by Captain Gibbons; formed up on the Fyzabad road and pushed forward through the trees and bushes.

General Walpole and his men slowly advanced, pushing the rebels ahead of them until they capture a large mosque with an extensive walled garden that commanded the approaches to the Iron Bridge.

Captain Henry Wilmot – Victoria Cross No. 244
Corporal William Nash – Victoria Cross No. 246
Private David Hawkes – Victoria Cross No. 247

Captain Wilmot, leading a small party of four men from the Rifle Brigade, scouting the approaches to the Iron Bridge, was passing through the suburbs when they entered a street and found a large number of mutineers encamped at the other end.

Almost immediately, the men of the Rifle Brigade came under heavy musket fire from the rebels and one of their number fell down, shot through both legs. Corporal Nash and Private Hawkes lifted up the wounded man and carried him off to safety while Captain Wilmot covered their retreat with fire from his pistol; during the escape Private Hawkes was also seriously wounded.

For this action which saved the life of their fallen comrade, Captain Wilmot, Corporal Nash and Private Hawkes were all later awarded the Victoria Cross.

Figure 78. The Iron Bridge

Figure 79. The Stone Bridge

At the same time, Colonel Pratt who commanded the left wing; comprising 23rd Royal Welsh Fusiliers and 2nd Punjab Infantry supported by two 24 pounder guns and a light Field Battery of three guns; also advanced towards the Iron Bridge along a road closer to the river.

Having left the 1st Bengal Fusiliers to occupy the mosque at the Iron Bridge, General Outram moved off with the remainder of the right wing towards the Fyzabad road where he met up with the cavalry and artillery of General Hope Grant.

With General Hope Grant's men covering his right flank, General Outram advanced through the trees towards the Stone Bridge but as they moved forward they came across the camp of the 15th Irregular Horse which they attacked, capturing their standards and two guns. Without much further opposition, General Outram advanced to the Stone Bridge but found that the enemy artillery still had command of the bridge approaches, so retired back to the mosque.

Jung Bahádur's men take the field

On 12th March, Jung Bahádur's force of 9,000 men with 25 field guns took their position within the British lines between Banks's House and the Char Bagh.

On the next day the army of Ghurkhas crossed the canal and began to clear the houses on the left of General Campbell's main line of march, providing protection to his flank.

Preparations for attack on Little Imambara

During the 12th and 13th March, Brigadier Napier continued to press forward along the intended route into the city, towards a small Imambara which lay between the Begum Kothi and the Kaiser Bagh. Keeping off the main road, which was heavily defended, the men used sappers and artillery to breach each house in their path which they cleared before moving on to the next, all the while under heavy musket fire from the neighbouring houses.

On the afternoon of the 13th March, General Lugard's troops occupying the Begum Kothi were relieved by General Franks and his troops.

Able Seaman Edward Robinson – Victoria Cross No. 248

Throughout the day and night of the 13th March, General Outram and General Campbell's artillery continued to bombard the city with fire directed at the Little Imambara and the Kaiser Bagh.

The work of the artillerymen was dangerous as they were the target for the enemy artillery as well as rebel sharpshooters who were often very close to their emplacements.

While manning a Naval Brigade battery with mutineers stationed only 50 yards away, Able Seaman Robinson noticed that some of the sandbags, used to construct the embrasure around his position, had caught fire and were endangering their post.

Despite heavy fire from the nearby rebels, Able Seaman Robinson climbed on top of the embrasure and extinguished the fire, receiving a serious wound in the process.

For this action Able Seaman Robinson was later awarded the Victoria Cross.

⁜

On 13th March, General Outram requested permission from General Campbell to storm the Iron Bridge so that he could mount an attack to the rear of the Residency and the Kaiser Bagh. The response from General Campbell was that Outram could only make the attack if it could be made without any loss of life to his men. As the Iron Bridge was still under fire from the rebel artillery, this was effectively a refusal. A less cautious General may have exercised some flexibility with the reply, however, the conservative General Outram followed his commander-in-chief's orders to the letter and did not attempt to cross the Iron Bridge, instead he erected a barricade across his end of the bridge. This would prove to be a costly mistake.

Capture of the Little Imambara and Kaiser Bagh

The British artillery kept up its bombardment during the night and by daybreak on 14th March two breaches were deemed to be large enough for the assault on the Little Imambara to take place.

The assault party, comprising two companies of the 10th Regiment of Foot together with 100 men from Major Brasyer's Sikhs were assembled behind a wall with only the width of a road separating them from the walls of the Imambara enclosure. A party of sappers, with scaling ladders and powder bags, was assembled just to their rear and Brigadier Russell's Brigade was nearby ready to support the assault. Lieutenant Beaumont of the Royal Engineers together with Major Brasyer and some of his Sikhs advanced to a house close to the Imambara and gained entry by blowing in the wall and driving out the rebels. The house was connected by a trench to the outer wall of the Imambara and this was used by the party to close on the wall and blow open a

Figure 80. The Little Imambara

breach. The assault parties, seeing that Major Brasyer had gained access threw themselves at the breaches and were soon in control of the Imambara. Openings in the walls were soon made and this allowed the assault force to occupy the Kings Coach house and the Kings Brother's house which overlooked the front of the Kaiser Bagh.

The second line of the mutineers' defences had now been turned and Colonel Harness, commander of the Royal Engineers advised Brigadier Russell to halt his advance and secure the ground that they had taken so far.

The Sikhs, however, could not be restrained and some of them had already pursued the fleeing mutineers into an outer courtyard of the Kaiser Bagh. From the roofs of the Coach house and Brothers house Major Brasyer with a number of his Sikhs, supported Lieutenant Havelock leading men from the 90th Regiment, and laid down a withering fire on the three nearest bastions in the Kaiser Bagh, such that the rebels abandoned their guns.

Following this success, Lieutenant Havelock called up men from the 10th Regiment to assist Major Brasyer and his Sikhs and despite heavy musket fire from the mutineers this force gradually cleared the houses to the right of the Kaiser Bagh.

After some time about 50 men had reached the Cheena Bazaar which flanked the Kaiser Bagh and were now well within the rebels third and last line of defence. Lieutenant Havelock and some of the Sikhs seized two adjoining bastions and turned the guns on a large body of rebels making for the Kaiser Bagh from the 2nd lines of defence.

Brigadier Napier and General Franks now came up with large numbers of men to provide support to the attack and at 11 o'clock General Campbell was advised that some of his men were inside the Kaiser Bagh.

This was unexpected news, as the British were expecting fierce resistance and had not planned to take the Kaiser Bagh until the following day.

After a brief discussion, with Brigadier Napier and General Franks, it was decided that the Kaiser Bagh could be taken now, so General Campbell issued orders for the assault to continue and for reinforcements to be called up. He also issued orders for the men at the Secundra Bagh to attack the right hand end of the second line of defence which was to their front.

Within short order these troops had cleared and occupied the Mess House, Tara Kothi, Moti Mahal and the Chatter Manzil and then pushed forward to the third line of defence.

When reinforcements arrived General Franks and his men restarted their advance on the Kaiser Bagh and managed, via the Cheena Bazaar, to enter the courtyard of Saidut Ali's Mosque at the rear of the complex.

Major Brasyer with 150 of his Sikhs and about 50 Highlanders from the 97th managed to drive the rebels from their guns and entered the main square of the Kaiser Bagh, where they met stiffer opposition. Despite being greatly outnumbered, Major Brasyer's force pushed the enemy back to the Badshah Manzil (the Kings main residence) but with the enemy now at their rear they fell back to a bronze gate in the north-west side of the Kaiser Bagh and took refuge.

The main storming parties had now reached the main square of the Kaiser Bagh and the massed mutineers were split into smaller parties who fled and occupied the various palaces each of which was like a small fortress.

The Badshah Manzil, which was filled with treasures and resplendent in its rich fittings, was plundered by the British forces, until night brought a halt to their activities.

The fighting continued the next morning, as the final palaces were cleared, after which guards were placed on all of the palaces to prevent further looting. Sappers were employed to putting out fires and destroying the large stores of gunpowder that had been found.

With their main citadel now in British hands, the rebels were fleeing to escape the city, which was relatively easy as, following the order regarding the Iron Bridge; General Outram's force was stuck on the other side of the river rather than in the city where he could have cut off the enemy retreat.

The situation was further compounded by another order from General Campbell which sent General Hope Grant and his cavalry off to Sitapur and Brigadier Campbell with his cavalry to Sundeela to cut off the rebel retreat.

However, this move was too late to stop a major force of 20,000 mutineers who dispersed into the countryside. The cavalry could have been much more effectively deployed closer to the city as many more rebels used the absence of the cavalry to affect their escape.

Capture of the Residency

After leaving General Walpole's division to guard the northern bank by the Iron and Stone bridges, General Outram finally crossed back to the south bank of the Gumti on 16th March.

With Brigadier Russell's 5th Brigade comprising; 23rd Fusiliers, 79th Highlanders and 1st Bengal Fusiliers; General Outram cross the river by a bridge of casks built opposite the Secundra Bagh. After reaching the Mess-House General Outram was joined by men of the 20th Regiment of Foot and Major Brasyer's Sikhs and the joint force made their way through the Kaiser Bagh, by a route blasted out by the Sappers & Miners, towards the Residency. Apart from some initially intensive musket fire, the assault on the Residency, was practically unopposed and in very short time was back under British control.

Two companies of men from 23rd Regiment, under the command of Lieutenant-Colonel Bell, pressed forward through the Residency and captured the gun that had been guarding the Iron Bridge and other batteries up to the Stone Bridge.

From the Residency, a field battery of the Madras Artillery bombarded the Macchi Bhawan citadel and the nearby Great Imambara and was joined by two large guns manned by the Naval Brigade.

After a period of bombardment the 1st Bengal Fusiliers and Major Brasyer's Sikhs had little difficulty in taking both places as the rebels retired abandoning the positions and 7 artillery pieces.

With these advances, General Outram's force had steadily been pushing the mutineers ahead of them and as they abandoned their positions they fled across the Stone Bridge and engaged General Walpole's men, the attack was repulsed but many of the rebels managed to make good their escape.

Attack on the Alum Bagh

While the main events were taking place in the city of Lucknow, at 9 o'clock in the morning of 16th March the mutineers made a determined attack against General Franklyn's small force of about 1,000 men stationed at the Alum Bagh.

The initial movement of the rebels was an attempt to turn the British left flank and attack their rear, however, General Franklyn

quickly countered by moving a force of guns and cavalry from the Military Train under Major Robertson to a position at the rear and a battery of guns commanded by Captain Olpherts to his left flank; which forestalled the rebel attack.

The main rebel force attacked towards the British front but the British artillery commanded by Colonel Eyre first halted their advance and then drove them back, the battle lasted some time and it was not until half past one in the afternoon that the rebels retired.

Further operations at Lucknow

To forestall further enemy attacks on the Alum Bagh, the force of Ghurkhas commanded by Jung Bahádur moved against the Char Bagh on the morning of 17th March, which they occupied and cleared all enemy positions up the Cawnpore road to the Alum Bagh.

In the afternoon of 17th March, Jung Bahádur's force was attacked by a large enemy force, however, the Maharaja himself led a force which turned their flank and they were completely defeated with the loss of 10 guns and a number of ammunition wagons.

On the morning of the 17th March, Outram's force continued its progress to the north west and without much resistance occupied the Huseni Mosque and the Daulat Khana palace (the house of happiness).

In the afternoon, Outram again advanced and with; a wing of the 20th Regiment of Foot, a wing of the 23rd Regiment of

Figure 81. The Alum Bagh

Foot, a wing of the 79th Highlanders, Brasyer's Sikhs, Middleton's field battery and a company of native sappers; proceeded to occupy a group of buildings known as the Sharif-ud-Daula's House, meeting very little resistance as the rebels were quick to evacuate the buildings.

In one of the palaces, the Jumma Musjid, nine cartloads of powder had been discovered, packed in tin boxes. It was decided that this should be destroyed by throwing it down a well. A line of men was formed and the boxes were passed from hand to hand, the first case thrown down the well struck the side causing a spark which ignited and exploded. The flame raced up the well and ignited the line of boxes being passed from hand to hand and exploded all of them, including the nine cartloads.

The terrific explosions killed 22 men in the working party, together with the two engineering officers (Captain Clarke and Lieutenant Brownlow) who were supervising; the only person to survive was the man who threw the first box down the well.

On the 18th March, General Outram continued to advance his forces, however, this was mainly moving additional forces up to reinforce his advanced piquets.

Battle of Musa Bagh

On the 17th and 18th March, General Campbell had received intelligence that a large number of rebels, between 8,000–9,000 were preparing to make a last stand at the Musa Bagh, a large palace with gardens and enclosures about four miles to the north west of the city.

With all of the major strong points within the city now under British control, General Campbell was determined to expel the mutineers from this last remaining stronghold. The general plan was that General Outram would make the main attack against the Musa Bagh, supported Hope Grant's cavalry on his right flank to the north of the River Gumti, while a force on the left flank commanded by Brigadier Campbell would cut off the rebel retreat as they were driven from the palace.

As planned, General Outram with his strong force; two squadrons of 9th Lancers, on company of Royal Engineers, one company of Native Sappers, Captain Middleton's Field Battery, Bombay artillery under the command of Captain Carleton, three companies of 20th Regiment, seven companies of 23rd Regiment, 79th Highlanders and the 2nd Punjab Infantry; advanced along the main road up the south bank of the river to make a frontal assault on the Musa Bagh.

Brigadier Campbell with a brigade of Infantry, some guns and 1,500 cavalry was posted to the left of the Musa Bagh with orders to cut down the enemy as they attempted to retreat.

Jung Bahádur's force of Ghurkhas from the army of Nepal was ordered to enter the city from their position at the Char Bagh Bridge and advance towards the rear of the Huseni Mosque to handle any rebels who might try to take refuge in the city.

As General Outram advanced on the Musa Bagh, he first had to take a house at Gao Ghat which had been the residence of the

Figure 82. The Musa Bagh

last prime minister of Oudh, the Nawab Ali Naki Khan who was now held prisoner at Calcutta.

Lieutenant Evereth led a company of 79th Highlanders to attack and clear the house, which was accomplished with little difficulty.

The force now advanced on the Musa Bagh but were delayed for a while until a wall at the suburbs was breached, the 23rd and 79th then stormed into the position while the 9th Lancers made a flanking movement to the enemy left and Captain Middleton's guns pounded the centre. Before long the mutineers abandoned their positions and guns, and retreated along the expected line which should have been guarded by Brigadier Campbell's men.

General Outram left Major Green with the 2nd Punjab Infantry to occupy the Musa Bagh and then withdrew the rest of his men back to their previous positions in the city.

The 9th Lancers, led by Captain Coles, set off in pursuit of the rebels chasing them for about four miles before they overtook and engaged them.

Troop Sergeant Major David Rush – Victoria Cross No. 250

During the engagement, Troop Sergeant-Major Rushe, accompanied by a private charged eight rebels hidden in a ravine, killing three of them.

For this action Troop Sergeant-Major Rushe was later awarded the Victoria Cross.

During the action, the Lancers killed about 100 of the rebel force and captured six guns before they fled and dispersed throughout the countryside. The Lancers then returned to the city.

Private Robert Newell – Victoria Cross No. 252

During the fighting one of the Lancers horse fell while riding over the rough ground and as he fell he was caught up beneath his ride. Surrounded by rebels he would have soon been despatched, however, Private Newell rode to his assistance and under a heavy musket fire brought him to safety.

For this action Private Newell was later awarded the Victoria Cross.

Brigadier Campbell's progress

Brigadier Campbell left his encampment at the Alum Bagh at about 2 o'clock in the morning and after slow progress due to the broken ground and skirmishing with rebels in the villages and woods in his path, the force came across a small mud fort at about 1 o'clock in the afternoon just as they halted for food.

Initially it was thought that this position was unoccupied until a patrol was fired upon, Colonel Charles Hagart with 'H' troop of the 7th Hussars, some of Hodson's Horse, some men from the 78th Highlanders and two of Major Tombs's guns was sent to dislodge the rebels.

Cornet William Bankes – Victoria Cross No. 251

After the guns had fired a few rounds at the fort, about 50 men rushed out of the fort and began to charge the guns.

Captain Slade the commander of 'H' troop was one of the first men to fall, however, Cornet Bankes led the troop in a charge against the rebels and shot three mutineers with his pistol.

Lieutenant Wilkin was now severely wounded by a sword cut that had nearly severed his foot, so command now fell to the young cornet who urged the troop to continue the attack.

A young mutineer, a mere boy, hamstrung Cornet Bankes horse with a slash from his sword and the Cornet crashed to the ground where being unable to draw his sword and with his pistol now empty he was unable to defend himself, was set upon by the rebels who slashed at him mercilessly.

For this action Cornet Bankes was later awarded the Victoria Cross, unfortunately he died of his wounds fifteen days later.

Brigadier Campbell continued his advance to the agreed position east of the Musa Bagh but at such a slow rate that by the time he arrived in position most of the mutineers had made their escape.

The recapture of Lucknow is complete

With the capture of the Musa Bagh, it only remained to stamp out the remaining rebels within the city; a strong force with two guns was occupying the Shadatganj a heavily fortified building in the very heart of the city. On 21st March Brigadier Lugard with men from the 93rd Highlanders and 4th Punjab Rifles were despatched to deal with this last bastion of resistance. The rebels defended their position stoutly but were eventually dislodged and were pursued by Brigadier Campbell's cavalry who inflicted a large number of casualties.

After a series of operations over a period of twenty days, Lucknow was now back under British command.

For such a protracted campaign against an enemy dug into formidable defences the British losses were relatively light; 16

British Officers, 3 Native Officers and 18 men were killed; 51 British Officers, 4 Native Officers and 540 men were wounded and 13 men were missing.

The losses inflicted on the mutineers was considerably higher, however, the most disappointing aspect of the campaign was the fact that large numbers of rebels had been allowed to escape into the country side and would continue to cause problems for a further year.

Action at Baroun

An example of the many actions required to quell the rebels who escaped Lucknow, but continued to cause considerable disruption in the region, was that which occurred on the 14th October 1858 against rebels in the village of Baroun near Lucknow.

Lieutenant Hanson Jarrett – Victoria Cross No. 288

A force of about 100 men of the 84th Regiment of Foot with about 150 men of the 20th Punjab Infantry were advancing across rice fields knee deep in mud and water towards the village.

Captain Wyatt, who was leading the column ordered up one company of the 20th to deal with a force of rebels who were holed up in a house. Lieutenant Jarrett of the 20th and Lieutenant Sadlier of the Madras Rifles led the men to the house which was defended by about 70 rebels. The only entrance was up a narrow entry but despite this Lieutenant Jarrett was prepared to make an assault. Calling for volunteers, Lieutenant Jarrett led the four men who stepped forward in a charge against the house and through a hail of bullets managed to scale a wall of the house but could not gain entry. With so few of his men having followed his lead the Lieutenant was forced to retire.

For his daring attempt, Lieutenant Jarrett was later awarded the Victoria Cross.

15

THE SUMMER CAMPAIGNS 1858

With the recapture of Lucknow, all of the major centres were now back under British control, however, due to a number of errors of judgement during the Lucknow campaign, large numbers of rebel troops had been allowed to escape and were now roaming free in the provinces of Oudh, Rohilkhand and Azamgarh.

The Confiscation Proclamation

On 3rd March, General Outram, in his capacity as Chief Commissioner of Oudh, had received a proclamation from Lord Canning, which was only to be enacted and published after Lucknow had been recaptured.

General Outram disagreed with the propositions of the "Confiscation Proclamation" but could not change Lord Canning's mind regarding the proposals, so it was published on 20th March 1858.

Under the terms of the proclamation all the lands of Oudh, except those belonging to six named individuals who had remained loyal to the crown, were now confiscated and became crown property. Landowners who laid down their arms and could prove that they had no involvement in the murder of Europeans would be considered for having their lands restored.

When the terms of the proclamation became generally known, the unsettled situation in Oudh became even worse, with many chiefs who had at worst remained neutral now becoming hostile.

Improvement of Lucknow defences

Before heading off to subdue the remaining rebels in the provinces, General Campbell decided that the defences of Lucknow required improvement in order to prevent any future occupation by the rebels.

A large fortification was constructed on the south side of the Gumti, opposite the stone bridge, which became known as the Macchi Bhawan Fort. This incorporated the old Macchi Bhawan citadel and the Grand Imambara; many native houses on the forts landward sides were demolished to provide clear fields of fire.

The original Residency position was surrounded by ramparts and converted into a separate detached fort.

In addition to the new defences, General Campbell established the Lucknow Field Force to garrison the city and to keep the mutineers in the immediate surrounding areas under control.

The field force, under the command of General Hope Grant, comprised: three troops of horse artillery, three light field batteries, three garrison batteries with siege train, one company of Royal Engineers, one company Madras Sappers, three companies of Punjab Sappers, the Delhi Pioneers; 2nd Dragoon Guards, one squadron Lahore Light Horse, 1st Light Cavalry, Hodson's Horse, 7th Hussars; 20th Regiment of Foot, 23rd Fusiliers, 38th and 53rd Regiment of Foot, 90th Light Infantry, 2nd and 3rd battalions Rifle Brigade, 1st Bengal Fusiliers, 1st Madras Fusiliers, 3rd Punjab Regiment and Ferozepur Regiment.

General Campbell was of the opinion that the subjugation of the rebels in Oudh was his next priority, however, this was not shared by Lord Channing the Governor General who thought that Rohilkhand should be the next province to be subdued.

As a partial compromise General Campbell sent a field force under the command of General Sir E. Lugard to subdue the rebels in the district of Azamgarh, in the east of Oudh, where the mutineers had besieged the town of Azamgarh which was only 55 miles from Benares and also sent a field force under the command of General Walpole to Rohilkhand.

General Hope Grant's operations in Oudh

On 9th April, General Hope Grant received orders from General Campbell to proceed to Bari, a town about 30 miles from Lucknow, to disperse rebels said to be congregating there, following this he was to march east towards Muhammadabad and following the course of the Ghogra river to Bitauli where the Begum of Lucknow was thought to be sheltering with 6,000 of his followers. After this he was to march to Ramnugger to cover the march of the army of Nepal as they returned home.

To carry out these orders, General Hope Grant left Lucknow on 11th April with a force comprising; horse, field and garrison artillery; cavalry units 7th Hussars, a squadron of 2nd Dragoon Guards and Wale's Punjab Horse and Infantry, 2nd Battalion Rifle Brigade, 38th Regiment of Foot, 1st Bengal Fusiliers, the 5th Punjab Corps supported by about 100 sappers and miners; in total about 3,000 men.

On the evening of the following day, while the force was camped at a point about 10 miles from Bari, a group of rebel cavalry entered the camp on an intelligence gathering mission; when challenged by the piquets they truthfully stated they were from the 12th Irregulars and were allowed to pass.

Battle of Bari

When the rebels returned to Bari, the rebel leader used their information to formulate his plans; he moved his whole force to a village about four miles from Bari on the expected route of the British force and established a strong position. Guarded by a river to the front, the rebels planned to hold the village with infantry while the cavalry would attack the British flanks as they came into the attack.

On the morning of 13th April, General Hope Grant and his men advanced on Bari, as planned, unaware that they were walking into a trap set by the rebels.

The enemy cavalry made good progress and avoiding the British line of march soon gained a position to the rear of the British column from where they could mount an attack on the baggage train made up of about 6,000 carts. Spotting two British guns, that were lightly guarded, the leader of the rebel cavalry decided to deviate from the agreed plan and tempted by such an easy target set out to capture the guns. They surrounded and captured the guns and were about to carry them off when they were spotted by a troop of the 7th Hussars, however, instead of facing the charging hussars, the rebels rode off and reverted to their original plan and began to mount an attack on the baggage train.

By now the rebels had lost their advantage of surprise and General Hope Grant reinforced the rearguard who despite two determined attacks managed to fight off the rebel cavalry who with their plans thwarted retreated.

General Hope Grant pressed forward with his troops but now on the alert noticed the well prepared enemy positions and proceeded with caution.

The rebel leader, with his plans now in disarray, evacuated his position without firing a shot and moved off to wait for a more suitable opportunity to attack the British.

The British force continued their advance and when they reach Bari they found that this town had also been abandoned by the mutineers.

Bitauli

Pressing on to his second objective, General Hope Grant and his force reached Muhammadabad on the 15th April and Ramnugger on the 19th April where they received the news that the Begum had evacuated Bitauli when she heard of the General's advance.

Protection of Jang Bahádur's force

General Hope Grant now set out to find Jang Bahádur and his army of Nepal and encountered them at Masauli; he now moved his force to protect the road between Cawnpore and Lucknow and eventually returned to Fort Jellalabad on the outskirts of Lucknow on 16th May.

Jang Bahádur and his men eventually crossed the border back into Nepal in early June 1858.

Battle of Nuwabgunge

At the beginning of June, General Hope Grant received news that a large body of mutineers was being assembled at Nuwabgunge, about 18 miles from Lucknow.

Determined to disperse the rebels, the General set out with a large force for Chinhut and joined up with Colonel Purnell who was camped there with a force of about 1,200 men. When he arrived at Chinhut, General Hope Grant learned that the rebels had taken up a strong position just outside Nuwabgunge on a small plateau with three sides protected by a stream and the fourth by jungle.

Hoping to make a surprise attack by interposing his force between that of the rebels and the jungle, General Hope Grant set out for Nuwabgunge at 11 o'clock on the evening of 12th June and after a night march of 12 miles reached his objective just before dawn.

After a short rest, the General sent four companies of the Rifles, a troop of Horse Artillery and some cavalry over the stream via a small stone bridge.

The enemy were taken completely by surprise but soon rallied and after bringing two guns to bear made a determined attack at the British rear, placing their guns in jeopardy. General Hope Grant ordered the 7th Hussars and a further four guns into the fray and after advancing to within 500 yards of the rebels the guns unleashed deadly volleys of grape shot, forcing them to retire leaving their guns behind.

The 7th Hussars mounted several charges at the retreating mutineers, causing many casualties and after about three hours of fighting the battle was over, with the 15,000 rebels scattered to all quarters.

Private Same (John) Shaw – Victoria Cross No. 274

During the battle one mutineer, having been separated from his comrades was determined to make a brave stand and with his back to a tree glared at the men who had confronted him.

Private Shaw decided to rush the man and end his fight, and despite having receiving a grievous blow to the head from the man's sword, managed to dispatch him with his own sword.

For this action, Private Shaw was later awarded the Victoria Cross.

The rebel leader Raja Balbhadra Singh was one of the over 600 rebels killed, over 400 were wounded. The British losses amounted to 36 killed and 62 wounded, however, a further 33 men died of sunstroke and about 250 men were hospitalised due to the effects of the sun.

After the battle, General Hope Grant returned to Lucknow for consultations with the Civil Commissioner while his troops remained encamped at Nuwabgunge.

Fyzabad

General Hope Grant soon returned to his force, with orders from the Commander-in-Chief to go to the aid of Raja Maun Singh a loyal native chief, who was besieged in his fort near Fyzabad.

On 22nd July, the General left Nuwabgunge and after a week of strenuous marching arrived at Fyzabad, occupied the city without opposition and relieved the siege of Raja Maun Singh's fortress.

With the approach of the British force, the 20,000 rebels had split into two columns, one retiring over the river Gogra and the other heading for Sultanpore.

Sultanpore

After relieving Raja Maun Singh, General Hope Grant was ordered to expel the rebels from Sultanpore, however, due to heavy rains it was not possible to start this venture until the 7th of August.

Brigadier Horsford was placed in command of a column made up of; the 1st Madras Fusiliers, the 5th Punjab Rifles, a detachment of the 7th Hussars, about 300 men from Hodson's Horse and a troop of Horse Artillery.

On 12th August, Brigadier Horsford's force was about three miles from Sultanpore and after a reconnaissance found the bridge over the River Sai to be well guarded by rebel guns and the force occupying the city was estimated to be 14,000 men.

Faced with this overwhelming force, Brigadier Horsford sent a message back to General Hope Grant requesting reinforcements.

On the morning of 19th August, General Hope Grant left Fyzabad with all of his guns and men, who had recently been augmented by a wing of the 53rd Regiment and arrived at Sultanpore four days later.

The General wanted to make a river crossing immediately but the rebels had removed all of the boats, however, the engineers and Madras Sappers managed to cobble together three substantial rafts from small boats that were found abandoned.

On the morning of the 25th August, in a matter of only two hours, the 1st Madras Fusiliers and 5th Punjab Infantry were ferried across the river, followed by the guns which had been dismounted from their carriages.

Colonel Galway was placed in command of this force and ordered to occupy two villages where the enemy had established a piquet. The advance force quickly occupied the villages, but were soon under heavy fire from the rebels, so the Punjab Rifles were sent across the river to provide support.

It took two further days for the main force to cross the river, the hospital and heavy guns were left behind under the guard of the wing of the 53rd Regiment of Foot.

On the evening of the 28th August, the rebels mounted an attack on the British position but after a brisk fight were repulsed, darkness prevented a British pursuit.

On the next morning, when the British advanced, the town was found to have been abandoned so Sultanpore was occupied without further opposition.

Preparations for the winter campaign

The capture of Sultanpore ended General Hope Grant's major operations for the summer, apart from minor operations to destroy some strategic forts and to disrupt the gathering of rebel forces in preparation for the upcoming winter campaign.

Ensign Patrick Roddy – Victoria Cross No. 283

It was on the 27th September 1858, while returning from such an operation, led by Major Hume against rebels at Kuthirga, that Ensign Roddy who was attached to the Kapurthala Contingent came across some retreating rebels.

The cavalry were reluctant to approach one large rebel, armed with a percussion musket, as before they could get within striking distance of their swords he would lose off a shot.

Undeterred, Ensign Roddy charged the man, who at a distance of about 6 yards discharged his musket killing Ensign Roddy's horse, which fell and trapped him on the ground.

The rebel immediately went in to attack the disadvantaged Roddy with his sword, however, Ensign Roddy managed to hold him off long enough for him to draw his own sword and kill the rebel.

For this action Ensign Roddy was later awarded the Victoria Cross.

It is said the Ensign Roddy had previously been offered a Victoria Cross, for actions at the Alum Bagh but had preferred to accept a commission instead.

The Rohilkhand Campaign

General Campbell's plan for operations against the Rohilkhand rebels, involved; General Walpole's brigade clearing the left bank of the Ganges up to the Rohilkhand border where he would be joined by a force from Futtehgur with as many troops as could be spared from Cawnpore, commanded by General Campbell himself. Major-General Penny was to advance from Meerut and join up with General Campbell's conjoined force at Miranpur Katra, mid way between Shahjehanpore and Bareilly. Brigadier-General Jones would invade Rohilkhand from the north west with a force that he was assembling at Roorkee. The three columns would then converge on Bareilly, where it was expected that they would engage and defeat the main rebel forces.

Major-General Seaton, in command of the forces at Futtehgur would patrol the Ganges to stop rebels assembling to the rear of the Rohilkhand Field Force.

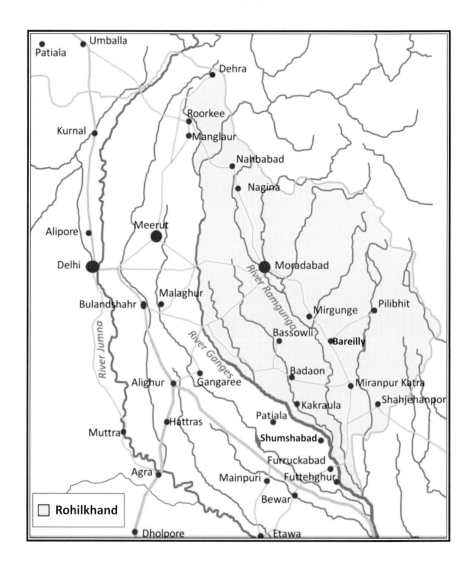

Figure 83. Rohilkhand province

General Walpole's Field Force

On 10th April 1858, General Walpole left Lucknow with his field force made up of; Infantry brigade commanded by Brigadier Adrian Hope with the 42nd, 79th and 93rd Highlanders and the 4th Punjab Rifles; Cavalry consisting of 9th Lancers and 2nd Punjab Cavalry and Artillery commanded by Major Brind with two troops of horse artillery, two 18 pounders, two 8" howitzers and nine mortars plus a few engineers and sappers.

A new fort being constructed by the rebels at Roheenadabad was destroyed by the field force on 11th April.

Fort Rooya

On the 15th April 1858, General Walpole and his force arrived at the village of Madhogunge about a mile from the jungle fort of Rooya which belonged to the rebel leader Nurput Sing.

Leaving his baggage, guarded by a strong force of cavalry and infantry, supported by two field guns, General Walpole advanced on the fort with the rest of his force.

Acting on intelligence, which proved to be incorrect, General Walpole advanced on the northern wall of the fort which he expected to be the weak point and only guarded by a few guns. On arrival at the fort it was discovered that the north and east sides of the fort, which were surrounded by thick jungle, were in fact the strong points with the walls, fronted by a deep ditch, having several gun bastions and loopholes for musket fire. General Walpole sent a small force of infantry to reconnoitre the south side and his cavalry to the west side which effectively encircled the fort. Units of the 42nd Regiment were sent forward towards a gate on the north side, it was generally expected that Major Wilkinson would be making an attack on the weaker south side and the 42nd were being positioned to prevent the rebels escaping from the gate in the north wall. This assumption proved to be incorrect as General Walpole ordered the small force, without the benefit of artillery support, to advance on the gate and engage the mutineers.

Captain Grove advanced as ordered and managed to reach the ditch in front of the fort, which offered some protection, however, under the withering fire from the fort his men were suffering heavy casualties and Captain Grove called up for reinforcements. Captain Cafe with a force of about 100 men from the 4th Punjab Rifles soon arrived and took up position with the men from the 42nd in the ditch at the front of the north wall.

An attempt to scale the parapet was made but was finally abandoned after a loss of two officers and 46 men killed or wounded.

Captain William Cafe – Victoria Cross No. 264
Lance Corporal Alexander Thompson – Victoria Cross No. 266
Private Edward Spence – Victoria Cross No. 270

Captain Cafe asked Captain Grove for permission to call for volunteers to retrieve Lieutenant Edward Willoughby[23] who had fallen during the attempt to scale the parapet. The Lieutenant who was on the sick list had left his sick bed to join in the fight.

Lance-Corporal Thompson and Private Spence, together with two native officers from the 4th Punjab Rifles volunteered to join Captain Cafe in this dangerous task. On reaching Lieutenant Willoughby, they found that he was dead but they still returned with his body to prevent it being mutilated.

During the action, Captain Cafe had his left arm broken and Private Spence received what would prove to be a mortal wound.

Captain Cafe, Lance-Corporal Thompson and Private Spence were all later awarded the Victoria Cross for their part in this action.

Quartermaster Sergeant John Simpson – Victoria Cross No. 265

After the attack on the parapet, Quartermaster-Sergeant Simpson advanced to within 40 yards of the north wall to bring Lieutenant Douglas, who had been badly wounded, back to a place of safety.

Quartermaster-Sergeant Simpson went out once again, under heavy fire, to bring a badly wounded Private back to safety.

For these actions Quartermaster-Sergeant Simpson was later awarded the Victoria Cross.

Private James Davis – Victoria Cross No. 267

Private Davis together with another Private from his regiment, volunteered to go out under heavy fire to rescue Lieutenant Bramley who was badly wounded. When the other Private was shot and killed, Private Davis continued on his own and brought Lieutenant Bramley to safety, unfortunately the Lieutenant's wound proved to be mortal.

Private Davis went out once again to bring back the body of the private who was killed during the rescue attempt.

For this action Private Davis was later awarded the Victoria Cross.

---

23 Lieutenant Edward Willoughby was the brother of Captain Willoughby one of the defenders of the Delhi Magazine

Soon after these events, Brigadier Adian Hope arrived at the front and almost immediately was shot dead. After enduring about six hours of intensive fire from the mutineers in the fort, General Walpole finally abandoned the assault and issued the order to retreat.

Unable to bring his heavy guns to bear on the north wall, General Walpole decided to withdraw his forces from the north wall and planned for an attack against the south wall during the next morning.

On the morning of the 16th April, it was discovered that the rebels had fled from the fort during the night, leaving their guns behind.

The next day, the column resumed their march and towards the end of the day they came across a large body of mutineers who were occupying some small villages near to the town of Alligunge.

After a brief artillery duel and a cavalry engagement, while the rebels tried to cover the removal of their guns, the mutineers were forced to retreat in much haste across the River Ramganga by the bridge of boats at Alligunge.

On the 18th April, General Walpole moved his heavy guns to the right bank of the river and secured the bridge in readiness for the crossing of the siege train, which would be required for the assault on Bareilly.

On the same day, General Campbell left Lucknow to join up with his forces at Cawnpore, three days earlier the siege train with 28 heavy guns and mortars left Cawnpore for Futtehgur, escorted by a squadron of Punjab Cavalry, the 75th Highlanders and the 2nd Punjab Infantry.

General Campbell's Field Force

As General Campbell arrived at Cawnpore, the Headquarters Staff left for Futtehgur but the General remained until the following day when, escorted by a squadron of 5th Punjab Cavalry, a squadron of Irregular Cavalry and the headquarters of the 80th foot, he also set out for Futtehgur. General Campbell's party caught up with the Headquarters Staff column on the 20th April, having performed a double days' march and together they proceeded towards Futtehgur, crossing the bridge at Kala Nuddee on 24th April. Wanting to have discussions with General Penny, General Campbell rode into Futtehgur that evening and was followed by his column the next morning.

Colonel Seaton, who had been left in charge of Futtehgur and surrounding districts in January, had been busy during the intervening period; strengthening the fort and moving the bridge of boats to a position where it was dominated by the fort.

In early April, large enemy forces were being assembled at Alligunge, Bargaum and Kankar with the intention of crossing the Ganges and invading the Doab via Rohilkhand.

On the night of 6th April, Colonel Seaton with a force of 1,000 infantry and 300 cavalry supported by 5 guns set out to disperse the forces gathering at Kankar. At daybreak the next morning, Colonel Seaton attacked and defeated the rebels, killing about 250 of their number and captured 3 guns.

This action seemed to postpone the planned invasion by the rebels.

On 27th April, General Walpole's column, together with the siege train joined General Campbell's forces gathered at Futtehgur.

On the next morning, the combined force set off for Jellalabad, which they reached later in the day and found the fort and town to have been recently abandoned by the mutineers.

The next day, the force marched to the town of Kanth and on the way received the sad new that Captain William Peel of the Naval Brigade was dead and on reaching the town were greeted with the further bad news that General Penny had also been killed.

On 30th April General Campbell's force crossed the Ramganga River by way of a bridge of boats and camped outside the city of Shahjehanpore where he set up a military post.

The column resumed its march on the 2nd May and reached Furreedpore on the outskirts of Bareilly on 4th May.

General Penny's Field Force

After his discussions with General Campbell at Futtehgur on 25th April, General Penny crossed the Ganges to carry out his part in the Rohilkhand Campaign and following intelligence proceeded to Oosait where a large force of rebels was said to be concentrating. General Penny sent his heavy guns and baggage, under a heavy escort, to the town of Kukerowlee.

Arriving near the town at midnight, General Penny received the news that the rebels had moved on to the town of Datagunge so continued the night march towards Kukerowlee.

On reaching the outskirts of the town, several horsemen were seen to their front and it was assumed that this was part of their own force sent to escort the heavy guns and baggage to the town. However, this was not the case, they had walked into a prepared rebel ambush and the enemy opened up with artillery fire from the right while cavalry attacked from the left and the rebel infantry open fire at their front. During the initial fusillade of grapeshot, General Penny was mown down and killed; Colonel Jones assumed command of the column and tried to deploy his artillery and cavalry but due to the excellent defensive positions of the enemy this was largely ineffective so the Colonel decided to hold his ground and await the arrival of the infantry.

With the arrival of Lieutenant-Colonel Bingham and men from the 64th Regiment of Foot, an attack was launched and the rebels were dislodged from their defences and forced back into the town; a cavalry charge induced the enemy to flee the town and they were pursued for some distance.

After spending the night at Kukerowlee, Colonel Jones now in command of the column set off again the next morning and after crossing the Ramganga joined up with General Campbell's force.

General Jones's Roorkee Field Force

On 13th April, Brigadier-General Jones left Roorkee with his field force to come at the rebels in Rohilkhand from the north west. His force consisted of: Cavalry, a squadron of 6th Dragoon Guards and the Multan Horse; Infantry, 60th Royal Rifles, 1st Punjab Rifles, 17th Punjab Infantry and 1st Sikh Infantry and Artillery comprising one light and one heavy battery.

General Jones's first objective was to get his men, guns and supplies across the River Ganges but when he heard that a large rebel force was encamped at Nargal, on the left bank of the river about 16 miles from Hardwar, he devised a plan to not only cross the river but at the same time inflict a defeat on the enemy.

The General moved his heavy guns and baggage to a point on the right river bank directly opposite the town of Nargal and deceived the rebels into thinking that this was where he would make his crossing. Meanwhile, he led his main force to a spot near Hardwar where they crossed the river and proceeded down the left bank which was covered in jungle. The advanced guard soon made contact with the enemy at Bhagneewalla where the rebels opened fire on them with six artillery pieces. The field artillery, commanded by Captain Austen was quick to return fire and the Multan Horse mounted several charges which dispersed the rebels who fled in great disorder. They were chased for several miles by the cavalry who inflicted heavy casualties and captured four guns.

The next morning, Captain Cureton of the Multan Horse sent out a patrol of his men, commanded by a native officer, Emam Buksh Khan, to investigate reports that rebels were concealed in the jungle near the village of Nujeejabad. On reaching the village, Emam Buksh Khan was informed that about 500 rebels were located nearby in the Khote Fort. Emam Buksh Khan proceeded to the fort with his men and after surrounding it called to the garrison to surrender or he would show no quarter. Without a fight, the gates to the fort were opened and the mutineers were disarmed.

Not being eligible for the award of the Victoria Cross, Emam Buksh Khan was awarded the Order of Merit 3rd class for this expedition.

On the 18th April, the force moved through Nujeejabad and pushed on to Fort Futtehgur, which they found had been recently abandoned by the rebels as eight guns, a store of ammunition and grain were still in place.

On 20th April, the heavy guns crossed the Ganges and rejoined the main force. On the same day, General Jones received news that 6,000 rebels were gathered at Nugeenah and set off with his force to engage them.

At 9 o'clock on the morning of 21st April, the British force arrived at Nujeejabad and found the enemy dug in by a canal which fronted the town. After a heated artillery exchange, the enemy artillery was driven out of the town by attacks from the British cavalry and with the loss of their artillery the mutineers were soon dispersed.

On the next day, General Jones continued his advance, making for the town of Moradabad which was on the direct route to Bareilly, his primary objective.

While on the road, the General received news that the town was being looted by Feroze Shar (one of the princes of Delhi) and 2,000 of his men, however, as he got closer Feroze Shar abandoned the town and retreated to Bareilly.

When General Jones reached Moradabad, he decided to set up camp and wait for news of General Walpole's column so that he could time his arrival at Bareilly to coincide with that of his fellow General.

The column resumed its march on 3rd May and two days later reached Meergunge about 14 miles from Bareilly where it again waited for news of the other advancing British Columns.

Battle of Bareilly

With his forces now assembled, General Campbell was ready to make his attack on Bareilly, the capital of Rohilkhand.

The forces at his disposal consisted of: Cavalry; 1st Brigade commanded by Brigadier Jones with 6th Dragoon Guards and the Multan Horse, 2nd Brigade commanded by Brigadier Hagart with 9th Lancers, 2nd Punjab Cavalry and detachments of Lahore Light Horse, 1st Punjab Cavalry and 17th Irregular Cavalry; Artillery under the command of Lieutenant-Colonel Brind with two troops of Bengal Horse Artillery, two batteries of Bengal Heavy field artillery, a battery of Bengal Light field artillery and the Siege train Company; Infantry was the Highland Brigade under the command of Lieutenant-Colonel Hay with 42nd, 78th, 79th and 93rd Highlanders, 4th Punjab Rifles, the Beluch Battalion, companies from 64th and 82nd Regiments of

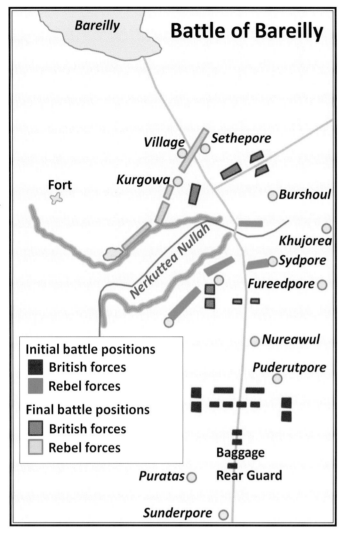

Figure 84. Battle of Bareilly

cavalry was followed by the infantry with the 78th Highlanders and a detachment of sappers and engineers moving down the road with the 93rd Highlanders to the right of the road and the 42nd Highlanders to the left of the road. In close support of the first line of troops were the 79th Highlanders and the Beluch battalion, with the 6th Dragoon Guards, the Multan Horse, 9th Lancers and a detachment of Punjab Cavalry.

The baggage and siege trains were protected by the 64th Regiment, a wing of the 82nd Regiment, the 2nd Punjab Infantry and the 4th Punjab Rifles.

A rear guard comprising 22nd Punjab Infantry, a troop of horse artillery, a squadron of 5th Punjab Cavalry and the 17th Irregular Cavalry, completed the force which numbered 7,636 men with 19 guns (excluding those with the siege train).

The mutineers had come out of the city and formed up along the banks of the Nuttea Nuddee with a stream between them and the city; at about 7 o'clock in the morning they opened up with artillery fire.

The British horse artillery and cavalry quickly advanced along both flanks and before long their guns were unlimbered and responding to the enemy fire, so accurate and telling was their fire that the rebels abandoned their guns and fled back over the stream towards the city. The heavy artillery and infantry now advanced down the road until they reached the ravine with the river at the bottom; part of the force took up position on the river bank while the remainder crossed the bridge and advanced towards the town. The heavy guns were quickly brought across the bridge and began to bombard the centre of the enemy line which was entrenched in houses and enclosures in the city suburbs.

General Campbell now called a temporary halt to the advance, to allow the siege and baggage train to catch up and to give his artillery time to cause havoc in the rebel defensive positions.

At about 11 o'clock in the morning, while the British attention was focused on the large enemy force in the suburbs, a large force of about 150 Rohilla Ghazees left the cover of some buildings and made a concerted attempt to turn the British left flank.

They first fell upon men of the 4th Punjab Rifles who had just occupied some of the old cavalry lines and pushed them back towards the 42nd Highlanders.

Colour Sergeant William Gardner – Victoria Cross No. 271

General Campbell, who was directing matters from a position close to his beloved Highlanders, immediately called the 42nd into line with fixed bayonets and they met the charge of the fanatical Ghazees head on.

Foot, 2nd and 22nd Punjab Infantry and a detachment of Bengal Sappers and Miners.

Long before first light on the 5th May 1858, General Campbell advanced with his force from Furreedpore and was informed by his cavalry patrols that the enemy were formed up in line of battle in front of his approach, supported by cavalry.

General Campbell formed up his own battle lines, with the Highland Brigade, 4th Sikhs and Beluch Battalion at the centre supported by cavalry and horse artillery on both flanks.

A second battle line was formed to protect the baggage and siege trains from attack by enemy cavalry.

As the battle began, the 2nd Punjab Cavalry formed up on the left of the main road with the Lahore Light Horse on the right of the road and across the road were the 9th Lancers, 1st Punjab Cavalry, a troop of horse artillery and several field guns. The

A band of rebels managed to get around the left flank and gain the rear of the formation where three of them dragged Colonel Alexander Cameron from his horse before he could draw his sword.

Seeing the plight of his Commanding Officer, Colour-Sergeant Gardiner rushed forward and bayoneted two of his assailants while Private Gavin shot the third.

Had it not been for the Colour-Sergeant's brave intervention Colonel Cameron would have been hacked to death.

For his part in this action, Colour-Sergeant Gardiner was later awarded the Victoria Cross.

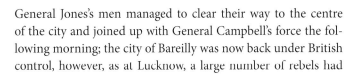

The Ghazee attack continued and came to within ten yards of the British guns, however, the 42nd held firm and at the end of the fight 133 rebel bodies surrounded the 42nd colours.

While the Ghazee attack took place, a large enemy cavalry force made a determined attack on the baggage train, however, fire from Captain Tombs's troop of horse artillery, followed up by a charge of two squadrons of the 6th Dragoon Guards and the Multan Horse soon dispersed them.

This was the last offensive action by the rebels and soon afterwards the 79th and 93rd Highlanders were ordered to seize the suburbs in the centre and the enemy retreated back into the city.

As his men had been fighting for over six hours, during the hottest part of the day, and as the next phase would involve hand to hand street fighting, General Campbell called a halt to the action and set up camp for the night to allow the men some well earned rest.

At dawn on the following morning, General Campbell advanced with his force into the cantonments and as they moved forward they heard the sound of guns in the distance, the General correctly assumed that the Roorkee Field Force had arrived to join in the battle.

On the morning of 6th May, General Jones with the Roorkee Field Force began his final advance on Bareilly and after a fierce artillery battle managed to carry a bridge and gain entry to the city.

Private Valentine Bambrick – Victoria Cross No. 272

Confused street by street fighting now took place in the warren of streets and alleyways that comprised this part of the city.

During the fighting, Private Bambrick together with his company commander Lieutenant Cromer Ashburnham were cornered in a serai by three mutineers, despite having been wounded twice Private Bambrick helped fight off the rebels, killing one in the process.

For this action, Private Bambrick was later awarded the Victoria Cross, having been nominated for the award by Lieutenant Ashburnham.

General Jones's men managed to clear their way to the centre of the city and joined up with General Campbell's force the following morning; the city of Bareilly was now back under British control, however, as at Lucknow, a large number of rebels had been allowed to escape.

Battle of Shahjehanpore

On 30th April, when General Campbell passed through Shahjehanpore on his way to Bareilly, where he had left a small garrison in place to provide some protection to his rear.

Lieutenant-Colonel Hale had been left with a wing of the 82nd Regiment of Foot, a detachment of artillery with two 24 pounder and two 9 pounders guns and De Kantzow's Irregular Horse.

When the rebel Nana Sahib had abandoned the town, all the roofs had been torn from the buildings so as to make them uninhabitable; Colonel Hale therefore made his camp under canvas, near the jail which he stocked with provisions and deployed his guns to make it a defensible position.

After learning that General Campbell would leave Shahjehanpore on the morning of 2nd May, a large force stationed at Muhammadi resolved to attack any garrison that had been left behind. Hoping to mount a surprise attack, the rebel force marched through the day and into the night arriving at a place just four miles from the town on the night of 2nd May; rather than press ahead with an attack, the rebel leaders decided to halt and rest their men before making an attack in the morning. This halt eliminated the considerable advantage of a surprise attack, as during the night native British spies reported the presence of the rebels to Colonel Hale.

The Colonel immediately moved all of his stores and camp equipment into the jail enclosure, guarded by four companies of the 82nd Regiment. He then moved out with Lieutenant De Kantzow's Horse to reconnoitre the situation and soon found a vast army of about 8,000 rebel cavalry resting on the plain. Lieutenant De Kantzow wanted to engage the enemy but Colonel Hale wisely overruled him and the party returned to Shahjehanpore, where he assembled all of his troops in the jail enclosure.

On the morning of 3rd May the rebels advanced on the town, which it occupied and plundered. Eight enemy guns were brought to bear on the jail enclosure and began a bombardment which would last for eight days and nights.

General Campbell first heard news of the siege at Shahjehanpore on 7th May when Bareilly was finally back in British hands. On hearing the news, General Campbell broke up the Roorkee Field Force and formed the Shahjehanpore Field Force under the command of Brigadier-General Jones to go to the rescue of Colonel Hale and his men.

The force was made up of Field Artillery commanded by Captain Austen, Heavy Artillery commanded by Lieutenant Stubbs, a company of sappers, two squadrons of the 6th Dragoon Guards, the Multan Horse, 60th Rifles, 79th Highlanders, a wing of the 82nd Regiment of Foot and the 22nd Punjab Infantry.

On the 8th May the field force left Bareilly and by 11th May was just outside Shahjehanpore. Instead of proceeding along the road from Bareilly and crossing the river Gogra by a stone bridge to enter the southern part of the town, which would have meant street fighting through the town, the force instead headed for the northern suburbs.

While looking for a place to ford the river, a large body of enemy cavalry came out of the town and crossed the river by the stone bridge to attack General Jones's right flank. The field force immediately formed up to face the enemy, with the 60th Rifles and 79th Highlanders forming the first line with the 22nd Punjab Infantry in support and the cavalry providing protection to their right flank. At a distance of about 1,200 yards Lieutenant Stubbs heavy artillery was deployed and after a few rounds managed to disperse the enemy cavalry. With the rebel cavalry in retreat, the British cavalry and Horse Artillery gave chase and pushed them across the river and back into the town.

The heavy artillery was now moved up and proceeded to bombard the main streets of the city and under cover of their fire the British infantry crossed the Gogra and moved into the eastern suburbs and skirting the main part of the town reached the old cantonment, near the jail, where they joined up with Colonel Hale's men.

It was soon discovered that the field force had been opposed by only a fraction of the rebel force, the main body of the enemy forces had been assembled at a fort on the other side of a small stream, the Kanhaut. On the 14th May, General Jones received intelligence that the rebels intended to mount an attack against his rear, so at about 2 o'clock in the morning he assembled his troops behind the stream in readiness.

As dawn broke, the rebel army was seen to be advancing and soon the British artillery opened fire under which the enemy retreated to the cover of nearby trees.

A group of rebel cavalry crossed the Kanhaut and charged the heavy guns, however, rounds of grape shot stopped their progress and the few that got through were charged by Lieutenant De Kantzow and two of his troopers while the guns resumed their bombardment of the rebel lines.

Despite having defeated a vastly superior force, General Jones was conscious of his vulnerability and sent a message to General Campbell for further reinforcements to secure his position.

During the next few days, until 14th May, General Jones spent most of his time in making preparations for an expected attack from the rebels; during the same period, a large number of mutineers reinforced the rebel army.

With his forces now enlarged, on the 15th May, the rebel leader launched an all out attack on the British force dug in at the jail enclosure.

The enemy mounted charge after charge against the British position but each was successfully repelled, however, due to his lack of cavalry, General Jones was not able to go on the offensive and contented himself with maintaining his position.

Garrison established at Bareilly

With the recapture of Bareilly, the province of Rohilkhand was back under British control, however, with large bands of rebels still in the area it was imperative to establish a strong garrison at Bareilly, so General Walpole was appointed to the command of the troops in the province.

A force comprising; Remington's Horse Artillery, a heavy field battery, the 2nd Punjab Cavalry, a wing of the 42nd Highlanders, the 78th and 93rd Highlanders and the 17th Punjab Infantry was selected to form the garrison.

For special operations, a moveable column under the command of Brigadier Coke was formed with Hammond's Light Field Battery, a Heavy Field Battery, 100 Pioneers, a squadron of the 17th Irregular Cavalry, a wing of the 42nd Highlanders, the 1st Punjab Infantry and the 1st Sikh Infantry.

On 11th May, the movable column moved off towards Pillebheet where the leader of the Rohilkhand rebels, Khan Bahadur Khan was said to have fled.

On 15th May, having made the above arrangements, General Campbell left Bareilly for Futtehgur where he would have a more central location to oversee the overall campaigning.

The General moved out with his; headquarters staff, Captain Tombs's Horse Artillery, some of the siege artillery, two squadrons of 9th Lancers, three squadrons of Punjab Cavalry, the 64th Regiment of Foot and the Beluch Battalion; and after a march of six hours made camp at Furreedpore.

Early the next morning the march resumed and the force reached Futtehgur where General Campbell received the message from General Jones, regarding his plight at Shahjehanpore.

General Campbell immediately sent messages for the remainder of the 9th Lancers at Bareilly and also to Brigadier Coke with his moveable column to come and join him as soon as possible. On the 17th May, the force was joined by the rest of the 9th Lancers, while they camped at Tilhour and after receiving news that the rebels were camped a few miles outside of Shahjehanpore set off that evening to intercept them.

After a night time march, the force crossed the bridge of boats and entered the city at about 9 o'clock in the morning and established their camp near the old cantonment where they could guard two fords and the bridge of boats. A strong piquet with two guns was posted in the village of Lohedpoor on the banks of the Kanhaut stream.

In the afternoon, Colonel Percy Herbert with a small unit of cavalry carried out a reconnaissance of the ground on the far side of the Kanhaut stream and about two miles from the British camp came across a mud fort occupied by a large rebel force.

When Colonel Herbert came within range, his cavalry were assailed by artillery fire from the fort, followed by the movement of a large rebel cavalry force which came onto the plain from behind the fort.

To face this threat, General Campbell placed the Rifle Brigade and 64th and 79th Regiments of Foot along his front, supported by Captain Tombs's Horse Artillery which was soon returning the enemy fire.

As the British infantry advanced, the rebels withdrew their guns back to the fort and their cavalry melted away, with insufficient cavalry at his disposal General Campbell chose not to pursue the enemy.

On the morning of 23rd May, Brigadier Coke's force joined up with General Campbell's force, however, with news that the River Ganges was rising and that access to Futtehgur by the bridge of boats might soon be impassable, General Campbell decided to make a dash for the town with a small escort and arrived there two days later.

General Jones was left with orders to attack the mutineers on the next morning.

Battle of Mohumdee

On 24th May, in accordance with his orders, General Jones advanced on Mohumdee, some 20 miles from Shahjehanpore, where the rebels had concentrated.

On approaching the village of Bunnai, the rebel artillery opened up on the column, however, a return barrage from the British Heavy guns kept their cavalry at bay.

As the British Cavalry and Horse Artillery advanced the enemy forces fell back and the main British column pushed forward.

When the British Cavalry passed a mango grove a small body of rebel cavalry, 20 in number, led by the rebel cavalry leader charged into the Multan Horse who were on the right flank. The rebels managed to kill and wound some of the Multan Horse, however, after a brief fight all of the rebels including their leader were killed.

The British cavalry chose this moment to charge the rebel force, which did not stand to meet the charge but instead fled across the plain and escaped with only minor losses.

On the next day, General Jones moved with his column to Mohumdee and found that it had been abandoned by the rebels, after blowing up the fort and a nearby fortified village the force returned to Shahjehanpore where they arrived on 29th May.

End of Rohilkhand Campaign

On the 1st June General Jones sent out an expedition which after a minor engagement captured the town of Shahabad, two weeks later on the 14th June the Shahjehanpore Field Force was disbanded and signalled the end of the Rohilkhand Campaign.

Much of the hard work had been done, with large armies having been defeated and dispersed, however, much still remained to drive the rebels out of Western Bengal, Oudh and Central India.

Continued unrest in Rohilkhand

Although the campaign had ended, turmoil still existed in the Rohilkhand and the bordering state of Oudh due to the dissatisfaction of many of the landowners, however, the dissidents could not agree on a coordinated resistance and began to act independently.

The Nizam Ali Khan with a large group of followers began to threaten the British post at Pillebheet (Hafizabad) and Khan Bahadur Khan with 4,000 followers, the Nawab of Farrukhabad with 5,000 followers and Walayat Shah with 3,000 followers were also active.

A small force under the command of Lieutenant De Kantzow was sent to protect the station at Powain, where the local Rajah was convinced to keep his 2,000 levies under training which proved successful in preventing an attack on the town.

By the end of August, Ali Khan Mewati, acting with Nizam Ali Khan was threatening the village of Nuriah, only 10 miles from the military post at Pillebheet. Captain Robert Larkins, in command at Pillebheet, sent a small force of 200 men commanded by Lieutenant Craigie to Nuriah on 28th August with instructions to hold the village against any rebel attacks. On the following morning the two rebel chiefs, with 300 infantry and

100 cavalry, supported by three guns, mounted an attack on the village. Lieutenant Craigie and his men met the rebels outside of the village and after some vicious hand to hand fighting repulsed the attack, after which the rebels retired to the nearby village of Sirpurah, three miles away. Hearing the noise of the fighting, Captain Larkins decided to send reinforcements to Lieutenant Craigie and despatched Captain Browne with a force of 150 men of the 2nd Punjab Cavalry and 100 Kumaon levies to Nuriah, which they reached at 4 o'clock that afternoon. After having reconnoitred the enemy position and finding that a direct attack would involve crossing about a mile of flooded ground, with water about 2 feet deep, Captain Browne decided to make a detour and attack the rebel flank and rear.

Battle of Sirpurah

At midnight, Captain Browne with; 230 Punjab Cavalry, 150 men of the 17th Native Infantry, 100 men of the 24th Pioneers and 100 Kumaon levies began to circle around the enemy right flank and by daybreak had reached a position to the left rear of the rebels.

After a strenuous journey through the night, Captain Browne halted his column for a much needed rest, however, this was short lived as the rebels soon noticed the British force and began to bring their artillery into action against the resting men. With their position having been discovered, Captain Browne had no alternative but to order his force to advance. With his front covered by skirmishers with fixed bayonets, Captain Browne and his infantry advanced under the cover of a grassy jungle.

Captain Samuel Browne – Victoria Cross No. 281

As the infantry advanced, the British cavalry on the left were advancing down the road and soon became the target for the enemy artillery.

Seeing a gun to his front, that was firing grape shot at the cavalry, Captain Browne with his orderly charged the gun and immediately set about the gunners in order to prevent them from firing their gun.

Captain Browne was soon surrounded by rebels and he was wounded in the knee and soon afterwards his left arm was severed at the shoulder by a sword blow, his horse was also struck down and fell, trapping the captain beneath him.

Despite his wounds, Captain Browne had prevented the rebels firing their gun and the advancing skirmishers soon capture the gun and slaughtered the gunners.

For this action Captain Browne was later awarded the Victoria Cross.

The infantry continued their advance and captured the enemy position, aided by the cavalry who swept up the left flank.

The battle was won with heavy losses having been inflicted upon the rebels, the two rebel leaders managed to escape, however, Nizam Ali Khan was wounded.

Sardar River Force

In November 1858, General Walpole despatched a small force from the garrison at Bareilly, under the command of Colonel Smythe to guard the river crossings at the Sardar River, which was the border between Oudh and Rohilkhand, with the intention of preventing the Oudh mutineers crossing into the province.

The force consisted of one company from the 42nd Regiment of Foot commanded by Captain William Lawson, a squadron of Native Cavalry and a detachment from the newly raised Kumaon Native regiment, the force was to be split between the major crossing points at the Maylah and Sissaya Ghats.

For some time this was a pleasurable posting, however things were soon to change drastically.

Private Walter Cook – Victoria Cross No. 293
Private Duncan Millar – Victoria Cross No. 294

On the morning of 15th January 1859, a force of about 2,000 rebels crossed the river Sardar at Maylah Ghat about three miles from Colonel Smythe's main camp.

In the dense jungle, the British cavalry could not be deployed and the Kumaon regiment was composed of raw recruits so could not be relied upon. The bulk of the resistance would have to fall on the shoulders of Captain Lawson and his men from No.6 Company of the 42nd Regiment. Unfortunately, as half of his men were on picket duty with Ensign Francis Coleridge, and secluded at some distance away, Captain Lawson was faced with the prospect of taking on the rebel force with only 37 men.

Late in the afternoon, Captain Lawson was severely wounded in the groin and taken to the rear; he later died from his wounds. The only other officer, Lieutenant Bayly was also wounded and the three NCOs a Colour-Sergeant and two Corporals were all killed.

Hearing the noise of the fighting, Colonel Smythe sent for reinforcements, however, the nearest detachment was at Madho Tanda a day's march away.

With no officers or NCOs to offer direction, Privates Cook and Millar moved to the front and began to direct the troops and provide encouragement. Against almost impossible odds, Ensign Coleridge managed to force his way through the jungle with the other half of the company and the rebels fearing further reinforcements began to back off, which allowed the small force to take up better positions. The small force managed to keep the rebels at bay for ten hours from dawn until dusk, 17 of the men were killed or wounded.

For their part in the action, Privates Cook and Millar were both awarded the Victoria Cross.

—— ✠ ——

Reinforcements from Madho Tanda arrived the next day and managed to drive the rebels back across the river.

In march 1859, the field force was disbanded and the units returned to their garrison duties at Bareilly.

Azamgarh Campaign

Following his defeat at Jugdeespore and the destruction of his citadel, Kunwar Singh with his force of mutineers and retainers moved off towards the state of Rewa, hoping to make his way eventually to Upper India or Delhi to join up with other forces of mutineers.

When Kunwar Singh attempted to cross the Rewa, the young Rajah of Rewa, who was related to Kunwar Singh, surprisingly refused him permission to cross his territory, so he abandoned the attempt.

For some months there was no news of Kunwar Singh, until it came to light that he had crossed the River Ganges into Oudh and on 17th March 1858 had captured the village of Atraulia about 20 miles from Azamgarh.

Colonel Milman, in command of the small garrison at Azamgarh, which was made up of 200 men of his own regiment the 37th Foot and 60 men of the 4th Madras Cavalry, supported by two light field guns, decided to move against Kunwar Singh when he heard about the occupation of Atraulia.

On 21st March, Colonel Milman left his camp at Koelsar and after marching through the night came across a band of rebels in some mango groves, after driving off the mutineers the party was ordered to stand down and have breakfast. While the force rested, news arrived that the main body of the rebels was advancing on their position. In danger of being encircled, Colonel Milman decided to fall back to their old camping ground at Koelsar. Leaving his baggage behind, Colonel Milman retired back to the entrenchment around the jail on the outskirts of Azamgarh and sent urgent requests for reinforcements to Benares, Allahabad and Lucknow.

On 26th March, Kunwar Singh with a force of 5,000 men with four guns occupied the town of Azamgarh, however, by this time the British force within the jail entrenchment had been reinforced by 46 men of the Madras Rifles and 280 men of the 37th Regiment from Ghazeepore. Colonel Dames, who came with the reinforcements, being the senior officer, assumed command.

On the following day, Colonel Dames decided to go on the offensive and mounted a sortie on the rebels gathered on the plain. His small force, of 200 men from the 37th supported by 60 men of the Madras Cavalry with two guns, managed to drive off some of the rebels and flushed with success the Colonel decided to attack the town but was easily repulsed and had to retire back to the jail.

On 27th March, Lord Canning was informed of the enemy occupation of Azamgarh and realised that if this was not countered then Kunwar Singh would probably mount an attack on Benares.

First relief of Azamgarh

General Lord Mark Kerr was at once ordered to march from his station at Allahabad and go to the relief of Azamgarh. That evening he left Allahabad with the left wing of his regiment the 13th Light Infantry, a total of 372 men and 19 officers, and arrived at Benares on 31st March.

At Benares General Kerr's force was augmented by 55 men and two officers of the 2nd Dragoon Guards and 17 men and one officer of the Royal Artillery with two guns and two mortars.

The Azamgarh Relief Force left Benares on 2nd April and by 5th April had arrived at a small village about ten miles outside the town. In the early hours of the 6th April, General Kerr began his advance into Azamgarh, somewhat hampered by his large supply of stores and ammunition being conveyed on elephants, camels and oxen drawn carts. While trying to clear the way for the supply train, an advanced party was assailed by heavy musket fire to their front and flanks from rebels hiding in the trees and nearby buildings. With his small number of guns, General Kerr tried to suppress the rebels with artillery fire but too little effect.

Private Patrick Carlin – Victoria Cross No. 263

During the action, Private Carlin was trying to carry a wounded native Corporal of 4th madras rifles off the battle field when he was fired upon by a mutineer.

After placing the wounded Corporal on the ground and borrowing his sword, Private Carlin fought off and killed the man and then carried the wounded Corporal off to safety.

For this action, Private Carlin was later awarded the Victoria Cross.

—— ✠ ——

With another rebel force advancing on their rear, the situation was becoming very dire so the artillery fire was concentrated on some of the buildings, in the hope that they would be abandoned by the mutineers and thus vacated would provide a place of refuge for the British force. As hoped, the artillery fire caused the rebels to abandon the buildings which they set on fire, however, they were still used as a launch platform for a renewed frontal attack which carried the enemy centre. The rear guard managed to fend off several determined attacks against the supply train which, after a march of about two miles, finally managed to reach the jail entrenchment and the relief was complete.

Sergeant William Napier – Victoria Cross No. 262

During the attacks on the baggage train, Private Benjamin Milner was severely wounded and despite being surrounded by rebels, Sergeant Napier stood by the Private, bandaged his wounds and carried him back to the safety of the convoy.

For this action, Sergeant Napier was later awarded the Victoria Cross.

A force of just over 460 men had managed to force their way through an enemy force estimated to be at least 4,000 strong with minimal casualties of 8 killed and 34 seriously wounded.

General Lugard's Azamgarh Field Force

On joining up with the force commanded by Colonel Dames, General Kerr received news of his orders to maintain a defensive position at Azamgarh and await the arrival of General Lugard's force which was on its way from Lucknow.

On 29th March, General Lugard left Lucknow, in command of the Azamgarh Field Force; 10th, 34th and 84th Regiments of Foot, 1,700 Sikh Cavalry, a portion of the military train acting as cavalry and three artillery batteries; to go to the relief of the besieged force at Azamgarh.

After reaching Sultanpore on 5th April and finding that the bridge of boats had been destroyed, General Lugard was forced to take a longer route, along the banks of the Gumti to Juanpore, instead of taking the direct route.

After six long days of marching, the force reached the village of Tigna, a few miles from Juanpore, where General Lugard received the news that the mutineers were besieging the town which was garrisoned by only a small force of Ghurkhas.

As the men had already marched 16 miles, General Lugard rested his men and sent out scouts to reconnoitre the enemy positions.

By early evening, the General received news that the rebels were on the move, so with 300 of his cavalry and three horse-artillery pieces he set off in pursuit, after ordering Brigadier Douglas to follow on with some of the infantry.

At about four miles from his camp, General Lugard came across a force of about 3,000 rebels who were in full retreat, he immediately sent his cavalry after them and following several charges they were dispersed, two of their guns were captured.

At daybreak on the 15th April, General Lugard advanced with his whole force on Juanpore.

A small force of four companies of the 10th Regiment of Foot supported by a squadron of cavalry and three guns carried a bridge of boats which they had reconnoitred the previous evening and after a determined fight gained a strong enemy position which had been held by 300 mutineers.

The main column, under the command of Brigadier Douglas crossed into the city via the city bridge and found that the rebels had fled.

General Lugard immediately ordered Major Michael with a force of cavalry and horse artillery to chase down the rebels and capture Kunwar Singh.

Private Samuel Morley – Victoria Cross No. 268
Farrier Michael Murphy – Victoria Cross No. 269

The rebels from Dinapore covered the rebel leaders retreat and each time the cavalry charged, they formed into a square forming a formidable defence.

It was during one of these charges that Lieutenant Hamilton, the Adjutant of the 3rd Sikh Cavalry fell from his horse seriously wounded. While on the ground, the mutineers began to lay into the Adjutant with their swords until Private Morley and Farrier Murphy rushed up and chased them off.

The pair stood guard over the Lieutenant, until help arrived, despite both having been wounded.

Unfortunately, Lieutenant Hamilton died from his wounds on the next day.

For this action Private Morley and Farrier Murphy were both awarded the Victoria Cross.

After pursuing the rebels for some time, Major Michael halted his force and set up camp for the night after sending a message back to Azamgarh requesting reinforcements.

The next day General Lugard sent Brigadier Douglas with a force; made up of a wing of the 37th Regiment of Foot, the 84th Regiment of Foot, a company of the Madras Rifles and artillery; to join Major Michael in his quest for the rebel leader. On the 17th April, Brigadier Douglas attacked the forces of Kunwar Singh at a place near Azimutghur and drove them from well prepared positions. The pursuit continued the next morning and as night fell, the British column made camp, only three to four miles from the rebel camp.

On learning of the British halt, Kunwar Singh took the opportunity to put some distance between his force and the British force, and after marching through the night crossed the river Gozogra at Sikandrapore and moved on to Mandhur in the Ghazeepore District. The rebels rest at Mandhur was short lived as at midnight on the 18th April, they received news that Brigadier Douglas was once again on their trail and, having marched nearly 120 miles in five days, was now in sight.

On coming in sight of the rebel force, Brigadier Douglas launched an immediate attack and scattered the enemy who left a cannon, large quantities of ammunition and some elephants behind in their haste to escape.

The mutineers were chased for about six miles but when they broke up into small units and scattered in all directions the British set up camp as night was falling.

Kunwar Singh was trying to cross the river Ganges and reach the shelter of the jungles in his homeland of Jugdeespore. Trying to disguise his intended crossing point he spread rumours that this would be at a spot 10 miles from where he intended to cross at the Theopore Ghat. Hearing that Brigadier Douglas had halted for the night, Kunwar Singh made a dash for Theopore Ghat, where he had boats concealed and they had nearly completed their crossing by the time that the British force arrived. The last boat was sunk and it was reported that Kunwar Singh was wounded and had to have his shattered arm amputated but the force managed to escape and on 21st April reached Jugdeespore where he was joined by his brother Ummeer Singh.

On 22nd April Captain LeGrand, in command of the garrison at Arrah, moved out with a force of 150 men of 35th Regiment of Foot, 50 men from the Naval Brigade and 150 men of Rattray's Sikhs supported by two 12 pounder howitzers, to attack Kunwar Singh.

On the morning of the 23rd April, the force came to a village about two miles from Jugdeespore, where a group of rebels was erecting a defensive breastwork.

The guns opened up fire on the village and the infantry marched forward and found it to be deserted so passed through to a road which was heading through a mango grove.

As they approached the grove of mangoes the skirmishers spotted a large body of mutineers moving into strong positions and fired upon them, this was soon taken up by the rest of the column.

Captain LeGrand called a halt and ordered the column to form up in line, the men at first ignored the command and eager to engage with the enemy began to charge, a bugle call was sounded for the men to fall back, which they did, however, this allowed the enemy to reach their prepared positions, from where they opened up a withering fire. After about an hour of exchanging fire, the numerical superiority of the rebels began to tell and

they were passing by on each flank trying to cut off the British retreat. With this development the order to retreat was sounded and leaving the guns, which had been spiked, behind they fell back through the jungle.

As the men emerged from the trees they made for a depression on the plain, which was full of stagnant water, and were soon attacked by the enemy cavalry which was driven off by determined volleys of rifle fire.

By the time that they reached the village, men were dropping dead from heat exhaustion and Captain LeGrand was mortally wounded, by the time they got to a point about three miles from Arrah the force which had numbered 199 Europeans was down to 80.

When news of the disaster reached Brigadier Douglas, he crossed the Ganges with a strong force of men from the 84th Regiment of Foot and arrived at Arrah on 1st May 1858.

Brigadier Douglas's force was not large enough to mount an attack against Kunwar Singh so he remained at Arrah to await the arrival of General Lugard and his force.

When General Lugard heard of the disaster which had struck Captain LeGrand, he set off from Azamgarh and after crossing the Ganges on 3rd May advanced towards Arrah and on 8th May had reached Behar.

After sending two companies of the 84th Regiment of Foot and detachments of the Madras Rifles and Sikh Horse supported by two guns of horse artillery to Arrah, General Lugard moved his force to the plain at the west of Jugdeespore where he expected to wait for reinforcements from Colonel Corefield's column, approaching from Sasseram.

On the afternoon of the 9th May, a large rebel force emerged from the jungle and began to advance towards Arrah but Lugard's cavalry supported by the artillery managed to drive them back into the jungle.

After another rebel force made an attack on his camp, as the men were erecting their tents, General Lugard decided to mount an attack against Jugdeespore and after some token resistance from the rebels, the town was taken and the rebels fell back to the village of Lutwarpore.

The British learned that Kunwar Singh was no longer leading the rebels as he had died from his wounds, soon after the rebels had arrived back at Jugdeespore.

After destroying the fortifications at Jugdeespore, General Lugard set off on 10th May in pursuit of the rebel force and on hearing news that they intended to disperse from their prepared positions into the jungle, decided to make a swift strike before they could do so.

With a force of 655 infantry and 115 cavalry, supported by artillery; carrying nothing but spare ammunition and field rations, however, essentially they were accompanied by elephants carrying large quantities of water; General Lugard headed into the thickest part of the jungle. As the force approached the rebel positions, the mutineers tried to outflank the British and attack their rear, however, determined fire from the 10th Regiment of Foot fought them off and the column managed to take the enemies prepared positions.

At the same time, Colonel Corfield attacked two villages on the southern edge of the jungle with men of the 6th Regiment of Foot, men of the Indian Naval Brigade and a detachment of Sikhs. During this attack, in the heat of the day, Colonel Corfield lost 7 men dead with heatstroke and of his 110 men 60 were incapacitated by the heat and had to be carried back to camp.

For the next few weeks, there was a period of guerrilla warfare as the rebels, who had split into small units, were chased through the jungle.

A set engagement took place on the 4th June when a large body of rebels were caught in the open and many of the enemy were slain.

On 15th June, General Lugard declared that the jungles had been cleared and suffering from ill health he resigned his command and returned to England.

The field force was split up, Brigadier Douglas with the 84th Regiment of foot and the military train went to Benares while Captain Rattray with his Sikhs remained in Jugdeespore. The remaining units were dispersed to various locations.

During July, the activity of the rebels in south Behar seemed to have been replaced by that of bandits whose only motivation seemed to be robbery and plunder.

On the 8th July, rebels entered Arrah and were only dislodged with the arrival of troops from Patna.

To help quell these disturbances, Brigadier Douglas was placed in charge of this part of Behar, from Dinapore to Ghazeepore which included the districts of Arrah and Jugdeespore.

Brigadier Douglas distributed his forces in small units across the region, so that he was in a position to respond quickly to any disturbance.

Many small bands of rebels were operating in the area led by Sikh leaders such as Meghur Singh and Joodhur Singh and after another leader, Sangram Singh, committed some atrocities in the area around Rotas, Captain Rattray sent a small party of his Sikhs to capture him.

On the 17th July, a party of eight of Rattray's Sikhs captured Sangram Singh at Dehra and after killing his brother, sons, nephew and grandsons brought him back for trial and subsequent execution.

Although Brigadier Douglas was in command of the district, Jugdeespore was still in rebels hands and at the beginning of

August was occupied by Ummer Singh with the main force of the Behar rebels.

To make a successful attack on the rebels at Jugdeespore would require Brigadier Douglas to concentrate all of his forces, however, due to the attacks of small marauding bands of rebels across the region during August, this proved to be impossible to arrange.

Battle of Suhejnee

One of Brigadier Douglas's main objectives was to ensure that the Grand Truck road was kept open to allow for free communications. On the 27th September Lieutenant-Colonel Turner was engaged in this activity with a small force, which included 54 men of the 3rd Sikh Irregular Cavalry commanded by Lieutenant Broughton and 68 men of Rattray's mounted police commanded by Lieutenant Baker.

While the rest of his column rested and had breakfast at the village of Khurona, Lieutenant-Colonel Turner despatched his cavalry against a band of rebels camped at the nearby village of Suhejnee on the banks of the river Peeroo.

Mr Chicken, an acting master in the merchant navy, who was currently attached to the Indian Naval Brigade, was at nearby Dehra, on his way to Buxar, attached himself to the cavalry force.

Lieutenant Charles Baker – Victoria Cross No. 283
Civilian George Chicken – Victoria Cross No. 285

Lieutenant Baker led his small force of cavalry against the rebels and in his own words described the events as follows; *"The enemy [at this time supposed to have mustered from 900 to 1,000 strong in infantry, with 50 cavalry] advanced. Without exchanging a shot, I at once retired slowly, followed up steadily by the rebel line for 100 yards clear of the village or jungle, when suddenly wheeling about my divisions into line with a hearty cheer, we charged into and through the centre of the enemy's line".*

"Lieutenant Broughton, with his detachment, immediately following up the movement, with excellent effect, from his position on the enemy's left. The rebel right wing, of about 300 men, broke at once, but the centre and left, observing the great labour of the horses in crossing the heavy ground, stood, and receiving the charge with repeated volleys, were cut down or broke only a few yards ahead of the cavalry".

"From this moment the pursuit was limited to the strongest and best horses of the force, numbering some sixty of all ranks, who dashing into and swimming a deep and wide nullah, followed the flying enemy through the village of Russowlee and its sugar cane khets, over 2 miles of swamp and 300 yards into the thick jungle near Peroo, when both men and horses being completely

exhausted, I sounded the halt and assembly, and collecting my wounded, returned to camp at Munjhaen about 6 p.m.".

During the attack and pursuit of the rebels, Mr Chicken found himself alone when he caught up with a party of about 20 fleeing rebels. Continuing his charge Mr Chicken killed five of the rebels before he was seriously wounded and dismounted from his horse. He would have certainly been killed had it not been for the intervention of four native troopers from the 1st Bengal Police and 3rd Sikh Irregular Cavalry who dispersed the rebels and rescued him.

For their actions in the battle, both Lieutenant Baker and Mr Chicken were later awarded the Victoria Cross. The four native troopers who rescued Mr Chicken were each awarded the Order for Merit.

———— ✠ ————

Several small engagements were fought during the remainder of the hot season and during the monsoon season were concentrated on guarding the lines of communication and keeping the rebels in check.

In October, when the rains had stopped, Brigadier Douglas decided to go back on the offensive, splitting his now 7,000 men into seven columns he directed four columns towards Buxar to sweep the rebels south down to Jugdeespore, two columns would stop the rebels moving off to the east and a further column would stop them moving west.

The move to surround the rebels began on 15th October and the net was slowly being closed until on the 17th October one of the columns was delayed for a few hours and the mutineers managed to escape to the east, looking to cross the River Soane.

With a lack of sufficient Cavalry, Brigadier Douglas was unable to move fast enough to catch the fleeing rebels, however, Captain Havelock proposed that 60 men from the infantry be mounted to supplement the cavalry.

The proposal was accepted and on the morning of the 18th October, Captain Havelock set out with his 60 mounted infantry, three mounted troops from the military train and 60 cavalry, reaching the River Soane ahead of the rebels on the morning of the next day.

Unable to cross the river, the rebels turned to the south west closely followed by Captain Havelock and his force.

The rebels tried to regain the safety of the jungles but were prevented by the native regiments, following the British cavalry force, and were eventually driven into the Kaimur Hills, where on the 24th November they were taken by surprise by the main British force commanded by Brigadier Douglas.

Many mutineers were killed and a large amount of ammunition was captured, the remaining rebels fled and dispersed and were unable to reorganise and pose any further threat.

By the end of the year Brigadier Douglas declared the campaign to be at an end, Western Behar was back under British control.

16

SUBJUGATION OF OUDH

Having subdued, Rohilkhand province to the west and the Azamgarh Districts to the east, General Campbell (now Lord Clyde) wanted to complete the subjugation of the Province of Oudh during a winter campaign of 1858/59.

The River Gogra running roughly parallel to the River Ganges divided the province into two parts and the southern part itself was divided into two by the road running from Cawnpore to Lucknow. General Campbell's plan was that each of these three parts would be a separate theatre of operations, with the two parts south of the Gogra being attacked first and simultaneously. The rebels that were not crushed by these first two operations would be driven into the districts north of the Gogra which would then be the final theatre of operations.

For the two southern Gogra theatres, General Campbell had three forces of men at his disposal; the Rohilkhand force to the west, the Azamgarh force to the east and the Cawnpore/Lucknow force at the centre.

Two columns from Rohilkhand were to advance into Oudh; one from Farrukhabad was to clear and secure the south west of the province; the other column from Shahjehanpore was to clear the north west driving the rebels north eastward towards the river Gogra and would reoccupy Sitapur.

At the same time, four brigades would set out from Sobraon, near Allahabad to sweep the Baiswarra district between the Rivers Ganges and Gumti; capture the many forts of the feudal landowners and drive them and their bands of followers across the Gogra.

A third column from Azamgarh in the east would cross the border and secure south Behar, driving the rebels north west towards the Gogra.

On having successfully driven the rebels in the southern districts over the River Gogra, the second part of General Campbell's plan would then come into play.

A strong force would be placed along the River Gogra, to prevent the rebels slipping back into the southern districts; the rebels would then be driven across the River Raptee towards the border with Nepal, where they would be captured or have to flee into the Himalayan foothills.

General Campbell communicated his plan to the Commander in Chief of the army, Prince George the Duke of Cambridge, in a letter dated 2nd October 1858, with the intention that it would start to be implemented in November, at the end of the monsoon season.

Battle of Sundeela

The campaign was brought forward, prompted by a rebel attack on the 4th of October, directed against the British post of Sundeela near Lucknow.

Captain Dawson commanded a garrison comprising; 600 men of the newly raised 7th Oudh Police Infantry, 740 men of the newly raised 2nd and 5th Oudh Police Cavalry, No. 12 Battery of the Bengal Artillery with two 9 pounder guns and a unit of the Royal Artillery with two 5½" mortars.

Faced by a rebel force of about 12,000 men supported by four guns, Captain Dawson placed his infantry into a small mud fort and sent his cavalry away; the British force kept the rebels at bay for two days until relieved by Major Maynard with a force of 120 men from the 88th Regiment of Foot which had been sent from Lucknow.

Brigadier G. R. Barker arrived at Sundeela on 7th October with 200 men from the 88th Regiment of Foot, 100 men from 3rd Battalion Rifle Brigade, 200 men from 2nd Dragoon Guards, 25 men from Hodson's Horse and a small battery of artillery with two guns.

On the following morning Brigadier Barker decided to attack the rebel force which was camped in a strong position at a nearby village. The rebel position was well chosen, with the village being on high ground and surrounded by jungle while the British would have to advance across an open plain.

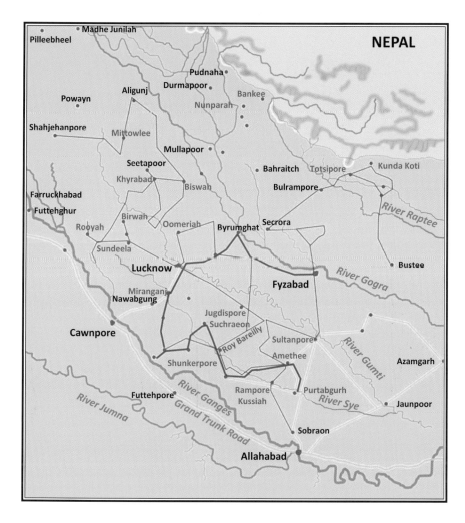

Figure 85. The Oudh winter campaign

The attack started with a gallant frontal attack by the men of the Rifle Brigade, immediately followed by an attack on the rebels left flank, in the face of this two pronged attack the rebels suffered heavy casualties and soon began to withdraw into the jungle.

Trumpeter Thomas Monaghan – Victoria Cross No. 286
Private Charles Anderson – Victoria Cross No. 287

During the pursuit of the enemy through the jungle of sugar cane, Lieutenant-Colonel Seymour was leading a small party of Dragoon Guards when he was attacked by about 30 to 40 mutineers.

After firing a volley of musket fire at short range, the rebels charged the Colonel with swords drawn and after taking two sword cuts Lieutenant-Colonel Seymour fell to the ground surrounded by the rebels.

Seeing the plight of Lieutenant-Colonel Seymour, Trumpeter Monaghan and Private Anderson immediately rushed to his aid and after killing rebels who were in the process of delivering what would have probably been fatal blows managed to keep the rest at bay until the rest of their party got involved in the fight.

Having been protected by Trumpeter Monaghan and Private Anderson, Lieutenant-Colonel Seymour was able to regain his feet and helped to dispatch the remainder of the rebel force.

For saving the life of Lieutenant-Colonel Seymour, Trumpeter Monaghan and Private Anderson were later awarded the Victoria Cross.

⸎

Although heavy casualties were inflicted on the rebels, during the battle and clear up operations, the British losses were also significant with 82 men killed or wounded.

Battle of Birwah

After the Battle of Sundeela, Brigadier Barker marched off towards Birwah where the rebels were sheltering in a strong fort surrounded by dense jungle.

The British reached the fort on 31st October and began an artillery barrage which lasted for eight hours before a breach was affected. While the Rifle Brigade stormed the breach, Lieutenant Carnegie of the Bengal Engineers laid a charge and blew up the main gate, which allowed Major Maynard with men of the 88th Regiment of Foot entry into the fort.

Although the British had gained entry to the main fort, the rebel leader Gholab Singh and some of his men had taken refuge within a house at the centre of the fort enclosure.

As the house was easily defended with many protected loop-holes and windows, Brigadier Barker did not wish to risk the lives of his men with a direct assault and instead directed his artillery to blow up the house and let it burn.

Posting men to guard the doors by which the enemy might escape, Brigadier Barker stood the rest of his men down.

During the night Gholab Singh and about ten of his supporters made a desperate dash to one of the bastions and managed to escape into the jungle.

The campaign against Oudh's western districts

Now that the rebels had started the winter campaigning, General Campbell's plan began to be initiated and General Seaton launched the two Rohilkhand columns against the southern districts of Oudh.

Capture of Rooya

On the 15th October a small column of men from the 82nd Regiment of Foot, under the command of Colonel Hall, left Farrukhabad, crossed into Oudh and began to advance on Sundeela to join up with Brigadier Barker's force.

On 28th October Brigadier Barker's force, now joined with the column led by Colonel Hall, attacked and recaptured the fort at Rooya.

During November, Brigadier Barker advanced towards Sundeela, clearing the rebels before him and by the end of the month had secured Khyrabad and Biswah.

Battle of Miranganj

While Brigadier Barker and Colonel Hall were operating in the west, Brigadier Evelegh was clearing the ground along the River Ganges moving up from the south towards Sundeela.

On the 5th October, Brigadier Evelegh engaged and inflicted heavy losses on the rebels at the Battle of Miranganj between Cawnpore and Lucknow.

After the battle Brigadier Evelegh continued his advance clearing the rebels between Brigadier Barkers and Brigadier Troup's forces and on 2nd December took the fort at Oomeria.

South West Oudh districts cleared

With the completion of the above two operations, the mutineers had been cleared from the south west theatre of operations in Oudh. The River Ganges, which had been unusable since the start of the mutiny, was once again available for use by the British forces.

North West Oudh operations

On the 18th October, the second Rohilkhand column, under the command of Brigadier Troup left Shahjehanpore and after two successful encounters with the rebel leader Badadur Ali Khan cleared the Rohilkhand border of rebels and advanced into Oudh.

On the 8th of November, Brigadier Troup advanced on the fort at Mittowlee which he bombarded with his artillery, in the morning he found the fort abandoned as the rebels had escaped during the night.

Continuing his march to the north east, Brigadier Troup engaged a large force of rebels at Mehunde on the 10th November and inflicted a heavy defeat.

After the battle, Brigadier Troup continued his advance northward driving the rebels towards Alligunge where after a short action on the 17th November, the majority of the rebels were driven across the Gogra.

The force continued its march along the banks of the Gogra and reached Biswah on the 2nd December where they joined up with Brigadier Barkers force.

Operations to clear the north west districts of Oudh had now been successfully completed and all of the rebel forces, with one exception, had been driven across the Gogra, as planned. The exception was Prince Feroze Shah with 1,500 men who, when hemmed in near Biswah, doubled back and managed to escape between the two British armies, eventually crossing the rivers Ganges and Jumna and joining up with the rebel army in Central India.

Operations in Baiswarra district

With the western districts under control, operations to clear the rebels from the Baiswarra district, the area between the rivers Ganges and Gumti, were now the next priority; these would take place under the personal guidance of General Campbell.

From previous operations, the British forces held a line from Sultanpore via Pertabgurh to Allahabad and from Sultanpore northwards to Fyzabad, however, before the start of his operations General Campbell wanted to strengthen the Sultanpore position to prevent rebels escaping back into the Azamgarh districts.

To accomplish this, the General despatched a force under General Hope Grant to protect the eastern flank and co-operate with a column commanded by Colonel Kelly who advanced from Azamgarh into Oudh.

Driving the rebels ahead of him Colonel Kelly captured Akbarpore and Tanda where on 30th October he halted and took up station to guard the flank during the ensuing operations.

Before leaving Allahabad, to go and join his troops, General Campbell issued a proclamation, announcing to the population of Oudh that he was coming to enforce the law and that to complete this without loss of life and property he expected the population to put up no resistance.

Where there was no resistance, lives and property would be protected, however, even the slightest sign of resistance would be met by the full force of his army and towns and villages would be plundered and burnt to the ground.

Capture of Rampore Kussiah

As a start to the campaign, General Hope Grant and Brigadier Wetherall were ordered, by General Campbell, to capture Rampore Kussiah, the stronghold of the powerful Khanpooria clan, in a joint operation.

A column commanded by Brigadier Wetherall, comprising; the 79th Highlanders, the Beluch Battalion, a wing of the 9th Punjab Infantry and the 1st Punjab Cavalry, supported by Horse Artillery and a Heavy Field Battery; left Soraou to move against Rampore Kussiah.

Brigadier Wetherall's force was to be part of a two pronged attack on Rampore Kussiah, with a force commanded by General Hope Grant due to attack from the north while he attacked from the south; to ensure a coordinated effort it was agreed that the attack would take place on the 4th November.

On the 3rd November, while General Hope Grant and his men were camped about six miles from the fort at Rampore Kussiah, he was surprised by the sounds of heavy fighting in the direction of the fort.

Brigadier Wetherall and his force arrived at the front of the fort at about 10 o'clock on the morning of the 3rd November and found, at a bend in the river Sai, an impressive entrenchment surrounding a fort at its centre.

The entrenchments which had a circumference of about three miles enclosed about 160 acres of dense bamboo and thorn jungle, with only a few covered ways giving access to its interior. The walls were of mud construction and rose to a height of 7 or 8 feet, this was fronted by a ditch which was between 8 and 20 feet wide and 12 to 18 feet deep, finally an abattis constructed from jungle thorns protected the far side of the ditch. The jungle came up almost to the walls of the enclosure on all sides apart from on the north and north east sides. The old fort inside the enclosure was of typical design being rectangular with rounded bastions at each corner, the curtain walls between the corners were also protected by more bastions. At the centre of the fort was a heavily defended stone building which was the residence of the tribal chief.

It seemed impossible that this formidable fortress could be carried by the small force that Brigadier Wetherall commanded, however, when he received intelligence that the defensive works had not been completed right down to the river the Brigadier decided to mount an immediate attack before this weakness in the defences could be closed.

Brigadier Wetherall secretly assembled his force behind the village and fort of Agaiya, about 1,500 yards from the stronghold and placed his heavy artillery battery on some high ground which was protected by the old fort. A company of the 79th Highlanders was also placed in the old fort and another company was placed in front of the battery to act as sharpshooters. The right wing of the 9th Punjab Infantry was placed on the right of his position with orders to force their way through the jungle and turn the left of the entrenchment. Troops of cavalry were placed on each flank to look for any fords that might cross the river and to be in position to prevent any rebel forces from crossing the river to attack their infantry.

Just as he had completed the disposition of his troops, but after his artillery had already commenced their fire, Brigadier Wetherall received a message from General Hope Grant that he was available to help with the assault at first light on the following morning.

However, as he had already started his assault, the Brigadier decided to continue the attack with the intention of carrying the outer works and then wait for the General's force to attack the interior defences.

Under the cover of the artillery fire, the Brigadier directed Captain Thelwall with the 9th Punjab Infantry to force his way through the jungle; which they did until they were halted by intense rebel fire from muskets and guns, at about 60 yards from the walls of the entrenchment.

With his position rapidly becoming untenable, Captain Thelwall launched an attack on the bastion from which most of the enemy fire was being directed at them. After crossing the ditch, the bastion was taken and two captured guns were immediately turned on the enemy.

With a force of 1,500 rebels now advancing to retake the bastion, Captain Thelwall and his men were once again in a desperate position but managed to hold on until reinforcements in the guise of two companies from the 79th Highlanders and four companies from the 1st Beluch Battalion, arrived to provide support.

For the next few hours the British force continued to capture the outer works until at about 2 o'clock in the afternoon the rebels decided to abandon the fort and entrenchments, escaping to the east via the north wall.

Brigadier Wetherall sent a message to General Hope Grant informing him that he had attacked the fort and requesting help to prevent the rebel escape; the General immediately despatched his cavalry and horse artillery but they arrived too late to intercept the rebels.

Although the fort had been captured, General Campbell was angry that as a result of his orders having been disregarded a large body of rebels had been allowed to escape. The enemy losses were only about 300 while the British killed and wounded numbered 78.

Capture of Amethi

After joining up with the British camp at the Biglah cantonment near Pertabghur, on the river Sai; General Campbell sent a letter to the Raja of Amethi, on the 2nd November, requesting him to surrender. The Raja was also sent a copy of Queen Victoria's proclamation that promised mercy and forgiveness to all but those that had committed the blackest of crimes. The letter concluded by informing the Raja that if he did not furnish proof of his allegiance by the 6th November, then an attack would be made against his stronghold at Amethi. Having received no satisfactory reply to his message, General Campbell despatch the Siege Train towards Amethi on the 7th November.

On the next morning, having left a detachment to guard Petabghur, Brigadier Pinkney set out with the Headquarters Column for Amethi, this was made up of ; a wing of the 5th Fusiliers, the 54th Regiment of Foot, the 1st Sikh Infantry, a regiment of Oudh Police Infantry, a squadron of Carabineers, a regiment of Oudh Police Cavalry, a squadron of 6th Madras Cavalry, a detachment of the Pathan Horse supported by a Royal Artillery light field battery, a Bengal Artillery Heavy Battery, a company of Royal Engineers and some Delhi Pioneers.

On the 9th November, the force halted at a small Hindu temple about three miles from Amethi and had just pitched their tents when General Hope Grant arrived to inform General Campbell that, in accordance with his orders his force was camped on the other side of Amethi about three miles from the stronghold. Soon afterwards Brigadier Wetherall also reported that his column was in position.

Having observed the arrival of the British forces and judging any resistance to be futile, the Raja sent a message to General Campbell offering to evacuate the fort with his men and then give up his arms; he stated that this applied only to the men of his own army as he had no power over the rebel forces. General Campbell replied that the fort must be surrendered with all men giving up their arms, or the fort would face a bombardment in the morning. During the night, the Raja left the fort and in the morning appeared in the British camp stating that the rebels had fled during the night.

A small party was sent to take possession of the stronghold and when the citadel was entered it was found to be occupied by about 3,000 of the Raja's own retainers with a few guns.

Capture of Shunkerpore

Leaving a strong force at Amethi, to dismantle the fort and clear the jungle, General Campbell turned his force towards Shunkerpore where Beni Mahdoo, the leader of the Rajputs in Oudh, had his stronghold.

With General Hope Grant's column on his right and that of Brigadier Wetherall on his left, the General with the Headquarters Column set off and on 15th November they had reached a position about three miles to the north and east of the fortress.

General Hope Grant's column moved to a position at the north face of the fort and Brigadier Evelegh was ordered to move in from the north west to complete the encirclement.

The outer ditch of the enclosure was almost eight miles in circumference, within which were four strongholds located within a dense jungle of thorns.

General Campbell sent a message to Beni Mahdoo advising him that if he surrendered then his claim to retain his land and possessions would be considered. The rebel leader replied only a few hours later, saying that he would not surrender, as he wished to remain loyal to his sovereign, however, he would abandon his fort and hope that his son would be allowed to keep his estates.

At about 2 o'clock in the morning, Beni Mahdoo with 10,000 troops, guns, treasure and baggage managed to leave the fort undetected, and after making a wide detour to the west, avoided General Hope Grant's right flank and escaped into the jungle near Bareilly. Due to the late arrival of his orders, Brigadier Evelegh and his force was not in position in time to prevent the rebels escape.

The British forces entered the enclosure and fort the next morning and found it to be totally deserted apart from a few old men and priests.

Moves to capture Beni Mahdoo

Following the evacuation of Shunkerpore, General Campbell redistributed his assault forces to chase down and capture Beni Mahdoo.

Colonel Taylor, appointed to succeed Brigadier Wetherall, was sent with his column to Fyzabad, with orders to cross the Gogra at that point, to prevent the rebel leader circling around to the east.

General Hope Grant was despatched towards Bareilly and then Jugdeespore to get closer to the rebel leader, should he decide to escape in that direction.

After leaving a detachment at Shunkerpore, to destroy the fort, General Campbell with Brigadier Pinkney's headquarters brigade (now commanded by Colonel Jones) also set out for Bareilly, with the intention of joining up with Brigadier Evelegh's force, which had been directed to follow the escaping rebels.

On the 17th November, Brigadier Evelegh's force managed to engage Beni Mahdoo's force near Doondea Khera, inflicted many casualties, captured three guns but was unable to stop the rebel movement to the west.

On the 19th November, after arriving at Bareilly, General Campbell received the news of Brigadier Evelegh's success and that the rebel army had been kept to the south between Doondea Khera and the river Ganges.

In the early morning of 20th November, after leaving a small force to hold Bareilly, General Campbell continued his march north westward, parallel to the Ganges, heading for Suchraon with the intention of intercepting the rebel force.

After arriving at Buchraon, General Campbell received further news from Brigadier Evelegh that the rebels were now held up in a fortress at Doondea Khera and from their disposition it appeared that they were intent on engaging in battle with the British forces. During the early morning of 24th November, General Campbell's force managed to join up with Brigadier Evelegh's force at Bidhoura, near the rebel stronghold and after a recognisance observed the enemy drawn up in line of battle with their right flank at the village of Buksur and their left flank at Doondea Khera. The rebels were in a strong position with the river Ganges protecting their rear and a thorny jungle to their front.

As soon as the rebel artillery opened fire, General Campbell moved his men to form a line of advance; Brigadier Evelegh's force was placed on the right, Colonel Jones's force on the left with cavalry out on both flanks with artillery between each of the units.

General Campbell began his attack with a line of skirmishers advancing into the jungle ahead of his main force, supported by fire from the British artillery. In the face of the advancing skirmishers the rebel line broke and the mutineers fled and were chased by the British cavalry who inflicted heavy casualties.

Once again the majority of the rebels, including Beni Mahdoo, managed to escape and headed off northwards; two movable columns were quickly formed and set off in pursuit.

These columns managed to drive the rebels across the Gumti and then the Gogra River thus clearing the vast Baiswarra district of rebels. With the eastern districts of Oudh, south of the river Gogra, now cleared of rebels General Campbell could now enact the final part of his plan to subdue the province of Oude.

Oudh Campaign finalé

Having successfully completed the first two parts of his plan, General Campbell returned to Lucknow with his Headquarters column, to make preparations for the final part of his plan to subdue the province of Oudh.

After arriving at Lucknow on the 28th November, two days later General Campbell sent out Brigadier Evelegh with his column, to capture the fort at Oomeriah, about 20 miles north east of the city. This fort, which for some time had effectively blockaded the road to the north east out of Lucknow, had been the source of much inconvenience to the British forces. Brigadier Evelegh's force reached the fort on the 2nd December and after a brief resistance managed to expel the rebels and occupy the fort. For the next three days, his men systematically levelled the fortress to the ground.

Also on the 2nd December, Brigadier Troup who had been marching down from Mehndee in the north joined up with Brigadier Barker, who had been marching north from Sundeela, at Biswah.

Prince Feroze Shah, with about 2,000 men, fearing that he was about to be boxed in near Biswah, doubled back towards the Ganges but General Campbell, anticipating such a move, sent a force of about 2,000 cavalry to support Brigadiers Barker and Troup, in their endeavours to intercept the rebel force. Unfortunately, the rebel leader, aided by intelligence from the local population, managed to evade the British forces and escaped across the Ganges into the Doab and marched off towards Etawah to attack the forts of two chiefs who had remained loyal to the Crown.

Final Oudh Campaign

On the 5th December, Lord Clyde left Lucknow for Fyzabad, with a strong column commanded by Brigadier Horsford and after reaching Nuwabgunge was joined by Purnell's Brigade.

That evening, the column received news that Beni Mahdoo was camped on the other side of the Gogra at Byram Ghat, about 20 miles away.

Lord Clyde set off the next morning at dawn, heading for Beyram Ghat and while halted for breakfast heard further news from his spies that the rebels were still trying to cross the river.

Seeing an opportunity to cause some disruption, Lord Clyde with his cavalry and four guns of horse artillery set off at a gallop for the river crossing, however, by the time that they arrived the enemy had completed their crossing.

The remainder of the column caught up with their commander and camped at the village of Gunespore, about a mile from the river.

General Hope Grant was advancing up the left bank of the Gogra towards Secrora and got to within 15 miles of the rebel force before he was spotted and the rebels retreated northward.

While Brigadier Purnell and his brigade were left at Gunespore, to gather material and boats to bridge the river Gogra, Lord Clyde with the remainder of the force moved on to Fyzabad which they reached on the 10th December.

Two days later they reached Secrora where they were joined by Colonel Christie and a small force of men from the 80th Regiment of Foot; General Hope Grant and his force had already pressed ahead and by the 18th December had arrived at Bulrampore only a few miles from the river Raptee.

On the 23rd December, Brigadier Rowcroft occupied Tulsepore where he was later joined by General Hope Grant and his force.

Meanwhile, Lord Clyde had received intelligence that Nana Sahib and the Begum of Oudh had taken up refuge at the city of Baraitch and had march off hoping to engage the rebels in a decisive battle.

Unfortunately, when the General arrived at Baraitch on the morning of the 17th December, he found the city to have been deserted by the rebels who had moved off the previous morning and were now thought to be at Nanparah about 20 miles away.

Lord Clyde was forced to delay his pursuit, due to heavy rains, until 23rd December when after leaving a small force to hold Baraitch; he set out for Nanparah and reached the village of Intha where his progress was again delayed by heavy rains.

After spending Christmas day in camp, the column set off again the following morning and received news that the rebels were still at Nanparah and were fully intent on defending the strong fort, however, when they reached the fort at noon they found it abandoned.

After a short halt, Lord Clyde continued his pursuit of the rebels and at about 3 o'clock in the afternoon found the rebel force drawn up in front of the village of Burordiah.

Action at Burordiah

As there were still some hours of daylight remaining, Lord Clyde decided to make an attack and formed his men into their battle lines.

The British advanced until they were within the range of the rebel guns, at which time Lord Clyde ordered a move to attack the enemy left flank and with their flank having been turned the rebels broke and fled across the plain.

While galloping to give orders for the pursuit, Lord Clyde's horse stumbled and the General was thrown and dislocated his shoulder. The pursuit of the rebels continued until nightfall at which time it was called off and the cavalry returned to camp.

Capture of Fort Musjidiah

At 10 o'clock on the morning of the 27th December, the British left Burordiah and after a march of about 2 hours they came across the Fort of Musjidiah, on the plain ahead of them.

Despite its strong defences, the fort was captured with some ease, after a bombardment of three hours and the British force set up camp, where they remained during the following day.

On the 29th December, after leaving some troops to destroy the fort, Lord Clyde moved off south to return to Nanarah by a different route. On the next afternoon he received the news that Nana Sahib and Beni Mahdoo with thousands of their followers had gathered at Bankee on the river Raptee, which was about 20 miles north of Nanarah.

Hoping to surprise the rebels, Lord Clyde decided on a night march and using a troop of about 150 elephants to carry his infantry in rotation, set off in the pitch black at 8:30 in the evening.

Battle at Bankee on the River Raptee

After a march of 15 miles the British force rested until first light, when they resumed their march and after a short time came across the enemy, stretched out in front of the River Raptee with a deep swamp to their front and the river and jungle to their rear.

As soon as the British began their advance with cavalry and horse artillery, the rebels fired a few desultory shots before making for the jungle to their rear.

The British force continued their advance passing to both sides of the swamp but could not move fast enough to prevent the rebels from retreating into the jungle.

After chasing the enemy through the jungle and reaching the high ground, the rebels were seen to be moving along the edge of the jungle making their way for the river.

The 7th Hussars and a squadron of the 1st Punjab Cavalry were the first to ride up and immediately began a charge towards the enemy, who were moving off to their right; they were soon followed by four further squadrons.

Six enemy guns on the far bank of the river began to lay down a covering fire while the rebels fled for the river; Captain Stisted leading the first squadron of British cavalry caught up with the fleeing enemy cavalry and a desperate fight took place in the river.

Major Charles Fraser – Victoria Cross No. 290

Major Herne, leading the left wing of the 7th Hussars was swept away by the fast flowing river and later in the day was found to have been drowned.

Captain Stisted and troopers of the 7th Hussars were also in difficulties due to the fast flowing waters.

Major Fraser, who had just returned to active duty with the regiment after having been seriously wounded in the hand on 13th June at the Battle of Nuwabgunge, plunged into the river and rescued Captain Stisted and two troopers who were being swept down the river and in great danger of being drowned.

For saving the lives of these men, despite being hampered by his wounded hand, Major Fraser was later awarded the Victoria Cross.

After the battle, the men set up camp and took a well earned rest; the cavalry had been in the saddle for almost 30 hours.

By the 1st January 1859, all of the Oudh factions had either surrendered or like Nana Sahib and the Nawab of Banda had escaped into Nepal.

Lord Clyde therefore declared that the campaign was at an end and returned to Lucknow.

Trans-Gogra operations

On 26th November 1858, Lieutenant-Colonel Simpson with the left wing of the 34th Regiment of Foot, currently operating with the Fyzabad Field Force, was sent to Fyzabad to help prevent the return of Oudh rebels who had fled to Nepal.

On the 7th January 1859, Colonel Kelly was despatched to the foothills with men of the 34th Regiment and on 14th February 1859 a force comprising; a battery of Royal Artillery, a wing of the 13th Regiment, the 3rd Sikhs and the Jat horse were despatched to the Trans-Gogra district with orders to seize two mountain passes that might be used by the returning rebels.

By the 13th March 1859, Colonel Kelly had taken up position with half of his force at Boggah on the east bank of the river

Gandak, while on the opposite bank at Nichnowl he had posted Lieutenant-Colonel Simpson with the rest of the force.

After a time both forces crossed the frontier and on the 26th March, Colonel Kelly attacked a rebel force at Bhootwul, drove them back into the jungle and captured four of their guns.

Continuing to follow the enemy through the jungle, Colonel Kelly engaged the rebels again on the 28th March and this time achieved a complete route.

The British column captured a further three guns, 6 elephants, 30 camels and 300 horses together with large amounts of baggage. Over 400 rebels were killed and the 34th did not suffer a single casualty.

Immediately after the action, one of the rebel leaders Mirza Nadir with 50 of his men came into the British camp and surrendered, however, Nana Sahib and Bala Rao with their men fled back into the hills of Nepal.

Satisfied with his achievements, Colonel Kelly began his return journey to Fyzabad but when he learned that rebels were congregating at Kewanee, he despatched a wing of the 34th Regiment, under the command of Captain Puget to deal with the mutineers.

Private George Richardson – Victoria Cross No. 295

On the 27th of April 1859, as the 34th advanced on Kewanee the rebels began to withdraw, one rebel, who seemed to be of some importance by his dress and armaments, posted himself behind a tree and at a range of about 20 yards began firing potshots at the advancing British force.

Private Richardson, from No. 6 Company, rushed to the head of the line and launched an attack at the man using his rifle as a club, as he had not had time to reload it.

When the private got to within three yards, the rebel fired his pistol, shooting him in the arm and shattering his elbow. Despite having one arm disabled, Private Richardson continued his assault and dragged the rebel to the ground and held him down until Lieutenant Dyson-Laurie came up and despatched the man.

For this action Private Richardson was later awarded the Victoria Cross.

The rebels were dispersed by the 34th, Private Richardson was the only man to be wounded, and Captain Puget returned with his men to Fyzabad where they arrived on the 30th May.

17

CENTRAL INDIA CAMPAIGN

Since 1854, the Central India Agency had managed, on behalf of the crown, the area of central India that was comprised of seven large states; Bundelkhand, Bagelkhand, Gwalior, Bhopal, Indore, Malwa and Bhopawar; the region also included nearly 150 smaller princely states and Jhansi, a part of Bundelkhand which was ceded to the crown in 1853 under the doctrine of lapse.

Nominally each of the states, which had mainly been acquired by the Honourable East India Company during the Anglo-Maratha wars, was ruled by a Maratha or Mogul prince, however, most of the power lay in the hands of residents or commissioners appointed by the Company.

The Central India Agency covered the lands between the Narmada and Jumna rivers, however, the central India mutinies also extended into the southern and eastern parts of Rajputana and the territories of Saugor and Narbada.

Initial operations in Central India

With outbreaks of mutiny having broken out across much of Central India, but with mainly only native troops at their disposal, actions to reverse the situation were slow to take place.

During the spring and summer of 1857, containing operations were carried out by columns led by Generals Stuart and Durand which established sufficient stability for a more structured campaign, to subdue Central India, to take place later in the year.

General Stuart and General Durand's column

In early July, General Stuart took over the command of troops at Aurangabad from General Woodburn who had been forced to retire due to ill health.

After receiving the ill-informed news that Mhow had fallen, it was decided to move against Mhow rather than Indore and

on the 12th July, General Stuart set forth with a force comprising men of the 14th Light Dragoon and the 25th Bombay Native Infantry, supported by a battery of field artillery.

By the 20th July, the force had reached the banks of the river Tapti, where they made camp and were struck with an outbreak of cholera which caused many deaths including that of Major Follett, the commanding officer of the 25th Bengal Native Infantry.

On the 22nd July, the column reached the fort at Assarghur where they were joined by Colonel Durand and after crossing the

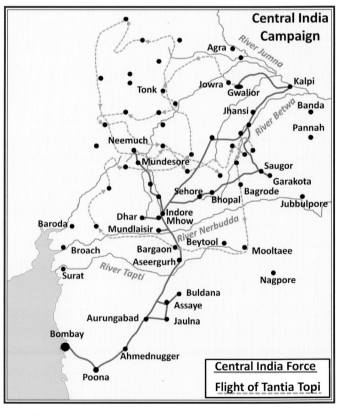

Figure 86. Central India campaign

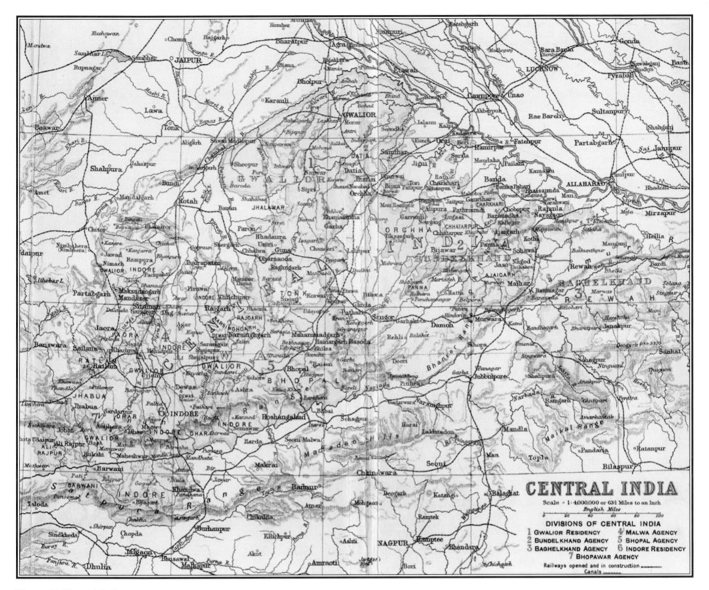

Figure 87. Central India

river Nerbudda, on 28th July, were joined by the 3rd Hyderabad Cavalry under the command of Captain Orr.

After camping at Simrol on the 1st August, the force began its last march to Mhow on the following morning and encountering no opposition they managed to reach the town and relieve the small garrison.

On the 5th August, General Stuart's force was strengthened by the arrival of 250 men from the 86th Regiment of Foot.

With the rainy season now in full flow and lacking the men to make an attack on Indore, the force remained at Mhow and prepared themselves for the upcoming dry weather operations. On the 12th October, just as the rains were easing, General Durant received news that the rebels intended to attack the town of Mandlesar and sent two troops of the 3rd Hyderabad Cavalry, under the command of Lieutenant Clarke, to the village of Goojeeree to intercept them.

The General also sent another detachment of cavalry direct to Mandlesar to support Captain Keatinge, the local political agent.

Two days later, on 14th October, three companies of the 25th Bombay Native Infantry, 50 men of the 14th Light Dragoons and three guns were sent to Goojeeree in support of Lieutenant Clarke.

After leaving a small garrison; comprising detachments of the 86th Regiment of Foot, 25th Bombay Native Infantry and the Bombay Sappers; to guard Mhow, General Stuart left the town on 19th October heading for Dhar, where a mutiny had broken out on 15th October. The siege train left Mhow on the following day.

Capture of Dhar

On 22nd October, the force arrived at Dhar and found the rebels arrayed in front of the fort, after a brief battle the rebels were driven back into the fort.

Due to the terrain and fortifications, an assault on the fort could only be successful if the walls were breached, so when the

Figure 88. Fort Dhar

siege train arrived two days later the heavy guns began the bombardment of the forts walls.

By the 31st October a useable breach had been made in the walls and a storming party was organised to enter the fort that evening. After darkness had fallen the storming party made their attack and gained entry to the fort with little difficulty, only to find the place deserted as the rebels had fled. General Durand ordered the fort to be destroyed.

Battle of Mundesore

On the 8th November, General Durand and his force, having destroyed the fort, set out for Mundesore where they arrived on 20th November and camped at a village just four miles from the town.

It was here that General Durand received the news that the rebels were raising the siege at Neemuch and the force of 5,000 men was intending to join the force at Mundesore. To prevent a junction of the two forces, the General crossed the river Chumbul the next morning and moved to the west of Mundesore, where his advance force of cavalry soon spotted the advancing rebels, about five miles distant. After advancing towards the rebels from Neemuch, the General was pressed by rebels who had left Mundesore to threaten his rear.

The forces met at the village of Goraria about five miles from Mundesore and the ensuing battle lasted throughout the night until the rebels finally fled the village after an intense artillery bombardment on the morning of the 21st November.

Lieutenant Harry Prendergast – Victoria Cross No. 232

During the battle on the 21st November, Lieutenant Prendergast saved the life of Lieutenant Dew of the 14th Light Dragoons when he attacked a mutineer who was about to discharge his musket into the back of Lieutenant Drew.

As Lieutenant Prendergast attacked, the rebel turned and shot him in the right side, seriously wounding him and but for the

action of Major Orr, who killed the rebel, he himself may have been killed by a follow up attack.

For this action, Lieutenant Prendergast was later awarded the Victoria Cross; his citation also makes reference to two further actions at Rathghur and Betwa where he was again wounded.

The rearguard of the British force chased the rebels, who had attacked the rear of the column, back into the city.

When the main force returned to Mundesore on the afternoon of the 21st November, they found the city to have been abandoned.

After the action at Mundesore, the column returned to Lahore.

Central India Campaign plan

In Calcutta, General Sir Colin Campbell and his Chief of Staff General Mansfield, together with Sir Robert Hamilton, formulated plans for the pacification of Central India which were based upon several columns to be formed from troops supplied by the Bombay and Madras presidencies.

The plan was for the Central India Field Force, raised in Bombay, commanded by General Sir Hugh Rose, and based in Mhow to march to Gwalior, Jhansi and then on to Kalpi; while the Madras force led by General Sir Patrick Grant and based at Jabalpur would clear the lines of communication with Allahabad and Mirzapur and cross Bundelkhand to Bandah.

Other forces to be involved were the Saugor and Nerbudda Field Force commanded by General Sir George Cornish Whitlock, the Rajputana Field Force commanded by General Henry Roberts and the Malwa Field Force commanded by General John Michel.

Having completed his role in the planning of the campaign to subdue Central India, Sir Robert Hamilton set off for Indore, where he arrived on 16th December 1857 and resumed his role as political agent for Central India and the Saugor and Nerbudda Territories.

Central India Field Force

Soon after the news of the outbreak of mutiny in India had reached London, Prince George the Duke of Cambridge and head of the British army, appointed Major-General Sir Hugh Rose to the command of the Poona Division of the Bombay Army, to replace Sir Charles Napier who had been sent to quell the insurrection in the Sindh province.

General Rose arrived at Bombay on 19th September 1857 and proceeded to Indore to take up his command. On the 17th December, the day after his arrival at Indore, the General was appointed to the command of the Central India Field Force.

The 1st Brigade, formerly the Malwa Field Force, which was stationed at Mhow and commanded by Brigadier C. S. Stuart of the Bombay Army was made up of; one squadron of 14th Light Dragoons, one troop of the3rd Bombay Light Cavalry, two regiments of the Hyderabad Contingent Cavalry, two companies of the 86th Regiment of Foot, the 25th Bombay Native Infantry, one regiment of the Hyderabad Contingent Infantry, a detachment from the Bombay Sappers and Miners and three Light Field Artillery batteries one from the Royal Artillery, one from the Bombay Army and the last from the Hyderabad Contingent.

The 2nd Brigade, stationed at Sehore and commanded by Brigadier Charles Steuart was made up of; the HQ of the 14th Light Dragoons, the HQ of the 3rd Bombay Light Cavalry, 3rd Bombay European Fusiliers, 24th Bombay Native Infantry, one regiment of Hyderabad Contingent Infantry, a company of Madras Sappers, a detachment of Bombay Sappers and Miners, a troop of horse artillery, a light field artillery battery and a battery of the Bhopal Artillery. A siege train would join the brigade on 15th January 1858.

On the 17th of December, the day that he assumed command, General Rose rode from Indore to Mhow and inspected the troops of his 1st Brigade and over the next few days made preparations to ready his force for operations.

Early in the New Year, General Rose received the happy news of the relief of Lucknow by Sir Colin Campbell, however, he also received the distressing news that a large force of mutineers was marching towards Saugor.

Saugor was a large and important arsenal protected by a small garrison of one company of European Infantry and about 40 officials who occupied the fort, together with about 170 European women and children. The station also had a native cantonment of about 1,000 men of the 31st Bengal Native Infantry and 100 Irregular Cavalry.

So far the native regiment had remained loyal, however, with the advance of a large force of mutineers their continued loyalty was placed in some doubt.

Brigadier Whitlock had been assigned the task of relieving Saugor, however, as this column was coming from Madras and was not expected to arrive for another two months, General Rose decided that it was expedient for his force to come to the aid of the station at Saugor instead.

On the 6th January 1858, General Rose left Mhow to join his 2nd Brigade at Sehore and two days later his siege train was despatched from Indore.

On the morning of the 16th January, after the arrival of the siege train the previous day, General Rose left Sehore at the head of his men to begin his advance to Saugor; reinforced by 700 men assigned to his force by the loyal Begum of Bhopal.

On the 10th January, the 1st Brigade left Mhow to clear the Grand Trunk road and take the fortress at Chanderi.

Siege and Battle of Rathghur

On 24th January General Rose and his column reached the fortress of Rathghur which was about 25 miles from Saugor, without much effort the British force managed to drive the mutineers from the town and their positions outside the fortress.

Taking the fortress was a more challenging matter, however, and after reconnoitring the area for suitable locations for his artillery batteries the General set up camp in the nearby jungle to await the arrival of the siege train.

On the next day, following the arrival of the siege train, General Rose deployed his force to surround the fortress and set about establishing his artillery batteries. Work on the batteries continued all day and through the night but by daybreak on the 27th they opened up a tremendous barrage on the fort such that by 10 o'clock in the morning on the following day a large breach had been made.

As two men were inspecting the breach, to see if it was viable for an assault, a commotion broke out towards the rear of the British Force, as a large force of mutineers from Saugor, under the leadership of the Rajah of Banpur, was assembling to attack the baggage train.

General Rose despatched a small force made up from the 14th Light Dragoons, the 3rd Bombay Cavalry, some horse artillery and the 5th Hyderabad Infantry to deal with the threat. As the cavalry advanced on the rebels their resolve dissipated and after throwing down their arms and ammunition they fled, hotly pursued by the British force and the mutineers attempt to relieve the fort had been thwarted.

The bombardment of the fort continued through the day and night and on the next morning, when the breach was reinspected the fort was found to be deserted, the occupants having fled during the night.

On the 30th January, the sappers and miners entered the fort and began to demolish the buildings.

Barodia

That day, General Rose received news that the rebel garrison from Rathghur, now strengthened by some rebels from Bundelkhand, had established a position at Barodia, a small village with a fort about 12 miles away.

Figure 89. Rathghur Fort

As the rebels were in a position to obstruct the British advance on Saugor or disrupt their lines of supply, the General felt that it was necessary to drive the mutineers out of Barodia.

At midday on 31st January, after leaving Brigadier Steuart in charge of the remaining forces to protect Rahatgarh, General Rose left Rahatgarh with a force made up of horse and field artillery, 3 troops of the 14th Light Dragoons, 2 troops of the 3rd Bombay Light Cavalry, the 3rd European Regiment, a detachment of the Hyderabad Contingent and a detachment of Madras Sapper and Miners; bound for Barodia.

At about 4 o'clock in the afternoon, the British force came across the rebels posted on the banks of the river Bina, guarding the ford. After a brief but intense battle, the rebels were driven back across the river and after leaving the detachment of the Hyderabad Contingent to guard the ford, General Rose advanced with his force on Barodia where the rebels were entrenched. Following a brief artillery barrage, General Rose unleashed his cavalry on the enemy positions who soon drove the rebels out of the village and into the surrounding jungle.

The enemy losses were estimated at 400 to 500 with their ablest commander, Anant Singh being killed and the Raja of Banpur being wounded. British casualties were light with two officers killed, six officers wounded and fifteen men wounded (two would later die from their wounds). General Rose's ADC Captain Neville of the Royal Engineers was one of the officers killed.

Immediately after the battle, General Rose and his men returned to Rathghur, where they arrived at 2 o'clock in the morning of the 1st February.

Relief of Saugor

The defeat of the rebels at Rathghur and Barodia had removed the threat to the rear of the British force and with their supply lines now secured; General Rose was once again ready to advance on Saugor.

On 3rd February, General Rose's force entered Saugor unopposed as the rebel forces had fled in front of their advance and the 370 Europeans, including 67 women and 130 children who had been besieged since 29th June 1857 were finally relieved.

Sanoda and Garrakota

With rebels now having been cleared to the north and west of his position, General Rose was now determined to clear a way to the east, to enable an advance on Jhansi.

His first major objective was the very strong fortress at Garrakota, about 20 miles from Saugor, which was occupied by the mutineers of the 50th and 52nd Bengal Native Infantry.

However, first he sent a small force to destroy the fort at Sanoda and establish a crossing over the river Beas for use by his siege train. The small fort at Sanoda was destroyed on the 8th February and the next day General Rose advanced with his force towards Garrakota where they arrived in the afternoon of the 11th February. After reconnoitring the enemy positions, a strong rebel force was found to be dug in around the village of Baseri, near the fort and guarding the main road. Despite the lateness of the hour, it was now 8 o'clock in the evening and dark, General Rose decided to attack and clear the position. After a barrage of fire from the horse artillery, the rebels were driven out of their positions and retreated back into the fort.

During the night a breaching battery was established facing the west wall of the fort and during all of the next day the British guns pounded the fort and managed to silence the enemy guns. Unfortunately, due to the size of his force, General Rose was unable to encircle the fort and as dawn broke the rebels could be seen streaming from the fort via an unguarded gate. The British cavalry pursued the retreating mutineers for almost 25 miles and inflicted heavy casualties before returning to the fort which was found to be full of supplies.

After destroying the west wall of the fort, General Rose returned with his men to Saugor where they arrived on the 17th February.

Advance on Jhansi

On arriving back at Saugor, General Rose was eager to advance on Jhansi, however, due to a lack of transportation he was forced to delay his advance for nine days while this problem was sorted out.

The General was also keen for news from the 1st Brigade, commanded by Brigadier Stuart, with whom he was expected to join forces, before any assault on Jhansi.

He was also awaiting news from Brigadier Whitlock, whose column was advancing from Jabalpur to Saugor.

Although frustrated by the delay, General Rose took full advantage of the time, resupplying the column with food and ammunition, repairing damage to the siege guns as well as securing the carts and wagons necessary to transport the supplies.

Having finally received the news that Brigadier Whitlock had left Jabalpur and that Brigadier Stuart with the 1st Brigade was expected to arrive at Goona on about the 28th February, General Rose felt that he was now ready to begin the advance on Jhansi.

On the evening of 26th February, General Rose despatched Major Orr's column of the Hyderabad contingent to march on a route parallel to his intended route, with the task to reconnoitre the passes and determine the best route for the force to join up with the 1st and 2nd Brigades.

A few hours later at 2 o'clock in the morning of 27th February, General Rose left Saugor with the remained of his troops on the way to Jhansi and the next day was joined by Major Orr's column, who having completed his reconnoitre of the passes recommended the pass of Mudinpore as the best route forward.

In order to secure his communications with Saugor, the fort at Barodia, which commanded to road to the pass needed to be captured, this was accomplished with little effort on 2nd March.

In an attempt to deceive the mutineers of his intentions, on the 3rd March General Rose despatched a force under the command of Major Scudamore to mount a distraction attack against the pass at Narut and the fort at Malthon which guarded the pass. Soon afterwards, the General set out with the bulk of his force, bound for his main objective the pass at Mudinpore.

As the advanced guard of the column reached the approach to the pass they came under fire from mutineers posted in the surrounding hills but this force was soon driven back by artillery fire from Major Orr's batteries. After clearing the hills, General Rose's column advanced steadily up the pass driving the main rebel force before them into the village of Mudinpore where many of the mutineers were either killed or captured. By the end of the day the British column had cleared the pass and exhausted by their efforts they camped at the village of Pepeeria near the fort of Sorai which commanded the surrounding plains.

Having forced the pass at Mudinpore, the British force now commanded a position to the rear of the rebel forces that were forced to abandon their positions at the pass of Malthon and the forts at Narut, Maraura, Sorai and Banpur.

Major Richard Keatinge – Victoria Cross No. 249

On the 11th March, the 1st Brigade, commanded by Brigadier Stuart, lay siege to the formidable fort at Chanderi and destroyed the palace of the Rajah of Banpur.

After pounding the walls of the fort with intense artillery fire for several days a breach in the defences was eventually achieved.

On the evening of the 16th March, Major Keatinge with his native servant reconnoitred the approaches and found a path across the defensive ditch leading straight to the breach.

At daybreak on the following morning, the 17th March, Major Keatinge volunteered to lead the assault on the fort, taking the route that he had reconnoitred the previous evening. The Major was one of the first men to gain the breach, where he was seriously wounded; despite his wounds Major Keatinge continued to lead his men to the eventual capture of the fort during which he was once again wounded.

For his part in this action Major Keatinge was later awarded the Victoria Cross.

After resting for a few days, General Rose's force continued their advance towards Jhansi on the 14th March. After having marched along the shore of lake Talbehat they crossed the river Betwa via a ford on the 17th March and by 20th March were encamped about eight miles from Jhansi.

Despite orders from the Governor General, that allowed General Rose to bypass the heavily defended town of Jhansi and proceed to Chirkaree, the General chose to lay siege to the town and for the next few days carried out extensive reconnaissances of the enemy defences in order to formulate a plan of attack.

During this time, the General established his artillery batteries and began an intense bombardment of the city which was to last for 17 days.

On the 24th March, the 1st Brigade, commanded by Brigadier Stuart, arrived from Chanderi and took their place in the lines.

On the 31st March, General Rose received intelligence that a large rebel force of some 22,000 men, with 28 guns, led by Tantia Topi was advancing from the north to come to the relief of the rebels besieged at Jhansi.

The General now faced a very difficult situation, with about 11,000 mutineers established in Jhansi in strongly defended positions; he was now confronted by a much larger enemy force advancing on his rear.

Decisive action was required and General Rose decided to continue the siege but at the same time launch an attack on the new enemy forces.

Battle of Betwa

A small force of 1,500 men with cavalry and artillery was sent to the ford across the river Betwa where they quickly established their lines; with the heavy guns in the centre, supported by the 3rd European Infantry, the 24th Regiment of Foot and men from the Hyderabad Infantry.

The right flank consisted of a company of 14th Dragoons and a company of the Hyderabad Cavalry supported by the Eagle troop of horse artillery. The left flank was composed of two troops of 14th Dragoons supported by Captain Lightfoot's Field battery, some men of the 25th and 85th regiments supported by cavalry and artillery were held in reserve.

At around midnight, the enemy force with large numbers of infantry, about 600–700 cavalry and all of their artillery advanced to within 600 yards of the British lines and began the battle with an artillery bombardment. As the enemy artillery was having some success against his heavy guns and Infantry in the centre, General Rose ordered the cavalry on each flank to attack the enemy guns, Lieutenant Clarke leading the Hyderabad Cavalry, charged the guns three times before being seriously wounded and lost most of his men.

With General Rose at the head of Captain Need's troop of Dragoons the cavalry continued to press on the enemy left flank while the troops commanded by Captains Prettyjohn and Mac-Mahon continued the fight against the right flank with their troops of Dragoons.

The ferocity of the British cavalry attacks caused much confusion in the enemy ranks and they began to retreat in disorder, now pursued by the British infantry, they were pushed back to the banks of the Betwa River.

It was at the river that the British cavalry, now in advance of the infantry, who could not keep up with their frantic charge, encountered the rebel reserve forces under the command of Tantia Topi himself.

Lieutenant James Leith – Victoria Cross No. 255

In the face of the charging cavalry, supported by artillery fire, the enemy reserve force also began their retreat across the river and Captain Need well in advance of his men entered the river and was immediately surrounded by the enemy.

Captain Need was on the point of being bayoneted to death by the rebels when Lieutenant Leith charged into the mêlée and dispersed the rebels thus saving his Captain's life.

For this action Lieutenant Leith was later awarded the Victoria Cross.

While General Rose was engaged with the main enemy force, Brigadier Stuart led the reserve force of the 25th and 86th regiments against a force of about 2,000 rebels, entrenched in the village of Kushabir who were defeated after a vigorous battle during which all the enemy guns and ammunition were captured.

Having completed their task of defeating the relieving force, which had fled off towards Kalpi, both battalions now returned to the siege lines at Jhansi.

Assault on Jhansi

While the force was defeating the enemy at the river Betwa, the bombardment of the city defences was kept up and minor forays were occasionally launched.

Lieutenant Hugh Cochrane – Victoria Cross No. 254

On the 1st of April, Lieutenant Cochrane was ordered to capture one of the mutineers' guns.

Being the officer in charge, the Lieutenant was the only man mounted, so was well ahead of his men when he charged forward under heavy artillery and rifle fire. On reaching the gun, he chased off the enemy gunners and retained possession of the gun until his company of men arrived on the scene.

For this action Lieutenant Cochrane was later awarded the Victoria Cross.

His gallantry during an attack on the enemy rearguard, during which he had three horses shot out from under him, is also mentioned in the Victoria Cross citation.

The scale of the bombardment was such that large numbers of mutineers attempted to leave the city via the northern gate, however, these were cut down by the British cavalry.

On the 2nd April, the Chief Engineer reported that all preparations for the assault were now complete and General Rose

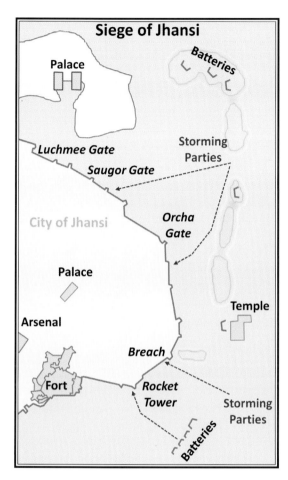

Figure 90. Assault on Jhansi

issued orders and a plan of attack which was to be launched the next day.

At 2 o'clock in the morning of the 3rd April, the men were woken and assembled at their designated positions to await the signal to begin the attack.

There were two main assault columns: the left attack commanded by Brigadier Stuart consisted of the following units from the 1st Brigade; the 21st Company Royal Engineers, the 25th Bombay Native Infantry and the 86th Regiment of Foot. The left attack was divided into two assault parties; Colonel Lowth commanding one party was to storm a breach made in the walls near the mound while Major Stuart leading the other party was to use ladders to escalade the rocket tower and the low curtain wall to the right of the tower. The second assault column, assigned to the right attack, was led by Brigadier Steuart consisting of the Madras and Bombay Sappers, the 3rd Bombay Europeans and the Hyderabad Infantry. The assault column of the right attack was also split into two assault parties; the right party was commanded by Colonel Liddell and the left by Captain

Robinson. These assault parties were to escalade the town walls using ladders.

A feint attack against the west wall was to be made by Major Gall and it was from here that Captain Ommaney was to fire three guns as the signal for the main assault columns to begin their attack.

While waiting for the signal to attack, the men of the left attack slowly advanced towards their objectives and despite the light of a full moon managed to get to within 350 yards of the walls, which were about 23 feet high, undetected.

The signal was finally fired just as dawn was breaking and when the men were about 100 yards from the Rocket Tower, Major Stuart ordered them to charge.

Private James Byrne – Victoria Cross No. 258
Captain Henry Jerome – Victoria Cross No. 261

In the face of very heavy fire, the ladders were placed against the walls and led by Lieutenant Dartnell the men scaled the walls but suffered many casualties.

Captain Jerome was with the party led by Captain Darby, storming the breach which was carried with few losses and after gaining the city proceeded to clear some houses which were occupied by the rebels, who had been driven from the top of the walls.

Many officers and men were severely wounded during the clearing of these houses, including Ensign Sewell, however, despite being wounded himself Private Byrne assisted Captain Jerome in carrying Ensign Sewell to safety through heavy musket fire, undoubtedly saving his life.

For this action Private Byrne and Captain Jerome were both awarded the Victoria Cross.

Captain Jerome's citation also mentions a second act of bravery on 28th May at Jumna when he was severely wounded with part of his head torn off.

⊹

Private Frederick Whirlpool – Victoria Cross No. 260

In the action of the left attack, Private Whirlpool twice volunteered to bring in wounded men from the walls of the fort while under heavy fire and for this action was later awarded the Victoria Cross.

Private Whirlpool's citation mentions a second act of bravery when on 6th May he went to the rescue of Lieutenant Doune at Lohari where he received 17 wounds, one of which nearly severed his head.

⊹

Private James Pearson – Victoria Cross No. 259

Also during the left attack, Private Pearson attacked a group of mutineers, killing one and bayoneting two others. Despite being severely wounded during this action he carried the wounded Private Burn to safety, regrettably Private Burn later died from his wounds.

For this action, Private Pearson was later awarded the Victoria Cross.

Bombardier Joseph Brennan – Victoria Cross No. 257

Bombardier Brennan managed to bring two guns to bear on the fort which was laying down intense fire on the British forces and due to the accuracy of his fire the enemy guns were silenced.

The act, which was carried out in the face of heavy enemy fire, later resulted in Bombardier Brennan being awarded the Victoria Cross.

Having gained the breach and scaled the Rocket Tower, the left attack now turned their attention to the royal palace which with fierce hand to hand fighting they managed to clear room by room.

With the sounding of the signal, the right attack also began their assault and had to cross about 200 yards of open ground under intense musket and artillery fire before they managed to place three ladders against the walls.

Many of the assault parties fell as they were bombarded by missiles thrown down from the top of the walls, however, the Sappers held firm and continued to steady the ladders as the men ascended.

About 100 men from the 3rd Bombay European, who were part of the reserve, were called forward to help provide protection to the men scaling the ladders.

Finding it almost impossible to scale the wall with ladders it was decided to blow a postern gate, with gunpowder, to gain entry.

Having gained entry to the city the men proceeded to clear the ramparts, to allow safe entry over the walls, and then proceeded towards the palace.

Corporal Michael Sleavon – Victoria Cross No. 256

On the route to the Palace was a street junction which was covered by heavy fire from the fort, many men were killed or wounded trying to cross this open space so the engineers suggested erecting a temporary barrier across the opening to give some protection.

A barrier was erected using planks, doors and furniture taken from the surrounding houses, despite the heavy fire from a distance of only 200 yards, Corporal Sleavon remained in place directing the construction until nightfall by which time the right attack had managed to reach the palace.

For his part in this action Corporal Sleavon was later awarded the Victoria Cross.

Having captured the palace, the troops began the process of clearing the surrounding houses and after a bloody battle managed to secure the palace stables which had been occupied by 30 to 40 of the Ranee's personal bodyguard.

After having unsuccessfully attempted to leave the city, a force of about 400 mutineers occupied a high rocky hill to the west of the fort. General Rose immediately ordered the hill to be surrounded and it was soon under heavy fire from the British artillery.

The artillery barrage failed to dislodge the mutineers, so the British infantry advanced up the hill killing many of the enemy, the Ranee's father, Mamu Sahib, was one of the wounded who were captured, he was hanged a few days later.

On the next day, the British continued their assault and captured the remainder of the city after extensive street fighting but it was not until the early hours of the morning of the 5th April that it was discovered that the fort had been abandoned by the rebels and that the Ranee had escaped during the night and fled to Bhandara about 21 miles away.

A force of cavalry was despatched to try and capture the Ranee, however, after catching up with her and her small force at Bhandara, she once again managed to escape.

Mopping up operations continued throughout the day but eventually the city was cleared of rebels and Jhansi was back under British control.

The fight for the city had resulted in British losses of 307 killed and wounded, however, the rebel losses were estimated at about 5,000.

Advance on Kalpi

With Jhansi back under British control, the next target for General Rose was the fortified arsenal at Kalpi, however, due to lack of food, transport and ammunition the General was forced to halt until his supplies could be replenished.

Before he could advance on Kalpi, the General also had to secure Jhansi from attack from the rebels who were now thought to be at Kotah, however, on hearing that Brigadier Smith with the Rajputana Field Force had secured Kotah this threat was dispelled.

On 22nd April, General Rose was once again ready to resume his advance and at about midnight he despatched a flying column, under the command of Major Gall to scout the road from Jhansi to Kalpi and collect information about enemy movements.

After leaving part of the 2nd Brigade, under the command of Lieutenant-Colonel Liddell, to garrison Jhansi, General Rose set out for Kalpi with the rest of his force on 25th April.

On the 1st May, General Rose joined up with Major Gall's force at Poonth, about 16 miles from Koonch where he was updated on the rebel forces located at Kalpi some 40 miles distant.

He also learned that Tantia Topi, after leaving a small garrison at Kalpi, had advanced with the bulk of his force to Koonch where he was entrenched and guarding the road from Jhansi.

On the evening of the 5th May, the 2nd Brigade with 400 men from the 71st Regiment joined the force at Poonth and General Rose issued orders for the 1st Brigade to proceed to the village of Lahorree while the 2nd Brigade was directed to Koonch.

Capture of Fort Lahorree

The 1st Brigade reached Lahorree the next morning and after hearing that the rebels held a strong fort about 7 mile away, despatched Major Gall with a wing of the 3rd European Infantry, some artillery and cavalry, to deal with the matter.

On reaching the fort, Major Gall determined that it was too strong to be quickly breached by his artillery, so, after blowing the main gate with powder, he ordered a direct assault.

Entry to the fort was quickly attained and all the male occupants were killed, it was during this assault that Private Whirlpool VC was severely wounded while saving the life of Lieutenant Doune.

In the evening, after allowing his men some much needed rest, Major Gall set out for Koonch about 6 miles away and at dawn rested his men at the village of Nagoopura to avoid the murderous heat of the day, 110°F in the shade.

Capture of Koonch

On the morning of the 7th May, having completed their flanking movements, the British forces were all situated close to Koonch; the 1st Brigade occupied the left flank at the village of Nagoopura to the north west and rear of the town and its fort; the 2nd Brigade under the command of Brigadier Stuart occupied the village of Chomair at the centre and faced the main rebel force, who in fortified positions guarded the Jhansi road and Major Orr at the village of Oomree occupied the right flank.

Koonch was a difficult place to attack, being surrounded by woods which provided the enemy with cover and the area was scattered with many small buildings and walled gardens which were easy to defend.

After checking on the disposition of his troops and a brief survey of the enemy positions, General Rose determined to clear a large body of enemy troops posted behind a low wall to his front and in a wood to the left of the wall.

After shelling both positions, Major Gall advanced into the wood and found that the rebels had abandoned their positions behind the wall and were retreating to the rear of the woods.

With this news, General Rose issued orders for a general assault on the town by first clearing the woods and buildings and after an artillery barrage; the houses at the front of the town were soon captured.

On the left flank, the 86th regiment with the 14th Light Dragoons, supported by horse artillery, drove through the north of the town and soon captured the fort.

With their defensive line cut in two and their right flank turned, the mutineers began to retreat across uneven ground towards Kalpi. Due to the heat of the day, 12 men had already died from heat stroke; General Rose called off the pursuit of the enemy by the infantry and instead directed the cavalry of both brigades supported by horse artillery to this task. The enemy retreat was covered by a large body of skirmishers who fell back in good order to cover their comrades, however, after having been pursued for about eight miles most of them were killed by the British forces.

The main body of rebel troops reached the road to Kalpi and continued their retreat unmolested as by this time the cavalry, exhausted by their efforts, had returned to Koonch.

Many of the fleeing mutineers also fell due to the ravages of the sun.

Assault on Kalpi

After the Battle of Koonch, General Rose rested his men while gathering forage and fresh water for the next stage of his journey.

General Rose left Koonch on the 9th May with the 1st Brigade and headed for the village of Golowlee on the river Jumna to rendezvous with Lieutenant-Colonel Maxwell, commanding a column of the Bengal army, who would resupply his force with ammunition.

The 2nd Brigade left Koonch on the 11th May, with the intention of marching to Banda, however, after getting lost they joined General Rose at Sucalee.

On the 14th May, General Rose managed to make contact with Lieutenant-Colonel Maxwell and a resupply of ammunition for his force was accomplished.

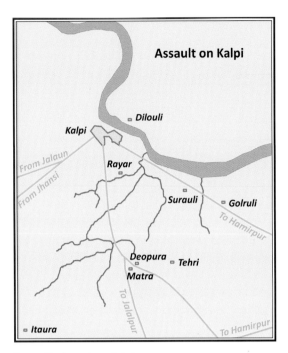

Figure 91. Assault on Kalpi

By the 17th May, Lieutenant-Colonel Maxwell had moved down the Jumna to Golowlee, where he set up his artillery batteries to bombard the fort and town of Kalpi.

For the next few days the mutineers were constantly conducting skirmishes against the British forces. The rebels deliberately carried out the majority of their raids during the heat of the day, when they knew the exertions on the European troops would be greatest.

With daytime temperatures reaching 120°F and at night seldom falling below 100°F, the men suffered greatly from the heat, with 21 dying from sunstroke in one week and over 310 being hospitalised.

By the 21st May, Colonel Maxwell's batteries were ready to begin their bombardment of the fort and town, which they did with vigour.

The approaches to the town and fort at Kalpi were well guarded by several steep ravines which offered good defensive positions to the mutineers.

On reaching the lower ground, the British would be confronted by a secondary line of defence; an array of 85, mainly stone built temples which again provided good positions for the rebel defenders.

Despite the strength of the enemy position, General Rose believed that he must make a direct attack soon, as he could not expose his troops to a long campaign during the heat of the season; he therefore decided to press home an attack on the 23rd May.

On the 22nd May, before General Rose could launch his attack, the mutineers launched their own attack, advancing along the Banda road to attack the British left flank, while their artillery pounded the British central positions. The attack on the left flank, led by Rao Sahib the nephew of Nana Sahib, was intended as a feint to draw British forces from the right flank which was their real objective. Fortunately, General Rose suspected this rebel ploy and kept the force protecting his right flank intact, despite the heavy attack on his left. This was just as well, as suddenly, the rebels using the ravines for cover made a concerted attack against the right flank. In the face of vastly superior enemy numbers, hindered by the heat of the day and the increasing misfires of their Enfield rifles, the British forces were slowly driven back until Brigadier C. S. Stuart took control of the situation. With the British field guns and mortar batteries providing covering fire, the 25th and 86th Native Infantry formed a line to dispute the enemy advance. Despite the stiff British resistance, it was likely that the line would have been overwhelmed by the larger rebel force, however, General Rose brought up the men of the Camel Corps and personally led them in a charge against the mutineers.

Such was the impact of this brave charge that the rebel force almost immediately began to retreat back into the ravines where they came under heavy fire from the British artillery. Seeing the failure of the main attack, the rebels attacking the left flank also fled.

With the rebels in full retreat, General Rose ordered the British forces to advance on all fronts until they reached the outskirts of Kalpi where they rested for the night.

On the following morning, the British resumed their advance and without opposition occupied the fort and town of Kalpi, which had been abandoned by the rebels during the night.

The heavy bombardment of the fort and town by Colonel Maxwell's batteries had forced most of the rebels to flee towards Jaloun.

A force, under the command of Major Gall, was directed to pursue the rebels and they advanced along the Kalpi to Jhansi road to accomplish this task.

Lieutenant Harry Lyster – Victoria Cross No. 273

It was on 23rd May, during this pursuit of the enemy, that Lieutenant Lyster, following orders for the cavalry to charge the enemy, came across a small force of mutineers that had formed up in a defensive square.

Without hesitation, the Lieutenant charged into the midst of the square which he dispersed, killing several mutineers in the process.

For this action, Lieutenant Lyster was later awarded the Victoria Cross.

With the capture of Kalpi, the Central India Force's objectives had been achieved and General Rose was ordered to split up his force and send his men to Gwalior and Jhansi where they were to form the garrisons for those towns.

On 25th May, Lieutenant-Colonel Robertson with one troop of the 14th Light Dragoons, one squadron of the 3rd Bombay Cavalry, the Hyderabad Contingency Cavalry, a light field battery and the 25th Bombay Infantry was sent along the Jalaun road in pursuit of the rebels who were fleeing towards Gwalior. After a short time, General Rose despatched a wing of the 86th Regiment of Foot and two further squadrons of the 14th Light Dragoons to reinforce Lieutenant-Colonel Robertson's column. A few days later, when it was confirmed that the rebels were indeed making for Gwalior, General Rose despatched another column to reinforce the pursuit column; Brigadier Stuart with a light field battery, some more troops of the 14th Light Dragoons, a wing of the 71st Regiment of Foot, four companies of the 25th Bombay Infantry and some Bombay Sappers and Miners.

General Rose, having suffered from several bouts of severe sun stroke and exhausted by the rigours of the campaign was advised by his medical officer to go to Bombay on sick leave. Taking this medical advice, the General applied for sick leave and resigned his position on 1st June.

The Gwalior Campaign

After the defeat of the mutineers at Koonch, Tantia Topi made his way to Gwalior where he plotted to get control of the province of Scindia, which still remained loyal to the British.

After the fall of Jhansi, the rebels last stronghold south of the river Jumna, the Ranee of Jhansi and the Nawab of Banda fled to a village some 15 miles from Gwalior and when Tantia Topi received this news he left Gwalior to join up with them.

On the 27th May, the three rebel leaders held a council of war and although no long term strategy was agreed, it was decided that the rebel force should proceed to Gwalior and try to recruit the Maharaja of Sindh's army to their cause.

On the following morning, after crossing the Scinde River, the rebel force entered Gwalior territory and halted at Amean where they were confronted by a small force from the Maharaja's army who delivered orders from the Maharaja that they should retire.

Ignoring the Maharaja's orders, the rebel force continued its advance into Scinde territory and set up camp just outside the city of Gwalior.

On the morning of the 1st June, the Maharaja led a force of 8,000 men against the rebel army, however, on reaching the rebel army the whole of his force, except his personal bodyguard, went over to the rebels.

It was only the brave resistance of his bodyguard, who lost 60 of their number that allowed the Maharaja to escape and make his way to Agra where he arrived on the 3rd June.

The rebels occupied the town and fort of Gwalior unopposed and installed Nana Sahib as Peshwa.

News of the fall of Gwalior reached General Rose at Kalpi on 4th June and despite having relinquished his command and requested to go on sick leave only days earlier, the General informed Lord Canning that he was willing to command a force to retake the city. Lord Canning gladly accepted his offer and Brigadier-General Napier, who had been appointed as his successor, agreed to serve as his second in command.

On the 6th June, after leaving the bulk of his force to garrison the town, General Rose left Kalpi with a small force of horse artillery and cavalry and making forced marches during the night, to avoid the heat of the day, set out to catch up with Brigadier Stuart's column. On the 11th June, General Rose caught up with Brigadier Stuart's column at fort Indoorkee, on the River Scinde, and it was here that he received the news that Colonel Riddell's column of Bombay troops escorting a siege train of heavy artillery and ammunition had left Agra and was bound for Gwalior to assist with a siege. The General also learnt that Lord Clyde had ordered Brigadier Smith, with a brigade of the Rajputana Field Force, to advance from Chanderi and make for Gwalior.

Conscious of the rapidly approaching monsoon season, General Rose was eager to avoid a full blown siege operation which would be a long drawn out affair, he instead put into action a plan for a direct assault on the town and fort.

Major Orr, commanding the Hyderabad Contingent, was ordered to move from Jhansi to Punier, about 12 miles from Gwalior, where he would hold the Bombay road and cut off a potential escape route for a rebel retreat. Brigadier Smith was ordered to advance from Sipree, along the Jhansi road to Kotah-ki-Serai about 7 miles from Gwalior and Colonel Riddell was ordered to advance to the Residency, 7 miles to the north of the city.

General Rose expected that these encircling forces would be in position by the 19th June and his force would advance on the weaker eastern side of the city to make the attack.

On 12th June, General Rose's column reached Amean where he received news that a force of Bombay troops had arrived to garrison Kalpi and that his 2nd Brigade was now on its way to join him.

On the arrival of the 2nd Brigade, Brigadier-General Robert Napier assumed command and on the morning of 16th June reached Bahadurpore about 4 miles from the cantonment at Morar.

Battle of Morar

Captain Abbott, with the Hyderabad Cavalry, was ordered to reconnoitre the cantonment and reported back that the rebels were established in strong positions, in front of the buildings, which appeared to be still in good condition.

After inspecting the enemy positions himself, General Rose decided on an immediate attack, if left to the following day, the rebels were likely to burn all of the cantonment bungalows and deprive the British forces of much needed shelter.

Private George Rodgers – Victoria Cross No. 275

The General quickly formed his men into two lines; Brigadier Stuart with the 1st Brigade occupied the 1st line while General Napier with the 2nd Brigade occupied the 2nd line.

With General Rose, leading the 1st line advanced on the centre of the rebel position and despite heavy fire from enemy artillery managed to drive the main body of the mutineers from the cantonment, which fled and joined their comrades in ravines to the right of the position.

Seeing the enemy retreating in large number to the ravines on the right, General Napier ordered Colonel Campbell, commanding the wing of the 71st regiment and supported by the 14th Dragoons, to clear the new enemy position.

The 71st regiment advanced in skirmishing order and after some fierce hand to hand fighting managed to clear the rebels from their well protected positions in the ravines.

During the fighting, Private Rodgers single handed charged a position defended by 7 well armed rebels and managed to drive them off, killing one of them in the process.

For this action Private Rodgers was later awarded the Victoria Cross.

✠

Having been cleared from the cantonment and the ravines, the rebels retreated back towards Gwalior and General Rose and his forces occupied the cantonment giving the British command of the Morar River and the road to Agra.

Battle of Kotah-ki-Serai

On the morning of the 17th June, Brigadier Smith reached the town of Kotah-ki-Serai which was about three miles south east of Gwalior.

The Brigadier had been ordered, by General Rose, to halt at the town, however, as large numbers of mutineers were in the vicinity, he thought the town was not a good place to halt. Leaving his large baggage train under guard at the nearby fort, Brigadier

Smith crossed the river, with the 8th Hussars scouting the way. After advancing for half a mile, the column came under fire from hidden rebel batteries which ran in a line under the hills across the road to Gwalior. The horse artillery was brought forward by Brigadier Smith and they quickly silenced the enemy guns.

With the guns silenced, Colonel Raines began to advance with the infantry and when they reached within 50 yards of the rebel defences they charged the position but were slowed down by a deep water filled ditch, they found the position deserted by the time they reached the rebel trenches.

Led by Colonel Raines, the infantry continued to pursue the retreating mutineers and began to advance along the road.

Captain Clement Heneage-Walker – Victoria Cross No. 276
Sergeant Joseph Ward – Victoria Cross No. 277
Farrier George Hollis – Victoria Cross No. 278
Private John Pearson – Victoria Cross No. 279

Having reached the crest of the hills, the wide plain between Morar and Gwalior lay before the British force with the Phoolbagh Palace occupied by Tantia Topi and defended by two batteries of guns, many other guns were located across the plain.

Having spotted a large force of enemy cavalry advancing up a ravine to the right of his position, Brigadier Smith ordered the 8th Hussars to intercept them.

Led by Colonel Hicks and Captain Heneage, the 8th Hussars charged the rebel cavalry and sweeping them before them drove on into the enemy camp at the Phoolbagh Palace, however, having outstripped all support they had to withdraw. The 8th Hussars returned to the British lines with two captured guns.

For their part in the action, Captain Heneage, Sergeant Ward, Farrier Hollis and Private Pearson were later awarded the Victoria Cross, having been nominated for the award by a ballot of their peers in the regiment.

During this action, the rebel leader the Ranee of Jhansi was killed.

✠

With his men exhausted by the battle and the heat of the day, Brigadier Smith retired to the shelter of the ravines in the hills and set up camp for the night. The 95th Regiment had lost five officers and 81 men due to heat stroke, having marched 26 miles during the day.

On the evening of the 17th June, General Rose, in response to a request for reinforcements from Brigadier Smith, sent a force of Light Dragoons, a light Field Battery and the 25th Bombay Infantry to Kotah-ki-Serai.

On the morning of the 18th June, the troops from Kalpi arrived at Morar and in the afternoon, after leaving a garrison, under the command of General Napier, to guard the town, General Rose departed for Kotah-ki-Serai with two troops of the 14th Light Dragoons, a Light Field Battery, a wing of the 71st Light Infantry, the 86th Regiment of Foot and a wing of the Hyderabad Infantry.

After a march of over 20 miles, the column crossed the river Morar and set up camp near to Brigadier Smith's camp. During the march, the men had suffered greatly from heat exhaustion with over 100 men struck down in the 86th Regiment alone.

On the next morning, General Rose reconnoitred the British position and found two strong enemy forces which threatened the British advance towards Gwalior. The first in the hills to the left of the position, was a force of artillery and infantry, protected by cavalry to their rear, positioned across the road; protected by a deep canal at their front. The second force was also to the left of the British position and was comprised of a large body of artillery and infantry stationed in a gorge guarding a road from the ford to Gwalior. As these forces threatened his left flank and rear, General Rose determined that this threat must be eliminated before he could continue his advance on the town and fort of Gwalior.

To carry out this endeavour, General Rose first instructed the Madras Sappers and Miners to construct a bridge across the canal, his plan being to use this to cross the canal and place his force between the two enemy positions and Gwalior.

He would then attack these positions from the rear, while Brigadier Smith and his force, concealed by the ravines, would attack their front and left flank.

Battle of Gwalior

By nightfall, the bridge was complete, however, when large numbers of rebels were observed leaving Gwalior to reinforce their forward positions, with the obvious intent of making an attack on the British left flank, General Rose changed his plan of attack.

Instead of interposing a force between the two rebel positions and Gwalior, the General instead set out to turn the rebel left flank.

Brigadier Stuart with the 86th Regiment of Foot and the 25th Bombay Native Infantry crossed the canal and headed to attack the enemy left flank, while Colonel Raines with the 95th Regiment, supported by the 10th Bombay Native Infantry, crossed the canal and headed towards the right of the rebel positions as a diversion.

Lieutenant-Colonel Lowth, leading the 86th regiment, advanced against the rebel left flank, who retired back to their guns on the ridge, however, being pressed hard by the British

force they continued their retreat, abandoning their guns which were captured.

Lieutenant Brockman, whose company had captured the guns, promptly turned them on the retreating mutineers and caused many casualties.

Lieutenant Roome, leading the 10th Bombay Native Infantry, supporting the 95th Regiment completed the capture of the ridge by clearing the hills on the left of the enemy line, again capturing rebels' guns and mortars which were turned on the rebels retreating across the plain to Gwalior.

With the high ground now in British hands, General Rose looked down at Gwalior, on his right was the Phoolbagh Palace, the old city and the fort on the rock of Gwalior. While on his left was the new town of Lashkar and the Grand Parade.

With the rebels fleeing across the plain in disarray and seeking cover wherever they could find it, General Rose resolved to take

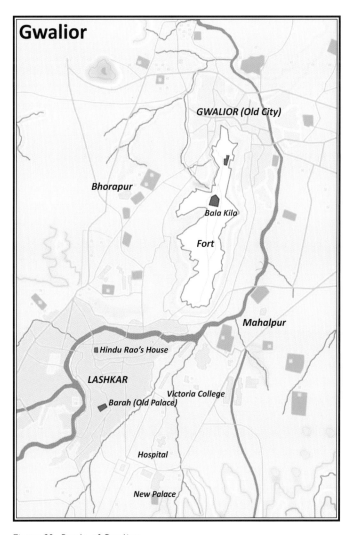

Figure 92. Battle of Gwalior

the town before nightfall and ordered an immediate advance of his forces.

The 3rd troop of the Bombay Horse Artillery with a troop of the 8th Hussars covered the extreme right flank while Colonel Owen leading the 1st Bombay Lancers descended the heights to attack the Grand Parade and the new city. With a battery of Light Field Artillery and two troops of the 14th Light Dragoons covering his advance, General Rose moved forward his infantry; with the 86th Regiment on the left flank and the 95th Regiment on the right flank.

The swift advance of the British forces caught the mutineers unaware and instead of mounting a defence of their positions seemed more intent on making their escape.

As the British infantry was approaching the plain, Colonel Owen and his lancers charged across the Grand Parade and chased the rebels into Lashkar and then drove them out of the new town.

Brigadier Smith and his force attacked the garden palace of Phoolbagh and after taking the palace continued to pursue the rebels until well after nightfall, capturing most of their guns.

By the night of the 19th of June, General Rose had capture all of Gwalior except the fort in the old town, with a loss of only 87 men killed or wounded and he set about securing his new positions.

Battle of Jaura Alipur

Early in the morning of 20th June, Brigadier-General Napier, at Morar, received orders from General Rose to pursue the rebels who had fled from Gwalior.

General Napier set off a few hours later with a force of about 480 cavalry with a troop of Horse Artillery in support. After a ride of 32 miles, General Napier's force caught up with the mutineers at Jaura Alipur just after sunrise on the 21st of June. The rebels were reported to have a force of about 12,000 men with 22 guns and were posted with their right flank on the village of Jaura Alipur, cavalry on both flanks and their infantry and artillery in the centre.

Concealed by rising ground, General Napier advanced to within 1,200 yards of the enemy position and observed that the ground to the enemy left was clear so advanced his horse artillery to within 300 yards of the enemy line from where they began to lay down an enfilading barrage. Within a few minutes, the fire from Captain Lightfoot's Horse Artillery had silenced the enemy guns and the rebel line was beginning to waver.

Captain Lightfoot re-limbered his guns and charged the enemy line, closely followed by Captain Prettyjohn leading the 14th Dragoons and Captain Abbott with the Hyderabad Cavalry.

Seeing the charge on the left, General Napier immediately followed up with the rest of his force and the rebels were driven back through their lines and out of the villages into open country.

The rebels were chase for about six miles, 25 guns and large quantities of ammunition were captured.

Capture of Fort Gwalior

The fort on the rock of Gwalior was a formidable fortress about a mile and a half in length and about 300 yards wide at its broadest point; during the operations so far, the guns in the fort had kept up a constant and heavy fire against the British troops.

On the morning of the 20th June, the guns in the fort continued their fire against the British positions.

Lieutenant William Waller – Victoria Cross No. 280

When the guns restarted their fire, Lieutenant Rose with a detachment of the 25th Bombay Native Infantry was in command near the main gate of the old fort and Lieutenant Waller with another detachment of the 25th was stationed nearby. Lieutenant Rose proposed to his fellow officer, that they should combine forces and attempt to force entry into the fort via the main gate. Lieutenant Waller readily agreed and the small band of men, accompanied by a blacksmith, crept up to the gate undetected. The blacksmith managed to force the gateway open, together with a further five gates which barred their progress. After forcing the sixth and final gate, the British party was eventually noticed by the defenders who brought a gun to bear on the gate, dashing forward the party was soon engaged in fierce hand to hand combat with the fort's garrison.

Just as the final and successful charge was made, Lieutenant Rose was shot by a mutineer and when he fell, the mutineer set about him with a sword. Lieutenant Waller rushed to the aid of his comrade and killed the rebel but too late to save the life of his friend, however, the fortress was now in British hands.

For his part in the capture of the fort, Lieutenant Waller was later awarded the Victoria Cross.

On the 20th June, British troops escorted the Maharaja of Scinde and installed him back in his palace at Gwalior where he was restored to govern his kingdom.

With the capture of Gwalior, the campaign was finally at an end and on 29th June General Rose, still suffering from ill health, handed over his command to General Napier and returned to Bombay to take command of the presidency army.

The Central India Field Force was now split up and assigned to other duties: the 95th highlanders took up garrison duties at the old fort in Gwalior; the 71st and 86th regiments together with the 25th Bombay Native Infantry with detachments of cavalry and artillery formed the garrison at Morar; General Napier with the 3rd Bombay Europeans and 24th Bombay Native Infantry were sent to Jhansi and Brigadier Smith's brigade was split between the stations at Gwalior, Sipri and Ghuna.

Berar Field Force

The Hyderabad Contingent had little involvement in the early days of the mutiny as the Madras presidency was little affected. However, in November of 1858, detachments of the Contingent from various locations were assembled at Amraoti as the Berar Field Force under the command of Brigadier W. Hill.

The purpose of the field force was to protect the Berar frontier and to pursue Tantia Topi should he come within their territory.

Operations in Gawilgarh Hills

On the 8th December 1858, while on patrol in the Gawilgarh Hills, Brigadier Hills came across a group of 30 to 40 rebel cavalry and assuming them to be the advanced party of a much larger force set of in pursuit with his 2nd Cavalry under the command of Captain Clogstoun.

Unfortunately, when the rebels spotted the British force, they quickly dispersed into the jungle and could not be followed, however, a few were captured and subsequently executed.

On the next morning Captain Clogstoun was sent out from the camp at Hindi to reconnoitre towards Sendwa and after having proceeded for about 15 miles came across the tracks of a large body of men where they had entered the jungle.

After following the tracks for eight miles, the enemy was seen to be moving through tall grass a short distance away from the British column.

Captain Clogstoun launched an immediate attack and managed to kill several of their number before they once again disappeared into the jungle.

Battle of Chichamba

On the 15th January, Brigadier Hills and his force was approaching the village of Wakhad, where he intended to camp following a day's march of 36 miles. However, when he arrived at the village he received a message from Captain Campbell, the commissioner in the neighbouring village of Rissod, that a large body of rebels had just entered his village and plundered it.

On receiving this news, Brigadier Hill with a detachment of his force set out immediately for Rissod and on reaching the village found that the rebels had fled, with their plunder, along the road to Jintur.

Captain Herbert Clogstoun – Victoria Cross No. 292

Captain Clogstoun, who was the first to arrive at the village with his squadron, set off in pursuit of the rebels and after a hard gallop of about seven miles caught up with them near the village of Chichamba.

Only a few of his men had been able to keep up with the Captain, however, seeing the need to delay the retreat of the rebels he charged at thm with eight of his men.

After driving the rebels into the village, Captain Clogstoun moved into the plain where he formed up with the rest of the detachment which was now arriving.

Unfortunately of the eight men who accompanied Captain Clogstoun in his charge, four were killed and three wounded, the Captain was also wounded by a musket shot.

For this action Captain Clogstoun was later awarded the Victoria Cross.

With the rebels now inside the village, with a small fort at its centre, Brigadier Hill ordered the village to be surrounded by his cavalry so as to contain them. When his infantry arrived, Brigadier Hill launched an attack in force but under the heavy enemy fire, especially from the fort, he was forced to retire after losing many of his officers and men. Reluctant to just allow the rebels to escape, the Brigadier posted piquets of cavalry around the village but in the dead of night the mutineers managed to effect their escape into the nearby hills, however, due to the alertness of the piquets who pursued them they suffered heavy losses.

The field force was involved in several other minor operations until March 1859, when the force was split up and sent back to their individual stations.

The Bundelkhand Campaign

Part of the planned Central India Campaign was the pacification of Bundelkhand by a column from the Madras Army, in November 1857 Major-General George Cornish Whitlock was appointed to the command of this column.

The Saugor Field force was to be assembled at Jubbulpore, in preparation for an advance on Banda.

General Whitlock; with his force of 12th Lancers, 4th, 6th and 7th Madras Light Cavalry, 2nd Hyderabad Contingency Cavalry,

3rd Madras European Infantry, 1st Madras Infantry, troops of European and Native Horse Artillery, detachments of Royal Artillery and Madras Foot Artillery and a detachment of the Madras Sappers and Miners; reached Kamptee on 1th January 1858.

After leaving Kamptee on 23rd January, the force reached Jubbulpore on 3rd February where the Nagpur Column; squadrons of 4th Madras and 2nd Hyderabad Cavalry, 33rd Madras Infantry, 1st Nagpur Irregular Infantry and 3rd Battalion Madras Artillery; led by Colonel Miller was waiting for them.

On 11th February, the 4th and 6th Madras Light Cavalry were ordered to proceed to Allahabad, however, when news that a large rebel force led by Nana Sahib had entered Bundelkhand, they were ordered to halt and await the arrival of the main force led by General Whitlock.

On 17th February, General Whitlock advanced, with the now combined Saugor & Nerbudda Field Force, from Jubbulpore and reached Jukehi on the 24th, finding that the place had been sacked by the rebels.

During the march to Jukehi, General Whitlock made no attempt to pacify the territory, despite the suggestions of his officers and left strongholds such as Ramnugger, Mardangarh and Ramgarh still occupied by rebel forces.

On the 5th of March, General Whitlock entered Saugor, which had been relieved by General Rose a month earlier; again the General ignored the advice of his senior officers and the rebel leader Kishor Singh was allowed to plunder the country between Damoh and Jubbulpore unmolested.

Having been ordered to march on Nagode and Panna, the force reached Panna on the 29th March 1858 where he remained until 2nd April when he was ordered to move to Jhansi.

After reaching Chatarpur on 9th April, the General was informed that a force of 2,000 rebels was congregating at Jhigan about 17 miles away and the General decided to mount a surprise attack.

Marching through the night of 10th April, the force reached Jhigan at about 5 o'clock in the morning of 11th April and immediately launched a successful attack which drove the rebels from their positions in the fortress and inflicted heavy casualties, while only two of his men were wounded.

The General now continued his advance towards Banda, where the Nawab Ali Bahadur had established positions at Goera Mughali intent on preventing General Whitlock's advance on his capital.

Battle of Banda

With a force of some 6,000 men and a further 3,000 in reserve, the Nawab occupied a good position, with his artillery having command of the main road and his men concealed in a maze of ravines and nullahs which would make it difficult for the British to mount a strong combined attack with their Cavalry and Horse Artillery.

The General had at his disposal less than 2,500 men; 1,899 men of his own force supplemented by 414 troops from the Rajah of Charhari.

On the morning of 18th April, the advanced guard commanded by Colonel Apthorp with the 3rd Madras Europeans and Captain Macintyre with a squadron of the 2nd Hyderabad Contingent Cavalry protecting his right flank advanced to within 600 yards of the enemy positions where they came under heavy artillery fire.

As the artillery was positioned to enfilade the advancing British infantry, Colonel Apthorp ordered Captain Macintyre to charge the guns, which he did with endeavour and captured one of the rebel guns.

The main body of British infantry now advanced to their left to support the hard pressed advanced guard and were soon engaged in fierce hand to hand combat. The British cavalry and artillery managed to turn the enemy left flank and Major T. Oakes leading the 12th Lancers charged the mutineers who fled in advance of the onslaught.

With the enemy force in retreat, but only falling back slowly, the British artillery was fully occupied in dislodging them from new positions but when the British forces reached the high ground the mutineers finally left the field after suffering heavy losses, with 800 killed and a further 200 wounded. British losses were slight with five killed and 29 wounded.

With the battle over, General Whitlock and his men marched a short distance and occupied the city of Banda where they captured many guns and supplies.

The defeated Nawab and his men continued their retreat towards Hamirpur where he crossed the river Ken, joined another body of his troops at Jalapur and then marched to Kalpi to join the rebels at Jhansi.

Despite the British victory at Banda, the rebels with an army of over 15,000 men still occupied Kalpi, Hamirpur, Jalapur and Kirwi and were in control of the eastern half of the district.

General Whitlock remained inactive at Banda, awaiting the arrival of the 2nd brigade commanded by Brigadier John MacDuff who left Jubbulpore, with his force of about 1,000 men, on 18th March but did not arrive at Banda until the 27th May.

On the 1st of June General Whitlock left Banda for Kirwi and with the approach of the British force the army of Narayan Rao retreated to the hills. The rebel leader Madhu Rao surrendered on 6th June, without a shot being fired and the British captured 42 guns and large amounts of treasure.

After the capture of Kirwi, General Whitlock's force was distributed to Mohaba, Jalaun, Banda, Kirka, Saugor, Damoh and other places, to maintain order in the Bundelkhand and Jamnah districts.

On the 1st January 1859, Lieutenant-Colonel Frederick Gottreux, the commander of a field detachment of General Whitlock's force, left their base at Punghuttee to deal with a body of mutineers based in the hills near the village of Surbhungah.

With the force, which was mainly composed of native soldiers, was a detachment of 30 men from the 43rd Light Infantry regiment under the command of Ensign Gerald Young.

The column marched until just after midnight and camped on an open plateau in the hills about three miles from Surbhungah, during the night a spy reported that the rebels had moved camp and were now in some dense jungle near Kurrereah. Just after this the head man from the village arrived, confirmed the rebels' new location and offered to guide the British force in the morning.

Action at Kurrereah

After leaving their baggage under a small guard, the force set out at 5:30 the next morning and soon came within sight of the rebel camp. On spotting the British force, the rebels immediately began to retreat, abandoning their baggage ponies.

Private Henry Addison – Victoria Cross No. 291

Lieutenant Gompertz was despatched with the cavalry and managed to cut off the enemy retreat and soon the infantry were engaged in hand to hand fighting with the rebels.

The mutineers were pushed back through the jungle and split into small groups that took up positions in the ravines, to continue their resistance.

It was during the attack on one of these small groups of mutineers that the political agent Lieutenant Osborne was wounded by a sword cut to the right hand.

Seeing the wounded Lieutenant fall to the ground, Private Addison rushed forward to defend and protect him. The private was successful in his endeavour and saved the Lieutenant's life, however, in the process he received two severe sword wounds, one to the left arm which caused a compound fracture and a more serious blow to the left leg which required a battle field amputation of his leg above the knee.

For this action Private Addison was later awarded the Victoria Cross.

Before long the rebels had retreated and dispersed further into the jungle and as pursuit was deemed to be pointless, the column returned to their camp at Surbhungah where they had breakfast before setting out to return to their base at Kothee.

The Rajputana Campaign

During the initial period of the mutiny, the state of Rajputana was relatively quiet while the adjoining districts of Central India were seething with the ravages of mutiny.

Brigadier-General George St. Patrick Lawrence, with only a small force of European soldiers that he could rely upon, concentrated his efforts on securing the important stations of Ajmer, Nasirabad and Neemuch rather than on offensive operations.

However, when the rebels established a large force at Awah, the General felt compelled to act and assembled a small force of about 650 men at Bewar to move against the rebels.

Although he had insufficient force to establish a siege, the General was confident that if the rebels could be drawn out into battle then he would be able to defeat them.

Action at Awah

After having been delayed by heavy rains, General Lawrence and his force reached Awah on 18th September 1857 and as he approached the walls his force was assailed by the enemy artillery to which his own artillery responded with their own fire.

Being unable to do little more than force the enemy artillery to withdraw behind the town walls, General Lawrence thought it expedient to withdraw his forces as it was clear that the enemy were not going to engage with him in battle.

After waiting at a nearby village for three days, to see if the situation changed, General Lawrence and his force finally returned to Ajmer and Nasirabad.

Mutiny at Kotah

On the 15th October 1857, the native troops at Kotah revolted and murdered the political agent Major Charles Burton and his two sons, this event prompted General Lawrence to send an urgent request to Bombay for reinforcements.

95th Regiment of Foot arrive in India

After spending less than a year at home, after their service in the Crimea, during June 1857 the regiment was despatched to service in the Cape Colonies on board *SS Polmaise* and *SS Beechworth*.

On arrival at the Cape, the *SS Polmaise* received news of the outbreak of mutiny in India and the 95th received orders to immediately divert to Bombay where they arrived on the 27th

September; the *SS Beechworth* arrived a month later on the 30th October.

On the 22nd November, the regiment boarded the HEIC steamer *Berenice* and set sail for Rajputana to become part of the Central India Field Force.

After arriving at Mandavie, the left wing of the regiment, some 400 men, was formed up as part of a field force commanded by Major Raines.

The field force, which also included the right wing of the 10th Bombay Native Infantry, 2 squadrons of the Scinde Horse a company of Royal Engineers and a field battery of artillery set out for Boojh (the capital of Cutch) where they arrived on 26th November 1857.

Four days later on the 30th November, the column set out for Deesa where they arrived on Christmas day.

Having to await the arrival of further British troops to replace them, the Right wing of the regiment some 480 men, did not leave Bombay until the 28th December. Leaving on board the steamships *Berenice* and *Lady Canning* they arrived at Deesa and Nusseerabad on the 5th of January 1858.

Two days earlier, on the 3rd of January, Major Raines with his field force left Deesa and halted at the village of Muddar for three days.

While resting his men, Major Raines received news of a rebel force at the fortified village of Rowa, some 12 miles away and on the 6th January he led a small force to clear the village.

Battle of Rowa

The British force consisted of 4 officers and 108 men from the 95th Regiment supported by two companies of the 10th Bombay Native Infantry and two field guns.

On reaching the village which was built on the side of a hill, it was found to be strongly defended by a ditch 9 feet deep which was surmounted by a mud wall forming a semi circular defence guarding the front of the village.

Observing that the wall and ditch was less formidable on the extreme flanks, Major Raines ordered the two companies of the 10th Bombay Native Infantry to make a wide detour, under the cover of heavily wooded ground to make an approach on the right flank.

The 95th, also partially covered by trees and bushes, advanced to within a 100 yards of the front of the village and began to lay down a heavy fire on the parapet of the enemy defences to distract the enemy from the movements on their flank.

Once the flank attack was fully engaged, the 95th made a frontal attack with bayonets attached.

Private Bernard McQuirt – Victoria Cross No. 236

The first officer over the walls at Rowa was Captain McGowan, commanding the 10th Bombay Native Infantry, who after becoming separated from his men was attacked by three rebels who cut him down.

While lying on the ground trying to defend himself, Private McQuirt rushed to his assistance. After shooting one of the assailants, Private McQuirt attacked the other two with his bayonet and managed to wound one.

During his bid to save the life of Captain McGowan, Private McQuirt was himself seriously wounded, suffering a shot to the arm and five sabre blows, two to the shoulders, two to the head and one which severed a thumb.

Private McQuirt was now in danger of losing his own life, until a native soldier, Suddoo Surpuray from the 10th, arrived and chased off the last assailant.

For this action, Private McQuirt was later awarded the Victoria Cross and for his part Suddoo Surpuray received a promotion to Naick, the equivalent of Corporal.

The enemy were completely surprised by the flank attack and coupled with the ferocity of the frontal attack by the 95th they were quickly defeated and suffered heavy losses.

An interesting aspect of the battle was that a large number of the rebel dead and wounded were as the result of arrows rather than the bullets of the British force; during the initial stage of the battle the British troops were joined by some native auxiliary troops armed with bows and arrows which they used to fire volley after volley into the rebels just behind their parapet with devastating effect.

After the battle, Major Raines received orders to proceed to Awah and join up with the field force commanded by Colonel Holmes; the junction of the columns occurred at Jaitpore, two miles outside of Awah on the 19th January 1858.

Recapture of Awah

Awah was one of the most strongly defended fortified towns in Rajputana, guarded by about 2,000 rebels with many cannons.

When Colonel Holmes column approached the town and his field artillery began their fire, the mutineers withdrew into the fort. Plans were made to assault the town on the 23rd January, however, during the night a severe storm broke with heavy rain, thunder and lightning and hurricane force winds so the attack was postponed. During the tempest, the mutineers managed to slip away and the next morning the fort was discovered to have been abandoned.

General Roberts takes command of the Rajputana Field Force

As seen above, some new troops began arriving in January 1858, however, the bulk of the force, under the command of Major-General Henry Gee Roberts did not arrive until March 1858. Taking up station at Nusseerabad, General Roberts, who was senior to General Lawrence, assumed command of the Rajputana Field Force, now numbering some 4,300 men.

Siege of Kotah

On the morning of 21st March 1858, General Roberts arrived at Kotah with his 1st Brigade commanded by Brigadier Macan and was joined by his 2nd Brigade commanded by Brigadier Parke and the siege train later in the day.

Having been released from imprisonment by the mutineers, the Maharaja, with some of his troops that had remained loyal, was in possession of the south west part of the city near the palace and a fortified wall that protected it from the rest of the city.

As there were no boats available, capable of carrying the heavy artillery across the river, batteries were established near the village of Suckutpoor and on the morning of the 24th March they began the bombardment of the rebel positions.

On the 25th and 27th March, the rebels made vigorous attacks against the Maharaja's troops but these were repulsed with the aid of British troops sent over the river as reinforcements; 300 men of the 83rd under the command of Major Heath.

On the 29th March, General Roberts also crossed the river with a further 600 men of the 95th as reinforcements.

Further batteries were established on both sides of the river over the next two days and on 29th March a sustained barrage commenced and in the early evening the rebels' main magazine was hit and exploded.

It was decided that an assault on the town would take place the next day and in preparation the engineers constructed rafts and the artillery maintained their bombardment throughout the night.

Assault on Kotah

The assault troops were organised into three columns; the first under the command of Lieutenant-Colonel Parke consisted of 250 of the 72nd Highlanders commanded by Major Thelluson and 250 men of the 12th Native Infantry commanded by Captain Adams; the second column under the command of Lieutenant-Colonel Holmes consisted of 250 men of the 83rd Regiment of Foot commanded by Major Steele and 250 men of the 12th Native Infantry commanded by Lieutenant Howinson and the third column commanded by Lieutenant-Colonel Raines consisted of 250 men of the 95th Regiment of Foot commanded by Major Massey and 250 men of the 10th Native Infantry commanded by Lieutenant Roome.

A reserve column, under the command of Brigadier Macan consisted of 250 men from the 83rd Regiment commanded by Lieutenant-Colonel Heatley and 250 men of the 13th Native Infantry commanded by Captain Stuart.

Engineers carrying powder bags and native sappers carrying scaling ladders accompanied each of the assault columns.

At 1 o'clock in the morning on 30th March, the columns began crossing the river by raft and by 7 o'clock the crossing was successfully completed.

The initial plan to blast holes in the defensive wall for the passage of the 1st and 2nd columns, while the 3rd column would advance via the Kittonpole Gate, which was to be blown. However, this plan had to be abandoned after the Engineers had inspected the old wall. Because of the thickness of the wall, it was decided that all columns would advance via the Kittonpole Gate and just after noon the gate was blown. With the gate blown, the three columns rushed through the gate; the first and second columns moved off to the right while the third column moved to the left.

In the face of the advancing British forces the mutineers steadily fell back and the first column reached the Pattadar bastion from where they made their way to the Zorawan bastion. After a brief fight the men captured the Soorujpole Gate with its large bastions, having now completely outflanked the rebels the first column now occupied a position to their rear.

Following in the wake of the first column, the second column also reached the Soorujpole Gate and the third column was directly to their left where they were able to cut down many of the mutineers as the they were driven back into the town.

Lieutenant Aylmer Cameron – Victoria Cross No. 253

After occupying the bastions, the first column began the process of clearing the houses while some of the rebels scaled the walls to escape.

During this hand to hand fighting, Lieutenant Cameron led a small party of men from the 72nd in an attack on a loop holed house occupied by mutineers. In the attack the Lieutenant killed three of the enemy but was severely wounded when half of his hand was sliced off by a sword blow.

For his part in this action Lieutenant Cameron was later awarded the Victoria Cross.

With the Soorujpole gate occupied by the first column, Colonel Holmes with the second column headed towards the north end of the town, which he found to have been abandoned by the rebels, and occupied the Rampoora and Lallpoora gates.

With the mutineers leaving the city in great numbers, the reserve entered the town and joined the third column at the Rampoora gate and the town was now totally under British control.

On the 20th April 1858, the British forces left Kotah, content that the Maharaja and his troops were now able to maintain control over the town and region.

Tantia Topi enters Rajputana

After Tantia Topi was defeated at the battle of Jaura Alipur on 21st June 1858 he moved off towards Bharatpur, however, this move was anticipated by Brigadier Showers and forced Tantia Topi to head for Jaipur instead where he believed he had many supporters.

Receiving news from Captain Eden, the political agent at Jaipur, regarding the advance of Tantia Topi; General Roberts set out with a force from Nusseerabad on 28th June and as a result of forced marches arrived at Jaipur while Tantia Topi was still about 60 miles from the city.

Foiled in his approach to Jaipur, Tantia Topi headed south towards the city of Tonk, the capital of a principality which was partly in Rajputana and partly in Central India.

Colonel Holmes flying column

On 8th July, as he approached the city of Tonk, General Roberts sent out a flying column under the command of Colonel Holmes to intercept the rebel army.

At Tonk, the Nawab, Wazir Muhammad Khan had taken refuge in the citadel which was defended by those of his troops that remained loyal, the remainder of his troops joined Tantia Topi's army who now moved off in the direction of Madhupura and Indragarh to the north east of Kotah pursued by Colonel Holmes and his column.

The river Chumbul, swollen by the rains, proved to be an impassable barrier to Tantia Topi and on the 13th of July, Colonel Holmes received news that the enemy force was now heading towards Kasthala, however, on reaching this place they could be seen moving up into the hills.

Tantia Topi headed up the Khatkar valley and moved to Boondee where the local Rajah, Ram Singh remained loyal to the British and closed the gates of his walled city to the rebels forcing them to cross the Boondee hills via the Keena Pass heading for Adeypoor where they had many friends.

Unable to cross the hills with his guns, Colonel Holmes continued his pursuit by a different route and by the 21st July had reached Maogaon where he camped on the banks of the river Mej where he waited for three days until the river became fordable.

On the 4th August, Colonel Holmes reached Jehazpore where he learned that Tantia Topi had reached Mandalgarh ahead of him and was now heading for Bheelwara.

Having received orders to join up with General Roberts force, Colonel Holmes's column crossed the Banas River on 8th August and arrived at Bheelwara the next day, to find that General Roberts had already defeated the rebels.

General Roberts movements

After hearing that Tantia Topi's force had crossed the Boondee hills, General Roberts moved his force westward towards Ajmer near where he took command of the Nusseerabad to Neemuch road near the village of Surwar and set up camp for 11 days due to the heavy rains.

When the rains ceased, the General began to advance his force towards Neemuch where he hoped to intercept the rebels and on the 7th August learned that Tantia Topi had taken up positions at Sanganeer near the river Kotaria which separated it from the town of Bheelwara.

Action at Sanganeer

In late afternoon of the 8th August, General Roberts with an advance force reached Sanganeer and found the rebels formed up in a horseshoe defence to the front of the town and nearby Bheelwara.

After quickly clearing Sanganeer, the General moved his artillery down to the river banks from where they opened up fire on the enemy right flank. The artillery fire quickly dispersed the rebels and allowed General Roberts to move his force across the river without much opposition and the 83rd Regiment stormed and occupied the village of Rowari.

The British guns which had now crossed the river, kept up a barrage on the rebel left until they retreated out of range; with darkness having fallen pursuit was called off until the next day.

The pursuit continues

On the 9th August, having been joined by Colonel Holmes and his force of cavalry, the pursuit of the rebels was continued and by 13th August the British force had reached Kunkrowlee where General Roberts received intelligence that Tantia Topi and his force were camped on the banks of the Banas river only 7 miles away.

As it was late in the day, General Roberts set up camp at Kunk-rowlee until 5 o'clock the next morning when after leaving troops to guard his baggage train and siege guns, he recommenced his advance.

Action at Banas River

After a march of only two hours, the British force came across the rebels drawn up in a strong position along a rocky ridge of hills which formed the bank of the river.

The enemy artillery was placed on their right flank and occupied a position from which they could lay down fire on the plain across which the British would have to advance.

After forming up his troops behind a low ridge, General Roberts ordered the advance, with the cavalry covering the left flank and were soon under fire from the enemy artillery.

Despite this fire, the British infantry crossed the plain, forded the river and soon drove the rebels from their ridge, capturing four artillery pieces.

The main body of the rebels was composed of cavalry and they quickly retreated out of sight but were pursued by Colonel Naylor with cavalry and some horse artillery. After a chase of about four miles, Colonel Naylor's force caught up with a large force of rebel infantry being escorted by a large number of cavalry. Having become detached from a large part of his force, Colonel Naylor followed the rebels at a distance until his men caught up, at which time they launched an attack against the enemy column rear-guard. Most of the rebel infantry threw down their muskets and sought refuge in the nearby jungle but were pursued by Colonel Naylor and his small force, by this time numbering only 150 men.

With darkness having fallen, his men being exhausted and the ground becoming very unsuitable for cavalry, Colonel Naylor called off the pursuit and returned to the British camp which he reached just before midnight, having been in the saddle for almost 18 hours.

Fort Paori

Having been once again defeated by the British, Tantia Topi moved off to join a new ally, Man Singh who on 2nd of August had captured the fort at Paori, just north of Sipree.

Brigadier Smith, with his brigade of the Rajputana Field Force was stationed at Sipree and when he heard of the rebel capture of fort Paori, he immediately set out to intervene, however, when he arrived he found the fort to be too heavily defended to be attacked by his force supported only by field guns.

Brigadier Smith sent off a request to General Napier for reinforcements and heavy artillery. General Napier responded in person and setting out from Gwalior, with the siege train and 600 men, reached Paori on the 20th August 1858 where he took up position next to Brigadier Smith's force, outside the range of the enemy guns.

General Napier carried out a reconnoitre of the enemy position, and used his experienced engineers eye to determine the best point for his attack. At sunset he sent four 8" mortars down to a temple recently captured by Major Vialls. The temple was located 400 yards from the main fort entrance which was comprised of three large gates with flanking bastions.

The mortars kept up a continuous fire during the night and while the enemy attention was concentrated on their front, breaching batteries were established on the east side of the fort.

From the next morning, the batteries and mortars kept up a barrage for the next thirty hours and on the night of the 23rd August, just before the British were about to storm the fort, it was discovered that the fort had been abandoned and was occupied unopposed.

On the 27th August, after having demolished the Paori fortifications and having despatched a column to pursue the rebels, General Napier returned to Sipree.

Colonel Robertson, with a column of just over 1,100 men supported by cavalry and horse artillery set off in pursuit of Man Singh and his men and after a first days march of 20 miles came across the track of the fleeing rebels just as they halted to make camp for the night.

Following the rebel tracks for five days, Colonel Robertson's force reached the village of Sangi where Man Singh's force had split and headed off in two directions. Colonel Robertson continued to follow the main tracks and learned that he was on the trail of a large column of the Gwalior Contingent with some Bengal Native Infantry regiments.

After reaching Berhampore on the 3rd of September, Colonel Robertson learned that the rebels were stationed at Beejapore, three miles away on the Chupet River.

Battle of Beejapore

After leaving the bulk of his force behind to protect the baggage train and artillery from a possible attack from Man Singh, Colonel Robertson set out with a force of about 540 men, which included 47 men from the 8th Hussars.

Just before daybreak on the 5th of September, Colonel Robertson and his column arrived just outside of the village of Beejapore. At first light the attack was ordered and the cavalry moved to the right of the village to attack the left flank of the enemy while the infantry made a head on approach.

Troop Sergeant Major James Champion – Victoria Cross No. 282

Early during the battle Captain Poore and Lieutenant Hanbury of the 8th Hussars were both put out of action by severe sword wounds and despite being seriously wounded, Troop Sergeant-Major Champion took over the command of the unit and led the men throughout the battle and the chase down of the rebels afterwards.

At the end of the day, when the 8th Hussars finally returned to camp, Troop Sergeant-Major Champion was able to receive medical attention.

The surgeon discovered that the musket ball to his chest had gone right through the Troop Sergeant-Major's body. Due to the lack of proper bandages, he used the Troop Sergeant-Major's own shirt tails to dress his wound.

For this action, Troop Sergeant-Major Champion was later awarded the Victoria Cross.

The mutineers suffered heavy losses during the battle and follow-up with the dead estimated at about 450; after the battle, Colonel Robertson moved off with his column to Goona.

The pursuit of Tantia Topi

After his defeat at the Banas River, Tantia Topi marched east towards Boondee, followed by General Roberts and his force.

On the 18th August General Roberts met up with Brigadier Parke and his Neemuch Brigade at Poona and after having reinforced Parke's cavalry, with men from the 8th Hussars and Beluch Horse, instructed the Brigadier to continue the pursuit.

Initially, Brigadier Parke headed south to Neemuch, to get remounts for his cavalry and then set out for Morasa in an attempt to intercept Tantia Topi as he looked for a viable crossing across the river Chumbul which was in flood.

Having made a swift dash south, Tantia Topi and his force managed to cross the river at Sagoodar on 20th August, ahead of Brigadier Parke's column and marched to Jhalrapatan, the capital of the Jhalwar State.

The ruler of Jhalwar, the Maharaja Rana Pirthi Sing, remained loyal to the British, however, most of his men deserted to the rebels and Tantia Topi was allowed to take the town unopposed and besieged the Maharaja in his palace.

The Maharaja was forced to hand over some of his treasure to the rebels, before he fled into the night, which was used to pay Tania's army. The rebel army, which now numbered about 10,000 men, plundered the Maharaja's arsenal and obtained vast amounts of much needed ammunition and about 30 artillery pieces.

With the river Chumbul now impassable, Tantia felt safe from immediate pursuit from Roberts or Parke and remained at Jhalrapatan until early September when he moved off with his force to Rajgurh on his way towards Indore where he expected to find plenty of sympathisers.

Major-General Michel, the commander of the Malwa Field Force, anticipating that Tantia Topi might make a dash for Indore, despatched a small force under the command of Colonel Lockhart to Oojein, a town just north of Indore.

On hearing that Tantia Topi was at Rajgurh, Colonel Lockhart moved off to Soosner, about thirty miles from the town where, having insufficient force to make an attack, he awaited the arrival of reinforcements; Colonel Hope had been despatched from Mhow.

Tantia Topi, with his vastly superior force, hesitated to attack Lockhart's small force which allowed Colonel Lockhart to join up with Colonel Hope's force at Nalkhara where on the 13th September; General Michel arrived to take command of the combined force.

With Brigadier Parke's force moving to cover Indore, General Michel moved his column, designated the Mhow Field Force, off to Rajgurh where he found the enemy army established on both sides of the river.

Battle of Biowra

At 5 o'clock the next morning, General Michel resumed his advance only to find that the rebel army had move off during the night, however, after crossing the river the rebels were discovered on the road to Biowra.

Moving ahead of the main column, the cavalry had a minor skirmish with the enemy rearguard during which the rebels abandoned three of their guns and after following them for four miles came across the main body of the rebel infantry drawn up across the road with their artillery on a ridge.

Confronting the main rebel force, the cavalry only numbering 260, had to fall back and await the arrival of the rest of the British column. When the column arrived they advanced in line of battle, with the artillery in the centre and the cavalry protecting the right flank. The rebels kept up a fire with eight of their guns, however, as the British advanced towards their position they began to retreat.

The British artillery dashed forward and began to fire at the retreating enemy, who when out of the range of the British guns stopped and returned the fire with their own guns which were of a larger calibre.

This stop start retreat continued for about three miles until the repeated fire of the British guns finally broke the enemy lines who dispersed in confusion.

The cavalry, under the command of Captain Sir William Gordon was now unleashed on the rebel force who were pursued for about four miles until the men and horses were exhausted, 27 rebel guns were brought back to the British camp together with vast amounts of ammunition. Rebel losses were heavy, with 400–500 killed or wounded, while the British losses were minor with 3 dying as a result of heat exhaustion and 3 were wounded.

The rebels divide their force

After the defeat at Biowra, the rebel force headed east towards the Betwa valley and after moving through densely wooded country halted at Seronge, where they stayed for a week, knowing that the heavy rains would impede General Michel's operations.

With Brigadier Smith's force from Sipree watching their movements and a column commanded by Colonel Liddell closing in from the north east, the rebel commanders decided to divide their forces.

Tantia Topi was to advance on Chanderi, while Rao Sahib was to cross the Betwa river and move to Jalbahat in the direction of Jhansi.

At Chanderi, Tantia Topi hoped that the garrison of Scindia's troops would join him, however, when he arrived the commander of the fort refused him entry and after wasting three days in a vain attempting to take the fort he moved south towards Mungrowlee.

Battle of Mungrowlee

Now that the monsoon rains had ceased, General Michel advanced up the Betwa valley looking for Tantia Topi's force and on the night of the 8th October received reliable intelligence that the rebel force was stationed just outside Mungrowlee.

On the next morning, before first light, General Michel moved out with his column to Mungrowlee where his scouts reported that the enemy force of 5,000 was only two miles away and moving towards him.

The General continued his advance and soon encountered the rebel advanced guard of about 1,000 men at the village of Barulpore, however, a few rounds of artillery fire drove them back to the main force in position at the village of Shajehan Mhow, which was at an elevated position, surrounded by scrub jungle.

The British continued their advance, with skirmishers leading the way, and as they got close the rebels abandoned the village

and attempted to outflank the British left on which they had brought their artillery to bear.

Because of the dense jungle, some of the enemy managed to get between the British main force and their rearguard, however, charges from the 17th Lancers, led by Sir William Gordon soon dispersed them before much damage was done.

The steady advance of the British line continued and charges by the 92nd and 71st Regiments captured some of the enemy guns, when all six of their guns had been captured the rebels fled in all directions.

With his cavalry limited to only 85 men of the 17th Lancers, General Michel decided not to give chase to the rebels.

Tantia Topi and Rao Sahib rejoin forces

That night, Tantia Topi, who had managed to escape with about 2,500 of his men, managed to cross the Betwa River and marched to Lullutpore where he joined back up with the forces of Rao Sahib and the Nawab of Banda.

On the next day the rebel force moved to the town of Sindwah and as there was 30 miles of dense jungle between the town and the Betwa River, the rebel leaders thought that they had escaped their pursuers.

General Michel had however anticipated the rebel moves and after instructing Brigadier Smith to bar Tantia Topi's route to the west, he crossed the river with his own force and headed through the jungle towards Tehree.

At midnight on the 18th October, the General received intelligence that the rebels were at Sindwah and were intending to cross the Jamni river and pass to the east of his force.

Battle of Sindwah

General Michel set out for Sindwah at 4o'clock in the morning and after four hours marching came across the rebels, who were indeed moving to the east, near Sindwah.

To prevent the rebels moving further eastward, the General advanced rapidly with some of his cavalry parallel to their left flank and the rebels seeing his intention launched an attack.

The 8th Hussars, 1st Bombay Lancers and the 17th Lancers managed to drive the enemy back and the remained of the British Cavalry and Horse Artillery were soon on the scene and opened fire.

The enemy now opened fire with their artillery and tried to turn both of the British flanks, however, the arrival of a Bengal Battery and the 19th Bombay Native Infantry together with the 92nd Highlanders managed to stave off the attack and drive the rebels back up the hill.

Lieutenant Henry Evelyn Wood – Victoria Cross No. 289

During the attack, Lieutenant Wood, who had volunteered to lead a troop from the 3rd Cavalry, was riding ahead of his troop when he spotted a body of rebels organising themselves to make a stand.

Almost single handed, Lieutenant Wood charged into the group dispersing them.

For this action, Lieutenant Wood was later awarded the Victoria Cross; the citation also mentions another act of bravery at Sindhora on 29th of December when he rescued a merchant from bandits.

The advance of the British infantry forced the rebels to retire and artillery fire dispersed their formations causing them to retreat. The British cavalry pursued the rebels for about nine miles until the difficulties of the ground brought a halt to the chase.

The rebel losses were heavy, with about 500 having been killed and their four guns were captured, the British losses were four killed and 19 wounded.

Tantia Topi, who was being hemmed in on all sides by the British columns, decided to make a dash south for the Nerbudda river but was headed off by Colonel Liddell and turned north eastwards to deceive his pursuer. The following day he retraced his steps and headed into the Jaclone jungles.

After the battle at Sindwah, General Michel also moved his forces to the north west to prevent Tantia Topi escaping to the south and on the 22nd October, after arriving at Lullutpore, received the news that the rebels had returned to the Jaclone jungles.

Without guns or wheeled carriages, the rebels were able to move more easily through the dense jungle but General Michel and his force had to take a more circuitous route.

Action at Kurai

At dawn of the 25th October, General Michel came across the rebel force near the village of Kurai.

The British infantry, under the command of Colonel Lockhart, who were operating in advance of the cavalry, moved against the rebel column cutting it in two and when the cavalry arrived on the scene the rebels were already dispersing.

The enemy had split into three columns and the British cavalry pursued two of these for about six miles; the infantry also pursued for about five miles, clearing the villages as they went.

Tantia Topi, who had passed through Kurai about two or three hours before his column was attacked, escaped with half of his men and continued on his journey south, however, the next day he stumbled into a force led by Colonel Beecher at Bagrode.

With only a small force, Colonel Beecher was able to inflict losses by his repeated charges at the column but was unable to halt the progress of the rebel column, which crossed the Nerbudda River into the province of Nagpur.

After crossing the Nerbudda, Tantia Topi moved to Futtehpore but when he received news that a column of the South Mahratta Horse led by Lieutenant Kerr had left Hoshangabad and was in hot pursuit, he set out for Mooltali on his way to Nagpur.

Finding that a British force was barring their direct route to Nagpur the rebels turned to the west, intending to cross the hills by a little known pass at Mul Ghat, but this way was blocked by a force of British cavalry, so they moved off south again.

On reaching Boorgaum, Tantia Topi tried to enlist the help of the Ranee of Bhopal but instead of helping, the Ranee informed the British of his location and more British columns began to converge on the rebel force.

By 19th November 1858, the rebels had reached Koregaon where Tantia Topi decided to rest his men and deliberate his next actions.

Movements of British intercept forces

After defeating the rebels at Kurai, General Michel continued his pursuit of the rebels and on 7th November reached Hosungabad where he met up with Brigadier Parke.

While General Michel and his force crossed the Nerbudda following the route taken by Tantia Topi, Brigadier Parke moved to Charwa hoping to intercept the rebels, however, when Parke and later Michel reached Charwa they found that Tantia Topi and his force has already passed through the town.

When Brigadier Edwardes, the commanding officer at Mhow, heard that Tantia Topi was heading west with his forces, he despatched two small infantry forces to guard the fords near Akerpore, where the Grand Trunk road crossed the Nerbudda river.

On receiving further intelligence, Major Sutherland, in command of one of the detachments comprising 100 men from the 92nd Highlanders and 100 men of the 4th Bombay Rifles, was ordered to cross the river and ensure that the Trunk Road was kept clear.

On 23rd November while halted at Tekree, Major Sutherland received the news that Tantia Topi and Rao Sahib were at Koregaon and on the following morning he moved his force to Jeelwana to cut off the route to the Sindwah Pass.

Before he set off, Major Sutherland was joined by a detachment of 50 men from the 71st Highland Light Infantry under the command of Lieutenant Lewis and a detachment of 150 men with the Camel Corps commanded by Lieutenant Barras.

Action at Rajpore

On the 25th November, Major Sutherland's force caught up with the rear guard of Tantia Topi's force of 3,000 to 4,000 men just as it was leaving Rajpore.

After following the rebels through dense jungle for about seven miles, they came across the rebels drawn up in a line across the road with two guns placed in the centre of their formation. Due to the rising ground on each side of the road, any flanking movement was out of the question, so despite the disparity in numbers, Major Sutherland's force was outnumbered by a factor of 10 to 1, the British force launched a frontal attack in the face of grape shot from the enemy guns. The ferocity of the charge was such that the British soon carried the guns and the rebels broke ranks and fled.

Being exhausted by the fight and the heat of the day, Major Sutherland chose not to give chase but retired to Rajpore where he rested for the night.

After the action at Rajpore, Tantia Topi moved off towards Baroda, followed at a greater distance by Major Sutherland and his force. Unknown to the rebel leader, he was in danger from a greater threat, Brigadier Parke with a flying column had covered 240 miles in nine days in an attempt to intercept him before he reached Baroda.

Action at Chota Oodeypore

On the 1st December 1858, Brigadier Parke and his force of 840 men caught up with Tantia Topi at Chota Oodeypore and engaged the 3,000 rebels in battle and inflicted a heavy defeat on the enemy.

Not surprising after their exertions of the last few days, Brigadier Parke did not give chase but rested at Chota Oodeypore for the next few days.

After his surprise defeat, and fearing pursuit by Brigadier Parke, Tantia Topi's force covered nearly 60 miles in the next 24 hours and crossed into the state of Rajputana once again and took refuge in the dense jungles of Baiswarra.

On Christmas Day, Tantia Topi's force emerged from the jungle near Pertabgarh, where he stumbled upon a small British force of 200 infantry with some guns and cavalry under the command of Major Roche who were camped nearby.

The small British force manage to delay the progress of the much larger rebel force for several hours but eventually they were side stepped and the rebels managed to reach Zirapore.

However, Colonel Benson commanding the 2nd Cavalry column received news of the rebel movements and immediately set out in pursuit and by the 29th December caught up with them as they camped at Zirapore.

Action at Zirapore

As dawn broke, Colonel Benson moved on the rebel camp only to find that they had moved out but two miles down the road they were lined up across the road.

The British guns were unlimbered and a fire was opened up on the rebels who began to retire into the jungle. The cavalry swept the rebels from the jungle and across a ravine, when they tried to turn the British left flank they were again attacked by the British cavalry and fled.

Action at Chapra Bursaud

On the day after the action at Zirapore, a force under the command of Colonel Somerset, which had marched 134 miles in five days, took up the pursuit of the rebels and on the morning of 31st December engaged the rebels at Chapra Bursaud.

After a brief exchange of intense and effective fire from the British Horse Artillery a charge by the British cavalry once again forced the rebels to retire. The cavalry pursued the enemy for 12 miles but when they dispersed in small groups the British returned to their camp at Chapra Bursaud.

After this defeat, Tantia Topi fled to Nahargarh where he halted and was joined by Man Singh but after leaving Man Sing on the banks of the Chumbul River, he headed north and affected a junction with Feroze Shah at Indurgurh.

Having suffered considerable losses during a defeat by General Napier, at Ranodde on the 17th December, Feroze Shah was now leading a much smaller and much discourage force; the combined forces of the two leaders now amounted to only about 2,000 men.

Action at Daosa

On the morning of 14th January 1859, Tantia Topi was again intercepted by a British column, this time it was Brigadier Showers who had come down from Agra with a light column to cover any move towards Jeypore or Bhurtpore.

After coming across the rebel force in the early hours of the morning, Brigadier Showers waited until first light and then launched an attack with his cavalry, catching the enemy by surprise as they were preparing to march off.

After the cavalry burst through their ranks, the rebels tried to rally, however, the cavalry charged again and drove them from the town onto the open plain, where they dispersed as they fled.

Over 300 rebels were killed during the attack.

Action at Sikar

On the 8th January, Colonel Holmes had set out from Nusseer-abad heading towards Tonk and Jeypore. On reaching Tonk, the British force received news that the rebels were heading for Jeypore and set off in pursuit.

In the early hours of 21st January, after having marched 54 miles in the last 24 hours, Colonel Holmes surprised the rebels in their camp at Sikar, about 64 miles from Jeypore.

As the British approached, the rebel cavalry rode off without making any attempt to engage the British force. The British artillery was quickly into action and completed the rout and the rebels fled the field.

Despite a chase of several hours by the British cavalry, the rebel leaders, Tantia Topi, Rao Sahib and Feroze Shah escaped with their men, however, the defeat had a great impact on the resolve of the rebel force and soon afterwards Tantia Topi was deserted by both Feroze Shah and Rao Sahib.

Action at Kooshana

On the 10th February 1859, Brigadier Honner left Goonah in pursuit of the combined forces of Rao Sahib and Feroze Shah who were heading for the seclusion of the Seronge jungles.

As the British force was approaching Kooshana, where the rebels were camped, their approach was noticed by the mutineers who immediately fled, with Rao Sahib's force moved off to the south west while Feroze Shah and his men headed south east.

The rearguard of the enemy where caught by the British cavalry and suffered losses of nearly 230 killed as they were pursued for about ten miles.

Both of the rebel forces managed to reach the relative safety of the dense Seronge jungle, however, General Michel ordered the pursuing British columns to guard strategic points on the border of the jungle.

Final defeat of Feroze Shah

Columns commanded by Colonel De Salis and Colonel Rich made their way to the south of the jungle and acting in concert managed to coral the rebel and inflict a final and heavy defeat on the rebel force who suffered losses of about 500 killed. Feroze Shah and Rao Sahib, however, managed to escape capture and disappeared for some time.

Paron Jungles

Meanwhile, General Napier and him men were clearing the Paron Jungles where Man Singh and Tantia Topi had gone to ground, building roads to give access to the previously inaccessible haunts of the rebels.

On the 2nd April 1859, Man Singh marched into the camp of Captain Meade and surrendered his force and five days later agreed to betray Tantia Topi.

Tantia Topi captured and executed

On the evening of the 7th April, Captain Meade selected a party of men from the 9th Bombay Native Infantry to go into the jungle, guided to the location where Tantia Topi was camped.

The small force managed to capture Tantia Topi while he slept and conveyed him back to the British camp and onward to Sipree where on 15th April he was tried by Court Martial on the charge of *"having been in rebellion, and having waged war against the British Government between January 1857 and December 1858, especially at Jhansi and Gwalior."*

Having been found guilty, Tantia Topi was hanged on 18th April on the parade ground near the fort at Sipree.

18

END OF THE MUTINY

Unlike a war which has a defined start, usually signified by a formal Declaration of War and a defined end, usually marked by a Peace Treaty, the Indian Mutiny, being a rebellion had neither; so the start and end dates are somewhat fluid. The start of the mutiny is generally accepted as being May 1857, at the time of the Meerut mutiny even though several acts of mutiny and rebellion had occurred before this date. Some sources use June 1858 as the end of the mutiny, following the defeat of the mutineers at Gwalior, however, the end is generally accepted as April 1859 with the capture and execution of Tantia Topi but again minor acts of rebellion and banditry occurred for several months after this date.

Aftermath of the Mutiny

Most of the changes in the aftermath of the mutiny were related to changes in the role of the Most Honourable East India Company in the administration of India.

The Company was blamed, in most quarters, for letting the conditions develop that led to the mutiny and even more so for allowing the mutiny to develop to the scale that it did rather than nipping it in the bud.

In August 1858, with the Government of India Act, the British Crown took over direct administration of affairs in India and created the India Office with the appropriate responsibilities.

The main reasons for the mutiny were determined to fall into two areas; religion and economics.

Many of the changes implemented by the Company prior to the mutiny had a direct impact on differing religious views and traditions to the extent that many of the population felt that the British intended to convert the country to Christianity.

Other changes made by the Company were made in order to try and implement a free and open market economy, without any regard to the affect on the day to day economics of local Indian traders and farmers.

With these problems in mind, the British Raj tried to manage India affairs in a more conservative fashion, taking into account local traditions and hierarchies.

With the demise of the Company's role as an administrator of Indian Affairs, their considerable armies were disbanded, however, most of the officers and men were absorbed into the British Army and continued to serve in India for the British Crown.

PART THREE

PORTRAITS OF VALOUR

Biographies of the 181 Indian Mutiny
Victoria Cross recipients

Dighton Macnaghten Probyn
Undated (VC No. 115)

Gazetted: 18th June 1858 22154/2960

Rank and Unit: Captain – 2nd Punjab Cavalry, Indian Army

Citation

Has been distinguished for gallantry and daring throughout this campaign. At the battle of Agra, when his squadron charged the rebel infantry, he was some time separated from his men, and surrounded by five or six sepoys. He defended himself from the various cuts made at him, and before his own men had joined him had cut down two of his assailants. At another time, in single combat with a sepoy, he was wounded in the wrist, by the bayonet, and his horse also was slightly wounded; but, though the sepoy fought desperately, he cut him down. The same day he singled out a standard bearer, and, in the presence of a number of the enemy, killed him and captured the standard. These are only a few of the gallant deeds of this brave young officer.
(Despatch from Major-General James Hope Grant, K.C.B., dated 10th January, 1858.)

Biography

On 21st January 1833, Dighton Macnaghten Probyn was born in Marylebone, London. His father was Captain George Probyn of the Royal Navy, who was an elder of Trinity House, his mother Alicia was the daughter of Sir Francis Workman Macnaghten of Bushmills, Co. Antrim in Ireland.

In 1849 Dighton joined the light cavalry arm of the East India Companies Bengal Army and was posted as a Cornet to the 6th Light Cavalry on 20th October 1849.

In 1852 Dighton was appointed as Adjutant to the newly formed 2nd Punjab Cavalry, commanded by Captain Sam Browne;[32] the regiment was part of the Punjab Irregular Force, responsible for maintaining control of the Trans-Indus Frontier and on 19th August 1853 was promoted to the rank of Lieutenant. During his tour of duty on the Trans-Indus Frontier, Dighton took part in the Bozdar Expedition during the early part of 1857. The Bozdar's, who were a Balochi tribe based in the Yusafzai district of Afghanistan had been making forays across the border into British territories for many years, however, after causing casualties to members of the Punjab Irregular Force during raids towards the end of 1856, the Chief Commissioner of the Punjab, Sir John Lawrence decided that a retaliatory expedition was in

Figure 93. Dighton Probyn

order. In March 1857, Brigadier-General Sir Neville Chamberlain led a force into the Bozdar lands burning crops, spoiling water sources and destroying homes until the Bozdar's sued for peace, with an agreement that the incursions would cease a peace was agreed on 16th March 1857. For his involvement in this action Dighton was awarded a North West Frontier clasp to the India General Service medal.

Dighton served throughout the India Mutiny during 1857 to 1858 and was present during the siege of Delhi (8th June – 21st September 1857) and actions at Nujjufghur, Bulandshahr and Allygurh. He was in command of the 2nd Punjab Cavalry during the final assault and capture of Delhi and for his actions during the Mutiny he was mentioned in despatches on four occasions.

Although his citation and recommendation for the Victoria Cross contains no dates and refers to general gallantry during the Mutiny, resulting in his Victoria Cross medal being undated,[33] his action at the battle of Agra is mentioned. Dighton and the 2nd Punjab Cavalry were serving as part of Colonel Greathed's 'Flying Column' when on 2nd August 1857; he displayed great courage and gallantry during the battle of Agra, this action was probably the main reason that Dighton was later awarded the Victoria Cross.

Probably as a result of his actions at the battle of Agra, Dighton was promoted to the rank of Captain on 21st August 1857 and took command of the 6th Bengal Light Cavalry upon the death of Captain Willock who was killed in action.

---

32 Inventor of the Sam Browne belt

33 Although rare an undated Victoria Cross is not unique

Dighton was present at the relief of Lucknow, on 27th November 1857, where he had temporary command of the 2nd Punjab Cavalry Brigade; this was made permanent after Lieutenant Nicholson was seriously wounded. On the 6th December 1857, Dighton was in action at the battle of Cawnpore. For these last two actions Dighton was mentioned in despatches and received the thanks of the Governor General, conveyed in General Orders dated 10th December 1857. In the final days of the mutiny, Dighton was constantly engaged with the cavalry in patrolling and chasing down small bands of mutineers, however, the rigours of campaigning were beginning to take their toll and acting on medical advice he set off on 18th March 1858 for his return to England. On 24th March 1858 Dighton was promoted to the Brevet rank of Major.[34] For his service during the mutiny, Dighton was awarded the India Mutiny Medal with clasps for Delhi, Relief of Lucknow and Lucknow.

Dighton was appointed to the military division as an ordinary member 3rd class, Companion, of the Most Honourable Order of the Bath on 18th June 1858,[35] it was on this same day (Waterloo Day) that Dighton was 'gazetted' for his Victoria Cross.

On 2nd August 1858, Dighton was presented with his Victoria Cross medal by Queen Victoria at an investiture held on Southsea Common.

In England, Dighton soon returned to good health and spent much of his time in the company of the royal family and fashionable society.

His regiment the 6th Bengal Light Cavalry was merged with the 4th regiment to form the 3rd European Light Cavalry and Dighton was transferred to the roll of this new regiment, however, as a further reward for his service during the mutiny, in January 1859 he was given command of Wale's Horse[36] – the 1st Sikh Irregular Cavalry. In January 1860, Dighton joined his new regiment in India, which soon became known as 'Probyn's Horse' and began lobbying for the corps to be included in the Anglo-French expedition to China (the second Opium War). On 28th January 1860, Sir James Hope Grant, who had been appointed to command the Anglo-India expeditionary force to China requested that each man of the 1st Sikh Cavalry sign a document to indicate his willingness to serve in China. To a man, the men of 'Probyn's Horse' signed the document.

In early February, Dighton proceeded with his regiment to the railhead at Raniganj, some 600 miles from Lucknow and entrained for Calcutta. At Calcutta, the regiment was issued government horses, temporarily suspending the system of Silladar,[37]

which was common to the irregular cavalry units in the Indian Army.

By 1st April, General Hope Grant's force was en route for Hong Kong, where they landed towards the end of the month. Probyn's Horse together with Fane's Horse and the Kings Dragoon Guards were billeted together at Kowloon. In early June, Dighton on board *HMS Queen of England*, set off as part of a fleet of 30 ships, on the final leg of the journey to China, however, due to heavy gales the fleet was forced to return to Hong Kong. The force finally managed to land at Pei-t'ang, near the Taku Forts, on 5th August. Dighton was involved in several actions, including the capture of Tangu and the taking of the Taku Forts and outside the walled town of Chang-kia-wan played a decisive part in the taking of the town when his force of only 100 men charged a Tartar force of over 2,000 horsemen. For his actions at Chang-kia-wan, Dighton was mentioned in the despatches of General Sir Hope Grant and those of Sir Garnet Wolseley. Probyn's Horse were again involved in a decisive cavalry charge, during the siege of Pa-li-chiao, when supporting Fane's Horse and the King's Dragoon Guards, they broke the spirit of the Tartar cavalry driving them from the field. In early October; Dighton was involved in the sacking of the Summer Palace, during which three huge enamelled bowls were 'acquired' by Probyn, and later presented to Queen Victoria as a gift from the Army. On 13th October 1860, the allies entered Peking, and the war was brought to a successful conclusion with the signing of a peace treaty. For his service in China, Dighton was later awarded the China War Medal 1857–60, with clasps for Taku Forts and Peking.

Dighton returned to India in January 1861, landing at Calcutta.

At the suggestion of Prince George the Duke of Cambridge, Dighton was promoted to the Brevet rank of Lieutenant-Colonel on 15th February 1861.[38]

In October 1863, Dighton and his regiment were part of a 5,600 strong force, under the command of Brigadier General Neville Bowles Chamberlain, despatched to the Umbeyla region on the border between the Emirate of Afghanistan and the Punjab province of British India. Rebels from the Pashtun Yusafzai tribes objected to British rule in the area and had for some time been raiding along the Chamla Valley; the purpose of the expedition was to oust the rebels from their stronghold at Malka. This was a small but costly campaign, the British casualties amounted to 1,000 men killed or wounded, however, it was ultimately successful and the rebels were driven out of the area during December 1863. For this action Dighton was awarded a second clasp, for Umbeyla, to his India General Service Medal.

---

34 *London Gazette* – 22117/1572
35 *London Gazette* – 22154/2956
36 Captain Wale was killed during the final days of operation at Lucknow.
37 The system of Sillidar required each cavalryman to provide his own horse and weapons.

---

38 *London Gazette* – 22480/655

At the end of the expedition, Dighton returned to Peshawar, arriving there on 27th December 1863.

In a memorandum from the India Office, dated 1st March 1864, officers who had a rank in the Indian Army on 15th February 1861 were given a rank in the British Army. Under this ruling, Dighton was given the rank of Lieutenant-Colonel with effect from 15th February 1861.[39]

During 1866, Dighton relinquished command of the Regiment and returned to England on furlough.

In a notice from the India Office, dated 28th March 1867, it was reported that under the terms of a Royal Warrant dated 31st January 1859, Dighton, having completed the qualifying period of service was to be promoted to the Brevet rank of Colonel, the promotion was to have an effective date of 15th February 1866.[40]

In 1869, Dighton was appointed as Commandant of the Central India Horse succeeding General Sam Browne. The Central India Horse, founded in 1861 by the merging of Mayne's Horse, Meade's Horse and Beatson's Horse was now organised into two regiments based 130 miles apart at Agra and at Goona. The responsibility of the regiments was to guard the Grand Trunk road against bandits.

Subsequent to the death of General Richard Podmore of the Madras Infantry on 24th July 1870, as part of the resulting promotions, Dighton was promoted to the Brevet rank of Major-General with effect from 25th July 1870[41] and was appointed as Aide-de-Camp to the Viceroy Lord Mayo.

It was in his role as ADC to the Viceroy that Dighton accompanied the 26 year old HRH Prince Alfred,[42] the Duke of Edinburgh on his royal tour of India during 1870 to 1871.

On 25th April 1872, at Milford in Surrey, Dighton married his first cousin Leticia, daughter of Thomas R. Thellusson, the marriage lasted 28 years until Leticia's death in 1900.

In a message from Marlborough House, dated 4th March 1872, it was announced that Dighton had been appointed as Equerry to HRH the Prince of Wales.[43]

On leaving India, in memory of his service to the regiment, Dighton was appointed as an honorary Sikh an appointment that he took most seriously such that he was never again to trim his beard.

Dighton returned to England to fulfil this new duty, embarking upon what would be a long relationship with the future king.

In March 1875, Dighton was back in India when he accompanied the Prince of Wales on a 17 week tour of the country.

On 7th March 1877, Dighton was appointed as an Extra Knight Commander of the Most Exalted Order of the Star of India.[44]

On 22nd March 1877, Dighton was appointed as Comptroller and Treasurer of the Prince of Wales's Household,[45] a choice which was with the full approval of Queen Victoria who wrote '... *his age and very high character would seem to fit him for a post of confidence*'.

In a memo from the War Office, dated 15th February 1878, it was reported that subsequent to several officers having been placed on the retired list and in order to complete the establishment of General Officers in the Indian Army, as specified under the terms of a Royal Warrant dated 28th January 1878, Dighton was to be promoted to the rank of Lieutenant-General with effect from 1st October 1877.[46]

On 13th March 1879, Dighton attended the wedding of HRH Arthur William Patrick Albert, Duke of Connaught and Strathearne, Earl of Sussex, Duke of Saxony, Prince of Saxe-Coburg and Gotha[47] to HRH Princess Louise Margaret Alexandra Victoria Agnes of Prussia, in St Georges Chapel, Windsor Castle.[48]

In a memorandum from the India Office, dated 9th August 1881, royal approval was given for the promotion of Dighton to the rank of Lieutenant-Colonel in the Cavalry of the Bengal Army, to be effective from 1st April 1881.[49]

On 27th April 1882, Dighton attended the wedding of HRH Leopold George Duncan Albert, Duke of Albany, Earl of Clarence, Baron Arklow, Duke of Saxony, Prince of Saxe-Coburg and Gotha[50] to HSH the Princess Helen Frederica Augusta[51] at St George's Chapel, Windsor Castle.[52]

On 1st July 1882, Dighton was transferred to the unemployed supernumerary list (i.e. retired).[53]

By an order from Queen Victoria, dated 10th November 1884, Dighton was appointed to a Commission, under the direction of its secretary Sir Francis Philip Cunliffe-Owen which was to organise an exhibition of Indian Products and culture to take place in London during 1886.[54]

In recognition of his role as Comptroller to His Royal Highness the Duke of Connaught and Strathearne,[55] Dighton attended

39 *London Gazette* – 22828/1344
40 *London Gazette* – 23236/2053
41 *London Gazette* – 23754/3145
42 Queen Victoria's second son
43 *London Gazette* – 23837/1312

44 *London Gazette* – 24303/1787
45 *London Gazette* – 24436/2194
46 *London Gazette* – 24552/750
47 Queen Victoria's third son
48 *London Gazette* – 24696/2225
49 *London Gazette* – 25003/4137
50 Queen Victoria's fourth son
51 Fourth daughter of His Serene Highness the reigning Prince of Waldeck and Pyrmont
52 *London Gazette* – 25102/1978
53 *London Gazette* – 25148/4303
54 *London Gazette* – 25415/4949
55 Queen Victoria's third son Prince Arthur

the wedding of Queen Victoria's fifth daughter Princess Beatrice to Prince Henry Maurice of Battenberg which took place at the Isle of Wight on 23rd July 1885.[56]

In his role as a member of the organising commission, on 4th May 1886, Dighton attended the opening ceremony of the Colonial and Indian Exhibition which took place at the Albert Hall, London.[57]

In the honours list celebrating the completion of her 50th year of reign, on 21st June 1887, Queen Victoria appointed Dighton as an ordinary member 2nd Class (Knight Commander) of the Civil Division of the Most Honourable Order of the Bath.[58] On 21st June 1887, Dighton attended the Golden Jubilee celebrations for Queen Victoria which were held in Westminster Abbey.[59]

While still on the unemployed supernumerary list, Dighton was promoted to the rank of General on 1st December 1888.[60]

In his role as Comptroller and Treasurer to His Royal Highness the Prince of Wales, Dighton attended the wedding of Princess Louise[61] to Alexander William George the Earl of Fife, which was held in the private chapel of Buckingham Palace on 27th July 1889.[62] And also in his role as Comptroller and Treasurer to HRH the Prince of Wales, Dighton attended the wedding of Her Highness the Princess Franzisca Josepha Louise Augusta Marie Christiana Helena[63] with His Highness the Prince Aribert Joseph Alexander of Anhalt, which was held in St George's Chapel, Windsor Castle on 6th July 1891.[64]

On 20th January 1892, Dighton was an attendant to HRH the Price of Wales at the Funeral of the Prince's eldest son HRH Albert Victor Christian Edward, Duke of Clarence and Avondale and Earl of Athlone and grandson of Queen Victoria; the remains were remove from Sandringham and buried in St George's Chapel, Windsor Castle.[65]

In a memorandum from the India Office dated 27th June 1893, Queen Victoria gave approval to the promotion of Dighton to the rank of Colonel in the cavalry of the Bengal Army, which was to be effective from 1st April 1893.[66]

In his role as Comptroller to HRH the Prince of Wales, Dighton attended the wedding of the prince's son HRH George Frederick Ernest Albert, Duke of York, Earl of Inverness and

Baron Killarnet to HSH the Princess Victoria Mary Augusta Louise Olga Pauline Claudise Agnes, daughter of the Duke and Duchess of Teck,[67] which took place at the Chapel Royal, St James's Palace on 6th July 1893.[68]

In an order from the Chancery of the Royal Victorian Order[69] at St James's palace, dated 25th May 1896, it was announced that Queen Victoria had appointed Dighton as a Knight Grand Cross in the Royal Victorian Order,[70] one of the Orders founding inductees.

On Wednesday 22nd July 1896, Dighton attended the wedding of HRH the Princess Maud Charlotte Mary Victoria, daughter of HRH the Prince and Princess of Wales, to HRH the Prince Christian Frederic Charles George Waldemar Axel of Denmark; the ceremony took place in the private chapel of Buckingham Palace.[71]

On 23rd June 1897, Dighton attended a ceremony in St Paul's Cathedral as part of the celebrations to recognise Queen Victoria's Diamond Jubilee, following the end of the 60th year of her reign.[72]

On 3rd November 1897, Dighton attended the funeral of HRH Princess Mary Adelaide Wilhelmina the Duchess of Teck (first cousin to Queen Victoria), which took place at St George's Chapel, Windsor Castle.[73]

On 2nd February 1901, Dighton attended the funeral of Queen Victoria, who had died on Tuesday 22nd January and had lain in state at Osborne House on the Isle of Wight until the funeral which took place at the St George's Chapel in Windsor Castle.[74] With the death of Queen Victoria, Dighton requested permission to retire, however, as he had been so successful in managing the financial affairs of the Prince and Princess of Wales, the new King was eager for Dighton to continue the management of his finances.

On 9th February 1901, at the Court of St James's, Dighton was sworn in as a member of the Most Honourable Privy Council, to the new king Edward VII.[75]

Following a command from Buckingham Palace on 22nd February 1901, Dighton was appointed as an Extra Equerry to King Edward VII[76] and on 14th March, following an order from

56 *London Gazette* – 25495/3530
57 *London Gazette* – 25586/2325
58 *London Gazette* – 25712/3363
59 *London Gazette* – 25773/112
60 *London Gazette* – 25884/7203
61 The eldest daughter of the Prince and Princess of Wales
62 *London Gazette* – 25962/4313
63 Grand daughter of Queen Victoria and the youngest daughter of the Prince and Princess Christian of Schleswig-Holstein
64 *London Gazette* – 26184/3862
65 *London Gazette* – 26254/599
66 *London Gazette* – 26416/3643

67 The Duchess was a first cousin to Queen Victoria
68 *London Gazette* – 26424/4112
69 Queen Victoria founded the order on 21st April 1896, so that she could bestow an honour, for distinguished personal service to herself or a member of her family, without the need for government minister approval.
70 *London Gazette* – 26743/3124
71 *London Gazette* – 26765/4496
72 *London Gazette* – 26947/1588
73 *London Gazette* – 26909/6224
74 *London Gazette* – 27316/3559
75 *London Gazette* – 27283/1057
76 *London Gazette* – 27288/1349

HRH the Duke of Cornwall and York, was appointed as Keeper of His Majesty's Privy Purse.[77]

On 11th July 1902, Dighton was appointed as an additional member first class (Knight Grand Cross) of the Civil Division of the Most Honourable Order of the Bath.[78]

Dighton attended the coronation of King Edward VII, on 9th August 1902, which was held at Westminster Abbey.[79]

On 22nd July 1903, Dighton was appointed as a Companion of the Imperial Service Order.[80] This new order had been created by King Edward VII, during August 1902, as a method for the recognition of long and meritorious service by Civil servants.

On 13th May 1904, Dighton was appointed as Honorary Colonel of the Prince of Wales's Own Lancers (Probyn's Horse).[81]

On 20th October 1909, Dighton was appointed as an ordinary member second class (Knight Commander) of the Military Division of the Most Honourable Order of the Bath.[82]

Dighton attended a Privy Council meeting at the Court of St James's on 7th May 1910, where the new king, George V announced the death of his father earlier that day and confirmed his accession to the throne.[83] On 17th May 1910, Dighton attended the funeral of Edward VII, which took place at Westminster Hall.[84] On the death of the King, Dighton now aged 77, could quite rightly have expected a well earned retirement, however, as one of the three people upon whom Queen Alexandra was now utterly dependent, he soldiered on and continued to manage the Queen's finances.

Dighton was appointed as an Ordinary member first class (Knight Grand Cross) of the Military Division of the Most Honourable Order of the Bath on 3rd June 1910, becoming the first person outside of the royal family to have been appointed to the highest level of both the Civil and Military divisions of the Order.[85]

On 10th June 1910, Dighton was appointed as an Extra Equerry to King George V[86] and on 23rd September was appointed as Comptroller to Queen Alexandra with effect from 7th May 1910.[87]

On 19th June 1911, Dighton was appointed as a Knight Grand Commander of the Most Exalted Order of the Star of India.[88]

In August 1911, Dighton became seriously ill with heart trouble, specialists predicted that he would not last out the year, however, despite these predictions he made a full recovery although by now he was suffering from the extreme effects of gout which had shortened his neck muscles, such that he was unable to raise his head from his chest.

Dighton's abilities in managing the finances of Queen Alexandra were stretched to almost breaking point during the years of the Great War during which the Queen's indulgence in charitable works knew no bounds.

In June of 1924, following an excursion where he caught a slight chill, Dighton became seriously ill and was confined to bed in a room previously occupied by Queen Victoria at Sandringham. Dighton succumbed to this illness and died aged 91 on 20th June 1924 at 6:00 am.

Following a memorial service which was held at the Chapel Royal in St James's palace on 24th June, he was buried in Kensal Green cemetery.

Queen Alexandra placed a cross of flowers on his coffin, together with a hand written note; *'For my beloved General*

77 *London Gazette* – 27294/1848
78 *London Gazette* – 27453/4441
79 *London Gazette* – 27489/6861
80 *London Gazette* – 27579/4665
81 *London Gazette* – 27676/3089
82 *London Gazette* – 28299/7745
83 *London Gazette* – 28365/3246
84 *London Gazette* – 28401/5486
85 *London Gazette* – 28380/3860
86 *London Gazette* – 28383/4075
87 *London Gazette* – 28418/6761
88 *London Gazette* – 28505/4593

Figure 93a. Grave of Dighton Probyn

Probyn, with thanks for all he has been to me all these years – 52 years. We shall miss him so much, but he will draw us up to Heaven, where he is sure to go. God bless. From his devoted Alexandria'.

Dighton's Victoria Cross medal is not on public display; it was bought at auction 24th September 2005 for £160,000 and is in the hands of a private collector.

John Buckley
11th May 1857 (VC No. 116)

Gazetted: 18th June 1858 22154/2959

Rank and Unit: Deputy Assistant Commissary of Ordnance – Bengal Veteran Establishment

Citation
For gallant conduct in the defence of the Delhi Magazine, on the 11th May, 1857.

Biography
John was born on 24th May 1813, at Cocker Hill, Stalybridge in Cheshire, to parents Thomas a labourer and Sarah.

His initial employment was in the local textile industry where he first worked at Harrison's Mill as a Piecer, which involved leaning over the spinning machine to repair broken threads. He then worked at Bayley's Mill, as a cotton carder.

Obviously not satisfied with a life of toil in the mills, John travelled to Manchester where on 28th January 1832, at the age of 18, he enlisted in the 4th/5th Bengal Artillery.

An as yet unconfirmed source, states that John may have had other reasons for joining the army and leaving the country. It is possible that John was married to Ann (née Woodall) shortly before he joined the army, the couple are thought to have had two (or possibly three children): Mary Ann born on 31st October 1829, Ann born some time in 1830 who only survived for one

Figure 94. John Buckley

day and Hannah. Mary Ann and Hannah were both christened on 6th February 1831 at Old St George in Stalybridge.

After a short spell at the Artillery barracks in Chatham, on 20th June 1832 John embarked on board *HMS Layton* at Gravesend bound for India where he joined up with the 2nd/4th battalion at Benares as a gunner.

John was promoted to the rank of Corporal on 1st November 1834 and shortly after, during 1835, was transferred to Fort William in Calcutta. It was while stationed in Calcutta that John met and on 28th July 1835, at Chunar, married Mary Ann (née Broadway) who was only 14 years of age. The couple would go on to have three children, however by 1845 Mary Ann and two of the children had succumbed to disease and died. On 16th May 1840, John was promoted to the rank of Sergeant. On 17th August 1846, at Allahabad John was remarried to Esther (née Hunter) and the couple would go on to have five children, three sons and two daughters. In 1852, the surviving daughter from his first marriage died and during the following year he lost two sons from his second marriage to the harsh climate and disease of the Indian sub-continent, which was proving to be a very hostile environment for the Europeans. By 1854, John was a sub-conductor in the Bengal Veterans Establishment and was promoted to Staff Conductor on 1st May 1856. During 1857, John was transferred to Delhi as Assistant Commissary of Ordnance and was employed at the Delhi magazine.

It was at Delhi on 11th May 1857, during the defence of the magazine that he performed the deeds for which he was later awarded the Victoria Cross.

During the action John was wounded and captured by the mutineers, it was during his imprisonment by the rebels that he learned that his wife Esther and their three children: Robert James, Jane Evelyn and Sarah Amanda, had all been slain by the rebels during their attack on Delhi. Having now lost two wives and eight children John did not wish to live any longer and begged his captors to kill him, however, because of the bravery John had shown during the defence of the magazine, his captors refused to do so. John eventually managed to escape and rejoin the Army, where now with no concern for his own life he volunteered for all manner of dangerous missions.

On 8th June 1857, John was present at the battle of Badli-ki-Serai and at some stage performed the duties of Provost Marshal at Meerut. Perhaps it was in this role that John oversaw the execution of 150 rebels, this was done by strapping the men to the muzzle of a cannon, which when fired blew them apart.[89]

---

89 This barbaric practice was in fact quite humane as it caused instant death, the main reason for using this method of execution was to instil fear in the local population who were forced to witness the punishment.

After falling ill, John embarked for England on 21st May 1858 where he arrived on 6th July, to begin a two year period of sick leave.

John was presented with his Victoria Cross medal by Queen Victoria at an investiture which took place on Southsea Common of 2nd August 1858 and less than two months later, on 18th October John was promoted to the rank of Lieutenant.

In 1859, after having completed his period of sick leave, John returned to the Veterans Establishment in Lucknow with the rank of Major and retired from the army with this rank on 1st October 1861.

Following his retirement from the Army, John returned to England where he lived out his remaining days in London. John died at his home, 213 East India Dock Road, Poplar in London on 14th July 1876 at the age of 63 and was buried in a pauper's grave in the City of London and Tower Hamlets Cemetery.

John's Victoria Cross medal is on public display at the Royal Logistic Corps Museum, Camberley in Surrey.

Figure 94a. Grave of John Buckley

George Forrest
11th May 1857 (VC No. 117)

Gazetted: 18th June 1858 22154/2959

Rank and Unit: Lieutenant – Bengal Veteran Establishment

Citation
For gallant conduct in the defence of the Delhi Magazine, on the 11th May, 1857.

Biography
George was the 2nd son of father Sir George William, who was Director of Records for the Government of India and wife Emma (née Viner), he was born is the parish of St Michael's in Dublin some time during 1800. Unfortunately very little is known about the life and career of George.

George was married to Ann (née Edwards) sometime in 1832 and they would have two sons, Robert Edward born in 1835 and George William who was born in 1845.

If was on 11th May 1857, as a lieutenant in the Bengal Veteran Establishment, that George performed the deeds, during the defence of the magazine at Delhi, for which he was later awarded the Victoria Cross.

In addition to the Victoria Cross, George was also awarded the Mutiny medal for his service in India.

George was presented with his Victoria Cross medal by Major Troup at a special ceremony held in Landour on 2nd November 1858.

At some stage George was promoted to the rank of Captain and transferred to the Bengal Ordnance department, it was with this rank that he was killed in action at Dehra Dun on 3rd November 1859 and was buried in the Dehra Dun cemetery.

The whereabouts of his Victoria Cross medal is unknown; it is believed to be held privately.

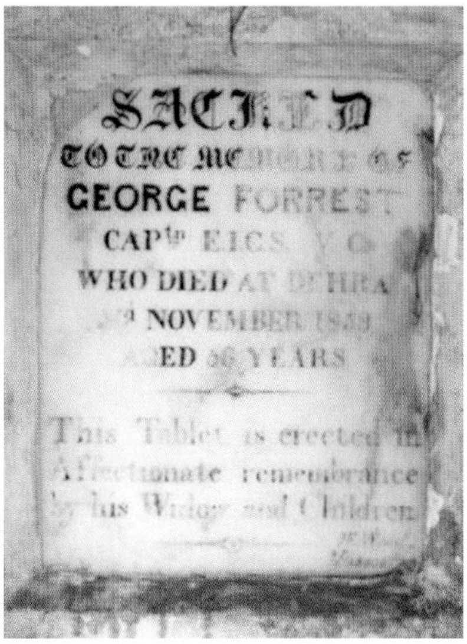

Figure 95b. Memorial at Royal Artillery Museum, Woolwich

Figure 95a. Grave of George Forrest

William Raynor
11th May 1857 (VC No. 118)

Gazetted: 18th June 1858 22154/2959

Rank and Unit: Lieutenant – Bengal Veteran Establishment

Citation

For gallant conduct in the defence of the Delhi Magazine, on the 11th May, 1857.

Biography

William was born in July 1795 at Plumtree near Keyworth in Nottinghamshire to father John and mother Elizabeth (née Tongue) and was baptised in Plumtree on 10th August 1796.

William had an older sister, Mary born in 1793 who died in June 1795 just before he was born.

Sometime late in 1812, William aged 17 enlisted in the army service of the Honourable East India Company. He arrived in India during February 1813, having been transported on board the HEIC ship *Hugh Inglis* to take up a position in the Bengal European Regiment.

William fought in the Gorkha or Anglo-Nepalese war of 1814 to 1816 and was awarded the Army of India Medal with clasp for Nepal for this service.

Sometime in 1818, William was promoted to the rank of Sergeant-Major.

On 8th October 1819, William married the widow Mary (née Wilkinson), however this was short lived as Mary died soon after the marriage.

On 6th November 1820, William was appointed as a Sub-Conductor in the Ordnance Commissariat department and was posted to the arsenal in Fort William at Calcutta.

On 14th January 1823, William was promoted to the rank of Conductor and was posted to the magazine at Cawnpore, a station where he would serve for over 20 years.

On 27th August 1823, William was married to Mary Anne (née Werril) at Cawnpore. The couple would go on to have five children, the first four: William Joseph born on 26th October 1826, Adelaide Louisa born on 14th July 1834, Richard John born on 8th October 1836 and Thomas Samuel born on 14th July 1839 were all born in Cawnpore and the last born was Albert Charles, born in Delhi on 18th September 1844.

On 6th October 1843, William was promoted to the rank of Deputy Assistant Commissary of Ordnance and was posted to the Delhi magazine where he would serve for 14 years and on 17th April 1845, William was promoted to the rank of Assistant Commissary of Ordnance.

On 17th August 1852, after 40 years of service William was promoted to the commissioned rank of Commissary of Ordnance and was appointed as a Lieutenant in the Bengal Veterans Establishment.

William was appointed to a position at the magazine in Ferozepur on 10th July 1855, however, was directed to continue working at the Delhi magazine under a temporary arrangement.

It was at Delhi on 11th May 1857, that William performed the deeds in defence of the magazine for which he would later be awarded the Victoria Cross. At the age of 61 years and 10 months William is the oldest person to have been awarded the Victoria Cross.

Shortly after this action, William was promoted to the rank of Captain a rank he would hold until his death.

In addition to the Victoria Cross, William was also awarded the India Mutiny medal for his service during the Mutiny.

William died from natural causes on 13th December 1860, aged 64 years and five months and was buried the next day in the Ferozepur Civil Cemetery.

In August 1865, William's wife Mary was granted 2,500 acres of forest at Dehra Dun, in the foothills of the Himalayas by way of an imperial warrant or *Sunnud*. Some of the land was used by Mary and her children to create a tea plantation, however, the bulk of the land was used to establish a leper colony which became known as Raynorpore.

William's Victoria Cross medal is held by the Royal Logistics Corps Museum in Camberley Surry and can be viewed by appointment.

Figure 96a. Grave of William Raynor

Everard Aloysius Lisle Phillipps
30th May 1857 (VC No. 119)

Gazetted: 21st October 1859 22318/3793
15th January 1907 27986/325

Rank and Unit: Ensign – 11th Bengal Native Infantry

Citation

21st October 1859

MEMORANDUM. Ensign Everard Aloysius Lisle Phillipps, of the 11th'Regiment of Bengal Native Infantry, would have been recommended to Her Majesty for the decoration" of 'the' Victoria Cross, had he survived; for many gallant deeds which he performed during the Siege of Delhi, during which he was wounded, three times. At the assault of that city, he captured the Water Bastion, with a small party of men; and was finally killed in the streets of Delhi on the 18th of September.

15th January 1907

The KING has been graciously pleased to approve of the Decoration of the Victoria Cross being delivered to the representatives of the under mentioned Officer's and men who fell in the performance of acts of valour, and with reference to whom it was notified in the London Gazette that they would have been recommended to Her late Majesty for the Victoria Cross had they survived.

Biography

Everard was born on 28th May 1835, at the family home Grace Dieu Manor, Colerton near Ashby de la Zouche in Leicestershire. He was the second son of father Ambrose Lisle March Phillipps de Lisle who was a justice of the peace and deputy Lieutenant of Leicestershire and mother Laura Maria (née Clifford).

Everard was part of a very large family with seven sisters: Winifreda Mary, Mary, Bertha Mary, Margaret Mary, Gwendoline Mary, Filumena Mary Anne, Alice Mary Elizabeth and eight brothers: Ambrose Charles, Reginald Bernard, Bernard Mary, Osmund, Francis, Edwin Joseph, Rudolph and Gerard.

Between 1847 and 1849 Everard was educated at St Edmund's College, Old Hall Green near Ware before completing his education at Oscott College in Sutton Coldfield near Birmingham, he was a keen sportsman who loved to play cricket. Following his time at College, Everard spent some time in Paris, together with his older brother, Ambrose where the pair were friends of Count de Montalembert, the celebrated religious writer and politician.

Figure 97. Everard Aloysius Lisle Phillipps

While in Paris they attended lavish parties held by Emperor Napoleon III and Empress Eugenie at their court in the Tuileries. During this time Everard learnt to speak Hindustani.

Sometime in 1854, at the age of 19, Everard decided on a career in the army and joined the forces of the Honourable East India Company. He set sail for India on 17th October 1854 as a commissioned officer (Ensign) in the 11th Bengal Native Infantry.

Although Everard was initially very homesick he settled down to the routine of army life and even found time to become infatuated with Agnes Rutherford, the daughter of his Colonel. The Colonel, however, was not keen for his daughter to become involved with a Catholic ensign who had no money.

On 4th May 1857, Everard was transferred with his regiment to the town of Meerut and it was here on the 10th of May that his regiment was one of the first to mutiny. Earlier in the day 85 members of the 3rd Bengal Light Cavalry refused to obey orders and were imprisoned. Because he could speak Hindustani, Everard was asked to read out an address to the remaining troops from his own regiment the 11th and the 20th Native Infantry – the troops chose this moment to mutiny and they stormed the prison and released the imprisoned men from the 3rd Bengal Light Cavalry. Everard was lucky to escape with his life as Colonel Finnis who was at his side was shot dead by the mutineers. After fierce fighting during which the mutineers set fire to the officer's bungalows and killed every European woman or child that they came across, they were eventually driven off and they made their way to Delhi.

After temporarily serving with the Carabineers for three days, Everard was assigned as orderly to Colonel Jones in the 60th regiment of foot.

Now totally disillusioned with service in the Honourable East India Company, Everard was desperate to receive a Queen's commission and wrote letters home to his father pleading for the purchase of a commission.

Finally on 27th March, Brigadier-General Wilson, commander of the Meerut garrison received orders to join the Field Force being assembled to march on Delhi and Everard marched off with the men of the 60th under the command of Lieutenant-Colonel Jones. By the 30th March, the force was encamped at Ghazeeooddeen-nuggar on the banks of the Hindun River about nine miles from Delhi and at 4:00pm a scout reported that the mutineers were forming up to attack. At this time of year the river was low and the advancing enemy on the other side of the river were only accessible via a causeway. Everard's part in the ensuing action is described in his own words, from a letter sent to his mother on the following day.

There's a causeway nearly a mile in length, at the end of which the enemy had placed one 9-pounder and one 8-inch howitzer which swept the causeway. On reaching the bridge the two companies extended, two more come in support and the long range of the rifles forced the enemy to abandon their guns. The Colonel sent me down to order the two leading companies to reform on the causeway and take the guns at the point of the bayonets. One of the 11th colours was with the guns – the sepoys carried it off on our taking the guns, one sepoy, Dars Singh of the 11th, fired his musket into a cart full of ammunition. Captain Andrews, Wilton and myself and about nine men were round a tumbrel when it blew up. Andrews was blown to pieces and four men killed. Wilton's head was bruised – God only knows how I escaped. I'm merely bruised, just a little blood drawn from about five places. The poor 'Creeper', the horse I was riding, was shot in four places, in the rear fore-leg, in off hock, in hip and a fearful wound in the body. The shot that gave him the last wound almost melted my scabbard, a narrow escape for my leg. A most fearful affair. When the explosion took place, I thought I was hit by a shell and expected to go to pieces every minute. When the smoke cleared up the enemy had retired to a village strongly walled, on rising ground about 200 yards off. We fire a few shots and cleared it at the point of a bayonet. The sepoys fought like fiends – in one place we left about 35 all dead in a heap, killed altogether 50 and lost five men of rifles … altogether it was a sharp little action.

Three days later, on 5th June, Ensign William Napier, who had lost a leg in the fighting on the causeway, died of his wounds and Colonel Jones took advantage of this unexpected vacancy to recommend Everard as his replacement.

The city of Delhi, which was occupied by about 20,000 mutineers, was now besieged by the British Field Force commanded by Sir Henry Barnard. The British forces occupied the high ground on a ridge which extended from Flagstaff Tower on the left, to Hindoo Rao's house on the right of the line. It was from these positions that some light artillery was brought to bear on the city and used to bombard the defenders and assault the approaches in an attempt to stem the flow of new mutineers into the city. There was much skirmishing and some full scale attacks by the mutineers as they tried to dislodge the British besiegers. It was during these actions that Everard was wounded twice, once on 12th June[90] and again in the shoulder on 19th June.[91]

By September the British forces were ready for a full scale assault against Delhi and by the 10th of September had advanced and established positions to within 200 yards of the defenders.

On 14th September, Everard distinguished himself once again when he led a small party of riflemen in an assault against the Water Bastion and having successfully gained the position Everard turned the guns on the retreating mutineers.

On 17th September, Colonel Jones advanced even further forward and occupied the Delhi Bank, where mortars were installed to bombard the King's Palace. During the advance on the Delhi Bank, Everard was tasked with an attack on a key position which was performed successfully. After the attack Everard retired with his men to a breastwork behind which they could recovery. A small hole was left in the breastwork, in order to maintain observation of the enemy, when Everard was looking through the hole he was shot in the eye and died instantly.[92]

On the very next day, the news that Everard was so desperate to hear, was published in the London Gazette, it was confirmed that effective from 5th June 1857 he was commissioned as an Ensign in the 60th Regiment of Foot.[93]

Everard was buried in Rajpura Cemetery in Delhi; a gravestone was erected by his fellow officers.

Letters from brother officers, Lieutenants Gough and Müller, to Everard's parents expressed the general view that had he survived Everard would have been recommended for the Victoria Cross in particular for his actions in the taking of the Water Bastion. At this time the Royal Warrant did not allow for posthumous award of the medal.

However, a recent proposal by Mr Pennington, the person responsible for the operation of the system of awards, did allow for a memorandum to be published indicating that the stated person would have received the award had he survived – in Everard's case this was duly published in the London Gazette on 21st October 1859. On 15th January 1907, King Edward VII issued a Royal Warrant that posthumously awarded the Victoria Cross to those persons who had been subject of the memorandum. It was thus that Everard became to first person to be the

90 *London Gazette* – 22073/4433
91 *London Gazette* – 22050/3407
92 *London Gazette* – 22095/673
93 *London Gazette* – 22041/3143

subject of a posthumous award of the Victoria Cross. The medal was presented to his oldest surviving brother Edwin on 17th September 1907 exactly fifty years after his death.

Recognition of a posthumous award of the Victoria Cross was not made official until the Royal Warrant was completely rewritten by George V and reissued in June 1920. A new clause 4, stated that the award could be made posthumously.

Everard's Victoria Cross medal is privately held by his family.

Alfred Spencer Heathcote
Undated (VC No. 120)

Gazetted: 20th January 1860 22347/178

Rank and Unit: Lieutenant – 60th Rifles

Citation
For highly gallant and daring conduct at Delhi throughout the Siege, from June to September, 1857, during which he was wounded. He volunteered for services of extreme danger, especially during the six days of severe fighting in the streets after the Assault. Elected by the Officers of his Regiment.

Biography
Alfred was born on 29th March 1832, in London to parents Henry Spencer and Anne (née Currie), he was baptised on 12th July of the same year at Old Church, St Pancras, London.

Alfred was the oldest of four children, a sister Caroline was born in 1833, brother Mark Henry was born on 4th February 1835 and brother Charles Graham was born during 1836. All three brothers would go on to achieve the rank of Colonel, however, Alfred's colonelcy was in the Australian Militia rather than the British army.

Alfred began his military career when he enlisted as an ensign in the 1st Regiment of the Royal Surrey Militia on 25th October 1855.[94]

Figure 98. Alfred Spencer Heathcote

94 *London Gazette* – 21815/4235

On 16th May 1856, Alfred was appointed as an ensign without purchase in the 1st Battalion of the 60th Rifles[95] and soon afterwards would have joined his regiment in India where they were stationed at Jullundur near to Delhi. Just under a year after Alfred arrived in India, the mutiny broke out and as he was stationed in northern India he was involved in many of the actions to quell the rebellion. In May 1857 Alfred was involved in action on the Hindun River and in June took part in the Battle of Badli-ki-Serai and the capture of the heights before Delhi, where on 17th June he was wounded. In September 1857, Alfred was involved in the siege operations and the assault and eventual capture of Delhi, including the attack on the Royal Palace. It was during this period that Alfred performed the deeds which so impressed his fellow officers that under clause 13 of the Royal Warrant he was recommended for the award of the Victoria Cross.

On 22nd June 1858, Alfred was promoted to the rank of Lieutenant.[96]

During the second half of 1858, Alfred was also involved in the Rohilkhand Campaign with actions at Bugawalla and Nugena, the relief of Moradabad and the capture of Bareilly, the relief of Shahjehanpore and the capture of Bunnai, Gumti and Shahabad. For his service during the mutiny Alfred was awarded the India Mutiny medal with clasp for Delhi.

While still in India, Alfred was married on 5th February 1859 to Mary Harriet (née Thompson).

It would seem that at some stage, probably in late 1859 or early 1860, that Alfred either transferred or was seconded to the 2nd Battalion of the regiment after having returned to England from India.

On 28th February 1860, the regiment was despatched to China where they landed on 29th June to take part in the later stages of the 2nd Opium War. During the war in China, Alfred was involved in the battle and taking of the Taku forts in August and the taking of Peking in September 1860. It was while serving in China, that on 11th January 1861, Albert was finally presented with his Victoria Cross medal by Lieutenant-General Sir J. Grant. On 28th February 1862, Alfred returned to England following his service in China, for which he was awarded the China War medal with clasps for Taku Forts and Peking.

On 11th August 1863, after the sale of his commission, Albert retired from the army with 7 years of service.[97]

It would appear that soon after leaving the British army, Albert immigrated to Australia where he took up a career within the Queensland Militia forces. At this time the British army were fighting the Maori in New Zealand and in Queensland,

left pretty much to their own devices, the colony was raising a militia to fight a frontier war against the indigenous aborigine population.

During his time in Australia, Alfred and his wife had three children: a son born on 10th November 1865 at Pike's Creek, Leyburn, Queensland and two daughters Beatrice and Mabel one of which was born at Warwick in Queensland.

At some stage Alfred raised and commanded the Queensland Volunteer Cavalry Corps.

On 6th August 1871, Alfred was appointed to the command of the First Infantry New South Wales, probably with the rank of Colonel.

Alfred died on 21st February 1912 at the age of 79 and was buried in St James Anglican Churchyard (Bowral Cemetery) in Sydney, New South Wales.

Alfred's Victoria Cross medal is on public display in the Victoria Barracks in Sydney.

Figure 98a. Memorial to Alfred Spencer Heathcote

95 *London Gazette* – 21884/1791
96 *London Gazette* – 22155/ 3014
97 *London Gazette* – 22761/3997

Peter Gill
4th June 1857 (VC No. 121)

Gazetted: 24th August 1858 22176/3903

Rank and Unit: Sergeant-Major – Ludhiana Regiment, Indian Army

Citation

This Non-Commissioned Officer also conducted himself with gallantry at Benares, on the night of the 4th of June, 1857. He volunteered, with Sergeant-Major Rosamond, of the 37th Regiment of Bengal Native Infantry, to bring in Captain Brown, Pension Paymaster, and his family, from a detached Bungalow to the Barracks, as above recorded, and saved the life of the Quartermaster-Sergeant of the 25th Regiment of Bengal Native Infantry, in the early part of the evening, by cutting off the head of the Sepoy who had just bayoneted him. Sergeant-Major Gill states, that on the same night he faced a Guard of 27 men, with only a Sergeant's sword; and it is also represented that he twice saved the life of Major Barrett, 27th Regiment of Bengal Native Infantry, when attacked by Sepoy's of his own Regiment.

Biography

Peter was born some time during 1816,[98] in St Paul's Parish Dublin and after leaving school he trained as a tailor.

At some stage Peter moved to London and in February 1842 enlisted for service with the Honourable East India Company in the Bengal Artillery.

Upon his arrival in India, on board the Honourable East India Company steamship *Henry*, Peter was assigned to the 5th company of the 3rd battalion of the Bengal Artillery as a gunner. Peter served with the Bengal Artillery during the first (1845–46) and second (1848–49) Anglo-Sikh wars for which he was awarded the Sutlej and Punjab medals. In April 1850, having been promoted to the rank of Sergeant-Major, Peter was transferred to the Ludhiana Regiment of Sikhs. It was with this regiment on 4th June 1857, during the mutiny at Benares that Peter performed the deeds for which he would later be awarded the Victoria Cross.

On 16th April 1858, Peter received a commission as Ensign in the Moradabad Infantry Levy and served with this regiment for the remainder of the mutiny until the conclusion of the Oudh campaign in April 1859. It was later in 1859 that Peter was presented with his Victoria Cross medal, however, details of this event are unknown.

Peter was promoted from the unattached list, to the rank of Lieutenant in the Indian Establishment on 22nd May 1863[99] and served as the duty lieutenant at Lucknow for the next four years.

On 21st October 1867, Peter was assigned as Barrack Master at Morar Gwalior, where about a year later on 24th October 1868 he was killed in action and was buried in the Artillery Lines Cemetery at Gwalior.

His Victoria Cross medal is held within a private collection.

---

98 Most sources quote September 1831 as his date of birth, however, it is recorded that Peter was awarded the Sutlej medal for service during the First Anglo-Sikh war in 1845–46; unlikely if he was only 14 or 15 years old.

99 *London Gazette* – 22738/2687

Matthew Rosamund (Rosamond)
4th June 1857 (VC No. 122)

Gazetted: 24th August 1858 22176/3903

Rank and Unit: Sergeant-Major – 37th Bengal Native Infantry

Citation

This Non-Commissioned Officer volunteered to accompany Lieutenant-Colonel Spottiswoode, Commanding the 37th Regiment of Bengal Native Infantry, to the right of the Lines, in order to set them on fire, with the view of driving out the Sepoys,—on the occasion of the outbreak at Benares, on the evening of the 4th of June, 1857; and also volunteered, with Serjeant-Major Gill, of the Loodiana Regiment, to bring off Captain Brown, Pension Paymaster, his wife and infant, and also some others, from a detached Bungalow, into the Barracks. His conduct was highly meritorious, and he has been since promoted.

Biography

Matthew was born on 13th July 1823 at East Socon, a district of St. Neots in Huntingdonshire, to father George and mother Elizabeth (née Bamber).

Unfortunately very little is known of Matthew's early life, however, it is likely that he enlisted in the service of the Honourable East India Company army at some time around his 18th birthday in 1841 when he took up a position with the 37th Bengal Infantry.

On 21st July 1851, Matthew was married to Bridget (née Mahoney) at Agra, West Bengal in India.

It was on 4th June 1857, at Benares that Matthew now with the rank of Sergeant-Major, performed the deeds for which he was later awarded the Victoria Cross.

On 16th April 1858, Matthew received a commission as Ensign in the Bengal Army.

Matthew was presented with his Victoria Cross medal some time during February 1859 while serving in India.

During 1863, Matthew was Barrack Master at Barrackpore and Dum Dum; on 9th September 1864 he was promoted to the rank of Lieutenant[100] and he saw service at Fort William in Calcutta.

During 1865, Matthew married Alice (née Wollen) at Serampore, Bengal in India.

Matthew died on 14th July 1866, while on board ship on a voyage in the Red Sea, he is presumed to have been buried at sea.

Figure 100. Matthew Rosamund

The whereabouts of Matthew's Victoria Cross medal is unknown, believed to be held in a private collection having been sold by Spinks in 1903.

Figure 100a. Memorial Matthew Rosamund

---

100 *London Gazette* – 22892/4363

John Kirk
4th June 1857 (VC No. 123)

Gazetted: 20th January 1860 22347/179

Rank and Unit: Private 2359 – 10th Regiment of Foot

Citation

*For daring gallantry at Benares, on the 4th of June, 1857,
on the outbreak of the mutiny of the Native Troops at
that station, in having volunteered to proceed with two
Non-commissioned Officers to rescue Captain Brown,
Pension Paymaster, and his family, who were surrounded
by rebels in the compound of their house; and having, at the
risk of his own life, succeeded in saving them.*

Biography

John Kirk was born in Liverpool on 18th July 1827, little is
known of his family or early life.

On 27th January 1846, John left his job as a labourer and
enlisted in the army at Liverpool where he joined the first battalion of the 10th Regiment of Foot. It is likely that John joined his
regiment in India just at the end of the first Anglo-Sikh war and
would have been stationed at Lahore in the Punjab.

John was involved with his regiment in the second Anglo-Sikh
war and for his service was awarded the Sikh War medal with
two clasps.[101] It was on 4th June 1857, that John performed the
deeds at Benares for which he would later be awarded the Victoria Cross.

The regiment returned to England, from service in India,
during 1859 and John was presented with his Victoria Cross
medal by Queen Victoria at an investiture held at Home Park,
Windsor Castle on 9th November 1860.

During 1862, the regiment was sent on garrison duties
to Ireland and it was here in Kilkenny on 10th May 1864 that
after 17 years and 278 days service, John was discharged from
the army. At a medical examination on 2nd April 1864, John
had been found to be unfit for service due to chronic (syphi-
litic) rheumatism. John had been far from an ideal soldier who
never rose above the rank of private and appeared 56 times in
the defaulter's book. John's main problem was with drink; he was
tried and convicted on 12 occasions for being drunk on duty.

On leaving the army, John returned to Liverpool to take up a
role of itinerant labourer, however, because of the drink it is not
likely that he did much work.

---

101 The first Anglo-Sikh war saw the start of clasps being awarded to campaign
    medals to indicate the recipients involvement in particular battles.

Figure 101. John Kirk

Less than a year and a half after his discharge, on 30th August
1865, while residing at the workhouse on Brownlow Hill in Liverpool, John died from tuberculosis and was buried in Anfield
cemetery.

John's Victoria Cross medal is on public display at the Museum
of Lincolnshire Life, Lincoln.

Figure 101a. Grave of John Kirk

Cornelius Coughlan
8th June 1857 (VC No. 124)

Gazetted: 11th November 1862 22680/5346

Rank and Unit: Colour Sergeant – 75th Regiment of Foot

Citation

For gallantly venturing, under a heavy fire, with three others, into a Serai occupied by the Enemy in great numbers, and removing Private Corbett, 75th Regiment, who lay severely wounded. Also for cheering and encouraging a party which hesitated to charge down a lane in Subzee Mundee, at Delhi, lined on each side with huts, and raked by a cross fire; then entering with the said party into an enclosure filled with the Enemy, and destroying every man. For having also, on the same occasion, returned under a cross fire to collect dhoolies, and carry off the wounded ; a service which was successfully performed, and for which this man obtained great praise from the Officers of his Regiment.

Biography

Cornelius was born on 27th June 1828 at Eyrecourt, Co Galway in Ireland to father Edward and mother Catherine.

Little is known of his early life, however, it is believed that Cornelius was educated locally in Eyrecourt.

At some stage, probably at the time of his 18th birthday in 1846, Cornelius in common with many of his compatriots joined the British army to escape the abject poverty that prevailed in Ireland. The 75th Regiment of Foot was serving in Ireland and as about three quarters of its strength was made up of Irish volunteers it was a logical regiment for Cornelius to join. From June 1846 the 75th was based at Athlone, less than 30 miles from where Cornelius was living so this is probably where he enlisted. In July 1847, the regiment moved to Dublin where it was quartered in the Royal Barracks. In July 1848, following troubles in Tipperary, known as the "Smith O'Brian Rebellion", the regiment was moved to Kilkenny where they remained until March 1849, when they moved to Fermoy to prepare for imminent deployment to India. It is thought that Cornelius was a private for only two years; if this was the case then he would have been promoted to the rank of Corporal before leaving Ireland for Foreign Service.

In early May 1849, the regiment left Ireland bound for service in India and after landing at Calcutta in August, they proceeded via Allahabad, to Umballa were they arrived on 21st December; this was to be their home until November 1853. Leaving Umballa

Figure 102. Cornelius Coughlan

the regiment moved to Peshawar until 1855 when they moved to Rawalpindi, until the mutiny broke out at Meerut on 10th May 1857.

Sometime in 1856, Cornelius was married to Margaret probably in Rawalpindi and the couple would go on to have two children, Margaret and Edward.

With news of the mutiny, the regiment was ordered to proceed to Umballa where they took their place as part of the Field Force and advanced to besiege Delhi. Cornelius must have made rapid progress through the ranks as by this time he held the rank of Colour-Sergeant (a rank that he held for 10 years). It was during the actions in and around Delhi, that Cornelius performed the deeds for which he would later be awarded the Victoria Cross. During the first deed on 8th June he was badly wounded in the left knee. The gallant conduct of Cornelius on 8th, 12th and 15th June was mentioned in Regimental Orders on 16th June. During the Mutiny, Cornelius saw further action at Cawnpore and Lucknow before the regiment was moved to Allahabad on 25th January 1860 and then a year later to Fort William in Calcutta. For his service during the Mutiny, Cornelius was awarded the India Mutiny medal with clasps for Delhi and the relief of Lucknow.

Cornelius left India during February 1862, after having spent 13 years on the sub-continent; the regiment arrived back in England, landing at Plymouth during June 1862 whereupon they were stationed at the Raglan Barracks in Devonport.

It was at Devonport, on 31st January 1863, that Cornelius was presented with his Victoria Cross medal by Major-General Sir William Hutchinson. Queen Victoria had sent him a personal letter complementing him on his bravery and lamenting the fact that she would not be able to personally present his medal.

Sometime during 1863, Cornelius was promoted to the rank of Sergeant-Major.

In December 1863, the regiment moved to Aldershot where they were stationed until 1866. In early March, in response to a Fenian conspiracy, the number of British troops in Ireland was increased and the regiment was despatched to Kingstown, Dublin where they occupied the Richmond barracks.

Sometime in 1867, after 21 years of exemplary service, Cornelius retired from the army and was awarded the Army Long Service and Good Conduct medal together with the Army Meritorious Service medal.

Cornelius remained in Ireland and at some stage joined the 3rd Battalion of the Connaught Rangers, where he served on the permanent staff[102] as a Sergeant-Major for 21 years.

In about 1875, Cornelius moved to Altamont Street in Westport, Co Mayo where he was to live until his death on 14th February 1915. He was buried in the Old Cemetery in Westport in an unmarked grave.

Cornelius's Victoria Cross medal is on public display at the National War Museum of Scotland in Edinburgh Castle.

Figure 102a. Grave of Cornelius Coughlan

---

102 The 3rd Battalion was a part time reserve battalion.

Alfred Stowell Jones
8th June 1857 (VC No. 125)

Gazetted: 18th June 1858 22154/2960

Rank and Unit: Lieutenant – 9th Lancers

Citation
The Cavalry charged the rebels and rode through them. Lieutenant Jones, of the 9th Lancers, with his squadron, captured one of their guns, killing the drivers, and, with Lieutenant-Colonel Yule's assistance, turned it upon a village, occupied by the rebels, who were quickly dislodged. This was a well-conceived act, gallantly executed. (**Despatch from Major-General James Hope Grant, K.C.B., dated 10th January, 1858.**)

Biography
Alfred was born on 24th January 1832 at 3 Husskisson Street in Liverpool, the youngest son of parents John who was a clergyman and mother Hannah (née Pares).

Alfred was educated at Liverpool College until 1849 when he continued his education at the Sandhurst military college. Following his graduation from Sandhurst, Alfred joined the army on 9th July 1852 by the purchase of a commission as Cornet in the 9th Light Dragoons.[103]

Alfred joined his regiment in India where they had been serving since 1841 and on 21st September 1855 was promoted to the rank of Lieutenant.[104] Throughout the siege of Delhi Alfred served in the role of Deputy Assistant Quartermaster to the

Figure 103. Alfred Stowell Jones

---

103 *London Gazette* – 21337/1917
104 *London Gazette* – 21786/3509

Cavalry and it was on the 8th June 1857, during the first engagement at Badli-ki-Serai, that he performed the deeds for which he would later be awarded the Victoria Cross.

While leading a charge on mutineers at Agra on 10th October 1857, Alfred was unseated from his horse when he was shot through the bridle arm, falling to the ground he was set about by mutineers wielding sabres and received 22 wounds one of which required an eye to be removed.

It is thought that Alfred was returned to England to recover from his wounds. For his service in India he was awarded the Indian Mutiny medal with clasps for Delhi and the Relief of Lucknow, he was also mentioned in despatches on three occasions.

On 16th March 1858, Alfred was promoted to the rank of Captain and joined the 18th Light Dragoons,[105] which had just been reformed in Leeds.

Alfred was presented by his Victoria Cross medal by Queen Victoria at an investiture held on Southsea Common, Portsmouth on 2nd August 1858.

Some years later Alfred commented on the lack of notice and his surprise at the award "... *I was startled by the date, June 18th, of the London Gazette, and began with my blue pencil, because in these days it seems ridiculous that I should not have known anything about it for more than a month. But I was very busy breaking in horse and teaching recruits to ride for the 18th Hussars, then being raised at Leeds, and I distinctly remember my surprise at receiving an order at Mess dinner to go down to Portsmouth one day at the very end of July, or nearly in August, for a Parade on Southsea Common, when twelve V.C.s were to be presented by Queen Victoria, and that was the first intimation I had that I had been recommended for the Cross. A young horse I was riding in the School at Leeds a few days before, had thrown up his head and bruised my blind eye-brow, so my appearance was shocking, and made the Queen so nervous that he pricked me in pinning the Cross through my tunic.*"

On 18th October 1859, Alfred exchanged with Captain John Payton and transferred to the 13th Regiment of Foot.[106]

Probably not long after moving to the 13th Regiment of Foot, Alfred was sent to the Staff College at Camberley in Surrey for training as a Staff Officer and on 30th November 1860 was given the brevet rank of Major.[107]

After graduating from the Staff College some time during 1861, Alfred was sent to serve on the Staff at the Cape Colony in South Africa where he stayed until 1867. While serving in South Africa, Alfred was married to Emily, Sicily (née Back) on 13th June 1863, at St James, Westminster Place. The couple would go

on to have six children, a daughter Margarita born on 7th September 1870 at Pool House, Graby in Leicestershire who married Arthur Watson the eldest son of General Sir John Watson VC a former comrade of Alfred at Delhi. All of his five sons chose careers in the military: Harry the eldest son was a Captain in the Royal Navy, Owen was a Captain in the Royal Navy Reserve, Tertius was a Lieutenant in the Royal Horse Artillery, Percy was a Captain in the 13th lancers, he was killed in action in Mesopotamia, and the youngest son was a lieutenant in the 11th Hussars, who died while playing polo in India.

On 29th May 1868, Alfred was placed on the supernumerary list when he was appointed to the role of Adjutant at the Staff College.[108] On 1st October 1871, Alfred received a brevet promotion to the rank of Lieutenant-Colonel,[109] this was later anti-dated to 28th August 1871[110] and finally was confirmed to be effective 13th September 1871.[111] Alfred was removed from the supernumerary list on 24th April 1872, when he left the Staff College and returned to the 13th Regiment of Foot as a Captain.[112] Having returned to the 13th only a few weeks before, Alfred sold his commission on 19th June 1872 and retired from the army after almost exactly 20 years service.[113]

Figure 103a. Grave of Alfred Stowell Jones

105 *London Gazette* – 22114/1455
106 *London Gazette* – 22317/3766
107 *London Gazette* – 22454/4786

108 *London Gazette* – 23385/3124
109 *London Gazette* – 23789/4388
110 *London Gazette* – 23794/4598
111 *London Gazette* – 23800/5146
112 *London Gazette* – 23855/2197
113 *London Gazette* – 23868/2803

On leaving the Army, Alfred pursued a career as a Civil Engineer specialising in environmental engineering. In 1878 he became a member of the Institute of Civil Engineers and was a founder member of the Royal Sanitary Institute. Alfred wrote two books and many articles in professional journals, regarding the treatment of sewage. From 1895 until 1912, when he retired, Alfred was manager of all of the 1st Army Corps sewage works at Aldershot.

For a period of time Alfred was a Justice of the Peace for Berkshire.

Alfred died at his home, Ridge Cottage, Finchampstead, Woking on 29th May 1920, aged 68 and was buried in St James's Churchyard, Finchampstead.

The location of Alfred's Victoria Cross medal is unknown.

Henry Hartigan
8th June 1857 (VC No. 126)

Gazetted: 19th June 1858 22386/2316

Rank and Unit: Pensioned Sergeant – 9th Lancers

Citation

For daring and distinguished gallantry in the following instances:—

At the battle of Budle-ke-Serai, near Delhi, on the 8th June, 1857, in going to the assistance of Serjeant H. Helstone, who was wounded, dismounted, and surrounded by the enemy, and at the risk of his own life, carrying him to the rear.

On the 10th October, 1857, at Agra, in having run unarmed to the assistance of Serjeant Crews, who was attacked by four rebels. Hartigan caught a tulwar, from one of them with his. right hand, and with the other hit him on the mouth, disarmed him, and then defended himself against the other three, killing one and wounding two, when he was himself disabled from further service by severe and dangerous wounds.

Biography

Henry was born during March 1826 in Drumlea, Enniskillen, Co Fermanagh, Ireland, unfortunately very little is known about his life story.

It is likely that Henry joined the army at some time around his 18th birthday, say during 1844. As his regiment, the 9th Lancers had been serving in India since 1841 he would have joined them in India soon after enlisting. Henry took part, with his regiment in the 2nd Sikh War (1848–1849) and was awarded the Punjab Medal with clasps for Chillianwala and Goojerat for this service. It was in the early stages of the siege of Delhi, during the Battle of Badli-ki-Serai on 8th June 1857, that Henry performed the deeds for which he was later awarded the Victoria Cross. Henry also performed a second act of bravery during the Battle of Agra on 10th October 1857 during which he was gravely wounded. Due to his recuperation from his wounds Henry took no part in the relief of Lucknow and as a result his Indian Mutiny medal only has one clasp for Delhi.

Henry was presented with his Victoria Cross medal by Lady Hersey, at an investiture which took place on 24th December 1860 at Fort William in Calcutta.

At some stage it is thought that Henry was commissioned and promoted to the rank of Lieutenant in the 16th Lancers. It is presumed that Henry continued his service with the 16th Lancers in

India, probably until his death at Calcutta on 29th October 1886 at 60 years of age. Henry was buried in an unmarked grave in Barrackpore New Cemetery, Calcutta.

Henry's Victoria Cross medal is on display at the Newcastle-under-Lyme Museum and Art Gallery in Staffordshire.

However, it should be noted that this medal is thought to be a forgery. Hancock's have confirmed that the style of engraving is not correct for the time the medal was issued.

Figure 104a. Memorial to Henry Hartigan

Thomas Cadell
12th June 1857 (VC No. 127)

Gazetted: 22nd April 1862 22621/2229

Rank and Unit: Lieutenant – 2nd European Bengal Fusiliers

Citation

For having, on the 12th of June, 1857, at the Flag-staff Piquet at Delhi, when the whole of the Piquet of Her Majesty's 75th Regiment and 2nd European Bengal Fusiliers were driven in by a large body of the enemy, brought in from amongst the enemy a wounded Bugler of his own regiment, under a most severe fire, who would otherwise have been cut up by the rebels. Also, on the same day, when the Fusiliers were retiring, by order, on Metcalfe's house, on its being reported that there was a wounded man left behind, Lieutenant Cadell went back of his own accord towards the enemy, accompanied by three men, and brought in a man of the 75th Regiment, who was severely wounded, under a most heavy fire from the advancing enemy.

Biography

Thomas was born on 5th September 1835 at Cockenzie House, Cockenzie, East Lothian, the youngest son of Hew Francis and Janet Marion (née Buchan-Syderff).

Born into a large family, Thomas had four brothers: John, Francis who would join the navy and become an explorer who navigated the sources of the Murray River in Australia, William and Robert who would pursue a career in the army becoming a General in the Royal Artillery. Thomas also had six sisters: Janet, Mary, Marion, Anne, Harriet and Martha.

Before pursuing a career in the army, Thomas was educated at the Edinburgh Academy, the Grange in Sunderland and also abroad.

On 17th April 1854, at the age of 18, Thomas enlisted as an Ensign in the 2nd Battalion of the European Bengal Fusiliers and joined his regiment in India. Thomas was promoted to the rank of Lieutenant on 23rd November 1856. It was during the siege of Delhi on 12th June 1857 that Thomas performed the deeds for which he would later be awarded the Victoria Cross. Thomas served throughout the Mutiny, being involved in the Oudh Campaign with the 4th Irregular Cavalry and in command of a flying column in the campaign in Bundelkhand fighting against the Bhel tribesmen where he gained a mention in despatches. For his service during the Mutiny Thomas was awarded the Indian Mutiny medal with clasp for Delhi. Under the terms of a Royal Warrant dated 16th January 1861, Thomas became part of the regular

Figure 105. Thomas Cadell

British Army when he was appointed as a Lieutenant in the Bengal Staff Corps;[114] this was advised in a memorandum from the India Office dated 27th November 1862. Thomas was presented with his Victoria Cross medal by Brigadier-General James Travers[115] on 29th December 1862 at an investiture in Bhopal, India. On 17th April 1866, Thomas was promoted to the rank of Captain.[116]

Thomas was married to Anne Catherine (née Dalmahoy) in Edinburgh on 18th April 1867; the couple would have four children: Hew Francis who would become a Major in the army, Patrick who would have a career in the India Civil service and become Chief Secretary to the Government of India. The couple also had two daughters.

On 17th April 1874, Thomas was promoted to the Rank of Major.[117] From 1879 until 1892, although still in the army, Thomas was in the employment of the Political Department in Central India. On 17th April 1880, Thomas was promoted to the rank of Lieutenant-Colonel[118] and became a Political Agent 1st Class in Mewar, a suburb of Bombay.

For some time Thomas held the appointment of Chief Commissioner of the Andaman and Nicobar Islands and at some stage received a brevet promotion to the rank of Colonel.

On the 50th anniversary of the military operations during the mutiny in India, in recognition for his services Thomas was appointed as an Ordinary Member third class Companion of the Military Division of the Most Honourable Order of the Bath effective 25th June 1907.[119]

On 5th September 1892, Thomas retired from the army when he was placed on the unemployed supernumerary list.[120]

Thomas died at home in Edinburgh on 6th April 1919, at the age of 83 and was buried four days later in the family vault at Tranent Parish Church, Dovecot Brae in Edinburgh.

Thomas, whose Victoria Cross medal is held in a private collection, was the cousin of Samuel Hill Lawrence who was also awarded the Victoria Cross.

Figure 105a. Grave of Thomas Cadell

114 *London Gazette* – 22686/6159
115 James Travers was himself a holder of the Victoria Cross, having been given the award for actions during July 1857.
116 *London Gazette* – 23161/4981
117 *London Gazette* – 24106/3098
118 *London Gazette* – 24857/3591

119 *London Gazette* – 28034/4431
120 *London Gazette* – 26327/5333

Thomas Hancock
19th June 1857 (VC No. 128)

Gazetted: 15th January 1858 22083/178

Rank and Unit: Private – 9th Lancers

Citation

The guns, I am happy to say, were saved, but a wagon of Major Scott's battery was blown up. I must not fail to mention the excellent conduct of a Sowar of the 4th Irregular Cavalry, and two men of the 9th Lancers, Privates Thomas Hancock and John Purcell, who, when my horse was shot down, remained by me throughout. One of these men and the Sowar offered me their horses, and I was dragged out by the Sowar's horse. Private Hancock was severely wounded, and Private Purcell's horse was killed under him. The Sowar's name is Roopur Khan. **(Extract of a letter from Brigadier J. H. Grant, C.B., Commanding Cavalry Brigade of the Field Force, to the Deputy Assistant-Adjutant – General of Division. Dated Camp, Delhi, June 22, 1857.)**

Biography

Thomas was born during July 1823 in Kensington, London.

In 1841, at the age of 18, Thomas joined the 3rd Light Dragoons and took up his duties in India. A year later, Thomas transferred to the 9th Lancers and was involved in the Gwalior Campaign of 1843 for which he was awarded the Gwalior Campaign Star (Punniar Star). Thomas was also involved in the 1st (1845–46) and 2nd (1848–49) Sikh wars for which he was awarded the Sutlej Medal (Sobraon) and the Punjab Medal with clasps for Chillianwala and Goojerat. Thomas served during the India Mutiny and it was during the siege of Delhi, on 19th June 1857, that he performed the deeds for which he was later awarded the Victoria Cross.

In addition to the letter, which was used as the basis for the Victoria Cross citation, Brigadier-General Hope wrote another letter to the Assistant Adjutant-General of the Army, Major H. W. Norman on 10th January 1858 in which he extols the virtues of Thomas; *"I had the sincere gratification of naming two privates of the 9th Lancers, who had displayed signal gallantry in the fight—Privates Thomas Hancock, who lost an arm on the occasion, and John Purcell, who had his horse shot under him, and was, I regret to say, afterwards killed at the assault of Delhi. Sir Henry Barnard was pleased to recommend that the Victoria Cross should be conferred on both."*

During this action, Thomas was severely wounded which resulted in his right arm having to be amputated. Being unfit

Figure 106. Thomas Hancock

for further service with his regiment, Thomas was returned to England and in 1858 received an honourable discharge after 17 years of service. Probably in recognition of his brave acts during the siege of Delhi, at some stage Thomas was promoted to the rank of Corporal. For his service in India, Thomas was awarded the Indian Mutiny medal with clasp for Delhi.

Thomas did not have an unblemished record in the army, having been tried on three occasions by a regimental court martial (twice for drink related offences) – however, his discharge papers stated that his character and conduct had been "latterly good".

While out of work and living in London, Thomas wrote to Captain Sir Edward Walter, regarding his plight. Captain Walter had recently created the Corps of Commissioners as a means of providing ex-servicemen with employment. Thomas was employed with the Corps on 12th March 1859 and set to work with Messrs Hunt and Roskell, silversmiths and jewellers to Queen Victoria, becoming one of the original eight Corps employees.

Thomas was presented with his Victoria Cross medal by Queen Victoria at an investiture held at Buckingham Palace on 8th June 1859.

Thomas remained employed by the Corps of Commissioners until he was discharged on 14th November 1865.

Little is known of his life after leaving the Corps until his death on 12th March 1871, while he was living in the workhouse at Kensington. At the age of 47, Thomas died after a long and painful illness, with death due to excess fluid in the body as a result of either a kidney or congestive heart failure.

He was buried in an unmarked grave in Brompton Cemetery on 20th March 1871.

Thomas's Victoria Cross medal is held as part of a private collection.

Figure 106a. Grave of Thomas Hancock

John Purcell
19th June 1857 (VC No. 129)

Gazetted: 15th January 1858 22083/178

Rank and Unit: Private – 9th Lancers

Citation

The guns, I am happy to say, were saved, but a wagon of Major Scott's battery was blown up. I must not fail to mention the excellent conduct of a Sowar of the 4th Irregular Cavalry, and two men of the 9th Lancers, Privates Thomas Hancock and John Purcell, who, when my horse was shot down, remained by me throughout. One of these men and the Sowar offered me their horses, and I was dragged out by the Sowar's horse. Private Hancock was severely wounded, and Private Purcell's horse was killed under him. The Sowar's name is Roopur Khan. **(Extract of a letter from Brigadier J. H. Grant, C.B., Commanding Cavalry Brigade of the Field Force, to the Deputy Assistant-Adjutant – General of Division. Dated Camp, Delhi, June 22, 1857.)**

Biography

Unfortunately very little is known regarding the life of John, who was born some time during 1814 at Kilcommon, Oughterard in Co Galway, Ireland.

John first comes onto the public radar during the Mutiny in India, where he took part in the siege and relief of Lucknow as well as the siege of Delhi, where on 19th June 1857 he performed the deeds for which he was later awarded the Victoria Cross.

In addition to the letter, which was used as the basis for the Victoria Cross citation, Brigadier-General Hope wrote another letter to the Assistant Adjutant-General of the Army, Major H. W. Norman on 10th January 1858 in which he extols the virtues of John; "*I had the sincere gratification of naming two privates of the 9th Lancers, who had displayed signal gallantry in the fight—Privates Thomas Hancock, who lost an arm on the occasion, and John Purcell, who had his horse shot under him, and was, I regret to say, afterwards killed at the assault of Delhi. Sir Henry Barnard was pleased to recommend that the Victoria Cross should be conferred on both.*"

Unfortunately, john would never be presented with his Victoria Cross medal as he was killed in action at Delhi on 19th September 1857, less than three months after his award winning action.

His Victoria Cross medal was sent by registered post to the Commanding Officer of the 9th Lancers and was later delivered to John's brother James.

For his service during the mutiny John was awarded the Indian Mutiny medal with clasps for Lucknow, Relief of Lucknow and Delhi.

John was buried in an unmarked grave in the Old Military Cemetery in Delhi.

The location of his Victoria Cross medal is unknown.

Samuel Turner
19th June 1857 (VC No. 130)

Gazetted: 20th January 1860 22347/179

Rank and Unit: Private – 1st Battalion, 60th Rifles

Citation

For having, at Delhi, on the night of the 19th of June, 1857, during a severe conflict with the Enemy, who attacked the rear of the Camp, carried off on his shoulders, under a heavy fire, a mortally wounded Officer, Lieutenant Humphreys, of the Indian Service. During this service, Private Turner was wounded by a sabre cut in the right arm. His gallant conduct saved the above named Officer from the fate of others, whose mangled remains were not recovered until the following day.

Biography

Samuel was born during February 1826 at Witnesham, near Ipswich in Suffolk.

Unfortunately very little is known of Samuel's life story, it is possible that he joined the 1st Battalion of the 60th rifles (either in 1843 when they were stationed in Manchester or in 1844 when stationed in Ireland) when he was about 18 years of age.

However, the 1st Battalion was involved in the 1st and 2nd Sikh wars which took place between 1845–46 and 1848–49 and as Samuel has no campaign medals it is probable that he joined his regiment some time in 1850, when they were stationed in India.

Figure 108a. Grave of Samuel Turner

It was on 19th June 1857 during the siege of Delhi that Samuel performed the deeds for which he would later be awarded the Victoria Cross medal. For his service during the mutiny, Samuel was awarded the Indian Mutiny medal with clasp for Delhi. Samuel was presented with his Victoria Cross medal at an investiture held in December 1860 at Simla on the North West Frontier in India. It is likely that Samuel left the army soon after receiving his Victoria Cross medal, there is some evidence that he worked as an hotelier and farrier in Simla.

Samuel died on 13th June 1868, aged 42, at Meerut near to Delhi and was buried in St John's Cemetery in Meerut.

The location of his Victoria Cross medal is unknown.

Stephen Garvin
23rd June 1857 (VC No. 131)

Gazetted: 20th January 1860 22347/178

Rank and Unit: Colour Sergeant – 1st Battalion, 60th Rifles

Citation
For daring and gallant conduct before Delhi on the 23rd of June, 1857, in volunteering to lead a small party of men, under a heavy fire, to the "Sammy House," for the purpose of dislodging a number of the Enemy in position there, who kept up a destructive fire on the advanced battery of heavy guns, in which, after a sharp contest, he succeeded. Also recommended for gallant conduct throughout the operations before Delhi.

Biography
Stephen was born on 2nd February 1826 at Cashel in Co Tipperary, Ireland to parents James and Francis (née Ryan).

Stephen began his career in the army at the tender age of 16, enlisting with the 64th Regiment on 6th July 1842. Probably sometime in 1846, Stephen transferred to the 60th Rifles and began a lengthy deployment to India.

With his new regiment, Stephen saw service in the Punjab Campaign from 1848–49 and was awarded the Punjab Medal with clasps for Mooltan and Goojerat. Stephen served throughout the Indian Mutiny and it was during the siege of Delhi that he performed the deeds for which he was later awarded the Victoria

Figure 109. Stephen Garvin

Cross. For his service during the siege of Delhi, Stephen was also awarded the Distinguished Conduct Medal.

While stationed in India, Stephen was married for the first of four occasions and despite his death at the relatively early age of 48 he would outlive all of his wives and one of his two daughters.

For his service during the mutiny Stephen was awarded the Indian Mutiny medal with clasp for Delhi and for his service in India was awarded the India General Service medal with clasp for North West Frontier.

In 1860, Stephen returned with the regiment to England where he was to take up garrison duties at Dover castle.

Stephen was presented with his Victoria Cross medal on 9th November 1860 by Queen Victoria at an investiture held at Windsor Castle.

At some time after 1861, Stephen was promoted to the rank of Regimental Sergeant-Major and was transferred to the 64th Regiment and after 23 years of service, retired from the army during 1865.

In recognition of his extensive and productive army career, Stephen was awarded the Army Long Service and Good Conduct medal.

Stephen died at home in Chesterton on 23rd November 1874, aged 48, and was buried in Chesterton Parish Churchyard. His Victoria Cross medal is privately held.

Figure 109a. Grave of Stephen Garvin

John McGovern[121]
23rd June 1857 (VC No. 132)

Gazetted: 21st June 1859 22278/2420

Rank and Unit: Private No.95 – 1st Bengal Fusiliers

Citation

For gallant conduct during the operations before Delhi, but more especially on the 23rd of June, 1857, when he carried into camp a wounded comrade under a very heavy fire from the enemy's battery, at the risk of his own life.

Biography

John was born on 16th May 1825 in the parish of Templeport in Tullyhaw, Co Cavan, Ireland.

At the age of 20, John left his work as a labourer and travelled to Limerick where on 18th November 1845, he enlisted for an initial period of ten years service in the army of the Honourable East India Company. Soon afterwards, John set sail for India on board the troopship *Cressy* where he arrived on 11th September 1846 and was posted as a private in the 1st Bengal Fusiliers. John was first involved in active service during the second Burmese War from 1852–53 and for this service was awarded the Burma War medal with clasp for Pegu.

John's service was not without problems, on several occasions he was punished for drunkenness and fighting with his comrades.

John served throughout the Indian Mutiny and it was during the siege of Delhi, on 23rd June 1857 that he performed the deeds for which he would later be awarded the Victoria Cross. John was also involved in the siege at Lucknow and on 16th December 1857 saw action at the Battle of Narnoul. It was during this battle that John performed another glorious deed – three mutineers had taken refuge in a small turret and their sniping was causing much difficulty when John volunteered to dislodge them, which he did successfully, killing all three men. For his service during the mutiny, John was awarded the Indian Mutiny medal with clasps for Delhi and Lucknow.

On 10th July 1860, John was presented with his Victoria Cross medal at a special parade held in India, with receipt of the medal John became a changed man and acted as an ideal soldier as he did not wish to bring any disgrace to the Victoria Cross.

In 1861, after the British Government disbanded the Honourable East India Company army, the 1st Bengal Fusiliers were

---

121 In official papers various spellings are used for his surname; McGaurun, M'Gaurun, M'Guarun appear in the Regimental Role and the Army List – he was also sometimes known as McGowan.

Figure 110. John McGovern

On 22nd November 1888, at the age of 63, John died from pneumonia at his home on Ferrie Street in Hamilton and was buried in the Holy Sepulchre Cemetery.

John's Victoria Cross medal is held by the National Army Museum at Chelsea and although not currently on public display can be viewed by appointment.

incorporated into the British Army as part of the 101st Fusiliers. Some of the new regiment left India, however, due to a badly wounded arm, John decided to remain in India rather than join the line regiment. In 1862, after 17 years of service, John was discharged from the army as one of his arms was practically useless due to the wounds it had received.

After leaving the army, John briefly returned to Ireland where he was married to Rosanna, the couple would go on to have eight children, four sons and four daughters.

In 1863, John immigrated to Canada where he took up residence in Hamilton, Ontario and worked at various times as a dockworker, clerk, messenger and peddler.

Figure 110a. Grave of John McGovern

William George Cubitt
30th June 1857 (VC No. 133)

Gazetted: 21st June 1859 22278/2420

Rank and Unit: Lieutenant – 13th Bengal Native Infantry

Citation

For having on the retreat from Chinhut, on the 30th of June, 1857, saved the lives of three men of the 32nd Regiment, at the risk of his own.

Figure III. William George Cubitt

Biography

William was born at Fort William in Calcutta on 19th October 1835, the only son of parents William who was a Major with the Honourable East India Company and Harriet (née Harcourt).

Little is known of William's early years, other than that he was educated privately at Laleham School on the Thames near London.

In 1853, on or around the date of his 18th Birthday, William followed in his father's footsteps when he enlisted as a Lieutenant with the Honourable East India Company and was placed with the 13th Native Infantry. During 1855 to 1856, William saw action in the Santhal Campaign which took place in the northern province of Bihar. William also served throughout the Indian Mutiny, being involved in plenty of action around Lucknow where on 30th June 1857, during the retreat from Chinhut; he performed the deeds for which he would later be awarded the Victoria Cross. William was also heavily involved in the defence of Lucknow and on 12th November 1857 was mentioned in despatches[122] by Brigadier J. Inglis the commander of the Lucknow garrison. During the defence of Lucknow, between 25th September and 10th November, William was wounded on two occasions.[123] On 21st October 1857, William was again mentioned in despatches by Lieutenant B. M. M. Aitken.[124]

For his service during the mutiny, William was awarded the Indian Mutiny medal with clasp for defence of Lucknow.

William was presented with his Victoria Cross medal by Queen Victoria at an investiture held at Windsor Castle on 4th January 1860.

On 19th May 1863, William was married to Charlotte Isabella (née Hills) at Fort William church in Calcutta.[125] Charlotte was the sister of General Sir James Hills-Johnes who was

also a recipient of the Victoria Cross[126] who was awarded his VC for deeds during the siege of Delhi only a few weeks after William. The couple would go on to have six children: William Martin born on 13th July 1864 at Dinapore, James Edward born on 6th October 1865 also at Dinapore, Ethel Mary born on 25th June 1868 at Benares, Louis Hills Court born on 20th September 1872 at Dana and Nellie born on 6th September 1874 at Calcutta.

In a memorandum from the India Office dated 1st March 1864, following the dissolution of the Honourable East India Company's army, William was appointed as a Lieutenant in the British Army with effect from 23rd November 1857.[127] A later memorandum from the India Office dated 28th June 1865, noted that William had been assigned to the Bengal Staff Corps also effective from 23rd November 1857.[128] On 26th July 1865, William was given a brevet promotion to the rank of Captain;[129] this would be made substantive on 16th July 1866.[130] William was promoted to the rank of Major on 26th July 1873.[131]

From 1874 to 1875 William was involved with the Dufla Expedition, which as part of the Trans Himalayan Survey was mapping the Dufla Hills on the North-East frontier; for his activities he was mentioned in despatches.

From 1878 to 1880, William saw action in the second Anglo-Afghan War and on 26th July 1879 was promoted to the rank of Lieutenant-Colonel.[132] For his service William was awarded the Afghanistan medal with clasp for Ali Musjid.

---

122 *London Gazette* – 22098/819
123 *London Gazette* – 22098/820
124 *London Gazette* – 22098/827
125 *Times* 24th July 1863

126 William was also uncle to another VC recipient, Lewis Pugh Evans who was so honoured for deeds in the Great War.
127 *London Gazette* – 22828/1352
128 *London Gazette* – 22985/3295
129 *London Gazette* – 23045/6400
130 *London Gazette* – 23192/6649
131 *London Gazette* – 24039/5505
132 *London Gazette* – 24780/6317

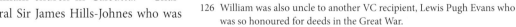

On 26th July 1883, William was promoted to the rank of Colonel[133] and joined another survey expedition, under the command of Sir Rowley Sale Sale-Hill, to the Akka on the north east frontier, which ended in 1885.

From 1886 until 1887, William saw action in the third Anglo-Burmese War where he commanded the 43rd Goorkha Light Infantry and received two mentions in despatches.[134] For his service in the war William was awarded the India General Service medal with clasp for Burma 1855–7 and on 25th November 1887 his service was further recognised when he was appointed as a Companion of the Distinguished Service Order to be effective from 1st July 1887.[135]

William retired from the army in1891 after 38 years of service and at some stage he returned to England to live out his remaining days.

William died at home at Eastfield in North Yorkshire on 25th January 1903, aged 67 and was buried on 28th January at St Peter's Churchyard, Frimley in Surrey.

William's Victoria Cross medal is in private hands.

Figure 111a. Grave of William George Cubitt

133 *London Gazette* – 25272/4675
134 *London Gazette* – 25735/4759 and 25735/4762
135 *London Gazette* – 25761/6374

William Oxenham
30th June 1857 (VC No. 134)

Gazetted: 21st November 1859 22328/4193

Rank and Unit: Corporal – 32nd Regiment of Foot

Citation

For distinguished gallantry in saving the life of Mr. Capper, of the Bengal Civil Service, by extricating him from the ruins of a Veranda which had fallen on him, Corporal Oxenham being for ten minutes exposed to a heavy fire, while doing so.

Biography

William was born on 15th October 1821 at St Peters, Tiverton in Devon to parents John and Charlotte (née Sharland). He was the second child and first son, having an older sister Mary Ann born in 1819 and two younger brothers, Ephraim born in1824 and James born in 1828.

Little is known of William's early life, however, it is thought that he began his life in the army sometime around 1841[136] when he enlisted in the 32nd Regiment of Foot.

Prior to joining the army, William was married to Hannah (née Harris) in the parish church at Tiverton, on 13th March 1841 and on the marriage certificate William gave his employment as Labourer. The couple would have a daughter, Charlotte born in 1842, however, by 1851 the couple had separated. Initially

Figure 112. William Oxenham

136 It is likely that William enlisted some time after 17th February 1841, when the regiment returned to England after a posting in Canada.

the regiment, which on its return from Canada was garrisoned at Portsmouth, spent time on United Kingdom duties being based in Leeds until 1844 and then Manchester until 1845 at which time the regiment moved to Ireland. In Ireland the regiment was based in Dublin, Mullingar and then Athlone, however, on 19th March 1846 they received orders to proceed to Fermoy where they were to make preparations for deployment to India.

On 29th May 1846, the regiment was embarked upon the transports: *British Sovereign, Duchess of Northumberland, Edinburgh, General Palmer* and *Abourkir* and set sail for India where they landed at Calcutta in early September 1846.

Initially intended to be stationed at Agra, the regiment proceeded by river from Calcutta to Chinsurah, however, this was changed to Meerut so they proceeded to Benares which they reach on 1st January 1847 and arrived at Meerut on 19th February where they were to be stationed until 14th February 1848. As the first Anglo-Sikh war had ended before their arrival, these first two years in India would have been relatively quiet, however, following the assassination of two British Commissioners on 20th April 1848, who were on a mission to the Multan district, things were soon to change. This incident would spark off the second Anglo-Sikh war and on receiving news of the event the 32nd was placed on alert and moved to Ferozepur where they arrived on 27th May 1848.

On 10th August 1848, the regiment was assigned to the Multan Field force and as part of this force was involved throughout the second Anglo-Sikh war being involved in the siege of Multan and the Battle of Gujarat. For his involvement in these hostilities, William was awarded the Punjab Medal with clasps for Mooltan and Goojerat.

Following the end of hostilities the regiment was stationed at Jullundur where they would remain until the end of 1851, at which time they moved to Peshawar where they arrived on 8th January 1852. On 11th November 1853, William was promoted to the rank of Corporal and shortly afterwards in December 1853 / January 1854 the regiment was moved to Kussowlie where they were to remain until March 1855 when they were sent to relieve the 52nd Regiment of Foot at Lucknow. For his service in Peshawar and Kussowlie, William was awarded the India General Service Medal with clasp for North West Frontier.

The regiment were still forming the garrison at Lucknow at the onset of the Mutiny and it was here on 30th June 1857 that William performed the deeds for which he was later awarded the Victoria Cross. A few weeks later, William received a serious wound to his forearm while defending the city against the mutineers. Following the evacuation of Lucknow, the regiment proceeded to Cawnpore where they arrived on 30th November 1857 and remained there until their transfer to Allahabad

in April 1858. In July 1858, the regiment joined the field force commanded by Brigadier Berkely for operations in the Oudh province and then returned to Allahabad on 27th January 1859. In early February 1859, the regiment began the slow process of preparing to leave India when they travelled by train to Chinsurah, from where on 24th April they set sail for England on board the troopship *Albuhera*, arriving at Portsmouth on 26th August 1859. On 6th August 1859, just prior to arriving back in England, William was promoted to the rank of Sergeant. For his service during the Mutiny, William was awarded the Indian Mutiny medal with clasp for Defence of Lucknow.

The day after arriving at Portsmouth, the regiment was transferred by train to Dover where they were to perform garrison duties until 6th August 1860.

On 4th January 1860, William was presented with his Victoria Cross medal by Queen Victoria at an investiture held at Windsor Castle.

Only a few weeks after receiving his medal, William was married to Caroline (née Pullman) on 13th February 1860 at the Parish Church in St. Edmunds, Exeter.[137]

After leaving Dover, the regiment served at Aldershot until 21st August 1861, Plymouth until 22nd August 1862 and Raglan Barracks Devonport until April 1863 when they began a deployment in Ireland. It is not known when William left the army, however, he was awarded the Long Service and Good Conduct medal which at the time required a service of 21 years, it is safe to assume that he was discharged some time in 1862 or early 1863 before the deployment to Ireland.

William died from Meningitis on 29th December 1875, while living in St Sidwell's Parish, Exeter and on 3rd January 1876 was buried in the Dissenters section of Higher Cemetery, in Exeter.

William's Victoria Cross medal is on public display at the Duke of Cornwall Museum, Bodmin, Cornwall.

Figure II2a. Grave of William Oxenham

---

137 As no record can be found of a divorce with his first wife it is possible that this marriage was bigamous.

Robert Hope Moncrieff Aitken
30th June 1857 (VC No. 135)

Gazetted: 17th April 1863 22727/2070

Rank and Unit: Lieutenant – 13th Bengal Native Infantry

Citation

For various acts of gallantry performed during the defence of the Residency of Lucknow, from the 30th of June to the 22nd of November, 1857.

1. On three different occasions, Lieutenant Aitken went into the garden under the enemy's loopholes in the "Captain's Bazaar." On two of these occasions, he brought out a number of bullocks which had been left in the garden; subsequently, on the 3rd of July, the enemy having set fire to the Bhoosa Stock in the garden, and it being apprehended that the fire would reach the Powder Magazine which had been left there, Lieutenant Aitken, accompanied by other Officers, went into the garden, and cut down all the tents which might have communicated the fire to the powder. This was done, close to the enemy's, loopholes, under a bright light from the flames. It was a most dangerous service.

2. On the night of the 20th of August, the Enemy, having set fire to the Bailey Guard Gate, Lieutenant Aitken was the first man in the gateway, and, assisted by some sepoys and a water-carrier of his Regiment, he partially opened the gate under a heavy, fire of musketry, and, having removed the burning wood and straw, saved the gate.

3. On the evening of the 25th of September, this Officer led on twelve sepoys of his Regiment, for the purpose of attacking two guns opposite the gate referred to, in order to prevent their being turned-on the late Major-General Havelock's second column. Having captured them, he attacked and took the Teree Kotee, with a small force.

4. On the morning of the 26th of September, with a small party of his Regiment, he assaulted and captured the barricaded gateway of the Furreed Buksh Palace, and the Palace itself. On this occasion, he sprang up against a small wicket gate on the right and prevented the enemy from shutting it until, with assistance, it was forced open, and the assaulting party were thus enabled to rush in. The complete success of the attack was solely owing to this Officer's distinguished bravery.

Figure 113. Robert Hope Moncrieff Aitken

5. In a subsequent sortie on the 29th of September, Lieutenant Aitken volunteered to take a gun which still continued firing, taking with him four soldiers through the houses and lanes to the gun. The enemy fired on this party from the houses, but they held their ground, until a "stronger party coming up, the gun was upset from its carriage, and taken into the Residency. Another gun was subsequently taken.

Biography

Robert was born on 6th February 1826 at Cupar in Fife, Scotland. The seventh child and fifth son of John Aitken. Robert had eight brothers: George, Andrew, John Christie, Charles, Alexander, Frank and James Lumsden, he also had two sisters, Margaret Jane and Janet Pouton.

Little is known of his early life, until on 2nd September 1847, Robert at the age of 21 was commissioned as an ensign in the Bengal Army, less than a year later, on 14th July 1848, he transferred to the 13th Bengal Native Infantry. With his new regiment, Robert took part in the Punjab Campaign (2nd Anglo/Sikh War) and was present at the Battle of Ramnugger on 22nd November 1848. Robert also took part in the Battle of Gujrat on 22nd February 1849 and was with the column commanded by Major General Sir Walter Gilbert which pursued the defeated Sikh and Afghan Armies. For his involvement in these actions Robert was awarded the Punjab Medal with clasp for Goojerat.

On 15th November 1853, Robert was promoted to the rank of Lieutenant.

During 1855 and early 1856, Robert was involved in putting down the Santhal rebellion. This was a rebellion in eastern India by the Santhal people (led by four brothers: Sindhu, Kanhu, Chand and Bhairav Murmu) against the British administration and the corrupt zamindari caste system. Major skirmishes took place between July 1855 and January 1856 and Robert, together with Lieutenant Loughman, was personally responsible for the capture of Koulea,[138] a Santhal chief.

Robert saw action at Chinhut, during the first few days of the Mutiny, however it is his conduct during the defence of the residency at Lucknow from 30th June to 22nd November 1857 that resulted in his being awarded the Victoria Cross – his citation mentions five separated deeds. His actions during the defence of Lucknow resulted in at least six mentions in despatches. Following the retreat from the residency, Robert was moved to Cawnpore and on 6th December was involved in the battle for Cawnpore. During the later days of the mutiny, in the Oude Campaign, Robert served as a member of the Oude Military Police and again received many mentions in despatches. For his service during the mutiny, Robert was awarded the Indian Mutiny Medal with clasp for Defence of Lucknow.

On 18th February 1861, Robert was promoted to the rank of Captain and the next day received a brevet promotion to the rank of Major.[139] On 1st January 1862, following the disbanding of the Honourable East India Company Army, Robert was transferred to the British Army, where he retained his rank of Captain in the Bengal Staff Corps. On 1st April 1863, Robert was appointed to the position of Inspector General of the Oude Police, a position that he was to hold for 13 years until his retirement in 1876.

During May 1865, Robert was presented with his Victoria Cross medal[140] by General Sir Hugh Rose, Commander in Chief of British forces in India. The presentation was unusual in that it took place almost on the exact spot where the deeds resulting in the award were performed – the Residency at Lucknow.

From 31st January 1865, Robert was a shareholder in the Elgin Cotton Spinning and Weaving Company Limited, Cawnpore.

On 2nd September 1867, Robert's brevet rank of Major was made substantive[141] and on 1st August 1869 was given a brevet promotion to the rank of Lieutenant-Colonel.[142]

In April 1871, Robert was recommended for the award of Companion of the Most Honourable Order of the Bath (CB) by Lord Napier GCB, Commander-in-Chief of the Indian army and Lord Mayo GCB, Governor General of India, however, no evidence exists to support the actual award of this honour to Robert.[143]

On 25th September 1873, Robert's brevet promotion of Lieutenant-Colonel was made substantive.[144]

Robert retired from the army with full pay on 25th April 1876 and on 12th August 1876 was promoted to the honorary rank of Colonel.[145]

At some stage, probably after his retirement and return to Scotland, Robert was married to Mary (née Anderson) and the couple had a daughter Ida.

On 18th September 1887, at the age of 61, Robert died at his home in Pilmour Cottage, St Andrews and was buried in the Old Cemetery, St Andrews.

His Victoria Cross medal is on public display at the National Army Museum in Chelsea.

Robert was the uncle of Lieutenant R. J. T. Digby-Jones who was awarded the Victoria Cross for deeds during the Boer War.

Figure 113a.
Grave of Robert
Hope Moncrieff
Aitken

---

138 Although the chief had a price of R 5,000 on his head, as a serving soldier Robert was unable to claim the reward.

139 *London Gazette* – 22697/121

140 Robert was not actually given his medal on this day, as at the time of the presentation it could not be found as it had been left behind at Simla. Instead, Robert was presented with a borrowed Companion of the Bath medal. As the medal in Simla could not be found, a duplicate was prepared and subsequently given to Robert. The original medal eventually turned up at an auction in 1900, where the widow of Major Judge of the 2nd Gurkha regiment was trying to sell it. Apparently her husband had purchased the medal in Simla some time during 1874 for £35-10s. However, as the medal had never been presented, it remained the property of the Crown and instead of being sold was returned to the War Office.

141 *London Gazette* – 23360/1588

142 *London Gazette* – 23582/594

143 No record of the award was posted in the *London Gazette*. His obituary in *The Times* (dated 22nd September 1887 makes no mention of the award of a CB, despite mentioning the award of the VC and his minor medals.

144 *London Gazette* – 24045/5938

145 *London Gazette* – 24353/4482

James Colthurst Travers
1st July 1857 (VC No. 136)

Gazetted: 1st March 1861 22485/1007

Rank and Unit: Colonel– 2nd Battalion, Bengal Native Infantry

Citation

For a daring act of bravery, in July, 1857, when the Indore Presidency was suddenly attacked by Holkar's Troops, in having charged the guns with only five men to support him, and driven the Gunners from the guns, thereby creating a favourable diversion, which saved the lives of many persons, fugitives to the Residency. It is stated that Officers who were present considered that the effect of the charge was to enable many Europeans to escape from actual slaughter, and time was gained which enabled the faithful Bhopal Artillery to man their guns. Colonel Travers's horse was shot in three places, and his accoutrements were shot through in various parts. He commanded the Bhopal Levy.

Biography

James was born on 6th October 1820 at the family home, Dyke House in Cork the third son of father Major-General Sir Robert Travers KCMG, CB of the 10th Regiment of Foot and mother Harriet Letitia (née Belford) the daughter of Major William Belford.

James was born into a large Anglo-Irish family with a distinguished Military history. His father was one of six brothers who all served in the military, three of whom (including his father) received knighthoods for their services. James had three older sisters: Harriet Matilda born in 1813, Isabella Eliza born in 1814, Julia Anna born in 1815 and one younger sister, Elizabeth Mary Colthurst born in 1829. James also had two older brothers: Robert William and Thomas Maitland who were both born in 1819 and five younger brothers: Eaton Joseph born 1823, Ernest Augustus Belford born 1824, John Nicholas born 1825, Horace Newman born in 1826 and Henry Fane born in 1828, all of the brothers would serve in the military (three were killed in India).

With this background it is not surprising that James was also destined for a career in the military and after completing his education at the Honourable East India Company Military Academy at Addiscombe in Surrey he was commissioned as a 2nd Lieutenant in the Bengal Infantry on 11th June 1838.

James arrived at Fort William, Calcutta in India, on 12th January 1839 to take up his position and was assigned to the 57th Native Infantry stationed at Barrackpore. After only a few months

Figure 114. James Colthurst Travers

he was transferred to the 2nd Native Infantry station at Ferozepur on 12th April 1839. James had his first active service when he saw action with his regiment during the first Anglo-Afghan war. On 3rd January 1841 he took part in the successful actions near Shakrak where under the command of Captain H. W. Farrington, the forces of Aktar Khan were dispersed. On 7th June 1841, James was promoted to the rank of 1st Lieutenant and following service under Captain John Griffin on 17th August 1841, when a force of 5,000 commanded by Aktar and Akram Khan was defeated at Sikandarabad, he received a mention in despatches. James also took part on 12th January 1842, in an action under the command of Major-General William Nott, when a force of 15,000 men commanded by Atta Muhammad and Suftar Jang were defeated near Kandahar. On 23rd February 1842, James was transferred to the 1st Irregular Cavalry (Skinner's Horse) where under the command of Captain Haldane he saw action at Tarnak, Argand-ab and Babawalli where n 25th March he was slightly wounded. On the march to Ghazni, James was involved in cavalry engagements on 28th August at Mukur and Ghoain on 30th August for which he again received a mention in despatches. James took part in the capture of Ghazni on 6th September and on the march to Kabul was involved in fighting at Beni-badain and Maidan during 14th to 15th September. James arrived at Kabul on 17th September where he remained until 12th October when he left with the united armies of Nott and Pollock for a battle at Haft Kotal which took place on 14th October. James finally arrived back at Ferozepur on 23rd December 1842. For his service in the war, James was awarded the Candahar, Ghuznee, Cabal Medal (1841–42) which was inscribed on the reverse with all three of the campaigns. He was also recommended for a brevet promotion to Major to become effective once he attained the rank of Captain.

In March 1843, James returned to regimental duties and on 15th March he was appointed to the role of Adjutant to the Bhopal Contingent. On 7th January 1846, James was promoted to the rank of Captain and in line with the recommendation made after the First Anglo-Afghan war received a brevet promotion to the rank of Major the next day.

During January, James was assigned to the Sutlej army and took part in the first Anglo-Sikh war (also known as the Sutlej Campaign). In command of a Nasiri battalion of Ghurkhas in the division of Sir Harry Smith, James took part in the Battle of Sobraon on 10th February 1846, for this action he received two mentions in despatches. On 24th March, James was appointed as second in command of the Bhopal Contingent. For his service in the First Anglo-Sikh war, James was awarded the Sutlej Campaign (1845–46) medal[146] which was inscribed on the reverse with Sobraon.

On 19th November 1849, James was married to Mary Isabella (née Macintyre)[147] the daughter of Donald Macintyre a merchant with a business in Calcutta.

James was appointed to the role of Postmaster at Sehore on13th February 1850 and on 20th June 1854 received a brevet promotion to the rank of Lieutenant-Colonel.[148] On 22nd August 1855, James was appointed as officiating commandant of the Bhopal Contingent and give full command on 15th February 1856. During 1856, James commanded the Bhopal Contingent in the field in operations against the forces of Sankar Sing, for this service he received the thanks of the Indian Government. On 6th December 1856, James was promoted to the rank of Colonel.[149]

Following the outbreak of the Mutiny, James was moved from Bhopal to Indur, in the middle of June to assume command of the forces where Colonel Henry Marion Durand was the resident. It was on the 1st July 1857, after some of the local Holkar troops mutinied and massacred occupants of the Residency, that James performed the deeds for which he would later be awarded the Victoria Cross, for this action James also received a mention in despatches. Although the troops under James's command did not mutiny they would not engage with the rebels so James was left with no alternative but to abandon the residency and move to Sehore where they arrived on 4th July. In addition to the Victoria Cross, James was awarded the Indian Mutiny Medal for his service during the mutiny.

In 1858, after the mutiny, James returned to his old regiment the 2nd Bengal Infantry where he was Political Agent with command of cavalry for Western Malwa, however, on 8th September 1860 he was appointed as the commandant of the Central India Horse and was Political Assistant to the Agent Governor-General of Central India. James's career in the army continued to advance and on 25th October 1861 he was appointed as Brigadier-General in command of the Sangor district.

James was finally presented with his Victoria Cross medal by General Sir Hugh Rose, Commander In Chief of the forces in India, on 3rd June 1862, at a ceremony in Gwalior.

On 23rd July 1865, James received a brevet promotion to the rank of Major-General[150] and the same year received a good conduct pension. James was appointed to the command of the Meerut division in Bengal on 5th August 1869, a position that he was to hold until the end of 1873. On 5th February 1873, James received a brevet promotion to the rank of Lieutenant-General[151] and a few weeks later on 24th May was appointed as an Ordinary Member 3rd Class (Companion) of the Military Division of the Most Honourable Order of the Bath.[152] On 1st January 1874, after having received a substantive promotion to the rank of Colonel,[153] James was appointed to a position in the Bengal Staff Corps and on 3rd July 1874 was permitted to reside outside of India.

In 1876, James wrote and had published a book "The Evacuation of Indore" to give his account of events and to refute certain statements contained within J. W. Kaye's book "History of the Sepoy War".

Figure II4a. Grave of James Colthurst Travers

---

146 This was the first medal to use clasps to denote participation in multiple battles. The first battle was inscribed on the reverse of the medal and subsequent battles were commemorated by the award of a clasp to clip on the medal ribbon.

147 General Donald Macintyre, Mary's brother was awarded a Victoria Cross for deeds performed on 4th January 1872 during the Looshai Campaign in North East India.

148 *London Gazette* – 21853/698

149 *London Gazette*- 22828/1347 – In a memo dated 1st March 1864, from the India Office, James was transferred to the British Army with the rank of Colonel effective 6th December 1856. This was following the dissolution of the East India Company armies.

150 *London Gazette* – 23016/4543

151 *London Gazette* – 23962/1714

152 *London Gazette* – 23979/2583

153 *London Gazette* – 24078/1772

On 1st October 1877, James received a brevet promotion to the rank of General.[154]

James retired from army life after 43 years service, when on 1st July 1881 he was placed on the Unemployed Supernumerary List.[155]

James died on 1st April 1884 at Pallanza, Lake Maggiore in Italy aged 62 and was buried in the old cemetery at Pallanza.

The whereabouts of James's Victoria Cross medal is unknown, believed to be held in a private collection.

---

154 *London Gazette* – 24552/750
155 *London Gazette* – 25049/6215 (Initial announcement under incorrect name James Fraser). Correction 25049/6711

William Dowling
4th July 1857 (VC No. 137)

Gazetted: 21st November 1859 22328/4193

Rank and Unit: Private – 32nd Regiment of Foot

Citation

For distinguished gallantry on the 4th of July, 1857, in going out with two other men, since dead, and spiking two of the Enemy's guns. He killed a Soubadar of the Enemy by one of the guns.

Also, for distinguished gallantry on the 9th of the same month, in going out again with three men, since dead, to spike one of the Enemy's guns. He had to retire, the spike being too small, but was exposed to the same danger.

Also, for distinguished bravery, on the 27th of September, 1857, in spiking an 18-pounder gun during a Sortie, he being at the same time under a most heavy fire from the Enemy.

Biography

William was born some time during 1825 at Thomastown in County Kilkenny, Ireland. Like many of his brave Irish compatriots who served with distinction in the British army, very little is known of his life story.

It is thought that William enlisted in the British army, with the 32nd Regiment of Foot, sometime during 1845. This is probably correct as the 32nd, after their tour of Canada and after spending some time in England at Leeds and Manchester, moved to Ireland in 1845, where they were based at Dublin, Mullingar and then Athlone. After spending time in Athlone, the regiment moved to Fermoy on 19th March 1846, where they prepared for deployment to India.

On 29th May 1846, the regiment was embarked upon the transports: *British Sovereign, Duchess of Northumberland, Edinburgh, General Palmer* and *Abourkir* and set sail for India where they landed at Calcutta in early September 1846. Initially intended to be stationed at Agra, the regiment proceeded by river from Calcutta to Chinsurah, however, this was changed to Meerut so they proceeded to Benares which they reach on 1st January 1847 and arrived at Meerut on 19th February where they were to be stationed until 14th February 1848. As the first Anglo-Sikh war had ended before their arrival, these first two years in India would have been relatively quiet, however, following the assassination of two British Commissioners on 20th April 1848, who were on a mission to the Mooltan district, things were soon to change.

This incident would spark off the second Anglo-Sikh war and on receiving news of the event the 32nd was placed on alert and moved to Ferozepur where they arrived on 27th May 1848.

On 10th August 1848, the regiment was assigned to the Mooltan Field force and as part of this force was involved throughout the second Anglo-Sikh war being involved in the siege of Mooltan and the battle of Goojerat. There is no record of William receiving the Punjab medal for these actions so was probably part of the force which was not involved. Following the end of hostilities the regiment was stationed at Jullundur where they would remain until the end of 1851, at which time they moved to Peshawar where they arrived on 8th January 1852. In December 1853 / January 1854 the regiment was moved to Kussowlie where they were to remain until March 1855 when they were sent to relieve the 52nd Regiment of Foot at Lucknow.

It was during the defence of Lucknow, on 4th July 1857, that William performed the deeds for which he would later be awarded the Victoria Cross.

For his service during the Mutiny, William was awarded the Indian Mutiny medal with clasp for Defence of Lucknow. In early February 1859, the regiment began the slow process of preparing to leave India when the travelled by train to Chinsurah from where on 24th April they set sail for England on board the troopship *Albuhera* arriving at Portsmouth on 26th August 1859. The day after arriving at Portsmouth, the regiment was transferred by train to Dover where they were to perform garrison duties until 6th August 1860.

On 4th January 1860, William was presented with his Victoria Cross medal by Queen Victoria at an investiture held at Windsor Castle.

After leaving Dover, the regiment served at Aldershot until 21st August 1861, Plymouth until 22nd August 1862 and Raglan Barracks Devonport until April 1863 when they began a deployment in Ireland.

At some stage, probably after his deployment to Ireland, William was married to Maria (née Colgan) and the couple would go on to have two children: Joseph Francis born in Dublin on 16th December 1863 and Maria, also born in Ireland, sometime around 1866.

At some stage William left the army and moved to Liverpool where he was employed as a Customs Officer, in 1881 he is recorded to be living at 2 Rokeby St., Everton where he was living with his wife and children.

William died from Bronchitis at Stanley Hospital, Liverpool on 17th February 1887, aged 63 and was buried in an unmarked grave in the Ford Roman Catholic Cemetery in Liverpool.

William's Victoria Cross medal is on public display at the Duke of Cornwall's Light Infantry Museum, Bodmin.

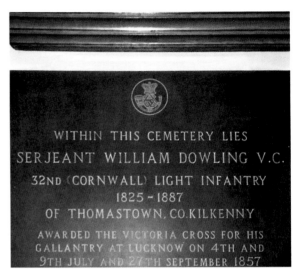

Figure 115a. Grave of William Dowling

William Connolly
7th July 1857 (VC No. 138)

Gazetted: 3rd September 1858 22179/4014

Rank and Unit: Gunner – Bengal Horse Artillery

Citation

This Soldier is recommended for the Victoria Cross for his gallantry in Action with the Enemy, at Jhelum, on the 7th of July, 1857. Lieutenant Cookes, Bengal Horse Artillery, reports "that about daybreak on that day, I advanced my half Troop at a gallop, and engaged the Enemy within easy musket range. The Sponge-man of one of my Guns having been shot during the advance, Gunner Connolly assumed the duties of 2nd Sponge-man, and he had barely assisted in two discharges of his Gun, when a musket ball, through the left thigh, felled him to the ground; nothing daunted by pain and loss of blood, he was endeavouring to resume his post, when I ordered a movement in retirement, and though severely wounded, he was mounted on his horse in the Gun-team, and rode to the next position which the Guns took up, and manfully declined going to the rear when the necessity of his so doing was represented to him. About eleven o'clock, A.M., when the Guns were still in Action, the same Gunner, whilst sponging, was again knocked down by a musket-ball striking him on the hip, thereby causing great faintness and partial unconsciousness, for the pain appeared excessive, and the blood flowed fast. On seeing this, I gave directions for his removal out of Action; but this brave man hearing me, staggered to his feet, and said, ' No, Sir, I'll not go there, whilst I can work here,' and shortly afterwards he again resumed his post as Sponge-man. Late in the afternoon of the same day, my three Guns were engaged at one hundred yards from the Walls of a Village with the defenders, viz., the 14th Native Infantry Mutineers, amidst a storm of bullets which did great execution. Gunner Connolly, though suffering severely from his two previous wounds, was wielding his sponge with an energy and courage which attracted the admiration of his comrades, and while cheerfully encouraging a wounded man to hasten in bringing up the ammunition, a musket ball tore through the muscles of his right leg but with the most undaunted bravery he struggled on and not till he had loaded six times, did this man give way, when, through loss of blood, he fell in my arms, and I placed him on a wagon, which shortly afterwards bore him in a state of unconsciousness from the fight".

Biography

William was born in Liverpool during May 1817, unfortunately very little is known of his life story other than the deeds for which he was awarded the Victoria Cross.

As a gunner with the Bengal Horse Artillery, it was on 7th July 1857, that William performed the deeds at Jhelum in the Punjab, for which he was later awarded the Victoria Cross.

William was presented with his Victoria Cross medal during February 1859, while still serving in India.

At some stage, William left the army and returned to England.

He was living at 14 Westminster Road, Kirkdale, Liverpool when on 31st December 1891 he died from bronchitis at the West Derby Hospital in Liverpool aged 74; William was buried in Kirkdale Cemetery in Liverpool in an unmarked grave.

William's Victoria Cross medal is on public display at the British in India Museum, Colne, Lancashire.

Figure 116a. Grave of William Connolly

Samuel Hill Lawrence
7th July 1857 (VC No. 139)

Gazetted: 22nd November 1859 22328/4193

Rank and Unit: Lieutenant – 32nd Regiment of Foot

Citation

For distinguished bravery in a Sortie on the 7th of July, 1857, made, as reported by Major Wilson, late Deputy-Assistant Adjutant-General of the Lucknow Garrison, "for the purpose of examining a house strongly held by the Enemy, in order to discover whether or not a mine was being driven from it." Major Wilson states that he saw the attack, and was an eye-witness to the great personal gallantry of Major Lawrence on the occasion, he being the first person to mount the ladder, and enter the window of the house, in effecting which he had his pistol knocked out of his hand by one of the Enemy:—also, for distinguished gallantry in a Sortie, on the 26th of September, 1857, in charging with two of his men, in advance of his Company, and capturing a 9-pounder gun.

Biography

Samuel was born on 22nd January 1831 at Cork in Ireland. His father, also called Samuel, was an officer in the 32nd Regiment of Foot his mother Margaret (née Macdonald) was of Scottish ancestry. The family were prominent Protestants in Ireland and Samuel Lawrence senior was thought to have been a master of the Orange Lodge in Nenagh in 1825.

Samuel began his army career when, just before his 17th birthday on 12th December 1847, he enlisted as an Ensign with his father's regiment the 32nd Regiment of Foot.[156]

Samuel would have joined his regiment in India at either Meerut or Ferozepur and soon after his arrival was involved in the First Anglo-Sikh War (Punjab Campaign) being involved in the siege and capture of the city and fortress at Mooltan. He was also present at the capture of the fort and garrison at Cheniote as well as the Battle of Goojerat. For his service in this war, Samuel was awarded the Punjab Medal (1848–49) with clasps for Mooltan and Goojerat.

Following the end of hostilities the regiment was stationed at Jullundur where, on 22nd February 1850 Samuel advanced his position in the regiment when he purchased a promotion to Lieutenant.[157] At the end of 1851, the regiment was moved to Peshawar where they arrived on 8th January 1852 and remained

Figure 117. Samuel Hill Lawrence

until December 1853 / January 1854 when they moved to Kussowlie. In March 1855, the regiment were sent to relieve the 52nd Regiment of Foot at Lucknow.

At the time of the Mutiny, Samuel was in command of the Headquarters at the old Fort Macchi Bhawan at Lucknow until it was evacuated on 1st July 1857 and troops were concentrated in the Residency for its defence. It was during the defence of the Residency at Lucknow, on 7th July 1857, that Samuel performed the deeds for which he would later be awarded the Victoria Cross. Samuel remained at the Residency, for most of the time commanding the Redan Battery, until on 24th November 1857 it was relieved by the force of Lord Clyde. On 17th July 1857, Samuel was promoted to the rank of Captain.[158] For his service during the Mutiny, Samuel was awarded the Indian Mutiny medal with clasp for Defence of Lucknow; he was also twice mentioned in despatches and on 24th March 1858 received a brevet promotion to the rank of Major.[159]

On 29th November 1859, Samuel transferred to the 25th Regiment of Foot by way of an exchange with Captain Edward Augustus Thurlow Cunynghame.[160]

Samuel was presented with his Victoria Cross medal by Queen Victoria at an investiture held at Windsor Castle on 4th January 1860.

On 23rd September 1862, Samuel transferred to the 8th Hussars again by way of exchange this time with Captain Peter Charles Gilles Webster.

Samuel finally left India on 13th January 1864 when he set sail on board the *St. Lawrence*; after calling at the Cape of Good Hope on 1st March and St. Helena on 12th March he landed at Portsmouth on 26th April 1864. After landing at Portsmouth, the 8th Hussars proceeded to York, however, soon after their arrival

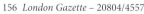

156 *London Gazette* – 20804/4557
157 *London Gazette* – 21070/496

158 *London Gazette* – 22077/4595
159 *London Gazette* – 22117/1571
160 *London Gazette* – 22330/4480

Samuel once again transferred regiments, this time to the 11th Hussars when he exchanged with Captain Horace Montague on 21st June 1864.[161] Following the exchange, Samuel was stationed with his new regiment in Ireland at Dublin where he remained until his retirement from the army on 24th January 1865 after 17 years of service.[162]

Tragically Samuel died on 17th June 1868 aged 37 in Montevideo, Uruguay and was buried in the old British Cemetery in the City, in 1884 his body was reinterred at the British Cemetery on the Avenue General Riviera.

Samuel's Victoria Cross medal is on public display at the Duke of Cornwall's Light Infantry Museum, Bodmin in Cornwall.

He was the cousin of Lieutenant Thomas Cadell VC, who was also awarded his medal for deeds performed during the Mutiny on 12th June 1857.

Henry Tombs
9th July 1857 (VC No. 140)

Gazetted: 24th April 1858 22131/2050

Rank and Unit: Major – Bengal Horse Artillery

Citation
For very gallant conduct on the part of Lieutenant Hills before Delhi, in defending the position assigned to him in case of alarm, and for noble behaviour on the part of Lieutenant-Colonel Tombs in twice coming to his subaltern's rescue, and on each occasion killing his man. **(See despatch of Lieutenant-Colonel Mackenzie, Commanding 1st Brigade Horse Artillery, dated Camp, near Delhi,. 10th July, 1857, published in the Supplement to the London Gazette of the 16th January, 1858.).**

Biography
Henry was born on board ship on route to India on 10th November 1824 to father John an officer in the Bengal Cavalry and mother Mary (née Remington). He was baptised in Calcutta on 10th January 1825. Henry was the youngest of eight children with six older brothers and a sister Mary Ann.

Henry was sent to England for his education and like his brothers before him initially attended Abingdon School where his father had been educated. At the tender age of 14 Henry began the preparations for his military career when on 12th February 1839 he was enrolled in the Royal Military College at Sandhurst. However, he only stayed at Sandhurst for a few months

Figure 118. Henry Tombs

161 *London Gazette* – 22865/3168
162 *London Gazette* – 22932/316

leaving on 30th June after which he enrolled at the Honourable East India Company's Military Seminary at Addiscombe on 9th August 1839. Henry graduated from Addiscombe on 11th June 1841 and was commissioned as a 2nd Lieutenant in the Bengal Artillery. Leaving to take up his post he arrived at Calcutta on 18th November 1841 and was posted to the foot artillery at Dum Dum.

In August 1842, Henry was posted with a detachment of artillery to the northern provinces of India and on 1st March 1843 was posted to the 3rd company of the 5th battalion of artillery at Saugor in the state of Madhya Pradesh.

On 23rd November 1843, Henry was assigned to the 6th company of the 6th battalion of artillery based at Jhansi and it was with this unit that he saw his first action in the Gwalior campaign. Henry was part of the force known as the 'Left Wing', under the command of Major-General Sir John Grey, which defeated a force of Marathas at Punniar on 29th December 1843. For his action at Punniar, Henry was mentioned in the despatches of Major-General Gray dated 30th December 1843 – *"Lt.Tombs, attached to the rearguard of the left wing of the army of Gwallior (sic), with 2 guns of No. 16 Light Field Battery, fired several shots with great precision and effect on the enemy's left in action near Punniar."*[163] For his involvement in the campaign, Henry was awarded the Gwalior Campaign Star (1843) with clasp for Punniar.

On 15th January 1844, Henry was promoted to the rank of 1st Lieutenant and on the 1st March was posted to the horse artillery at Ludiana.

As a member of the 1st troop of the 1st brigade of the horse artillery, Henry took part in the Sutlej campaign (first Anglo-Sikh war) and took part in the Battle of Mudki on 18th December 1845; he was also involved in the Battle of Ferozeshah, which took place on 21st December. During the actions which took place in January 1846, Henry served as Aide-de-Camp to Sir Harry George Wakelyn Smith and was involved at the action at Badhowal on 21st January and the decisive battle at Aliwal on 28th January. For his service as Aide-de-Camp, Henry was mentioned in the despatches of Sir Harry Smith dated 30th January 1846.[164] For his service in the war, Henry was awarded the Sutlej Medal (1845–46) engraved on the reverse with Moodkee 1845 and with clasps for Ferozeshuhur and Aliwal.

Henry served as deputy assistant quartermaster-general of the artillery division during the Punjab Campaign (2nd Anglo-Sikh war) and was present at the action at Ramnugger on 22nd November 1848, the battle at Chillianwala on 13th January 1849 and the decisive Battle of Goojerat on 21st February. For his service during the campaign, Henry received two mentions in despatches, from General Gough on 16th January 1849[165] and Brigadier-General Tennant on 22nd February 1849.[166] He was also recommended for a brevet promotion to the rank of Major (once he attained the rank of Captain) and received the Punjab Medal with clasps for Chillianwala and Goojerat.

For the remainder of 1849 and early in 1850, Henry was deployed on special duty, until on 12th March 1850 he was appointed as a member of a special committee of artillery officers at Umbeyla.

On 30th October 1850, Henry was appointed as adjutant and quartermaster of the 2nd brigade of horse artillery and on 13th November was appointed as adjutant to the Umballa artillery division. He served in these roles until 30th November 1853 when he was transferred to the foot artillery.

Henry was promoted to the rank of Captain, in the Bengal artillery on 25th July 1854 and in accordance with the recommendation made after the Punjab Campaign received a brevet promotion to the rank of Major on 1st August 1854[167] and on 27th November 1855 returned to the horse artillery.

At the outbreak of the mutiny in 1857, Henry was in command of the 2nd troop of the 1st brigade of the horse artillery based at Meerut and on 27th May moved with the columns of Brigadier-General Archdale Wilson to join up with a force coming down from Umbeyla. On 30th May, while approaching Ghaziud-din-Nagar, the column was attacked by rebels and Henry, with his troop, repulsed a rebel attack and secured the bridge across the river Hindun, during this action his horse was shot out from under him.[168] During an action the next day, to clear the village of Ghazi, Henry again had his horse shot out from under him. For the actions on the 30th and 31st May, Henry received a mention in the despatches of Brigadier Wilson.[169] On 7th June General Wilson's column finally joined up with the Umballa force of Sir H. Bernard at Paniput and the combined force set off for Delhi. On the following day, Henry was involved, as part of the force of General Hope Grant in the Battle of Badli-ki-Serai, where despite fierce resistance the rebels were routed, during the battle he had two horses shot out from under him. The way was now clear to Delhi, which was held by the mutineers and the column lay siege to the city, Henry would be present throughout the siege. On 17th June Henry commanded a column which captured a rebel gun battery located between

163 *London Gazette* – 20323/826
164 *London Gazette* – 20588/1172

165 *London Gazette* – 20952/746
166 *London Gazette* – 20969/1300
167 *London Gazette* – 21641/4096
168 *London Gazette* – 22050/3399
169 *London Gazette* – 22050/3398

the Lahore Gate and the Garstin Bastion, which was threatening to enfilade the British positions. During this action he again had two horses shot out from under him and was slightly wounded,[170] for this deed Henry was mentioned in the despatches of Major F. Gaitskell,[171] Major C. Reid and Major-General Sir H. Barnard.[172] It was during the siege, on 9th July 1857, that Henry performed the deeds for which he would later be awarded the Victoria Cross. For this action Henry was mentioned in the despatches of Lieutenant Colonel M. Mackenzie and Major-General T. Reed.[173] On 25th August, Henry commanded the artillery of the force commanded by Brigadier-General John Nicholson at the Battle of Najafgarh, which successfully prevented the rebels from intercepting the siege train coming from Ferozepur. During September 1857, Henry commanded the 4th (Mortar) battery in siege operations at Delhi and on 17th September commanded the horse artillery in an assault on the city during which he was slightly wounded. For his part in this action, Henry received a mention in the despatches of Brigadier J. Hope Grant[174] and a mention in the General Orders of the Governor-General of India (dated 4th December 1857).[175] For his service during the siege and relief of Delhi (8th June to 21st September 1857), Henry received a brevet promotion to the rank of Lieutenant-Colonel on 19th January 1858[176] and two days later was appointed as an extra member 3rd Class (Companion) of the Military Division of the Most Honourable Order of the Bath.[177]

Lord Roberts,[178] who was a Lieutenant in the horse artillery during the siege of Delhi, eulogised the efforts of Henry, during the siege, with two entries in his autobiography "Forty-One Years in India" as follows:

It was impossible for me to describe my pleasure at finding myself a member of a force which had already gained imperishable fame. I longed to meet and know the men who names were in everyone's mouth. The hero of the day was Henry Tombs, of the Bengal Horse Artillery, an unusually handsome man and a thorough soldier. His gallantry in the attack on the Idgah (a Mahomedan place of worship and sacrifice) and wherever he had been engaged was the general talk of the camp. I had always heard of Tombs as one of the best officers in the regiment, and it

170 *London Gazette* – 33073/ 4432 & 4455
171 *London Gazette* – 22073/4446–7
172 *London Gazette* – 22084/224–5
173 *London Gazette* – 22084/246–7
174 *London Gazette* – 22073/4450–1
175 *London Gazette* – 22084/243
176 *London Gazette* – 22085/272
177 *London Gazette* – 22086/310
178 Lord Roberts was himself awarded the Victoria Cross for deeds performed at Khudaganj, India on 2nd January 1858

was with feelings of respectful admiration that I made his acquaintance a few days later.

Jeremy Hills, one of the subalterns in Tomb's troop, was an old Addiscombe friend of mine; he delighted in talking of his Commander, in dilating on his merits as a soldier and his skill in handling each arm of the service. As a cool, bold leader of men, Tombs was unsurpassed; no fire, however hot, and no crisis, however unexpected, could take him by surprise ; he grasped the situation in a moment and issued his orders without hesitation, inspiring all ranks with confidence in his power and capacity. He was somewhat of a martinet, and was more feared than liked by his men until they realized what a grand leader he was, when they gave him their entire confidence and were ready to follow him anywhere and everywhere.

And;

On the 17th (September, 1857) we were attacked from almost every direction— a manoeuvre intended to prevent our observing a battery which was being constructed close to an Idgah situated on a hill to our right, from which to enfilade our position on the Ridge. As it was very important to prevent the completion of this battery, Barnard ordered it to be attacked by two small columns, one commanded by Tombs, of the Bengal Horse Artillery, the other by Reid. Tombs, with 400 of the 60th Rifles and 1st Bengal Fusiliers, thirty of the Guides Cavalry, twenty Sappers and Miners and his own troop of Horse Artillery, moved towards the enemy's left. … Tombs drove the rebels through a succession of gardens, till they reached the Idgah, where they made an obstinate but unavailing resistance. The gates of the mosque were blown open and thirty-nine of its defenders were killed. Tombs himself was slightly wounded and had two horses killed, making five which had been shot under this gallant soldier since the commencement of the campaign.

After the fall of Delhi, Henry's troop was so run down after their exertions that, in October, they were ordered to Meerut for a refit and in January 1858 they joined up with the force of Sir Colin Campbell at Cawnpore.

In March 1858, Henry, commanding the 2nd troop of the 1st Brigade of Bengal Horse Artillery was involved in the siege and ultimate capture of Lucknow, for which he received an honourable mention in General Orders.

Following the capture of Lucknow on 21st March, Henry and his troop were involved in operations in Oudh and Rohilkhand. After leaving Lucknow on 7th April, Henry was present at the taking of the fort at Rooya on 15th April and the action at

Alligunge on 22nd April. Henry commanded the artillery at the Battle of Bareilly on 5th May and took part in the relief of Shahjehanpore on the 18th May 1858; he was also involved in actions at Mohamed on 24th May and at Shahabad on 31st May. On 4th June, after the rebels had been driven from Rohilkhand, the field force to which Henry's unit was assigned was broken up and in August he returned with his troop to Meerut.

For his service during the mutiny, Henry received the Indian Mutiny Medal with clasps for Delhi and Lucknow and on 20th July 1858 was promoted to the brevet rank of Colonel.[179]

Henry was also mentioned by name in a eulogy by Lord Panmure, secretary of state for war, in the House of Lords when he proposed a vote of thanks to the army for their service in India.

It was some time during 1858, in India that Henry was presented with his Victoria Cross medal; unfortunately the details of the ceremony are unknown.

On 29th April 1861, Henry was promoted to the rank of Lieutenant-Colonel,[180] with the promotion Henry relinquished command of his troop and was transferred to the 2nd Brigade of the Royal Horse Artillery with command of the artillery at Meerut. In a War Office memorandum dated 29th April 1862, it was formally recorded that, following the dissolution of the armies of the Honourable East India Company, Henry was transferred from the Bengal Artillery to the Royal Regiment of Artillery with the rank of Captain to be effective 25th July 1854.

On 16th May 1863, Henry was appointed as Brigadier-General to command the Artillery Brigade at Gwalior and for the period of February to April 1865 was given command of the right column of the Bhutan field force, by Sir Hugh Rose, which recaptured Dewangiri. For his service in this campaign, Henry was awarded the India General Service Medal with clasp for Bhootan; he was also awarded a good conduct pension.

On 11th March 1867, Henry received a brevet promotion to the rank of Major-General,[181] relinquished his command of the Gwalior district artillery and returned to England.

In recognition of his service in India, Henry was appointed as an ordinary member 2nd class (Knight Commander) of the Military Division of the Most Honourable Order of the Bath on 14th March 1868.[182]

At some time during 1869, Henry was married to Georgina Janet (née Stirling), the youngest daughter of Admiral Sir James Stirling. The couple would have three children, Dorothea Gwladys, Mabel and son Henry Edwin Stirling who was born at

Lucknow on 27th October 1873 but who unfortunately died at Suez on 2nd December 1874 soon after his father died.

Henry returned to service in India when on 30th August 1871 he was appointed to the command of the Allahabad Division, where he commanded the 3rd division on military manoeuvres from December 1871 until January 1872 and soon afterwards on 1st April 1872 was transferred to the Oudh Division. On 1st August 1872, Henry became a regimental Colonel in command of the 1st Division, however after taking ill over the Christmas period in 1873, he had to relinquish his command and on 11th February 1874 left India to return to England on sick leave.

On his journey home, when he reached Marseilles he became very ill and had to have an operation in Paris; during his hospitalisation he was informed that his illness was incurable.

Henry died at Newport on the Isle of Wight on 2nd August 1874 aged 48 and was buried at Mount Joy Cemetery, Carisbrooke on the Isle of Wight. His Victoria Cross medal is on public display at the Royal Artillery Museum at Woolwich.

Figure 118a. Grave of Henry Tombs

179 *London Gazette* – 22164/3379
180 *London Gazette* – 22649/3829 giving date as 30th October 1861,
      22720/1688 changed date to 29th April 1861
181 *London Gazette* – 23250/2758 and 23427/5167
182 *London Gazette* – 23362/1703

Figure 119. James Hills

Louise - 07979 191 561.

f
ltern's
tch
Horse
in the
.).

e, Bengal,
d mother

hat would
ibald born
Scott born
n 1851 and
Emma Savi..., John born
on 19th August 1834, George Scott born on 16th September 1835, Robert Savi born on 8th May 1837, Elliot Mcnaghten born on 8th February 1842 and Charles Richard born on 28th March 1847, all of the children were born in India.

During his early years, James spent most of his time in Scotland being educated at the Edinburgh Academy from 1843 to 1847 and then the Edinburgh Military Academy from 1847 to 1851. James was sent to complete his education at the Honourable East India Company military seminary at Addiscombe from 1851 to 1853.

On graduating from Addiscombe, on 11th June 1853, James enlisted as a 2nd Lieutenant in the Bengal Artillery.

James saw service throughout the Indian Mutiny, serving as a subaltern with the 2nd troop of the 1st brigade of the Bengal Horse Artillery. On 30th to 31st May 1857, James was involved with the troop in the action on the Hindun River, which secured a vital bridge across the river. On 8th June 1857, James was involved in the Battle of Badli-ki-Serai and the subsequent occupation of the Delhi Ridge and defence of the post at Hindoo Rao's house. It was on 9th July 1857, during the siege of Delhi, that James, together with his troop commander Major Tombs, performed the deeds for which he would later be awarded the

Victoria Cross. During this action, which was mentioned in the despatches of Lieutenant-Colonel Mackenzie on 10th July, James was severely wounded.[183] On 25th August James took part in the Battle of Nujeefghar and on 8th September was promoted to the rank of 1st Lieutenant. James was involved in the assault and recapture of Delhi on 20th September and the siege and capture of Lucknow during 2nd to 16th March 1858. Following the capture of Lucknow on 21st March, James was involved in operations in Oudh and Rohilkhand, taking part in the capture of the fort at Rooya on 15th April and the action at Alligunge on 22nd April. James also saw action at the Battle of Bareilly on 5th May and took part in the relief of Shahjehanpore on the 18th May 1858. He was also involved in actions at Mohamdi on 24th May and at Shahabad on 31st May.

For his service during the Mutiny, James was awarded the Indian Mutiny Medal with clasps for Delhi and Lucknow.

James was presented with his Victoria Cross medal by Lord Clyde, Commander In Chief India, at some time during 1859.

From September 1859 to March 1862, James served in the capacity of Aide-de-Camp to Lord Canning, the Governor General of India. From April 1862 until March 1863, James served as Assistant Resident of Nepal, following which on 24th March 1863 he was promoted to the rank of 2nd Captain.[184]

In April 1863, James resumed his service with the Bengal Horse Artillery and on 19th January 1864 received a brevet promotion to the rank of Major;[185] during 1863–64 he was involved in the Eusufzai Expedition.

In September 1864, James was appointed as Brigade Major, of the Northern Division, a position that he would hold for five

183 *London Gazette* – 22084/247
184 *London Gazette* – 22720/1688
185 *London Gazette* – 22809/236

years until 1869, only interrupted by his service in the Abyssinian Expedition. During the Abyssinian Expedition (December 1867 to May 1868), James commanded a mortar battery and was present at the capture of Magdala. For his service in Abyssinia, James was awarded the Abyssinian War Medal and received a mention in despatches. On 15th August 1868 he received a brevet promotion to the rank of Lieutenant-Colonel.[186]

On 9th October 1869, James was appointed as Commandant of the Peshawar Mountain Battery and while stationed at Kohat from February 1870 until April 1871 was also the garrison and district commander. James was promoted to the rank of Captain on 28th August 1871[187] and to Major on 5th July 1872.[188] From December 1871 until March 1872, James commanded the Peshawar Mountain Battery in the Lushai Campaign as part of the Chittagong column commanded by Brigadier-General Charles H. Brownlow, for this service James was awarded the India General Service medal with clasp for Looshai. On 1st August 1872, James was appointed to the command of 'C' Battery in 'F' Brigade of the Royal Horse Artillery, a position that he would hold until 1875.

James was appointed as an Ordinary Member 3rd Class (Companion) of the Military Division of the Most Honourable Order of the Bath on 10th September 1872.[189]

James was appointed to the position of Assistant Adjutant General of the Lahore Division on 9th February 1876 and a few days later on 14th February he received a brevet promotion to the rank of Colonel.[190]

On 12th October 1878, James was assigned as Assistant Adjutant General to the Kandahar Field Force and in this capacity took part in the first phase of the 2nd Anglo-Afghan War, for his actions he was twice mentioned in the despatches of Lieutenant-General Sir Donald Stewart on 24th June and 22nd July 1879. On 31st December 1878, James was promoted to the rank of Lieutenant-Colonel[191] and on 10th July 1879 received a brevet promotion to the rank of Major-General.[192] On receiving his promotion to Major-General, James was assigned to the force of Sir F. S. Roberts in the Kurram Valley, to take up this position he had to make a monumental journey of over 450 miles; leaving Kandahar on 9th September he arrived in time to join up with the force on their advance to Kabul. James was present at the Battle of Charasiah on 6th October 1879 and the assault and occupation of Kabul which occurred on 9th October 1879

and on 13th October until 17th January 1880 (when the role was dispensed with) he acted as the Military Governor of Kabul. Although he commanded no forces during the campaign, James did such good service in assisting the Commissariat with logistics that he received a favourable mention in the despatches of Sir Roberts on 20th November 1879.[193]

After a short period of unemployment, during which he worked in committee on compensation issues, James was appointed to the command of the 3rd Division of the Northern Afghanistan Field Force on 16th May, a position that he held until the force was disbanded in September 1880. For this service, James was once again mentioned in despatches and on 5th May was formally thanked for his service by both houses of parliament. For his service in the 2nd Anglo-Afghan War, James was awarded the Afghanistan Medal (1878–80) with clasps for Kabul and Charasiah and on 22nd February 1881 was appointed as an Ordinary Member 2nd Class (Knight Commander) of the Military Division of the Most Honourable Order of the Bath.[194]

On 15th December 1881, James was awarded a Good Service pension.

At some stage in 1881, James left India and took up residence at Abermade, Llanilar, Cardigan, Wales before moving to Dolaucothy, near Llandilo in Carmarthenshire.

On 16th September 1882, James was married to Elizabeth (née Johnes) in Westminster Abbey and on 6th September 1883 he received royal accent to change his name to Hills-Johnes.[195]

James was promoted to the rank of Lieutenant-General on 31st December 1883.[196]

On 14th November 1884, James was appointed as a Sheriff of Carmarthenshire[197] and a year later on 13th November 1885 was reappointed[198] to the position.

On 7th September 1885, James was places on the army unemployed supernumerary list.

James was very active in local government being a county councillor and Chairman of the Joint Counties Association and on 10th April 1886 he was appointed as Deputy Lieutenant for the county of Carmarthenshire.[199] For his service to local government he was awarded the freedom of the Borough and County of Carmarthenshire in 1910.

On 30th June 1888, James was finally retired from the army,[200] however, he did continue to support the volunteer and reserve

---

186 *London Gazette* – 23412/4512
187 *London Gazette* – 23794/4598
188 *London Gazette* – 23876/3193
189 *London Gazette* – 23895/3969
190 *London Gazette* – 24362/4963
191 *London Gazette* – 24668/173
192 *London Gazette* – 24748/4752

193 *London Gazette* – 24801/218
194 *London Gazette* – 24994/975
195 *London Gazette* – 25267/4400 & 25275/4790
196 *London Gazette* – 25312/380
197 *London Gazette* – 25414/4889
198 *London Gazette* – 25529/5187
199 *London Gazette* – 25578/1839
200 *London Gazette* – 25843/4190

forces and for a time served as Chairman of the Carmarthenshire County Association of Territorial Forces.

James was appointed as an honorary Colonel of the Carmarthenshire Artillery on 25th February 1891.[201]

On 3rd June 1893, James was appointed as an Ordinary Member 1st Class (Knight Grand Cross) of the Military Division of the Most Honourable Order of the Bath.[202]

James was appointed as an honorary Colonel of 1st Pembroke Volunteer Battalion on 4th October 1905[203] and as honorary Colonel of the Carmarthen Royal Field Reserve Artillery on 31st May 1908;[204] on the following day he was made honorary Colonel of the 4th Battalion Welsh Regiment.[205]

During the war in South Africa, James accompanied Lord Roberts (in a private capacity) on a visit to Kronstad and Diamond Hill.

In addition to supporting the Volunteer movement, James was also active with the University College of Wales, serving as a Council Member and Treasurer, for his service with the University he was awarded a doctorate of law (LL.D).

James died at his home in Dolaucothy, from Influenza on 3rd January 1919, aged 85 and was buried in the family vault at Caio Churchyard.

His Victoria Cross medal is on public display at the Royal Artillery Museum in Woolwich, London.

James had strong associations with two other recipients of the Victoria Cross: Lieutenant William George Cubitt, who was awarded his Victoria Cross for deeds during the Indian Mutiny on 30th June 1857, was his brother in law and he was a great uncle of Lieutenant-Colonel Lewis Pugh Evans who was awarded a Victoria Cross for actions on 26th November 1917 in Belgium during the Great War.

Some sources incorrectly cite that James was murdered by his butler; it was in fact his father-in-law who was the victim, as described in the following newspaper article.

The Western Mail, Monday August 21st, 1876.
   Mr. John Johnes, formerly judge of the county court for the counties of Carmarthen, Cardigan and Pembroke, chairman of the Carmarthenshire quarter sessions, and recorder of the borough of Carmarthenshire, was assassinated on Saturday at his seat, Dolaucothy, near Llandilo, by his butler, Henry Tremble.
   The murder, which appears to have been carried out with the utmost deliberation, took place in the library and in

making his escape Tremble shot Mrs. Cookman, the eldest daughter of Mr. Johnes, whose injuries are not, however, likely to prove fatal. He then proceeded to his cottage, and, after writing a letter to the vicar, in which he is reported to have made a confession, he committed suicide.

It seems that the relationship between Henry Tremble and his employer had been deteriorating for some time, and the last straw for the increasingly surly butler had been when John Johnes refused his application for the vacant lease of the Dolaucothy Arms. The arguments that followed resulted in Tremble being dismissed from service.

Figure 119a. Memorial to James Hills

201 *London Gazette* – 26137/1007
202 *London Gazette* – 26409/3251
203 *London Gazette* – 27842/6708
204 *London Gazette* – 28200/9031
205 *London Gazette* – 28261/4661

James Thompson
9th July 1857 (VC No. 142)

Gazetted: 20th January 1860 22347/179

Rank and Unit: Private – 1st Battalion 60th Rifles

Citation

*For gallant conduct in saving the life of his Captain
(Captain Wilton), on the 9th of July, 1857, by dashing
forward to his relief, when that Officer was surrounded by
a party of Ghazees, who made a sudden rush on him from
a Serai, and killing two of them before further assistance
could reach.*

*Also recommended for conspicuous conduct throughout the
Siege. Wounded.*

Elected by the Privates of the Regiment.

Biography

James was born in 1829 (possibly in December)[206] at Hadley,
near Yoxall, Burton in Staffordshire to father Edward who was a
farm labourer and mother Lydia.

James had four brothers, Richard who was born in 1826,
William born in 1833, Thomas born in 1835 and Edward born
in 1839.

For a time James worked as a form labourer, like his father,
however, on 30th January 1852 he took up a career in the army
and enlisted, at Derby, as a private in the 60th Rifles.

James would have joined his regiment, which had been serving
in India for some time, at Jullundur sometime in 1852 and would
have spent a relatively quiet time at Jullundur and Meerut, where
the regiment relocated in 1855, until the outbreak of the Mutiny.
It was on 9th July 1857, during the siege of Delhi, that James
performed the deeds for which he was later awarded the Victoria Cross – it was under rule 13 that James was elected for the
award by a ballot of the Privates of the regiment. Some months
later, on 14th September 1857, during the assault on Delhi, James
was severely wounded and his left arm was amputated. Because
of his wounds James was repatriated to England and in August
1858 was discharged from the army at Chatham Docks. For his
service in India, James was awarded the Indian Mutiny Medal
with clasp for Delhi.

After leaving the army, James was employed by Captain
Wilton as a gamekeeper at his estate in Scotland.

During March 1859, James was married to Dinah (née Gilbert).

Figure 120. James Thompson

James was presented with his Victoria Cross medal by Queen
Victoria at an investiture held at Windsor Home Park on 9th
November 1860.

It appears that James returned to the Midlands some time in
1865 and was employed in the recently established coalfields as
a colliery watchman.

By 1871 James was living at Sheep Wash, Slitting Mill near
Rugeley in Staffordshire and seems to be in a new marriage with
wife Hannah, the couple have three children George, John and
Minnie.

It is probable that James was employed by the Fair Oak
Mining Company, which had sunk mine shafts less than a mile
from where James lived at Slitting Mill.

By the 1880's James had moved his family to Walsall, where
they lived in Dudley Street.

It was while living in Walsall that James died on 5th December 1891 aged 61, he was buried in an unmarked grave at the
Queen Street Cemetery in Walsall.

James's Victoria Cross medal is on public display at the Royal
Green Jackets museum in Winchester.

---

206 Baptised on 25th December 1829 at St Peter's Church, Yoxall

William Alexander Kerr
10th July 1857 (VC No. 143)

Figure 121. William Alexander Kerr

Gazetted: 27th April 1858 22131/2050

Rank and Unit: Lieutenant – 24th Bombay Native Infantry

Citation

On the breaking out of a mutiny in the 27th Bombay Native Infantry in July, 1857, a party of the mutineers took up a position in the stronghold, or pagu, near the town of Kolapore, and defended themselves to extremity.

Lieutenant Kerr, of the Southern Mahratta Irregular Horse, took a prominent share of the attack on the position, and at the moment when its capture was of great public importance, he made a dash at one of the gateways, with some dismounted horsemen, and forced an entrance by breaking down the gate. The attack was completely successful, and the defenders were either killed, wounded, or captured, a result that may with perfect justice be attributed to Lieutenant Kerr's dashing and devoted bravery. **(Letter from the Political Superintendent at Kolapore, to the Adjutant-General of the Army, dated 10th September, 1857.)**

Biography

William was born on 18th July 1831 at The Holmes, near Melrose in Roxburghshire, Scotland. His father was Loraine McDowell and mother Marianne (née White), the daughter of Admiral White.

From 1840 until 1845, William was educated at the Loretto School near Musselborough.

In June 1849, just before his 18th birthday, William joined the army of the Honourable East India Company as a Lieutenant in the 24th Bombay Native Infantry and left to join his regiment in India.

At some stage, possibly after the 24th were disarmed at Peshawar on 22nd May 1857, William was seconded to the South Mahratta Horse, part of the Bombay Irregular Cavalry and it was with this unit that he served out the remainder of his army career. William served throughout the Mutiny, and it was on 10th July 1857 at Kolapore, while subduing the 27th Bombay Native Infantry, who had mutinied, that he performed the deeds for which he was later awarded the Victoria Cross; during this action William was wounded.

William was presented with his Victoria Cross Medal on 4th September 1858 at Belgaum by Major General F. T. Farrell, commander of the Southern Division.

In December 1858, William succeeded in defending the town of Bhilsa against a large force of rebels under the command of Tantia Topi which led to the capture of the rebel leader. For his service during the mutiny, William was awarded the Indian Mutiny Medal with clasp for Central India. And at some stage was promoted to the rank of Captain, second in charge of the South Mahratta Horse.

On 4th January 1860, William was married to Harriet (née Atty) at the parish church in Rugby; the couple would have no children.

Sometime in 1860, on hearing that the South Mahratta Horse was to be disbanded, William resigned his commission and left the army.

Very little is known regarding William's later life other than he did much to promote horse racing in India and wrote several books on the riding and purchasing of horses.

William died on 19th May 1919 at Folkestone in Kent, aged 88 and was buried in the Cheriton Road Cemetery in Folkestone.

William's Victoria Cross medal is on public display as part of the Lord Ashcroft collection held by the Imperial War Museum, London.

Figure 121a. Grave of William Alexander Kerr

Abraham Boulger
12th July 1857 (VC No. 144)

Gazetted: 18th June 1858 22154/2957

Rank and Unit: Lance-Corporal no. 2860 – 84th Regiment of Foot

Citation

For distinguished bravery and forwardness; as a skirmisher, in all the twelve actions fought between 12th July, and 25th September, 1857. **(Extract from Field Force Orders of the late Major-General Havelock, dated 17th October, 1857.)**

Biography

Abraham was born on 4th September 1833 at Kilcullen, Co Kildare in Ireland.

After two years service as a boy cadet, Abraham enlisted in the British Army on 15th February 1851, just before his 18th birthday and joined the 84th Regiment of Foot as a Private.

On 18th December 1851, Abraham was sent to India with his regiment and served throughout the Indian Mutiny. With the start of the mutiny, Abraham and his regiment were part of the force of Major-General Havelock and were in the advanced party which was sent to the relief of Cawnpore, where they arrived on 2nd June. General Wheeler, in command at Cawnpore, was so confident in the loyalty of his troops[207] that he despatched the relieving troops, columns from the 84th and 32nd, to assist with the relief of Lucknow. It was during the first relief of Lucknow, on 12th July that Abraham, now a Lance-Corporal, performed the first of the deeds for which he was later awarded the Victoria Cross. Abraham was involved in many actions during the remainder of July, August and September and was present at the second relief of Lucknow on 25th September when he was wounded while entering the city; he received a mention in despatches for this action. While part of a storming party at Lucknow on 29th September, Abraham was seriously wounded being shot in the left thigh and the right hand, losing his middle finger. In the defence of the residency at Lucknow while storming the Hirn Khana on 16th November 1857, Abraham was again wounded. For his service during the mutiny, Abraham was awarded the Indian Mutiny medal with clasp for Lucknow, he was also awarded an additional years service towards his pension.[208] Abraham and his regiment left India on 30th June 1858 returning to England for garrison duties.

Figure 122. Abraham Boulger

Abraham was presented with his Victoria Cross medal by Queen Victoria at an investiture at Buckingham Palace on 8th June 1859.

Abraham served on garrison duties in Halifax, Nova Scotia from 24th December 1869 until 11th January 1871. On 2nd November 1872, Abraham now a Sergeant-Major was appointed as Quartermaster of the regiment.[209] On 1st July 1881, the 84th Regiment was disbanded and reformed as 2nd Battalion, York and Lancaster regiment.

From 5th August until 6th November 1882, Abraham was involved in the Anglo-Egyptian War. The York and Lancaster regiment was part of the 2nd Brigade commanded by Major-General Gerald Graham VC.[210] Abraham was present at the actions at El Magfar, Tel-el-Mahuta, Kassassin and on 13th September 1882 the Battle of Tel-el-Kebir. For his service in the war, James was awarded the Egypt Medal with clasp for Tel-el-Kebir, he was also awarded the Khedive Star and on 2nd November 1882 was appointed to the rank of honorary Captain.[211] On 7th March 1883, Abraham was appointed to the honorary rank of Major for his service in Egypt.[212]

From 17th October 1883, Abraham served as part of the garrison force at Bermuda and after over 20 years of service retired from the army on 19th November 1887; on retirement he was

---

207 Misplaced as it turned out.
208 War Office letter dated 11th April 1861

209 *London Gazette* – 23915/5108
210 Gerald Graham was awarded his VC for actions at Sevastopol, in the Crimea on 18th June 1855.
211 *London Gazette* – 25168/5109
212 *London Gazette* – 25209/1261

awarded the Long Service and Good Conduct medal and was made honorary Lieutenant-Colonel.[213]

Following his retirement from the army, Abraham returned to Ireland where he lived at Moate, near Athlone in Co Westmeath.

At some stage, Abraham was married to Mary, nearly 30 years his junior, thought to be the daughter of a local and wealthy landowner. As he was a Protestant, he had to change his religion in order to marry the Catholic Mary. The couple would have three children: Alice-Ellen born in 1897, Agnes and William Abraham.

Abraham died at home on 23rd January 1900, from Influenza and was buried in the Ballymore Roman Catholic Churchyard.

Abraham's Victoria Cross medal is on public display at The York & Lancaster Regimental Museum, Rotherham, South Yorkshire.

Figure 122a. Grave of Abraham Boulger

Patrick Mylott
12th July 1857 (VC No. 145)

Gazetted: 24th December 1858 22212/5513

Rank and Unit: Private – 84th Regiment of Foot

Citation

For being foremost in rushing across a road, under a shower of balls, to take an opposite enclosure; and for gallant conduct at every engagement at which he was present with his Regiment, from 12th of July, 1857, to the relief of the garrison.

Elected by the private soldiers of the Regiment.

Biography

Patrick was born during June 1820 in Kilcommon Parish, Hollymount, Claremorris in Co Mayo, Ireland. Unfortunately, in common with many of his compatriots of this era, his life story is lost to the mist of times.

It is probable that Patrick joined the army at some time close to his 18th birthday, say in 1838, in which case he would have served his first four years in England until 1842 when the regiment was posted to Burma.

Figure 123a. Grave of Patrick Mylott

The regiment was posted to India during 1845 and was therefore fully acclimatised at the time of the mutiny. Patrick served throughout the mutiny, taking part in the relief of Cawnpore and Lucknow. It was during the siege of Lucknow that he performed the deeds for which he would later be awarded the Victoria Cross – being elected by the privates of the regiment, under the terms of rule 13 of the founding warrant. Patrick would have returned to England with the regiment on 30th June 1858 spending several years on garrison duties. For his service during the mutiny, Patrick was awarded the Indian Mutiny medal with clasps for Lucknow and Defence of Lucknow.

Patrick was presented with his Victoria Cross medal by Queen Victoria on 4th January 1860 at an investiture held at Windsor Castle.

It is unknown when Patrick left the army, however, he served at least 20 years as he was awarded the Good Conduct and Long Service medal. He had attained the rank of Sergeant by the time he retired.

At some stage, Patrick was married to Mary (née Higgins) and in 1871 they had a daughter named Julia.

On 22nd December 1878, at the age of 58, Patrick died at the Workhouse Hospital, Brownlow Hill in Liverpool and was buried in the Anfield Cemetery in Liverpool.

The location of Patrick's Victoria Cross medal is unknown.

Henry Marshman Havelock
16th July 1857 (VC No. 146)

Gazetted: 15th January 1858 22083/178

Rank and Unit: Lieutenant – 10th Regiment of Foot

Citation

In the combat at Cawnpore, Lieutenant Havelock was my Aide-de-Camp. The 64th Regiment had been much under artillery fire, from which it had severely suffered. The whole of the infantry were lying down in line, when, perceiving that the enemy had brought out the last reserved gun, a 24-pounder, and were rallying round it, I called up the regiment to rise and advance. Without any other word from me, Lieutenant Havelock placed himself on his horse, in front of the centre of the 64th, opposite the muzzle of the gun. Major Stirling, commanding the regiment, was in front, dismounted, but the Lieutenant continued to move steadily on in front of the regiment at a foot pace, on his horse. The gun discharged shot until the troops were within a short distance, when they fired grape. In went the corps, led by the Lieutenant, who still steered steadily on the gun's muzzle until it was mastered by a rush of the 64th. **(Extract of a telegram from the late Major-General Sir Henry Havelock to the Commander-in-Chief in India, dated Cawnpore, August 18th, 1857.)**

Biography

Henry was born on 6th August 1830 at Chinsurah, Bengal, India the first son and fifth of eight children born to father Lieutenant Henry Havelock serving in 13th Regiment of Foot and mother Hannah Shepard (née Marshman), the youngest daughter of missionaries serving in India.

Little is known regarding Henry's four older sisters, however, his three younger brothers were Joshua born on 11th December 1831, Ettrick born on 5th August 1833 and George Broadfoot born on 5th June 1847.

Following an education at Rev. Dr. Cuthbert's School in St. John's Wood, London, Henry was commissioned as an Ensign in the 39th Regiment of Foot on 31st March 1846,[214] some months short of his 16th birthday.

Henry would have joined his regiment which was serving in India some time in 1846, where they were stationed at Dinapore until October when they moved to Calcutta where they arrived in January 1847. Henry's first stay in India was short lived as the

---

214 *London Gazette* – 20589/1180

Figure 124. Henry Marshman Havelock

regiment returned to garrison duties in England during June/July 1847.

On 23rd June 1848, Henry purchased a commission as Lieutenant in the 86th Regiment of Foot which was stationed in India, however, on his journey to join the regiment he suffered from a severe bout of sunstroke and had to return to England. On completing his sick leave, Henry did join the 86th in India, however on 13th February 1852 he transferred to the 10th Regiment of Foot to take up the post of Adjutant.[215] After a few years in India, Henry returned to England hoping to take part in the Crimean War but as this was unsuccessful he enrolled at the staff college during 1856.

Towards the end of 1856, Henry left the staff college and once again set out to the East arriving in time to take part in the Anglo-Persian War.

On 22nd January 1857, Henry was appointed as Deputy Assistant Quartermaster-General on the staff of the division commanded by his father, who by now had the rank of Major-General. During the war, Henry was involved in the bombardment and capture of Mohamra, for which he was mentioned in despatches.[216] For his service during the war, Henry was awarded the India General Service Medal (1854–95) with clasp for Persia.

After the war Henry accompanied his father to Calcutta where they arrived on 17th June 1857, after the start of the mutiny. When Henry's father was appointed as commander of a column to go to the relief of Cawnpore and Lucknow, Henry was appointed as his -de-camp on 23rd June and proceeded to Allahabad in Bengal, with the column. On the march to Cawnpore,

Henry took part in the battles at Futtehpore on 12th July and at Aong and Pandoo-Nadi on the 15th July 1857. It was during the attack on Cawnpore on 16th July that Henry performed the deeds for which he was later awarded the Victoria Cross, having been recommended for the award by his father. On 21st July 1857, Henry was appointed as deputy assistant adjutant-general for the force which now advanced on Lucknow. In this capacity, Henry was present at the action at Oonoa on 29th July, Bashiratganj on 5th August (where his horse was shot out from under him) and at Bithoor on 16th August. Henry took part in the second advance on Lucknow, after the column was reinforced by a force under the command of Lieutenant-General Sir James Outram, taking part with distinction at the Battle of Mangalwar on 21st September and at the Alam Bagh on 23rd September, where it is said that he saved the life of Lieutenant-General Outram on two occasions. On 25th September, Henry performed with distinction during an attack on the Char-Bagh Bridge, which successfully gained entry into the city of Lucknow, for this action he was once again , recommended for the award of the Victoria Cross, this time by Lieutenant-General Outram. During this action, Henry was severely wounded, having been shot through the left elbow and once again his horse was shot out from under him.[217] On 9th October 1857, Henry was promoted to the rank of Captain,[218] in the 18th Regiment of Foot. Once he recovered from his wounds, Henry took part in the defence of the Residency at Lucknow until the relief of the garrison by the force of General Sir Colin Campbell, on 17th November 1857, during which action Henry was again seriously wounded.[219] Despite his wounds, Henry was at his father's side on 24th November when he died from dysentery and attended his funeral at the Alam Bagh two days later. On the death of his father, Henry relinquished his role as Aide-de-Camp, however, despite still suffering from his wounds, in December 1857, he was appointed, at his own request, as deputy assistant adjutant-general to the Azamgarh and Janpur field force under the command of Brigadier-General Thomas Harte Franks.

With effect from 18th January 1858, Henry was confirmed as a Baronet with an annual pension of £1,000. This honour was due to be bestowed upon his father for his distinguished service in India, however, upon his death the honour was handed down to his eldest son, Henry.[220]

On 19th January 1858, Henry received a brevet promotion to the rank of Major.[221] As part of the Janpur field force, Henry was

215 *London Gazette* – 21290/408
216 *London Gazette* – 22032/2821

217 *London Gazette* – 22073/4435
218 *London Gazette* – 22049/3356
219 *London Gazette* – 22095/665
220 *London Gazette* – 22085/261
221 *London Gazette* – 22085/272

involved in operations against the rebel leader Mahudi Haisan and saw action at Nasratpur on 23rd January, Chanda and Hamirpur on 19th February, Sultanpur on 23rd February and at Dhaurahra on 4th March. After joining up with a column commanded by General Sir Colin Campbell, Henry was involved in the siege and capture of Lucknow which took place on 19th March. On 29th March 1858, Henry was appointed as assistant deputy adjutant general to the field forces of the Behar and Ghazipore districts and in this capacity accompanied the force led by Brigadier-General Sir Edward Lugard on its mission to relieve Azamgarh. During the campaign, Henry was involved in actions at Metahi on 11th and 5th April after which the rebels were driven into the jungles of Jagdispur and in October he formed a mounted infantry unit to chase the rebels from the jungle into the Kaimur Hills, he was wounded during this operation. On 25th November 1858, Henry was appointed to the command of the 1st Regiment of Hodson's Horse in the Oude campaign taking part in several actions: including Bajadua on 26th December, the capture of Masjadua on the next day and at Bandi on 31st December, until the end of the campaign in March 1859. For his service during the mutiny, Henry was awarded the Indian Mutiny Medal with clasps for the Relief of Lucknow and Lucknow. He was also awarded an additional year's pensionable service for his actions in the defence of Lucknow.

After the mutiny, Henry returned to England where he joined up with his regiment at the Shorncliffe Army Camp near Cheriton in Kent. On 26th April 1859, Henry received a brevet promotion to the rank of Lieutenant-Colonel.[222]

Henry was presented with his Victoria Cross medal by Queen Victoria on 8th June 1859 at an investiture held at Buckingham Palace.

On 1st October 1861, Henry was appointed as deputy assistant adjutant general at Aldershot, however, in less than two years he was back on active service when in August 1863 he accompanied his regiment to New Zealand to take part in the campaign to invade Waikato. On 25th October 1863, Henry was appointed as Deputy Assistant Quartermaster General to the forces in New Zealand, a position that he would hold until January 1865. During the campaign, Henry was present at the capture of Rangiriri on 20th & 21st November and commanded troops during the Waiari affair in January 1864 where he saw action at Paterangi and Rangiawhia on 20th and 21st February and the siege and capture of Orakau on 2nd April. On 28th June 1864, Henry became a Major by purchase, however, as this was on the unattached list,[223] he returned to England from New Zealand

during early 1865. For his service in New Zealand, Henry was mentioned several times in despatches and was awarded the New Zealand Medal (1860–66).

On 10th May 1865, Henry was married to Lady Alice Moreton, daughter of the 2nd Earl of Dulcie, the couple would have three children: daughter Ethel born in Montreal, Canada on 1st November 1867, Henry Spencer Moreton who was born in Dublin, Ireland on 30th January 1872 and Alan who was born on 30th March 1874 in London.

On 10th August 1866, Henry was appointed as an ordinary member 3rd class (Companion) of the Military Division of the Most Honourable Order of the Bath.[224]

From 13th March 1867 until 31st March 1869, Henry served as Assistant Quarter-Master General in Canada, during the Fenian Uprising. On 17th June 1868, while serving in Canada, Henry was promoted to the brevet rank of Colonel, having completed the qualifying period as a Lieutenant-Colonel.[225]

Following his return to England from Canada, on 1st August 1869 Henry was appointed as Assistant Quarter-Master General for Ireland and took up his post on the General Staff at Dublin, which he retained until 30th September 1872. During this posting Henry took a temporary leave of absence and visited France as a war correspondent during the Franco-German War (1870–71) and was present at the surrender of the French Army under the command of Emperor Napoleon III on 2nd September 1870 at Sedan.

In January 1874, Henry was defeated in his attempt to become the Liberal MP for Stroud, however, a few weeks later on 6th February he was elected to serve as the Member of Parliament for the borough of Sunderland.[226]

For several months in 1877, Henry acted as a war correspondent attached to the Russian army during the Russo-Turkish (1877–78) and was present at the siege of Plevna during July and operations in the Shipka Pass in August.

On 17th March 1880, Henry was granted a Royal Licence to change his name by the addition of Allen to his surname – this was required in order to comply with the terms of the will of his cousin, Robert Henry Allen who had bequeathed him his estate at Blackwell Grange Darlington subject to this condition.[227]

On the following day, Henry was promoted to the rank of Major-General.

On 2nd April 1880, Henry was re-elected as the Member of Parliament for the borough of Sunderland,[228] however, on 12th

---

222 *London Gazette* – 22255/1727
223 *London Gazette* – 22868/3275

224 *London Gazette* – 23149/4423
225 *London Gazette* – 23431/5385
226 *London Gazette* – 24064/592
227 *London Gazette* – 24825/2190
228 *London Gazette* – 24829/2358

April 1881 he accepted the Chiltern Hundreds and resigned from Parliament,[229] in order to take up the command of the 2nd Infantry Brigade at Aldershot, which was to be effective from the 1st April.

On 9th December 1881, Henry was placed on the retirement list with the honorary rank of Lieutenant-General.[230]

In 1882, Henry made an unofficial visit to Egypt during the Anglo-Egyptian war where he visited Lieutenant-General Sir Garnet Wolseley at his headquarters at Ismailia. Ever keen for action he took part in the assault on Tel-el-Kebir with the Highland Brigade commanded by General Sir Archibald Alison. It is said that an insurance company, hearing of his exploits, decided to cancel his life insurance policy.

On 15th December 1885, Henry was elected as the Member of Parliament for the South-Eastern Division of County Durham[231] and he retained his seat at the election of 20th July 1886.[232]

On 7th May 1887, Henry was appointed as honorary Colonel of the Northern Division, 2nd Brigade of the Royal Artillery militia.[233]

To celebrate the completion of the 50th year of the reign of Queen Victoria, Henry was appointed as an Ordinary Member 2nd Class (Knight Commander) of the Military Division of the Most Honourable Order of the Bath on 21st June 1887.[234]

On 17th October 1888, Henry was appointed to the command of the Tyne and Tees Brigade which was one of the Infantry Volunteer Brigades.[235]

In the Parliamentary election of 1892, Henry lost his seat to a small majority, however, on 7th August 1895 he was re-elected as Member of Parliament for the South Eastern Division of County Durham.[236]

In addition to being a Member of Parliament, Henry also served as Alderman on the Durham County Council, Justice of the Peace for North Riding of Yorkshire and Co. Durham and also as Deputy Lieutenant for county Durham.

On 27th November 1895, Henry was appointed as Colonel-in-Chief of the Royal Irish Regiment.[237]

In celebration of the completion of the 60th year of the reign of Queen Victoria, Henry was appointed as an additional member of the 1st Class (Knight Grand Cross) of the Military Division of

the Most Honourable Order of the Bath on 22nd June 1897.[238] Henry also received the Queen Victoria Diamond Jubilee Medal.

During the parliament recess of 1897, Henry in his role as chairman of the parliamentary Naval and Military Service Committee set off on a visit to India. The purpose of his visit was twofold: first he was to investigate concerns being voiced regarding discipline within his regiment the Royal Irish, second he was to visit the troops engaged in fighting hill tribes on the border with Afghanistan.

While in India, Henry was attached to the forces of General Sir William Lockhart who had provided him with an escort and had extracted a promise from Henry that he would not take any unnecessary risks. On 30th December 1897, while moving down from Ali Masjid (the narrowest point of the Khyber Pass) following a visit to Landi Kotal, Henry got into difficulties with a fresh horse and moved well ahead of his escort where he became a target for a small band of rebel Afridi tribesmen. It is believed that the rebels were attempting to capture Henry for ransom, however, when they shot his horse the bullet passed through his leg severed an artery and he bled to death. When his body was discovered it was taken to Rawalpindi where his regiment the Royal Irish were quartered.

Henry was buried in the New Cemetery, Harley Road in Rawalpindi.

The location of his Victoria Cross medal is unknown.

Figure 124a. Grave of Henry Marshman Havelock

229 *London Gazette* – 24961/1791
230 *London Gazette* – 25064/277
231 *London Gazette* – 25541/6133
232 *London Gazette* – 25609/3497
233 *London Gazette* – 25698/2522
234 *London Gazette* – 25712/3361 & 25773/212
235 *London Gazette* – 25866/5649
236 *London Gazette* – 26651/4480
237 *London Gazette* – 26699/233

238 *London Gazette* – 26867/3567 & 26947/1681

Richard Wadeson
18th July 1857 (VC No. 147)

Gazetted: 24th December 1858 22212/5518

Rank and Unit: Lieutenant – 75th Regiment of Foot

Citation

For conspicuous bravery at Delhi on the 18th of July, 1857, when the Regiment was engaged in the Subjee Mundee, in having saved the life of Private Michael Farrell, when attacked by a Sowar of the enemy's Cavalry, and killing the Sowar.

Also, on the same day, for rescuing Private John Barry, of the same Regiment, when, wounded and helpless, he was attacked by a Cavalry Sowar, whom Lieutenant Wadeson killed.

Biography

Richard was born on 31st July 1826 at Bay Horse (Gaythorse?) near Lancaster, it is possible that his father was the local Station Master.

On 17th November 1843, at the age of 17, Richard enlisted in the 75th Regiment of Foot at Plymouth, the regiment had returned from garrison duties in South Africa only a few weeks earlier and were recruiting to bring the regiment back up to strength. In July 1844, the regiment was moved to duties in South Wales and were stationed at Newport. Just over a year later in September 1845 the regiment was moved to Ireland where they were initially stationed at Birr. In June 1846, the regiment was transferred to Athlone and soon afterwards on 27th August 1846, Richard was promoted to the rank of Corporal. In July 1847, the regiment was once again on the move, this time to Dublin, however, after a year, on 31st July 1848 the regiment was moved to Kilkenny in response to troubles in Tipperary which became known as the 'Smith O'Brian Rebellion'. From August to September the regiment was part of the field force commanded by Major-General John MacDonald which was tasked with putting down the rebellion.

At some stage, Richard was married to Susan of Alphington in Devon, the couple would have a least two children. The youngest, Edith Evangeline was born some time in 1869 at Dandgate in Kent.

Richard was promoted to the rank of Sergeant on 7th November 1848.

In March 1849, the regiment was told to prepare for immediate deployment to India and on 29th March they moved to Fermoy in readiness for their deployment.

Figure 125. Richard Wadeson

In early May, the regiment embarked on board 5 ships and set sail for India, arriving at Calcutta during the second half of August. From Calcutta, the regiment proceeded by ship to Allahabad where they set off on a march to Umballa, where they arrived on 21st December. In November 1853, the regiment was moved to Peshawar, during their stay in Umballa they lost over 90 men to the ravages of cholera and fever. On 24th February 1854, Richard was promoted to the rank of Sergeant-Major. In 1855, the regiment was moved to Rawalpindi and in December 1856 were moved to the outpost of Kasauli in the foothills of the Himalayas. On hearing news of the mutiny the regiment was ordered back to Umballa where, in May 1857, they formed up as part of the force sent to the relief of Delhi, which was now in the hands of the mutineers.

On 2nd June 1857, Richard was commissioned as an Ensign in the 75th Regiment of Foot.[239]

Richard was involved in the Battle of Badli-ki-Serai on 8th of June and on 16th of June was mentioned in Regimental Orders for his 'Gallant Conduct' during actions on the 8th, 12th and 15th June. It was a few weeks later on 18th July, during the taking of the Sabzee Mundee village outside Delhi, that Richard performed the deeds for which he would later be awarded the Victoria Cross. Richard was promoted to the rank of Lieutenant, without purchase, on 19th September 1857.[240] The regiment was involved in the siege and ultimate relief of Delhi and took part in actions at Agra, Cawnpore and Lucknow. Following the death of General Havelock on 24th November 1857, the regiment

---

239 *London Gazette* – 22041/3143
240 *London Gazette* – 22083/184

was moved to the 1st division under the command of Sir James Outram and were posted to the Alam Bagh. On 14th February 1858, the regiment were posted to Cawnpore as part of the reserve and were able to take a well earned rest. On 11th March 1859, Richard was appointed as adjutant for the regiment, a position that he would hold for over five years.[241]

For his service during the mutiny, Richard was awarded the Indian Mutiny Medal (1857–58) with clasp for Delhi.

In early 1860, the regiment set out for Allahabad, arriving on 25th January, where they would form the garrison for the next year. On 26th January 1861, the regiment was again on the move, this time to Calcutta, where on 9th March they occupied Fort William. After a 12 year deployment to India, the regiment finally made preparations to their return to England and between 24th February and 1st March 1862 embarked on the transports *Malabar*, *Salamanca* and *Dartmouth*. The regiment was landed at Portsmouth in late June and took up residence in the Raglan Barracks in Devonport.

Richard was promoted to the rank of Captain on 9th December 1864, at which time he relinquished his position as adjutant of the regiment.[242]

On 10th April 1865, the regiment was assigned to the South West district where they established headquarters at Fort Grange and Fort Pouncer, detachments were located at Gosport, Weymouth and Portland where they constructed defensive works.

On 2nd March 1866, the regiment were sent to Ireland as part of the reinforcements despatched to quell the 'Fenian Rebellion'. Disembarking from the troopship *Tamor* at Kingstown on 6th March, the regiment took up station in Richmond Barracks until they were assigned to Kilkenny in September.

After an arduous tour in Ireland, on 20th March 1867, the regiment were despatched to garrison Gibraltar, where they were ultimately to occupy the Buena Vista Barracks.

In July 1868, the regiment were told to make ready for a deployment to Singapore and Hong Kong, however, it was not until 8th October that they boarded the troopship *Himalaya* bound for Hong Kong where they arrived on 21st December.

On 25th September 1871, the regiment departed for the Cape Colony, where they arrived at East London on 10th October and were stationed at King William's Town, Pietermaritzburg and Durban. On 17th July 1872, Richard was promoted to the rank of Major.[243] During January 1875, the regiment started preparations for their return to the United Kingdom and on 26th March arrived at Queenstown, Belfast and established detachments at Armagh, Newtownards and Drogheda.

Following the retirement of Colonel Thomas Milles, Richard was promoted to the rank of Lieutenant-Colonel on 18th December 1875 and was given command of the regiment,[244] becoming only the third person to rise through the ranks to regimental command.

In April 1876, the regiment moved to the Curragh, where they were to remain for just over a year and on 28th May 1877 boarded *HMS Assistance* bound for their next posting to Guernsey and Alderney. This posting was of short duration and in just a year they boarded *HMS Orontes* bound for England, after landing in Portsmouth they took up residence at Aldershot. On 30th October 1880 the regiment was posted to Chatham. On 18th December 1880, having completed five years with the rank of regimental Lieutenant-Colonel, Richard was retired on half-pay and given a brevet promotion to the rank of Colonel.[245]

On 26th March 1881, in recognition of his exemplary military service, Richard was appointed as Major and Lieutenant-Governor of the Royal Hospital at Chelsea, where he took up residence.[246]

Richard died in the hospital on 24th January 1885 at the age of 58 and was later buried in Brompton Cemetery, London with full military honours.

Richard's Victoria Cross medal is on public display at the Gordon Highlanders Museum in Aberdeen.

Figure 125a. Grave of Richard Wadeson

241 *London Gazette* – 22274/2319
242 *London Gazette* – 22919/6485
243 *London Gazette* – 23882/3441

244 *London Gazette* – 24281/3
245 *London Gazette* – 24915/6800
246 *London Gazette* – 24954/1360

Andrew Cathcart Bogle
29th July 1857 (VC No. 148)

Gazetted: 2nd September 1859 22303/3302

Rank and Unit: Lieutenant – 78th Regiment of Foot

Citation
For conspicuous gallantry on the 29th July, 1857, in the attack at Oonao, in leading the way into a loop-holed house, strongly occupied by the enemy, from which a heavy fire harassed the advance of his regiment. Captain Bogle was severely wounded in this important service.

Figure 126. Andrew Cathcart Bogle

Biography
Andrew was born on 20th January 1829, at Govern in Glasgow to parents Archibald and Janet (née Bogle).[247] He was the second son and third child, with three brothers and two sisters, all born in Govan: Robert born on 14th September 1826,[248] Mary born on 15th October 1827, Margaret Agnes born on 25th August 1830, Archibald George born on 20th April 1832 and Michael James born on 19th March 1835.

From August 1842 until December 1847, Andrew was educated at Cheltenham College.

Andrew began his career in the army on 28th December 1849 when he purchased a commission as Ensign in the 72nd Regiment of Foot.[249] On 15th February 1850, Andrew transferred by way of exchange to 78th Regiment of Foot,[250] soon afterwards he would have joined his regiment in either Colabba, Bombay or in Aden, the regiment having been split into two wings during 1849. The left wing were ordered to Poona were they arrived from Bombay on 18th February 1853 and the right wing were also despatched from Aden, arriving at Poona on 5th March thus reuniting the regiment for the first time in over 3 years. On 18th March 1853, Andrew advanced his career by the purchase of a promotion to the rank of Lieutenant.[251]

On 1st November 1856, in response to threats to Afghanistan and possible incursions into India, the Governor-General of India, Viscount Charles Canning, declared war on Persia.

A naval expedition, under the command of Major-General Stalker was quickly despatched to the Persian Gulf and on 10th

December, the significant port of Busheer was captured and placed under British administration.

On 19th January 1857, Andrew and the regiment set sail from Bombay in three transports, as reinforcements to the first expedition, and landed at Busheer on 1st February. On 7th February, Andrew and the regiment were involved in the Battle of Khushab, where the Persian army were defeated with heavy losses. After an intense naval bombardment of the fortress at Mohammrah, Andrew and the regiment were disembarked from the transport *Berenice* on 26th March and occupied the port. On 2nd April, the regiment was involved in the Battle of Ahvaz and on their return to Mohammrah on the 5th April received the news that a peace treaty had been signed in Paris on 4th March, the Anglo-Persian war was now at an end. For his service during the war, Andrew was awarded the India General Service medal with clasp for Persia.

With the end of the war, on 10th May the regiment set sail from Mohammrah, for their return to India, landing at Bombay on 23rd May. On their arrival at Bombay, they received news of the Mutiny and the rebels capture of Delhi and were immediately despatched to Calcutta where they arrived on 10th June 1857. On 13th June the regiment received urgent orders to proceed to Barrackpore where they disarmed to the native troops. Arriving back at Calcutta on 16th June, the regiment were immediately redirect to Allahabad, where Brigadier-General Havelock was assembling a force to march to the relief of Cawnpore and Lucknow. On 7th July the force left Allahabad on route to Cawnpore, on the way they fought battles at Futtehpore on 10th, Aong on 14th and Pandoo-Nuddee on 16th. After some fierce fighting, the city of Cawnpore was recaptured on 16th July 1857. On 25th July, after leaving a detachment to defend Cawnpore, General Havelock set off with his force towards Lucknow and on 29th July faced a large number of mutineers at the heavily

---

247 They were cousins
248 Robert, who was a Captain in the 78th, was killed in action at Lucknow, during the Indian Mutiny
249 *London Gazette* – 21054/3944 – It was previously reported that he joined the 78th on 23rd November 1849 (LG 21040/3526) however, this was later rescinded (LG 21042/3648).
250 *London Gazette* – 21068/424
251 *London Gazette* – 21422/811

fortified village of Oonoa. It was during the taking of the village that Andrew performed the deeds for which he would later be awarded the Victoria Cross, during the action he was severely wounded. Andrew was also mentioned in the despatches of General Havelock for his part in the action.[252] After some setbacks, General Havelock's force eventually accomplished the 1st Relief of Lucknow on 25th September and would defend the residency until relieved by the force of Sir Colin Campbell on 17th November. Andrew was appointed as Adjutant on 24th February 1858.[253] On 26th April 1858, Andrew and the regiment joined the Rohilkhand field force at Cawnpore, which had been formed on 29th March under the command of Brigadier-General Walpole. Andrew was involved with the regiment at the Battle of Bareilly on the 5th May and after successfully ejecting the rebels, the 78th occupied the town and formed the garrison. On 31st August 1858, Andrew was promoted to the rank of Captain and transferred to 13th Regiment of Foot[254] and a year later on 30th August 1859 was transferred to the 10th Regiment of Foot by way of an exchange.[255] Andrew returned to England during 1859, after having spent almost ten years in India. The regiment was stationed in Plymouth with headquarters at Devonport. For his service in India, Andrew was awarded the Indian Mutiny medal with clasps for Defence of Lucknow and Lucknow.

At some stage, probably after his return from India, Andrew married Effield (née Messiter), the couple would not have any children.

On 4th January 1860, Andrew was presented with his Victoria Cross medal by Queen Victoria at an investiture held at Windsor Castle.

In 1862, the regiment was deployed to Ireland, where they were based at the Curragh Army Camp in County Kildare.

On 25th April 1865, Andrew purchased a commission of Major and was placed on the half pay list,[256] for some time he served as Aide-de-Camp to Lieutenant-General Sir J. L. Pennefather at Aldershot.

Andrew was assigned from the half pay list as a Major with the 23rd Regiment of Foot,[257] however, instead of taking up this appointment it appears that he resigned from the army by way of the sale of his commission.

Little is known of Andrew's life after the army other than he moved to Dorset where he died at his home, Sherborne House, Sherborne on 11th December 1890, after a long illness.

Andrew was cremated at Woking, a few days later on 16th December, probably the first Victoria Cross recipient to be cremated.[258]

Andrew's Victoria Cross medal is on public display at the Regimental Museum of The Queen's Own Highlanders at Fort George near Inverness.

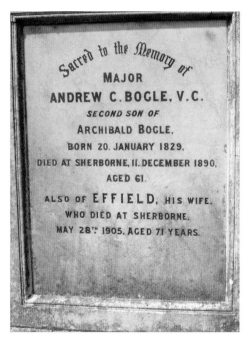

Figure 126a. Grave of Andrew Cathcart Bogle

252 *London Gazette* – 22050/3416
253 *London Gazette* – 22132/2095
254 *London Gazette* – 22178/3983
255 *London Gazette* – 22302/3239
256 *London Gazette* – 22961/2188
257 *London Gazette* – 23415/4630

258 Andrew was the 151st person to have been cremated in the whole of the United Kingdom.

George Lambert
29th July 1857 (VC No. 149)

Gazetted: 18th June 1858 22154/2957

Rank and Unit: Sergeant Major – 84th Regiment of Foot

Citation

For distinguished conduct, at Onao, on the 29th of July; at Bithoor, on the 16th of August; and at Lucknow, on the 25th of September. **(Extract from Field Force Orders of the late Major-General Havelock, dated 17th October, 1857.)**

Biography

George was born on 16th December 1819 at Market Hill in Co. Armagh, Ireland. His father, also named George was a farmer.

On 6th June 1840, George enlisted in the British army as a private in the 84th Regiment of Foot, probably at Dublin where a few days earlier the regiment had arrived for a tour of duty in Ireland. George spent his first two years of service in Ireland, initially based at Dublin then from 5th August 1841 in Naas and finally in Limerick from 3rd September 1841.

George was sent off on foreign service to the East Indies on 8th August 1842 and would spend the next 17 years in Burma and India. His first posting was to Moulmein, in Burma, where the regiment was stationed from 6th September 1842, this was followed by a series of postings in India: Madras from 28th March 1845, Secunderabad from 20th February 1847, and Trichinopoly from 21st January 1850. From 15th January 1854, the regiment was once again stationed in Burma, this time in Rangoon. By the time of the mutiny, George had risen through the ranks to the rank of Sergeant-Major and the regiment was rushed from Rangoon to India, where they joined the Field Force of General Havelock.

It was at the Battle of Oonoa, on 29th July 1857, that George performed the first of the deeds for which he would later be awarded the Victoria Cross. George was also involved in the two battles at Busherut-gunge which took place on 29th July and 5th August 1857 and in the action at Boorbeake Chowkee on 12th August. It was at the Battle of Bithoor on 16th August, that George performed the second deed mentioned in his Victoria Cross citation. The regiment was also involved in action at Mungawar on 21st September just before their involvement in the assault and capture of Lucknow on 25th September 1857. It was during this action that George performed the deed for which he received his third Victoria Cross citation and where he was seriously wounded in the head. From 26th November 1857, the regiment was station in Alum Bagh and on 12th December 1857, George

received a commission as Ensign.[259] In early 1858, the regiment were assigned to the Azamgarh Field Force under the command of Sir Edward Layard and on 15th April 1858 were involved in the second relief of Azamgarh. The regiment were stationed at Buxar from 9th June 1858 and on 2nd July George was appointed as Adjutant to the regiment.[260] George was promoted to the rank of Lieutenant on 17th September 1858.[261] From 14th March 1859, the regiment was stationed at Dum Dum and it was from here, a few months later that they began their return journey to England, after 17 years in the East Indies. For his service during the mutiny, George was awarded the Indian Mutiny medal with clasps for The defence of Lucknow and Lucknow.

On their return from India, the regiment was based at Hillsborough Barracks in Sheffield from 3rd September 1859 and it was here on the parade ground that George died from an aortic aneurism on 10th February 1860.

There is no record of the details of any presentation of George's Victoria Cross medal, perhaps because he died so soon after his return from India it was never actually presented.

George was buried at Wardsend Cemetery in Sheffield on 18th February, his Victoria Cross medal is on public display at the York and Lancaster Regiment Museum in Rotherham.

Figure 127a. Grave of George Lambert

259 *London Gazette* – 22090/498
260 *London Gazette* – 22158/3137
261 *London Gazette* – 22194/4577

Ross Lowis Mangles
30th July 1857 (VC No. 150)

Gazetted: 6th July 1859 22283/2629

Rank and Unit: Civilian – Bengal Civil Service

Citation

Mr. Mangles volunteered and served with the Force, consisting of detachments of Her Majesty's 10th and 37th Regiments, and some Native Troops, despatched to the relief of Arrah, in July, 1857, under the Command of Captain Dunbar, of the 10th Regiment.

The Force fell into an Ambuscade on the night of the 29th of July, 1857, and, during the retreat on the next morning, Mr. Mangles, with signal gallantry and generous self-devotion, and notwithstanding that he had himself been previously wounded, carried for several miles, out of action, a wounded soldier of Her Majesty's 37th Regiment, after binding up his wounds under a murderous fire, which killed or wounded almost the whole detachment and he bore him in safety to the boats.

Biography

Ross was born on 14th April 1833 in Calcutta, India. His father was Ross Donnelly a member of the Bengal Civil Service[262] and mother Harriett (née Newcombe).

Ross was educated at Bath Grammar School and the Honourable East India Company College at Haileybury.

In 1853, Ross followed in the steps of his father and joined the Bengal Civil Service and served as assistant Magistrate at Patna until 1857.

During 1857, he accompanied the 45th regiment (Rattray's Sikhs) and helped to quell a disturbance in Patna City. Ross volunteered to join the Arrah Relief Force, made up of units from the 10th Regiment of Foot and 37th Regiment of Foot, commanded by Captain Dunbar of the 10th. The force proceeded to Arrah and it was during a failed attempt to gain entry to the city on the night of 29th/30th July that Ross performed the deeds for which he would later be awarded the Victoria Cross.

It was Sir James Outram who recommended Ross, together with Mr. W. McDonell, for the award of the Victoria Cross, however, as both men were civilians this was initially rejected. It was only after extensive lobbying to London, by the India

Figure 128. Ross Lowis Mangles

Governor-General Lord Canning, that on 10th August 1858 a Royal Warrant was issued to amend the original warrant and allow the award to be made to civilians in certain circumstances. With the award having been confirmed Ross became the first of only five civilians to have been awarded the Victoria Cross.

In early August 1857, after the mutineers had been cleared from Arrah, Ross was appointed as Magistrate to the Chumparan District of North Behar and in early 1858 moved to Jenan in the Churpah district, after the mutineers returned to Behar. For his service during the mutiny Ross was awarded the Indian Mutiny Medal.

In September 1858, Ross returned to England on sick leave and did not return to India until January 1860. It appears that the last few weeks of Ross's stay in England was very busy as on 4th January 1860 he was presented with his Victoria Cross medal by Queen Victoria at Windsor Castle.

Sometime in January Ross also married Henrietta Anne (née More-Molyneux), the couple would go on to have five children: Ross Donnelly born in November 1861 at Tiparah in Bengal who died on 21st December 1862 at 13 months old: Walter James born in India on 13th September 1862:[263] Mary Harriet born on 26th January 1864 at Chittagong in India: Arthur Edward Ross born in 1867 at Pirbright and Rowland Henry born on 9th February 1874 in Guildford.

On his return to India, Ross had several roles within the Bengal Civil Service: Commissioner, 2nd Class, Revenue and Circuit, Residency Division, Bengal: Judicial Commissioner of Mysore and Coorg in Madras: Secretary to the Government of Bengal and Member of the Board of Revenue, Lower Provinces.

---

262 After his retirement from the Civil Service, he served as Member of Parliament for Guildford and was a Director and Chairman of the East India Company.

263 Became a Major in the army and was awarded the Distinguished Service Order (DSO)

Ross retired from the Bengal Civil Service during 1883 and returned to England where he took up residence at The Lodge, Pirbright near Woking in Surrey.

Ross died at home on 28th February 1905 at the age of 71, and was buried in Brookwood Cemetery near Woking.

Ross's Victoria Cross medal is on public display at the National Army Museum in Chelsea.

Figure 128a. Grave of Ross Lowis Mangles

William Fraser McDonell
30th July 1857 (VC No. 151)

Gazetted: 17th February 1860 22357/557

Rank and Unit: Civilian – Bengal Civil Service

Citation

For great coolness and bravery on the 30th of July, 1857, during the retreat of the British Troops from Arrah, in having climbed, under an incessant fire, outside the Boat in which he and several Soldiers were, up to the rudder, and with considerable difficulty cut through the lashing which secured it to the side of the boat. On the lashing being cut, the boat obeyed the helm, and thus thirty-five European Soldiers escaped certain death.

Biography

William was born on 17th December 1829 at Pittville House in Cheltenham. His father was Aeneas Ranald, who was a member of the Madras Civil Service, his mother was Juliana Charlotte (née Wade).

William was educated at Cheltenham College from 1841 until he completed his education at the Honourable East India Company College at Haileybury from 1847 until 1849, graduating with the classification of First Class, Highly Distinguished.

In 1849, William joined the Bengal Civil Service and from 1852 until 1855 performed the role of Assistant Magistrate and Collector at Sarun until he was promoted to the position of Magistrate of Sarun.

With the outbreak of the mutiny, the Civil Officers of the outlying districts were concentrated at Patna and William found himself temporarily without a job. With time on his hands, William joined the Arrah Relief Force which departed from Dinapore on 29th July 1957 to go to the assistance of the small force of about 70 which was beleaguered within the town. It was on 30th July during the retreat from Arrah that William performed the deeds for which he would be awarded the Victoria Cross becoming only the second civilian to receive the award. With the end of the mutiny in Behar, William returned to his position of Magistrate at Sarun and until June 1860 was involved in the settling of the confiscated estates of the rebel leader Koer Kahn. After completing the task of settling the estates, William began a leave of absence and returned to Europe.

William was presented with his Victoria Cross medal by Queen Victoria on 9th November 1860 at an investiture held at Windsor Castle.

Figure 129. William Fraser McDonell

On his return to India in 1863, William was Magistrate and Collector at Nadia until he was appointed as a Judge. William took another leave of absence during 1870. William held the position as judge until 1874, at which time he was appointed as a Judge on the High Court at Fort William in Calcutta. Initially the appointment was on a temporary basis but was made permanent in 1878, William held this position until his retirement on 29th April 1886.

Following his retirement, William returned to England where he lived in London until 1890.

At some stage William married Alice (née Phelps) at the cathedral in Cape Town, the couple would have four daughters: Jane Louise was the first born and Helen Grant was the youngest.

In 1890, William moved to Cheltenham where he was a member of the Council and a governor of Cheltenham College until his death.

In 1893, William spent the winter in Malta due to his failing health.

During 1894, while watching a cricket match in Cheltenham, William caught a chill which developed into pneumonia and after a short illness he died on 31st July 1894. He was buried in St Peter's Churchyard at Leckhampton near Cheltenham.

William's Victoria Cross medal is on public display at the Imperial War Museum in London, as part of the Lord Ashcroft collection. It should be noted that the medal is an official replacement as the original medal was stolen.

Figure 129a. Grave of William Fraser McDonell

William Sutton
13th September 1857 (VC No. 152)

Gazetted: 20th January 1860 22347/178

Rank and Unit: Bugler No. 2578 – 1st Battalion 60th Rifles

Citation

For gallant conduct at Delhi on the 13th of September, 1857, the night previous to the Assault, in volunteering to reconnoitre the breach. This Soldier's conduct was conspicuous throughout the operations, especially on the 2nd of August, 1857, on which occasion, during an attack by the Enemy in force, he rushed forward over the trenches, and killed one of the Enemy's Buglers, who was in the act of sounding.

Elected by the Privates of the Regiment.

Figure 130. William Sutton

Biography

Unfortunately very little is known about the life of William, who was born some time during 1830[264] in Ightham near Sevenoaks in Kent.

If we assume that William enlisted in the army at some time around his 18th birthday, say in 1848–1850 then he would have joined the 1st Battalion of the 60th Rifles in India.

The regiment spent the years leading up to the mutiny garrisoned at various stations in the Punjab and at the start of the mutiny were at Meerut where it all started. The regiment moved on to Delhi and it was here on 13th September 1857, during an assault on the city, that he performed the deeds that would later result in the award of the Victoria Cross. William was selected for the award under the terms of rule 13, as a result of a ballot of the privates of the regiment. The regiment was involved throughout the mutiny taking part in the Rohilkhand campaign in the district of Oude. The regiment left India from Calcutta in 1860 and arrived in Dover where they formed the garrison. For his service during the mutiny, William was awarded the India Mutiny Medal with clasp for Delhi.

William was presented with his Victoria Cross medal by Queen Victoria on 9th November 1860 at an investiture held in Windsor Castle.

William was stationed in Aldershot and London until the regiment were posted to Ireland in 1864, taking up posts at Dublin, Newry, Enniskillen and Derry until 1866 when the regiment had a short posting to Malta.

In 1867, the regiment was posted to Canada and after spending some time in Montreal and Quebec, were posted to Halifax Nova Scotia where they would remain until 1877.

On their return to England in 1877, the regiment was stationed at Portsmouth and Winchester until 1879 and it is likely that William retired from the army during this period as during 1881 it is recorded that he was employed as a Bricklayer's labourer.

Some time prior to 1881, William was married as in this year it is recorded that he was a widower.

William died on 16th February 1888 in Ightham, at the age of 57 and was buried in an unmarked grave in St Peter's Parish Church, Ightham on 20th February.

William's Victoria Cross medal is on public display at the Royal Green Jackets Museum in Winchester.

It should be noted that the medal on display is not the original as this was lost and William purchased a replacement on 20th January 1872.

---

264 Perhaps his date of birth was 1831, the 1881 census gives his age as 49, also it is recorded that a William Sutton was baptised at Igtham on 1st May 1831.

Joseph Petrus Hendrik Crowe
12th August 1857 (VC No. 153)

Gazetted: 15th January 1858 22083/178

Rank and Unit: Lieutenant – 78th Regiment of Foot

Citation

For being the first to enter the redoubt at Bourzekee Chowkee, the entrenched village in front of the Busherut-gunge, on the 12th of August. **(Telegram from the late Major- General Sir Henry Havelock to the Commander- in- Chief in India, dated, Cawnpore, 18th August, 1857.)**

Biography

Joseph was born on 12th January 1826, at Vermaak's Military Post, near Uitenhage in the Cape Colony, South Africa. He was the youngest son of father Joseph who was a Lieutenant in the 60th Regiment of Foot and mother Classina Magdalena (née Vermaak), who was Afrikaans.

Joseph had an older sister Maria Margaret, an older brother Thomas Coenraad and a younger sister Doretheya Susanna. In 1826, the family moved to 34 Cuyler Street in Uitenhage and in 1839 moved to 2 Caledon Street, it is likely that Joseph, like his brother before him, was educated by Mr James Rose Innes.

It is possible that Joseph served with local levies (Provisional Companies attached to British Regiments) before, on the recommendation of Governors Sir George Napier and Sir Henry Pottinger, he received a commission as Ensign in the 78th Regiment of Foot on 27th October 1846.[265]

Joseph left the Cape Colony during February 1847, bound with his regiment for a tour of duty in India. The regiment was stationed in Bombay until the outbreak of the Anglo-Persian War. On 17th September 1850, Joseph was promoted to the rank of Lieutenant.[266]

Following the declaration of War against Persia, Joseph and the 78th were despatched to the war zone on 19th January 1857 and landed to occupy the port of Busheer on 1st February. On 7th February, Joseph was involved in the Battle of Khushab, where the enemy suffered heavy losses. After a heavy naval bombardment, the 78th occupied the fortress of Mohammrah on 26th March and on 2nd April took part in the Battle of Ahwaz. For his service in the War, Joseph was awarded the India General Service Medal with clasp for Persia.

Figure 131. Joseph Petrus Hendrik Crowe

With the end of the war, on 4th March the regiment set sail from Mohammrah on 10th May, for their return to India and landed at Bombay on 23rd May. On their arrival at Bombay, they received news of the Mutiny and the rebels capture of Delhi and were immediately despatched to Calcutta where they arrived on 10th June 1857.

On 13th June the regiment received urgent orders to proceed to Barrackpore where they disarmed the native troops. Arriving back at Calcutta on 16th June, the regiment were immediately redirected to Allahabad, where Brigadier-General Havelock was assembling a force to march to the relief of Cawnpore and Lucknow. On 7th July the force left Allahabad on route to Cawnpore, on the way they fought battles at Futtehpore on 10th, Aong on 14th and Pandoo-Nuddee on 16th. After some fierce fighting, the city of Cawnpore was recaptured on 16th July 1857. On 25th July, after leaving a detachment to defend Cawnpore, General Havelock set off with his force towards Lucknow and on 29th July faced a large number of mutineers at the heavily fortified village of Oonoa. It was on 12th August 1857, in the attack on the fortified village of Boozeke Chowkee on the outskirts of Cawnpore, that Joseph performed the deeds for which he would later be awarded the Victoria Cross. After some setbacks, General Havelock's force eventually accomplished the 1st Relief of Lucknow on 25th September, during which Joseph was slightly wounded.[267] The regiment would defend the residency until relieved by the force of Sir Colin Campbell on 17th November. Joseph was promoted to the rank of Captain on 8th January 1858 and was transferred to the 10th Regiment.[268]

265 *London Gazette* – 20653/3766
266 *London Gazette* – 21136/2516
267 *London Gazette* – 22112/1400
268 *London Gazette* – 22082/145

For his service during the mutiny, Joseph was awarded the Indian Mutiny medal with clasps for Defence of Lucknow and Lucknow.

On 18th March 1859, Joseph left India after 12 years on the sub-continent and landed at Plymouth on 13th July and then moved to Ireland.

On 20th December 1859, Joseph received a brevet promotion to the rank of Major.[269]

In 1860, Joseph was posted to the Cape Colony in South Africa and for a few months in 1862 commanded the regiment at Port Elizabeth. At some stage the regiment moved to Fort Beaufort where they were stationed until their return to India on 21st November 1864.

On 28th August 1866, Joseph was promoted to the rank of Major[270] as a result of this a promotion scheduled for 22 January 1867 was cancelled.

In 1868, Joseph began a deployment to Japan which lasted until 1871, during this tour, on 2nd January 1871 Joseph received a brevet promotion to the rank of Lieutenant-Colonel[271] and was given command of a brigade.

From Japan, the regiment was deployed to Hong-Kong and Singapore and from this station were deployed to the Perak War in Malaya from 1875 until 1876.

On 23rd October 1875, Joseph was promoted to the rank of Lieutenant-Colonel and was given command of the 2nd Battalion.[272]

On 8th March 1876, after a career of 29 years, Joseph retired from the army on full pay and was given the honorary brevet rank of Colonel.[273]

On his return to England, Joseph caught a chill while shooting snipe in Ireland and died on 12th April 1876 at his home in Penge, Surrey from congestion of the lungs and heart disease.

Joseph was buried in West Norwood Cemetery in London, however, in 1976 almost exactly 100 years after his death, his body was exhumed on the instruct of relatives and on 5th February 1977 was reinterred in the Old Moths section of the Old Anglican Cemetery in Uitinhage, South Africa.

Upon his death, Josephs Victoria Cross medal was inherited by his older sister Maria Margaret where it was stored with his other medals at the family home "Firlands", Rondebosch in South Africa where they were unfortunately destroyed in a fire during 1942.

Figure 131a. Grave of Joseph Petrus Hendrik Crowe

---

269 *London Gazette* – 22338/4779
270 *London Gazette* – 23250/2758
271 *London Gazette* – 23669/249
272 *London Gazette* – 24265/5378
273 *London Gazette* – 24303/1790

James Blair
12th August 1857 (VC No. 154)

Gazetted: 25th February 1862 22601/956

Rank and Unit: Captain – 2nd Bombay Light Cavalry

Citation

For having on two occasions distinguished himself by his gallant and daring conduct.

1. On the night of the 12th of August, 1857, at Neemuch, in volunteering to apprehend 7 or 8 armed mutineers who had shut themselves up for defence in a house, the door of which he burst open. He then rushed in among them, and forced them to escape through the roof; in this encounter, he was severely wounded. In spite of his wounds he pursued the fugitives, but was unable to come up with them, in consequence of the darkness of the night.

2. On the 23rd of October, 1857, at Jeerum, in fighting his way most gallantly through a body of rebels who had literally surrounded him. After breaking the end of his sword on one of their heads, and receiving a severe sword cut on his right arm, he rejoined his troop. In this wounded condition, and with no other weapon than the hilt of his broken sword, he put himself at the head of his men, charged the rebels most effectually, and dispersed them.

Biography

James was born on 27th January 1828 at Nimach in the Gwalior State, India to father Edward Macleod[274] who was a Captain in the Bengal Cavalry and mother Susanna (née Kennedy).

James was the second son and third of ten children with an older brother Edward Robert born on 25th May 1825 and an older sister Eliza born on 4th October 1826. He also had four younger brothers: Thomas Hawkes born on 4th November 1829, Robert born on 1st August 1835, Charles Renny born on 14th February 1837 and Henry born on 23rd June 1841 together with three younger sisters: Charlotte born on 11th September 1831, Isabella born on 8th May 1833 and Susan born on 18th January 1840. All of the children were born in India.

James was educated in England, for some time attending the Reverend Daniel Godfrey school in Walcot near Bath in Somerset.

On 10th June 1844, James followed in his father's footsteps when, at the age of 16, he enlisted with the Bengal Cavalry as an

Figure 132. James Blair

Ensign. On 19th March 1848, James was promoted to the rank of Lieutenant.

James was married to Francis Belinda Emily (née Halhed) on 2nd January 1851 at Bath in Somerset, the couple would have two children: James Edward born in Bath on 4th November 1851 and Emily Jessie Ellen born on 11th May 1853 at Raijhkote in India.

At the start of the mutiny, James and his regiment were stationed at Nasirabad where despite the rebellion of the Artillery and Infantry the Cavalry remained loyal and took part in the campaign to pacify Central India. It was during actions at Neemuch in Bengal on 12th August 1857, that James performed the first of the deeds for which he would later be awarded the Victoria Cross, where he was severely wounded. The regiment were involved in the Battle of Nimbhara on 19th September 1857. The second deed mentioned in James's Victoria Cross citation, took place on 23rd October 1857 where he was again severely wounded, this time by a sword cut to his right arm. For his service during the mutiny, James was awarded the Indian Mutiny Medal with clasp for Central India, he also received a mention in despatches.

James was presented with his Victoria Cross Medal by Lieutenant-General Sir W. Mansfield the GOC at Bombay, sometime during 1862.

Following the dissolution of the Honourable East India Company and its armies, in an India Office memo dated 1st march 1864, James was appointed as a Captain in the British Army pre-dated to 23rd October 1857.[275] On 10th June 1864, James was promoted to the rank of Major[276] and exactly six years later on 10th June 1870 received a brevet promotion to the rank of Lieutenant-Colonel.[277] James's brevet promotion

---

274 E. M. Blair was killed in action on 12th January 1842 in the retreat from Kabul during the 1st Anglo-Afghan War.

275 *London Gazette* – 22828/1368
276 *London Gazette* – 22952/1751
277 *London Gazette* – 23705/487

to the rank of Lieutenant-Colonel was made substantive on 30th July 1874[278] and on 10th June 1875 he received a brevet promotion to the rank of Colonel.[279] In 1880, James was given command of the 1st Regiment Bengal Cavalry and from 1882 until 1885 served as the Political Resident in Aden with the rank of Brigadier-General. On 2nd July 1885, James was promoted to the rank of Major-General.[280] Sometime in early 1889, James was promoted to the rank of Lieutenant-General and on 25th May 1889 was appointed as an ordinary member 3rd Class (Commander) of the Military Division of the Most Honourable Order of the Bath.[281]

On 2nd July 1890 was placed on the Unemployed Supernumerary List,[282] effectively bringing his active army career to an end.

It is presumed that after his retirement from army life, James returned to England, where for a time he lived in Thorpe Hall, Wycliffe in Darlington before moving to The Pavilion in Melrose.

On 1st April 1894, while still on the Unemployed Supernumerary List, James was promoted to the rank of General.[283]

James died at his home in Melrose on 14th January 1905, aged 77 and was buried on 22nd January in Trinity Churchyard, Melrose.

James's Victoria Cross medal is believed to be in private hands.

It should be noted that James was the cousin of Robert Blair of the 2nd Dragoon Guards, who also was awarded a Victoria Cross for deeds performed on 28th September 1857 at Bulandshahr during the Indian Mutiny.

Figure 132a. Grave of James Blair

---

278 *London Gazette* – 24152/5409
279 *London Gazette* – 24253/4770
280 *London Gazette* – 25494/3476
281 *London Gazette* – 25939/2873
282 *London Gazette* – 26072/4046
283 *London Gazette* – 26519/3257

Denis Dempsey
12th August 1857 (VC No. 155)

Gazetted: 17th February 1860 22357/557

Rank and Unit: Private No. 2134 – 10th Regiment of Foot (1st Battalion)

Citation

For having, at Lucknow, on the 14th March, 1858, carried a Powder Bag through a burning village, with great coolness and gallantry, for the purpose of mining a passage in rear of' the enemy's position. This he did, exposed to a very heavy fire from the enemy behind loop holed walls, and to an almost still greater danger from the sparks which flew in every direction from the blazing houses.

Also, for having been the first man who entered the village of Jugdeespore on the 12th August, 1857, under a most galling fire.

Private Dempsey was likewise one of those who helped to carry Ensign Erskine, of the 10th Regiment, in the retreat from Arrah, in July, 1857.

Biography

Denis was born some time during 1826 in Rathmichael Bray in Co Wicklow, Ireland.

It is probable that Denis enlisted in the army at or around the time of his 18th birthday, say in 1844, if this was the case then he would have joined his regiment the 10th Foot on foreign service in India where they had been stationed since 1842.

Denis first saw action when he was involved in the 2nd Anglo-Sikh war, during which he was involved in the siege and capture of Multan – this lasted from August 1848 until 22nd January 1849 when the town surrendered. Denis was also involved in the decisive Battle of Goojerat which took place on 21st February 1849. For his service in the 2nd Anglo-Sikh war, Denis was awarded the Punjab Medal with clasps for Mooltan and Goojerat.

At the start of the mutiny, the regiment were stationed at Dinapore with responsibility for guarding the communications between Calcutta and Delhi, so could not take part in the siege of Delhi. On 25th July 1857, fearing that the local troops would rebel, the commander at Dinapore attempted to disarm them. In response, the local troops numbering almost 2,000 deserted and fled to Arrah where they besieged the small garrison of about 70 Sikh's. On 29th July, Denis was part of the force of 400 men from the 10th and 37th regiments, under the command of Captain Dunbar, sent to relieve the town.

Figure 133. Denis Dempsey

The Arrah Relief Force was ambushed by the mutineers just outside of the town and after suffering heavy losses they were forced to retreat. It was during this retreat that Denis performed one of the deeds mentioned in his Victoria Cross Citation he helped carry the seriously wounded Ensign Erskine for more than two miles under constant fire from the enemy. Unfortunately, Ensign Erskine died from his wounds the next day. A force of men and artillery from the 5th Fusiliers, commanded by Major Vincent Eyre, managed to relieve Arrah on 3rd August 1857.

On 12th August 1857, Denis performed the 2nd deed to appear in his Victoria Cross citation, when he was the first man of the regiment to enter the town of Jugdeespore, despite heavy fire from the enemy, during the successful assault on the town. Denis and the 10th Regiment were part of the force of about 2,000 men, under the command of Sir Colin Campbell sent to the relief of Lucknow.

From the 1st March 1858, the force was engaged in assaults on Lucknow and it was on 14th March during a successful attack on the town that Denis performed the deed for which he would later be awarded the Victoria Cross. Lucknow was relieved two days later.

For his service during the mutiny, Denis was awarded the Indian Mutiny Medal with clasp for Lucknow.

On 18th March 1859, Denis left India after 15 years of duty in the sub-continent, the regiment arrived at Portsmouth on 13th July and were garrisoned at Devonport.

Denis was presented with his Victoria Cross medal by Queen Victoria on 9th November 1860 at an investiture held at Windsor Castle.

In 1862, the regiment were sent to Ireland where they remained until 1864 when they left for the Cape Colony in South Africa to relieve the 2nd battalion which had formed the garrison since 1860.

In 1868, Denis was off to Japan where he was stationed until the regiment moved to Hong Kong in 1871.

From Hong Kong the regiment moved to Singapore in 1872 and from 1875 to 1876 were involved in the Perak War in Malaysia.

Denis left Singapore in January 1877 and arrived in England during late April, having completed a 15 year tour of foreign service.

It is believed that Denis retired from the army upon his return to England. At some time he emigrated to Canada where he settled in Toronto.

At some stage it is believed that Denis was married, however the details are unknown.

On 10th January 1886, Denis died at his home, 103 Simcoe Street, Toronto, Canada, from congestion of the lung. He was buried in St Michael's Cemetery, Yonge Street in Toronto.

Denis's Victoria Cross Medal is believed to be in private hands.

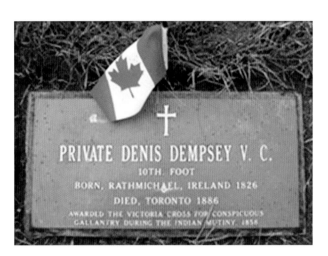

Figure 133a. Grave of Denis Dempsey

Charles John Stanley Gough
15th August 1857 (VC No. 156)

Gazetted: 21st October 1859 22318/3792

Rank and Unit: Major[284] – 5th Bengal European Cavalry

Citation

First, for gallantry in an affair at Khurkowdah, near Rhotuck, on the 15th of August, 1857, in which he saved his brother, who was wounded, and killed two of the Enemy.

Secondly, for gallantry on the 18th of August, when he led a Troop of the Guide Cavalry in a charge, and cut down two of the Enemy's Sowars, with one of whom he had a desperate hand to hand combat.

Thirdly, for-gallantly on the 27th of January, 1858, at Shumshabad, where, in a charge, he attacked one of the Enemy's leaders and pierced him with his sword, which was carried out of his hand in the melee. He defended himself with his revolver, and shot two of the Enemy.

Fourthly, for gallantry on the 23rd of February, at Meangunge, where he came to the assistance of Brevet-Major O. H. St. George Anson, and killed his opponent, immediately afterwards cutting down another of the Enemy in the same gallant manner.

Biography

Charles was born on 28th January 1832 at Chittagong in India, to father George who worked in the British Colonial Service and mother Charlotte Margaret (née Beecher). Charles had a younger brother, Hugh Henry who was born on 14th November 1833 at Calcutta. Henry would also be awarded the Victoria Cross,[285] both sons would also become Knights of the Realm.

Charles was educated in England, however, soon after his 16th birthday he returned to India and on 20th March 1848 was commissioned as a Cornet in the 8th Bengal Light Cavalry.

Almost as soon as he joined the army, Charles was involved in the 2nd Anglo-Sikh war in the Punjab. On 22nd November 1848, Charles was involved in the Battle of Ramnugger on the banks of the river Chenab. Charles was also involved in the action known

Figure 134. Charles John Stanley Gough

as the Passage of the Chenab which culminated with the Battle of Sadulpur on 3rd December 1848. He was also involved in the decisive battles of the war which took place at Chillianwala on 13th January 1849 and Goojerat on 21st February 1849. For his service during the war, Charles was awarded the Punjab Medal with clasps for Chillianwala and Goojerat.

At the time of the outbreak of the mutiny, Charles was a Lieutenant in the Corps of Guides and was part of the force sent to the relief of Delhi which had been occupied by the mutineers.

It was on 15th August 1857, at Kurkowdah on the way to Delhi, that Charles performed the first of the deeds for which he would later be awarded the Victoria Cross, during this action he saved the life of his brother Hugh. It was only three days later, on 18th August, that Charles performed the second deed mentioned in his Victoria Cross citation. During September 1857, Charles with the Corps of Guides was involved in the siege at Delhi. On 6th December 1857, Charles was promoted to the rank of Captain and transferred to Hodson's Horse and soon afterwards joined the forces of Sir Colin Campbell advancing to the relief of Lucknow. It was on 27th January 1858 at the Battle of Shumshabad that Charles performed the 3rd deed mentioned in his Victoria Cross citation and soon afterwards on 23rd February 1858 performed the 4th deed at the storming and capture of Meergunge. Charles returned with the regiment to Cawnpore and was part of the force sent to reinforce Sir James Outram in the defence of the Alum Bagh where he was wounded. With the death of William Stephen Raikes Hodson, Hodson's Horse was split up and assigned to three regiments, Charles and his brother

---

284 For the first two deeds in his Victoria Cross citation, Charles was a Lieutenant and for the next two was a Captain – the rank of Major backdated to 20th July 1858 was only granted on 1st March 1864, following the dissolution of the East India Company Armies.

285 On 12th November 1857, Sir Hugh Henry Gough,when a Lieutenant in the 1st Bengal Light Cavalry, performed the deeds at Alum Bagh, during the Indian Mutiny for which he would later be awarded the Victoria Cross.

Hugh joined 19th Hussars. Charles was also involved in the 2nd relief of Lucknow when the city was finally cleared of mutineers on 21st March 1858. During the siege and relief of Lucknow, Charles was mentioned three times in despatches and in General Orders issued by the Governor-General. On 20th July 1858, Charles received a brevet promotion to the rank of Major[286] in the Bengal Native Cavalry. For his service during the mutiny, Charles was awarded the Indian Mutiny Medal with clasps for Delhi and Relief of Lucknow.

Charles was presented with his Victoria Cross medal by Queen Victoria at an investiture held at Windsor Castle on 4th January 1860.

On 1st March 1864, following the dissolution of the Honourable East India Company Armies, Charles was commissioned in the British Army (Bengal Cavalry) with the rank of Major, effective 20th July 1858.[287]

Charles was appointed as Commandant of the 5th Regiment of the Bengal Cavalry on 26th May 1864 and it was in this capacity that he would serve in the Bhutan or Duar War, which lasted from November 1864 until 11 November 1865, ended by Treaty of Sinchula. For his service in the war, Charles was awarded the India General Service Medal with clasp for Bhutan.

On 12th February 1867, Charles received a brevet promotion to the rank of Lieutenant-Colonel.[288]

Charles was married to Harriet Anastasia (née de la Poer – Power) on 16th June 1869, at Kildalcon Church, Clonmel in Ireland. The couple would go on to have three children, Hubert born on 12th August 1870, John Edmund[289] born on 25th October 1871 and Annie Frances Harriette born during April 1873 (who would die before her seventh birthday).

On 29th May 1875, Charles was appointed as an Ordinary Member 3rd Class (Companion) of the Military Division of the Most Honourable Order of the Bath.[290]

Charles received a brevet promotion to the rank of Colonel on 28th November 1875[291] and on 16th July 1876 was promoted to the substantive rank of Lieutenant-Colonel.[292]

With the outbreak of the first phase of the 2nd Anglo-Afghan war in September 1878, Charles was given command of a cavalry Brigade in the Peshawar Valley Field Force which was commanded by Lieutenant-Colonel Sir Samuel Browne.[293] In this phase of the war, which ended with the treaty at Gandamak in May 1879, Charles was involved in the Battle of Ali Masjid on 21st November 1878 and commanded troops in action at Futteabad. During this period, Charles was mentioned in despatches on several occasions. After a massacre at the British Mission in Kabul on 3rd September 1879, the second phase of the war began and on 1st December 1879, Charles was given command of the 1st Brigade in the force of Major-General Bright, charged with securing the communication lines between the Khyber Pass and Kabul. For the last months of the war, which ended in September 1880, Charles was involved in various actions around Kabul. For his service during the war, Charles was awarded the Afghanistan Medal with clasps for Ali Masjid and Kabul.

At the end of the war, Charles returned to India where he was given command of the Hyderabad Contingent and on 22nd February 1881 was appointed as an Ordinary Member 2nd Class (Knight Commander) of the Military Division of the Most Honourable Order of the Bath.[294]

Figure 134a. Grave of Charles John Stanley Gough

286 *London Gazette* – 22164/3379
287 *London Gazette* – 22828/1344
288 *London Gazette* – 23360/1587
289 Like his father and uncle before him John would be awarded a Victoria Cross on 22nd April 1903 for deeds performed at Daratoleh during the war in Somaliland.
290 *London Gazette* – 24213/2852
291 *London Gazette* – 24354/4534
292 *London Gazette* – 24396/7058

293 Of "Sam Browne" belt fame, who would also be awarded a Victoria Cross for deeds performed on 31st August 1858 at Seerporah, during the Mutiny.
294 *London Gazette* – 24944/975

Figure 134b. Grave of Charles John Stanley Gough

Henry George Gore-Browne
21st August 1857 (VC No. 157)

Gazetted: 20th June 1862 22636/3152

Rank and Unit: Captain – 32nd Regiment of Foot

Citation

For conspicuous bravery in having, on the 21st of August, 1857, during the Siege of the Lucknow Residency, gallantly led a Sortie at great personal risk, for the purpose of spiking two heavy guns, which were doing considerable damage, to the defences. It appears from the statements of the non-commissioned officers and men who accompanied Captain Browne on the occasion, that he was the first person who entered the Battery, which consisted of the two guns in question, protected by high palisades, the embrasures being closed with sliding shutters. On reaching the Battery, Captain Browne removed the shutters, and jumped into the Battery. The result was, that the guns were spiked, and it is supposed that about one hundred of the enemy were killed.

Biography

Henry was born on 29th September 1830, in Newtown, Roscommon, Ireland to father Arthur and mother Anna Elizabeth (née Clements).

Henry was educated at Trinity College in Dublin and on 31st August 1855 enlisted in the British army as an Ensign with 32nd Regiment of Foot.[301]

Soon after enlisting, Henry would have set sail for India where his regiment had been stationed at Kussowlie for some time. On 15th October 1856, Henry was promoted to the rank of Lieutenant[302] and shortly afterwards on 30th October, the regiment was transferred to Lucknow where they were to relieve the 52nd Regiment of Foot. On 3rd May 1857, in the build up to the mutiny, Henry with the 32nd were sent to disarm the 7th Oudh Infantry, who were based just 7 miles outside Lucknow, as they had refused to use the new rifles.

On 16th May, with the mutiny having broken out in several places, units were sent from the barracks in the fort at Lucknow to occupy the Residency in the city and on 1st July the fort was abandoned and all troops were moved to the Residency. With Lucknow now besieged by a large force of mutineers, over the next few weeks the 32nd fought many actions in the defence of

On 2nd July 1885, Charles was promoted to the rank of Major-General[295] and had to relinquish command of the Hyderabad Contingent until in 1886 he was given command of a 1st Class District in Bengal. Charles was promoted to the rank of Lieutenant-General on 5th June 1889[296] and to General on 1st April 1894[297]. On 31st March 1895, Charles was placed on the Unemployed Supernumerary List,[298] which effectively brought his army career to an end after 47 years of service. In recognition of his exemplary service, Charles was made an Honorary Colonel of the 5th Cavalry in the Indian Army.

With his retirement from the army, Charles returned to Ireland where he lived at Innislonagh, near Clonmel in Co Tipperary and lived the life of a country gentleman.

On 25th May 1895, in recognition of his distinguished army service, Charles was appointed as an Ordinary Member 1st Class (Knight Grand Cross) of the Military Division of the Most Honourable Order of the Bath.[299]

In 1897, Charles book "The Sikhs and Sikh Wars" was published.

On 21st June 1908, Charles was appointed as Honorary Colonel of the Tipperary Royal Field Reserve Artillery.[300]

Charles died at his home in Innislonagh on 6th September 1912 and was buried in St Patrick's Cemetery in Clonmel.

His Victoria Cross medal is privately held.

---

295 *London Gazette* – 25494/3476
296 *London Gazette* – 25950/3534
297 *London Gazette* – 26519/3257
298 *London Gazette* – 26618/2354
299 *London Gazette* – 26628/3079
300 *London Gazette* – 28200/9032

301 *London Gazette* – 21773/3284
302 *London Gazette* – 21951/4247

Figure 135. Henry George Gore-Browne

the Residency and it was on 21st August that Henry performed the deeds for which he would later be awarded the Victoria Cross. On 25th September 1857, a force commanded by Sir H. Havelock managed to break though the lines of mutineers and join up with their besieged colleagues, the siege would continue until 22nd November when the Residency was eventually evacuated.

After briefly helping out in the defence of Cawnpore, Henry and the 32nd joined a force, commanded by Lieutenant-General Maxwell, in operations at Mysore during the first half of 1858.

For his service during the mutiny, Henry was awarded the Indian Mutiny Medal with clasp for Defence of Lucknow. He was also mentioned in despatches on several occasions and was awarded an extra years service for his service at Lucknow. He was also wounded twice, once quite seriously.

On 1st June 1858, Henry was promoted to the rank of Captain[303] and posted to the newly reformed 100th Regiment of Foot. The new regiment 'Royal Canadians' had been raised in Canada and on 1st July 1858 arrived at Liverpool from where they moved to their base camp at Shorncliffe. Henry would have joined his new regiment at Shorncliffe and after a period of training they moved to Aldershot in March 1859, for further training prior to their deployment to Gibraltar in May 1859.

On 10th April 1862,[304] Henry was married to Jane Anne (née Seeley), the couple would have two children, Charles Henry Arthur born on 3rd December 1876 and Annie Claudine Mary

born during 1878. Both children were born at Cowes on the Isle of Wight.

It was on Gibraltar, during June 1862, that Henry was presented with his Victoria Cross Medal, by the Governor of Gibraltar, Lieutenant-General Sir William Codrington.

The regiment formed the garrison in Gibraltar until the autumn of 1863 when they were sent on garrison duties to Malta.

With the escalating Fenian threat in Canada, the regiment left Malta on 15th October 1866 and arrived back in Quebec, where the majority of the men had been recruited, on 3rd November. On arriving in Montreal, the regiment was split into two detachments, one remaining in Montreal while the other was posted to Ottawa. In 1868, many of the men and officers had completed their initial ten year enlistment and left the regiment, Henry took the opportunity to purchase a commission as Major on 1st February 1868.[305] On 31st October 1868, the regiment returned home to the United Kingdom and from 12th November were based in the Gallowgate Barracks in Glasgow.

Soon after arriving back in the United Kingdom, on 23rd December 1868, Henry retired from the army on half pay.[306]

Figure 135a. Grave of Henry George Gore-Browne

303 *London Gazette* – 22147/2714
304 Many sources state a date of 1st April 1882, however, if this was the case then both children would be illegitimate (unlikely for a man of his position) – also the 1881 census states that he is married. Possible explanation is that the 1882 date refers to a change in his wife's married name to Gore-Browne after Henry changed his name by deed poll. The 1862 date is also problematic as there is a 13 year gap before the first child is born.

305 *London Gazette* – 23348/475
306 *London Gazette* – 23452/6778

Upon leaving the army, Henry moved to the Isle of Wight where he managed the estates of his brother-in-law Sir Charles Seeley.

On 27th February 1877, Henry was honoured with a brevet promotion to the rank of Lieutenant-Colonel.[307]

During his retirement, Henry was very active in local politics and society on the Isle of Wight where at various times he held the following appointments: President of the IoW Horticultural Society, Justice of the Peace for Hampshire and IoW, Member of IoW Board of Guardians, Highway Commissioner, Member of the IoW Hunt, Member of the IoW Conservative Association and Chairman of the Shanklin Conservative Club.

At some stage, possibly in 1882, Henry changed his name to Gore-Browne, by Deed Poll.

On 9th May 1912, Henry reached the pinnacle when he was appointed as Deputy Governor of the Isle of Wight.[308]

Henry died at his home Monteagle, Popham Road, Shanklin on the Isle of Wight on 15th November 1912 aged 82 and was buried four days later in St Mary the Virgin Churchyard, Brook on the Isle of Wight.

Henry's Victoria Cross Medal is on public display at the Duke of Cornwall's Light Infantry Museum, Bodmin, Cornwall.

---

307 *London Gazette* – 24438/2266
308 *London Gazette* – 28609/3587

John Divane
10th September 1857 (VC No. 158)

Gazetted: 20th January 1860 22347/178

Rank and Unit: Private No. 2820 – 60th Rifles

Citation

For distinguished gallantry in heading a successful charge made by the Beeloochee and Seikh Troops on one of the Enemy's trenches before Delhi, on the 10th of September, 1857. He leaped out of our trenches, closely followed by the Native Troops, and was shot down from the top of the Enemy's breastworks.

Elected by the Privates of the Regiment.

Biography

John was born sometime in November 1823, at Carrabane, Loughrea, Co Galway in Ireland.

He would have had very little education and was illiterate during his life, this caused problems with his identity on official records as his signature was often interpreted as DEVINE as well as DIVANE; in fact it is probable that his name was actually DUANE.

John worked as a labourer until on 18th September 1847, he enlisted in the 1st Battalion, 60th Rifles at Kilkenny aged 24.

On 4th February 1849, John arrived in India to join the bulk of his regiment which had been serving in the sub-continent since 1846 and by May was stationed in the barracks at Peshawar. In 1850 the regiment moved from Peshawar to Kussowlie and following spells in Subattoo and Jullundur moved to Meerut where they were stationed at the start of the mutiny. Following the outbreak of the mutiny in 1857, the regiment moved from Meerut to Delhi where they were part of the force which lay siege to the city after it was occupied by the mutineers.

It was during the siege of Delhi, on 10th September 1857, that John performed the deeds that under the terms of rule 13, he would be selected by a ballot of the privates of the regiment for the award of the Victoria Cross. During the action, John was severely wounded in the right leg which had to be amputated. Due to his incapacity as a result of the amputation, John was invalided out of the army on 31st December 1857. For his service in India, John was awarded the Indian Mutiny Medal with clasp for Delhi.

John's short military service was not always exemplary, he was subject to courts martial on two occasions and served a total of three weeks in prison.

Figure 136. John Divane

John was presented with his Victoria Cross medal by Queen Victoria on 9th November 1860 at an investiture held in Windsor Castle.

On leaving the army, John returned to his home town in Ireland, where he lived until sometime in 1880 when he moved to Penzance in Cornwall.

At some stage John was married and fathered several children.

For a time John worked as a fish hawker in Penzance until he died from senile decay on 1st December 1888 at home in 35 New Street, Penzance at the age of 65. He was buried a few days later in an unmarked pauper's grave in St Clare's Churchyard in Penzance.

The whereabouts of John's Victoria Cross Medal is unknown.

Patrick Green
11th September 1857 (VC No. 159)

Gazetted: 26th October 1858 22194/4574

Rank and Unit: Private – 75th Regiment of Foot

Citation

For the Act of Bravery recorded in a General Order, issued by the Commander-in-Chief in India, of which the following is a copy:

Head-Quarters, Allahabad, July 28, 1858. GENERAL ORDER, "The Commander-in-Chief in India is pleased to approve that the under mentioned Soldier be presented, in the name of Her Most Gracious Majesty, with a Medal of the Victoria Cross, for valour and daring in the field, viz.: Private Patrick Green, Her Majesty's 75th Foot, for having, on the 11th of September, 1857, when the piquet at the Koodsia Baugh at Delhi was hotly pressed by a large body of the Enemy, successfully rescued a comrade, who had fallen wounded as a skirmisher.

(Signed) C. CAMPBELL, General, Commander-in-Chief, East Indies.

Biography

Patrick was born some time during 1824 at Ballinasloe near Roscommon, County Galway in Ireland.

Figure 136a. Grave of John Divane

Figure 137. Patrick Green

It is likely that Patrick enlisted, as a Private, in the 75th Regiment some time during 1845 to 1848 as the regiment was stationed in Ireland and actively recruiting to bring the regiment up to strength following their recent return from South Africa.

The regiment arrived in Ireland during September 1845 and were initially stationed at Birr, moving to Athlone in June 1846 and Dublin in July 1847. On 31st July 1848 the regiment moved to Kilkenny and in March 1849 were placed on standby for an imminent posting to India. On 29th March they proceeded to Fermoy where in early May they set sail for India were they landed at Calcutta in August 1849 and took up their station at Umballa on 21st December.

In November 1853 the regiment moved to Peshawar and in February 1854 were sent to erect a fort at the Kohat Pass. In 1855 they moved to Rawalpindi and in December 1856 to Kasauli.

It was while based at Kasauli, that the regiment heard news of the outbreak of mutiny and on 12th May 1857 were ordered to Umballa, where on 16th May they joined a Field Force raised to go to the relief of Delhi. On the road to Delhi, the regiment took part in the Battle of Badli-ki-Serai on 8th June. On reaching Delhi, the regiment formed part of the force besieging the city and it was during the siege on 11th September 1857 that Patrick performed the deeds for which he would later be awarded the Victoria Cross.

Following the relief of Delhi on 20th September, the regiment were ordered to Agra and on 28th September, soon after leaving Delhi were involved in an action at Bulandshahr. The regiment reached Agra on 10th November and after the safety of the city was assured, on 13th October set out to the assistance of Cawnpore where they arrived on 26th October. After ensuring that the communication lines were re-established between Delhi and Agra the regiment were sent to Lucknow where they assisted with the safe withdrawal from the Residency on 20th November 1857. After Lucknow the regiment took part in operations in the province of Oudh but by February 1858 were taking a well earned rest. For his service in the Mutiny, Patrick was awarded the Indian Mutiny Medal with clasps for Delhi and Relief of Lucknow.

Patrick was presented with his Victoria Cross medal some time during February 1859, while stationed in India.

In late 1859, the regiment was moved from Meerut to Allahabad where they arrived on 26th January 1860. Exactly one year later, the regiment was moved to Calcutta where they formed the garrison at Fort William from 9th March until their departure for England which took place during February 1862.

After 13 years service in India, Patrick arrived back in England, landing in Portsmouth during June 1862. For the next few years the regiment saw service in England stationed at Devonport and Aldershot, however, in February 1866 the regiment were despatched to Ireland to help deal with the Fenian Conspiracy. It is not known when Patrick left the army, however, the regiment left Ireland for a tour of duty in Gibraltar on 2nd March 1866 and I think that it is highly likely that he took this opportunity to leave the army and remain in Ireland.

Patrick left the army with the rank of Colour-Sergeant and was awarded the Long Service and Good Conduct medal.

Patrick died in Cork on 19th July 1889 at the age of 75 and was buried in the Aghada Cemetery in Cork.

The location of Patrick's Victoria Cross medal is unknown.

Duncan Charles Home
14th September 1857 (VC No. 160)

Gazetted: 18th June 1858 22154/2961

Rank and Unit: Lieutenant – Bengal Engineers

Citation

Memorandum

Lieutenants Duncan Charles Home- and Philip Salkeld, Bengal Engineers, upon whom the Victoria Cross was provisionally conferred by Major-General Sir Archdale Wilson, Bart., K.C.B., for their conspicuous bravery in the performance of the desperate duty of blowing in the Cashmere Gate of the Fortress of Delhi, in broad daylight, under a heavy fire of musketry, on the morning of the 14th September, 1857, preparatory to the assault, would have been recommended to Her Majesty for confirmation in that distinction, had they survived.

Biography

Duncan was born at Jubbulpore in the Central Provinces of India on 10th June 1828 the third son of Major-General Richard who was Colonel of the 43rd Bengal Native Infantry and Frances Sophia (née Fraser).

He was educated at Elizabeth College in Guernsey from January 1841 until 1843 when he was privately educated by Messrs. Soton and Mayor at Wimbledon. In 1845, Duncan continued his education at the East India Military Seminary at Addiscombe in Surrey until his graduation on 11th December 1846 when he was commissioned as a 2nd Lieutenant in the Bengal Engineers. On leaving Addiscombe, Duncan attended the Royal Engineers College at Chatham for field instruction in the art of Sapping and Mining, under the command of Lieutenant Colonel Sir Frederick Smith and on 1st January 1847 was given the temporary and local rank of Ensign for the duration of his studies.[309]

Upon completion of his studies at Chatham, Duncan set sail on *HMS Barham* for India on 20th June 1848 and landed at Calcutta in November 1848, just in time to take part in the later stages of the second Anglo-Sikh war. Duncan was present during the final stages of the siege of Multan which lasted from 19th April 1848 until 22nd January 1849 and also at the decisive Battle of Gujarat on 21st February 1849. For his service during the war, Duncan was awarded the Punjab Medal with clasps for Mooltan and Goojerat.

309 *Edinburgh Gazette – 5606/6*

Figure 138. Duncan Charles Home

Following the war, Duncan was posted to the 3rd Company of Sappers based at Lahore until in October 1849 he was appointed as an Assistant Executive Officer in the Public Works Department and was assigned to the third division, Ganges Canal. In April 1852, Duncan was placed at the disposal of the Superintending Engineer, Punjab Circle and was employed in the Civil Engineers Department as an Assistant to the Executive Engineer of the Bari Doab Canals at Malikpur. In early 1853, Duncan was appointed as Executive Engineer of the first Division of the Bari Doab canal and on 15th February 1854 was promoted to the rank of Lieutenant.

When the mutiny broke out in May 1857, Duncan was based at Madhopur and was requested to raise three companies of Punjab Sappers, from the Sikh workmen working on the Grand Trunk Road, for duties at the siege of Delhi. This task was quickly accomplished and the three companies of newly raised sappers were soon marched off to Delhi under the command of Lieutenant H. W. Gulliver of the Bengal Engineers. In early July, due to the lack of Engineering Officers available at Delhi, Duncan raised a further two companies of Punjab Sappers and led this new detachment to Delhi where he arrived during August and on 22nd August was appointed as a Field Engineer.

It was on 14th September, while blowing a breach in the Kashmir gate, in preparation for the final assault on the City, that Duncan performed the deeds for which he would later be awarded the Victoria Cross.

Unfortunately, Duncan would never be presented with his Victoria Cross medal as on 1st October 1857 he was killed in action at Fort Malagarh. Apparently Duncan had laid a mine to breach the walls of the fort and after this had not exploded within the usual time after having lit the slow burning fuse he returned to the mine with the intention of relighting the fuse, however, the mine exploded and he was killed immediately.

Duncan was buried in the Bulandshahr Cemetery near Aligarh.

For his service during the mutiny, Duncan was awarded the Indian Mutiny Medal with clasp for Delhi.

His Victoria Cross Medal was posted to his father on 7th July 1858.

Unfortunately the medal was lost some time in the 1920s when the son of the owner took the medal to take part in his game of soldiers and it was lost in a field.

Figure 138a. Grave of Duncan Charles Home

Philip Salkeld
14th September 1857 (VC No. 161)

Gazetted: 18th June 1858 22154/2961

Rank and Unit: Lieutenant – Bengal Engineers

Citation

Memorandum

Lieutenants Duncan Charles Home- and Philip Salkeld, Bengal Engineers, upon whom the Victoria Cross was provisionally conferred by Major-General Sir Archdale Wilson, Bart., K.C.B., for their conspicuous bravery in the performance of the desperate duty of blowing in the Cashmere Gate of the Fortress of Delhi, in broad daylight, under a heavy fire of musketry, on the morning of the 14th September, 1857, preparatory to the assault, would have been recommended to Her Majesty for confirmation in that distinction, had they survived.

Biography

Philip was born in the rectory at Fontmell Magna near Shaftsbury in Dorset on 13th October 1830, he was the seventh of thirteen[310] children born to Reverend Robert who was rector at St Andrew's Parish Church and Elizabeth Henrietta (née Wilson). Philip was the couple's fourth son, his younger brothers Richard Henry and Charles Edward would both serve with distinction in the Indian Army.

Initially Philip was educated at Dr. Bridgman's School in Blandford, Dorset, then at Kings College School in London where he was a classmate of Robert Haydon Shebbeare who would be awarded a Victoria Cross for actions performed on the same day as Philip's Victoria Cross deeds. From 1846, Philip attended the Honourable East India Company Military Seminary at Addiscombe in Surrey, where after excelling in mathematics and modern languages he was selected for an appointment in the Engineers. On graduation Philip was given the rank of 2nd Lieutenant on 9th June 1848 and for the next two years continued his studies at the Royal Engineer College at Chatham.

After graduating from Chatham, Philip was ordered to travel overland to India where after arriving in Calcutta during June 1850 he joined his regiment the Corps of Sappers and Miners, Bengal Establishment. Philip's gift with languages stood him in good stead and he soon acquired a working knowledge of Hindustani.

Philip was sent to Meerut as an Engineer in June 1853 and later in the year was appointed as the officer in charge of the

---

310 Two of the children would die in their infancy

Figure 139. Philip Salkeld

Grand Trunk Road, he was promoted to the rank of Lieutenant on 1st August 1854. In December 1856, his role as officer in charge of the Grand Trunk Road came to an end and Philip was transferred to Delhi as an Executive Engineer in the Department of Public Works.

Philip was still stationed at Delhi at the start of the mutiny and on 10th May 1857, managed to escape from the city as it was captured by the mutineers. On leaving Delhi, Philip joined up with the force of Major-General Sir Henry William Barnard which would lay siege to Delhi.

It was on 14th September, during preparations for the final assault on the city that Philip performed the deeds for which he would later be awarded the Victoria Cross. He was one of three engineering officers to volunteer to blow the Kashmir Gate in preparation for an attack by the 32nd Regiment of Foot. The Kashmir Gate was successfully blown open, however, during the action Philip was mortally wounded and eventually died from his wounds on 10th October 1857. Philip was buried in the Old Military Cemetery in Delhi.

The Victoria Cross was awarded to Philip almost immediately after the attack on the Kashmir Gate by Major General Sir Archdale Wilson who ordered his Aide-de-Camp Lieutenant Turnbull to pin a Victoria Cross medal ribbon on the chest of Philip as he lay on his death bed, in the hope that it might revive his spirits. It is reported that Philip's response was "… it will be gratifying to send it home".

On 7th July 1858, Philip's Victoria Cross medal was sent by post to his father.

For his service during the mutiny, Philip was awarded the Indian Mutiny Medal with clasp for Delhi.

Philip's Victoria Medal is in private hands and not on public display.

Robert Haydon Shebbeare
14th September 1857 (VC No. 162)

Gazetted: 21st October 1859 22318/3792

Rank and Unit: Lieutenant – 60th Bengal Native Infantry

Citation

For distinguished gallantry at the head of the Guides with the 4th column of assault at Delhi, on the 14th of September, 1857, when, after twice charging beneath the wall of the loop holed Serai, it was found impossible, owing to the murderous fire, to attain the breach. Captain (then Lieutenant) Shebbeare endeavoured to reorganize the men, but one-third of the Europeans having fallen, his efforts to do so failed. He then conducted the rearguard of the retreat across the canal most successfully. He was most miraculously preserved through the affair but yet left the field with one bullet through his cheek, and a bad scalp wound along the back of the head from another.

Biography

Robert was born on 13th January 1827 at Clapham in London to father Charles John and mother Louisa Matilda (née Wolfe).

Robert was the second son and third of ten children, having an older brother Charles Hooper born in August 1824, an older sister Matilda Margaret born in August 1825 and five younger sisters and two younger brothers: twins Henrietta Francis and Henry Francis born in July 1828, Margaret Louisa born February

Figure 140. Robert Haydon Shebbeare

1831, Emma Jane born in May 1832, Helen Charlotte born in February 1834, Reginald John born in April 1839 and Alice May born in January 1845.

Robert was educated at Kings College School in London where he was the classmate of Philip Salkeld who would be awarded a Victoria Cross for deeds performed on the same day as the Victoria Cross deeds performed by Robert.

In 1844 Robert joined the Honourable East India Company as a Subaltern Cadet and joined the 60th Bengal Native Infantry in India. Little is known of Robert's early years in India other than at some stage he was promoted to the rank of Lieutenant.

At the time of the mutiny, Robert was stationed at Delhi and managed to escape when the mutineers captured the city. When his own regiment mutinied on 10th July, Robert was attached to the Corps of Guides where he was second in command. Robert was involved in the siege of Delhi and was slightly wounded three times on 14th July[311] and he was mentioned in the despatches of Major Reid on 12th August.[312] It was on the 14th September, during the final assault on Delhi, while attacking the breach in the Kashmir Gate, that Robert performed the deeds for which he would later be awarded the Victoria Cross. During the assault Robert was wounded in three places[313] and was mentioned in the despatches of Captain D. D. Muter on 17th September.[314] For his service during the mutiny, Robert was awarded the Indian Mutiny Medal with clasp for Delhi.

After the relief of Delhi, Robert raised a new regiment the 15th Punjab Pioneers, in Lahore which was exclusively recruited from the Mazhabi Sikh community and volunteered the force for service in China. Robert, with the 15th Punjab Pioneers took part in the Second Opium War and was involved in the taking of the Taku Forts in May 1858 and during the second phase of the war in the Battle of Taku Forts on 21st August 1860. Due to illness, Robert did not take part in the final march on Peking but set sail on *SS Emau* for passage home to England after an absence of 16 years service in India and China.

It was while at sea, somewhere between Shanghai and Point de Galle, on 16th September 1860 that Robert died from his illness[315] and was buried at sea.

Robert was never formally presented with his Victoria Cross medal, it was sent to him by registered post. The medal is still in the hands of family members.

---

311 *London Gazette* – 22050/3410
312 *London Gazette* – 22066/4012
313 *London Gazette* – 22073/4433
314 *London Gazette* – 22073/4454
315 Thought to have been Malaria

James McGuire
14th September 1857 (VC No. 163)

Gazetted: 24th December 1858 22212/5519

Rank and Unit: Sergeant No. 1863 – 1st European Bengal Fusiliers

Citation

At the assault on Delhi on the 14th September, 1857, when the Brigade had reached the Cabul Gate, the 1st Fusiliers and 75th Regiment, and some Sikhs, were waiting for orders, and some of the Regiments were getting ammunition served out (three boxes of which exploded from some cause not clearly known, and two others were in a state of ignition), when Serjeant McGuire and Drummer Ryan rushed into the burning mass, and, seizing the boxes, threw them, one after the other, over the parapet into the water. The confusion consequent on the explosion was very great, and the crowd of soldiers and native followers, who did not know where the danger lay, were rushing into certain destruction, when Serjeant McGuire and Drummer Ryan, by their coolness and personal daring, saved the lives of many at the risk of their own.

Biography

James was born in Largy, Lack, Enniskillen in Co. Fermanagh, Northern Ireland some time during 1827.

James worked as a labourer until on 29th March 1849 he enlisted at Enniskillen for ten years service with the Honourable East India Company and was enrolled as a Private in the 1st Bengal European Fusiliers.

James set sail aboard the troopship *Ellenborough* and after landing in India on 10th October 1849 joined his regiment at Cawnpore where it had just arrived following its participation in the 2nd Anglo Sikh War.

In March 1850 the regiment moved to Lahore, where due to the lack of space in the barracks they were quartered in the Royal Gardens. In September 1850, after a flood the regiment were laid low by an epidemic of Malaria which affected about 80% of the officers and men. In order to escape the breeding ground of the mosquitoes, the regiment moved to a new camp on high ground outside the city and in October moved to Meerut. By February 1851, 75% of the regiment were still suffering from the effects of the disease.

In early 1852 rumours abounded regarding the probability of war in Burma, these proved to be true and war was declared on 10th February 1852.

In April 1852, the regiment moved to Calcutta and in November boarded the frigate *HMS Sphynx* and Honourable East India Company vessels *Muzuffor* and *Feraze* bound for Rangoon. On 19th November the regiment set sail on river steamers as part of the expedition commanded by Brigadier McNeill to capture the town and fort at Pegu. The expedition accomplished its mission on 21st November and after leaving a small garrison at Pegu returned to Rangoon the next day. Almost as soon as the main force had left, the town was besieged by a large force of insurgents. Word of the new attack on Pegu soon reached Rangoon and on 7th December a relief force departed and arrived at the town on 15th December. By the 20th December, the rebels had been vanquished and after leaving a much larger garrison of 700 men the force again returned to Rangoon.

During early January 1853, the regiment boarded Honourable East India Company transports *Moozuffur*, *Zenobia* and *Bernice* bound for Martaban where they arrived on 5th January. At Martaban was a heavily fortified British fort, known as the "Gibraltar" of Burma due to its strategic position and fortifications. On 20th January 1853, the war was effectively ended with a proclamation covering the annexation of further Burma territories. Over the next few months the regiment took part in local operations until 11th April when they started on their journey to return to Rangoon. The regiment was then split into a number of smaller commands which were sent to garrison several newly acquired frontier towns.

Towards the end of 1854, the regiment was relieved by the 29th Regiment of Foot and the various commands were reunited at Rangoon. The regiment embarked on Honourable East India Company transports and after an absence of over two years returned to India, arriving in Calcutta during February 1855.

For his service in the 2nd Anglo-Burmese War, James was awarded the India General Service Medal with clasp for Pegu.

After spending a few weeks in Calcutta, the regiment boarded river steamers and departed for Dinapore where they were stationed until January 1856 when they moved to Cawnpore. At some stage, James was promoted to the rank of Sergeant. The right wing and headquarters of the regiment moved to the newly constructed outpost at Dugshai, in the Himalayan foothills until in December 1856 the regiment was reunited at Umballa. In March 1857, the whole regiment moved to Dugshai, where they were stationed at the outbreak of the mutiny. On 13th May the regiment was ordered back to Umballa to await further orders and on 21st May were moved to Kurnaul.

On 7th June, the regiment set out on the role to Delhi, as part of a force sent to recapture the City and on the 8th June was involved in the Battle of Badli-ki-Serai. After the battle, the regiment took their place in the siege lines before Delhi. They were involved in the successful action to dislodge mutineers from the defensive works at Subzi Mundi on 14th July and the Battle of Nujjufghur on 24th August 1857. It was during an attack on the Kabul Gate during the final attacks on the city on 14th September, that James performed the deeds for which he would later be awarded the Victoria Cross. The city finally fell to the British onslaught on 20th September 1857. On 10th November, the regiment marched as part of a force of 2,500 men, commanded by Colonel Gerrard, in an operation against several strongholds held by the mutineers to the west of the city. The only major action was the Battle of Narnoul, which took place on 16th November and the regiment returned to Delhi on 29th November.

On 9th December, the regiment were ordered to proceed towards Lucknow where they arrived on 3rd March 1858 after spending some time at Cawnpore and the Alum Bagh. As part of General Outram's Brigade the regiment was involved in the capture of the "Yellow House", a rebel stronghold on the outskirts of the city, on 9th March and were also involved in the final actions which resulted in the capture of Lucknow on 21st March. During April the regiment was part of Major-General Sir Hope Grant's column on operations in the Fyzabad district and operations on the Gogra River in September 1858.

On 31st October, as part of a force commanded by Captain Trevor Wheler, the regiment fought their last action at Sahadit-Gunge. With the dissolution of the East India Army, by the British Government, the regiment was disbanded and reformed in the British army designated as 101st Bengal Fusiliers. In March 1859, the regiment returned to their headquarters at Dugshai where they arrived on 18th April after two years of almost constant campaigning. For his service during the mutiny, James was awarded the Indian Mutiny Medal with clasps for Delhi and Lucknow.

On 16th May 1859, after having completed his 10 year enlistment, James was discharged from the army with a pension of a shilling per day and returned to Ireland.

At some stage, possibly before he joined the army in 1849, James was married and is reported to have fathered four children.

James was presented with his Victoria Cross medal on 4th January 1860, by Queen Victoria in an investiture held at Windsor castle.

On 12th July 1862, James was convicted at Drum Duff, Enniskillen of stealing a cow and was sentenced to nine months imprisonment in Derry jail. Apparently, James lent a neighbour (possibly his Uncle) some money from his annual £10 Victoria Cross endowment to purchase a cow and when the money was not returned he took the cow as payment. As James had been convicted of a felony, he was stripped of his VC medal and pension under rule 15 of the founding Royal Warrant (later rescinded in

1920 by King George V) to become the second of only eight men to forfeit their medal under this rule.

James died in prison on 22nd December 1862 and was buried in Donagh Cemetery, Lisnaskea in County Fermanagh. James was buried in an unmarked grave, however the burial was under the name of Patrick Joseph Donnelly (his wife's maiden name). This burial under another name leads me to speculate that perhaps James took his own life which if this was the case would prevent burial in consecrated ground and the name change was used to get around this issue.

James's Victoria Cross medal is on public display at the National Army Museum in Chelsea, London.

Figure 141a. Memorial to James McGuire

John Smith
14th September 1857 (VC No. 164)

Gazetted: 27th April 1858 22131/2051

Rank and Unit: Sergeant – Bengal Sappers & Miners

Citation

For conspicuous gallantry, in conjunction with Lieutenants Home and Salkeld, in the performance of the desperate duty of blowing in the Cashmere Gate of the fortress of Delhi in broad daylight, under a heavy and destructive fire of musketry, on the morning of the 14th September, 1857, preparatory to the assault. **(General Order of Major-General Sir Archdale Wilson, Bart., K.C.B., dated Head Quarters, Delhi City, September 21, 1857.)**

Biography

John was born at Ticknall in South Derbyshire during February 1814 and had two brothers and five sisters.

John was apprenticed to his Uncle as a cobbler and shoe maker, however, at the age of 23 joined the army of the Honourable East India Company as a private in the Bengal Sappers and Miners in 1837.

John would have joined his regiment in India soon after he enlisted. He was promoted to the rank of Sergeant in 1839.

John was involved in the 1st Anglo-Afghan war which took place from 1839 until 1842 and took part in the siege and battle to take Kabul in September 1842. For his service during the war, John was awarded the Candahar, Ghuznee, Cabul Medal (1841–42) which was inscribed with "Cabul" on the reverse.

John was also involved in the 1st Anglo-Sikh war, which took place during 1845 and 1846, and he saw action at the Battle of Sobraon on 10th February 1846. For his service during this war, John was awarded the Sutlej Medal (1845–46), inscribed with "Sobraon" on the reverse.

From 1848 to 1849, John was involved in the 2nd Anglo-Sikh war and took part in the decisive battles at Multan on 22nd January 1849 and Goojerat on 21st February 1849. For his service in this war, John was awarded the Punjab Medal (1848–49) with clasps for Mooltan and Goojerat.

Prior to the outbreak of the mutiny, John was working in the Punjab Public Works Department and was assigned to the Delhi Field Force when the mutiny broke out.

It was on 14th September 1857, during the siege of Delhi while blowing the Kashmir gate in preparation for the final attacks, that John performed the deeds for which he would later be awarded the Victoria Cross. For his service during the

Mutiny, John was awarded the Indian Mutiny Medal with clasp for Delhi.

John was presented with his Victoria Cross medal sometime 1859, while still serving in India.

At some stage, John was married to the widow of a trooper in the 12th Dragoons, the couple would have four daughters.

During 1860, John received a commission as Ensign in the Bengal Sappers and Miners.

John died from dysentery on 26th June 1864 at Jullunder in India aged 50, and was buried in the Artillery Cemetery in Jullunder.

His Victoria Cross medal is held as part of a private collection.

Figure 142a. Memorial to John Smith

Henry Smith
14th September 1857 (VC No. 165)

Gazetted: 27th April 1858 22131/2051

Rank and Unit: Lance Corporal No. 2764 – 52nd Regiment of Foot

Citation

Lance-Corporal Smith most gallantly carried away a wounded comrade under a heavy fire of grape and musketry on the Chaundee Chouck, in the city of Delhi, on the morning of the assault on the 14th September, 1857.
(General Order of Major-General Sir Archdale Wilson, Bart., K.C.B., dated Head Quarters, Delhi City, September 21, 1857.)

Biography

Henry was born at Thames Ditton, near Surbiton in Surrey some time during 1825.

On 9th February 1853, at the age of 28, Henry enlisted at Thames Ditton, in 52nd Regiment of Foot.

Soon after joining the army, Henry would have moved to India with his regiment and was stationed initially at Allahabad until sometime in 1854 they moved to Umballa. During the mutiny, Henry was involved in the siege of Delhi and it was here during the final attacks on the city on 14th September 1857 that he performed the deeds for which he would later be awarded the Victoria Cross. For his service during the mutiny, Henry was awarded the Indian Mutiny Medal with clasp for Delhi and at some stage received a promotion to the rank of Sergeant.

Henry was presented with his Victoria Cross medal some time during 1860, while still serving in India.

Henry died from cholera on 18th August 1862 at Gwalior in India and was buried in an unmarked mass grave in Gwalior Cemetery, along with many other men who had died from the disease.

His Victoria Cross medal was purchase by the officers of the 52nd Regiment in July 1896, for £70 and is now on public display at the Royal Green Jackets Museum in Winchester.

Robert Hawthorne
14th September 1857 (VC No. 166)

Figure 144. Robert Hawthorne

Gazetted: 27th April 1858 22131/2051

Rank and Unit: Bugler – 52nd Regiment of Foot

Citation

Bugler Hawthorne, who accompanied the explosion party, not only performed the dangerous duty on which he was employed, but previously attached himself to Lieutenant Salkeld, of the Engineers, when dangerously wounded, bound up his wounds under a heavy musketry fire, and had him removed without further injury. **(General Order of Major-General Sir Archdale Wilson, Bart., K.C.B., dated Head Quarters, Delhi City, September 21, 1857.)**

Biography

Robert was born some time during 1822 at Maghera, Co Londonderry in Northern Ireland.

From the age of ten Robert worked as a labourer until at the age of 14 on 15th February 1836, he enlisted in the British Army at Athlone in Co. Roscommon and joined the 52nd Regiment of Foot.

The regiment, who had been in Ireland since 1832, were head-quartered at Athlone and were recruiting in preparation for a posting overseas. Towards the end of March 1836, the regiment left Athlone and by 4th April were assembled at Cork where on 16th May they embarked upon the transport *HMS Parmelia* and set sail for Gibraltar. They landed at Gibraltar on 1st June and by the 8th June were quartered in the West Casement Barracks.

On 11th October 1838, the regiment boarded the transport *HMS Hercules* and set sail for Barbados where they arrived on the 6th November and occupied the Brick Barracks in St Anne's. The regiment had to temporarily vacate the Brick Barracks during late 1839 due to an outbreak of Yellow Fever which decimated the officers of the regiment and only returned after the barracks had been thoroughly cleaned and fumigated. From February to July 1840, the regiment left Barbados and were split into small detachments which formed the garrisons at St Vincent where headquarters were established at Kingston, Grenada and St Lucia. In April 1841, the regiment were all brought back together at Demerara where they remained until 24th March 1842 when they boarded *HMS Java* and set sail for Canada. The regiment arrived at St John's in New Brunswick on 18th April 1842 and in September 1843 one wing was moved to Halifax, Nova Scotia the remainder of the regiment followed in June 1844. In August 1844 the regiment moved to Quebec and in May 1845 moved on to Montreal where they were to remain until July 1847. On 20th July the regiment was moved by river steamer to Quebec and on 22nd July boarded *HMS Apollo* and set sail for England where they arrived at Portsmouth on 12th August 1847.

In March 1848, the regiment was moved from Portsmouth to Preston New Barracks and in April were moved to Liverpool, detachments were deployed at several towns throughout the North West District: Preston, Burnley, Manchester and Stockport: to assist the civil authorities during the Chartist troubles.

On 27th June 1850, Robert was arrested in Liverpool after being involved in a serious brawl and after spending 19 days in hospital was court marshalled and sentenced to 48 days detention with his pay docked by 1p per day for six months.

On 8th October 1850, the regiment was told to make ready for deployment to Ireland and in early January 1851 set sail from Liverpool to Dublin. On 9th January the 1st Division left Dublin for Limerick and by 28th February were joined at Limerick by the headquarters and other divisions.

During March 1852 the regiment moved back to Dublin and on 23rd May 1853 were told to make ready for deployment to India. In June the regiment moved to Cork and in small detachment set sail for India at regular intervals during the month arriving at Calcutta at various times during October. During the later part of October 1853, the regiment moved in stages to Chinsurah by river steamers and eventually were reunited by 19th December and on 6th February 1854 moved to Umballa. On 13th March 1855 the regiment moved to Meerut and in January 1856 moved to Cawnpore where on 31st January they formed up as part of the Oude Field Force sent to annex the district of Oude. On 18th February 1856, they arrived at Lucknow and on 20th March occupied barracks within the city until 18th July when they had to abandon the barracks due to an outbreak of cholera.

On 27th December the regiment moved to Sealkote in the Punjab and upon hearing news of the outbreak of mutiny moved to Wuzeerabad on 25th May 1857 where they joined the Punjab mobile column. Throughout the month of March the column moved to various locations across the region, to make the local population aware that a large European force was active in the Punjab, in the hope that this would prevent further mutiny. The column was also active in disarming several native regiments to prevent further trouble; on 25th June at Phillour the 33rd and 35th Native Infantry regiments were disarmed and at Amritsar on the 8th and 9th July the 59th Native Infantry and 9th Bengal Light Cavalry were also disarmed. On 12th July, the regiment intercepted and engaged in battle the mutineers from Sealkote at Revée in an action which became known as the action at Trimmoo Ghat, the first battle they had fought for over 40 years.

On 22nd July the regiment left Amritsar for Delhi where they arrived on 14th August, however, due to fever and the ravages of cholera only 240 of the 680 men were fit for service. It was on 14th September, during the blowing of the Kashmir Gate in preparation for the final assaults on the city, that Robert performed the deeds for which he would later be awarded the Victoria Cross. The much weakened regiment left Delhi on 5th October and returned to the Punjab arriving at Jullundur on 1st November 1857 and in March 1858 move to Sealkote. For his service during the mutiny, Robert was awarded the Indian Mutiny Medal with clasp for Delhi. It is thought that he was presented with his Victoria Cross medal, sometime during 1859, while still serving in India.

Robert returned to England some time during 1859 and saw out the remaining days of his army service at Chatham. He was discharged from the army, at his own request, on 20th April 1861 after 21 years of adult service during which he had been awarded four Good Conduct badges.

On leaving the army, Robert moved to Manchester where he was employed as a Bank Porter by Cunliffes, Brookes and Company.

At some stage, Robert was married to Christina (née Neale) and the couple had five children: Robert, Charles, Jane, Lily and Jessie.

Robert died at his home, 1 Huntington Street, Chorlton-on-Medlock from rheumatic fever and was buried in Ardwick Cemetery in Manchester (now a sports field).

His Victoria Cross Medal, was purchased by officers of the 52nd Regiment during 1909 and is now on public display at the Royal Green Jackets Museum in Winchester.

Figure 144a. Memorial to Robert Hawthorne

Miles Ryan
14th September 1857 (VC No. 167)

Gazetted: 24th December 1858 22212/5519

Rank and Unit: Drummer No. 1874 – 1st European Bengal Fusiliers

Citation

At the assault on Delhi on the 14th September, 1857, when the Brigade had reached the Cabul Gate, the 1st Fusiliers and 75th Regiment, and some Sikhs, were waiting for orders, and some of the Regiments were getting ammunition served out (three boxes of which exploded from some cause not clearly known, and two others were in a state of ignition), when Serjeant McGuire and Drummer Ryan rushed into the burning mass, and, seizing the boxes, threw them, one after the other, over the parapet into the water. The confusion consequent on the explosion was very great, and the crowd of soldiers and native followers, who did not know where the danger lay, were rushing into certain destruction, when Serjeant McGuire and Drummer Ryan, by their coolness and personal daring, saved the lives of many at the risk of their own.

Biography

Miles was born some time during 1826 at Londonderry in Northern Ireland, he worked as a blacksmith until 29th September 1848 when he enlisted at Banbridge in the army of the Honourable East India Company as a drummer and was assigned to the 1st European Bengal Fusiliers.

It was some time before Miles was sent out to India to join his regiment, he left Ireland on board the Honourable East India Company transport *Ellenborough*[316] and arrived in India on 10th October 1849. Miles joined the regiment at Cawnpore, just after they had returned from fighting in the 2nd Anglo-Sikh war. In March 1850 the regiment moved to Lahore and then in October to Meerut.

Following the declaration of war with Burma on 10th February 1852, the regiment were moved to Calcutta in April 1852 and set sail for Rangoon to take part in the 2nd Anglo-Burmese War. On 19th November 1852, Miles was involved in the capture of the town and Fort at Pegu and was part of the relief force which drove away a besieging force at Pegu on 20th December. In January 1853, the regiment moved to the fortress at Martaban

where they formed the garrison and took part in local operations until their return to Rangoon on 11th April where the regiment was split into small detachments and sent to garrison some of the newly acquired frontier towns. Towards the end of 1854, the regiment was reunited at Rangoon and returned to India, arriving at Calcutta during February 1855. For his service in the 2nd Anglo-Burmese War, Miles was awarded the India General Service Medal with clasp for Pegu.

After spending a few weeks in Calcutta, the regiment boarded river steamers and departed for Dinapore where they were stationed until January 1856 when they moved to Cawnpore. The right wing and headquarters of the regiment moved to the newly constructed outpost at Dugshai, in the Himalayan foothills until in December 1856 the regiment was reunited at Umballa. In March 1857, the whole regiment moved to Dugshai, where they were stationed at the outbreak of the mutiny. On 13th May the regiment was ordered back to Umballa to await further orders and on 21st May were moved to Karnal.

On 7th June, the regiment set out on the road to Delhi, as part of a force sent to recapture the City and on the 8th June was involved in the Battle of Badli-ki-Serai. After the battle, the regiment took their place in the siege lines before Delhi. They were involved in the successful action to dislodge mutineers from the defensive works at Subzi Mundi on 14th July and the Battle of Nujjufghur on 24th August 1857. It was during an attack on the Kabul Gate during the final attacks on the city on 14th September, that Miles performed the deeds for which he would later be awarded the Victoria Cross. The city finally fell to the British onslaught on 20th September 1857.

On 10th November, the regiment marched as part of a force of 2,500 men, commanded by Colonel Gerrard, in an operation against several strongholds held by the mutineers to the west of the city. The only major action was the Battle of Narnoul, which took place on 16th November and the regiment returned to Delhi on 29th November.

On 9th December, the regiment were ordered to proceed towards Lucknow where they arrived on 3rd March 1858 after spending some time at Cawnpore and the Alum Bagh. As part of General Outram's Brigade the regiment was involved in the capture of the "Yellow House", a rebel stronghold on the outskirts of the city, on 9th March and were also involved in the final actions which resulted in the capture of Lucknow on 21st March. During April the regiment was part of Major-General Sir Hope Grant's column on operations in the Fyzabad district and operations on the Gogra River in September 1858. On 31st October, as part of a force commanded by Captain Trevor Wheler, the regiment fought their last action at Sahadit-Gunge. With the dissolution of the East India Army, by the British Government, the

---

316 Miles travelled to India with James McGuire who would be involved in the same deeds which resulted in both being awarded the Victoria Cross.

regiment was disbanded and reformed in the British army designated as 101st Bengal Fusiliers. In March 1859, the regiment returned to their headquarters at Dugshai where they arrived on 18th April after two years of almost constant campaigning. For his service during the mutiny, Miles was awarded the Indian Mutiny Medal with clasps for Delhi and Lucknow.

On 16th May 1859, after having completed his 10 year enlistment, Miles was discharged from the army with a pension of a shilling per day and decided to remain in India.

Miles died during January 1887, somewhere in Bengal, his place of burial is unknown.

The whereabouts of his Victoria Cross medal is also unknown.

Herbert Taylor Reade
14th September 1857 (VC No. 168)

Gazetted: 5th February 1861 22477/449

Rank and Unit: Surgeon – 61st Regiment of Foot

Citation

During the siege of Delhi, on the 14th of September, 1857, while Surgeon Reade was attending to the wounded, at the end of one of the streets of the city, a party of rebels advanced from the direction of the Bank, and having established themselves in the houses in the street, commenced firing from the roofs. The wounded' were thus in very great danger, and would have fallen into the hands of the enemy, had not Surgeon Reade drawn his sword, and calling upon the few soldiers who were near to follow, succeeded, under a very heavy fire, in dislodging the rebels from their position. Surgeon Reade's party consisted of about ten in all, of whom two were killed, and five or six wounded. Surgeon Reade also accompanied the regiment at the assault of Delhi, and, on the morning of the 16th September, 1857, was one of the first up at the breach in the magazine, which was stormed by the 61st Regiment and Belooch Battalion, upon which occasion he, with a serjeant of the 61st Regiment, spiked one of the enemy's guns.

Biography

Herbert was born in Perth, Upper Canada on 20th September 1828. His father was Staff Surgeon George Hume who was Colonel of the 3rd Regiment of Leeds Militia in Upper Canada.[317]

Figure 146. Herbert Taylor Reade

---

317 He died in 1854 at Scutari during the Crimean War

Herbert had a younger brother John who, also became a Doctor of Medicine and rose to the rank of Surgeon General in the army.[318]

Herbert was initially educated in Quebec and then in Ireland. In 1850 he graduated as a Doctor of Medicine at Dublin and enlisted as an acting Assistant Surgeon in the 61st Regiment of Foot.

On 8th November 1850, Herbert was appointed as Assistant Surgeon in the 61st Regiment of Foot.[319] Herbert joined up with his regiment in India where they had been serving since 1845 and was stationed at Ferozepur. When the mutiny broke out in 1857, Herbert was still stationed at Ferozepur where the 57th Native Infantry were disarmed, unfortunately the 45th Native Infantry mutinied and fled to join the mutineers at Delhi. Herbert moved with the regiment to Delhi, as part of the Delhi Relief force and it was here on 14th September 1857 that he performed the deeds for which he would later be awarded the Victoria Cross. On 3rd November 1857, Herbert was promoted to the rank of Staff-Surgeon 2nd Class.[320] For his service during the mutiny, Herbert was awarded the Indian Mutiny Medal with clasp for Delhi.

Herbert left India in 1859 and after a short period of duty in Mauritius returned to England in 1860.

On 31st December 1861, Herbert transferred from the 61st Regiment to a position of Staff Surgeon in the Medical Department.[321]

Herbert was presented with his Victoria Cross Medal during July 1862 by Major General Sir Robert Percy Douglas the Lieutenant Governor of Jersey.

On 12th May 1863, Herbert was placed on half pay,[322] however, he was reinstated to full pay within a year on 19th April 1864.[323]

On 7th September 1871, under the terms of article 342 of the Royal Warrant dated 27th December 1870, Herbert was promoted to the rank of Staff Surgeon Major, having completed 20 years service on full pay.[324]

Herbert was promoted to Brigade Surgeon on 27th November 1879[325] and only a few months later on 27th March 1880 to the rank of Deputy Surgeon General.[326] On 30th November 1886, Herbert was promoted to the rank of Surgeon General[327]

and based at Colchester was the principle medical officer for the Eastern Division. Herbert was appointed as an Ordinary Member 3rd Class (Companion) of the Military Division of the Most Honourable Order of the Bath on 21st June 1887.[328]

Having completed over 37 years of service, Herbert retired from the army on 31st December 1887.[329]

On his retirement Herbert initially lived at Highbury Villa, Villiers Road in Southsea and then moved to Sunnylands, Park Gardens, Weston, Bath.

On 27th November 1895, Herbert was appointed as honorary Surgeon to Queen Victoria.[330]

Herbert died at his home in Bath on 23rd June 1897 at the age of 68 and was buried in Locksbrook Cemetery in Bath.

His Victoria Cross medal is on public display at the Soldiers of Gloucestershire Museum in Gloucester.

Figure 146a. Grave of Herbert Taylor Reade

318 John was also Knight Commander of the Bath, Knight of St John and
      Honorary Surgeon to Queen Victoria and King George V.
319 *London Gazette* – 21151/2911
320 *London Gazette* – 22057/3650
321 *London Gazette* – 22585/5633
322 *London Gazette* – 22735/2527
323 *London Gazette* – 22845/2172
324 *London Gazette* – 23782/4166
325 *London Gazette* – 24814/835
326 *London Gazette* – 24847/3176
327 *London Gazette* – 25661/5

328 *London Gazette* – 25712/7302
329 *London Gazette* – 25771/7302
330 *London Gazette* – 26683/6672

George Waller
14th September 1857 (VC No. 169)

Gazetted: 20th January 1860 22347/178

Rank and Unit: Colour Sergeant No. 2391 – 60th Rifles

Citation

For conspicuous bravery at Delhi on the 14th of September, 1857, in charging and capturing the Enemy's guns near the Cabul Gate; and again, on the 18th of September, 1857, in the repulse of a sudden attack made by the Enemy on a gun near the Chaudney Chouk.

Elected by the Non-Commissioned Officers of the Regiment.

Biography

George was born on 1st June 1827 at West Horsley, near Guildford in Surrey to father Charles and mother Martha.

George enlisted in the army on 12th October 1843 at the age of 16 at Great Bookham in Surrey and joined the 39th Regiment of Foot. His stay with the 39th was short lived as he transferred to 60th Rifles on 30th June 1844 and joined his regiment in Ireland.

In 1845 the regiment was deployed to India and were initially stationed at Poona until they moved to Kurrachee sometime in 1846. With the outbreak of the 2nd Anglo-Sikh war, the regiment was deployed to the Punjab where they were involved in the siege at Multan which lasted from 7th September 1848 until 22nd January 1849 when the town was taken. George was also involved in the decisive battle of the war which took place at Goojerat on 21st February 1849. For his service in the war, George was awarded the Punjab Medal (1848–49) with clasps for Mooltan and Goojerat.

From the Punjab the regiment moved to Peshawar and then Kussowlie. In 1852 the regiment was moved to Jullundur and then in 1855 were stationed at Meerut where they were serving when the mutiny broke out. By this time George had the rank of Colour-Sergeant.

George was involved in the siege at Delhi and it was on 14th September 1857, during the attack on the Kabul Gate that he performed the deeds for which he would later be awarded the Victoria Cross. George was elected for the award by a ballot of the non-commissioned officers of the regiment, under rule 13 of the origination Royal Warrant. On 18th September, during another attack on Delhi, George was wounded by a bullet in his right thigh. Following the siege at Delhi, the regiment were involved as part of the Rohilkhand Field Force in the subduing of the province of Oude. For his service during the mutiny, George

was awarded the Indian Mutiny Medal with clasp for Delhi. During 1859, the regiment were variously stationed at Benares, Allahabad, Dum-Dum and finally Calcutta from where early in the New Year they set sail for their return to England.

In 1860, after 15 years service in India, George was to spend the remainder of his army career on garrison duties in the England and Ireland, initially at Dover.

George was presented with his Victoria Cross medal on 9th November 1860, by Queen Victoria at an investiture held in Windsor Castle.

After spending a year at Dover, the regiment moved to the new camp at Aldershot in 1861 where they spent two years before spending a year in London. In 1864 the regiment was posted to Ireland where they were stationed at Dublin, it was during this tour in Ireland, sometime during 1865, that George retired from the army after 22 years of service. For his army service, George was awarded the Army Long Service and Good Conduct medal.

Following his retirement, George moved back to Sussex and it was on 10th January 1877, a few months short of his 50th birthday that he died while living at Cuckfield, near Haywards Heath.

George was buried on 14th January at Holy Trinity Churchyard, Hurstpierpoint in an unmarked grave next to where his mother was buried.

George's Victoria Cross medal is on public display at the Royal Green Jackets Museum in Winchester.

Figure 147a. Grave of George Waller

George Alexander Renny
16th September 1857 (VC No. 170)

Figure 148. George Alexander Renny

Gazetted: 12th April 1859 22248/1483

Rank and Unit: Lieutenant – Bengal Horse Artillery

Citation

Lieutenant-Colonel Farquhar, Commanding the 1st Belooch Regiment, reports that he was in command of the troops stationed in the Delhi magazine, after its capture on the 16th of September, 1857. Early in the forenoon of that day, a vigorous attack was made on the post by the enemy, and was kept up with great violence for some time, without the slightest chance of success. Under cover of a heavy cross fire from the high houses on the right flank of the magazine, and from Salimgarh and the Palace, the enemy advanced to the high wall of the magazine, and endeavoured to set fire to a thatched roof. The roof was partially set fire to, which was extinguished at the spot by a Sepoy of the Belooch Battalion, a soldier of the 61st Regiment having in vain attempted to do so. The roof having been again set on fire, Captain Renny with great gallantry mounted to the top of the wall of the magazine, and flung several shells with lighted fuses over into the midst of the enemy, which had an almost immediate effect, as the attack at once became feeble at that point, and soon after ceased there.

Biography

George was born on 12th May 1825 at Riga in Livonia, Russia. His father Alexander was a merchant whose family had been settled in Russia for over a century.

Soon after his birth, George's father died and his mother moved the family, George and his older sister, to Scotland where they settled in Montrose, Forfarshire to be closer to relatives.

George was initially educated at Montrose Academy followed by a period at the Honourable East India Company Military Seminary at Addiscombe.

On his graduation from Addiscombe, George was commissioned as a 2nd Lieutenant in the Bengal Horse Artillery on 7th June 1844 and in December went out to India to join his regiment.

From 24th January 1846, George was involved in the 1st Anglo-Sikh War, also known as the Sutlej Campaign and on 10th February 1846 was present at the Battle of Sobraon. For his service in the war, George was awarded the Sutlej Medal (1845–46) engraved on the reverse with Sobraon 1846.

On 6th October 1846, George was promoted to the rank of 1st Lieutenant and spent the next 11 years on duty on the plains of India.

Sometime during 1849, George was married to Flora Hastings (née Macwhirter) in India, the couple would go on to have six children, three sons and three daughters.

At the time of the mutiny, George was in command of the 5th Troop (Native) of the 1st Brigade Bengal Horse Artillery and was stationed at Jalandhar. On 7th June 1857, the loyalty of George's troop was tested when they were ordered to fire on Infantry and Cavalry that were joining in with the mutiny. The troop rose to the challenge and carried out their orders impeccably and ultimately they were the only battery of native artillery to remain loyal throughout the mutiny. After subduing the mutiny at Jalandhar, George joined the Relief Force going to the aid of Delhi and arrived on the outskirts of Delhi on 26th June to take part in the siege of the city which had been captured by the mutineers. Following an attack by rebel cavalry on the British positions on Delhi Ridge on 9th July, the guns and horses were taken away from the men in George's troop as a precautionary measure, however, they continued to operate the mortars of no 4 Siege Battery, throughout the siege. The siege train, with a large supply of heavy guns and ammunition, finally arrived at the city on 4th September and preparations began for the final assault on the city, which following an immense bombardment began on the 14th September. It was on 16th September 1857, during an attack to retake the Delhi Magazine with its vast store of guns and ammunition, that George performed the deeds for which he was later awarded the Victoria Cross. His actions prompted a mention in the despatches of Major-General Archdale Wilson commander of the Delhi Field Force.[331] Following the recapture of the city on 20th September, George and his troop were involved in operations in the Moozuffernuggur District. On 27th

---

331 *Edinburgh Gazette* – 6793/661

April 1858, George was promoted to the rank of Captain[332] and a few months later on 20th July 1858 received a brevet promotion to the rank of Major.[333] George commanded the native horse artillery during the campaign in Rohilkhand which was led by Brigadier General Robert Walpole and the unit was involved in their final action of the campaign at Sisseah on 15th January 1859. For his part in this action, George was mentioned in the despatches of General Walpole[334] and his conduct and that of his troop were mentioned in the General Orders of both the General and of Lord Clyde. For his service during the mutiny, George was awarded the Indian Mutiny Medal with clasp for Delhi, he also received a commendation from the Indian Government. The loyalty of his men was also recognised, each native officer was awarded the Order of British India and each non-commissioned officer and other rank received the Indian Order of Merit for their services.

George was presented with his Victoria Cross medal on 9th November 1860 by Queen Victoria at an investiture held at Windsor Castle.

On 1st June 1867, George received a brevet promotion to the rank of Lieutenant-Colonel.

During the Hazara and Black Mountain campaign during 1868, George commanded D battery of F brigade in the field force led by Brigadier-General Alfred Wilde, because of the terrain the guns were carried by elephants rather than horses. George also had command of the 94th Brigade of Royal Artillery. For his service in this campaign, George was awarded the India General Service Medal (1854–95) with clasp for North West Frontier. For his action on 4th October 1868, George received a mention in the despatches of Lieutenant-Colonel Atlay.[335]

On 28th August 1871, George was promoted to the regimental rank of Lieutenant-Colonel[336] and on 28th August 1876 received a brevet promotion to the rank of Colonel,[337] which was made substantive on 1st April 1877.[338]

As Colonel, George commanded the Royal Artillery in the Máu Division of Sindh province and also commanded the station at Ahmednagar.

On 31st December 1878, George retired from the army and received the honorary rank of Major-General.[339]

After 34 years of army service, spent exclusively in India, George returned to England where he took up residence at 24 Rivers Street in Bath, where on 5th January 1887, he died at the age of 61.

George was buried in the Locksbrook Cemetery in Bath.

In 1978, George's Victoria Cross medal was stolen during a burglary at the home of relative Mrs Margo Renny in Waldringfield, Suffolk. Amazingly, five years later in March 1983 the medal was discovered on Sheen Common by a person with a metal detector. Following a report in the local press about the find, the medal was reunited with its owner and is currently on loan to the Royal Artillery Museum at Woolwich.

Figure 148a. Grave of George Alexander Renny

332 *London Gazette* – 22621/2231
333 *London Gazette* – 22238/1089
334 *London Gazette* – 22251/1616
335 *London Gazette* – 23507/3399
336 *London Gazette* – 23794/4598
337 *London Gazette* – 24388/6532
338 *London Gazette* – 24445/2676
339 *London Gazette* – 24668/174

Edward Talbot Thackeray
16th September 1857 (VC No. 171)

Gazetted: 29th April 1862 22621/2229

Rank and Unit: 2nd Lieutenant – Bengal Engineers

Citation

For cool intrepidity and characteristic daring in extinguishing a fire in the Delhi Magazine enclosure, on the 16th of September, 1857, under a close and heavy musketry fire from the enemy, at the imminent risk of his life from the explosion of combustible stores in the shed in which the fire occurred.

Figure 149. Edward Talbot Thackeray

Biography

Edward was born on 19th October 1836 at Broxbourne in Hertfordshire to father Reverend Francis St. John and mother Mary Anne (née Shakespear). Edward was the fourth born of five children having and older sister Mary Augusta who was baptised on 12th May 1830; two older brothers, Francis Talbot who was baptised on 22nd September 1831, Francis St. John baptised on 13th February 1833 and a younger brother Frederic David Aitken born on 24th October 1845.

Edward was 1st cousin of William Makepeace Thackeray the renowned author.

From August 1845, Edward was educated at Marlborough College until the summer of 1850 when he was enrolled in the Honourable East India Company Military Seminary at Addiscombe. After graduating from Addiscombe, Edward was commissioned with the local and temporary rank of Ensign on 22nd December 1854, while he undertook field instruction in the art of Sapping and Mining at the Royal Engineering College at Chatham.[340]

On graduating from Chatham, Edward was commissioned as 2nd Lieutenant in the Bengal Engineers on 9th December 1856 and moved out to India to join his regiment. Following the outbreak of mutiny in May 1857, Edward was assigned to the Delhi Field Force and during the march towards Delhi was involved in the action at the Hindun River on 30th to 31st May and the Battle of Badli-ki-Serai on June 8th. It was during the final battles to regain Delhi, on 16th September 1857 in the attack to recapture the Delhi Magazine, that Edward performed the deeds for which he would later be awarded the Victoria Cross. After Delhi was safely back under British Control, Edward was part of a force commanded by Lieutenant Colonel Thomas Seaton which

engaged the rebels at the Battle of Gungeree on 14th December and the Battle of Puttialee on 17th December. Edward was involved throughout the Rohilkhand campaign taking part in the siege at Lucknow which culminated with the relief on 21st March 1858. He also took part in the Battle of Fort Rooya on 15th April, the Battle of Alligunge on 22nd April and the Battle of Bareilly on 5th May 1858. On 27th April 1858, Edward was promoted to the rank of Lieutenant.[341] Edward was also involved throughout the Oude Campaign during 1858 to 1859. For his service during the mutiny, Edward was awarded the Indian Mutiny Medal with clasps for Delhi and Lucknow.

Edward was presented with his Victoria Cross medal by Major-General Arthur Dalzell in July 1862 at Dover, during the year he was married to Amy Mary Anne (née Crowe) and the couple would have two daughters: Amy Margaret Ritchie born on 30th August 1863 at Debroghur in India and Anne Wynne born in 1865/66 also born in India. Edward's wife Amy died in 1866, possibly during the birth of their second child.

On 24th March 1865, Edward was promoted to 2nd Captain.[342]

On 2nd December 1869, Edward married Elizabeth (née Playdell), the couple would have four sons and a daughter: Edward Francis born on 2nd November 1870 in London,[343] Richmond Clive born 19th September 1873, Charles Bouverie born on 20th December 1875 in Bath,[344] Constance Elizabeth born during 1877 and Henry St John born on 6th October 1879.

---

340 *London Gazette* – 21643/4182

341 Harts Army List

342 *London Gazette* – 22951/1677

343 Edward Francis would have a distinguished career in the army, attaining the rank of Lieutenant-Colonel and being awarded the DSO during the Great War. He was also recommended for the Victoria Cross by General H. T. Lukin.

344 Charles Bouverie would also attain the rank of Lieutenant-Colonel and was also awarded the DSO during the Great War.

On 14th December 1870, Edward was promoted to the rank of Captain[345] and 18 months later on 5th July 1872 received a promotion to the rank of Major.[346]

In 1879, Edward was given command of the Bengal Sappers and Miners and was involved in the 2nd Anglo-Afghan War from 1879 to 1880. During the war, Edward was part of the Kabul Field Force which advanced on Kabul and was mentioned in despatches three times[347] for his actions on 17th December 1879 and on 24th December during the action at Jagdalak Kotal where he was seriously wounded. For the remainder of the war, Edward was in command of Fort Jagdalak, which occupied a strategic position in the Hindu Kush, between Kabul and Jellalabad. On 25th November 1880, Edward was promoted to the rank of Lieutenant-Colonel[348] and for his service during the war was awarded the Afghanistan Medal (1878–80).

Edward was promoted to the rank of Colonel on 25th November 1884.[349]

On 29th May 1886, Edward was appointed as an ordinary member 3rd Class (Companion) of the Military Division of the Most Honourable Order of the Bath.[350]

On 12th August 1886, having completed five years service as a regimental Lieutenant-Colonel, Edward was placed on the Indian Army Supernumerary List,[351] effectively bring his army career to a close. He was officially retired from the army on 9th April 1888, after 34 years of service which was all spent on the Indian sub-continent.[352]

In his retirement Edward returned to England and was very active in the St John's Ambulance Brigade, being Chief Commissioner of the Order of St John of Jerusalem from 1893 until 1898. On 12th August 1896, Edward was appointed as a Knight of Grace in the Grand Priory of the Order of the Hospital of St John of Jerusalem in England[353] and in 1897 was awarded the St John's Ambulance Brigade issue of the Queen Victoria Jubilee Medal.

Edward was appointed as an additional member 2nd Class (Knight Commander) of the Civil Division of the Most Honourable Order of the Bath on 22nd June 1897,[354] being inducted into the order by Queen Victoria on 14th March 1898.[355]

Sometime during 1898 or 1899, Edward moved to Italy where he would spend his remaining years.

During the Great War, Edward was Commissioner of the Bordighera Branch of the British Red Cross, in Italy from 1917 until 1919 and for his service was mentioned in the despatches of General F. R. Earl of Covan on 18th January 1919.[356] For his service, Edward was also awarded the British War Medal (1914–20) and the Victory Medal (1914–19) with mentioned in despatches Oak leaf clasp.

Edward wrote three books about his army experiences in India; "Two Indian Campaigns", "Biographies of Officers of the Bengal Engineers" and "Reminiscences of the Indian Mutiny and Afghanistan".

Edward died at his home in Garassio, Italy on 3rd September 1927 at the age of 90 and was buried in the English Cemetery at Bordighera.

Edward's Victoria Cross Medal is on public display at the South Africa National Museum of Military History in Johannesburg.

Figure 149a. Grave of Edward Talbot Thackeray

345 *London Gazette* – 23687/5748
346 *London Gazette* – 23876/3194
347 *London Gazette* – 24841/2863, 24841/2859 & 24841/2860
348 *London Gazette* – 24912/6674
349 *London Gazette* – 25417/5194
350 *London Gazette* – 22592/2633
351 *London Gazette* – 25630/4785
352 *London Gazette* – 25804/1990
353 *London Gazette* – 26725/1961
354 *London Gazette* – 26867/3568
355 *London Gazette* – 26947/1669

356 *London Gazette* – 31384/7213

Patrick Mahoney
21st September 1857 (VC No. 172)

Gazetted: 18th June 1858 22154/2957

Rank and Unit: Sergeant – 1st Madras Fusiliers

Citation

For distinguished gallantry (whilst doing duty with the Volunteer Cavalry) in aiding in the capture of the Regimental Colour of the 1st Regiment Native Infantry, at Mungulwar, on the 21st of September 1857. (**Extract from Field Force Orders of the late Major-General Havelock, dated 17th October, 1857.**)

Biography

Patrick was born during 1827 in Waterford in Ireland.

At some stage, Patrick joined the army of the Honourable East India Company and was assigned to the 1st Madras Fusiliers.

By the time of the mutiny, Patrick was a Sergeant and based with his regiment at Fort George in Madras. After the mutiny of his regiment, Patrick joined a small force of irregular cavalry, formed from the Officers and NCO's from regiments that had mutinied. This small unit joined the force of General Havelock which marched from Allahabad to the relief of Lucknow. It was on the journey to Lucknow, on 21st September 1857, in a Battle at Mangalwar that Patrick performed the deeds for which he would later be awarded the Victoria Cross.

Patrick was killed in action just over a month later on 30th October 1857 aged 30, during the siege at Lucknow. It is not known where Patrick was buried, presumably close to where he was killed.

Due to his untimely death, Patrick was never presented with his Victoria Cross medal.

For his service during the mutiny, Patrick was awarded the Indian Mutiny Medal with clasp for Lucknow.

Patrick's Victoria Cross medal is part of the Oriental and India Office Collection, held by the British Library in London.

William Rennie
21st September 1857 (VC No. 173)

Gazetted: 24th December 1858 22212/5518

Rank and Unit: Lieutenant – 90th Perthshire Regiment

Citation

For conspicuous gallantry in the advance upon Lucknow, under the late Major-General Havelock, on the 21st of September, 1857, in having charged the enemy's guns in advance of the skirmishers of the 90th Light Infantry, under a heavy musketry fire, and prevented them dragging off one gun, which was consequently captured.

For conspicuous gallantry at Lucknow on the 25th of September, 1857, in having charged in advance of the 90th column, in the face of a heavy fire of grape, and forced the enemy to abandon their guns.

Biography

William was born on 31st October 1822 at Elgin in Morayshire, Scotland.

At some stage, probably at a time around his 18th birthday, William enlisted in the army and joined the 73rd Regiment of Foot as a private. The 73rd returned to England in July 1841, from a tour of Canada and it is likely that William joined the regiment at this time. The regiment were stationed at Gosport, Woolwich and Bradford before moving to Newport in Monmouthshire in September 1842. In August 1844, the regiment left Wales for a deployment in Ireland and from December they formed the garrison at the Royal Barracks in Dublin.

On 29th September 1845, the regiment embarked on board the troopship *HMS Apollo*, bound for duties in the Cape Colony, however, mid-way through the voyage they were diverted to Argentina landing at Montevideo in January 1846. The regiment remained in Argentina until July 1846, where they were protecting British interests during the Uruguayan Civil War (1839–52), when they finally set sail for the Cape Colony.

The regiment arrived in South Africa during August and were despatched to Waterloo Bay on the Fish River where they were deployed with other troops against the Xhosa tribe during the 7th Cape Frontier War (also known as the 'War of the Axe' or 'Amatola' war). The war was concluded in December 1847 with the creation of the British Kaffraria Colony as a Crown dependency. In January 1848, the regiment was moved to Cape Town. William and the regiment were involved in the 8th Cape Frontier War which took place between December 1850 and February 1853. As part of a

Figure 151. William Rennie

actions that became known as the 2nd relief of Lucknow which culminated in the evacuation of the Residency on 20th November. William was also involved as part of the force of General Outram which resulted in the recapture of Lucknow on 21st March 1858. During April 1858, the regiment was part of the force of General Hope Grant on operations in Rohilkhand and were involved in the Battle of Bareilly on 13th May 1858. For his service during the mutiny, William was awarded the Indian Mutiny Medal with clasps for Defence of Lucknow and Lucknow.

William was presented with his Victoria Cross Medal in February 1859 while stationed at Sitapur.

William spent the next ten years on service at various stations throughout India and on 9th January 1863 received a promotion to the rank of Captain.[359]

On 31st September 1869, William set sail from Bombay on board *HMS Jumna* bound for England, after changing to *HMS Serapis* at Suez, the regiment arrived at Portsmouth on 3rd November 1869 after over 13 years of foreign service. On 7th November 1869, the regiment formed the garrison at Edinburgh Castle where they remained until their transfer to Glasgow in June 1871. William's final posting was to Dover, where the regiment arrived on 6th September 1873, a few weeks later on 10th December 1873, he received a promotion to the rank of Major.[360] On 28th March 1874, William retired from the army on full pay after over 30 years of service, he was granted the brevet honorary rank of Lieutenant-Colonel.[361]

force commanded by Major General Cathcart, William and the regiment took part in the Battle of Berea on 20th December 1852. William's conduct during this battle resulted in a battlefield commission to the rank of Ensign from his current rank of Sergeant Major; the commission was made official with an effective date of 11th August 1854.[357] For his service during the Cape Frontier Wars, William was awarded the South Africa Medal (1834–53).

On 30th November 1855, William transferred to the 90th Regiment of Foot when he was promoted to the rank of Lieutenant and given the role of Adjutant.[358] William probably joined up with his new regiment at Aldershot, where they were stationed from July 1856, following their return from the Crimea. In February 1857, the regiment moved to Portsmouth and occupied the Anglesey Barracks. Almost immediately they received orders for a deployment to India, however, at the end of March, they received further orders changing their destination to China. On 16th April 1857, William together with the Headquarters staff of the 90th set sail from Portsmouth on board *HMS Himalaya* bound for China. Part way through the journey, the regiment received new order to proceed to India, in light of the outbreak of mutiny, and arrived at Calcutta on 21st July. From Calcutta the regiment proceeded by river steamers to Allahabad and on the journey, on 1st August, disarmed the 11th Native Cavalry Regiment and the 63rd Native Infantry Regiment at Berhampore. The regiment joined up with the field force of General Havelock and advanced towards Lucknow, it was at Mangalwar on 21st September that William performed the deeds for which he would later be awarded the Victoria Cross. William was involved in the

Figure 151a. Grave of William Rennie

357 *London Gazette* – 21581/2469
358 *London Gazette* – 21822/4536

359 *London Gazette* – 22705/645
360 *London Gazette* – 24043/5780
361 *London Gazette* – 24081/1875

On his retirement, William spent some time living in London before returning to his home town of Elgin where on 27th August 1887 he died aged 75 and was buried in Elgin Cemetery.

William's Victoria Cross medal is on public display at the Cameronians Regimental Museum in Hamilton.

Figure 151a. Grave of William Rennie

Robert Grant
24th September 1857 (VC No. 174)

Gazetted: 19th June 1860 22396/2316

Rank and Unit: Corporal – 5th Regiment, 1st Battalion

Citation

For conspicuous devotion at Alum Bagh, on the 24th September, 1857, in proceeding under a heavy and galling fire to save the life of Private E. Deveney, whose leg had been shot away, and eventually carrying him safe into camp, with the assistance of the late Lieutenant Brown, and some comrades.

This gazette entry was erroneously attributed to Sergeant Robert Ewart, corrected by an entry on 12th October 1860 (22434/3679)

VICTORIA CROSS. Erratum in the London Gazette of Tuesday, June 19, 1860.

In the notification of Her Majesty's intention to confer the Victoria Cross on three soldiers of Her Majesty's Army, For, 1st Battalion, 5th Regiment, Serjeant Robert Ewart, Read, 1st Battalion, 5th Regiment, Serjeant Robert Grant.

Biography

Robert was born in Harrogate, Yorkshire at some time during 1837.

It is probable that Robert enlisted in the army some time in 1853 or 1854, leaving his job as a labourer, and after joining the 1st Battalion of the 5th Regiment of Foot would have served some time in Ireland before his first overseas posting to Singapore.

While serving in Singapore, the regiment received orders to proceed to India to help subdue the Mutiny. The regiment arrived in Calcutta on 4th July 1857 and a month later on 2nd August saw their first action when they were involved in the relief of Arrah. As part of the Oudh Relief Force, under the command of General Havelock, Robert was involved in the attempt to break through the mutineers besieging Lucknow which commenced on 21st September. It was during attacks on the Alum Bagh on 24th September that Robert performed the deeds for which he was later awarded the Victoria Cross. For this action Robert was promoted to the rank of Sergeant. The regiment was part of the force that finally gained entry into the Residency on September 25th and successfully mounted a defence until relieved by the force of Sir Colin Campbell on 17th March 1858. On 31st March 1858, the regiment left Lucknow for Cawnpore where they were based for the next year, involved in subduing the rebellion in the Oudh Province. In early 1859, the regiment moved to Allahabad where

Figure 152. Robert Grant

Robert was buried in an unmarked paupers grave (his wife could not afford the burial costs so these were born by the Parish council), in Highgate Cemetery in London.

His Victoria Cross Medal is on public display at the Fusilier's Museum, Alnwick Castle, Alnwick, Northumberland.

they suffered from cholera and moved to Calcutta in March 1860. For his service during the Mutiny, Robert was awarded the Indian Mutiny Medal with clasps for Defence of Lucknow and Lucknow.

Robert was presented with his Victoria Cross medal on 12th December 1860 by Lady Hersey at a ceremony held in Fort William at Calcutta, soon afterwards he returned to England with the regiment.

It is thought that Robert left the army during 1864 (after ten years service) and in August 1864 joined the Metropolitan Police as constable 306 in "Y" Division, Holloway. There is some doubt regarding this date as, from photographic evidence, it appears that Robert was awarded the Army Long Service and Good Conduct Medal, which at the time required 20 years of service. This also cast doubt on his date of death, quoted by some sources as being 7th March 1867. It is more probable that Robert died on 23rd November 1874, from pneumonia, while living at home in Islington, London and still serving as a Police Constable.

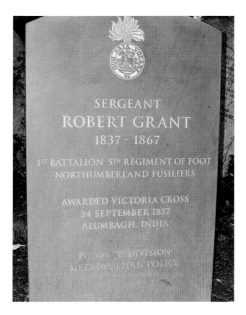

Figure 152a. Grave of Robert Grant

Joseph Jee
25th September 1857 (VC No. 175)

Gazetted: 8th November 1860 22445/4126

Rank and Unit: Surgeon – 78th Regiment of Foot

Citation

For most conspicuous gallantry and important Services, on the entry of the late Major- General Havelock's relieving force into Lucknow, on the 25th September, 1857, in having during action (when the 78th Highlanders, then in possession of the Char Bagh, captured two 9-pounders at the point of the bayonet), by great exertion and devoted exposure, attended to the large number of men wounded in the charge, whom he succeeded in getting removed on cots and the backs of their comrades, until he had collected the Dooly bearers who had fled. Subsequently, on the same day, in endeavouring to reach the Residency with the wounded men, Surgeon Jee became besieged by an overwhelming force in the Mote-Mehal, where he remained during the whole night and following morning, voluntarily and repeatedly exposing himself to a heavy fire in proceeding to dress the wounded men who fell while serving a 24-pounder in a most exposed situation. He eventually succeeded in taking many of the wounded, through a cross fire of ordnance and musketry, safely into the Residency, by the river-bank, although repeatedly warned not to make the perilous attempt.

Biography

Joseph was born on 9th February 1819 at Harthill, Atherstone in Warwickshire, his father was Christopher Preston and mother Elizabeth (née Edens).

Joseph was educated at medical schools and universities in London and Edinburgh and spent some time at the Ecole de Medicine in Paris, in 1841 he qualified as a Member of the Royal College of Surgeons.

On 15th April 1842, Joseph was commissioned as an assistant surgeon in the 57th Regiment of Foot[362] and just over a year and a half later on 22nd December 1843 transferred to the 15th Light Dragoons by way of exchange with assistant surgeon Bisset.[363]

Joseph was promoted to the rank of Surgeon on 23rd June 1854 and was assigned to the 78th Regiment which was serving in India, stationed at Poona.[364]

362 *London Gazette* – 20091/1048
363 *London Gazette* – 20298/4475
364 *London Gazette* – 21565/1949

Figure 153. Joseph Jee

Following the declaration of war against Persia, on 1st November 1856, early in January 1857, Joseph with his regiment left Poona for Bombay where they arrived on 19th January and set sail for Persia where they arrived off Busheer on 1st February. On 3rd February, the regiment was attached to a force commanded by General Outram and marched off to tackle a large enemy force that was being assembled about 40 miles away in preparation for an attack on the British held town and fort at Busheer. By the 7th February it appeared that the enemy force had dispersed, so the column set out to return to Busheer, however, outside the village of Khushab the force was ambushed and a savage battle ensued. After the battle the column returned to Busheer, where the recently arrived General Havelock now took command of the force. On 24th March a large force, under General Havelock, which included Joseph and the 78th set sail for the major Persian fortress at Mohammrah where they arrived on 26th March. Following a prolonged bombardment from the fleet, the fort and town were taken by the British forces on 27th March, during the battle Joseph had his horse shot out from under him. This was the last significant action of the war as news of the peace treaty signed in Paris on 4th March finally reached the British commanders. For his participation in the first Anglo-Persian War, Joseph was awarded the India General Service Medal (1854–95) with clasp for Persia. The regiment would not be presented with these medals until 18th February 1860 when they were stationed at Fort-George near Inverness.

With the end of the war, the regiment embarked on ships at Mohammrah and on 10th May 1857, set sail for their return to India. When they arrived at Bombay on 23rd May, the regiment received the unbelievable news of the mutiny of the native troops in Bengal and were immediately despatched to Calcutta where they arrived on 10th June. After a brief expedition to Barrackpore, where on 13th June they disarmed the native regiments, the regiment proceeded to Allahabad to join up with the force of General Havelock being assembled to go to the relief of Lucknow. On the march to Lucknow, Joseph was involved in the battles at Futtehpore on 10th July and Aherwa on 16th July before occupying Cawnpore on 17th July, which had been abandoned by the mutineers. After leaving a garrison at Cawnpore, the force set off again for Lucknow on 25th July and fought battles at Mangalwar on 26th July, Oonoa on 29th July and Bithoor on 16th August. The force depleted by casualties and the ravages of cholera now returned to Cawnpore for rest and recovery and to await reinforcements.

Following the arrival of General James Outram, who took command of the Cawnpore Garrison, on 21st September Joseph set out with another expedition going to the relief of Lucknow. The main attacks to relieve Lucknow took place on 25th September and it was on this day at the village of Cher Bagh, just outside the city, that Joseph performed the deeds for which he would later be awarded the Victoria Cross medal. By the 28th September 1857, the force had gained entry to the beleaguered Residency and continued the defence until it was decided to evacuate the Residency on 22nd November. Following the evacuation of the Residency at Lucknow, Joseph and the regiment proceeded to Alum Bagh where they remained until 28th April 1858 when they joined up with the Rohilkhand Field Force, under the command of Sir Colin Campbell, at Cawnpore. On 7th May, the regiment was involved in the Battle of Bareilly and following the capture of the town would form part of the garrison until 20th February 1859 when they moved to Agra. On 4th March 1859, the regiment left Agra to start the long journey home and after arriving at Bombay on 28th April set sail for England on 18th May. For his service during the mutiny, Joseph would be awarded the Indian Mutiny Medal with clasps for Defence of Lucknow and Lucknow. The regiment would be presented with their Indian Mutiny Medals on 9th August 1861 by Lady Havelock (the widow of General Sir Henry Havelock) in Edinburgh.

On 16th May 1859, Joseph was appointed as an Extra Member 3rd Class (Companion) of the Military Division of the Most Honourable Order of the Bath.[365]

The regiment arrived at Gravesend in mid-September and immediately set out for Fort George near Inverness which was to be their base until mid-February 1860 when they moved to Edinburgh.

On 9th November 1860, Joseph was presented with his Victoria Cross Medal by Queen Victoria at an investiture held in Windsor Castle.

A few weeks later, on 25th November 1860, Joseph was married to Nora Carola (née Riley) at the church of St. Mary of the Angels in London.

In April 1861, the regiment was moved to Aldershot.

On 13th December 1861, Joseph appeared as a witness, at Winchester Crown Court, in the trial of Private Thomas Jackson who was accused of the murder of Sergeant John Dickson in the barracks at Aldershot on 23rd November 1861. Private Jackson was found guilty and was hanged for his crime.[366]

Under the provisions of a Royal Warrant dated 1st October 1858, having completed 20 years service on full pay, Joseph was promoted to the rank of Surgeon Major on 15th April 1862.[367] On 15th May 1862, the regiment moved to Shorncliffe and almost exactly a year later on 26th May 1863 moved to Dover. From Dover the regiment were posted to Ireland and from 5th August 1864 were in barracks in Dublin. Soon after the move to Ireland, on 20th September 1864, Joseph transferred to the 1st Regiment of Dragoons,[368] moved back to England and joined his

Figure 153a. Grave of Joseph Jee

365 *London Gazette* – 22264/1988

366 *The Times* – 14th December 1861
367 *London Gazette* – 22629/2733
368 *London Gazette* – 22895/4507

regiment at Aldershot. After spending almost a year at Aldershot, on 8th August 1865 the regiment moved to Manchester and on 16th April 1867 moved to Ireland where they were stationed at Dublin.

Joseph retired from the army on half pay on 4th March 1868 and was awarded the honorary brevet rank of Deputy Inspector General of Hospitals.[369]

For some period, Joseph was a director of the Fullers Reef Gold Mining Co. which operated a gold mine in New South Wales, Australia.

On 15th April 1887, Joseph survived the sinking of the steamship *Victoria* which sank in the English Channel off Dieppe with a loss of 26 crew and passengers.

On 8th March 1899, Joseph received the honorary appointment of Surgeon to Queen Victoria.[370]

Joseph died on 17th March 1899 aged 80 at his home in Queniborough Old Hall, Queniborough near Leicester and was buried in the cemetery of Radcliffe Roman Catholic College in Queniborough.

His Victoria Cross medal is on public display at the Army Medical Services Museum in Aldershot.

Valentine Munbee McMaster
25th September 1857 (VC No. 176)

Gazetted: 18th June 1858 22154/2957

Rank and Unit: Assistant Surgeon – 78th Regiment of Foot

Citation

For the intrepidity with which he exposed himself to the fire of the enemy, in bringing in, and attending to, the wounded, on the 25th of September, at Lucknow. **(Extract from Field Force Orders of the late Major-General Havelock, dated 17th October, 1857.)**

Biography

Valentine was born on 16th May 1834 at Trichinopoly in India, his father was born in Belfast and his mother whose maiden name was Munbee, was born in Londonderry.

He was educated in Scotland and graduated from the University Of Edinburgh Medical School in 1854 as an MD and Licentiate of the Royal College of Surgeons, Edinburgh (LRCSE).

Valentine was appointed as an Assistant Surgeon to the 78th Regiment of Foot on 27th March 1855[371] and joined his regiment in Poona, India.

In January 1857, Valentine set sail from Bombay to Busheer to take part in the 1st Anglo-Persian War, taking part in the Battle of Khushab on 7th February and the Siege and Battle of Mohammrah on 26th to 27th March 1857. For his service during the war, Valentine was awarded the India General Service Medal (1854–95).

On 23rd May 1857, Valentine returned to Bombay, India and with the unexpected news of the mutiny were despatched to join up with the Lucknow Relief Force being assembled under the command of General Havelock at Allahabad. While serving with this force, Valentine was involved in the capture of Cawnpore on 17th July and the relief of Lucknow on 25th September, during which he performed the deeds for which he would later be awarded the Victoria Cross.

Valentine was presented with his Victoria Cross medal some time during 1858 by Lieutenant-General Sir Henry Somerset the Commander in Chief of the Bengal Army.

In April 1858, the regiment was assigned to the Rohilkhand Field Force, commanded by Sir Colin Campbell and was involved in the Battle of Bareilly on 7th May. Following the capture of Bareilly, the regiment formed the garrison until 20th February 1859 when they departed for Agra to begin the long journey home to England.

369 *London Gazette* – 23358/1437
370 *London Gazette* – 27060/1589

371 *Edinburgh Gazette* – 6575/208

Figure 154. Valentine Munbee McMaster

boarded the troopship *HMS Orontes* and set sail for Ireland, where they arrived at Queenstown on 17th December. By 20th December, the regiment was installed in the North Queen Street Barracks in Belfast and it was here on 22nd January 1872 at the age of 37 that Valentine died of heart failure. Valentine was buried in the City of Belfast Cemetery.

His Victoria Cross medal is on public display at the National War Museum of Scotland in Edinburgh Castle.

Figure 154a. Grave of Valentine Munbee McMaster

For his service during the mutiny, Valentine was awarded the Indian Mutiny Medal with clasps for Relief of Lucknow and Lucknow and was awarded an additional year of service towards his pension.

The regiment set sail from Bombay on 28th April and arrived at Gravesend during September, from where they proceeded to garrison Fort George near Inverness in Scotland until February 1860 when they moved to Edinburgh.

On 25th September 1860, Valentine transferred to the 6th Dragoons[372] and joined up with his regiment in India. With the 6th Dragoons, Valentine took part in the Umbeyla Campaign (1863–64), commanded by Neville Bowles Chamberlain and for this service was awarded the clasp for Umbeyla to his Indian General Service Medal.

At some stage, Valentine was married[373] and had a son Bryce who was born some time in 1866.

On 3rd June 1864, Valentine transferred to the 18th Hussars[374] and continued his service in India until 14th March 1868 when he was promoted to the rank of Surgeon and assigned to a staff position in the Medical Department.[375]

On 6th March 1869, Valentine moved back to his original regiment, the 78th as Surgeon[376] and joined up with the regiment who were on overseas duty in Halifax, Nova Scotia. Valentine remained in Canada until on 25th November 1871, the regiment

---

372 *Edinburgh Gazette* – 7053/1186

373 At some time after his death, his widow married Campbell Mellis Douglas, an assistant surgeon in the 24th Regiment of Foot, who was awarded a Victoria Cross for actions in India on 7th May 1867.

374 *Edinburgh Gazette* – 7438/750

375 *London Gazette* – 23361/1648

376 *London Gazette* – 23476/1515

Francis Cornwallis Maude
25th September 1857 (VC No. 177)

Gazetted: 18th June 1858 22154/2957

Rank and Unit: Captain – Royal Artillery

Citation

This officer steadily and cheerily pushed on with his men, and bore down the desperate opposition of the enemy, though with the loss of one-third of his Artillerymen. Sir James Outram adds, that this attack appeared to him to indicate no reckless or foolhardy daring, but the calm heroism of a true soldier, who fully appreciates the difficulties and dangers of the task he has undertaken and that, but for Captain Maude's nerve and coolness on this trying occasion, the Army could not have advanced. **(Extract from Field Force Orders of the late Major-General Havelock, dated 17th October, 1857.)**

Biography

Francis was born on 28th October 1828 in London, the oldest son of father Francis a Captain in the Royal Navy and mother Frances (née Brooking).

Francis was the oldest of eight children, with younger brothers; Charles Henry born on 21st August 1830, James Arthur born on 10th April 1832, Cecil William de Latham born 21st April 1850, Gerald Edward born on 12th June 1851 and Raymond William de Latham born on 27th June 1852; and two younger sisters, Blanche Emily Isabella born 10th July 1855 and Olivia Georgiana Elizabeth born on 1st March 1857. The five youngest children were born to his father's 2nd wife Georgiana (née Bushe) who he married on 28th June 1849.

Francis was educated at the Blackheath Preparatory School and then Rugby before being enrolled as a gentleman cadet at the Royal Military Academy in Woolwich on 9th May 1844. On graduation from the Royal Military Academy, Francis was commissioned as 2nd Lieutenant in the Royal Regiment of Artillery on 1st October 1847.[377]

Francis was promoted to the rank of 1st Lieutenant on 30th June 1848[378] and on 13th December 1854 was promoted to the rank of 2nd Captain.[379]

In Early 1855, Francis as the commander of a Royal Artillery battery, set sail on the troopship *Jullundur* bound for Trincomalee in Ceylon, where they arrived in late July. The posting in

Figure 155. Francis Cornwallis Maude

Ceylon was quite uneventful until on 6th June 1857, the Honourable East India Company frigate *Semiramis* arrived at Trincomalee with news of the outbreak of mutiny in India and orders for all European troops to proceed to India post haste.

Francis, with his artillery battery, set sail almost immediately and arrived in Calcutta on 13th June where they joined the garrison at Fort William. On 18th June, Francis was part of the force that was being assembled at Allahabad, under the command of General Havelock, to go to the aid of the garrison at Cawnpore. The Relief Force set out on 7th July, not knowing that on 27th June Major-General Sir Hugh Wheeler had been forced to surrender the garrison following which, in contradiction to the guarantees of safe passage, the mutineers murdered large numbers of women and children in the city. On the march towards Cawnpore, the force fought the Battle of Futtehpore on 12th July, where Francis took control of one of his artillery pieces and laid down a shot killing an elephant and tumbling its rider, said to have been Tantia Topi,[380] to the ground.

Francis was also involved in the battles at Aong and Pandoo Nuddee on 14th July and the Battle of Cawnpore on 15th July which culminated in the capture of the city on the 17th July. After settling a force to garrison Cawnpore (under the command of General Neill), the force of General Havelock set out to the relief of Lucknow, however, after the Battle of Oonoa on 29th July they returned to Cawnpore where they arrived on 13th August. Following the arrival of General Outram at Cawnpore, on 5th September a second attempt was made to go to the relief of Lucknow. After arriving at Lucknow on 17th September and following intense fighting, Francis and part of the force managed to break

377 *Edinburgh Gazette* – 5688/516

378 *Edinburgh Gazette* – 5778/415

379 *Edinburgh Gazette* – 6459/78

380 One of the most capable rebel leaders

through the line of besiegers and reinforce the British troops in the Residency. It was on 25th September 1857, during the final push to reinforce the defenders at the Lucknow Residency, that Francis performed the deeds for which he was later awarded the Victoria Cross. Francis was now part of the force besieged in the Residency and remained there until 19th November when a force commanded by Sir Colin Campbell dispersed the mutineers and the Residency was evacuated. On 19th January 1858, Francis received a brevet promotion to the rank of Major.[381] Francis was part of the force commanded by General Sir James Outram which recaptured Lucknow on 21st March 1858.

On 24th March 1858, Francis was appointed as an Extra Member 3rd Class (Companion) of the Military Division of the Most Honourable Order of the Bath[382] and on 20th July 1858 received a brevet promotion to the rank of Lieutenant-Colonel.[383]

Francis was presented with his Victoria Cross medal, sometime during 1858, while still serving in India, for his service during the mutiny he was awarded the Indian Mutiny Medal with clasps for Defence of Lucknow and Lucknow. He was also awarded an additional year of pensionable service.

Following the mutiny, Francis returned to Ceylon where on 24th January 1860 he was married to Paulina Susannah (née Stirling), the daughter of a Ceylon Supreme Court Judge. The couple would go on to have four children; Iona Isabella born on 8th October 1862, Georgiana Ivy born on 10th March 1864, Francis Stirling de Montalt born on 12th April 1867 and Mabel Matilda born on 10th March 1871.

On 1st April 1860, Francis was promoted to the rank of Captain.[384]

From Ceylon, Francis was transferred to Corfu where he remained until his transfer to Malta in 1864.

On 20th July 1866, under the terms of a Royal Warrant dated 3rd February 1866 and having completed the qualifying period in the rank of Lieutenant-Colonel, Francis received a brevet promotion to the rank of Colonel.[385]

Only a few weeks later on 29th August 1866, Francis retired from the army on half pay after nearly 20 years service[386] and returned to England where he initially lived in Brighton and then Emsworth in Hampshire.

On 17th December 1867, as Honorary Secretary of the Free Labour Registration Society and proprietor of the Malta Ice Works in Malta, Francis was declared bankrupt.[387]

Francis was permitted to commute his Retirement Allowance on 6th June 1870.[388]

In 1871, Francis moved to Sussex Place in South Kensington and in 1874 moved to 9 St Helen's Park Crescent in Southsea.

On 21st September 1876, Francis was appointed as Consul-General to Warsaw in Poland, a position that he would hold until 1886.

In 1895, Francis was appointed as a Military Knight of Windsor which gave him a pension and accommodation in Windsor Castle. This was not a heraldic order but was rather a means of help for impoverished retired military officers, the order was originally known as Alms Knights or colloquially as 'the poor Knights'.

Francis died on 19th October 1900, after a fall in one of the yards of Windsor Castle and was buried on 23rd October at St Leonards Road Cemetery in Windsor.

Francis's Victoria Cross medal is privately held. It should be noted that his cousin Lieutenant-Colonel Frederick Francis Maude was also a recipient of the Victoria Cross for deeds performed on 5th September 1855 at Sebastopol during the Crimean War.

Figure 155a. Grave of Francis Cornwallis Maude

381 *London Gazette* – 22085/272
382 *Edinburgh Gazette* – 6791/636
383 *London Gazette* – 22164/3378
384 *London Gazette* – 22377/1475
385 *London Gazette* – 23151/4541
386 *London Gazette* – 23169/5289
387 *London Gazette* – 23336/7051

388 *London Gazette* – 23723/1765

William Olpherts
25th September 1857 (VC No. 178)

Figure 156. William Olpherts

Gazetted: 18th June 1858 22154/2957

Rank and Unit: Captain – Bengal Artillery

Citation

For highly distinguished conduct on the 25th of September, 1857 when the troops penetrated into the city of Lucknow, in having charged on horseback, with Her Majesty's 90th Regiment, when gallantly headed by Colonel Campbell, it captured two guns in the face of a heavy fire of grape, and having afterwards returned, under a severe fire of musketry, to bring up limbers and horses to carry off the captured ordnance, which he accomplished. (**Extract from Field Force Orders of the late Major-General Havelock, dated 17th October, 1857.**)

Biography

William was born at Dartrey Lodge, Blackwater Town in Co. Armagh, Ireland on 8th March 1822, the third son of father William, a lawyer, and mother Rosanna (née Macartney).

He attended Gracehill School in Ballymena, Co Antrim and the Royal School in Dungannon, Co Tyrone before enrolling at the Honourable East India Company Military Seminary at Addiscombe in 1837.

On graduating from Addiscombe, William was commissioned as a 2nd Lieutenant in the Bengal Artillery on 11th June 1839. In August, William set sail for India and after arriving at Calcutta on 24th December 1839 joined his regiment at their headquarters in Dum Dum in the north of the city.

On 17th August 1841, William was promoted to the rank of Lieutenant.

In October 1841, William was posted to Moulmein in the Tenasserim district in Burma, where he commanded a battery of four guns.

After nine months in Burma, William returned to Dum Dum where he remained until October 1842 when he was sent to a battery at Saugor, in the state of Madhya Pradesh in Central India, which was in a state of insurrection.

In November 1842, William commanded two guns in a force commanded by Colonel Blackhall which defeated the rebels at Jhirrna Ghat on 12th November, for this action he was mentioned in despatches.

After the battle William returned to Saugor where he qualified as an interpreter in Indian languages.

In April 1843, William was given command of the 16th Bengal Light Field Battery and was stationed at Nowgong in the Bundelkhand region of central India.

In November 1843, William with his unit was part of the force commanded by General Sir Hugh Gough which took part in the Gwalior Campaign and took part in the Battle of Punniar on 29th December under the command of General Grey. For his service in the Gwalior Campaign, William received mentioned in despatches and was awarded the bronze Gwalior Campaign Star.

In May 1844, William was selected by the Governor-General Lord Ellingborough to raise a battery of horse artillery in the Bundelkhand Region.

Following the 1st Anglo-Afghan war (known as Auckland's Folly), which ended in 1842, the Muslim leaders in the Sindh Provence remained hostile to the British and in 1844 when this got out of hand, a force commanded by General Sir Charles Napier was despatched to quell the insurrection. When the local sepoys refused to travel to Sindh, William volunteered his newly assembled battery for this service and after a march of 1,260 miles across central India joined up with Napier on 15th October 1844 and was involved in several actions against the tribes occupying the hills on the border of the province. On 13th December 1845, the Governor-General of India, Lord Hardinge declared war on the Sikhs thus starting the 1st Anglo-Sikh war which lasted until ended by the treaty at Amritsar on 16th March 1846. As a volunteer, William was involved in the war and took part in operations against the fort at Kote Kangara. His conduct, having favourably attracted the attention of General Henry Montgomery Lawrence, William was appointed to raise an artillery battery from the men of the disbanded Sikh Army.

Soon after completing this task, William departed for Deccan where he commanded an artillery battery in the service of the Nizam of Hyderabad.

In February 1848, William was appointed as commandant of the artillery with the Gwalior contingent a position that he held until November 1851 when he resigned from his post and rejoined his regiment at Peshawar.

In 1852, William was part of the forces of General Sir Colin Campbell which undertook operations in the Peshawar Valley against the cross border Pathan tribes, for this service he was later awarded the India General Services Medal with clasp for North West Frontier.

In May 1852, under the terms of a medical furlough, William returned to England and in June was appointed as an orderly officer at the Honourable East India Company Military Seminary at Addiscombe. William was promoted to the rank of Captain on 3rd March 1853. In October 1854, William left his post at Addiscombe and with war underway in the Crimea was selected in November 1854 to serve under the command of Sir Fenwick Williams at Kars and Erzurum in Armenia.

On 15th December 1854, William received a brevet promotion to the rank of Major for the duration of his employment on special services in Turkey.[389] William set sail for the Crimea in December 1854 and made his way via the Black Sea and Zigana mountains to take up his command. He was assigned to the command of 7,000 Turkish troops who were tasked with the mission to prevent the advance of Russian troops from Erivan along the River Araxes. William had to fall back in the face of superior force, however, after making a stand at Devi Bournoo managed to successfully defend the positions at Erzurum. In October 1855, William was called back to Constantinople where he was assigned by Colonel William Ferguson Beatson to command the Bashi-Bazoukhs, a brigade of Turkish irregular troops, which he led until peace was declared.

With war at an end in the Crimea, William returned to England until January 1857 when he set sail for India, arriving at Bombay on 6th February. Proceeding by river and overland, William arrived at Benares in April where he took up command of a battery of horse artillery. On 4th June, William and his battery, under the command of General James Neill were instrumental in putting down the mutiny of three native regiments at Benares, following which he was assigned to the force of General Sir Henry Havelock which was going to the relief of Cawnpore and Lucknow. On 17th July, William was involved in the Battle of Bithoor during the retaking of Cawnpore.

William was involved in the 1st Relief of Lucknow (which was actually a reinforcement of the beleaguered troops) taking part in the Battle of Mangalwar on 21st September and was part of the force which broke through to the Residency on 25th September, during which he performed the deeds for which he would later

be awarded the Victoria Cross – elected for the award under rule 13 by a ballot of the regiment. From 25th September until 21st November, when the Residency was evacuated by the relieving forces of Sir Colin Campbell, William commanded the artillery of the besieged force. From 22nd November 1857 until 17th March 1858, William commanded a battery at the defence of Alum Bagh under the command of Sir James Outram. On 19th January 1858, William received the brevet promotion to the rank of Major.[390] William was part of the force of Sir Colin Campbell which recaptured Lucknow on 21st March 1858 and received the brevet promotion to the rank of Lieutenant-Colonel on 24th March 1858.[391] For his service during the mutiny, William was awarded the Indian Mutiny Medal with clasps for Defence of Lucknow and Lucknow, he also received several mentions in despatch.

For his courage, valour and eccentric behaviour in battle William earned the nickname of 'Hell Fire Jack'.

After the capture of Lucknow, William took command of a battery of horse artillery in district of Oude.

On 27th July 1858, William was appointed as an Ordinary Member 3rd Class (Companion) of the Military Division of the Most Honourable Order of the Bath.[392]

William was presented with his Victoria Cross medal on 4th May 1859 by Major-General Sir Sydney John Cotton at Lucknow.

During late 1859 until 1860, William served as a volunteer in the force of Brigadier Sir Neville Chamberlain in an expedition against the Wazir tribe on the North West frontier.

On 18th February 1861, William was promoted to the rank of Lieutenant Colonel.[393]

William was married to Alice Maria (née Cautley), the eldest daughter of Major-General George Cautley of the 5th Bengal European Light Cavalry, on 3rd June 1861. The couple would have four children, three daughters and a son William Cautley.

From 1861 until 1868, William commanded the artillery at Peshawar and then at Rawalpindi.

William received the brevet promotion to Colonel, to be effective 25th April 1864,[394] however, this was later backdated to 26th February 1864.[395]

On 26th June 1868, William received the brevet promotion to the rank of Major General.[396]

In 1868, William returned home to Ireland on Furlough and during his visit was awarded the Sword of Honour by the City and County of Armagh.

389 *London Gazette* – 21641/4096

390 *London Gazette* – 22085/273
391 *London Gazette* – 22117/1572
392 *London Gazette* – 22166/3475
393 *London Gazette* – 22587/75
394 *London Gazette* – 22863/3075
395 *London Gazette* – 23349/536
396 *London Gazette* – 24267/5453

William returned to India in 1870 and until his return to England in 1875 commanded the artillery in the districts of Gwalior, Rohilkhand, Sirkind and Oude.

William was promoted to the rank of Colonel on 17th July 1872.[397]

On 1st October 1877, William received the brevet promotion to the rank of Lieutenant General.[398]

On 1st July 1881, under the terms of articles 106III and 107 of Royal Warrant dated 25th June 1881, William was placed on the Unemployed Supernumerary List.[399]

William was promoted to the rank of General on 31st March 1883.[400]

On 4th August 1888, William was appointed as Colonel Commandant of the Royal Artillery.[401]

On 29th May 1886, William was appointed as an Ordinary Member 2nd Class (Knight Commander) of the Military Division of the Most Honourable Order of the Bath.[402]

On 23rd May 1900, William was appointed as an Ordinary Member 1st Class (Knight Grand Cross) of the Military Division of the Most Honourable Order of the Bath.[403]

William died at his home, Wood House, Upper Norwood in London on 30th April 1902 and was buried with full military honours at Richmond Cemetery on 3rd May 1902.

His Victoria Cross medal is on public display at the National Army Museum, Chelsea.

Figure 156a. Grave of William Olpherts

---

397 *London Gazette* – 23883/3488
398 *London Gazette* – 24508/5458
399 *London Gazette* – 24999/3676
400 *London Gazette* – 25232/2664
401 *London Gazette* – 25865/5605
402 *London Gazette* – 25592/2633
403 *London Gazette* – 27195/3327

Herbert Taylor MacPherson
25th September 1857 (VC No. 179)

Gazetted: 18th June 1858 22154/2957

Rank and Unit: Lieutenant – 78th Regiment of Foot

Citation

For distinguished conduct at Lucknow, on the 25th September, 1857, in setting an example of heroic gallantry to the men of the regiment, at the period of the action, in which they captured two brass nine-pounders at the point of the bayonet. **(Extract from Field Force Orders of the late Major-General Havelock, dated 17th October, 1857.)**

Biography

Herbert was born on 22nd January 1827 at Ardersier in Inverness-shire to father Duncan, a former Lieutenant-Colonel in the 78th Regiment of Foot and mother Ann Brodie (née Campbell).

He was the youngest of 9 children having four older brothers; James Duncan born in 1811, Aeneas McIntosh born in 1817, William Gordon born in 1819 and Alexander Campbell born in 1821 and four older sisters; Margaret born in 1809, Louisa born in 1812, Mary Ann born in 1814 and Sophia Brodie born in 1823.

Following the completion of his education at Nairn Academy, Herbert was eager to follow his father and uncles in a career in the army, however, lacking the funds to purchase a commission and lacking influential friends to recommend his application he was having little success. In 1844, Herbert reluctantly moved to London and took up an office job, however, fate was soon to present an opportunity as news reached London of the desperate position of the 78th regiment which had suffered greatly from an epidemic of cholera. On hearing the news, Herbert made a direct application for a commission in the 78th, to Lord Fitzroy Somerset, the Adjutant-General who was so impressed that he granted the request.

Herbert was commissioned as an Ensign in the 78th Regiment on 28th February 1845[404] and soon afterwards joined his regiment at Bombay, India where they were stationed at Fort George.

On 13th July 1848, Herbert was promoted to the rank of Lieutenant and soon afterwards was appointed to the role of Adjutant.[405] On 14th February 1846, the regiment moved to Poona then Kirkee and Belgaum until 1849 when the wings of the regiment set off in different directions, one wing going to Aden while Herbert and the other wing returned to Bombay where

---

404 *London Gazette* – 20449/679
405 *London Gazette* – 20907/3764

Figure 157. Herbert Taylor MacPherson

they arrived on 16th November 1849. In November 1850, the wings of the regiment were switched and Herbert was posted to Aden. While in Aden, Herbert was on a hunting trip with two colleagues during March 1851 and while sleeping in a hut was attacked during the night by assassins. One of his companions was mortally wounded, however, despite being stabbed 7 or 8 times, Herbert survived the attack. In January 1853, Herbert left Aden and reunited with the other wing of the regiment at Poona on 5th March 1853 and at some stage he was appointed to the post of Adjutant to the Regiment.

On 1st November 1856, the Governor General of India declared war on Persia and despatched troops to the Persian Gulf. On 7th/8th January 1857, Herbert and the 78th, as part of the secondary force, left Poona and on 19th January set sail from Bombay bound for the Persian Gulf where they arrived off Busheer on 1st February. Herbert, now serving as adjutant to the regiment, was involved in the Battle of Khushab on 7th February and was present at the bombardment and capture of Mohammrah on 26th March 1857. For his service during the first Anglo-Persian War, Herbert was awarded the India General Service Medal with clasp for Persia.

Following the cessation of hostilities, the 78th set sail from Mohammrah on 10th May bound for Bombay where they arrived on 22nd/23rd May only to hear the unexpected news of the outbreak of mutiny and orders to proceed to Calcutta where they arrived on 10th June.

From Calcutta, the regiment moved to Allahabad, to form up as part of the field force under the command of General Have-lock that was charged with securing the relief of Cawnpore and Lucknow. On 7th July, Herbert and the 78th left Allahabad for

Cawnpore and as part of General Havelock's field force was involved in the recapture of the city on 16th July. On 19th July, General Havelock's column left Cawnpore bound for Lucknow and Herbert was involved in the Battle of Oonoa on 29th July, during which he was wounded. Despite his wounds, Herbert was involved in the Battle of Busherut-gunge on 5th August, the Battle of Boorbeake Chowkee on 12th August and the Battle of Bithoor on 16th August. It was on 25th September 1857, during an action which successfully reinforced the garrison at Lucknow, that Herbert performed the deeds for which he would later be awarded the Victoria Cross. Following the reinforcement of Lucknow, Herbert served as part of the force commanded by General Outram which defended the Alum Bagh until 21st November, when the force of Sir Colin Campbell relieved the city and the Residency was evacuated. Herbert was promoted to the rank of Captain on 6th October 1857.[406] Herbert was also part of Sir Colin Campbell's force, serving as a Brigade Major, which managed to recapture Lucknow on 21st March 1858, however, just before the decisive action he was severely wounded on 14th March.[407]. By 26th April the regiment was at Cawnpore where they joined up with the Rohilkhand Field Force commanded by Brigadier General Walpole. On 7th May Herbert took part in the Battle of Bareilly and after the town was captured the regiment formed part of the garrison.

On 20th July 1858, Herbert received a brevet promotion to the rank of Major.[408]

Herbert was presented with his Victoria Cross medal during a ceremony at Shinde in India during November 1858.

For his service during the mutiny, Herbert was awarded the Indian Mutiny Medal with clasps for Defence of Lucknow and Lucknow.

On 20th February 1859, the regiment left Bareilly at the start of their journey to return to England, however, Herbert chose to stay in India and transferred to the 82nd Regiment of Foot, by way of an exchange on 26th February 1859.[409]

Sometime during 1859, Herbert was married to Maria Eliza-beth Henrietta (née Eckford), the daughter of Lieutenant-General James Eckford and the couple would go on to have three children; twins Clare and Neil born in Lahore on 17th December 1863 and son Duncan Haldane born in London on 8th August 1869.

On 28th February 1865, Herbert was promoted to the rank of Major[410] and became one of the first officers to transfer to the

---

406 *London Gazette* – 22083/184 & 22145/2639 – date of commission was altered from 5th to 6th October
407 *London Gazette* – 22140/2451
408 *London Gazette* – 22164/3379
409 *London Gazette* – 22253/1662
410 *London Gazette* – 23021/4686

new Indian Army following the break-up of the Honourable East India Company armies.

Herbert received a brevet promotion to the rank of Lieutenant-Colonel on 25th March 1867 and took up a position on the general staff of the Bengal Army.[411]

In October 1868, as part of the North West Frontier Wars, Herbert took part in the Hazara or Black Mountain Campaign. For his service during this campaign, Herbert was awarded the North West Frontier clasp to his Indian General Service medal.

On 30th August 1869, Herbert was appointed as an Ordinary Member 3rd Class (Companion) of the Military Division of the Most Honourable Order of the Bath.[412]

Herbert was promoted to the rank of Lieutenant-Colonel on 28th February 1871.[413]

From 1871 until 1872, Herbert took part in further frontier wars, this time on the North East frontier of India, in a campaign known as the Lushai Expedition. For his service in this action, Herbert was awarded the Looshai clasp to his India General Service medal.

On 13th March 1872, having completed the qualifying period with the rank of Lieutenant-colonel, Herbert received a brevet promotion to the rank of Colonel.[414]

On 14th April 1876, Herbert was appointed to the command of the Lahore Division with the local rank of Brigadier-General.

From August 1877 until January 1878, Herbert took part in the Jowaki Campaign[415] on the North West Frontier of India in an action to quell the Afridi tribesmen. He took part in the decisive action of the campaign, which was to force the Bori Pass. For his service in the campaign, Herbert was awarded the Jowaki clasp to his India General Service medal.

On 25th May 1878, Herbert, while in command of a brigade, was given the temporary rank of Brigadier-General.[416] With the outbreak of the 2nd Anglo-Afghan war in September 1878, Herbert was appointed to the command of the 1st Brigade in the 1st Division of the Peshawar Valley Field force commanded by Lieutenant-General Sir Samuel J. Browne. In this capacity he was present at the Battle of Ali Musjid on 21st November 1878 and subsequently was involved in expeditions to the Lughman and Kama valleys. The first phase of the war was concluded with the treaty of Gangamak in May 1879, however, following an uprising in Kabul on 3rd September 1879, hostilities were resumed and

Herbert was appointed by Lord Roberts to the command of the 1st Brigade of the Kandahar/Kabul Field Force. It was in this capacity that Herbert was involved in the Battle of Charasiah on 6th October 1879 and the assault and occupation of Kabul on 13th October. In December 1879, Herbert was involved in operations around Kabul, including the defeat of the Kohistanis in the Battle of Karez Mir on 10th December and the Battle of Takhi-i-Shah on 12th/13th December. On 26th April 1880, Herbert's 1st Division came to the aid of Colonel Jenkins and won a decisive victory against the forces of Mohammed Jan at the second Battle of Charasiah. In August 1880, Herbert with the 1st Division took part in the march from Kabul to relieve Kandahar which culminated in the Battle of Kandahar on 1st September 1880. For his service in the war, Herbert was awarded the Afghanistan Medal with clasps for Ali Musjid, Charasiah, Kabul and Kandahar; he was also awarded the Kabul to Kandahar Star.

Effective from 26th October 1880, Herbert received a brevet promotion to the local rank of Major-General[417] and was appointed to the Divisional Staff of the Army in Bengal to replace Lieutenant-General Sir D. M. Stewart who had resigned his commission.[418]

On 22nd February 1881, Herbert was appointed as an Ordinary Member 2nd Class (Knight Commander) of the Military Division of the Most Honourable Order of the Bath.[419]

Herbert was promoted to the rank of Major-General on 1st July 1882[420] and on 10th July was appointed to the command of the Indian Division sent to the war in Egypt. On 13th September 1882, Herbert and the Indian Contingent were involved in the Battle of Tel-El-Kabir and soon afterwards seized and occupied the important town of Zagazig. For his service in the Anglo-Egyptian War, Herbert was awarded the Egypt Medal with clasp for Tel-el-Kabir and the Khedive Star.

On 17th November 1882, Herbert was appointed as an Extra Knight Commander of the Most Exalted Order of the Star of India[421] and also as a member 2nd Class of the Order of the Medjidie.[422] Herbert also received the thanks of both houses of Parliament.

On his return to India from Egypt, Herbert took up a position on staff of the Bengal army.

Herbert was appointed as a member of the Council of the Governor of the Presidency of Fort St George on 15th January 1886.[423]

---

411 *London Gazette* – 23360/1588
412 *London Gazette* – 23531/4845
413 *London Gazette* – 23768/3645
414 *London Gazette* – 23865/2667
415 It was during this campaign that an early form of field telephone, developed by Captain J. W. Savage of the Royal Engineers, was used for the first time.
416 *London Gazette* – 24585/3244

417 *London Gazette* – 24918/6969
418 *London Gazette* – 24919/7010
419 *London Gazette* – 24944/975
420 *London Gazette* – 25148/4303
421 *London Gazette* – 25169/5167
422 *London Gazette* – 25169/5168
423 *London Gazette* – 25550/267

In 1886, Herbert was appointed as commander in chief of the Madras Army as the successor of Lord Roberts, the government was informed of this appointment on 13th August 1886.

In light of unrest in Upper Burma, following the conclusion of the third Anglo-Burmese war the previous year, Herbert was requested to lead an expeditionary force to put down the insurgents and on 9th September arrived in Rangoon to take up his command. Herbert set out with a large flotilla of river boats, which carried the reinforcements he had brought from India, and proceeded up the River Irrawaddy arriving at Mandalay on 17th September. While stationed at Mandalay, Herbert fell ill with a fever which was raging throughout the town and in October his doctors suggested a short sea cruise to aid his recovery. On 20th October 1886, Herbert boarded the Steamer *Irrawadi* at Prome, with the intention of sailing to Rangoon, however, soon after leaving Prome he succumbed to the fever and died at the age of 59. His body was taken by special train to Rangoon, where he was buried in the Military Cantonment Cemetery on 21st October 1886.

Herbert's Victoria Cross medal is on public display at the Highland Regimental Museum in Fort George near Inverness.

Joel Holmes
25th September 1857 (VC No. 180)

Gazetted: 18th June 1858 22154/2958

Rank and Unit: Private 1455 – 84th Regiment of Foot

Citation
For distinguished conduct in volunteering to assist in working a gun of Captain Maude's Battery, under heavy fire, from which gun nearly all the Artillerymen had been shot away. (**Extract from Field Force Orders of the late Major-General Havelock, dated 17th October, 1857.**)

Biography
Joel was born during February 1821 in Great Gomersal near Halifax in Yorkshire.

On 12th June 1839, soon after his 18th birthday, Joel enlisted as a private in the 84th Regiment of Foot; the regiment having recently returned to England after a posting to the West Indies.

Joel and the regiment left England on 8th August 1842 for Burma where they arrived at Moulmein on 6th September. In 1845 Joel and the regiment left Burma for India, where they began the first of many postings at Madras on 28th March. On 15th January 1854, Joel returned to Burma being posted to Rangoon and it was here that the regiment received news of the mutiny and orders to proceed to India as soon as possible.

On 2nd June, the regiment arrived at Allahabad, to form up as part of the field force under the command of General Havelock that was charged with securing the relief of Cawnpore and Lucknow.

On 7th July, Joel and the 84th left Allahabad for Cawnpore and as part of General Havelock's field force was involved in the recapture of the city on 16th July. On 19th July, General Havelock's column left Cawnpore bound for Lucknow and Joel was involved in the Battle of Oonoa on 29th July, the Battle of Busherut-gunge on 5th August, the Battle of Boorbeake Chowkee on 12th August and the Battle of Bithoor on 16th August. It was on 25th September 1857, during an action which successfully reinforced the garrison at Lucknow, that Joel performed the deeds for which he would later be awarded the Victoria Cross. From 26th November 1857, the regiment was station in Alum Bagh and in early 1858, the regiment were assigned to the Azamgarh Field Force under the command of Sir Edward Layard. On 15th April 1858, the regiment were involved in the second relief of Azamgarh.

Joel was presented with his Victoria Cross medal by Queen Victoria at an investiture held in Portsmouth on 2nd August 1858.

The regiment were stationed at Buxar from 9th June until 14th March 1859 when they moved to Dum Dum. Joel and the regiment left Calcutta in September 1859, to begin their return journey to England, after 17 years service in the East Indies. For his service during the mutiny, Joel was awarded the Indian Mutiny Medal with clasps for Defence of Lucknow and Lucknow.

On 13th November 1860, Joel retired from the army after just over 21 years of service, he was awarded the Long Service and Good Conduct medal.

Joel died on 27th July 1872, aged 51, while living in Halifax and was buried in an unmarked grave in the All Souls Cemetery, Halifax.

Joel's Victoria Cross Medal is on public display at the York and Lancaster Museum in Rotherham.

Figure 158a. Grave of Joel Holmes

Henry Ward
25th/26th September 1857 (VC No. 181)

Gazetted: 18th June 1858 22154/2958

Rank and Unit: Private – 78th Regiment of Foot

Citation

For his gallant and devoted conduct in having on the night of the 25th, and morning of the 26th of September, 1857, remained by the dooly of Captain H. M. Havelock, 10th Regiment, Deputy Assistant-Adjutant-General, Field Force, who was severely wounded, and on the morning of the 26th of September, escorted that Officer and Private Thomas Pilkington, 78th Highlanders, who was also wounded, and had taken refuge in the same dooly, through very heavy cross fire of ordnance and musketry. This soldier remained by the side of the dooly, and by his example and exertions kept the dooly bearers from dropping their double load, throughout the heavy fire, with the same steadiness as if on parade, thus saving the lives of both, and bringing them in safety to the Bailey Guard. **(Extract from Divisional Orders of Major-General Sir James Outram, G.C.B., dated 27th October, 1857.)**

Biography

Henry was born during 1823, baptised on 12th October 1823, in Harleston, Norfolk to father James and mother Mary (née Reeve).

It is probable that Henry enlisted as a private in the 78th regiment, in Liverpool or Manchester, sometime around his 18th birthday in 1841 and if this is the case then his career would have been as follows.

In July 1840 the regiment was stationed in Liverpool with its headquarters in Burnley until 23rd June 1841 when they moved to Manchester. Between 19th November and 1st April 1842 the regiment had a short stay in Ireland, stationed at Dublin. Leaving Ireland the regiment was stationed at Canterbury from 8th April, with orders to make ready for a deployment to India. In late May, the regiment embarked upon six ships and set sail for India, arriving at Bombay on 30th July and then moving to their station at Poona. On 7th April 1843, the regiment were ordered to the Sindh province[424] where from 20th May they were stationed at Kurrachee. In December 1844, the regiment moved to Hyderabad and then during February/March 1845 moved to Bombay where they were stationed at Fort George before moving to

---

424 During their stay in Sindh (and for some time afterwards) the regiment were beset by disease and lost 535 men including 3 officers as well as over 200 women and children.

Figure 159. Henry Ward

Poona where they arrived on 18th April 1845. On 14th February 1846, the regiment moved from Poona to Kirkee and then Belgaum until 1849 when the wings of the regiment set off in different directions, one wing going to Aden while the other wing returned to Bombay where they arrived on 16th November 1849. In November 1850, the wings of the regiment were switched but were finally reunited at Poona on 5th March 1853.

On 1st November 1856, the Governor General of India declared war on Persia and despatched troops to the Persian Gulf. On 7th/8th January 1857, Henry and the 78th, as part of secondary force, left Poona and on 19th January set sail from Bombay bound for the Persian Gulf where they arrived off Busheer on 1st February. Henry, was involved in the Battle of Khushab on 7th February and was present at the bombardment and capture of Mohammrah on 26th March 1857. For his service during the first Anglo-Persian War, Henry was awarded the India General Service Medal with clasp for Persia. Following the cessation of hostilities, the 78th set sail from Mohammrah on 10th May bound for Bombay where they arrived on 22nd/23rd May only to hear the unexpected news of the outbreak of mutiny and orders to proceed to Calcutta where they arrived on 10th June.

From Calcutta, the regiment moved to Allahabad, to form up as part of the field force under the command of General Havelock that was charged with securing the relief of Cawnpore and Lucknow.

On 7th July, Henry and the 78th left Allahabad for Cawnpore and as part of General Havelock's field force was involved in the recapture of the city on 16th July. On 19th July, General Havelock's column left Cawnpore bound for Lucknow and Henry was involved in the Battle of Oonoa on 29th July, the Battle of Busherut-gunge on 5th August, the Battle of Boorbeake Chowkee on 12th August and the Battle of Bithoor on 16th August. It was

on the night of 25th/26th September 1857, during an action which successfully reinforced the garrison at Lucknow, that Henry performed the deeds for which he would later be awarded the Victoria Cross. Having saved the life of General Havelock, Henry served as the General's personal servant until his death during the siege of Lucknow on 24th November 1857.

Returning to normal duties, Henry, as part of Sir Colin Campbell's force, took part in the action which managed to recapture Lucknow on 21st March 1858. By 26th April the regiment was at Cawnpore where they joined up with the Rohilkhand Field Force commanded by Brigadier General Walpole. On 7th May Henry took part in the Battle of Bareilly and after the town was captured the regiment formed part of the garrison.

Henry was presented with his Victoria Cross medal during a ceremony at Shinde in India during November 1858.

For his service during the mutiny, Henry was awarded the Indian Mutiny Medal with clasps for Defence of Lucknow and Lucknow.

On 20th February 1859, the regiment left Bareilly at the start of their journey to return to England, and departing from Bombay on 28th April arrived at Gravesend during mid-September. The regiment was stationed at Fort George near Inverness until February 1860 when they moved to Edinburgh. From April 1861, the regiment was stationed at Aldershot beginning a number of assignments in England. It is probable that Henry retired from the army at some time during 1861 or 1862, having completed the 21 years of service which qualified him for the Long Service and Good Conduct medal and having risen to the rank of Quartermaster Sergeant.

Figure 159a. Grave of Henry Ward

Henry died at Great Malvern in Worcestershire on 21st September 1867 at the age of 44 and was buried in the Great Malvern Cemetery.

Henry's Victoria Cross Medal is on public display at the Highlanders Regimental Museum in Fort George near Inverness.

Anthony Dickson Home
26th September 1857 (VC No. 182)

Gazetted: 18th June 1858 22154/2959

Rank and Unit: Surgeon – 90th Regiment of Foot

Citation

For persevering bravery and admirable conduct in charge of the wounded men left behind the column, when the troops under the late Major-General Havelock, forced their way into the Residency of Lucknow, on the 26th September, 1857. The escort left with the wounded had, by casualties, been reduced to a few stragglers, and being entirely separated from the column, this small party with the wounded were forced into a house, in which they defended themselves till it was set on fire. They then retreated to a shed a few yards from it, and in this place continued to defend themselves for more than twenty-two hours, till relieved. At last, only six men and Mr. Home remained to fire. Of four officers who were with the party, all were badly wounded, and three are since dead. The conduct of the defence during the latter part of the time devolved therefore on Mr. Home, and to his active exertions previously to being forced into the house, and his good conduct throughout, the safety of any of the wounded, and the successful defence, is mainly to be attributed.

Biography

Anthony was born on 30th November 1826, in Dunbar, East Lothian, Scotland to father George a shoemaker and mother Margaret (née Millingham).

After spending his early years in Berwickshire and Stirling, Anthony graduated from St Andrew's as an MD in 1847 and after a further year of training in Paris was made a Member of the Royal College of Surgeons in 1848.

On 17th March 1848, Anthony enlisted as an Assistant Surgeon, and was assigned to the 3rd West Indies Regiment[425] who had vacancies due to a recent outbreak of Yellow Fever. Soon after his enlistment, Anthony left England on a steamer bound for Barbados arriving at the capital Bridgetown about a month later and was immediately despatched to Demerara in British Guiana to join his regiment. In August 1848, Anthony was despatched to Trinidad to act as Assistant Surgeon to the 88th Regiment of Foot until a replacement arrived from England a few weeks later, at which time he returned to George Town in

425 *London Gazette* – 20837/1086

Figure 160. Anthony Dickson Home

British Guiana. While en-route to George Town, Anthony was transferred to the 72nd Regiment of Foot in Barbados, on 8th December 1848, as a replacement for the incumbent who had died from Yellow Fever.[426]

In early 1851, Anthony was posted with the regiment to Halifax, Nova Scotia in Canada for a short tour which lasted until the end of the year. On return from Canada, Anthony spent time in Guernsey and Ireland (Fermoy and Clare Castle) before serving the garrison at Gibraltar for 18 months.

On 10th December 1852, Anthony was transferred as an assistant Surgeon to a staff position.[427] Anthony transferred from his staff position to the 8th Hussars as an assistant surgeon on 15th August 1854[428] and joined his regiment in Malta, preparatory to embarking for Varna on the way to the Crimea. Anthony arrived at Balaklava on 28th September 1854, only two days after the British Expeditionary force had secured the town and harbour as their supply base. Apart from a brief stay in the hospital at Scutari, soon after the Battle of Inkerman, Anthony spent the war in the camp of the Light Division at Kadakai, just outside Balaklava. On 9th February 1855, Anthony was promoted to the rank of Surgeon and joined the 13th Light Dragoons.[429] For his service in the Crimea, Anthony was awarded the Crimea Medal with clasps for Balaklava and Sevastopol and the Turkish Crimean Medal.

In mid-April 1856, Anthony left the Crimea and after landing in Portsmouth was soon despatched to Cork in Ireland.

Anthony transferred by way of exchange to the 90th Regiment of Foot on 6th February 1857[430] and soon afterwards was despatched with his new regiment to China as part of an expeditionary force intended to take part in the Opium War. While standing too off Java, the expeditionary force was intercepted by a Royal Navy vessel and given news of the outbreak of mutiny in India and relayed orders that they were to proceed at once to Calcutta rather than Hong Kong. Arriving at Calcutta on 21st July, the regiment spent a week at Chinsurah before embarking on river steamers for Cawnpore. On 1st August, the regiment arrived at Berhampore where they disarmed the local garrison of Native Infantry, they now had orders to join the field force of General Havelock and proceeded to Allahabad where they arrived on 1st September.

The regiment was part of the force which recaptured Cawnpore on 15th September, after which they set out towards Lucknow. It was on 26th September 1857, after Lucknow had been successfully reinforced, that Anthony performed the deeds for which he would later be awarded the Victoria Cross. Anthony remained within the Residency until it was evacuated on 19th November 1857. Following the evacuation of the residency, Anthony was part of the force at Alum Bagh and was also part of General Sir Colin Campbell's force which recaptured Lucknow on 21st March 1858. On 31st March 1858, Anthony was promoted to the rank of Staff Surgeon 2nd Class,[431] however, due to failing health he returned to England on sick leave during April 1858, arriving on 4th June. For his service during the mutiny, Anthony was awarded the Indian Mutiny Medal with clasps for Defence of Lucknow and Lucknow.

Sometime in 1858, after his return from India, Anthony was married to Jessey Elizabeth (née Hallet) the daughter of a barrister. The couple would go on to have two sons and six daughters.

Anthony was presented with his Victoria Cross medal by Queen Victoria on 8th June 1859 at an investiture held in Buckingham Palace.

On 3rd December 1859, after having been appointed to the China Expeditionary Force commanded by Lieutenant-General Sir James Hope Grant, Anthony set sail for the Far East where he arrived at Hong Kong on 30th January 1860. Initially, Anthony worked in the hospital in Victoria, under the command of W. M. Muir, the Deputy Inspector General of the Army Medical Department until at the end of March he was assigned as Medical Officer on the staff of General Grant. Almost immediately, Anthony accompanied General Grant and his staff officers on a trip on board *HMS Grenada*, to Shanghai where the General wanted to make a firsthand assessment of the situation. Following the rejection of the allied commander's demands, by the Emperor of China on the 10th April the General discussed the

426 *London Gazette* – 20924/4473
427 *London Gazette* – 21390/3611
428 *London Gazette* – 21583/2531
429 *London Gazette* – 21660/489
430 *London Gazette* – 21965/424

431 *London Gazette* – 22149/2759

situation with the French commanders before returning to Hong Kong on 27th April.

With conflict now unavoidable, the 2nd phase of the 2nd Opium (or Arrow) war now commenced and Anthony accompanied the General and his troops which left Hong Kong on 11th June and arrived at Shanghai on 22nd June. With the British force now having joined up with the French force, Anthony was present at the taking of the Taku Forts on 21st August and the march to Peking which was occupied on 6th October 1860. Following the peace treaty which was signed on 18th October, Anthony accompanied the party of Lord Elgin on the long journey back to England. The party left Shanghai on 3rd of December arriving at Hong Kong on 3rd January 1861, where they stayed for one month. For his service in China, Anthony was awarded the 2nd China War Medal, with clasps for Taku Forts and Peking. In February 1861, Anthony left Hong Kong for the final leg of the journey home, taking a detour via the Philippines and arrived in England on 4th April 1861.

During the second week of December 1861, Anthony set sail from Liverpool bound for Canada, as part of the force being sent in response to the "Trent Affair" where it looked like the American Civil War conflict might spill over into Canada. After arriving in Halifax, Nova Scotia on 26th December 1861, Anthony was despatched to the town of Riviere du Loup, in lower Canada near the border with Maine, with instructions to arrange hospital accommodation for the troops being sent from England. Anthony made the necessary arrangements in time for the arrival of the last detachment of troops which arrived on 9th March 1862. Having completed his assignment, Anthony was ordered to Montreal on 13th March where he was attached to a small hospital, however, with the prospect of war receding he requested and was granted a leave of absence to visit the USA.

During his brief visit Anthony visited; Buffalo, Baltimore, New York and Washington before setting sail for England from Portland and arriving in Liverpool sometime in April.

In January 1863, Anthony was posted to India where he served in Bengal until October when he was sent to New Zealand to join the force of Lieutenant-General Cameron, which was engaged in the later stages of the 1863–64 Maori War. For his service during the war, Anthony was awarded the New Zealand (1860–66) medal.

In September 1865, Anthony left New Zealand and returned to Bengal where he took up his post within the Presidency.

On 5th July 1865, Anthony was appointed as an Ordinary Member 3rd Class (Companion) of the Military Division of the Most Honourable Order of the Bath.[432]

On 14th September 1866, for his service in New Zealand, Anthony was promoted to the rank of Surgeon-Major.[433]

Anthony transferred to the 35th Regiment of Foot on 3rd April 1867[434] and returned with his new regiment to England in January 1868.

On 15th February 1868, Anthony was, once again, transferred to a staff position.[435]

On 30th August 1871, Anthony was placed on the seconded list,[436] while he was employed as an Inspector by the Privy Council, until 1st November 1872 when the role ended and he was removed from the seconded list and took up a staff position.[437]

On 24th May 1873, Anthony was given the local rank of Deputy Surgeon-General while he served on the West Coast of Africa[438] and was assigned as Principle Medical Officer to the force of Sir Garnet Wolseley being sent to the Gold Coast of Africa. Anthony served in the campaigns of the 3rd Ashanti (or Sargenti) War until December 1873 when he contracted "Coast Fever" and was invalided home. For his service in the war, Anthony was awarded the Ashantee Medal (1873–74).

On 24th December 1873, Anthony was confirmed in the rank of Deputy Surgeon General but without the pay and allowances.[439]

Anthony was appointed as an Ordinary Member 2nd Class (Knight Commander) of the Military Division of the Most Honourable Order of the Bath on 31st March 1874.[440]

On his return to England, Anthony served as Head of Statistical Department of the Army Medical Department in the War Office until 12th July 1878 when he was appointed as Principal Medical Officer to Cyprus.

While serving as Principal Medical Officer in Cyprus, Anthony was given the local rank of Surgeon-General[441] and on 9th April 1879 this was converted to Acting Surgeon-General.[442]

On his return to England in April 1879, Anthony was stationed in York and was promoted to the rank of Surgeon General on 4th April 1880.[443]

From March 1880 until March 1882, Anthony served as Principle Medical Officer in Madras which was immediately followed by a term as Principle Medical Officer in Bengal which lasted until April 1885.

---

432 *London Gazette* – 22988/3425

433 *London Gazette* – 23162/5031
434 *London Gazette* – 23236/2052
435 *London Gazette* – 23352/721
436 *London Gazette* – 23771/3804
437 *London Gazette* – 23922/5453
438 *London Gazette* – 23991/2944
439 *London Gazette* – 24047/6077
440 *London Gazette* – 24082/1921
441 *London Gazette* – 24607/4265
442 *London Gazette* – 24741/4340
443 *London Gazette* – 2486/3808

On his return to England in April 1885 until his retirement, Anthony served as Principle Medical Officer to the Southern Military District and was based in Plymouth, Anthony left the army after over 38 years of service on 30th November 1886.[444]

Anthony's memoirs "Service Memories" were published in 1912.

On 10th August 1914, Anthony died at his home in Kensington, London at the age of 87 and was buried on 12th August in Highgate Cemetery in London.

Anthony's Victoria Cross Medal is on public display at the Army Medical Services Museum in Aldershot.

Figure 160a. Grave of Anthony Dickson Home

William Bradshaw
26th September 1857 (VC No. 183)

Gazetted: 18th June 1858 22154/2959

Rank and Unit: Assistant Surgeon – 90th Regiment of Foot

Citation
For intrepidity and good conduct when, ordered with Surgeon Home, 90th Regiment, to remove the wounded men left behind the column that forced its way into the Residency of Lucknow, on the 26th September, 1857. The dooly bearers had left the dhoolies, but by great exertions, and notwithstanding the close proximity of the sepoys, Surgeon Home, and Assistant-Surgeon Bradshaw got some of the bearers together, and Assistant-Surgeon Bradshaw with about twenty dhoolies, becoming separated from the rest of the party, succeeded in reaching the Residency in safety by the river bank.

Biography
William was born on 12th February 1830 at Thurles, Co. Tipperary in Ireland.

Soon after graduating as a Fellow of the Royal College of Surgeons, having been educated in Ireland, William was appointed as an Assistant-Surgeon on the Hospital Staff of the British Army on 15th August 1854.[445]

Figure 161. William Bradshaw

---

444 *London Gazette* – 25657/6436

445 *London Gazette* – 21583/2531

On 29th June 1855, William was transferred to the 50th Regiment of Foot, as an Assistant-Surgeon[446] and joined his regiment in the Crimea in time for the final assault on Sevastopol in September 1855. William boarded ship in Balaklava in mid July 1856 and returned home to England with his regiment. For his service in the Crimea, William was awarded the Crimea Medal with clasp for Sevastopol and the Turkish Crimea Medal.

Soon after his return to England, William was placed on the Supernumerary List on 1st August 1856.[447]

William was transferred to the 90th Regiment of Foot on 10th December 1856[448] and soon afterwards on 16th April 1857 was despatched with his new regiment to China as part of an expeditionary force intended to take part in the Opium War. While standing too off Java, the expeditionary force was intercepted by a Royal Navy vessel and given news of the outbreak of mutiny in India and relayed orders that they were to proceed at once to Calcutta rather than Hong Kong.

Arriving at Calcutta on 21st July, the regiment spent a week at Chinsurah before embarking on river steamers for Cawnpore. On 1st August, the regiment arrived at Berhampore where they disarmed the local garrison of Native Infantry; they now had orders to join the field force of General Havelock and proceeded to Allahabad where they arrived on 1st September. The regiment was part of the force which recaptured Cawnpore on 15th September, after which they set out towards Lucknow. It was on 26th September 1857, after Lucknow had been successfully reinforced, that William performed the deeds for which he would later be awarded the Victoria Cross. William was slightly wounded in this action.[449] William remained within the Residency until it was evacuated on 19th November 1857. For his service during the mutiny, William was awarded the Indian Mutiny Medal with clasp for the Defence of Lucknow.

On 8th October 1858, William was transferred to the 32nd Regiment of Foot and took part in operation in the provinces of Oudh and Roy Bareilly.

On 28th March 1859, William and the regiment boarded the troopship *Albuhera* at Chinsurah and on 24th April set sail for England where on 26th August 1859 they landed at Portsmouth.

William was presented with his Victoria Cross medal by Queen Victoria on 8th June 1859, at an investiture held in Buckingham Palace.

From Portsmouth, the regiment moved to Dover where they would form the garrison for the next year, however, on 13th January 1860, William was transferred to a staff position.[450]

On 16th October 1860, now suffering ill health, William was placed on half pay and retired from the army after only six years service.

William died on 9th March 1861 at his home in Thurles, Ireland at the age of 31 and was buried in St Mary's Church of Ireland Churchyard in the town.

William's Victoria Cross medal is on public display at the Royal Army Medical Corps Museum in Aldershot.

Figure 161a. Grave of William Bradshaw

---

446 *Edinburgh Gazette* – 6506/800
447 *London Gazette* – 21908/2667
448 *London Gazette* – 21949/4188

449 *London Gazette* – 22098/813
450 *Edinburgh Gazette* – 6980/50

Stewart McPherson
26th September 1857 (VC No. 184)

Gazetted: 12th April 1859 22248/1483

Rank and Unit: Colour Sergeant – 78th Regiment of Foot

Citation

For daring gallantry in the Lucknow Residency on the 26th September, 1857, in having rescued, at great personal risk, a wounded Private of his Company, who was lying in a most exposed situation, under a very heavy fire. Colour-Serjeant McPherson was also distinguished on many occasions by his coolness and gallantry in action.

Biography

Stewart was born in Culross, near Dunfermline sometime during 1822, the only son of Mungo and Mary. He was educated at the Geddes Public School in Culross until he left at the age of 15 to become an apprentice weaver in Dunfermline.

On 17th December 1839, Stewart enlisted in the 78th regiment of foot at Stirling and joined his regiment who were forming the garrison at Edinburgh Castle. On 17th July 1840 the regiment moved to Liverpool until 23rd June 1841 when they moved to Manchester. Between 19th November and 1st April 1842 the regiment had a short stay in Ireland, stationed at Dublin. Leaving Ireland the regiment was stationed at Canterbury from 8th April, with orders to make ready for a deployment to India. In late May, the regiment embarked upon six ships and set sail for India, arriving at Bombay on 30th July and moving to their station at Poona.

On 7th April 1843, the regiment were ordered to the Sindh province where from 20th May they were stationed at Kurrachee. In December 1844, the regiment moved to Hyderabad and then during February/March 1845 moved to Bombay where they were stationed at Fort George before moving to Poona where they arrived on 18th April 1845.

On 14th February 1846, the regiment moved from Poona to Kirkee and then Belgaum until 1849 when the wings of the regiment set off in different directions, one wing going to Aden while the other wing returned to Bombay where they arrived on 16th November 1849.

Stewart was married to a local Culross girl, Elizabeth (née Haig), in 1848 and the couple went on to have five children – Sarah, Eliza, Robina, Ferguson and McGregor.

In November 1850, the wings of the regiment were switched but were finally reunited at Poona on 5th March 1853.

On 1st November 1856, the Governor General of India declared war on Persia and despatched troops to the Persian

Figure 162. Stewart McPherson

Gulf. On 7th/8th January 1857, Stewart and the 78th, as part of the secondary force, left Poona and on 19th January set sail from Bombay bound for the Persian Gulf where they arrived off Busheer on 1st February. Stewart, was involved in the Battle of Khushab on 7th February and was present at the bombardment and capture of Mohammrah on 26th March 1857. For his service during the first Anglo-Persian War, Stewart was awarded the India General Service Medal with clasp for Persia. Following the cessation of hostilities, the 78th set sail from Mohammrah on 10th May bound for Bombay where they arrived on 22nd/23rd May only to hear the unexpected news of the outbreak of mutiny and orders to proceed to Calcutta where they arrived on 10th June.

From Calcutta, the regiment moved to Allahabad, to form up as part of the field force under the command of General Havelock that was charged with securing the relief of Cawnpore and Lucknow. On 7th July, Stewart and the 78th left Allahabad for Cawnpore and as part of General Havelock's field force was involved in the recapture of the city on 16th July. On 19th July, General Havelock's column left Cawnpore bound for Lucknow and Stewart was involved in the Battle of Oonoa on 29th July, the Battle of Busherut-gunge on 5th August, the Battle of Boorbeake Chowkee on 12th August and the Battle of Bithoor on 16th August. It was on 26th September 1857, following the successful reinforcement of the garrison at Lucknow, that Stewart performed the deeds for which he would later be awarded the Victoria Cross. By this time he had been promoted to the rank of Colour Sergeant. After the Residency was abandoned in November 1857, Stewart was part of the force defending the Alum Bagh until, as part of Sir Colin Campbell's force, he took part in the action which managed to recapture Lucknow on 21st

March 1858. By 26th April the regiment was at Cawnpore where they joined up with the Rohilkhand Field Force commanded by Brigadier General Walpole. On 7th May Stewart took part in the Battle of Bareilly and after the town was captured the regiment formed part of the garrison. For his service during the mutiny, Stewart was awarded the Indian Mutiny Medal with clasps for Defence of Lucknow and Lucknow.

On 20th February 1859, the regiment left Bareilly at the start of their journey to return to England, and departing from Bombay on 28th April arrived at Gravesend during mid-September.

Stewart was presented with his Victoria Cross medal by Queen Victoria during an investiture held at Windsor Castle on 4th January 1860.

The regiment was stationed at Fort George near Inverness until February 1860 when they moved to Edinburgh.

On 8th January 1861, having completed 21 years and 22 day of service, Stewart retired from the army and was awarded the Good Conduct and Long Service Medal.

After leaving the army, Stewart returned to his home town of Culross for a short time until he was appointed as the superintendant of Glasgow Industrial Schools and moved to Bailieston in Glasgow.

About ten years later, Stewart retired from his job in Glasgow and again returned to Culross where he bought a house which he named Lucknow Villa; it was here that he died on 7th December 1892 at the age of 70/71. He was buried in the Culross Abbey Cemetery.

Stewart's Victoria Cross Medal is on public display at the Highlander's Museum in Fort George near Inverness.

Figure 162a. Grave of Stewart McPherson

Thomas Duffy
26th September 1857 (VC No. 185)

Gazetted: 18th June 1858 22154/2958

Rank and Unit: Private – 1st Madras Fusiliers

Citation
For his cool intrepidity and daring skill, whereby a 24-pounder gun was saved from falling into the hands of the enemy. **(Extract from Divisional Orders of Major-General Sir James Outram, G.C.B., dated 16th October, 1857.)**

Biography
Thomas was born in Mount Temple (Caulry) near Athlone, Co Westmeath in Ireland, sometime during 1806. Unfortunately, very little is known of the life story of this Irishman.

At some stage, Thomas enlisted as a private in the 1st Madras Fusiliers which was a regiment of the Honourable East India Company army in India.

Thomas would have spent his entire army career in India, with possible assignments in Burma.

It was on 26th September 1857, during operations to reinforce the garrison at Lucknow, that Thomas performed the deeds for which he would later be awarded the Victoria Cross.

For his service during the mutiny, Thomas was awarded the Indian Mutiny Medal with clasp for Relief of Lucknow.

Thomas was presented with his Victoria Cross Medal by Lieutenant-Colonel M. Beresford at a ceremony in Mysore, India some time during 1859.

After leaving the army, Thomas returned to Ireland and was living on Upper Dorset Street, Dublin when he died on 24th December 1868 at the age of 62. Thomas was buried in the Glasnevin Cemetery in Dublin.

Thomas's Victoria Cross medal is on public display at the National Army Museum in Chelsea, London.

Figure 163a. Grave of Thomas Duffy

James Hollowell
26th September 1857 (VC No. 186)

Gazetted: 18th June 1858 22154/2958

Rank and Unit: Private – 78th Regiment of Foot

Citation

A party, on the 26th of September, 1857, was shut up and besieged in a house in the city of Lucknow, by the rebel sepoys. Private James Hollowell, one of the party, behaved, throughout the day, in the most admirable manner ; he directed, encouraged, and led the others, exposing himself fearlessly, and by his talent in persuading and cheering, prevailed on nine dispirited men to make a successful defence, in a burning house, with the enemy, firing through four windows. **(Extract from Divisional Orders of Major-General Sir James Outram, G.C.B., dated 14th October, 1857.)**

Biography

James was born in Lambeth, South London some time during 1823.

It is probable that James enlisted as a private in the 78th Regiment of Foot some time in 1841/42, on or around the time of his 18th birthday.

On 17th July 1840 the regiment moved to Liverpool until 23rd June 1841 when they moved to Manchester. Between 19th November and 1st April 1842 the regiment had a short stay in Ireland, stationed at Dublin. Leaving Ireland the regiment was stationed at Canterbury from 8th April, with orders to make ready for a deployment to India. In late May, the regiment embarked upon six ships and set sail for India, arriving at Bombay on 30th July and moving to their station at Poona.

On 7th April 1843, the regiment were ordered to the Sindh province where from 20th May they were stationed at Kurrachee. In December 1844, the regiment moved to Hyderabad and then during February/March 1845 moved to Bombay where they were stationed at Fort George before moving to Poona where they arrived on 18th April 1845. On 14th February 1846, the regiment moved from Poona to Kirkee and then Belgaum until 1849 when the wings of the regiment set off in different directions, one wing going to Aden while the other wing returned to Bombay where they arrived on 16th November 1849. In November 1850, the wings of the regiment were switched but were finally reunited at Poona on 5th March 1853.

On 1st November 1856, the Governor General of India declared war on Persia and despatched troops to the Persian Gulf. On 7th/8th January 1857, James and the 78th, as part of

Figure 164. James Hollowell

the secondary force, left Poona and on 19th January set sail from Bombay bound for the Persian Gulf where they arrived off Busheer on 1st February. James was involved in the Battle of Khushab on 7th February and was present at the bombardment and capture of Mohammrah on 26th March 1857. For his service during the first Anglo-Persian War, James was awarded the India General Service Medal with clasp for Persia.

Following the cessation of hostilities, the 78th set sail from Mohammrah on 10th May bound for Bombay where they arrived on 22nd/23rd May only to hear the unexpected news of the outbreak of mutiny and orders to proceed to Calcutta where they arrived on 10th June.

From Calcutta, the regiment moved to Allahabad, to form up as part of the field force under the command of General Havelock that was charged with securing the relief of Cawnpore and Lucknow. On 7th July, Stewart and the 78th left Allahabad for Cawnpore and as part of General Havelock's field force was involved in the recapture of the city on 16th July. On 19th July, General Havelock's column left Cawnpore bound for Lucknow and James was involved in the Battle of Oonoa on 29th July, the Battle of Busherut-gunge on 5th August, the Battle of Boorbeake Chowkee on 12th August and the Battle of Bithoor on 16th August. It was on 26th September 1857, following the successful reinforcement of the garrison at Lucknow, that James performed the deeds for which he would later be awarded the Victoria Cross. After the Residency was abandoned in November 1857, James was part of the force defending the Alum Bagh until, as part of Sir Colin Campbell's force, he took part in the action which managed to recapture Lucknow on 21st March 1858. By 26th April the regiment was at Cawnpore where they joined up with the Rohilkhand Field Force commanded by Brigadier General Walpole. On 7th May, James took part in the Battle of

Bareilly and after the town was captured the regiment formed part of the garrison. For his service during the mutiny, James was awarded the Indian Mutiny Medal with clasps for Defence of Lucknow and Lucknow.

James was presented with his Victoria Cross medal by Lieutenant-General Sir James Outram, at a ceremony in India some time during 1858.

On 20th February 1859, the regiment left Bareilly at the start of their journey to return to England, and departing from Bombay on 28th April arrived at Gravesend during mid-September.

The regiment was stationed at Fort George near Inverness until February 1860 when they moved to Edinburgh.

It is probable that James retired from army life soon after arriving back in England, before the 20 year qualifying period for the Long Service and Good Conduct medal, with the rank of Lance-Corporal.

On leaving the army, James returned to London and was employed by the Corps of Commissioners.

He was living at 20 Gloucester Place, Holburn, London when he died from heart disease on 4th April 1876 at the age of 53.

James was buried in an unmarked grave, in the Corps of Commissioners section of Brookwood Cemetery, Woking, Surrey on 12th April 1876.

James's Victoria Cross Medal is on public display at the Highlanders Regimental Museum in Fort George near Inverness.

Figure 164a. Grave of James Hollowell

Peter McManus
26th September 1857 (VC No. 187)

Gazetted: 18th June 1858 22154/2958

Rank and Unit: Private – 5th Regiment of Foot

Citation

On the same occasion, Private McManus kept outside the house, until he was himself wounded, and under cover of a pillar, kept firing on the sepoys and preventing their rushing on the house. He also, in conjunction with Private John Ryan, rushed into the street, and took Captain Arnold, of the 1st Madras Fusiliers, out of a dooly, and brought him into the house in spite of a heavy fire, in which Captain Arnold was again wounded. **(Extract from Divisional Orders of Major-General Sir James Outram, G.C.B., dated 14th October, 1857.)**

Biography

Peter was born at Tynan, Co Armagh, Ireland some time during March 1829.

It is probable that Peter enlisted as a private in the 1st Battalion of the 5th Regiment of Foot in 1847 sometime near to his 18th birthday, the regiment was stationed in Ireland at this time.

Not long after joining the regiment, Peter saw overseas service when they were posted to Mauritius. The regiment were stationed at Singapore at the outbreak of the mutiny and upon receiving the news were immediately dispatched to India, arriving at Calcutta on 4th July 1857.

The regiment were ordered to make their way to Lucknow and join up with the relief force of General Havelock. On the way the regiment were involved in the relief of Arrah on 2nd August. It was on 26th September 1857, during the successful operation to reinforce Lucknow, that Peter performed the deeds for which he would later be awarded the Victoria Cross, having been nominated for the award by the Privates of the regiment under Rule 13. During this action Peter was wounded. The regiment remained in the Alum Bagh, defending Lucknow until 16th November when the Residency was evacuated by the force of Sir Colin Campbell. Peter was also part of the force commanded by Sir Colin Campbell which recaptured Lucknow in March 1858. For his service in the mutiny, Peter was awarded the Indian Mutiny Medal with clasps for Defence of Lucknow and Lucknow.

In January 1859, Peter was with the regiment at Allahabad and it was here on 27th April 1859, at the age of 30, that he died from smallpox. The location of Peter's burial is unknown, however, it is likely that he was buried with other victims of smallpox somewhere in Allahabad.

Peter's Victoria Cross Medal is on public display at the Fusiliers Museum of Northumberland in Alnwick Castle.

John Ryan
26th September 1857 (VC No. 188)

Gazetted: 18th June 1858 22154/2958

Rank and Unit: Private – 1st Madras Fusiliers

Citation

In addition to the above act, Private Ryan distinguished himself throughout the day by his intrepidity, and especially devoted himself to rescuing the wounded in the neighbourhood from being massacred. He was most anxious to visit every dooly. **(Extract from Divisional Orders of Major-General Sir James Outram, G.C.B., dated 14th October, 1857.)**

Biography

John was born in Kilkenny, Ireland some time during 1823.

It is probable that John enlisted in the army of the Honourable East India Company some time in 1841, around the time of his 18th birthday.

John would have joined his regiment 1st Madras Fusiliers in India and would spend his entire army career in India or Burma.

John was part of the force of General Havelock which reinforced the residency at Lucknow and it was on 26th September 1857, the day after this successful action that he performed the deeds for which he was later awarded the Victoria Cross. He was also promoted to the rank of Sergeant.

John was part of the force which defended the residency until it was relieved and evacuated on 16th November 1857.

For his service during the mutiny, John was awarded the Indian Mutiny Medal with clasps for Defence of Lucknow and Lucknow.

John was presented with his Victoria Cross Medal by Lieutenant-General Sir James Outram at a ceremony in India, soon afterwards he was killed in action at Cawnpore on 4th March 1858 aged 34. John was buried in the Old British Cemetery in Cawnpore.

John's Victoria Cross medal is on public display at the National Army Museum in Chelsea, London.

Jacob Thomas
27th September 1857 (VC No. 189)

Gazetted: 24th December 1858 22212/5519

Rank and Unit: Bombardier – Bengal Artillery

Citation

For distinguished gallantry at Lucknow on the 27th September, 1857, in having brought off on his back, under a heavy fire, under circumstances of considerable difficulty, a wounded soldier of the Madras Fusiliers, when the party to which he was attached was returning to the Residency from a sortie, whereby he saved him from falling into the hands of the enemy.

Biography

Jacob was born some time during February 1833 at Coed-Y-Bwddy Farm in Llanwinio near Carmarthen, Wales. His father, also called Jacob was a farmer and carpenter.

Prior to joining the army, Jacob worked as a "fitter-up", this job was probably in the leather trade, perhaps in the manufacture of shoes.

At the age of 20, on 6th July 1853 at Cardiff, Jacob enlisted in the artillery of the Honourable East India Company army for a term of 12 years. Later that year he moved to India and joined up with his unit which was part of the 4th Battery of the 1st Battalion of the Bengal Artillery.

When the mutiny broke out, Jacob was stationed at Lucknow and was one of the original defenders caught up in the siege of the Residency. On 1st August 1857, Jacob was promoted to the rank of Bombardier and it was soon afterwards on 27th September that he performed the deeds for which he would later be awarded the Victoria Cross. Jacob remained in Lucknow until the city was abandoned on 16th November, however, he was part of the force commanded by Sir Colin Campbell which retook the city in March 1858. For his service during the mutiny, Jacob was awarded the Indian Mutiny Medal with clasps for Defence of Lucknow and Lucknow.

On 6th August 1858, Jacob received a promotion to the rank of Corporal and to Sergeant on 29th March 1859.

Jacob was married to Margaret Hamilton (née Taggart) a widow on 14th March 1859 at St James's Church in Delhi.

Jacob was presented with his Victoria Cross medal by Queen Victoria on 4th January 1860, at an investiture held in Windsor Castle.

As part of the breakup of the armies of the Honourable East India Company, on 12th June 1861 Jacob was transferred to the 4th Battery of the 16th Brigade of the Royal Artillery regiment.

Jacob was promoted to the rank of Hospital Sergeant on 1st February 1862, to Battery Sergeant on 7th March 1863 and to Quartermaster Sergeant on 23rd March 1863.

On 30th October 1866, Jacob's army career was cut short after sustaining injuries when a horse fell on him. Being judged to be unfit for duty he was discharged, with a pension, at Darjeeling after only 13 years of service.

After leaving the army, Jacob was employed in the local police force and by the time of his death on 3rd March 1911, at the age of 78 had attained the rank of Inspector.

Jacob was buried in an unmarked grave in Bendel Churchyard, Hooghly near Darjeeling.

Jacob's Victoria Cross medal is on public display at the Royal Artillery Museum in Woolwich, London.

Figure 167a. Memorial at Royal Artillery Museum, Woolwich

Robert Blair
28th September 1857 (VC No. 190)

Gazetted: 15 June 1858 22154/2960

Rank and Unit: Lieutenant – 2nd Dragoon Guards

Citation

A most gallant feat was here performed by Lieutenant Blair, who was ordered to take a party of one serjeant and twelve men and bring in a deserted ammunition wagon. As his party approached, a body of fifty or sixty of the enemy's horse came down upon him, from a village, where they had remained unobserved: without a moment's hesitation he formed up his men, and, regardless of the odds, gallantly led them on, dashing through the rebels. He made good his retreat without losing a man, leaving nine of them dead on the field. Of these he killed four himself; but, to my regret, after having run a native officer through the body with his sword, he was severely wounded, the joint of his shoulder being nearly severed. **(Despatch from Major-General James Hope Grant, K.C.B., dated 10th January, 1858.)**

Biography

Robert was born on 13th March 1834 at Aventoun, Linlithgow, West Lothian in Scotland to father William who was a barrister and mother Isabell, Cornelia (née Halkett).

Robert graduated with a degree in Law from Glasgow University and under a Snell Exhibitioner scholarship completed post graduate work at Balliol College, Oxford.

At the age of 19, Robert purchased a commission as Cornet in the 16th Light Dragoons on 16th December 1853,[451] however, only a few days later on 23rd December 1853 transferred to the 9th Light Dragoons[452] and joined his regiment in India. Robert advanced his career when on 2nd November 1855 he purchased a commission as Lieutenant which had become vacant in the 9th Light Dragoons.[453] On 26th December 1856, Robert transferred by way of exchange to the 2nd Dragoons, however remained on attachment to the 9th Lancers.[454]

At the time of the mutiny, Robert was stationed at Umballa but with the mutiny was assigned as part of the cavalry brigade commanded by James Hope Grant which was part of the force commanded by Lord Roberts to go to the relief of Delhi.

Figure 168. Robert Blair

Robert was present during the siege of Delhi which was established on 8th June 1857 and during the final assault which resulted in the capture of the city on 21st September. It was on the 28th September 1857, during operations in the Bulandshahr district, to the east of Delhi, that Robert performed the deeds for which he would later be awarded the Victoria Cross. During the action Robert was severely wounded by a sabre blow to the shoulder which nearly severed his arm, as a result of this wound he was sent to the hospital in Meerut. For his service during the mutiny, Robert was awarded the Indian Mutiny Medal with clasp for Delhi.

On 7th July 1858, Robert was promoted to the rank of Captain.[455]

Robert was presented with his Victoria Cross medal by Queen Victoria on 2nd August 1858, at a ceremony on Southsea Common in Portsmouth.

Having returned to India, Robert died from smallpox on 28th March 1859 at the age of 25, while stationed at Cawnpore and was buried in the Old British Cemetery.

Robert's Victoria Cross medal is on public display at the 1st Queens Dragoon Guards Regimental Museum in Cardiff Castle, Wales.

Robert was the cousin of James Blair who also was awarded a Victoria Cross during the mutiny, for deeds performed at Neemuch on 12th August 1857.

---

451 *London Gazette* – 21503/3683
452 *London Gazette* – 21505/3746
453 *London Gazette* – 21808/4037
454 *London Gazette* – 21953/4325

455 *London Gazette* – 22183/4194

Bernard Diamond
28th September 1857 (VC No. 191)

Gazetted: 27th April 1858 22131/2051

Rank and Unit: Sergeant – Bengal Horse Artillery

Citation

For an act of valour performed in action against the rebels and mutineers at Bulandshahr, on the 28th September, 1857, when these two soldiers evinced the most determined bravery in working their gun under a very heavy fire of musketry, whereby they cleared the road of the enemy, after every other man belonging to it had been either killed or disabled by wounds. **(Despatch of Major Turner, Bengal Horse Artillery, dated Bulandshahr, 2nd October, 1857.)**

Biography

Bernard was born in Portglenone, Co Antrim in Ireland sometime in January 1827.

In 1847, Bernard enlisted in the army of the Honourable East India Company and soon afterwards joined his regiment the Bengal Horse Artillery in India.

Not long after arriving in India, Bernard was involved in the 2nd Anglo-Sikh war which started in April 1848 and continued until a treaty was signed in March 1849. During the war, Bernard was involved in the Battle of Chillianwala on 13th January 1849 and the decisive Battle of Gujarat on 21st February 1849. For his service during the war, Bernard was awarded the Punjab Medal with clasps for Chillianwala and Goojerat.

Sometime during 1854, Bernard married Mary Collins, a widow, and the couple would have three children all of whom were born in India.

Bernard was part of the force commanded by Lord Roberts which laid siege to Delhi from June until the city was recaptured on 21st September 1857. It was a few days later on 28th September that Bernard, who by now had the rank of Sergeant, performed the deeds for which he would later be awarded the Victoria Cross during a battle to take the village of Bulandshahr a few miles to the east of Delhi. Bernard was also part of the force commanded by Sir Colin Campbell, which facilitated the evacuation of the Residency at Lucknow on 19th November and recaptured Lucknow on 21st March 1858. For his service during the mutiny, Bernard was awarded the Indian Mutiny Medal with clasps for Delhi, Relief of Lucknow and Lucknow.

 Bernard was presented with his Victoria Cross Medal some time during 1858 in India.

Figure 169. Bernard Diamond

Sometime in 1866, Bernard was discharged from the army after nearly 20 years of service due to blindness in one eye, as a result of wounds he had sustained, he was awarded the Long Service and Good Conduct Medal.

Sometime in 1875, Bernard and his family emigrated to New Zealand and it was at Masterton on the North Ireland that he died on 24th January 1892 at the age of 65 and was buried in Masterton Cemetery.

Bernard's Victoria Cross medal is on public display at the Queen Elizabeth II Army Memorial Museum, in Waiouru, New Zealand.

Figure 169a. Memorial at Royal Artillery Museum, Woolwich

Robert Kells
28th September 1857 (VC No. 192)

Gazetted: 24th December 1858 22212/5517

Rank and Unit: Lance Corporal – 9th Lancers

Citation

For conspicuous bravery at Bulandshahr, on the 28th of September, 1857, in defending against a number of the enemy his commanding officer, Captain Drysdale, who was lying in a street with his collar-bone broken, his horse having been disabled by a shot, and remaining with him until out of danger. (**Despatch from Major-General Sir James Hope Grant, K.C.B., dated 8th April, 1858.**)

Biography

Robert was born in Meerut India on 7th April 1832.

On 22nd October 1844, at the age of 12 years and 6 months, Robert joined the 9th Lancers.

In November 1848, Robert saw his first active service at the age of 16, when he took part in the 2nd Sikh war and was involved in the Passage of Chenab and the Battle of Chillianwala on 13th January 1849. On 1st February, Robert was promoted to the rank of Trumpeter and less than three weeks later on 21st February he took part in the Battle of Goojerat. For his involvement in the war, Robert was awarded the Punjab Medal with clasps for Chillianwala and Goojerat.

At the outbreak of the mutiny, Robert and the 9th Lancers were stationed at Umballa and were assigned to the Delhi Field Force commanded by Major General George Anson, who was replaced by Major General Sir Henry Barnard when Anson died from cholera on 27th May.

The force set out from Umballa on 17th May and after joining forces with the Meerut Brigade, commanded by Brigadier Archdale Wilson fought the Battle of Badli-ki-Serai on 8th June and established positions on the Delhi Ridge. Robert was part of the besieging force and was involved in the final capture of Delhi on 21st September 1857. Following the recapture of the city, Robert and the 9th Lancers were assigned to a Flying Column commanded by Colonel Edward Greathed and on 24th September moved out to patrol the Gangetic Goab, the area of land between the Ganges and Yamuna rivers.

It was on the 28th September, during the Battle of Bulandshahr, that Robert, now with the rank of Lance-Corporal, performed the deeds for which he would later be awarded the Victoria Cross.

Robert took part in the Battle of Agra on 10th November 1857 and was part of the force which evacuated the Residency at

Figure 170. Robert Kells

Lucknow on 19th November; he was also present when Lucknow was finally recaptured on 21st March 1858. On 24th May 1858, Robert was promoted to the rank of Trumpet-Major. For the remainder of the mutiny, Robert was involved in the campaigns in the Rohilkhand and Oudh provinces. For his service during the mutiny, Robert was awarded the Indian Mutiny Medal with clasps for Delhi, Relief of Lucknow and Lucknow.

Wishing to remain in India after the mutiny, Robert transferred to the 1st Bengal European Light Cavalry on 1st March 1859, as the 9th Lancers were returning home to England.

On 19th February 1859, Robert's Victoria Cross Medal was one of 15 despatched by the Secretary of War for presentation in India, however, when they arrived in India the 9th Lancers had already left for England so the medals for the Lancers were returned to London. Eventually, Robert's Victoria Cross medal was returned to India where it was presented to him at Allahabad sometime in the second half of 1860.

With the dissolution of the Honourable East India Company Army in 1862, Robert's regiment was transferred to the British Army and renamed as the 19th Hussars.

Robert was discharged from the army at Benares on 14th November 1868, being unfit for service due to a fall from his horse and "disease due to the climate". With over 24 years service in the army, Robert was awarded the Long Service and Good Conduct Medal, on his retirement he stated that he was returning to London to reside in Blackfriars Road.

On 1st January 1881, Robert was appointed as a Yeoman of the King's Body-Guard with the rank of Yeoman Bed Hanger and resided at the Tower of London. In this capacity, Robert attended many state occasions, including the visit of Kaiser Wilhelm to London in 1891.

At some stage Robert was married to Sara Ann (née Matthews) and the couple had a son Frederick who was born in 1889.

Robert was awarded the Queen Victoria Jubilee Medal (1887) and clasp (1897) as well as the King Edward VII Coronation Medal 1902. Robert was also awarded the Royal Victoria Medal (1896), which was presented to him by King Edward VII on 25th June 1901, during an inspection of the Yeoman at the Tower of London.

Robert died on 14th April 1905, a week after his 73rd birthday and was buried in Lambeth Cemetery in London.

Robert's Victoria Cross Medal is on public display at the 9th/12th Royal Lancers Regimental Museum in Derby.

Figure 170a. Grave of Robert Kells

Patrick Donohoe
28th September 1857 (VC No. 193)

Gazetted: 24th December 1858 22212/5517

Rank and Unit: Private – 9th Lancers

Citation

For having, at Bulandshahr, on the 28th of September, 1857, gone to the support of Lieutenant Blair, who had been severely wounded, and, with a few other men, brought that officer in safety through a large body of the enemy's cavalry.
(Despatch from Major-General Sir James Hope Grant, K.C.B., dated 8th April, 1858.)

Biography

Patrick was born on 28th September 1820, in Nenagh, Co Tipperary in Ireland. Little is known of Patrick's family or early life, however, he had a younger brother Timothy[456] who was born on 17th March 1825.

It is likely that Patrick joined the army on or around his 18th birthday, in 1838 and would have joined his regiment the 9th Lancers in India soon afterwards.

In December 1843, Patrick saw his first active service when he took part in the Gwalior Campaign in northern India against the Maratha army and fought in the Battle of Punniar on 29th December 1843. For his service during this campaign, Patrick was awarded the Gwalior Campaign Star, engraved on the rear with the battle honour for Punniar. Patrick next saw action, in the 1st Anglo-Sikh War which started in December 1845 and was concluded by the Treaty of Lahore on 9th March 1846. During the war, Patrick took part in the decisive Battle of Sobraon on 10th February 1846. For his service during the war, Patrick was awarded the Sutlej Medal (1845–46) engraved with the battle honour for Sobraon. In November 1848, Patrick again saw active service, when he took part in the 2nd Anglo-Sikh war and was involved in the Passage of Chenab and the Battle of Chillianwala on 13th January 1849 and the Battle of Goojerat on 21st February. For his involvement in the war, Patrick was awarded the Punjab Medal with clasps for Chillianwala and Goojerat.

At the outbreak of the mutiny, Patrick and the 9th Lancers were stationed at Umballa and were assigned to the Delhi Field Force commanded by Major General George Anson, who was replaced by Major General Sir Henry Barnard when Anson died from cholera on 27th May. The force set out from Umballa

---

456 Timothy would be awarded the highest American military award, the Medal of Honour, for action at Fredricksburg in Virginia during the American Civil War, when he served with the 69th New York Infantry.

on 17th May and after joining forces with the Mccrut Brigade, commanded by Brigadier Archdale Wilson fought the Battle of Badli-ki-Serai on 8th June and established positions on the Delhi Ridge. Patrick was part of the besieging force and was involved in the final capture of Delhi on 21st September 1857. Following the recapture of the city, Patrick and the 9th Lancers were assigned to a Flying Column commanded by Colonel Edward Greathed and on 24th September moved out to patrol the Gangetic Goab, the area of land between the Ganges and Yamuna rivers. It was on the 28th September, during the Battle of Bulandshahr, that Patrick, performed the deeds for which he would later be awarded the Victoria Cross. Patrick took part in the Battle of Agra on 10th November 1857 and was part of the force which evacuated the Residency at Lucknow on 19th November; he was also present when Lucknow was finally recaptured on 21st March 1858. For the remainder of the mutiny, Robert was involved in the campaigns in the Rohilkhand and Oudh provinces.

At some stage during his time in India, Patrick was married at Bombay to Mary Anne (née Glosscott) the widow of Sergeant Thomas Edwards and became stepfather to her daughter Anna.[457]

For his service during the mutiny, Robert was awarded the Indian Mutiny Medal with clasps for Delhi, Relief of Lucknow and Lucknow.

Patrick arrived back in England, after his tour in India, during September 1859 and a few weeks later on 4th January 1860, he was presented with his Victoria Cross Medal by Queen Victoria at a ceremony at Windsor Castle.

It is not known when Patrick left the army, however, his regiment returned to Ireland in 1864 before returning to India in 1875, and it is likely that he left the army during this tour of Ireland. Having served for more than 20 years, Patrick was awarded the Army Long Service and Good Conduct Medal.

Patrick died aged 56 on 16th August 1876 at his home in Ashbourne, Co Meath in Ireland and he was buried in an unmarked grave in the Donaghmore RC Churchyard.

Patrick's Victoria Cross Medal is part of a private collection held in Canada.

Figure 171a.
Grave of
Patrick
Donohoe

---

457 As Anna Leonowens (having herself married a soldier in India), she was governess to the children of the king of Siam and her journals were the inspiration for the book "Anna and the King of Siam", which itself was the inspiration for the film "The King and I".

Richard Fitzgerald
28th September 1857 (VC No. 194)

Gazetted: 24th April 1858 22131/2051

Rank and Unit: Gunner – Bengal Horse Artillery

Citation

For an act of valour performed in action against the rebels and mutineers at Bulandshahr, on the 28th September, 1857, when these two soldiers evinced the most determined bravery in working their gun under a very heavy fire of musketry, whereby they cleared the road of the enemy, after every other man belonging to it had been either killed or disabled by wounds. (**Despatch of Major Turner, Bengal Horse Artillery, dated Bulandshahr, 2nd October, 1857.**)

Biography

Richard was born some time during December 1831 at St Finbars in Co Cork, Ireland.

On 17th December 1851, Richard enlisted at Cork in the army of the Honourable East India Company as a Gunner in the Bengal Horse Artillery, having previously been employed as a carpenter.

Richard arrived in India, at Calcutta on 15th November 1852 on board the troopship *Soubahdar* and joined up with his regiment. Richard was part of the force commanded by Lord Roberts which laid siege to Delhi from June until the city was recaptured on 21st September 1857. It was a few days later on 28th September that Richard, performed the deeds for which he would later be awarded the Victoria Cross during a battle to take the village of Bulandshahr a few miles to the east of Delhi. For his service during the mutiny, Richard was awarded the Indian Mutiny Medal with clasp for Delhi.

Richard was presented with his Victoria Cross Medal some time during 1858 in India.

Little is known of Richard's life after the Mutiny, however, it is believed that he remained in India where he died some time in 1884 at the age of 53, based upon the fact that this was when he stopped drawing his Victoria Cross pension.

Richard's Victoria Cross Medal is on public display at the Bristol Museum and Art Gallery in Bristol.

Figure 172a. Memorial at Royal Artillery Museum, Woolwich

James Reynolds Roberts
28th September 1857 (VC No. 195)

Gazetted: 24th December 1858 22212/5517

Rank and Unit: Private – 9th Lancers

Citation

For conspicuous gallantry at Bulandshahr, on the 28th of September, 1857, in bringing a comrade, mortally wounded, through a street under a heavy musketry fire, in which service he was himself wounded. **(Despatch from Major-General Sir James Hope Grant, K.C.B., dated 8th April, 1858)**

Biography

James was born some time during 1826, in Bow, London.

It is probable that James enlisted in the army of the Honourable East India Company some time on or around his 18th birthday, in 1854 and would have joined his regiment the 9th Lancers in India soon afterwards.

At the outbreak of the mutiny, James and the 9th Lancers were stationed at Umballa and were assigned to the Delhi Field Force commanded by Major General George Anson, who was replaced by Major General Sir Henry Barnard when Anson died from cholera on 27th May. The force set out from Umballa on 17th May and after joining forces with the Meerut Brigade, commanded by Brigadier Archdale Wilson fought the Battle of Badli-ki-Serai on 8th June and established positions on the Delhi Ridge. James was part of the besieging force and was involved in the final capture of Delhi on 21st September 1857. Following the recapture of the city, James and the 9th Lancers were assigned to a Flying Column commanded by Colonel Edward Greathed and on 24th September moved out to patrol the Gangetic Goab, the area of land between the Ganges and Yamuna rivers. It was on the 28th September, during the Battle of Bulandshahr, that James, performed the deeds for which he would later be awarded the Victoria Cross; during the action he was severely wounded. James took part in the Battle of Agra on 10th November 1857 and was part of the force which evacuated the Residency at Lucknow on 19th November; he was also present when Lucknow was finally recaptured on 21st March 1858. For the remainder of the mutiny, James was involved in the campaigns in the Rohilkhand and Oudh provinces and returned to England sometime in early 1859. For his service during the mutiny, James was awarded the Indian Mutiny Medal with clasps for Delhi, Defence of Lucknow and Lucknow.

Not long after arriving back in England, James was admitted to the Middlesex Hospital, Marylebone, London where he died on 1st August 1859 at the age of 33 and was buried in an unmarked grave in Old Paddington Cemetery.

Due to his early death, James was never presented with his Victoria Cross Medal, which on 21st September 1859 was sent by registered post to his brother.

James's Victoria Cross Medal is on public display at the 9th/12th Royal Lancers Regimental Museum in Derby.

Figure 173a. Grave of James Reynolds Roberts

Figure 173b. Grave of James Reynolds Roberts

Augustus Henry Archibald Anson
28th September 1857 (VC No. 196)

Gazetted: 24th December 1858 22212/5517

Rank and Unit: Captain – 84th Regiment

Citation

For conspicuous bravery at Bulandshahr, on the 28th September, 1857. The 9th Light Dragoons had charged through the town, and were reforming in the Serai; the enemy attempted to close the entrance by drawing their carts across it, so as to shut in the cavalry and form a cover from which to fire upon them. Captain Anson, taking a lance, dashed out of the gateway, and knocked the drivers off their carts. Owing to a wound in his left hand, received at Delhi, he could not stop his horse, and rode into the middle of the enemy, who fired a volley at him, one ball passing through his coat.

At Lucknow, at the assault of the Secundra Bagh, on 16th November, 1857, he entered with the storming party on the gates being burst open. He had his horse killed, and was himself slightly wounded. He has shown the greatest gallantry on every occasion, and has slain many enemies in fight. **(Despatch from Major-General Sir James Hope Grant, K.C.B., dated 12th August, 1858)**

Biography

Augustus was born on 5th March 1835 at Slebech Hall, Pembroke in Wales, the seventh child and third son of Thomas William, the 1st Earl of Lichfield and Louisa Barbara Catherine (née Philips). He had four older sisters: Louisa Mary Anne, Gwendoline Isabella Anna Maria, Anne Frederica and Harriet Francis Maria: two older brothers Thomas George and William Victor Leopold Horatio and a younger brother Adelbert John Robert.

Augustus began his army career on 27th May 1853, when he purchased a commission as Ensign in the 44th Regiment of Foot.[458] On 28th October 1853, Augustus was transferred to the 4th Regiment of Foot[459] but his stay was short lived as he purchased a commission as 2nd Lieutenant in the Rifle Brigade on 2nd December 1853.[460] Augustus was promoted to the rank of Lieutenant in the Rifle Brigade on 8th December 1854[461] and soon afterwards on the 8th January was sent out to the war in

Figure 174. Augustus Henry Archibald Anson

the Crimea where he served in the siege of Sevastopol. For his service during the war, Augustus was awarded the Crimea Medal with clasp for Sevastopol, he would also be awarded the Sardinian Medal and the Turkish Crimea Medal.

On 6th July 1855, Augustus advanced his career in the Rifle Brigade with the purchase of a commission of Captain.[462] Augustus transferred to the 84th Regiment of Foot, by way of exchange, on 8th January 1856[463] and joined his regiment in India, where he was appointed as Aide de Camp to his uncle General George Anson, who was the Commander in Chief of the forces in India. On 27th May 1857, on the outskirts of Delhi, while leading a force going to the relief of the city following the outbreak of mutiny, General Anson died from cholera, leaving Augustus without a role. Captain Richard Curzon, knowing that General Sir James Hope Grant was without an Aide-de-Camp recommended Augustus for the position and the General gladly accepted him for the role. In this role, Augustus was part of the Delhi Field Force which was sent to the relief of Delhi and following the siege, he was involved in the recapture of Delhi on 18th September 1857, during which action he was wounded in the hand.[464] It was a few days later on 28th September 1857, during the Battle of Bulandshahr while attached to the 9th Lancers, that Augustus performed the deeds for which he was later awarded the Victoria Cross. On 16th November 1857, Augustus was present at the relief of Lucknow, where the Residency was evacuated, during this action he was wounded again and his horse was killed,[465] Augustus's conduct during this action is also mentioned in his Victoria Cross citation. Following the relief of Lucknow, Augustus was allowed to continue with the 9th

458 *London Gazette* – 21443/1482
459 *London Gazette* – 21489/2897
460 *London Gazette* – 21499/3551
461 *London Gazette* – 21638/3988

462 *London Gazette* – 21741/2598
463 *London Gazette* – 21835/71
464 *London Gazette* – 22073/4455
465 *London Gazette* – 22079/45

Lancers and General Grant found himself a new Aide-de-Camp. With the 9th Lancers, Augustus was involved in many actions during the mutiny, including operations at Agra, the capture of Meangunje and on 21st March 1858 the capture of Lucknow. On 2nd March 1858, Augustus was awarded the Order of the Medjidie (5th Class), by the Turkish government for his service during the Crimean War.[466] Augustus saw further action with the 9th Lancers at Koorsee, Baree and Nuwabgunge before being transferred to the 10th Light Dragoons on 24th August 1858.[467] With the 10th Dragoons, Augustus took part in the campaign to subdue the Oudh province and was involved in the Passage of the Goomtee. For his service during the mutiny, Augustus was awarded the Indian Mutiny Medal with clasps for Delhi, Defence of Lucknow and Lucknow.

On 7th December 1858, Augustus transferred to the 7th Light Dragoons by way of exchange[468] and returned to England.

Augustus was elected as Member of Parliament for the City of Litchfield on 30th April 1859 for the new session due to start on 31st May 1859.[469]

On 28th May 1859, Augustus was rewarded with a brevet promotion to the rank of Major, for his service in India during the mutiny.[470]

Augustus was presented with his Victoria Cross Medal by Queen Victoria on 8th June 1859 at a Ball in Buckingham Palace.

In 1860, Augustus was assigned to the joint British and French force sent to China to take part in the 2nd Opium War. After landing at Pei-Tang on 1st August, Augustus was reunited with General Sir James Hope Grant and once again served as his Aide-de-Camp. Augustus was one of the first men through the gates in the taking of the Taku Forts on 21st August 1860 and took part in the capture of Peking on 6th October. Soon after the taking of Peking, Augustus returned to England to deliver a despatch from General Sir James Hope Grant to the War Office, which he did on 28th December 1860.[471] For his service in China, Augustus was awarded the China War Medal (1857–60) with clasps for Taku Forts and Peking. Also for his service in China, Augustus was offered the choice of a brevet promotion to the rank of Lieutenant-Colonel or a substantive promotion to the rank of Major, however, this was on the unattached list. Augustus chose the promotion to Major,[472] unfortunately this would prove to effectively end his army career as despite several applications he was never able to secure another regimental position.

Having been placed on the unattached list allowed Augustus the freedom to participate more fully in his role as Member of Parliament for the City of Litchfield and he was very active in the debates during formulation of the Bill to abolish the practice of purchasing rank in the army. Augustus was eager to gain adequate compensation for those who would be financially disadvantaged by such a change.

On 1st December 1863, Augustus was married to Amelia Maria (née Claughton)[473] at Kidderminster in Worcestershire and the couple took up residency at Shugborough Hall near Tamworth in Staffordshire.

On 15th February 1867, Augustus, an avid supporter of the Volunteer Force was appointed as a Major in the London Scottish Rifle Volunteer Corps,[474] where his old friend Sir James Hope Grant was honorary Colonel.

In the General Election of 1868, the number of MPs for the City of Lichfield was reduced from two to one and Augustus lost his seat as Member of Parliament. Augustus's career as an MP was not over however, as he gained the seat of Bewdley in unusual circumstances. The election for the seat in the 1868 General Election was declared void on 16th February 1869 and a by-election was held on 11th March 1869. The incumbent, Sir Richard Attwood Glass did not contest the by-election and was replaced by John Cuncliffe Pickersgill Cuncliffe the new Conservative candidate. However, Cuncliffe was unseated by petition on 30th April 1868 and Augustus was installed as the Liberal Member for Parliament.

On 23rd July 1870, Augustus received a brevet promotion to the rank of Lieutenant-Colonel.

Augustus continued to champion the causes of army officers in his duties as Member of Parliament and in 1873 published a pamphlet "The Supersession of the Colonels of the Royal Army" in which he outlined the case against the practice of promoting officers to the rank of Colonel over the heads of officers with greater seniority.

Due to failing health as a result of respiratory problems, Augustus resigned his commission with the 15th Middlesex Rifle Volunteer Corps on 4th June 1873[475] and retired from the army days later on 31st June 1873[476] after 20 years service during which he was mentioned in despatches on 17 different occasions (14 times during the Indian Mutiny).

Since 1872, due to his failing health, Augustus had spent each winter in the south of France and it was in Cannes on 17th

---

466 *London Gazette* – 22107/1264
467 *London Gazette* – 22176/3904
468 *London Gazette* – 22207/5349
469 *London Gazette* – 22258/1815
470 *London Gazette* – 22275/2363
471 *London Gazette* – 22465/5305
472 *London Gazette* – 22480/654

473 Amelia was the daughter of Reverend Thomas Leigh Claughton the Bishop of Rochester and niece of William the Earl of Dudley.
474 *London Gazette* – 23225/1476
475 *London Gazette* – 23983/2688
476 *London Gazette* – 24008/3825

November 1877 that he died at the age of 42 and was buried in the Cimitiére Protestant du Grand Jas in Cannes.

Augustus's Victoria Cross Medal is on public display at Shugborough Hall in Staffordshire.

In his memory, the Anson Memorial Sword is presented to the leading cadet at the Royal Military College at Sandhurst each year.

Figure 174a. Grave of Augustus Henry Archibald Anson

Denis Dynon[477]
2nd October 1857 (VC No. 197)

Gazetted: 25th February 1862 22601/957

Rank and Unit: Corporal No. 2165 – 53rd Regiment

Citation

Lieut. Daunt, 11th Bengal Native Infantry and Sergt. Dynon, are recommended for conspicuous gallantry in action, on the 2nd October 1857, with the mutineers of the Ramgurh Battn. At Chota Behar, in capturing two guns, particularly the last, when they rushed at and captured it by pistolling the gunners, who were mowing the detachment down with grape, one-third of which was hors de combat at the time.

Biography

Denis was born during September 1822 near the town of Rosenallis in the Parish of Kilmannon in Queen's County, Ireland.

At the age of 19, Denis left his job as a labourer and on 8th September 1841, joined the army at Mountrath in Queen's County where he was enlisted as a Private in the 44th Regiment of Foot.

Denis would have joined his regiment, who were serving in India at Cawnpore, Delhi or Ferozepur where they were station in November 1841, December 1841 or January 1842 respectively. The bulk of the regiment was fighting in Afghanistan and during a retreat from Kabul in January 1842 they were almost wiped out at Gundamuck in the Khoord Cabul Pass. The detachment of the 44th with which Denis served was on its way to Afghanistan when news of the disaster reached them and they abandoned the mission of reinforcement and returned to Karnal. In February 1843, the regiment left India for their return to England and joined up with the remainder of their comrades at Deal in June.

After short periods at Chichester, Gosport and Winchester the regiment moved to Devonport in May 1844 and it was here on 1st July 1844 that Denis transferred to the 53rd Regiment of Foot who were serving in India. Denis served with the regiment during the 1st Anglo-Sikh War (Sutlej Campaign) which lasted from December 1845 until ended by the Treaty of Lahore which was signed on 9th March 1846. During the war he took part in the Battle of Aliwal on 28th January 1846 and the Battle of Sobraon on 10th February 1846. For his part in the war, Denis was awarded the Sutlej Medal inscribed on reverse with Aliwal and clasp for Sobraon.

---

477 Denis's surname could have been Dynan as this is the name used within his army papers and enscribed on his Victoria Cross Medal.

From November 1848, Denis served with the regiment during the 2nd Anglo-Sikh War (Punjab Campaign) and was present at the Battle of Gujarat on 13th February 1849. For his service in this war, Denis was awarded the Punjab Medal with clasp for Goojerat. Denis would probably have served during the frontier wars on the North West Frontier during 1852 and 1853, however, there is no record of his being awarded the relevant campaign medals.

At the start of the mutiny in May 1857, Denis and the 53rd were stationed at Fort William in Calcutta. They were initially deployed to guard public and commercial properties in the city and in disarming the native Indian Regiments based around the arsenal at Dum Dum. On 1st July 1857, Denis received a promotion to the rank of Corporal. On 27th August, Denis and the Left Wing of the regiment were dispatched to the north of India and headed for Allahabad, where forces were being concentrated for operations against the mutineers. During their march, the mutiny had spread throughout the Chota Nagpur district and the military station at Hazaribagh was under threat. Following requests from Captain Dalton, the commissioner, in late September the 53rd were diverted towards Hazaribagh to provide assistance. On the way to Hazaribagh, the regiment received intelligence that a major rebel force of 3,000 men, the Ramghur Battalion, was occupying the town of Chattra. On 2nd October 1857, Major English with a small force of about 350 men from the 53rd attacked and defeated the mutineers in the Battle of Chattra, it was during this action that Denis performed the deeds for which he would later be awarded the Victoria Cross.

Now that the threat to Hazaribagh had been eliminated, Denis and the 53rd joined the force of Sir Colin Campbell and took part in the evacuation of the Residency at Lucknow on 19th November. The regiment were also involved in the recapture of Lucknow which was completed on 21st March 1858. In July 1858, Denis was promoted to the rank of Sergeant. After Lucknow the regiment was involved in operations in the Rohilkhand and Oudh provinces. For his service during the mutiny, Denis was awarded the Indian Mutiny Medal with clasps for Relief of Lucknow and Lucknow.

Denis returned to England during late 1860 and was stationed at Devonport until February 1861 when he was discharged from the army being unfit for the ordinary duties of a soldier as a result of illness due to his 16 years service in India. At the time of his discharge, Denis was a seriously ill man with Pulmonary and Hepatic disease and immediately entered the Royal Military Hospital at Kilmainham in Dublin as an in-pensioner. It was at the hospital, on 2nd May 1862, that Denis was presented with his Victoria Cross Medal by the Master of the hospital.

On 1st June 1862, Denis was discharged from the Hospital giving his intended place of residence as Clonaslee in Queen's County, however, it is believed that he was living in Dublin when he died on 16th February 1863 at the age of 40. The location of his grave is unknown but believed to be in Dublin.

Denis's Victoria Cross Medal is on public display at the Imperial War Museum as part of the Lord Ashcroft collection.

John Charles Campbell Daunt
2nd October 1857 (VC No. 198)

Gazetted: 25th February 1862 22601/957

Rank and Unit: Lieutenant – 11th Bengal Native Infantry

Citation

*Lieut. Daunt, 11th Bengal Native Infantry and Sergt.
Dynon, are recommended for conspicuous gallantry in
action, on the 2nd October 1857, with the mutineers of the
Ramgurh Battn. At Chota Behar, in capturing two guns,
particularly the last, when they rushed at and captured it
by pistolling the gunners, who were mowing the detachment
down with grape, one-third of which was hors de combat at
the time.*

*Lieut. Daunt is also recommended for chasing, on the 2nd
Nov. following, the mutineers of the 32nd Bengal Native
Infantry across a plain into a rich cultivation, into which
he followed them with a few of Rattray's Sikhs. He was
dangerously wounded in the attempt to drive out a large
body of these mutineers from an enclosure, the preservation
of many of his party on the occasion being attributed to his
gallantry.*

Biography

John was born in Autranches, Normandy, France on 8th November 1832, his father Richard an Iron Merchant and mother Bridget (née Hughes) were both born in Ireland. John was born into a large family having 3 older brothers and one younger brother as well as 7 older sisters. In 1851, John was living with his family in Manchester and listed his employment as a merchant.

At the age of 20, John enlisted in the army of the Honourable East India Company and was commissioned as an Ensign in the 70th Bengal Native Infantry on 20th July 1852.

Soon after the start of the mutiny, John was promoted to the rank of Lieutenant on 20th July 1857 and was assigned as Baggage-Master to the 27th Madras Infantry but soon afterwards was assigned to Major English of the 53rd Regiment of Foot as an interpreter with the Intelligence Department. It was in this role, during the Battle of Chattra on 2nd October 1857, that John performed the deeds for which he would later be awarded the Victoria Cross. On 2nd November 1857, John was involved in the defeat of mutineers from the 32nd Native Infantry at Nowadah Behar during which he was seriously wounded. For his service during the mutiny, John was awarded the Indian Mutiny Medal, with no clasps.

Figure 176. John Charles Campbell Daunt

Having recovered from his wounds, John rejoined the 70th Native Infantry at Canton in China on 1st April 1858 which was on active service during the 2nd Opium War. John took part in the affair with the Braves at the White Cloud Mountains in June 1858 and the repulse of the Chinese at the Landing Pier and Magazine Hill in Canton. For his service during the war, John was awarded the 2nd China War Medal (1857–60) with no clasps.

After returning to India from China, John although still employed by the army was appointed to the civil position of District Superintendent in the Bengal Police Department at Lohordugga, a position that he would hold until his death.

It was while on leave in England, when he was living at Brighton that John was married to Jane Alice Maddison (née Philpott) at Holmwood Church, Dorking in Surrey on 13th May 1863. The couple would go on to have 7 children; Emma Eveleen born in 1864, John Hubert Edward born in 1865, Walter Dickens born on 2nd June 1867 at Arrah in Bengal, Maude Seeley born on 29th July 1869 at Dundee in Scotland, Bertram Rochfort born on 30th September 1871 at Ranchie in Bengal, Guy Bushby[478] born on 18th February 1874 at Ranchie in Bengal and Laura Florence born on 20th March 1877 also at Ranchie in Bengal.

During his leave in England, John received news of his Victoria Cross presentation due to take place in India, the medal was later sent to him via. Registered Post.

John received a brevet promotion to the rank of Captain on 20th July 1864[479] which was made substantive on 12th September 1866.[480]

While still performing his role with the Bengal Police department, John continued to receive army promotions; to brevet

---

478 Guy died on 16th April 1879 at the age of 5 in Notting Hill, London.

479 *London Gazette* – 22952/1745

480 *London Gazette* – 23225/1469

Major on 17th September 1871 which was made substantive on 20th July 1872,[481] to Lieutenant-Colonel on 20th July 1878[482] and finally to brevet Colonel on 20th July 1882.[483]

John returned to England on sick leave and from 1st July 1885 resided at Overy House, Clifton in Bristol where on 15th April 1886 he died at the age of 53. He was buried with full military honours on 20th April at Redland Green Chapel Graveyard in Bristol.

John's Victoria Cross Medal is on public display at the Imperial War Museum as part of the Lord Ashcroft collection.

Figure 176a. Grave of John Charles Campbell Daunt

Patrick McHale
2nd October 1857 (VC No. 199)

Gazetted: 19th June 1860 22396/2316

Rank and Unit: Private No. 2626 – 1st Battalion, 5th Regiment of Foot

Citation

For conspicuous bravery at Lucknow on the 2nd October, 1857, when he was the first man at the capture of one of the guns at the Cawnpore Battery,—and again, on the 22nd December, 1857, when, by a bold rush, he was the first to take possession of one of the enemy's guns, which had sent several rounds of grape through his company, which was skirmishing up to it.

On every occasion of attack, Private McHale has been the first to meet the foe, amongst whom he caused such consternation by the boldness of his rush, as to leave little work for those who followed to his support. By his habitual coolness and daring, and sustained bravery in action, his name has become a household word for gallantry among his comrades.

Biography

Patrick was born some time during 1826 at Killala in Co. Mayo, Ireland, he obviously had little schooling as he could not read or write.

On 18th December 1847, at the age of 21, Patrick enlisted as a Private with the 5th Regiment of Foot at Parkhurst Barracks on the Isle of Wight and a few months later on 8th May 1848, set sail on the *Lady Edmonsbury* for Mauritius to join up with his regiment on garrison duties. Patrick landed at Mauritius on 19th August 1848 and served for nine years in the garrison.

Figure 177. Patrick McHale

---

481 *London Gazette* – 23939/217
482 *London Gazette* – 24641/5998 & 25152/4210 (to correct date of promotion)
483 *London Gazette* – 25152/4469

At the outbreak of the mutiny, Patrick was stationed with the regiment at Singapore and were immediately despatched to India where they arrived at Calcutta on 4th July 1857 and were assigned to the force of General Havelock going to the relief of Lucknow.

Patrick first saw action during the relief of Arrah on 2nd/3rd August, when the 5th under the command of Major Vincent Eyre used their new Enfield rifles to devastating effect. The regiment was involved in operations in the Jugdeespore District culminating in the Battle of Mangalwar on 21st September. Patrick and the 5th were part of the force which captured the Alum Bagh, on the outskirts of Lucknow and effected the reinforcement of the garrison besieged in the Residency. Patrick remained within the residency helping with the defence of Lucknow until it was evacuated by the force of Sir Colin Campbell on 16th November 1857. It was during the defence, on 2nd October that Patrick performed the deeds for which he would later be awarded the Victoria Cross. Under Rule 13, Patrick was elected for the award by a ballot of the Privates of the regiment. As part of the force commanded by Sir Colin Campbell, Patrick was involved in the recapture of Lucknow on 21st March 1858. On 31st March 1858, the regiment left Lucknow for Cawnpore where as part of the Oude Field Force they were involved in subduing the mutiny in the province. For his service during the mutiny, Patrick was awarded the Indian Mutiny Medal with clasps for Defence of Lucknow and Lucknow.

Patrick was presented with his Victoria Cross Medal by Lady Hersey on 12th December 1860, at a ceremony held at Fort William in Calcutta.

During March 1861, the regiment left India for England and Patrick returned home after 12 years of overseas duties.

At some stage, Patrick was awarded the Good Conduct Medal and the Regimental Medal of Merit.

The remainder of Patrick's army service was at bases in England and it was at the military camp at Shorncliffe in Kent that on 26th October 1866 he died at the age of 40 and was buried in the camp's military cemetery.

Patrick's Victoria Cross Medal is on public display at the Fusiliers Museum of Northumberland in Aln-wick Castle, Alnwick.

Figure 177a. Grave of Patrick McHale

John Sinnott
6th October 1857 (VC No. 200)

Gazetted: 24th December 1858 22212/5514

Rank and Unit: Lance Corporal – 84th Regiment of Foot

Citation

For conspicuous gallantry at Lucknow, on the 6th of October, 1857, in going out with Serjeants Glinn and Mullins and private Mullins, to rescue Lieutenant Gibaut, who, in carrying out water to extinguish a fire in the breastwork, had been mortally wounded, and lay outside. They brought in the body under a heavy fire. Lance-Corporal Sinnott was twice wounded. His comrades unanimously elected him for the Victoria Cross, as the most worthy. He had previously repeatedly accompanied Lieutenant Gibaut when he carried out water to extinguish the fire. **(Despatch from Lieutenant-General Sir James Outram, Bart., G.C.B., dated 2nd December 1857.)**

Biography

John was born in Wexford, Ireland some time during 1829 and at the age of 20 on 24th October 1849 enlisted at Dublin, as a Private in the 84th Regiment of Foot.

John joined his regiment in India, where they had been serving since 1845, sometime early in 1850 and at some stage was promoted to the rank of Corporal.

With the onset of mutiny, John was part of the force sent to the relief of Cawnpore on 2nd June and afterwards was assigned to the force of General Havelock being sent to the relief of Lucknow. On 25th September 1857, John was part of the force which effected a reinforcement of the garrison besieged in the Residency at Lucknow and remained to help with its continued defence. It was during the defence, on 6nd October that John performed the deeds for which he would later be awarded the Victoria Cross during which he was twice wounded. Under Rule 13, John was elected for the award by a ballot of the Non-Commissioned Officers of the regiment. John remained within the residency helping with the defence of Lucknow until it was evacuated by the force of Sir Colin Campbell on 16th November 1857. As part of the force commanded by Sir Colin Campbell, John was involved in the recapture of Lucknow on 21st March 1858. For his service during the mutiny, John was awarded the Indian Mutiny Medal with clasps for Defence of Lucknow and Lucknow.

John returned to England from India during September 1859 after nine years on the sub-continent.

Figure 178. John Sinnott

John was presented with his Victoria Cross medal by Queen Victoria on 4th January 1860 at an investiture held at Windsor Castle.

In 1863, John was deployed to garrison duties in Ireland, followed by a posting to Malta in 1865 and Jamaica in 1867. At some stage John received a promotion to the rank of Sergeant.

On 22nd March 1870, after over 21 years of service, John was discharged from the army with a pension of 14 shillings per week. For his exemplarily military service, John was awarded the Army Long Service and Good Conduct Medal.

John died on 20th July 1896 at the age of 67 in his home at Clapham in London and was buried on 24th July in an unmarked grave in Battersea New Cemetery in Morden, Surrey.

John's Victoria Cross Medal is on public display at the York & Lancaster Regimental Museum in Rotherham, however there is some question regarding if this medal is the original or a replica. On 9th February 1886, the medal was sold at auction by Spink's

Figure 178a. Grave of John Sinnott

to a Mr Partridge for the meagre sum of £23 and 10 shillings. At some stage the medal arrived back in the possession of John's family, however, it was stolen from the family home some time during World War I. Hancock's issued an official replacement medal which presumably was sent to the family, however, perhaps this was also lost because at some time in the 1950's the family purchased a VC at auction for about £2,000 which remains in the family possession in Canada. The York and Lancaster Regimental Museum also purchased their medal via auction but which is the original and which is the replica?

Figure 178b. Memorial to John Sinnott

John Freeman
10th October 1857 (VC No. 201)

Gazetted: 24th December 1858 22212/5517

Rank and Unit: Private – 9th Lancers

Citation

For conspicuous gallantry on the 10th of October, 1857, at Agra, in having gone to the assistance of Lieutenant Jones, who had been shot, killing the leader of the enemy's cavalry, and defending Lieutenant Jones against several of the enemy. **(Despatch from Major-General Sir James Hope Grant, K.C.B., dated 8th April, 1858.)**

Biography

John was born in Sittingbourne, Kent some time in 1832 or 1833.

It is not known when John enlisted in the 9th Lancers as a Private, however, due to the lack of earlier campaign medals it was probably sometime around 1850. John would have joined his regiment in India, soon after his enlistment, where they had been serving since 1841. At the outbreak of the mutiny, John and the 9th Lancers were stationed at Umballa and were assigned to the Delhi Field Force commanded by Major General George Anson. General Anson died from cholera on 27th May, soon after he took command of the Delhi Field Force and was replaced by Major General Sir Henry Barnard. The force set out from Umballa on 17th May and after joining forces with the Meerut Brigade, commanded by Brigadier Archdale Wilson fought the Battle of Badli-ki-Serai on 8th June and established positions on the Delhi Ridge. John remained as part of the besieging force and was involved in the final capture of Delhi on 21st September 1857, following which they were assigned to a Flying Column commanded by Colonel Edward Greathed. On 24th September the flying column moved out to patrol the Gangetic Goab, the area of land between the Ganges and Yamuna rivers. On the 28th September, John took part in the Battle of Bulandshahr and on 10th November 1857 in the Battle of Agra, during which he performed the deeds for which he was later awarded the Victoria Cross. John was part of the force which evacuated the Residency at Lucknow on 19th November and was also present when Lucknow was finally recaptured on 21st March 1858. For the remainder of the mutiny, John was involved in the campaigns in the Rohilkhand and Oudh provinces. During the Battle of Bareilly during 5th to 7th May 1858, John was dangerously wounded.[484] For his service during the mutiny, John was

---

484 *London Gazette* – 22170/3628

awarded the Indian Mutiny Medal with clasps for Delhi, Relief of Lucknow and Lucknow.

John returned to England with his regiment in May 1858 and on 4th January 1860 was presented with his Victoria Cross Medal by Queen Victoria at an investiture in Windsor Castle.

John died on 1st July 1913 at the age of 79 while living at Hackney in London and was buried three days later at Abney Park Cemetery, Stoke Newington in London.

John's Victoria Cross Medal is on public display at the Imperial War Museum in London as part of the Lord Ashcroft collection.

Figure 179a. Grave of John Freeman

James William Miller
10th October 1857 (VC No. 202)

Gazetted: 25th February 1862 22601/957

Rank and Unit: Conductor – Bengal Ordnance Department

Citation

For having, on the 28th of October, 1857, at great personal risk, gone to the assistance of, and carried out of action, a wounded Officer, Lieutenant Glubb, of the late 38th Regiment of Bengal Native Infantry. He was himself subsequently wounded and sent to Agra.

Conductor Miller was at the time employed with Heavy howitzer and Ordnance stores attached to a detachment of troops, commanded by the late Colonel Cottop, C.B., in the attack on the above mentioned date on the rebels who had taken, up their position in the Serai at Futtehpore Sikra near Agra.

Biography

James was born on 5th May 1820, in Glasgow, possibly Kirkwall and may have been raised by an uncle who was a minister in the church.

At the age of 21, James left his job as a candle maker and on 22 June 1841 enlisted in the army of the Honourable East India Company. After some initial induction at Chatham, James set

Figure 180. James William Miller

sail for India where he landed at Calcutta in January 1842 and resided for a short time at Fort Dum Dum on the outskirts of the city. In February 1842, James left Dum Dum and arrived at Agra in May 1842 where he joined up with his regiment 1st Company of 3rd Brigade of the Bengal Artillery. James was promoted to the rank of Bombardier on 3rd May 1844, to the rank of Corporal on 27th August 1844 and to the rank of Sergeant on 12th August 1845. On 20th June 1846, James was transferred to the Arsenal at Fort William in Calcutta and was appointed as acting Staff Sergeant.

James was married to Agnes (née Forsyth) on 24th October 1849, the couple would go on to have eight children; five daughters, Emily, Alice, Frances, Seraphina and Eva and three sons, Andrew, Frank and Henry.

In 1849, James was promoted to Staff Sergeant and was transferred to the Magazine at the Arsenal at Dum Dum. Having become acquainted with the workings of the Arsenal Workshop James was transferred from the magazine to the workshop on 31st January 1851 as Blacksmith Sergeant. In 1853, when Dum Dum was reduced to a depot, James was moved to the arsenal at Fort William in Calcutta as Carpenter Sergeant and at the end of the year was moved to the workshops at the Agra magazine. In 1856, James was sent to the Artillery Depot of Instruction at Madras to study for the Lieutenant's examination which he passed within two months instead of the six months which were allowed.

In 1857, James was posted back to the Magazine at Agra. With the outbreak of mutiny, James was assigned to Ordinance Store of a regiment and it was while performing these duties at Futtehpore on 28th October 1857 that he performed the deeds for which he would later be awarded the Victoria Cross. During this action James was wounded and sent back to the Depot at Agra. For his service during the mutiny, James was awarded the Indian Mutiny Medal with no clasps. From June 1858 until October 1859, James was in charge of the Ordnance Depot at Bareilly following which he was assigned to the Timber Department of the Gun Carriage Agency based at Cossipore in Calcutta.

James was presented with his Victoria Cross Medal at a ceremony somewhere in India during 1862, instead of travelling to London to receive the medal from Queen Victoria he used the money to buy a watch for his wife which he had specially made in Edinburgh.

In 1863, James was appointed as Store Keeper in the Gun Carriage Agency at Futtehpore. On 11th March 1864, James was promoted to the rank of Conductor by the Governor General of India backdated to 1st October 1857 and to the rank of Deputy Assistant Commissary on 27th October 1873. James received an honorary promotion to the rank of Ensign in the British Army

on 8th April 1874. On 28th April 1875, James received an honorary promotion to the rank of Lieutenant in the British Army.[485] James was promoted to the rank of Assistant Commissary by the Governor General of India on 27th October 1877. On 29th May 1879, James was promoted to the rank of Deputy Commissary by the Governor General of India and was appointed to the command of the Truallam Depot, on the same day he received an honorary promotion to the rank of Captain in the British Army.[486] On 10th August 1882, James retired from the Gun Carriage Agency of the Bengal Establishment and was given an honorary promotion to the rank of Major in the British Army.[487]

James died on 12th June 1892 at the age of 72 at Simla and was buried in Simla Churchyard.

The whereabouts of James's Victoria Cross in unknown, it is believed to have been stolen during a train journey while the family was living in India.

Figure 180a. Memorial to Glaswegians awarded the Victoria Cross

485 *London Gazette* – 24203/2287
486 *London Gazette* – 24842/2919
487 *London Gazette* – 25205/1124

Thomas Henry Kavanagh
9th November 1857 (VC No. 203)

Gazetted: 8th July 1859 22283/2629[488]

Rank and Unit: Assistant Commissioner in Oude – Bengal Civil Service

Citation

On the 8th of November, 1857. Mr. Kavanagh, then serving under the orders of Lieutenant-General Sir James Ottram, in Lucknow, volunteered on the dangerous duty of proceeding through the City to the Camp of the Commander-in-Chief, for the purpose of guiding the relieving Force to the beleaguered Garrison in the Residency,—a task which he performed with chivalrous gallantry and devotion.

Figure 181. Thomas Henry Kavanagh

Biography

Thomas was born on 15th July 1821 at Mulligar, Co. Westmeath in Ireland.

On 1st April 1849, Thomas joined the Indian Civil Service, moved out to India and served as part of the Punjab Commission.

At some stage, Thomas was married to Agnes Mary (née Courtney) and the couple would eventually have 14 children. Thomas moved to Lucknow, where he was performing the duties of a quite lowly clerk and his wife and children were spending the summer at Cawnpore. After a falling out with persons at Cawnpore, Agnes and the four oldest children (Baron, Blanche, Kathleen and Cecil),[489] joined her husband at Lucknow. Agnes was fortunate to leave Cawnpore when she did, soon afterwards the mutiny started and the town was besieged by mutineers. After a promise of safe conduct, General Wheeler evacuated the town on 27th July, however, the rebels captured 120 women and children who were subsequently massacred and thrown down a well at Bibigarh.

Following the fall of Cawnpore, the mutineers moved to besiege Lucknow which was defended by a small force commanded by Henry Montgomery Lawrence. After an unsuccessful attempt to attack and disperse the mutineers, the much reduced force and the civilian population consolidated their defence of the city in the Residency. Between the 23rd and 25th September 1857, a force led by Generals Outram and Havelock attempted to relieve Lucknow but were only successful in breaking through to reinforce the Residency on 27th September. Thomas volunteered

to serve with the Cornish miners of the 32nd Regiment of Foot, during the defence who were engaged in disrupting the mutineer's attempts to place mines and blow up the British defences. He was so enthusiastic in his efforts that he earned the nickname of "Assistant Field Engineer" from General Outram.

During early November 1857, a second relief force commanded by General Sir Colin Campbell approached the town and reached the Alum Bagh defence. Thomas realising that the first relief attempt failed because the relieving force lacked detailed knowledge of the mutineers defences volunteered to leave the town and direct the force into the town. It was for this action that Thomas was later awarded the Victoria Cross, the third of only five civilians to have been honoured with the award. On the night of 9th November, Thomas disguised as a native, left the town passing through a force of many thousand mutineers undetected and joined up with General Campbell. With the help of Thomas the force managed to fight through to the Residency by 17th November. On 23rd November, Sir Colin Campbell's force managed to successfully evacuate the Residency. For his service during the mutiny, Thomas was awarded the Indian Mutiny Medal with clasp for Defence of Lucknow.

Thomas was presented with his Victoria Cross Medal by Queen Victoria on 4th January 1860 at a ceremony held in Windsor Castle.

Thomas wrote a book about his exploits "How I Won the Victoria Cross", which was published in 1860.

In 1872, Thomas was appointed as Deputy Commissioner of Purtalgurh in Oudh province.

Thomas died on 13th November 1882, aged 61, at Gibraltar and was buried in the North Front Cemetery.

---

488 *London Gazette* – 22382/1705 corrects the date of deed originally quoted.
489 Cecil would die during the Siege and Agnes was wounded – *London Gazette* 22112/1406.

The whereabouts of Thomas's Victoria Cross Medal is unknown – thought to be held in a private collection, it was sold by Sotheby's in 1864 for £750.

Figure 181a. Grave of Thomas Henry Kavanagh

Hugh Henry Gough
12th November 1857 (VC No. 204)

Gazetted: 24th December 1858 22212/5516

Rank and Unit: Lieutenant – 1st Bengal European Light Horse

Citation

Lieutenant Gough, when in command of a party of Hodson's Horse, near Alum Bagh, on the 12th of November, 1857, particularly distinguished himself by his forward bearing in charging across a swamp, and capturing two guns, although defended by a vastly superior body of the enemy. On this occasion he had his horse wounded in two places, and his turban cut through by sword cuts, whilst engaged in combat with three Sepoys.

Lieutenant Gough also particularly distinguished himself, near Jellaiabad, Lucknow, on the 25th February, 1858, by showing a brilliant example to his Regiment, when ordered to charge the enemy's guns, and by his gallant and forward conduct, he enabled them to effect their object. On this occasion he engaged himself in a series of single combats, until at length he was disabled by a musket ball through the leg, while charging two Sepoys with fixed bayonets. Lieutenant Gough on this day had two horses killed under him, a shot through his helmet, and another through his scabbard, besides being severely wounded.

Biography

Hugh was born on 14th November 1833 at Calcutta in India, the third son of father George who worked for the British Colonial Service and mother Charlotte Margaret (née Beecher).

His older brother Charles John Stanley would also be awarded a Victoria Cross for deeds during the Indian Mutiny as would his uncle John Edmund Gough on 22nd April 1903 at Daratoleh in Somaliland, the three would also receive knighthoods.

Hugh was educated privately and at the Honourable East India Company College at Haileybury. Having graduated from Haileybury, Hugh enlisted in the army of the Honourable East India Company on 4th September 1853 and joined his regiment the 3rd Bengal Cavalry in India as a Cornet. On 9th August 1855, Hugh was promoted to the rank of Lieutenant.

At the outbreak of the mutiny, Hugh was stationed with his regiment at Meerut and his regiment was one of the first to mutiny after which they moved to Delhi where they were part of the force that captured the city.

Hugh joined up with the Delhi Field Relief Force and on 8th

Figure 182. Hugh Henry Gough

June was part of the British force which commenced the siege of Delhi. In July 1857, Hugh was appointed as Adjutant of Hodson's Horse, an irregular Light Cavalry unit which was part of the 1st Bengal European Light Horse. Hugh's first major action with his new regiment was at Rohtuk on 17th/18th August, when they followed a group of mounted mutineers which had left Delhi and engaged the enemy outside the villages of Samplah and Kurkowdah. During this action Hugh was wounded.

The regiment saw no further action until on 14th September, when following a five day artillery barrage the British launched an overwhelming attack which recaptured the city on 19th September.

On 27th September 1857, a force led by Brigadier Greathed, left the city to pursue rebels heading for Rohilkhand, Hugh commanded a detachment of 200 from Hodson's Horse. The force of mutineers was engaged and destroyed at the Battle of Bulandshahr on 28th September. As Delhi was now back in British hands, a field force was raised to go to the relief of Lucknow, on 14th October the force was joined by General Hope Grant who took over command from Brigadier Greathed. By the 12th of November 1857, the force was joined by Sir Colin Campbell who took over command and the assault on Lucknow began. It was during action at the Alum Bagh on 12th November, that Hugh performed the deeds for which he would later be awarded the Victoria Cross. Between 19th and 21st November 1857, the Residency at Lucknow was successfully evacuated by the force of Sir Colin Campbell. Hugh took part in the Battle of Futtehgur on 2nd January 1858 and was involved in the campaign to recapture Lucknow. It was at Jellalabad on 25th February 1858, that Hugh performed the deeds which formed the second entry

in his Victoria Cross citation, during this action he was severely wounded. A few days later, Hugh left Hodson's Horse to recover from his wounds. His actions during the recapture of Lucknow earned Hugh five Mentions in Despatches. For his service during the Mutiny, Hugh was awarded the Indian Mutiny Medal with clasps for Delhi, the Relief of Lucknow and Lucknow.

Hugh was presented with his Victoria Cross medal at a ceremony in India some time during 1859.

On 4th January 1861, Hugh was promoted to the rank of Captain and a day later received a brevet promotion to the rank of Major[490] and joined the 19th Hussars.

Hugh was married to Annie Maud Margaret (née Hill) at Simla on 8th September 1863, the couple would go on to have eight children; four daughters, Charlotte Elise, Mary Gertrude and two other daughters; four sons, Charles Hugh Henry born at Rawalpindi on 14th December 1878, Hugh Augustus Keppel and another son born in India and George Francis Bloomfield born in London on 22nd May 1880.

In August 1867, Hugh transferred to the 12th Bengal Cavalry and on 20th September took over command of the regiment. Almost immediately, Hugh took his command to Abyssinia for the war which took place between December 1867 and May 1868. The regiment was involved in the decisive battle of the war at Magdala on 10th April 1868. For his service during the war, Hugh was awarded the Abyssinian War Medal (1867–68).

On 14th August 1868, Hugh was appointed as an Ordinary Member, Third Class (Companion) of the Military Division of the Most Honourable Order of the Bath.[491]

Hugh received a brevet promotion to the rank of Lieutenant-Colonel on 30th March 1869.[492] On 4th September 1873, Hugh was promoted to the rank of major[493] and on 1st October 1877 received a brevet promotion to the rank of Colonel.[494]

In November 1878, Hugh with the 12th Cavalry was part of the Kuram Field Force commanded by Major General Sir Frederick Roberts which entered Afghanistan in the 2nd Anglo-Afghanistan war. Hugh was present at the Battle of Peiwar Kotal on 2nd December 1878 and the pursuit of the Afghans over the Shutargardan Pass into central Afghanistan. He was subsequently involved in operations in Khost. In 1879, Hugh was appointed as Commanding Officer of communications for the Kabul Field Force and in this role was present at the Battle of Charasiah on the 6th October 1879 and the occupation of Kabul

490   *London Gazette* – 22626/2551
491   *London Gazette* – 23412/4511
492   *London Gazette* – 23582/594
493   *London Gazette* – 24045/5938
494   *London Gazette* – 24664/7433

two days later. During the siege of the Sherpur Cantonment near Kabul from 15th to 22nd December 1879, Hugh, commanding the cavalry, was wounded. Hugh commanded the cavalry on Major General Sir Frederick Robert's famous march from Kabul to Kandahar which took place between 8th and 31st August 1880 and took part in the Battle of Kandahar on 1st September 1880. For his service during the war, Hugh was awarded the Afghanistan Medal (1878–80) with clasps for Peiwar Kotal, Charisiah, Kabul and Kandahar. He was also awarded the Kabul to Kandahar Star. This was Hugh's last period of active service.

On 22nd February 1881, Hugh was appointed as an Ordinary Member, 2nd Class (Knight Commander) of the Military Division of the Most Honourable Order of the Bath.[495]

On 6th June 1884, Hugh was given the command of a Brigade and promoted to the rank of Brigadier-General.[496] Hugh was promoted to the rank of Major General on 6th February 1887 and was given command of the Lahore Division of the Bengal

Army,[497] a position that he would hold until 1892. On 13th June 1891, Hugh was promoted to the rank of Lieutenant-General[498] and on 16th May 1894 he was promoted to the rank of General.[499]

Hugh was appointed as an Ordinary Member, 1st Class (Knight Grand Cross) of the Military Division of the Most Honourable Order of the Bath[500] on 20th May 1896.

On 1st April 1897, Hugh was placed on the unemployed supernumerary list,[501] ending 44 years of army service, the same year he published an account of his experiences during the Indian Mutiny in a book entitled "Old Memories".

In recognition of his outstanding military career, Hugh was appointed by Queen Victoria to the role of Keeper of the Crown Jewels on 1st February 1898[502] and he took up residence in the Tower of London. Hugh was confirmed in this role, now called Keeper of the Jewel House by King Edward VII on 23rd July 1901.[503]

Hugh died on 12th May 1909, at the age of 75, while living in St Thomas's Tower, in the Tower of London.

Hugh was buried with full military honours in Kensal Green Cemetery in London and two recipients of the Victoria Cross (Earl Roberts and Sir James Hills-Johnes) were amongst the pallbearers.

Hugh's Victoria Cross Medal is believed to be in a private collection.

Figure 182a. Grave of Hugh Henry Gough

495 *London Gazette* – 24944/975
496 *London Gazette* – 25387/3679

497 *London Gazette* – 25677/1002
498 *London Gazette* – 26178/3532
499 *London Gazette* – 26521/3383
500 *London Gazette* – 26741/3053
501 *London Gazette* – 26848/2369
502 *London Gazette* – 26935/668
503 *London Gazette* – 27336/4838

John Watson
14th November 1857 (VC No. 205)

Gazetted: 18th June 1858 22154/2960–1

Rank and Unit: Lieutenant – 1st Punjab Cavalry

Citation

Lieut. Watson, on the 14th November, with his own squadron, and that under Captain, then Lieutenant, Probyn, came upon a body of the rebel cavalry. The Ressaldar in command of them, a fine specimen of the Hindustani Mussulman, and backed up by some half dozen equally brave men, rode out to the front. Lieutenant Watson singled out this fine looking fellow, and attacked him. The Ressaldar presented his pistol at Lieutenant Watson's breast, at a yard's distance and fired; but, most providentially, without effect; the ball must, by accident, have previously fallen out. Lieutenant Watson ran the man through with his sword, and dismounted him; but the native officer, nothing daunted, drew his tulwar, and with his Sowar's renewed his attack upon Lieutenant Watson, who bravely defended himself until his own men joined in the melée, and utterly routed the party. In this rencontre Lieutenant Watson received a blow on the head from a tulwar, another on the left arm, which severed his chain gauntlet glove, a tulwar cut on his right arm, which fortunately only divided the sleeve of the jacket, but disabled the arm for some time; a bullet also passed through his coat, and he received a blow on his leg, which lamed him for some days afterwards.

(Despatch from Major-General James Hope Grant, K.C.B., dated 10th January, 1858.)

Biography

John was born on 6th September 1829 at Chigwell Row in Essex to father William George and mother Harriet (née Atkins).

On 3rd February 1848, at the age of 18, John enlisted in the Bombay Army and was commissioned as an Ensign and posted to the Bengal Fusiliers serving in India.

Not long after joining his regiment, John was involved in his first active service when he saw action in the 2nd Anglo-Sikh War or Punjab Campaign. He was involved in the siege and capture of Multan between 7th September 1848 and 22nd January 1849 and carried the Regimental Colours through the breach when the city was taken. On 21st February 1849, as part of the force commanded by Lord Gough, John took part in the Battle of Goojerat and the subsequent occupation of Peshawar. For his service

Figure 183. John Watson

during the war, John was awarded the Punjab Medal with clasps for Mooltan and Goojerat.

Soon after returning to India, after the war, John was transferred to the 28th Bombay Infantry and after a short stay was transferred to the 1st Baluchis where he had an equally short stay.

John's career as a cavalry officer began when he was transferred to the 1st Punjab Cavalry and probably at the time he was promoted to Lieutenant on 27th July 1852 he was given the role of adjutant to the regiment.

In January 1857, John saw action again, when as part of the Punjab Field Force commanded by Brigadier Neville Chamberlain he was involved in the Bozdar Campaign and during March helped in the forcing of the Khan Bund Pass which effectively ended the opposition.

Following the outbreak of mutiny at Meerut and the subsequent capture of Delhi by the mutineers, Sir John Lawrence sent a large contingent of troops from the Punjab to Delhi to assist with its relief and recapture, John's regiment was part of this force. After Delhi was successfully recaptured on 19th September 1857, John, as part of the force commanded by Brigadier Greathed, fought at the Battle of Bulandshahr on 28th September. John was now assigned to the Lucknow Relief force, commanded by Brigadier General Hope Grant and on the way to Lucknow fought in the Battle of Agra on 10th October. It was on 14th November 1857, during the fighting to relieve the Residency at Lucknow, that John performed the deeds for which he would later be awarded the Victoria Cross, during the action at Lucknow he was wounded three times. Following the evacuation of the Residency on 19th November, John was part of the force of Sir Colin Campbell sent to the Relief of Cawnpore and following the siege to part in the Battle of Cawnpore on 6th December 1857 which recaptured the city. John was also part of Sir Colin Campbell's force when it recaptured Lucknow on 21st March 1858. For his service during the mutiny, John was awarded the Indian Mutiny Medal with clasps for Delhi, Relief of Lucknow and Lucknow.

While recovering from his wounds, John together with Lieutenant Cattley raised a regiment of irregular cavalry at Lahore in 1858. Originally designated as the 4th Sikh Irregular Cavalry it would be designated as the 13th Bengal Cavalry in 1861 and in 1904 became the 13tg Duke of Connaught's Lancers (Watson's Horse). Although John was appointed as commandant of the regiment, he would not actually join it until 1861.

John was presented with his Victoria Cross Medal by Queen Victoria on 8th June 1859 at an investiture held at Buckingham Palace.

Sometime in 1860, John was married to Eliza Jesser (née Davis) and the couple would go on to have three sons, each of which would have a distinguished career in the army like their father; William Arthur who was born in Delhi on 25th September 1860, Harry Davis also born in India on 18th July 1866 and John Hugh. William attained the rank of Major General in the Central India Horse, was knighted and served with distinction in North Africa during World War I; he also married Margurite Audrey Jones the daughter of Victoria Cross recipient Lieutenant-Colonel Alfred Stowell Jones. Harry also attained the rank of Major General and also received a knighthood. John's 3rd son, also called John reached the rank of Major and served in the 13th Lancers, the regiment created by his father in 1858.

On 18th February 1861, John was promoted to the rank of Captain and joined his regiment the 13th Bengal Lancers. On the following day, John received a brevet promotion to the rank of Major.[504]

On 15th May 1863, John was appointed as an Ordinary Member 3rd Class (Companion) of the Military Division of the Most Honourable Order of the Bath.[505]

In October 1863, John was part of the Eusufzai Field Force commanded by Brigadier General Neville Chamberlain in the Umbeyla Campaign which was sent to the North West Frontier region of India to quell border conflicts with the Pashtun and Yusufzai tribes. For his service during this campaign, John was awarded the India General Service Medal (1854–95) with clasp for North West Frontier.

On 3rd February 1868, John was promoted to the rank of Major.[506] John received a brevet promotion to the rank of Lieutenant-Colonel on 22nd July 1869[507] and during the year he performed the role of Political Agent at Gwalior. John received a

brevet promotion to the rank of Colonel on 28th May 1870 and was appointed as Aide de Camp to Queen Victoria in Bengal.[508] In 1871, John was given command of the Central India Horse. And during 1873 was promoted to the rank of Colonel. On 3rd February 1874, John was promoted to the rank of Lieutenant- Colonel[509] and in 1877 served as Assistant Governor General of Central India. John was awarded the Empress of India Medal (1877).

Following the secret Cyprus Convention of 4th June 1878, by which the Ottoman Empire granted Great Britain control over the island, John commanded the cavalry brigade of the British force sent to occupy Cyprus.

During 1879 to 1880, John took part in the 2nd Anglo-Afghan war. During the first phase of the war he commanded the Punjab Chiefs Contingent and during the 2nd phase commanded the cavalry in the Kurram Field Force. For his service during the war, John was awarded the Afghanistan Medal (1878–1880) and received the thanks of both Houses of Parliament.

On 1st July 1881, John was promoted to the rank of Major-General[510] and given command of a division on the North West Frontier, he was also appointed as the Governor-General's agent at Baroda a position that he would hold until 1886.

John was appointed as an Ordinary Member 2nd Class (Knight Commander) of the Military Division of the Most Honourable Order of the Bath on 29th May 1886.[511]

On 14th January 1887, John was placed on the Unemployed Supernumerary List with the rank of Lieutenant-General.[512] While still on the Unemployed Supernumerary List, John was promoted to the rank of General on 1st March 1891.[513]

On 26th June 1902, John was appointed as an Ordinary Member 1st Class (Knight Grand Cross) of the Military Division of the Most Honourable Order of the Bath.[514]

John was appointed as Honorary Colonel of the Duke of Connaught's Lancers (Watson's Horse) on 13th May 1904.[515]

At some time around 1907, John returned to England and took up residence at North Court in Finchampstead, Berkshire where for the next 13 years he served as Rectors Warden at the local church of St James's.

John died on 23rd January 1919, at the age of 89, at his home at North Court and was buried in St James's Churchyard, Finchampstead.

504 *London Gazette* – 22724/1939
505 *London Gazette* – 22736/2570
506 *London Gazette* – 23392/3530
507 *London Gazette* – 23582/594

508 *London Gazette* – 23619/2746
509 *London Gazette* – 24091/2352
510 *London Gazette* – 25034/5402
511 *London Gazette* – 25592/2633
512 *London Gazette* – 25672/726
513 *London Gazette* – 26144/1482
514 *London Gazette* – 27448/4190
515 *London Gazette* – 27672/3089

John's Victoria Cross Medal is on public display at the Imperial War Museum in London as part of the Lord Ashcroft collection.

Figure 183a. Grave of John Watson

Hastings Edward Harington
14th November 1857 (VC No. 206)

Gazetted: 24th December 1858 22212/5516

Rank and Unit: Lieutenant – Bengal Artillery

Citation
Elected respectively, under the 13th clause of the Royal Warrant of the 29th of January, 1856, by the Officers and non-commissioned officers generally, and by the private soldiers of each troop or battery, for conspicuous gallantry at the relief of Lucknow, from the 14th to the 22nd of November, 1857.

Biography
Hastings was born on 9th November 1832 at Hinton Parva in Wiltshire, his father John was the local Reverend.

Hastings was educated at Reading School until 1849 when he completed his education at the Honourable East India Company Military Academy at Addiscombe in Surrey. On graduating from Addiscombe, Hastings was commissioned as a 2nd Lieutenant in the Bengal Artillery on 12th June 1852 and joined his regiment in Peshawar in India.

After his initial posting, Hastings was transferred to the post at Sealkote and was on leave in Cashmere when he heard the

Figure 184. Hastings Edward Harington

news regarding the outbreak of mutiny. On receiving the news, Hastings rushed back to his regiment in time to join the column of General Nicholson which had been deployed to quell the Sealkote mutineers. The rebels were successfully engaged at Trimmoo Ghat on 9th July 1857, where Hastings was wounded in the right foot. Hastings was involved in the siege of Delhi, through to its recapture on 21st September following which he joined up with the force of General Greathed going to the relief of Lucknow. He took part in the Battle of Bulandshahr on 28th September and now with the force commanded by General Sir Hope Grant was also present at the Battle of Agra on 10th October 1857. It was during the 2nd relief of Lucknow, between 14th and 22nd November 1857, that Hastings performed the deeds for which he would later be awarded the Victoria Cross. He was elected for the award by his fellow officers, under rule 13 of the originating Victoria Cross Warrant. On 20th November, during the above action, Hastings was seriously wounded.

Hastings was transferred to the Royal Horse Artillery and promoted to the rank of Lieutenant.

As part of the force of Sir Colin Campbell, Hastings was involved in the relief and recapture of Cawnpore on 6th December and the recapture of Lucknow on 21st March 1858, during this action he was wounded by a musket ball in the right thigh. On 14th April 1858, during action to take Fort Rooya in Oude, Hastings was seriously wounded in the back and left thigh and was moved to convalesce in the Himalayas. For his service during the mutiny, Hastings was awarded the Indian Mutiny Medal with clasps for Delhi, Relief of Lucknow and Lucknow.

Failing to recover from the bullet which remained in his back, Hastings returned to England in January 1859 where he underwent an operation to remove the bullet.

On 8th June 1859, Hastings was presented with his Victoria Cross Medal by Queen Victoria at an investiture held in Buckingham Palace.

Having recovered his health following his operation, Hastings returned to India on board *SS Colombo* and resumed his duties during October 1860. Soon after his arrival in India, Hastings was involved in the Sikkim Expedition to Tibet.

In June 1861, Hastings was promoted to the rank of 2nd Captain and appointed as adjutant of the 6th Battalion Bengal Artillery based in Agra.

It was in Agra on 20th July 1861 that Hastings died from cholera and was buried in Agra Cemetery.

The location of Hastings Victoria Cross Medal is unknown, believed to have been stolen.

Edward Jennings
14th November 1857 (VC No. 207)

Gazetted: 24th December 1858 22212/5516

Rank and Unit: Rough-Rider – Bengal Artillery

Citation

Elected respectively, under the 13th clause of the Royal Warrant of the 29th of January, 1856, by the Officers and non-commissioned officers generally, and by the private soldiers of each troop or battery, for conspicuous gallantry at the relief of Lucknow, from the 14th to the 22nd of November, 1857.

Biography

Edward was born during 1815[516] at Ballinrode, Co Mayo in Ireland, however at a young age he moved to the North-East of England and lived in North Shields.

Very little is known of his army career or life story other than that told by his medals.

It is probable that Edward enlisted in the army of the Honourable East India Company at some time around his 18th birthday in 1833 and he would have joined up with his regiment, the Bengal Artillery, in India soon afterwards.

Edward's first active service was during the 1st Anglo-Afghan War of 1839 to 1842 (also known as Auckland's Folly). He took part in the storming of Fort Guznee which took place between 12th and 23rd July 1839 and culminated in the Battle of Ghazni. For his service during the war, Edward was awarded the Ghuznee Medal (1839).[517]

From 1845 to 1846, Edward took part in the 1st Anglo-Sikh war and was involved in the Battle of Aliwal which took place on 28th January 1846. For his service in this war, Edward was awarded the Sutlej Medal (1845–46) inscribed on the rear with Aliwal.

On 2nd September 1850, Edward was married to Jane (née Morris) at Gateshead, it is not known whether the couple had any children.

At the outbreak of the mutiny, Edward was probably stationed at Sealkote and would have been part of the column commanded by General Nicholson which defeated the Sealkote mutineers at Trimmoo Ghat on 9th July 1857. Edward was involved in the

---

516 There is some confusion over his year of birth, with some sources stating 1820, however the 1881 census gives his age as 67 so I have accepted 1815 as year of birth.

517 This was only the second campaign medal to be awarded to all members of the army regardless of rank, the first was the Waterloo Medal.

Figure 185. Edward Jennings

girl; it is presumed that his first wife had died while in India. The couple would have five children; Margaret born on 12th July 1866 at Ballinrode, Ireland; Edward born during 1868 in Ireland; Bridget born in Ireland during 1871; Thomas born in North Shields during 1874 and Catherine born in North Shields in 1877.

From the birth place of his children, it appears that Edward returned to North Shields sometime between 1871 and 1874 and was working as a scavenger (road sweeper) for North Shields Council.

Edward died on 10th May 1889, aged 74, while living at 1 King George Stairs, North Shields in Northumberland and was buried in a pauper's grave in Preston Cemetery, North Shields.

Edward's Victoria Cross Medal is on public display at the Royal Artillery Museum in Woolwich, part of the Troop F collection.

Figure 185a. Grave of Edward Jennings

siege of Delhi, through to its recapture on 21st September following which he joined up with the force of General Greathed going to the relief of Lucknow. He took part in the Battle of Bulandshahr on 28th September and now with the force commanded by General Sir Hope Grant was also present at the Battle of Agra on 10th October 1857. It was during the 2nd relief of Lucknow, between 14th and 22nd November 1857, that Edward performed the deeds for which he would later be awarded the Victoria Cross. He was elected for the award by his fellow NCOs, under rule 13 of the originating Victoria Cross Warrant. During the action, Edward had saved the life of an officer and was offered a commission, however, being illiterate he chose not to accept the offer. The officer rewarded Edward with a payment of 1,000 rupees. As part of the force of Sir Colin Campbell, Edward was involved in the relief and recapture of Cawnpore on 6th December and the recapture of Lucknow on 21st March 1858. After Lucknow, Edward would have taken part in the campaign in the province of Oudh. For his service during the mutiny, Edward was awarded the Indian Mutiny Medal with clasps for Delhi, Relief of Lucknow and Lucknow.

In 1859, Edward after more than 25 years service spent in India, was discharged from the army to pension and returned to the United Kingdom.

Edward crossed paths with his Victoria Cross Medal when he returned to the United Kingdom, he was scheduled to be presented with his medal by Queen Victoria at the investiture at Windsor Castle on 9th October 1860, however, the medal did not arrive from India in time for the ceremony – it is assumed that the medal was sent to Edward at a later date by registered post.

It would appear that at some stage, Edward returned to his home town in Ireland and was remarried to Catherine, a local

Thomas Laughnan
14th November 1857 (VC No. 208)

Gazetted: 24th December 1858 22212/5516

Rank and Unit: Gunner – Bengal Artillery

Citation

Elected respectively, under the 13th clause of the Royal Warrant of the 29th of January, 1856, by the Officers and non-commissioned officers generally, and by the private soldiers of each troop or battery, for conspicuous gallantry at the relief of Lucknow, from the 14th to the 22nd of November, 1857.

Biography

Unfortunately very little is known regarding Thomas's life story.

Thomas was born at Kilmadaugh, Gort, Co Kildare in Ireland during August 1824.

At some stage he enlisted in the army of the Honourable East India Company and was assigned to the Bengal Artillery as a Gunner.

It was during the 2nd Relief of Lucknow between 14th and 22nd November 1857, that Thomas performed the deeds for which he was later awarded the Victoria Cross, having been nominated for the award under rule 13 by his peers in the regiment. For his service during the mutiny, Thomas was awarded the Indian Mutiny Medal with clasp for Relief of Lucknow.

Thomas was presented with his Victoria Cross Medal some time during 1859 while serving in India.

Thomas died on 23rd July 1864, just before his fortieth birthday in Co Galway, Ireland. His place of burial is unknown.

Thomas's Victoria Cross Medal is on public display at the Royal Artillery Museum in Woolwich, London.

Figure 186a. Memorial at Royal Artillery Museum, Woolwich

Hugh McInnes
14th November 1857 (VC No. 209)

Gazetted: 24th December 1858 22212/5516

Rank and Unit: Gunner – Bengal Artillery

Citation

Elected respectively, under the 13th clause of the Royal Warrant of the 29th of January, 1856, by the Officers and non-commissioned officers generally, and by the private soldiers of each troop or battery, for conspicuous gallantry at the relief of Lucknow, from the 14th to the 22nd of November, 1857.

Biography

Hugh was born on 16th January 1816[518] in Anderson, Glasgow to father Donald (or Daniel) and Agnes (née McKinnon). Hugh was one of four children with an older sister Flora, an older brother Archibald and a younger brother Angus.

At some stage Hugh enlisted in the army of the Honourable East India Company and was assigned to the Bengal Artillery as a Gunner. It was during the 2nd Relief of Lucknow between

Figure 187a. Memorial to Glaswegians awarded the Victoria Cross

---

518 Various dates of birth are cited in the sources including October 1815 and October 1835.

14th and 22nd November 1857, that Hugh performed the deeds for which he was later awarded the Victoria Cross, having been nominated for the award under rule 13 by his peers in the regiment. For his service during the mutiny, Hugh was awarded the Indian Mutiny Medal with clasp for Relief of Lucknow.

Hugh was presented with his Victoria Cross Medal some time during 1859 while serving in India.

After his service in India, Hugh returned to Glasgow where he worked as an engineering labourer.

On 8th March 1876, Hugh was married to Helen (née Wilson) a widow at St Margaret's Chapel, Kinning Park, Glasgow.

Hugh died at the age of 63 on 7th December 1879, at 61 Cathcart Street, Kinning Park in Glasgow and was buried two days later in a pauper's grave in St Peter's Cemetery, Dalbeth, Glasgow.

The location of Hugh's Victoria Cross Medal is unknown.

James Park
14th November 1857 (VC No. 210)

Gazetted: 24th December 1858 22212/5516

Rank and Unit: Gunner – Bengal Artillery

Citation

Elected respectively, under the 13th clause of the Royal Warrant of the 29th of January, 1856, by the Officers and non-commissioned officers generally, and by the private soldiers of each troop or battery, for conspicuous gallantry at the relief of Lucknow, from the 14th to the 22nd of November, 1857.

Biography

James was born during January 1835 in Barony, Glasgow.

At some stage James enlisted in the army of the Honourable East India Company and joined his regiment the Bengal Artillery as a gunner in India.

At the outbreak of the mutiny, James was probably stationed at Sealkote and would have been part of the column commanded by General Nicholson which defeated the Sealkote mutineers at Trimmoo Ghat on 9th July 1857. James was involved in the siege of Delhi, through to its recapture on 21st September following which he joined up with the force of General Greathed going

Figure 188a. Memorial to Glaswegians awarded the Victoria Cross

to the relief of Lucknow. He took part in the Battle of Buland-shahr on 28th September and now with the force commanded by General Sir Hope Grant was also present at the Battle of Agra on 10th October 1857. It was during the 2nd relief of Lucknow, between 14th and 22nd November 1857, that James performed the deeds for which he would later be awarded the Victoria Cross. He was elected for the award by his fellow gunners, under rule 13 of the originating Victoria Cross Warrant. As part of the force of Sir Colin Campbell, James was involved in the relief and recapture of Cawnpore on 6th December and the recapture of Lucknow on 21st March 1858. Soon after the relief of Lucknow, on 14th June 1858 during continued operations against the mutineers, James was killed in action near Lucknow. The location of where he was buried is unknown. For his service during the mutiny, James was awarded the Indian Mutiny Medal with clasps for Delhi, Relief of Lucknow and Lucknow.

James was never presented with his Victoria Cross Medal, which is now believed to be in the hands of a private collector.

William George Drummond Steuart (Stewart) 16th November 1857 (VC No. 211)

Gazetted: 24th December 1858 22212/5514

Rank and Unit: Captain – 93rd Regiment

Citation

For distinguished personal gallantry at Lucknow, on the 16th November, 1857, in leading an attack upon and capturing two guns, by which the position of the mess house was secured.

Elected by the Officers of the Regiment.

Biography

William, known for most of his life as George, was born during February 1831 at Grantully in Perthshire, the only son of Captain Sir William Drummond Stewart 19th Laird of Grantully and 7th Baronet of Murthly and his wife Maria Christina (née Battersby).

On 2nd June 1848, George began his army career when he purchased a commission as Ensign in the 93rd Regiment of Foot.[519] George joined with his regiment at Stirling Castle during August 1848, when they returned to Scotland from a tour in Canada. During the summer of 1849 the regiment performed the duties of Honour Guard to Queen Victoria and on 5th April 1850 were transferred to Edinburgh castle on garrison duties. On 21st February 1852, George was promoted to the rank of Lieutenant.[520]

On 27th February 1854, George and the regiment left Edin-burgh for Plymouth where the set sail for the Crimea. After landing on the Crimean peninsula on 14th September 1854, as part of the allied Expeditionary Force, George was involved in the battle of Alma which took place on 20th September. After their march south towards Sevastopol, the regiment took part in the Battle of Balaklava on 25th October where their action against the charge of Russian cavalry became known as the 'Thin Red Line'. George also served in the Siege of Sevastopol spending the winter of 1854 to 55 in the trenches, where he was wounded. On 29th December 1854, George was promoted to the rank of Captain.[521] On 16th June 1856, George left the Crimea with his regiment and returned to England where they arrived at Portsmouth on 15th July and proceeded to the new camp at Aldershot. For his service during the war, George was awarded

---

519 *London Gazette* – 20863/2089
520 *London Gazette* – 21298/698
521 *London Gazette* – 21645/4259

the Crimean Medal with clasps for Alma, Balaclava and Sevastopol. He was also awarded the Turkish Crimean Medal and was appointed as a member 5th class of the Order of the Medjidie by the Ottoman Emperor.

On 6th March 1857, the regiment received orders to make ready for a deployment to China and in two detachments left Plymouth on 1st June and Gosport on 16th June bound for China. When the regiment arrived at the Cape Colony, they received the news of the mutiny in India and with new orders were immediately despatched to India, arriving at Calcutta on 20th September 1857.

On arrival in India, the regiment became part of the Force commanded by Sir Colin Campbell and by 31st October 1857 had reach Cawnpore where a force was being assembled to go to the relief of Lucknow. On 14th November, George was involved in the start of the 2nd Relief of Lucknow and on 16th November 1857 during the storming of the Secundra Bagh he performed the deeds for which he would later be awarded the Victoria Cross, having been selected for the award by a ballot of the officers of the regiment under rule 13 of the originating warrant. On the same day, the 93rd were involved in the taking of the Shah Nujeef fortification where a regimental flag was raised as a signal to the beleaguered garrison in the Residency. Between the 18th and 22nd November, the Residency was evacuated and George with the 93rd helped cover the retreat. From 29th November 1857 until 6th December 1857, George and the 93rd were involved in the action which culminated in the successful Battle of Cawnpore.

On 1st February 1858, as part of the force of Sir Colin Campbell, the advance towards Lucknow began afresh and on 1st March the battle to retake Lucknow began. On the 9th March, the 93rd stormed the Martinière defences and on 11th March stormed the Kaiser Baugh defences following which fighting continued until Lucknow fell to the British on 21st March 1858. After a short rest, George and the 93rd joined the force of Brigadier Adrian Hope in operations in Rohilkhand on 7th April and on 20th April took part in the Battle of Alligunge. George took part in further battles at Bareilly on 5th May 1858 and Russoolpore on 26th October before the regiment was assigned to the force of General Troup which was directed to quell the rebels in the Oudh region during the early part of 1859. For his service during the mutiny, George was awarded the Indian Mutiny Medal with clasps for Relief of Lucknow and Lucknow.

On 6th May 1859, George purchased a commission as Major, however, as this was on the unattached list this effectively ended his military career.[522]

George was presented with his Victoria Cross Medal on 6th December 1859 by Sir Robert Garrett at a ceremony held at Umbeyla in Peshawar, India.

George returned to England in 1860 and resided at the family home in Hythe, Kent where on 19th October 1868, while performing a sword swallowing trick, things went tragically wrong and he died from internal injuries a week later on 26th October 1868 at the age of 37.

George was buried in the family vault, next to his mother at St Mary's Church in Grantully.

The location of George's Victoria Cross Medal is unknown, believed to have been lost by George.

Figure 189a. Grave of William George Drummond Steuart

---

522 *London Gazette* – 22260/1870

Francis David Millet Brown
16th November 1857 (VC No. 212)

Gazetted: 17th February 1860 22357/557

Rank and Unit: Lieutenant – 1st European Bengal Fusiliers

Citation

For great gallantry at Narrioul, on the 16th November, 1857, in having, at the imminent risk of his own life, rushed to the assistance of a wounded soldier of the 1st European Bengal Fusiliers, whom he carried off, under a very heavy fire from the enemy, whose cavalry were within forty or fifty yards of him at the time.

Figure 190. Francis David Millet Brown

Biography

Francis was born on 7th August 1837 at Bhagalpur in India, the 2nd son of father George Francis a Commissioner of Revenue and Circuit of Bhagalpur in the Bengal Civil Service and mother Catherine Jemima (née Gane). Francis had two sisters; Lucy and Fanny and three brothers, George, George Peploe and Horace.

Francis was educated at Grosvenor College in Bath from 1852 until 1854 and privately by Rev Brisco Morland Gane (his maternal grandfather?).

On 8th December 1855, just after his 18th birthday, Francis enlisted in the army of the Honourable East India Company and was commissioned as an Ensign in the 11th Bengal Native Infantry. Francis joined his regiment at Cawnpore in India and on 7th March 1856 was transferred to the 1st European Bengal Fusiliers and promoted to the rank of 2nd Lieutenant.

In March 1857, Francis moved with his regiment to Dugshai where they were stationed when the mutiny broke out at Meerut.

On 13th May, the regiment received orders to proceed to Umballa where they arrived on 15th May and were assigned to the 1st Brigade under the command of Brigadier Showers. On 7th June 1857, Francis was promoted to the rank of Lieutenant and the same day the regiment was ordered to proceed to Delhi, and on 8th June they were involved in the Battle of Badli-ki-Serai.

From the middle of June, the regiment took up position on the 'Ridge' overlooking Delhi helping to enforce the siege. During the siege, the regiment took part in several actions, the most notable being the Battle of Nuzzufghur on 25th August 1857 where they were part of a flying column commanded by General Nicholson. On 14th September 1857, Francis and his regiment were part of the force of Brigadier-General Nicholson involved in the final assault and the recapture of Delhi which was achieved on 20th September. Francis left Delhi on 10th November as part of a flying column commanded by Colonel Gerrard sent to

pursue the retreating mutineers. On 16th November 1857, the mutineers were engaged in the Battle of Narnoul and during the action Francis performed the deeds for which he would later be awarded the Victoria Cross. The column returned to Delhi on 29th November and on the following day, as part of a force commanded by Colonel Thomas Seaton, was ordered to the relief of Lucknow. On the way to Lucknow, Francis and the regiment were involved in the Battle of Gungeree on 14th December, the Battle of Puttialee on 17th December and the Battle of Mynpoorie on 27th December. As part of Sir Colin Campbell's force, Francis was involved in the siege and recapture of Lucknow on 21st March 1858.

Francis was the officer in charge of a troop of Hodson's Horse during the regiment's last action of the mutiny which took place at Sahadit on 30th October 1858.

For his service during the mutiny, Francis was awarded the Indian Mutiny Medal with clasps for Delhi and Lucknow.

In March 1859, the regiment returned to their base at Dugshai where they arrived on 18th April after two years of continuous campaigning.

Francis was presented to Queen Victoria at a Levee held at St James's Palace on 24th April 1860.

Francis was presented with his Victoria Cross Medal during December 1860 by Sir Hugh Rose, Commander in Chief of forces in India at Multan.

On 2nd May 1861, following a proclamation by Queen Victoria which disbanded the armies of the Honourable East India Company, Francis was transferred as a Lieutenant into the 101st Royal Bengal Fusiliers.

From November to December 1863, Francis was part of the Ensufyze Field Force commanded by Sir Neville Chamberlain involved in the Umbeyla Campaign on the North West frontier of India and took part in the forcing of the Umbeyla Pass. On 20th December 1863, the regiment returned to their headquarters at Dugshai. For his service during the campaign, Francis was awarded the India General Service Medal (1854–95) with clasp for Umbeyla.

From 17th January 1864, Francis attended Thomason's Civil Engineering College at Roorkee where on 23rd August 1864 he was promoted to the rank of Captain.[523] After graduating from Thomason College, Francis was transferred to the Bengal Staff Corps on 14th September 1865 and assigned as assistant Instructor of Survey to the Public Works Department of the North West Frontier Province. In 1868, Francis was appointed as assistant Principle of the Thomason Civil Engineering College in Roorkee.

On 13th February 1869, Francis began an extended period of leave, which would extend to almost a year, and returned to England. Just before his return to India on 29th January 1871, Francis was married to Jessie Rhind (née Russell) on 27th December 1870 at St Luke's Church in Cheltenham. The couple would go on to have two sons; Frank Russell born on 24th March 1872 and Claude Russell born on 11th April 1873. Both of the children were born in India, both joined the army and served in the South African War, Frank was killed in action at Bloemfontein on 4th April 1900 while Claude was seriously wounded. Claude continued his army career with the Royal Engineers during World War I.

In March 1871, Francis was promoted to the rank of Executive Engineer 4th Grade in the North West Frontier Province, then to 3rd Grade in September 1872 when he was posted to Allahabad and finally to 2nd Grade on 1st March 1874 when he was transferred to Meerut. On 7th December 1875, Francis was promoted to the rank of Major and transferred back to a position on the staff of the Bengal Army.

From 1st January 1880 until 22nd December 1881, Francis who by now was a widower was on extended leave in England; it was probably during this stay in England that he was remarried to Jessie Doris (née Childs). The couple would go on to have five children; a daughter Jessie Vera Lawford born in 1889 and four sons who all made a career in the army; Eric Carmichael who attained the rank of Lieutenant-Colonel, Wynyard Keith born in 1888 who was a Captain when he was killed in action at Gallipoli on 4th June 1915 during World War I, Vincent Christopher who was a colonel in the Royal Marines when he was killed in action in Belgium on 28th May 1940 during World War II and Reginald Llewellyn who was born on 23rd July 1895 and attained the rank of Major-General.

On 8th December 1881, just before his return to India, Francis was promoted to the rank of Lieutenant Colonel and took up a position within the Bengal Staff Corps.[524] Francis was promoted to the rank of Colonel on 8th December 1885.[525] In 1891, Francis was appointed as the Principle of the Thomason Civil Engineering College at Roorkee, a position that he would hold until August 1892, when he was transferred back to a Military Depot. On 9th August 1894, Francis was transferred to the Unemployed Supernumerary List,[526] ending his military career of nearly forty years.

After his retirement, Francis returned to England and on 21st November 1895 died at the age of 58 while residing at Sandown on the Isle of Wight.

After a service in Winchester Cathedral, Francis was buried in West Hill Cemetery, Winchester on 25th November 1895.

Francis's Victoria Cross Medal was stolen in 1900 from Rugby and was never recovered, however, a medal which is probably a replacement, is held by Wellington College.

Figure 190a. Grave of Francis David Millet Brown

523 *London Gazette* – 22887/4125

524 *London Gazette* – 25075/771
525 *London Gazette* – 25561/851
526 *London Gazette* – 26546/5005

Alfred Kirke Ffrench
16th November 1857 (VC No. 213)

Gazetted: 24th December 1858 22212/5513

Rank and Unit: Lieutenant – 53rd Regiment of Foot

Citation

For conspicuous bravery on the 16th of November, 1857, at the taking of the Secundra Bagh, Lucknow, when in command of the Grenadier Company, being one of the first to enter the building. His conduct was highly praised by the whole Company.

Elected by the Officers of the Regiment.

Figure 191. Alfred Kirke Ffrench

Biography

Alfred was born on 25th February 1835 in Meerut, India; his father was Lieutenant-Colonel Thomas FFrench of the 53rd Regiment of Foot.

Alfred was privately educated and attended the Royal Military College at Sandhurst in Camberley, following his graduation he purchase a commission as Ensign on 10th February 1854[527] in his father's regiment the 53rd Regiment of Foot. His brother, Thomas Charles was also an officer in the same regiment. Alfred joined his regiment in India at Dugshai during June 1854. On 21st October 1855, Alfred was promoted to the rank of Lieutenant.[528]

At the start of the mutiny, Alfred and his regiment were based in Calcutta and were assigned to the force of Sir Colin Campbell that was directed to go to the relief of Lucknow. Alfred was part of the force which attacked Lucknow during November 1857, in an attempt to relieve the garrison besieged within the Residency. It was on 16th November during the taking of the Secundra Bagh that Alfred performed the deeds for which he would later be awarded with the Victoria Cross, having been selected for the award by a ballot of the officers under rule 13 of the originating warrant. On 6th December 1857, Alfred was present at the battle of Cawnpore and from 1st March 1858 until 21st March was involved in the operation which led to the recapture of Lucknow. Following Lucknow, Alfred was involved in operations to subdue the mutineers in the province of Oudh. For his service during the mutiny, Alfred was awarded the Indian Mutiny Medal with clasps for Relief of Lucknow and Lucknow. The details regarding any presentation of his Victoria Cross Medal are Unknown.

In April 1860, Alfred left India and was posted with his regiment to garrison duties in Canada during which, on 3rd September 1863 he received a promotion to the rank of Captain.[529]

In May 1869, Alfred and his regiment were posted to garrison duties in Bermuda. During his stay in Bermuda, Alfred was taken ill and returned to England on a leave of absence where he took up residence at "The Manor House" in Chiswick, London.

Alfred died at the family home, 41 Grove Place, Brompton on 28th December 1872 at the age of 37 and was buried in the family plot at Brompton Cemetery on 4th January 1873.

Figure 191a. Grave of Alfred Kirke Ffrench

---

527 *London Gazette* – 21520/387
528 *London Gazette* – 21832/4865

---

529 *London Gazette* – 22773/4607

Alfred's retirement from the army, with the award of full value for his commission, was announced on 1st January 1873,[530] after his death.

Alfred's Victoria Cross Medal is on public display at the King's Shropshire Light Infantry Museum, Shrewsbury, Shropshire.

Nowell Salmon
16th November 1857 (VC No. 214)

Gazetted: 24th December 1858 22212/5512

Rank and Unit: Lieutenant – Royal Navy (Naval Brigade)

Citation

For conspicuous gallantry at Lucknow, on the 16th of November, 1857, in climbing up a tree, touching the angle of the Shah Nujjiff, to reply to the fire of the enemy, for which most dangerous service, the late Captain Peel, K.C.B., had called for volunteers.

Biography

Nowell was born on 20th February 1835 at the Vicarage, Swarraton in Hampshire where his father Henry was the rector, his mother Emily (née Nowell) was the daughter of a Vice-Admiral in the Navy.

From August 1846 until Easter 1847, Nowell was educated at Marlborough.

On 10th May 1847, only weeks after his 12th birthday, Nowell enlisted as a Cadet (Volunteer 1st Class) in the Royal Navy. From July 1851 until February 1854, Nowell served on board *HMS Thetis* under the command of Captain Augustus Leopold Kuper, on operations off the south east coast of America and in the Pacific. On 1st March 1854, Nowell was promoted to the rank of Mate and on 18th March was assigned to *HMS James Watt*, under the command of Captain George Augustus Elliot and served in the Baltic Campaign during the Crimean War. For his service during the War, Nowell was awarded the Baltic Medal (1854–55).

Figure 192. Nowell Salmon

On 4th February 1856, Nowell arrived in Devonport from the Baltic having been promoted to the rank of Lieutenant on 5th January 1856. Nowell took command of the newly launched gunboat *HMS Ant* on 7th March 1856 with the rank of Lieutenant Commander.

On 16th September 1856, Nowell was assigned to *HMS Shannon*, under the command of Captain William Peel. On board *HMS Shannon*, Nowell set sail for China on 17th March 1857 and after making port at Cape Town on 7th May arrived off Singapore on 11th June where the ship was joined by Lord Elgin and his staff. On 23rd June they set sail for Hong Kong where they arrived on 2nd July and disembarked Lord Elgin and his party.

When news of the deteriorating situation in India reached Hong Kong, *HMS Shannon* was ordered to India and after leaving on 16th July arrived at Calcutta on 6th August 1857. On arrival in India, Captain Peel immediately offered the Governor General, the services of his men and guns, to operate as a Naval Brigade. This offer was accepted and the resulting force, commanded by Captain Peel, became known as the "Shannon Brigade". On 14th August, Nowell accompanied Captain Peel and the first detachment of the Shannon Brigade when they departed on the river steamer *Chunar* bound for Allahabad where they arrived on 25th September 1857. The second detachment of the Shannon Brigade arrived at Allahabad on 20th October and three days later Nowell departed for Lucknow as part of an advanced party led by Captain Peel. On 1st November, Nowell was involved in the Battle of Khujwa during the advance on Lucknow.

On reaching Lucknow the Shannon Brigade were involved in the 2nd Relief, taking part in the Battle of Alum Bagh on 12th November and actions at Dilkusha and Martinière on the outskirts of the city on 14th November. It was during an action at the Shah Najaf Mosque on 16th November 1857 that Nowell performed the deeds for which he would later be awarded the Victoria Cross. During this action, Nowell severely wounded in the thigh and sent back to Allahabad where he arrived on 26th November. Nowell was involved in the siege and recapture of Lucknow from 1st March 1858 until the eventual fall of the city on 21st March. On 23rd March 1858, Nowell was promoted to the rank of Commander, in recognition of his gallantry during the mutiny and for his service he was awarded the Indian Mutiny Medal with clasps for Relief of Lucknow and Lucknow.

After a long journey, the Shannon Brigade finally returned to *HMS Shannon* at Calcutta on 5th August and on 15th September set sail for England where they arrived on 29th December 1858 and were paid off on 15th January 1859.

On 8th June 1859, Nowell was presented with his Victoria Cross Medal by Queen Victoria during an investiture held at Buckingham Palace.

Nowell assumed command of the newly commissioned *HMS Icarus* on 1st November 1859 and was assigned to the West Indies and North American Station. In mid 1860, Nowell arrested the famous American filibuster William Walker at Trujillo in Honduras. Walker, with a band of mercenaries had for the last decade been trying to subvert and assume control of various Central American States[531] and on 6th August 1859 he landed on Honduras and captured the city of Trujillo. Walker's actions were incompatible with British interests as they were destabilising to the area and Britain was trying to promote the construction of a canal through Central America to link the Atlantic and Pacific oceans'. As Britain controlled the neighbouring regions of British Honduras and the Mosquito Coast, Walker's attempt to take control of Honduras was the final straw, hence his arrest. Rather than return Walker to America, Nowell handed him over to the Honduran authorities and under their instruction he was executed by firing squad on 12th September 1860; for his actions Nowell was awarded a Gold Medal by the Central American States.

In April 1861, Nowell returned to England when *HMS Icarus* was assigned to the Channel Squadron. In February 1862, *HMS Icarus* was assigned to the Mediterranean squadron until 24th May 1864 and Nowell was promoted to the rank of Captain on 12th December 1863.

Nowell was awarded the Order of St Bento d'Avis, by the Portuguese Government on 2nd August 1865, however was not granted permission from the Admiralty to wear the order.

On 11th January 1866, Nowell was married at the parish church in Upway, Dorset to Emily Augusta (née Saunders); the couple would go on to have two children, a son Geoffrey[532] who was born in Naples on 26th November 1871 and a daughter Eleanor.

Nowell was assigned as Captain to *HMS Defence* on 25th March 1869 and took up operations on the Mediterranean Station where he was based at Malta and Naples.

On 29th April 1874, Nowell was appointed as Captain of *HMS Valiant* and served as part of the Coast Guard deployed in the River Foynes in Ireland.

Nowell was appointed as an Ordinary Member 3rd Class (Companion) of the Military Division of the Most Honourable Order of the Bath on 29th May 1875[533] and on 12th December of the same year was appointed as Naval Aide-de-Camp to Queen Victoria,[534] a position that he would hold until 2nd August 1879.

---

531 On 12th July 1856, Walker was elected as president of Nicaragua, after a fraudulent election.

532 As a colonel in the Rifle Brigade, Geoffrey would serve in the Boer War and World War I.

533 *London Gazette* – 24213/2852

534 *London Gazette* – 24282/57

On 28th November 1877, Nowell was assigned as Captain to *HMS Swiftsure*, for service on the Mediterranean Station.

Nowell was promoted to the rank of Rear-Admiral on 2nd August 1879.[535]

On 11th April 1882, Nowell was appointed as Commander-in-Chief of the Cape of Good Hope and West Africa Coast Station where he adopted *HMS Boadacea* as his flag ship. He served in this position until 6th March 1885.

Nowell was promoted to the rank of Vice-Admiral on 11th July 1885.[536]

During 1887, Nowell served as a member of a Royal Commission into the Civil Service and on 21st June 1887 was appointed as an Additional Member 2nd Class (Knight Commander) of the Military Division of the Most Honourable Order of the Bath.[537]

From 17th December 1887 until September 1891, Nowell served as Commander-in-Chief of the China Station and assigned *HMS Audacious* (later renamed as *Imperieuse*) as his flag ship.

Nowell was promoted to the rank of Admiral on 10th September 1891[538] and three years later on 22nd June 1894 was appointed as Commander-in-Chief of Portsmouth, where he lived in Admiralty House; he nominated his flag ship as *HMS Victory*.

On 22 June 1897, Nowell was appointed as an Additional Member 1st Class (Knight Grand Cross) of the Military Division of the Most Honourable Order of the Bath.[539]

Nowell commanded the fleet on 26th June 1897 during Queen Victoria's Diamond Jubilee Fleet Review with *HMS Renown* as his flag ship. Nowell was awarded the Queen Victoria Diamond Jubilee Medal (1897).

On 23rd August 1897, Nowell was appointed as First and Principle Aide-de-Camp to Queen Victoria.

Nowell was appointed to the rank of Admiral of the Fleet on13th January 1899,[540] replacing Sir John Edmund Commerell VC who had retired.

During 1899, Nowell was a County Magistrate for the Division of Droxford in Hampshire.

Nowell was awarded the King Edward VII Coronation Medal (1902) and the King George V Coronation Medal (1911).

On 20th February 1905, Nowell retired from the navy[541] and seven years later died aged at his home 44 Clarence Parade, Southsea on 14th February 1912, six days before his 77th

birthday. Nowell was buried in St Peter's Churchyard, Curdridge in Hampshire.

Nowell's Victoria Cross Medal is on public display at the Imperial War Museum as part of the Lord Ashcroft Collection.

Figure 192a. Grave of Nowell Salmon

---

535 *London Gazette* – 24749/4805
536 *London Gazette* – 25490/3240
537 *London Gazette* – 25712/3362
538 *London Gazette* – 26203/4987
539 *London Gazette* – 26867/3567
540 *London Gazette* – 27043/298
541 *London Gazette* – 27772/1845

Thomas James Young
16th November 1857 (VC No. 215)

Gazetted: 1st February 1859 22225/414

Rank and Unit: Lieutenant – Royal Navy (Naval Brigade)

Citation

Lieutenant (now Commander) Young, late Gunnery Officer of Her Majesty's ship "Shannon," and William Hall, "Captain of the Foretop," of that Vessel, were recommended by the late Captain Peel for the Victoria Cross, for their gallant conduct at a 24-Pounder Gun, brought up to the angle of the Shah Nujjiff, at Lucknow, on the 16th of November, 1857.

Figure 193. Thomas James Young

Biography

Thomas was born some time during 1827 at Chelsea in London. It appears that he joined the navy at an early age sometime around 1840.

On 7th December 1848, Thomas was promoted to the rank of Mate/Sub-Lieutenant and sometime during 1851 to the rank of Lieutenant.

On 27th March 1852, Thomas was assigned as Lieutenant to *HMS Excellent* a gunnery ship at Portsmouth commanded by Captain Henry Ducie Chads.

Thomas served as Lieutenant on board *HMS Agamemnon*[542] under the command of Captain Thomas Maitland in the Channel Squadron from 27th September 1852 until 22nd October 1853. From 22nd October 1853 until 1st January 1854, Thomas continued to serve as Lieutenant on board *HMS Agamemnon*, now under the command of Captain William Robert Mends which was deployed as the flag ship for Rear-Admiral Sir Edmond Lyons commander of the Black Sea fleet during the Crimean War. On 3rd January 1854, now under the command of Captain Thomas Matthew Charles Symonds, *HMS Agamemnon* entered the Black Sea and carried out operations along the eastern shore. *HMS Agamemnon* returned to Varna on 28th July 1854, however on 7th September left Varna bound for Balaklava. On 27th November 1854, command of *HMS Agamemnon* was passed to Captain Thomas Sabine Pasley and on 17th October 1854 she was involved in the 1st bombardment of Sevastopol. After taking part in the siege and bombardments of Sevastopol, Thomas and *HMS Agamemnon* were involved in operation at Kertch during May 1855. On 10th February 1856, command of *HMS Agamemnon*

---

542 *HMS Agamemnon* was the first Royal Navy warship to be designed for screw propulsion.

was passed to Captain James John Stopford and the ship returned to England where the crew were paid off at Portsmouth on 12th July 1856. For his service during the Crimean War, Thomas was awarded the Crimean War Medal with clasps for Azov and Sevastopol. He was also awarded the Turkish Crimea Medal and the Order of the Medjidie (5th Class) by the Ottoman Emperor.

On 1st September 1856, Thomas was assigned as Lieutenant to *HMS Inflexible*, however, before he could take up this post he was reassigned as Gunnery Officer to *HMS Shannon* under the command of Captain William Peel, taking up this post on 16th September 1856. On board *HMS Shannon*, Thomas set sail for China on 17th March 1857 and after making port at Cape Town on 7th May arrived off Singapore on 11th June where the ship was joined by Lord Elgin and his staff. On 23rd June they set sail for Hong Kong where they arrived on 2nd July and disembarked Lord Elgin and his party.

When news of the deteriorating situation in India reached Hong Kong, *HMS Shannon* was ordered to India and after leaving on 16th July arrived at Calcutta on 6th August 1857. On arrival in India, Captain Peel immediately offered the Governor General, the services of his men and guns, to operate as a Naval Brigade. This offer was accepted and the resulting force, commanded by Captain Peel, became known as the "Shannon Brigade". On 14th August, Thomas accompanied Captain Peel and the first detachment of the Shannon Brigade when they departed on the river steamer *Chunar* bound for Allahabad where they arrived on 25th September 1857. The second detachment of the Shannon Brigade arrived at Allahabad on 20th October and three days later Thomas departed for Lucknow as part of an advanced party led by Captain Peel. On 1st November, Thomas was involved in the Battle of Khujwa during the advance on Lucknow. On reaching Lucknow the Shannon Brigade were involved in the 2nd Relief, taking part in the Battle of Alum Bagh on 12th November and actions at Dilkusha and Martinière on the outskirts of the city on 14th November. It was during an action at the Shah Najaf Mosque on 16th November 1857 that Thomas performed the deeds for which he would later be awarded the Victoria Cross. Thomas was involved in the siege and recapture of Lucknow from 1st March 1858 until the eventual fall of the city on 21st March. On 22nd March 1858, Thomas was promoted to the rank of Commander, in recognition of his gallantry during the mutiny and for his service during the war he was awarded the Indian Mutiny Medal with clasps for Relief of Lucknow and Lucknow. After a long journey, the Shannon Brigade finally returned to *HMS Shannon* at Calcutta on 5th August and on 15th September set sail for England where they arrived on 29th December 1858 and were paid off on 15th January 1859.

On 8th June 1859, Thomas was presented with his Victoria Cross Medal by Queen Victoria during an investiture held at Buckingham Palace.

Thomas was married to Louisa Mary (née Boyes)[543] on 10th January 1860 at St James Church in Paddington. The couple would have one child, a daughter Amy Isabella who was born at Bognor on 16th November 1869, eight months after her father's death.

From 16th September 1863 until 12th January 1867, Thomas was 2nd in Command to first Captain James Charles Prevost and then Captain Robert Coote on board *HMS Gibraltar* while on operations on the Mediterranean Station.

On 11th April 1866, it is reported that Thomas was promoted to the rank of Captain, however, there are no details of his being given a command.

Thomas died at Caen in France on 20th March 1869 at the age of 41 and was buried in the Protestant Cemetery in Caen.

Thomas's Victoria Cross Medal is on public display at the National Maritime Museum, Greenwich.

Figure 193a. Grave of Thomas James Young

---

543 Louisa's brother, midshipman Duncan George Boyes was awarded the Victoria Cross for services at Shimonoseki in Japan on 6th September 1864.

James Munro
16th November 1857 (VC No. 216)

Figure 194. James Munro

Gazetted: 8th November 1860 22445/4126

Rank and Unit: Colour-Sergeant – 93rd Regiment of Foot

Citation

For devoted gallantry, at Secunderabagh, on the 16th November, 1857, in having promptly rushed to the rescue of Captain E. Walsh, of the same corps, when wounded, and in danger of his life, whom he carried to a place of comparative safety, to which place the Serjeant was brought in, very shortly afterwards, badly wounded.

Biography

James was born on 11th October 1826 at Easter Rariche, Nigg, Easter Ross in Scotland to father James a Wright and mother Effie (née McKenzie).

James had two older brothers; Kenneth baptised on 5th June 1821 and Angus baptised on 15th August 1825 both born at Nigg; a younger brother Andrew born on 20th January 1829 at Nigg and three younger sisters; Jane born on 7th March 1831 at Feam in Ross and Cromarty and twins Catherine and Helen Baptised on 4th March 1834 and both also born in Feam.

It is believed that James enlisted in the army at the age of 20, in1846 and would have joined his regiment the 93rd Highlanders in Montreal, Canada where the regiment had been on service since 1838. In 1847, the regiment moved to Quebec and on 1st August 1848, having been relieved by the 79th Highlanders, boarded the troopship *Resistance* bound for Portsmouth where they arrived on 30th August. After landing in Portsmouth, the regiment returned to Leith in Scotland and posted detachments at Stirling Castle, Perth and Dundee.

From 1849 until 1853 the regiment served short postings in Scotland and England ending up at Devonport on 15th July 1853. On 12th February 1854, the regiment received orders to prepare for overseas active service and on the 27th February moved to Portsmouth. At some stage during 1854, James was promoted to the rank of Sergeant.

On 28th February 1854, the regiment boarded the troop ship *Himalaya* and set sail for Malta where they arrived on 7th March. During the regiments short stay in Malta they were encamped at the Bomba Horn Works where they carried out extensive target practice with their newly issued Minié rifles. On 4th April 1854, news reached Malta of the declaration of war against the Russian Empire and on 6th April the regiment embarked upon the steamer *Kangaroo* bound for Gallipoli, where they landed on

11th April. On 6th May the regiment boarded the steamer *Andes* bound for Scutari, where they landed on 9th May and were assigned to the 2nd Brigade commanded by Sir Colin Campbell. On 13th June after the arrival of the 79th and 42nd Regiments, which completed the complement of the Highland Brigade, the regiment boarded the Steamer *Melbourne* and set sail for Varna where it landed with the rest of the brigade on 15th June.

At Varna, the regiment were stricken with outbreaks of cholera and were forced to move camp on three occasions in an attempt to avoid the sickness, eventually returning to Varna on 21st August. On 31st August, after leaving the sick behind, the regiment boarded *HMS Terrible* and set sail for Baltchik Bay where they boarded a fleet of six sailing vessels and on 7th September set out for the Crimean Peninsula where they landed as part of the Anglo-French Expeditionary force on 14th September. The regiment was involved in the battles at Alma, Balaklava and Inkerman, however, the fact that James has no clasps for these battles suggests that he was one of the sick left behind at Varna.

It is likely that James was part of the detachment that joined the regiment, from Varna, in the entrenchments of Sevastopol on 26th December 1854. On 22nd May 1855, James was involved in the expedition which captured Kertch on 25th May and returned to Balaklava on 14th June. On 18th June, James was involved in the 1st unsuccessful attack on the Redan. For his service during the war, James was awarded the Crimean War Medal with clasp for Sevastopol and the Turkish Crimean Medal.

On 16th June 1856, James with the regiment boarded *HMS Sidon* and set sail for England where they arrived at Portsmouth on 15th July and proceeded to the new camp at Aldershot.

The regiment moved by rail to Dover on 23rd July and on 30th September 1856, occupied Dover Castle relieving the 79th regiment as the garrison. On 31st January 1857, the regiment received orders to make ready for deployment to India, however on 6th March these were rescinded and they were ordered to China. At some stage during 1857, James was promoted to the rank of Colour-Sergeant. The regiment moved to Portsmouth on 23rd May and in two detachments boarded *HMS Belleisle* on 3rd of June and *SS Mauritius* on 16th June and set sail for China. The two ships were reunited on 11th August, at Simon's Bay just off the Cape of Good Hope and it was here that they received news of the mutiny and orders to proceed to Calcutta. Leaving South Africa on 16th August, the regiment arrived at Calcutta on 20th September where they were welcomed by the newly appointed Commander-in-Chief Sir Colin Campbell.

From 28th September until 9th October, the regiment left Calcutta bound for Cawnpore which was over 600 miles away. The regiment was reunited at Cawnpore on 10th November and on the 14th November began the assaults on Lucknow, which became known as the 2nd Relief. It was during an attack on the walled fortification Secundra Bagh on 16th November 1857, that James performed the deeds for which he would later be awarded the Victoria Cross. Having taken a wounded officer to a place of safety, James returned to the fight and was severely wounded by two musket balls which pierced his upper thighs and shattered his lower vertebrae. Being severely wounded, James took no further part in the war and was repatriated to England, for his service during the mutiny he was awarded the Indian Mutiny Medal with clasp for Relief of Lucknow.

On his return to England, sometime during 1858, James was declared unfit for further duty and was discharged from the army after over 12 years of service.

James was presented with his Victoria Cross Medal by Queen Victoria on 9th November 1860 at an investiture held in Home Park at Windsor Castle.

At some stage it is believed that he was married to Jessie (née Ross).

James never recovered from his wounds which continued to affect him both physically and mentally.

While working as a ranger in Queen's Park in Edinburgh, he came to the attention of the police because of his kleptomania and dementia brought on by his wounds and the large amounts of alcohol that he consumed to stem the pain.

At some time in 1869, James was admitted to the Edinburgh Asylum at Craigdunin Hospital as "a married soldier, not epileptic, nor suicidal but dangerous".

James died at Craigdunin Hospital on 15th February 1871, at the age of 44, and was buried in the hospital cemetery in a pauper's grave.

James's Victoria Cross Medal is on public display at the Argyll & Sutherland Highlanders Museum in Stirling Castle.

Figure 194a. Grave of James Munro

John Paton
16th November 1857 (VC No. 217)

Gazetted: 24th December 1858 22212/5514

Rank and Unit: Sergeant – 93rd Regiment of Foot

Citation

For distinguished personal gallantry at Lucknow, on the 16th of November, 1857, in proceeding alone round the Shah Nujjiff under an extremely heavy-fire, discovering a breach on the opposite side, to which he afterwards conducted the Regiment, by which means that important position was taken.

Elected by the non-commissioned officers of the Regiment.

Figure 195. John Paton

Biography

John was born on 23rd December 1833 at Stirling in Scotland to father Matthew who was a soldier and mother Isabella (née Bell).

Probably at around the time of his 18th birthday in 1851, John enlisted in his local regiment the 42nd Regiment of Foot (Black Watch), based at Perth, however, just prior to the Crimean War he transferred to the 93rd Regiment of Foot.

On 28th February 1854, John and the regiment boarded the troop ship *Himalaya* and set sail for Malta where they arrived on 7th March. On 4th April 1854, news reached Malta of the declaration of war against the Russian Empire and the regiment was ordered east, where they landed at Scutari on 9th May and were assigned to the 2nd Brigade commanded by Sir Colin Campbell. Sailing from Varna on 31st August the regiment landed on the Crimean Peninsula, as part of the Anglo-French Expeditionary force, on 14th September. On 19th September, the allied army began its march south towards the Russian stronghold at Sevastopol and the next day John saw his first action during the Battle of Alma. Continuing their march towards Sevastopol, the regiment reached the town and harbour of Balaklava on 26th September and were deployed to defend what was to be the British base of operations. On 25th October 1854, John fought in the Battle of Balaklava, where the regiment famously earned the title of "the Thin Red Line". Although the regiment was involved in the Battle of Inkerman on 5th November and the expedition to Kertch in May/June 1855 it appears that John spent the rest of the war in the trenches around Sevastopol. For his service during the war, John was awarded the Crimean Medal with clasps for Alma, Balaclava and Sevastopol. He also received the Turkish Crimea Medal.

On 16th June 1856, John and the regiment boarded *HMS Sidon* and set sail for England where they arrived at Portsmouth on 15th July and proceeded to the new camp at Aldershot. The regiment were moved by rail to Dover on 23rd July and on 30th September 1856, occupied Dover Castle relieving the 79th regiment as the garrison.

On 31st January 1857, the regiment received orders to make ready for deployment to India, however on 6th March these were rescinded and they were ordered to China. The regiment moved to Portsmouth on 23rd May and in two detachments boarded *HMS Belleisle* on 3rd of June and *SS Mauritius* on 16th June and set sail for China. The two ships were reunited on 11th August, at Simon's Bay just off the Cape of Good Hope and it was here that they received news of the mutiny and orders to proceed to Calcutta.

Leaving South Africa on 16th August, the regiment arrived at Calcutta on 20th September where they were welcomed by the newly appointed Commander-in-Chief Sir Colin Campbell. From 28th September until 9th October, the regiment left Calcutta bound for Cawnpore which was over 600 miles away. The regiment was reunited at Cawnpore on 10th November and on the 14th November began the assaults on Lucknow, which became known as the 2nd Relief. It was during the assault on the Shah Najaf Mosque on 16th November 1857, that John performed the deeds for which he would later be awarded the Victoria Cross, having been elected for the award by a ballot of the NCO's of the regiment under rule 13 of the originating warrant. Following the evacuation of the Residency on 23rd November, John and the 93rd helped cover the retreat of the rescue columns. On 6th December 1857, John was involved in the Battle of Cawnpore, which recaptured the city from the mutineers. From 2nd March 1858, John was involved in the siege of Lucknow which culminated in the final recapture of the city on 21st March. On

6th April 1858, the regiment were formed up as part of the force to conduct a campaign to clear the province of Rohilkhand of mutineers during which they took part in an action at Fort Rooya on 16th April and the Battle of Bareilly on 5th May. Following the capture of Bareilly, the regiment formed the garrison of the city until mid October when they were assigned to operation to quell the rebels in the Oudh province. For his service during the mutiny, John was awarded the Indian Mutiny Medal with clasps for Relief of Lucknow and Lucknow.

In February 1859, the regiment set off for the post of Sabathu near Simla where they arrived during the middle of April.

John was presented with his Victoria Cross Medal by Major-General Sir Robert Garrett on 6th December 1859 at Umbeyla, Peshawar in India.

In November 1859 the regiment moved to Umballa and on 21st January 1860 to Lahore where they stayed until 9th March 1861 when they moved to Rawalpindi.

It is during this period in early 1861, that John left the army after ten years of service and emigrated to Australia. On 28th May 1861, John began his new career in the New South Wales prison service when he employed as a prison warder at Darlinghurst Gaol. In September 1865, John was appointed as chief Warden at Port Macquarie and during 1866 was married to Mary (née Miller) at Gouldburn. The couple would have two children, twin girls Bella and Tina unfortunately the marriage was short lived as Mary died in 1869.

John was remarried to Amelia Martha Crook (née Spurling) at Sydney in 1872.

In 1875, John was appointed as Chief Gaoler at Deniliquin Gaol and his wife was employed as a matron. John was appointed as Governor of Berrima Gaol on 15th November 1888 and on 1st July 1890 was appointed to succeed Peter Herbert as Governor of Goulbburn Gaol. John retired from the prison service on 29th February 1896 after a career of almost 30 years and went to live in Sydney at Verona, 19 Prospect Road, Summer Hill.

John died at his home in Sydney on 1st April 1914 aged 80 and was buried in Rookwood Cemetery with full military honours.

John's Victoria Cross Medal is on public display at the Argyll & Sutherland Highlanders Museum in Stirling Castle.

Figure 195a. Grave of John Paton

John Dunlay
16th November 1857 (VC No. 218)

Gazetted: 24th December 18581859 22212/5514

Rank and Unit: Lance-Corporal – 93rd Regiment of Foot

Citation

For being the first man, now surviving, of the Regiment, who, on the 16th November, 1857, entered one of the breaches in the Secundra Bagh, at Lucknow, with Captain Burroughs, whom he most gallantly supported against superior numbers.

Elected by the private soldiers of the Regiment.

Biography

John was born during 1831 at Douglas, Co Cork in Ireland, he probably enlisted in the army at around the time of his 18th birthday in 1849, however, there is no record of his having served with the regiment in the Crimea.

The regiment set sail for China in June 1857, however with news of the outbreak of mutiny they were diverted to India where they landed at Calcutta on 20th September. John proceeded across country with the regiment to Cawnpore and was involved in the second relief of Lucknow and it was during the battle to take the Secundra Bagh on 16th November 1857 that he performed the deeds for which he would later be awarded the Victoria Cross, having been nominated for the award by a ballot of the privates of the regiment. Following the evacuation of the Residency on 23rd November, John and the 93rd helped cover the retreat of the rescue columns. On 6th December 1857, John was involved in the Battle of Cawnpore, which recaptured the city from the mutineers. John was involved in the siege and recapture of Lucknow, on the march to Lucknow he recovered the Regimental Colours which had briefly fallen into the hands of the enemy and was wounded in the knee during this action. Although wounded it is said that John carried the Colours into Lucknow when the city was recaptured on 21st March 1858. For his service during the mutiny, John was awarded the Indian Mutiny Medal with clasps for Relief of Lucknow and Lucknow.

Because of his wounds, John was sent back to England and was discharged to pension at some time during 1858, being unfit for further duties.

On leaving the army, john returned to Ireland and lived in the city of Cork.

John was presented with his Victoria Cross Medal by Queen Victoria on 4th January 1860 at an investiture held in Windsor Castle.

On 16th October 1890, John fell from a hay loft and died from his injuries the next day at the Southern Infirmary in Cork, he was buried in St Josephs Cemetery, Cork.

John's Victoria Cross Medal is part of the Sheesh Mahal Collection which is held at a museum in Patialia, Punjab in India.

Peter Grant
16th November 1857 (VC No. 219)

Figure 197. Peter Grant

Gazetted: 24th December 1858 22212/5515

Rank and Unit: Private – 93rd Regiment of Foot

Citation

For great personal gallantry, on the 16th of November, 1857, at the Secundra Bagh, in killing five of the enemy with one of their own swords, who were attempting to follow Lieutenant-Colonel Ewart, when that officer was carrying away a colour which he had captured.

Elected by the private soldiers of the Regiment.

Biography

Peter was born somewhere in Ireland during 1824.

It is probable that Peter joined the army at some time around his 18th birthday in 1842 and as such would have joined his regiment the 93rd Regiment of Foot in Canada where they had been stationed since 1838.

In 1847, the regiment moved to Quebec and on 1st August 1848, having been relieved by the 79th Highlanders, boarded the troopship *Resistance* bound for Portsmouth where they arrived on 30th August.

After landing in Portsmouth, the regiment returned to Leith in Scotland and posted detachments at Stirling Castle, Perth and Dundee. From 1849 until 1853 the regiment served short postings in Scotland and England ending up at Devonport on 15th July 1853. On 12th February 1854, the regiment received orders to prepare for overseas active service and on the 27th February moved to Portsmouth.

On 28th February 1854, the regiment boarded the troop ship *Himalaya* and set sail for Malta where they arrived on 7th March.

On 4th April 1854, news reached Malta of the declaration of war against the Russian Empire and on 6th April the regiment embarked upon the steamer *Kangaroo* bound for Gallipoli, where they landed on 11th April. On 6th May the regiment boarded the steamer *Andes* bound for Scutari, where they landed on 9th May and were assigned to the 2nd Brigade commanded by Sir Colin Campbell. On 13th June after the arrival of the 79th and 42nd Regiments, which completed the complement of the Highland Brigade, the regiment boarded the Steamer *Melbourne* and set sail for Varna where it landed with the rest of the brigade on 15th June.

At Varna, the regiment were stricken with outbreaks of cholera and were forced to move camp on three occasions in an attempt to avoid the sickness, eventually returning to Varna on 21st August.

On 31st August, after leaving the sick behind, the regiment boarded *HMS Terrible* and set sail for Baltchik Bay where they boarded a fleet of six sailing vessels and on 7th September set out for the Crimean Peninsula where they landed as part of the Anglo-French Expeditionary force on 14th September.

The regiment was involved in the battles at Alma, Balaklava and Inkerman, however, the fact that Peter has no clasps for these battles suggests that he was one of the sick left behind at Varna. It is likely that Peter was part of the detachment that joined the regiment, from Varna, in the entrenchments of Sevastopol on 26th December 1854. On 22nd May 1855, Peter was involved in the expedition which captured Kertch on 25th May and returned to Balaklava on 14th June and the trenches around Sevastopol. For his service during the war, Peter was awarded the Crimean War Medal with clasp for Sevastopol and the Turkish Crimean Medal.

On 16th June, Peter with the regiment boarded *HMS Sidon* and set sail for England where they arrived at Portsmouth on 15th July and proceeded to the new camp at Aldershot.

The regiment moved by rail to Dover on 23rd July and on 30th September 1856, occupied Dover Castle relieving the 79th regiment as the garrison. On 31st January 1857, the regiment received orders to make ready for deployment to India, however on 6th March these were rescinded and they were ordered to China. The regiment moved to Portsmouth on 23rd May and in two detachments boarded *HMS Belleisle* on 3rd of June and *SS Mauritius* on 16th June and set sail for China. The two ships were reunited on 11th August, at Simon's Bay just off the Cape of Good Hope and it was here that they received news of the mutiny and orders to proceed to Calcutta.

Leaving South Africa on 16th August, the regiment arrived at Calcutta on 20th September where they were welcomed by the newly appointed Commander-in-Chief Sir Colin Campbell. From 28th September until 9th October, the regiment left Calcutta bound for Cawnpore which was over 600 miles away. The regiment was reunited at Cawnpore on 10th November and on the 14th November began the assaults on Lucknow, which became known as the 2nd Relief. It was during an attack on the walled fortification Secundra Bagh on 16th November 1857, that Peter performed the deeds for which he would later be awarded the Victoria Cross. Peter was elected for the award by a ballot of the private soldiers of the regiment under rule 13. Following the evacuation of the Residency on 23rd November, Peter and the 93rd helped cover the retreat of the rescue columns. On 6th December 1857, Peter was involved in the Battle of Cawnpore, which recaptured the city from the mutineers. From 2nd March 1858, Peter was involved in the siege of Lucknow which culminated in the final recapture of the city on 21st March. On 6th April 1858, the regiment were assigned as part of the force to conduct a campaign to clear the province of Rohilkhand of mutineers during which they took part in an action at Fort Rooya on 16th April and the Battle of Bareilly on 5th May. Following the capture of Bareilly, the regiment formed the garrison of the city until mid October when they were assigned to operation to quell the rebels in the Oudh province. For his service during the mutiny, Peter was awarded the Indian Mutiny Medal with clasps for Relief of Lucknow and Lucknow.

In February 1859, the regiment set off for the post of Subathoo near Simla where they arrived during the middle of April.

Peter was presented with his Victoria Cross Medal by Major-General Sir Robert Garrett on 6th December 1859 at Umbeyla, Peshawar in India.

In November 1859 the regiment moved to Umballa and on 21st January 1860 to Lahore where they stayed until 9th March 1861 when they moved to Rawalpindi. On 11th November 1861 the regiment moved to the Peshawar district and despite moving camp on several occasions suffered badly from outbreaks of cholera, loosing over 90 men to the disease in just over a year. On 30th December 1862, the regiment moved to the station at Sealkote and it was from here towards the end of 1863 that Peter returned home where he was initially based at Aberdeen.

In May 1865, the depot company of the regiment moved to Stirling Castle however by June 1866 they were back in Aberdeen. On 10th January 1868, while on leave from Aberdeen, Peter was visiting with friends at Wheatley's public house, Overgate in the centre of Dundee when he went missing. His body was found floating in the River Tay on 13th January by Constable Bremner a little to the east of Craig Harbour. At the age of 43, Peter was buried in a common grave in the Eastern Necropolis in Dundee.

Despite it being reported that his Victoria Cross Medal, together with other medals was pinned on his uniform tunic when his lodging room was cleared after his death – there was no sign of his medals, the location of his Victoria Cross is unknown, perhaps it was buried with him.

Figure 197a. Memorial to Peter Grant

Charles Irwin
16th November 1857 (VC No. 220)

Gazetted: 24th December 1858 22212/5513

Rank and Unit: Private No. 3168 – 53rd Regiment of Foot

Citation

For conspicuous bravery at the assault of the Secundra Bagh, at Lucknow, on the 16th of November, 1857. Although severely wounded through the right shoulder, he was one of the first men of the 53rd Regiment, who entered the buildings under a very severe fire.

Elected by the private soldiers of the Regiment.

Biography

Charles was born some time during 1824 in Manorhamilton, Co Leitrim in Ireland, he had a brother Edward.

On 4th September 1842, at the age of 18, Charles abandoned his trade as a cutler and enlisted with the 18th Regiment of Foot at Sligo.

Charles would have joined his regiment at Chusan in China, where they were stationed since October 1842, following the end of the 1st Anglo-China (Opium) War. Although the regiment suffered few casualties in combat during the war, their numbers were severely depleted due to sickness and Charles was part of the draft recruited to bring the regiment back to strength. Soon after his arrival in China, Charles moved to the Island of Kulangsu as part of the occupying force until April 1844 when the regiment moved back to Chusan and then to Hong Kong[544] where they formed the garrison.

On 1st April 1847, as part of Sir John Davis's response to the ill treatment of British and Europeans in Canton, the 18th were part of a substantial force sent to the Canton River with the intention of capturing the city. Faced with such an overwhelming force, the Canton mandarins made full reparations and the 18th returned to Hong Kong.

On 20th November 1847, the regiment boarded the troopship *Balcarres* and set sail for India where they landed at Calcutta on 10th January 1848 and occupied Fort William. In March 1849, the regiment moved to Umballa where they remained until the end of the year at which point they moved to Meerut. In the winter of 1850, the regiment moved back to Calcutta and once again occupied Fort William.

At the start of 1852, the regiment were expecting to return to

Figure 198. Charles Irwin

England, however on 19th January 1852 they received orders to proceed to Burma to help enforce some minor treaty issues. By the time that the 18th arrived on the scene, Commodore George Lambert had managed to escalate matters into a full scale war, later to be known as the 2nd Anglo-Burmese war. During the war, Charles and the Regiment, as part of the force commanded by Major-General Henry Godwin, took part in the capture of the Port of Martaban on 5th April 1852, the capture of Rangoon on 11th April, the capture of Pegu on 3rd June and the capture of Prome on 9th October 1852. The war was ended by a proclamation of Annexation issued on 20th January 1853. For his part in the war, Charles was awarded the India General Service Medal (1854–1895) with clasp for Pegu.

Charles and the regiment returned to Calcutta from Burma in November 1853 and soon afterwards the regiment was returned to England, however, wishing to remain in India, Charles transferred to the 53rd Regiment of Foot.

Charles and his new regiment were based at Calcutta when the mutiny broke out and were initially involved in disarming the native regiments in and around the city, when this was accomplished the regiment were ordered to join up with the force of Sir Colin Campbell. With the Lucknow Relief Force, Charles and the 53rd were involved in a skirmish at Bunnee on 2nd November 1857 and the Relief of Lucknow from 13th to 24th November, during which the defenders in the Residency were evacuated. It was on 16th November 1857, during the assault on the Secundra Bagh, that Charles performed the deeds for which he would later be awarded the Victoria Cross, having been nominated for the award by a ballot of the Privates of the regiment – under rule 13 of the Royal Warrant. During this action, Charles was severely wounded in the right shoulder. On 6th December 1857, Charles

---

544 As part of the treaty of Nanking, which ended the 1st Anglo-China War, Hong Kong was ceded to the British.

was involved in the Battle of Cawnpore which recaptured the city and at actions at; Sheerghat on 9th December, Kalla Nuddee on 2nd January 1858, Shumshabad on 28th January and the storming of Meergunge on 23rd February 1858. Charles returned with the 53rd to Lucknow taking part in the siege from 2nd March until the city was retaken on 21st March 1858. After the recapture of Lucknow, Charles and the 53rd were assigned to a force under the command of Major-General Sir Hope Grant and were involved in actions at Courcy on 22nd March, the passage of Gumti at Sultanpore on 27th August, the passage of the Gogra on 25th November and the skirmish at Bungeon on 3rd December 1858. For his service during the mutiny, Charles was awarded the Indian Mutiny Medal with clasps for Relief of Lucknow and Lucknow.

Charles was presented with his Victoria Cross Medal at a ceremony in India some time during 1859.

When his regiment left India in 1860, Charles transferred to the 87th Regiment of Foot which was under orders for deployment to Hong Kong. After spending a short time in Hong Kong, Charles and the 87th returned to England for garrison duties and in 1864, he was discharged from the army at his own request after just over 21 years of service. On 2nd August 1864, Charles was accepted as an out-pensioner of the Royal Hospital at Chelsea and was awarded a life time pension of 8 pence per day.

At some stage, Charles moved back to Ireland and was living in Newton Butler in Co. Fermanagh when he died on 8th April 1873 at the age of 49. He was buried in St, Mark's Churchyard, Magheraveely in Co. Fermanagh.

Charles's Victoria Cross medal is on public display at the King's Shropshire Light Infantry Museum in Shrewsbury, Shropshire.

Figure 198a. Memorial to Fermanagh Victoria Cross recipients

James Kenny
16th November 1857 (VC No. 221)

Gazetted: 24th December 1858 22212/5513

Rank and Unit: Private No. 1841 – 53rd Regiment of Foot

Citation

For conspicuous bravery at the taking of the Secundra Bagh, at Lucknow, on the 16th of November, 1857, and for volunteering to bring up ammunition to his Company, under a very severe cross fire.

Elected by the private soldiers of the Regiment.

Biography

It is believed that James was born in Dublin, Ireland at some time during 1824.

Due to the lack of surviving service records, very little is known of the life of James, however, it is probable that he joined the army at some time around his 18th birthday in 1842 or he may have been enlisted in the 53rd regiment at some time during 1847/48 as part of the intake to replace losses during the first Anglo-Sikh War.

James was involved with the 53rd Regiment in the 2nd Anglo-Sikh war from September 1848 until March 1849 and took part in the decisive Battle of Goojerat on 13th February 1849. For his service during the war, James was awarded the Punjab Medal (1848–49) with clasp for Goojerat.

James and his regiment were based at Calcutta when the mutiny broke out and were initially involved in disarming the native regiments in and around the city, when this was accomplished the regiment were ordered to join up with the force of Sir Colin Campbell.

With the Lucknow Relief Force, James and the 53rd were involved in a skirmish at Bunnee on 2nd November 1857 and the Relief of Lucknow from 13th to 24th November, during which the defenders in the Residency were evacuated. It was on 16th November 1857, during the assault on the Secundra Bagh, that James performed the deeds for which he would later be awarded the Victoria Cross, having been nominated for the award by a ballot of the Privates of the regiment – under rule 13 of the Royal Warrant. On 6th December 1857, James was involved in the Battle of Cawnpore which recaptured the city and at actions at; Sheerghat on 9th December, Kala Nuddee on 2nd January 1858, Shumshabad on 28th January and the storming of Meeangunge on 23rd February 1858. James returned with the 53rd to Lucknow taking part in the siege from 2nd March until the city was retaken on 21st March 1858. After the recapture of Lucknow, James and the 53rd were assigned to a force under the command of Major-General Sir Hope Grant and were involved in actions at Courcy on 22nd March, the passage of Gumti at Sultanpore on 27th August, the passage of the Gogra on 25th November and the skirmish at Bungeon on 3rd December 1858. For his service during the mutiny, James was awarded the Indian Mutiny Medal with clasps for Relief of Lucknow and Lucknow.

James was presented with his Victoria Cross Medal at a ceremony in India, probably at some time during 1859.

When his regiment left India in 1860, James transferred to the 6th Bengal European Fusiliers in order to remain in India. In 1861, with the disbanding of the East India Company armies, James transferred to the 101st Regiment of Foot.

While serving with the regiment at Multan in the Punjab, James died from disease on 2nd October 1962 at the age of 33 and was buried in an unmarked grave in the European Cemetery at Multan.

The whereabouts of James's Victoria Cross Medal is unknown, perhaps it was buried with him.

David Mackay
16th November 1857 (VC No. 222)

Gazetted: 24th December 1858 22212/5515

Rank and Unit: Private – 93rd Regiment of Foot

Citation

For great "personal gallantry in capturing an enemy's colour after a most obstinate resistance, at the Secundra Bagh, Lucknow, on the 16th of November, 1857". He was severely wounded afterwards at the capture of the Shah Nujjiff.

Elected by the private soldiers of the Regiment.

Biography

David was born on 23rd November 1831 at Alterwell, Howe, Lyth, Caithness in Scotland the second child to father Angus, a farm labourer and mother Christina (née Nicholson).

He was born into what would become a large family with 6 brothers; Hugh born on 7th April 1830, Donald born on 3rd September 1835, Adam born on 3rd April 1838, William born on 19th December 1844, John born on 26th September 1849 and George a twin born on 15th September 1853: 6 sisters; Janet born on 25th October 1833, Christina born on 1st September 1841, Ann born on 14th April 1843, Margaret born on 27th January 1847 and Barbara a twin born on 15th September 1853.

Just after his 19th birthday, on 23rd December 1850, David enlisted as a private in the 93rd Regiment of Foot at Thurso and joined his regiment at Edinburgh where they had been serving as the garrison since 5th April 1850.

On 15th April 1851, David moved with the regiment to Glasgow where he served until 23rd February 1852 when the regiment moved to Weedon in Buckinghamshire. On 11th August 1852, the regiment left Weedon for Portsmouth where they arrived on 14th August and remained there until 14th June 1853 when they left for Cobham Camp where they took part in manoeuvres. After the manoeuvres, the regiment moved to Devonport on 15th July 1853, where on 12th February 1854 they received orders to make ready for active service deployment.

On 27th February 1854, the regiment moved to Portsmouth where they boarded the steamship *Himalaya* and the next day set sail for Malta where they arrived on 7th March. On Malta, David and the regiment were encamped at the fortifications known as the Bomba Horn Works and spent most of their time at target practice with their recently issued Minié rifles.

On 6th April 1854, following news of the declaration of war against the Russian Empire, David and the regiment boarded the steamship *Kangaroo* and set sail for Gallipoli where they arrived on 11th April and set up camp at Bulair.

On 6th May the regiment boarded the steamer *Andes* and set sail for Scutari where they arrived on 9th May and were assigned to the 2nd Brigade (Highland) of the 1st Division, under the command of Sir Colin Campbell.

On 13th June, the highland brigade set sail for Varna, on board the steamer *Melbourne*, where they arrived on 15th June.

Following several changes of camp, in a vain attempt to escape illness from cholera, the regiment set sail from Galata on board *HMS Terrible* on 31st August bound for Baltchik Bay where they boarded six sailing ships; *Caducems*, *Her Majesty*, *City of Carlisle*, *Palmerston*, *Edendale* and *Arndale* and on 7th September set sail for the Crimean Peninsula. Arriving off Eupatoria on 13th September, the regiment landed the next day as part of the Anglo/French expeditionary force and on 19th September they began their march towards Sevastopol.

On 20th September 1854, David took part in the Battle of Alma and on 23rd September, the regiment resumed its march to Sevastopol.

After arriving at Balaklava on 26th September, the bulk of the army moved to the south of Sevastopol to begin the siege of the city. After drawing lots within the Highland Brigade, the 93rd were assigned to the defence of Balaklava and were stationed at the village of Kadikoi. In addition to their defensive duties the regiment was used to unload munitions and other supplies and transport them to the first supply depot for the Sevastopol siege. On 25th October, David and the regiment were involved in the Battle of Balaklava, where they famously received the accolade of "the thin Red Line".

On 5th November 1854, David took part in the Battle of Inkerman, following which the regiment resumed their duties ferrying supplies to the Sevastopol siege lines.

The regiment was assigned to the force of Major-General Sir George Browne which on 22nd May 1855 boarded *HMS Sphynx* and *HMS Stromboli* and set forth on an expedition to Kertch. The regiment was landed near Kertch on 24th May, however, the Russian troops had retired and the town surrendered the next day.

On 12th June the regiment boarded *HMS Terrible* and returned to Balaklava where they landed on 14th June and took up position at their camp on the heights before Sevastopol on 16th June.

On 18th June the regiment took part in the unsuccessful attack on the Redan and afterwards spent time in the trenches as part of the Right Attack until 23rd August when they moved to Kamara to provide support to the Sardinian troops. On 8th September 1855, the regiment returned to their camp on the Sevastopol heights and formed part of the reserve during the 2nd failed attack on the Redan, however with the fall of the city on the following day they returned to Kamara. For his service during the war, David was awarded the Crimea Medal with clasps for Alma, Balaklava and Sevastopol.

On 16th June 1856, David and the regiment boarded *HMS Sidon* and set sail for England and after landing at Portsmouth on 15th July, they took up station at Aldershot on the same day. On 23rd July, the regiment moved to Dover and on 30th September relieved the 79th Regiment as garrison and occupied Dover castle. On 6th March 1857, the regiment received orders to make ready for a deployment to China and on 23rd May they moved to Portsmouth where they were quartered in the Clarence Barracks.

After boarding *HMS Belleisle* on 1st June, the regiment set sail for China on 3rd June and by 9th August were anchored off Simons Bay near Cape Town.[545] It was here that they received the news of the mutiny in India, together with orders to proceed to India with the utmost urgency.

The regiment arrived at Calcutta, on board *SS Mauritius*, on 20th September 1857 and were deployed to the force sent to the relief of Lucknow where they arrived on 9th November. It was on 16th November 1857, during the taking of the Secundra Bagh defence, that David performed the deeds for which he would later be awarded the Victoria Cross, having been nominated for the award by the Privates of the regiment. Later the same day, during the attack on the Shah Najaf Mosque, David was severely wounded. In March 1858, David was returned to England and was awarded the Indian Mutiny Medal with clasp for Relief of Lucknow for his service during the mutiny.

David was presented with his Victoria Cross medal by Queen Victoria on 8th June 1859 at a ceremony held in Buckingham Palace.

On 25th August 1859, David was married to Mary (née Stevenson) at Holburn Free Church, Hardgate, Old Macher in Aberdeen. The couple would go on to have five children; Alexander Hugh born in Aberdeen on 9th September 1861, Mary Jean born in Stonehaven on 17th January 1863, David born in Hardgate on 6th July 1864, John George Andrew born at Newhills on 12th August 1866 and James born on 12th September 1868 at Dalkeith near Edinburgh.

On 17th November 1859, David was promoted to Sergeant and was deployed as a recruiting Sergeant in and around Aberdeen.

Due to his wounds, David was discharged from the army, on medical grounds, on 24th January 1861 upon the completion of 10 years service.

---

545 Some sources state that David was promoted to the rank of Corporal, during this journey, on 24th July, however, this conflicts with his stated rank of Private at the time he performed the deeds for which he was awarded the Victoria Cross.

On leaving the army, David moved to Auchinheath, Lesmagow and was employed with a Manufacturer, from 1861 until 1866 initially as a storekeeper, then as a Tape Machine operator and finally as a paper cutter and after leaving this employment he worked as a casual labourer.

His wife Mary died on the 3rd July 1879 at Auchinheath, aged 49 years, suffering from a tumour of the colon and now being unable to work, David sold his Victoria Cross medal for £20 in order to feed his children.

David died at his home in Auchinheath, Lesmagow on 18th November 1880 at the age of 48 from a valvular disease of the heart.

The whereabouts of David's Victoria Cross medal is unknown, believed to be held by a private collector, it was sold at auction in June 1901 for £75.

Figure 200. Grave of David McKay

John Smith
16th November 1857 (VC No. 223)

Gazetted: 24th December 1858 22212/5515

Rank and Unit: Private – 1st Madras Fusiliers

Citation

For having been one of the first to try and enter the gateway on the north side of the Secundra Bagh. On the gateway being burst open, he was one of the first to enter, and was surrounded by the enemy. He received a sword-cut on the head, a bayonet wound on the left side, and a contusion from the butt end of a musket on the right shoulder, notwithstanding which he fought his way out, and continued to perform his duties for the rest of the day.

Elected by the private soldiers of the Regiment.

Biography

John was born in the St Luke's parish of London some time during July 1822.

In 1841, John enlisted in the army of the Honourable East India Company and joined his regiment 1st Madras Fusiliers at Secunderabad. In February 1843, soon after joining the regiment, John was involved with the European Officers and men of the regiment in putting down a revolt of the native soldiers in the regiment.

On 7th September 1852, John and the regiment were embarked upon *HMS Sphynx*, *SS Moozuffer* and transport *Graham* and set sail for Rangoon to take part in the 2nd Anglo-Burma war.

In February/March 1856 the regiment returned to India where they were stationed at Fort St George in Madras.

On 17th March 1857, the regiment left for the war in Persia, however, after reaching the Persian Gulf and hearing news of the signing of a peace treaty they returned to India, arriving at Calcutta on 20th April.

During the mutiny, John served in the Lucknow relief force and it was during the taking of the Secundra Bagh on 16th November 1857 that he performed the deeds for which he would later be awarded the Victoria Cross, following a ballot of the Privates of the Regiment. During this action, John was wounded by a sabre cut to the head, a bayonet thrust to his left side and by a musket blow to his right shoulder. For his service during the mutiny, John was awarded the Indian Mutiny Medal with clasp for Relief of Lucknow.

John was presented with his Victoria Cross Medal at a ceremony which took place in India at some time during 1859.

After 20 years of service, John was discharged to pension during 1861 and remained in India.

John died on 6th May 1866 at Taujore, Trichinopoly in India and was buried in an unmarked grave in the Taujore Cemetery.

The location of John's Victoria Cross Medal is unknown, believed to be in a private collection as it was sold at auction on 11th May 1989.

John Harrison
16th November 1857 (VC No. 224)

Gazetted: 24th December 1858 22212/5512

Rank and Unit: Leading Seaman – Royal Navy – Naval Brigade

Citation

For conspicuous gallantry at Lucknow, on the 16th of November, 1857, in climbing up a tree, touching the angle of the Shah Nujjiff, to reply to the fire of the enemy, for which most dangerous service, the late Captain Peel, K.C.B., had called for volunteers.

Biography

John was born at Castleboro in Co Wexford, Ireland on 24th January 1832, his father was a carpenter on the nearby Carew Estate.

John joined the navy as a boy 2nd Class in 1850 at the age of 18. As part of the Baltic Fleet, John took part in the Crimean War and was involved in operations in the sea of Azov and the bombardment of Sevastopol. For his service during the war, John was awarded the Baltic Medal, the Crimea Medal with clasps for Azov and Sebastopol and the Turkish Crimea Medal.

John was involved in the early stages of the 2nd Anglo-China (Arrow) war and for his service was awarded the Second China War Medal.

At some stage, John joined *HMS Shannon* as a Leading Seaman, probably when she docked at Hong Kong on 27th June 1857. *HMS Shannon* was on her way to join the fleet engaged in the 2nd Anglo-China war when, after receiving news of the outbreak of mutiny they were diverted to India. John was part of the 1st Detachment of the Naval Brigade (known as the Shannon Brigade), led by Captain William Peel that left Calcutta on 14th September 1857 to join the forces in the relief of Lucknow. It was on 16th November 1857, during an attack on the Shah Najaf Mosque at Lucknow, that John performed the deeds for which he would later be awarded the Victoria Cross – John was seriously wounded during the action. John also took part in the final recapture of Lucknow on 21st March 1858. For his service during the mutiny, John was awarded the Crimea Medal with clasps for Relief of Lucknow and Lucknow.

On 12th August 1858, John rejoined the crew of *HMS Shannon* and three days later set sail for England where they arrived at Spithead on 29th December.

A few days later on 13th January 1859, John who was now a Boatswain's Mate and Petty Officer was discharged from the Navy, probably being unfit for service as a result of his wounds.

John was presented with his Victoria Cross Medal by Queen Victoria at a ceremony held at Windsor Castle on 4th January 1860.

Following his time in the Navy, John managed to find a position within Customs and Excise.

John died at his home 5 Stafford Place, Westminster on 27 December 1865 and was buried at Brompton Cemetery, West London.

John's Victoria Cross Medal is on public display at the National Maritime Museum in Greenwich, London.

Figure 202. Grave of John Harrison

William Edward Nelson Hall[546]
16th November 1857 (VC No. 225)

Gazetted: 1st February 1859 22225/414

Rank and Unit: Able Seaman – Royal Navy – Naval Brigade

Citation

Lieutenant (now Commander) Young, late* Gunnery Officer of Her Majesty's ship "Shannon," and William Hall, "Captain of the Foretop," of that Vessel, were recommended by the late Captain Peel for the Victoria Cross, for their gallant conduct at a 24-Pounder Gun, brought up to the angle of the Shah Nujjiff, at Lucknow, on the 16th of November, 1857.

Biography

William was born at Horton's Bluff, Minas Basin, Nova Scotia, Canada on 28th April 1827. His father Jacob was a slave who was one of a cargo of slaves being transported to America, who was freed by *HMS Leopard* and taken to Nova Scotia in 1812. His mother, Lucy or Lucinda, was also a slave who escaped when British forces attacked and destroyed Washington in 1814. On arriving in Nova Scotia, Jacob was given a job by Peter Hall on his farm at Centerville and in a token of gratitude towards his

Figure 203. William Edward Nelson Hall

---

546 Gravestone gives Edward as a middle name but birth certificate gives Nelson

benefactor he assumed Hall as his surname. Jacob moved to Horton's Bluff and worked at a shipyard in Hantsport owned by Abraham Cunard, the father of Samuel Cunard the famous shipping magnet.

After a basic education, William also worked in the shipyards until in 1844 at the age of 17 he began his life as a sailor, working in the merchant Navy's of Nova Scotia and America and also for a short time from 1847 until 1849 in the American Navy.

On 2nd February 1852, William enlisted in the Royal Navy at Red Cross Street in Liverpool and was assigned to *HMS Rodney* which at this time was operating as part of the Channel Squadron. From 11th February 1853, *HMS Rodney* was assigned to the Mediterranean station until the outbreak of the Crimean War when she was redeployed as part of the Black Sea fleet. In September 1854, William landed on the Crimean Peninsula as part of the Naval Brigade, under the command of Captain Henry Keppel and was involved in the siege of Sevastopol where he helped man a battery of naval guns. During the siege, on 18th November 1854, William witnessed the deed of William Peel which would later result in him being awarded the Victoria Cross. On 5th November 1854, William took part in the Battle of Inkerman where he manned a battery of Naval guns. At the end of the war, William returned to England with *HMS Rodney* and landed at Portsmouth on 21 Jan 1856. For his service during the war, William was awarded the Crimea Medal with clasps for Inkerman and Sevastopol and the Turkish Crimea Medal.

On leaving *HMS Rodney* in January, William joined *HMS Victory* which was being used as a training ship in Portsmouth and remained until he joined *HMS Shannon* in October 1856 and was reunited with Captain William Peel who was in command of the vessel.

Following commissioning, *HMS Shannon* was on station with the Channel Squadron until she was sent to join the fleet engaged in the 2nd Anglo-China war. However, after arriving at Hong Kong in June 1857 and receiving news of the outbreak of mutiny they were diverted to India. William was part of the 1st Detachment of the Naval Brigade (known as the Shannon Brigade), led by Captain William Peel that left Calcutta on 14th September 1857 to join the forces in the relief of Lucknow. It was on 16th November 1857, during an attack on the Shah Najaf Mosque at Lucknow, that William performed the deeds for which he would later be awarded the Victoria Cross, the first coloured man to be so honoured. William took part in operations at Cawnpore during October 1857 and also took part in the final recapture of Lucknow on 21st March 1858. For his service during the mutiny, William was awarded the Crimea Medal with clasps for Relief of Lucknow and Lucknow. On 1st February 1858, William was

promoted to Leading Seaman and in July was promoted to the positions of Captain of the Mast and Captain of the Foretop. On 12th August 1858, William rejoined the crew of *HMS Shannon* and three days later set sail for England where they arrived at Spithead on 29th December.

In June 1859, William joined *HMS Donegal* and while anchored in the harbour at Queenstown in Ireland was presented with his Victoria Cross medal by Rear-Admiral Charles Talbot on 28th October 1859.

William served in several other Royal Navy ships; *HMS Hero, HMS Canopus, HMS Bellerophon, HMS Impregnable* and *HMS Peterel* until his final posting to *HMS Royal Adelaide*. On 10th June 1876, after serving for over 24 years, William retired from the Royal Navy with the Petty Officer 1st Class rank of Quartermaster.

On his retirement from the Navy, William returned to Canada where he went to live with his two sisters Rachel and Mary on a small farm at Avonport in King's County, Nova Scotia.

William died as a result of paralysis, at his home on 27th August 1904, and was buried in the Baptist Church Cemetery, Stonet Hill, Lockhartville but in 1945 his remains were reinterred in the Hantsport Baptist Church Cemetery.

William's Victoria Cross Medal is on public display at the Nova Scotia Museum in Halifax, Nova Scotia.

Figure 203a. Grave of William Edward Nelson Hall

John Christopher Guise
16th/17th November 1857 (VC No. 226)

Gazetted: 24th December 1858 22212/5514

Rank and Unit: Major – 90th Regiment of Foot

Citation

For conspicuous gallantry in action on the 16th and 17th of November, 1857, at Lucknow.

Elected by the Officers of the Regiment.

Biography

John was born at Littledean, near Gloucester, on 27th July 1826, the youngest of five children born to General Sir John Wright and Charlotte Diana (née Vernon). John had three brothers; William Vernon born on 19th August 1816, Henry John born on 25th August 1817 and Francis Edward born on 24th April 1820; he also had a sister Jane Elizabeth born some time in 1825.

After having graduated from the Royal Military College at Sandhurst, John purchased a commission of Ensign in the 90th Regiment of Foot on 6th June 1845.[547]

It is probable that John remained in England to be united with the bulk of the regiment which returned to England in February 1846 after a ten year deployment to Ceylon. On 13th October 1848, John purchased a commission of Lieutenant in the regiment.[548] In early 1851, John moved with the regiment to Ireland where they were initially stationed at Cork until early 1852 when they moved to Dublin. On 6th June 1854, John was promoted to the rank of Captain.[549]

Soon after the declaration of war against Russia, which heralded the start of the Crimean War, the regiment received orders to make ready for a deployment to India early in 1855.

However, following a request from Lord Raglan for reinforcements, the regiment received orders on 12th November to proceed to the Crimea with utmost urgency. A week later on 19th November, the regiment embarked upon *SS Europa* at Kingston and set sail for the Crimea where they were landed at Balaklava on 5th December 1854. John was only on active duty until 24th December, when he fell seriously ill and on 1st January 1855 was evacuated back to England. Despite only spending a short time on the Crimean peninsula, John was awarded the Crimea Medal with clasp for Sevastopol and the Turkish Crimea Medal for his part in the war. The regiment left the Crimea in June 1856, on

Figure 204. John Christopher Guise

board *HMS Queen* (towed for part of the way by *HMS Terrible*) and arrived back at Portsmouth in July, and were stationed at the new camp at Aldershot.

On 1st October 1856, John was appointed as Instructor of Musketry to the regiment.[550]

In February 1857, the regiment was moved to Portsmouth where they occupied the Anglesey Barracks and shortly after their arrival they received orders to make ready for deployment to India, however, at the end of March they received further orders to proceed to China instead.

In early April, John and three companies of the regiment boarded *HMS Transit* and set sail for China, the remainder of the regiment set sail on board *HMS Himalaya* on 16th April. *HMS Transit* had an inauspicious start, after an accident near the Needles she had to return to Portsmouth for repairs, however, the delay was short and during June both ships were reunited at the Cape Colony. John and the regiment set off once again for China on board *HMS Transit*, a few days after the departure of *HMS Himalaya*, however, once again they were beset by misfortune, as with their sails shredded during a cyclone, the *Transit* ran aground on a coral reef on 10th July. John, with the regiment and ship's crew managed to wade ashore to the nearby island of Banka, close to Sumatra, at the time a part of the Dutch East Indies.

On 18th July a British gunboat *HMS Dove* arrived on the island with news of the outbreak of mutiny in India and a few days later *HMS Actaeon* arrived and took the regiment to Singapore where they arrived on 23rd July and received orders to proceed to India with the utmost haste.

At Singapore the regiment boarded *HMS Shannon* and *HMS Pearl* and on 29th July set sail for India where they arrived at

547 *London Gazette* – 20477/1693
548 *London Gazette* – 20905/3692
549 *London Gazette* – 21559/1726

550 *London Gazette* – 21934/3467

Calcutta on 28th August 1857. After spending some time being refitted, after losing all their gear when *HMS Transit* was abandoned, they set out for Benares where they arrived on 10th September by the end of October John was reunited with the rest of the regiment at Cawnpore where a force was being assembled to go to the relief of Lucknow. On 13th November 1857, John was promoted to the rank of Major.[551] It was on 16th/17th November 1857, during the attacks on Lucknow that John performed the deeds for which he would later be awarded the Victoria Cross, having been elected for the award by a ballot of the officers of the regiment in accordance with rule 13 of the originating Royal Warrant. John was also involved with the regiment in the action which resulted in the recapture of Lucknow on 21st March 1858. John received a brevet promotion to the rank of Lieutenant-Colonel on 24th March 1858.[552] From 23rd April until 21st May the regiment were part of the force of Sir Hope Grant which was chasing down mutineers in the region around Bareilly. For his part in the mutiny John was awarded the Indian Mutiny Medal with clasps for Relief of Lucknow and Lucknow.

After the end of the Mutiny, John and the regiment continued to serve in India, being stationed at various outposts; Chinhut, Sitapur, Allahabad, Meerut, Lahore, Meean Meer, Peshawar, Nowshera, Subathoo and Kamptee.

During this time, in February 1859, John was presented with his Victoria Cross Medal probably at Sitapur and on 13th January 1860, he purchased the commission of Lieutenant-Colonel in the regiment.[553]

On 18th September 1861, John was married to Isabella (née Newcombe), the couple would go one to have four children; Catherine Isabella, Mary Emily, John Henry Wingfield born on 7th December 1865 and Arthur St Valery Beauchamp born on 20th February 1868.

John received a brevet promotion to the rank of Colonel on 7th August 1863[554] and a few months later on 3rd June 1864 was placed on the half pay list.[555]

On 2nd June 1869, John was appointed as an Ordinary Member, 3rd Class (Companion) of the Military Division of the Most Honourable Order of the Bath.[556]

The regiment left Kamptee on 27th September 1869 for Nagpur where they left for Bombay by rail and on 30th September boarded *HMS Jumna* to begin their journey back to England. After changing to *HMS Serapis* at Alexandria, the

regiment arrived back home at Portsmouth on 3rd November 1869 after nearly 13 years foreign service. On the next day, after having been joined by the depot companies from Winchester, the regiment boarded *HMS Orontes* and set sail for Edinburgh where they were established as the garrison at Edinburgh Castle on 9th November 1869. On 3rd September 1873, the regiment moved to Dover and shortly afterwards were deployed to the war in South Africa, however, it is unknown if John was part of this deployment.

On 14th September 1877, subsequent to the death of Major General Robert Newport Tinley, John received a brevet promotion to the rank of Major General which was backdated to 23rd March 1869.[557] On 1st July 1881, John was placed on the retired list[558] after 36 years of service and was granted the honorary brevet rank of Lieutenant-General.[559]

After leaving the army, John went to stay with his sister Jane and his brother-in-law at Addington Park in Kent before moving to Ireland where he set up home at St Waleran House, Gorey in Co Wexford where for a time he was a Justice of the Peace.

On 8th April 1890, John was appointed as the Honorary Colonel of the Leicestershire Regiment.[560]

John died at his home in St Waleran House on 5th February 1895, the same day as Major General Montresor Rogers VC, at

Figure 204a. Grave of John Christopher Guise

551 *London Gazette* – 22093/571
552 *London Gazette* – 22117/1571
553 *London Gazette* – 22345/110
554 *London Gazette* – 22820/725
555 *London Gazette* – 22860/2871
556 *London Gazette* – 23503/3180

557 *London Gazette* – 24503/5235
558 *London Gazette* – 24999/3675
559 *London Gazette* – 25014/4688
560 *London Gazette* – 26061/3298

the age of 68 and was buried in the Gorey Churchyard on 8th February.

John's Victoria Cross Medal is on public display at the Imperial War Museum in London, part of the Lord Ashcroft collection.

Samuel Hill
16th/17th November 1857 (VC No. 227)

Gazetted: 24th December 1858 22212/5514

Rank and Unit: Sergeant – 90th Regiment of Foot

Citation

For gallant conduct on the 16th and 17th of November, 1857, at the storming of the Secundra Bagh at Lucknow, in saving the life of Captain Irby, warding off with his firelock a tulwar cut made at his head by a sepoy, and in going out under a heavy fire to help two wounded men. Also for general gallant conduct throughout the operations for the relief of the Lucknow garrison.

Elected by the non-commissioned officers of the Regiment.

Biography

Samuel was born at Glenavy, Co Antrim in Northern Ireland during 1826.

In December 1844, at the age of 18, Samuel enlisted in the army and joined the 67th Regiment of Foot who had just arrived in Dublin after a move from Manchester. In January 1846, Samuel moved with the regiment to Limerick and a few months later in May moved to Cork. In January 1848, Samuel saw his first period of overseas service when the regiment was deployed to the garrison at Gibraltar; this was followed by a posting to the West Indies in 1851.

Figure 205. Samuel Hill

In 1856, Samuel transferred to 90th Regiment of Foot and after being based in the camp at Aldershot moved to Portsmouth in February 1857 to make ready for a deployment to China. In April 1857, the regiment set sail for China, however, upon receiving news of the outbreak of mutiny in India they were ordered to the sub-continent and on arrival were assigned to the Lucknow Relief Force.

It was on 16th/17th November 1857, during the attacks on Lucknow that Samuel, now with the rank of Sergeant, performed the deeds for which he would later be awarded the Victoria Cross, having been elected for the award by a ballot of the Non-Commissioned officers of the regiment in accordance with rule 13 of the originating Royal Warrant. Samuel was also involved with the regiment in the action which resulted in the recapture of Lucknow on 21st March 1858. From 23rd April until 21st May the regiment were part of the force of Sir Hope Grant which was chasing down mutineers in the region around Bareilly.

For his part in the mutiny Samuel was awarded the Indian Mutiny Medal with clasps for Relief of Lucknow and Lucknow.

After the end of the Mutiny, Samuel and the regiment continued to serve in India, being stationed at Sitapur during 1859, where in February 1859 he was presented with his Victoria Cross Medal.

After moving to Allahabad in 1861 the regiment moved to Meerut on 31st December 1862 and it was here on 21st February 1863 that Samuel was killed in action and buried in an unmarked grave at St John's Cemetery in Meerut.

Samuel's Victoria Cross Medal is on public display at the Tolson Memorial Museum in Huddersfield, Yorkshire.

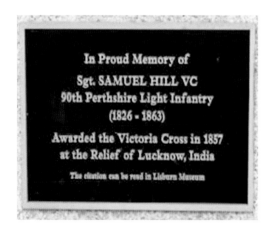

Figure 205a. St John's Church Meerut

Charles Pye
17th November 1857 (VC No. 228)

Gazetted: 24th December 1858 22212/5513

Rank and Unit: Sergeant Major – 53rd Regiment of Foot

Citation

For steadiness and fearless conduct under fire at Lucknow, on the 17th of November, 1857, when bringing up ammunition to the Mess House, and on every occasion when the Regiment has been engaged.

Elected by the non-commissioned officers of the Regiment.

Biography

Charles was born some time during 1820 at Rickerscote in Staffordshire and was baptised on 24th September 1820 at Forebridge also in Staffordshire. He was the eldest son and one of five children born to Thomas a brick and tile maker and Alice (née Hall). He had three younger brothers; Timothy, Philip and Peter as well as an older sister.

In 1826, the family moved to Birmingham and it was here ten years later that his father Thomas was convicted of housebreaking and was transported to Australia for life. It is believed that Charles, now an orphan as his mother had died giving birth to his youngest brother, moved back to Rickerscote with his brother and sister to be cared for by his Uncle.

On 18th November 1840, at the age of 20, Charles enlisted in the army at Coventry and began his army career as a Private in the 40th Regiment of Foot.

Charles left England on 1st February 1841 to join his regiment which was serving in India, he arrived in June 1841 and was initially stationed at Quetta until October when the regiment was moved to Kandahar. In December 1843, Charles served with the regiment in the Gwalior Campaign and was present at the Battle of Maharajpore on 29th December 1843. For his service during the campaign, Charles was awarded the Gwalior Campaign Star engraved with Maharajpoor Star.

In November 1844, Charles transferred to the 31st Regiment of Foot and saw action with the regiment during the Sutlej Campaign (1st Anglo-Sikh War). During the war, Charles was involved in the Battle of Mudki on 18th December 1845, the Battle of Ferozeshah on 21st December 1845, the Battle of Aliwal on 28th January 1846 and the Battle of Sobraon on 10th February 1846. For his service during the war, Charles was awarded the Sutlej Medal, engraved Moodkee 1845 and with clasps for Ferozeshuhur, Aliwal and Sobraon.

Figure 206. Charles Pye

On 1st April 1846, now a Corporal, Charles transferred to the 53rd Regiment of Foot as he wished to remain in India and the 31st Regiment were returning home to England.

During 1848 to 1849, Charles now with the rank of Sergeant, served with his new regiment in the Punjab Campaign (2nd Anglo-Sikh War), however, the regiment took no part in the major battles hence for his service during the war, Charles was awarded the Punjab Medal without any clasps.

In 1852, Charles saw service on the North West Frontier and was in action against the hill tribes in Peshawar. In 1855, Charles who was an avid Freemason, was appointed as the Grand Master of his Lodge. Charles was promoted to the rank of Sergeant-Major on 26th September 1856.

On 3rd January 1857, Charles married the widow of a fellow soldier Mary Ann Farrell (née Casey) in Calcutta and set up home with Mary and her two children.

At the start of the mutiny in May 1857, Charles and the 53rd were stationed at Fort William in Calcutta. They were initially deployed to guard public and commercial properties in the city and in disarming the native Indian Regiments based around the arsenal at Dum Dum.

On 27th August, Charles and the regiment were dispatched to the north of India and headed down the Grand Trunk Road for Allahabad, where forces were being concentrated for operations against the mutineers. After joining the Lucknow Relief Force commanded by Sir Colin Campbell, the regiment were involved in an action at Khujwa on 1st November 1857, where Charles was seriously wounded.[561]

Despite still recovering from his wounds, Charles took part in the action which resulted in the evacuation of the Residency on 19th October and it was two days early that Charles performed the deeds for which he would later be awarded the Victoria Cross, having been nominated for the award following a ballot of the non-commissioned officers of the regiment. Following the relief of Lucknow, Charles took part in the Battle of Cawnpore on 6th December 1857 and was involved in operations to pursue the Gwalior Contingent. During these operations, Charles was involved in; the Battle of Kallah Nuddee on 2nd January 1858 and the occupation of Futtehpore on the same day, the Battle of Shumshabad on 27th January 1858 and the Battle of Meeangunge on 23rd February 1858. Charles was also involved in the action which resulted in the final recapture of Lucknow on 21st March 1858. Following the capture of Lucknow, Charles was involved with his regiment in operations in the province of Oudh, as part of the force commanded by General James Hope Grant, taking part in the occupation of Sultanpore. On 2nd July 1858, Charles received a commission as Ensign as reward for his service in India.[562]

From 28th October 1858 until 19th May 1859, Charles served as to adjutant to the Oudh Military Police force and following this assignment was appointed as adjutant to the 53rd Regiment on 30th May 1859.[563]

Charles was presented with his Victoria Cross Medal, sometime during 1859, while still serving in India.

For his service during the mutiny, Charles was awarded the Indian Mutiny Medal with clasps for Relief of Lucknow and Lucknow.

Charles returned to England with the regiment on 14th April 1860 after nearly 19 years of service abroad and was stationed at Aldershot. On 9th April 1861, Charles was promoted to the rank of Lieutenant and continued in his role as Adjutant to the Regiment.[564] Charles resigned from his position as Adjutant on 18th March 1862[565] and a few weeks later on 27th May 1862, sold his commission and resigned from the army[566] after over 21 years of service.

On 27th August 1862, Charles with his wife and step-children boarded the SS *African* and left England for a new life in New Zealand, settling at Papakura near Auckland. Not long after arriving in New Zealand, Charles was caught up in the Maori Wars which had been raging since 1860, and in July 1863 was appointed as a Captain in the Auckland Militia and the following

561 *London Gazette* – 22084/259

562 *London Gazette* – 22158/3137
563 *London Gazette* – 22301/3205
564 *London Gazette* – 22500/1494
565 *London Gazette* – 22609/1478
566 *London Gazette* – 22629/2733

year was transferred as a Captain to the Colonial Defence Force. During the war, Charles saw action at Rangiawhia and Orakau in 1864 and for his service was awarded the New Zealand Medal (1860–66).

When the Colonial Defence Force was disbanded in October 1867, Charles tried his hand at farming but without much success and afterwards owned a gold mine and produce store in the Thames District of the North Island.

In 1875, Charles sailed to Australia for a reunion with his father at Kirkstall, near Melbourne in the state of Victoria.

As Charles had purchased a plot of land from his father, it appears that he intended to settle in Australia with his family, however on 12th July 1876 at the age of 56, died from bronchitis while staying with his father at Kirkstall and was buried in the Tower Hill Cemetery at Koroit.

Charles's Victoria Cross Medal is on public display at the Auckland Institute and Museum in Auckland, New Zealand.

Figure 206a. Memorial at Springvale Botanical Cemetery, Victoria

Patrick Graham
17th November 1857 (VC No. 229)

Gazetted: 24th December 1858 22212/5514

Rank and Unit: Private 3829 – 90th Regiment of Foot

Citation

For bringing in a wounded comrade under a very heavy fire, on the 17th of November, 1857, at Lucknow.

Elected by the private soldiers of the Regiment.

Biography

Patrick was born some time during 1837 in the St Michael's Parish of Dublin, Ireland.

On 5th December 1854, at the age of 17, Patrick left his job as a confectioner and enlisted in the army at Dublin. He became a Private in the 90th Regiment of foot, coincidentally on the same day that the bulk of the regiment were landing at Balaklava in the Crimea.

Sometime in August 1855, Patrick joined his regiment in the Crimea and was assigned to duties in the trenches around Sevastopol. For his service in the Crimea, Patrick was awarded the Crimea Medal with clasp for Sevastopol and the Turkish Crimea Medal. In June 1856, Patrick boarded *HMS Queen*, with the regiment, to begin the journey back to England and arrived at Portsmouth at the end of July.

From Portsmouth the regiment were sent to the new camp at Aldershot where they remained until February 1857 when they were sent back to Portsmouth with orders to make ready for deployment to China. In April 1857, the regiment set sail for China, however, upon receiving news of the outbreak of mutiny in India they were ordered to the sub-continent and on arrival were assigned to the Lucknow Relief Force.

It was on 17th November 1857, during the attacks on Lucknow that Patrick, performed the deeds for which he would later be awarded the Victoria Cross, having been elected for the award by a ballot of the private soldiers of the regiment in accordance with rule 13 of the originating Royal Warrant. Patrick was also involved with the regiment in the action which resulted in the recapture of Lucknow on 21st March 1858. From 23rd April until 21st May the regiment were part of the force of Sir Hope Grant which was chasing down mutineers in the region around Bareilly. For his part in the mutiny Patrick was awarded the Indian Mutiny Medal with clasps for Relief of Lucknow and Lucknow.

After the end of the Mutiny, Patrick and the regiment continued to serve in India, being stationed at Sitapur during 1859, where in February 1859 he was presented with his Victoria Cross Medal.

After moving to Allahabad in 1861 it appears that Patrick returned to England during July of 1861, however, after re-engaging at Manchester for a further 13 years service on 27th June 1863 he rejoined the regiment at Meean Meer in India during January 1864. In December 1864, the regiment moved to Peshawar and a year later in December 1865 moved to Nowshera where they remained until December 1866 when they moved to Subathoo. It was while stationed at Subathoo that Patrick became one of the many casualties of cholera and on 29th October 1867 he was declared unfit for further military service and was sent back to England.

On 1st September 1868, Patrick was discharged from the army after over 12 years service and took up residence at 198 North King Street in Dublin.

Patrick died on 3rd June 1875, at the age of 37 and was buried in an unmarked grave in the Arbour Hill Cemetery in Dublin, subsequently the cemetery records were destroyed and the exact location of Patrick's grave is unknown.

Patrick's Victoria Cross Medal is on public display at the Cameronians Regimental Museum, Hamilton, Lanarkshire.

Thomas Bernard Hackett
18th November 1857 (VC No. 230)

Gazetted: 12th April 1859 22248/1482

Rank and Unit: Lieutenant – 23rd Regiment of Foot

Citation
For daring gallantry at Secundra Bagh, Lucknow, on the 18th November, 1857, in having with others, rescued a Corporal of the 23rd Regiment, who was lying wounded and exposed to very heavy fire. Also, for conspicuous bravery, in having, under a heavy fire, ascended the roof, and cut down the thatch of a Bungalow, to prevent its being set on fire.

This was a most important service at the time.

Biography
Thomas was born on 15th June 1836 at Riverstown, Birr, Co Tipperary in Ireland. He was the 9th of 11 children born to Thomas, a landowner and the High Sheriff of Kings County and his wife Jane Bernard (née Shaw). Thomas had 7 older sisters, one older brother and two younger brothers.

Thomas began his career in the army on 7th June 1854 when he purchased a commission of Ensign in the 6th Light Dragoons.[567] On 3rd November 1854, Thomas was transferred to the 23rd Regiment of Foot with the rank of Ensign[568] and a

Figure 208. Thomas Bernard Hackett

567 *London Gazette* – 21559/1721
568 *London Gazette* – 21617/3312

few months later on 9th February 1855 was promoted to the rank of Lieutenant.[569] From 5th June 1855 until 6th September 1855, Thomas served with his regiment in the Crimea and on 18th June 1855 was involved in the assault on the Redan. He was also involved in the siege of Sevastopol. For his service in the Crimea, Thomas was awarded the Crimea Medal with clasp for Sevastopol and the Turkish Crimea Medal.

In May 1857, the regiment set sail from Portsmouth bound for India where they arrived at Calcutta in September and moved across country to join the Lucknow Relief Force. It was on the 18th November 1857, during the attack on Lucknow that resulted in the successful evacuation of the garrison from the Residency, that Thomas performed the deeds for which he would later be awarded the Victoria Cross. Thomas was involved in the Battle of Cawnpore on 6th December 1857 and a few weeks later on 26th January 1858, he advanced his position in the regiment when he purchased a commission as Captain.[570] Thomas was present during the action which resulted in the recapture of Lucknow on 21st March 1858 and subsequently took part in operations in the Baiswarra district, including the affairs at Jubrowlie, Foornab and Doondikiara. For his service during the mutiny, Thomas was awarded the Indian Mutiny Medal with clasps for Relief of Lucknow and Lucknow.

Thomas was presented with his Victoria Cross Medal by Lord Clyde the Commander in Chief of forces in India at a ceremony in Lucknow during May 1860.

Thomas remained in India until 1869 and arrived back in England on 9th November 1869. On 3rd September 1870, Thomas purchased the commission of Major in the regiment[571] and on 1st April 1874 received a brevet promotion to the rank of Lieutenant-Colonel.[572]

Thomas married Josephine (née Marshall) on 9th June 1974, the couple would be childless.

After 20 years of service, Thomas sold his commission and retired from the army on 19th August 1874.[573]

On leaving the army, Thomas returned to Ireland set up home at Arrabeg in Co Tipperary, where he was a landowner and became a Justice of the Peace for Tipperary.

On 4th October 1880, while on a partridge shoot, Thomas was involved in a tragic accident; his gun got caught up in a thicket and was accidental discharged causing mortal wounds.

Thomas died of his wounds on the following day and on 8th October 1880 he was buried in the Marshall family vault at Lockeen Churchyard, Borriskone near Riverstown in Co Tipperary, Ireland.

Thomas's Victoria Cross Medal is on public display at the Imperial War Museum in London as part of the Lord Ashcroft collection.

Figure 208a. Grave of Thomas Bernard Hackett

569 *London Gazette* – 21660/490
570 *London Gazette* – 22087/366
571 *London Gazette* – 23653/4037
572 *London Gazette* – 24082/1924
573 *London Gazette* – 24123/4072

George Monger
18th November 1857 (VC No. 231)

Gazetted: 12th April 1859 22248/1482

Rank and Unit: Private 5202 – 23rd Regiment of Foot

Citation

*For daring gallantry at Secundra Bagh, Lucknow, on
the 18th of November, 1857, in having volunteered to
accompany Lieutenant Hackett, whom he assisted in
bringing in a Corporal of the 23rd Regiment, who was lying
wounded in an exposed position.*

Biography

George was born on 3rd March 1840 at Woodmancott, near Basingstoke in Hampshire.

On 10th November 1855, at 15 years of age, George enlisted at Winchester as a drummer boy in the 23rd Regiment of Foot.

In May 1857, the regiment set sail from Portsmouth bound for India where they arrived at Calcutta in September and moved across country to join the Lucknow Relief Force. It was on the 18th November 1857, during the attack on Lucknow that resulted in the successful evacuation of the garrison from the Residency, that George aged 17, performed the deeds for which he would later be awarded the Victoria Cross. George was involved in the Battle of Cawnpore on 6th December 1857. George was present during the action which resulted in the recapture of Lucknow on 21st March 1858 and subsequently took part in operations in the Baiswarra district, including the affairs at Jubrowlie, Foornab and Doondikiara. For his service during the mutiny, George was awarded the Indian Mutiny Medal with clasps for Relief of Lucknow and Lucknow.

George was presented with his Victoria Cross Medal by Lord Clyde the Commander in Chief of forces in India at a ceremony in Lucknow during May 1860.

George remained in India until 1869 and arrived back in England on 9th November 1869 and having completed his initial enlistment period of 10 years was discharged from the army at his own request. On leaving the army, George moved to North Waltham in Hampshire, where he worked as a labourer.

In 1871, George married Mary Ann (née Love) and the couple would go one to have 6 children: Leavina born in 1874, Joseph born in 1878 and Earnest John born in 1881; three other children died soon after they were born.

On moving to St Leonards-on-Sea, Sussex sometime around 1878, George worked as a plasterer for Mr J. C. Kenwood until he was forced to stop working due to severe Asthma. Unable to

Figure 209. George Monger

work and having to support a wife and three children, George lived in abject poverty until his plight came to the attention of Major-General Sherer who helped to raise funds to support the family.

On 9th August 1887, at the age of 47, George died at his home Bohemia, in St Leonards-on-Sea from tuberculosis and was buried with full military honours, four days later at Hastings Borough Council Cemetery.

George's Victoria Cross Medal is on public display at the Regimental Museum the Royal Welch Fusiliers in Caernarfon Castle in Wales.

Figure 209a. Grave of George Monger

Harry North Dalrymple Prendergast
21st November 1857 (VC No. 232)

Gazetted: 21st October 1859 22318/3793

Rank and Unit: Lieutenant – Madras Engineers

Citation

For conspicuous bravery on the 21st of November, 1857, at Mundisore, in saving the life of Lieutenant G. Dew, 14th Light Dragoons, at the risk of his own, by attempting to cut down a Velaitee, who covered him (Lieutenant Dew) with his piece, from only a few paces to the rear. Lieutenant Prendergast was wounded in this- affair by the discharge of the piece, and would probably have, been cut down, had not the rebel been killed by Major Orr.

He also distinguished himself by his gallantry in the actions at Ratgurh and Betwa, when he was severely wounded.

Major-General Sir Hugh Rose, in forwarding his recommendation of this Officer, states: "Lieutenant Prendergast, Madras Engineers, was specially mentioned by Brigadier, now Sir Charles Stuart, for the gallant act at Mundisore, when he, was severely wounded.

Secondly, he was specially mentioned by me when acting voluntarily as my Aide-de-Camp in the action before besieging Ratgurh, on the Beena River, for gallant conduct. His horse was killed on that occasion.

Thirdly, at the Action of the Betwa, he again voluntarily acted as my Aide-de-Camp, and distinguished himself by his bravery in the charge, which I made with Captain Need's Troop, Her Majesty's 14th Light Dragoons, against the left of the so-called Peishwa's Army, under Tantia Topi. He was severely wounded on that occasion."

Biography

Harry was born on 15th October 1834 at Madras in India, the youngest of three children born to Thomas who worked for the Madras Civil Service and Lucy Caroline (née Dalrymple). Thomas had a sister Fanny Elizabeth Strachan born on 27th September 1829 and a brother Hew Lindsay born on 29th April 1831; Hew would also have a successful army career and attained the rank of Major-General. When his mother died, on 15th November 1839, Harry and his brother Hew were sent to live with their Grandfather, Major-General Sir Jeffery Prendergast, in Brighton.

During 1849 and 1850, Harry was educated at Brighton College and afterwards at Cheam School until he attended the Honourable East India Company's Military Seminary at Addiscombe from

Figure 210. Harry North Dalrymple Prendergast

August 1852. Harry graduated from Addiscombe on 8th June 1854 and was granted the local and temporary rank of Ensign when on 23rd June 1854 he was placed under the command of Colonel H. D. Jones of the Royal Engineers, at Chatham for field instruction in the art of Sapping and Mining.[574] After graduating from Chatham, Harry set out to join his regiment in India and arrived at Madras in October 1856 and was posted to Godavari.

On 1st November 1856, the Governor General of India declared war on Persia and Harry was transferred to B Company of the Sappers in readiness for deployment to the war. On 19th January 1857, Harry boarded the Honourable East India Company ship *Victoria* at Coconada and set sail for the Persian Gulf where they landed at Bushire at the end of March. The Madras Engineers transferred over to the Bengal Marine vessel *SS Hugh Lindsay* on 26th March and proceeded up the Shat-el-Arab River and took part in the bombardment and occupation of Mohammrah on the next day. On 4th April, the British force received news that a peace treaty had been signed in Paris on 4th March and began preparations for their return to India, the Sappers set sail for Bombay on 1st June 1857. For his service during the war, Harry was awarded the India General Service Medal with clasp for Persia.

Despite having just returned from the war in Persia, on hearing news of the mutiny, the Sappers volunteered for service against the mutineers and Harry was assigned to the Deccan and Mhow Field Force under the command of Major-General Woodburn, which was part of the Malwa Field Force commanded by Brigadier-General Stuart which in turn was within the Central India Field Force under the command of Sir Hugh Rose.

---

574 *London Gazette* – 21565/1949

The Sappers set off from Bombay on 16th June and headed for Aurangabad where they joined up with the Deccan Field Force on 5th July. On 23rd July, the force relieved Asseerghur and then Mhow on 2nd August. Due to the poor condition of the roads during the monsoon, the Sappers remained in Mhow until 20th October when they set off for Dhar. Harry was acting as Brigade-Major, second in command to Major Boileau who was the command engineer. After a siege which lasted for just over a week, Dhar was taken and occupied on 1st November and the field force now moved on to Mundesore where they arrived on 21st November. From Mundesore, the objective was to relieve Neemuch which was 30 miles to the North. Requiring intelligence, Harry was sent with Captain Mayne and 300 Cavalry to perform a reconnaissance and when they came upon and charged a force of mutineers, harry performed the deeds for which he would later be awarded the Victoria Cross. During this action Harry was severely wounded by a Musket ball through the chest, which just missed his heart.[575]

While acting as Aide-de-Camp to Major-General Sir Hugh Rose, Harry saw action during the siege of Rathghur from 25th to 29th January 1858 for which he received a second mention in his Victoria Cross citation. During this action Harry had his horse shot out from under him. At the Battle of Betwa on 1st April, Harry while still acting as Aide-de-Camp to Major-General Rose, performed the deeds which resulted in the third mention in his Victoria Cross citation. During the battle Harry was again severely wounded with sabre cuts to the left arm and hand which nearly severed his left thumb. On 4th April 1858, Harry was invalided at Jhansi, due to the wounds rendered to his left arm which left it almost useless, and was sent home on 2 years sick leave. On 27th April 1858, just before boarding ship for home at Calcutta, Harry was promoted to the rank of Lieutenant. For his service during the mutiny, Harry was awarded the Indian Mutiny Medal with clasp for Central India.

Despite his infirmity, Harry was not content to spend his time in "idle recuperation" in England and volunteered for active service on two occasions, first in 1859 to fight for Austria in the war against Italy and France and secondly in 1860 when he volunteered to fight in the 2nd Opium War. Harry was extremely disappointed to be rejected for active service on both occasions, saying *"I can play cricket so I can fight"*.

Harry was presented with his Victoria Cross Medal by Queen Victoria at a ceremony held at Windsor Castle on 4th January 1860.

Harry returned to service in India during 1860 and initially served as an Assistant Engineer in the Department of Public Works after which he served as commandant of the Western Division. On 7th April 1863, Harry was promoted to the rank of 2nd Captain in the Royal Engineers[576] and on the next day received a brevet promotion to the rank of Major[577] and was appointed to the position of Governor General's agent in the state of Baroda. Following the death of Lord Elgin on 20th November 1863, Sir William Thomas Denison was appointed as interim Governor of India and Harry accompanied him on a tour which took in Agra, Delhi, Lucknow and Benares before arriving at Calcutta. On his return to Madras, Harry was appointed as assistant commissioning Engineer of railways.

On 11th October 1864, Harry was married to Amelia Rachel (née Simpson) at Bangalore in India, the couple would go on to have 8 children all born in India; Maude Dora Josephine, Amy Louisa Caroline born in 1866, Fanny Bertha born on 8th January 1867, Teresa Ella Drummond born on 25th June 1869, Harry Young born on 7th December 1870, George William Yelverton born on 17th July 1872, Herbert Hew Loraine born on 15th March 1878 and Arthur Frederick Claude Vereker born on 14th August 1887.

In late 1867, Harry was appointed as field engineer to the Abyssinian expedition, commanded by Sir Robert Napier, and after sailing from Baypore with three companies of sappers was involved in the campaign which lasted from December 1867 to May 1868. On 10th April 1868, Harry was involved in the decisive battle at Magdala and received a mention in despatches. For his service during the expedition, Harry was awarded the Abyssinian War Medal (1867–68).

On his return from Abyssinia, Harry continued as assistant commissioning Engineer for the railways and on 15th August 1868, Harry received a brevet promotion to the rank of Lieutenant-Colonel.[578]

Soon after his promotion, Harry was appointed to the command of the Madras Sappers, a position that he would hold until 1st September 1880. His service in command of the Madras Sappers was interrupted for two years from 1874 until 1876, when Harry was on extended leave, during this time his brother Major Hew Prendergast acted as commander in his place.

Harry was placed on the Supernumerary List on 24th March 1871.[579] On 5th July 1872, Harry was promoted to the rank of Major.[580] Harry received a brevet promotion to the rank of Colonel on 30th January 1875.[581]

575 *London Gazette* – 22112/1390

576 *London Gazette* – 22752/3453
577 *London Gazette* – 22772/4608
578 *London Gazette* – 23412/4512
579 *London Gazette* – 23745/2697
580 *London Gazette* – 23876/3195
581 *London Gazette* – 24238/4188

On 29th May 1875, Harry was appointed as an Ordinary Member 3rd Class (Companion) of the Military Division of the Most Honourable Order of the Bath.[582]

Harry was promoted to the rank of Lieutenant-Colonel on 17th April 1878.[583] In April 1878, Harry taking command of 4 companies of the Madras & Bombay Sappers, was part of a force of some 7,000 men despatched by Lord Beaconsfield from India to the Mediterranean. After spending a month at Malta, the force was ordered to Cyprus where they arrived off Larnica on 16th July 1878. Harry returned to India on 25th August and resumed command of the Sappers.

In 1879, Harry spent 3 months in England on sick leave and missed opportunities to be involved in the 2nd Anglo-Afghan war having initially been named as the commanding engineer to the division commanded by General Primrose. In September 1880, Harry was appointed to the command of the Malabar and Kanara districts of South West India with the rank of Brigadier-General and in 1881 was transferred to the command of the Bellary District. On 16th September 1882, Harry was promoted to the rank of Major-General,[584] had to relinquish his district command and was appointed as Quartermaster General by Sir Frederick Sleigh Roberts and took up his post at Secunderabad.

After a short vacation in England, Harry was transferred to the staff of the Indian Army on 3rd April 1883, with the rank of Major-General and was placed in command of the Burma division.[585] Soon after taking up his new command, Harry undertook a tour of Burma with the Chief Commissioned Sir Charles Hawkes Todd Crosthwaite, to familiarise himself with the country as the possibility of war was in the air. On his return to India, Harry was offered the command of the Hyderabad Subsidiary Force, however, for a few months he returned to Burma in case war was declared but when this possibility receded he returned to India and took up the offered command at Secunderabad.

The British government issued an ultimatum to the King of Burma on 22nd October 1885 and in anticipation of a refusal the Viceroy of India, George Robinson the 1st Marques of Ripon appointed Harry as commander of the Burmese Expeditionary Force. Harry travelled to Burma and on 7th November 1885 inspected his force of 9,000 troops at Rangoon and following the rejection of the British ultimatum on 9th November made ready to invade Burma and depose the King. By 14th November, the invasion force had been assembled at the British Frontier post at Thayelmyo and after boarding river steamers proceeded up the River Irrawaddy, taking the defences at Minhla on 17th

November 1885. Over the next few days the force continued up the river and subdued the river defences at Nyaung-U, Pakokku and Myingyan before reaching the capital city of Ava on 26th November, where Harry met with envoys of King Thibow, who approached the British fleet under a flag of truce. On 27th November, acting on orders from their King, the Burma forces in Ava laid down their arms and surrendered. The next day the British forces reached Mandalay and peacefully occupied the city and following discussions with Harry, King Thirbow accepted unconditional terms of surrender and the 3rd Anglo-Burma war was at an end.

On 28th November 1885, Harry was promoted to the rank of Lieutenant-General.[586]

Harry was appointed as an Extra Member 2nd Class (Knight Commander) of the Military Division on the Most Honourable Order of the Bath on 8th December 1885.[587]

On 6th December 1885, Harry despatched a brigade to the town of Bhamo, to forestall any moves by China, who were also engaged in border disputes with Burma and after completion of the occupation of the town on 28th December, Harry returned to Mandalay where he arrived on 12th January 1886. Burma, with a land area greater than that of France, was formally annexed as part of the British Empire on 1st January 1886 and on 18th February, Harry was given command of all British forces in Burma. On 25th March 1886, Harry was informed that due to his promotion to the rank of Lieutenant-General he would have to relinquish his command as his rank now exceeded that required for the post. For his service during the war in Burma, Harry was awarded the clasp for Burma 1885–87 for his India General Service Medal.

After relinquishing command of the forces in Burma in April 1886, Harry returned to England for three months and then returned to India where he resided at the Ootacamund Hill Station in the state of Tamil Nadu and waited for his next position.

Harry was promoted to the rank of General on 22nd February 1887.[588] Harry spent over a year without employment, until he was appointed as the Acting Resident at Travancore and Chief Commissioner at Cochin, a position that he held from 7th July 1887 until October 1887. Over the next few years further political appointments followed; from 10th October 1887 until 15th January 1889 Harry served as Resident of Mysore and from 18th January 1889 until April 1890 served as the Resident of Baroda (apart from the period 3rd April to 8th October 1889 when he stood in for Sir Robert Sandeman as Chief Commissioner for

---

582 *London Gazette* – 24213/2852
583 *London Gazette* – 24572/2573
584 *London Gazette* – 25150/4383
585 *London Gazette* – 25266/4359

586 *London Gazette* – 25542/6193
587 *London Gazette* – 25537/5934
588 *London Gazette* – 25677/1002

Baluchistan). From July 1890 until 6th February 1891 Harry was again Resident of Baroda and from 1st June 1891 until 16th April 1892 was Resident of Mysore and Chief Commissioner of Coorg.

On 1st April 1891, Harry was placed on the unemployed supernumerary list[589] and at the early age of 57, his army career was over.

After completing his role as Resident of Mysore, Harry left India for the final time and returned to England in April 1892. On 30th March 1901, Harry was appointed as President of the Association of Old Brightonians, his old school.

Harry was appointed as an Ordinary Member 1st Class (Knight Grand Cross) of the Military Division on the Most Honourable Order of the Bath on 26th June 1902.[590]

On 13th May 1903, Harry was appointed Honorary Colonel of the 2nd Queen's Own Sappers and Miners.[591] Harry was appointed as Colonel Commandant of the Royal Engineers on 1st October 1908.[592]

On 24th July 1913, Harry died from pneumonia at his home, 2 Heron Court, Richmond-on-Thames in Surrey and was buried four days later at the Richmond Cemetery.

Harry's Victoria Cross Medal is on public display at the Royal Engineers Museum, Chatham in Kent.

Figure 210a. Grave of Harry North Dalrymple Prendergast

589 *London Gazette* – 26163/2683
590 *London Gazette* – 27448/4190
591 *London Gazette* – 27676/3089
592 *London Gazette* – 28199/8700

Arthur Mayo
22nd November 1857 (VC No. 233)

Gazetted: 25th February 1862 22601/958

Rank and Unit: Midshipman – Indian Navy – Naval Brigade

Citation
For-having headed the charge on the 22nd of November, 1857, in the engagement between the Indian Naval Brigade and the mutineers of the 73rd Native Infantry, and Bengal Artillery, when the former was ordered to charge 2 sixpounders which were keeping up a heavy fire. Mr. Mayo was nearly 20 yards in front of any one else during the advance.

Biography
Arthur was born on 18th May 1840 at St. Giles in Oxford, the 5th son born to Herbert and Sarah (née Harman). One of his older brothers served with the 38th Regiment of Foot at the Relief of Lucknow.

After completing his education at Berkhampstead School, which he attended from 1847 until 1854, Arthur joined the Royal Navy and as a midshipman was assigned to *HMS Wellesley* in 1855 and set sail for India. On 18th February 1857, Arthur joined the Indian Navy and for a short time served on the steam frigate *Punjab*, which was employed in the task of ferrying the 64th Regiment of Foot from Bombay to Calcutta.

In June 1857, following the outbreak of mutiny, Arthur with several of his comrades from the *Punjab* and men from the

Figure 211. Arthur Mayo

Zenobia, was assigned to the 4th Indian Naval Brigade and was sent from Calcutta to Dacca on a mission to disarm the Bengal Artillery and 73rd Native Infantry who had mutinied. It was on 22nd November 1857, in the action at Dacca at the age of 17½, that Arthur performed the deeds for which he would later be awarded the Victoria Cross. In response to an urgent request from the Commissioner of Assam, Francis Jenkins, Arthur and the Naval Brigade were despatched to northern Bengal and via Sylhet arrived at Debroghur on 2nd October 1858 where they helped subdue the unrest. On 14th February 1859, Arthur and the Naval Brigade were part of a force commanded by Lieutenant-Colonel Hannay of the 1st Assam Infantry which was despatched on a mission to the Abor Hills to quell the unrest of the local tribes. Arthur was wounded in the hand by a poisoned arrow on 27th February 1859,[593] during an action against villages in the Abor Hills, however, despite his wound he completed his objectives and received two mentions in despatches for his actions. For his service during the mutiny, Arthur was awarded the Indian Mutiny Medal (without clasps).

In 1860, Arthur was invalided home and was discharged from the Navy to pension on 28th November 1862 after 8 years of service.

On 2nd May 1862, Arthur continued his education when he enrolled at Oxford University (Magdalen Hall) from where he graduated with a BA on 18th June 1865.

It is believed that Arthur received his Victoria Cross Medal by Registered post, however, on 22nd June 1864 at a levee held at St James Palace he was presented to Albert HRH the Price of Wales[594] in recognition of his award.

A month after his graduation, Arthur was married to Ellen Horser (née Baker) at Oxford on 18th July 1865. The couple would go on to have six children; Mary who was born on 20th April 1866 would become a Dominican Nun at Adelaide in Australia, Arthur who was born in May 1867 only survived for six months. There were three other sons, Edward, Francis and Raymond all of whom would become Jesuit priests and finally Margaret who was born on 18th March 1880.

On 25th February 1866, Arthur was ordained as a Deacon for the Bishop of Exeter at Salisbury and served as assistant curate of St Peter's Church in Plymouth until October 1867. Arthur was received into the Catholic Church on 5th November 1867, at Farm Street by Father P. Galway of the Society of Jesus. After spending some years at St Mary's, Torquay in Devon in 1892 Arthur went to live in Malta where he remained until 1901.

In 1901, Arthur returned to England and went to live with his youngest daughter Margaret at 23 Rosebury Road in Bournemouth where he became an active member of the Corpus Christi Church at Boscombe.

As a talented musician with a very fine voice, Alfred served for many years as the organist for the church.

Arthur died at home on 18th May 1920, during a small celebration for his 80th birthday and was buried with full military honours at Boscombe East Cemetery.

The location of Arthur's Victoria Cross Medal is unknown.

Figure 211a. Grave of Arthur Mayo

---

593 *London Gazette* – 22287/2746
594 Who would succeed to the throne as King Edward VII

Thomas Flynn (Flinn)
28th November 1857 (VC No. 234)

Gazetted: 12th April 1859 22248/1483

Rank and Unit: Drummer No. 3406 – 64th Regiment of Foot

Citation
For conspicuous gallantry, in the charge on the Enemy's guns on the 28th November, 1857, when, being himself wounded, he engaged in a hand to hand encounter two of the Rebel Artillerymen.

Biography
Thomas was born during August 1842 at Athlone, Co Westmeath in Ireland; the only son of William who was a soldier in the 64th Regiment of Foot, probably serving with the depot companies who were stationed in Ireland while the bulk of the regiment were deployed to Canada. In October 1843, Thomas would have moved to Plymouth where the depot companies were reunited with the bulk of the regiment on their return from service in Nova Scotia. In September 1845, the regiment returned to Ireland where they were stationed at Dublin until the end of 1848 when they were moved to Cork and told to make ready for deployment to India.

At the end of 1848, the regiment departed for India and on their arrival were stationed at Poona, it is thought that Thomas enlisted in the regiment, as a drummer, in 1855 at the age of 13.

Following the declaration of war against Persia on 1st November 1856, Thomas and the regiment were sent from Bombay to the Gulf of Persia and were involved in all of the major battles of the war; at Bushire on 5th December which resulted in the capture of the city on the 10th December, the siege and capture of Mohammrah on 27th March and the Battle of Ahvaz on 1st April 1857. After receiving news of the signing of a peace treaty in Paris on 4th March 1857, the expeditionary force to Persia was disbanded and Thomas and the 64th returned to India, arriving at Bombay on 4th June 1857.

Immediately on arriving at Bombay, as a result of the outbreak of mutiny, the regiment was transferred to another ship and set sail for Calcutta with orders to join the forces of Sir Colin Campbell which was being assembled to go to the relief of Lucknow. On arrival in Calcutta, the regiment was initially deployed to the task of disarming the native regiments in and around the city until on 3rd July 1857 they were ordered to make their way to Cawnpore to meet up with the Lucknow Relief Force. As part of the force commanded by Sir Colin Campbell, the regiment took part in the siege of Cawnpore on 19th November which culminated in the capture of the city on 6th December 1857. It

Figure 212. Thomas Flynn

was on 28th November 1857, during the action at Cawnpore, that Thomas, despite being wounded, performed the deeds for which he would later be awarded the Victoria Cross at the age of 15 years and 3 months he was one of the youngest to receive the award.[595] Due to the fact that he received no clasps to his Indian Mutiny Medal, and that he was wounded during the battle at Cawnpore, it is likely that Thomas was part of the detachment left to garrison Cawnpore rather than part of the force which was sent to the relief of Lucknow. After the relief of Lucknow, the regiment returned to Cawnpore and was assigned to the first infantry brigade under the command of Brigadier Greathed and fought in operations in the province of Oude under General Sir Hope Grant. Following operations in Oudh, the regiment was involved in operations in Rohilkhand before they returned to their base in Kurrachee in 1858. For his service during the mutiny, Thomas was awarded the Indian Mutiny Medal without clasps.

Thomas was presented with his Victoria Cross Medal by Brigadier Hall at a garrison parade held during March 1860.

In March 1861, the regiment left India after a deployment of 12 years and arrived back in England during July 1861 where they formed the garrison at Dover.

For the next few years Thomas served at several posts in England; Aldershot in 1863, Gosport in 1864, Portsmouth in 1865, Manchester in 1866 and Parkhurst in 1867; before being posted to Malta in 1867.

After 14 years of service, Thomas was discharged from the army in 1869 and returned to his home town of Athlone in Ireland.

---

595 Andrew Fitzgibbon was also 15 years and 3 months old when he performed actions at the Taku Forts on 21st August 1860, during the 3rd Anglo-China War, that resulted in the award of the Victoria Cross.

During his time in the army, Thomas had a very bad disciplinary record mainly due to excessive and persistent drunkenness and served a total of 586 days imprisonment for 14 separate charges of habitual drunkenness. Unfortunately, after leaving the army his problems with drink continued and unable to support himself he was soon committed to the Athlone Workhouse.[596]

In April 1892, not long before his death, his local Member of Parliament, Donal Sullivan raised the plight of Thomas in the Houses of Parliament when he directed the following question to St John Brodrick, the Financial Secretary to the War Office: "… whether he is aware that Flinn was awarded a pension of £10 a year for his valorous conduct, which sum the Guardians of the Athlone Union appropriate towards his maintenance; and whether some small increase could be made, so as to enable him in his old age to end his days more comfortably than in a workhouse?" The reply from Brodrick summed up Thomas's desperate situation: "This case is well known at the War Office. Flynn did very gallant service and was awarded the Victoria Cross, but I regret to say that he was discharged with a very bad character, he having been entered in the defaulter-book 47 times, and tried by Court Martial 15 times. The poor man is a victim to drink to such an extent that when he

had the control of his money he only left the workhouse for the purpose of drinking up his annuity as soon as received. It would consequently be useless to consider his case for an increase".

Soon after this intervention on his behalf, Thomas died on 10th August 1892, while residing at the Athlone Workhouse aged 50 and was buried in an unmarked pauper's grave in Cornamach Roman Catholic Cemetery.

Thomas's Victoria Cross Medal is believed to be held in a private collection.

Figure 212a. Memorial to Thomas Flynn, South Staffordshire Regimental Chapel

596 Hansard, House of Commons debate 1st April 1892 vol 3 c 466

Frederick Sleigh Roberts
2nd January 1858 (VC No. 235)

Gazetted: 24th December 1858 22212/5516

Rank and Unit: Lieutenant – Bengal Artillery

Citation

Lieutenant Roberts' gallantry has on every occasion been most marked.

On following up the retreating enemy on the 2nd January, 1858, at Khodagunge, he saw in the distance two Sepoys going away with a standard. Lieutenant Roberts put spurs to his horse, and overtook them just as they were about to enter a village. They immediately turned round, and presented their muskets at him, and one of the men pulled the trigger, but fortunately the caps snapped, and the standard-bearer was cut down by this gallant young officer, and the standard taken possession of by him. He also, on the same day, cut down another Sepoy who was standing at bay, with musket and bayonet, keeping off a Sowar. Lieutenant Roberts rode to the assistance of the horseman, and, rushing at the Sepoy, with one blow of his sword cut him across the face, killing him on the spot.

Biography

Frederick was born on 30th September 1832 in Cawnpore, India where his father Lieutenant-Colonel Abraham Roberts was in command of the 1st Bengal European Regiment, his mother was Isabel (née Bunbury) the widow of Major Hamilton George Maxwell and his father's second wife. Frederick was brought up in a large family with two older half sisters; Francis Eliza and Maria Isabella and an older half brother George Rickett[597] born on 8th February 1827 from his father's first marriage to Frances Isabella Poyntz (née Ricketts). Frederick also had an older half brother Hamilton[598] and half sister Innes Lloyd from his mother's first marriage as well as a younger sister Harriet Mercer who was born in 1833 at Cawnpore. Frederick received his middle name of Sleigh, in honour of the Cawnpore garrison commander Major-General William Sleigh.

When he was only a year old, Frederick almost died from a raging fever, it was only when his father, in desperation, held him under flowing spring water (in line with a local Indian custom)

---

597 George would also persue a military career and attained the rank of Major-General

598 Like his father, Hamilton had a military career and achieved the rank of Colonel

Figure 213. Frederick Sleigh Roberts

that his fever broke and his health slowly returned, however as a result of the fever he lost the sight in one eye.

In 1834, Frederick's father returned to England for a while and the family were settled at 23 Royal York Crescent, Clifton, Bristol in Somerset.

Frederick was initially educated at Clifton and Eton before he was enrolled at the Sandhurst Military Academy in January 1847, with the intention of purchasing a commission in the British Army when he graduated. Due to the financial constraints of his father, this plan was abandoned and his father decided that Frederick should look to a career in the Indian Army so he left Sandhurst in June 1848 and attended the private school of Stoton and Mayer's at Wimbledon until 1st February 1850 when he was enrolled at the Honourable East India Company Military Seminary at Addiscombe near Croydon. On graduating from Addiscombe, Frederick was commissioned as a 2nd Lieutenant in the Bengal Artillery on 12th December 1851 and on 1st April 1852 joined his regiment at Dum Dum near Calcutta.

In August 1852, Frederick was posted to the 1st Mountain battery at Peshawar and for a time he acted as Aide-de-Camp to his father who commanded the Peshawar division and at the end of 1854 joined the Bengal Horse Artillery. Frederick was appointed to the position of Deputy Assistant Quartermaster General to the Peshawar Division on 25th March 1856 and was performing this role at the outbreak of mutiny. On 12th May 1857, when news of the mutiny at Meerut reached Peshawar, Frederick accompanied General Reed to Rawalpindi and on 20th May was appointed as Quartermaster to a column commanded by General Nicholson directed to operations against the mutineers in the Punjab. On

8th June 1857, Frederick was promoted to the rank of Lieutenant. On 25th June, this column disarmed the 33rd and 35th Native Infantry Regiments and on the following day Frederick applied to join the army at Delhi, where on 28th June he was appointed as the Deputy Assistant Quartermaster General to the artillery. During the siege at Delhi, Frederick was involved in the defence of Hindoo Rao's house on 30th June and during action on the 14th July was wounded when a bullet struck his cap pouch and caused severe bruising to his spine.

After having been restricted to light duties for a month, Frederick rejoined the staff of Major General Archdale Wilson and as part of Colonel Greathed's column took part in the final assault and recapture of Delhi on 21st September 1857. Frederick remained with Colonel Greathed's column during the march to Cawnpore and was involved in the actions at Bulandshahr, Aligarh, Agra, Bithoor and Kanauji before the column reached Cawnpore on 26th October 1857.

On 30th October, Frederick was assigned as Quartermaster General to the division of Brigadier Hope Grant as part of the force commanded by Sir Colin Campbell which was sent to the relief of Lucknow and was involved in the actions which resulted in the evacuation of the Residency on 27th November 1857. On 6th December 1857, Frederick was involved in the Battle of Cawnpore and in the subsequent pursuit and defeat of the Gwalior contingent during which on the 2nd January 1858 at Khudaganj he performed the deeds for which he would later be awarded the Victoria Cross. Still with the force of Sir Colin Campbell, Frederick took part in the action which resulted in the recapture of Lucknow on 21st March 1858, he also took part in the action at Koorsie the next day which was his last action before leaving India on 3rd May 1858 to return to England on sick leave. For his service during the mutiny, Frederick was awarded the Indian Mutiny Medal with clasps for Delhi, Relief of Lucknow and Lucknow, he was also mentioned in dispatches on seven occasions.

On 17th May 1859, Frederick married Nora Henrietta (née Bews) at Waterford in Ireland, the couple would go on to have six children. Nora Frederica was born in Mean Mir on 10th March 1860 but she would die on 3rd March 1861 at Simla, just before her 1st birthday; Eveleen Soutelle was born at Clifton on 18th July 1868 but she would die on 8th February 1869 at sea during the families return to India, aged just over 6 months; Frederick Henry born on 27th July 1869 at Simla however he would die at Simla on 20th August 1969, less than a month old; Aileen Mary was born on 20th September 1870 at Simla; Frederick Hugh Sherston[599] was

born on 8th January 1872 at Umballa and Ada Edwina Stewart was born in Simla on 28th March 1875.

Frederick was presented with his Victoria Cross Medal, by Queen Victoria at an investiture at Buckingham Palace on 8th June 1859.

In June 1859, soon after receiving his Victoria Cross Medal, Frederick returned to India and in July 1859 was assigned to take charge of the organisation of the Camps of Charles Canning the 1st Viceroy of India, during his extensive tour through Oudh, the North West Provinces, the Punjab and Central India. On 12th November 1860, Frederick was promoted to the rank of 2nd Captain[600] and on the following day received a brevet promotion to the rank of Major.[601] During the winters of 1861/62 and 1862/3, Frederick accompanied the Commander in Chief of the Indian Army Sir Hugh Rose on his tours of Derajat and Central India.

During December 1863, Frederick took part in the later stages of the Umbeyla campaign under the command of Major General John Garvock and was involved in the storming of Lalu, the capture of Umbeyla on 17th December and the subsequent destruction of Mulka. For his service during the campaign, Frederick was awarded the Indian General Service Medal with clasp for Umbeyla.

In February 1865, Frederick once again left India for England on sick leave, returning during April 1866 when he was appointed as Assistant Quartermaster General to the Bengal Army.

In October 1867, Frederick was appointed as Quartermaster General to the Bengal Brigade under the command of Brigadier Donald Stewarts and was responsible for the logistical arrangements for the expedition to Abyssinia. On 9th February 1868, Frederick arrived at Zulla, the expedition's base on the Red Sea, where he remained as senior base officer during the four month campaign. On 15th August 1868, Frederick received a brevet promotion to the rank of Lieutenant-Colonel.[602] Frederick was promoted to the rank of Captain on 18th November 1868[603] this was later backdated to 20th October 1868.[604] For his service during the campaign, Frederick was awarded the Abyssinian War Medal and was mentioned in despatches on three occasions he was also offered the position of 1st Assistant Quartermaster General to the army in India which he took up on 10th March 1869 on his return to India.

Frederick held this position, under the command of Colonel Peter Stark Lumsden until 15th September 1871 when he was

---

599 Frederick Hugh Sherston Roberts, was awarded a Victoria Cross like his father, for deeds performed during the Battle of Colenso on 15th December 1899 during the 2nd Boer War, he would die of his wounds two days later at the age of 27.

600 *London Gazette* – 22621/2232
601 *London Gazette* – 22480/665
602 *London Gazette* – 23412/4517
603 *London Gazette* – 23442/5924
604 *London Gazette* – 23449/6593

appointed as Quartermaster General to the Looshai Expeditionary Force and was responsible for fitting out the two columns to be commanded by General's Brownlow and Bourchier. After fitting out the two columns, Frederick was appointed as senior staff officer to the Cachar Column under the command of Brigadier-General Bourchier on 3rd November 1871. The objective of the expedition was to free British subjects, including a 6 year old girl Mary Winchester, who were being held captive by the hill tribes. On 15th December 1871, General Bourchier's force left Cachar while General Brownlow's force set out from Chittagong – the expedition was a complete success and Frederick returned to Cachar on 10th March 1872. For his service during the expedition, Frederick was awarded the clasp for Looshai to his Indian General Service Medal.

Frederick returned to India during March 1872 and was appointed as Deputy Quartermaster General to the Bengal Army and during the winter of 1872/73 accompanied the Viceroy Lord Napier on a tour of the Punjab.

On 5th July 1872, Frederick was promoted to the rank of Major.[605]

Frederick was appointed as an Ordinary Member 3rd Class (Companion) of the Military Division of the Most Honourable order of the Bath on 10th September 1872.[606]

In February 1873, after the incumbent, General Peter Stark Lumsden, had returned to England, Frederick performed the role of Quartermaster General for five months until July 1873 and from 11th March 1874 he again performed the role on an acting basis. Frederick could not be permanently appointed to the role, as he did not hold the qualifying rank of full colonel. When Frederick received a brevet promotion to the rank of Colonel on 30th January 1875,[607] Lord Napier confirmed him as Quartermaster General. In January 1876, Frederick had responsibility for the arrangements of a camp at Delhi, to cater for the visit to India by HRH the Prince of Wales and accompanied the Prince at the manoeuvres organised for his visit. In the winter of 1876/77, Frederick accompanied Sir Frederick Haines, the Commander-in-Chief of forces in India on an inspection tour of the Punjab and Scinde regions. On 1st January 1877, Frederick supervised the arrangements for the Great Durbar at Delhi, when Queen Victoria was proclaimed Empress of India.

When General Sir Charles Patton Keyes retired, Frederick was offered his command of the Punjab Frontier Force and special Commissioner of the Scinde- Punjab frontier by the viceroy Lord Lytton and took up his post, based at Abbottabad on 15th March 1878.

In October 1878, with tensions once again rising in Afghanistan, it was agreed that three columns would be raised in preparation for an invasion and Frederick was given command of the Kurram Valley Field Force being raised at Kohat. Frederick took up his command on 9th October and by 18th October the Kurram force had reached the border town of Thull where they awaited orders for the advance into Afghan territory. On 21st October, following the expiry of the Viceroy's ultimatum to Sher Ali Khan, the force entered Afghanistan and by 25th October had occupied the fort at Kurram. On 2nd December 1878, the Kurram Force fought an action at Piewer Kotal and successfully secured strategic mountain passes from the Kurram Valley. On 31st December 1878, Frederick was promoted to the rank of Major-General.[608] On 2nd January 1879, Frederick advanced with his force into the Khost Valley and on 7th December defeated the Mangals and occupied the fort at Matwi. Returning to Ali Kheyl, Frederick began preparations for an advance on Kabul which were completed by 29th April, however before the advance could begin in earnest he received news on 13th May that the Treaty of Gandamak had been signed by Mohammad Yaqub Khan (son and successor of Sher Ali Khan) thus ending the hostilities of the first phase of the 2nd Anglo-Afghan War.

At the end of June 1879, Frederick received a communication from the Viceroy, Lord Lytton appointing him as a member of a Commission of Enquiry into army expenditure and organisation which was about to be convened at Simla. After handing over his command to Brigadier-General Massey, Frederick made his way back to Simla, accompanied by his wife.

Frederick was appointed as an Ordinary Member 2nd Class (Knight Commander) of the Military Division of the Most Honourable order of the Bath on 25th July 1879.[609]

On 1st August, Frederick started his work on the Army Commission which was presided over by Sir Ashley Eden. During the commission, Frederick was a strong advocate of the abolition of the three Presidency Armies and their replacement by four army corps.[610]

On 3rd September 1879, an uprising in Kabul led to the slaughter of the British representative, Sir Louis Cavagnari his staff and guards which resulted in the start of the 2nd phase of the 2nd Anglo-Afghan War. On receipt of this news, the viceroy Lord Lytton ordered Frederick to return to his force in the Kurram Valley and then proceed with haste to Kabul and put down the rebellion. Frederick left Simla on 6th September and joined up with his newly named Kabul Field force and by 19th September had advanced to the Shulargardan Pass which

605 *London Gazette* – 23876/3193
606 *London Gazette* – 23895/3969
607 *London Gazette* – 24188/1588

608 *London Gazette* – 24668/174
609 *London Gazette* – 24747/4697
610 These measures would eventually be implemented 16 years later.

opened up the way to central Afghanistan. On the 6th October 1879, the Afghan army was defeated at Char Asaib and two days later the Kabul Field Force occupied Kabul, and on 12th October Mohammad Yaqub Khan abdicated and was deported to India.

On 11th November 1879, Frederick received a brevet promotion to the local rank of Lieutenant-General while serving in Afghanistan.[611]

Frederick was appointed as an Ordinary Member 1st Class (Knight Grand Cross) of the Military Division of the Most Honourable order of the Bath on 11th November 1879.[612]

In November, the Mullahs declared a religious war against the British and on 23rd December, Frederick's force was attacked at Sherpur by an Afghan army of 100,000 men. The attack was driven off with the Afghan's suffering heavy losses. On 5th May 1880, Sir Donald Stewart arrived at Kabul, with his men from Kandahar and assumed supreme command of all forces in Afghanistan. Frederick retained command of the two Kabul divisions. On 22nd July 1880, Abdur Rahman Khan, a cousin of Mohammad Yaqub Khan was installed as Emir instead of Mohammad Yaqub's brother Ayub Khan. Frederick was preparing to withdraw his troops back to India, via the Kurram Valley when news arrived that a brigade commanded by Brigadier-General George Burrows had been defeated by Afghan forces commanded by Ayub Khan at the Battle of Maiwand on 27th July and that Lieutenant-General Primrose was now besieged at Kandahar.

Frederick was ordered to go to the relief of Kandahar and left Kabul on 9th August 1880 to begin his famous march. His column of 10,000 men arrived at Kandahar on the morning of 31st August having covered 313 miles in just 22 days. On the next day, 1st September 1880, Frederick defeated the forces of Ayub Khan at the Battle of Kandahar and ended the revolt and war, soon afterwards the new Emir reconfirmed the Treaty of Gandamak formally ending hostilities. For his service during the war, Frederick was awarded the Afghanistan Medal (1878–80) with clasps for Peiwar Kotal, Charasiah, Kabul and Kandahar. He was also awarded the Kabul to Kandahar Star (1880) and received the thanks of both houses of Parliament, the Government of India and the Governor-General in Council.

On 21st September 1880, Frederick was appointed as an Ordinary Member 1st Class (Knight Grand Cross) of the Military Division of the Most Honourable Order of the Bath.[613]

Frederick left Kandahar on 9th September and proceeded to Quetta where he remained until 12th October when he moved to Sibi and following a request to be relieved relinquished his

command of the Kabul Field Force on 15th October 1880 and proceeded to Simla.

On 30th October 1880, Frederick left India for a well earned period of leave in England, where he arrived at Dover on 17th November 1880 after an absence of 12 years.

In late February 1881, when news of the defeat at Majuba Hill and the death of Sir George Pomeroy Colley, CIC of British forces in the 1st Boer War reached London, Frederick was appointed as his replacement. Frederick set sail for the Transvaal on board *HMS Balmoral Castle* on 6th March, however on 23rd March he received a telegraph from the government advising that a treaty had been signed with the Boer's and that he should not proceed further than Cape Town. On 30th March 1881, Frederick was appointed Governor and Commander-in-Chief of the colony at Natal and the Transvaal Provinces, he was also appointed as Her Majesties High Commissioner of South East Africa.[614] On the same day, Frederick was placed on the army staff, with the local rank of Lieutenant-General while commanding troops in Natal and Transvaal.[615] On his arrival in South Africa, Frederick was met with instructions to return to England and after only 24 hours in the colony set sail on his return and arrived back in England on 19th April 1881 after an abortive and unwanted 6 week intrusion into his home leave.

Frederick was granted the dignity of a Baronet by Queen Victoria on 11th June 1881.[616]

In August 1881, Frederick spent three weeks as the guest of His Imperial Majesty the Emperor of Germany at Army manoeuvres at Hanover and Schleswig-Holstein.

In October 1881, Frederick was offered the command of troops in the Madras Presidency which he accepted, however, before his departure for India, Mr Childers the Secretary of State for War offered him the office of Quartermaster General in succession to Sir Garnet Wolseley. Frederick was tempted by the offer, however as his arrangements for a return to India were complete he asked leave to take up his new command but would consider the post of Quartermaster General when it was closer to being vacated. Frederick left London for India on 26th October 1881 and arrived at Madras to take up his new command, on 27th November. On 16th November 1881, during his journey to India, Frederick was formally appointed to the command of troops in the Madras Presidency with the local rank of Lieutenant-General.[617]

In early 1882, Frederick visited Burma on a tour with the Viceroy of India George Frederick Samuel Robinson the 1st Marquis of Ripon. During the visit Frederick advised on

611 *London Gazette* – 24837/2658
612 *London Gazette* – 24886/5069
613 *London Gazette* – 24886/5069

614 *London Gazette* – 24947/1071
615 *London Gazette* – 24946/1019
616 *London Gazette* – 24984/3002
617 *London Gazette* – 25034/5401

preparations for improvements to the defences of Rangoon and before leaving Burma was once again offered the post of Quartermaster General by Mr Childers which he declined.

Frederick was promoted to the rank of Lieutenant-General on 26th July 1883.[618]

In April 1885, Frederick attended a meeting at Rawalpindi with Emir Abdur Rahman and the new Viceroy Frederick Hamilton-Temple-Blackwood the 1st Marquis of Dufferin and Ava regarding threats to the integrity of the Afghanistan border following the Panjdeh incident on 30th March 1885 when Russian troops crossed the border. As a result of the meeting the 1st and 2nd Indian Army Corps were ordered to make ready for war and Sir Donald Stewart the Commander-in-Chief of forces in India appointed Frederick to the command of the 1st Corps.

On 23rd June 1885, there was a change of British Government and Lord Salisbury took over a Prime Minister, the more robust diplomacy by the new government avoided war and Russia agreed to respect the borders of Afghanistan.

On 8th July 1885, Frederick received a telegram from the Viceroy Lord Dufferin advising him of the Royal Assent to his appointment as Commander-in-Chief of forces in India, however it also granted him leave to visit England before taking up this appointment. Frederick left Bombay on 18th August and spent time in Italy and Switzerland as well as England before returning to India at the end of November. Frederick was appointed as the replacement to Sir Donald Stewart in the role of Commander-in-Chief East India on 28th November 1885 with the local rank of General.[619]

Soon after his appointment, Frederick had to turn his attention to the situation in Burma which had been escalating while he was absent from India. In 1833 the King of Burma had sent a mission to Paris and by mid 1885 had concluded a "Commercial Convention" with the French Government which threatened British Trade in Burma. Following Burmese sanctions against a British Trading company an ultimatum to King Thebaw was issued by the Indian Viceroy on 22nd October 1885 and to cover the events should this be rejected, a force of 10,000 men commanded by Lieutenant-General Harry North Dalrymple Prendergast VC was dispatched to Rangoon. When a less than positive reply to the ultimatum was received on 14th November, General Prendergast advanced on Mandalay and by 29th November had captured the city and received the surrender of King Thebaw thus ending the 3rd Anglo-Burma war. Upper Burma was formally annexed as part of the British Empire on 1st January 1886 and in February Frederick made a visit to Mandalay with the Viceroy Lord

Dufferin. On his return to India, Frederick spent much of the year organising improvements to communications on the North-West Frontier and improving the security of this strategic border.

On 15th January 1886, Frederick was replaced as a member of the council of the Governor and President of Fort George[620] as it was incompatible with his new position as CIC India.

In November 1886, Frederick returned to Mandalay and assumed command of the forces in Burma and set about to subdue the remaining resistance of the Dacoit tribesmen. For his service during the conflict, Frederick was awarded a third clasp for Burma 1885–87 to his Indian General Service Medal.

In February 1887, Frederick returned to Calcutta and over the next few years did much to improve the organisation of the army in India including the formation of a Transport Department and the Regimental Institute to provide better services to the serving men and officers of the regiments.

Frederick was appointed as a Knight Commander of the Most Eminent Order of the Indian Empire on 15th February 1887[621] and on 21st June 1887 he was appointed as a Knight Grand Commander of the Order.[622]

On 24th September 1887, Frederick was appointed as honorary Colonel of the 2nd London Voluntary Rifle Corps.[623]

In November 1888, Lord Dufferin left India and was replaced as Viceroy by Henry Charles Keith Petty-Fitzmaurice Lord Lansdowne on 10th December 1888.

Frederick was appointed as honorary Colonel to the 5th Battalion Sherwood Foresters Militia on 29th December 1888.[624]

In early 1889, Frederick accompanied the new Viceroy Lord Lansdowne on a tour of the North-West frontier.

On 1st January 1890, Frederick welcomed Prince Albert Victor on his arrival at Calcutta for a visit to India and presented the Prince to the Army at a camp and manoeuvres at Muridki.

During his journey to Calcutta, Frederick received a telegram from Mr Edward Stanhope, the Secretary of State for War stating that Lord Cross the Secretary of State for India wished to extend his tenure as Commander-in-Chief India past the usual term, however he also asked Frederick to consider an appointment to the role of Adjutant-General in succession to Lord Wolseley which was due to become vacant on 1st October 1890. Although Frederick was still enjoying his role in India, he gladly accepted the offer of position as Adjutant-General as this would be based at Horse Guards in London however he advised that the new Viceroy wished that he remained in India during

618 *London Gazette* – 25268/4452
619 *London Gazette* – 25546/65

620 *London Gazette* – 25550/267
621 *London Gazette* – 25673/787
622 *London Gazette* – 25712/3365
623 *London Gazette* – 25741/5101
624 *London Gazette* – 25888/7421

the winter of 1890/91. In April 1890, Frederick was informed by Mr Stanhope that due to the fact that a suitable replacement could not be found, he was requested to continue in his post as Commander-in-Chief in India.

On 28th November 1890, Frederick received a brevet promotion to the rank of General.[625]

In 1891, Frederick had to deal with some minor campaigns to the Zhoab Valley, to the Kohat Region, against the Black Mountain Hill tribes and into Assam.

In the winter of 1891, Frederick had to manage the more extensive Hunza-Nagar Campaign to quell disturbances on the northern Kashmir boundary which had been stirred up by Russian incursions.

Frederick was promoted to the rank of General on 31st December 1891.[626]

On 1st January 1892, Frederick received a request to further extend his term as Commander-in Chief India, which he would have been happy to accept if he was allowed a few months leave in England, however, under current regulations the CIC was not allowed any leave, so he reluctantly requested that he be allowed to resign his command in the spring of 1893.

On 23rd February 1892, Frederick was granted the dignity of Baron and took the title of Baron Roberts of Kandahar and the City of Waterford.[627]

On 7th April 1893, Frederick relinquished his command of forces in India and after serving for 41 years on the sub-continent returned to England.

Frederick was appointed as an Extra Knight Grand Commander of the Most Exalted Order of the Star of India on 3rd June 1893.[628]

In 1895, Frederick had published his biography of the famous Duke, entitled "Rise of Wellington".

Frederick was promoted to the rank of Field Marshal on 25th May 1895.[629]

On 1st October 1895, Frederick was appointed to the command of British Forces in Ireland in succession to Lord Wolseley.[630]

Frederick was appointed to the position of Colonel Commandant of the Royal Artillery on 7th October 1896.[631]

In recognition of his attendance at the Diamond Jubilee celebrations for Queen Victoria on 20th June 1897, Frederick was awarded the Queen Victoria Diamond Jubilee Medal.

In 1897, Frederick published an autobiography entitled "Forty-one year's in India".

On 20th August 1897, Frederick was appointed as one of the 22 Knights of the Most Illustrious Order of St Patrick.

On 11th October 1899, the Boer's of the South African Republic and the Republic of the Orange Free State declared war on Britain thus starting the 2nd Anglo-Boer War. From the British point of view the started badly, with the Boers invading the Cape Colony and laying siege to Mafeking on 13th October and Kimberley on 14th October, they also invaded Natal and besieged Ladysmith on the 2nd November. Worse was to come, during "Black Week", British forces were defeated at the Battle of Stormberg on 10th December, the Battle of Magersfontein on 11th December and the Battle of Colenso on 15th December 1899.[632] Following this disastrous start to the war, Frederick was appointed as the Commander-in-Chief of the forces in South Africa[633] on 23rd December 1899, replacing General Redvers Henry Buller VC.[634]

Frederick arrived in Cape Town on 10th January 1900 and with his Chief of Staff, Lord Kitchener made preparations for an advance on Bloemfontein, the capital of the Orange Free State. Improvements in the British position were rapidly achieved with the siege at Kimberly being raised on 15th February and the sieges at Ladysmith and Mafeking being raised afterwards on 28th February and 18th May respectively. On 10th March 1900, Frederick was appointed as honorary Colonel of the City of London Imperial Volunteers.[635] On 13th March 1900, Bloemfontein was taken and on 28th May the Orange Free State was annexed and renamed the Orange River Colony. On 31st May, Johannesburg was taken and on 5th June, the capital Pretoria was also taken, Transvaal was annexed on 1st September 1900. Frederick was appointed to the honorary position of Colonel of the Irish Guards on 17th October 1900.[636] On 12th December 1900, now that both Boer States had been annexed, Frederick handed over the role as the Commander-in-Chief of the forces in South Africa to Lieutenant-General Horatio Herbert Lord Kitchener of Khartoum and returned to England where he arrived at Portsmouth on 2nd January 1901. For his service in South Africa, Frederick was awarded the Queen's South Africa Medal (1899–1902) with clasps for Cape Colony, Paardeberg, Driefontein, Johannesberg, Diamond Hill and Belfast.

---

625 *London Gazette* – 26109/6463
626 *London Gazette* – 26239/4
627 *London Gazette* – 26260/990
628 *London Gazette* – 26409/3252
629 *London Gazette* – 26628/3080
630 *London Gazette* – 26667/5406
631 *London Gazette* – 26791/608

632 During this battle, Frederick's only son, Frederick Hugh Sherston VC would receive he wounds from which he would die two days later.
633 *London Gazette* – 27146/8541
634 General Buller was awarded a Victoria Cross for deeds performed on 28th March 1879 during the Anglo-Zulu War.
635 *London Gazette* – 27172/1632
636 *London Gazette* – 27286/1227

On 7th January 1901 was sworn in as Commander-in Chief of the British Army[637] a position that he would hold until 11th February 1904 when the post was abolished.

Frederick had an audience with Queen Victoria at Osborne House on 14th January 1901 where he was elevated to an Earldom, this was the last audience granted by the Queen before her death eight days later on 22 January 1901.

On 24th January 1901, Frederick was appointed as a Knight Commander of the Most Noble Order of the Garter.[638]

Frederick was granted the dignities of Viscount and Earl by King Edward VII on 11th February 1901 and assumed the titles of Viscount St Pierre and Earl Roberts of Kandahar in Afghanistan and Pretoria in the Transvaal Colony and the City of Waterford.[639]

On 11th March 1901, Frederick was appointed as a Knight of Grace of the Order of the Hospital of St John of Jerusalem in England.[640]

On 3rd May 1901, Frederick was granted licence to wear the decoration of a Knight of the Order of the Black Eagle, which had been confirmed on him by the German Emperor the King of Prussia, when he visited London for the funeral of Queen Victoria.[641] At a later date, Frederick was also appointed as a Knight Grand Cross of the Order of the Red Eagle by the Emperor.

On 27th June 1901, Frederick was appointed to the Privy Council of King Edward VII.[642]

On 3rd July 1901, Frederick was appointed as a Knight of Justice of the Order of the Hospital of St John of Jerusalem in England.[643]

Frederick was appointed as the first president of the Pilgrim Society which was formed on 16th July 1902 for the "promotion of Anglo-American Good Fellowship".

On the occasion of the coronation of King Edward VII, on 9th August 1902, Frederick was one of the first to be appointed to the Chancery of the Order of Merit[644] he was also awarded the Edward VII Coronation Medal (1902) to commemorate his attendance at the coronation.

On 11th February 1904, after 52 years of service, Frederick was retired from the army when his post as Commander-in-Chief of the British Army was abolished following recommendations by Lord Esher into army reforms.

In 1904, Frederick was appointed as Master Gunner of St James's Park and became the ceremonial head of the Royal Regiment of Artillery.

In his retirement, Frederick was a strong advocate of the introduction of conscription, to help prepare the nation for what was generally thought to be an impending war in Europe. In 1905, Frederick became president of the National Service League, which was founded in 1902 under the presidency of Lord Raglan. He also did much to promote the mass training of civilians in the skills of rifle shooting through membership of shooting clubs.

On 28th February 1908, in recognition of his services to the volunteer service, Frederick was awarded the Volunteer Officers Decoration.[645]

The Emperor of Austria awarded Frederick the Franz Joseph Diamond Jubilee Medal (1908) in celebration of his 60 year reign following his succession to the throne at the age of 18 on 2nd December 1848.

Frederick was appointed as honorary Colonel to the 1st Wessex Brigade and the North Somerset territorial regiments on 1st April 1908[646] and also as a Lieutenant-Colonel in the Special Reserve of Officers to the 6th Battalion of the Gloucestershire Regiment.[647] Frederick was appointed as honorary Colonel to the following Territorial Reserve Forces; The Waterford Royal Field Reserve Artillery on 2nd August 1908, the 3rd Battalion the Sherwood Foresters on 26th July 1908 and the 3rd Battalion the Loyal North Lancashire also on 26th July 1908.[648] Frederick was appointed as a Knight 1st Class of the Order of Carol I, the order was created on 10th May 1909 to celebrate the forty year reign of the King of Rumania. At some stage Frederick was appointed as a Knight 1st Class of the Order of Paulownia Sun by the Japanese government.

Frederick was awarded the George V Coronation Medal in commemoration of his attendance at the coronation on 22nd June 1911.

On 5th August 1911, Frederick was appointed as a Colonel of the National Reserve.[649]

Frederick provided advice regarding the Ulster Volunteer Force which was founded in January 1913.

Following the declaration of war against Germany, Frederick was appointed as Colonel-in-Chief of Overseas and Indian Forces in the United Kingdom. It was in this capacity, that he was visiting Indian troops on the battle fields of France and on

637 *London Gazette* – 27264/157
638 *London Gazette* – 27290/1498
639 *London Gazette* – 27283/1058
640 *London Gazette* – 27293/1763
641 *London Gazette* – 27311/3124
642 *London Gazette* – 27327/4327
643 *London Gazette* – 27330/4469
644 *London Gazette* – 27470/5679

645 *London Gazette* – 28114/1402
646 *London Gazette* – 28180/6946 & 6944
647 *London Gazette* – 28253/3874
648 *London Gazette* – 28200/9032 & 9033
649 *London Gazette* – 28520/5919

14th November 1914 at the age of 82 he died from pneumonia at St Omer in France. For his brief service during the 'Great War', Frederick was awarded the 1914 Star (with clasp 5th August – 22nd November 1914, the British War Medal (1914–20) and the Victory Medal (1914–1919).

A small ceremony was held at the army General HQ in St Omer on 15th November, before Frederick's body was transported to Boulogne and then onward to Folkestone and by train to Ascot where a private family ceremony was held. Following this ceremony the body was conveyed, on the gun carriage that his son had tried to save when he died at the Battle of Colenso, to Ascot Station and onwards to Charing Cross station and then to St Paul's Cathedral where a state funeral was held on 20th November 1914.

After lying in state in Westminster Hall,[650] Frederick was interred in a vault within St Paul's, all of the pall bearers were high ranking General's including Lord Kitchener.

Frederick's Victoria Cross Medal is on public display at the National Army Museum, Chelsea.

Rudyard Kipling, a friend of Frederick for over thirty years wrote three poems about his friend and hero; "Bob's",[651] "Lord Roberts" and "A General Summary".

Figure 213a. Grave of Frederick Sleigh Roberts

---

650 One of only two non-Royals to be granted this honour in the 20th century, the other being Winston Churchill.

651 The name by which Frederick was affectionately known by the men in his command.

Bernard McQuirt
6th January 1858 (VC No. 236)

Gazetted: 11th November 1859 22324/4032

Rank and Unit: Private No. 3380 – 95th Regiment of Foot

Citation

For gallant conduct on the 6th of January 1858, at the capture of the entrenched town of Rowa, when he was severely and dangerously wounded in a hand to hand fight with three men, of whom he killed one and wounded another. He received five sabre cuts and a musket shot in this service.

Biography

Bernard was born during 1829 (possibly in September) at the small village of Donaghcloney near Lurgan, Co Armagh in Ireland.

On 3rd October 1854, at the age of 25, Bernard left his job as a labourer and enlisted in the army at Lurgan and joined the 95th Regiment of Foot as a Private.

In April 1855, Bernard was sent as part of a draft of reinforcements to join his regiment in the Crimea. After spending a month in Malta, he arrived on the Crimean peninsula in May, after all of the major battles and was deployed to the lines around Sevastopol. Towards the end of his stay in the Crimea, Bernard was convicted by Courts Martial for being drunk on duty and was sentenced to 42 days of hard labour which he served between 9th March 1856 and 23rd April 1856. On 18th June 1856, the regiment boarded *HMS Brunswick* and set sail for England; after stops at Constantinople, Malta and Gibraltar they disembarked at Portsmouth on 19th July and moved to the new camp at Aldershot.

The regiment were moved to Dublin in Ireland on garrison duties until June 1857 when they were ordered to make ready for deployment to the Cape Colony in South Africa.

On 18th June 1857, exactly one year after leaving the Crimea, the Headquarters and Right Wing of the regiment set sail from Kingstown on *HMS Polmaise* bound for Cape Town and on arrival received orders to proceed at once to Bombay where they arrived on 27th September 1857. On 26th June Bernard, with the Left Wing of the regiment set sail from Kingstown on board *HMS Beechworth* and on arrival at Cape Town also received orders to proceed to India where they landed at Bombay on 30th October. On 22nd November, Bernard and the Left Wing, under the command of Major Raines boarded the Honourable East India Company steamer *Berenice* and set sail by river to join the

Central India Field Force in the state of Rajputana. The regiment occupied Boojh, the capital city of Cutch state in the Gujarat region on 29th November and were involved in several minor operations against the mutineers.

It was on 6th January 1858, during the action at Rowa, that Bernard performed the deeds for which he would later be awarded the Victoria Cross. During this action Bernard was dangerously wounded with a musket shot to the arm and five sabre cuts; two to the head, two to the shoulder and the last nearly severing his thumb. On 30th October 1858, at a camp in Mulharghur, Bernard was declared unfit for further service due to the wounds that he had sustained and was sent back to England. For his service in India, Bernard was awarded the Indian Mutiny Medal with clasp for Central India.

Bernard was discharged from the army, on medical grounds on 5th July 1859 after 4 years and 231 days of service at the age of 29 years and 10 months.

On 4th January 1860, Bernard was presented with his Victoria Cross Medal by Queen Victoria at a ceremony in Windsor Castle.

On leaving the army, Bernard returned to Ireland and took up residence at 72 Urney Street in Belfast, just off the Falls Road. It was here that Bernard died on 5th October 1888 from chronic bronchitis and was buried two days later at Belfast City Cemetery in an unmarked pauper's grave.

His burial was registered under the name of McCourt.

The whereabouts of Bernard's Victoria Cross Medal is unknown; it is believed that he was buried wearing his medals.

Figure 214a. Grave of Bernard McQuirt

David Spence
17th January 1858 (VC No. 237)

Gazetted: 24th December 1858 22212/5512

Rank and Unit: Troop Sergeant-Major No. 606 – 9th Lancers

Citation

For conspicuous gallantry on the 17th of January, 1858, at Shumsabad, in going to the assistance of Private Kidd, who had been wounded, and his horse disabled, and bringing him out from a large number of rebels. **(Despatch from Major-General Sir James Hope Grant, K.C.B., dated 8th April, 1858.)**

Biography

David was born some time during 1818 at Inverkeithing, Fife in Scotland to father Robert, a stone mason and mother Agnes (née Anderson).

In 1835 (when David was 17 and Elspet only 16), David was married to Elspet (née Mathieson) and the couple would go on to have 12 children; Agnes born in Cawnpore during 1842, Eliza born in Cawnpore in 1844, Anne born in Cawnpore in 1845, Isabella born in Wuzeerabad in 1850, Agnes born in Umballa in

Figure 215. David Spence

1852 and Charles born in Umballa in 1856. Of the children born in India, only 3 would survive to maturity.

At the age of 20, David left his job as an Anchor Smith and enlisted in the army at Belfast on 1st June 1838 and joined his regiment the 9th Lancers at Leeds soon afterwards.

David's initial army service was spent in England, stationed at Leeds and Nottingham during 1838, Ipswich from April 1839, Hounslow from April 1840 and Dorchester from April 1841. Towards the end of 1841, David began what would be a long deployment to India and on 1st April 1842 he was promoted to the rank of Corporal.

When the couple left for India, they had already had three children but two had died in infancy; the third Robert was left in Scotland to be cared for by Elspeth's grandmother.

In December 1843, David saw his first active service when he was involved in the Gwalior Campaign and on 29th December took part in the Battle of Punniar near Mangore. For his involvement in the campaign, David was awarded the Gwalior Campaign Star with star for Punniar.

On 17th January 1843, David was promoted to the rank of Sergeant.

Following a breakdown of diplomatic relations between the Honourable East India Company in India and the bordering Sikh Empire at the end of 1845, hostilities broke out during December 1845 and so began the Sutlej Campaign (First Anglo-Sikh War). With his regiment, David took part in the campaign in the Punjab and on 10th February 1846, was involved in the decisive Battle of Sobraon. The war was concluded with the Treaty of Lahore on 9th March 1846 under the terms of which the Sikh Empire ceded the region of Jullundur Doab to the Honourable East India Company. For his part in the campaign, David was awarded the Sutlej Medal (1845–46) engraved on the reverse with Sobraon 1846.

On 25th February 1848, David was promoted to the rank of Troop Sergeant-Major.

Peace in the Punjab was short lived, within three years hostilities with the Sikh Empire were resumed with the Punjab Campaign (Second Anglo-Sikh War) in November 1848. David took part in the campaign and was involved in the Passage of Chenab on 4th December 1848, the Battle of Chillianwala on 12th January 1849 and the decisive Battle of Goojerat on 21st February 1849. On 30th March 1849, the Punjab region was annexed and became part of the British Empire in India. For his service during the war, David was awarded the Punjab Medal (1848–49) with clasps for Chillianwala and Goojerat.

On 1st October 1850, David resigned from his role of Troop Sergeant-Major and reverted back to the rank of Sergeant

however on 1st July 1851 he was again promoted to the rank of Troop Sergeant-Major.

Following the outbreak of mutiny at Meerut and the mutineers subsequent capture of Delhi, General Anson began assembling troop at Simla and on 17th May 1857 the Delhi Field Force left Umballa and advanced on Delhi. On 27th May 1857 General Anson died from cholera at Karnal and was replaced by Major-General Sir Henry Barnard.

David and the 9th Lancers were part of the Cavalry division of the Delhi Field Force under the command of Colonel James Hope Grant when they took part in their first action during the mutiny in the Battle of Badli-ki-Serai on 8th June 1857. After advancing on Delhi, the field force besieged the city and David was involved in the siege and final assault on the city which began on 14th September and resulted in the recapture of the city on 20th September 1857. On 24th September, David with the 9th Lancers left Delhi as part of a force commanded by Brigadier Edward Greathed which was charged with securing the route between Delhi and Cawnpore and on 10th October was involved in the Battle of Agra. Greathed's column joined up with the force of Sir Colin Campbell and David was involved in the relief of Lucknow which started on 14th November and culminated in the evacuation of the Residency on 21st November 1857. After Lucknow, Sir Colin Campbell's force advanced on Cawnpore and on 6th December 1857, David was part of the 600 strong cavalry division which defeated the forces of Tantia Topi in the 3rd Battle of Cawnpore. It was during the advance towards Lucknow on 17th January 1858, at Shumshabad, that David performed the deeds for which he would later be awarded the Victoria Cross. David was part of Sir Colin Campbell's force which besieged Lucknow from 2nd March 1858 and the recapture of the city on 21st March. Towards the end of the mutiny, David served in the Rohilkhand and Oudh campaigns taking part in the Battle of Bareilly on 5th May 1858 and other actions. For his service during the mutiny, David was awarded the Indian Mutiny Medal with clasps for Delhi, Relief of Lucknow and Lucknow.

David and the 9th Lancers returned to England in September 1858, after a tour of over 16 years and on 1st October 1859 he was promoted to the rank of Regimental Sergeant-Major.

David was presented with his Victoria Cross Medal by Queen Victoria at a ceremony in Windsor Castle on 4th January 1860.

On 24th October 1862, after over 24 years of service, Henry was discharged to pension at his own request in Brighton. He was awarded the Army Long Service and Good Conduct Medal.

After leaving the army, David was appointed as a Yeoman of the Guard and moved to London.

It was while living in Lambeth that David died on 17th April 1877 at the age of 58, after collapsing in the street having suffered a heart attack and was buried in the Lambeth Cemetery, Blackshaw Road, Tooting in London.

David's Victoria Cross Medal is on public display at the 9th/12th Royal Lancers Museum in Derby.

Figure 215a. Grave of David Spence

John Adam Tytler
10th February 1858 (VC No. 238)

Gazetted: 23rd August 1858 22176/3903

Rank and Unit: Lieutenant – 66th Bengal Native Infantry

Citation

On the attacking parties approaching the enemy's position under a heavy fire of round shot, grape, and musketry, on the occasion of the Action at Choorpoorah, on the 10th February last, Lieutenant Tytler dashed on horseback ahead of all, and alone, up to the enemy's guns, where he remained engaged hand to hand, until they were carried by us; and where he was shot through the left arm, had a spear wound in his chest, and a ball through the right sleeve of his coat. **(Letter from Captain C. C. G. Ross, Commanding 66th (Goorkha) Regiment, to Captain Brownlow, Major of Brigade, Kemaon Field Force.)**

Biography

John was born at Monghyr, Bengal in India on 29th October 1825, the 3rd son of father John who was a Surgeon employed by the Honourable East India Company and mother Anne (née Gillies).

At the age of five, John was sent home to England for his education and lived with his mother's sisters until his parents returned from India in 1835. The family remained in London for a year and then moved to Jersey, where John attended a school near St Helier run by Mr de Joux. After John's father died in March 1837, his mother move the family to Edinburgh to be

Figure 216. John Adam Tytler

closer to her family and John attended the Edinburgh Academy until he reached his 17th birthday in 1842 at which time he was moved to the Lisle School where he spent the next year completing his education.

In the autumn of 1844, John returned to India and with the support of Sir Jeremiah Bryant a friend of his father and a Major-General in the Bengal Army, was commissioned as an Ensign in the 1st Bengal Native Infantry Regiment on 10th December 1844. On 19th July 1848, John was promoted to the rank of Lieutenant.

John saw his first period of active service when he took part in the Mohmand Expedition from March 1851 until April 1852. Under the command of Sir Colin Campbell the expedition fought the Pashtun Mohmand tribe on the Peshawar frontier. John was also involved in the Ranizai and Utman Kel Expedition in May 1852. For this service, John was awarded the India General Service Medal (1854–95) with clasp for North-West Frontier.

On 19th October 1853, John was appointed to the position of Adjutant to the regiment.

John was to remain for some years on the North West Frontier and saw active service during the Bori Valley Expedition, under the command of Colonel S. B. Boileau, which occurred between 29th November 1853 and 24th February 1854. During the majority of the mutiny, John was serving with his regiment in the Kumaon foothills in the state of Uttakakhand on the North West Frontier of India and had little involvement until the regiment were attacked by a large force of rebels at Churpurah on 10th February 1858. It was during this action that John performed the deeds for which he would later be awarded the Victoria Cross Medal and was seriously wounded with a shot in his left arm and a spear to the chest.

On 5th June 1858, John was married to Adelaide Ann (née Ross)[652] at Nainital and the couple would go on to have five daughters; Eliza Christianna born in Edinburgh on 25th March 1861, Anne Gilles born in Edinburgh on 3rd June 1862, Matilda Henrietta born on 29th December 1863 at Peshawar, Adelaide Mary born on 31st October 1865 at Almorah in Bengal and a further daughter born on 16th October 1869 in Aberdeen.

John and the regiment were involved in the Oudh Campaign and saw action at Pusegaon, the capture of Fort Mittowlee, the Battle at Russoolpore on 25th October 1858 and the Battle of Biswah on 18th November 1858. For his service during the mutiny, John was awarded the Indian Mutiny Medal without clasps.

On 2nd April 1859, John was promoted to the rank of Captain and on 18th July 1862 was appointed as second in command of the 3rd Goorkha (Kemaon) Regiment.

In 1863, John was in command of the 4th Goorkha Regiment during the Umbeyla Campaign as part of the Umbeyla Field Force commanded by Brigadier General Neville Bowes Chamberlain. The campaign which lasted from 22nd October 1863 until 23rd December 1863 was which charged with subduing the Pashtun Yusufzai tribesmen who were concentrated at Malka in the buffer zone between the Empire of Afghanistan and the Punjab region of British India. For his service during the campaign, John was awarded the clasp for Umbeyla to be added to his India General Service Medal.

On 10th December 1864, John received a promotion to the rank of Major[653] and two days later was appointed as 2nd in command of the 4th Goorkha Regiment, a year later on 4th December 1865 he was appointed as Commandant of the regiment, a position that he would hold until his death.

During October 1868, John commanded the regiment as part of the Hazara Field Force, under the command of Brigadier-General Alfred Wilde in the Black Mountain Campaign. On 10th December 1870, John was promoted to the rank of Lieutenant-Colonel.[654] From 9th December 1871 until 20th February 1872, John led his regiment as part of the Chittagong column commanded by General Brownlow in the Lushai Expedition and for his service during the campaign he was awarded the Looshai clasp to his India General Service Medal.

On 10th September 1872, John was appointed as an Ordinary Member 3rd Class (Companion) of the Military Division of the Most Honourable Order of the Bath.[655]

John received a brevet promotion to the rank of Colonel on 10th December 1875.

At the start of the 2nd Anglo-Afghan War, John was given command of the 2nd Brigade of the Peshawar Valley Field force, with the rank of Brigadier-General, which was commanded by Lieutenant-General Sir Samuel Browne. After the Treaty of Gandamak in May 1879 ended the first phase of the war, John was given command of the forces in the newly acquired territory between Londi Kotal and the old border, however, due to ill health it was not long before he had to resign this command. The 2nd phase of the war was sparked off in September 1879 with an uprising in Kabul and John immediately offered his services, despite his continued ill health. As part of the Kurram Valley Field Force, John was given the task of conducting operations against the Kaimusht border tribes in order to divert rebel forces away from Kabul.

---

652 Daughter of Colonel Hugh Ross and the sister of General Sir Campbell Claye Grant Ross

653 *London Gazette* – 23021/4686
654 *London Gazette* – 23768/3645
655 *London Gazette* – 23895/3969

It was at Thal in the Kurram Valley, on 14th September 1880 that John died from pneumonia and was buried the next day at Kohat Cemetery.

John's Victoria Cross Medal is on public display at the Ghurkha Museum in Winchester.

Figure 216a. Memorial to John Adam Tytler

James John McLeod Innes
23rd February 1858 (VC No. 239)

Gazetted: 24th December 1858 22212/5518

Rank and Unit: Lieutenant –Bengal Engineers

Citation

At the action at Sultanpore, Lieutenant Innes, far in advance of the leading skirmishers, was the first to secure a gun which the enemy were abandoning. Retiring from this, they rallied round another gun further back, from which the shot would, (in another instant) have ploughed through our advancing columns, when Lieutenant Innes rode up, unsupported, shot the gunner who was about to apply the match, and, remaining undaunted at his post, the mark for a hundred matchlock men, who were sheltered in some adjoining huts, kept the Artillerymen at bay, until assistance reached him. **(Letter from Major-General Thomas Harte Franks, K.C.B., of 12th March, 1858.)**

Biography

James was born on 5th February 1830 at Baghulpur in India, his father James was a Surgeon in the Bengal Army and his mother Jane Alicia (née McLeod) was the daughter of Lieutenant-General Duncan McLeod (Bengal Engineers).

James spent his childhood in Scotland and after a private education he attended Edinburgh University, on graduation he

Figure 217. James John McLeod Innes

joined the Honourable East India Company Military Seminary at Addiscombe in February 1847. James graduated from Addiscombe in December 1848 after receiving the Pollock Medal for the most distinguished cadet in the senior year. After leaving Addiscombe, James received a commission in the Bengal Engineer Regiment of the Honourable East India Company Army on 8th December 1848 and with the local and temporary rank of Ensign enrolled at Chatham for field instruction in Sapping and Mining.[656]

After graduating from Chatham, James left for India where he arrived during November 1850 and was initially employed in the Public Works Department where he worked as an Engineer on the construction of the Bari Doab Canal in the Punjab. James was promoted to the rank of Lieutenant on 1st August 1854.

On 30th October 1855, James married Lucy Jane (née MacPherson)[657] at Jullundur; the couple would go on to have four children; James Edgeworth born on 17th March 1859, Hugh McLeod born on 22 March 1862, Arthur Donald born on 15th September 1863 and Alicia Sibella born on 10th July 1873.

In February 1856, the King of Oudh was deposed and his territories were annexed by the Honourable East India Company, soon afterwards James was sent to the new province as Assistant Chief Engineer in the Public Works Department. At the outbreak of the mutiny, James was stationed at Lucknow (the capital of Oudh province) and was assigned to improving the defences of the Old Fort Macchi Bhawan. After the disaster of the Battle of Chinhut on 30th June 1857, where a British force of 600 men led by Colonel William Case, faced a mutineer force of 6,000 and were slaughtered almost to a man, Sir Henry Lawrence the Chief Commissioner of Oudh ordered the Old Fort to be abandoned and concentrated his forces in the Residency.

On 1st July, James was ordered to blow up the Old Fort, so that it could not be used by the mutineers, which he accomplished under difficult circumstances before joining his comrades in the Residency, which was now besieged by the mutineers.

During the siege, James was mainly employed in mining operations where he had some notable success. On 20th July he exploded a mine near the Redan battery helping to drive back a mass attack by the mutineers and on 21st August he blew up Johannes's House which was being used by rebel snipers. On 25th September 1857, Major-General Henry Havelock managed to break through the rebel lines and reinforce the defenders of the Residency with his force of 1,500 men, following which James was placed in charge of the mining operations in support of Havelock's force which occupied palaces on the banks of the

Gumti River. A second relief force, under the command of Sir Colin Campbell reached the city on 14th November and after reaching the Residency began an evacuation of the besieged forces on 19th which was completed successfully by the 21st November 1857 thus ending the siege which had lasted for 148 days. Following the evacuation of Lucknow, James was assigned to the 4th Infantry Division of the Juanpore Field Force, commanded by Brigadier-General Sir Thomas Harte Franks for operations against the rebels in Oudh. James was involved in actions at Miranpur, Chanda and Amirpur before taking part in the Battle of Sultanpore on 23rd February 1858 during which he performed the deeds for which he would later be awarded the Victoria Cross. On 4th March 1858, James was severely wounded during an attack on the Fort at Dhaurahra, just after General Franks's division had met up with the forces of Sir Colin Campbell for the final advance to recapture Lucknow. For his service during the mutiny, James was awarded the Indian Mutiny Medal with clasps for Defence of Lucknow and Lucknow. His service during the defence of Lucknow earned him an extra year of service towards his pension and the praise and thanks of Major-General Sir John Eardley Wilmot Inglis, who commanded the Lucknow Garrison for the first 87 days of the siege, for his *"arduous duties"* and *"gallant bearing"*.

After the mutiny, James was appointed as the garrison engineer at Fort William in Calcutta and on 27th August 1858, was promoted to the rank of 2nd Captain, on the following day he received a brevet promotion to the rank of Major.

It was while serving at Fort William that James was presented with his Victoria Cross Medal on 1st July 1859 by the Governor General Lord Canning. During the presentation Lord Canning paid tribute to James and the Bengal Engineers:

… I must add that it is a peculiar pleasure to me to present this Cross to an Officer of the Bengal Engineers, for I say to you—not as a compliment but in the words of sober truth—that I do not believe that there has ever existed in any army a body of men who have rendered, individually and collectively, more constant and valuable service to their country than the Engineers of her Majesty's Indian Forces. Men, all of them, of proved ability and highly cultivated intellect, they have been unceasingly called upon in peace, as much as in war, to achieve great tasks for the protection and advancement of India, and they have never been found wanting. That, when summoned to meet an enemy in the field, they can carry their lives in their hands as lightly as any man, your own deeds and those of many of your brother-officers have abundantly proved.

It is in itself a distinction to belong to such a Corps,

---

656 *London Gazette* – 20929/4625
657 Youngest daughter of Professor Hugh MacPherson of Aberdeen

and you, Major Innes, have the proud satisfaction to know that while you have derived honour from being enrolled among the Engineers of the Army of Bengal, you have done all that a gallant soldier can do to repay that honour, in augmenting by your own acts the lustre and reputation of your distinguished regiment.

In June 1861, when the Honourable East India Company Military Academy at Addiscombe was closed James was specially mentioned by Henry Pelham-Clinton 5th Duke of Newcastle, the Secretary of State, and the Address of Lord Canning to him (James Innes) on the occasion of the presentation of the VC was read to the assembled cadets at the final Public Examination.

After Fort William, James served in the Public Works Department of the Central Provinces and the Punjab and was promoted to the rank of 1st Captain on 29th February 1864. In 1868, James was appointed to the commission to investigate the failure of the Bank of Bombay and following this worked as an engineer on construction of the upper section of the Indus Valley Railway. On 14th June 1869, James received a brevet promotion to the rank of Lieutenant-Colonel.[658] On 10th November 1869, James was placed on the Seconded List[659] and soon afterwards in 1870 was appointed as Accountant General of the Public Work Department, a position that he was to hold for the next 7 years.

James was promoted to the rank of Major on 5th July 1872[660] and on 1st April 1874, was promoted to the rank of Lieutenant-Colonel.[661]

James was returned to the Supernumerary List on 4th September 1877[662] and on 1st October 1877 received a brevet promotion to the rank of Colonel.[663] In 1881 James was appointed as Inspector General of Military Works at Simla and was responsible for the design of new coastal and frontier defences, he was also appointed as a member of the Indian Defence Committee. On 26th May 1883, James was promoted to the rank of Colonel[664] and on 28th November 1885 was promoted to the rank of Major-General.[665] On 16th March 1886 after 37 years of service, James was retired to pension with the honorary rank of Lieutenant-General.[666]

In his retirement, James devoted his time to literary pursuits and published the following works; two histories of the mutiny, *Lucknow and Oude in the Mutiny* (1895) and *The Sepoy Revolt*

of 1857 (1897) as well as two biographies, *Sir Henry Lawrence* (1898) and *Sir James Browne* (1905).

James was appointed as an Ordinary Member 3rd Class (Companion) of the Military Division of the Most Honourable Order of the Bath on 28th June 1907, in celebration of the 50th anniversary of the Siege of Lucknow.[667]

After a long illness, James died at his home, 5 Pemberton Terrace, Cambridge on 13th December 1907 at the age of 67. He was buried in the New Cambridge Cemetery in Cambridge.

James's Victoria Cross Medal is on public display at the Royal Engineers Museum in Chatham.

Figure 217a. Grave of James John McLeod Innes

658 *London Gazette* – 23511/3693
659 *London Gazette* – 23553/5976
660 *London Gazette* – 23876/3194
661 *London Gazette* – 24082/1923
662 *London Gazette* – 24500/5098
663 *London Gazette* – 24521/6186
664 *London Gazette* – 25239/2929
665 *London Gazette* – 25542/6193
666 *London Gazette* – 25579/1900

667 *London Gazette* – 28034/4431

Frederick Robertson Aikman
1st March 1858 (VC No. 240)

Gazetted: 3rd September 1858 22179/4014

Rank and Unit: Lieutenant –4th Bengal Native Infantry

Citation

This Officer, Commanding the 3rd Sikh Cavalry on the advanced Piquet, with one hundred of his men, having obtained information, just as the Force marched on the morning of the 1st of March last, of the proximity, three miles off the high road, of a body of 500 Rebel Infantry, 200 Horse, and 2 Guns, under Moosahib Ali Chuckbdar, attacked and utterly routed them, cutting up more than 100 men, capturing two guns, and driving the survivors into, and over, the Gumti. This feat was performed under every disadvantage of broken ground, and partially under the flanking fire of an adjoining Fort. Lieutenant Aikman received a severe sabre cut in the face in a personal encounter with several of the enemy.

Biography

Fredrick was born on 6th February 1828 at Ross House on the outskirts of Hamilton in Scotland, the sixth and youngest son of father George who was a ship's Captain employed by the Honourable East India Company Maritime Service and mother Sarah (née Cumby).

Fredrick was the 2nd youngest of nine children, with two older sisters; Georgina born on 1st December 1815 and Rose Bella born on 19th January 1824; five older brothers, George born on 22nd January 1817, Hugh Henry born on 5th March 1819, John born on 19th December 1820, William born on 12th March 1822 and Charles born on 24th February 1826. He also had a younger sister Sarah Eliza born on 6th December 1829.

On 18th January 1845, just before his 17th birthday, Frederick entered the service of the Most Honourable East India Company and was enlisted as an Ensign in the 4th Bengal Native Infantry.

Frederick saw his first active service with the regiment during the 1st Anglo-Sikh war (Sutlej Campaign) from December 1845 until 9th March 1846 when the conflict was ended with the signing of the Treaty of Lahore. On 10th February, Frederick took part in the Battle of Sobraon and for his service during the war he was awarded the Sutlej Medal (1845–46) engraved on the reverse with Sobraon 1846.

Frederick was promoted to the rank of Lieutenant on 7th July 1848 and soon afterwards was involved in the 2nd Anglo-Sikh War (Punjab Campaign) as part of General Hugh Wheeler's Field

Figure 218. Frederick Robertson Aikman

Force. For his service during the war, Frederick was awarded the Punjab Medal (1848–49).

During the mutiny, Frederick continued to serve with the 4th Bengal Native Infantry (one of the few native regiments of the Bengal Army that did not mutiny) and from 8th June 1857 was at the siege of Delhi until the city was recaptured on 21st September 1857. Frederick was involve at the Battle of Bulandshahr on 28th to 30th September and during October and November 1857 raised the Julandhar Cavalry (3rd Sikh Irregular Regiment). It was with this new regiment, as part of the force of Sir Colin Campbell advancing on Lucknow, that Frederick performed the deeds on 1st Match 1858, near Amethi that would later result in the award of the Victoria Cross medal. During this action Frederick was severely wounded by a sabre cut to the face. On 7th May 1858, Frederick returned to England on sick leave. For his service during the mutiny, Frederick was awarded the Indian Mutiny Medal with clasps for Lucknow and Central India.

On 26th April 1858, Frederick was promoted to the rank of Captain.[668] From 15th May 1858 until 4th February 1859, Frederick served as 2nd in command of the 3rd Sikh Irregular Cavalry Regiment.

Frederick was presented with his Victoria Cross Medal on 8th June 1859 by Queen Victoria at an investiture held at Buckingham Palace.

On 21st November 1860, after over 15 years of service, Frederick was forced to resign from the army on half-pay as a result of the wounds that he sustained during his Victoria Cross action.

Following his retirement, Frederick took up residence at 7 Queen's Gate in London.

---

668 *London Gazette* – 22828/1350

Frederick was married to Louisa Grace (née Hargreaves) at St Stephens, Bayswater in London on 4th March 1862.

On 15th March 1865, Frederick was appointed as a Major in the 2nd London Rifle Volunteer Corps.[669]

Frederick, on the nomination of Lord Foley, was appointed as a Member of the Honourable Corps of Gentleman-at-Arms, the Body Guard of the Sovereign, on 13th May 1865. He would hold this position until his death.[670]

On 20th October 1865, Frederick was appointed as Lieutenant-Colonel of the Royal East Sussex Militia / East Middlesex Militia.[671]

On 4th January 1867, Frederick applied for a patent and was granted provisional protection for the invention of *"… Improvements to rifles for the purpose of instructing soldiers to fire with precision over long ranges, and for obtaining a correct register of the shooting by showing the result of each shot".*[672] This was automatically voided on 9th July 1870 when Frederick failed to make the payment of stamp duty required to continue his patent application.[673]

Frederick was appointed as Lieutenant-Colonel Commandant of the Royal East Sussex Militia / East Middlesex Militia on 28th July 1871.[674] On 22nd July 1882, Frederick was appointed as Honorary Colonel of 4th Battalion Duke of Cambridge's Own Regiment,[675] he resigned this commission on 28th July 1886,[676] however was reappointed on 10th September 1887.[677]

Frederick died suddenly on 5th October 1880, when at about 1:00 am he collapsed on the ballroom floor at the County Ball in Hamilton and despite immediate medical attention died a few minutes later at the age of 60. He was buried in the family vault at Kensal Green Cemetery in London.

His Victoria Cross Medal is believed to be still in the hands of the family and is not on public display.

Figure 218a. Grave of Frederick Robertson Aikman

669 *London Gazette* – 22949/1568
670 *London Gazette* – 22969/2550
671 *London Gazette* – 23234/1983
672 *London Gazette* – 23228/1607
673 *London Gazette* – 23634/3403
674 *London Gazette* – 23770/3763

675 *London Gazette* – 25129/3406
676 *London Gazette* – 25610/3566
677 *London Gazette* – 25737/4887

William Goate
6th March 1858 (VC No. 241)

Gazetted: 24th December 1858 22212/5512

Rank and Unit: Lance Corporal No. 2017 – 9th Lancers

Citation

For conspicuous gallantry at Lucknow, on the 6th of March, 1858, in having dismounted, in the presence of a number of the enemy, and taken up the body of Major Smyth, 2nd Dragoon Guards, which he attempted to bring off the field, and after being obliged to relinquish it, being surrounded by the enemy's cavalry, he went a second time under a heavy fire to recover the body. (**Despatch from Major-General Sir James Hope Grant, K.C.B., dated 8th April, 1858.**)

Figure 219. William Goate

Biography

William was born on 12th January 1836 at Fritton near Long Stratton, Norwich in Norfolk to father John and mother Lucy Anne.

William's father died when he was quite young so he left school at an early age and started work as a farm labourer, which is where he learned about horses.

On 22nd November 1853, at the age of 19, William left his job as a labourer and enlisted in the army at Westminster where he was enrolled as a Private in the 9th Lancers. After almost exactly a year of service, William began his one and only period of Foreign Service when he was deployed with the regiment to India on 27th November 1854.

At the outbreak of the mutiny, William and the 9th Lancers were stationed at Umballa and were assigned to the Delhi Field Force commanded by Major General George Anson. General Anson died from cholera on 27th May, soon after he took command of the Delhi Field Force and was replaced by Major General Sir Henry Barnard.

The force set out from Umballa on 17th May and after joining forces with the Meerut Brigade, commanded by Brigadier Archdale Wilson fought the Battle of Badli-ki-Serai on 8th June and established positions on the Delhi Ridge. William remained as part of the besieging force and was involved in the final capture of Delhi on 21st September 1857, following which they were assigned to a Flying Column commanded by Colonel Edward Greathed. On 24th September the flying column moved out to patrol the Gangetic Goab, the area of land between the Ganges and Yamuna rivers and on the 28th September, William took part in the Battle of Bulandshahr and on 10th November 1857 in the Battle of Agra. At some stage, prior to Lucknow, it appears that

William was promoted to the rank of Lance-Corporal. William was part of the force which evacuated the Residency at Lucknow on 19th November and as part of the force that finally recaptured Lucknow on 21st March 1858, was involved in an action on the outskirts of Lucknow on 6th March where he performed the deeds for which he would later be awarded the Victoria Cross. For the remainder of the mutiny, William was involved in the Rohilkhand and Oudh campaigns. For his service during the mutiny, William was awarded the Indian Mutiny Medal with clasps for Delhi, Relief of Lucknow and Lucknow.

William returned to England with his regiment in May 1859 and on 4th January 1860 was presented with his Victoria Cross Medal by Queen Victoria at an investiture in Windsor Castle.

In 1864, William was deployed with the regiment to Ireland and it was here, in Dublin on 22nd November 1864, that William now with the rank of Corporal,[678] was discharged from the army at his own request having completed his initial enlistment period of 11 years.[679]

On leaving the army, William moved back to Norfolk and set up home at Bungay near Norwich where he worked as a railway porter and then warehouseman.

William was married to Sarah (née Ling) while living at Bungay and the couple had one child, a son also called William born in Bungay sometime during 1867.

At some time around 1878, William moved to Jarrow-on-Tyne and for the next 22 years worked for Palmers Shipbuilders.

---

678 Although the ranks of Lance-Corporal and Corporal are attributed to William in some official papers, his discharge papers (WO97-2890-032) contain no record of these promotions.

679 William's pensionable service was 12 years as he was credited, in error, an additional year of service for service during the defence of Lucknow.

During his time in Jarrow, William served for 18 years in the Jarrow Company Volunteers with the rank of Lance-Corporal.

In May 1900, William moved to Southsea in Hampshire where he lived at 22 Leopold Street. It is thought that William moved to Southsea to be close to his son William, his wife Sarah and his grandson Robert Henry who was born on 9th August 1899.

William died at his home in Southsea, from gastric cancer, on 24th October 1901 at the age of 64 and was buried in an unmarked common grave in the Highland Road Cemetery in the Eastney district of Southsea.

His Victoria Cross Medal is on public display at the 9th/12th Royal Lancers Museum in Derby.

Figure 219a. Grave of William Goate

Thomas Adair Butler
9th March 1858 (VC No. 242)

Gazetted: 6th May 1859 22260/1867

Rank and Unit: Lieutenant – Bengal European Fusiliers

Citation

Of which success the skirmishers on the other side of the river were subsequently apprised by Lieutenant Butler, of the Bengal Fusiliers, who swam across the Gumti, and, climbing the parapet, remained in that position for a considerable time, under a heavy fire of musketry, until the work was occupied. (**Extract of Lieutenant-General Sir James Outram's memorandum of operations carried on under his command at the siege of Lucknow, published in the Governor-General's Gazette Extraordinary, of the 5th April, 1858, and republished in General Orders by the Commander-in-Chief in India, on the 27th of December, 1858.**)

Biography

Thomas was born on 12th February 1836, at Soberton in Hampshire; he was the youngest of four children born to father Stephen who was the curate at the local church and mother Mary Anne (née Thistlethwaite). Thomas had two older sisters; Mary Mary-Anne baptised on 25th October 1829 and Catherine Lian baptised on 3rd March 1833 and an older brother George Stephen

Figure 220. Thomas Adair Butler

baptised on 4th January 1835. On 21st May 1838, when Thomas was only two years old his mother Mary died at the age of 31 and sometime afterwards his father was remarried to Caroline (née Linton) whose only child Caroline, born on 27th October 1826 became his step sister. In 1848, at the age of 10, Thomas moved to Southampton following his father's appointment as the curate for the Holy Trinity Church in the city.

Thomas was initially educated privately and then attended the Royal Academy at Gosport, which was established in 1791 by Dr William Burney as a preparatory school for pupils wishing to take the Royal Navy entrance examinations. At the time that Thomas attended the Academy, it was run by Reverend Edward Burney, the son of the founder, and had a wider brief to see that *"Young Gentlemen are educated for the Navy, Army and the Civil Service, the Learned Professions, Public Schools etc."*

On 9th June 1854, at the age of 18, Thomas enlisted in the Bengal Army of the Honourable East India Company and was commissioned as an Ensign in the 1st Bengal Fusiliers. Thomas probably joined his regiment in Calcutta during February 1855 where they had just arrived back in India after over two years in Burma. In March, the regiment moved to Dinapore until January 1856 when they moved to Cawnpore. On 23rd November 1856, Thomas was promoted to the rank of Lieutenant.

In March 1857, the regiment moved to Dugshai which is where they were stationed at the outbreak of the mutiny. On 13th May the regiment received orders to join the Delhi Field force being assembled at Alipore and on arrival were assigned to the 1st Brigade under the command of Brigadier-General Showers.

Thomas, who had been on leave, arrived at Alipore on 7th June, just before the force departed for Delhi, after covering 110 miles on horseback in 40 hours. On 8th June, Thomas and the regiment were involved in the Battle of Badli-ki-Serai and two days later were part of the forces which occupied "The Ridge" at the start of the siege of Delhi. Thomas was involved in the action at Subzi Mundi on 14th July, which cleared the rebels out of the fortress and on 24th to 26th August was involved in the Battle of Nujjufghur. He was also involved in the final assault on the city which resulted in its recapture on 20th September 1857.

Following the capture of Delhi, Thomas left the city on 10th November as part of a field force commanded by Colonel Gerrard on operations to clear the outlying district of mutineers, the only significant action before the force returned to the city on 29th November was the Battle of Narnoul which took place on 16th November 1857.

Thomas left Delhi again on 6th December as part of the escort for a convoy of stores and cattle moving to join up with the field force going to the relief of Lucknow. On the journey, the force fought actions at Gungehri on 14th December and Puttialee on

17th December before occupying the town of Mynpoorie on 21st December.

On 31st December the convoy joined up with the Brigade of General Walpole at Bewar and the combined force reached Futtehpore, the HQ of the Lucknow Field Force commanded by Sir Colin Campbell, on 4th January 1858.

On 27th January, the force left Futtehpore escorting a column of supplies to Cawnpore which they reached on 3rd February and three day later, as part of the Highland Division commanded by Brigadier General Douglas began the advance on Lucknow.

After the division took part in the Battle of Jellalabad, on 25th February, and occupied the old fort they took up their position in the encampment of Sir Colin Campbell's troops near the Alum Bagh, as part of the force besieging the city. On 3rd March, Thomas was directed to the Mohammed Bagh as part of a force sent to defend the artillery batteries in that location. On 9th March Thomas was part of the force which successfully captured the "Yellow House" and afterward during an escort duty for artillery; it was on the banks of the Gumti River that he performed the deeds for which he would later be awarded the Victoria Cross.

On 16th March, the assault to retake Lucknow was in full swing and Thomas was involved in attacks on the Kaiser Bagh, the Residency and the taking of the Macchi Bhawan old fort, by 21st March 1858 the city was cleared of mutineers and back in British hands.

In April 1858, Thomas and the regiment were part of a flying column commanded by Major-General Sir Hope Grant sent to subdue the rebels in the Fyzabad district and on 13th April were involved in the Battle of Baree.

In September 1858, the regiment dispersed a large force of mutineers who were occupying a large island on the River Gogra near to Durriabad where the regiment were quartered. The regiment were engaged again with this force on 6th November and inflicted heavy losses on the mutineers.

Tomas and the regiment saw their final action during the mutiny at the Battle of Nawab Gunge on 30th October 1858.

For his service during the mutiny, Thomas was awarded the Indian Mutiny Medal with clasps for Delhi and Lucknow.

In March 1859, after two years of almost non-stop campaigning the regiment set out on the journey to return to their base in Dugshai which they reached on 18th April 1859.

Thomas was presented with his Victoria Cross Medal by Queen Victoria at an investiture held at Buckingham Palace on 8th June 1859.

On 2nd May 1861, following the breakup of the Honourable East India Company armies, the regiment was disbanded and reformed as 101st Royal Bengal Fusiliers within the British Army.

On 30th July 1862, Thomas was appointed as regimental Instructor of Musketry.[680] Thomas was promoted to the rank of Captain on 16th January 1863.[681]

From October to December 1863, Thomas and the regiment took part in the Umbeyla Campaign as a unit within the Ensufyze Field Force and took part in actions at "Craig Piquet" on 13th November and Conical Hill on 15th December. The rebel hill tribes surrendered on 17th December 1863 and on 1st January 1864 the field force was split up and Thomas and the regiment were sent to Rawalpindi where they arrived on 11th January. For his service during the campaign, Thomas was awarded the India General Service Medal with clasp for Umbeyla.

On 20th December 1864, Thomas and the regiment returned to Dugshai and then in 1868 to Cawnpore where they remained for a short time before beginning their journey to England.

After setting sail from Bombay at the end of 1868, the regiment arrived at Portsmouth on 3rd February 1869 and moved to their station at Gosport and then in June 1870 moved to Aldershot.

At some stage, Thomas was married to Anna Maria who was born in Dublin.

Thomas was in command of the honour guard on 18th June 1871, when the regimental colours of the 1st Bengal European Regiment were deposited in Winchester Cathedral.

After spells at Bury from September 1871, Manchester from July 1872 and Preston from September 1873 the regiment returned to Aldershot in July 1874.

On 30th September 1874, after 19 years of service, Thomas retired from the army and was granted the Honorary rank of Major.[682]

Thomas's first wife Anna Maria died in 1887 and some time afterwards he was married for a second time to Harriet Annie (née Davidson) from the Isle of Man.

Little is known of Thomas's life after he left the army other than that in 1889 he founded the Portsmouth Brigade which offered a home to boys.

On 17th May 1901, Thomas died from heart disease at his home in Lyndale, Yorktown, Camberley and was buried three days later in St Michael's Churchyard, Camberley.

Thomas's Victoria Cross medal is on public display at the Royal Military Academy, Sandhurst in Berkshire.

Figure 220a. Grave of Thomas Adair Butler

680 *London Gazette* – 22667/4679
681 *London Gazette* – 22699/270
682 *London Gazette* – 24135/4535

Francis Edward Henry Farquharson
9th March 1858 (VC No. 243)

Gazetted: 16th June 1859 22278/2420

Rank and Unit: Lieutenant – 42nd Regiment of Foot

Citation

For conspicuous bravery, when engaged before Lucknow, on the 9th March, 1858, in having led a portion of his Company, stormed a bastion mounting two guns, and spiked the guns, by which the advanced position, held during the night of the 9th of March, was rendered secure from the fire of Artillery.

Lieutenant Farquharson was severely wounded, while holding an advanced position, on the morning of the 10th of March.

Biography

Francis was born on 25th March 1837 at Glasgow in Scotland to father Henry Hubert[683] a Lieutenant-Colonel in the 1st Regiment of Foot and mother Elizabeth Anne (née Reynolds).

On 19th January 1855, at the age of 18, Francis was commissioned as an Ensign in the 42nd Regiment (later to be The Black Watch – Royal Highlanders)[684] and was promoted to the rank of Lieutenant on 24th April 1855.[685]

Soon after enlisting, Francis was off to war and joined his regiment in the siege of Sevastopol on 14th July 1855. After the fall of Sevastopol on 9th September 1855, the regiment moved to Kamara where they remained until the peace was signed and on 15th June 1856 embarked at Kamiesch and set sail for England where they landed at Portsmouth on 24th July 1856. For his service during the war, Francis was awarded the Crimea Medal with clasp for Sevastopol and the Turkish Crimea Medal.

From Portsmouth the regiment moved to the new camp at Aldershot where they were reviewed by Queen Victoria before moving to Dover where they formed the garrison.

On 4th August 1857, the regiment was again reviewed by Queen Victoria before leaving England in six transports on 14th August arriving at Calcutta during October and November 1857. On 24th November the regiment joined the force of Sir Colin Campbell and began their advance on Cawnpore, the final push started on 3rd December when they marched from Cheemee

Figure 221. Francis Edward Henry Farquharson

to Cawnpore, a distance of 80 miles in 56 hours which was an extraordinary feat in the tropical heat. Francis was involved in the Battle of Cawnpore on 6th December 1857, where the Gwalior Contingent of mutineers was defeated with heavy losses. After Cawnpore was secured, Francis and his regiment were assigned to the field force of General Sir Hope Grant for operations in Rohilkhand and on 2nd January were involved in the Battle of Khodagunge on the Kala Nuddee River.

As part of the force of Sir Colin Campbell, Francis and the regiment were involved in the siege of Lucknow which resulted in the recapture of the City on 21st March. It was during the assault on the Martinière and Banks's House on 9th March 1858, that Francis performed the deeds for which he would later be awarded the Victoria Cross. On the following day, Francis was seriously wounded[686] and it is presumed that he took no further part in the actions against the mutineers. For his service during the Mutiny, Francis was awarded the Indian Mutiny Medal with clasp for Lucknow.

Francis was presented with his Victoria Cross Medal by Queen Victoria at an investiture held at Windsor Castle on 4th January 1860.

On 1st January 1861, Francis and the regiment were stationed at Bareilly where they were presented with new regimental colours by Sir Hugh Rose, Commander-in-Chief of forces in India and in September the ancient name of "Black Watch" was again assigned to the regiment.

Francis was promoted to the rank of Captain on 28th June 1862.[687]

---

683 Henry would later be appointed as Usher of the Black Rod to the first Victoria State Parliament.
684 *London Gazette* – 21652/210
685 *London Gazette* – 21699/1574

686 *London Gazette* – 22139/2399
687 *London Gazette* – 22658/4307

On 5th September 1867, Francis was married to Harriet Charlotte Henrietta (née Lowe) at Murree in the Punjab, India; the couple would have a daughter Beatrice Eleanor born in Edinburgh on 15th November 1869.

In March 1868, after a tour of ten years, the regiment left India and after arriving back at Portsmouth were immediately sent by rail to Edinburgh where they formed the garrison at Edinburgh Castle.

In 1871, Britain purchased the Gold Coast from the Dutch and when the Ashanti invaded the Abirem district and occupied Elmina the district capital, this prompted the start of the 3rd Anglo-Ashanti War. Francis served in the war as a staff officer to Colonel McLeod who commanded the advanced guard as part of the force commanded by Sir Garnet Wolseley which arrived in the Gold Coast during January 1874. Francis was present at the Battle of Borobassi on 26th January, the Battle of Amoaful on 31st January, the Battle of Brequah where he was wounded and the Battle of Ordah-su and capture of Coomassie on 4th February 1874. After contracting a serious disease, in the inhospitable climate, Francis was invalided home to England. On 1st April 1874, Francis received a Brevet promotion to the rank of Major.[688] For his service during the war, Francis was awarded the Ashantee Medal (1873–74) with clasp for Coomassie.

On 12th September 1875, after a long and painful illness resulting from the disease that he contracted during the Ashanti Campaign, Francis died at Harberton Vicarage in Devon at the age of 38 and was buried in the Harberton Parish Churchyard.

Francis's Victoria Cross Medal is on public display at the Black Watch Museum in Balhousie Castle in Perth, Scotland.

Figure 221 b. Grave of Francis Edward Henry Farquharson

Figure 221 a. Grave of Francis Edward Henry Farquharson

---

688 *London Gazette* – 24082/1925

Henry Wilmot
11th March 1858 (VC No. 244)

Gazetted: 24th December 1858 22212/5515

Rank and Unit: Captain – Rifle Brigade, 2nd Battalion

Citation

For conspicuous gallantry at Lucknow on the 11th March, 1858. Captain Wilmot's Company was engaged with a large body of the enemy, near the Iron Bridge. That officer found himself at the end of a street with only four of his men, opposed to a considerable body. One of the four was shot through both legs, and became utterly helpless: the two men lifted him up, and although Private Hawkes was severely wounded, he carried him for a considerable distance, exposed to the fire of the enemy, Captain Wilmot firing with the men's rifles, and covering the retreat of the party.

(Despatch of Brigadier-General Walpole, C.B., dated 20th of March, 1858.)

Biography

Henry was born on 3rd February 1831 at Chaddesden in Derbyshire, the 2nd son of father Henry Sachevrel a Lieutenant in the Royal Navy and 4th Baronet of Chaddesden and mother Maria (née Mundy).

Henry had one older brother, Robert Edward Eardley born on 29th January 1830 and two younger brothers; Edward born on 12th March 1833[689] and Arthur Alfred born on 14th February 1845 who was ordained as a minister in the Church.

After completing his education at Rugby School, Henry at the age of 18, joined the army when he purchased the commission of Ensign in the 43rd Regiment of Foot on 29th May 1849.[690]

Henry served his initial years with the regiment stationed in Ireland, however, when the regiment set sail for South Africa in September 1851 and took part in the eighth Kaffir War, he was not part of their number and presumably remained in Ireland with the Depot Company.

On 17th October 1851, Henry purchased a commission of Lieutenant in the regiment.[691]

Following the war in South Africa, the regiment moved to India arriving at Bangalore on 30th January 1854 but again Henry remained in Ireland.

Figure 222. Henry Wilmot

On 1st May 1855, Henry purchased a commission as Captain[692] in the 43rd Regiment of Foot.

Probably in frustration at missing out on active service, Henry was transferred as Captain in the Rifle Brigade on 10th August 1855[693] and may have been posted to the Crimea. If Henry did spend time in the Crimea then it would have been very brief and after hostilities had ended so he did not receive the Crimean War Medal. The 2nd Battalion boarded *HMS King Philip* at Balaklava on 8th June 1856 bound for England, where they landed at Portsmouth on 11th July and were immediately transported by rail to Aldershot where they were reviewed by Queen Victoria on 20th July 1856.

Henry and his battalion remained at Aldershot until June 1857 when they moved to London and were in attendance at the first investiture of the Victoria Cross held at Hyde Park on 26th June, where eight members of the regiment were presented with their Victoria Cross medals by Queen Victoria.

On the evening of the 26th June, the regiment were transported by rail to Liverpool and the next day set sail for Dublin where they occupied the Beggars Bush and Linen Hall barracks.

In August 1857, following the outbreak of the mutiny, the 2nd Battalion were ordered to make ready for deployment to India and in three divisions set sail from Cork on 3rd August on board *SS Lady Jocelyn*, on 4th August on board *HMS United Kingdom* and on 7th August on board the transport *Sussex*. After landing at Calcutta on 3rd November, the first detachment proceeded by river steamer up the Ganges and reached Allahabad on 20th November and after being joined by the 2nd detachment on 24th

---

689 Edward, following in his father's footsteps, rose to the rank of Commander in the Royal Navy and was killed in action on 15th August 1863 in Japan while serving on board *HMS Euryalus*.
690 *London Gazette* – 20982/1763
691 *London Gazette* – 21254/2586

692 *London Gazette* – 21704/1667
693 *London Gazette* – 21760/3033

November set out for Cawnpore as part of a force commanded by General Windham. On 6th December 1857, the regiment were involved in the Battle of Cawnpore and on 18th December, after the city had been secured, was part of Oude Field Force which set off in pursuit of the Gwalior Contingent of mutineers. During this time Henry served on the staff of Sir James Hope Grant as Deputy Judge-Advocate-General. The regiment took part in the capture of the Fort at Etawah on 29th December and then proceeded to Futtehgur where they met up with the force of Sir Colin Campbell on 4th January 1858 but returned to Cawnpore.

On 27th February 1858, the regiment left Cawnpore to rejoin the force commanded by Sir Colin Campbell which was now advancing on Lucknow. From 6th March, Henry and the regiment were involved in the siege and assault on Lucknow and on 7th March took part in the capture of the "Yellow Bungalow". It was on the 11th March, during an action in Lucknow, that Henry performed the deeds for which he would later be awarded the Victoria Cross. Following the recapture of Lucknow on 21st March, Henry and the Battalion were part of the Lucknow Field Force commanded by General Sir James Hope Grant and took part in the Battle of Nuwabgunge on 13th June 1858 and occupied the city. On 20th July 1858, Henry received a brevet promotion to the rank of Major[694] and two days later left Nuwabgunge for Fyzabad and then on to Sultanpore, taking part in some minor skirmishes as the mutiny came to an end. For his service during the mutiny, Henry was awarded the Indian Mutiny Medal with clasp for Lucknow.

Henry was presented with his Victoria Cross Medal at some time in 1859, while still serving in India.

In the summer of 1860, Henry took part in the 2nd Anglo-China War (2nd Opium War) where he served as Judge Advocate-General, he took part in the taking of the Taku Forts on 21st August and the capture of Peking on 6th October 1860. For his service during the war, Henry was awarded the 2nd China War Medal (1857–60) with clasps for Taku Forts and Peking.

Not long after returning from China, Henry was appointed as a Major in the 1st Battalion of the Derbyshire Rifle Volunteers[695] on 1st December 1861 and after over 13 years of service retired from the army on 4th February 1862.[696]

On 15th July 1862, Henry was married to Charlotte Cecilia (née Pare).

Henry was appointed as Lieutenant-Colonel commander in the 1st Battalion of the Derbyshire Rifle Volunteers[697] on 22nd April 1863.

On 15th January 1868, Henry was appointed as a Deputy Lieutenant for the county of Derbyshire.[698]

At the bye-election resulting from the death of Sir Thomas Gresley, Henry was elected as Member for Parliament for the South Division of the county of Derbyshire on 18th January 1869.[699]

Following the death of his father on 11th April 1872, Henry became the 5th Baronet of Chaddesden.

In 1874, Henry was appointed as a Governor of Repton School, a position that he would hold until 1901.

Henry was re-elected to serve as the Member of Parliament for South Derbyshire on 6th February 1874[700] and again on 2nd April 1880.[701]

On 24th May 1881, Henry was appointed as an Ordinary Member 3rd Class (Companion) of the Civil Division of the Most Honourable Order of the Bath.[702]

Henry received the honorary rank of Colonel in the 1st Battalion of the Derbyshire Rifle Volunteers on 1st July 1881,[703]

Figure 222a. Grave of Henry Wilmot

694 *London Gazette* – 22164/3379
695 *London Gazette* – 22583/5580
696 *London Gazette* – 22595/592
697 *London Gazette* – 22729/2188

698 *London Gazette* – 23343/213
699 *London Gazette* – 23460/291
700 *London Gazette* – 24066/693
701 *London Gazette* – 24829/2358
702 *London Gazette* – 24976/2674
703 *London Gazette* – 25026/5090

however a few months later on 14th December 1881 he resigned and was appointed as Honorary Colonel of the Corps.[704] On 11th July 1888, Henry was appointed to the command of the North Midland Volunteer Infantry Brigade (Sherwood Foresters)[705] with the rank of Colonel. He served until 19th June 1895 when he resigned and was appointed as Honorary Colonel of the Regiment.[706]

During 1895, Henry served as Chairman and Alderman of Derbyshire County Council, he also served as a Justice of the Peace.

For his service to the army volunteer service, Henry was awarded the Volunteer Officer's Decoration (1892). At some stage he was also appointed as an Honorary Associate of the Order of St John of Jerusalem in England.

On 22nd June 1897, Henry was appointed as an Additional Member 2nd Class (Knight Commander) of the Civil Division of the Most Honourable Order of the Bath.[707]

Henry died of pneumonia on 7th April 1901 at his home "Chaddesden" in Bournemouth, Hampshire aged 70 years and was buried at St Mary's Churchyard in Chaddesden.

Henry's Victoria Cross Medal is on public display at the Royal Green Jackets Museum in Winchester.

---

704 *London Gazette* – 25048/6663
705 *London Gazette* – 25836/3765
706 *London Gazette* – 26635/3464
707 *London Gazette* – 26947/1685

William McBean
11th March 1858 (VC No. 245)

Gazetted: 24th December 1858 22212/5515

Rank and Unit: Lieutenant – 93rd Regiment of Foot

Citation

For distinguished personal bravery in killing eleven of the enemy with his own hand in the main breach of the Begum Bagh at Lucknow, on the 11th March, 1858.

Biography

William was born on 1st January 1818[708] at Inverness, the son of a shoemaker.

On 3rd February 1835 at the age of 17 and much against the wishes of his parents, William left his job as a ploughman and enlisted in the army joining the 93rd Regiment of Foot as a Drummer Boy.

William was initially stationed at Weedon in Northamptonshire before moving to Blackburn in May 1835. As a new soldier, William was continually barracked by the drill instructors for having a "rolling gait" and after a particularly harsh drill it was suggested by a friend that he should take the instructor behind the canteen and give him a good thrashing. William is said to have replied *"Man, that would ne'er do. I intend to be in command of this regiment before I leave it. It would be an ill beginning to be brought before the Colonel for thrashing the drill Corporal"*; a most prophetic pronouncement.

In October 1835, William and the regiment moved to Liverpool where they boarded transports and set sail for Dublin where they performed garrison duties.

On reaching his 18th birthday on 1st January 1836 William was given the rank of Private.

In early October 1836, after spending a year on duty in Dublin the regiment was moved to Newry until 19th – 22nd May 1837 when they moved to Belfast and received orders to make ready for deployment to Gibraltar in the autumn. On 26th November 1837, the regiment moved to Cork in readiness for setting sail to Gibraltar, however, due to an insurrection in Canada their departure was deferred and they were informed that they would now be deployed to Canada.

The regiment was despatched to Canada in two deployments; the Right Wing left Cork on board *HMS Inconstant* on 26th January 1838 and arrived at Halifax, Nova Scotia on 29th

---

708 At this time it was not a legal requirement to register births and when noted the birth date was often recorded as 1st January of the year of birth.

Figure 223. William McBean

January; the Left Wing departed on board *HMS Pique* on 23rd January, however, due to severe storms did not arrive at Halifax until 5th March 1838. During their time in Canada, the regiment was stationed at Halifax, Montreal, Kingston and Toronto and on 16th November 1838 were involved in the Prescott Affair. William was promoted to the rank of Corporal on 7th November 1839 and was promoted to the rank of Sergeant on 22nd March 1844.

On 1st August 1848, after serving for ten years in the province, the regiment boarded *HMS Resistance* at Quebec and set sail for England and after landing at Portsmouth travelled to Stirling Castle where they took up the garrison duties on 31st August 1848 and established bases at Perth and Dundee.

On 5th April 1850, the regiment moved to Edinburgh where they were established as the garrison in the castle until 15th April 1851 when they moved to Glasgow. On 23rd February 1852, William and the regiment were moved to Weedon and on 25th June 1852, he was promoted to the rank of Colour-Sergeant. William moved to Portsmouth on 11th August 1852 and occupied the Anglesey Barracks until 14th June 1853 when the regiment moved to Chobham Camp for a month of manoeuvres after which they moved to Devonport on 15th July with detachments at Plymouth and Dartmouth Prison.

On 12th February 1854, the regiment received orders to make ready for deployment on active service and on 28th February boarded *HMS Himalaya* bound for Malta where they arrived on 7th March 1854. While stationed on Malta, the regiment were engaged in extensive practice with their newly issued Minié rifles.

On 4th April 1854, after receiving news of the declaration of war against Russia the regiment boarded the steamer *Kangaroo*

and on 6th April set sail for Gallipoli where they arrived on 11th April. On 6th May 1854, the regiment boarded the Steamer *Andes* and set sail for Scutari where they landed three days later and on 13th June boarded the Steamer *Melbourne* and departed for Varna where the Anglo/French Expeditionary Force was being assembled, arriving on 15th June. At Varna the regiment was struck down by cholera and moved to various camps including Aladyn and Givrakla in a vain attempt to escape the ravages of the disease. At the age of 36 and after 20 years of exemplary good conduct, William was commissioned as Ensign on 10th August 1854 by Colonel William Bernard Ainslie.[709]

On 31st August 1854, while the regiment departed for the Crimean peninsula, William was placed in charge of the 102 NCO's and men who were sick, the 20 soldiers wives and 83 baggage ponies, and remained in Varna. It was during his time at Varna that William struck up a friendship with Florence Nightingale being very impressed with her care of the sick men. On 8th December 1854, William was promoted to the rank of Lieutenant.[710] William finally landed at Balaklava on 26th December, having returned to the regiment with a contingent of the sick NCO's and men who had by now recovered from their illness.

On his arrival on the Crimean peninsula, William was deployed to the siege lines at Sevastopol, having missed all of the iconic battles which were waged before his arrival. During the early part of 1855, William was involved in a reconnaissance of the Tchernaya River and was appointed as adjutant to the regiment on 16th February 1855.[711] From 3rd to 8th May William and the regiment briefly left the lines at Sevastopol to take part in the first expedition to Kertch which was aborted by the French Command upon orders from Emperor Napoleon.

On 22nd May 1855, William and the regiment boarded *HMS Sphynx* and *HMS Stomboli* and as part of the joint French/Turkish and English force set sail for Kertch to secure the access to the Sea of Azov. On 25th May the town of Kertch surrendered and the force commanded by Major-General Sir George Browne occupied the fortress at Yenicale unopposed, the Russians having fled. William and the regiment left Kertch on board *HMS Terrible* on 12th June and landed at Balaklava on 14th June where they returned to their former position in the lines around Sevastopol. On 18th June, William and the regiment were involved in the first unsuccessful attack on Sevastopol as part of the force which attempted to capture the Great Redan and were also involved in the second attack on the 8th September 1855. On 9th September, William with ten men volunteered to leave the advanced trenches and investigate the Redan which appeared to have been

709 *London Gazette* – 21581/2470
710 *London Gazette* – 21638/3988
711 *London Gazette* – 21664/606

abandoned by the Russians. On entering the Redan, William found that this was indeed the case; the Russians had fled to the Northern part of the city. On 16th June 1856, William and the regiment boarded *HMS Sidon* and finally left the Crimea bound for England where they landed at Portsmouth on 15th July and proceeded to the new camp at Aldershot. For his service during the war, William was awarded; the Crimea Medal with clasp for Sevastopol, the Turkish Crimean Medal and the Imperial Order of the Medjidie 5th Class.[712]

On 23rd July 1856, William and the regiment left Aldershot by rail for Dover where they camped on the Western Heights until 30th September when they relieved the 79th Highlanders as the garrison and occupied Dover Castle and the Shaft Barracks.

On 31st January 1857, the regiment received orders to prepare for immediate embarkation for India, however on 6th March these were replaced with orders to prepare for deployment to China. The regiment was finally despatched to China from Portsmouth in two detachments, the first left on board *HMS Belleisle* and set sail on 23rd May, William was with the second detachment which set sail on board *HMS Mauritius* on 16th June. On 11th August *HMS Mauritius* arrived at Simon's Bay in the Cape Colony and after meeting up with officers on board *HMS Belleisle*, which had arrived a few days earlier, received news of the mutiny and new orders to proceed at once to India. Leaving the Cape of Good Hope on 16th August 1857, William set sail on *HMS Mauritius* and arrived at Calcutta on 20th September and once again the regiment was reunited.

From the 28th September 1857, the regiment left Calcutta in small detachments on the 600 mile journey along the Grand Trunk Road towards Cawnpore, William was in the last detachment which left on the 9th October and by 11th November the regiment had formed up as part of the Lucknow Relief Force.

On 15th November, after fierce hand to hand combat the regiment captured the Secundra Bagh and the Shah Najaf Mosque from the mutineers. On the morning of 17th November, William, Sergeant Hutchinson and Drummer Ross (a boy 12 years old) volunteered to climb the dome of the mosque and hoist the regimental colours as a signal to the garrison besieged in the Residency that help was close at hand.

From the 19th to 21st November, the garrison in the Residency was evacuated and William and the 93rd regiment covered their retreat. William took part in the Battle of Cawnpore on 6th December and afterwards, as part of the force of General Hope Grant, pursued the Gwalior contingent of rebels and inflicted a heavy defeat at Serai Ghât on 9th December 1857.

On 2nd March 1858, William and the regiment formed up as part of the force of Sir Colin Campbell for the final assault on Lucknow. As part of Major-General Lugard's division William was involved in the storming of the Martinière on the 9th March. It was during the storming of the Begum's Palace on 11th March that William performed the deeds for which he would later be awarded the Victoria Cross and after the city was finally in British hands on 27th March the regiment took a well earned rest at Dilkusha.

William was mentioned in the Roll of Officers deemed deserving of honourable mention for their service at Lucknow, which was issued by Brigadier-General Sir Edward Lugard on 24th March 1858.[713] After his service at Lucknow, William was offered the command of his army by one of the Indian Prince's, however, this generous offer was declined.

On 7th April 1858, the regiment was assigned to the Rohilkhand Field Force and during the campaign was involved in actions in this province and later in the province of Oudh. On 16th April 1858, William was promoted to the rank of Captain[714] and took part in the taking of Fort Rooya on the same day. William took part in the action at Alligunge on 22nd April and the Battle of Bareilly on the 5th May 1858. After the battle, William and the regiment occupied the town of Bareilly and served as the garrison until mid November when they took part in the campaign to subdue the Oudh province where they were involved in actions at Pusegaon on 19th November, Russoolpore on 26th November and the taking of the fort at Mittowlee. In early December all elements of the regiment were reunited at Biswah. For his service during the mutiny, William was awarded the Indian Mutiny Medal with clasps for Relief of Lucknow and Lucknow.

William was presented with his Victoria Cross Medal by Major-General Sir Robert Garrett on 6th February 1859 at a special parade at Umbeyla, Peshawar in India.

On 20th February 1859, William and the regiment were ordered to the hill station at Subathoo where they arrived in mid April and stayed until November when they moved to Umballa for drill and musket training.

On 21st January 1860, William and the regiment were employed as part of the escort for Governor General Lord Canning's tour of the North West provinces and the Punjab. After arriving at Lahore the regiment received new orders directing them to Rawalpindi where they arrived on 9th March 1860.

William received a brevet promotion to the rank of Major on 10th August 1860.[715]

712 *London Gazette* – 22107/1265

713 *London Gazette* – 22143/2583
714 *London Gazette* – 22155/3014
715 *London Gazette* – 22493/1244

The regiment moved to Peshawar on 14th November 1861 and were beset by repeated outbreaks of cholera which over the coming months would result in 93 deaths.

On 30th December 1862 the regiment moved to Sealkote and remained until 3rd November 1863 when they joined the field force of Sir Neville Chamberlain and took part in the Eusufzai Campaign.

William remained in Sealkote, in charge of the invalids and the time expired men about to return to Europe and at some stage returned to England and took command of the Depot Company stationed at Aberdeen.

At some stage after his return to Scotland, William was married to Miss Beveridge from Kirkaldy. His wife and only child, a son, both predeceased him.

In May 1865, the Depot Company was moved to Stirling Castle however returned to Aberdeen in June 1866.

On 27th December 1869, the regiment began its journey to return to England and on 15th February 1870 set sail on board the troopship *Jumna* at Bombay and after transferring to *HMS Himalaya* at Alexandria arrived at Portsmouth on 21st March and then Leith on 28th March and established detachments at Aberdeen, Perth and Stirling.

On 15th June 1871, the Regimental Head Quarters was moved to Edinburgh Castle and William was in command of G Company. On 14th July 1871, William received a brevet promotion to the rank of Lieutenant-Colonel[716] and was promoted to the rank of Major on 8th June 1872.[717]

The regiment left Edinburgh on board *HMS Himalaya* and sailed to Portsmouth on 12th May 1873 and then moved to the camp at Aldershot on their arrival two days later.

On 29th October 1873, William was promoted to the rank of Lieutenant-Colonel[718] and succeeded Colonel Burroughs as commander of the regiment, only one of a handful of men to have risen through the ranks to the command of a regiment. On 1st July 1874 the regiment moved to Woolwich and then soon afterwards to the camp at Shorncliffe. William and the regiment moved to Dublin on 26th March 1876 where they formed the garrison until 17th May 1877 when they move to Curragh Camp. William received a brevet promotion to the rank of Colonel on 1st October 1877.[719]

On 16th February 1878, after 44 years of service, William retired from the army with a pension of £420/year plus an additional £100 good service pension and was awarded the honorary rank of Major-General.[720]

After only a few months of retirement, William died following a short period of illness at Herbert Military Hospital, Shooters Hill at Woolwich on 22nd June 1878 at the age of 59.

Following a brief ceremony, with full military honours, William's body was transported by rail to Edinburgh where on 2nd July 1878 he was buried in the Grange Cemetery.

William's Victoria Cross Medal is on public display at the Argyll and Sutherland Highlanders Museum in Stirling Castle.

Figure 223a. Grave of William McBean

---

716 *London Gazette* – 23774/3903
717 *London Gazette* – 23868/2804
718 *London Gazette* – 24036/5030
719 *London Gazette* – 24525/6438
720 *London Gazette* – 24570/2452

William Nash
11th March 1858 (VC No. 246)

Gazetted: 24th December 1858 22212/5515

Rank and Unit: Corporal No. 1218 – Rifle Brigade – 2nd Battalion

Citation

For conspicuous gallantry at Lucknow on the 11th March 1858. Captain Wilmot's Company was engaged with a large body of the enemy, near the Iron Bridge. That officer found himself at the end of a street with only four of his men, opposed to a considerable body. One of the four was shot through both legs, and became utterly helpless the two men lifted him up, and although Private Hawkes was severely wounded, he carried him for a considerable distance, exposed to the fire of the enemy, Captain Wilmot firing with the men's rifles, and covering the retreat of the party.

(Despatch of Brigadier-General Walpole, C.B., dated 20th of March, 1858.)

Biography

William was born at Newcastle in County Limerick, Ireland on 23rd April 1824.

At the age of 14½, William left his job as a labourer and enlisted in the army on 2nd June 1838 at Portsmouth and joined the 2nd battalion of the Rifle Brigade as a Private.

Just after his enlistment, on 16th June 1838, William and the battalion marched in three divisions from Portsmouth to Chelsea where they were barracked to take part in the coronation of Queen Victoria on 28th June during which they lined Piccadilly from Hyde Park Corner to the corner of St James's Street. On 10th July 1838, William and the battalion marched to Woolwich where they relieved the 1st Battalion until 9th October 1840 when they were moved to Windsor and from 12th October were quartered in the Infantry Barracks. William was appointed as a bugler on 1st June 1839 a position that he would hold until 30th April 1841 when he reverted to Private.

The battalion was ordered to make ready for overseas deployment and moved to Bristol on 30th August 1842 from where they proceeded by rail to Deptford, boarded the transport *Abercrombie Robinson* and on 3rd September set sail for Bermuda where they arrived at St George's on 5th November 1842. On 30th July 1843, the battalion boarded the transport *Java* and set sail for Halifax Nova Scotia where they arrived on 12th August 1843. William was promoted to the rank of Corporal on 21st February 1845. After spending three years in Halifax, on 1st August 1846,

Figure 224. William Nash

William and the battalion boarded *HMS Belleisle* and set sail to Montreal where they arrived on 22nd August. After spending a year in Montreal, on 10th August 1847 the battalion was posted to Kingston in Upper Canada and established detachments in Toronto and Quebec. On 15th December 1848, William was promoted to the rank of Sergeant. In May 1852 all elements of the battalion were assembled at Quebec and on 3rd June set sail for England on board *HMS Simoom*, they arrived at Portsmouth on 26th June after an absence from home of almost ten years.

On arrival at Portsmouth, the battalion were moved to their station at Canterbury.

On 17th November 1852, the battalion was moved to Chelsea in readiness for participation in the funeral of their Colonel-in-Chief the Duke of Wellington. During the funeral, which took place the next day, the battalion marched at the head of the procession from Horse Guards to St Paul's Cathedral. The next day they returned to barracks at Canterbury.

On 13th June 1853, William and the battalion left Canterbury for the camp at Chobham where they worked on constructing facilities at this new training station until 14th July when they were transferred to Portsmouth and took up quarters in the Clarence barracks and were told to make ready for foreign deployment.

On 24th February 1854 the battalion boarded *HMS Vulcan* at Portsmouth *HMS Himalaya* at Southampton and set sail for Malta and by 11th March both detachments were occupying the Ropewalk barracks.

The battalion boarded the steamship *Golden Fleece* on 30th March and set sail for Gallipoli where they arrived on 6th April 1854. On Gallipoli, the battalion were employed making roads, digging wells and preparing the British lines near the Gulf of Xeros. On 6th May the battalion again boarded the *Golden Fleece* and left for Scutari where they arrived on the following day and were assigned to the Light Division commanded by Sir George Browne. On the 29th May, the battalion yet again boarded the *Golden Fleece* and set sail for Varna where the Anglo/French Expeditionary force was being assembled for the invasion of the Crimea. While based at Varna, the battalion was beset by cholera and it is thought that William was one of the inflicted as it appears that he was not present when the battalion landed on the Crimean peninsula on 14th September 1854. It would further appear that he must have had a serious dose of the disease, sufficient for him to be sent back to England, as his records show no service in the Crimea.

William was promoted to the rank of Colour Sergeant on 8th February 1855. On 8th June 1856, the 2nd battalion boarded the transport *King Phillip* at Balaklava and set sail for England, where they arrived at Portsmouth on 11th July and were immediately transported by rail to the camp at Aldershot at which point William was presumably reunited with his comrades.

In late June 1857 the battalion moved to London and were present at the first investiture held in Hyde Park on 26th June where eight men from the 2nd battalion were presented with their Victoria Cross medals by Queen Victoria. After taking part in the review, the battalion were transported to Liverpool and on the 27th June set sail for Dublin, where they were quartered in the Beggar's Bush and Linen-Hall barracks.

In the aftermath of the mutiny in India, the battalion was ordered to proceed to India with haste and they departed Ireland in three divisions; the first leaving Cork on 3rd August on board *Lady Jocelyn*; the second leaving Kingstown on 4th August on board *United Kingdom* and the last, also from Kingstown on 6th August on board *Sussex*. The first detachments arrived at Calcutta on 3rd November and began their long journey to join General Windham at Cawnpore.

During the journey to India, on 27th September 1857, William was reduced in rank to Sergeant and soon after arriving in India faced a regimental court martial, served 3 days imprisonment (from 6th to 8th November) and was reduced back to Private.

As part of the force commanded by General Windham, the battalion took part in the 2nd Battle of Cawnpore on 6th December 1857 and on 29th December were involved in the capture of the fort at Etawah. On 8th January 1858, the battalion moved to Futtehgur where they formed up as part of the field force commanded by Sir Colin Campbell and under the command of Brigadier Walpole took part in operations along the Ramganga River before returning to Cawnpore on 11th February 1858. On 22nd January 1858, William was promoted back to the rank of

Corporal. William and the battalion left Cawnpore on 3rd March 1858, as part of the field force sent to recapture Lucknow and were involved in the taking of the Yellow House on 9th March. It was during the defence of the iron bridge on the road from Fyzabad to Lucknow, on 11th March 1858, that William performed the deeds for which he would later be awarded the Victoria Cross. Lucknow was finally recaptured on 21st March and on 11th April William and the battalion left the city as part of the field force commanded by Sir Hope Grant and took part in operations in the province of Oudh to the north of the city. On 1st April 1858, William was promoted to the rank of Sergeant. William took part in the Battle of Nuwabgunge on 13th June 1858 and from 5th December took part in the trans-Gogra Campaign under the command of Lord Clyde seeing action at Medjidie and Raptee before returning to Lucknow during July 1859 at the end of the mutiny. For his service during the mutiny, William was awarded the Indian Mutiny Medal with clasp for Lucknow.

From Lucknow William and the regiment were moved to Subathoo and it was probably while stationed here that he was presented with his Victoria Cross Medal.

In 1860 William was tried for the second time by regimental court martial and after serving two days imprisonment from 11th to 12th September 1860 was reduced in rank back to Private.

In December 1861, the battalion was sent to Umballa for three months of musketry training following which they returned to Subathoo until 2nd February 1863 when they were transferred to Delhi.

On 17th February 1863, William was again promoted to the rank of Corporal and on 3rd April was promoted to the rank of Sergeant, however this was to be short lived as for the 3rd time he was tried by Regimental Court Martial, served ten days in prison

Figure 224a. Grave of William Nash

(from 24th June until 3rd July 1863) and was once again reduced in rank to Private.

It was while serving at Delhi, that on 30th October 1863, William was declared unfit for further service due to ailments resulting from the rigours of over 18 years foreign service.

William was returned to England and finally discharged from the army at Netley on 24th May 1864 after over 22 years of service.

Despite his having been tried by court martial on three occasions, William's conduct was generally very good and he was also in receipt of three good conduct badges.

Unfortunately, little is known of William's life after the army other than he died at his home in Hackney on 29th April 1875 at the age of 50 and was buried in St John's Churchyard, Hackney.

The whereabouts of William's Victoria Cross Medal is unknown.

David Hawkes
11th March 1858 (VC No. 247)

Gazetted: 24th December 1858 22212/5515

Rank and Unit: Private – Rifle Brigade – 2nd Battalion

Citation

For conspicuous gallantry at Lucknow on the 11th March 1858. Captain Wilmot's Company was engaged with a large body of the enemy, near the Iron Bridge. That officer found himself at the end of a street with only four of his men, opposed to a considerable body. One of the four was shot through both legs, and became utterly helpless the two men lifted him up, and although Private Hawkes was severely wounded, he carried him for a considerable distance, exposed to the fire of the enemy, Captain Wilmot firing with the men's rifles, and covering the retreat of the party.
(Despatch of Brigadier-General Walpole, C.B., dated 20th of March, 1858.)

Biography

David was born in 1822 at Witham in Essex to father William who was a labourer and mother Sarah (née Joice), he was baptised at St Nicholas Church in Witham on 23rd June 1822. David had two older brothers William born in 1814 and Stephen born in 1818, he also had a younger sister Sarah Ann born in 1833.

Unfortunately as David died in service, very little information is available regarding his time in the army as no discharge or pension records were retained.

Assuming that David joined the army on or around the time of his 18th birthday, his army life would have started in 1840 and his movements would have been similar to those of William Nash with whom he shared the deed for which he was awarded the Victoria Cross.

David was killed in action at Fyzabad on 14th August 1858 at the age of 36, no details of his burial location have survived.

David was never presented with his Victoria Cross Medal as he died before the award was formally approved by Queen Victoria and even before the details were published in the London Gazette – the medal was sent by registered post to his father on 10th February 1859.

For his service during the mutiny, David was awarded the Indian Mutiny Medal with clasp for Lucknow.

David's Victoria Cross Medal is on public display at the Fitzwilliam Museum in Cambridge.

Figure 225a. Memorial to David Hawkes, Winchester Cathedral

Edward Robinson
13th March 1858 (VC No. 248)

Gazetted: 24th December 1858 22212/5512

Rank and Unit: Able Seaman – Royal Navy (Naval Brigade)

Citation

For conspicuous bravery, in having at Lucknow, on the 13th of March, 1858, under a heavy musketry fire, within fifty yards, jumped on the sand bags of a battery, and extinguished a fire among them. He was dangerously wounded in performing this service.

Biography

Edward was born on 17th June 1838 at Portsea, Portsmouth to father James who was a mariner and mother Sophia; he had a younger brother born around 1841.

On 11th August 1852, just after his 14th birthday, Edward joined the Royal Navy as a Boy 2nd Class and was assigned to *HMS Victory*, commanded by Captain George Bohun Martin, which was the flagship of Admiral Thomas Briggs and was based at Portsmouth.

In September 1856, Edward was transferred as an able seaman to the newly commissioned *HMS Shannon* commanded by Captain William Peel. On 17th March 1857, Edward set sail from Plymouth on board *HMS Shannon* bound for China and were anchored off Singapore on 11th June when they first heard the news of the outbreak of mutiny in India. Lord Elgin and his staff boarded *HMS Shannon* at Singapore and set sail to Hong Kong where after arriving on 2nd July, they heard of the worsening situation in India and received orders to proceed to Calcutta. On

Figure 226. Edward Robinson

16th July 1857, after boarding detachments of Royal Marines and men from the 90th Regiment of Foot, *HMS Shannon* set sail for Calcutta where she arrived on 6th August. After arriving in Calcutta, Captain William Peel offered the services of himself and his men to the Governor General, an offer that was gratefully accepted. With the first detachment of the newly formed Naval Brigade, Captain Peel left Calcutta by river steamers on 14th August, bound for Cawnpore. After recruiting additional men from merchant ships in the harbour, Edward with the second detachment left Calcutta on 12th September and was reunited with the first detachment at Futtehpore on 31st October.

As part of the force commanded by Sir Colin Campbell, Edward and the Naval Brigade took part in the 2nd relief of Lucknow, which on 19th to 21st November resulted in the evacuation of Residency. After leaving Lucknow, Edward and the Naval Brigade played a decisive part in the 2nd Battle of Cawnpore when on the 6th December the city was recaptured from the mutineers. On 2nd January 1858, the Brigade was involved in action at the Kallee-Nuddee River while on their way to Futtehgur, which they reached on the following day. Here they waited until 12th February when they began their journey towards Lucknow, only to be halted at Oonoa on 17th February awaiting clarification of their orders.

Eventually on the 25th February their journey was resumed and on 3rd March they took their place in the lines of Sir Colin Campbell's force which was besieging Lucknow. It was on 13th March, during operations in preparation for the final assault on the city that Edward performed the deeds for which he would later be awarded the Victoria Cross, being seriously wounded in the shoulder during the action.

Due to his wounds, Edward took no further part in the fighting and by 12th May was back on board *HMS Shannon* at Calcutta with other sick and wounded from the Naval Brigade. It was not until September 1858, that the crew finally returned to *HMS Shannon* and with a new Captain, Acting Captain Francis Marten, following the death of Captain Peel, she set sail from Calcutta on 15th September and landed at Spithead on 29th December 1858. For his service during the mutiny, Edward was awarded the Indian Mutiny Medal with clasps for Relief of Lucknow and Lucknow.

Due to his wounds, Edward was discharged from the Royal Navy but immediately enlisted in the Coast Guard service, where over the next ten years he was stationed at Dover until 1860, Portsmouth until 1861, followed by short stays at Dublin and Sligo before returning to Dover in 1862.

Edward was presented with his Victoria Cross Medal by Queen Victoria at a ceremony held at Windsor Castle on 4th January 1860.

Edward was married to Annie (née Goldsack) at Dover during September 1865, the couple would go on to have five sons; Edward born in Folkestone *c.*1866, Thomas born in Battersea *c.*1873, Alfred born in Battersea *c.*1875, Walter born in St Martin's *c.*1876 and Archbald also born at St Martin's *c.*1881; the couple also had three daughters, Annie born at Folkestone *c.*1868, Matilda born in Battersea *c.*1870 and Florence born at St Martin's *c.*1878.

On 13th December 1865, Edward moved to his final Coast Guard station at Folkestone where he remained until he left the service and joined the Office of the Naval Reserve in London during 1868.

Edward remained with the Naval Reserve Office for 10 years and lived in Battersea in London.

In 1878, Edward was appointed as a gardener at Windsor Castle and when this job became too difficult he was appointed as the Gatekeeper at the Old Windsor entrance to Windsor Home Park and with his family he took up residence at Albert Bridge Lodge, Windsor.

Edward died on 2nd October 1896 at the age of 58 and was buried in St Peter and St Andrew's Church cemetery in Windsor on 8th October 1896. On 15th May 2000, HRH The Duke of Edinburgh unveiled a reconditioned headstone over his grave.

Edward's Victoria Cross Medal is on public display at the National Maritime Museum in Greenwich.

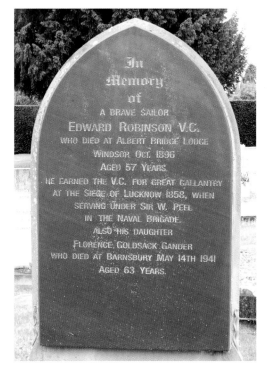

Figure 226a. Grave of Edward Robinson

Richard Harte Keatinge
17th March 1858 (VC No. 249)

Gazetted: 25th February 1862 22601/956

Rank and Unit: Captain – Bombay Artillery – Indian Army

Citation

For having rendered most efficient aid at the assault of Chanderi; in voluntarily leading the Column through the breach, which was protected by a heavy cross fire. He was one of the foremost to enter, and was severely wounded in the breach. The Column was saved from a serious loss that would probably have resulted, but for Major Keatinge's knowledge of the small path leading across the ditch, which had been examined during the night by himself and a servant, who declined, when required, to lead the column, without his master. Having cleared the breach; he led into the Fort where he was struck down by another dangerous wound. The Commander-in-Chief in India states that the success at Chanderi was mainly owing to this Officer, whose gallantry, really brilliant, he considers was equalled by his ability and devotion. **(Major Keatinge was at the time a Political Officer with the 2nd Brigade of the Central India Field Force.)**

Biography

Richard was born on 17th June 1825 at Dublin in Ireland to father the Right Honourable Richard who was a Privy Councillor, Kings Council (barrister) and a Judge in the Court of Probate in Ireland and mother Harriet Augusta (née Joseph). Richard had an older brother Maurice who was born ten years earlier in 1815.

After being privately educated at schools in Dublin, Richard was commissioned as a 2nd Lieutenant in the army of the Honourable East India Company on 11th June 1842, six days before his 17th birthday.

Richard joined his regiment, the Bombay Artillery 3rd Troop, in India on 15th November 1843 and was promoted to the rank of Lieutenant on 3rd July 1845.

In 1846, Richard was married to Harriet (née Pottinger) the sister of Major General J. Pottinger, the couple would go on to have six children; four sons, Eldred, Henry, Maurice and one other and two daughters Annie Harriet born in 1848 in India and Fanny.

In 1847, Richard was appointed as the assistant political superintendant at Namur in the south west region of the Madhya Pradesh State in the west of central India. From 24th December 1851, Richard was transferred to civil employ in the Political

Figure 227. Richard Harte Keatinge

Department and served as Political Agent to Mundlaiser and from 20th February 1852 as Commandant of the Namur Police Corps. On 10th December 1856, Richard received a brevet promotion to the rank of Captain.

Richard was promoted to the rank of Captain on 3rd January 1857[721] and in July joined the column of Major-General Sir Henry Marion Durand at Malwa, as Political Officer.

As part of this force, Richard was involved in the siege and capture of the fort at Dhar from 22nd to 29th November 1857, the Battle of Mundesore on 21st November 1857 and the Battle of Neemuch on 25th November 1857. In December 1857, Richard was appointed as the Political Agent to West Malwa and joined the 1st Brigade of the Central India Field Force being assembled at Indore as Political Officer. It was with this force, commanded by General Sir Hugh Rose, that on 17th March 1858, during the Battle of Chanderi, Richard performed the deeds for which he would later be awarded the Victoria Cross. During this action he received two serious wounds. On 20th July 1858, Richard received a brevet promotion to the rank of Major[722] in the Bombay Staff Corps. Richard commanded a force of irregular troops against Seeta Ram Holkar in the Sathpoora Hills in October 1858 and served with Brigadier Parke's Brigade in the pursuit of Tantia Topi during November 1858 and operations against insurgents in the Sathpoora Hills during 1859. For his service during the mutiny, Richard was awarded the Indian Mutiny Medal with clasp for Central India. In 1860, Richard was appointed as Political Agent to Namur, a role that he was to perform until April 1862. During this period, on 18th February 1861, Richard was

---

721 *London Gazette* – 22621/2236
722 *London Gazette* – 22223/296

transferred to the Bombay Staff Corps. Richard was appointed as Political Agent to Gwalior in April 1862 and continued in the position until February 1863. On 11th June 1862, Richard was promoted to the rank of Major.[723]

Richard was presented with his Victoria Cross Medal on 1st January 1863 by Lieutenant-General Sir William Mansfield, the General Officer Commanding at Bombay.

In February 1863, Richard was appointed as the Political Agent to Kathiawar and from 1865 to 1866 commanded field detachments against rebel Wagher tribesmen. He was commended for his actions in the General Orders of 28th January 1866. Richard was appointed as a Companion of the Most Exalted Order of the Star of India on 24th May 1866.[724] On 13th November 1866, Richard received a brevet promotion to the rank of Lieutenant-Colonel.[725] In November 1867, left Kathiawar and was appointed as the Governor General's agent to the Rajputana States. Richard was promoted to the rank of Lieutenant-Colonel on 11th June 1868.[726]

In 1868, Richard founded the Rajkumar College at Rajkot, which opened its doors as a school for boys in 1870 and was described in some quarters as the India Eton.

From 8th July 1870 to 1871, Richard was appointed to the role of acting Chief Commissioner of the Central Provinces during the absence of Sir Henry Morris. Richard was Chief Commissioner of Ajmer-Merwara from 1st April 1871 until 21st June 1873. On 11th June 1873, Richard received a brevet promotion to the rank of Colonel.[727] In June 1873, Richard was reappointed as the Governor General's Agent to the Rajputana States, a post that he held until February 1874.

Richard's first wife, Harriet died in 1874.

On 7th February 1874, Richard was appointed as the first Chief Commissioner to the state of Assam a post that he held until 12th June 1878. At some time after leaving this post, Richard returned to England and lived in London.

In 1882, Richard was married to Julia Anna (née Alderson) the widow of Mr. E. C. Fox.

Richard was placed on the unemployed supernumerary list on 1st January 1884[728] and after 42 years of service was effectively retired. On the same day he also received a promotion to the rank of Major-General.[729] On 1st July 1887, while still on the unemployed supernumerary list, Richard was promoted to the rank of Lieutenant-General.[730] Richard was promoted to the rank of General, while on the unemployed supernumerary list, on 1st April 1894.[731]

In his retirement, Richard lived at "Lynwod", North Parade in Horsham which is where he died on 24th May 1904 at the age of 78 and was buried in the Hill Street Cemetery in Horsham.

Richard's Victoria Cross Medal is in the hands of his family.

Figure 227a. Grave of Richard Harte Keatinge

723 *London Gazette* – 22698/221
724 *London Gazette* – 23119/3129
725 *London Gazette* – 23360/1587
726 *London Gazette* – 23450/6658
727 *London Gazette* – 24033/4905
728 *London Gazette* – 25342/1716
729 *London Gazette* – 25342/1715

730 *London Gazette* – 25725/4136
731 *London Gazette* – 25519/3256

David Rush (Rushe)[732]
19th March 1858 (VC No. 250)

Gazetted: 24th December 1858 22212/5512

Rank and Unit: Troop Sergeant-Major No. 1218 – 9th Lancers

Citation

For conspicuous bravery, near Lucknow, on the 19th of March, 1858, in having, in company with one other private of the troop, attacked eight of the enemy, who had posted themselves in a nullah, and killed three of them. **(Despatch from Major-General Sir James Hope Grant, K.C.B., dated 8th April, 1858.)**

Figure 228. David Rush

Biography

David was born on 28th April 1827 at Woburn in Bedfordshire to father William and mother Elizabeth.

On 26th May 1842, a month after his 18th birthday, David enlisted in the army at London and joined his regiment the 9th Lancers as a Private. It would appear that David did not join the regiment in India until sometime in April 1843, and did not serve in the Gwalior Campaign which ended on December 1843.

David saw his first active service during the 1st Anglo-Sikh War which started in December 1845 and was concluded by the Treaty of Lahore on 9th March 1846. During the war, David took part in the decisive Battle of Sobraon on 10th February 1846. For his service during the war, David was awarded the Sutlej Medal (1845–46) engraved with the battle honour for Sobraon.

In November 1848, David again saw active service, when he took part in the 2nd Anglo-Sikh war and was involved in the Passage of Chenab, the Battle of Chillianwala on 13th January 1849 and the Battle of Goojerat on 21st February. For his involvement in the war, David was awarded the Punjab Medal with clasps for Chillianwala and Goojerat.

On 14th October 1849, David was promoted to the rank of Corporal and on 1st February 1851 was promoted to the rank of Sergeant. David was promoted to the rank of Troop Sergeant-Major on 5th March 1857.

At the outbreak of the mutiny, David and the 9th Lancers were stationed at Umballa and were assigned to the Delhi Field Force commanded by Major General George Anson, who was replaced by Major General Sir Henry Barnard when Anson died from cholera on 27th May. The force set out from Umballa on 17th May and after joining forces with the Meerut Brigade,

commanded by Brigadier Archdale Wilson fought the Battle of Badli-ki-Serai on 8th June and established positions on the Delhi Ridge. David was part of the besieging force and was involved in the final capture of Delhi on 21st September 1857. Following the recapture of the city, David and the 9th Lancers were assigned to a Flying Column commanded by Colonel Edward Greathed and on 24th September moved out to patrol the Gangetic Goab, the area of land between the Ganges and Yamuna rivers. On the 28th September, David and the 9th Lancers were involved in the Battle of Bulandshahr. David also took part in the Battle of Agra on 10th November 1857 and was part of the force which evacuated the Residency at Lucknow on 19th November.

It was on 19th March 1858, during the action that resulted in the recapture of Lucknow on 21st March 1858, that David performed the deeds for which he would later be awarded the Victoria Cross.

For the remainder of the mutiny, David was involved in the campaigns in the Rohilkhand and Oudh provinces. For his service during the mutiny, David was awarded the Indian Mutiny Medal with clasps for Delhi, Relief of Lucknow and Lucknow.

David arrived back in England, after his tour in India, during September 1859, having been absent for over 16 years and was sent to the camp at Aldershot.

A few weeks later on 4th January 1860, David was presented with his Victoria Cross Medal by Queen Victoria at a ceremony at Windsor Castle.

At some time, probably in 1861, David was married to Sarah (née Bellews) and the couple would go on to have six children, four sons and two daughters.

On 29th October 1862, David was promoted to the rank of regimental Sergeant Major. In 1864, David and the 9th Lancers began a tour of Ireland where they were initially stationed at

---

732 Most sources quote surname as Rushe, however, his military discharge papers refer to David as Rush

Dublin and later at Dundalk. On 9th April 1867, after nearly 25 years of service, David was discharged from the army to pension, at his own request and was awarded the Good Conduct and Long Service medal.

On leaving the army, David moved with his family to Great Marlow in Buckinghamshire and in 1881 was residing on the High Street in Great Marlow and was employed as a brewery clerk.

David died at his home in Great Marlow on 6th November 1886 at the age of 59 and was buried in the Marlow Parish Churchyard in an unmarked grave.

Not long after his death, David's Victoria Cross Medal was sold by his wife Sarah, however in 1959 the medal was bought back by the Rush family and is now on loan to the 9th/12th Royal Lancers Museum in Derby.

Figure 228a. Grave of David Rush

William George Hawtrey Bankes
19th March 1858 (VC No. 251)

Gazetted: 24th December 1858 22212/5519

Rank and Unit: Cornet – 7th Hussars

Citation
Cornet William George Hawtrey Bankes, 7th Hussars, upon whom the Commander-in-Chief in India has reported that the Decoration of the Victoria Cross has been provisionally conferred, for conspicuous gallantry, in thrice charging a body of infuriated fanatics, who had rushed on the guns employed in shelling a small mud fort in the vicinity of Moosa-Bagh, Lucknow, on the 19th of March, 1858,—of the wounds received on which occasion he subsequently died,-and-would have been recommended to Her Majesty for confirmation in that distinction, had he survived.

Biography
William was born on 11th September 1836 in Kingston Lacy, Dorset the 5th child born to father George a Member of Parliament and mother Georgina Charlotte (née Nugent).

William's older siblings were Georgina Charlotte Francis born in 1825, Edmund George born on 24th April 1826, Henry Hyde born on 11th April 1828 and Edward Dee born on 12th January 1831. William also had three younger sisters, Adelaide born in 1838 and twins Augusta Anne and Octavia Elizabeth born in 1840.

After attending the preparatory school at Temple Grove, William attended Westminster School. Instead of going on to University he chose to pursue a career in the army and after purchasing a commission as Cornet on 3rd March 1857 joined his regiment the 7th Hussars at Aldershot.

In August 1857, the regiment was ordered to India to help quell the mutiny and on 27th August set sail on board the clipper *Lightning* and arrived at Calcutta 88 days later on 25th November.

After disembarking on 1st December, William and the 7th Hussars moved into barracks at Fort William and then were moved by rail to Rannegaige and then marched to Allahabad which they reached on 13th December. At Allahabad, the regiment took possession of their horses which had been secured by an advanced party led by the Commanding Officer Colonel Hagart and his Veterinary Surgeon Barker. After breaking in the horses, which took about two weeks, the regiment rode to Cawnpore.

Elements of the regiment were involved in escort duties on the road between Cawnpore and Lucknow, the Battle of

Figure 229. William George Hawtrey Bankes

Meeangunge and repulsing the mutineers attack on the Alum Bagh, however, it is not known if William was involved in any of these engagements.

From early March 1858, William and the regiment were involved, as part of the force of Sir Colin Campbell, in the siege and assaults which resulted in the recapture of Lucknow on 21st March 1858. It was on the 19th March 1858, during an attack on the Moosa Bagh that William performed the deeds for which he would later be awarded the Victoria Cross. During this action William was very seriously wounded with 11 sword wounds, and was taken to the field hospital at Trucknelo near Lucknow.

At the field hospital, William received the best treatment possible and received care from the Surgeon General himself; however, this required his right arm and right leg to be amputated. Sir Colin Campbell, Colonel Hagart and the Surgeon General each wrote letters to William's parents at Kingston Lacy informing them of his condition and expected recovery. An account of his condition at the field hospital reads as follows "... *one leg is lopped off above the knee; the other is nearly severed; one arm is cleft to the bone; the other has gone entirely, and about the body are many slashes. When Dr. Russell*[733] *went to see him afterwards, the brave youngster was quite cheerful and is reputed to have said 'they tell me, if I get over this I can go yachting …'*".

Unfortunately on April the 6th 1858, William at the age of 21, died from an infection to his wounds, 18 days after his brave

deeds at the Moosa Bagh. It is presumed that he was buried near to the hospital, however, no records of the location of his grave exist.

On 5th May 1858, Queen Victoria wrote of William's plight in a letter to the Princess Royal "*... There is a poor young man – of the name Bankes – who has been cut almost to pieces – he fell and was surrounded by a set of fanatics who cut at him, his thigh was nearly severed from his body – and so was his arm! Besides six other desperate wounds! He has had his right leg and his right arm amputated – and yet they hope he will live. This is, they say, the pattern of patience and fortitude*".

It is unclear how William was awarded his Victoria Cross at this time as posthumous awards were not covered by the Originating Royal Warrant and the mention of his award in the London Gazette on 24th December 1858 was a memorandum "... had he survived." entry not the fully approved by Queen Victoria entry. On 15th January 1907, King Edward VII issued a Royal Warrant that posthumously awarded the Victoria Cross to those persons who had been subject of such memorandum entries. Recognition of a posthumous award of the Victoria Cross was not made official until the Royal Warrant was completely rewritten by George V and reissued in June 1920. A new clause 4, stated that the award could be made posthumously.

However, despite all of the above, it does appear that William's relatives received his Victoria Cross soon after his gazetting; some sources state that it was sent to his mother by registered post on 25th December 1858 other sources state that it was personally presented to his mother by Queen Victoria at the family home in Kingston Lacy in Dorset. It is quite likely that the award of the medal was as a direct result of the intervention of Queen Victoria.

Figure 229a. Grave of William George Hawtrey Bannkes

---

733   It is possible that the Dr Russell was in fact William Howard Russell *The Times* correspondent.

William's Victoria Cross Medal is on public display at the Queen's Own Hussars Museum in Warwick.

For his service during the Mutiny William was also awarded the Indian Mutiny Medal with clasp for Lucknow.

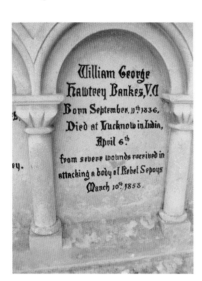

Figure 229b. Grave of William George Hawtrey Bannkes

Robert Newell
19th March 1858 (VC No. 252)

Gazetted: 24th December 1858 22212/5512

Rank and Unit: Private – 9th Lancers

Citation

For conspicuous gallantry at Lucknow, on the 19th of March, 1858, in going to the assistance of a comrade whose horse had fallen on bad ground, and bringing him away, under a heavy fire of musketry from a large body of the enemy. **(Despatch from Major-General Sir James Hope Grant, K.C.B., dated 8th April, 1858.)**

Biography

Robert was born some time during 1835 at Seaham in county Durham, unfortunately because of his death in service little information is available regarding his life or army career as no discharge papers or pension records exist.

Assuming that Robert enlisted in the army at or around his 18th birthday, say in 1853, then his time in the army would have been as follows.

After enlisting as a Private in the 9th Lancers, Robert would have been sent to join his regiment in India. At the outbreak of the mutiny, Robert and the 9th Lancers were stationed at Umballa and were assigned to the Delhi Field Force commanded by Major General George Anson, who was replaced by Major General Sir Henry Barnard when Anson died from cholera on 27th May. The force set out from Umballa on 17th May and after joining forces with the Meerut Brigade, commanded by Brigadier Archdale Wilson fought the Battle of Badli-ki-Serai on 8th June and established positions on the Delhi Ridge.

Robert was part of the besieging force and was involved in the final capture of Delhi on 21st September 1857.

Following the recapture of the city, Robert and the 9th Lancers were assigned to a Flying Column commanded by Colonel Edward Greathed and on 24th September moved out to patrol the Gangetic Goab, the area of land between the Ganges and Yamuna rivers. On the 28th September, Robert and the 9th Lancers were involved in the Battle of Bulandshahr. Robert also took part in the Battle of Agra on 10th November 1857 and was part of the force which evacuated the Residency at Lucknow on 19th November.

It was on 19th March 1858, during the action that resulted in the recapture of Lucknow on 21st March 1858, that Robert performed the deeds for which he would later be awarded the Victoria Cross.

Unfortunately, only a few weeks later on 11th July 1858, Robert died from acute diarrhoea while the regiment were station at Umballa and was buried the next day at the Umballa Cemetery in an unmarked grave.

For his service during the mutiny, Robert was awarded the Indian Mutiny Medal with clasps for Delhi, Relief of Lucknow and Lucknow.

Due to his untimely death, Robert was never presented with his Victoria Cross Medal which is now on public display at the Imperial War Museum in London, part of the Lord Ashcroft Collection.

Apparently the medal was sent to India for presentation, however, on receipt was sent by post to his widow.

Aylmer Spicer Cameron
30th March 1858 (VC No. 253)

Gazetted: 11th November 1859 22324/4032

Rank and Unit: Lieutenant – 72nd Regiment of Foot, 1st Battalion

Citation

For conspicuous bravery on the 30th of March, 1858, at Kotah, in having headed a small party of men, and attacked a body of armed fanatic rebels, strongly posted in a loop-holed house, with one narrow entrance. Lieutenant Cameron stormed the house, and killed three rebels in single combat. He was severely wounded, having lost half of one hand by a stroke from a tulwar.

Biography

Aylmer was born on 12th August 1833 at Christchurch in Hampshire to father William Neville Gordon[734] and mother Caroline (née Edwards). Aylmer was the fifth of eleven children and had one older brother, William Gordon born on 16th October 1827 in Paris, France and three younger brothers; Orford Summerville born on 17th October 1836 in Christchurch, George Gervis born in 1840 also in Christchurch and Abney Hastings born in 1842 on the Isle of Wight.

Figure 231. Aylmer Spicer Cameron

734 William was a Lieutenant-Colonel in the Grenadier Guards who had lost his right arm during the Battle of Waterloo.

All five of the brothers would be commissioned as officers in the armed services; William received a GCB, became a General and commanded the Kings Own Royal Regiment; Orford was a Captain in the Royal Navy and took part in the capture of the Taku forts during the war with China; George was a page of honour to Queen Victoria and a Lieutenant in the Coldstream Guards and Abney was a Captain in the 19th Regiment of Foot and was killed in 1877 during the Ashanti Wars.

Aylmer also had three older sisters; Charlotte Maria born on 10th May 1829, in Christchurch; Louisa born on 22nd September 1830 at Camberwell and Caroline born on 19th February 1832 at St Marylebone. He also had three younger sisters; twins Ellen Maria and Emma Brownmille born on 6th March 1835 and Alice Amelia born on 16th July 1838.

After completing his education at the Royal Military College at Sandhurst, Aylmer continued the family tradition when at the age of 18 he purchase a commission as Ensign in the 72nd Regiment of Foot on 9th July 1852.[735]

Soon after enlisting, Aylmer would have joined his regiment which was on service in Halifax Nova Scotia where he remained until late 1854, at which time the regiment set sail for Ireland where they arrived on 12th October 1854. During his time in Canada, Aylmer advanced his position in the regiment when he purchased the commission of Lieutenant on 1st September 1854.[736]

After a short stay in Ireland, the regiment set sail on 1st December for Malta where they arrived on 5th January 1855. Aylmer's time in Malta was also short lived as on 22nd May 1855, they set sail for the Crimea where they arrived on 13th June 1855 and took up positions in the trenches of Sevastopol as part of the Highland Brigade. Aylmer and the regiment were involved in the unsuccessful attacks on the Great Redan on 18th June and 8th September and from 9th October 1855 until 8th March 1856, he served as an assistant Engineer with the Highland Division. On 6th July 1856, Aylmer left the Crimea and after landing at Portsmouth on 31st July was immediately deployed to the Channel Islands. For his service during the war, Aylmer was awarded the Crimean War Medal with clasp for Sevastopol and the Turkish Crimea Medal.

In April 1857, Aylmer and the regiment left the Channel Islands and returned to England where they took up station at the Shorncliffe Camp in Kent.

On 4th September 1857, the regiment were despatched to India, as reinforcements to help quell the mutiny; they arrived at Bombay in January 1858 and served in the Central India Campaign.

It was on 30th March 1858, during the battle at Kotah, that Aylmer performed the deeds for which he was later awarded the Victoria Cross. During the action, Aylmer was seriously wounded losing half of his left hand from a sword strike; he also received two bayonet wounds. Aylmer also took part in the pursuit of Tantia Topi and the Gwalior contingent of mutineers and was involved in the Battle of Bunass on 14th August 1858 and the Battle of Pertabghur on 24th December 1858. For his service during the mutiny, Aylmer was awarded the Indian Mutiny Medal with clasp for Central India; he also received a mention in despatches.

On 13th December 1859, Aylmer was promoted to the rank of Captain[737] and joined the newly formed 2nd battalion of his new regiment the 25th Regiment of Foot at Preston, Lancashire.

Aylmer was presented with his Victoria Cross Medal by Queen Victoria at a ceremony held in Windsor Castle on 9th November 1860.

In May 1862, the regiment moved to Edinburgh until 28th July 1863 when they boarded *HMS Himalaya* and set sail for Ceylon where they remained until January 1868 at which time they were moved to India.

On 30th September 1865, Aylmer was married to Arabella Piercy (née Henderson) at St John's Episcopal Church in Edinburgh. The couple would go on to have eight children; Charles Lockart Aylmer born on 2nd August 1866 at Colerain in Northern Ireland, Amy Piercy born on 2nd May 1869 in York Town Surrey,

Figure 231a. Grave of Aylmer Spicer Cameron

735 *London Gazette* – 21337/1918
736 *London Gazette* – 21589/2701

737 *London Gazette* – 22336/4712

Rose Aylmer born on 17th October 1874 at the North West Provinces in India, Neville Gordon born on 29th September 1876 at Ripon in Yorkshire, Orford Somerville born on 23rd May 1878 at Armbrae in Halifax Nova Scotia, Cyril St Clair born on 22nd July 1879 at Armbrae in Halifax Nova Scotia, Esme Gordon born on 16th January 1881 at Armbrae in Halifax Nova Scotia and Cecil Aylmer born on 17th September 1883 at Croydon in Surrey. Four of Aylmer's five sons would follow their father and serve their country with military service: Charles served as a Lieutenant in the Royal Navy, Orford served in the Royal Field Artillery reached the rank of Brigadier and was awarded the DSO, Cyril served in the Royal Navy reached the rank of Vice-Admiral and was awarded a CBE and Cecil[738] also served in the Royal Field artillery, reached the rank of Major and was awarded the DSO and CBE.

In December 1870, Aylmer passed out from the Staff College and on 21st June 1871 purchased a commission of Major in the 25th Regiment of Foot.[739]

In 1872, Aylmer was appointed to the role of Garrison Instructor at Umballa in India and in 1874 was appointed to the role of Chief Instructor in Bengal, a position that he would hold until 14th July 1876 when he resigned[740] and moved from the supernumerary list back to a regimental role. On 1st October 1877, Aylmer received a brevet promotion to the rank of Lieutenant-Colonel.[741]

From 1878 until 1881, Aylmer performed the role of Assistant Adjutant-General in Canada.

Aylmer was promoted from half pay to the rank of Lieutenant-Colonel on 15th July 1881[742] and was transferred to the King's Own Borderers. On 1st October 1881, Aylmer was promoted to the rank of Colonel and was appointed to the command of the King's Own Borderers.[743]

Aylmer was appointed to the staff position of Assistant Quartermaster General of the Intelligence Branch on 27th June 1883[744] and was placed on half pay.[745]

On 1st January 1886, Aylmer was appointed as Commandant and Secretary of the Royal Military College at Sandhurst.[746]

Aylmer was appointed as an Ordinary Member 3rd Class (Companion) of the Military Division of the Most Honourable Order of the Bath on 29th May 1886.[747]

On 12th August 1888, after 36 years of service, Aylmer retired from the army and settled in Hampshire.

Aylmer died at his home 'Alvara' in Alverstoke, Gosport on 10th June 1909 at the age of 75 and was buried in St Mark's Churchyard at Christchurch in Hampshire.

Aylmer's Victoria Cross Medal is on public display at the Highlanders Regimental Museum at Fort George near Inverness.

738 Cecil had a very interesting life, not only did he serve in the Royal Artillery as a staff officer during World War I but under the codename Evelyn he served as a spymaster running operatives in German occupied France and Belgium. In 1911, Cecil and his wife Ruby were convicted of fraud at Edinburgh and sentenced to three years in prison for attempting to defraud Lloyds by falsely claiming for the theft of Ruby's pearl necklace. Cecil refused to give any evidence in his defence and served the full sentence, during her incarceration Ruby confessed that she was soley responsible for the crime and that her husband had remained silent in order to protect her. After his release from prison a petition was raised calling for his pardon, which amongst others was signed by 5 Dukes, 20 Privy Councillors and 126 Generals. Cecil received a full pardon and was restored to his rank in the army. After the Great War, Cecil who was a fluent Russian speaker was transferred to the War Office and served as Chief Intelligence Officer with the British Military Mission in Siberia during the Russian Revolution. In 1924, Cecil killed himself with a gun at Hillsborough Barracks in Sheffield.
739 *London Gazette* – 23748/2848
740 *London Gazette* – 24367/5200
741 *London Gazette* – 24508/5462
742 *London Gazette* – 25032/5305
743 *London Gazette* – 25026/5087

744 *London Gazette* – 25241/3039
745 *London Gazette* – 25245/3266
746 *London Gazette* – 25544/6300
747 *London Gazette* – 25592/2633

Hugh Stewart Cochrane
1st April 1858 (VC No. 254)

Gazetted: 24th December 1858 22212/5518

Rank and Unit: Lieutenant and Adjutant – 86th Regiment of Foot

Citation

For conspicuous gallantry near Jhansi, on the 1st of April, 1858, when No. 1 Company of the Regiment was ordered to take a gun, in dashing forward at a gallop, under a heavy musketry and artillery fire, driving the enemy from the gun, and keeping possession of it till the Company came up. Also for conspicuous gallantry in attacking the rear-guard of the enemy, when he had three horses shot under him in succession. **(Despatch from Major-General Sir Hugh Henry Rose, G.C.B., dated 23rd April, 1858.)**

Biography

Hugh was born on 4th August 1829 at Kilmallie, Fort William in Scotland, the 4th of 5 children born to father George and mother Susan (née McColl). Hugh had two older brothers; Thomas John born on 7th November 1823 and Donald born on 3rd November 1826. He also had an older sister, Hope Spread born on 18th March 1825 and a younger sister, Ann Stewart born on 25th May 1831.

Hugh began his career in the army when on 13th April 1849, at the age of 19, he purchased the commission of Ensign in the 86th Regiment of Foot[748] and soon afterwards would have joined his regiment in India where they had been serving since 1842.

On 15th October 1852, Hugh advanced his standing in the regiment when he purchased a commission of Lieutenant.[749] Hugh saw service at Deeja and Poona in Bombay and was serving at Kurrachee at the outbreak of the mutiny. On 18th April 1856, Hugh was appointed as adjutant to the regiment.[750] From December 1857, Hugh and the regiment took part in the Central India Campaign under the command of General Sir Hugh Rose.

On 17th March 1858, Hugh took part in the storming and capture of the hill fort at Chanderi and was slightly wounded during the action. Hugh was also present at the Battle of Betwa on 1st April 1858 and later on the same day in actions around the city of Jhansi, he performed the deeds for which he would later be awarded the Victoria Cross. Between 3rd and 6th April 1858, Hugh was involved in the siege, storming and capture of

Figure 232. Hugh Stewart Cochrane

the city and fortress at Jhansi, where under heavy fire from the fort he planted the British Flag on the palace. On 6th May 1858, Hugh took part in the Battle of Kunch and ten days later in the Battle of Kalpi. Hugh was also involved in the Battle of Morar on 1st June and the Battle of Gwalior on 19th June 1858. During the pursuit of Tantia Topi through the jungles of Central India, Hugh commanded Irregular Cavalry as part of the force of Sir Robert Napier. For his service during the mutiny, Hugh was awarded the Indian Mutiny Medal with clasp for Central India, he was also mentioned in despatches on two occasions.

On 24th August 1858, Hugh was promoted to the rank of Captain and transferred to the 16th Regiment of Foot.[751] He left India and joined his new regiment at Dublin in Ireland.

Hugh transferred to the 7th Regiment of Foot, by way of an exchange with Captain Twemlow, on 21st March 1859 and joined his new regiment at Jhelum in the Punjab, India[752] or at Peshawar where the regiment moved to in April 1859.

In early 1862, the regiment moved to Ferozepur and in November of the following year were moved to the Peshawar border in preparation for action against Afghan Pashtun and Yusufzai hill tribes who were making incursion across the borders. On 5th December 1863, the regiment crossed the border and moved to the Umbeyla Pass where they formed up as part of the 1st Brigade of the Eusufzai Field Force, commanded by Major-General Garvock and took part in the North West Frontier War that became known as the Umbeyla Expedition. Hugh took part in the Battle of Conical Hill on 14th December and after the burning of the rebel stronghold Malka by a force commanded by Brigadier-General Neville Bowles Chamberlain

---

748 *London Gazette* – 20967/1204
749 *London Gazette* – 21367/2684
750 *London Gazette* – 21873/1466

751 *London Gazette* – 22176/3904
752 *London Gazette* – 22270/2180

on 23rd December the war was all but over and the regiment returned to Ferozepur. For his service during the war, Hugh was awarded the Indian General Service Medal with clasp for Umbeyla.

On 19th January 1864, Hugh received a brevet promotion to the rank of Major.[753]

Hugh was married to Amy (née Bell) on 23rd August 1865 at St George's in Hanover Square, London.

On 1st November 1865, the regiment began the 662 mile journey from Ferozepur to their new base at Saugor which they reached on 11th January 1866.

On 2nd December 1869, the regiment left Saugor for Bombay and on 21st November 1870 began their long journey home when they boarded *HMS Euphrates* and set sail for Aden where they arrived on 30th November. From Aden the regiment proceeded by rail to Alexandria where they boarded *HMS Serapis* and set sail for England, arriving at Portsmouth on 28th December 1870.

Hugh advanced his position within the regiment when he purchased the commission of Major on 21st October 1871 and transferred to the 2nd Battalion.[754]

On 30th December 1871, Hugh and the battalion boarded *HMS Simoon* and set sail for Ireland where they were installed at the Curragh Camp until August 1872 when they moved to Cork.

Hugh received a brevet promotion to the rank of Lieutenant-Colonel on 7th January 1874.[755]

On 30th September 1874, the battalion boarded the Indian troopship *Seraphis* at Queenstown and set sail for India. After landing at Bombay on 1st November, they transferred by rail to Poona and occupied the Ghorpuri Lines district. Hugh was the Commandant at the camp at Khandala until 1875 when he was appointed as the Commanding Officer of the transit camp at Deolali[756] a position that he held until 1877 when he moved to Belgaum in Bombay.

On 16th February 1878, Hugh was promoted to the rank of Lieutenant-Colonel[757] and appointed to the command of the 43rd Regiment of Foot based at Fort St George in Madras.

Hugh received the brevet promotion to the rank of Colonel on 7th January 1879[758] and at some time during the year served with the regiment at Thayetmyo in Burma.

Some time prior to 1881 and presumably after the death of his first wife, Hugh was married to Mary Arden (née Maitland), probably in India where Mary was born and Hugh was serving.

On 27th July 1881, Hugh retired from the army after 32 years of service,[759] due to ill health and returned to England where he initially settled in Somerset.

On 18th April 1884, at the age of 55, Hugh died at his home on Villiers Road in Southsea and was buried in the Highland Road Cemetery at Eastney five days later.

Hugh's Victoria Cross Medal is believed to be held privately by his family.

Figure 232a. Grave of Hugh Stewart Cochrane

753 *London Gazette* – 22809/236
754 *London Gazette* – 23789/4386
755 *London Gazette* – 24062/492
756 The inhospitable conditions at the camp at Ddeolali and the fact that many men suffered psychological problems, gave rise to the infamous phrases *"gone doolally"* and *"doolally tap"* meaning to have lost ones mind. Tap is the Urdu word for malarial fever.
757 *London Gazette* – 24552/747
758 *London Gazette* – 24672/413

759 *London Gazette* – 24999/3688 – Hugh sold his commission and received the full value for the sale

James Leith
1st April 1858 (VC No. 255)

Figure 233. James Leith

Gazetted: 24th December 1858 22212/5517

Rank and Unit: Lieutenant – 14th Light Dragoons

Citation

For conspicuous bravery at Betwah, on the 1st of April, 1858, in having, charged alone, and rescued Captain Need, of the same Regiment, when surrounded by a large number of rebel Infantry. **(Despatch from Major-General Sir Hugh Henry Rose, G.C.B., dated 28th April, 1858.)**

Biography

James was born on 26th May 1826 at Glenkindie House, Glenkindie in Aberdeenshire, the 3rd son of father Sir Alexander a General in the army and mother Maria (née Thorp).

James had two older brothers; Alexander born 19th December 1817 and Robert William Disney born on 28th February 1819; an older sister, Ann Katherine born on 17th July 1821; a younger sister Mary Sarah born on 21st January 1829 and a younger brother Thomas born on 2nd September 1830.

Following his secondary education at the Blackheath Preparatory School, James enrolled at Trinity College, Cambridge on 7th July 1843 and graduated with a BA in 1849. While at Cambridge, James played cricket for the University, his first match was on 14th May 1846 and his last on 14th June 1849, and was awarded his 'Blue' some time in 1848. On 4th May 1849, having graduated from Cambridge, James was commissioned as a Cornet in the 14th Hussars.[760] James did not join his regiment at Lahore in India until November 1849, when he was part of a new draft of replacements needed to bring the regiment back up to strength following their recent participation in the 2nd Anglo-Sikh war. On 19th January 1851, James and the regiment moved from Lahore to Meerut, where they arrived on 6th March. James advanced his position within the regiment when on 27th May 1853 he purchased a commission as Lieutenant.[761]

On 30th December 1854, the regiment were placed under orders to prepare for deployment to Turkey and on 8th January 1855 the orders were confirmed to proceed to Bombay in order to embark for the Crimea. Just after beginning their journey to Bombay, the deployment to Crimea was countermanded and the regiment returned to Meerut. On 19th January, the day that they arrived back at Meerut, new orders were received to march to the military base at Kirkee, some 884 miles away where they arrived on 21st April 1855.

The regiment remained at Kirkee, just to the south of Bombay, until February 1857 when as part of the Persian Expeditionary Force they marched by squadron to Bombay and set sail for Bushire on the Persian Gulf where they landed during March 1857. Only a small part of the regiment, 'H' troop (89 men), was involved in the action, taking part in the capture of Mohammrah on 26th March. For his service during the Anglo Persian War, James was awarded the Indian General Service Medal with clasp for Persia. At the end of the war, following the treaty of Paris which was signed on 4th March, the regiment returned to Kirkee where they arrived during May 1857.

Following the outbreak of mutiny, James and the regiment were assigned to a force commanded by Major-General Alexander Woodburn, which was charged with the task of securing the road and communications between Bombay and Agra. On 8th June 1857, the force left Kirkee on the road towards Mhow and on 23rd June was involved in suppressing the mutiny of the garrison at Aurangabad. News of mutinies at Mhow and Indore reached the force at Aurangabad on 9th July and three days later marched off for Central India, now under the command of Major F. W. Follett, and reached Mhow on 1st August 1857. With travel being impossible due to the monsoon rains, it was not until 20th October that the Malwa Field Force, now under the command of Brigadier-General Charles Sheppard Stuart, left Mhow on operations to clear up pockets of mutineers in the surrounding area.

On 22nd October 1857, James was involved in the siege of the fort and town at Dhar which was finally captured on 31st October.

---

760 *London Gazette* – 20975/1474
761 *London Gazette* – 21443/1481

On hearing of the mutineer's siege of Neemuch, the Malwa Field Force left Dhar on the way to the relief of the city and on 21st November were involved in the Battle of Mundesore during which James was slightly wounded.[762] James was involved in the Battle of Goraria on 23rd November, when the mutineers from Mundesore tried to attack the rear of the force as it approached Neemuch and by 25th November the Malwa Field Force managed to relieve the garrison at Neemuch.

By 14th December the regiment was established in Indore and following the appointment of Major-General Sir Hugh Rose to the command of the Central India Field Force on 17th December 1857, were assigned to the 2nd Brigade of the force.

James and 'H' troop of the regiment formed part of the escort to the 2nd Brigade Siege Train on their journey from Mhow to Indore, where they arrived on 15th January 1858. Following the arrival of the Siege Train, the 2nd Brigade set off the next day with the objective of relieving Saugor. On 24th January, the force laid siege to the fort and town at Rathghur and on 28th January occupied the fort after the mutineers had abandoned their position. With the fall of Rathghur, the way was now clear to go to the relief of Saugor which had been besieged for 8 months. The relief was accomplished on 3rd February 1858.

On 9th February, Sir Hugh Rose led the 2nd Brigade to Garrakota where the fort was captured on the 13th and the escaping mutineers were pursued across the River Bias and engaged at the village of the same name.

The next objective of the force was the capture of Jhansi and they set out on this mission on 26th February, capturing the fort at Barodia on the next day. After forcing the pass at Muddenpore on 4th March, the brigade advanced on Jhansi and on 22nd March began the siege of the town. At this point the force was joined by the 1st Brigade under the command of Brigadier Stuart. On 1st April 1858 a substantial force, under the command of Tantia Topi, attacked the besiegers but were routed at the Battle of Betwa. It was during this battle that James performed the deeds for which he would later be awarded the Victoria Cross. After the fall of Jhansi on 5th April, James was part of the force which pursued the rebels as they fled towards Kalpi which was a major rebel stronghold and arsenal; this was captured on 23rd May. The surviving mutineers from Kalpi, fled to their last major stronghold at Gwalior which was captured on 20th June and effectively ended the campaign in central India. Soon after the action at Gwalior, the Central India Field Force was dismantled and the various regiments were dispersed to stations across India. For his service during the mutiny, James was awarded the Indian Mutiny Medal with clasp for Central India he was also mentioned in despatches on two occasions.

On 20th July 1858, James received a brevet promotion to the rank of Major,[763] however this was later changed to be effective from 28th July 1858.[764] James was promoted to the rank of Captain on 27th July 1858 and transferred to the 6th Dragoons.[765] On 18th January 1859, James transferred to the 2nd Dragoons by way of exchange with Captain Swindley[766] and would have joined his new regiment in Dublin soon afterwards.

On 8th June 1859, James was presented with his Victoria Cross Medal by Queen Victoria at an investiture held at Buckingham Palace.

It was while serving in Ireland that James was retired to half pay on 31st December 1861,[767] probably due to ill health, and returned to live in England. On the recommendation of Lord Foley, James was appointed to the Honourable Corps of Gentlemen of Arms to Queen Victoria on 5th May 1863.[768]

James was married to Isabella (née Shaw) on 8th September 1863 at St John's Church in Paddington London, the couple would go on to have three daughters; Ella born in 1865 at Bournemouth, May born on 21st Jul 1866 at Malvern Wells and Elsie born on 22nd February 1869 at Hyde Park.

On 13th May 1869, at the age of 42, James died at his home 35 Gloucester Place, Hyde Park from liver disease and was buried in the Towie Churchyard near Glenkindie, Aberdeenshire in Scotland.

Figure 233a.
Grave of James Leith

762 *London Gazette* – 22112/1390

763 *London Gazette* – 22180/4060
764 *London Gazette* – 22345/111
765 *London Gazette* – 22166/3480
766 *London Gazette* – 22220/173
767 *London Gazette* – 22585/5631
768 *London Gazette* – 22733/2461

James's Victoria Cross medal is on public display at the 14th/20th Hussars Museum, Preston in Lancashire.

Figure 233b. Grave of James Leith

Michael Sleavon (Slevin)[769]
3rd April 1858 (VC No. 256)

Gazetted: 11th November 1859 22324/4032

Rank and Unit: Corporal No. 2416 – Royal Engineers, 21st Field Company

Citation

For determined bravery at the attack of the Fort of Jhansi, on the 3rd of April, 1858, in maintaining his position at the head of a sap, and continuing the work under a heavy fire, with a cool and steady determination worthy of the highest praise.

Biography

Michael was born some time during 1826 at Magherculmoney, Co Fermanagh in Ireland.

On 7th April 1847, Michael left his job as a stone mason (working for a Mr William Archdale) and enlisted in the army at Lowtherstown, where he was assigned as a Gunner and Driver in the Royal Artillery. Once his building skills were recognised by the army, Michael was transferred to the Royal Sappers and Miners on 1st September 1849 and given the rank of Private.

In 1851, Michael was posted on his first tour of overseas duty to Bermuda and on 1st April 1855 was promoted to the rank of 2nd Corporal and exactly one year later on 1st April 1856 was promoted to Corporal. After just over four years in Bermuda, Michael returned to England until 1857 when as a result of the mutiny he was posted to India.

It was on 3rd April 1858, during preparations for the assault on the fort at Jhansi, that Michael performed the deeds for which he would later be awarded the Victoria Cross. On 8th May 1858, Michael was promoted to the rank of Sergeant. For his service during the mutiny, Michael was awarded the Indian Mutiny Medal with clasp for Central India.

Michael was presented with his Victoria Cross Medal some time during 1860 while still serving in India.

On his return from India, where he served for 19 months, Michael spent some time in England before serving his last overseas deployment at Fort George in Mauritius, which lasted for nearly six years. During this posting, Michael was tried by Regimental Court Martial and on 16th April 1862 was reduced in rank to Sapper. On 25th April 1871, after serving for just over 24 years, Michael was discharged from the army to pension, at

---

769 Various spellings of his surname exist in the official records – Slevin, Sleavin, Sleevin and Sleavon

Figure 234. Michael Sleavon

Joseph Charles Brennan
3rd April 1858 (VC No. 257)

Gazetted: 11th November 1859 22324/4032

Rank and Unit: Bombardier – Royal Regiment of Artillery

Citation

For marked gallantry at the assault of Jhansi, on the 3rd of April, 1858, in bringing up two guns of the Hyderabad Contingent, manned by Natives, lying each under a heavy fire from the walls, and directing them so accurately as to compel the Enemy to abandon his battery.

Biography

Joseph was born during August 1836 at St Probus, Truro in Cornwall.

his own request. After leaving the army, Michael returned to Ireland and settled down at a farm on the Archdale property near Dromard in Co Fermanagh.

Michael married Margaret (née McGoldrick) and the couple had two children; Edward and Bridget.

On 15th August 1902, at the age of 76, Michael died from heart disease at his home in Dromard and was buried in St Mary's Churchyard, Bannagh, near Ederney in Co Fermanagh.

Michael's Victoria Cross Medal was sold on 23rd January 1903, soon after his death, and is believed to be held privately.

On 27th December 1855, at the age of 19, Joseph left his job as a clerk and enlisted in the Royal Regiment of Artillery, at Newport in Monmouthshire, Wales. After the outbreak of mutiny, Joseph was despatched to India and landed at Bombay on 4th August 1857.

On 6th January 1858, Joseph was part of the Central India Field Force, commanded by Major-General Sir Hugh Rose, which left Mhow to go to the relief of Saugor. On 24th January, Joseph was part of the force which lay siege to the fort and town at Rathghur and on 28th January occupied the fort after the mutineers had abandoned their position. With the fall of Rathghur, the way was now clear to go to the relief of Saugor which had been besieged for 8 months. The relief was accomplished on 3rd February 1858.

The next objective of the force was the capture of Jhansi and they set out on this mission on 26th February, capturing the fort

Figure 234a. Grave of Michael Sleavon

Figure 235. Joseph Charles Brennan

at Barodia on the next day. After forcing the pass at Muddenpore on 4th March, the brigade advanced on Jhansi and on 22nd March began the siege of the town. At this point the force was joined by the 1st Brigade under the command of Brigadier Stuart. On 1st April 1858 a substantial force of mutineer's, under the command of Tantia Topi, attacked the besiegers but were routed at the Battle of Betwa. It was on 3rd April 1858, during the assault on Jhansi, that Joseph performed the deeds for which he would later be awarded the Victoria Cross; the city was captured two days later. For his bravery at Jhansi, Joseph was promoted to the rank of Bombardier.

After the fall of Jhansi on 5th April, Joseph was part of the force which pursued the rebels as they fled towards Kalpi which was a major rebel stronghold and arsenal and was involved in the Battle of Kunch on 7th May and the Battle of Kalpi on 23rd May 1858. At some time in 1858, Joseph was promoted to the rank of Sergeant. The surviving mutineers from Kalpi, fled to their last major stronghold at Gwalior which was captured on 20th June and effectively ended the campaign in central India. Soon after the action at Gwalior, the Central India Field Force was dismantled and the various regiments were dispersed to stations across India. For his service during the mutiny, Joseph was awarded the Indian Mutiny Medal with clasp for Central India.

Joseph was presented with his Victoria Cross Medal on 20th April 1860, at a ceremony held in Gwalior, India.

In October 1863, Joseph was tried by regimental court martial at Delhi for being absent at a commanding officer's parade some days earlier. Having been found guilty, Joseph who by now had the rank of Quartermaster Sergeant was reduced in rank to Gunner and Driver.

From early 1864 until November 1865, Joseph took part in the Bhutan (Duar) war in Bengal and for his service was awarded the India General Service Medal with clasp for Bhootan.

At some stage Joseph was married, however the details are unknown and before he returned to England in 1872 he had regained the rank of Sergeant.

On 24th September 1872, soon after his return to England from India, Joseph died from pneumonia at Elham, near Folkestone and was buried in the Shornecliffe Military Cemetery two days later.

Joseph's Victoria Cross Medal was sold at auction in 1975 and is believed to be held in a private collection.

Figure 235a.
Grave of Joseph
Charles Brennan

James Byrne
3rd April 1858 (VC No. 258)

Gazetted: 11th November 1859 22324/4032

Rank and Unit: Private – 86th Regiment of Foot

Citation

For gallant conduct on the 3rd of April, 1858, at the attack of the Fort of Jhansi, in carrying Lieutenant Sewell, who was lying badly wounded, to a place of safety, under a very heavy fire, assisted by Captain Jerome, in the performance of which act he was wounded by a sword cut.

Biography

James was born some time during 1822 at Newtown, Mount Kennedy in Co Wicklow, Ireland.

Unfortunately very little is known of the life and army career of James.

It is possible that James enlisted in the army during 1840, at some time on or around his 18th birthday and joined the 86th regiment of foot who were stationed in Ireland at this time. In 1842, James and his regiment were deployed to overseas service in India and were stationed at Bombay.

At the outbreak of the mutiny James and the regiment were still serving in India and were assigned to the Central India Field

Figure 236. James Byrne

Force under the command of Major-General Sir Hugh Rose. The regiment served throughout the campaigns in Rajputana and Central India and it was on 3rd April 1858 during the assault on the fort at Jhansi that James performed the deeds for which he would later be awarded the Victoria Cross. During this action, James was wounded by a sword cut.

James returned to England in August 1859, after 17 years of service in India and on 4th January 1860 he was presented with his Victoria Cross Medal by Queen Victoria at an investiture held at Windsor Castle. At some stage James was promoted to the rank of Sergeant.

It is probable that James was discharged to pension some time in 1860, after having completed 20 years of service, however, if this was not the case then he could have served in the garrison at Gibraltar from 1864 to 1867 and Mauritius from 1867 until 1870. It is unlikely that James would have served with the regiment in South Africa from 1870.

On 6th December 1872, James died at Dublin, aged 50 and was buried in the same grave as his mother in Glasnevin Cemetery in Dublin.

James's Victoria Cross Medal was sold at Sotheby's on 17th June 1903 for £35 but is now on public display at the Royal Ulster Rifles Museum in Belfast, Northern Ireland.

Figure 236a. Grave of James Byrne

James Pearson
3rd April 1858 (VC No. 259)

Gazetted: 28th April 1860 22381/1642

Rank and Unit: Private No. 1882 – 86th Regiment of Foot

Citation

For having gallantly attacked a number of armed rebels, on the occasion of the storming of Jhansi, on the 3rd April, 1858, one of whom he killed, and bayonetted two others.' He was himself wounded in the attack.

Also, for having brought in, at Kalpi, under a heavy fire, Private Michael Burns, who afterwards died of his wounds.

Biography

James was born on 2nd October 1822 at Rathdowney, in Queens County, Ireland.

On 13th February 1840, at the age of 18, James left his job as a labourer and enlisted in the army at Nenagh in Tipperary where he joined the 36th Regiment of Foot as a Private. From 22nd April 1840 until 30th April 1840, James was absent without leave; he was tried and convicted of desertion by a regimental court martial and sentenced to 20 days solitary confinement which he served from 30th April to 28th May 1840. James deserted again and was absent from 24th May 1841 until 22nd June 1841, he was again convicted by a regimental court martial and sentenced to four months imprisonment, which he served from 22nd June 1841 until 25th October 1841.

On 1st April 1842, while still serving in Ireland, James was transferred to the 86th Regiment of Foot and soon afterwards was deployed on overseas service to India, arriving at Bombay in August 1842. James was again tried by regimental court martial and from 26th May 1857 until 25th July 1857 he served his third period of imprisonment.

At the outbreak of the mutiny James and the regiment were still serving in India and were assigned to the Central India Field Force under the command of Major-General Sir Hugh Rose. The regiment served throughout the campaigns in Rajputana and Central India and it was on 3rd April 1858 during the assault on the fort at Jhansi that James performed the deeds for which he would later be awarded the Victoria Cross. During this action, James received bayonet wounds to his left wrist and left side. For his service during the mutiny, James was awarded the Indian Mutiny Medal with clasp for Central India. On 1st April 1859, James volunteered to transfer to the 56th Regiment of Foot, perhaps because the 86th were due to return to England and he wished to remain in India. James again volunteered to transfer regiments and on 1st July 1860 moved to the 83rd Regiment of Foot which was stationed at Belgaum. It was on 6th November 1860, at Belgaum, that James was discharged from the army, after 20 years of service, on medical grounds due to disability resulting from over 18 years of service in India. On leaving the army, James took up residence at Poona and pursued a career in the prison service, eventually serving as a prison governor at Madras.

James was presented with his Victoria Cross Medal by Lieutenant-General Sir William Mansfield, General Officer Commanding, Bengal in January 1861.

On 23rd October 1861, James was married to Sophia Banner (née Payne) a widow at Poonamallee in Madras.

James died on 23rd January 1900, aged 77, at Madras the site of his burial is not recorded, perhaps he was buried in the same cemetery as his wife, St Thomas's Cemetery, Pursewal Kum in Madras.

The location of James's Victoria Cross Medal is unknown.

Frederick Whirlpool (Conker, James)
3rd April 1858 (VC No. 260)

Gazetted: 21st October 1859 22318/3793

Rank and Unit: Private – 3rd Bombay European Regiment

Citation

For gallantly volunteering on the 3rd of April, 1858, in the attack of Jhansi, to return and carry away several killed and wounded, which he did twice under a very heavy fire from the wall; also, for devoted bravery at the Assault of Lohari oh the 2nd of May, 1858, in rushing to the rescue of Lieutenant Doune, of the Regiment, who was dangerously wounded. In this service, Private Whirlpool received seventeen desperate wounds, one of which nearly severed his head from his body. The gallant example shewn by this man is considered to have greatly contributed to the success of the day.

Biography

Frederick was born as Frederick Humphrey Conker some time in 1829 at Liverpool to father Humphrey James and mother Lavina (née Murphy) and was the 3rd of ten children, his siblings being William, Thomas, Susannah, Elizabeth, Benjamin, Dinah, Deborah, Josia and Samuel.

While still a child, the family moved back to Ireland where his father was the postmaster at Dundalk in Co. Louth. Frederick was an angry young man and after an argument with his father he left home, returned to Liverpool and worked as a clerk.

In 1854, Frederick joined the Honourable East India Company under the assumed name of Whirlpool, apparently his father had said that he had a temper like a whirlpool. Frederick left England on 26th November 1855 and after arriving at Bombay on 26th March 1856 joined his regiment the 3rd Bombay European Regiment. For a time, Frederick worked as an assistant army teacher, however, following the outbreak of mutiny was assigned to the Central India Field Force. It was during the assault on Fort Jhansi on 3rd April 1858, that Frederick performed the first of the deeds for which he would later be awarded the Victoria Cross. A month later on 2nd May 1858, Frederick performed the 2nd deed which appears on his Victoria Cross citation, during the assault on Lohari, during which he was severely wounded receiving 17 wounds, one of which nearly resulted in decapitation. After spending 5 months in hospital, Frederick miraculously recovered from his wound, however, being considered unfit for further military service he was discharged to pension.

In December 1859, Frederick emigrated to Australia and settled in the state of Victoria where he changed his name by deed poll to Frederick Humphrey James. Initially Frederick was employed as a teacher and applied unsuccessfully to join the police force. He later joined the Hawthorne and Kew Volunteer Rifles and it was here that a drill instructor discovered his true identity which led to his being presented with his Victoria Cross Medal.

On 20th June 1861, at a Volunteer Review at Melbourne to celebrate Queen Victoria's birthday, Frederick was presented with his Victoria Cross Medal by Lady Berkly, the wife of Sir Henry Barkly the governor of Victoria. This was the first public presentation of a Victoria Cross on Australian soil.

Soon after receiving his Victoria Cross Medal, Frederick was offered a job in the police force however this was declined and for a time he moved to Tasmania. Frederick moved to New South Wales in 1865 and after attending a teacher training course began work at a school near Wisemans ferry. Despite being a good teacher, Frederick still plagued by his injuries became a heavy drinker and after 3 years was dismissed by the school. After losing his job, Frederick moved to McGrath's Hill near Windsor in New South Wales, where he lived the life of a hermit.

After a while, Frederick was befriended by the local grocer John Dick Smith and confided his true identity, John supported his friend with free groceries which were delivered to his shanty on a weekly basis.

Frederick died at his home in McGrath's Hill on 24th June 1899, for heart disease at the age of 70 and Mr Smith arranged for his burial at the Presbyterian Cemetery in McGrath's Hill two days later.

Frederick's Victoria Cross Medal is on public display at the Australian War Memorial, Hall of Valour in Canberra.

Figure 238a. Memorial to Frederick Whirlpool in Liverpool

Henry Edward Jerome
3rd April 1858 (VC No. 261)

Gazetted: 11th November 1859 22324/4032

Rank and Unit: Captain – 86th Regiment of Foot

Citation

For conspicuous gallantry at Jhansi, on the 3rd of April, 1858, in having, with the assistance of Private Byrne, removed, under a very heavy fire Lieutenant Sewell, of the 86th Regiment, who was severely wounded, at a very exposed point of the attack upon the Fort; also, for gallant conduct at the capture of the Fort of Chandairee, the storming of Jhansi, and in action with a superior Rebel Force on the Jumna, on the 28th of May, 1858, when he was severely wounded.

Figure 239. Henry Edward Jerome

Biography

Henry was born on 2nd February 1830 at Antigua in the West Indies to father Joseph and mother whose maiden name was Walker.

After graduating from the military college at Sandhurst, Henry was commissioned as an Ensign in the 86th Regiment of Foot on 21st January 1848[770] and would have joined his regiment in India soon afterwards.

On 30th April 1852, Henry was promoted to the rank of Lieutenant.[771]

At the outbreak of the mutiny Henry and the regiment were still serving in India and were assigned to the Central India Field Force under the command of Major-General Sir Hugh Rose. Henry was involved in the Battle of Chanderi on 16th March 1858, which resulted in the capture of the fort. It was on 3rd April 1858, during the assault on Jhansi, which resulted in the capture of the fort 2 days later, that Henry performed the first of the deeds for which he would later be awarded the Victoria Cross. After the taking of Jhansi, Henry was involved in chasing down the mutineers who were escaping towards their major arsenal at Kalpi and on 7th May 1858 took part in the Battle of Kunch. Henry was involved in the siege and Battle of Kalpi which resulted in the capture of the fort on 23rd May 1858. It was on 28th May 1858, during the Battle of Jumna that Henry performed the second of the deeds for which he would later be awarded the Victoria Cross and was seriously wounded during the action. For his service during the mutiny, Henry was awarded the Indian Mutiny Medal with clasp for Central India.

Henry was promoted to the rank of Captain and transferred to 19th Regiment of Foot on 23rd July 1858[772] and joined his new regiment at Dacca. In October 1858, the regiment moved to Dinapore where they arrived on 24th November where they were stationed until February 1860 when they moved to Benares arriving on 12th March 1860. On 1st July 1859, Henry received a brevet promotion to the rank of Major.[773]

Henry was presented with his Victoria Cross Medal by Queen Victoria on 4th January 1860 at an investiture held at Windsor Castle.

In 1862, Henry and the regiment were moved to Jullundur.

Henry was married to Inez Temple Frances (née Cowper) on 18th April 1863 at St Thomas's, Portman Square in London; the couple would have one child, Lucien Joseph who was appointed as Consul-General to Ecuador in 1913.

On 1st November 1865, the regiment left Jullundur and moved to Peshawar where they arrived on 8th December and remained until February 1867 when they moved to Nawshera. After leaving Nawshera, the regiment arrived at Rawalpindi on 4th February 1868 where they remained until late September when they received orders to proceed to Oghee where the Hazara Field Force was being assembled. On their arrival at Oghee, the regiment were assigned to the 1st brigade, commanded by Brigadier-General Robert Bright, of the Hazara Field Force commanded by Brigadier-General Alfred Wilde. On 3rd October 1868, Henry and the regiment took part in the only significant battle against the Hassanzai tribesmen in the short Hazara or Black Mountain Campaign. Peace was declared on 9th October and the Field Force was disbanded on the 25th October 1868, following which, Henry and the regiment returned

770 *London Gazette* – 20817/198
771 *London Gazette* – 21314/1212

772 *London Gazette* – 22165/3412
773 *London Gazette* – 22281/2552

to Rawalpindi where they arrived on 4th November 1868. For his service during the Hazara Campaign, Henry was awarded the Indian General Service Medal with clasp for North West Frontier.

Henry received a brevet promotion to the rank of Lieutenant-Colonel on 15th September 1870.[774]

On 24th November 1871, Henry boarded *HMS Crocodile* at Bombay and began the return journey to England after having spent 23 years in India.

On 16th August 1873, Henry was promoted to the rank of Major and transferred to the 62nd Regiment of Foot.[775] Henry was placed on half pay on 15th July 1876[776] and took up a Staff appointment. On 15th May 1879, Henry was appointed as Fort Major at Guernsey and on 31st July 1879 received a brevet promotion to the rank of Colonel.[777] Having served 5 years as a substantive Major on the Staff, Henry was promoted to the rank of Lieutenant-Colonel on 15th May 1884.[778]

On 9th September 1885, after 37 years of service, Henry was retired to pension with the honorary rank of Major-General.[779]

On leaving the army, Henry moved to Bath and it was while living at 3 Sion Hill in Bath that he died from heart failure after a short illness on 25th February 1901, just 3 days short of his 71st birthday and was buried in the Lansdowne Cemetery in Bath.

Henry's Victoria Cross Medal is on public display as part of the Lord Ashcroft Collection at the Imperial War Museum in London.

Figure 239a. Grave of Henry Edward Jerome

Figure 239b. Grave of Henry Edward Jerome

774 *London Gazette* – 23667/4416
775 *London Gazette* – 24008/3825
776 *London Gazette* – 24345/4006
777 *London Gazette* – 24834/2557
778 *London Gazette* – 25370/2797
779 *London Gazette* – 25509/4227

William Napier
6th April 1858 (VC No. 262)

Gazetted: 24th December 1858 22212/5517

Rank and Unit: Sergeant – 13th Regiment of Foot

Citation

For conspicuous gallantry near Azamgarh, on the 6th of April, 1858, in having defended, and finally rescued, Private Benjamin Milnes, of the same Regiment, when severely wounded on the Baggage Guard. Serjeant Napier remained with him at the hazard of his life, when surrounded by Sepoys, bandaged his wound under fire, and then carried him in safety to the convoy. **(Despatch from Colonel Lord Mark Kerr, C.B., dated 2nd August, 1858.)**

Biography

William was born in 1828[780] at Bingley in Yorkshire to father Samuel and mother Mary (née Hartley).

Educated at a private school, William was brought up in a military family; his uncle, also called William served in the Grenadier Guards and fought at the Battle of Waterloo, he gave his Waterloo Medal to William. It was therefore no surprise that William left his job as a labourer, enlisted in the army at Leeds on 11th December 1846 and joined the 13th Regiment of Foot as a Private.

Soon after enlisting, William set sail on 12th January 1847 from Portsmouth bound for a deployment to Ireland where he was stationed at Dublin, Birr, Newry and Belfast until 26th April 1850 when the regiment set sail from Belfast for Fort George near Inverness where they arrived three days later. William was promoted to the rank of Corporal on 13th November 1850 and during the month the regiment was deployed to Stirling with detachments established at Dundee and Perth. In March 1851, the regiment received orders to make ready for deployment overseas and were transported by rail to Winchester.

On 24th May, William and the regiment boarded the freight ship *Hereford* and set sail for Gibraltar where after their arrival on the 5th June 1851 they were quartered in the Casemate Barracks. William was promoted to the rank of Sergeant on 1st March 1854.

In the summer of 1855, the regiment were told to make ready for deployment to the Crimea and on 7th July, under the

Figure 240. William Napier

command of Lord Mark Kerr they boarded the *SS Robert Lowe* and set sail for the Russian War, landing at Balaklava on 29th June 1855. As part of the 4th Division the regiment were quartered near the village of Kadikoi until August when as part of the 2nd Brigade of the 1st Division they were moved to the lines around Sevastopol. On 8th August 1855, the regiment took part in the second attack on the Great Redan, following which the Russians withdrew from the south of the city and hostilities were virtually at an end. After spending the winter in huts around Sevastopol, on 24th May 1856 the regiment boarded the steam transport *Khersonese* at Balaklava and set sail for Gibraltar, where they landed on 7th June. For his service during the war, William was awarded the Crimea Medal with clasp for Sevastopol and the Turkish Crimea Medal. William and the regiment were destined to spend only a short time in Gibraltar; soon after their return following reports that another Kaffir war was imminent they boarded *SS Imperatriz* and set sail for the Cape Colony, arriving at Port Elizabeth on 24th September 1856. After spending almost a year as the garrison at Graham's Town, the regiment received an urgent request for reinforcements to be sent to India to help quell the mutiny. On 22nd August 1857, William and the regiment boarded the *SS Madras* at Port Elizabeth and set sail for Calcutta where they arrived on 3rd October. The regiment left Calcutta on 15th October and proceeded by rail to Raneegunge and then marched via Allahabad and Futtehpore to Cawnpore where from 22nd December 1857 they were to form the garrison.

---

780 According to William's army discharge papers he was underage (i.e. not yet 18) until 10th February 1847 which would give a date of birth of 10th February 1829.

On receiving news that a strong rebel force, led by Koer Sing was besieging Azamgarh and with the danger that he could capture the un-garrisoned city of Benares, William and the regiment were despatched as part of a relief force on 27th March 1858. It was on 6th April 1858, during the battle to relieve Azamgarh, that William performed the deeds for which he would later be awarded the Victoria Cross. Lord Mark Kerr is said to have offered William a commission as a reward for his action, this was declined however on 20th November 1858 he was promoted to the rank of Colour-Sergeant.

As part of the Sarun Field Force, William and the regiment were involved in several battles and actions at; Belwah on 17th and 25th April, Captaingunge on 27th April and Nuggur on 29th April 1858. After resting at Bustee on 8th May they fought the Battle of Bustee on 9th June followed by actions at; Hurryah on 18th June, Debreheah on 29th August, Jugdeespore and Bhanpore on 26th October, Domereagunge on 26th November and Toolsepore on 23rd December 1858. For his service during the mutiny, William was awarded the Indian Mutiny Medal, however, as the regiment had not been involved in the major actions it was awarded with no clasp. On 13th February 1859, the Sarun Field Force was disbanded and William and the regiment returned to Goruckpore.

William was promoted to the rank of Sergeant-Major on 11th September 1860. In February 1861, the regiment moved to Gonda in the province of Oude and on 16th November moved to Morar, Gwalior where they arrived on 23rd December. Sometime in 1862, William was presented with his Victoria Cross Medal, probably while stationed at Morar. It was on 21st October 1862, while stationed at Morar, that William made his application to retire from the army. After nearly 16 years of service William retired from the army on 8th December 1862 at Fort William in Calcutta.

William had left the army with the intention of making a new life for himself in Australia and on 21st December he boarded SS *Madras* at Calcutta and set sail for Melbourne where he arrived sometime in January 1863.

Soon after his arrival, William found work as a clerk and on 16th September 1863 was married to Elizabeth (née Slater), the couple would have two children; Alfred Stephen Slater and Mary Elizabeth, both of whom died in infancy. Elizabeth died on 25th April 1867 at the age of 37.

On 5th November 1869, William married Ruth Ann Hirst (née Booth) a widow, at Bendigo in the state of Victoria and adopted Ruth's daughter Eliza.

After spending time working as a clerk and for a short time as a miner, William established a business manufacturing cordials at Rochester and became a pillar of the community, serving as treasurer to the Rochester branch of the Freemasons.

William moved to Melbourne after his home was destroyed by fire, however after a period of sickness he returned to Rochester in 1907.

On 2nd June 1908, William died at his home in Rochester and was buried in the General Cemetery at Bendigo.

William's Victoria Cross Medal is on public display at the Somerset Military Museum, Taunton in Somerset.

Figure 240a. Grave of William Napier

Patrick Carlin
6th April 1858 (VC No. 263)

Gazetted: 26th October 1858 22194/4574

Rank and Unit: Private No. 3611 – 13th Regiment of Foot

Citation

For the Act of Bravery recorded in a General Order, issued by the Commander-in-Chief in India, of which the following is a copy:

(Head-Quarters, Allahabad, June 29, 1858.)

GENERAL ORDER. The Commander-in-Chief in India directs that the undermentioned Soldier, of the 13th Foot, be presented, in the name of Her Most Gracious Majesty, with a Medal of the Victoria Cross, for valour and daring in the field, viz.: Private Patrick Carlin, No. 3611, of the 13th Foot, for rescuing, on the 6th of April, 1858, a wounded Naick of the 4th Madras Rifles, in the field of battle, after killing, with the Naick's sword, a mutineer sepoy, who fired at him whilst bearing off his wounded comrade on his shoulders.

((Signed) C. CAMPBELL, General, Commander-in-Chief, East Indies.)

Biography

Patrick was born during 1832 in Belfast, Northern Ireland.

On 5th December 1854, Patrick was a Private in the Antrim Rifles Volunteer force, however, on 8th May 1855 he left his job as a labourer and enlisted as a Private in the 13th Regiment of Foot at Belfast.

Soon after his enlistment, probably in June 1855, Patrick was deployed to the garrison at Malta where he spent the next 7 months.

Around February 1855, Patrick was sent to join the regiment in the Crimea and spent the remainder of the winter in huts on the outskirts of Sevastopol. On 24th May 1856, Patrick and the regiment boarded the steam transport *Khersonese* at Balaklava and set sail for Gibraltar, where they landed on 7th June. Since Patrick arrived in the Crimea after the end of the war he was not awarded any medals.

Patrick and the regiment spent a short time in Gibraltar as soon after their return, reports that another Kaffir war was imminent were received and they boarded *SS Imperatriz* bound for the Cape Colony, where they arrived at Port Elizabeth on 24th September 1856. After spending almost a year as the garrison at Graham's Town, the regiment received an urgent request for reinforcements to be sent to India to help quell the mutiny. On 22nd August 1857, Patrick and the regiment boarded the *SS*

Figure 241. Patrick Carlin

Madras at Port Elizabeth and set sail for Calcutta where they arrived on 3rd October.

The regiment left Calcutta on 15th October and proceeded by rail to Raneegunge and then marched via Allahabad and Futtehpore to Cawnpore where from 22nd December 1857 they were to form the garrison.

On receiving news that a strong rebel force, led by Koer Sing was besieging Azamgarh and with the danger that he could capture the un-garrisoned city of Benares, Patrick and the regiment were despatched as part of a relief force on 27th March 1858. It was on 6th April 1858, during the battle to relieve Azamgarh, that Patrick performed the deeds for which he would later be awarded the Victoria Cross.

As part of the Sarun Field Force, Patrick and the regiment were involved in several battles and actions at; Belwah on 17th and 25th April, Captaingunge on 27th April and Nuggur on 29th April 1858. After resting at Bustee on 8th May they fought the Battle of Bustee on 9th June followed by actions at; Hurryah on 18th June, Debreheah on 29th August, Jugdeespore and Bhanpore on 26th October, Domereagunge on 26th November and Toolsepore on 23rd December 1858. For his service during the mutiny, Patrick was awarded the Indian Mutiny Medal, however, as the regiment had not been involved in the major actions it was awarded with no clasp.

Patrick was presented with his Victoria Cross Medal by the Commander in Chief India General Sir Colin Campbell on 29th June 1858 at a ceremony in Allahabad.

On 13th February 1859, the Sarun Field Force was disbanded and Patrick and the regiment returned to Goruckpore. In February 1861, the regiment moved to Gonda in the province of

Oude and on 16th November moved to Morar, Gwalior where they arrived on 23rd December. On 22nd December 1862, the regiment was moved to Dum Dum and on 8th October 1863 moved to Fort William at Calcutta where they served as the garrison. On 13th/15th January 1864, the regiment set sail on board *HMS Newcastle* and *HMS Shannon* bound for England and after arriving at Gravesend in April were transported by rail to Dover where they formed the garrison.

It would seem that a return to England signalled the end of Patrick's good conduct as starting on 26th April 1864 he would be sentenced to short periods of imprisonment for drunkenness at regular intervals for the remained of his army career.

On 4th November 1864, while stationed at Dover, Patrick signed on for a further 11 years of service, having completed his initial period of engagement. Patrick and the regiment were transported by rail from Dover to Aldershot on 21st February 1865 and on 26th May moved by rail to Devonport. On 1st September 1865, the regiment were deployed to Ireland and took up station at Cork until August 1867 when they were deployed to Gibraltar.

Patrick was involved in an accident on 28th March 1871, while working on the defences at Gibraltar, when scaffolding collapsed he fell and broke the femur and ankle on his right leg.

On 31st July, despite having recovered from his fall, Patrick was declared unfit for further duty and on 19th September 1971 was discharged to pension and returned to Belfast after just over 16 years of service.

Over the years after leaving the army, Patrick fell on hard times and was resident at the Union Infirmary Belfast (the Old City Hospital and Workhouse) when he died on 11th May 1895 from exhaustion. He was initially buried within the grounds of the Workhouse but when this was developed he was reburied in the Friar's Bush Cemetery in Belfast.

Patrick's Victoria Cross Medal is on public display at the Somerset Military Museum, Taunton in Somerset.

William Martin Cafe
15th April 1858 (VC No. 264)

Gazetted: 17th February 1860 22357/557

Rank and Unit: Captain – 56th Bengal Native Infantry

Citation

For bearing away, under a heavy fire, with the assistance of Privates Thompson, Crowie, Spence, and Cook, the body of Lieutenant Willoughby, lying near the ditch of the Fort of Ruhya, and for running to the rescue of Private Spence, who had been severely wounded in the attempt.

Biography

William was born on 23rd April 1826, in London, the 3rd son of father Henry Smith and mother Sarah (née Waine).

William enlisted in the army of the Honourable East India Company and was commissioned as an Ensign with the 56th Bengal Native Infantry on 11th June 1842 and was promoted to the rank of Lieutenant on 12th April 1843.

In December 1843, William saw his first active service during the Gwalior Campaign and was involved in the Battle of Maharajpore on 29th December 1843. For his service during the campaign, William was awarded the Gwalior Campaign Star with star for Maharajpoor.

From November 1848, William was involved in the 2nd Anglo-Sikh war (Punjab Campaign) and took part in the Battle of Ramnugger on 22nd November, the Battle of Chillianwala on 13th January 1849 and the decisive Battle of Gujarat on 21st February 1849. On 29th January 1849, William was promoted to the rank of Captain. For his service during the war, William

Figure 242. William Martin Cafe

was awarded the Punjab Medal with clasps for Chillianwala and Goojerat.

William was stationed at Cawnpore at the outbreak of the mutiny and his regiment was one of the last in the city to join the mutineers, which they did on 5th June 1857 and then fled to join the forces at Delhi. William was now assigned to the 4th Regiment of Infantry (Punjab Rifles) which was a part of the Punjab Irregular Force. During the suppression of the mutiny, William took part in the Battle of Meeangunge on 23rd February 1858 and with the force of Sir Colin Campbell was involved in the siege and ultimate recapture of Lucknow from 1st to 21st March 1858.

It was as part of the Rohilkhand Field Force commanded by Brigadier-General Walpole that on 15th April 1858 during the assault on the Fort at Rooya that William performed the deeds for which he was later awarded the Victoria Cross. During the attack on Fort Rooya, William was seriously wounded and on 29th July 1859 left for England on sick leave to recover from his wounds. For his service during the mutiny, William was awarded the Indian Mutiny Medal with clasp for Lucknow.

In 1860, after returning to India from his sick leave, William was assigned to the Adjutant General department.

William was presented with his Victoria Cross Medal at a ceremony during December 1860, while stationed in India.

Following the transfer of the Honourable East India Companies forces to the British Army after its dissolution, William was confirmed in the rank of Captain in the Bengal Army Infantry with an effective date of 27th January 1849.[781] During 1861, William served in the Sikkim Expedition on the North East Frontier of India. William was promoted to the rank of Major effective 14th November 1861,[782] this was later changed to be effective from 29th August 1861.[783] In 1863, William was Deputy Assistant Adjutant General at Moradabad and in 1864 performed the same role at Delhi. William served as Assistant Adjutant General at Benares during 1869 until December when he served in the same capacity with the Sirhind Brigade. On 16th July 1864 William was promoted to the rank of Lieutenant-Colonel in the Bengal Army.[784] William received a brevet promotion to the rank of Colonel on 21st March 1873.[785]

At some stage prior to 1881, William was married to Isabella Mary.

On 28th November 1882, William was promoted to the rank of Major-General.[786] William was transferred to the supernumerary unemployed list on 16 July 1883.[787] On 25th December 1886, while still on the unemployed supernumerary list, William was promoted to the rank of Lieutenant-General.[788] While still on the unemployed supernumerary list, William was promoted to the rank of General on 1st April 1894.

William died at his home, 16 Wetherby Place, South Kensington in London on 6th August 1906 at the age of 80 and was buried in Brompton Cemetery in London.

William's Victoria Cross Medal is on public display at the National Army Museum in Chelsea, London.

Figure 242a. Grave of William Martin Cafe

781 *London Gazette* – 22828/1348
782 *London Gazette* – 22597/724
783 *London Gazette* – 22625/2496
784 *London Gazette* – 22952/1734
785 *London Gazette* – 24012/3994
786 *London Gazette* – 25191/399

787 *London Gazette* – 25264/4228
788 *London Gazette* – 25665/276

John Simpson
15th April 1858 (VC No. 265)

Gazetted: 27th May 1859 22268/2106

Rank and Unit: Quartermaster Sergeant – 42nd Regiment of Foot

Citation
For conspicuous bravery at the attack on the Fort of Rooya, on the 15th April, 1858, in having volunteered to go to an exposed point within forty yards of the parapet of the Fort, under a heavy fire, and brought in, first, Lieutenant Douglas, and afterwards a Private soldier, both of whom were dangerously wounded.

Biography
John was born in Edinburgh, Scotland on 29th January 1826.

On 8th June 1843, at the age of 17, John enlisted as a Private in the army and probably joined the reserve battalion, of his regiment the 42nd Regiment of Foot, which was stationed at Stirling. Sometime later in the year the reserve battalion were reunited at Malta with the 1st Battalion and were absorbed within their strength. In 1847, John and the regiment moved to the West Indies and were stationed at Bermuda until they moved to Nova Scotia in 1851. After a short stay in Canada, John and the regiment returned to England in 1852.

In early 1854 the regiment received orders for deployment to the East and landed at Scutari in Turkey on 9th June 1854. As part of the Highland Brigade commanded by Major-General Sir Colin Campbell, John and the regiment were landed on the Crimean peninsula with the Anglo/French Expeditionary force on 14th September 1854. On 19th September the Expeditionary Force began its march on Sevastopol and on the following day, John and the regiment took part in the Battle of Alma. John and the regiment played a minor role in the Battle of Balaklava on 25th October 1854 and in March 1855 took part in the Exped ition to secure the straits of Kertch following which they returned to the siege lines at Sevastopol. The regiment was involved in the unsuccessful attacks on the Great Redan on 18th June and 8th September 1855 and after the fall of Sevastopol moved to Kamara until the peace was signed. For his service during the war, John was awarded the Crimea Medal with clasps for Alma, Balaklava and Sevastopol and also the Turkish Crimea Medal. At the end of the war, John and the regiment embarked at Kamiesch and set sail for England where they arrived at Portsmouth on 24th July 1856. After a short stay at the camp at Aldershot, John and the regiment were deployed to garrison duties at Dover.

Figure 243. John Simpson

At some stage John was promoted to the rank of Quartermaster Sergeant.

On 14th August 1857, the regiment set off for India to help quell the mutiny and arrived in Calcutta during October and November.

John and the regiment saw their first action during the battle to recapture Cawnpore on 6th December 1857 and afterwards were part of the force sent in pursuit of the Gwalior contingent of mutineers which had fled the city. During the advance to relieve Futtehgur the regiment where involved in the Battle of Serai Ghat on 9th December and the Battle of Khodagunge on 1st January 1858. From 1st to 21st March 1858, John and the regiment were part of the force of Sir Colin Campbell which lay siege to Lucknow and eventually recaptured the city. During the assault on the city the regiment were involved in the capture of the Martinière barracks and Banks bungalow. After the fall of Lucknow, John and the regiment were part of the Rohilkhand Field Force commanded by Brigadier-General Sir Robert Walpole. It was on 15th April 1858, during the attack on Fort Rooya, that John performed the deeds for which he would later be awarded the Victoria Cross. John was involved in the Battle of Sirsa on 22nd April and the Battle of Bareilly on 5th May 1858, after which they formed the garrison of the town. For his service during the mutiny, John was awarded the Indian Mutiny Medal with clasp for Lucknow.

On 7th October 1859, John was commissioned as Quartermaster in the 42nd Regiment of Foot, while still serving in India.[789]

John was presented with his Victoria Cross Medal by Brigadier-General Sir Robert Walpole on 7th April 1860 at a special parade in Bareilly, India.

In March 1868, after over ten years of service in India, John and the regiment landed at Portsmouth and were despatched to Edinburgh on garrison duties. Following the creation of Brigade Depots, John was appointed as Quartermaster of the 55th Brigade Depot at Fort George near Inverness on 26th July 1873.[790] In November 1874, John was transferred to the 58th Brigade Depot at Stirling. On 1st April 1879, John transferred to the Royal Perth Militia and it was confirmed that while performing this role he would have the temporary rank of Quartermaster in the army.[791] John was appointed as Quartermaster to the 3rd Battalion at the Queen's Barracks in Perth on 1st July 1881 and received the honorary rank of Captain.[792] On 10th October 1883, John was retired to pension after 40 years of service and received the honorary rank of Major.[793] John was appointed as Quartermaster of the 2nd Perth Highland Volunteers on 8th December 1883.[794]

At some stage, John was married to Lydia Georginea.

On 27th October 1884, at the age of 58, John died at his home in St Martin's near Perth and was buried with full military honours at Balbeggie Churchyard, St Martin's.

John's Victoria Cross Medal is on public display at the County Museum of Natural History, Los Angeles, California in the USA.

Figure 243a. Grave of John Simpson

789 *London Gazette* – 22315/3668
790 *London Gazette* – 24001/3494
791 *London Gazette* – 24668/172
792 *London Gazette* – 25007/4346
793 *London Gazette* – 25276/4833
794 *London Gazette* – 25294/6314

Alexander Thompson
15th April 1858 (VC No. 266)

Gazetted: 27th May 1859 22268/2106

Rank and Unit: Lance-Corporal No. 1559 – 42nd Regiment of Foot

Citation

For daring gallantry, on the 15th April, 1858, when at the attack of the Fort of Rooya, in having volunteered to assist Captain Groves, Commanding the 4th Punjab Rifles, in bringing in the body of Lieutenant Willoughby, of that Corps, from the top of the Glacis, in a most exposed situation, under a heavy fire.

Biography

Alexander was born in the Parish of Tolbooth, in Edinburgh during 1824.

At the age of 18, Alexander left his job as a weaver and on 2nd March 1842, enlisted as a Private in the 42nd Regiment of Foot at Stirling. In 1843, Alexander was deployed on his first foreign service to Malta where he served as part of the garrison for just over 4 years. In 1847, Alexander and the regiment were transferred to Bermuda where they remained for a further 4 years, until they moved to Nova Scotia in 1851; after a short stay in Canada, Alexander and the regiment returned to England in 1852.

In early 1854 the regiment received orders for deployment to the East and landed at Scutari in Turkey on 9th June 1854. As part of the Highland Brigade commanded by Major-General Sir Colin Campbell, Alexander and the regiment were landed on the Crimean peninsula with the Anglo/French Expeditionary force on 14th September 1854. On 19th September the Expeditionary Force began its march on Sevastopol and on the following day, Alexander and the regiment took part in the Battle of Alma. Alexander and the regiment played a minor role in the Battle of Balaklava on 25th October 1854 and in March 1855 took part in the Expedition to secure the straits of Kertch following which they returned to the siege lines at Sevastopol. The regiment was involved in the unsuccessful attacks on the Great Redan on 18th June and 8th September 1855 and after the fall of Sevastopol moved to Kamara until the peace was signed. On 10th September 1855, Alexander was promoted to the rank of Corporal. For his service during the war, Alexander was awarded the Crimea Medal with clasps for Alma, Balaklava and Sevastopol and also the Turkish Crimea Medal. In May 1856, Alexander was tried by regimental court martial and was imprisoned from 18th May

Figure 244. Alexander Thompson

until 17th June; he was also reduced back to the rank of Private. At the end of the war, Alexander and the regiment embarked at Kamiesch and set sail for England where they arrived at Portsmouth on 24th July 1856.

After a short stay at the camp at Aldershot, Alexander and the regiment were deployed to garrison duties at Dover.

At some stage Alexander was promoted to the rank of Lance-Corporal.

On 14th August 1857, the regiment set off for India to help quell the mutiny and arrived in Calcutta during October and November. Alexander and the regiment saw their first action during the battle to recapture Cawnpore on 6th December 1857 and afterwards were part of the force sent in pursuit of the Gwalior contingent of mutineers which had fled the city. During the advance to relieve Futtehgur the regiment where involved in the Battle of Serai Ghat on 9th December and the Battle of Khodagunge on 1st January 1858. From 1st to 21st March 1858, Alexander and the regiment were part of the force of Sir Colin Campbell which lay siege to Lucknow and eventually recaptured the city. During the assault on the city the regiment were involved in the capture of the Martinière barracks and Banks bungalow. After the fall of Lucknow, Alexander and the regiment were part of the Rohilkhand Field Force commanded by Brigadier-General Sir Robert Walpole. It was on 15th April 1858, during the attack on Fort Rooya, that Alexander performed the deeds for which he would later be awarded the Victoria Cross. Alexander was involved in the Battle of Sirsa on 22nd April and the Battle of Bareilly on 5th May 1858, after which they formed the garrison of the town. On 1st July 1858, Alexander was promoted to the rank of Corporal. For his service during the mutiny, Alexander was awarded the Indian Mutiny Medal with clasp for Lucknow.

Alexander was presented with his Victoria Cross Medal by Brigadier-General Sir Robert Walpole on 7th April 1860 at a special parade in Bareilly, India.

On 3rd February 1861, Alexander was promoted to the rank of Sergeant.

While still serving in India, Alexander was declared medically unfit for further service on 31st October 1862 and was sent back to England. On his return to England, Alexander was examined again and it was confirmed that he was unfit for further service due to bad health resulting from his time in India and a fever which he contracted at Agra in 1861. After over 21 years of service, Alexander was discharged to pension at Netley on 21st July 1863.

On 22nd July 1864, Alexander was married to Isabella (née Speed) at Manimail in Fife Scotland; the couple would go on to have seven children: twins James and Isabella born on 10th May 1865 at Cupar who both died in infancy, George Speed born on 12th June 1866 at Cupar, Alexander Anderson born on 18th July 1868 at Perth, Thomas born on 13th October 1870 at Perth who died at the age of 4 years, Robert Milne born on 28th May 1876 at Perth and William Speed.

On leaving the army, Alexander returned to live in Scotland and at the age of 56 died at his home in Perth on 29th March 1880 and was buried in Wellshill Cemetery, Perth on 2nd April 1880.

Alexander's Victoria Cross Medal is on public display at the Black Watch Museum in Perth, Scotland.

Figure 244a. Grave of Alexander Thompson

James Davis (Kelly)[795]
15th April 1858 (VC No. 267)

Gazetted: 27th May 1859 22268/2106

Rank and Unit: Private No. 3159 – 42nd Regiment of Foot

Citation

For conspicuous gallantry, at the attack on the Fort of Rooya, when, with an advanced party, to point out the gate of the Fort to the Engineer Officer, Private Davis offered to carry the body of Lieutenant Bramley, who was killed at this point, to the Regiment. He performed this duty, of danger and affection under the very walls of the Fort.

Biography

James was born in the Parish of Canongate, in Edinburgh during February 1835.

At the age of 17, James left his job as a shoemaker and on 2nd November 1852, enlisted as a Private in the 72nd Regiment of Foot at Edinburgh. On 1st March 1854, James transferred to the 42nd Regiment of Foot and soon afterwards was deployment to the East and landed at Scutari in Turkey on 9th June 1854.

As part of the Highland Brigade commanded by Major-General Sir Colin Campbell, James and the regiment were landed on the Crimean peninsula with the Anglo/French Expeditionary force on 14th September 1854. On 19th September the Expeditionary Force began its march on Sevastopol and on the following day, James and the regiment took part in the Battle of Alma. James and the regiment played a minor role in the Battle of Balaklava on 25th October 1854 and in March 1855 took part in the Expedition to secure the straits of Kertch following which they returned to the siege lines at Sevastopol. The regiment was involved in the unsuccessful attacks on the Great Redan on 18th June and 8th September 1855 and after the fall of Sevastopol moved to Kamara until the peace was signed. For his service during the war, James was awarded the Crimea Medal with clasps for Alma, Balaklava and Sevastopol and also the Turkish Crimea Medal. At the end of the war, James and the regiment embarked at Kamiesch and set sail for England where they arrived at Portsmouth on 24th July 1856.

After a short stay at the camp at Aldershot, James and the regiment were deployed to garrison duties at Dover.

Figure 245. James Davis

On 14th August 1857, the regiment set off for India to help quell the mutiny and arrived in Calcutta during October and November.

James and the regiment saw their first action during the battle to recapture Cawnpore on 6th December 1857 and afterwards were part of the force sent in pursuit of the Gwalior contingent of mutineers which had fled the city. During the advance to relieve Futtehgur the regiment where involved in the Battle of Serai Ghat on 9th December and the Battle of Khodagunge on 1st January 1858. From 1st to 21st March 1858, James and the regiment were part of the force of Sir Colin Campbell which lay siege to Lucknow and eventually recaptured the city. During the assault on the city the regiment were involved in the capture of the Martinière barracks and Banks bungalow. After the fall of Lucknow, James and the regiment were part of the Rohilkhand Field Force commanded by Brigadier-General Sir Robert Walpole. It was on 15th April 1858, during the attack on Fort Rooya, that James performed the deeds for which he would later be awarded the Victoria Cross. James was involved in the Battle of Sirsa on 22nd April and the Battle of Bareilly on 5th May 1858, after which the regiment formed the garrison of the town. For his service during the mutiny, James was awarded the Indian Mutiny Medal with clasp for Lucknow.

James was presented with his Victoria Cross Medal by Brigadier-General Sir Robert Walpole on 7th April 1860 at a special parade in Bareilly, India.

On 12th March 1863, while serving at Umballa, James re-engaged for a further 11 years of service. In March 1868, after

---

795 James was born as James Davis Kelly, however, when he enlisted in the army he dropped the name Kelly and became James Davis – supposedly this was because he thought that with the name of Kelly people would think that he was Irish.

over ten years of service in India, James and the regiment landed at Portsmouth and were despatched to Edinburgh on garrison duties. In 1873, the regiment were moved to Portsmouth, in preparation for deployment on further overseas service, however, before departure James was examined on 30th October and declared unfit for military service due to ailments arising from his long service in India. On 25th November 1873, James was discharged from the army to pension after nearly 21 years of service and at the age of 38 returned to his home town of Edinburgh.

At some stage, prior to 1881, James was married to Elizabeth and the couple had two daughters Ann and Janet.

In 1881, James was working as a paper bleacher at the local paper mill in Lasswade, Edinburgh.

James died on 2nd March 1893, at his home in Edinburgh, at the age of 58 and was buried in the North Merchiston Cemetery in the city.

James's Victoria Cross Medal is on public display at the Imperial War Museum, in London as part of the Lord Ashcroft collection.

Figure 245a. Grave of James Davis

Samuel Morley
15th April 1858 (VC No. 268)

Gazetted: 7th August 1860 22411/2934

Rank and Unit: Private No. 3850 – Military Train, 2nd Battalion

Citation

On the evacuation of Azamgarh by Koer Sing's Army, on the 15th of April, 1858, a Squadron of the Military Train, and half a Troop of Horse Artillery, were sent in pursuit. Upon overtaking them, and coming into action with their rear-guard, a Squadron of the 3rd Seikh Cavalry (also detached in pursuit), and one Troop of the Military Train, were ordered to charge, when Lieutenant Hamilton, who commanded the Seikhs, was unhorsed, and immediately surrounded by the Enemy, who commenced cutting and hacking him whilst on the ground. Private Samuel Morley, seeing the predicament that Lieutenant Hamilton was in, although his (Morley's) horse had been shot from under him, immediately and most gallantly rushed up, on foot, to his assistance, and in conjunction with Farrier Murphy, who has already received the Victoria Cross for the same thing, cut down one of the Sepoys, and fought over Lieutenant Hamilton's body, until further assistance came up, and thereby was the means of saving Lieutenant Hamilton from being killed on the spot.

Figure 246. Samuel Morley

Biography

Samuel was born in December 1829 at Radcliffe-on-Trent in Nottinghamshire.

At some stage, Samuel left his job as a labourer and enlisted in the army where he served as a Private in the 8th Hussars.

With the 8th Hussars, Samuel was involved in the Crimean War from September 1855 until March 1856 and transferred to the 2nd Battalion of the Military Train sometime in September 1856.

Samuel served with the Military Train in India during the mutiny and was part of the forces of Sir Colin Campbell which effected the evacuation of the Residency at Lucknow in November 1857 and the recapture of the city in March 1858. It was during an action at Azamgarh on 15th April 1858 that Samuel performed the deeds for which he would later be awarded the Victoria Cross. During the action, Samuel was wounded with sabre cuts to his scalp and left elbow. For his service during the mutiny, Samuel was awarded the Indian Mutiny medal with clasps for Relief of Lucknow and Lucknow.

Having learned that Farrier Murphy had been awarded the Victoria Cross for the action at Azamgarh, Samuel asked General Paget why he had not received the award for his part in the action, when the General was inspecting the regiment at Aldershot some time in 1860. After investigating the matter, General Paget agreed that Samuel should also receive the Victoria Cross and he was presented with his medal by Queen Victoria on 9th November 1860 at an investiture held at Windsor Castle.

On 14th June 1864, Samuel enlisted for a further term of service at Norwich and at some time served for 6 months in Canada.

On 14th March 1870, after nearly 15 years of service, Samuel was discharged from the army at Dublin when the battalion was disbanded. Samuel had a rather blemished career in the army, being somewhat prone to going absent without leave, for which he was tried by court martial and appeared in the regimental defaulters book on 16 occasions.

After leaving the army, Samuel returned to his home town, Radcliffe-on-Trent where he found work at the local Gas-works.

Samuel died at his home, 13, Garnett Street in Nottingham on 16th June 1888 at the age of 59 and was buried in the General Cemetery in Nottingham two days later.

Samuel's Victoria Cross medal is on public display at the Royal Logistic Corps Museum, Camberley, Surrey.

Figure 246a. Grave of Samuel Morley

Michael Murphy
15th April 1858 (VC No. 269)

Figure 247. Michael Murphy

Gazetted: 27th May 1859 22268/2106

Rank and Unit: Farrier Private – Military Train, 2nd Battalion

Citation

For daring gallantry on the 15th April, 1858, when engaged in the pursuit of Kooer Singh's Army from Aziraghur, in having rescued Lieutenant Hamilton, Adjutant of the 3rd Sikh Cavalry, who was wounded, dismounted and surrounded by the enemy. Farrier Murphy cut down several men, and, although himself severely wounded, he never left Lieutenant Hamilton's side, until support arrived.

Biography

Michael was born in Cahir, Tipperary in Ireland some time during 1832,[796] his father also called Michael was a blacksmith.

On 27th August 1855, Michael left his job as a blacksmith and enlisted in the army at Cork, joining the 17th Lancers as a Private. As the 17th Lancers were still taking part in the Crimean War, Michael began his training with the 16th Lancers who were stationed at the Portobello Barracks in Dublin. On 18th October 1856, instead of joining his regiment who were now on their way to India from the Crimea, Michael transferred to the 2nd Battalion of the Military Train and remained in Ireland.

In March 1857, Michael and the battalion left the Curragh Camp and boarded the steamer *Calypso* at Dublin bound for Woolwich and on 28th April set sail for Hong Kong. After reaching Hong Kong, the battalion received orders to proceed to India to help subdue the mutiny and on 27th August 1857 they landed at Calcutta.

Michael served with the Military Train in India during the mutiny and was part of the forces of Sir Colin Campbell which effected the evacuation of the Residency at Lucknow in November 1857 and the recapture of the city in March 1858. On 29th March 1858, the battalion was assigned to the Azamgarh Field Force. It was during an action at Azamgarh on 15th April 1858 that Michael performed the deeds for which he would later be awarded the Victoria Cross and during the action he was severely wounded. To recover from his wounds, Michael was sent to Calcutta and from there was returned to England where he spent time being treated at the Invalid Depot in Great Yarmouth. For his service during the mutiny, Michael was awarded

the Indian Mutiny medal with clasps for Relief of Lucknow and Lucknow. Michael returned to normal duties on 14th May 1859 at the depot in Aldershot and on 1st October 1859 rejoined the 2nd battalion.

On 4th January 1860, Michael was presented with his Victoria Cross Medal by Queen Victoria at an investiture held at Windsor Castle.

Michael was married to Mary Fox, a widow, at the Farnham Register Office near Aldershot on 7th April 1860 and husband and wife together with two children aged 1 year and 5 years established a home at Aldershot camp. The couple would go on to have three children; Edward John, born on 10th January 1864 at Aldershot Camp, George Frederick William born on 15th December 1875 at Scotswood, Newcastle upon Tyne and Mary Ann born on 15th May 1878 at Murton Colliery in Co Durham.

Michael was promoted to Farrier Sergeant and moved with the regiment to Woolwich. In January 1862, Michael was attached to the 1st Battalion and served for five months in Canada, returning to Woolwich on 14th June 1862 and moved back to Aldershot soon afterwards. Michael transferred to the 6th Battalion on 21st March 1865 and saw service at the Royal Military Academy at Sandhurst. On 6th September 1866, Michael rejoined the 2nd Battalion of the Military Train and was based at the Curragh Camp in Ireland, however, in 1868 he was back at Woolwich. By the time that the Military Train became the Army Service Corps in 1869, Michael had been promoted to the rank of Farrier-Major and was once again stationed at Aldershot. On 1st July 1871, Michael was transferred to the 7th Hussars.

On 26th January 1872, Mr James Green, a civilian, was stopped by Farrier-Major Knott at the camp in Aldershot, with a wagon containing sacks of oats and hay. When asked to explain how he had come by these goods, Mr Green explained that Michael had

---

796 Michael's army records indicate a birth year of 1831 or 1832, however later documentation refers to a birth year ranging from 1837 to 1840. 1832 is the birth year shown on his gravestone.

given him permission to remove the oats and hay. Michael and Mr Green were subsequently arrested for the theft of 10 bushels of oats and hay and were tried for the offence at Winchester; Mr Green was acquitted and released, however, Michael was found guilty and sentenced to 9 months hard labour at the Hampshire House of Correction. On 5th March 1872, under the terms of clause 15 of the originating Victoria Cross Warrant, an order for the forfeit of Michael's Victoria Cross was issued and he became the fourth of only eight men to be served with an order of forfeit. Despite having been worn by Michael during every day of his trial, the Victoria Cross Medal could not be found and returned to the War Office as required by the Forfeit Notice, the medal would eventually reappear some 26 years later. Michael was released from prison on 30th November 1872 and he returned to the regiment, now based at Hownslow.

During 1873, Michael served with the regiment at Wimbledon and then Maidstone, however, when the regiment moved to Norwich in June 1874 Michael was in hospital so did not make this move. Michael transferred to the 9th Lancers on 7th December 1874, however, when his new regiment was posted to India

in January 1875 he transferred to the 6th Lancers who were just returning from India. Michael was discharged from the army, after almost 20 years of service, at Colchester on 1st February 1875.

On leaving the army, Michael took up residence at Bellingham in Northumberland but by early 1876 was working as an industrial blacksmith at Scotswood, Newcastle upon Tyne.

In mid-1878, Michael moved to Murton in Co Durham and by 1881 was living in the village of Heworth near Newcastle upon Tyne. In 1889, while living at Wilton Lodge in Darlington, Michael's wife Mary was admitted to Winterton Asylum, Sedgefield where she would reside until her death on 3rd March 1900. By 1891, Michael had moved to a cottage on the Blackwell Grange Estate, on the outskirts of Darlington; the estate was owned by Sir Henry Havelock-Allan who was also a Victoria Cross recipient.

At some time later, Michael moved to Darlington where he worked in a local iron works as a labourer.

Michael died of pneumonia on 4th April 1893, while living at 22 Vulcan Street in Darlington and was buried in the North Road Municipal Cemetery, in Darlington; Sir Henry Havelock-Allan and comrades from his campaign in India arranged for the erection of a headstone.

In July 1920, 27 years after his death, the royal warrant covering the rules of the Victoria Cross were changed to exclude the clause regarding forfeiture and Michael was reinstated in the Victoria Cross register.

Michael's Victoria Cross medal is on public display at the Royal Logistic Corps Museum, Camberley, Surrey.

Figure 247a. Grave of Michael Murphy

Figure 247b. Grave of Michael Murphy

Edward Spence
15th April 1858 (VC No. 270)

Gazetted: 27th May 1859 22268/2106
15th January 1907 27986/325

Rank and Unit: Private – 42nd Regiment of Foot

Citation

MEMORANDUM.

Private Edward Spence, 42nd Regiment, would have been recommended to Her Majesty for the decoration of the Victoria Cross, had he survived. He and Lance-Corporal Thompson, of that Regiment, volunteered, at the attack of the Fort of Rooya, on the 15th April, 1858, to assist Captain Groves, commanding the 4th Punjab Rifles, in bringing in the body of Lieutenant Willoughby from the top of the Glacis. Private Spence dauntlessly placed himself in an exposed position, so as to cover the party bearing away the body. He died on the 17th of the same month, from the effects of the wound which he received on the occasion.

War Office, January 15, 1907. The KING has been graciously pleased to approve of the Decoration of the Victoria Cross being delivered to the representatives of the undermentioned Officer's und men who fell in the performance of acts of valour, and with reference to whom it was notified in the London Gazette that they would have been recommended to Her late Majesty for the Victoria Cross had they survived.

Biography

Edward was born on 28th December 1830 at Dumfries in Scotland.

Unfortunately, as Edward died in service, very little information exists regarding the details of his life and brief army career.

It is probable that Edward enlisted in the army and joined the 42nd Regiment of Foot as a Private some time in 1856, after the regiment returned to England from the Crimea. After a short stay at the camp at Aldershot, Edward and the regiment were deployed to garrison duties at Dover.

On 14th August 1857, the regiment set off for India to help quell the mutiny and arrived in Calcutta during October and November. Edward and the regiment saw their first action during the battle to recapture Cawnpore on 6th December 1857 and afterwards were part of the force sent in pursuit of the Gwalior contingent of mutineers which had fled the city. During the advance to relieve Futtehgur the regiment where involved in the

Battle of Serai Ghat on 9th December and the Battle of Khodagunge on 1st January 1858. From 1st to 21st March 1858, Edward and the regiment were part of the force of Sir Colin Campbell which lay siege to Lucknow and eventually recaptured the city. During the assault on the city the regiment were involved in the capture of the Martinière barracks and Banks bungalow. After the fall of Lucknow, Edward and the regiment were part of the Rohilkhand Field Force commanded by Brigadier-General Sir Robert Walpole. It was on 15th April 1858, during the attack on Fort Rooya, that Edward performed the deeds for which he would later be awarded the Victoria Cross. During the action Edward was seriously wounded and died two days later on 17th April 1858, aged 27 and was buried in an unmarked grave in the Fort Rooya Cemetery. For his service during the mutiny, Edward was awarded the Indian Mutiny Medal with clasp for Lucknow.

At the time of his action at Fort Rooya, the Royal Warrant did not allow for the posthumous award of the Victoria Cross and Edward received a "had he survived" mention in the London Gazette on 27th May 1859. Following a change in the rules by King Edward VII, Edward was one of the first posthumous awards noted in the London Gazette of 15th January 1907. As the confirmation of the award of the Victoria Cross was almost 50 years after his death there was no medal presentation, however, the medal was sent to Richard Lyn, the son of Edward's cousin in July 1907.

Edward's Victoria Cross Medal is on public display at the Royal Highland Regimental Museum, Balhousie Castle, Perth in Scotland.

William Gardner
5th May 1858 (VC No. 271)

Gazetted: 23rd August 1858 22176/3903

Rank and Unit: Colour-Sergeant No. 1469 – 42nd Regiment of Foot

Citation

For his conspicuous and gallant conduct on the morning of the 5th of May last, in having saved the life of Lieutenant-Colonel Cameron, his Commanding Officer, who during the Action at Bareilly on that day, had been knocked from his horse, when three Fanatics rushed upon him. Colour-Serjeant Gardner ran out, and in a moment bayonetted two of them, and was in the act of attacking the third, when he was shot down by another soldier of the Regiment. **(Letter from Captain Macpherson, 42nd Regiment, to Lieutenant-Colonel Cameron, Commanding that Regiment.)**

Biography

William was born on 3rd March 1821 at Nemplar, near Lanark in Scotland.

On 10th February 1841, William left his job as a gardener and enlisted as a Private in the 42nd Regiment of Foot at Glasgow. William was promoted to the rank of Corporal on 1st March 1842 and just 75 days later on 15th May 1842 was promoted to the rank of Sergeant. In 1843, William was deployed on his first foreign service to Malta where he served as part of the garrison for just over 4 years. In 1847, William and the regiment were transferred to Bermuda where they remained for a further 4 years, until they moved to Nova Scotia in 1851; after a short stay in Canada, William and the regiment returned to England in 1852.

In early 1854 the regiment received orders for deployment to the East and landed at Scutari in Turkey on 9th June 1854. As part of the Highland Brigade commanded by Major-General Sir Colin Campbell, William and the regiment were landed on the Crimean peninsula with the Anglo/French Expeditionary force on 14th September 1854. On 19th September the Expeditionary Force began its march on Sevastopol and on the following day, the regiment took part in the Battle of Alma, as William did not receive the clasp for this battle it is assumed that he one of the many men who were laid low by illness. The regiment played a minor role in the Battle of Balaklava on 25th October 1854 but again William did not receive the clasp for this battle so was still probably incapacitated due to illness. In March 1855, William and the regiment took part in the Expedition to secure the straits of Kertch following which they returned to the

Figure 249. William Gardner

siege lines at Sevastopol. William was promoted to the rank of Colour-Sergeant on 25th July 1855. The regiment was involved in the unsuccessful attacks on the Great Redan on 18th June and 8th September 1855 and after the fall of Sevastopol moved to Kamara until the peace was signed. On 26th September 1855, William was awarded the Distinguished Conduct Medal and on 22nd October 1855 received a £20 annuity for distinguished conduct in the field. For his service during the war, William was awarded the Crimea Medal with clasp for Sevastopol and also the Turkish Crimea Medal. At the end of the war, William and the regiment embarked at Kamiesch and set sail for England where they arrived at Portsmouth on 24th July 1856.

After a short stay at the camp at Aldershot, William and the regiment were deployed to garrison duties at Dover.

On 14th August 1857, the regiment set off for India to help quell the mutiny and arrived in Calcutta during October and November. William and the regiment saw their first action during the battle to recapture Cawnpore on 6th December 1857 and afterwards were part of the force sent in pursuit of the Gwalior contingent of mutineers which had fled the city. During the advance to relieve Futtehgur the regiment were involved in the Battle of Serai Ghat on 9th December and the Battle of Khodagunge on 1st January 1858. From 1st to 21st March 1858, William and the regiment were part of the force of Sir Colin Campbell which lay siege to Lucknow and eventually recaptured the city. During the assault on the city the regiment were involved in the capture of the Martinière barracks and Banks bungalow. After the fall of Lucknow, William and the regiment were part of the Rohilkhand Field Force commanded by Brigadier-General Sir Robert Walpole. William was involved in the Battle of Sirsa on

22nd April and during the Battle of Bareilly on 5th May 1858, he performed the deeds for which he would later be awarded the Victoria Cross. During the battle William was slightly wounded in the left hand. After the town was taken, the regiment formed the garrison at Bareilly. For his service during the mutiny, William was awarded the Indian Mutiny Medal with clasp for Lucknow.

On 2nd December 1859, William was promoted to the rank of 2nd Master-Sergeant.

William was presented with his Victoria Cross Medal sometime in February 1860, probably at Bareilly, India.

William returned to England some time in 1861 and after over 21 years of service was discharged to pension at his own request on 4th March 1862 at Stirling Castle. His exemplary record resulted in the award of the Army Long Service and Good Conduct Medal.

At some stage William was married to Margaret (née Watson) and the couple had four children.

After leaving the army William returned to Lanarkshire with his wife and children and established a home at Anchorage Cottage in Bothwell.

On 9th March 1864, William took up the position of Sergeant Instructor with the 2nd Lanarkshire Rifle Volunteer Corps, a post he held for 20 years until 24th March 1884 when he was discharged due to old age.

William died at his home in Bothwell on 24th October 1897 at the age of 76 and was buried in the Bothwell Park Cemetery.

William's Victoria Cross Medal is on public display at the Imperial War Museum in London as part of the Lord Ashcroft collection.

Figure 249a. Grave of William Gardner

Valentine Bambrick
6th May 1858 (VC No. 272)

Gazetted: 24th December 1858 22212/5513

Rank and Unit: Private No. 3244 – 60th Regiment of Foot, 1st Battalion

Citation
For conspicuous bravery at Bareilly, on the 6th of May, 1858, when in a Serai, he was attacked by three Ghazees, one of whom he cut down. He was wounded twice on this occasion.

Biography
Valentine was born in Cawnpore on 13th April 1837 to father John and mother Harriette. He was born into a family with a strong military tradition with his father, uncle and younger brother all seeing service with the 11th Light Dragoons.

It is likely that Valentine began his own military career in 1855, on or around the time of his 18th birthday, when he joined the 60th Regiment of Foot who were stationed at Meerut. Valentine was stationed at Meerut when the mutiny broke out on 10th May 1857. Frome June 1857, Valentine and the regiment were involved in the siege of Delhi which culminated in the recapture of the city on 21st September 1857, during the final assault, detachments of the regiment preceded the main attack columns acting as skirmishers. Following the recapture of Delhi, the regiment were assigned to the Rohilkhand Field Force and were involved in the capture of Nugeelabad on 19th April 1858.

It was at the Battle of Bareilly on 6th May 1858, that Valentine performed the deeds for which he would later be awarded the Victoria Cross, during the action he was twice wounded. Valentine and the regiment were also involved in the Relief of Shahjehanpore on 11th May 1858, the capture of the forts at Bunnai and Mehundee on 26th May 1858 and the capture of Shahabad on 31st May 1858. From 18th October 1858, Valentine and the regiment took part in the Oude Campaign and saw action at the Battle of Russoolpore on 25th October, the capture of Fort Mittowlee on 7th November, actions at Mehundee and Biswah on 1st December and the decisive Battle of Toolespore on 23rd December 1858. For his service during the mutiny, Valentine was awarded the Indian Mutiny Medal without clasp.

Valentine was presented with his Victoria Cross medal some time in 1859, possibly at Benares where the regiment were stationed before moving to Allahabad, Dum Dum and Calcutta where they prepared for their return to England.

On 17th March 1860, the 60th Rifles set sail from Calcutta bound for England, however, prior to this date Valentine transferred to the 87th Regiment of Foot as he wished to remain in India. Despite his transfer to a new regiment, Valentine's time in India was soon to come to an end and by 1861 he was stationed at Buttevant in Ireland. After Ireland Valentine was stationed at Aldershot and it was here on the 16th November 1863 that he was discharged from the army.

On the evening of the 15th November, the day before his discharge, Valentine accompanied Charlotte Johnson, a local prostitute, to her lodgings at Pickford Street in Aldershot and the couple were involved in an altercation with Private (Lance-Corporal?) Henry Milner Russell of the Commissariat Corps. The couple left the scene but after Russell made a report to the police, they were both arrested later in the day and charged with assault and the theft of four of the five medals which Russell had pinned to the front of his tunic. Despite a search of their persons and lodgings none of the medals were found in the possession of Valentine or Charlotte, however, on the evening of the assault two of the medals were found in the corridor outside Charlotte's room in the boarding house. It is understood that three of the medals were; the Punjab, Sutlej and Crimea campaign medals and it was widely reported that the fourth was a Victoria Cross, however this seems very unlikely. Private Russell was never awarded the Victoria Cross so was not entitled to wear the medal, the Police estimated the worth of the medals to be 30 shillings and at the time a Victoria Cross would have been worth at least £5 and in his evidence at trial, Valentine stated *"… that if his better feelings would not have prevented him committing such a paltry robbery, his interest would, for he was in possession of a medal more prized by the British soldier than all those possessed by the prosecutor – the Victoria medal, which conferred £10 annually upon him, and also a pension, all of which he would lose if convicted."* At his trial at Winchester Assizes on 3rd December 1863, Valentine refuted the evidence of Russell who asserted that he had been throttled by Valentine while Charlotte ripped the medals from his chest. Valentine claimed that as he entered the lodging house Haley, another prostitute, called out for help as she was being assaulted by Russell and that his assault on Russell was an attempt to protect Haley. Unfortunately Haley could not be found and pressed to give evidence and Valentine was convicted and sentenced to three years penal servitude, Charlotte was also found guilty and sentenced to 1 year hard labour. From his arrest until trial, Valentine was confined in Winchester Gaol and after sentencing, the Governor, convinced of his innocence tried to get a commutation of his sentence. After sentence was passed, Valentine was incarcerated in the new model prison at Pentonville, where the Governor Captain Craig was also convinced of his

innocence. On 5th December 1863, following his conviction and in accordance with clause 15 of the originating Victoria Cross Warrant, a forfeit notice was issued by the Secretary of State and Valentine was removed from the Victoria Cross register and lost his pension.

Although he was aware of the consequences of his conviction, Valentine was inconsolable when he received the forfeiture notice and on 1st April 1864, two weeks before his 27th birthday, he committed suicide by hanging himself in his prison cell.

Valentine was the second of only eight men required to forfeit their Victoria Cross medal.

Valentine was vehement about his innocence right up to the end, as the letter that was found written on a slate in his cell when his body was found confirms.

My dear dear Friends and Family – Becoming quite tired of my truly miserable existence, I am about to rush into the presence of my Maker uncalled and unasked. To you I appeal for forgivness and pardon for all the unhappiness I have ever caused you. I dare not ask for mercy of God. I am doing that which admits no pardon; but if He will hear my prayer, I pray to Him to grant you consolation in your hour of affliction, for I know that, notwithstanding all my faults, that love which you always manifested towards me is not withheld yet, and therefore the news of my unfortunate fate will make time sorrowful. Pray for your unfortunate son. Val Bambrick. PS – Before I die, I protest solemnly my entire innocence of the charges for which I was punished, all but the assault, and that was done under the circumstances before mentioned to you in my letter. God bless you all. Love to all my relations. Pity even while you condemn Poor Val.

Valentine was buried in an unmarked grave in Islington Cemetery in London.

Following a letter from King George V in 1920, no further forfeit notices were issued and following a revision of the Warrant signed by the king on 5th February 1831, clause 12 allowed for the 8 forfeited medals to be reinstated.

There is no record of Valentine's Victoria Cross having been returned to the War Office as required by the forfeiture notice or of its return to relatives after reinstatement and the current location of the medal is unknown.

Harry Hammon Lyster
23rd May 1858 (VC No. 273)

Gazetted: 21st October 1859 22318/3792

Rank and Unit: Lieutenant – 72nd Bengal Native Infantry

Citation

For gallantly charging and breaking, singly, a skirmishing square of the retreating rebel army from Kalpi, and killing two or three Sepoys, in the conflict. **(Major-General Sir Hugh Henry Rose, G.C.B., reports that this Act of Bravery was witnessed by himself and by Lieutenant-Colonel Gall, C.B., of the 14th Light Dragoons.)**

Biography

Harry was born on 24th December 1830, at Blackrock, Dublin in Ireland to father Anthony Lionel and mother Marcia Deborah (née Tate). Harry had two older sisters; Emily Sophia Jenkinson born in 1825 and Georgina Celicia Sertoris born in 1827; two younger brothers and a younger sister, William George born in 1834, Louisa Charlotte born in 1837 and John born in 1838.

Harry served as a Special Constable in London in 1847, during the time of the Chartist Riots.

Harry joined the Honourable East India Company Army and was commissioned as Ensign in the 48th Native Infantry Regiment on 20th September 1848, just before his 18th birthday. Harry arrived in India on 9th November 1848 and was assigned to the 72nd Native Infantry Regiment rather than the 48th.

Some sources state that Harry served in the 2nd Anglo/Sikh war and was present during the siege at Multan which occurred between 7th September 1848 and 22nd January 1849. While this is possibly true it cannot be confirmed and there is no record of his having been awarded the Punjab Medal with the relevant clasp for Molten.

Harry was promoted to the rank of Lieutenant on 13th November 1854 and after the absorption of the East India Company army into the British Army this rank was reconfirmed.[797]

At the start of the mutiny, Harry was based with his regiment at Neemuch and it was here on 3rd June 1857 that his regiment joined the mutineers. Having no regiment, Harry was appointed to the staff of Major-General Sir Hugh Rose, as his Aide-de-Camp and interpreter, after he was appointed to the command of the Central India Field Force on 17th December 1857. Harry and the Field Force left Mhow on 6th January 1858 with the intention of advancing on the rebel stronghold and arsenal at Gwalior. After

a short siege, the Field Force captured the Fort at Rahatgarh on 26th January and on 31st January fought the Battle of Barodia during which Harry was wounded by a deep sword cut to the inner part of his right forearm while engaged in hand to hand combat with the nephew of Mahomed Fazil Khan (a rebel chieftain) who was killed during the fight.[798] After reaching Sehore on 2nd February 1858, the force advanced to the relief of Saugor which had been besieged since 29th June 1857, the town was relieved on the following day. The Fort and town of Garrakota was captured after a brief siege on 12th February 1858. After a short rest at Saugor, the force resumed its advance on 27th February with the objective of forcing a passage into Bundelkhand via the Mudanpur Pass after several diversionary attacks this was achieved on 3rd March 1858.

The next objective of the Central India Field Force was the capture of the major fort at Jhansi. On the march to Jhansi, the forts at Surahi and Maraura were captured before the Fort at Chanderi was taken on 17th March 1858. On 20th March the force lay siege to Fort Jhansi, on 31st March 1858 the force fought the Battle of Betwa when a large rebel army attempted to relieve the siege. The Fort and town at Jhansi was finally captured on 3rd April 1858. During the Battle of Kunch on 7th May 1858, Harry's charger was wounded by two sabre cuts and a bayonet thrust. The Field Force continued its advance on Gwalior, fighting the Battle of Morar on 12th June. It was at the Battle of Kalpi on 22nd May 1858, that Harry performed the deeds for which he was later awarded the Victoria Cross. The decisive battle of the campaign was fought on 19th June when the town and Fort of Gwalior

---

797 *London Gazette* – 22828/1351

798 *London Gazette* – 22138/2343

were captured. In July 1858, after Major-General Rose handed over command of the Field Force to his second in command Robert Napier, Harry relinquished his role as Aide-de-Camp. For his service during the mutiny, Harry was awarded the Indian Mutiny Medal with clasp for Central India.

On 12th November 1858, Harry was appointed as officiating, sub-assistant in the Bengal Stud Department.

In July 1860, Harry was appointed as Aide-de-Camp to the Commander in Chief India, General Sir Colin Campbell who was replaced by Lieutenant-General Sir Hugh Rose on 4th June 1861.

At some time during 1860, Harry was presented with his Victoria Cross Medal at a ceremony held in Calcutta.

Harry received the brevet promotion to Captain on 18th February 1861.[799] On 23rd December 1862, Harry was promoted to the rank of Captain in the Bengal Army.[800] Harry relinquished his role as Aide-de-Camp to Lieutenant-General Sir Hugh Rose, in August 1863. Harry received a brevet promotion to the rank of Major on 19th January 1864[801] and was appointed to the 3rd Goorkha (Kumaon) Regiment.

On 12th December 1865, Harry was married to the widow Caroline Matilda Underdown (née Davies) at Calcutta.

On 12th September 1866, Harry was promoted to the rank of Major on the Bengal Army Staff Corps.[802] Harry received a brevet promotion to the rank of Lieutenant-Colonel on 26th March 1870,[803] this was later predated to be effective from 18th March 1870.[804] On 8th April 1872, Harry was appointed as temporary 2nd in Command of the 3rd Goorkha regiment, a position that was made permanent on 23rd June 1873. On 20th September 1874, Harry was promoted to the rank of Lieutenant-Colonel.[805] Harry received the brevet promotion to the rank of Colonel on 20th September 1879[806] this was later antedated to be effective from 1st October 1877.[807]

From 1878 until 1880, Harry was involved in the 2nd Anglo/Afghan War, the 3rd Goorkha Regiment was part of the 2nd Brigade, of the Kandahar Field Force, commanded by Brigadier-General W. Hughes. The three field forces entered Afghanistan on 20th November 1878 and the Kandahar Field Force entered Kandahar on 8th January 1879. On 1st December 1879, Harry was appointed to the command of the 3rd Goorkha Regiment. Harry led his regiment during the Battle of Ahmed Khel on 19th April 1880. For his service during the war, Harry was awarded the Afghanistan Medal with clasp for Ahmed Khel.

On 22nd February 1881, Harry was appointed as an Ordinary Member 3rd Class (Companion) of the Military Division of the Most Honourable Order of the Bath.[808]

On 1st July 1887, Harry was promoted to the rank of Major-General[809] and relinquished command of the 3rd Goorkha regiment to take up a position with the Bengal Army Staff Corps. Harry was promoted to the rank of Lieutenant-General on 1st September 1891.[810] On 1st July 1892, after nearly 44 years of service, Harry was effectively retired from the army when he was placed on the Unemployed Supernumerary List.[811]

Following the death of his first wife Caroline in 1895, Harry married Ada Emily (née Cole) at Eastbourne on 25th July 1901.

Harry died on 1st February 1922 at the age of 91, while living at 1 St. Mark's Square, Gloucester Gate in London and was buried in the same grave as his first wife at St James the Less Churchyard, Stubbing near Maidenhead in Berkshire.

Harry was the uncle of Hamilton Lyster Reed who was awarded a Victoria Cross for deeds performed during the Battle of Colenso, on 15th December 1899, in the 2nd Boer War.

Harry's Victoria Cross Medal is on public display at the Imperial War Museum in London as part of the Lord Ashcroft collection.

Figure 251a. Grave of Harry Hammon Lyster

799 *London Gazette* – 22952/1743
800 *London Gazette* – 22747/3190
801 *London Gazette* – 22809/263
802 *London Gazette* – 23266/3477
803 *London Gazette* – 23636/3480
804 *London Gazette* – 23705/488
805 *London Gazette* – 24176/401
806 *London Gazette* – 24786/6751
807 *London Gazette* – 25026/5087

808 *London Gazette* – 24944/975
809 *London Gazette* – 25725/4136
810 *London Gazette* – 26203/4990
811 *London Gazette* – 26308/4128

Same (John) Shaw
13th June 1858 (VC No. 274)

Gazetted: 26th October 1858 22194/4574

Rank and Unit: Private – Rifle Brigade, 3rd Battalion

Citation

*For the Act of Bravery recorded in a despatch from
Major-General James Hope Grant, K.C.B., Commanding
the Lucknow Field Force, to the Deputy Adjutant-General of
the Army, of which the following is an extract:*

"Nowabgunge, 17th June, 1858.

*I have to bring to notice the conduct of Private Same Shaw,
of the 3rd Battalion, Rifle Brigade, who is recommended by
his Commanding Officer for the Victoria Cross, an armed
rebel had been seen to enter a tope of trees. Some officers
and men ran into the tope in pursuit of him. This man was
a Ghazee. Private Shaw drew his short sword, and with that
weapon rushed single-handed on the Ghazee. Shaw received
a severe tulwar wound, but after a desperate struggle, he
killed the man.*

*I trust his Excellency will allow me to recommend this
man for the Victoria Cross, and that he will approve of my
having issued a Division Order, stating that I have done so."*

Biography

Same (Samuel?) who was known as John was born in Preston-pans, East Lothian in Scotland, unfortunately his date of birth is unknown.

John was probably enlisted into the 1st battalion of the Rifle Brigade, and having been ordered to make ready for deployment to the East boarded *HMS Orinoco* on 13th July 1854 at Portsmouth and set sail for Malta the next day. On 24th July they received orders at Malta to proceed to Varna where the Anglo French Expeditionary force was being assembled. On 14th September 1854, after having spent many weeks in Varna, John and his battalion were landed on the Crimean Peninsula. John and the 1st Battalion were held in reserve during the Battle of Alma on 20th September, however, the 2nd battalion took part in the battle. After having advanced to the south of Sevastopol, John and the battalion were part of the forces besieging the city. On 25th October 1854, as part of the 4th Infantry Division and 2nd Infantry Brigade, commanded by Brigadier A. Torrens, John and the battalion took part in the Battle of Balaklava. On 5th November 1854, John and the battalion took part in the Battle of

Inkerman as part of the 4th Division commanded by Sir George Cathcart.For the remained of the war, John and the Battalion were deployed to the trenches around Sevastopol where they were engaged in working parties or in providing cover to working parties. On 4th June 1856, John and the battalion boarded *HMS Apollo* at Balaklava and set sail for England where they arrived at Portsmouth on 7th July and were immediately sent by rail to the camp at Aldershot. For his service during the war, John was awarded the Crimean Medal with clasps for Balaklava, Inkerman and Sevastopol and the Turkish Crimean Medal. He was also awarded the Distinguished Conduct Medal.

On 30th September 1856, John was one of the 170 men transferred from the 1st and 2nd battalions to the 3rd battalion which had been created on 1st April 1855.

On 1st July 1857, John and his new battalion boarded *HMS Barnham* and set sail for India, after a horrendous journey of four months due to bad weather, they finally landed at Calcutta on 8th November. After disembarking on the 13th November, the battalion proceeded by rail to Raneegunge where they arrived on 15th November and the next day set out to march to Allahabad which they reached on 27th November 1857. On 30th November, the battalion departed Allahabad by rail, bound for Cheenee which was the end of the line as the railway was still under construction and after a short march reached Futtehpore on 1st December. At Futtehpore the battalion received orders from Sir Colin Campbell to proceed to Cawnpore as soon as possible as he was about to engage the Gwalior contingent of mutineers. They set out immediately and after a gruelling march reached Cawnpore on 4th December 1857.

On 6th December 1857, John and the battalion were involved in the Battle of Cawnpore and the recapture of the city. On 18th December, John and the battalion left Cawnpore as part of a force commanded by Brigadier Walpole which was sent in pursuit of the Gwalior Contingent that had fled the city. The rebels were defeated at the Battle of Etawah on 28th December and the force joined up with the rest of Sir Colin Campbell's force at Futtehgur on 4th January 1858. On 1st February, John and the 3rd battalion were despatched to Oonoa to secure the road from Cawnpore to Lucknow and on 3rd March 1858 were part of Sir Colin Campbell's force which now was advancing on Lucknow. John and the battalion were involved in the siege and fighting which resulted in the recapture of Lucknow on 21st March 1858 and on 29th March were part of the force commanded by Sir Hope Grant sent in pursuit of the fleeing rebels. It was at the Battle of Nuwabgunge on 13th June that John performed the deeds for which he would later be awarded the Victoria Cross, during which he was severely wounded. At some stage after the battle, John was promoted to the rank of Corporal. On 21st June the battalion moved to Chinhut where they left the sick and wounded, presumably including John. John may have rejoined the battalion when they returned to Lucknow, however, he was with the regiment when they moved to Agra in February 1859 and it was probably here that John was presented with his Victoria Cross Medal. For his service during the mutiny, John was awarded the Indian Mutiny Medal with clasp for Lucknow.

John died on 27th December 1859, on board ship off India while on route home to England and was buried at sea.

John's Victoria Cross Medal is on public display at the Royal Green Jackets Museum in Winchester.

Figure 252a. Same John Shaw memorial

George Rodgers
16th June 1858 (VC No. 275)

Gazetted: 11th November 1859 22324/4033

Rank and Unit: Private – 71st Regiment of Foot

Citation
For daring conduct at Marar, Gwalior, on the 16th of June, 1858, in attacking by himself a party of seven Rebels, one of whom he killed. This was remarked as a valuable service, the party of Rebels being well armed and strongly posted in the line of advance of a detachment of the 71st Regiment.

Biography
George was born during January 1829 at Govan, Glasgow in Scotland.

It is probable that George enlisted with the 71st Regiment at some time around July 1847, when the regiment were stationed at Glasgow after their recent return from duties in Canada. On 21st December 1847, the regiment moved to Edinburgh where they formed the garrison at the castle. In April/May 1848 the regiment were moved to Ireland and were stationed at Dublin until April 1851 when they moved to Mullingar followed by moves to Newry in July 1851 and Kilkenny in August 1852. On 1st November 1852, the regiment received orders to make ready for deployment to the Mediterranean and in February/March 1853 they moved to the island of Corfu.

George and the regiment boarded the transport *Medway* on 26th January 1855 and set sail for the Crimea where they landed at Balaklava on 7th February and took up positions in the trenches around Sevastopol. On 22nd May 1855, the regiment boarded *HMS Sidon* and *HMS Valorous* as part of the expedition to secure the town and port of Kertch to secure the sea route between the Black Sea and the Sea of Azov, which was a major supply route used by the Russians. After taking control of the abandoned town of Kertch, the regiment moved on to Yenical where they established themselves as the garrison and remained until 30th May 1856 when they returned to the town of Kertch. On 22nd June 1856, the regiment handed over the administration of the town to Russian officials and set sail for Malta on board *HMS Sidon* and *HMS Valorous* after arriving on 29th June the occupied the Floriana, Ricasoli and Verdala barracks. For his service during the war, George was awarded the Crimean Medal with clasp for Sevastopol and the Turkish Crimean Medal.

On 2nd January 1858, the regiment received orders to proceed to India and George with the left wing of the regiment

Figure 253. George Rodgers

landed at Bombay on 6th February and proceeded by bullock cart to Mhow which they reach on 17th March 1858. On 30th March, the regiment left Mhow for Moti to join up, as part of the 2nd Brigade, with the Central India Field Force commanded by Major-General Sir Hugh Rose. After their arrival at Moti on 3rd May they proceeded towards Kalpi with the field force, fighting actions at Koonch on 7th May, Muttra on 16th May, Deapoora on 17th May and Gwalior on 22nd May before occupying Kalpi on 23rd May 1858. It was during the Battle of Morar on 16th June 1858 that George performed the deeds for which he would later be awarded the Victoria Cross. On 19th to 20th June the regiment was part of the force which captured and occupied Gwalior. After the city was occupied the regiment returned to Marar for some rest and recuperation. For his service during the mutiny, George was awarded the Indian Mutiny Medal with clasp for Central India.

The regiment returned to Gwalior on 12th August 1858 but returned again to Morar on 6th June 1859.

George was presented with his Victoria Cross Medal at Gwalior on 11th April 1860.

On 20th December 1860, the regiment were relieved by the 27th Regiment of Foot and were moved to the camp at Sealkote in the Punjab. George and the regiment remained at Sealkote until 1st November 1862 when they were relieved by the 93rd Regiment and moved to Nawshera where they arrived on 21st November. On 14th October 1863, the regiment joined the Field Force commanded by Brigadier-General Sir Neville Chamberlain at Nawakilla on the North West Frontier to take part in what was known as the Umbeyla Campaign against the Yusufzai tribesmen. The force took the Umbeyla Pass on 20th October and after various skirmishes fought a major engagement known as 'Craigs Picket' on 20th November 1863. On 15th December

1863, after having received reinforcements and a new commander Major-General Gorvock (appointed after the wounding of Sir Neville Chamberlain), the revitalised force made short work of the rebel resistance and soon achieved all the objectives. The regiment returned to Nonshera on 30th December and on 4th January 1864 moved to Peshawar. For his service during the campaign, George was awarded the India General Service Medal with clasp for Umbeyla.

On 23rd October 1864, the regiment departed for Calcutta where they were to get ready for their return to England, after leaving Calcutta on 14th February 1865 the regiment arrived at Gravesend on 19th June 1865 and joined their comrades from the right wing at Edinburgh Castle soon afterwards.

In February 1866, the regiment departed for Aldershot where they arrived on the 19th February and remained in the camp until December when the boarded *HMS Tamar* at Portsmouth and set sail for Ireland where they arrived on 14th December 1866 and took up station at Fermoy. With the possibility of a Fenian rebellion, the regiment were deployed in detachments across Ireland until 30th April 1868 when they were brought back together at Dublin. On 22nd July 1868, the regiment moved to Curragh Camp and on 17th October 1868 set sail for deployment to Gibraltar.

It is likely that George was discharge from the army, prior to the move to Gibraltar as he had completed his 21 years of service and was now eligible for pension.

Figure 253a. Glasgow memorial to George Rodgers

On leaving the army, George returned to Glasgow and it was here on 9th March 1870 at his sister's house at 20 Govan Street that he died as the result of a tragic accident.

George arrived at his sister's house on the morning of the 9th March and asked he for some alcohol to drink, after being refused on several occasions his sister persuaded him to lie down for a rest and left the house. In her absence, George found a bottle in the kitchen which he thought contained alcohol and promptly swallowed the contents. Unfortunately the bottle contained Vitriol drain cleaner which was mainly sulphuric acid and George died a painful death later in the day.

George was buried in an unmarked paupers grave at the Southern Necropolis in Glasgow.

George's Victoria Cross medal is on public display at the Royal Highland Fusiliers Museum in Glasgow.

Clement Heneage-Walker
17th June 1858 (VC No. 276)

Gazetted: 26th January 1859 22223/294

Rank and Unit: Captain – 8th Hussars

Citation

Selected for the Victoria Cross by their companions in the gallant charge made by a squadron of the Regiment at Gwalior, on the 17th of June, 1858, when, supported by a division of the Bombay Horse Artillery, and Her Majesty's 95th Regiment, they routed the enemy, who were advancing against Brigadier Smith's position, charged through the rebel camp into two batteries, capturing and bringing into their camp two of the enemy's guns, under a heavy and converging fire from the Fort and Town. **(Field Force Orders by Major-General Sir Hugh Henry Rose, G.C.B., Commanding Central India Field Force, dated Camp, Gwalior, 28th June, 1858.)**

Biography

Clement was born on 6th March 1831 at Compton Bassett in Wiltshire to father George[812] who was a Justice of the Peace and Member of Parliament and mother Harriet Sarah (née Weber).

Clement was the third of five children with and older brother Alan who was born in 1826 but died at the age of two, an older sister Matilda Harriet born in 1829, a younger sister Alice born in 1833 and a younger brother Michael born in 1835.

After his education at Eton School and Christ Church, Oxford Clement started his military career on 19th August 1851 when he purchased the commission as Cornet in the 8th Hussars regiment.[813]

Clement was stationed in England until the regiment received orders for their deployment in detachments to the east. The first detachment set sail on 19th April 1854 from Exeter, on board the transports *Echunga*, *Mary Anne* and *Shooting Star* and after a brief stopover at Constantinople landed at Varna in Bulgaria on 30th May 1854. The second detachment set sail on 1st May 1854 from Plymouth, on board the transports *Medora* and *Wilson Kennedy* and landed at Varna in Bulgaria on 10th June 1854. The regiment was reunited at Varna and formed up as part of the Light Brigade which set sail on 31st August 1854 for Kalamatia Bay off the coast of the Crimea.

---

812 On 29th August 1818, George assumed the name of Walker Heneage in lieu of Wyld by Royal Licence.

813 *London Gazette* – 21237/2127

Figure 254. Clement Heneage-Walker

Clement was promoted to the rank of Lieutenant on 3rd September 1854,[814] just before landing on the Crimean peninsula as part of the Anglo/French Expeditionary force on 16th September 1854.

On 19th September the allied force set out on their march towards Sevastopol and on the next day Clement and his regiment were involved in the Battle of Alma. On the way south to Sevastopol, Clement and the regiment were also involved in the action at MacKenzie's Farm on 25th September 1854, when elements of Russian Cavalry tried to disrupt the allied armies march south. On 25th October 1854, Clement was involved in the Battle of Balaklava and was one of the survivors of the Charge of the Light Brigade. Clement was also involved in the Battle of Inkerman on 5th November 1854. On 22nd May 1855 Clement and the regiment were involved in the expedition to Kertch, however, after the town was secured they returned to Balaklava and took up position in the lines around Sevastopol. The regiment was involved in the Battle of Tchernaya on 16th August 1855. Clement was promoted to the rank of 2nd Captain on 22nd November 1855. On 26th April 1856, the regiment boarded the transports *Oneida* and *Norman* and set sail for England, arriving at Portsmouth on 11th May 1856. Soon after their arrival, the regiment was sent to Ireland where they were stationed at Dundalk.

For his service in the Crimea, Clement was awarded the Crimea Medal with clasps for Alma, Balaklava, Inkerman and Sevastopol. He also received the Turkish Crimea Medal. In letters home during the war, Clement was less than complementary to the commanding officers, writing in a letter to his mother that *"We like Cardigan and get on well with him, Lucan is a ruffian and Sir G. Brown a thundering snob who will not allow us to have any porter served out, though there are thousands of gallons of it at Varna."* After the war, writing in response to the recriminations and accusations concerning the losses of the Light Brigade, Clement made his thoughts clear *"It is wonderful to observe the way that fool the 'British public' kicks a man directly he is down, as in the instance of unlucky Lucan. I always hated him, and so did the whole Cavalry Division, but for heaven's sake let a man have fair play – here is this unfortunate man catching it over the head and ears, merely because he obeyed an order given by the thick-headed Raglan through his still more stupid Q.M. (quartermaster) General Airey, who is about the worst of the whole headquarters staff".*

On 12th May 1857, Clement advanced his position within the regiment when he purchased the commission as Captain.[815]

After a short time in Ireland, the regiment were ordered to India to help quell the mutiny and set sail from Cork on 8th October 1857 on board the *SS Great Britain* bound for Bombay where they landed on 17th December 1857. Clement and the regiment served with the Rajputana Field Force, commanded by General Henry Roberts, during the mutiny. The regiment were involved in the Battle of Kotah on 30th March 1858, the Battle of Chanderi on 28th May when after a short siege the city was recaptured from the rebels and the Battle of Kotah-ki-Serai on 17th June 1858. It was at the Battle of Gwalior on 17th June that Clement performed the deeds for which he would later be awarded the Victoria Cross after a ballot of the officers of the regiment under clause 13 of the originating Royal Warrant. Following the fall of Gwalior on 20th June, Clement and the regiment were involved in further actions at Sindwah on 19th October, Koorai on 25th October 1858 and Naharghur on 17th January 1859. On 20th July 1858, Clement was awarded a brevet promotion to the rank of major.[816] For his service during the mutiny, Clement was awarded the Indian Mutiny Medal with clasp for Central India.

Clement was presented with his Victoria Cross Medal by General Officer Commanding Sir Henry Somerset on 18th June 1858 at a ceremony in Bombay.

Clement advanced his position within the regiment when he purchased a commission as Major on 16th November 1860. In February 1861, Clement and the regiment were stationed

---

814 *London Gazette* – 21613/3187

815 *London Gazette* – 22000/1686
816 *London Gazette* – 22207/5351

in Meerut. On 12th January 1864, Clement and the regiment boarded *HMS Renown* and set sail for England where after their arrival they were stationed at Brighton from 2nd May 1864.

Clement was married to Henrietta Letitia (née Vivian) on 7th December 1865 at St Paul's Church at Sketty in South Wales. The couple would go on to have five children; Godfrey Clement born on 17th May 1868 who would have a career in the army with the Grenadier Guards reaching the rank of Major and being awarded the DSO, John Vivian born on 27th May 1869, Algernon Vivian born on 4th February 1871 who would have a career in the Royal Navy and reach the rank of Rear-Admiral, Claude born on 24th April 1875 who pursued a career as a barrister and Ailine Dulcie born on 18th August 1877.

Clement resigned from the army on 21st March 1868 after the sale of his commission.[817]

After leaving the army, Clement returned to the family home, Compton House at Compton Basset and following the death of his father on 21st September 1875 succeeded to the family estates and devoted himself to the life of a country gentleman.

On 7th March 1887, Clement was appointed as the High Sheriff of Wiltshire[818] and also served in the capacity of Justice of the Peace.

Clement died suddenly at his home in Compton Bassett on 9th December 1901 at the age of 70 and was buried in the family vault at St Swithin's Church in Compton Bassett.

The location of Clement's Victoria Cross Medal is unknown, believed to be in the hands of a private collector.

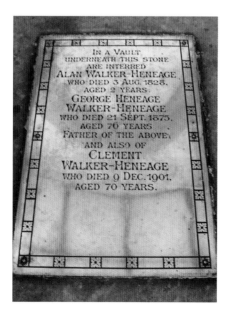

Figure 254a. Grave of Clement Heneage-Walker

---

817 *London Gazette* – 23363/1768
818 *London Gazette* – 25680/1222

Joseph Ward
17th June 1858 (VC No. 277)

Gazetted: 26th January 1859 22223/294

Rank and Unit: Sergeant No. 1584 – 8th Hussars

Citation

Selected for the Victoria Cross by their companions in the gallant charge made by a squadron of the Regiment at Gwalior, on the 17th of June, 1858, when, supported by a division of the Bombay Horse Artillery, and Her Majesty's 95th Regiment, they routed the enemy, who were advancing against Brigadier Smith's position, charged through the rebel camp into two batteries, capturing and bringing into their camp two of the enemy's guns, under a heavy and converging fire from the Fort and Town. **(Field Force Orders by Major-General Sir Hugh Henry Rose, G.C.B., Commanding Central India Field Force, dated Camp, Gwalior, 28th June, 1858.)**

Biography

Joseph was born during 1834 a Kinsale, Co Cork in Ireland.

Leaving his job as a clerk, Joseph enlisted as a Private in the 8th Hussars at London on 27th November 1854. Joseph joined his regiment in the Crimea on 14th July 1855 and took up position in the lines around Sevastopol. The regiment was involved in the Battle of Tchernaya on 16th August 1855. Joseph was promoted to the rank of Corporal on 4th December 1855 and two weeks later he was appointed as probationary Orderly Room Clerk. On 26th April 1856, the regiment boarded the transports *Oneida* and *Norman* and set sail for England, arriving at Portsmouth on 11th May 1856. Soon after their arrival, the regiment was sent to Ireland where they were stationed at Dundalk. For his service in the Crimea, Joseph was awarded the Crimea Medal with clasp for Sevastopol. He also received the Turkish Crimea Medal.

After a short time in Ireland, the regiment were ordered to India to help quell the mutiny and set sail from Cork on 8th October 1857 on board the *SS Great Britain* bound for Bombay where they landed on 17th December 1857. Joseph and the regiment served with the Rajputana Field Force, commanded by General Henry Roberts, during the mutiny. The regiment were involved in the Battle of Kotah on 30th March 1858, the Battle of Chanderi on 28th May when after a short siege the city was recaptured from the rebels and the Battle of Kotah-ki-Serai on 17th June 1858. Joseph was promoted to the rank of Sergeant on 1st May 1858. It was at the Battle of Gwalior on 17th June that Joseph performed the deeds for which he would later be awarded the Victoria Cross after a ballot of the NCO's of the regiment under clause 13 of the originating Royal

Warrant. During the action, Joseph was wounded. On 14th August 1858, Joseph was severely wounded in an action at Kattara. Following the fall of Gwalior on 20th June, Joseph and the regiment were involved in further actions at Sindwah on 19th October, Koorai on 25th October 1858 and Naharghur on 17th January 1859. For his service during the mutiny, Joseph was awarded the Indian Mutiny Medal with clasp for Central India.

Joseph was presented with his Victoria Cross Medal by General Officer Commanding Sir Henry Somerset on 18th June 1858 at a ceremony in Bombay.

On 6th April 1860, Joseph was appointed to the local rank of Troop Sergeant-Major. In February 1861, Joseph and the regiment were stationed in Meerut. On 26th March 1862, Joseph was tried by a Regimental Court Martial and was convicted of an unknown offence and reduced in rank back to Private. On 12th January 1864, Joseph and the regiment boarded *HMS Renown* and set sail for England where after their arrival they were stationed at Brighton from 2nd May 1864 but moved to York in June 1864.

Joseph re-enlisted for a further 12 years of service on 19th January 1866 at Birmingham and on 6th June was promoted again to the rank of Corporal. This new rank was only retained for a few days as after being confined for three days between 17th and 19th June, Joseph was convicted again by Regimental Court Martial and was reduced in rank back to Private.

In 1869 the regiment were despatched to duties in Ireland and it was here at Longford, on 23rd November 1872, that Joseph died at the age of 38 and was buried in St John's Church of Ireland in Longford.

The location of Joseph's Victoria Cross Medal is unknown, believed to be in the hands of a private collector.

Figure 255a. Grave of Joseph Ward

George Hollis
17th June 1858 (VC No. 278)

Gazetted: 26th January 1859 22223/294

Rank and Unit: Farrier No. 1298 – 8th Hussars

Citation

Selected for the Victoria Cross by their companions in the gallant charge made by a squadron of the Regiment at Gwalior, on the 17th of June, 1858, when, supported by a division of the Bombay Horse Artillery, and Her Majesty's 95th Regiment, they routed the enemy, who were advancing against Brigadier Smith's position, charged through the rebel camp into two batteries, capturing and bringing into their camp two of the enemy's guns, under a heavy and converging fire from the Fort and Town. **(Field Force Orders by Major-General Sir Hugh Henry Rose, G.C.B., Commanding Central India Field Force, dated Camp, Gwalior, 28th June, 1858.)**

Biography

George was born during October 1833 at Chipping Sodbury in Gloucestershire to father Edward and mother Ruth.

At the age of 20, George left his job as a smith and on 28th April 1854 enlisted as a Private in the 8th Hussars at Exeter. George joined his regiment in the Crimea in late September 1854, too late to qualify for the Crimea War Medal. On 26th April 1856, the regiment boarded the transports *Oneida* and *Norman* and set sail for England, arriving at Portsmouth on 11th May 1856. Soon after their arrival, the regiment was sent to Ireland where they were stationed at Dundalk.

After a short time in Ireland, the regiment were ordered to India to help quell the mutiny and set sail from Cork on 8th October 1857 on board the *SS Great Britain* bound for Bombay where they landed on 17th December 1857. George and the regiment served with the Rajputana Field Force, commanded by General Henry Roberts, during the mutiny. The regiment were involved in the Battle of Kotah on 30th March 1858, the Battle of Chanderi on 28th May when after a short siege the city was recaptured from the rebels and the Battle of Kotah ki Serai on 17th June 1858.

It was at the Battle of Gwalior on 17th June that George performed the deeds for which he would later be awarded the Victoria Cross after a ballot of the Private's of the regiment under clause 13 of the originating Royal Warrant. On 19th June 1858, during the action to capture the town of Gwalior, George received a gunshot wound to his right hand which required the amputation of his ring and middle fingers. On 29th March 1859, at Rajurghur, George was declared unfit for further service due to his wounded hand and was sent back home to England. For his service during the mutiny, George was awarded the Indian Mutiny Medal with clasp for Central India. George was finally discharged from the army, on medical grounds, on 1st November 1859 at Chatham after just over 5 years of service.

George was presented with his Victoria Cross Medal by Queen Victoria at an investiture held at Windsor Castle on 9th November 1860.

After leaving the army George moved to Exwick near Exeter in Devon, where he was employed by Messer's Snow and Company, Wine Merchants.

At some stage George was married to Catherine.

It was at his home 85, Cowick Street in Exwick that George died on 16th May 1879, from congestion of the lungs at the age of 45 and was buried at Exwick Cemetery four days later.

The location of George's Victoria Cross Medal is unknown, believed to be in the hands of a private collector.

Figure 256a. Grave of George Hollis

John Pearson
17th June 1858 (VC No. 279)

Gazetted: 26th January 1859 22223/294

Rank and Unit: Private No. 861 – 8th Hussars

Citation

Selected for the Victoria Cross by their companions in the gallant charge made by a squadron of the Regiment at Gwalior, on the 17th of June, 1858, when, supported by a division of the Bombay Horse Artillery, and Her Majesty's 95th Regiment, they routed the enemy, who were advancing against Brigadier Smith's position, charged through the rebel camp into two batteries, capturing and bringing into their camp two of the enemy's guns, under a heavy and converging fire from the Fort and Town. (**Field Force Orders by Major-General Sir Hugh Henry Rose, G.C.B., Commanding Central India Field Force, dated Camp, Gwalior, 28th June, 1858.**)

Biography

John was born on 19th January 1825 at Seacroft, Leeds in Yorkshire to father Stephen and mother Elizabeth (née Darley).

On 11th January 1844 (a week before his 18th birthday), John enlisted in the 8th Hussars at Leeds, having left his job as a gardener.

John was married to Selina (née Smart) at the General Baptist Church in Trowbridge, Wiltshire on 6th April 1851. The couple would go on to have 7 children; Stephen born in Meerut 1858, died on 1st August 1861 from cholera, Edward born at Meerut on 7th October 1862, Albert born in 1865 in Bengal, Frank born in 1867 in Bengal, Selina born on 10th January 1870 at Halifax, Ida born in 1872 at Halifax and Mary born on 17th January 1874 also at Halifax.

John was stationed in England until the regiment received orders for their deployment in detachments to the east. The first detachment set sail on 19th April 1854 from Exeter, on board the transports *Echunga*, *Mary Anne* and *Shooting Star* and after a brief stopover at Constantinople landed at Varna in Bulgaria on 30th May 1854. John was with the second detachment which set sail on 1st May 1854 from Plymouth, on board the transports *Medora* and *Wilson Kennedy* and landed at Varna in Bulgaria on 10th June 1854. The regiment was reunited at Varna and formed up as part of the Light Brigade which set sail on 31st August 1854 for Kalamatia Bay off the coast of the Crimea and was part of the Anglo/French Expeditionary force which landed on 16th September 1854.

On 19th September the allied force set out on their march towards Sevastopol and on the next day the regiment was

Figure 257. John Pearson

Figure 257a. Grave of John Pearson

involved in the Battle of Alma, it is assumed that John did not take part (perhaps due to illness) as he was not awarded the clasp for this battle. On 25th October 1854, John was involved in the Battle of Balaklava and was one of the survivors of the Charge of the Light Brigade, having been part of the 2nd Line. On 26th April 1856, the regiment boarded the transports *Oneida* and *Norman* and set sail for England, arriving at Portsmouth on 11th May 1856. Soon after their arrival, the regiment was sent to Ireland where they were stationed at Dundalk. For his service in the Crimea, John was awarded the Crimea Medal with clasps for Balaklava and Sevastopol. He also received the Turkish Crimea Medal.

After a short time in Ireland, the regiment were ordered to India to help quell the mutiny and set sail from Cork on 8th October 1857 on board the *SS Great Britain* bound for Bombay where they landed on 17th December 1857. During the mutiny John and the regiment served with the Rajputana Field Force, commanded by General Henry Roberts.

The regiment were involved in the Battle of Kotah on 30th March 1858, the Battle of Chanderi on 28th May when after a short siege the city was recaptured from the rebels and the Battle of Kotah-ki-Serai on 17th June 1858. It was at the Battle of Gwalior on 17th June that John performed the deeds for which he would later be awarded the Victoria Cross after a ballot of the Private's of the regiment under clause 13 of the originating Royal Warrant. During the action, John was wounded by a sword cut to his right shoulder. Following the fall of Gwalior on 20th June, John and the regiment were involved in further actions at Sindwah on 19th October, Koorai on 25th October 1858 and Naharghur on 17th January 1859. For his service during the mutiny, John was awarded the Indian Mutiny Medal with clasp for Central India.

John was presented with his Victoria Cross Medal by General Officer Commanding Sir Henry Somerset on 18th June 1858 at a ceremony in Bombay.

On 23rd July 1859, John was promoted to the rank of Corporal. In February 1861, John and the regiment were stationed in Meerut. On 1st November 1863, John transferred to the 19th Hussars (taking the new regimental number 668) and reverted back to the rank of Private, however, a month later on 1st December he was once again promoted to the rank of Corporal. John was promoted to the rank of Sergeant on 6th August 1865 and on 22nd September 1865 after over 21 years of service was awarded the Army Long Service and Good Conduct Medal and received an annual annuity of £5. On 3rd September 1867, John was awarded the Meritorious Service Medal and received an annual annuity of £15. After an examination at Meerut on 1st October 1867, John was declared unfit for further service due to Asthenia (a debilitating weakness) and was sent home to England where he was to spend a short time in the hospital at Netley. It was at Netley on 9th June 1868, after over 24 years of service that John was discharge from the army to pension and he went to live in Halifax, Yorkshire.

At some time, probably late 1881 or early 1882, John and his family emigrated to Canada to start a new life and settled in Ontario; by 1888 he owned a small farm near Little Pike Bay which was nine miles west of Lion's Head on the Bruce Peninsular in Ontario.

John died on the 18th April 1892 at his farm in Bruce County at the age of 67 and was buried in Eastnor Township Cemetery, Lion's Head.

John's Victoria Cross Medal is on public display at the Imperial War Museum in London as part of the Lord Ashcroft Collection.

William Francis Frederick Waller
20th June 1858 (VC No. 280)

Gazetted: 25th February 1862 22601/957

Rank and Unit: Lieutenant – 25th Bombay Light Infantry

Citation

For great gallantry at the capture by storm of the fortress of Gwalior, on the 20th June, 1858. He and Lieutenant Rose, who was killed, were the only. Europeans present, and, with a mere handful of men, they attacked the fortress, climbed on the roof of a house, shot the, gunners opposed to them and carried all before them and took the fort, killing every man in it.

Figure 258. William Francis Frederick Waller

Biography

William was born on 20th August 1839 at Daloolee near Bombay to father Thomas and mother Alicia Anne (née Gilbert).

On 20th February 1857, William joined the army of the Honourable East India Company and was commissioned as an Ensign with the 25th Bengal Native Infantry.

Sir Hugh Rose was appointed to the command of the Central India Field Force on 17th December 1857 and William with the 25th Bombay Native Infantry was assigned to the 1st Brigade of this force under the command of Brigadier Stuart. With the 1st Brigade, William took part in the siege and capture of Chanderi on 17th March 1858 and the siege and capture of Jhansi between 25th March and 3rd April 1858. William also took part in the Battle of Betwa on 31st March when a strong rebel force attacked the Brigade while it was besieging Jhansi. The Brigade took part in the Battle of Kunch on 7th May and the Battle of Kalpi on 22nd May 1858. On 3rd June 1858, William was promoted to the rank of Lieutenant. It was on 20th June 1858, during the battle to capture Gwalior, that William performed the deeds for which he would later be awarded the Victoria Cross. For his service during the mutiny, William was awarded the Indian Mutiny Medal with clasp for Central India.

William was presented with his Victoria Cross Medal by the General Officer Commanding Lieutenant-General Sir W. Mansfield at Bombay some time in 1862.

On 16th June 1864, William was married to Mary Anne (née Grierson) at Bombay, some sources state that the couple went on to have nine sons, however, this has not been confirmed.

William was promoted to the rank of Captain on 20th February 1869[819] and was transferred to the Political Department,

Sawunt Warre Local Corps. On 20th February 1877, William was promoted to the rank of Major.[820] Sometime during 1880, William was appointed as 2nd in Command of the Sawunt Warre Local Corps and in 1882 was appointed as Political Agent to the South Mahratta County. On 20th February 1883, William was promoted to the rank of Lieutenant-Colonel[821] and during the

Figure 258a. Grave of William Francis Frederick Waller

819 *London Gazette* – 23494/2624

820 *London Gazette* – 24471/3617
821 *London Gazette* – 25220/1900

next year was appointed as 2nd Assistant to the Political Agent at Kathiawar and joint Administrator at Sangli.

In August 1884, William returned to England on leave and while living at his home 1 Lansdown Terrace in Bath he died at the age of 45 on 29th January 1885 and was buried in Lockswood Cemetery in Bath.

William's Victoria Cross Medal is on public display at the Imperial War Museum as part of the Lord Ashcroft Collection.

Figure 258b. Grave of William Francis Frederick Waller

Samuel James Browne
20th June 1858 (VC No. 281)

Gazetted: 1st March 1861 22485/1007

Rank and Unit: Captain – 46th Bengal Native Infantry[822]

Citation

For having at Seerporah, in an engagement with the Rebel Forces under Khan Allie Khan, on the 31st of August, 1858, whilst advancing upon the Enemy's position, at day break, pushed on with one orderly Sowar upon a nine-pounder gun that was commanding one of the approaches to the enemy's position, and attacked the gunners, thereby preventing them from reloading, and firing upon the Infantry, who were advancing to the attack. In doing this, a personal conflict ensued, in which Captain, now Lieutenant-Colonel, Samuel James Browne, Commandant of the 2nd Punjab Cavalry, received a severe sword-cut wound on the left knee, and shortly afterwards another sword-cut wound, which severed the left arm at the shoulder, not, however, before Lieutenant- Colonel Browne had succeeded in cutting down one of his assailants. The gun was prevented from being reloaded, and was eventually captured by the Infantry, and the gunner slain.

Figure 259. Samuel James Browne

---

822 Samuel was actually in command of the 2nd Punjab Irregular Cavalry; the 46th had mutinied at Sealkote on 9th July 1857.

Biography

Samuel was born on 3rd October 1824 at Barrackpore in India to father John a surgeon in the Bengal Medical Service and mother Marie Charlotte (née Swinton).

He was the eighth born of nine children, having two older brothers; John Swinton born on 30th August 1806 and Clement Reid born on 11th January 1812; five older sisters, Felicite Anne born in1808, Charlotte Isabella born on 15th Feb 1810, Georgina Fortescue born in 1816, Jessie Simpson, Mary Anne born on 20th May 1822 and a younger brother Montague George born in 1829.

In October 1840, at the age of 16, Samuel set sail from Portsmouth returning to India after having presumably completed his education in England. On 22nd December 1840, Samuel joined the army of the Honourable East India Company and was commissioned as an Ensign in the 46th Bengal Native Infantry. Samuel was promoted to the rank of Lieutenant on 26th October 1844.

In September 1848, Samuel and the regiment were assembled at Ferozapore and assigned to the 3rd Brigade commanded by Brigadier Hoggan of the 3rd Division commanded by Major-General Sir Joseph Thackwell of the Punjab Army commanded by Sir Hugh Gough ready to take part in the 2nd Anglo Sikh War or Punjab Campaign. During the war, Samuel saw action at the Battle of Ramnugger on 22nd November 1848, the Battle of Sadoolapore on 2nd December, the Battle of Chillianwala on 13th January 1849 and the decisive Battle of Gujarat on 21st February 1849. For his service during the war, Samuel was awarded the Punjab Medal with clasp for Chillianwala and Goojerat.

In May 1849, after the Punjab Campaign, Samuel was charged with the task of raising an irregular cavalry force at Lahore, this was designated the 2nd Punjab Irregular Cavalry (the unit was later incorporated into the regular force and in 1904 was designated as the 22nd Sam Browne's Cavalry). Following the annexation of the Punjab, Samuel and the 2nd Punjab Cavalry served as part of the Punjab Frontier Force on the Derajat and Peshawar borders and were involved in several actions against the warring Pashtun tribesmen. After being 2nd in Command since its formation, Samuel was appointed to the command of the 2nd Punjab Irregular Cavalry on 8th January 1851 and led his unit during the Waziri Expedition in 1852. On 10th February 1855, Samuel was promoted to the rank of Captain. In March 1857, Samuel took part in the Bozdar Belooch expedition and in July 1857 was involved in operations against the Narinjee on the Eusufzai border. For his service in the frontier wars, Samuel was awarded the Indian General Service Medal with clasp for North West Frontier.

Towards the end of 1857, Samuel and his cavalry were moved from the defence of the North West Frontier to aid with the suppression of the mutiny. After joining the forces of Sir Colin Campbell the unit was involved in the siege which resulted in the recapture of Lucknow on 21st March 1858. Following Lucknow, Samuel and his unit were part of the Rohilkhand Field Force which fought the Battle of Koorsee on 23rd March, the Battle of Fort Rooya on 15th April and the Battle of Bareilly between 5th and 6th May 1858. On 20th July 1858, Samuel was awarded the brevet promotion to the rank of Major.[823] It was during the Battle of Seerporah that Samuel performed the deeds for which he would later be awarded the Victoria Cross. During the battle, Samuel was severely wounded with a sword cut to the left knee and another cut which severed his left arm at the shoulder. For his service during the mutiny, Samuel was awarded the Indian Mutiny Medal with clasp for Lucknow. Samuel received a brevet promotion to the rank of Lieutenant-Colonel on 26th April 1859.[824]

Sometime during the 2nd quarter of 1860, Samuel was married to Lucy (née Sherwood) at Cheltenham. The couple would go on to have five children; three daughters, Emily Sophie born in India on 8th April 1861, Charlotte Lawrence and Violet Adriana; and two sons, Sherwood Dighton born on 25th May 1862 who would attain the rank of Brigadier-General in the Royal Artillery and Alan Percy who would attain the rank of Lieutenant-Colonel in the Central India Horse.

Samuel was promoted to the rank of Major on 18th February 1861.

On 1st March 1861, Samuel was appointed as an Extra Member 3rd Class (Companion) of the Military Division of the Most Honourable Order of the Bath.[825]

In December 1862, Samuel was presented with his Victoria Cross Medal by Major-General Sir S. Cotton at a ceremony in Peshawar.

Samuel received a brevet promotion to the rank of Colonel on 26th April 1864.[826] On 22nd December 1864, Samuel was appointed as the officiating Commandant of the Guides Cavalry; the position was made substantive on 8th February 1865. On 22nd December 1866, Samuel was promoted to the rank of Lieutenant-Colonel.[827] Samuel left his post as Commandant of the Guides Cavalry on 18th March 1869 to take over the command of the Central India Horse, however, he would only hold this post for two months as he was appointed to the command of the Peshawar District. Samuel received a brevet promotion to the rank of Major-General on 8th February 1870; this was later post-dated to be effective 6th February 1870.[828] In May 1875,

823 *London Gazette* – 22164/3379
824 *London Gazette* – 22293/2935
825 *London Gazette* – 22486/1006
826 *London Gazette* – 22889/4237
827 *London Gazette* – 23270/3772
828 *London Gazette* – 23598/1738 & 23622/2878

Samuel was appointed as President of the Stud Commission and in March 1876 was appointed as Director of Remounts.

During 1875 and 1876, Samuel was on special duties as part of the party with HRH the Prince of Wales during his tour of India.

On 7th March 1876, Samuel was appointed as an Extra Knight Commander of the Most Exalted Order of the Star of India.[829]

Samuel received a brevet promotion to the rank of Lieutenant-General on 1st October 1877.[830] From April 1878, Samuel commanded the Lahore Division until 9th August 1878 when he was appointed as a Military Member of the Supreme Council.

Samuel served as a member of the Supreme Council until 5th November 1878 when he was appointed to the command of the Peshawar Valley Field Force and led the unit in the 2nd Anglo/Afghan war. After forcing the Khyber Pass, the field force captured the fort at Ali Musjid and with the road to Kabul now clear of rebels the force occupied Jellalabad where they spent the winter months. The force were only involved in minor operations up until the end of the war, however, they received the thanks of the Indian Government and both Houses of Parliament for their contribution. For his service during the war, Samuel was awarded the Afghanistan Medal with clasp for Ali Musjid.

On 25th July 1879, Samuel was appointed as an Ordinary Member 2nd Class (Knight Commander) of the Military Division of the Most Honourable Order of the Bath.[831]

In September 1880, Samuel left India and returned to England where he initially resided in London. Samuel was placed on the Unemployed Supernumerary List on 20th September 1884.[832] On 10th November 1884 Samuel was appointed to the commission for organising the Colonial and India Exhibition and attended its opening on 4th May 1886. While on the Unemployed Supernumerary List, Samuel was promoted to the rank of General on 1st December 1888.[833]

On 30th May 1891, Samuel was appointed as an Ordinary Member 1st Class (Knight Grand Cross) of the Military Division of the Most Honourable Order of the Bath.[834]

Samuel was the inventor of the "Sam Browne Belt", receiving patent No. 397 on 4th January 1900. He first thought of the belt in 1852 (some six years before he lost his arm) as, like many of his fellow officers he found that the official issue waist belt and slings were unsuitable for carrying a sword and revolver into action. Samuel's design incorporated a shoulder brace which distributed

the load more evenly and included space on the belt for a holster to safely carry a pistol. The newly designed belt became popular with many officers during the 2nd Anglo Afghan War but was not adopted for official army issue until 1899 (via army order 151).

Samuel died at his home, The Wood, Ryde on the Isle of Wight on 14th March 1901 at the age of 76 and after cremation at Woking on 21st March his ashes were buried in Ryde Cemetery.

Samuel's Victoria Cross Medal is on public display at the National Army Museum in Chelsea, London.

Figure 259a. Grave of Samuel James Browne

Figure 259b. Grave of Samuel James Browne

829 *London Gazette* – 24303/1787
830 *London Gazette* – 24508/5458
831 *London Gazette* – 24747/4697
832 *London Gazette* – 25397/4169
833 *London Gazette* – 25884/7203
834 *London Gazette* – 26167/2921

James Champion
8th September 1858[835] (VC No. 282)

Gazetted: 20th January 1860 22347/178

Rank and Unit: Troop Sergeant-Major No.1194 – 8th Hussars

Citation

*For distinguished bravery at Beejapore on the 8th of
September, 1858, when both the Officers attached to the
Troop were disabled, and himself severely wounded at the
commencement of the action by a ball through his body,
in having continued at his duty forward, throughout the
pursuit, and disabled several of the Enemy with his pistol.*

Also recommended for distinguished conduct at Gwalior.

Biography

James was born in 1834, baptised on 25th May, at Hammersmith in London to father William and mother Mary Ann (née Wake).

On 15th September 1851, James left his job as a servant and enlisted in the 8th Hussars at Westminster, giving his age as 19 when he was in fact 17 years old. James joined his regiment at Hounslow where he received his horse riding training. James remained in England until his regiment received orders for deployment to the East. He was part of the first detachment and set sail on 19th April 1854 from Exeter, on board the horse transport *Shooting Star* and after a brief stopover at Constantinople landed at Varna in Bulgaria on 30th May 1854.

The regiment was reunited at Varna and formed up as part of the Light Brigade which set sail on 31st August 1854 for Kalamatia Bay off the coast of the Crimea and was part of the Anglo/French Expeditionary force which landed on 16th September 1854.

On 19th September the allied force set out on their march towards Sevastopol and on the next day James and the regiment were involved in the Battle of Alma. James was in hospital from 5th October 1854 until 23rd November, probably as a result of cholera contracted while in Turkey, so was not present at the Battle of Balaklava or the Battle of Inkerman. On 15th December 1854, James was promoted to the rank of Corporal and just over two months later on 28th February 1855 was promoted to the rank of Sergeant. Over the next few months James served as Regimental Post Orderly and with his troop was part of Lord Raglan's escort. On 12th March 1856, James was promoted to

Figure 260. James Champion

the rank of Troop Sergeant-Major. On 26th April 1856, the regiment boarded the transports *Oneida* and *Norman* and set sail for England, arriving at Portsmouth on 11th May 1856. Soon after their arrival, the regiment was sent to Ireland where they were stationed at Dundalk. For his service in the Crimea, James was awarded the Crimea Medal with clasps for Alma and Sevastopol. He also received the Turkish Crimea Medal.

On 11th November 1856, James was married to Sarah (née Hamblin) at St Stephen, Shepards Bush, London. The couple would go on to have nine children; Henry James born on 18th September 1857, Emma Laura May born on 3rd December 1861 at Beejapore, F. F. born on 18th January 1863, William E. born in 1865, Alma Victoria born October 1866, Lavina born in 1869, Alice born in 1871, Ada M. born in May 1874 and Rodolph de Salis[836] born on 28th January 1877.

After a short time in Ireland, the regiment were ordered to India to help quell the mutiny and set sail from Cork on 8th October 1857 on board the *SS Great Britain* bound for Bombay where they landed on 17th December 1857.

James and the regiment served with the Rajputana Field Force, commanded by General Henry Roberts, during the mutiny. The regiment were involved in the Battle of Kotah on 30th March 1858, the Battle of Chanderi on 28th May when after a short siege the city was recaptured from the rebels and the Battle of Kotah-ki-Serai on 17th June 1858. During the Battle of Gwalior on 17th June, James was involved in a charge against

---

835 Discharge papers indicate he was wounded on 5th September not 8th as indicated by citation.

836 Named after the commander of the 8th Hussars, whose life was saved by James during his Victoria Cross deed.

the rebels, that some say rivalled that at Balaklava. For his part in this action, James was awarded the Meritorious Service Medal with an annual annuity of £15. On 31st August 1858, James was promoted to the rank of Regimental Sergeant-Major. Following the fall of Gwalior on 20th June, James and the regiment were involved in further actions and it was at Beejapore on 8th September 1858 that he performed the deeds for which he would later be awarded the Victoria Cross. During the action James was seriously wounded by a musket ball which struck him in the chest and passed right through his body. As a reward for his actions, James was offered a Commission, however, this was refused as it had been on two previous occasions. For his service during the mutiny, James was awarded the Indian Mutiny Medal with clasp for Central India.

At some stage, while still serving in India, James was presented with his Victoria Cross Medal.

In February 1861, James and the regiment were stationed in Meerut. Having completed his initial period of service, James re-engaged for a further 11 years on 19th September 1863. On 12th January 1864, James and the regiment boarded *HMS Renown* and set sail for England where after their arrival they were stationed at Brighton from 2nd May 1864 but moved to York in June 1864. In December 1867, James and the regiment were stationed in Manchester until 12th May 1868 when they moved to Edinburgh.

In April 1869 the regiment were despatched to duties in Ireland and it was here at Longford, on 23rd December 1873, that James was discharged to pension at his own request after over 22 years of service. Just prior to leaving the army, James was awarded the Army Long Service and Good Conduct Medal on 16th November 1869 together with an annual annuity of £10.

On leaving the army James moved with his family from Dublin to Gloucester.

While residing in Gloucester, James enlisted in the Royal Gloucestershire Hussars Yeomanry and was Regimental Sergeant-Major of the Cheltenham Troop from 1873 until 1883.

At some stage James was awarded the Empress of India Medal.

Sometime after leaving the Yeomanry, James returned to London and it was at his home 37 Dewhurst Road in South Hammersmith that he died on 4th May 1904 at the age of 69 and was buried in an unmarked grave in the Margrave Road Cemetery in Hammersmith.

James's Victoria Cross Medal is on public display at the Combined Service Museum, Redoubt Fortress, Eastbourne in Sussex.

Figure 260a. Grave of James Champion

Charles George Baker
27th September 1858 (VC No. 283)

Gazetted: 25th February 1862 22601/956

Rank and Unit: Lieutenant – Bengal Military Police Battalion

Citation

For gallant conduct on the occasion of an attack on the rebels at Suhejnee, near Peroo, on the 27th September, 1858, which is thus described in this officer's own words.

"The enemy (at the time supposed to have mustered from 900 to 1000 strong in infantry, with 50 cavalry,) advanced. Without exchanging a shot, I at once retired slowly, followed up steadily by the rebel line for 100 yards clear of village or jungle, when, suddenly wheeling about my divisions into line, with a hearty cheer, we charged into and through the centre of the enemy's line, Lieutenant Broughton, with his detachment, immediately following up the movement, with excellent effect, from his position upon the, enemy's left. The rebel right wing, of about 300 men, broke at once, but the centre and left, observing the great labour of the horses in crossing the heavy ground, stood and receiving the charge with repeated volleys, were cut down, or broke only a few yards ahead of the cavalry. From this moment, the pursuit was limited to the strongest and best horses of the force, numbering some 60 of all ranks, who dashing into and swimming a deep and wide nullah, followed the flying enemy through the village of Russowlee, and its sugar-cane kheta, over two miles of swamp, and 500 yards into the thick jungles near Peroo, when, both men and horses being completely exhausted, I sounded the halt and assembly, and, collecting my wounded, returned to camp at Munjhaen about 6 pm."

The charge ended in the utter defeat of the enemy, and is referred to by Lord Clyde, "as deserving of the highest encomium, on account both of conception and execution."

It is also described as having been as gallant as any during the war.

Biography

Charles was born on 8th December 1830 at Noacolly in northern India to father John who was a doctor in the service of the Honourable East India Company and mother Lydia.

Charles spent his early years in England where he was educated at Halesworth and Lowestoft and on his return to India

Figure 261. Charles George Baker

he joined the Maritime Service of the Honourable East India Company as a midshipman.

At some stage Charles joined the P&O Company where he served as an officer on ships plying their Eastern Route. Charles was serving as the 2nd Officer on the P&O Mail Steamer *Doura* in 1854 when the ship was involved in a shipwreck on shoals off the Paracel Islands in the South China Sea. Charles was placed in command of a small open boat which was despatched from the *Doura* to find help and after a perilous journey of over 500 miles, returned 8 days later with two P&O steamers which rescued the passengers and crew and saved the mail; the *Doura* broke up on the shoal the same evening. In 1855, Charles was promoted to Chief Officer.

Charles left the employment of P&O and joined the army of the Honourable East India Company when he was commissioned as a Lieutenant in the Bengal Military Police Battalion[837] on 15th April 1856 at Calcutta. It was after arriving at Calcutta and being reunited with friends that he discovered that his death due to smallpox had been widely circulated.

At the outbreak of the mutiny, Charles was stationed at Behar and when the Dinapore Brigade mutinied and his regiment was one of the few that remained loyal. It was for an action at Suhejnee, near Peroo, that on 27th September 1858, Charles performed the deeds for which he would later be awarded the Victoria Cross. In 1859, as a reward for his service at Suhejnee,

---

837 The regiment was raised in January 1856 by Captain Thomas Rattray and would later be designated 45th Rattray's Sikh's

Charles was appointed as commandant of the 1st Battalion Cavalry. For his service during the mutiny, Charles was awarded the Indian Mutiny Medal without clasp.

Charles was never presented with his Victoria Cross Medal, it was sent to him by registered post.

In 1863, Charles was appointed as the Officiating Deputy Inspector of Police in Dacca but soon afterwards had to leave the post due to illness and returned to England.

At some stage Charles was married to Charlotte and the couple had five children.

Charles and his family spent some time in the United States of America where some members of his family had settled.

At some stage, Charles joined the Turkish Imperial Ottoman Gendarmerie and in 1877 was appointed as Inspector of Brigade and served for Turkey in the Russia-Turkey war of 1877 to 1878, taking part in the Balkan's Campaign; during the war he spent time as a Russian prisoner.

In 1882, Charles transferred to the Egyptian Gendarmerie and at the time of his retirement in 1885 was Chief of the Public Security Department of the Egyptian Ministry of the Interior with a rank of 'Lewa Pasha' (Major-General).

Following his retirement, Charles returned to England and was residing at the Southcliffe Hotel, Southbourne-on-Sea when at the age of 75 he died on 19th February 1906 and was buried three days later in the Christchurch Cemetery.

The location of Charles's Victoria Cross Medal is unknown, believed to be in the hands of a private collector.

Figure 261a. Grave of Charles George Baker

Patrick Roddy
27th September 1858 (VC No. 284)

Gazetted: 12th April 1859 22248/1483

Rank and Unit: Ensign – Oudh Military Police Cavalry

Citation

Major-General Sir James Hope Grant, K.C.B., Commanding Oudh Force, bears testimony to the gallant conduct of Lieutenant Roddy, on several occasions. One instance is particularly mentioned.

On the return from Kuthirga of the Kuppurthulla Contingent, on the 27th of September, 1858, this officer, when engaged with the enemy, charged a Rebel (armed with a percussion musket), whom the Cavalry were afraid to approach, as each time they attempted to do so, the Rebel knelt and covered his assailant; this, however, did not deter Lieutenant Roddy, who went boldly in, and when within six yards, the Rebel fired, killing Lieutenant Roddy's horse, and before he could get disengaged from the horse, the Rebel attempted to cut him down. Lieutenant Roddy seized the Rebel until he could get at his sword, when he ran the man through the body. The Rebel turned out to be a subadar of the late 8th Native Infantry, a powerful man, and a most determined character.

Biography
Patrick was born on 17th March 1827 at Elphin, Co. Roscommon in Ireland.

Figure 262. Patrick Roddy

At the age of 20, Patrick left his job as a labourer and enlisted in the army of the Honourable East India Company at Liverpool on 2nd February 1848 and took up a position as Gunner with the Bengal Artillery. By 1851, Patrick had been promoted to the rank of Sergeant and was serving with the 2nd Company of the 3rd Battalion of the Bengal Artillery. Patrick's initial service during the mutiny was as part of the force of Major-General Sir James Outram in operations against the rebels in the province of Oudh.

It was with this force, that Patrick took part in operations at Lucknow which resulted in the evacuation of the residency on 22nd November 1857 during which he was slightly wounded and received a mention in despatches for his actions. Patrick was also involved in operations to defend the Alum Bagh in December 1857 and January 1858 during which on 22nd December he captured two guns at Guilee. Patrick received a further two mentions in despatches for these actions and on 24th February 1858 was rewarded with a commission as Ensign; the commission was not attached to any regiment and he continued to serve with the Bengal Artillery. Patrick served as part of the forces of Sir Colin Campbell which lay siege to Lucknow and eventually recaptured the city on 21st March 1858. On 14th May 1858, Patrick was assigned to the Oudh Military Police Cavalry and continued to serve in operations against the rebels as part of the Oudh Relief Force. Patrick was slightly wounded for a second time on 31st August 1858, however, this did not dampen his endeavours as he received two more mention in despatches in October 1858 and a mention in the General Orders of the Governor-General of India on 18th November 1858. It was near Kuthirga, on 27th September, operating as part of the Kupperthula Contingent, that Patrick performed the deeds for which he would later be awarded the Victoria Cross. On 3rd December 1858, Patrick was promoted to the rank of Lieutenant[838] and in 1859 was appointed as the Divisional Adjutant to the Oudh Military Police. For his service during the mutiny, Patrick was awarded the Indian Mutiny Medal with clasps for Defence of Lucknow and Lucknow.

Patrick was presented with his Victoria Cross Medal some time during 1860 at Lucknow.

In 1861, Patrick was placed on the Unattached List. On 11th January 1867, Patrick was promoted to the rank of Captain[839] and given employment with the Barracks Department. From December 1867 until May 1868, Patrick served with the forces of Sir Robert Napier during the war in Abyssinia and for this service was awarded the Abyssinian War Medal (1867–68) as well as receiving a mention in despatches.

At some stage Patrick married Margaret, probably in India and the couple had nine children; Thekla and two other daughters, Edwin Louis born c.1874, James Morris killed in action on North West Frontier in India on 8th November 1897 and four other sons.

In 1875, Patrick served as Station Staff Officer at Amritsar. On 9th February 1876, Patrick was promoted to Major[840] and was posted to Roorkee as Station Staff Officer. From 1878 until 1880, Patrick served as part of the Peshawar Valley Field Force, commanded by Sir Samuel James Browne, in the 2nd Anglo-Afghan War during which he fought at the Battle of Ali Masjid on 21st November 1878. For his service during the war, Patrick was awarded the Afghanistan Medal (1878–80) with clasp for Ali Musjid.

During 1881, Patrick was employed as the Station Staff Officer at Morar.

On 1st March 1882, Patrick was awarded a brevet promotion to the rank of Lieutenant-Colonel[841] this was confirmed as a substantive promotion on 24th February 1886.[842] Patrick retired from the army after nearly 40 years of service on 24th February 1887 and was promoted to the rank of Colonel.[843]

On leaving the army, Patrick settled at Jersey in the Channel Islands and it was here on 21st November 1895 that he died at the age of 75 and was buried in Mount A'Labbe Cemetery, St Helier, Jersey.

The location of Patrick's Victoria Cross Medal is unknown, believed to be in the hands of his family.

Figure 262a. Grave of Patrick Roddy

---

838 *London Gazette* – 22828/1354
839 *London Gazette* – 23207/199

840 *London Gazette* – 24291/529
841 *London Gazette* – 25150/4384
842 *London Gazette* – 25640/5328
843 *London Gazette* – 25710/3287

George Bell Chicken
27th September 1858 (VC No. 285)

Gazetted: 27th April 1860 22380/1596

Rank and Unit: Civilian volunteer – Indian Naval Brigade

Citation

For great gallantry on the 27th September, 1858, at Suhejnee, near Peroo, in having charged into the middle of a considerable number of the rebels, who were preparing to rally and open fire upon the scattered pursuers. They were surrounded on all sides, but, fighting desperately, Mr. Chicken succeeded in killing five before he was cut down himself. He would have been cut to pieces, had not some of the men of the 1st Bengal Police and 3rd Seikh Irregular Cavalry, dashed into the crowd to his rescue/and routed it, after killing several of the Enemy.

Biography

George was born on 2nd March 1833 at Howden Pans in the parish of Wallsend, near Newcastle-upon-Tyne to father George a Master Mariner and Elizabeth (née Bell) he was christened at St Peter's Church in Wallsend on 12th December 1833.

Having probably spent his early childhood in or around Howden Pans, in 1847 at the age of 14, George was serving as an apprentice on board the Brig *Darlington* under the command of master R. Smith and owned by Bell & Co. George learnt his trade on board *Darlington*, which was plying its trade between London and the Mediterranean, until he received his Mate's Register Ticket at Sunderland on 20th February 1852, just before his 19th birthday. On 24th February 1852, just days after receiving his ticket, George signed on as 2nd Mate on board *Anna* at Tynemouth and set sail for a voyage to the west coast of America, returning in May 1852. In July 1852, George set sail from Hull on a voyage to Valparaiso in Chile and returned to North Shields. In 1853, George returned to his first ship the *Darlington* as 1st Mate and sailed on various voyages to Copenhagen and other ports in the Baltic. In February 1854, George was granted his Master's ticket and he was appointed as Captain of the *Darlington* and sailed on further Baltic voyages. On 22nd May 1855, George set sail as 1st Mate on board *Hastings* and on 25th July 1855 was discharged at Calcutta.

It is unclear what George did for the next three years, however, after volunteering to serve with the Indian Naval Brigade he was appointed by Captain Campbell (for administrative purposes) as acting Master on the books of *HMS Calcutta* on 31st July 1858. George was proceeding to Buxar, to join up with the No. 3

Detachment of the naval brigade, commanded by Commander Batt (*HMS Zenobia*), when on 27th September 1858 after joining up with a force of the Bengal Military Police he performed the deeds at Suhejnee for which he was later awarded the Victoria Cross. During the action George was seriously wounded. For his service during the mutiny, George was awarded the Indian Mutiny Medal without clasps.

On 30th November 1859, George arrived back at Calcutta and on 12th March 1860 was given the command of the Schooner *Emily*. Soon after setting out on her voyage from Calcutta, the *Emily* floundered in a violent squall off Sandheads in the Bay of Bengal on 12th May 1860 and George together with all hands on board lost their lives.

George was the fourth of five civilians to be awarded the Victoria Cross, which was allowed under an amendment to the original warrant issued on 13th December 1858 which stated *"… that Non-Military Persons who, as Volunteers, have borne arms against the Mutineers, both at Lucknow and elsewhere, during the late operations in India, shall be considered as eligible to receive the decoration of the Victoria Cross, subject to the rules and ordinances already made and ordained for the government thereof, provided that it be established in any case that the person was serving under the orders of a General or other Officer in Command of Troops in the Field, when he performed the Act of Bravery for which it is proposed to confer the decoration".*

As George had been lost at sea before his award was sanctioned, his Victoria Cross medal was posted to his father on 4th March 1862.

George's Victoria Cross Medal is on public display at the Imperial War Museum in London as part of the Lord Ashcroft collection.

Thomas Monaghan
8th October 1858 (VC No. 286)

Gazetted: 11th November 1862 22680/5346

Rank and Unit: Trumpeter No. 1158 – 2nd Dragoon Guards

Citation

For saving the life of Lieutenant-Colonel Seymour, C.B., commanding the regiment, in an attack made on him on the 8th of October, 1858, by mutinous sepoys, in a dense jungle of sugar canes, from which an attempt was made to dislodge them. The mutineers were between 30 and 40 in number. They suddenly opened fire on Lieutenant-Colonel Seymour and his party at a few yards distance, and immediately afterwards rushed in upon them with drawn (native) swords. Pistolling a man, cutting at him, and emptying with deadly effect at arm's length every barrel of his revolver, Lieutenant- Colonel Seymour was cut down by two sword cuts, when the two men above recommended, rushed to his rescue, and the Trumpeter shooting a man with his pistol in the act of cutting at him, and both Trumpeter and Dragoon driving at the enemy with their swords, enabled him to arise, and assist in defending himself again, when the whole of the enemy were dispatched. The occurrence took place soon after the action fought near Sundeela, Oudh, on the date above mentioned.

Biography

Thomas was born on 18th April 1833 at Abergavenny, Monmouthshire in Wales.

On 3rd July 1849, at the age of just over 14 years, Thomas enlisted in the army at Westminster and joined the 3rd Dragoon Guards. Thomas initially served in England and on 6th March 1851 was given the rank of Trumpeter. In 1852, Thomas was sent to Ireland with the regiment and on 1st January 1853 he transferred to the 2nd Dragoon Guards. At some stage, probably during 1854/55, Thomas served for nearly a year with the Osmurli Irregular Cavalry in Turkey.

In July 1857, the regiment left for India, sent to help quell the mutiny and after arriving in Calcutta in late November were immediately despatched to Allahabad to join the Cavalry Division commanded by General Sir James Hope Grant, which was part of the force of Sir Colin Campbell. The journey from Calcutta to Allahabad was a trip of 500 miles, 400 miles of which were covered by the regiment on their newly issued horses.

From late January 1858, the regiment were involved with General Hope Grant's force in various mopping up operations

Figure 264. Thomas Monaghan

until in March they were part of Sir Colin Campbell's force which lay siege to Lucknow, culminating in the recapture of the city on 21st March 1858. Following the recapture of Lucknow, the regiment were involved in operation to suppress the rebels in the province of Oudh and it was on 8th October 1858 at Jamo near Sundlee that Thomas performed the deeds for which he would later be awarded the Victoria Cross. For his service during the mutiny, Thomas was awarded the Indian Mutiny Medal with clasp for Lucknow.

Thomas was presented with his Victoria Cross Medal by Sir Hugh Rose, Commander in Chief of forces in India at a ceremony held at Benares on 5th January 1863.

For some inexplicable reason, soon after Thomas was presented with his Victoria Cross Medal his up to now unblemished service record was marred on 25th February 1863 by the first of what would be four periods of imprisonment and two courts martial. His offences appear to be all related to being drunk on duty. On 10th March 1863, Thomas re-engaged for a further period of service in the army. In May 1870, the regiment returned to England after a service in India of over 12 years. On 28th June 1870, after another offence, Thomas was reduced in rank to Private.

On 10th June 1873, after over 22 years of service, Thomas was discharge to pension at his own request at Woolwich and stated that his intention was to move to Norwich and gain work as a Groom.

At some stage Thomas was married but the details are unknown.

Thomas died at his home 1 Pellipar Road in Woolwich on 10th November 1895 at the age of 62 and was buried 6 days later in an unmarked grave in Woolwich Cemetery, in London; a year after his death his widow managed to purchase the plot in which he was buried and in 1967 the regiment erected a headstone over his grave.

Thomas's Victoria Cross Medal is on public display at the Queen's Dragoon Guards Regimental Museum in Cardiff Castle, Wales.

Figure 264a. Grave of Thomas Monaghan

Charles Anderson
8th October 1858 (VC No. 287)

Gazetted: 11th November 1862 22680/5346

Rank and Unit: Private No. 875 – 2nd Dragoon Guards

Citation

For saving the life of Lieutenant-Colonel Seymour, C.B., commanding the regiment, in an attack made on him on the 8th of October, 1858, by mutinous sepoys, in a dense jungle of sugar canes, from which an attempt was made to dislodge them. The mutineers were between 30 and 40 in number. They suddenly opened fire on Lieutenant-Colonel Seymour and his party at a few yards distance, and immediately afterwards rushed in upon them with drawn (native) swords. Pistolling a man, cutting at him, and emptying with deadly effect at arm's length every barrel of his revolver, Lieutenant- Colonel Seymour was cut down by two sword cuts, when the two men above recommended, rushed to his rescue, and the Trumpeter shooting a man with his pistol in the act of cutting at him, and both Trumpeter and Dragoon driving at the enemy with their swords, enabled him to arise, and assist in defending himself again, when the whole of the enemy were dispatched. The occurrence took place soon after the action fought near Sundeela, Oudh, on the date above mentioned.

Figure 265. Charles Anderson

Biography

Charles was born some time during 1827 at Liverpool in Lancashire.

On 11th December 1845, at the age of 18, Charles left his job as a labourer and enlisted in the army at Dublin, where he joined the 2nd Dragoon Guards as a Private. After being tried by regimental court martial, Charles was imprisoned from 1st January 1855 until 19th June 1855 for an unknown offence. Charles was promoted to the rank of Corporal on 20th June 1856, however, after another trial by court martial and a period of imprisonment from 7th to 10th March 1857 he was reduced in rank back to Private.

In July 1857, the regiment left for India, sent to help quell the mutiny and after arriving in Calcutta in late November were immediately despatched to Allahabad to join the Cavalry Division commanded by General Sir James Hope Grant, which was part of the force of Sir Colin Campbell.

The journey from Calcutta to Allahabad was a trip of 500 miles, 400 miles of which were covered by the regiment on their newly issued horses.

From late January 1858, the regiment were involved with General Hope Grant's force in various mopping up operations until in March they were part of Sir Colin Campbell's force which lay siege to Lucknow, culminating in the recapture of the city on 21st March 1858. Following the recapture of Lucknow, the regiment were involved in operation to suppress the rebels in the province of Oudh and it was on 8th October 1858 at Jamo near Sundlee that Charles performed the deeds for which he would later be awarded the Victoria Cross. For his service during the mutiny, Charles was awarded the Indian Mutiny Medal with clasp for Lucknow.

On 16th August 1860, Charles was again promoted to the rank of Corporal, however, again after trial by court martial and a period of imprisonment from 1st to 18th June 1862 he was reduced in rank back to Private.

Charles was presented with his Victoria Cross Medal by Sir Hugh Rose, Commander in Chief of forces in India at a ceremony held at Benares on 5th January 1863.

On 15th February 1869, Charles was promoted to the rank of Corporal for the third time. In May 1870, after over 12 years in India, Charles returned with the regiment to England and soon after arrival at Colchester was discharged from the army to pension at his own request on 28th June 1870, having completed 24 years of service. Although he stated at the time of his discharge that he intended to go to Dublin, it appears that at some stage he moved to Seaham Harbour near Sunderland in County Durham and took up employment as a coal miner.

On 19th April 1899, at the age of 73, while living at Swinbank Cottage in Seaham Harbour, Charles fell from the cliffs and died from a fractured skull. He was buried in the Princess Road Cemetery in Seaham Harbour.

Charles's Victoria Cross Medal is on public display at the Queen's Dragoon Guards Regimental Museum in Cardiff Castle, Wales.

Figure 265a. Grave of Charles Anderson

Hanson Chambers Taylor Jarrett
8th October 1858 (VC No. 288)

Gazetted: 18th June 1859 22278/2420

Rank and Unit: Lieutenant – 26th Bengal Native Infantry

Citation

For an act of daring bravery at the village of Baroun, on the 14th of October, 1858, on an occasion when about 70 Sepoys were defending themselves in a brick building, the only approach to which was up a very narrow street, in having called on the men of his regiment to follow him, when, backed by only some four men, he made a dash at the narrow entrance, where, though a shower of balls was poured upon him, he pushed his way up to the wall of the house, and beating up the bayonets of the rebels with his sword, endeavoured to get in.

Biography

Hanson was born on 22nd March 1839 at Madras in India, the son of father Thomas a barrister and mother Eliza Julia (née Chambers).

After his education in England, at Prior Park College near Bath, Hanson returned to India and on 13th June 1854 enlisted in the army of the Honourable East India Company and was commissioned as an Ensign in the 26th Bengal Native Infantry.

At the time of the mutiny, Hanson was stationed at Meean Meer and on 13th May 1857 the regiment was disarmed as a precaution; this was to no avail as a few weeks later on 30th July 1857, while at Lahore the regiment did mutiny. With his regiment now in the ranks of the mutineers, Hanson was assigned to the 20th/28th Punjab Infantry which had been formed at Ferozepur on 1st July 1857. On 27th August 1857, Hanson was promoted to the rank of Lieutenant.[844]

Hanson served with the regiment throughout the mutiny and it was at the village of Baroun on 14th October 1858 that he performed the deeds for which he would later be awarded the Victoria Cross. For his service during the mutiny, Hanson was awarded the Indian Mutiny Medal without clasp.

On 19th May 1859, Hanson was appointed as adjutant of the regiment.

Hanson was presented with his Victoria Cross Medal some time during 1860, while still serving in India.

On 31st January 1865, Hanson was appointed as a Wing Officer of the regiment. Hanson was promoted to the rank of Captain on 10th June 1866 and took up a position within the Bengal Staff Corps.[845] In 1867, Hanson transferred to the Public Works Department where he took up a position within the Forests Department; this gave him the time and opportunity to indulge in his passion of big game hunting. Hanson was promoted to the rank of Major on 10th June 1874[846] and on 10th June 1880 was promoted to the rank of Lieutenant-Colonel and given the post of Deputy Conservator of Forests.[847] On 18th June 1884, Hanson was appointed as Conservator of Forests and was promoted to the rank of Colonel.[848]

Hanson was married to Nina Louise (née de Dombasle) at Allahabad cathedral on 26th March 1890.

Sadly, Hanson died at his home in Saugor on 11th April 1890, just over two weeks after his marriage and was buried in the Saugor New Cemetery.

The location of Hanson's Victoria Cross Medal is unknown, believed to be in the hands of a private collector.

---

844 *London Gazette* – 22686/6160

845 *London Gazette* – 23192/6649
846 *London Gazette* – 24124/4118
847 *London Gazette* – 24880/4801
848 *London Gazette* – 25401/4333

Henry Evelyn Wood
19th October 1858 (VC No. 289)

Gazetted: 4th September 1860 22419/3257

Rank and Unit: Lieutenant – 17th Lancers

Citation

For having, on the 19th of October, 1858, during Action at Sindwaho, when in command of a Troop of the 3rd Light Cavalry, attacked with much gallantry, almost single handed, a body of Rebels who had made a stand, whom he routed. Also, for having subsequently, near Siudhora, gallantly advanced with a Duffadar and Sowar of Beatson's Horse, and rescued from a band of robbers, a Potail, Chemmum Singh, whom they had captured and carried off to the Jungles, where they intended to hang him.

Biography

Although christened Henry, for most of his life he was known by his middle name Evelyn.

Evelyn was born on 9th February 1838 at the All Saints Vicarage, Cressing near Braintree in Essex to father Reverend Sir John Page Baronet who was the vicar at Cressing and mother Emma Caroline (née Mitchell).

Evelyn was the youngest of 8 children with sisters; Emma, Katherine, Evelyn, Maria, Anna Caroline and brothers Francis and Charles Page. At the age of 9, Evelyn was sent to school at Marlborough College in Wiltshire where he attended the "Grammar School" until February 1849 when he graduated to the College. After over three years at the college, Evelyn left in Easter 1852 following what he judged to be an unwarranted beating.

A few months after his 14th birthday, Evelyn sat and passed the Naval Cadet Examination on 15th April 1852 and joined his first ship *HMS Victory* a month later on 15th May. This posting only lasted for five days and on 20th May Evelyn was transferred to *HMS Queen* commanded by Captain Charles Wise, which had just returned from the Mediterranean.

On 2nd July 1852, Evelyn's uncle Captain Frederick Thomas Mitchell took over command of *HMS Queen*. At the end of 1853, *HMS Queen* joined the rest of the fleet at Constantinople and in January 1854 sailed into the Euxine Sea in response to the destruction of the Turkish fleet at Sinope by the Russian fleet. In April 1854, *HMS Queen* was involved in the bombardment of Odessa and on 15th April 1854, Evelyn was certified as a Midshipman. From May to August 1854, *HMS Queen* was on patrol off Sevastopol, helping to prevent the Russian navy leave the

Figure 267. Henry Evelyn Wood

harbour and on 14th to 15th September supported the disembarking of troops at Eupatoria.

On 1st October 1854, Evelyn was one of the men taken from various ships to form the Naval Brigade, commanded by Captain Stephen Lushington from *HMS Albion* in response to the request from Lord Raglan for reinforcements. *HMS Firebrand* collected the volunteers from the fleet and delivered them to Balaklava the next day, Evelyn was assigned to Captain William Peel's brigade and it was with his squadron of the Naval Brigade that he served during the campaign on the Crimean peninsula. The brigade was involved in manning guns for the bombardment of Sevastopol and it was on 17th October 1854 that Evelyn volunteered with Captain Peel's Aide-de-Camp midshipman Edward St John Daniel to bring up powder for the guns. During this action Evelyn was wounded, Daniel was later awarded the Victoria Cross for this action. On 5th November 1854, Evelyn took part in the Battle of Inkerman as commander of a gun battery. On 2nd April 1855, Evelyn was appointed as acting Aide-de-Camp to Captain Peel. During the 2nd bombardment of Sevastopol on 9th April 1855, Evelyn helped rebuild the defences around his battery during heavy enemy fire. During the assault on the Redan on 18th June 1855, Evelyn was part of a ladder party and was the only Naval Brigade officer to reach the defences of the Redan and place his ladder; during the action he was seriously wounded. For the above three actions, Captain Lushinton recommended Evelyn for the Victoria Cross, however this was inexplicably not granted.

Following the sounding of the retreat after the failed attack on the Redan, Evelyn was brought back to the British lines where the doctors wanted to amputate his left arm due to the severe nature of his wound. Evelyn refused this treatment and was transported, in Lord Raglan's personal carriage (which the Lord had placed at his disposal) to *HMS Queen* which was in harbour at Kazatch. On 10th July 1855, Evelyn was sent to the hospital at Therapia on the Bosporus and on 19th July boarded *SS Great Britain* for transport back to England, however, after *SS Great Britain* sprang a leak he was transferred to *HMS Perseverance* and arrived back at the family home in Essex sometime in early August.

Evelyn resigned from the navy on 7th September and wishing to continue serving in the war in the Crimea enlisted in the army as a Cornet with the 13th Light Dragoons[849] on the same day at Dorchester. Having previously requested a posting to the regiment serving in the Crimea, Evelyn was one of two Cornets sent East at the request for replacements, after leaving England on 3rd January 1856 he arrived at Scutari on 22nd January. On 1st February 1856, Evelyn purchased the commission of Lieutenant in the 13th Light Dragoons.[850] Evelyn was admitted to the hospital at Scutari on 21st February suffering from typhoid and pneumonia and the doctors gave little hope for his survival. Having been informed of his terminal condition, Evelyn's parents set sail from England and arrived at Constantinople on 19th March where his mother immediately set about managing his treatment and nursing. On 15th April, despite the advice of his doctors, Evelyn and his parents boarded *SS Great Western* for the return to England and after a brief stop at Malta arrived at Folkestone on 1st May 1856. For his service in the war, Evelyn was awarded the Crimean Medal with clasps for Inkerman and Sevastopol and the Turkish Crimean Medal. For his service as a midshipman during the war in Crimea, Evelyn was appointed by the French Government as a Knight 5th Class of the Imperial Order of the Legion of Honour on 2nd August 1856.[851]

Evelyn's recovery was a slow process, he spent some time in France during his recuperation and it was not until 31st December 1856 that he rejoined his regiment at Cahir in Ireland. During his time in Ireland, Evelyn was experiencing difficulties in meeting the expenses of life as an officer in a cavalry regiment and in May, while stationed at Newbridge, considered a transfer to an Infantry Regiment or indeed service with the French Foreign Legion in order to reduce his cost of living.

However, with the outbreak of mutiny in India, Evelyn's attitude changed and he eagerly sought a place in a regiment to serve in India. On 7th August 1857, Evelyn instructed an agent in London to arrange a regimental transfer and took a three month leave of absence to study at a Military College in Richmond. Soon after his arrival back in Ireland, Evelyn received an offer to join the 17th Lancers who were on standby for deployment to India and on 9th October 1857, he transferred to the 17th Lancers retaining his rank as Lieutenant[852] and joined his new regiment at Cork. Evelyn immediately set sail, with his regiment, on board *SS Great Britain* bound for India and landed at Bombay on 21st December, soon afterwards they moved to Kirkee near Poona where they spent the next few weeks awaiting the delivery of their horses.

On 3rd April 1858, Evelyn was appointed to the 5th Class of the Imperial Order of the Medjidie by the Turkish Government for his service as a midshipman during the Crimean War.[853]

On 25th May 1858, Evelyn was assigned to the troop of Captain Sir William Gordon and was despatched to Mhow, a journey of over 500 miles, which they reached on 20th July. Evelyn, now in command of a troop of the 3rd Light Infantry, was part of a force in pursuit of the forces of rebel leader Tantia Topi, which were engaged on several occasions. It was during a battle near the village of Sindwah on 19th October 1858 that Evelyn performed the deeds for which he was later awarded the Victoria Cross; his citation also makes reference to a second deed at Siudhara where he rescued a loyal merchant from the rebels. On 9th November 1858, while recovering from a bout of illness, Evelyn was appointed as staff officer to Colonel Benson, within the role he also acted as interpreter and Bazaar Master. Evelyn was appointed to the role of Brigade-Major, with Somerset's Brigade on 12th January 1859. Evelyn was part of the force that continued to pursue Tantia Topi until his eventual capture on 7th April 1859 and his execution by hanging on 18th April 1859. For his service during the mutiny, Evelyn was awarded the Indian Mutiny Medal without clasp.

On 13th May 1859, Evelyn rejoined the 17th Lancers at Gwalior, however after reaching Mhow on 11th June he discovered that he had been appointed as Brigade-Major to the Irregular Cavalry known as "Beatson's Horse" and commanded by Colonel William Ferguson Beatson. Evelyn passed examinations at Bombay on 15th October, to obtain his qualification as an interpreter and soon after returning to the regiment was given command of "Beatson's Horse" on 1st December 1859. Evelyn was involved with the regiment in operations against bandits in the Sironj jungle until 4th October 1860 when he handed over command of the regiment to Captain Martin. On 24th October 1860 Evelyn set sail from Calcutta to return to England and arrived at his father's house in Essex on 28th December 1860.

Unfortunately Evelyn was never presented with his Victoria Cross Medal; it was sent to the Commander-in-Chief in

849 *London Gazette* – 21778/3362
850 *London Gazette* – 21845/366 – paid for by his uncle Vice-Chancellor Sir William Page Wood
851 *London Gazette* – 21909/2700

852 *London Gazette* – 22049/3356
853 *London Gazette* – 22122/1738

India but arrived after his departure for England. The medal was returned to the War Office and subsequently forwarded to Evelyn via Registered Post.

Evelyn attended a Military Medical Board in London during January 1861 which concluded that with his recurring ear problems he should not return to duty in India for at least two years. Evelyn purchased a commission as Captain in the 17th Lancers on 16th April 1861.[854] In September 1861, Evelyn went to stay with Captain Lendy at Sunbury on Thames to study for the entrance examination to the army Staff College, in early 1862 he spent two months in Heidelberg as part of his studies and took his examinations in July 1862. On 19th August 1862, Evelyn received a brevet promotion to the rank of Major.[855] Having passed the entrance examination, Evelyn had to overcome one more hurdle before he could enter the Staff College. The rules dictated that only one officer from a regiment could attend the college at any one time and as an officer from the 17th Lancers was already at the college Evelyn had to change regiments, he transferred by way of exchange to the 73rd Regiment of Foot on 21st October 1862.[856] Evelyn entered the Staff College at Camberley in January 1863 and after graduating in December 1864 was appointed as Aide-de-Camp to General William Napier, commander of the Dublin Division.

On 10th November 1865, Evelyn transferred by way of exchange to the 17th Regiment of Foot.[857]

After General Napier was appointed to the post of Governor General Military Education on 31st March 1866, Evelyn relinquished his position as the General's Aide-de-Camp and returned to his regiment stationed at Aldershot. Due to his ill health from double pneumonia, the army Medical Board would not let Evelyn join his regiment at Aldershot until 30th June 1866 and before he could get into his regimental duties he was appointed as Deputy Assistant Quartermaster General in charge of the Instructional Kitchen of Cookery. This appointment was short lived as on 19th August 1866, Evelyn was appointed as Brigade-Major to the North Camp at Aldershot, under the command of General Sir Alfred Horsford.

In December 1866, Evelyn joined General Horsford at Dublin in Ireland following rumours of a pending Fenian Rebellion, however with little activity the pair returned to Aldershot in March 1867.

Despite her family's objections to a mixed marriage (he was Protestant and his wife to be was Catholic) Evelyn was married to Mary Paulina Anne (née Southwell) on 19th September 1867.

The couple would have six children, three sons; Evelyn Fitzgerald Mitchell born on 16th November 1869, Charles Mitchell Aloysius born on 2nd April 1873 and Arthur Herbert born on 26th April 1877; and three daughters, Anna Paulina Mary, Marcella Caroline Mary and Victoria Eugene Mary.

On 14th November 1868, Evelyn was appointed as Deputy Assistant Adjutant General to the South Camp at Aldershot. With his recurring bouts of ill health, Evelyn thought that it would be prudent to prepare for a life outside of the army and enrolled as a Law Student with the Middle Temple in April 1869. On 22nd June 1870, Evelyn advanced his position within the regiment by the purchase of a commission as Major at half pay.[858] Evelyn transferred by way of exchange to the 90th Regiment of Foot on 29th October 1871[859] and joined his new regiment at Stirling Castle. In the spring of 1872, Evelyn returned to Aldershot where he performed the role of Commandant of the School of Instruction for Auxiliary Forces. On 19th January 1873, after over ten year's service as a brevet Major, Evelyn received a brevet promotion to the rank of Lieutenant-Colonel.[860] In August 1873, Evelyn was appointed as Deputy Assistant Quartermaster General at Cannock Chase, on the staff of General Sir Daniel Lysons.

On 12th September 1873, Evelyn set sail from Liverpool for the Gold Coast to take part in the third Anglo-Ashanti war, having been appointed to special service on the Force commanded by Sir Garnet Wolseley. The force arrived at Cape Coast Castle on 2nd October 1873 and Evelyn was assigned to the command of the Old Dutch Fort at Elmina. Evelyn saw action at Essainan on 15th October and at Faisowah on 27th November and towards the end of the year raised an irregular native regiment, known as "Wood's Regiment". Evelyn took part in the Battle of Amoaful on 31st January 1874 where he was wounded by a nail head fired into his chest and the Battle of Ordahsu on 4th February following which the city of Coomassie was occupied. Peace was concluded with the treaty of Fommanah which was signed on 13th February 1874. For his service during the war, Evelyn received several mentions in despatches and was awarded the Ashantee Medal with clasp for Coomassie. During March 1874, Evelyn returned to England on board *SS Manitoban* and was granted three months leave to recover his health.

Evelyn was appointed as an Ordinary Member 3rd Class (Companion) of the Military Division of the Most Honourable Order of the Bath on 31st March 1874[861] and on the next day received a brevet promotion to the rank of Colonel.[862]

854 *London Gazette* – 22502/1616
855 *London Gazette* – 22654/4111
856 *London Gazette* – 22673/4990
857 *London Gazette* – 23035/5247

858 *London Gazette* – 23626/3041
859 *London Gazette* – 23789/4387
860 *London Gazette* – 23947/587
861 *London Gazette* – 24082/1921
862 *London Gazette* – 24082/1924

At the end of his leave, Evelyn expected to join the regimental headquarters at Dover, however, his commanding officer felt that there was no need for a full Colonel at HQ so on 1st July 1874 he took up duties at the Depot in Hamilton. At some time during 1874, Evelyn qualified as a Barrister with the Middle Temple. On 10th September 1874, Evelyn was appointed as the Superintending Officer of Garrison Instruction at Aldershot Camp a position that he would hold until 27th March 1876. Evelyn was appointed as Assistant Quartermaster General at Aldershot on 23rd April 1876 a post that he would hold until 1st February 1878. In August 1877, Evelyn was offered the position of Commandant of the Military College at Sandhurst by the Governor General William Napier. After much deliberation Evelyn declined the offer as his regiment was at the top of the list for foreign deployment and he still wished to command a brigade. On 11th January 1878, Evelyn's regiment set sail for South Africa to take part in the 9th Xhosa (Gaika) War;[863] as the regiment had its full complement of senior officers and with Evelyn being the most senior, he did not sail with the regiment. Evelyn's frustration was short lived as he was assigned to the force on "Special Service" and set sail a month later, arriving at East London on 4th March 1878. By the time Evelyn arrived in the Cape Colony the initial Transkei Campaign had been concluded, however the Gaika tribe were still causing trouble in the Buffalo Range of the Amatola Mountains and he was placed in command of a column of 3,000 men to conduct operations against them. Evelyn successfully commanded the column in operations until the threat was eliminated by 27th May 1878, he was mentioned in despatches for his actions.

Having returned to King Williams Town, Evelyn was appointed to the command of the Natal Column on 26th June 1878 with orders to proceed to Utrecht in the Natal. After a journey of over 500 miles, which required the crossing of over 100 un-bridged rivers the column arrived at Utrecht on 17th September 1878 and following orders moved to Luneberg on 16th October to provide protection to the German settlers who had been ordered to leave by the Zulu chief Cetshwayo.

In October 1878, Evelyn was appointed as the Political Agent for North Zululand and Swaziland by the High Commissioner and on 13th November 1878, he was promoted to the rank of Lieutenant-Colonel and appointed to the command of the regiment.[864]

Following incidents on the border between Natal and Zululand the High Commissioner Sir Henry Bartle Frere issued an ultimatum to the Zulu chief Cetshwayo on 11th December 1878. On 16th December 1878, Evelyn was appointed to the command of the 4th Column, a force of just over 2,000 men, and on 6th January in anticipation of the war crossed the Blood River into Zululand. When the ultimatum expired on 10th January 1879, without a positive response from the Zulu nation, the Anglo-Zulu war had begun. Evelyn's force proceeded along the Umvolosi River valley and on 24th January faced down a force of about 20,000 Zulu's, who on seeing the organisation of the British troops refused to engage. On 31st January the force established a position on Kambula Hill where they remained awaiting reinforcements and transportation; on 14th March Evelyn despatched some officers to the Orange Free State to purchase some wagons. On 28th March, the column suffered a defeat from a vastly superior force of Zulu at Hlobane Mountain with many losses, however on the next day they defeated the Zulu's at Kambula.

Evelyn was appointed to the local rank of Brigadier-General on 3rd April 1879.

On 23rd June 1879, Evelyn was appointed as an ordinary member 2nd Class (Knight Commander) of the Most Honourable Order of the Bath.[865]

Evelyn with his column, now renamed the "Flying Column" led the advance and took part in the decisive Battle of Ulundi (the Zulu capital) on 4th July 1879 which effectively ended the war. On 18th July 1879, Evelyn took leave of the "Flying Column" and proceeded to Maritzburg from where a few days later he set sail on his return to England, landing at Portsmouth on 26th August. For his service during the wars in the Cape Colony, Evelyn was awarded the South Africa Medal with clasp 1877-8-9, denoting the years that he served.

Evelyn received a temporary brevet promotion to the rank of Brigadier-General (to be effective while serving on the staff in Ireland) and was placed on half pay on 15th December 1879[866] and assumed command of the Belfast District on 22nd December. The above appointment was strange as on 29th October 1879, Evelyn had been offered and accepted the command of the Chatham District.

Evelyn received a temporary brevet promotion to the rank of Brigadier General on 9th January 1880[867] (to be effective while in command of the Chatham District) and took up his command on 12th January 1880.

At the request of Queen Victoria, Evelyn and his wife accompanied Her Imperial Majesty Empress Eugénie of France on a visit to South Africa to visit the site of her son's death. Prince Imperial Louis Napoleon was killed in action on 1st June 1879

---

863 This was part of the Cape Frontier Wars also known as Africa's 100 years war.
864 *London Gazette* – 24651/6696

865 *London Gazette* – 24737/4086
866 *London Gazette* – 24792/7416–7417
867 *London Gazette* – 24799/102

during the Zulu War. The party set sail from Southampton on board *SS German* on 25th March 1880 and arrived at Capetown on 16th April. Following a tour of the places where the Prince Imperial had been stationed and the place of his death, the party left Durban on board the *SS Asiatic* on 23rd June and after transhipping to the *SS Trojan* at Algoa Bay on 26th June set sail for England where they arrived at Plymouth on 27th July 1880.

On his return from the visit to South Africa, Evelyn resumed his duties as commander of the Chatham District.

Following the outbreak of the 1st Boer War (Transvaal War) on 16th December 1880, Evelyn was requested by the War Office to return to South Africa and serve on the staff of Major-General Sir George Pomeroy Colley. Evelyn received his letter of service on 6th January and on 15th January 1881, received a brevet promotion to the rank of Brigadier-General while serving on the staff of the army in South Africa.[868] Evelyn set sail for the Cape colony on 14th January and after landing at Cape Town on 7th February arrived at Government House in Durban on 9th February 1881. Major-General Sir George Pomeroy Colley was killed in action at the Battle of Majuba Hill on 27th February and on the following day Evelyn was sworn in as acting Governor of Natal and Administrator of the Transvaal and received a brevet promotion to the local rank of Major-General, while serving in Natal and the Transvaal.[869] Ironically, Stephanus Johannes Paulus Kruger (known as Paul Kruger) the Boer Leader had agreed the previous day to a negotiated peace settlement suggested by Lord Kimberley. Evelyn signed an armistice to end the war on 6th March and on 23rd March a peace treaty was signed with Peter Kruger at O'Neil's Cottage which officially ended the war.

On 8th April 1881, Evelyn was appointed as a Commissioner together with Sir John Henry deVilliers, and the High Commissioner Sir Hercules Robinson to enquire and report on all matters relating to the future settlement of the Transvaal Territory.[870] The result of the commission's work was the Pretoria Convention, which was signed on 3rd August 1881 and ratified by the Transvaal Government on 25th October ceded self government of the Transvaal to the Boers under British suzerainty.

Evelyn was promoted to the rank of Major-General on 30th November 1881.[871]

In December 1881, Evelyn left South Africa and resumed his duties at Chatham on 14th February 1882, although he was not formally appointed to the command until 17th February 1882.[872]

On 17th February 1882, Evelyn was appointed as an Ordinary Member 1st Class (Knight Grand Cross) of the Most Distinguished Order of St Michael and St George.[873]

Soon after his return to England, Evelyn was offered the post of Governor of the Isle of Man by Sir William Vernon Harcourt which he regrettably declined.

Following a nationalist uprising against the Government of Khedive Tewfic Pasha (governor of Egypt and Sudan), Evelyn left England on 4th August 1882 on board *SS Catalonia* in command of the 4th Brigade, part of the British Expeditionary Force sent to Egypt. Evelyn arrived at Alexandria on 15th August and set up his quarters in a convent school at Ramleh. The 4th Brigade was assigned by Major-General Garnet Wolseley to the task of keeping the insurgents under control in and around Alexandria and was involved in the capture of Kafr Dowar on 19th August and the port of Damietta on 24th September 1882. For his service during the Anglo-Egypt War, Evelyn was awarded the Khedives Star, was appointed to the 2nd Class of the Imperial Order of the Medjidie and received mentions in despatches and the thanks of both Houses of Parliament.

Following his return from Egypt Evelyn was appointed to the command of troops in the Chatham District on 1st November 1882.[874]

On 29th November, Evelyn received a letter from Lord Granville, passing on the wish from the Prime Minister William Ewart Gladstone that he proceed to Egypt to recreate the Egyptian Army which had been disbanded after the nationalist rebellion. Evelyn accepted the appointment and after joining Lord Dufferin in Cairo was appointed as Sirdar (commander-in-chief) of the Egyptian Army on 21st December 1882 and given a budget of £200,000 to recreate the army. After only three months, Evelyn had a force ready to be inspected by the Khedive. In June 1883, Evelyn was granted two months leave to recover from illness and left for Suez in mid-July, however, with news of an outbreak of cholera which threatened to turn into an epidemic he returned to Cairo to help manage the situation. In the middle of August, with the cholera outbreak now under control, Evelyn was finally able to return to England on leave.

On his return to Egypt, Evelyn was appointed to the command of the Sudan Bureau by the Consul General and also acted as his Staff Officer for Political Affairs.

On 13th March 1884, during the Mahdist War in the Sudan, Major-General Charles George Gordon was besieged in Khartoum and in August, the British Government bowing to public pressure, finally agreed to send a relief force to rescue Gordon.

868 *London Gazette* – 24924/180
869 *London Gazette* – 24947/1072
870 *London Gazette* – 24960/1734
871 *London Gazette* – 25042/6215
872 *London Gazette* – 25074/709

873 *London Gazette* – 25073/653
874 *London Gazette* – 25166/4983

General Garnet Wolseley was appointed to the command of the relief force and on 15th September 1884 Evelyn was appointed to the command of communications for the Nile Expedition, with the brevet rank of Major-General.[875] General Wolseley's force arrived at Khartoum on 28th January 1885, only to find that two days earlier the city had fallen and General Gordon and his men had been slain. Now without purpose, the relief force retired back along the Nile towards Egypt and Evelyn and his men managed the logistics of a safe withdrawal. For his service during the Nile Expedition, Evelyn was awarded the Egypt Medal (1882–89) with clasp for The Nile 1884–85, he was also mentioned in despatches.

On 31st March 1885, Evelyn handed over command of the Egyptian Army to Sir Francis Grenfell and in recognition of his service in the role was appointed as a member 1st class (Grand Cordon) of the Order of the Medjidie on 8th July 1885.[876]

Evelyn returned to England on 19th June 1885, however, it was not until 1st April 1886 that he was appointed to the Staff in command of the troops in the Eastern District.[877] During his time at Colchester, Evelyn spent much of his time helping Lord Wolseley draft and implement changes to modernise the army. On the recommendation of Lord Wolseley, Evelyn was appointed to the command of Aldershot on 1st January 1889 with the local rank of Lieutenant-General.[878] Evelyn was promoted to the rank of Lieutenant-General on 1st April 1890.[879]

On 31st May 1891, Evelyn was appointed as an Ordinary Member 1st Class (Knight Grand Cross) of the Military Division of the Most Honourable Order of the Bath.[880]

During his time in command at Aldershot, Evelyn implemented many reforms which included improvements to the accommodation, the method of training, an increase in manoeuvres on the Berkshire Downs and improved marksmanship. His early success in achieving improvements was demonstrated by the response from the Adjutant-General Viscount Wolseley to the suggestion that Evelyn consider the Command of the Army in Bombay when he stated in a letter *"… it would be a real calamity to the Army that should you leave it."*

On 9th October 1893, Evelyn was appointed as Quartermaster General to the Army.[881] Two months after his appointment, Evelyn was offered the position of Governor of Malta, which he declined. During his tenure as Quartermaster General, Evelyn was responsible for the War Department purchasing a large plot of land on Salisbury Plain to be used for Army exercises and manoeuvres. Evelyn greatly improved the transportation of the British soldier by negotiating new rail and shipping contracts. On 26th March 1895, Evelyn was promoted to the rank of General.[882]

In 1897, Evelyn was awarded the Queen Victoria Diamond Jubilee Medal.

Evelyn was appointed as Deputy Lieutenant to the county of Essex on 10th August 1897.[883]

On 1st October 1897, Evelyn was appointed as Adjutant-General to the Army, replacing a fellow Victoria Cross recipient General Sir Redvers Henry Buller.[884]

At the outbreak of the 2nd Boer War (South African War) on 7th November 1899 Evelyn was responsible for the mobilisation of the troops. Despite volunteering for command in the war zone, Evelyn was not permitted to take an active part in the war in which three of his sons were serving. On 30th November 1900, Lord Wolseley retired as Commander-in-Chief of the Army and for just over a month Evelyn performed the role in an acting capacity until 3rd January 1901 when Lord Roberts took up the command.

Like many of his contemporaries, Evelyn was devastated by the death of Queen Victoria on 22nd January 1901 and took part in her funeral procession on 2nd February.

On 1st February 1901, Evelyn was asked by the Military Secretary if he would consider serving in South Africa under Lord Kitchener. Although Kitchener was junior in rank Evelyn said that he would serve as his country saw fit. This did not happen due to a telegram from Lord Kitchener which stated that while he would be delighted to serve under Sir Evelyn Wood, if he were sent out, he felt that he ought not to have him under his command.

On 1st October 1901, Evelyn was appointed as a General on the Staff with command of the 2nd Army Corps.[885]

In celebration of the new king coming to the throne, Evelyn was awarded the King Edward VII Coronation Medal in 1902.

Evelyn was promoted to the rank of Field Marshal on 28th April 1903.[886]

After nearly 50 years service, Evelyn retired from the army on 31st December 1904 at the age of 66.

In his retirement, Evelyn continued to pursue his passion for hunting and riding with hounds and also continued his writing

During his service in the army Evelyn had written and had published several books; *"Cavalry in the Waterloo Campaign"* (1895), *"The Crimea in 1854 & 1894"* (1896) and *"Achievements of Cavalry"* (1897). Following his retirement Evelyn was even

875 *London Gazette* – 25431/122
876 *London Gazette* – 25489/3178
877 *London Gazette* – 25568/1281
878 *London Gazette* – 25882/7079
879 *London Gazette* – 26040/2100
880 *London Gazette* – 26167/2921
881 *London Gazette* – 26446/5554

882 *London Gazette* – 26622/2632
883 *London Gazette* – 26884/4674
884 *London Gazette* – 26895/5321
885 *London Gazette* – 27360/6400
886 *London Gazette* – 27547/2693

more prolific writing the following books in addition to numerous contributions to military magazines; *"From Midshipman to Field Marshal"* (1906) his autobiography (from which much of the detail of this biography is taken), *"The Revolt in Hindustan"* (1908), *"Our Fighting Services and how they made the Empire"* (1916) and *"Winnowed Memories"* (1917) – he also edited the book *"British Battles on Land and Sea"* (1915).

On 16th November 1907, Evelyn was appointed as Colonel of the Royal Horse Guards and the ceremonial role of Gold Stick (bodyguard to the monarch).[887] Evelyn was appointed as Chairman of the City of London Territorial Force Association on 14th January 1908.[888] On 1st April 1908, Evelyn was appointed as Honorary Colonel of the 5th Battalion of the Essex Regiment[889] and Honorary Colonel of the Inns of Court Officer Training Corps.[890]

In celebration of the new King attaining the throne, Evelyn was awarded the King George V Coronation Medal in 1911.

Evelyn was appointed as a Constable of the Tower of London on 11th March 1911,[891] a position that he would hold until 23rd July 1919.[892]

Evelyn died at his home in Harlow, Essex on 2nd December 1919 at the age of 81 and was buried with full military honours at the Aldershot Military Cemetery four days later.

Evelyn's Victoria Cross Medal is on public display at the National Army Museum, Chelsea in London.

Figure 267a. Grave of Henry Evelyn Wood

887 *London Gazette* – 28080/7683
888 *London Gazette* – 28099/319
889 *London Gazette* – 28213/234
890 *London Gazette* – 28271/5468
891 *London Gazette* – 28477/2320
892 *London Gazette* – 31488/9948

Charles Craufurd Fraser
31st December 1858 (VC No. 290)

Gazetted: 8th November 1860 22445/4126

Rank and Unit: Major – 7th Hussars

Citation

For conspicuous and cool gallantry, on the 31st December, 1858, in having volunteered, at great personal risk, and under a sharp fire of musketry, to swim to the rescue of Captain Stisted, and some men of the 7th Hussars, who were in imminent danger of being drowned in the River Raptee, while in pursuit of the rebels. Major Eraser succeeded in this gallant service, although at the time partially disabled, not having recovered from a severe wound received while leading a Squadron in a charge against some fanatics, in the Action of Nuwabgunge, on the 13th June, 1858.

Biography

Charles was born on 31st August 1829 in Fitzwilliam Street, Dublin to father James John 3rd Baronet of Leadclune, who had served on the staff of Wellington at the battle of Waterloo, and Charlotte Ann (née Craufurd). He was baptised on 15 October 1829 at St. Peter's Church, Dublin and was rebaptised on 13 October 1832 at Hampreston, Dorset.

Charles was the 2nd of three sons, with an older brother William Augustus born on 10th February 1826 and a younger brother James Keith born in 1832.

After completing his education at Eton, Charles began his career in the army just after his 18th birthday when on 3rd December 1847 he purchased a commission as Cornet in the 7th Hussars,[893] his father's former regiment. On 14th June 1850, Charles advanced his position in the regiment when he purchased the commission of Lieutenant.[894] Charles again advanced his position in the regiment when on 21st April 1854 he purchased a commission as Captain.[895] After having spent nearly ten years on home service, with the outbreak of the mutiny in India, Charles and the regiment were about to be deployed on foreign and active service.

On 9th August 1857, the regiment handed over their horses at Aldershot and departed by rail for Canterbury where the regiment was brought up to strength by drafting in over 180 men from 15 different regiments.

Now up to strength, the regiment boarded *HMS Lightning* at Gravesend and on 27th August set sail for India; after a three

893 *London Gazette* – 20802/4480
894 *London Gazette* – 21104/1665
895 *London Gazette* – 21545/1253

Figure 268. Charles Craufurd Fraser

month journey due to adverse trade winds they landed at Calcutta on 27th November 1857. From Calcutta the regiment moved to Allahabad where they waited to be allocated horses from the depot at Calcutta. During the wait at Allahabad, Charles served for a short time as Orderly Officer to the recently arrived Commander-in-Chief Sir Colin Campbell and was present at the affair at Munseata on 5th January 1858.

On 18th January 1858, after training up the horses from Calcutta, the regiment moved off towards Cawnpore, crossing the Ganges in early February.

While one half of the regiment performed escort duties on the road to Cawnpore, Charles and the remainder of the regiment were attached to the Cavalry Division commanded by General Sir James Hope Grant and took part in the Battle of Meeangunge on 23rd February 1858. On 25th February 1858, the regiment was part of a force commanded by Sir James Outram which took part in the Battle of Alum Bagh, a fortification to the south of Lucknow. Still with Sir James Hope Grant's cavalry division, Charles and the regiment took part in the siege of Lucknow from 2nd March until the city was recaptured on 21st March 1858. During the attack on Lucknow the regiment, on 19th March, were responsible for the capture of the Musa Bagh fortification. Following the fall of Lucknow, Charles and the regiment remained with the force of General Sir Hope Grant and pursued the mutineers across the Oudh province. Charles took part in the action at Barree on 13th April and the Battle of Nuwabgunge on 13th June 1858 where he was severely wounded in the hand. For his conduct during the Battle of Nuwabgunge, Charles was mentioned in the despatch of Sir Hope Grant for "most conspicuous gallantry" and on 20th July 1858 he received a brevet promotion to the rank of Major.[896]

Due to the severity of his wound, Charles did not return to duty with the regiment until December 1858 and it was

soon afterwards on 31st December, during the Battle on the River Raptee that he performed the deeds for which he would later be awarded the Victoria Cross; despite being somewhat disabled by his wounded hand. Charles continued in the pursuit of the rebels until they fled into Nepal and the campaign came to an end. For his service during the mutiny, Charles was awarded the Indian Mutiny Medal with clasp for Lucknow.

Although the bulk of the regiment was to remain in India for several years, Charles was part of a detachment that returned to England in March 1859.

Charles was once again advanced within the regiment when he purchased the commission of Major on 13th May 1859[897] and on 16th August 1859, was transferred to the 11th Hussars by way of an exchange.[898]

In addition to the Victoria Cross, Charles was also awarded the Royal Humane Society Medal for his action on the Raptee River. The Royal Humane Society Treasurer Benjamin Hawkes recommended the award of a silver gilt medal on 11th January 1860 and this was later approved. The award of the silver gilt medal is extremely rare with only one other known recipient; Midshipman Charles Lucas, the first Victoria Cross recipient.

Charles was presented with his Victoria Cross Medal on 9th November 1860 by Queen Victoria at a ceremony held at Windsor Castle.

Charles purchased the commission of Lieutenant-Colonel on 18th January 1861[899] and was appointed to the command of the 11th Hussars. On 18th January 1866, having completed the period of qualifying service as Lieutenant-Colonel, Charles received a brevet promotion to the rank of Colonel.[900] In 1866, Charles was deployed with his regiment to India.

In October 1867, Charles was appointed as Commandant to the Headquarters of the force of Sir Robert Napier which was sent on the campaign to Abyssinia. During the war, Charles was present at the Battle of Arogie Ravine on 9th April 1868 and the decisive Battle of Magdala on 15th April. For his service during the war, Charles was awarded the Abyssinian War Medal (1867–68) and was mentioned in despatches for "his unceasing vigilance". At the end of the war, Charles returned to England, landing at Portsmouth in mid-June.

Charles was appointed as an Ordinary Member 3rd Class (Companion) of the Military Division of the Most Honourable Order of the Bath on 14th August 1868.[901]

---

896 *London Gazette* – 22201/4854

897 *London Gazette* – 22262/1940
898 *London Gazette* – 22298/3111
899 *London Gazette* – 22472/201
900 *London Gazette* – 23067/714
901 *London Gazette* – 23412/4511

On 25th July 1870, Charles was promoted to the rank of Major-General. On 16th July 1873 Charles handed over command of the 11th Hussars to Lieutenant-General Arthur Lyttleton-Annesley after having been appointed as Aide-de-Camp to His Royal Highness the Duke of Cambridge a position that he would hold until October 1877. In 1880 Charles was appointed as Inspector-General of Cavalry in Ireland, which he held until 1884. Charles was appointed as Inspector-General of Cavalry in Great Britain on 1st April 1884 and was posted to Aldershot in command of the Cavalry Brigade.[902]

Charles was elected as a Conservative Member of Parliament for the North Lambeth constituency in the general election on 15th December 1885[903] and would serve as their MP until 1892.

On 25th June 1886 Charles was appointed as Colonel to the 8th Hussars.[904] Charles was promoted to the rank of Lieutenant-General on 1st October 1886.[905] After 43 years of service, Charles was retired on full pay on 1st January 1890.[906]

On 30th May 1891, Charles was appointed as an Ordinary Member 2nd Class (Knight Commander) of the Military Division of the Most Honourable Order of the Bath.[907]

Charles died at his home in Sloan Street, London on 7th June 1895 at the age of 65 and was buried in Brompton Cemetery.

The location of Charles's Victoria Cross Medal is unknown.

Figure 268a. Grave of Charles Craufurd Fraser

902 *London Gazette* – 25329/1305
903 *London Gazette* – 25541/6135
904 *London Gazette* – 25604/3189
905 *London Gazette* – 25637/5160
906 *London Gazette* – 26010/8
907 *London Gazette* – 26167/2921

Henry Addison
2nd January 1859 (VC No. 291)

Gazetted: 2nd September 1859 22303/3302

Rank and Unit: Private No.3232 – 43rd Regiment of Foot

Citation

For gallant conduct on the 2nd of January, 1859, near Kurrereah, in defending, against a large force, and saving the life of Lieutenant Osborn, Political Agent, who had fallen on the ground wounded. Private Addison received two dangerous wounds, and lost a leg, in this gallant service.

Biography

Henry was born in February 1821 at the village of Bardwell in Suffolk to father David and mother Mary Anne (née Stevens), he was the youngest of four sons with brother George born in 1809, David born in 1813 and William born in 1816.

On 9th February 1841, Henry left his job as a labourer and enlisted in the army with the 94th Regiment of Foot at Bury St Edmunds in Suffolk.

On 10th March 1841, Henry was despatched to join his regiment in Indian where he would serve with them for the next 13 years, being stationed at Trichinopoly, Madras, Calcutta and Cannapore. During this time the only action that Henry experienced was during the suppression of the Moplah Revolt in 1849. Wishing to stay in India and with the 94th due to return to England, Henry transferred to the 43rd Regiment of Foot on 1st March 1854 and joined his new regiment at Fort St George in Madras.

At some stage Henry was married to Charlotte (née Dixon) who had been born in Madras and the couple had a son William who was born in 1859, unfortunately he died on 8th August 1862 after they had returned to England.

Due to being stationed in Madras, the regiment was not immediately involved in the mutiny and it was not until late in 1857 that they became part of the Madras Column and were sent to join the Central India Field Force commanded by Sir Hugh Rose. After a march of over 600 miles the column reached Kamptee on 28th March 1858, by 17th April they had reached Jubbulpore and after completing an overall journey of 1,300 miles arrived at Kalpi on 7th June 1858. Due to the excessive heat, nearly 50 men had died from heatstroke, and the exhaustion of the march the regiment rested for some time at Kalpi where they also waited the passing of the monsoon season. With the improvement of conditions after the monsoon, the regiment continued their journey towards Saugor.

Figure 269. Henry Addison

nearby until the fitting was completed. Henry complied with the Queen's wishes and then returned to Bardwell with his new leg where he lived for the remainder of his life.

Henry died at his home on Up Street, Bardwell on 18th June 1887 at the age of 66 and was buried in St Mary's Churchyard, Bardwell.

Henry's Victoria Cross Medal is on public display at the Royal Green Jackets Museum in Winchester.

Figure 269a. Grave of Henry Addison

It was on 2nd January 1859, in the Punnah jungle near Kurrereah that Henry performed the deeds for which he would later be awarded the Victoria Cross. During the action, Henry received a severe sword wound to his left arm and an even worse wound to his left leg which required a battle field amputation. For his service during the mutiny Henry was awarded the Indian Mutiny Medal without clasp. After having recovered from his wounds and having been fitted with a temporary wooden leg, Henry and his family set sail from Madras in March 1860 and returned to Chatham in England. On 7th August 1860, after 19 years of service all of which was spent in India, Henry was discharged to pension on medical grounds at Chatham. For his service Henry was awarded the Good Conduct and Long Service Medal.

After leaving the army, Henry and his family returned to his home town of Bardwell. Lieutenant Willoughby Osborne (the man whose life Henry saved at Kurrereah) kept in touch with the family for the rest of his life and paid Henry a pension of £20 per year.

Henry was presented with his Victoria Cross Medal on 9th November 1860 by Queen Victoria at an investiture held at Windsor Castle.

Soon after receiving his medal, Henry received a letter from Sir Charles Phipps acting on behalf of Queen Victoria, requesting that Henry order a new artificial leg from Mr Biggs of Leicester Square, in her name and that he should reside in lodgings

Herbert Mackworth Clogstoun
15th January 1859 (VC No. 292)

Gazetted: 21st October 1859 22318/3792

Rank and Unit: Captain – 19th Madras Native Infantry

Citation

For conspicuous bravery in charging the, Rebels into Chichumbah with only eight men of his Regiment (the 2nd Cavalry Hyderabad Contingent), compelling them to re-enter the Town, and finally to abandon their plunder. He was severely wounded himself, and-lost, seven out of the eight men who accompanied him.

Biography

Herbert was born on 13th June 1820 at Port of Spain, Trinidad in the West Indies to father Samuel Matthew and mother Caroline Jane (née Walcott).

On 15th January 1838, some months before his 18th birthday, Herbert joined the army of the Honourable East India Company and was commissioned as an Ensign in the 19th Madras Native Infantry. Herbert was promoted to the rank of Lieutenant on 29th February 1840. In August 1852, Herbert saw his first active service when he was sent as part of a force of reinforcements to the 2nd Anglo-Burmese War. On 29th August 1852, Herbert was promoted to the rank of Captain. Herbert saw service as part of the Madras Division commanded by Brigadier-General S. W. Steel and on 23rd February 1853 received a mention in his despatches. For his service during the war Herbert was awarded the India General Service Medal with clasp for Pegu.

Herbert was married to Mary Julia Blanche (née Mackenzie) on 8th January 1856 at Melison Chapel, Blacktown, Bolarum Cannamore in India. The couple would go on to have five children; Herbert Cunningham Standish born on 24th January 1857, Cuthbert George Wilder born 10th March 1858, Mary Adeline born in 1859, Blanche Margaret Standish born in 1861 and Adeline Grace Hill born in 1862.

On 7th August 1856, Herbert was attached as 2nd in Command of the 2nd Cavalry of the Hyderabad Contingent. It would appear that Herbert remained with some troops of the 2nd Cavalry at their base in Bolarum for most of the mutiny, while the commander Captain A. W. Macintire and the remaining troops were attached to the force of Brigadier General Whitelock.

In November 1858, Herbert and his troops moved to Amraoti where Brigadier Hill was assembling the Berar Field Force to pursue the rebel leader Tantia Topi and protect the Berar frontier.

Figure 270. Herbert Mackworth Clogstoun

Herbert was involved in an action against the rebels in the Gwalighar Hills on 8th December 1858 and for his deeds he received a mention in despatches. It was on 15th January 1859 during action at the village of Chichumbah that Herbert performed the deeds for which he would later be awarded the Victoria Cross; during the action he was seriously wounded. For his service during the mutiny Herbert was awarded the Indian Mutiny Medal without clasp.

Herbert was presented with his Victoria Cross Medal by the General Officer Commanding Madras Lieutenant-General Sir P. Grant, at Madras on 19th January 1860.

On 13th March 1860, Herbert received a brevet promotion to the rank of Major[908] and on 12th September 1861 was appointed to the command of the 2nd Cavalry of the Hyderabad Contingent.

Herbert was killed in action at Hingoli on 6th May 1862, aged 41, and was buried in St George's Cathedral Cemetery in Madras.

His Victoria Cross Medal is on public display at the National Army Museum in Chelsea.

---

908 *London Gazette* – 22366/1058

Walter Cook
15th January 1859 (VC No. 293)

Gazetted: 18th June 1859 22278/2420

Rank and Unit: Private – 42nd Regiment of Foot

Citation

In the action at Maylah Ghaut, on the 15th January, 1859, Brigadier-General Walpole reports that the conduct of Privates Cook and Millar deserves to be particularly pointed out. At the time the fight was the severest, and the few men of the 42nd Regiment were skirmishing so close to the enemy (who were in great numbers), that some of the men were wounded by sword cuts, and the only officer with the 42nd was carried to the rear, severely wounded, and the Color-Serjeant was killed, these soldiers went to the front, took a prominent part in directing the Company, and displayed a courage, coolness, and discipline, which was the admiration of all who witnessed it.

Biography

Walter was born on 18th June 1834 at Cripplegate in London.

On 15th June 1856, the 42nd Regiment of Foot left the Crimea for England arriving at Portsmouth on 24th July and moved to the camp at Aldershot and it is probably at around this time that Walter left his job as a moulder and joined the army.

In August 1857, Walter and the regiment were despatched to India to help with the suppression of the mutiny. They arrived at Calcutta in six transports during October and November 1857 and on 3rd December march to Cawnpore to join the relief force commanded by Sir Colin Campbell. On 6th December 1857, the regiment took part in the Battle of Cawnpore which recaptured the city and two days later joined the force of General Sir James Hope Grant in pursuit of the rebels arriving at Bithoor on 9th December, where they destroyed much of the rebel's artillery and ammunition. Walter and the regiment were part of the force of Sir Colin Campbell which laid siege to Lucknow from 2nd March 1858 until the city was recaptured on 21st March. During the assault on the city the regiment was involved in the actions at the Martinière, Banks Bungalow and Begum Kotee.

In April the regiment moved to Dilkusha where they formed up as part of the Rohilkhand Field Force commanded by Brigadier Walpole. The regiment took part in the Battle of Fort Rooya on 15th April 1858 and the Battle of Bareilly on 5th/6th May. After the capture of Bareilly the regiment formed the town garrison until November 1858 when they moved to the banks of the River Sarda where they were tasked in preventing rebel forces crossing from Oudh into Rohilkhand. It was on 15th January 1859 at Maylah Ghat (a crossing on the River Sarda) that Walter performed the deeds for which he would later be awarded the Victoria Cross. For his service during the mutiny, Walter was awarded the Indian Mutiny Medal with clasp for Lucknow. On 1st September 1859, Walter transferred to the 90th Regiment of Foot.

Walter was presented with his Victoria Cross Medal some time during 1860 while serving in India.

It was while serving with his new regiment that he died some time in 1864, having been drowned in the River Ravi.

There is no record of a place of burial, presumably because he body was never found.

The location of Walter's Victoria Cross Medal is unknown.

Duncan Millar
15th January 1859 (VC No. 294)

Gazetted: 18th June 1859 22278/2420

Rank and Unit: Private No. 1802 – 42nd Regiment of Foot

Citation

In the action at Maylah Ghaut, on the 15th January, 1859, Brigadier-General Walpole reports that the conduct of Privates Cook and Millar deserves to be particularly pointed out. At the time the fight was the severest, and the few men of the 42nd Regiment were skirmishing so close to the enemy (who were in great numbers), that some of the men were wounded by sword cuts, and the only officer with the 42nd was carried to the rear, severely wounded, and the Color-Serjeant was killed, these soldiers went to the front, took a prominent part in directing the Company, and displayed a courage, coolness, and discipline, which was the admiration of all who witnessed it.

Biography

Duncan was born on 19th June 1824 at Kilmarnock in Ayrshire, Scotland.

Three months before his 18th birthday, Duncan left his job as a labourer and enlisted in the army on 19th March 1842 at Glasgow and became a Private in the 64th Regiment of Foot. Duncan's stay with the 64th Regiment was very short lived, as on 1st April 1842 he volunteered and joined the 42nd Regiment of Foot.

In 1843, Duncan began his first overseas deployment when the regiment was sent to Malta to serve as the garrison. After spending just over 4 years at Malta, the regiment was sent to Bermuda in 1847 where they would serve another 4 years as the garrison until 1851 when they were sent to Halifax Nova Scotia. In 1852, Duncan and the regiment returned to England after an overseas tour of almost 9 ½ years. In early 1854, Duncan and the regiment were deployed to the East to take part in the war with Russia.

After landing at Scutari on 9th June 1854, Duncan and the regiment landed on the Crimean Peninsula on 14th September as part of the Anglo/French Expeditionary force. On 20th September 1854 the regiment was involved in the Battle of Alma and afterwards continued their journey south and took part in the siege of Sevastopol. On 25th October 1854, Duncan served with the regiment at the Battle of Balaklava as part of the Highland Brigade. After taking part in the expedition to Kertch where they helped secure the towns of Kertch and Yenical, the regiment

Figure 272. Duncan Millar

returned to the siege lines at Sevastopol until its fall on 9th September 1855. On 15th June 1856, the regiment left the Crimea for England arriving at Portsmouth on 24th July and moved to the camp at Aldershot. For his service in the Crimea, Duncan was awarded the Crimea War Medal with clasps for Alma, Balaklava and Sevastopol as well as the Turkish Crimea Medal.

In August 1857, Duncan and the regiment were despatched to India to help with the suppression of the mutiny. They arrived at Calcutta in six transports during October and November 1857 and on 3rd December marched to Cawnpore to join the relief force commanded by Sir Colin Campbell. On 6th December 1857, the regiment took part in the Battle of Cawnpore which recaptured the city and two days later joined the force of General Sir James Hope Grant in pursuit of the rebels arriving at Bithoor on 9th December, where they destroyed much of the rebel's artillery and ammunition. Walter and the regiment were part of the force of Sir Colin Campbell which laid siege to Lucknow from 2nd March 1858 until the city was recaptured on 21st March. During the assault on the city the regiment was involved in the actions at the Martinière, Banks Bungalow and Begum Kotee.

In April the regiment moved to Dilkusha where they formed up as part of the Rohilkhand Field Force commanded by Brigadier Walpole. The regiment took part in the Battle of Fort Rooya on 15th April 1858 and the Battle of Bareilly on 5th/6th May. After the capture of Bareilly the regiment formed the town garrison until November 1858 when they moved to the banks of the River Sarda where they were tasked in preventing rebel forces crossing from Oudh into Rohilkhand. It was on 15th January 1859 at Maylah Ghat (a crossing on the River Sarda) that Duncan performed the deeds for which he would later be awarded the Victoria Cross. For his service during the mutiny, Duncan was awarded the Indian Mutiny Medal with clasp for Lucknow.

Following the end of the mutiny, Duncan served in the garrison at Bareilly and it was here on 7th April 1860 that he was presented with his Victoria Cross Medal by Brigadier-General Sir R. Walpole.

In March 1861, the regiment left Bareilly for Futtehgur where they were plagued by outbreaks of cholera, to escape the disease they moved to Secundra Bagh at the end of July. At the beginning of December 1861, the regiment was moved to the hill station at Dugshai and it was here on 21st October 1862 that Duncan was declared unfit for further military service due to an impaired constitution as a result of his service in India. Duncan was returned home to England and on 21st July 1863, while a patient at the Royal Victoria Hospital in Netley, after over 21 years of service he was discharged from the army on medical grounds.

At some stage, Duncan was married to Rebecca.

After leaving the army, Duncan returned to Glasgow and it was here on 7th July 1881 at the age of 57 that he died and was buried in the Anderston Burial Ground, Glasgow.

Duncan's Victoria Cross Medal is on public display at the National War Museum in Edinburgh Castle.

George Richardson
27th April 1859 (VC No. 295)

Gazetted: 11th November 1859 22324/4032

Rank and Unit: Private No. 4318 – 34th Regiment of Foot

Citation

At Kewanie, Trans-Gogra, on the 27th of April 1859, for determined courage in having, although severely wounded,—one arm being disabled,—closed with and secured a Rebel Sepoy armed with a loaded revolver.

Biography

George was born on 1st August 1831 at Derrylane, Killashandra in Co. Cavan, Ireland, the youngest son of father John a linen weaver and mother Anne. He was baptised on 19th July 1834 in Kilishandra.

On 4th December 1855, while serving with the Cavan Militia, George volunteered at Dublin to join the British Army and was enlisted as a Private in the 34th Regiment of Foot. On 23rd June 1857, while serving in Edinburgh George was reported as a deserter, being absent without leave and when he returned to the regiment on 18th September he was sentenced to three months imprisonment which he served at Colchester. After completing his prison term, George was sent out to join his regiment who had left for India from Portsmouth on board *HMS Golden Fleece* on 24th August and arrived at Calcutta on 17th October 1857.

Figure 273. George Richardson

As George was not awarded the clasp for Lucknow it is safe to assume that he was not reunited with his regiment until after Lucknow was recaptured on 21st March 1858 – it was probably during April while stationed at Juanpore or Azamgarh that he rejoined the regiment.

On 12th September 1858, the regiment, now part of the Azamgarh Field Force left the town for Fyzabad where they were tasked with preventing the return to Oudh of the rebels who had fled to Nepal. The regiment left Fyzabad on 14th February for the Trans-Gogra district in order to secure two mountain passes that could be used by the returning rebels. The rebels were successfully engaged on 26th and 28th February near Bhootwul and the regiment began their return to Fyzabad. It was on 27th April 1859, at Kewanie, that George performed the deeds for which he would later be awarded the Victoria Cross. During the action George was seriously wounded, with his right arm fractured by a bullet and severe sabre wounds to his left leg and hand. For his service during the mutiny, George was awarded the Indian Mutiny Medal without clasp.

George was presented with his Victoria Cross Medal some time during 1860, while still serving in India.

Due to his wounds, George was sent home to England on the *SS Startled Fawn* and on 2nd August 1860 after only five years of service was discharged from the army on medical grounds.

After leaving the army, George returned to his home town in Ireland and in 1861 he joined the Orange Order.

At some stage George was married to Elizabeth and in 1862 they emigrated to Canada and initially settled in Montreal where George worked as a coachman.

In 1865, in anticipation of a possible Fenian invasion of Canada, George enlisted with the Prince of Wales Rifles, serving at Sandwich in Ontario; at some point he was promoted to the rank of Sergeant. For his military service, George was granted some homestead land near Lindsay in Ontario by the State Government where he settled with his wife Elizabeth.

In 1916, George's house was destroyed by fire and despite his advanced age of 85, he carried his wife out of the house suffering burns which resulted in the partial loss of sight in one eye. Unfortunately, his wife Elizabeth died as a result of the shock of this experience. George's medals were destroyed during the fire, however, in 1918 these were replaced by the War Office.

In 1921, George placed the Canadian wreath on the tomb of the unknown soldier in Arlington Cemetery in Washington, USA.

Due to his military service and continued involvement with the Orange Order, George became a personal friend of the Canadian Defence Minister, Sir Sam Hughes.

George died from pneumonia on 28th January 1923, aged 92, while a patient at the Westminster Township Hospital in London, Ontario and was buried in the Veteran's Section of Prospect Cemetery with full military honours.

George's Victoria Cross Medal is believed to be in the hands of a private collector in Canada.

Figure 273a. Grave of George Richardson

BIBLIOGRAPHY AND SOURCES

Wherever possible I have tried to use contemporary or near contemporary sources during the research for this book, a task made very much easier in this Internet Age. I have also made use of official records, Regimental Histories, newspapers and other sources too numerous to mention here.

Bibliography

History of the Indian Mutiny (Ball 1912)

Dictionary of Indian Biography (Buckland 1906)

History of the Hyderabad Contingent (Burton 1905)

History of the Indian Revolt (Dodd 1859)

History of the Indian Mutiny (Forrest 1904)

Heroes of the Indian Empire (Foster 1890)

Life of General Havelock (Headley 1859)

History of the Indian Mutiny (Holmes 1898)

History of the India (Hunter 1907)

Lucknow and Oude in the Mutiny (Innes 1895)

Sepoy Revolt (Innes 1897)

Kaye's and Malleson's History of the Indian Mutiny (Kaye, Malleson 1914)

Incidents in the Sepoy War (Knollys 1873)

Life of General Hope Grant (Knollys 1894)

Central India during the Rebellion of 1857–58 (Lowe 1860)

Indian Mutiny of 1857 (Mall 1891)

Memories of the Mutiny (Maude 1894)

Sepoy Revolt (Mead 1894)

Fourty-one years in India (Lord Roberts of Kandahar 1901)

Indian Mutiny of 1857 (Sedgwick 1920)

Addiscombe – its Heroes and Men of Note (Vibart 1894)

Life of General Sir Henry Evelyn Wood (Williams 1892)

Ledger and Sword (Willson 1903)

From Midshipman to Field Marshal (Wood 1906)

Sources

Archive.org – provides on-line access to an extensive library of out of copyright books that was indispensible to my research efforts. All of the books listed in the Bibliography were downloaded from this library.

Annals of Indian Administration – various editions

Memorialstovalour.co.uk – is an excellent site for general facts about VC recipients

Victoriacross.org.uk – is an excellent site run by Iain Stewart, about VC matters

Victoriacrossonline

Other on-line resources that have been indispensible to my research are:

Hansard – for a verbatim account of parliament deliberations

London Gazette – excellent government on-line archive which is easy to search for military promotions, military despatches, etc.

The National Archives – for service records

The *Times* newspaper archive for a contemporary account of events

INDEX